OCEAN YEARBOOK 20

OCEAN
YEARBOOK 20

Pacem in Maribus

Sponsored by the
International
Ocean Institute

DALHOUSIE
UNIVERSITY

**MARINE &
ENVIRONMENTAL
LAW INSTITUTE**

Sponsored by the Marine &
Environmental Law Institute
of Dalhousie Law School

Edited by
Aldo Chircop, Scott Coffen-Smout, and Moira McConnell

 Transnational Publishers   New York

Sponsored by the
International Ocean Institute

Transnational Publishers, New York

©2006 by Transnational Publishers
All rights reserved. Published 2006.
Printed 2006 in the United States of America

International Standard Book Number: 1-57105-351-4
Library of Congress Catalog Card Number: 79:642855
International Standard Serial Number: 0191-8575

Contents

Appendices

The International Ocean Institute

Pacem in Maribus

The International Ocean Institute (IOI) was created to promote education, capacity building, and research as a means to enhance the peaceful and sustainable use and management of ocean and coastal spaces and their resources, as well as the protection and conservation of the marine environment, guided by the principle of the Common Heritage of Mankind. Professor Elisabeth Mann Borgese founded the IOI in 1972 as an independent, non-profit, non-governmental organization headquartered at the University of Malta.

For 30 years the IOI has stood at the forefront of organizations in addressing these issues with the concern of future generations through an interdisciplinary and comprehensive approach. The IOI has also prepared working papers for the Third United Nations Conference on the Law of the Sea (UNCLOS III: 1973–1982), the Preparatory Commission for the International Seabed Authority, and for the International Tribunal for the Law of the Sea (1982–1994), as well as for various governments. It has provided consultants to UNEP, the World Bank, the United Nations Industrial Development Organization (UNIDO), and the Asian-African Legal Consultative Committee (AALCC). It contributed to the formulation of recommendations of the World Summits in Rio de Janeiro (1992) and Johannesburg (2002) and of the World Water Forum in Japan (2003) on oceans, coasts and islands, as well as to the review of the developments in ocean affairs through the United Nations open-ended informal consultative process.

The goals of the IOI are to:

- contribute to the evolving process of ocean governance through its functions and activities;
- monitor the implementation of international conventions and agreements as they relate to the oceans;
- mobilise the political will to implement national and regional plans and international agreements on the management and sustainable use of the ocean, coasts and islands through a global network of operational centres;

- raise awareness of the peaceful uses of the ocean, its protection and conservation, as well as the sustainable development of its resources, and in accordance with the principle of the common heritage of humankind;
- engage in the dissemination, the sharing and transfer of knowledge and experience; and
- respond to the needs of developing countries, particularly coastal communities and the role of women by increasing their abilities to develop and manage the ocean and coastal resources sustainably.

The International Ocean Institute achieves its goals through:

- education and training;
- research and analysis;
- organization of conferences and meetings;
- institution-building and partnership;
- promotion and communication; and
- fundraising in support of the activities of the Institute and its network.

The IOI's activities include training projects, information dissemination, conferences, research and publications:

- Training of hundreds of decision-makers and professionals, mainly from developing countries, through short and long duration interdisciplinary courses in ocean and coastal management;
- Ocean governance advocacy within the United Nations system through participation in and contribution to intergovernmental meetings and conferences;
- Development work among coastal communities with the objective of improving their livelihood while restoring and preserving coastal ecology;
- Information dissemination to international organizations and national institutions through the global IOI Network and the IOI web site;
- Organization of the biennial *Pacem in Maribus* Conference and other seminars and workshops;
- Research on a variety of ocean-related areas such as international and regional agreements and policies on oceans and the coastal zone; on regional and sub-regional co-operation and on scientific and technological approaches to sustainable management of living and nonliving marine resources;
- Education and awareness-creation about ocean resources, marine and coastal environments, and the need to care for them;

- Publication of the *Ocean Yearbook* in collaboration with the Dalhousie University Law School, Canada;
- Maturing IOI's website (www.ioinst.org) and publication of an electronic newsletter IOInforma by the IOI HQ. Regional operational centres also publish their own newsletters, research papers and reports; and
- Services include advice, consultancy, and information regarding ocean and coastal environments.

The IOI gained a worldwide respect and reputation through its contribution to the codification and implementation of the Law of the Sea Convention, and to the subsequent development of the concept of sustainable development as it applies to the ocean. Furthermore, through the launching of such projects as the coastal and eco-villages projects, dedicated women and youth programmes, training in ocean governance, risk assessment and others, the IOI has contributed positively to the implementation of ocean governance, with a particular focus on developing nations.

The IOI is now developing an international ocean governance and capacity building education programme, OceanLearn, that will consist of a network of education, training and research centres with expertise in ocean, coastal and marine-related affairs and governance. The Centres will be joined together in a partnership so as to provide for an interdisciplinary and comprehensive coverage of the subject areas. The overall objective will be to enhance the abilities of developing countries to develop and govern their own marine and coastal resources and environment sustainably.

The IOI scope and presence is truly international with 25 Operational Centres around the globe and with several new Centres in the development stage. The IOI network provides a flexible mechanism with a governing and co-ordinating structure that generates synergism and strategic planning of the network of semiautonomous nodes. This cohesive and comprehensive mechanism is capable of co-operating equally well with other intergovernmental systems and the private sector. The current centres and their host institutions are:

IOI—Canada, Dalhousie University; IOI—China, National Marine Data and Information Service, State Oceanic Administration, China; IOI—Costa Rica, Universidad Nacional, Costa Rica; IOI—India, Indian Institute of Technology, Madras, India; IOI—Japan, Yokohama City University, Japan; IOI—Malta, University of Malta, Malta; IOI—Black Sea, National Institute of Marine Geology and Geoecology, Romania; IOI—Senegal, Centre de Recherches Oceanographiques de Dakar—Thiaroye, Senegal; IOI—Southern Africa, University of Western Cape, South Africa; IOI—Eastern Africa, Kenya Marine and Fisheries Research Institute, Mombasa, Kenya; IOI—Ukraine, Institute of Biology of the Southern Seas, Sevastopol, Ukraine; IOI—Russia, State Institute of Oceanography; IOI—Western Africa, Nigerian Institute for Oceanography and Marine Research, Lagos, Nigeria; IOI—Thailand, Office of Thai Marine Policy and Restoration Committee, Bangkok, Thailand; IOI—Caspian Sea, Astrakhan State Technical University, Astrakhan, Russia; IOI—Volga River Basin, Nizhny Novgorod State University of Architecture and Civil Engineering, Russia; IOI—Indonesia, Centre for Marine Studies, University of Indonesia; IOI—South Western Atlantic Centre for Marine Studies, Brazil; IOI—Germany, Centre for Tropical Marine Ecology, Germany; IOI—Regional Centre for Australia and the Western Pacific, International Marine Project Activities Centre, Australia; IOI—Baltic, University of Kalmar, Sweden; IOI—Islamic Republic of Iran, Iranian National Centre for Oceanography (INCO), Tehran, Iran; IOI—Slovenia, Marine Biology Station at the Institute of Biology, Piran, Slovenia; IOI—Pacific Islands, University of the South Pacific; IOI—Egypt, National Institute of Oceanography and Fisheries (NIOF), Egypt.

Each Operational Centre is autonomous, identifying its own priorities for research, capacity building and development within the broad mission of the IOI, while benefiting from the support of the overall IOI Network. Regional approaches to research and capacity building enable the Institute to draw upon the different strengths of the Operational Centres to cater to the needs identified within each region. A director, generally supported by a small staff with a large number of experts and volunteers on call, runs each Centre.

Fifteen directors are members of the IOI Committee of Directors, which meets annually. The IOI is governed by a Board that takes decisions on policy, programme and budget matters. Growing steadily and responding to global changes, the IOI Network is now aiming at a multiplier effect to its spectrum of activities. It plans to move from direct training to training-the-trainers; from direct implementation of projects to offering advisory and consultative services; from a network of centres to a network of regional clusters and affiliates.

Marine & Environmental Law Institute
Dalhousie Law School

Established in 1883, Dalhousie Law School is the oldest common law school in Canada. As a leading law school, Dalhousie has traditionally played a critical role in the development of national legal education in Canada, in servicing the needs of the Atlantic region and as a focal point for graduate level education globally. The Law School offers the full breadth of undergraduate and graduate level education and is home to the Marine & Environmental Law Institute (http://www.dal.ca/law/MELAW), the Indigenous Blacks and Mi'kmaq Programme, the Health Law Institute, the Commonwealth Judicial Institute, and the Law and Technology Institute. Dalhousie Law School is pleased and honoured to support and provide a home for the *Ocean Yearbook* in its Marine & Environmental Law Institute.

Dalhousie Law School, with its location in the vibrant port city of Halifax, is internationally recognized for excellence in marine and environmental law research and teaching. Since its establishment in 1974 as an area of specialization for Dalhousie LL.B. students, the Marine & Environmental Law Programme (MELP) has provided LL.B. and post-graduate students (LL.M. and Doctoral) with one of the most extensive academic course offerings in these two fields in the world. With more than 12 full and part-time faculty members currently teaching in the Programme, students have a unique opportunity to learn about public and private law practice in marine (including shipping) and environmental law taught from domestic and international perspectives. Students wishing to specialize in these fields have the option of obtaining a certificate of specialization in either Marine or Environmental Law or both, while completing the three-year LL.B. degree. In addition, a joint LL.B. and Masters degree in Resource and Environmental Management (MREM) with the School for Resource and Environmental Studies, Faculty of Management, has been developed and should be offered in 2006.

The 30 years of research excellence of the Dalhousie Law School MELP faculty was formally recognized by the Dalhousie Board of Governors in 2004 with the creation of a Marine & Environmental Law Institute. The

Institute, which is housed in the Law School, carries out research and consultancy activities and also directs the MELP academic specialization. Its primary researcher is the holder of an appointment as a senior Canada Research Chair in Ocean Law & Governance. In addition to their scholarly research and publication activities, faculty and staff associated with the Institute carry out research projects and provide advisory services to agencies of the United Nations, international non-governmental organizations, and regional organizations as well as assisting government departments and non-governmental organizations in Canada and overseas.

The Marine & Environmental Law Institute is also the editorial office of the *Ocean Yearbook*, a major international interdisciplinary annual, devoted to ocean affairs. Dalhousie law students have the chance to gain experience working as research assistants on the Institute's research projects and workshops, and assisting with editing the *Ocean Yearbook*.

The Marine & Environmental Law Institute also works closely with on-campus student groups such as the Environmental Law Students' Society. It frequently collaborates closely with other disciplinary and interdisciplinary graduate programmes, such as the Marine Affairs Program (MAP) and other scholars at Dalhousie University and elsewhere and with marine and environmental organizations in the Maritimes.

Acknowledgments

The editors are grateful for the ongoing administrative and substantive support provided by the Marine & Environmental Law Institute and the Sir James Dunn Law Library at Dalhousie University Law School. The financial support for the editorial office provided by Dalhousie Law School and by the International Ocean Institute though its headquarters is gratefully acknowledged. We wish to extend thanks to Patrick Canning for research and editing assistance, to Susan Rolston for compiling the volume index and for revising the directory of oceans-related organizations, and to Lauri MacDougall for administrative support. As in past issues, warm thanks also go to members of the Board of Editors for continuing support.

We are very pleased to be working with Transnational Publishers of New York effective with the publication of this volume. Special thanks are extended to Heike Fenton and her staff at Transnational for editorial and infrastructural support.

THE EDITORS

Essay: Tsunami—26 December 2004

Awni Behnam
President, International Ocean Institute

William Langewiesche, in his book *The Outlaw Sea*, wrote:

> [I]t is easy to forget that our world is an ocean world, and to ignore what in practice that means. Some shores have been tamed, however temporarily, but beyond the horizon lies a place that refuses to submit. It is the wave maker, an anarchic expanse, the open ocean of the high seas. Under its many names, and with variations in color and mood, this single ocean spreads across three-fourths of the globe. Geographically, it is not the exception to our planet, but by far its greatest defining feature. By political and social measures it is important too—not merely as wilderness that has always existed or as a reminder of the world as it was before, but also quite possibly as a harbinger of a larger chaos to come. That is neither a lament nor a cheap forecast of doom, but more simply an observation of modern life in a place that is rarely seen. At a time when every last patch of land is claimed by one government or another, and when citizenship is treated as an absolute condition of human existence, the ocean is a realm that remains radically free.[1]

December 26, 2004, is a day that will live in infamy in the annals of natural disasters. It is not an exaggeration to consider the appalling loss of life and massive destruction that followed the earthquake and resultant tsunami in the Indian Ocean on that fatal day as a wake-up call to the international community. The whole world was shocked and surprised by the tragic events and watched with horror the events unfolding live on our television screens. The faces of both those who lost loved ones and the terrified children orphaned will forever haunt us. One does not remain neutral during natural disasters of this scale and certainly the outpouring of goodwill was immediately evident.

---

1. W. Langewiesche, *The Outlaw Sea: A World of Freedom, Chaos, and Crime* (New York: North Point Press, 2004): 3.

Ocean Yearbook 20: 1–5.

The natural phenomena of the movement of tectonic plates and the collision of ocean and continental plates result in the seabed deforming and displacing seawater, thus unleashing destructive waves (tsunami). Tsunamis often result in devastation, loss of life and environmental degradation. The tsunami waves can happen everywhere on the coast and may become dangerous due to the specifics of the shoreline and seabed. It has been with us since creation. So then one might well ask, why were we, the inhabitants of our planet, so surprised and taken aback on that fatal day?

No one can ignore the huge impact and scale of the damage caused in 11 countries with such a tragic loss of life, approaching a quarter of a million souls. At that time, there was an important part of the international community actively engaged in the development and operation of tsunami early warning systems. In fact, it is already a reality. Japan and the USA were well ahead of others in the international community in the development of tsunami early warning and mitigation systems. An active warning system for the Pacific Ocean had long been established and proven its worth. However, contrary to common belief, the other parts of the world's ocean were not neglected by the scientific community. In fact, in the 1990s the Intergovern-mental Oceanographic Commission (IOC) of UNESCO looked actively into the creation of an early warning system for the Indian Ocean to mitigate marine natural hazards. However, the scarcity and lack of commitment of resources by governments and international organizations was the main reason for protracted discussions, delays and inaction. Finally, the combina-tion of a lack of funding and low policy priority did not permit the establishment of an effective warning system.

The tsunami warning system for the Caribbean Region suffered the same fate. Governments decided not to make it a priority issue. The tsunami danger was marginalized; one may well ask why? Was it because of the infrequency of tsunami events? Low casualties? Or pure apathy? In the final analysis, it is clear there was a failure shared by the international community. I believe that it was not a "Tsunami"-related failure, but one of a much wider cause, namely the neglect of the oceans.

The issues of the ocean subsequent to the adoption of the United Nations Law of Sea Convention and its entry into force in 1994 were "placed on the back-burner."[2] The oceans simply fell from governments' priorities. Similarly, the civil society movement became understandably distracted as the challenges of priority-setting focused on poverty, civil strife, hunger and diseases, and consequently diverted their attention from the issues of oceans.

---

2. See "Emerging Institutional Framework for Ocean Governance," *Pacem in Maribus* 2000, XXVIII (Hamburg, December 2000).

Oceans have consistently escaped the attention of bureaucrats and representatives of States in multilateral diplomatic fora. It is equally regrettable that the Millennium Development Goals adopted by the United Nations General Assembly in 2000 did not contain the slightest mention of the oceans. The Review of the Development Goals will take place in September 2005. The Heads of State and Government of the developing countries of the Group of 77 met in Doha in June 2005, in part to prepare a collective stand for the September Summit in New York. While for the first time natural disaster figured in their declaration and on their agenda, they failed to pay the required attention to the issues of the ocean. This neglect in the broader context of multilateral governance diplomacy is truly unfortunate, if not unforgivable. One may also recall that the 2002 Johannesburg Summit on Sustainable Development that reviewed Agenda 21 met with a draft preparatory document that ignored completely the issues of the ocean. It was only due to the personal efforts of committed individuals such as Dr. Biliana Cicin-Sain, Dr. Patricio Bernal, Dr. Gunnar Kullenberg, Dr. Veerle Vanderweerd and a few other activists, that the oceans found a humble place in the agenda outcome of the Summit.

By continually deciding to neglect the issues of the oceans and keep them from entering the multilateral development and diplomacy agenda, there have been unforeseen repercussions, namely the reduction of awareness and public knowledge of the issues leading to a national and international governance deficit. It also weakens the linkages between specific ocean phenomena and natural disasters, many of which are ocean-related.

With the benefit of hindsight one cannot help but wonder how it was possible that so many lives were lost on 26 December when there was ample time for many to reach safe ground away from the shore. Far beyond the absence of an early warning system referred to earlier, there were simply no national or local disaster and risk reduction measures in place. People did not know what was in progress, what was to be done and where to go. This lacuna became evident when the World Conference on Disaster Reduction (WCDR) met in Kobe, Japan, only a few weeks after the December tsunami, where we learned of the urgent need to implement multi-hazards preparedness and awareness measures at all levels, with priority placed on education and building a culture of awareness at the local level. In simple words, what to do when a tsunami occurs!

The one encouraging sign in this sad episode was the manner in which the United Nations system responded with efficacy in the post-tsunami relief and mitigation. Organizations such as the Intergovernmental Oceanographic Commission (IOC), the World Meteorological Organization (WMO) and the Inter-agency Secretariat of the International Strategy for Disaster Reduction (ISDR) were commended for their leadership roles and for

adopting a long-term strategy for natural disasters prevention and mitigation programmes.[3]

History is full of examples that called for a comprehensive approach to
mitigating the impact of marine natural hazards worldwide. Yet only
recently the coastal degradation suffered by many countries as a result of
tidal waves, storm surges, hurricanes and cyclones, went almost unnoticed.

The recent tragedy of the Asian Tsunami brought out the best in our
humanity. The solidarity and commendable response by governments,
NGOs and institutions, in particular the United Nations system, has been
unique and unsurpassed in recent history. However, how many of us who
were touched in one way or another by the pictures of the unfolding
tsunami tragedy remembered that half a million souls perished in Bangladesh from a storm surge in 1970? In fact, another cyclonic storm surge
killed 138,000 on the coast southeast of Dacca, Bangladesh in 1991. It is
regrettable that no similar international mobilization took place at that time
to create an early warning system, nor was there an outcry for awareness and
mitigation or rapid response. The difference between the two events, the
Asian Tsunami and the storm surge that devastated Bangladesh, is telling in
itself and reflects our complex relationships in the international community.

For this and other valid reasons, the International Ocean Institute
(IOI) in an open letter on 17 January 2005 set out policy recommendations
warning that a hasty development of a tsunami warning system in a 1-year
time-frame may not be the best solution. In fact, the IOI recalled that,

> At the end of the nineties, IOC jointly with WMO, IHP of UNESCO
> developed a project proposal on Storm Surges Reduction in the
> northern part of the Indian Ocean. The objective was to develop the
> infrastructure necessary for providing effective and timely storm surge
> forecasts and warnings. The proposal was approved by the IOC, IHP
> and WMO governing bodies in 1999 and negotiations started with
> funding agencies. However no funds were made available. That
> proposal contained such components as sea level observation network,
> communication scheme, training and awareness. As far as it can be
> remembered there was a reference for the need to make a system multi-
> purpose in order to be able to deal with other marine disasters.[4]

---

3. As a testimony to the leadership of the United Nations Secretary-General,
Mr. Kofi Annan, in the mobilization of the international community, the IOI Board
of Governors awarded him the first Elisabeth Mann Borgese Medal, which he
accepted in April 2005.

4. Open Letter from the IOI: Indian Ocean Tsunami Warning System, IOIHQ/
ES02/05, 17 January 2005.

For all of the above reasons, the IOI has been strongly urging the development of a multipurpose system based on regional sub-systems for marine-related disasters that encompass early warning, awareness, preparedness and mitigation measures.

There is a need to build upon the goodwill that exists at this time and in particular the worldwide understanding of what natural hazards such as the tsunami can bring, and the public must understand they can happen anywhere and at any time. Thus the need to mobilize resources for a truly global system that is anchored in human awareness.

One would also hope that the mitigation of the effects of the Asian Tsunami on the livelihood of the affected coastal communities will bring a fresh start to a sustainable coastal management regime. For example, destroyed fishing boats are currently being replaced by better and larger ones. While this may seem desirable, they will only add to the vicious circle of poverty, as it will contribute to the continued depletion of fish stocks leading to impoverishment of the coastal communities concerned. Perhaps a good start would have been rehabilitation and alternative sources of employment through uses of oceans-related resources, mangroves, seashells for conversion into lime, aquaculture, etc. This itself is indicative of the need for a long-term strategy and vision for the future of vulnerable coastal communities.

An early warning system, no matter how excellent or technologically efficient, is not sufficient. The approach to awareness preparation and mitigation of marine-related disasters needs to be comprehensive and coherent and based on a human scope of understanding and knowledge.

It is my hope that this volume of the *Ocean Yearbook* will help the international ocean community to take this opportunity to re-examine current policies. While we will never be able to prevent natural phenomena, we can learn to live with the ocean and respect its majesty.

Response of Governmental and Non-Governmental Organizations to Marine Natural Disasters: The IOC and IOI Case

Iouri Oliounine

Executive Director, International Ocean Institute Headquarters, Malta

Tsunamis may happen in many parts of the world's ocean where strong underwater earthquakes and volcanic explosions may occur, or where there is a danger of underwater landslides. The 26 December 2004 tsunami disaster in the Indian Ocean devastated coastal areas in 11 countries and took a huge number of human lives among local communities and tourists. The economic losses were of a few billion dollars. The scientific community had issued warnings and international organizations took action long before the disaster to make governments ready, however, due to different reasons there was no or very limited response given and the warnings were in many cases ignored.

The Indian Ocean tsunami shifted the focus of governments around the world to the threat of marine natural disasters. The creation of the tsunami warming system for the Indian Ocean, and globally, has become a top priority on the political agenda. Necessary steps have been taken by the United Nations (UN) and other organizations for establishing a plan of action to combat tsunamis and other marine disasters. It is expected that the International Ocean Institute (IOI) as a global non-governmental organization will play a role in creating preparedness of coastal communities against marine disasters. Examples are given of the IOI Network activities that can be useful for marine natural disaster mitigation.

PROLOGUE TO THE FUTURE

The end of the 19th century was marked by deadly and disastrous tsunami events: the explosion of the Krakatoa volcano in 1883 generated a tsunami that devastated the East Indies with a death toll of more than 36,000; and the Sanriku tsunami, caused by an earthquake in the Japan Trench, took more than 27,000 lives.

Ocean Yearbook 20: 7–19.

In the 20th century the death toll due to tsunamis was relatively small at 15,000 lives.[1] In the middle of the last century tsunamis were frequent in the northern part of the Pacific Ocean. Some were Pacific-wide, with the most disastrous in 1952 (Kamchatka), 1960 (Chile), and 1964 (Alaska) caused by earthquakes. The analysis showed that a tsunami generated in one part of the ocean easily reached within a few hours the most remote places of the ocean, striking distant coasts and creating large-scale damage. It was also clear that there is no linear correlation between earthquake magnitude and tsunami intensity as not all of the strong earthquakes generated waves.

As a follow-up to the disastrous tsunamis of the 1950s and 1960s, the Pacific Tsunami Warning System was established, and international coopera-tion started, led by the Intergovernmental Oceanographic Commission (IOC) of UNESCO. From time-to-time Mother Nature reminded people of the tsunami danger in the Celebes Sea in 1976 or in Papua New Guinea in 1998. Though the death toll was quite large (10,000 lives total), they were considered local tsunamis, far away from civilization and looked at by many as more exotic than dangerous. The losses were much lower than those of hurricanes, floods and other natural disasters (Table 1).

There was no surprise that in the International Decade on Natural Disaster Reduction (IDNDR) agenda the tsunami as a natural disaster was marginalized and was hidden in the IDNDR statistics as "others" among natural disaster events, with the priority attention given to storms, earth-quakes, floods and draughts. In fact, since 1999 two-thirds of the recorded disasters were floods and storms.[2]

Surprising is the fact that in May 1994 at the Yokohama Conference on IDNDR, there was no or very little reference to tsunamis in the promotional materials, even from such countries as Canada, Russia or the USA, who were among the pioneers for the establishment of the Tsunami Warning System in the Pacific Ocean and were always supportive of the tsunami programme of the IOC. Of course, there were always some "crazy" scientists in the International Union of Geodesy and Geophysics (IUGG) and IOC circles who were warning of potential danger, but their views were easily ignored on the basis that nothing would happen. And then the 21st century arrived! 26 December 2004 will be in the memory of humankind and in its legends and myths for centuries to come. It was a nice, sunny Sunday morning with people on the beaches when an undersea earthquake measuring 9.0 on the

1. This number does not include the death toll of 58,000 caused by the Messina earthquake in Sicily, Italy in 1908 as a large percentage of this number were earthquake victims. *GEO Yearbook, An Overview of Our Changing Environment, 2004/5*, P. Harrison ed., (Nairobi: UNEP, 2005), available online: http://www.unep.org/GEO/yearbook/(Date accessed: 4 July 2005).

2. Preview of the Yokohama Strategy and Plan of Action for a Safer World, Kobe Conference, A/Conf.206/L.1, para 12, p. 5.

Richter scale shook the ocean bottom off the west coast of Northern Sumatra, Indonesia. The earthquake created tsunami waves that started propagating across the Indian Ocean with the speed of a jet plane, and in two and a half hours reached the shores of India and Sri Lanka and in 7 hours reached the shores of Africa, 7,000 km from the earthquake's epicenter (Figure 1). Millions of people were affected with billions of dollars of livelihood damage. The tsunami took the lives of around 300,000 people. In total, 320,000 people were killed by all natural disasters, including tsunamis, in 2004.[3]

The December 26th tsunami was sobering for all and the time of mourning came. The tragedy brutally reminded us all of the awesome destructive power of the ocean. Live television brought to us the sufferings of thousands of people, the destruction of property and the pictures of environmental damage. The most affected were indigenous groups of society—women, youth and old people. The effect of the waves on the economy could have been even worse if it happened in a more economically developed region. The very high death toll was to a large degree due to the very dense population in the coastal areas of the affected region and the poor living conditions.

There was another very special feature of this disaster. To say that it was the largest natural disaster during the last 100 years would be a mistake. Storm surges and floods in Bangladesh in the 1970s took double the number of lives. However, these disasters only affected Bangladesh and only had national or regional effects. With the December 2004 tsunami it was for the first time that the vulnerable were not only people from the region but also many foreign tourists in Thailand, Indonesia and Sri Lanka—a few thousand of them perished. The Indian Ocean tsunami disaster revealed an alarming level of vulnerability. Death came into many European, Japanese and American families. The tsunami became a global issue of high political, social, and human priority. It showed how vividly events in one place could profoundly affect people thousands of miles away.

The response of the international community to the disaster was also unique. Governments, governmental and non-governmental international organizations, businesses and industries, groups and individuals united in their readiness to provide support to the region and those suffering due to the tsunami disaster.

The absence of a tsunami warning system in the Indian Ocean has been widely questioned after the event, as a lack of awareness, communication and forecasting accounted for a large percentage of the casualties. Without

3. Figures announced in Geneva by the Centre for Research on the Epidemiology of Disasters, Brussels, 21 March 2005.

Table 1.—Total Number of People Reported Affected, By Type of Phenomenon and By Year (1994–2003) (In Thousands)

	1994	1995	1996	1997	1998	1999	2000	2001	2002	2003	Total
Avalanches/landslides	298	1,122	9	34	209	15	208	67	771	459	3,194
Droughts/famines	20,515	30,431	5,836	8,016	24,495	38,647	176,477	86,757	338,536	70,274	799,985
Earthquakes	730	3,029	2,018	634	1,878	3,893	2,458	19,307	548	3,956	38,452
Extreme temperatures	1,108	535	n/a	615	36	725	28	213	104	1,840	5,205
Floods	127,688	198,233	178,451	44,956	290,073	150,167	62,506	34,500	167,186	166,828	1,420,587
Forest/scrub fires	3,067	12	6	53	167	19	39	6	26	9	3,404
Volcanic eruptions	236	26	7	7	8	34	119	78	298	25	837
Windstorms	38,311	13,771	28,144	13,594	26,784	21,153	15,459	30,645	110,709	10,781	309,354
Other natural disasters (1)	n/a	n/a	n/a	29	10	1	17	n/a	2	ndr	59
Subtotal hydro-meteorological disasters	190,988	244,105	212,446	67,297	341,775	210,727	254,734	152,189	617,334	250,191	2,541,786
Subtotal geographical disasters	966	3,055	2,025	641	1,886	3,928	2,577	19,386	845	3,981	39,290

	1994	1995	1996	1997	1998	1999	2000	2001	2002	2003	Total
Total natural disasters	191,954	247,160	214,470	67,939	343,661	214,655	257,312	171,574	618,180	254,171	2,581,076
Industrial accidents	19	27	16	163	63	3	17	19	2	555	885
Miscellaneous accidents	11	19	18	20	52	12	15	30	56	14	249
Transport accidents	3	3	3	3	4	5	6	3	5	4	41
Total technological disasters	34	50	36	186	119	21	38	53	63	574	1174
Total	191,988	247,210	214,507	68,125	343,780	214,675	257,350	171,627	618,243	254,745	2,582,251

Source: EM-DAT: The OFDA/CRED International Disaster Database; http://www.em-dat.net - Université Catholique de Louvain–Brussels.

(1) Insect infestations and waves/surges

Note: "n/a" signifies "no data available"; "ndr" signifies "no disaster reported". See "caveats" for more information

During the decade, hydrometeorological disasters were accountable for 98 per cent of the total of people reported affected by disasters. Floods are the disasters that affect most people, accounting for 55 per cent of the total for 1994–2003. However, during the years 2000–2002, the number of people affected by droughts were in greater number than those affected by floods.

The number of people affected by technological accidents is far behind those affected by natural disasters. However, in Brazil, the spill of 1.2 billion liters of toxic materials into two rivers left 550,000 people without regular water supply in April 2003.

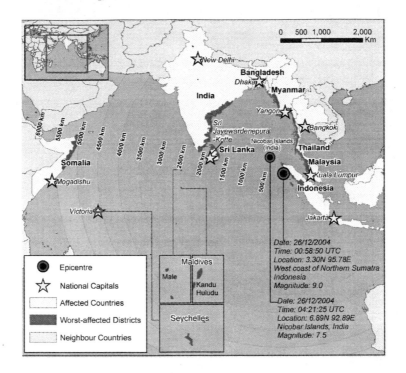

FIG. 1.—Indian Ocean Earthquake Epicenter and Human Impacts. Map provided courtesy of the ReliefWeb Centre, United Nations Office for the Coordination of Humanitarian Affairs.

losing time, mass media started looking for those responsible, for those whom to blame. The most frequently asked questions were: Where were the UN and other international organizations and governments? Why is there an operational tsunami warning system only in the Pacific Ocean? Why is there no such system in other oceans? Could a warning system prevent the large scale of destruction? Fortunately, mass media quickly understood that looking for a scapegoat was not a constructive approach. It would lead nowhere and would not help much to improve the situation. The key question has become: What should we do and how?

With 20 years of experience of coordinating activities of the IOC Tsunami Programme in the Pacific, I will try to give an answer to some of these questions and present a view on the role of a non-governmental organization such as the IOI in assisting others in marine natural hazards prevention and mitigation.

It would be a mistake to think that the scientific community and international organizations did not understand the danger of tsunamis in other parts of the ocean than the Pacific. In the scientific literature we find many references to a high probability of a tsunami occurrence in the Indian

Ocean, Caribbean Basin, and the Mediterranean Sea. There were calls for action and there was a response from the international organizations.

In the IOC Annual Report for 2000 it is stated that IOC was looking to extend the warning system in the Pacific Ocean to other tsunami-threatened areas, including the Caribbean, the Mediterranean and the Indian Ocean. In 2001, the IOC Assembly at its 21st Session recommended "that careful consideration of all related aspects (of extending responsibilities of the International Coordination Group for the Tsunami Warning System in the Pacific to other than the Pacific Regions) should be carried out and the findings reported to the next Executive Council Meeting."[4] Several projects were formulated related to marine natural hazards mitigation for different parts of the world ocean that have never seen the light of day.

At the end of the 1980s, the IOC, jointly with Japan, organized a mission to the southern part of the Pacific Ocean to recommend what should be done to extend the Pacific Tsunami Warning System, which is operational in the northern part, for the entire Pacific Ocean. The project proposal for the sub-regional Pacific Tsunami Warning System was drafted, but has never been implemented.

At the end of the 1990s, the IOC jointly with the World Meteorological Organization (WMO), and the International Hydrological Programme (IHP) of UNESCO developed a project proposal on Storm Surges Preparedness for the northern part of the Indian Ocean. The objective was to develop a mechanism necessary for providing effective and timely storm surge forecasts and warning. The proposal included data collection and analysis, communication and information dissemination, as well as awareness and educational components. It was planned as a multi-purpose system to be used for the prevention not only of storm surge effects, but also of tsunamis and other natural disasters. The proposal was approved by the IOC, the IHP and the WMO Governing Bodies in 1999 and negotiations started with funding agencies. However, governments of the region, excluding India, were reluctant to give priority to the project funding and did not support international organizations in their negotiations with funding agencies like UNDP and the World Bank. Later in 2004 it was reanimated in the form of the Marine Impacts on Lowland Agriculture and Coastal Resources (MILAC) plan, which was discussed at the IOC Executive Council meeting in June 2004.

The proposal for the Tsunami Warning System in the Caribbean Region saw the same fate. The regional meeting on the Intra-American Sea (IAS) Tsunami Warning System was organized with the support of the IOC in December 2000 in Puerto Rico. Based on the findings of this meeting, the

4. Summary Report of the 21st Session of IOC Assembly, IOC-XXI/2, p. 11.

IAS Project proposal was drafted. In spite of all the optimistic expectations, no funds were provided for the development of the project.

In Europe, the European Commission funded Genesis and Impact on the European Coast (GITEC) and Genesis and Impact on the European Coast, Tsunami Warning and Observation (GITEC TWO) projects with the objective to improve our knowledge of tsunamis in Europe and estimate the potential danger of this hazard for European coastal states. Interesting tsunami research and modeling results were received and tsunami catalogues were assembled and published. There was a general opinion that the tsunami threat was real and necessary measures should be taken. However, the results of the projects never materialized into a tsunami warning system development proposal, and still today there is no strategy in Europe for effective integration of vulnerability and risk assessment into early warning.

From these examples, one can see that the scientific community and international organizations have implemented good efforts. Unfortunately, these efforts have never been well acknowledged and appreciated by the governments and funding agencies. Why were the governments reluctant in giving priority to these projects in their national planning policies?

As Dr. V. Gusiakov mentioned in his March 2005 presentation, a "tsunami is a typical example of a low probability-high consequence hazard, having, as a rule, a long recurrence interval (from 10–20 to 100–150 years) for a particular coastal location..."[5] A low frequency of hazard occurrence has always given governments an excuse to postpone the expensive system development for tomorrow, as there were other political, social and economic priorities and more dangerous and disastrous hazards of higher frequency.

What happened also presents a typical situation when the freedom of scientists to speak, present their views, and give a warning does not necessarily mean that they are heard by the decision-makers.

The Indian Ocean tsunami changed the views of many skeptics, but even today there is a need to fight for a global Tsunami Warning System. Before the Indian Ocean tsunami, the voices of the opponents to the expansion of the Pacific Tsunami Warning System to other regions were much stronger. It was one of the reasons why the Marine Natural Disaster Programme of the IOC was so badly funded and till 2005 survived only because of extra budgetary contributions of some Member States, such as the USA, Japan, France, Canada, and a few others.

The Indian Ocean tsunami has become a wake-up call for governments. Marine natural hazards have become a high priority issue on the political

5. "Tsunami as Destructive Aftermath of Submarine Earthquakes and Volcanic Eruptions," International Coordination Meeting for the Development of a Tsunami Warning and Mitigation System for the Indian Ocean within a Global Framework, 3–8 March 2005, UNESCO, Paris, France.

agendas. The disaster urged governments to move from words to action. The way forward was chalked out after several high-level international, regional and national meetings. The IOC and the International Strategy for Disaster Reduction (ISDR) were given a responsibility to lead and coordinate the efforts in marine natural hazards mitigation, with a focus on the creation of a tsunami warning system in the Indian Ocean using the experience of the operations of the tsunami warning system in the Pacific. The system will be composed of prevention, monitoring and mitigation elements and should meet the needs to respond effectively to both local and distant tsunamis. The system will be complemented by robust models and scenarios of potential tsunami events that can be used in the formation and dissemination of warnings.

There was a general opinion that there is a need to design a global warning and mitigation system, as there is a global threat from marine natural disasters. There was a clear understanding that the system will not be implemented without the involvement of all governments concerned, international organizations, industries, the private sector, and civil society organizations.

There was a call to "all Member States to provide financial, technical and other kinds of assistance in order to promote national capacity and cooperation as well as preparedness, mitigation and prevention."[6] As Mr. Jan Egeland, the UN Under-Secretary General for Humanitarian Affairs, stated in his welcoming address to the World Conference on Disaster Reduction, 18–22 January 2005, Kobe, Hyogo, Japan, "Through the interaction between governments, international organizations, NGOs, experts and the public, the international community will have a unique opportunity to move determinately in building the resilience of nations and communities to disasters."

The role of NGOs in the partnership is indispensable as many of them are working directly with local least developed communities and have gained valuable experience in creating awareness, enhancing contacts between the scientific community and grass roots movements in the field of community vulnerability reduction and risk assessment, and providing public education and training.

A policy document based upon observations and lessons learned during 1990–1996, entitled "Towards practical and pragmatic natural disaster reduction by the year 2000," Geneva, December 1996, contains a diagram which is valid for the present situation (Figure 2). A global effort is needed

6. IOC Workshop Report no. 196, 2005, Communiqué of the International Coordination Meeting for the development of a tsunami warning and mitigation system for the Indian Ocean within a global framework, UNESCO, France, 3–8 March 2005.

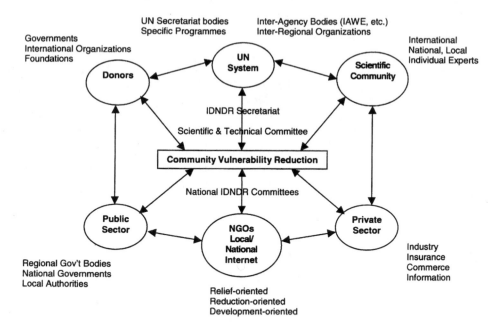

FIG. 2.—"The Decade"

by all partners and on all scales to put in place prediction, warning, notification, and community response mechanisms to save lives and communities in the future. The NGOs should play the role of equal partners with responsibility for the fields of activities where their knowledge and expertise is the highest.

WHAT CAN IOI DO, WHEN AND HOW?

The IOI network of Operational Centres and existing networks of other organizations should work together to meet the objectives formulated during the marine hazards meetings within and outside the UN. Though the primary focus will be on the Indian Ocean, the target audience should be global. The cooperation will help foster a dialogue between different community groups for the purpose of developing recommendations for a coordinated plan of action as follows:

- identify urgent local communities' needs;
- obtain a specification of which kind of warning-forecasting products various recipients-users can utilize;
- define the primary recipients;

- increase marine disaster risk awareness and foster public awareness of such risks;
- integrate the total knowledge of tsunami phenomena in the reduction of risks and human vulnerability; and
- initiate programmes of education and training.

The achievements of the IOI in the field of education and training are known worldwide. The experience in risk management is less well known. However, in 1999–2001 the IOI in partnership with Swiss Re implemented a project on risk management with the objective to effect change at the coastal community level so as to reduce the exposure of these communities to the risks associated with living in marine disaster-prone areas. The project included the establishment of proper emergency planning and response and changing settlement practices and fishing approaches with the aim to reduce exposure and vulnerability to risks, thereby allowing the insurance industry to come in at the micro-level and provide insurance at an acceptable risk.

There are five IOI Centres in the ocean area affected by the December 2004 tsunami, namely, in India (Madras), Thailand (Bangkok), Indonesia (Jakarta), Kenya (Mombassa), and Australia (Townsville). All of these Centres are ready to contribute and are contributing to the development of the tsunami warning system in the Indian Ocean, and particularly to improving preparedness of coastal communities to marine natural disasters. Preparedness here does not mean construction of protection walls. It means education, awareness and planning. They are all not very costly efforts but can be, if wisely implemented, very effective.

IOI–Australia is ready to contribute to the better management of Marine Protected Areas (MPAs) by organizing training courses and providing training packages. The rational management of MPAs is an important aspect of disaster mitigation, especially where conservation of mangroves and coral reefs is involved. The Centre is also targeted to assist the International Marine Protected Areas Congress with the delivery of post-tsunami projects in Thailand and Indonesia through training and awareness-raising activities. The IOI OceanLearn strategy, for which several international organizations have expressed an interest in its implementation, can respond to training needs in the marine disaster preparedness area. The IOI–Australia is working with UNEP/GPA and IOI–Pacific Islands on the adaptation of their waste management course for the Pacific Islands, and hopefully IOI will adapt the course for the Eastern Asian Seas in a year or two. Proper waste management would have greatly reduced the impacts of the recent tsunami, as much of the habitat damage was caused by debris washed over reefs and lagoons by the waves. The Centre will also be ready to provide its expertise in marine biodiversity. Any survey work associated with the identification of vulnerable areas would be of interest to the Centre.

IOI–Thailand is already assisting the Government of Thailand in the establishment of a national center on disaster prevention and warning. It contributes to the training programme carried out by the Department of Marine and Coastal Resources within the Coastal Habitats and Resources Management (CHARM) project, with the emphasis on coastal reef and seagrass protection, mangrove restoration and conservation, and a fish conservation programme for fishermen. The Centre provides support to the projects related to community livelihood development and restoration and implements adaptive learning in water resource management for the community fisheries development. IOI–Thailand is involved in the restoration of ecotourism in southern Thailand, which was seriously damaged by the December 2004 tsunami.

IOI–India made an assessment of the tsunami impact on the coastal communities of the Tamil Nadu region where IOI has been implementing in recent years the eco-villages project within the Women/Youth and the Sea Programme. The project is focused on assisting coastal communities in the Tamil Nadu region, home to some of the most impoverished segments of Indian society. It turned out that one village, where the major occupation is the collection of seashells and conversion into lime, was especially damaged. The tsunami took away in a few minutes the entire shell collection of a few months, all the kilns where the shells were being fired have been destroyed, fishing catamarans damaged, and all the villagers lost their livelihoods. The Children's Centre that was providing much needed supplementary education to the village children was also washed away.[7] To help the coastal community in reconstruction, a project proposal was formulated under the title "Rehabilitation and Remuneration of Women's Livelihood in a Tsunami affected Village in South India" and submitted to UNDP for funding within the South-South Grants Facility.

There are more IOI Centres located worldwide in the marine disaster-prone areas. They are in Costa Rica, Malta, Ukraine, Japan, Fiji, and China. These Centres will be ready to cope with disasters by assisting in developing and implementing national strategies for preparedness and resilience building, and in developing emergency preparedness plans so that the plans will reflect the risks that poor communities identified as their priorities.

As Mr. Raymond Forde stated, "Warning Systems by themselves are ... of little value unless communities understand how they work and how warning should be transmitted."[8] Communities should also know what to do

---

7. From the report of Prof. R. Rajagopalan, India, IOI Governing Board Member.

8. Mr. Raymond Forde, Federation Governing Member and President of the Barbados Red Cross Society, Statement at the Mauritius International Meeting for SIDS, January 2005.

when the disaster comes. In all these training and awareness efforts, the IOI could be a reliable partner. Some components of the future marine natural hazards programme can be implemented now, without waiting for the creation of a fully operational tsunami warning system. They include training and education, awareness and promotion. The IOI offers its services to the international community in these fields.

The human memory is short and new priorities may appear. There is a need to act urgently to make people ready to effectively confront future disasters and develop comprehensive and strategic approaches to diminishing the effects of disasters. Though we cannot give answers to all concerns now, we need, as a higher priority, to give answers to what to do, when and how.

After the Tsunami—Restoring the Livelihoods of Coastal Fishers and Enhancing Their Role in Coastal Fisheries Management and Conservation Practices in the Future

Uwe Tietze*

Fisheries Department, Food and Agriculture Organization of the United Nations, Rome, Italy

INTRODUCTION

The tsunami waves of 26 December 2004 were caused by the largest earthquake in nearly half a century, which originated off the coast of Sumatra, Indonesia. The waves struck at least 12 countries in Asia and Africa and destroyed the livelihoods of about 5 million people in coastal communities. Some 1.5 million were fishermen and their family members. They suffered death, injury, loss of assets and equipment. Fisheries and aquaculture appear to have been the sectors most seriously hit by the disaster.

In the aftermath of the tsunami, national governments have led relief efforts supported by widespread global solidarity, the United Nations (UN) agencies, bilateral donors, international financial institutions (IFIs), numerous non-governmental organizations (NGOs) and civil society. These efforts appear to have been somewhat successful in the delivery of emergency food, shelter and medical supplies to most of the survivors. Widespread famine was prevented. The feared outbreak of serious disease was cut off. While relief efforts continue to be required for the hundreds of thousands of displaced people, the challenge for the affected countries and the international community is now the longer-term rehabilitation of the millions of livelihoods that were affected by the tsunami.

---

* The views expressed in this article are those of the author and not the expression of any opinion whatsoever on the part of the Food and Agriculture Organization of the United Nations (FAO).

Ocean Yearbook 20: 21–40.

DAMAGE TO LIVES AND LIVELIHOODS

Current information suggests that the tsunami waves caused more than 60,000 deaths in the fisheries sector alone, of the more than 222,000 people who died together. About 110,000 fishing vessels were destroyed or damaged[1] with an estimated replacement cost in excess of US$101 million. Some 36,000 fishing vessel engines were lost or damaged with an estimated replacement cost of US$574 million and over 1.5 million units of fishing gear were destroyed with an estimated replacement cost of US$111 million. The damage to fishing harbors and landing sites was estimated at about US$33 million. Direct damages to aquaculture installations such as fish-ponds, cages and hatcheries were estimated at about US$85 million. As a result of these damages, the livelihoods of approximately 1.5 million members of fishing households are threatened.

Indonesia is the worst affected country. The tsunami devastated the coastal areas of two entire districts in the north Sumatra province, in particular the northern and western regions of Banda Aceh. The number of dead or missing persons is estimated at 230,000 and the number of displaced people in Aceh at over 400,000.

Damages and losses caused by the tsunami in Indonesia are estimated at about US$4.5 billion, of which nearly two-thirds in the private sector, including housing, commerce, agriculture, fisheries and transport. Some two-thirds of fishing implements, such as boats and gear and half of the fisheries and aquaculture infrastructure, were destroyed or damaged by the tsunami waves. The fisheries sector output in the affected districts is expected to decline by as much as 60 percent in the short- and medium-term as a consequence of physical losses and damages and the numbers of fishermen killed. Direct damage of fishing and aquaculture assets has been estimated at about US$140 million.

In India, the tsunami waves caused extensive damage in the Andaman and Nicobar Islands and in the coastal areas of Andhra Pradesh, Kerala, Pondicherry and Tamil Nadu. More than 10,000 people lost their lives and over 2 million livelihoods were affected. In Tamil Nadu, the worst affected Indian state, the tsunami killed about 8,000 people, of whom more than four-fifths were members of fishing communities.

Twenty of the 198 inhabited islands of the Maldives were devastated by the tsunami waves. Over one-third of the total population of 280,000 was severely affected, their homes destroyed and their water and food supply

---

1. The estimates were prepared by the Fishing Technology Service of FAO based upon reports of national fisheries administrations and government agencies, reports of FAO experts and consultants and on various assessment reports by multi-agency missions of the staff of UN agencies, IFIs and bilateral donors.

interrupted. Eighty people were killed and 20 remain missing. About 12,000 people were displaced. Tourism and fisheries, which are the most important economic sectors in the Maldives, were severely affected by the tsunami. In relative terms, the Maldives was the worst hit country since the damage to productive assets, housing and infrastructure, estimated at US$470 million, was equivalent to nearly two-thirds of the country's gross domestic product (GDP). The direct damage to fishing and fish processing implements and indirect income losses in the fishery sector have been estimated at US$25 million.

In Sri Lanka, the tsunami waves struck 12 of its 14 coastal districts, killed over 31,000 people, destroyed some 140,000 houses and damaged natural ecosystems and coastal infrastructure. Vulnerable groups, such as poor fishing communities living close to the shore in simple houses and shelters, suffered the most. The overall economic damage is estimated at close to US$1 billion, which is about 4.5 percent of Sri Lanka's GDP, with losses concentrated in the housing, tourism, fisheries and transport sectors.

Most of the people killed were fishermen and their family members. In addition, some 90,000 fishers were displaced. More than 20,000 fishing vessels, i.e., two-thirds of the country's fishing fleet of about 28,000 vessels, were destroyed or damaged as were fishing infrastructure and inputs— fishing harbors, cold storages, fishing gear and outboard motors. The total damage to the fisheries sector, excluding damage to housing and personal effects of the fishermen, is estimated at US$120 million.

In southern Thailand along the coast of the Andaman Sea, more than 5,000 people were killed by the tsunami waves, about half of them foreign tourists. People working in fishing and allied activities, and in tourism, were the most affected. The livelihoods of several hundred thousand people were affected by the tsunami. Severe damage was inflicted on some 400 fishing villages, including damage or destruction of 4,500 fishing boats. About 30,000 mostly poor households that depended on fisheries lost their means of livelihood.

In Africa, the northeastern coastline of Somalia was badly struck by the tsunami waves. The people there had already suffered from civil war, chronic droughts and floods. An estimated 150 people died and more than 50,000 were directly affected through damage and destruction of their houses, boats, wells and water reservoirs. Because the tsunami coincided with the height of the fishing season, the impact on livelihoods was particularly severe.

The Seychelles suffered severe flooding and widespread damage to roads, fishing infrastructure and tourism resources. The overall damage was estimated at about 4 percent of the country's GDP while the estimated loss in fishing infrastructure was estimated in the order of US$7 million. Myanmar, Kenya and the United Republic of Tanzania also suffered damages, although to a lesser extent.

SHORT-TERM RELIEF MEASURES

In the aftermath of the tsunami, national governments have led relief efforts supported by national disaster and relief management structures, widespread global solidarity, the UN agencies, bilateral donors, IFIs, NGOs and civil society. These efforts have been successful in the delivery of emergency food, shelter and medical supplies to most of the survivors, thereby preventing the outbreak of famine and disease. Relief efforts continue to be required for the hundreds of thousands of displaced people who still live in temporary housing and are dependent on food assistance.

There has been an unprecedented level of solidarity with and support to the affected countries and people by the international community. The United Nations Flash Appeal in early January raised more than US$700 million for UN agencies for relief and early recovery efforts. The aggregate amount of public donor commitments to relief and rehabilitation, as reported by the United Nations Office for the Coordination of Humanitarian Affairs (OCHA), is over US$5.5 billion. This amount does not yet include relief and rehabilitation commitments from the Asian Development Bank (ADB) and the World Bank and also excludes US$1–2 billion of donations from private parties as estimated by the World Bank.

As far as the relief efforts for the affected fisheries and aquaculture sectors are concerned, FAO and its Fisheries Department took the lead in close cooperation with the UN Development Group, OCHA, other UN organizations, IFIs, fisheries networks, intergovernmental organizations, NGOs and civil society.

Staff and consultants of the FAO Fisheries Department, together with other FAO departments, participated in damage and needs assessment missions and reported their findings and responses on a daily basis to OCHA. These included reports in the OCHA Situation Reports on Earthquakes and Tsunamis. In order that the benefits of FAO's expertise and resources reach the largest number of fishermen, fish farmers and their families, staff of FAO's Fisheries Department assisted those who were responsible for planning and implementing relief and rehabilitation activities at national and regional levels. At the national level, staff and consultants of the Department formed part of national task forces, established by governments, to coordinate all tsunami-related assessment, relief and rehabilitation measures and efforts.

With regard to fisheries and aquaculture, these efforts focused primarily on the supply of fishing gear, repair and replacement of boats, rehabilitation and restocking of fish ponds, early rehabilitation of harbors, anchorages, fish storage and processing, with the purpose of resuming fish production and thereby incomes and employment of affected fishermen and fish farmers, and the supply of fish and food for the coastal population.

As part of the overall FAO efforts to assist the affected countries, close collaboration was maintained with IFIs such as the World Bank, Asian Development Bank (ADB) and Islamic Development Bank in the areas of needs and damage assessments in the agriculture and fisheries sectors, formulation of rehabilitation and recovery strategies, participation in missions to help design project/program interventions and in facilitating the exchange of technical and operational information.

With an orientation toward medium- and long-term rehabilitation efforts, the FAO Fisheries Department contributed to the development of country-driven program frameworks for tsunami-affected countries. These frameworks are developed by governments with multi-agency assistance provided by the IFIs and the UN system. Each country framework has a fisheries component and incorporates a livelihoods-based approach and other cross-cutting issues such as food security, gender and the protection of the coastal and marine environment, noting that fisher and farmer livelihoods constituted the largest group affected in most countries.

The FAO Fisheries Department has developed and operates a web site on fisheries and aquaculture interventions in tsunami-affected areas that seek to provide consolidated information on needs in the fisheries and aquaculture sector, relief and rehabilitation measures, and to serve as a focal point for all stakeholders and donors. This web site forms part of the overall FAO tsunami web site and is connected to the UN Atlas of the Oceans web site maintained by FAO on behalf of UN agencies. The site assists in the coordination of information for all agencies on ocean-related activities and intense activity is now developing around the tsunami issue.[2]

With the emergency relief phase largely completed, the challenge for affected countries and the international community is to use the available assistance for the long-term rehabilitation of the millions of livelihoods that were affected by the tsunami and restore the capacity of the national, regional and local economies for sustained and equitable development. In this context, there is an urgent need for coordination, guidance and consensus building on the priority issues for the governments of these countries, together with the UN, FAO, IFIs, bilateral donors, NGOs and civil society.

2. See http://www.fao.org/tsunami/fisheries/index.htm.

ISSUES AND CONSTRAINTS IN THE REHABILITATION OF FISHERIES AND AQUACULTURE AND MEDIUM- AND LONG-TERM OPTIONS FOR RESTORING LIVELIHOODS AND ENHANCING COASTAL CONSERVATION AND PROTECTION

A major issue and possible constraint to the long-term sustainable rehabilitation of the fisheries and aquaculture sectors of the tsunami-affected countries is the danger of reinstitutionalizing the factors of vulnerability and unsustainable exploitation of aquatic and fisheries resources. This includes the danger of replacing fishing craft and gear used for fishing practices and methods that, in the past, contributed to the overexploitation of fisheries resources and had a negative impact on the coastal and marine ecosystem. The same is true for aquaculture practices, many of which have had negative impacts on the coastal and aquatic environment.[3]

Care must be taken to provide responsible and sustainable fishing and fish farming inputs and to modify existing fishing and fish farming practices as needed.[4] The provision of training, advice and other support, including financial aid in the form of microfinance and rural credit is required if people are to change their fishing and fish farming practices to responsible and sustainable ones. To lessen the pressure on aquatic and fisheries resources, alternative livelihoods need to be promoted in coastal communities, not only related to fisheries and fish farming but also outside the sector. Hence, supporting vocational training and micro-enterprise support programs are needed as well as access to microfinance and credit sources to meet start-up capital and working capital requirements.

Furthermore, it is necessary to assess the extent of environmental destruction in fisheries/aquaculture habitats and sites caused by the tsunami waves and the effect on production potential, and to advise on actions that may be required to rehabilitate both these habitat/sites and productivity.

Another important issue in preventing and reducing the negative impact of future natural disasters such as tsunami waves and tropical storms

---

3. D. J. Nickerson, "Trade-offs of Mangrove Area Development in the Philippines," *Ecological Economics*, 28 (1999): 279–298; J. H. Primavera, "A Critical Review of Shrimp Culture in the Philippines," *Reviews of Fisheries Science*, 1 (1993): 151–201; P. Ronnback and J. H. Primavera, "Illuminating the Need for Ecological Knowledge in Economic Valuation of Mangroves under Different Management Regimes—A Critique," *Ecological Economics*, 35 (2000): 135–141.

4. The principles and international standards of behavior for responsible practices with a view to ensuring the effective conservation, management and development of living aquatic resources are set out in the *Code of Conduct for Responsible Fisheries* (Rome: FAO, 1995); the *FAO Technical Guidelines for Responsible Fisheries 1—Fishing Operations* (Rome: FAO, 1996); and the *FAO Technical Guidelines for Responsible Fisheries 2—Aquaculture Development* (Rome: FAO, 1997).

is related to the settlements of coastal and fishing communities and their location which are, in many cases, extremely vulnerable and unprotected. The consistent involvement of these hitherto quite marginalized communities in identifying future coastal and land-use planning needs to be strengthened as well as their use of, and property rights to, the land.

Closely related to this is the issue of coastal conservation and protection. Measures urgently need to be taken to prevent further soil erosion in coastal areas, rehabilitate mangrove forests and use natural and other means of soft armoring and protecting coastlines against destruction by tsunami waves, floods and storms. All of these measures must be designed and implemented in close consultation and involvement with local authorities and communities.

The introduction of community-based, integrated coastal and aquatic resource management structures offers an opportunity to address most of the issues mentioned above in an integrated and participatory manner. While the focus of medium- and long-term rehabilitation programs will certainly need to be adjusted, the following elements are considered essential:

- promoting sustainable and environmentally friendly fishing, fish farming, fish preservation and processing practices compatible with the state of fishery resources;
- rehabilitation and conservation of the coastal environment and fisheries resources;
- better governance and more effective community-based planning in coastal areas[5] and coastal protection and conservation measures with the active participation of the coastal fishers and population;
- creation and diversification of sustainable livelihoods of traditional fishing and fish farming communities and supporting training;
- micro-enterprise support, microfinance and rural credit programs and facilities;
- linking the fisheries and aquaculture sectors to emerging early warning systems for natural disasters; and
- measures to improve safety at sea and the introduction of mutual insurance programs for fisheries and aquaculture, which also cover the risk of natural calamities.

5. The principles and international standards of behavior for responsible practices with regard to the integration of fisheries into coastal area management are set out in the *FAO Technical Guidelines for Responsible Fisheries 3—Integration of Fisheries into Coastal Area Management* (Rome: FAO, 1996).

Enhancing the Role of Coastal Fishing Communities in Coastal and Fisheries Management and Conservation

The livelihoods of coastal fishing communities in the tsunami-affected countries can only be rehabilitated and safeguarded in the long-term if the communities are empowered to play an informed and active role in coastal and fisheries management and conservation in their respective areas of residence, i.e., at the local as well as the national level. All efforts to achieve this need to consider the situation that existed prior to the impact of the tsunami waves on the coastal environment of these countries.

The situation prior to the tsunami was characterized in all the tsunami-affected countries by the full overexploitation of fisheries resources and by a deterioration of the coastal environment. This was caused not only by industrialization and urbanization in coastal areas but also by an increase in the number of fishermen as a result of population growth and migration to coastal areas.

The findings of recent empirical studies carried out in the framework of an FAO interregional project suggest,[6] however, that the number of coastal fishermen has started to decline or stagnate in recent years in many developing countries. The findings further suggest that artisanal fisheries, in many cases, are no longer a "last resort employment" for people in coastal areas. Access to alternative employment opportunities and increased occupational mobility, as a result of higher levels of education, general economic development and government policies aiming to reduce fishing effort and conserve the coastal environment, are among the reasons that have contributed to the change.

These new demographic trends of stagnating and declining numbers of fishers and occupational diversification are creating a more conducive environment for the participation of fishing communities in coastal and aquatic resource management and conservation. Another positive factor shown by the studies is that fishermen are generally well aware of and acknowledge the fact that catches and variety of fish caught have declined over the past decades and that pollution of coastal waters has considerably increased, partly as a result of population pressure and an increase in the number of fishermen.

Fishermen in Southeast and South Asia and in East Africa who were interviewed in the course of the studies readily supported the introduction of strict fishing regulations to ensure the recovery of over-fished and depleted stocks. At the same time, many fishermen felt that governments

6. See U. Tietze, G. Groenewold and A. Marcoux, *Demographic Change in Coastal Fishing Communities and its Implications for the Coastal Environment.* FAO Fisheries Technical Paper 403 (Rome: FAO, 2000).

had not taken adequate steps for the conservation and protection of fisheries resources.

As in other parts of the world, defining basic principles and effective processes for improved governance of coastal areas is a prerequisite for sound economic investment and environmental conservation.[7] This holds true also for the tsunami-affected countries. Important elements of a framework for improved governance and management are the introduction of management mechanisms that allow the involvement of all stakeholders in the governance process as well as the use of clear and transparent systems for monitoring and evaluation and measuring the impact and success of management systems, including the impact on the socio-economic well-being of coastal and fishing communities. These elements create a climate for reasonable and less adversarial approaches to resolving conflicts.

Unfortunately, the findings of the FAO studies also reflect a lack of consultation and involvement of coastal fishing communities in the management and conservation of fisheries resources and the coastal environment and a lack of recognition of their social, economic and occupational concerns.

Some of the tsunami-affected developing countries[8] have in fact already introduced decentralized fisheries management and coastal conservation mechanisms, such as in the Philippines.[9] They have introduced community-based fisheries and aquatic resource management structures or involved fishermen's organizations in fisheries management and conservation, as in Malaysia. However, the consideration of socio-economic issues in coastal fisheries management in most Asian and Pacific countries is rather limited.[10] Other countries such as Thailand operate community-based fisheries management programs only as pilot projects and on a geographically very limited scale. One example is the program in Phang-Nga Bay,[11] an area seriously affected by the recent tsunami waves.

7. Committee on Marine Area Governance and Management, Marine Board, Commission on Engineering and Technical Systems, National Research Council, *Striking a Balance: Improving Stewardship of Marine Areas* (Washington D.C.: National Academy Press, 1997): 4–5.

8. D. Menasveta, *Fisheries Management Frameworks of the Countries Bordering the South China Sea* (Bangkok: FAO Regional Office for Asia and the Pacific, 1997).

9. See J. C. Muñoz, "Fisheries and Coastal Resource Management in the Philippines," in *Guidelines on the Collection of Demographic and Socio-economic Information on Fishing Communities for Use in Coastal and Aquatic Resources Management*, ed., L. V. Villareal (Rome: FAO, 2004): 81–97. Bangkok, Regional Office for Asia and the Pacific, FAO, 1993.

10. Indo-Pacific Fishery Commission, 1994: Proceedings of the Symposium on Socio-economic Issues in Coastal Fisheries Management, Bangkok, 23–26 November 1993.

11. D. J. Nickerson ed., *Community-Based Fisheries Management in Phang-Nga Bay, Thailand.* Proceedings of the National Workshop on Community-Based Fisheries

Although pockets of community-based fisheries management exist in the region, a widespread lack of the consideration of socio-economic concerns and community-based fisheries and coastal management and conservation is also documented in a recent FAO publication.[12] This summarizes the proceedings and recommendations of a regional workshop held in 2002 at the University of the Philippines in the Visayas on the use of demographic data in fisheries and coastal development and management in the Philippines and other Southeast and South Asian countries.

Following the workshop, guidelines were prepared and field tested. These can be used for the collection of demographic and socio-economic information on fishing communities for use in coastal and aquatic resource management. The guidelines specify key indicators for the identification of demographic issues in coastal area management and for monitoring the impact of management measures on the socio-economic well-being of coastal and fishing communities. They also identify data sources and methods for the collection of data, using the case of the Philippines as an example. As far as possible, in order to avoid duplication of data collection and reduce costs, data sources are identified as censuses and surveys, which are routinely carried out. These include population and housing censuses, national demographic surveys, maternal and child mortality surveys, labor force surveys, functional literacy, education and mass media surveys, family income and expenditure surveys, and family planning and similar surveys.

Case studies on the use of demographic data in coastal area management in Italy and the United States of America and the case studies from Asian countries presented at the regional workshop on the use of demographic data in coastal area management in the Philippines and other Southeast and South Asian countries provide practical examples of how demographic indicators are actually used in coastal and fisheries management.

The use of such types of guidelines for the preparation of coastal and aquatic resource and fisheries management plans and for the monitoring of their impact on the well-being of coastal populations can theoretically result in the concerns of coastal populations, including fishing communities, being more seriously taken into consideration, quite apart from conservation concerns and coastal commercial interests such as the tourism and property development industry.

Management, organized by the Department of Fisheries of Thailand, FAO and the Bay of Bengal Programme, Phuket, Thailand, 14–16 February 1996. Bangkok, Regional Office for Asia and the Pacific, FAO, 1998.

12. L. V. Villareal, V. Kelleher and U. Tietze eds., *Guidelines on the Collection of Demographic and Socio-economic Information for Use in Coastal and Aquatic Resources Management*, FAO Fisheries Technical Paper 439 (Rome: FAO, 2004).

In countries where it might be difficult to break entrenched patterns of resource overuse and misuse, to overcome layers of dysfunctional procedures within government and the business community and to tackle national-scale issues, which have been identified when preparing coastal profiles, a "special area management" approach might be appropriate, i.e., focusing the program's efforts on selected areas that illustrate conditions typical of the coast as a whole.[13]

The specific approach used in each country and community will vary according to many factors, including cultural, political, institutional and socio-economic considerations. Comprehensive approaches have been in place for enough time, and in enough parts of the world not only to be able to glean lessons from individual experiences, but systematically to assess and learn across international resource management experiences.[14]

The close involvement of coastal and fishing communities in the management and conservation of coastal areas and aquatic resources is a key prerequisite to linking the fisheries and aquaculture sectors of the tsunami-affected countries to emerging early warning systems for natural disasters.

As endorsed by the recent World Conference on Disaster Reduction Framework for Action 2005–2015 in Kobe, Japan, the international community is challenged to apply all available knowledge about risk reduction and recovery in the wake of a disaster of this magnitude. It was emphasized at the conference that the international community must be responsible for how it rebuilds so as not to reconstruct risk, leaving populations equally vulnerable in any subsequent wave of disasters in the region. The countries bordering the Bay of Bengal and the Indian Ocean are already making efforts to establish an early warning system for earthquakes and tsunami waves. They have already had considerable experience through their cyclone early warning systems. The development of an early warning system for tsunami waves and for floods and tropical storms requires inputs particularly on environmental and socio-economic aspects, including training and extension support, integration of early

13. S. B. Olsen, "Can Community-Based Management Be Made Operational?," *Intercoast Network. International Newsletter of Coastal Management*, 19 (Naragansett, Rhode Island, United States: University of Rhode Island, Coastal Resources Center, Fall 2003).

14. D. Nickerson and S. B. Olsen, *Collaborative Learning Initiatives in Integrated Coastal Management*. Coastal Management Report #2239. (Narragansett, Rhode Island, United States: University of Rhode Island, Coastal Resources Center, 2003); S. B. Olsen and D. Nickerson, *The Governance of Coastal Ecosystems at the Regional Scale: an Analysis of the Strategies and Outcomes of Long-Term Programs*, Coastal Management Report #2243 (Narragansett, Rhode Island, United States: University of Rhode Island, Coastal Resources Center, 2003).

warning mechanisms into fisheries and coastal planning and management, and the involvement of fishers' associations in the operation of early warning systems. Essentially, the communities have to recognize their own key roles as stakeholders in their own preservation.

Promoting the Diversification of Livelihoods and Micro-enterprise Development and Supporting Training, Extension, Rural Credit and Microfinance Services

The creation and diversification of sustainable livelihoods of traditional fishing and fish farming communities in the tsunami-affected and other developing countries, and supporting programs and facilities need to be seen in the context of ongoing trends and changes that are occurring in the coastal and small-scale fisheries sectors of many developing countries.

Recent studies[15] reveal a trend of diversification of livelihoods in fishing communities as well as that of polarization within the small-scale fisheries sectors of developing countries. The diversification of livelihoods is reflected by the changing sources of income of fisher households, which now include occupations outside the fisheries sector in service industries, agriculture, transport, construction and elsewhere. The polarization within the small-scale fisheries sector in developing and developed countries is indicated by fishermen, who previously worked full-time and are now reducing their level of fishing to the level of part-time or occasional fishing while at the same time seeking employment outside the fisheries sector, often of a seasonal nature.

Others who remain in the small-scale fisheries sector are using more technologically advanced fishing craft, gear and fishing and fish-finding methods to increase the economic efficiency and profitability of their fishing operations. The short-term rate of return on invested capital of small-scale fishing boats in developing and developed countries likewise can be relatively high as shown by a recent global study carried out by FAO.[16] These trends of diversification of livelihoods and techno-economic and occupational polarization in small-scale and coastal marine fishing are also reflected by the fact that globally, the number of full-time fishing

15. See A. Poonnachit-Korsieporn, *Coastal Fishing Communities in Thailand*, Bangkok, Regional Office for Asia and the Pacific (FAO, 2000): 185–186; also U. Tietze, G. Groenewold and A. Marcoux, *Demographic Change in Coastal Fishing Communities and its Implications for the Coastal Environment*, FAO Fisheries Technical Paper 403 (Rome: FAO, 2000): 76, 96.

16. See U. Tietze, J. Prado, J.-M. Le Ry and R. Lasch, *Techno-economic Performance of Marine Capture Fisheries*, FAO Fisheries Technical Paper 421 (Rome: FAO, 2001): 5–10.

households is declining, while the number of part-time and occasional fishing households is increasing.[17]

Diversification trends and processes, coupled with conservation safeguards, need to be supported and strengthened by any new projects and programs to be implemented in the context of medium- and long-term tsunami rehabilitation efforts. Such programs might also draw and build upon lessons from the ongoing pilot initiatives in this field. These could usefully serve as comparative examples for other tsunami-affected countries.

In micro-enterprise development and supporting microfinance and training/extension services, FAO recently assisted the Indian Government in organizing a national workshop on best practices in microfinance programs for women in coastal fishing communities in India.[18] The main workshop objective was to analyze and document recent experiences with microfinance programs and micro-enterprise programs for women in coastal fishing communities in India and to draw conclusions with regard to best practices in this field.

All major stakeholders (i.e., senior representatives of central and state fisheries administrations, financial institutions, fisheries research, extension and training institutions and foundations, fishermen's and women's associations, and a sample of NGOs) participated in the workshop. A number of viable fisheries and non-fisheries micro-enterprises, which are and can be undertaken by women in coastal fishing communities in India, were identified in terms of activity, location, investment cost and credit needs, the number of women to be involved in each activity, training requirements and linkages with organizations and institutions that can provide the necessary support.

These enterprises include marine aquaculture activities (i.e., mussel culture, oyster culture and crab fattening); freshwater aquaculture activities (i.e., backyard hatcheries for giant freshwater prawns and carp seed nurseries); fish processing activities (i.e., fish smoking, fish drying, preparation of "Maldives fish," preparing battered and breaded fish products for bakeries, caterers and restaurants); the preparation of silage from fish waste; shell craft production; provision of services (i.e., fish vending stalls, fish fast food counters, setting up and maintenance of aquariums, contract cleaning of fish and other markets, net making); and agricultural activities (i.e., organic growing of vegetables on leased land, ornamental plant nurseries and the preparation of compost).

---

17. See *Numbers of Fishers 1970-1997*, FAO Fisheries Circular No. 929, Revision 2 (Rome: FAO, 1999).

18. L. V. Villareal and M. A. Upare, *Report of the National Workshop on Best Practices in Microfinance Programmes for Women in Coastal Fishing Communities in India.* Panaji, Goa, India, 1–4 July 2003, FAO Fisheries Report No. 724 (Rome: FAO, 2003).

As one follow-up to the workshop, the Indian Government established a core group, which is coordinating and monitoring the implementation of the workshop's recommendations. These include the preparation of location-specific action plans for the large-scale introduction of micro-enterprises and alternative income-generating activities in coastal fishing communities in India, with a special focus on women. The work in progress in India could serve as an example for other tsunami-affected countries.

The diversification of livelihoods and promotion of alternative income-generating activities and micro-enterprises require the availability of start-up and working capital and thus the access to microfinance and rural credit services. The UN has declared the year 2005 as the International Year of Micro-credit. The United Nations General Assembly Resolution 52/94 of 18 December 1997 acknowledged the important contribution that microfinance programs have made to poverty eradication and empowerment of the poor. It called upon the organizations of the UN system to include a microfinance approach in their programs. Microfinance is defined as the provision of a broad range of services, including loans, savings and insurance. Perhaps the best known example of such a system is that of the Grameen Bank and Muhammad Yunus' own critique, while perhaps a bit starry-eyed, nevertheless warrants careful examination.[19]

Microfinance programs can be a powerful tool in poverty alleviation and in the medium- and long-term rehabilitation of the tsunami-affected fishing communities in the countries bordering the Indian Ocean. In the case of fishing and fish-farming communities, the alleviation of poverty is an important precondition for their participation in efforts to rehabilitate and conserve the aquatic environment and fisheries resources. This again is likely to create conducive conditions for the implementation of the FAO Code of Conduct for Responsible Fisheries and the sustainable use of fisheries resources.

Recent experiences with microfinance in fisheries and aquaculture have been documented by FAO and guidelines and case studies have been published.[20] The guidelines set out general principles and basic consider-ations for those involved in providing microfinance services to fisheries and aquaculture and for those who intend to include fishing and fish-farming communities as part of the client base of their operation. The guidelines further elaborate on lending models, methodologies and policies that have applicability to fisheries and address concerns that are particular to the sector, while adhering to best practices in the microfinance field.

19. M. Yunus, "The Grameen Bank Story: Rural Credit in Bangladesh," in A. Krishna, N. Uphoff, and M. J. Esman eds., *Reasons for Hope* (West Hartford, Conn.: Kumarian Press, 1997): 9–24.

20. U. Tietze and L. V. Villareal, *Microfinance in Fisheries and Aquaculture. Guidelines and Case Studies,* FAO Fisheries Technical Paper 440 (Rome: FAO, 2003).

The publication also contains a summary of the proceedings and recommendations of the Report of the Regional Workshop on Microfinance Programmes in Support of Responsible Aquaculture and Marine Capture Fisheries in Asia. This workshop was held in Chiang Mai, Thailand from 16 to 20 December 2002. An overview of recent experiences with microfinance programs in fisheries and aquaculture in Asia is given and conclusions are drawn regarding future directions and initiatives in this field. The workshop was attended by 31 participants from eight South and Southeast Asian countries: Bangladesh, India, Malaysia, Nepal, the Philippines, Sri Lanka, Thailand and Viet Nam. It brought together experts representing fisheries government institutions, financial institutions, academic and research institutions, NGOs, cooperatives, women's unions, fishermen's associations and technical staff of foreign-assisted projects in aquaculture in the region.

The publication concludes with two examples of successful FAO-executed projects that incorporated microfinance programs in fishing community development in the Philippines and in small-scale aquaculture development in Viet Nam, with a special focus on gender and poverty alleviation. The case studies provide practical examples of how micro-credit can contribute to the empowerment of women in fishing and fish-farming communities, help alleviate poverty and contribute to the socio-economic well-being and food security of fishers and fish farmers. The lessons learnt from such guidelines and case studies could well be useful for those who are designing similar programs for the tsunami-affected countries.

Risk Management and Protection against the Effects of Natural Disasters through Mutual Insurance Programs

Future long-term rehabilitation efforts in the tsunami-affected countries should certainly include the introduction of mutual insurance programs, which give protection against the effects of natural disasters. However, these efforts have to acknowledge past experiences in Asia with insurance programs in fisheries and aquaculture.[21]

The management of risks inherent in fisheries and aquaculture is an important element of the overall management of fisheries and aquatic resources. In the past, a number of countries, including most of those affected by the recent tsunami waves, have taken steps to provide a measure of protection against part of the risks inherent in fisheries and aquaculture by setting up insurance schemes of various kinds.

21. M. Hotta, *Fisheries Insurance Programs in Asia—Experiences, Practices and Principles,* FAO Fisheries Circular No. 948 (Rome: FAO, 1999).

In response to this interest on the part of governments in the region and the agencies concerned with fisheries insurance, the Regional Conference on Insurance and Credit for Sustainable Fisheries Development in Asia was held at Nihon University in Tokyo in November 1996 under the auspices of FAO, the Asia and Pacific Rural and Agricultural Credit Association (APRACA) and the National Federation of Fishery Cooperative Associations of Japan (Zengyoren). The conference provided a forum for interaction between policy-makers and technicians on matters relating to fisheries insurance and an opportunity to discuss the experiences of the countries involved in the insurance practices. The conference was attended by participants from Bangladesh, India, Indonesia, the Islamic Republic of Iran, Malaysia, Federated States of Micronesia, Nepal, the Philippines, Republic of Korea, Sri Lanka, Thailand, Viet Nam, Japan and Norway as well as by observers from Bolivia, Brazil, Senegal and Tunisia.

There was a growing consensus among the countries of the Asian region regarding the importance of fisheries insurance, even in countries where insurance schemes had yet to be implemented (such as Nepal, the Philippines, Thailand and Viet Nam). Existing insurance schemes, however, had only limited success. Yet there are exceptions such as accident and life insurance programs for fishermen in India, which have been successfully implemented, with the help of fishermen's cooperatives, where they exist; such programs have in fact contributed to strengthening fishermen's cooperatives.

The performance of past fisheries and aquaculture insurance programs in the tsunami-affected countries and other developing countries in Asia had been poor and at best mixed, particularly with regard to financial viability, as a result of high loss ratios, high administrative costs and inadequate coverage of insurance needs in tsunami-affected countries such as Indonesia, Sri Lanka, Malaysia and India.

Participants observed that government financial support is critical to introduce such programs and sustain them during their initial operation. They noted that, without this support, the private sector is not in a position to absorb the costs of establishing such programs on its own. The importance of fisheries to national economies, in terms of food security, employment and foreign exchange earnings, all justify some level of government support in order to establish insurance programs. Donors and IFIs might want to assist governments of the tsunami-affected countries in their efforts.

It should be noted that while, initially at least, government subsidies may be necessary to encourage participation in new insurance programs by offering insured parties affordable premium rates, financial support may also be required for a reinsurance plan. Such assistance, however, must be within the terms of the Agreement on Subsidies and Countervailing

Measures of the World Trade Organization (WTO).[22] This is especially important for countries that are major exporters of raw and processed fish such as all of the tsunami-affected countries in Asia.

The conference stressed further that fisheries insurance should be viewed from the perspective of small-scale fishermen and fish farmers, who comprise the majority of the fishing population in developing countries, as well as in those particularly affected by the tsunami. These fishermen need protection against losses caused by natural disasters, particularly in areas where typhoons and tropical storms are common and often damage or destroy the investments of small-scale fishermen and fish farmers as has just happened again on an unprecedented scale with the tsunami disaster. The conference also recognized that government support to insurance schemes should not only include financial aspects, formulation of insurance policy and setting up schemes, but should also motivate industry and the private sector to participate.

Participants noted that, in addition to financial constraints, a number of technical and institutional issues need to be addressed, which can not only affect program implementation but also hinder the establishment of insurance schemes. Among these issues are the following: inadequate benchmark data on the extent of damage to vessels, gear, catches and production, ponds and installations; a wide variety of diverse fishing and aquaculture practices; little apparent demand for insurance; lack of a government policy with respect to insurance; lack of an institutional arrangement to connect village-level participants with the programs; lack of trained personnel familiar with insurance programs; lack of coordination among relevant agencies; long delays in settling claims; lack of an appropriate legal and regulatory framework; and lack of necessary infrastructure.

Whether insurance is voluntary or compulsory is often an issue for fisheries management. In Malaysia the fishermen's personal accident insurance scheme worked reasonably well, partly because it had been made compulsory and linked to the licensing of fishing vessels.

In many countries, including Sri Lanka, India and Thailand, insurance is linked to bank credit programs. Financial institutions, which lend to the fisheries and aquaculture sector, have an incentive to lend when assets financed by the loans are insured, thus reducing the risk to the institution and making possible increases in lending and investment in the fisheries sector.

22. The Agreement on Subsidies and Countervailing Measures ("SCM Agreement") addresses multilateral disciplines regulating the provision of subsidies, and the use of countervailing measures to offset injury caused by subsidized imports; available online: <http://www.wto.org/english/docs_e/legal_e/24-scm.pdf>.

The advantages and benefits of fisheries insurance can be summarized as protecting fishermen and fish farmers against accidents and natural hazards beyond their control; providing basic compensation for the loss of or damage to fishing vessels, gear and catch (or harvest), thus contributing to the stabilization of incomes within the fisheries sector; reducing the risk to financial institutions, which provide credit to fishermen and fish farmers, in relation to fisheries credit; reducing the risk for fishermen and fish farmers in investing their own resources in the adoption of new technologies and acquiring improved equipment; fostering mutual assistance and cooperation among fishermen, fish farmers and their organizations; reducing the unpredictable burden on governments of providing emergency assistance in the wake of natural disasters; promoting stability in fishery enterprises; contributing to the general welfare of fisheries communities; and stabilizing the contribution of the fisheries sector to national economies.

While it should be noted that the information and case studies, upon which the conference's conclusions and recommendations were based, date from the early 1990s, the main observations and conclusions would probably have considerable validity for current times.

CONCLUSION

The rehabilitation, in the long-term, of the livelihoods of the tsunami-affected fishermen, fish farmers and their family members will only be successful if past omissions and mistakes are rectified. Above all, coastal fishing and fish-farming communities must be efficiently linked to the emerging early warning systems for natural disasters in countries bordering the Bay of Bengal and the Indian Ocean, with particular attention to earthquakes and related tsunami waves.

It will not be possible to achieve a close linkage of coastal communities and early warning systems unless these communities are far more closely involved in the management and conservation of coastal areas, including coastal lands, intertidal lands and inshore waters, where people live and pursue their occupations. This means that fishermen need ready access to all information that affects their livelihood as well as a strong voice in land-use decisions that affect their community. These include new developments such as the construction of hotels and tourist facilities, jetties and ports, power plants and infrastructure, especially when in or near mangrove areas.

Another important precondition for the long-term sustainable rehabilitation of livelihoods is the reversal of unsustainable fishing and fish-farming practices and capacities and the adoption of environmentally friendly and sustainable ones. This again can only realistically be achieved if fishermen and fish farmers are actually involved—at various levels—in the management of fisheries and aquaculture resources and fishing and fish-farming efforts and—equally important—if their social, economic, local community and occupational concerns are seriously taken into consideration. This is particularly important when coastal area profiles are being prepared, management issues are being identified, management measures and projects are being designed and implemented to address the issues, and monitoring mechanisms are put into place to assess the impact of these measures and projects on the issues identified. The FAO guidelines on the collection of demographic and socio-economic information on fishing communities for use in coastal and aquatic resource management referred to above, can be used in this process.

The pilot testing of the guidelines in the Philippines, carried out in close cooperation with the University of the Philippines in the Visayas and the Banate Bay and Southern Iloilo Resources Management Councils, shows that information collected with the concerned government agencies—which play a role in rural development, planning, health care, housing, employment, etc.—not only serves the purpose of cost- and time-efficient collection of information, but also fosters a close cooperation between local communities and these agencies in the identification and monitoring of important issues to be addressed by management measures and projects and in the implementation of the measures and projects themselves.

Likewise, when the impact of management and conservation measures and regulations is being monitored, it is crucial that in addition to environmental, biological and ecological indicators, indicators also for the social and structural economic well being of coastal households and communities are used for monitoring and evaluation purposes. This makes the management and conservation processes and their results more transparent, guides the processes toward providing social and economic benefits to coastal populations and, at the same time, assures these populations that their social, economic and occupational concerns are taken into consideration when important resource management decisions are made. This again can only encourage active participation.

Risk management in the form of the introduction of mutual insurance programs that also cover, to a large extent, damages caused by natural disasters such as the recent tsunami, needs to be made an integral part of coastal fisheries and aquaculture management rather than relying on occasional government interventions in the form of welfare measures and grants to victims. While governments need to play a role in the field of legislation and provide financial support through reinsurance or otherwise, it is essential that the insured also have to make a contribution and are aware of and share risks related to the location of their houses, landing sites and fish farms, and the adoption of safety-at-sea measures, for example.

As described above, many of the tsunami-affected countries have experience, on a limited scale and sometimes on a pilot scale, with, among others, community-based coastal fisheries management programs, insurance programs, safety-at-sea programs, environmental conservation programs and programs in support of the introduction of responsible fishing and aquaculture practices. Lessons have been learnt and shared and there are many good reasons for a large-scale introduction of many of the programs previously operated on a pilot scale.

The need to implement long-term livelihoods and fisheries and aquaculture rehabilitation with global and donor support, which is at present available and was endorsed by the Twenty-sixth Session of the FAO Committee on Fisheries, held in Rome from 7 to 11 March 2005, should make it more urgent and opportune to apply the lessons learnt on a large scale for the benefit of coastal fishermen and fish farmer communities.

Last, but not least, the recent demographic trend of a stagnation and even a decline in the numbers of fishermen in many coastal areas together with the trend of livelihood diversification, including seeking employment outside the fisheries sector, and the awareness of communities of the problems of over-fishing and degradation of the environment shown in recent studies, should create a conducive environment for endeavors to involve these communities in a more meaningful and comprehensive way in coastal fisheries management and conservation and ultimately in the long-term rehabilitation of their livelihoods.

Delineation and Delimitation of Sub-National Maritime Boundaries: Insights from the Philippines

Jay L. Batongbacal
JSD Candidate, Dalhousie University Law School, Halifax, Canada

BACKGROUND

Since the early 1900s, Philippine law has recognized the concept of "municipal waters," a maritime zone appurtenant to coastal municipalities and cities over which they exercise fisheries licensing powers. In subsequent decades, and three iterations of the Fisheries Act, the breadth and scope of this maritime zone was extended and modified. The current Philippine Fisheries Code of 1998 (hereafter the Fisheries Code) defines municipal waters as follows:

> Municipal waters—include not only streams, lakes, inland bodies of water and tidal waters within the municipality which are not included within the protected areas defined under Republic Act No. 7586 (The NIPAS Law), public forest, timber lands, forest reserves or fishery reserves, but also marine waters included between two (2) lines drawn perpendicular to the general coastline from points where the boundary lines of the municipality touch the sea at low tide and a third line parallel with the general coastline including offshore islands and fifteen (15) kilometres from such coastline. Where two (2) municipalities are so situated on opposite shores that there is less than thirty (30) kilometres of waters between them, the third line shall be equally distant from the opposite shore of the respective municipalities.[1]

The sundry provisions of the Fisheries Code, combined with scattered sections of the Local Government Code of 1991,[2] grant more than 800 coastal municipalities and cities local powers to generate revenues from the

---

1. *Philippine Fisheries Code of 1998*, Republic Act No. 8550, 10th Cong. (Philippines), 5th special sess., 17 February 1998, Sec. 4(58).
2. *Local Government Code of 1991*, Republic Act No. 7160, 5th Cong. (Philippines), 5th sess., 10 October 1991.

Ocean Yearbook 20: 41–78.

use of fisheries and aquatic resources, enforce fisheries and environmental laws, allocate municipal fisheries and aquatic resources among local residents, and exercise considerable control over the geographically-included waters for the purposes of fisheries and environmental management. Especially in the late 1990s, the allocation of fisheries and environmental jurisdiction in favor of coastal municipalities and cities has been a welcome event for non-governmental organizations (NGOs) and international development agencies, providing a window for partnership with local governments in all kinds of community-based co-management projects.

However, in spite of nearly a century of being in the law books, the provisions on municipal waters had never been actually implemented in terms of clear technical rules and guidelines of delineation and delimitation. Ironically, the ambiguous concept of municipal waters had become the main obstacle to effective management, due to the absence of local maritime jurisdictional boundaries. This proved fatal to many attempts at law enforcement, which was seen as the solution to massive problems of illegal fishing. Since violations of the Fisheries Code and municipal fisheries ordinances were technically criminal offences, proof beyond reasonable doubt required clear evidence of the geographical boundaries within which the offence was committed. Only the national government, with a handful of fisheries law enforcement officers based in the national capital region, and the occasional Deputized Fish Wardens, were tasked with the duties of policing the waters along the country's more than 17,800 km of coastline and 7,107 islands. It was only by seeking assistance from the national government, exercising general law enforcement powers, that the local governments could take action against violations. Almost every case of a fisheries law violation was mired in legal technicalities and jurisdictional issues, more often ending in acquittal of the violator.[3]

THE BATTLE FOR MUNICIPAL WATERS

In 1999, the Coastal Resource Management Project (CRMP) being implemented by the Department of Environment and Natural Resources (DENR) identified the lack of municipal water boundaries as a primary stumbling block to its implementation of the project in its pilot municipalities. At the First Conference of Coastal Municipalities of the League of Municipalities of

---

3. For more information on the challenges faced by local fisheries law enforcement, see R. F. Sievert and D. A. D. Diamante-Fabunan, "People Power vs. Illegal Fishing: Can It Work?," *Overseas: The Online Magazine for Sustainable Seas* 3: 2 (February 2000), available online: <http://www.oneocean.org/overseas/200002/people_power_vs_illegal_fishing.html>.

the Philippines held that May, the League of Municipalities of the Philippines (LMP), the umbrella organization of municipal local government units, issued Resolution No. 1, Series of 1999, requesting then-President Joseph Estrada to direct the proper government agencies to finally establish the municipal water boundaries.[4] The Coastal Resource Management Project then sponsored a series of meetings of an *ad hoc*, inter-agency group together with the National Mapping and Resource Information Authority (NAMRIA) to focus on drafting technical guidelines to delineate and delimit municipal waters. As part of this group, I had undertaken the task of drafting the technical guidelines, and after at least five revisions, we arrived at a consensus document that was taken for field-testing in September 1999. Several workshops were sponsored by the Bureau of Fisheries and Aquatic Resources (BFAR) to test the implementation of the guidelines in the provinces of Surigao del Norte, Surigao del Sur, Masbate, Bohol, Davao Oriental, and the municipalities surrounding Davao Gulf.

    The guidelines drew upon the provisions of the United Nations Convention on the Law of the Sea,[5] and provided for the establishment of municipal water boundaries using normal and straight baselines. Since the Philippines is an archipelagic country, and a number of cities and municipalities were also comprised of islands, the guidelines also provided for the establishment of "municipal archipelagic baselines." The procedure for delineation and delimitation was fairly straightforward: upon the request of a local government unit, the National Mapping and Resource Information Authority would schedule a preliminary delineation workshop in the requesting local government unit's area. The preliminary results would then be officially charted and transmitted to the local government unit for purposes of publication and public hearing. The publication was required to be made particularly for the other adjacent, opposite, or otherwise affected local government units. At the hearings, comments and objections would be noted, and if necessary, negotiations for adjustment of the boundaries could be undertaken with the affected municipalities or cities. Based on the inputs, the delineation and delimitation would be validated, finalized, and certified by the National Mapping and Resource Information Authority. The coordinates and charts would then be sent back to the local government units, in order for them to enact a municipal ordinance that

    4. League of Municipalities of the Philippines (LMP), "A Resolution Calling for the Enactment/Implementation of Measures Empowering the Local Government Units for Integrated Coastal Development." *LMP Resolution No. 01, Series of 1999* (28 May 1999). Also available online: <http://www.oneocean.org/overseas/may99/resolution_01.html>.

    5. United Nations Convention on the Law of the Sea, 1982, entered into force, November 1994, available online: <http://www.un.org/Depts/los>.

defined their municipal waters. Included in the guidelines was an annex produced by the National Mapping and Resource Information Authority for the workshops, which provided instructions on how a simple delineation and delimitation could be drawn by ordinary citizens of the municipalities and cities using a transparent sheet with concentric circles printed on it, the appropriate chart, and pencils. The purpose of this was to make the initial process of delineation and delimitation transparent, participatory, and less technical. Any inaccuracies could be checked and corrected by the National Mapping and Resource Information Authority through more sophisticated means later, but at least the general configuration of the boundaries could already be seen and more importantly, accepted by the participants. This simple method was pivotal in demonstrating to the representatives of the local government units how the resulting configuration of their municipal water boundaries was created purely on the basis of the guidelines.[6]

The guidelines were then taken to the Secretary of Environment and Natural Resources, under whose administrative supervision the National Mapping and Resource Information Authority fell, for signature. As it turned out, this was not an easy task. There was reluctance on the part of then-Secretary Antonio Cerilles, and it became necessary for the Coastal Resource Management Project to engage in coalition-building and endorsement-seeking among people's organizations, non-government organizations, and local government units in order for the document to be given attention. It found its most prominent ally in the NGOs for Fisheries Reform, or NFR, a long-standing coalition of non-government organizations who were instrumental in lobbying for the passage of the Fisheries Code in 1998 and who were actively campaigning for its full implementation. This was followed by resolutions from many municipal legislative councils requesting the National Mapping and Resource Information Authority to delineate their municipal waters;[7] some provincial governments also urged the promulgation and implementation of the guidelines.[8] Political wran-

6. See Annex 1.
7. See, for example, Resolution No. 170, Series of 2000 of the Municipality of Sibonga, Province of Cebu (16 November 2000); Resolution No. 01–006, Series of 2001 of the Municipality of Loon, Province of Bohol (15 January 2001); and Resolution No. 2001–09, Series of 2001 of the Municipality of Tubigon, Province of Bohol (23 January 2001).
8. See, for example, in January 2000 Governor Antonio Kho of Masbate Province wrote a letter officially endorsing the guidelines and urged Secretary Antonio Cerilles to formally issue them as an administrative order of the Department of Environment and Natural Resources. At the same time, the Provincial Legislative Council of Bohol Province issued Resolution No. 2001–039, also requesting Secretary Cerilles to promulgate the guidelines. Both the Masbate and Bohol Provinces were areas wherein the procedures in the draft guidelines were initially tested.

gling and changes in administration also intervened, notably the ousting of President Joseph E. Estrada and his replacement by President Gloria Macapagal-Arroyo in 2000. After the transitory period of the fledgling government, it took more than 2 years of lobbying through 3 different Secretaries of Environment and Natural Resources before the guidelines were signed and promulgated as DENR Administrative Order No. 17, Series of 2001 (hereafter DENR Administrative Order 17) on June 11, 2001, by Secretary Heherson Alvarez.[9]

Within days of publication, the commercial fishing sector, which operated under national government licenses that did not apply to municipal waters, held a press conference and denounced the Order for "closing" lucrative fishing grounds. The problem is that under the Fisheries Code, municipal waters are reserved for the municipal fishermen, i.e., those fishing in boats weighing 3 gross tons or less, and commercial fishers were prohibited from engaging in fishing within the 15 kilometer band of municipal waters. The delineation and delimitation of municipal water boundaries essentially established with clarity the limits within which commercial fishing boats could not operate, and thus eliminated the legal loopholes that previously protected their operations close to shore. The commercial fishing sector also decried the provisions of DENR Administrative Order 17, which provided for the use of municipal archipelagic baselines in the case of municipalities and cities comprised partly or wholly of islands. They argued that this resulted in an unacceptable extension of the municipal waters, depriving the commercial fishers of even more fishing grounds. The sector called for the immediate revocation of the delineation and delimitation guidelines, and warned that even the poor man's fish would disappear if the call was not heeded.[10]

In response, the coalition of NGOs and people's organizations, led by the NGOs for Fisheries Reform, that had built up around the endorsement of the Order issued a Unity Statement that contradicted the commercial fishing sector's claims.[11] The NGOs inaugurated a broad-based alliance composed of over 100 NGOs and grass roots people's organizations from across the country, publicized a strong statement of support for DENR Administrative Order 17, and initiated a campaign to quickly implement the guidelines and protect it from revocation.[12] They linked up with the League of Municipalities of the Philippines, which officially represented all the municipalities and cities of the country, and the League of Vice-Governors

9. See Annex 1.
10. R. Villanueva, "'Galunggong' May Soon Disappear," *Today* (15 June 2001).
11. CERD, et al., *Unity Statement* (10 July 2001).
12. "Ipatupad ang DAO 17! (Implement DAO 17!)" *Overseas: The Online Magazine for Sustainable Seas* 5: 10 (October 2001), available online: <http://oneocean.org/overseas/200110/appeal.html>.

of the Philippines comprised of the Vice Governors of the 78 provinces, both of which issued resolutions expressing support.[13] Soon, they consolidated into a multi-sectoral coalition called Movement for DAO-17 (DENR Administrative Order 17), or M-17. Very few other coalitions in the Philippines had such a broad-based composition bound by a common interest.

The commercial fisheries sector had its own campaign, undertaken at the highest levels of government. Meetings with the President were reportedly held asking her to intervene.[14] The Department of Agriculture, particularly the Bureau of Fisheries and Aquatic Resources (BFAR) supported the commercial fisheries sector's cause, but could not do so openly in deference to inter-departmental courtesy.[15] Implementation of the guidelines was in fact suspended for a time, purportedly in deference to seeking a legal opinion from the Secretary of Justice on the validity of the guidelines, only to resume again when he declined to issue an opinion.[16] The commercial fisheries sector brought the issue to the Committee on Appropriations of the House of Representatives, which first tried to pressure Secretary Alvarez to revoke DENR Administrative Order 17, and then later, together and the Office of the Legal Counsel of the House, issued unusual separate legal opinions that "declared" the existence of "legal infirmities" in DENR Administrative Order 17, particularly its use of the archipelagic doctrine, and in the issuance of the guidelines by DENR rather than the Department of Agriculture.[17] The commercial fishers filed cases in local

13. See LMP, "ND Resolution 05–2001: Resolution of Support to the DENR Administrative Order No. 17 Series of 2001 Entitled Delineating/Delimiting Municipal Waters," *Overseas: The Online Magazine for Sustainable Seas* 4: 10 (08 October 2001), available online: <http://www.oneocean.org/overseas/200110/lmp_resolution.html>. See also "Chronology of Events Related to DAO 17: History of the Struggle," *Overseas: The Online Magazine for Sustainable Seas* 6: 3 (March 2003), available online: <http://www.oneocean.org/overseas/200303/chronology_of_events_related_to_dao17.html>.

14. R. Basilio, "NGOs Support AO Defining New Limit of Municipal Waters," *Cyberdyaryo* (06 November 2001), <http://www.cyberdyaryo.com/features/f2001_1106_01.htm>.

15. See "Chronology of Events Related to DAO 17: History of the Struggle," n. 13 above.

16. Department of Justice (Philippines), *Opinion No. 62 s. 2001* (23 October 2001).

17. See "Chronology of Events Related to DAO 17: History of the Struggle," n. 13 above. The issuance of these legal opinions is unusual since the Government of the Philippines is modelled after the American system, and therefore these opinions patently violate the principle of separation of powers between the Legislature and the Judiciary.

courts seeking the annulment of the guidelines, but failed to secure a restraining order.[18]

These political maneuverings were not without impact; over the next few months, key members of M-17 had to deal with an almost constant see-sawing of opinions and commitments among various officials of the national government. M-17 and Secretary Alvarez held fast to a "no-compromise" stance, linked the delineation and delimitation issue to the establishment of effective fisheries management and law enforcement to enable local governments to protect their marine resources and food security, and emphasized the need to apply the archipelagic principle not merely as a matter of technicality but also a matter of legal principle. This forced the commercial fisheries sector to back off from their original aim of outright revocation, and shift to a less drastic solution. Attempts were made to negotiate amendatory guidelines, and a special formula was proposed for delineation with respect to municipalities with islands. But both sides of the debate eventually dug into their respective positions and reached an impasse.

With the political struggle taking place within the national offices and the resumption of implementation after the Secretary of Justice declined to issue a legal opinion, the Coastal Resource Management Project, the National Mapping and Resource Information Authority, the League of Municipalities of the Philippines, the NGOs for Fisheries Reform, and elements of M-17 coordinated a veritable race to undertake the delineation and delimitation of municipal water boundaries. Aside from the Coastal Resource Management Project areas, provinces acting through their provincial governments or congressional representatives, and the Fisheries Resource Management Project (FRMP) of the BFAR, became the springboards for delineation and delimitation activities. Using the simplified and participatory methods of technical delineation and delimitation devised by the National Mapping and Resource Information Authority, representatives[19] and constituents[20] of the municipalities and cities were called to bay-wide or province-wide meetings at which they were fully briefed on the guidelines, provided with charts and tools, and asked to jointly carry out the preliminary delineation of their waters. Normally, within a day, the

---

18. *Alliance of Philippine Fishing Federations, et al. v. Hon. Heherson Alvarez, et al.,* Civil Case No. 01–102-MM, Regional Trial Court of Malabon, Metro Manila (17 July 2001) and *Pablo Sarabia, Sr. v. Heherson Alvarez, et al.,* Civil Case No. 669-C, Regional Trial Court of Negros Occidental (9 May 2002).

19. These were usually comprised of either the mayor or vice-mayor, members of the local legislative councils, and representatives from the municipal planning and development office.

20. Normally, these were comprised of members of local fishermen's cooperatives, associations, and NGOs operating in the area.

participants were able to draw the limits of their respective waters themselves, and have them validated by the National Mapping and Resource Information Authority staff. These workshops were held under a cooperative and problem-solving setting, and not only provided the local government units with a venue to carry out maritime boundary delineation, but also the opportunity for actual boundary negotiations. In most cases, contentious issues such as fishery disputes between local government units were resolved and settled through these sessions, and only in a few cases were disputes left undecided. Generally, the workshops were good opportunities for the local government units to discuss common problems in fisheries management and discuss ways and means of further cooperation.[21]

By March 2002, implementation of DENR Administrative Order 17 had resulted in boundary delineations and delimitations on a wide scale, as shown in Table 1 by the statistics compiled by the National Mapping and Resource Information Authority. But that same month, a newly appointed Secretary of Environment and Natural Resources, Elisea Gozun, replaced Heherson Alvarez, and was confronted by the Committee on Appointments in Congress with a legal opinion, issued by an Acting Secretary of Justice (a new Secretary was set to be appointed), declaring that it was the Department of Agriculture, not the Department of Environment and Natural Resources, which had the authority to issue guidelines for delineation and delimitation of municipal waters.[22] She immediately issued an order revoking DENR Administrative Order 17,[23] and suspending implementation until new guidelines were issued by the Department of Agriculture. The National Mapping and Resource Information Authority was directed to stop entertaining further requests for delineation and delimitation of municipal waters, but finalize all reports and charts for those municipalities whose municipal waters had already been delineated and delimited.

The likewise newly appointed Secretary of Agriculture, Luis Lorenzo Jr., took an eminently practical approach. He viewed the contentious issues as revolving mainly around local government units with islands. He accepted in principle that municipal waters had to be delineated and delimited for law enforcement purposes, that the national government's poverty alleviation program based on agriculture required the definition of the marine municipal jurisdictions, and that the archipelagic principle could not be dispensed with. The main issue for him was how to accommodate the commercial fishing sector's imminent loss of fishing grounds.

21. Mr. Mar Guidote, Coordinator, Coastal Law Enforcement Alliance—Region 7 (CLEAR-7), CRMP, pers. comm., (8 March 2002).
22. Department of Justice, *Opinion No. 100 s. 2002* (27 November 2002).
23. Department of Environment and Natural Resources, *Administrative Order No. 2003–07* (17 March 2003).

Table 1.—Status of Implementation of DENR Administrative
Order 17 as of March 2003

Status	Coastal provinces	Coastal Cities			
		W/o islands	W/islands	Opposite/ adjacent	Sub-total
Delineated	65	39	22	12	73
Validated	41	30	19	11	60
To be validated	24	9	3	1	13
Status	Coastal Towns				
	W/o island	W/island	Opposite/ adjacent	Sub-total	TOTAL
Delineated	393	279	170	842	915
Validated	317	194	102	613	673
To be validated	76	85	68	229	242

Source: National Mapping and Resource Information Authority

One of the Secretary's trusted assistants, Assistant Secretary Benjamin Tabios Jr., was tasked to convene an inter-agency group and consider new guidelines, this time divided between a set of guidelines for those local government units with islands, and another set of guidelines for those local government units without islands. The draft of the first set of guidelines was a verbatim copy of DENR Administrative Order 17, except for the portions providing for the rules of delineation for local government units with islands and the application of the archipelagic principle. A draft of the second set of guidelines applicable to municipalities with islands was fairly similar, but provided islands other than the mainland of the municipality with municipal waters either only 3 kilometers wide, or based on the 7-fathom isobath. Multi-sectoral consultations were arranged in different cities of the country at which public input was sought on the new guidelines.[24]

M-17 mobilized its constituents to repeatedly and prominently demand the re-enactment of DENR Administrative Order 17 *in toto* at every consultation. The League of Municipalities of the Philippines expressed in no uncertain terms at every forum, and were echoed by the various groups of NGOs and POs who managed to get themselves invited to participate.[25]

24. R. Dela Cruz, "Public say in fishery measure in the wraps." *The Manila Times* (25 March 2004). Also available online: <http://www.manilatimes.net/national/2004/mar/25/yehey/business/20040325bus6.html>.

25. Critics of the consultations complained that they were not given sufficient publicity and the invitations to them were selective. The M-17 network, however, was able to monitor the consultations, regularly update its members, and mobilize the necessary constituents through an electronic mailing list. Informal reports on what

The Department of Agriculture revised its proposal by providing for a differential application of the archipelagic principle, which it promoted as a "win-win" formula. This complicated formula treated islands in different ways: those within 5 kilometers of the mainland were to be enclosed in municipal archipelagic baselines, those between 5.01 to 15 kilometers did not generate their own municipal waters, while those beyond 15 kilometers from the mainland generate 3 to 5 kilometers of municipal waters subject to agreement between the local government unit concerned and the Department of Agriculture.[26]

In January 2004, the Department of Agriculture issued the "guidelines for delineation and delimitation of municipal water boundaries of cities and municipalities without offshore islands."[27] But despite an announcement the following month that the second set of guidelines covering municipalities with islands had been prepared,[28] continuing controversy has prevented its promulgation,[29] and over a year later as of this writing, the Department of Agriculture has still not moved forward on the matter.

REFLECTIONS AND LESSONS LEARNED

This article synthesizes reflections and observations of the author over the process in which he took an active part. Little information is available on any similar process of sub-national and participatory maritime boundary delineation and delimitation activities in other countries, although examples abound of local fisheries disputes between local communities and municipal units. Having been at the center of the policy-making and policy-implementation process in this instance, some insights drawn directly from the author's experience might prove useful for other nations considering decentralized and devolved fisheries management jurisdictions. Especially

occurred during these consultations were provided to the author. Mr. Buddy dela Cruz of the NGOs for Fisheries Reform (NFR), separate e-mails to the author, 13 July 2003, 17 November 2003, and 25 November 2003.

26. Mr. Mar Guidote, Coordinator, Coastal Law Enforcement Alliance for Region-7, CRMP, pers. comm. (12 March 2004).

27. Department of Agriculture. *Administrative Order No. 1, Series of 2004* (14 January 2004). Full text also available at *OneOcean:* <http://www.oneocean.org/download/db_files/DAO–2004–01.pdf>.

28. R. Dela Cruz, "DA Says Fishing Area Limits to Hurt Sector." *The Manila Times* (16 February 2004), available online: <http://www.manilatimes.net/national/2004/feb/16/yehey/business/20040216bus 10.html>.

29. R. Dela Cruz, "Heated discussions delay issuance of second set of fishery guidelines," *The Manila Times* (04 March 2004), available online: <http://www.manilatimes.net/national/2004/mar/04/yehey/business/20040304bus7.html>.

for advocates of community-based co-management, the author hopes that the Philippines' experience with the basic task of drawing legally recognized local maritime boundaries as a basic step in establishing the management regime may be particularly helpful and valuable.

1. *Local communities can be capacitated to directly undertake even the technical task of maritime boundary delineation and delimitation. There is a process of self-realization inherent in this activity that enables them to arrive at mutually acceptable results that not only comply with technical requirements but also satisfy perceptions of justice.*

Although the technical rules contained in the DENR Administrative Order 17 drew upon the language of the Law of the Sea Convention in setting forth rules for basepoints and baselines, the task of delineation was not left to the geodetic engineers alone. Indeed, the preliminary delineation task was directly and deliberately given over to members of the coastal communities concerned, comprised of local fishermen, local legislative council members, and local people from different walks of life. This was done through a simplified system using pencils, charts, compasses, rulers, and a plastic sheet of concentric circles. Members of adjacent and opposite municipalities were asked to undertake the delineation exercise in groups. This enabled a uniform and transparent application of the technical rules that was understandable to all, sidelining issues that may arise from scientific or "expert" interventions. The visual and manual procedure of delineation allowed even those who had not passed secondary school to participate in a highly technical undertaking.

The advantage posed by this simple process is that it also provided the opportunity for the participants to immediately discuss concrete problems and issues that the establishment of the local maritime boundaries posed for their own constituents. By undertaking the delineation and delimitation themselves, the participants establish a common appreciation of the situation and are able to use the activity as a starting point for discussing and negotiating ways and means of addressing the needs of those who are perceived to be disadvantaged. Since they themselves participated in the process of drawing those boundaries, there was little dispute about who should be entitled to a particular extent of municipal waters; rather, the discussion turned to questions of how neighbors could accommodate each others' citizens, given the configuration and circumstances of the municipal waters before them.

It is of course inevitable that maritime boundary delimitations may result in some municipalities acquiring more expansive municipal waters than others, especially in the case of municipalities that have the misfortune of being located inside the curve of a bay or gulf. This also means that maritime boundary delineations inevitably raise questions of justice in allocation, which are most important for local community groups who may be directly dependent on the resources that are affected by such boundaries. Rather than side-stepping the issue of justice by throwing it to outside technical expertise, a participatory method of delineation such as the one outlined in this article allows those stakeholders to directly appreciate and then try to resolve those issues themselves. The joint process of delineation and delimitation undertaken face-to-face also provided the venue for negotiations and accommodation of the interests of disadvantaged municipalities.

2. *The revelation of local maritime boundaries through a participatory process of delineation and delimitation enables local communities to concretely identify and characterize their own fishery disputes, and establishes a common ground which can open the way for their amicable settlement.*

In instances where there were fishery disputes between municipalities, the delineation and delimitation workshops allowed the participants to concretize their fishery disputes and appreciate its geographic scope clearly. Having identified the geographic extent of the dispute, the municipalities concerned were able to establish the parameters of their common problems and focus their thoughts and discussions more concretely toward more effective and mutually acceptable solutions. In a sense, the problem became more manageable and solvable, as it was no longer perceived as a problem of "keeping outsiders away" from some unseen border through "more effective law enforcement." This standard approach was no longer the only solution available, and alternatives such as establishment of buffer zones or fish sanctuaries in problem areas, became much more attractive against undelineated fishery boundary disputes.

Prior to the delineation and delimitation exercises, local fisheries disputes were often known to exist but could not be immediately resolved due to threshold issues such as the entitlement to resources and extent of legal jurisdiction; these threshold issues often took on a "legal" character that could only be resolved through litigation, which was uncommon and excluded practical considerations such as the impacts of the delineation on the community. A more inclusive approach to management of municipal waters, i.e., one that accommodated both residents and non-residents, became possible with the process outlined above. This provided the opportunity for resort to extra-judicial means of resolving the disputes.

3. The establishment of local maritime boundaries may themselves provide the incentive and basis for reforms in fisheries legislation.

The issuance of the DENR Administrative Order 17 led to the clear polarization and consolidation of fishers interest groups across the country. By consolidating around their respective policy positions, each sector found a clearer voice, and their opinions became more accessible and concise, allowing the policy debate to be shorn of clutter and expressed more understandably for the wider public. Both sectors became more visible and their sectoral solidarity and respective positioning allowed for a clearer appreciation of the sides of the dispute.

The alliances brought to the fore by this event helped to reinforce the networks of local fishing communities and their organizations around a central rallying point. It also galvanized the formerly amorphous and disjointed commercial fisheries sector on the other end of the debate. The commercial fisheries sector, which normally operates from communities other than those in whose waters they operate, found itself isolated and marginalized, and for all its power and influence over the political elite, it could not convincingly push its hard-line agenda of ensuring unfettered and open access to municipal waters. Arrayed against it was a coalition of local governments, NGOs, people's organizations, and even some national government officials, and a compromise solution appears inevitable.

At the time of this writing, the government's tardiness in issuing a second set of guidelines applicable to local government units with islands seems to be understandable. Its greater dilemma is how to allow access to the commercial fisheries sector to waters from which they are actually legally barred, since the Fisheries Code definition does not allow for anything less than a 15 kilometer zone from the shoreline. Implementing the letter of the law will likely either decimate the commercial fisheries sector, which reportedly cannot operate beyond the municipal water limits, or require a complete restructuring of the commercial fishing industry into smaller and less efficient fleets of municipal fishing boats. This problem cannot be resolved within the current framework of the Fisheries Code, and requires major legislative reforms, some of which are now pending in the legislature. Among the options are to reduce the municipal waters zone to less than 15 kilometers, change the definition of municipal fishing to accommodate commercial fishing vessels, expressly allow certain types of commercial fishing within the 15-kilometer zone, and to devolve regulatory jurisdiction over commercial fishing to local governments. It remains to be seen which of the many possible solutions will actually be adopted in legislation.

4. Agency capture by the commercial fishery sector need not necessarily be an irresolvable situation, and the process of local coalition-building and networking among affected and disempowered local fisher communities and allied parties can provide a means for effectively engaging against vested interests.

While the commercial fishers may have found their ally in the BFAR in a typical example of agency capture, the resulting outcome was not as one-sided and partisan as would have been expected. The establishment of the broad-based M-17 alliance, founded upon a clear understanding and implementation of the delineation and delimitation process and its basis in science and law, generated sufficient counterforce even against national government agencies or their officials at the highest levels. Although the revocation of the DENR Administrative Order 17 was ultimately a frustrating outcome, things are not as terrible as they seem because the majority of the municipalities still retain the maximum extent of their waters as defined under the DENR Administrative Order 17.

Even the compromise formula offered by Department of Agriculture in its second set of guidelines, with its differential application of the archipelagic principle, may still establish waters not so far removed from what would have resulted from a straightforward application of the DENR Administrative Order 17. Out of 915 coastal municipalities and cities, only 301 had islands as part of their territories. Of these, 75 percent had islands less than 5 kilometers from the mainland, 18 percent had islands within 5.1 to 10 kilometers, and 10 percent had islands beyond 10 kilometers.[30] This means that less than 10 percent of the total number of municipalities in the Philippines would fit the situation feared by the commercial fisheries sector, that of a municipality whose municipal waters would be extended so far and expanded so much as to deny them significant fishing grounds. For the remaining 90 percent of the coastal local government units, the delineation and delimitation exercise was still a substantial victory.

5. A participatory process of delineating and delimiting local maritime boundaries can become a process of promoting further cooperation among the affected local governments.

The participatory process of the delineation and delimitation process under the DENR Administrative Order 17 was an enabling and empowering process that allowed local stakeholders not only to concretely appreciate the limits of their jurisdictional boundaries, but also realize that such boundaries were an important first step in fully understanding the issues

30. Mr. Mar Guidote (n. 26 above).

concerning their management of the coastal fisheries, and the appropriate means to resolve them. Despite the division of their coastal waters, participants quickly recognized that additional measures need to be undertaken to manage the activities occurring around the boundaries, including the need for inter-municipal cooperation, coordination, and at times, compromise for such matters as licensing, monitoring, and law enforcement.

The joint determination of jurisdiction also encouraged a sense of joint implementation and enforcement, initiating further collaboration between the participants. This "good neighbor" policy leads to a greater solidarity and cooperative spirit among most concerned communities in the management of their marine areas. In some provinces such as Cebu and Bohol, the delineation exercise strengthened the practice of establishing and maintaining joint law enforcement operations and facilitating the operations of teams of multi-sectoral fisheries law enforcement officers and deputies against commercial fishers illegally operating in their waters. This promoted efforts to pool scarce resources and further cooperation among cash-strapped municipalities in managing their coastal resources.

CONCLUSION

The establishment of sub-national maritime boundaries may provide a means for more effective management of coastal fisheries. However, the delineation and delimitation exercise need not be undertaken through a centralized and top-down approach in which the national government, through agency experts, unilaterally divides the coastal waters between the coastal municipalities and cities. The Philippine experience with sub-national maritime boundary-making demonstrated that the process is a very important social issue, because it can affect the perceived allocation of resources among resource users and bring conflicts among competing groups into much sharper focus. This makes it even more imperative that the delineation and delimitation process be perceived as transparent and its results be seen as mutually acceptable. An expert-driven, highly technical approach to delineation and delimitation may not necessarily be conducive to these conditions.

The sub-national maritime boundary-making attempted in the Philippines may provide a good example of how to establish a transparent and participatory process that could produce mutually acceptable outcomes and at the same time provide the opportunity for competing resource users to clarify their concerns, and perhaps encourage them to start resolving them. A participatory approach provides the added benefits of promoting solidarity and cooperation among the concerned stakeholders, and allows the delineation and delimitation process to be more than a mere technical procedure. It makes maritime boundary-making a more profound and empowering process of building social unity among commonly-situated community groups, and of clarifying festering issues between competing sectors in order to prepare them for broader consideration, and hopefully, eventual resolution.

ANNEX 1.—DENR ADMINISTRATIVE ORDER
(NO. 2001–17), JUNE 11, 2001

SUBJECT: GUIDELINES FOR DELINEATING/DELIMITING MUNICIPAL
WATERS

Pursuant to Article 1 on National Territory of the 1987 Constitution, Presidential Decree No. 1599 dated June 11, 1978, Section 123 of Republic Act 8550, otherwise known as the Philippine Fisheries Code of 1998, and Executive Order No. 192 dated June 10, 1987, the following regulations and guidelines governing the delineation and delimitation of municipal waters of the country are hereby promulgated:

Section 1.   Basic Policy

It is the policy of the State to protect the rights of the people, especially the local communities with priority to marginal fisherfolks, in the preferential use of the municipal waters. The delineation/delimitation of municipal waters will define the geographic extent of the city or municipality's taxation or revenue-generating powers, its law enforcement jurisdiction, resource allocation, and general management powers.

Section 2.   Definition of Terms

For the purposes of this manual, the following definition of terms shall be used:

Adjacent municipalities—coastal municipalities sharing a common land boundary point on the coast

Archipelago—a group of islands, including parts of islands, interconnecting waters and other natural features which are so closely related that such islands, waters, and other features form an intrinsic geographical, economic, and political entity, or which historically have been regarded as such

Awash—flush with or washed by waves

Baseline—the line from which the outer limits of municipal waters are projected

Basepoint—a point on land from which baselines are drawn

Cay—a low, flat island of sand, coral, or other material which is awash or dries during low water

Coast—the edge or margin of land next to the sea

Coastal terminal point—a boundary point on the coast, common to two adjacent municipalities

Coastline—the line where the shore and water meet

Construction line—a temporary drawing line used in determining a final line, e.g., a boundary line, or points used to determine that final line

Delimitation—the determination of boundaries of municipal waters between adjacent or opposite municipalities where the delineation of their respective waters show that their respective municipal waters overlap

Delineation—the determination of the outer limits of the municipal waters of a municipality

Drying reef—a reef or part of it which dries at low tide

Fringing reef—a reef directly attached to the shore or located in its immediate vicinity

General coastline of the municipality—refers to the coastline of the mainland and offshore and/or fringing islands of the municipality

High water or high tide—refers to the highest level reached at a place by the water surface in one oscillation

Island—a naturally formed area of land, surrounded by water, provided that where the island is surrounded by the sea, the same should also always be above the water at high tide

Lateral boundary—the municipal water boundary between two adjacent municipalities

Low water or low tide—refers to lowest level reached at a place by the water surface in one oscillation

Low water line or low water mark—the intersection of the plane of low water with the shore; the line along a coast or beach to which the sea recedes at low water

Mainland of the city or municipality—the land area of the municipality within which the municipal capitol is located

Median line or *equidistance line*—a line every point of which is equidistant from the nearest points on the coasts of two municipalities

Municipal archipelagic baseline—a baseline used in cases where the municipality is composed of islands or has offshore and/or fringing islands

Normal baseline—the baseline described by the coastline of a municipality, where such coastline is relatively smooth and simple and there are no outlying or fringing islands, reefs, rocks, pinnacles, or other abutting features

Opposite municipalities—municipalities not sharing land boundaries but having coastlines which face each other and are less than thirty (30) kilometers apart

Pinnacle rock—a sharp pointed rock rising from the bottom, which may extend above the surface of the water

Reef—a mass of rock or coral which either reaches close to the sea surface or is exposed at low tide

Rock—a formation of natural origin that constitutes an integral part of the lithosphere, which may or may not always be above high tide

Rock awash—rock awash according to chart datum (usually low water)

Sandbar—a shallow portion of the coast, largely made of loose sand that is near the surface of the water

Shoal—an offshore hazard to navigation on which there is a depth of ten (10) fathoms or twenty (20) meters or less, composed of unconsolidated material except coral or rock

Straight baseline—a baseline used in cases where the coastline is deeply indented or cut into

Tidal water—any water the level of which changes periodically due to tidal action

Section 3. Coverage

The coverage of this administrative order shall be all the municipal waters as defined by Sec. 4(58) of RA 8550, which include, not only streams, lakes, inland bodies of water and tidal waters within the municipality which are not included within the protected areas as defined under RA 7586 (The NIPAS Law), public forest, timber lands, forest reserves or fishery reserves, but also marine waters included between two (2) lines drawn perpendicular to the general coastline from points where the boundary lines of the municipality touch the sea at low tide and a third line parallel with the general coastline including offshore islands and fifteen (15) kilometers from such coastline. Where two (2) municipalities are situated on opposite shores that there is less than thirty (30) kilometers of marine waters between them, the third line shall be equally distant from opposite shore of the respective municipalities. This administrative order shall not be construed to preclude special agencies or offices in exercising their jurisdiction over municipal waters by virtue of special laws creating these agencies such as, but not limited to, the Laguna Lake Development Authority and the Palawan Council for Sustainable Development, pursuant to Sec. 17 of RA 8550.

Section 4. Role/Responsibility of Agencies

In order to have an efficient and effective flow of activities in the delineation/delimitation of municipal waters, the role of the agencies involved are herein provided:

1. Department of Environment and Natural Resources (DENR)

    1. As the mother agency, oversee the activities being conducted by NAMRIA;

    2. Provide the implementation mechanism for the delineation/delimitation;

    3. Provide assistance/support and participate in the conduct of public hearing through its field offices, units, agencies, programs, and projects.

2. National Mapping and Resource Information Authority (NAMRIA)

   1. Delineate or delimit the boundaries of municipal waters on maps or charts of appropriate scale as requested by the local government units;

   2. Provide the local government units proposed maps and technical descriptions of the maps before the conduct of the public hearing;

   3. Approve the maps, charts, and technical descriptions as a result of the delineation/delimitation of municipal waters;

   4. Participate in public hearings and consultations conducted in relation to the delineation/delimitation of municipal waters and take note of comments, inputs, suggestions, reactions or objections to the proposed delineation/delimitation;

   5. Revise maps, charts, or technical descriptions as a result of the public hearing;

   6. Approve an official copy of maps, charts, and technical descriptions and provide the approved maps to the municipality/city concerned;

   7. Provide technical assistance relevant to delineation and delimitation of municipal waters;

   8. Act as the repository of all technical descriptions and corresponding original maps or charts of all municipal waters;

   9. Conduct actual verification of boundary limits as required.

3. Local Government Units

   1. Request the NAMRIA to delineate/delimit the boundaries of their municipal waters;

   2. Conduct public hearings and consultations in relation to the proposed delineation/delimitation;

   3. Settle disputes with adjacent or opposite municipalities arising from the delineation/delimitation through the *Sangguniang Bayan/Panglungsod* or *Panlalawigan* or in any appropriate body;

   4. Enact ordinances setting forth the extent of its municipal waters, incorporating thereof the maps or charts and technical descriptions.

4. Other Agencies and/or Entities

   Other agencies and/or entities that are involved in the management and development of municipal waters should assist in the delineation/delimitation of municipal waters. Information (map, technical descriptions, etc.) of areas under their administrative jurisdiction should be provided.

Section 5.   Systems and Procedures

A.   Requirements to Start Delineation Process

1.   Filing of Request for Delineation

All requests for delineation and delimitation of municipal waters shall be directed to the Administrator of the NAMRIA, through the Director of the Coast and Geodetic Survey Department.

A request may be made by any of the following:

a) a city or municipality individually or jointly with other cities/municipalities with whom common boundaries are shared, through a resolution of the *Sangguniang Panglung-sod* or *Sangguniang Bayan*;

b) a province on behalf of all of its coastal municipalities, through a resolution of the *Sangguniang Panlalawigan*;

c) a national government agency on behalf of any city or municipality, through a formal letter/request signed by the head of the agency, but only with the conformity of the affected local government unit/s, expressed in form of a resolution of the *Sanggunian* concerned which shall be attached to the letter/request.

A copy of the resolution or letter/request shall be furnished by the NAMRIA to:

a) the DENR Community Environment and Natural Resources Office (CENRO) and/or the relevant DENR Regional Office;

b) the BFAR;

c) any adjacent or opposite municipality which may be affected by the delineation and/or delimitation;

d) the Regional Office of the Philippine National Police Maritime Group (PNP-MARIG);

e) any special agency having jurisdiction over coastal waters which may be excluded from municipal waters in accordance with the Fisheries Code (e.g., the Protected Area Management Board (PAMB) with respect to areas under the NIPAS Act);

f) any affected private parties or sectors which the city or municipality may deem fit to notify.

2. Basic Technical Requirements for Requesting Entity

The filing of request for delineation must include basic technical requirements such as:

a) a list of known or named islands and maps of said islands under the jurisdiction of the municipality whose municipal waters are to be delineated and delimited; and

b) a copy of the legislation/proclamation creating the municipality or city.

3. Response

The NAMRIA through the Director of the Coast and Geodetic Survey Department shall schedule the delineation and delimitation of the municipal waters of the municipality. A copy of the response shall also be furnished to any adjacent or opposite municipality, which may be affected by the delineation and/or delimitation.

B. Procedure for Delineation and Delimitation of Municipal Waters

1. Delineation of Municipal Waters

a) *Use of normal baselines*

i. Where the coastline is not deeply indented or cut into, and there are no outlying or fringing islands, reefs, or rocks, the normal baseline shall be the low water line.

ii. The normal baseline shall determine the general coastline of the municipality for purposes of delineation and delimitation.

iii. The outer limits of the municipal waters of the municipality shall be determined by a line parallel to the normal baselines and fifteen (15) kilometers therefrom.

b) *Use of straight baselines*

i. Where the coastline is deeply indented and/or there are outlying or fringing reefs or rocks, the outermost points of the coastline may be connected by straight baselines, provided that the length of such baselines does not exceed thirty (30) kilometers.

ii. In such cases, the straight baselines shall determine the general coastline of the municipality for purposes of delineation and delimitation.

iii. Reefs, rocks, cays, shoals, sandbars, and any other features which are submerged during high tide shall not be used as basepoints. Neither shall they have their own coastlines.

iv. The outer limits of the municipal waters of the municipality shall be determined by a line parallel to the straight baselines and fifteen (15) kilometers therefrom.

c) *Use of municipal archipelagic baselines*

i. Where the territory of a municipality includes several islands, the outermost points of such islands shall be used as basepoints and connected by municipal archipelagic baselines, provided that the length of such baselines shall not exceed thirty (30) kilometers.

ii. The municipal archipelagic baselines shall determine the general coastline of the municipality for purposes of delineation and delimitation.

iii. Islands, isles, or islets located more than thirty (30) kilometers from the mainland of the municipality shall have their own separate coastlines.

iv. Rocks, reefs, cays, shoals, sandbars, and other features which are submerged during high tide shall not be used as basepoints for municipal archipelagic baselines. Neither shall they have their own coastlines.

v. The outer limits of the municipal waters of the municipality shall be enclosed by a line parallel to the municipal archipelagic baselines and fifteen (15) kilometers therefrom.

d) *Combination of baselines*

A combination of normal and straight baselines, or normal and municipal archipelagic baselines, may be used depending on the circumstances and in the interest of simplicity in determining the general coastline and delineating municipal waters.

2. Delimitation of Adjacent Municipal Waters

a) Where the general coastline is not curved or irregularly shaped at the coastal terminal point of the land boundary common to two (2) adjacent municipalities, the lateral boundary shall be determined by a line perpendicular to the general coastline at the terminal point.

b) Where the general coastline at the point where the land boundary touches the sea is curved or irregularly shaped, making the determination of a perpendicular line impossible, the lateral boundary between two (2) adjacent municipalities may be determined by either of the following methods, depending on the complexity of the coastline:

i. Simplified bisection

The lateral boundary shall be determined as follows:

i.a) Examine the direction of the general coastline on both sides of the common coastal terminal point. On each side of the common point, draw a straight line, a short baseline, whose length shall be limited to the point where the direction of the general coastline changes significantly or veers to another quadrant (see Fig. 1 for illustration).

FIG. 1. Lateral Boundary.

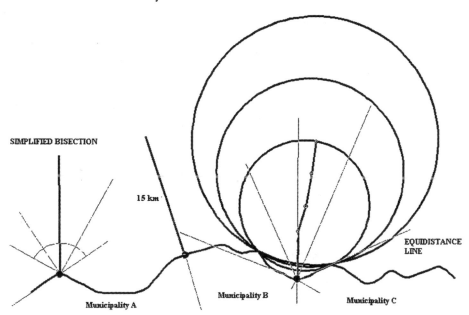

Source: National Mapping and Resource Information Authority (NAMRIA).

i.b) Draw perpendicular lines to the coastlines on both sides of the common terminal point, passing through this common terminal point. Bisect the angle formed by the two perpendicular lines. The bisector is the lateral boundary of the municipal waters between the adjacent municipalities. The bisector will extend to fifteen (15) kilometers if the coastlines beyond the short baselines will no longer affect its equidistance from both coastlines; otherwise, it will extend only up to a distance beyond which the equidistance line method shall already be applied (see Fig. 1 for illustration).

i. *Equidistance line*

The lateral boundary shall be determined by a line equidistant from the coastlines of the adjacent municipalities, as determined through the use of the baselines under Paragraphs 1a through 1d of Section 5B.

3. Delimitation of Opposite Municipal Waters

In the case of opposite municipalities which are less than thirty (30) kilometers apart, the municipal water boundaries between them shall be determined by the median or equidistance line between the general coastlines of the respective municipalities, as determined through the use of the baselines under Paragraphs 1a through 1d of Section 5B.

4. Delimitation of Municipal Waters of Three or More Adjacent and Opposite Municipalities

In cases where three or more municipalities are so situated that they have overlapping municipal waters, the delimitation of the lateral and offshore boundaries of their municipal waters shall be determined by the equidistance line method. The lateral boundaries will usually end at a point which is common to three or more municipalities, at the offshore boundary.

5. Municipal Water Boundary Delimitation Prior to Republic Act No. 8550

Where two municipalities have actually delimited the boundaries of their municipal waters prior to the enactment of Republic Act No. 8550 in 1998, in accordance with the law prevailing at the time, and pursuant to the procedure prescribed therein, such previous boundary delimitation shall be respected and given effect as far as may be practicable in the light of the provisions of the Fisheries Code of 1998 and the application of the guidelines in this manual in order to respect prior vested rights.

6. Finalization Only After Approval

The technical description of municipal waters shall be deemed final only after the boundaries of municipal waters have been duly approved by the concerned city or municipality as evidenced by a final and executory ordinance embodying the same. Each boundary corner common to two (2) adjacent or opposite municipalities shall have exactly the same geographic position.

7. Depth Curve

Where practicable, the seven (7) fathom depth curve within the municipal waters shall be clearly indicated on the charts provided by the NAMRIA.

8. Demarcation of Marine Reserves, Sanctuaries, or Other Special Areas

If within or overlapping with the municipal waters, there is a marine reserve, sanctuary, or other special area under the exclusive jurisdiction of an entity other than the municipality, a clearance shall be obtained by the NAMRIA from said entity prior to the inclusion of the boundaries of such reserve, sanctuary, or special area, or such part thereof which overlaps with the municipal waters so as to effectively exclude the same from the computation of the area of municipal waters. Provided that the protected seascape or marine reserve area shall be managed by local governments according to the mandate and responsibilities as provided in the NIPAS Law. Nothing in this provision shall prevent the National Government from declaring any portion of municipal waters as Protected Areas or Marine Reserves.

C. Publication and Public Hearing

1. Public Hearing

The NAMRIA shall submit to the requesting city or municipality a preliminary delineation of the municipal waters, and delimitation thereof with respect to any adjacent or opposite municipality, drawn on maps or charts of appropriate scale, and accompanied by a technical description. Such delineation and/or delimitation shall be in accordance with the technical guidelines set forth in Section 5B hereof.

The requesting city or municipality shall cause the publication of the map or chart clearly showing the delineation and/or delimitation of municipal waters, through

  a) posting in prominent places in the city or municipality;

  b) dissemination of copies of the same to all the component *barangays*; and *c)* furnishing copies, through regular channels, to any cities or municipalities affected.

In accordance with regular processes and practices, the requesting city or municipality shall conduct the same for public hearing and consultation for the purpose of receiving comments, inputs, suggestions, reactions, or objections to the proposed delineation and/or delimitation. The NAMRIA shall be present at the public hearing to document and consider such comments, inputs, suggestions, reactions, or objections.

Adjacent or opposite municipalities may, if they so decide for purposes of convenience and practicality, jointly hold the public hearings.

2. Disputes with Adjacent or Opposite Municipalities

If adjacent or opposite municipalities, as well as agencies having jurisdiction over defined coastal waters, or any interested parties, raised any objection to the preliminary delineation and/or delimitation of municipal waters, such objection shall be made in writing, in the form of a Resolution of the *Sangguniang Bayan* or *Panglungsod* concerned, or an official letter from the responsible officer or person, and officially presented at public hearing.

a) Amicable Settlement Encouraged

In case of boundary conflict, this guideline shall not prevent the municipalities concerned from negotiating or mutually agreeing to common municipal water boundaries provided there is substantial compliance with the provisions of the law. Such negotiated boundaries shall be submitted to the NAMRIA for verification. The NAMRIA may also provide technical assistance and advice to the municipalities in the course of their negotiations.

The delimitation of municipal water boundaries in accordance with a negotiated settlement shall be certified by the NAMRIA prior to its finalization and submission for enactment as an ordinance. Certification of such negotiated boundaries shall not be denied under normal circumstances.

b) Irreconcilable Differences

In case the municipalities cannot settle their differences amicably through negotiation, and the differences are based on the proper application of technical rules and guidelines, they shall jointly submit the issue to the NAMRIA for decision. The NAMRIA shall inform the municipalities of its decision within thirty (30) days from the submission of the issue.

c) Disputes Before Other Fora

Where at the time of the delineation and/or delimitation, the dispute is pending before another forum on account of substantial issues that go beyond the application of technical rules and guidelines (e.g., when there is a pending case before a regular court over ownership and/or jurisdiction over islands or other features), the NAMRIA may, in the meantime, delineate and determine the temporary municipal water boundaries between the contesting municipalities, without considering the contested islands or features, provided that the affected municipalities agree to such temporary delimitation, provided further that the temporary delimitation shall be subject to the outcome of the dispute as determined by the concerned forum.

D. Revision and Finalization

1. Certification of Final Map

The NAMRIA, after considering the inputs from the public hearing, or the outcome of the dispute settlement mechanisms set forth in Paragraph 2 of Section 5C, shall revise the delineation and/or delimitation, and within thirty (30) days from the date of the last public hearing, or last meeting under Paragraph 1 of Section 5C, provide an official copy of the revised maps, charts, and technical descriptions to the requesting city or municipality. Such maps, charts, and technical description shall be duly certified by the NAMRIA Administrator as comprising the final and definitive delineation and/or delimitation of municipal waters.

2. Enactment of Ordinance

After the receipt of the revised and certified delineation or delimitation, if any, or of the date of the last public hearing if no revision was necessary, the requesting city or municipality shall enact an ordinance setting forth the extent of its municipal waters, incorporating the maps, charts, and technical descriptions prepared and verified by NAMRIA as an integral part of the ordinance, provided that in enacting the ordinance, no amendments shall be made to the maps, charts, or technical descriptions prepared and approved by NAMRIA.

Once the ordinance has become final and executory, the original copy must be submitted to the NAMRIA and official copies thereof shall be provide to the following:

a) any adjacent or opposite municipalities affected by the delimitation;

b) the BFAR;

c) the Regional Office of the PNP-MARIG;

d) any concerned special agency having jurisdiction over coastal waters which may be excluded from municipal waters;

e) any affected party or sector the city or municipality may deem fit to notify;

f) the DENR field office.

3. Repository Function

The NAMRIA shall be the repository of all technical descriptions and corresponding maps or charts of all municipal waters. An official copy of such technical descriptions and maps or charts shall be provided to the municipality concerned.

Section 6. Fees and Costs

For the delineation of municipal waters that would be conducted by NAMRIA, each city/municipality shall be charged with a service fee of PhP 5,000.00 plus PhP 50.00 per kilometer of coastline of the municipality exclusive of field expenses. NAMRIA shall likewise charge a verification fee of PhP 5,000.00, wherever applicable.

Section 7. Transitory provision

These guidelines shall be immediately effective in delineating municipal waters in all cities and municipalities except those which have offshore islands or islets for which the delineation process shall start six (6) months from the effectivity of these guidelines.

Section 8. Repealing Clause

All orders, rules, and regulations inconsistent with or contrary to the provisions of these Guidelines are hereby repealed or modified accordingly.

Section 9. Effectivity

This Administrative Order shall take effect fifteen (15) days after its publication in newspaper of general circulation.

Signed: HEHERSON T. ALVAREZ
Secretary of Environment and
Natural Resources

TECHNICAL ANNEX
METHODS/PROCEDURES FOR DELINEATING
MUNICIPAL WATERS

A. USING NORMAL BASELINES

The normal baseline is the baseline described by the coastline of a city or municipality, where such a coastline is relatively smooth and simple and there are no outlying or fringing islands, reefs, rocks, pinnacles, or other abutting features (see Fig. 2).

FIG. 2. Normal Baseline. Only protruding points usually count or have impact on the offshore limit.

1. Using fifteen (15) kilometers (on a scale of the chart or map where the municipal waters will be delineated) as radius and a point on the coastline at low tide as center of circle, draw arcs of circles from different points on the coastline of the municipality. Allow these arcs to intersect.

2. Select the outermost arcs that have been drawn. These arcs form the offshore limit of the municipal waters. Note that not all points along the coastline contribute to the delineation of this offshore limit. Usually, only the protruding points of the coastline do count and have the most impact.

B. USING STRAIGHT BASELINES

A straight baseline is the baseline used in cases where the coastline is deeply indented or cut into (see Fig. 3).

1. Join protruding points along the coastline by straight lines, the length of which should not exceed thirty (30) kilometers.

FIG. 3. Straight baselines on irregular, deeply indented coastline.

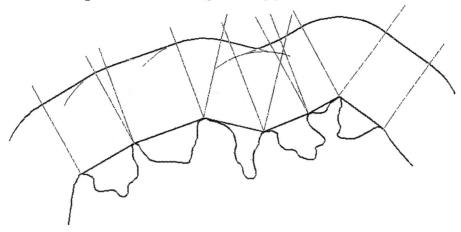

2. Draw perpendicular lines passing through the basepoints of each baseline.

3. From the basepoints, measure fifteen (15) kilometers offshore along the perpendicular lines. Connect the offshore points on the perpendiculars of each baseline. The line joining these offshore points is parallel to the baseline.

4a. When the exterior angle formed by two consecutive baselines is more than 180 degrees, draw an arc of circle, using fifteen (15) kilometers as radius and the common basepoint of the two baselines as center of circle, from one perpendicular to the other perpendicular. The offshore limit of the municipal waters, measured from these two baselines, is the line consisting of the arc and the two parallel lines.

4b. When the exterior angle formed by two consecutive baselines is less than 180 degrees, no arc of circle is drawn. The offshore limit of the municipal waters, measured from these two baselines, is the line consisting of the intersecting two parallel lines.

5. The offshore limit of the entire municipal waters consists of the lines determined in (4a) and (4b).

C. USING ARCHIPELAGIC BASELINES

Archipelagic baselines are straight lines joining the outermost points of islands of a municipality.

1. Municipality with offshore islands

Join the outermost points of the municipality by straight lines, beginning from one coastal terminal point (a boundary point on the coast, common to two municipalities) on the mainland of the municipality; then to the outermost islands; then to the other coastal terminal point of the municipality; provided that the length of each line shall not exceed thirty (30) kilometers; provided further that an isolated island of the municipality, if any, distant more than thirty (30) kilometers from any of the other islands of the municipality, shall generate its own municipal waters. More than one point on an island can be used as basepoint (see Fig. 4).

Fig. 4. Archipelagic Baseline. Municipality with offshore islands.

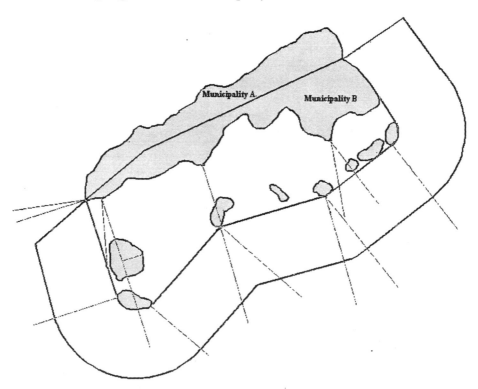

2. Municipality composed of islands

   a. Join the outermost points of the outermost islands by straight lines; provided further that the length of each line shall not exceed thirty (30) kilometers; provided further that an isolated island of the municipality, if any, distant more than thirty (30) kilometers from any of the other islands of the municipality,

FIG. 5. Archipelagic Baselines. Municipality composed of islands distant not more than 30 KM from each other are joined by straight lines.

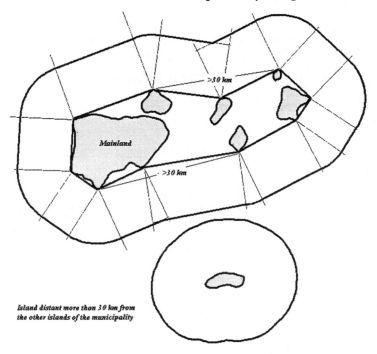

shall generate its own municipal waters. More than one point on an island can be used as basepoint (see Fig. 5).

Common to 1 and 2:

b. Draw perpendicular lines passing through the basepoints of each baseline.

c. From the basepoints, measure fifteen (15) kilometers offshore along the perpendicular lines. Connect the offshore points on the perpendiculars of each baseline. The line joining these offshore points is parallel to the baseline.

d1. When the exterior angle formed by two consecutive baselines is more than 180 degrees, draw an arc of circle, using fifteen (15) kilometers as radius and the common basepoint of the two baselines as center of circle, from one perpendicular to the other perpendicular. The offshore limit of the municipal waters, measured from these two baselines, is the line consisting of the arc and the two parallel lines.

d2. When the exterior angle formed by two consecutive baselines is less than 180 degrees, no arc of circle is drawn. The offshore limit of the municipal waters, measured from these two baselines, is the line consisting of the intersecting two parallel lines.

e. The offshore limit of the entire municipal waters consists of the lines determined in (d1) and (d2).

MANUAL METHOD/PROCEDURE FOR DELIMITING MUNICIPAL WATERS

When the delineation of municipal waters of adjacent or opposite municipalities produce overlapping areas, it is necessary to delimit municipal waters in order to allocate the overlapping areas between the municipalities concerned. Considering the archipelagic nature of the country, and the many configurations of the Philippine coastline, it is very likely that delimitation will be required by most coastal municipalities. In these cases, it is necessary to use a simple method of delimiting the municipal waters in a convenient and cost-effective manner.

The Enrique A. Macaspac Concentric Circles Method of Determining an Equidistance Line in Boundary Delimitation

The Enrique A. Macaspac Concentric Circles Method of Determining an Equidistance Line in Boundary Delimitation is based on the theory that the center of a circle is equidistant from any other point on the circumference of that circle. To use this method, concentric circles are drawn on a stable, transparent medium such as acetate paper. For municipal waters, the radius of the largest circle should be made equal to fifteen (15) kilometers on the scale of the nautical chart or topographical map where the municipal waters will be delineated and delimited. For convenience, the incremental radius of each circle shall be five (5) millimeters regardless of scale of chart or map.

The equidistance line is determined by connecting the equidistant points identified by the center of each circle whose circumference touches at least one point (point of tangency) on both coastlines of the neighboring municipalities, whether adjacent or opposite, whose municipal water boundaries are being determined. The use of this method facilitates the delimitation of the waters.

This method also offers the following advantages:

1. Convenience. Since the instruments used are simple and easily available (map or chart, compass, transparent medium like acetate paper, and pen or pencil), there is no need for expensive computer software or experts.

2. Simplicity. The method is very simple, requiring only patience and a sharp eye. Since even an ordinary person can use it, neighboring municipalities can easily check each other's work.

3. Speed. It eliminates the construction lines of other manual methods; thus it is faster.

4. Reasonable accuracy. This method is based on theory. There is no difference in the results using this method (E. A. Macaspac Concentric Circles Method) and the method which uses construction lines, described by A. L. Shalowitz in the Manual on the Technical Aspects of the United Nations Convention on the Law of the Sea. It also agrees very closely with computer-generated results from the software DELMAR (DELimitation of MARitime Boundaries). As long as the user is familiar with the use of maps, charts, and scales, the results produced will be reasonably accurate.

This method has been tested in pilot activities delineating and delimiting the municipal waters of the coastal municipalities in the provinces of Davao Oriental, Masbate, and Bohol.

FIG. 6. Lateral Boundary. E.A. Macaspac concentric circles method.

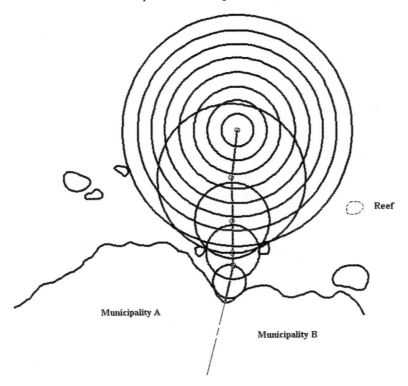

Procedure for Adjacent Municipalities

The delimitation of lateral boundaries starts from either the common coastal terminal points of the land boundaries of the adjacent municipalities, or from the offshore end of the lateral boundary fifteen (15) kilometers from the coastline (see Fig. 6).

1. Move the concentric circles to a point where the circumference of the circle touches at least one point each on both coastlines of the adjacent municipalities. No other points on the coastlines should be within that circle. Mark the center of the circle on the chart or map. This point on the chart or map now is equidistant from those two or more points on the coastlines of the two municipalities.

2. Repeat this step progressively, using the varying radii, until the coastal terminal point (if starting from the offshore end) or the fifteen (15) kilometer limit (if starting from the coastal terminal point) is reached.

3. Connect the marked points. The line represents the delimited lateral boundary of the municipal waters of the adjacent municipalities.

Procedure for Opposite Municipalities

The delimitation of the offshore boundary starts from one end of the common waters of opposite municipalities, to the other end (see Fig. 7).

FIG. 7. Concentric Circles Method—Opposite Municipalities.

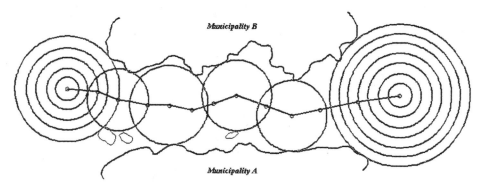

1. Move the concentric circles to a point where the circumference of a circle touches at least one point each on both coastlines of the opposite municipalities. No other points on the coastlines should be within that circle. Mark the center of the circle on the chart or

map. This point on the chart or map now is equidistant from those two or more points on the coastlines of the two municipalities.

2. Repeat this step progressively, using the varying radii, until the other end of the common waters is reached.

3. Connect the marked points. The line represents the delimited offshore boundary of the municipal waters of the opposite municipalities.

Procedure for Three or More Adjacent and Opposite Municipalities

The delimitation of the boundaries among three or more adjacent and opposite municipalities having overlapping municipal waters essentially follows the procedures for adjacent or opposite municipalities.

1. Delimit the lateral boundaries, two municipalities at a time. The lateral boundaries will usually end at a point which is common to three or more municipalities, at the offshore boundary.

2. Delimit the offshore boundaries. Between two tri-points is the delimited offshore boundary between two opposite municipalities. Tri-points are points along the median line equidistant from three points from the coastlines of three municipalities.

Confronting the Oceans Crisis: A Pacific Strategy

Laurence Cordonnery
Visiting Fellow, East-West Center, Hawaii, USA

In 2002, the Pacific Islands Forum leaders adopted the Pacific Islands Regional Ocean Policy (PIROP). Its goal is to "ensure the future sustainable use of our ocean and its resources by Pacific Islanders communities and external partners."[1] This Policy acknowledges the following essential facts: the ocean is a transboundary and dynamic resource; threats to the ocean's long-term integrity are increasing in both number and severity; and sustainable economic and social development in the region is dependent on wise use of the ocean and its resources.

More recently, in February 2004, the Pacific Islands Region Oceans Forum, held in Fiji, was the first step to envisage practical ways of implementing the Policy. This article aims to discuss the issues raised by the implementation of PIROP both at regional and national levels, and its potential as a tool to solve the oceans crisis. Although not legally binding, PIROP provides a framework for the formulation and implementation of sustainable development in the region. It is expected to provide the basis for articulating future national ocean policies and to harmonize national and regional actions for its implementation. Incidentally, it is the first attempt in the world to adopt such an integrated policy framework at an oceanic scale. In the global context of the oceans crisis, PIROP is therefore unique in its proactive approach to secure sustainable uses of the Pacific Ocean. Given the critical importance of marine resources to Pacific Islanders such proactiveness is not coincidental.

PROACTIVENESS AS A SURVIVAL STRATEGY FOR PACIFIC ISLAND COUNTRIES

Pacific Island Countries (PICs) are known to be ecologically fragile and vulnerable to natural disasters. Their small sizes, limited land resources,

---

1. The Pacific Islands Regional Ocean Policy is online at: <http://www.spc.int/piocean/forum/New/policy2.htm>.

Ocean Yearbook 20: 79–92.

geographic dispersion and isolation from markets, place them at a disadvantage economically, and prevent economies of scale. Indeed, one of their specificities is the reliance on a subsistence economy in parallel to a developing import-dominated cash economy. This, in turn, explains the major importance of coastal resources to local communities since fish and shellfish from inshore waters are the primary source of protein available. Insofar as offshore resources are concerned, the Western and Central Pacific Ocean provides the habitat for the world's largest and most valuable tuna resources, contributing 48 percent of the world's 4-million-tonne tuna catch in 2003.[2] According to the Secretariat of the Pacific Community, the Exclusive Economic Zones (EEZs) of PICs yield 78 percent of the Western and Central Pacific Ocean tuna catch,[3] with an estimated value of US$1.3 billion in 1999.[4] Given the limited economic development options available, the importance of tuna resources and their exploitation to the economic security and sustainable development of PICs are considerable and cannot be overstated. PICs have traditionally exploited tuna resources for local consumption; however, artisanal fisheries in comparison with industrial fishing activities undertaken by Distant-Water Fishing Nations (DWFNs) represent less than 10 percent of the total tuna catch. The negotiation of access agreements with DWFNs (USA, Japan, Taiwan, Korea, and China mainly) has therefore been the main strategy sought by PICs to obtain benefits from the foreign exploitation of tuna stocks present in their EEZs. Created in 1979, the Forum Fisheries Agency (FFA) has been mandated to promote regional cooperation and co-ordination amongst PICs in the management, conservation, legislation and fisheries policies for the tuna resources of its member countries.[5] FFA has also played a pivotal role in the elaboration of a regional regulatory framework for ensuring the long-term sustainability of tuna resources involving all stakeholders, including DWFNs.

2. In 2003, the total catch of the four main tuna species (albacore, bigeye, skipjack, and yellowfin) in the Western and Central Pacific Ocean was 1,973,665 tonnes, while the worldwide total catch was of 4,099,840 tonnes. T. A. Lawson ed., *Tuna Fishery Yearbook 2003* (Nouméa, New Caledonia: Secretariat of the Pacific Community, 2004).

3. A. D. Lewis, "The Status of Pacific Tuna Stocks: The Interaction of Biological, Boundary and Legal Issues in the Conservation and Management of Highly Migratory Species," (Paper presented at the *Pacem in Maribus XXVII* Conference, University of the South Pacific, Suva, Fiji, 7–12 November 1999).

4. G. Van Santen and P. Muller, "Working Apart or Together: The Case for a Common Approach to Management of the Tuna Resources in Exclusive Economic Zones of Pacific Island Countries," (Pacific Islands Discussion Paper Series, No. 10, The World Bank, Washington, D.C., 2000).

5. The FFA Convention is online at: <http://www.ffa.int>. This founding document details the FFA's origin, operation and role in regional fisheries cooperation.

This long series of dialogue between FFA Member States and DWFNs lead to the adoption of the Convention on the Conservation and Management of Highly Migratory Fish Stocks in the Western and Central Pacific in Honolulu, in 2000.[6] Another illustration of regional coordination can be found in the continued support of the Secretariat of the Pacific Community as a provider of scientific advice for the management of tuna stocks.[7]

RATIONALE FOR A REGIONAL OCEAN POLICY

Despite the regional cooperation achievements described above, a more fully integrated approach to ocean management is required in order to address crosscutting issues and avoid duplication of activities. Collaboration among regional organizations certainly needs to be strengthened, but, as membership is not uniform, disparities remain in the delivery of programs. This is precisely why the geographical scope of the PIROP coincides with the broadest of all regional organizations, that of the South Pacific Regional Environment Programme (SPREP) membership, which includes 22 PICs and territories and five metropolitan countries.[8] National capacities, infrastructure development and availability of resources differ among PICs and must be considered along with the geographic diversity of the islands, ranging from low-lying atolls to high islands of volcanic origin. National priorities in ocean management differ as a result, despite the existence of common issues. PIROP is thus envisaged to provide a template that PICs could adopt and modify when developing their own national ocean policies. With rapid population growth and changing aspirations of Pacific Islanders as a result of their participation in the cash economy, there is now a collective awareness of the need to address pressing issues that have become common to all PICs. Unsustainable use of fisheries, habitat degradation, pollution of coastal waters from land-based as well sea-based sources, waste management, climate change, sea level rise and threats due to invasive species are examples of such common issues that are to be examined under a Regional Ocean Policy.

6. Also known as and referred to hereafter as the Western and Central Pacific Fisheries Convention (WCPFC).

7. See SPC's Oceanic Fisheries Programme web site: <http://www.spc.int/OceanFish>.

8. The members of SPREP are: American Samoa, Australia, Cook Islands, Federated States of Micronesia, Fiji, France, French Polynesia, Guam, Kiribati, Marshall Islands, Nauru, New Caledonia, New Zealand, Niue, Northern Marianas, Palau, Papua New Guinea, Pitcairn Island, Samoa, Solomon Islands, Tokelau, Tonga, Tuvalu, United Kingdom, United States of America, Vanuatu, and Wallis and Futuna.

The Policy itself is articulated around five guiding principles: 1) improving our understanding of the ocean; 2) sustainably developing and managing the use of ocean resources; 3) maintaining the health of the ocean; 4) promoting the peaceful use of the ocean; and 5) creating partnerships and promoting cooperation. Each of the principles identified in the Policy is further developed in the framework for Integrated Strategic Action (ISA) through a series of priority initiatives and actions. The ISA Framework is designed to serve as a guide for implementation rather than a prescriptive workplan, and is intended to be inclusive, allowing for participation by governments, non-governmental organizations, non-state actors, the private sector, and civil society. Both the Policy and the Framework are focused at the regional level, but implementation will necessarily involve actions at all levels (i.e., local, national, regional and international). The ISA Framework also provides guidance to national governments in implementing sustainable development and managing ocean, coastal and island resources, in partnership with local communities.[9]

The Pacific Islands Regional Oceans Forum[10] held in Fiji in February 2004 was the first step to implement the Policy through the ISA. Participants to this Forum were requested to propose and prioritize strategic actions for implementing each of the PIROP's principles. These strategic actions will be examined here along with implementation issues.

IMPROVING OUR UNDERSTANDING OF THE OCEAN

Knowledge about the ocean remains incomplete and sometimes uncertain; but the need to protect the resource is pressing. The challenge is to apply what we do know to ensure sustainable use of ocean resources. Purely scientific approaches to resource management in the region have been costly and have had limited success. Therefore, Forum participants advocated a dual strategy: "co-management," involving customary resource owners and their traditional knowledge in decisions about the ocean, and parallel efforts to improve access by all decision-makers to scientific information on ocean and coastal processes and ecosystems. One model of co-management can be found in Samoa, where villages have the legal right to regulate their own fisheries. So far, 57 communities have put village fisheries by-laws in

9. For further information on the Integrated Strategic Action Framework and the Pacific Islands Regional Oceans Forum, see <http://www.spc.int/piocean/forum/New/welcome.htm>.

10. Participants to this Forum included representatives of governments and of regional organizations, members of the private sector and of non-governmental organizations and academics, each in their informal expert capacity.

place.[11] The main advantage of village by-laws over the regular laws is that, in this case, rules are created by people with a real interest in the management and conservation of fishery resources. The success of the village by-law model in Samoa is linked to community participation in the management of resources based on customary ownership. This model integrates one of the most important yet easily forgotten aspects of development—culture, as reflected in customary land and marine tenure systems. The extent to which the Samoan model would be replicable across the Pacific, with its great variety of traditional authority structures, still needs to be tested. The transposability of the Samoan village by-law model will be determined by the extent to which customary law is given legal recognition in the country considered and the extent to which cultural and social customary practices have been maintained in society generally. Transposing the Samoan village by-law model to Melanesian countries may present additional difficulties due to the greater cultural and linguistic diversity and the erosion in some parts of Vanuatu and the Solomon Islands, of the chiefly system and the questioning of chiefs' decisions and authority.

The co-management strategy is to be pursued in parallel with improving access to scientific information related to ocean and coastal processes and ecosystems as a support to decision making. Partnerships between international and regional organizations, the public and private sectors will be required to implement this strategic action. Regional Oceans Forum participants proposed to address the issue of enhancing knowledge management by establishing a regional network and procedures for information and data collection, maintenance and sharing and for coordination of research. It is worth noting that such procedures are already in place for managing tuna resources in the region but need further elaboration under the new WCPFC. The network of locally managed marine areas in the Western Pacific may also be used as a model for enhancing knowledge management. This network has a systematic approach to the collection and sharing of information in order to determine the conditions in which locally managed marine areas work in practice across different sites.[12] Yet, access to the Internet remains difficult for communities in remote areas, which prevents an effective use of the network web site and

11. The by-laws must follow the provisions of the 1988 Fisheries Act of Samoa and can cover any issue related to management and conservation of fisheries. They are legally recognized in court. For more information, see U. Fa'asili, 2001, "Review of the Village Fisheries Management Plan of the Extension Programme in Samoa," Field Report No. 7, Secretariat of the Pacific Community, pp. 1–56. Also available online at: <http://www.spc.int/coastfish/sections/community/english/publications/samoa-review.pdf>.

12. See <http://www.lmmanetwork.org>.

discussion forum. This particular issue would need to be addressed so that incentives in knowledge management benefit local communities in priority.

SUSTAINABLY DEVELOPING AND MANAGING THE USE OF OCEAN RESOURCES

Assuming that most, if not all, ocean uses are currently unsustainable, what might be the most appropriate approach to change this pattern? Regional Oceans Forum participants agreed that in order to be sustainable, development and management of coasts and the ocean must be integrated, precautionary and ecosystem-based. Engaging all stakeholders, including local communities, in resource management decision making is a central element to the implementation of this principle. It must be considered as part of the need to ensure equitable sharing of resource access and benefits at local, national and regional levels.

At the regional level, PICs are currently receiving about 3 percent of the value of the tuna fished from their waters and therefore need to explore more suitable ways of getting a better return from foreign access granted to their tuna fisheries.[13] As a result, it might be preferable to harvest tuna resources at the maximum economic yield (i.e., the harvest rate that maximizes economic returns from the fishery) instead of the maximum sustainable yield.[14] This would prevent current risks of over-exploitation whereby harvests may be beyond the maximum sustainable yield level as a result of poor enforcement of regulations or lack of information to determine what the maximum sustainable yield is. Increased commercial exploitation of tuna stocks by Pacific Island countries themselves, also referred to as the domestication of the tuna industry, is another option for getting the full benefit out of the resource. This will require the acquisition of competitive ships, extensive training of local officers and crew and the upgrading of landing facilities. Such capacity building represents a long-term commitment that has been acknowledged by Forum participants.

13. See M. Bertignac, H. F. Campbell, J. Hampton and A. J. Hand, "Maximising Resource Rent from the Western and Central Pacific Tuna Fisheries," *Marine Resource Economics* 15, 3 (2000): 151–77.

14. It is now widely recognized that using maximum sustainable yield as a management tool has led to many biological variables being ignored in catch allocation decisions, in fact in species being overexploited. To avoid this, the precautionary approach adopted under the WCPFC requires the setting of reference points as target levels of fishing effort designed to ensure that the abundance of fish stocks is maintained at a level above that which can produce maximum sustainable yield. This translates the idea that caution is required when information is uncertain, unreliable, or inadequate.

However, almost all of the public fishing ventures initiated by PICs since the early 1990s have failed financially, giving rise to the following question, how should fishing revenue be invested so as to maximize sustained economic development?[15]

At the local and national levels, equitable access to resources and sharing of benefits require the establishment and protection of traditional knowledge and intellectual property rights. At present, PICs do not have adequate legislation to regulate bioprospecting nor to obtain financial benefits (such as royalties) for the commercialization of products derived from the use of their genetic resources. Existing intellectual property rights have a limited life, give priority to individual ownership and impose strict interpretations of invention. This is in contrast with traditional knowledge that is characterized by collective ownership held in perpetuity, but yet subject to change over time. The Secretariat of the Pacific Community (SPC), the Pacific Islands Forum Secretariat (PIFS) in partnership with UNESCO have attempted to address this issue by developing a Pacific Regional Framework for the Protection of Traditional Knowledge and Expressions of Culture.[16] This regional framework focuses on a draft model law establishing a new range of statutory rights for traditional owners of traditional knowledge and expressions of culture. It defines the meaning of traditional cultural rights by listing the different uses of traditional knowledge that require prior and informed consent of the traditional owners. The procedure for obtaining prior and informed consent as well as terms and conditions attached are detailed. Offences, civil action claims and remedies are incorporated as part of the enforcement process. The model law provides a basis for Pacific Islands countries wishing to enact legislation for the protection of traditional knowledge and expressions of culture. It may be relevant to protect marine-related intellectual property and related traditional knowledge from unauthorized exploitation. Traditional fishing techniques and traditional uses of marine resources for specific purposes such as healing may be examples of knowledge currently not protected by law. Countries wishing to enact the model law are free to adapt its provisions in accordance with its national needs, the wishes of traditional communities, legal drafting conditions and so on.

15. For possible options to this issue, see M. Pretes and E. Peterson, "Rethinking Fisheries Policy in the Pacific," *Marine Policy* 28 (2004): 297–309.

16. See *Pacific Regional Framework for the Protection of Traditional Knowledge and Expressions of Culture,* produced by the Secretariat of the Pacific Community, the Pacific Islands Forum Secretariat and the UNESCO Pacific Regional Office, available online: <http://www.spc.int/Culture/activities_legal.htm>. This document was endorsed by the Ministers of Culture of member countries of the Pacific Islands Forum Secretariat in 2002.

The aim of equitable sharing of resource access also means that social, environmental and cultural impacts of significant policies and development initiatives will have to be assessed prior to their implementation. At present, mechanisms such as environmental impact assessments (EIAs) are not systematically in place throughout the region. Where EIAs are mandatory, the process often presents significant flaws preventing informed decision making and consideration of possible alternatives. In addition, socio-economic valuation and assessment of resources as well as biological processes and pollution is not included as a legal requirement in most of the EIAs undertaken in the region. The need for EIAs is particularly apparent for any major tourism, industrial or infrastructure development in the region.[17] For instance, the construction of major resorts may create coastal changes that, if not carefully planned, may result in permanent damage as in the case of the Denauru Island resort in Fiji where the tidal patterns have been modified as a result of a sea wall construction, thus making the artificial beach unattractive to tourists, the very purpose for which it was built. Such permanent damage might have been avoided had a proper EIA been undertaken in this case.

EIAs may also be a relevant tool in the process of acknowledging and enhancing the ecological importance of mangroves, which have commonly been used as landfills and which continue to be perceived as 'wasteland' throughout the region. This could be achieved by incorporating such ecological valuation in the scoping of sites subject to EIAs and by proposing, if necessary, alternative locations to the development proposed.

Applied to the Pacific region, the EIA process necessarily requires a minimum institutional capacity that needs to be located at the appropriate level of government (whether central, provincial or local) where development and sectoral policies, programmes and projects, are evaluated. The EIA review process must also ensure that there is sufficient evidence showing that people affected by the project have been consulted and that members of the local community understand the information contained in the environmental impact statement. In other words, community participation in development decisions must be established as a legally enforceable right.

From a mitigation perspective, EIAs could address issues of soil erosion by developing mitigation measures such as erosion control practices like terracing or recommending the use of ponds to control sediment run-off

17. For further discussion about the need and relevance of EIAs in the Pacific region, see L. Cordonnery, "Environmental Legal Issues in the South Pacific and the Quest for Sustainable Development and Good Governance," in A. Jowitt and T. Newton-Cain eds., *Passage of Change: Law, Society and Governance in the Pacific* (Canberra: Pandanus Books, Research School of Pacific and Asian Studies, Australian National University, 2003): 233–249.

around construction projects involving earth works. Through the EIA process the erodability of soil in areas to be logged could also be determined and sensitive areas could be mapped out. Similarly, it is notable that the impacts of sedimentation on coral reefs can be easily monitored by establishing monitoring sites where the percentage of live cover of coral is measured, and that such a monitoring measure can be incorporated into the EIA process. Addressing coastal pollution resulting from land-based activities is also within the scope of the EIAs by determining whether the receiving waters (stream, river and/or bay) can accommodate the additional nutrient load that will result from the proposed activity. The answer will depend on the amount of dilution that can be expected. For example, in the case of a river, the dilution is controlled by the volume of flow. In the case of a marine discharge, dilution will be determined by the amount of flushing, a function of the tidal range and the water currents. If there is insufficient dilution to reduce the nutrient loading to near background levels within 100 m of the outfall, then the EIA should recommend sewage treatment to reduce the nutrient loading.

MAINTAINING THE HEALTH OF THE OCEAN

Maintaining the health of the ocean requires preserving ecosystem integrity and minimizing the harmful impacts of human activities. The strategy advocated by Forum participants for the preservation of ecosystem integrity is to enhance biodiversity conservation at local, national and regional scales by establishing networks of marine protected areas that are representative of the coastal and marine ecosystems present in the region. This strategic action extends to the high seas and offshore fisheries as well. For example, research is currently undertaken by the author on the identification of potential marine reserves in the Western and Central Pacific Ocean as a tool for managing tuna stocks.[18] This project research aims to conduct numerical simulations with ecosystem models such as SEAPODYM (spatial ecosystem and population dynamics model) that include the main tuna species present in the Western and Central Pacific Ocean (skipjack, yellowfin, albacore and bigeye). Areas that will be tested for potential identification as marine reserves are international waters within the Western and Central Pacific Tuna Commission convention area located within a

18. See L. Cordonnery, (Cordonnery_L@eastwestcenter.org) and P. Lehodey, Fisheries Scientist at the Secretariat for the Pacific Community (PatrickL@spc.int) for more information on the research project on ''The Potential Impacts and Relevance of Marine Reserves on Tuna Stocks and Fisheries in the Tropical Pacific Ocean.''

band between 10° N and 10° S. These areas have been selected because of their importance for fisheries statistical data and also because they are currently unregulated, or not subject to any specific management measure. The first simulation will rely on data already integrated within the SEAPODYM model, which has the following parameters: wind, phyto-zooplankton, temperature, oxygen, and spawning habitat, excluding data on fishing effort in order to determine the natural tendency of the stocks as a baseline.

The second simulation aims to compare areas to be tested with and without fishing effort data in order to determine areas that would be the most relevant to protect. Relocation of fishing effort and its impact on the fisheries as a result of establishing marine reserves will be calculated and integrated in the simulation as well. The third simulation aims to determine if there is any spawning gradient within the areas to be tested and to identify the most relevant areas for the distribution of larvae, juveniles and young tunas. Candidate areas identified in the course of this research will be proposed to the members of the Western and Central Pacific Tuna Commission for designation.[19]

In order to preserve ecosystem integrity, the PICs must also be able to enforce national controls on the introduction of alien species and must have the capacity to prevent, detect, monitor and respond to invasive alien species. Indeed, given the fragility of island ecosystems, endemic species on islands can be lost within a very short time span due to the introduction of insect pests, diseases, predators or destruction of critical habitat. Environmental management of ports, planning and response to marine spills are capacity-building issues that need to be addressed.

At the regional level, Forum participants advocated an annual assessment of marine pollution issues to identify the various sources of marine pollution (from marine to land-based sources) and assess their respective impacts upon the marine environment. Degradation of coastal environments is now widespread throughout the Pacific. This is typically a result of development activities that are either unsustainable by nature, as in the case of clear-cut logging, or for which no EIAs were conducted and therefore no monitoring, mitigation or alternative development options were devised. The most common types of impacts from development activities include soil erosion, impacts of sedimentation on coral reefs, mangrove reclamation and degradation, and pollution by sewage and industrial effluents.

The Forum participants proposed to establish a Regional Global Programme of Action for the Protection of the Marine Environment from

19. Results of the simulations are still pending. However, information on the project has been disseminated at the Pacific Islands Regional Oceans Forum held in Suva, in February 2002. A number of Pacific Islands Countries are already supportive of the concept of using marine protected areas for tuna management purposes.

Land-based Activities in order to increase national capacity to address monitoring, enforcement and clean-up of land-based pollution. This issue has not yet been addressed despite having important environmental implications on both fisheries and coastal environments, both locally and regionally. For example, the impacts of Ok Tedi copper mine discharges released into the Fly River in Papua New Guinea on the northern Australian coasts is a typical illustration of the transboundary nature of land-based sources of marine pollution. The Ok Tedi copper mine is situated in the headwaters of the Ok Tedi, which is a tributary of the Fly River. The river system, with its huge estuary and massive flood plains, lakes and tributaries, supports one of the richest fish, aquatic and wetland fauna in the Pacific region. An average of 90 million tonnes per year of tailings and mine-induced erosion are discharged to the Ok Tedi each year from the Ok Tedi mine. About 30 million tonnes of this reaches the Fly River.[20]

PROMOTING THE PEACEFUL USE OF THE OCEAN

In order to discourage illicit and criminal activities that contradict national, regional and international agreements, PICs have to exercise control and enforcement over their maritime zones. At present this is difficult to achieve given the maritime boundaries overlapping claims and disputes. Forum participants have thus identified maritime boundary delimitations and the settlement of disputes as prerequisites. This may be a slow process since some PICs might be able to claim continental shelf extension,[21] such as the Federated States of Micronesia, Papua New Guinea, Fiji, Solomon Islands and Tonga. But these countries have little marine scientific research capacity of their own and are reliant on regional assistance from the South Pacific Applied Geosciences Commission (SOPAC) for the delineation of potential continental shelf extension, which is geologically and legally complex.

Lack of consistency between national legislation and international law needs to be addressed. This process has started with the enactment of new

---

20. For further information on the human and environmental impacts of the Ok Tedi Mine, see "Ok Tedi Mine: Unearthing Controversy," in *Report Series: World Resources 2002–2004: Decisions for the Earth: Balance, Voice and Power*, United Nations Development Programme, United Nations Environment Programme, World Bank, World Resources Institute, available online: <http://pubs.wri.org/pubs_content_text.cfm?ContentID=1860>.

21. A geologically and legally complex procedure under Article 76 of the 1982 United Nations Convention of the Law of the Sea that enables a coastal state to extend its sovereignty over mineral resources of the seabed beyond the 200-nautical-mile Exclusive Economic Zone.

fisheries legislation encompassing resource conservation issues and the adoption of national tuna management plans in most PICs. Compliance with international agreements needs to be strengthened while monitoring and enforcement mechanisms already in place for fishing activities need to be fully implemented. Collaboration with shipping and fishing nations as well as naval powers is required to alleviate the lack of capacity within PICs. Australia and France have already concluded a number of bilateral arrangements with PICs for the aerial surveillance of their maritime zones. The geographical coverage of such arrangements would need to be extended and the involvement of other naval powers to be sought. A Vessel Monitoring System (VMS) is part of the minimum terms and conditions for gaining fisheries access in any of the FFA Member States' exclusive economic zones, but this requirement has yet to be implemented in some member countries.

CREATING PARTNERSHIPS AND PROMOTING COOPERATION

Capacity building is a major issue for PICs and improved ocean governance in the areas of security, monitoring, enforcement and sustainable use of resources is highly dependent on partnerships and cooperation with donor countries and metropolitan powers. This realization explains why PIROP has been presented at the 2002 World Summit on Sustainable Development in Johannesburg as a partnership initiative on Small Islands Developing States.[22] Yet, moving beyond the current level of cooperation and partnerships might be difficult in some cases as some aid-donor countries are also naval powers or fishing nations in the region, thus pursuing short-term as well as long-term interests that may not always coincide with the strategic actions advocated in the Policy. The transboundary movement of hazardous wastes such as plutonium illustrates such divergences of interests between the aid-donor countries involved in this trade, namely UK, France and Japan, and the PICs, whose legal positions range from seeking exclusion of the ship's route from their EEZs to advocating a strict liability regime in case of an accident. On the other hand, donor countries involved maintain that there is no need for an additional liability regime specific to this issue while the freedom of navigation should not be restrained.[23]

22. Partnership initiatives presented at the Johannesburg Summit are to strengthen the implementation of Agenda 21 and related international instruments. Partnerships are voluntary multi-stakeholder initiatives, intended to be a complement to and not a substitute for these commitments.

23. On April 7, 2005, the Secretary General of the Pacific Islands Forum made a declaration expressing the concerns of Member States regarding the passage into their EEZs of the cargo ship *Pacific Sandpiper* carrying radioactive wastes treated in La Hague, France and whose final destination is Japan. The ship is scheduled to pass through the Tasman Sea and the EEZs of New Caledonia, Vanuatu, Solomon Islands

In other instances, strengthening partnerships and cooperation seem achievable, particularly when it comes to learning from past experience in the implementation of national ocean policies as in the case of Australia[24] or Canada.[25] Some opportunities for cooperation in the management of inshore marine resources remain untapped, particularly regarding the transfer of technology and of research methodology from the French Pacific Territories whose linguistic isolation partly explains the absence of substantial partnerships with PICs until now.

Regarding the management of tuna resources, cooperation with DWFNs may prove difficult, particularly when determining the allocation of total allowable catches in relation to gear type within the new convention area of the WCPFC. Similarly, the regulation of high seas fishing within the convention area and the implementation of the compatibility requirement between in-zone and high seas management measures remains uncertain. Insofar as security is concerned, the international focus on the prevention of terrorism and in particular the Proliferation Security Initiative (PSI)[26] may provide some opportunities for PICs to enhance their maritime surveillance capacity through cooperation. This, in turn, might increase the leverage of PICs as a regional power bloc and give rise to trade-offs with the USA.[27]

Current diplomatic efforts by Australia, New Zealand and France to address the issue of illegal fishing in the Pacific Ocean are worth noting here in that they provide an illustration of this new trend in regional maritime cooperation. A new agreement between the three countries is to be concluded in the near future, in the spirit of the existing "FRANZ" agreement, which currently facilitates natural disasters emergency response towards PICs. The aim of the new agreement will be to facilitate intelligence networking and to gather logistic and military resources (mainly maritime

and the Federated States of Micronesia. The lack of a specific liability regime in case of an accident was once again highlighted, along with the threats such cargo potentially represent for the economy of PICs mostly reliant on tourism and fishing. Source: *Oceania Flash*, 7 April 2005, ed. P. A. Decloître, available online: <http://newspad-pacific.info/>.

24. *Australia's Ocean Policy*, Environment Australia, Commonwealth of Australia, 1998, 52 pp. Available online: <http://www.environment.gov.au/net/oceanspo.html>.

25. *Canada's Oceans Strategy*, Fisheries and Oceans Canada, Ottawa, 2002, 33 pp. Available online: <http://www.cos-soc.gc.ca/doc/publications_e.asp>.

26. For more information on the Proliferation Security Initiative, see the U.S. Department of State web site: <http://www.state.gov/t/np/rls/fs/23764.htm>.

27. For example, in March 2005, financial assistance from the U.S. Embassy in Fiji was given to the Pacific Islands Forum Secretariat (US$60,000) in order to combat terrorism and money laundering in the region. *Oceania Flash*, ed. P. A. Decloître (15 March 2005), available online: <http://newspad-pacific.info/>.

and aerial surveillance patrols) undertaken by the three countries in order to combat illegal fishing and to monitor the exclusive economic zones of PICs.[28]

CONCLUSION

PICs have been visionary on a number of occasions related to ocean governance in the past, from their support for extended coastal state jurisdiction during the negotiations of the United Nations Convention on the Law of the Sea (UNCLOS), to the more recent adoption of a regional approach to managing tuna resources in the wake of the 1995 Agreement on the UNCLOS provisions relating to the conservation and management of highly migratory fish stocks.[29] The Policy demonstrates, at least on paper, the proactiveness of PICs as a united voice advocating an improved management of the largest and last commercially sustainable ocean on earth. Within the region, political willingness and leadership to commit and raise adequate resources will be essential if the foreseeable implementation difficulties outlined in this article are to be overcome. This challenge will determine whether the Policy can be used as a model for ocean governance as it promises to be. For regional powers within the Pacific Rim who were not part of the inception and endorsement phases of the PIROP, their commitment to PIROP will be determined by their willingness to act as partners and to cooperate with the PICs in the implementation process.

28. *Oceania Flash*, ed. P. A. Decloître (18 March 2005), available online: <http://newspad-pacific.info/>.

29. Agreement for the Implementation of the Provisions of the United Nations Convention on the Law of the Sea of 10 December 1982 relating to the Conservation and Management of Straddling Fish Stocks and Highly Migratory Fish Stocks, UN Doc. A/CONF. 164/33 (1995) 34, *International Legal Materials*, 1542.

The U.S. Commission on Ocean Policy: An Historical Overview (1997–2005)

Marc J. Hershman*

Professor of Marine Affairs and Adjunct Professor of Law, University of Washington, Seattle, Washington, U.S.A.

John R. Hansen*

Master's Candidate, School of Marine Affairs, University of Washington, Seattle, Washington, U.S.A.

INTRODUCTION

On September 20, 2004, the U.S. Commission on Ocean Policy (hereinafter "Commission") officially delivered its final report to the President of the United States and to major officials of the Bush administration.[1] The hour-long presentation occurred in the Roosevelt Room of the White House, and was witnessed by about 20 members of the administration, including cabinet secretaries and White House and agency officials. Later that day the Commission delivered its report to Senators Ernest Hollings and Ted Stevens, the leading proponents for ocean policy reform in the U.S. Senate.

* Professor Hershman was a member of the U.S. Commission on Ocean Policy during its existence from July 2001 until December, 2004. Mr. Hansen was primarily responsible for the legislative history in Part I and the review of policy responses to the Commission's report in Part IV.

Acknowledgements: Thanks to the School of Marine Affairs, University of Washington, for in-kind support, and for the assistance and encouragement of many colleagues among the Commissioners and staff of the U.S. Commission on Ocean Policy. Additional gratitude to Terry Schaff and Margaret Spring for their assistance in the preparation and review of this article. Further thanks to Eli Weissman for his valuable input and use of his personal files on the legislative history of the Oceans Act.

1. U.S. Commission on Ocean Policy. *An Ocean Blueprint for the 21st Century.* Final Report. Washington, DC, 2004 [hereinafter Commission Report] Available online: <http://www.oceancommission.gov/documents/full_color_rpt/000_ocean_full_report.pdf>.

Ocean Yearbook 20: 93–145.

These actions culminated a three-year comprehensive study into virtually all aspects of U.S. ocean policy. In the view of Commissioners, commission staff and advisors, and all the people who participated in and followed the Commission's work, this was a very important moment. Thirty-five years had passed since the Stratton Commission issued its influential report in 1969[2] and now the U.S. had a new "blueprint" for its ocean affairs for the next decades.[3]

The purpose of this article is to begin to describe the history of the Commission's work. The assumption is that the Commission's report will influence measurably how the U.S. approaches its ocean and coastal resources, and for this reason it is important to document the Commission and its work. The Commission went out of business officially on December 19, 2004, and the work of implementation passed to others. Part IV of this article shows how federal and state actions have already begun in response to the recommendations of the report.

There are many dimensions to this story—historical, legislative, and political. Prior to the initiation of the Commission's work there was a considerable literature outlining ocean and coastal problems and suggesting approaches to an overhaul of U.S. ocean policy.[4] Over the years there will be lots of commentary in reaction to the Commission report. Debates will ensue over the value of some policy recommendations, over the process followed by the Commission, over the pace and direction of implementation efforts, and over the ultimate question of the state of the ocean and coastal environment and the pace of improvement and/or the rate of decline. An important question will be whether the Commission's work made a difference in the development of U.S. ocean policy.

This article presents an initial first step in the analytical process of determining the Commission's efficacy. What actually happened? The focus is on the Commission itself—how it came about, what work it did, and the results of its labors in the year after the report was initially released.

2. U.S. Commission on Marine Science, Engineering and Resources, *Our Nation and the Sea*, Washington, D.C.: U.S. Government Printing Office, 1969. This Commission is almost always referred to as the "Stratton Commission" after its chairman, Julius Stratton.

3. The PEW Ocean Commission operated approximately during the same timeframe as the U.S. Ocean Commission, and issued its report in April 2003. Pew Ocean Commission, *America's Living Oceans: Charting a Course for Sea Change*. Available online: <http://www.pewtrusts.org/>. The two reports are very similar, although the scope of the PEW report is somewhat narrower than the U.S. Commission. This article does not address the PEW report.

4. See B. Cicin-Sain and R. W. Knecht, *The Future of U.S. Ocean Policy* (Washington, D.C.: Island Press, 2000), for a recent review of major natural resource and environmental policy issues affecting oceans and coasts of the U.S., including a valuable reference list.

Attention is given primarily to the official documented record that is widely available and would be of use to future researchers.

What is not done in this article, but which we hope will interest writers in the future, are the detailed stories of certain discrete issues and the individuals and interest groups behind them. For example, the Commission operated at a time when fisheries management issues were hotly debated in the U.S. and around the world. How did the Commission contribute to the understanding and resolution of that issue? Another set of concerns dealt with the future of oceanographic science and its infrastructural, technological and data management needs. Did the Commission's work make a difference? And the problems of global climate change that are inextricably linked to the sea were often raised in testimony before the Commission. To what extent did the Commission try to foresee longer-term problems and prepare society for addressing them?

Another set of stories are needed that address the human dimension of the Commission's work. How did 16 diverse members come together on such a broad set of issues? What were the compromises that had to be reached? How did the Commissioners interact with their staff, science advisors, Congressional and administration leaders? In due course "memoirs" of the years on the Commission ought to be produced by members and those who watched the Commission closely.

Finally, it must be pointed out that the first author of this article was a member of the Commission. The article therefore presents a positive and hopeful perspective. The experience of serving on the Commission was exciting and educational. The Commission heard about the progress that was being made by individuals and groups at all levels of society, the problems that persisted and the damage that resulted, and the many suggestions for improvement that were made. There was a sense that issues could be addressed and problems resolved; that positive opportunities awaited people through better understanding, protection and use of the sea.

The article is organized in four parts. Part I outlines the legislative history of the Oceans Act of 2000 that set up the U.S. Ocean Commission. For almost four years a Commission bill was debated in the Congress. A variety of issues had to be resolved before the bill became law. Interestingly, with the benefit of hindsight, the compromises reached on most of these issues strengthened the Commission and improved its ability to function. Part II deals with that short period of time between the effective date of the law and the first meeting of the Commission. It was at this time that Commissioners were selected, a chair elected, operating procedures established, and an important tone of cooperation and collegiality set for the duration of the Commission's work. Part III deals with an overview of the Commission's output—the Final Report and the supporting materials. Fortunately, there is an excellent record of the Commission's activities and products that is readily available. This section provides some broad themes advanced by the Commission and a brief review of the "regional ocean governance" recommendation as an illustration of one important issue addressed by the Commission. Part IV addresses the initial reaction of policy-makers in the Executive Office of the President, Congress and the States to the Commission's work. Although the outcome of this initial flurry of enthusiasm cannot be predicted, one important conclusion is that the Commission was noticed![5]

PART I—LEGISLATIVE HISTORY (1997–2000)

The Oceans Act of 2000 was signed into law by President Bill Clinton on August 7, 2000, officially establishing the U.S. Commission on Ocean Policy. On the 20th of January, 2001, the law became effective and the process began to conduct the first comprehensive federal review of the ocean and coastal activities and policies of the United States in over thirty years. While the Oceans Act became law in the summer of 2000, the legislative activities that led to the creation of the U.S. Commission on Ocean Policy had begun almost three years earlier. Senator Fritz Hollings of South Carolina formally initiated these activities in September 1997, with the introduction of the Oceans Act of 1997. Over the next four sessions of Congress, six additional versions of the Oceans Act were introduced in both the House of Representatives and the Senate.

The following section will provide a summary and discussion of the legislative history of the Oceans Act during the 105th and 106th U.S. Congresses. First, we provide a description of the seven Oceans Acts introduced during this period. A comparison of the bills will highlight some of the changes to the language of the legislation over time. Second, we present a more thorough discussion of the central issues that arose during the progression of the Oceans Act, drawing attention to some of the concerns that supplied a great deal of debate and exchange between all parties involved. While the discussion of these topics is not meant to be comprehensive, it will provide insight into those issues and disputes that were the most passionately debated in Congress, and how these disagreements were resolved in order to allow the Oceans Act to become law.

5. As measured by media attention alone, the Commission captured considerable attention—especially when the Preliminary report was issued for comment in April 2004. Consultants to the Commission reported approximately 1000 "media hits" (print and electronic) when the Preliminary Report was announced.

History of Oceans Act Legislation

The first Oceans Act, introduced by Senator Hollings, was modeled after the Marine Resources and Engineering Development Act of 1966.[6] One part of this early piece of legislation formed the Stratton Commission, which provided the most recent comprehensive federal review of ocean policy in the United States. The Act created a 15-member Commission on Marine Science, Engineering, and Resources appointed by the President, as well as National Marine Council to aid the Commission's work and oversee all related federal activities. The Commission was charged with the task of a comprehensive investigation of marine science in the United States, concluding with the submission of a report of their findings within 18 months.[7] The Act called for the Commission and Council to be terminated shortly after the submission of the Commission's final report. It also required the President to respond by providing an annual report to Congress, including an evaluation of United States marine science activities and recommendations on ocean-related legislation.

The Oceans Act of 1997[8] used many of the same legislative components of the 1966 Act, including the creation of a 15-member commission and a National Ocean Council. However, rather than a commission focusing on Marine Science, Engineering and Resources, the Oceans Act of 1997 called for a Commission on Ocean *Policy*, with the charge of creating a national ocean and coastal policy for the United States. The language of the Act expanded the Commission's focus beyond marine science, showing the need for comprehensive study of all aspects of ocean and coastal activities.[9]

A day after the Oceans Act was introduced in the Senate by Senator Hollings, another version of it was also introduced into the House of Representatives.[10] Sponsored by Congressman Sam Farr of California, this version of the Oceans Act was similar to Senator Hollings in many ways, with some distinguishing characteristics. Congressman Farr's version did not create a National Ocean Council, but did create a Commission on Ocean Policy. However, Congressman Farr's version had no termination of the Commission, but rather called for the Commission to continue indefinitely while reporting to the President at least once every five years. Despite some

6. Marine Resources and Engineering Development Act, Pub. L. No. 89–454, 33 U.S.C. §§ 1101–1108 (1966).

7. See Stratton Commission, n. 2 above.

8. S. 1213, 105th Cong. (1997).

9. This reflected the earlier work of the Stratton Commission, which had examined all aspects of U.S. ocean policy despite their legislatively stated focus on scientific endeavors (Marine Resources and Engineering Development Act of 1966, § 5(b)).

10. H.R. 2547, 105th Cong. (1997).

other minor differences, the two versions of the Oceans Act of 1997 were somewhat similar in their central goal of federal ocean policy review.

The final version of the Oceans Act introduced during the 105th Congress was the Oceans Act of 1998,[11] sponsored by Congressman Jim Saxton of New Jersey. Similar to the earlier House version, this Oceans Act legislation created a Commission on Ocean Policy while omitting the creation of a National Ocean Council. This bill called for a commission report within 18 months followed by the termination of the commission within 30 days, the same as Senator Hollings' bill.

These three bills, from Senator Hollings and Congressmen Farr and Saxton, were considered at a hearing before the House Subcommittee on Fisheries Conservation, Wildlife and Oceans, on March 19, 1998. Senator Hollings' original Oceans Act bill had passed the Senate in the previous year,[12] and was being considered by the House Committee on Resources along with the two House versions that had been introduced. Statements were given by Committee members, Federal Agency members, and representatives of non-governmental organizations. After this hearing, Congressman Farr's bill had no further action, and Senator Hollings' bill had one additional hearing before the House Subcommittee on Water Resources and Environment followed by no further House action. Meanwhile, Congressman Saxton's bill was passed by the House of Representatives in September of 1998. However, once received in the Senate, the Saxton Oceans Act had no further action taken upon it. While none of these bills were passed out of Congress, this early legislation provided the foundation in both the Senate and House for the forthcoming Oceans Act that would eventually become law during the 106th Congress.

Senator Hollings initiated Oceans Act legislation during the 106th Congress with his introduction of the Oceans Act of 1999.[13] This version was a reintroduction of the Oceans Act of 1997 that had passed the Senate two years earlier. However, unlike its earlier version, this Oceans Act received no action in the Senate and was later succeeded by a revamped Oceans Act from Senator Hollings that would eventually be signed into law. However, before this would happen, Congressmen Farr and Saxton would again introduce their own versions of the Oceans Act in the House of Representatives, the Oceans Acts of 1999[14] and 2000,[15] respectively. While all three of these bills were similar to their predecessors from the 105th Congress, none of them received very much on-the-record action during the 106th

---

11. H.R. 3445, 105th Cong. (1998).
12. S. 1213 was passed by the Senate on November 13, 1997.
13. S. 959, 106th Cong. (1999).
14. H.R. 2425, 106th Cong. (1999).
15. H.R. 4410, 106th Cong. (2000).

Congress. Rather, many features of these bills were combined to create what would be the final Oceans Act, Senator Hollings' Oceans Act of 2000.[16] Before introduction of the final version of the Oceans Act, the Senate and House had pre-conferencing[17] meetings to ensure that the views and concerns of both houses of Congress were attended to in this final piece of legislation. This resulted in a bill with a combination of language originating from the earlier Oceans Acts of Senator Hollings, Congressman Saxton, and to a lesser extent Congressman Farr. This conglomeration ultimately resulted in the bill passing Congress and being sent to the President within four months of introduction. The specifics of this process and the changes that occurred will be discussed in detail in the next section.

The final Oceans Act created a U.S. Commission on Ocean Policy with sixteen members all appointed by the President, twelve of which came from lists provided by Congressional leadership, resulting in a Commission with high geographical and institutional diversity. There was no creation of a National Ocean Council, but a Science Advisory Panel was instituted to aid the Commission in their subsequent work. Appropriated with $9,500,000[18] over three years, the Commission was required to report by June 20th, 2003[19] with findings and recommendations relating to the ocean and coastal policies of the United States. The Commission was to be terminated within 90 days of submission of their final report.[20] Following the submission of the final report, the Act called upon the President to respond to the Commission's findings within 90 days.[21] The Act called for the President to respond by submitting to Congress a statement of proposals to implement or respond to the Commission's recommendations. Further, the President was required to provide a biennial report to Congress summarizing all

16. S. 2327, 106th Cong. (2000).

17. Pre-conferencing refers to the attempt by the staffs of relevant committees in both the House and Senate to agree on the terms of a bill before it is introduced in Congress, so that it may be passed more quickly following introduction without further need for conferencing between the House and Senate versions.

18. Amended by Pub. L. 107–372 (2002); original language appropriated $6,000,000 over three years. $9,500,000 refers to $8,500,000 in amendment and initial $1,000,000 from NOAA appropriations. See n. 90 below.

19. Amended by Pub. L. 107–206 (2002); original language called for a Final Report within 18 months. The Commission submitted their final report on September 20th, 2004, delayed due to the extensive time needed to complete their findings and formulate comprehensive recommendations.

20. Amended by Pub. L. 107–372 (2002); original language terminated the Commission within 30 days.

21. Amended by Pub. L. 107–372 (2002); original language allowed 120 days for Presidential response to the Commission's findings.

federal programs related to the oceans and coasts. On August 7, 2000, President Bill Clinton signed the Oceans Act 2000 into law.[22]

Important Issues in Oceans Act Legislation

While the preceding was a summary of the legislative history of the Oceans Act, the following will highlight five issues that were central to the changes made to the Oceans Act during the 105th and 106th Congress. The five issues to be discussed are the process for appointing Commissioners to the U.S. Commission on Ocean Policy, the proposal to establish a National Ocean Council, the decision not to exclude geographic areas to be considered by the Commission, the creation of a Science Advisory Panel for the Commission, and finally the domestic focus of the Commission's work.[23]

Procedure for Appointing Commission Members

Early drafts of Senator Hollings' Oceans Act called for a U.S. Commission on Ocean Policy that would have been created in an almost identical manner to that of the Stratton Commission, with fifteen members appointed by the President, coming from federal and State government and other ocean-related institutions. However, a federal commission appointed entirely by the President was not as politically feasible as it had been three decades earlier. Senator Olympia Snowe of Maine, a co-sponsor of Hollings' original Oceans Act, was concerned by Hollings' draft versions of the legislation that created a commission coming only from the President without any input from Congress.[24] As a result, Senator Hollings' bill,[25] as introduced, created a 15-member commission, but only seven of the fifteen members came directly from the President. The final eight members came from the Congressional leadership, with two members each being appointed directly by the Senate majority and minority leaders, and the Speaker of the House and House minority leader.

22. Pub. L. No. 106–256.
23. While these particular five issues were selected by the authors for discussion, numerous other issues were involved to a lesser extent with the passage of the Oceans Act. These include the proposal to exclude military activities, the President's role in initiating ocean and coastal legislation, a Congressional advisory committee for the Commission, and representation of industry on the Commission, among others.
24. 143 Cong. Rec. S 9893, Vol. 143, No. 129 (September 24, 1997) (statement of Sen. Snowe).
25. S. 1213, 105th Cong. (1997).

This process for establishing the Commission was amended once Hollings' bill was considered by the Senate Committee on Commerce, Science, and Transportation. Senator Kay Bailey Hutchinson of Texas expressed concern over the balance of Democrat and Republican nominees on the Commission, and wanted to ensure that one party's nominees alone could not control the Commission, especially with the possibility of a Democratic President in the White House.[26] In response, Senator John McCain of Arizona offered an amendment for Hollings' bill. The amendment increased the size of the Commission to sixteen members and required the President to select twelve of the sixteen members from lists provided by Congressional leadership.[27] Four members were to come from lists of eight provided by the Senate majority leader and the Speaker of the House, while two members were to come from lists provided by the minority leaders of the Senate and the House. The final four members were appointed by the President without Congressional input. Thus, the resulting legislative language that was later passed by the Senate created a commission with all members being appointed by the President, but with the majority of commissioners coming from Congressional nominees. Similarly, another provision of the bill that was changed in the 106th Congress after pre-conferencing activities addressed the issue of geographic balance of commissioners.[28] A commission coming from Congressional nominees, combined with a requirement for geographic balance, led to a bill that created a commission with members from all regions of the country, with strong ties to Congressional leaders on ocean issues. Conversely, Congressman Farr's Oceans Act of 1997 called for a 15-member commission appointed entirely by the President without Congressional participation, as discussed in draft versions of Hollings bill. This fact might have contributed to Farr's Oceans Act being the only version that was not passed by the House or the Senate during the 105th Congress. As a result, the method for appointing the Commission as amended by Senator McCain in 1997 was adopted in later versions of the Oceans Act, including Hollings' Oceans Act of 2000,[29] which became law and officially established the U.S. Commission on Ocean Policy.

Proposal to Establish a National Ocean Council

While the Stratton Commission was the most visible outcome of the Marine Resources and Engineering Development Act of 1966, another important

26. Margaret Spring, Senate Committee on Commerce, Science, and Transportation, in Seattle, Wash., pers. comm. (Mar. 11, 2005).
27. S. Rep. No. 105–151 (1997).
28. S. 2327 § 3(a)(1), 106th Cong. (2000).
29. S. 2327, 106th Cong., Pub. L. No. 106–256 (2000).

federal group that was formed by the Act was the National Council on Marine Resources and Engineering Development. The Council, formed in the Executive office of the President, was chaired by the Vice President and was composed of eight additional members who came from the President's cabinet and other federal agencies. This council was charged with overseeing federal marine science activities, the creation of a comprehensive national marine science plan, and providing recommendations for resolving differences between all federal departments and agencies as related to marine science.[30]

In the tradition of following the earlier Stratton Commission legislation, Senator Hollings' original Oceans Act of 1997[31] called for the creation of a similar National Ocean Council, with twelve members coming from the President's cabinet and numerous federal agencies. While the idea of an independent policy commission was agreed upon between all those in support of an Oceans Act, the prospect of creating a National Ocean Council had a cooler reception. There was a high degree of worry throughout many federal agencies as to how a cabinet-level Ocean Council could affect their activities.[32] There was also concern among fellow Senators about the role of a Council as created concurrently with an Ocean Policy Commission. Within two months of Hollings' introduction of the Oceans Act of 1997, an amendment was offered to respond to these concerns.[33] Senator Lincoln Chafee of Rhode Island provided insight into his apprehension with the original version of the bill with a floor statement regarding the need for an amendment: "[T]he creation of a National Ocean Council raised two concerns. First, how would the National Ocean Council affect the execution of existing environmental laws? Second, is it timely now to create a permanent Council prior to the report of the independent National Ocean Commission created in the bill?"[34] The amendment responded to these fears by adding language that the Council's primary function would be to aid the National Ocean Commission, and requiring the Council to take the Commission's final report into consideration when forming a national ocean policy. Further, a clause was added to the amendment terminating the Council within one year of submission of the Commission's final report.

Despite these changes to the legislation, the idea of a National Ocean Council never achieved the same level of acceptance as that of an independent commission. While a commission would form recommendations after extensive study and then go out of business, a National Council

30. Marine Resources and Engineering Development Act of 1966, § 4.
31. S. 1213 § 5, 105th Cong. (1997).
32. Margaret Spring, pers. comm. (n. 26 above).
33. Amendment No. 1639, 105th Cong. (1997).
34. 143 Cong. Rec. S 12700, Vol. 143, No. 160, Part II (Nov. 13, 1997) (statement of Sen. Chafee).

instantly created an additional level of bureaucracy that was unpopular among many members of Congress and the Executive branch. Senator Hollings' statement in regard to the previously discussed amendment sheds some light on why many were worried about such a council, "[I]f, based on experience and the Commission recommendations, the Council proves to be an effective long term mechanism for coordinating federal ocean activities, it could be extended either administratively or legislatively."[35] The formation of a national ocean council that could possibly be continued indefinitely proved unacceptable to many members of Congress. Congressman Saxton did not include such a council in his Oceans Act legislation[36] that was passed by the House during the 105th Congress, and while Congressman Farr did so during the 106th Congress,[37] that bill received no action. Senator Hollings kept language for creating a Council in his first Oceans Act bill[38] introduced during the 106th Congress, as it was a reintroduction of the amended Oceans Act of 1997.[39] However, this bill received no action during this session of Congress. Instead, after pre-conferencing activities with the House regarding Hollings' later Oceans Act of 2000,[40] the language creating a National Ocean Council was removed altogether, and the bill passed both houses of Congress within four months.

Proposals to Exclude Geographic Areas from Commission Consideration

The Stratton Commission, when formed, was given the freedom to study all areas of the marine environment under United States' jurisdiction. These included public and private coastal waters, offshore areas out to a depth of 200 meters, and all States' shorelands and inland waters.[41] The Stratton Commission was free to formulate recommendations that would apply to all lands and waters in these areas. The political atmosphere in Congress between 1997 and 2000 did not automatically allow for the same level of freedom. Instead, the divergent political agendas of the Senate and House of Representatives led to much discussion over the effect the Commission would have on private property, the inclusion of inland waters and estuaries in the Commission's recommendations, and the role coastal States would play with a federal commission.

35. *Id.* at S 12701 (statement of Sen. Hollings).
36. Oceans Act of 1998, H.R. 3445, 105th Cong. (1998).
37. Oceans Act of 1999, H.R. 2425, 106th Cong. (1999).
38. Oceans Act of 1999, S. 959, 106th Cong. (1999).
39. S. 1213, 105th Cong. (1997).
40. S. 2327, 106th Cong. (2000).
41. Marine Resources and Engineering Development Act of 1966, § 8.

Senator Hollings, using the Stratton Commission as his model, did not include any language restricting the findings and recommendations of the ocean commission created by his first Oceans Act.[42] Nowhere in the bill was there any reference to exclusion of States, language regarding private property, or the restriction on studying inshore waters and estuaries. In contrast, the Oceans Act of 1998[43] introduced in the House of Representatives had language expressly addressing all of these. Many of these provisions of the House bill reflect amendments offered in subcommittee and committee markup sessions. These include a section requiring the Commission's final report to consider effects on private property and requiring that no recommendations have a negative impact on coastal economies.[44] A second section eliminated specific recommendations for selected States, saying none shall be aimed at Alaska or Idaho.[45] Finally, the bill also required that the views of all Governors of coastal States shall be reflected in the final Commission report.[46] These amendments, while offered by Congressman Saxton,[47] reflect the overall conservative makeup of the House Resources Committee. While this language was quite restrictive when compared to Hollings' original Oceans Act, it did not include further restrictions that had been proposed by other members of the House. Congressman Billy Tauzin of Louisiana, a state with extensive estuarine acreage, had proposed removing all estuarine zones, the regions where inland rivers approach and meet marine waters, from the areas to be studied by the Commission.[48] This amendment would have forced the Commission to only study offshore waters, effectively eliminating the majority of coastal zones and greatly reducing any effects of the Commission's recommendations on States. This amendment failed by a vote of 24 to 12.[49]

This contrast between the expansive nature of Hollings' Senate Oceans Act and Saxton's more restrictive House Oceans Act were reflections of the political views of a leading Democratic Senator and a majority Republican House of Representatives. While the Senate was anxious to follow the lead of Senator Hollings and form a commission free to study all areas of the marine environment, the House was wary of a federal commission infringing on private property rights and States' autonomy. As a result, a compromise was reached during the 106th Congress in order to allow the

---

42. Oceans Act of 1997, S. 1213, 105th Cong. (1997).
43. H.R. 3445, 105th Cong. (1998).
44. *Id.* at § 4(b)(5).
45. *Id.* at § 4(b)(6).
46. *Id.* at § 4(b)(4).
47. H.R. Rep. No. 105–718 (1998).
48. *Id.* at 15.
49. *Id.*

bill to pass. Hollings' first Oceans Act of the 106th Congress[50] did not reflect any of the concerns over private property and States' rights, but his final version implemented much of the language coming from the House during the 105th Congress, most likely a direct result of pre-conferencing activities. The Oceans Act of 2000[51] added a section stating that the Commission's final report shall not be specific to any one State,[52] and another section stating that the Commission shall give equal consideration to environmental, technical, scientific and economic factors.[53] The bill also included requirements for all Governors of coastal States to receive a draft version of the Commission report, and for their views regarding any Commission recommendations to be considered by the Commission and published in the final report.[54]

Use of a Science Advisory Panel

One area of concern within Congress surrounded the scientific data that an ocean commission would use, and how selective use of information might lead to the Commission reaching biased conclusions. In the scientific community, a widely-accepted method of ensuring that information is unbiased and is the best available is to have it peer reviewed, meaning other experts in the field evaluate the information or study it for any flaws. While not addressed in early Oceans Act legislation, concerns about this issue eventually led to the Commission having its own scientific advisory panel when the Oceans Act of 2000 became law.

The Oceans Act of 1997,[55] as introduced by both Senator Hollings and Congressman Farr, had no mention of scientific peer review or a scientific advisory group. Congressman Saxton addressed this concern in the language of his Oceans Act bill[56] during the 105th Congress. In July of 1998, Congressman Saxton introduced an amendment in full committee to his bill that included language requiring all data used by the Commission to be peer reviewed.[57] This was the first sign that review of the scientific information used by the ocean policy commission was a crucial aspect of any Oceans Act that would be enacted.

50. Oceans Act of 1999, S. 959, 106th Cong. (1999).
51. S. 2327, 106th Cong. (2000).
52. *Id.* at § 3(f)(4).
53. *Id.* at § 3(f)(3).
54. *Id.* at §§ 3(g)(1–2).
55. S. 1213, H.R. 2547, 105th Cong. (1997).
56. Oceans Act of 1998, H.R. 3445, 105th Cong. (1998).
57. H.R. Rep. No. 105–718 (1998).

When Hollings first reintroduced his Oceans Act legislation into the 106th Congress,[58] there was still no mention of a requirement for peer review or any other type of oversight of the data that the ocean commission would use in its work. Even in the initial version of the Oceans Act of 2000 introduced into the Senate,[59] any provision requiring peer review was lacking. However, concern was expressed in Congress over the absence of such a requirement.[60] As a result, this facet of the legislation was changed dramatically. Instead of including a simple requirement for peer reviewed data, as with Congressman Saxton's earlier legislation, Hollings' final version of the Oceans Act of 2000[61] added a science advisory panel for the Commission. Included in the section covering resources for the Commission on Ocean Policy, the bill called for the establishment of a multidisciplinary science advisory panel, formed through consultation with the Ocean Studies Board of the National Research Council of the National Academy of Sciences. The advisory board was required to assist the Commission in preparing its report, and ensuring that the scientific information considered by the Commission was based on the best scientific information available.[62]

Role of International Affairs in United States Ocean Policy

A persistent issue with the language of the numerous Oceans Acts during this period was the role of international policy in a review of U.S. ocean policy. While the ocean commission would be constructed by the federal government and made up of U.S. citizens, the international nature of the oceans and the extensive role of the U.S. in use of the seas suggested to some that international policy concerns should not be overlooked. As a result, some lawmakers included language stressing this belief in their versions of the Oceans Act. However, many of these direct legislative references to international policy were removed in the final version of the Oceans Act of 2000,[63] leading some to believe that the U.S. Commission on Ocean Policy was compelled to have a strongly domestic focus.

Senator Hollings' Oceans Act of 1997[64] had multiple references to international law and policy when describing the findings and recommendations the Commission was to produce. In this version of his bill, Senator

---

58. Oceans Act of 1999, S. 959, 106th Cong. (1999).
59. S. 2327, 106th Cong. (2000).
60. Pers. comm., Margaret Spring, n. 26 above. The Senate Energy Committee put a hold on the bill until this issue was resolved.
61. S. 2327, 106th Cong. (2000).
62. *Id.* at § 3(c)(3).
63. S. 2327, 106th Cong. (2000).
64. S. 1213, 105th Cong. (1997).

Hollings made specific reference to the United States' National Ocean Policy being "consistent with the obligations of the United States under international law."[65] Later in the same section, the language of the Act instructs the Commission "to consider the relationship of the ocean and coastal policy of the United States to the United Nations Convention on the Law of the Sea and other international agreements."[66] Finally, the bill lists as one of its objectives the preservation of the role of the United States as a leader in ocean and coastal activities, and cooperation with international bodies when it is in the best interest of the country.[67] Further evidence for Congressional concern over the importance of international ocean policy comes from the House of Representatives, in floor statements regarding Congressman Saxton's Oceans Act of 1998.[68] In September of 1998, Congressman Robert Underwood of Guam stated his support for international policy having a strong role in a U.S. ocean commission by calling for the ratification of the UN Convention on the Law of the Sea:

> This international arrangement, and collaboration with other developed nations that this treaty represents, goes hand in hand with the national policy we are seeking to create. It is possible to have one without the other, but to only develop a national policy and not address the need for international cooperation in our new global village is not quite responsible.[69]

References to international policy and the UN Convention on the Law of the Sea were also included in Congressman Farr's Oceans Act of 1997, found in the same section that discussed the report the ocean commission was to produce. This language was also included in Senator Hollings' Oceans Act of 1999,[70] introduced in the 106th Congress, with identical references to the United States' obligations under international law and the UN Convention on the Law of the Sea. However, the Oceans Act of 2000[71] that became law was noticeably lacking in these references. Despite the inclusion of explicit references to international law and agreements in earlier legislation, the Oceans Act of 2000 had no mention of international laws, agreements, or the UN Convention on the Law of the Sea when discussing the required matter of the commission on ocean policy's final

---

65. *Id.* at § 6(b)(1).
66. *Id.* at § 6(b)(8).
67. *Id.* at § 2(b)(9).
68. H.R. 3445, 105th Cong. (1998).
69. 144 Cong. Rec. H 7757, Vol. 144, No. 122 (September 15, 1998) (statement of Rep. Underwood).
70. S. 959, 106th Cong. (1999).
71. S. 2327, 106th Cong. (2000).

report.[72] Instead, only the objective of preserving the United States' role as a leader in ocean and coastal activities and international cooperation when in the national interest remained in the final bill. Interestingly, this simple clause took on a large role in the Commission's work when dealing with international issues. The Commission devoted a full chapter of its final report to international affairs,[73] and made numerous references to U.S. international obligations and programs in other chapters of the report.

Conclusion

The history of the Oceans Act of 2000 can be traced back to 1966, with the passage of the Marine Resources and Engineering Development Act and the formation of the Stratton Commission. While the legislation that created the Stratton Commission was revived for modern times, the political atmosphere of the 1960s differed greatly from that of the late 1990s and the 105th and 106th Congresses. The Oceans Act legislation of Senator Fritz Hollings reflected the political principles of Democrats in the Senate, who were ready for a comprehensive review of U.S. ocean policy with few restrictions. However, the legislation emerging from the House, introduced by Congressmen Sam Farr and Jim Saxton reflected the more conservative Republican makeup of the House of Representatives. While these two representatives were not directly responsible for the conservative nature of their bills, their legislation reveals a House that was more apprehensive about the effects of a federal commission without any constraints. Thus, the Oceans Act of 2000 that was passed by Congress reflected the views of both Democrats and Republicans.

The five issues discussed in this section led to a U.S. Commission on Ocean Policy that had some different characteristics than the Stratton Commission. To start, there was more Congressional involvement in the selection process, leading to a Commission with a diverse geographic base as well as diverse expertise. It also resulted in the appointment of Commissioners with closer political ties to elected officials in certain regions of the country. Secondly, the rejection of a National Ocean Council from the onset resulted in a connection to the Administration through the Council on Environmental Quality, an advisory body within the White House, rather than through line agencies. This led to greater independence for the Commission from the "path dependent" thinking of the bureaucracy that might have resulted from a Council.

72. *Id.* at § 3(f)(2).
73. Commission Report, Chapter 29, n. 1 above.

While geographic areas were not excluded in the final bill, the clauses requiring equal consideration of environmental, economic, scientific and technical factors, and the section allowing States to review a draft report, were valuable to the work of the Commission. The former clause was frequently cited during the Commission deliberations and kept the concept of a balanced policy on the agenda. The latter clause proved invaluable in improving the report and gaining allies at the State and local levels. The inclusion of a science advisory panel for the Commission was very helpful because it allowed the panel to be integrated into the Commission's work, proving far better than creating a potentially contentious separate peer review process. Finally, while international policy was somewhat downplayed in the final law, the inclusion of the objective to preserve the United States' role as a world leader in ocean and coastal activities created a "backdoor" for the Commission to consider aspects of international policy it deemed important. However, for reasons organic to the Commission process, such as Commissioner backgrounds and required hearings around the U.S. where domestic issues were given overwhelming prominence, the Commission gave much greater attention to domestic rather than international affairs.

PART II—INITIATING THE COMMISSION AND ITS WORK: JANUARY TO SEPTEMBER 2001

Choosing the Commissioners

The Oceans Act created a complicated process for choosing commissioners, some of which was discussed in Part I.[74] Specific roles were assigned to 13 political leaders to choose the 16 commissioners. This differed markedly from the Stratton Commission process that gave the job of choosing commissioners to the President. Despite this rather decentralized process, described below, the 16 were officially announced by the President on June 15, 2001,[75] after a process that got underway January 21, 2001, the effective date of the Act.

As discussed above, the Republican controlled House wanted to assure that the commissioners chosen represented a balance among nominees by the Republican and Democratic members of Congress. This resulted in a process that required the President to choose 12 of the 16 commissioners from four lists containing a total of 24 names submitted by the majority and minority leadership of the two houses of Congress (eight names on the

74. See n. 24–29 above.
75. News release, The White House, Release of June 15, 2001, available online: <http://www.whitehouse.gov/news/releases/2001/06/20010615-14.html>.

majority lists and four names on the minority lists). But the Act went further than this by requiring consultation with the majority and minority leadership of the primary subject matter committees concerned with ocean and coastal affairs. In the Senate the subject matter committee with jurisdiction was the Senate Committee on Commerce, State and the Judiciary. In the House three committees split jurisdiction over ocean issues: Resources, Science, and Transportation and Infrastructure. Thus, in addition to the Majority leader of the Senate, the Speaker of the House, and the minority leaders in each chamber, the respective chairs and ranking minority members of four substantive committees were part of the process. Thus, twelve members of Congress and the President had the duty to come up with the names of the Commissioners.

In this process it must be noted that the majority party had twice the number of names to nominate as the minority party, and ultimately the President got to choose the commissioners so long as they were nominated. In addition, he had four "picks" of his own. Because the Republicans controlled both houses of Congress and the Presidency in 2001, some commentators argued that the Commission was a "Bush commission," and a "Republican commission," and predicted certain policy results because of that.[76] Throughout the deliberation of the Commission the chairman and commissioners referred to the commission as "non-partisan," even though the selection process involved political partisans. This characterization is the correct one. As the Chairman often said in his presentations, each commissioner had views and opinions on the issues, but they were based on their expertise and experience, not on a political agenda established from the outside.

A number of staffers for congressional committees and key interest groups that watched the process closely referred to the selection of commissioners as inherently a staff-driven, low-visibility, political process.[77] The Administration and the Congress was new and still getting organized. The issue was a tiny one compared to other issues facing the Congress and the Administration. The members were not deluged with nominees. Attempts to "beat the bushes" for names, and to seek high-level people from outside the ocean community (as was done in the case of the Stratton

76. This comment was most frequently heard from environmental interest organizations.

77. The observations on the Congressional selection processes are based on interviews with Margaret Spring, Senate Committee on Commerce, March 11, 2005; David Jansen, House Resources Committee (minority) March 9, 2005; Terry Schaff, Woods Hole Oceanographic Institution, March 15, 2005; Penny Dalton, Committee on Ocean Research and Education, March 2, 2005; Ellen Athas, formerly with CEQ, April 15, 2005; Margaret Davidson, Director NOAA/NOS Coastal Services Center, July 1, 2005.

Commission with Julius Stratton, a University and Foundation President) were not productive. Congressional leaders of substantive committees solicited their members for names, and attempts were made to construct a list that distributed among members (i.e., each interested member gets a name). Lists of preferred members submitted by key ocean-related organizations ultimately had little influence. Some industry groups had "favorites" that they advanced such as in the oil and gas and ports industries. However, in the words of one key staffer, the process was difficult to control and ultimately became political.

No attempt was made for this article to research the nomination strategy and selection process for each successful Commissioner. In many cases individuals with a special interest in serving may have sought to become a "favorite son" candidate. To illustrate the process in one case, here is the story of one commissioner, the first author of this article.

Since U.S. coastal zone management and ocean policy is my academic field of interest and expertise, I was well aware of the move to establish a Commission and decided in late 2000 and early 2001 to seek to become a member. I consulted with colleagues and started a little campaign. I asked Washington State fishery, shipping and port industry lobbyists, University lobbyists, and others to lobby the Washington State Congressional delegation to support my candidacy. They made calls and sent letters. I made direct contact with coast and ocean staffers in the Washington delegation. Both Washington State Senators signed letters of support. One House staffer did the hard work of getting a co-signed letter from all 9 House members (Republicans and Democrats) supporting me, and sending it on to the House Resources Committee, minority side, since 6 of the 9 members from Washington State are Democrats and two of the Democrats were on that committee. (Only one other person from Washington was seeking appointment.) With the co-signed letter in hand, a former student of mine who was the staffer for the minority on House Resources, argued my case to the staff of the ranking minority leader on House Resources, who then wrote a supportive letter to Congressman Gephardt, the Ranking Democrat in the House. This worked, and the next thing I knew I was on his list and my name was submitted as one of four coming from the minority side of the House of Representatives.[78]

78. Personal statement of Marc Hershman as relayed to Frank Muller-Karger, a fellow Commissioner in an e-mail message dated April 7, 2005.

The four Congressional lists were submitted to the White House Office of Personnel on March 3, 2001.[79] The process after this is harder to document. The White House staff was still being organized and the "cognizant agency" with which the Commission would coordinate was not yet clearly established, and the leadership of that office was not in place as yet. (By June 2001, the Council of Environmental Quality (CEQ) had assumed cognizant agency responsibility and Jim Connaughten became CEQ chairman.)

According to the Oceans Act, Commissioners should be:

... knowledgeable in ocean and coastal activities, including individuals representing State and local governments, ocean-related industries, academic and technical institutions, and public interest organizations involved with scientific, regulatory, economic, and environmental ocean and coastal activities. The membership of the Commission shall be balanced by area of expertise and balanced geographically to the extent consistent with maintaining the highest level of expertise on the Commission.[80]

Thus there were a variety of criteria spelled out in the Oceans Act, as well as considerations special to the administration as the basis for choice.[81] However, the Administration had four picks of its own and this added to the calculations since they could make up for "holes" in the coverage based on geography, areas of expertise, and other factors.[82]

As it turned out a big hole related to diversity—no women or minorities were on the lists submitted through the Congressional process. This is an interesting failing in this form of constructing a Commission. None of the four Congressional leaders had the responsibility of considering the makeup of the entire group—from their perspective that would be someone else's responsibility. It fell to the Administration to seek some level of gender and ethnic diversity. To the Administration's credit they ended up appointing two women with special expertise and a Hispanic person to the Commission. In the case of the Commissioner with Hispanic roots, the

79. Pers. Comm., from Arthur Nowell to Marc Hershman, dated March 7, 2001, forwarding information on submitted names from Scott Sparks of Consortium for Oceanographic Research and Education (CORE).

80. Pub. L. No. 106–256, § 3(b)(1).

81. A special assistant to the incoming Bush administration, John Howard, was overseeing CEQ while the Administration was being organized and represented the political perspective in making choices. His criteria for selection are not known. Interview with Ellen Athas, April 15, 2005.

82. CEQ convened an interagency panel to suggest names for the President's four picks. Since this panel was aware of the names being considered by Congressional leaders, there was an attempt to use the four to balance the Congressional nominees. Margaret Davidson, pers. comm., July 1, 2005.

administration actively solicited for nominees through Hispanic networks and an oceanographer with special expertise in ocean observation applied and was selected.[83]

The 16 Commissioners

As noted above, the names of the 16 Commissioners were announced by the White House on June 15, 2001,[84] and official appointments followed shortly thereafter. Table 1 presents summary information about the Commissioners. A brief biography of each Commissioner is posted on the Commission's web site.[85] As envisioned in the Oceans Act, the group came from different regions of the country—New England (2), mid-Atlantic (3), Great Lakes (1), Washington DC (1), Southeast (1), Gulf of Mexico (4), West coast (3) and Alaska (1). The diversity of expertise among Commissioners was also evident, including marine academic scientists and explorers, fisheries managers, marine transportation experts, marine educators, offshore oil and gas operators and analysts, environmental lawyers and policy experts, bankers, local government officials, and Naval officers (retired).

Most striking is the senior level policy and administrative leadership experience of so many of the Commissioners. The leadership experience included major assignments in the Navy, federal government agencies, State resource and port agencies, major corporations, industry associations, local governments, and academic departments, institutes and colleges. The majority of Commissioners have been in charge of large organizations in public and private life, with extensive experience at organizational management, budgeting, policy development, and organizational change. They were savvy at dealing with external constituents, with political forces, and with financial pressures. Most importantly, they understood how large organizations and government agencies operated.

83. Commissioner Frank Muller-Karger is of Puerto Rican, Venezuelan and German descent. In an e-mail message to the author dated April 7, 2005, Muller-Karger described the way in which he heard about the Commission opportunity through an e-mail message circulated within the Hispanic Community, and after replying was sent application forms and interviewed by telephone before being nominated by the President.

Congressional leaders also were concerned about diversity on the Commission when the list of names became public. There was a meeting in Spring 2001 to discuss the potential to amend the Oceans Act to require that minority, women, fisheries and environmental group categories be considered even if the number of commissioners increased. When counter-proposals came forward requiring that certain additional groups be represented, the process became unwieldy and the attempt to amend the law was dropped. See n. 26 above.

84. White House Press Release of June 15, 2001. See n. 75 above.

85. Available online: <http://www.oceancommission.gov/commission/commissionbios.html#top>.

Table 1.—U.S. Ocean Commissioners

Name	Geographic Region	Commission Working Group	Expertise	Experience
Admiral James. D. Watkins, U.S.N. (Ret.)	Wash., D.C.	Chairman (ex-officio on all committees)	U.S. governmental affairs, Navy operations, ocean research policy	Chief of Naval Operations, Chair of U.S. Aids Commission; Sec'y of Energy; President of CORE
Robert Ballard, Ph.D.	New England (RI)	Research, Education, Operations	Oceanography, ocean exploration, marine education	Director of ocean exploration labs; developer of ROV systems; founder of ocean education programs; professor of Oceanography
Ted A. Beattie	Great Lakes (ILL)	Research, Education, Operations	Marine education	CEO of Shedd Aquarium; past president American Zoo and Aquarium Society
Lillian Borrone	Mid-Atlantic (NJ)	Governance	Port development and administration, maritime policy	Former Port Commerce Director, Port Authority NY/NJ; Board Chair, Eno Transportation Foundation
James M. Coleman, Ph.D.	Gulf of Mexico (LA)	WG Chmn., Research, Education, Operations; Investment and implementation	Oceanography; marine research administration/operations	Boyd Professor, LSU; former chair, Marine Board, NAS; member, National Academy of Engineering
Ann D'Amato	West Coast (CA)	Stewardship	Local government administration	Chief of Staff to Los Angeles City Atty; former Deputy Mayor, Los Angeles

Name	Region	Category	Focus area	Biography
Lawrence Dickerson	Gulf of Mexico (Tx)	Governance	Oil and gas operations	COO Diamond Offshore Drilling; Executive Comm. Nat'l Ocean Industries Ass'n
V.Admiral Paul G. Gaffney II, USN (Ret.)	Mid-Atlantic (NJ)	Stewardship; Investment and implementation	Ocean Engineering, U.S. Navy operations/administration	President, Monmouth U.; former Pres., Nat'l Defense U.; former chief of Naval research
Marc J. Hershman	West Coast (WA)	Governance	U.S. coast and marine law; coastal zone management	Professor and former Director, UW School of Marine Affairs; editor, Coastal Mgmt Journal
Paul L. Kelly	Gulf of Mexico (Tx)	Stewardship; Investment and implementation	Marine resources law; oil and gas policy	Sr. V.P., Rowan Cos; former Chair, U.S. DOI OCS Policy Comm.
Christopher Koch	Mid-Atlantic (VA)	Governance; Investment and implementation	Maritime law and policy; U.S. fisheries law and policy	CEO, World Shipping Council; former Chair, FMC; former Gen. Counsel, Sea-Land Svc.
Frank Muller-Karger, Ph.D.	Gulf of Mexico (Fl)	Stewardship	Oceanography; remote sensing	Prof. of biological oceanography; Director of nst. for Marine Remote Sensing
Edward B. Rasmuson	West Coast (AK)	Research, Education, Operations; Investment and implementation	Banking; commercial fisheries policy	Former CEO, Nat'l Bank of Alaska; philanthropist, formerly Bd. of Regents, U. of Alaska

Name	Geographic Region	Commission Working Group	Expertise	Experience
Andrew A. Rosenberg, Ph.D.	New England (NH)	Governance	Fisheries science; fisheries management/administration	Prof., UNH; former Dean, Coll. of Life Sciences, UNH; formerly Reg. Dir. and Deputy Dir., NMFS
William D. Ruckelshaus	West Coast (WA)	WG Chmn., Governance; Investment and implementation	Environmental law and policy; fisheries restoration policy	Dir., Madrona Venture Group; chair World Resources Inst.; former Admin U.S. EPA
Paul A. Sandifer, Ph.D.	Southeast (SC)	WG Chmn, Stewardship; Investment and implementation	Fisheries Science; aquaculture; fisheries management and administration	Sr. Scientist, NOAA; former Dir., SC Dept. Natural Resources
Thomas R. Kitsos, Ph.D.	Wash., D.C.	Executive Director	U.S. Congressional leadership, minerals management, public administration and political science	Former Acting Dir., MMS; former staff member for Merchant Marine Fisheries Comm. of U.S. House of Representatives

Choosing the Chairman

The statute was clear that the Chair of the Commission was to be selected by the Commissioners.[86] This differed from the Stratton Commission that called for the chair and vice chair to be chosen by the President. In an initial conversation by telephone among a number of the Commissioners in early August 2001, the choice of Chair was discussed. Although no formal decision could be made until a first official meeting, it was clearly a crucial step in the process and nominations for Chairman were taken.

It was no secret that Admiral James Watkins was a frontrunner. No communication to the Commissioners about chairmanship came from the White House or Congressional leaders. Nor was there a "campaign" or lobbying of Commissioners by the Admiral or any other Commissioners on his behalf. As it turned out Admiral Watkins was the only official nominee and was elected unanimously during the first official meeting on September 17, 2001. His extensive experience in national policy and administrative affairs (Chief of Naval Operations, Chair of the AIDS Commission, Secretary of Energy, President of the national Consortium on Oceanographic Research and Education), his seniority (four star Admiral, colleague to many members of Congress and the Administration), his technical knowledge in ocean research and leadership in advancing the National Ocean Partnership Act in 1996, and in lobbying for the Ocean Policy Commission, made him a logical choice. Furthermore, he wanted the job and was available to provide virtually his full time to the effort. Almost every other Commissioner had a "day job" of some significance.

During initial discussions in August of 2001, Bill Ruckelshaus was nominated for chair as well. His credentials were powerful—twice administrator of the Environmental Protection Agency (EPA), leadership in the Nixon administration in the early 1970s (CIA Director and a very brief stint as U.S. Attorney General), member of the Brundtland Commission that reshaped environmental affairs for the world, CEO of a major corporation, U.S. representative to negotiate the Salmon Treaty with Canada, leader in salmon restoration in the Pacific Northwest, and Board member for many corporations and national and international environmental and natural resources NGOs. His skill as a lawyer and national policy leader in environmental affairs would be extremely valuable to the Commission in dealing with its extensive mandate to address governance issues in U.S. ocean affairs.

After a few days' reflection and discussion with Admiral Watkins and other Commissioners, Ruckelshaus declined consideration as chair and urged all Commissioners to support the Admiral. His reasoning was that the Commission should not start out its work with a "contest" for leadership, but rather begin its work with unanimous support behind its leader. He argued that the Admiral's skills and knowledge, his investment in the ocean issues, his willingness to give it the time needed, his willingness to rely on

---

86. Pub. L. No. 106–256, § 3(b)(3).

other Commissioners for the expertise he did not possess, and his residence in Washington D.C. would serve all of us well.

Thus, the very first, and perhaps one of the most important initial decisions of the Commission, was done through open and reasoned discussion involving virtually all Commissioners, and resulted in a common understanding and consensus support for the nomination of chairman. This established a "tone" for open deliberation, for acting in unison when the case was clear, and for seeing the importance of the collective effort over individual aspirations.

Preparing the First Meeting

Those first unofficial telephone conversations among Commissioners also addressed a variety of substantive and procedural issues—how to structure and run the Commission's day-to-day affairs. This included the issues of how to choose the Executive Director and other staff, establishing an office for the Commission, complying with a wide range of official rules of the U.S. government on budget, personnel, ethics, and financial disclosure, and deciding on meeting protocols and relations with the public. It also dealt with how the Commissioners would organize themselves into sub-committees or work groups to undertake consideration of the issues laid out in the Oceans Act. Much of this was done to prepare for the first official meeting of the Commission on September 17 and 18, 2001.[87] The discussion and resolution of these issues between August and November of 2001 set a tone for openness and dialogue between the Chairman and the Commissioners on many aspects of the management of the Commission's work.

With regard to procedural matters, the statute provided little guidance. The chairman is responsible for hiring the Executive Director (subject to confirmation by a majority of Commissioners), hiring other staff as needed, assigning duties to the staff, and for budget expenditures.[88] Open meetings, advanced notice in the Federal Register, public participation at meetings, record keeping and availability, are addressed as well.[89]

Fortunately for the Commission advance steps were taken to assure that the Commission had a rapid start. In 1998, the National Oceanic and Atmospheric Administration (NOAA) received a $1 million appropriation to help prepare for the Commission's work.[90] Since a bill had passed the Senate that year, it was anticipated that start-up work would be needed. Between then and 2001 when the Commission was a reality, NOAA/NOS used part of the funds for substantive work such as producing reports about the Stratton Commission, issues analysis, future challenges, and an interac-

---

87. The record of the first official meeting of the Commission is available online: <http://oceancommission.gov/meetings/sep17_18_01/sep17_18_01.html>.
88. Pub. L. No. 106–256 §§ 3(b)(3) and (d).
89. *Id.* at § 3(e).
90. Pub. L. No. 105B235 at 150.

tive web page.[91] Once the Commissioners were appointed, NOAA staff spent three or four months from August 2001 to October/November 2001 helping with a transition phase while the Commission got organized. NOAA's National Ocean Service (NOS) officials facilitated the first telephone discussions among Commissioners, handled administrative arrangements for the first meeting on September 17 and 18, 2001, and assisted with details such as office space, posting notices for meetings and staff positions, arranging for recording and transcribing the minutes of the meeting, and establishing a web presence.[92]

In addition to NOAA's role, two other organizations assisted the Commission in its start-up. The first was CEQ, designated as the "cognizant agency" for the Bush administration on matters of policy.[93] A number of meetings were held at CEQ involving NOAA and the Admiral after he secured the nomination as Chair. CEQ provided initial assistance for recruiting an Executive Director by drafting a job description, and determined that the Commission should hold its first meeting as planned on September 17, so close after the 9/11 terrorist attacks.[94]

The second agency helping in the start-up phase was the U.S. General Services Administration (GSA), the official body charged with supporting independent commissions. GSA officials and lawyers discussed such issues as Commissioner compensation, Commissioner financial disclosure, proper procedures for meetings, security clearances, ethics rules for special government employees, and application of Federal Advisory Committee Act (FACA) rules.[95] According to staff assisting the Admiral at this juncture, these meetings were crucially important.[96] The Admiral wanted the Commission to fully and accurately comply with the rules so that no criticism could be leveled in the future. It was already apparent that environmental organizations were watching closely because they had written to the President and the Commission in May and June 2001, protesting the lack of a member of the Commission representing the national environmen-

---

91. "NOAA Activities of the National Ocean Service in support of the Commission on Ocean Policy," memorandum circulated at the first meeting of the Commission, on file with the first author.

92. Pers. comm., Glenn Boledovich to Marc Hershman, dated March 11, 2005.

93. Pers. comm., Ellen Athas, April 15, 2005. Ms. Athas suggests that the choice of CEQ as the cognizant agency was probably a joint decision among the primary interested federal agencies rather than a top-down directive since the agencies already had been working on the issue and were the only ones with a strong interest.

94. Pers. comm., Terry Schaff, March 15, 2005.

95. Federal Advisory Committee Act, 86 Stat. 770. See Commission on Ocean Policy Inaugural Meeting Briefing Book for Commissioners, September 17 and 18, 2001.

96. Pers. comm., Terry Schaff, March 15, 2005. Mr. Schaff assisted the Admiral closely during the organizational phase of the Commission. He was adamant in expressing the Admiral's determination that administrative details be handled accurately and thoroughly to avoid any criticism of the Commission.

tal organizations.[97] Similarly, the national fishing organizations, both commercial and recreational, were cautious because none of their members had a seat on the Commission.[98]

One indication of the desire to comply as fully as possible was the Admiral's decision that the Commission would comply with all relevant FACA rules even though the law said that many of those provisions of administrative law were not applicable to the Commission.[99] This resulted in more detailed record keeping and availability of information than the Oceans Act itself would require.[100]

Another indication of the desire to go beyond the terms of the law was the Admiral's desire to involve all Commissioners in the choice of Executive Director and the make-up of subcommittees of Commissioners. The statute allowed him to move forward independently on the choice of Executive Director so long as a majority would concur. In the early telephone conversations the Commissioners and the Admiral encouraged NOAA and CEQ to move ahead with describing a position and advertising it so that applications might be available for the first official meeting of the Commission. That worked and an initial eight qualified applicants (out of 73 received) were available on September 17 and the Commission was able to discuss a procedure for interviews. Eight Commissioners volunteered to conduct the interviews and provide advice to the Admiral and all Commissioners as soon as possible. This expedited process allowed for the choice of an Executive Director to become official at the November meeting.

The decision to establish sub-committees of Commissioners was an important initial step in addressing substantive issues. The agenda for the first meeting included a proposal for three committees—governance, research and marine operations, and investment.[101] Review by the full Commission noted the need for an additional subcommittee on steward-ship, dealing with the use and protection of natural resources. This was accepted and added, and the leaders of each subcommittee were identified, thus spreading the leadership wider than the chair. Again, a pattern of dialogue and discussion, and willingness to adjust, was established early in the Commission's work.

97. A coalition of 13 environmental groups argued in a letter to the President, dated May 14th 2001, that the Commission should include "strong representation from the national marine conservation community." Another letter of concern was later sent protesting the failure to include such a representative. Once the Commission was organized, the Chairman met with representatives of the coalition to assure them that the process would include ample opportunity for their participation (Terry Schaff, pers. comm., March 15, 2005). In general, the national marine conservation community was very pleased with the final report.

98. Pers. comm., Terry Schaff, *id.*.

99. Pub. L. No. 106–256 § 3(a).

100. See n. 96 above.

101. See n. 87 above.

PART III—THE WORK OF THE U.S. COMMISSION ON OCEAN POLICY (2001-2004)

Overview of the USCOP Products

The output of the USCOP is well documented. This was particularly required in the Oceans Act,[102] and is required for all advisory bodies to the federal government under the Federal Advisory Committee Act (FACA).[103] In addition to its Final Report, the Commission produced 14 appendices, a video illustrating the work of the Commission, and a voluminous set of archived materials filed with the Library of Congress and the NOAA library in Silver Spring, Maryland. The official web site of the Commission, which contains all of the reports, interim reports, record of meetings, and other materials, will be maintained for the forseeable future, remaining in its static state as of the end of 2004, after which a CD-ROM of the web site will be added to the archives.[104]

The Final Report of the Commission, which is available in hard copy, CD and on the Commission's official web site, is 522 pages, containing 31 chapters and 212 recommended actions.[105] (See Table 2) To make it more user friendly the report includes a 26-page Executive Summary, a text box on page 25 titled "Critical Actions Recommended by the U.S. Commission on Ocean Policy" that puts the major themes on one page, and a final chapter listing all the recommendations categorized by individual or organization directed to take action as well as by chapter. The report is organized into nine parts addressing the following areas: ocean assets and challenges, improved governance, education, coastal resources, water quality, ocean uses and preservation, science, international policy, and implementation. Table 2 displays the nine parts, the chapters within each part, and a brief description of the scope of each chapter and its recommendations. Thus, the Final Report is a lengthy document, covering a great many topics, each of which includes background information, discussion of problems and issues, and recommendations for change.

102. Pub. L. No. 106–256, § 3(e)(2).
103. Pub. L. 92–463, 86 Stat. 770, 5 USCA App. 2.
104. "A Guide to the Archives of the U.S. Commission on Ocean Policy," memorandum to Commissioners sent electronically by the Executive Director, Tom Kitsos, October 12, 2004.
105. See n. 1 above, and <http://www.oceancommission.gov>.

Table 2.—Content and Scope of USCOP Report

Part I: Our Oceans: A National Asset	
Ch. 1 Recognizing Ocean Assets and Challenges	The value of the ocean and coastal economy; employment; lost value from environmental degradation; reduced resource base; losses from land use, hazards, climate change
Ch. 2 Understanding the Past to Shape a New National Ocean Policy	History of U.S. ocean policy from WWII to present; the USCOP mandate, members, process and products
Ch. 3 Setting the Nation's Sights	The vision for the future; guiding principles; putting principles into policy
Primer on Ocean Jurisdictions: Drawing Lines in the Water	Defining offshore zones: the baseline, seaward boundaries of states; territorial sea; contiguous zone; exclusive economic zone; continental shelf; high seas
Part II: Blueprint for Change: A New National Ocean Policy Framework	
Ch. 4 Enhancing Ocean Leadership and Coordination	Proposal for National Ocean Council; Assistant to the President for Oceans; Presidential Council of Advisors (non-federal)
Ch. 5 Advancing a Regional Approach	Bottom-up regional ocean councils; federal support for regional efforts; regional research and information services; regional ecosystem assessments
Ch. 6 Coordinating Management in Federal Waters	Expanding uses of offshore waters; clarifying offshore management responsibilities; creating a coordinated offshore management regime; gaining fair return from the offshore; using marine protected areas as a management tool
Ch. 7 Strengthening the Federal Agency Structure	Reorganization proposals of the past; strengthening NOAA (phase 1); consolidating some ocean and coastal programs (phase 2); managing all natural resources through an ecosystem-based approach (phase 3)
Part III: Ocean Stewardship: The Importance of Education and Public Awareness	
Ch. 8 Promoting Lifelong Ocean Education	Strengthening the nation's ocean awareness; building a collaborative ocean education network through a new national ocean education office; linking the research and education communities; incorporating ocean education into K–12 curriculum; investing in higher education and the future ocean workforce; advancing informal education for all Americans
Part IV: Living on the Edge: Economic Growth and Resource Conservation Along the Coast	
Ch. 9 Managing Coasts and their Watersheds	Population and tourism growth in the coastal zone; need for a stronger CZMA addressing watersheds, smart growth and offshore management; focus attention on coastal watersheds; Consolidation needed in area-based coastal management programs

Ch. 10 Guarding People and Property against Natural Hazards	Assessing the growing cost of natural hazards; changing inappropriate federal incentives; changes needed in the national flood insurance program
Ch. 11 Conserving and Restoring Coastal Habitat	Dedicated funding needed for coastal land conservation; regional ocean councils should set priorities for habitat conservation and restoration; coastal wetlands require a comprehensive protection framework
Ch. 12 Managing Sediment and Shorelines	Sediment as resource or problem; changing sediment quantities and quality; sediment management at a regional level; costs and benefits of dredging; improved implementation of dredged material management plans by national and regional dredging teams; improve management capabilities for contaminated sediments
Ch. 13 Supporting Marine Commerce and Transportation	Prepare the U.S. Marine transportation system for future growth; design a new national freight transportation strategy; upgrade emergency preparedness planning
Part V: Clear Waters Ahead: Coastal and Ocean Water Quality	
Ch. 14 Addressing Coastal Water Pollution	Improve control of point source pollution through advanced treatment, better on-site treatment and improved infrastructure, incentives and enforcement; increase attention to non-point sources of pollution and introduce enforceable management measures; improve controls of atmospheric sources of water pollution
Ch. 15 Creating a National Monitoring Network	Expand and better coordinate the existing monitoring network; include coastal areas in monitoring and link to the emerging ocean observing system; develop an effective system design that includes goals, periodic review and user input
Ch. 16 Limiting Vessel Pollution and Improving Vessel Safety	Use incentives to develop a culture of vessel safety, security and environmental compliance; work to enhance flag state oversight and compliance and strengthened port state control programs; Congress should act to manage waste water discharges from cruise ships; improve management of air emissions and sanitary waste; reduce risk of oil spills through better prevention programs and places of refuge
Ch. 17 Preventing the Spread of Invasive Species	Assess status of the problem and existing diverse approaches; identify and control pathways for introduction of non-native species; better coordinate and streamline efforts to control already introduced species

Ch. 18 Reducing Marine Debris	Sources and consequences of marine debris; adding a NOAA-based marine debris management program; expanding the EPA and NOAA efforts at enforcement and outreach; improve programs to address derelict fishing gear and port reception facilities for waste
Part VI: Ocean Value and Vitality: Enhancing the Use and Protection of Ocean Resources	
Ch. 19 Achieving Sustainable Fisheries	Upgrade use of scientific findings and capacity of scientific and statistical committees in fisheries management; require that harvest limits be at or below the ABC set by the SSC; expand cooperative research programs between scientists and fishers; authorize additional interstate fishery management plans; broaden membership and improve appointment process for fishery management councils; authorize use of dedicated access privileges and establish national guidelines; repeal programs that encourage overcapitalization; expand cooperative fisheries enforcement programs; maximize use of vessel monitoring systems and other technologies in enforcement; further advance ecosystem-based management through enhanced attention to essential fish habitat and by-catch reduction; aggressive steps to advance the Fish Stocks Agreement and the FAO Code of Conduct for Responsible Fishing
Ch. 20 Protecting Marine Mammals and Endangered Species	Assess the threats to marine mammals, sea turtles, salmonids and seabirds; place protection of all marine mammals under NOAA; enhance cooperation among jurisdictions under the ESA; clarify the definitions of "take" and "harassment"; implement programmatic permitting for activities affecting marine mammals; expand programs that mitigate human impacts on marine mammals and endangered species including effects of noise; apply ecosystem-based regional approaches as appropriate
Ch. 21 Preserving Coral Reefs and Coral Communities	Congress should pass a comprehensive law for coral reef protection, management and restoration; NOAA should take the lead for the management of deep water coral communities; establish standards that ensure sustainable harvest of coral reef resources
Ch. 22 Setting a Course for Sustainable Marine Aquaculture	Minimize the multiple environmental impacts potentially caused by marine aquaculture; develop a new marine aquaculture legal framework led by NOAA; create the Office of Sustainable Marine Aquaculture for regulation, guideline development, R&D and education

Ch. 23 Connecting the Oceans and Human Health	Enhance interagency and private sector work to discover new marine micro-organisms; improve understanding, detection and prevention of harmful algal blooms, harmful marine bacteria and viruses, and contaminated seafood; improve methods for monitoring and identifying pathogens and chemical toxins; apply new knowledge in work of regional ocean councils
Ch. 24 Managing Offshore Energy and Other Mineral Resources	Assess trends in offshore oil and gas production including deep-water oil production, natural gas from shallow water, and LNG carriers and offshore LNG ports; share federal oil and gas revenues from the OCS with all coastal states for investment in renewable coast and ocean resources; expand the MMS Environmental Studies Program and integrate the offshore oil and gas industry into the ocean observing program; review gas hydrates research for future potential in meeting national needs; Congress should establish an offshore renewable energy regime
Part VII: Science-Based Decisions: Advancing our Understanding of the Oceans	
Ch. 25 Creating a National Strategy for Increasing Scientific Knowledge	Make the oceanographic partnership program an integral part of the new ocean policy framework; double the ocean and coastal research budget over the next five years; design a national research strategy for basic and applied research, including a specific program for social science and economic research; expand the national ocean exploration program; better coordinate federal ocean and coastal mapping and charting activities; re-establish the Congressional Office of Technology Assessment
Ch. 26 Achieving a Sustained, Integrated Ocean Observing System (IOOS)	Promote development of IOOS through strong partnerships; create a national lead office and regional associations that includes user participation; establish core variables, incorporate research observatories and new technologies; incorporate added satellite observing into IOOS; insure production of useful end products; insure that IOOS can be integrated in global Earth Observing System
Ch. 27 Enhancing Ocean Infrastructure and Technology Development	Develop a national infrastructure strategy for facilities, new technology and technology transfer; ensure dedicated funding for critical infrastructure needs including the UNOLS fleet, fisheries research vessels, ocean exploration infrastructure, and others; support technology needs essential for ocean and coastal management; create virtual marine technology centers

Ch. 28 Modernizing Ocean Data and Information Systems	Establish a lead federal organization for ocean and coastal data and information management; NOAA and the Navy should establish an information management and communications partnership; improve access to ocean data including use of the National Virtual Ocean Data System; clarify requirements for accessing data from federally funded academic research and newly declassified naval oceanographic data
Part VIII: The Global Ocean: U.S. Participation in International Policy	
Ch. 29 Advancing International Ocean Science and Policy	Accede to the UN Convention on Law of the Sea; review Convention on Biological Diversity for possible ratification; establish an interagency committee to support ocean-related international policy; enhance support for international research in ocean science and management
Part IX: Moving Ahead: Implementing a New National Ocean Policy	
Ch. 30 Funding Needs and Possible Sources	Congress should establish the Ocean Policy Trust Fund using unallocated revenues from offshore uses; disburse trust resources to state and federal agencies to support new or expanded ocean and coastal management activities; produce the biennial report on ocean funding called for in the Oceans Act of 2000
Ch. 31 Summary of Recommendations	[Listing of all recommendations in the report; index of recommendations organized by primary implementing entity: Congress, Executive branch, Federal government agencies, interagency groups, regional bodies, states, international]

The 14 appendices contain considerable additional useful information. Some appendices can be characterized as "data" on which recommendations were based, e.g., inventories of marine educators, academic infrastructure, ocean and coastal facilities, ocean and coastal laws, and Congressional Committees with jurisdiction (Appendices 3, 4, 5, 6 and F, respectively). Others are an elaboration of particular parts of the report such as a paper on demographic trends and ocean and coastal economic value, an expansion of the proposed structure for federal coordination, and detailed costs associated with implementation (Appendices C, E and G, respectively). An especially valuable set of appendices present syntheses of testimony before the Commission organized by topic and by presenter, and a volume including the comments from 37 Governors who responded to the draft report of the Commission (Appendices 1 and 2, respectively, and a "Special Addendum" for the Governors' comments). Taken together the Report and the appendices provide a small library of published information serving as a baseline for U.S. ocean policy development.

Finally the archives of the Commission, including documents and the CD of the official web site, contain such information as mid-term and preliminary reports, briefing books and transcripts from each official Commission meeting, all testimony presented, follow-up written questions and answers between the Commission and presenters, official public comments, reports on Commission site visits, summaries of Commissioner working groups and their draft policy options, press releases, public statements and official correspondence between Commissioners and the Commission Chairman on substantive matters.

This record provides future researchers and historians a wealth of information as U.S. ocean policy evaluation and development moves forward.

Highlights from the Report—Major Themes and Regional Ocean Governance

Major Themes

The following discussion focuses on the major themes and the regional ocean governance recommendation of the USCOP. The discussion first focuses on major themes[106] and then discusses the specific recommendations of Chapter 5 "Advancing a regional approach" and related chapters that refer to the regional ocean governance concept. The regional ocean governance recommendation is but one of many. It is of particular interest to the first author of this article. It also illustrates how a number of the broader themes of the report might be applied.

The first theme that permeates the report is a desire to substantially upgrade and provide focus to the attention the nation gives to its oceans and coasts. The nation's public policy agenda is crowded with so many worthy issues that it takes hard work to make the case for greater attention, increased resources and reform. At virtually every step in the analysis— economic contribution, resource depletion and degradation, governance, education, technology, international affairs, and others—the Commission showed why society needed to pay more attention to this extensive resource area.

Secondly, the Oceans Act calls for a "coordinated and comprehensive" ocean policy. The call for increased "coordination" occurs throughout the

---

106. The discussion of major themes is an interpretation of the entire report by the authors, in the style of an essay rather than an account of specific provisions. For this reason detailed references are omitted since the observations are derived from many aspects of the report.

report, but receives direct attention organizationally in Chapters 4–7 dealing with an improved governance structure for ocean and coastal affairs. This concept recognizes that many governmental and non-governmental organizations now pay attention to virtually every issue raised in the report, but the degree of overlap, redundancy, and sometime conflicting approaches leads to inadequate results and increased costs. Further, the Commission called for an "integrated" ocean policy as well as one that is "coordinated and comprehensive." This means that the parts of an ocean policy connect to, and support, one another. A conscious effort was made to link the recommendations to one another as much as possible. This is most apparent in the linkage of marine science to management and policy. This is expressed strongly in the fisheries recommendations, in the promotion of regional ocean governance, in the recommendations that ocean observing and monitoring serve management, and in many others.

Thirdly, and related to the above, the chapters of the report are divided fairly equally between proposals for "capacity building" and attention to "problem-solving." "Capacity-building" looks to the future and addresses preparation for the problems to come, even if they are not clearly on the policy agenda as yet. This perspective led to the major governance and financial recommendations as well as to those relating to science, ocean observing and monitoring, and education. A more coordinated and robust governance framework, a more educated workforce, and better information prepares us for dealing with tomorrow's issues. On the other hand, 16 chapters deal with "problem-solving" and how management can achieve better results. The problems normally are specific to the issue and often are concerned with contradictory or overlapping laws and management standards, a need to better coordinate or combine efforts of agencies, the need for improved research on a specific issue, or the recognition that trends will require adjustments in management philosophy.

Fourthly, the report reflects a balanced view toward resource protection and the need for economic development. A specific section of the Oceans Act requires that equal consideration be given to environmental, technical feasibility, economic and scientific factors in the Commission's assessment and recommendations.[107] This part of the bill was occasionally mentioned in Commission deliberations, but the diversity of interests and expertise among the Commissioners insured that this breadth of view would be maintained. As explained earlier, economic, scientific, technical and governmental experts were represented among the Commissioners and virtually all discussions reflected those perspectives.

Fifthly, an explicit theme articulated throughout the report is the need to approach coastal and ocean management from an ecosystem-based

---

107. Pub. L. 106–256, § 3(f)(3).

perspective, and to apply management within areas defined by ecosystems, rather than jurisdictional criteria. This concept is defined in Chapter 3 and related closely to other principles such as the use of the precautionary approach, adaptive management, biodiversity goals, application of scientific information, and others.

Finally, the Commission had a healthy respect for the work of the many professionals currently engaged in coastal and ocean affairs. This led to a preference for finding ways to make the system work better by overcoming obstacles, resolving identified problems, and creating mechanisms for improvement. Rarely did the notion of "wipe the slate clean and start over" arise. In this sense the Commission kept a keen eye on recommendations that could be implemented by building on activities already underway or for which there was a clear precedent for change.

Regional Ocean Governance

The concept of regional ocean governance is outlined in Chapter 5 of the report. The focus of the first part of that chapter is on the establishment of voluntary, flexible regional ocean councils that are formed from the "bottom-up," and initiated by Governors of States. They do not supplant existing authorities but are squarely aimed at the challenge of coordination among many diverse players with authority and interest in the issues. Regional ocean councils are an integral part of a new "National Ocean Policy Framework" that is discussed throughout the report as the vehicle for implementing many of the recommendations.

Regional ocean councils could perform a number of tasks, take on a variety of shapes, and define themselves in ways most suited to the identified problems of the region. They may be built on existing regional initiatives, or regional leaders could create new entities. The rationale is that the regions of the U.S. differ radically on many dimensions and they have to decide for themselves the appropriate structure, scope and functions for their region. The report suggests some minimum characteristics for regional ocean councils:[108]

- Boundaries that approximate Large Marine Ecosystems or other appropriate ecosystem-based areas;
- Geographic area that extends from coastal watersheds to the offshore boundary of the exclusive economic zone (EEZ);
- Agenda that considers a wide range of ocean and coastal issues; and

108. See Commission Report, n. 1 above, at 59, Box 5.2.

- Membership that includes all levels of government and non-governmental interests.

The report also outlines some core functions of regional ocean councils:

- Defining regional goals and priorities;
- Facilitating coordinated and collaborative responses to regional issues; and
- Communicating regional concerns to the federal government entities overseeing ocean affairs.

The formation of regional ocean councils can be seen as one possible structure for effective State, local and interest group participation in ocean affairs. But the report recommends a number of other mechanisms to support a regional perspective to ocean affairs. One is a more coordinated set of federal agencies operating within a region. The report called for a Presidential Executive Order to require improved coordination and outreach by federal agencies within regions. Another is the formation of a multi-organizational regional ocean information program to provide research, data collection, product development and outreach. This program is to be closely linked with regional ocean observing systems proposed in Chapter 26. Further, regional ecosystem assessments, to be coordinated by NOAA and EPA, are to be developed for each region. These assessments, to be updated periodically, are to be integrated with the National Environmental Policy Act guidelines for environmental impact statements within regions. Finally, as outlined in Chapter 6, and discussed further in Chapter 9, increased use of the offshore federal waters, from 3–200 nautical miles is becoming increasingly common yet there are many regulatory gaps, agency overlaps and conflicts. The report calls "for a broad dialogue among stakeholders at the national, regional, and State levels on a more coordinated and deliberate approach to managing activities in offshore areas."[109]

This vision for a regional approach to ocean and coastal management brings together a number of the themes developed within the report. As noted above, if the regions of the U.S. had a regional ocean council that defined and characterized the region as well as articulated its goals and objectives it would do much to advance the visibility of the ocean as an integral part of our area of responsibility as a nation within the world community. The existence of the councils, and the products, information and discussion they stimulate would add immeasurably to the "ocean literacy" goal advanced in the report.

109. Commission Report, n. 1 above, at 102.

Further, regional ocean councils embody the notion of building a coordinated, comprehensive and integrated ocean policy. It is clear that the primary purpose of the regional approach is to build a bridge among jurisdictions and to advance toward common goals and objectives. The aim is to consider many coastal and ocean uses within a common framework within the region, and to advance the region's needs at the federal level.

The regional structure combines capacity building and problem solving in its conception. The capacity comes from the development of the regional ocean information system that is linked with the region's ocean observation system. Related is the call for regional ecosystem assessments to establish an information baseline. The products from these efforts, if designed to meet the goals and objectives laid out by the regional ocean councils, create opportunities for an integration between science and policy that can serve the region in many ways as it addresses existing, and new, unanticipated marine problems.

Regional ocean councils also can be the vehicle for considering multiple uses of the seas and coasts within an ecosystem-based framework. If the membership includes multiple levels of government and all major stakeholders, then the economic and environmental interests of the local communities, state coastal zone and submerged land managers and federal agencies can be considered jointly. If such a broad-based plan includes the region's goals and objectives, occurs within a defined ecosystem, and is preceded by an ecosystem assessment, then the result can be a comprehensive, coordinated and integrated regional ocean and coastal policy, as laid out in the USCOP report.

Further, the regional ocean council mechanism becomes a vehicle for the integration of a wide range of the USCOP recommendations. The regional ocean council mechanism is specifically mentioned in nine chapters of the report in addition to its detailed treatment in Chapter 5. It is referenced in Chapter 6 dealing with offshore uses including marine protected areas; Chapter 9 addressing linkages between coastal and offshore uses; Chapter 11 calling for regional input on priorities for conserving and restoring resource habitat; Chapter 19 dealing with linking fisheries management with other regional concerns including essential fish habitat; Chapter 20 suggesting the need for a regional ecosystem-based approach for marine mammal and endangered species management; Chapter 21 suggesting that regional ecosystem-based plans for coral reef protection and management; Chapter 23 noting the importance for regional ecosystem assessments to assess algal blooms and bacteria particular to their area; Chapter 26 concerning melding regional ocean observing systems with ocean information systems proposed for U.S. regions; and Chapter 28 discussing priority needs for ocean information programs.

Although the vision of a regional approach to ocean and coastal affairs is described in the report, and can provide a goal, a potential structure and a set of criteria by which to assess progress, there are formidable obstacles in the path of actual implementation.[110] Conceptual and practical issues arise around the question of institutional change. Governmental or behavioral institutions and practices do not change easily. It takes tremendous pressure (economic, political, legal, or social), compelling reasons and strong positive or negative incentives (for example, funding, power advantages and/or threat of sanctions) to bring it about. Additionally, designing new institutions, especially in ocean and coastal affairs, requires analysis of three dimensions of institutional change—the fit of the institution to the problem being addressed, the interplay of the new institution with other institutional players within vertical or horizontal relationships, and the question of the appropriate scale at which to design the institution.[111] These are challenging analytical tasks.

Applying the regional ocean governance concept in places around the U.S. will be a long-term and challenging exercise. Some regions have a head start, such as the Gulf of Maine Council on the Marine Environment,[112] the many regional institutions that have emerged in the Great Lakes,[113] and the Gulf of Mexico that has an intergovernmental EPA/Gulf of Mexico Program[114] addressing water quality issues. Other regions are just beginning to examine regionalism in ocean affairs, including the Pacific Northwest and the mid-Atlantic States.

PART IV—POLICY RESPONSE TO THE COMMISSION REPORT (2004–2005)

The following section will discuss governmental responses to the final report of the U.S. Commission on Ocean Policy by the Executive Office of the President, by the Congress, and by the U.S. coastal States. President George W. Bush released the U.S. Ocean Action Plan, and signed an executive order creating a federal Committee on Ocean Policy. Numerous bills have been introduced into Congress regarding many aspects of ocean gover-

110. See P. Hoagland and A. R. Solow, "Regional Ocean Governance: A Critique of Two Recent Proposals," *Marine Technology Society Journal* 38, 4 (2005): 61–68; for a response article, see also M. Hershman and F. Muller-Karger, "Crosstalk: A Dialogue on Regional Ocean Governance: Moving Toward Ecosystem-based Management," *Marine Technology Society Journal* 39, 1 (2005): 3–5.

111. See O. R. Young, *The Institutional Dimensions of Environmental Change: Fit, Interplay and Scale* (Cambridge, MA: MIT Press, 2002).

112. See <http://www.gulfofmaine.org>.

113. See <http://www.glc.org/> and <http://www.glfc.org/> for discussion of two of the Great Lakes regional efforts, the Great Lakes Commission and the Great Lakes Fishery Commission.

114. See <http://www.epa.gov/gmpo>.

nance, all directly related to the recommendations of the Commission. Finally, many coastal States have responded to the Commission's report by initiating new ocean policy and governance activities. While many of these programs are in their very early stages, the large volume of action highlights the wide range of ocean policy activities directly responding to the Commission's work.

Executive Office of the President Ocean Policy Activities

On December 17th 2004, President George W. Bush submitted to Congress his response to the Commission's final report, the U.S. Ocean Action Plan.[115] Coinciding with the release of the Action Plan, President Bush also signed an executive order[116] establishing a national ocean policy for the U.S. and forming a cabinet-level Committee on Ocean Policy. The national ocean policy set forth in the executive order calls for improved coordination of federal ocean-related activities and facilitated coordination among federal, State, tribal, and local governments, along with the private sector, foreign governments and international organizations. The majority of the executive order is devoted to the creation of the Committee on Ocean Policy. The Committee was created as a part of the Council of Environmental Quality (CEQ), and is chaired by the Chairman of the CEQ. The Committee is to consist of 24 designated members, including the Secretaries of State, Defense, the Interior, Agriculture, Health and Human Services, Commerce, Labor, Transportation, Energy and Homeland Security. The Committee will also include the Attorney General, the Administrators of the EPA and the National Aeronautics and Space Administration (NASA), the Directors of the Office of Management and Budget, National Intelligence, Office of Science and Technology Policy and the National Science Foundation, and the Chairman of the Joint Chiefs of Staff.

The Committee on Ocean Policy is charged with the duty of overseeing policies related to ocean-related matters for the President, as well as advising heads of executive departments. Included in the plan is a diagram outlining the new coordinated governance structure to be established by the Committee on Ocean Policy within the Executive Branch (Figure 1). The Committee is also responsible for obtaining advice and information from State, local and tribal representatives on ocean and coastal matters. These activities are in place to allow the Committee to facilitate certain activities

115. U.S. Ocean Action Plan: The Bush Administration's Response to the U.S. Commission on Ocean Policy [hereinafter Action Plan], available online: <http://ocean.ceq.gov/actionplan.pdf>.

116. Exec. Order No. 13,336. 69 Fed. Reg. 76,591 (Dec. 17, 2004).

Fig. 1.—Bush Action Plan Ocean Governance Structure

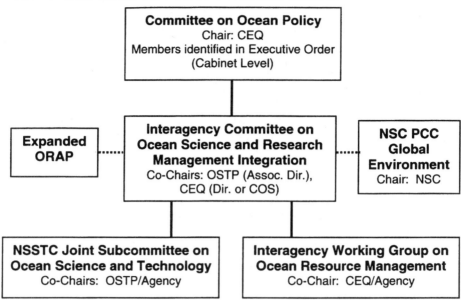

Source: See Action Plan, n. 115 above, at 10. More information available at: <http://ocean.ceq.gov/about/welcome.html>.

relating to U.S. Ocean Policy. These include the development and implementation of common ocean-related goals, the use of science in establishment of ocean-related policy, and the overall efficient exchange of ocean-related information.

The U.S. Ocean Action Plan covers a wide range of ocean and coastal topics, totaling almost forty pages. Such topics as market-based fisheries and ocean observation and research are highlighted by the Action Plan, however, there are few explicit policy statements or calls for new funding found within the plan. Regional Ocean Governance, as discussed in Part three of this article, is addressed in both the Executive Order and the U.S. Ocean Action Plan. The Executive Order calls for voluntary regional approaches to be used with ocean-related matters.[117] Within the Action Plan, there are three specific regional activities identified for further attention: Great Lakes Regional Collaboration,[118] Regional Partnership in the Gulf of Mexico,[119] and the Southeast Aquatic Resources Partnership.[120] Additionally, the plan calls for the establishment of an Interagency

117. *Id.* § 4(d)(ii), at 45.
118. See Ocean Action Plan, n. 115 above, at 10.
119. *Id.*, Action Plan, at 11.
120. *Id.*

Committee on Ocean Science and Resource Management Integration, with duties that include resolving statutory and regulatory redundancies on the regional level, as well as conflict resolution and recognition of emerging ocean issues for national and regional benefit.[121] Finally, regional ocean management is also mentioned in a recommendation regarding the advancement of the use of Large Marine Ecosystem-based (LME) management within the United Nations Environment Programme's Regional Seas Programmes.[122]

The Committee on Ocean Policy had its first official meeting on April 5, 2005.[123] The organizational structure and initial priorities for the three working committees of the Committee on Ocean Policy has recently been developed and published.[124] Meanwhile, the Legislative branch has been very active in responding to the U.S. Commission on Ocean Policy by introducing a wide range of ocean-related legislation.

Federal Ocean Legislation

Once the U.S. Commission on Ocean Policy released its Preliminary report, and in some cases preceding it, Congressional supporters have responded by introducing numerous bills related to ocean policy (See Table 3). These bills, beginning in the 108th Congress, cover a wide array of issues, but have mainly fallen into three main areas of ocean policy: governance, stewardship, and science. These three areas reflect the main areas of findings and recommendations of the final Commission report. Governance is reflected in bills such as the NOAA Organic Act,[125] Office of Ocean and Coastal Policy Creation Act of 2003,[126] the National Ocean and Policy Leadership Act,[127] and the Oceans Conservation, Education, and National Strategy for the 21st Century Act,[128] also known as the "Big Ocean Bill." Stewardship is

121. *Id.*, Action Plan, at 7.
122. *Id.*, Action Plan, at 36.
123. A reference to this meeting is a press release from the Office of the Governor of Rhode Island; available online: <http://www.governor.ri.gov/pr.php?ID=398>.
124. Information and membership for the Interagency Committee on Ocean Science and Resource Management Integration, NSTC Joint Subcommittee on Ocean Science and Technology, and the Subcommittee on Integrated Management of Ocean Resources are available online: <http://ocean.ceq.gov/about/welcome.html>.
125. H.R. 50, 109th Cong. (2005).
126. H.R. 3627, 108th Cong. (2003).
127. S. 2647, 108th Cong. (2004).
128. H.R. 4900, 108th Cong. (2004).

highlighted in bills concerning estuarine land protection,[129] oceans and human health,[130] ballast water,[131] and marine debris,[132] and aquatic invasive species.[133] Marine science is the focus of many bills, regarding both ocean observation[134] and exploration.[135]

In the 108th Congress, Senator Hollings introduced the Oceans and Human Health Act, which was the only bill passed by Congress directly relating to the Commission's report.[136] Senator Hollings also introduced a bill calling for a national ocean policy and additional partnerships to further advance ocean policy throughout the U.S.,[137] among others. However, this bill did not pass, and Senator Hollings, the chief proponent in the Senate for ocean policy reform, retired at the end of the 108th Congress. Table 3 provides a summary of ocean-related bills introduced in the 108th and 109th Congresses.

Table 3.—Federal Ocean Legislation Introduced in the 108th and 109th Congresses in Response to USCOP Recommendations[138]

Bill #	Title	Sponsor
Governance		
H.R. 3627 (108th Cong.)	Office of Ocean and Coastal Policy Creation Act of 2003	Saxton (R-NJ)
Establishes in the Executive Office of the President the Office of Oceans and Coastal Policy. Directs Office of Oceans and Coastal Policy to develop comprehensive ocean and coastal policy, and to advise President on ocean and coastal policy.		
S. 2647 (108th Cong.)	National Ocean Policy and Leadership Act	Hollings (D-SC)
Establishes a national ocean policy, sets forth the missions of NOAA, and ensures effective interagency coordination. Directs the Administrator of NOAA to report to Congress on status of nation's oceans and atmosphere, and establishes a Council on Ocean Stewardship in the Executive Office of the President.		

129. S. 861, 108th Cong. (2003).
130. S. 1218, 108th Cong. (2003); see n. 133 below.
131. S. 363, 109th Cong. (2005).
132. S. 362, 109th Cong. (2005).
133. H.R. 1592, 109th Cong. (2005).
134. S. 361, H.R. 1489, H.R. 1584, 109th Cong. (2005); S. 2489 108th Cong. (2004).
135. S. 39, 109th Cong. (2005).
136. Passed as Title IX of H.R. 4818, Consolidated Appropriations Act, 2005, 108th Cong. (2004). See n. 129 above.
137. National Ocean Policy and Leadership Act, S. 2647, 108th Cong. (2004).
138. This table summarizes those bills introduced in the 109th Congress, many of which are reintroductions of earlier bills from the 108th Congress, as well as bills from the 108th Congress that have not as yet been reintroduced. This list is current as of June 16, 2005.

Bill #	Title	Sponsor
H.R. 4900 (108th Cong.)	Oceans Conservation, Education, and National Strategy for the 21st Century Act	Greenwood (R-PA)
Establishes a national policy for the oceans, establishes national standards for any Federal ocean-related activities. Directs President to submit to Congress recommendations for reorganizing functions of existing federal agencies, and establishes a National Oceans Advisor, Council, and Council of Advisors.		
H.R. 50 (109th Cong.)	National Oceanic and Atmospheric Administration Act	Ehlers (R-MI)
Reestablishes the National Oceanic and Atmospheric Administration (NOAA) in the Department of Commerce. Among other requirements, the bill creates programs to support ongoing operations of data collection of information regarding ocean, coastal, and Great Lakes information.		
Stewardship		
S. 861 (108th Cong.)	Coastal and Estuarine Land Protection Act	Hollings (D-SC)
Permanent acquisitions of coastal lands through federal grants, given to coastal States or to the National Estuarine Research Reserve in that State. Amends the Coastal Zone Management Act of 1972 to allow the Secretary of Commerce to implement management strategies based on input from outside sources.		
S. 1218 (108th Cong.)	Oceans and Human Health Act	Hollings (D-SC)
Provides for Presidential support and coordination of interagency ocean science programs and development and coordination of a comprehensive and integrated U.S. research and monitoring program. Authorizes the Secretary of Commerce to establish an Oceans and Human Health Initiative.		
S. 362 (109th Cong.)	Marine Debris Research Prevention and Reduction Act	Inouye (D-HI)
Establishes within NOAA a Marine Debris Prevention and Removal Program of project grants to reduce and prevent the occurrence and adverse impacts of marine debris on the marine environment and navigation safety.		
S. 363 (109th Cong.)	Ballast Water Management Act of 2005	Inouye (D-HI)
Amends the Non-indigenous Aquatic Nuisance Prevention and Control Act of 1990 to revise certain aquatic invasive species prevention requirements to apply them to certain U.S. and foreign vessels using U.S. ports, and to establish ballast water and sediment management standards for vessels of the armed forces.		
H.R. 1431 (109th Cong.)	Fisheries Science and Management Act of 2005	Rahall (D-WV)
Amends the Magnuson-Stevens Fishery Conservation and Management Act to revise requirements for the appointment and training of the voting members of the eight Regional Fishery Management Councils. Requires each science and statistical committee established by a Council to include a fishery and marine science subcommittee.		

Bill #	Title	Sponsor
H.R. 1592 (109th Cong.)	Aquatic Invasive Species Research Act	Ehlers (R-MI)
Establishes marine and freshwater research, development, and demonstration programs to support efforts to prevent, control, and eradicate invasive species, as well as to educate citizens and stakeholders, and restore ecosystems.		
S. 1195 (109th Cong.)	National Offshore Aquaculture Act of 2005	Stevens (R-AK)
Support and provide for an offshore aquaculture industry in the Exclusive Economic Zone of the United States, by providing the necessary authorities, procedures, and permitting processes to encourage investment in aquaculture operations, demonstrations, and research while protecting marine ecosystem quality.		
S. 1224 (109th Cong.)	National Oceans Protection Act of 2005	Boxer (D-CA)
An act to secure, for present and future generations of people of the United States, the full range of environmental, economic, educational, social, cultural, nutritional, and recreational benefits of healthy marine ecosystems.		
H.R. 2939 (109th Cong.)	Oceans Conservation, Education, and National Strategy for the 21st Century Act	Weldon (R-PA)
Establishes a national policy to protect, maintain, and restore the health of marine ecosystems and national standards for implementing the policy to ensure that federal agency actions are consistent with the policy.		
Marine Science		
S. 2489 (108th Cong.)	Coastal and Ocean Mapping Integration Act	Inouye (D-HI)
Directs the Administrator of NOAA to establish an integrated coastal and ocean mapping program for the Great Lakes, coastal State waters, territorial sea, the exclusive economic zone, and the U.S. continental shelf, in hopes of furthering U.S. conservation, management and research efforts in these areas.		
S. 39 (109th Cong.)	National Ocean Exploration Program Act	Stevens (R-AK)
Directs the Secretary of Commerce to establish a national ocean exploration program within NOAA. Among other requirements, the bill calls for the program to promote development of oceanographic research, conduct education and outreach activities that improve public understanding of ocean science, resources, and processes.		

Bill #	Title	Sponsor
S. 361 (109th Cong.)	Ocean and Coastal Observation System Act of 2005	Snowe (D-ME)
Directs the President, acting through the National Ocean Research Leadership Council, to establish and maintain an integrated system of ocean and coastal observations, data communication and management, analysis, modeling, research and education.		
H.R. 1489 (109th Cong.)	Coastal Ocean Observation System Integration and Implementation Act of 2005	Gilchrest (R-MD)
Directs the Secretary of Commerce to establish within NOAA a Coastal Ocean Observation System to support coastal and fishery management activities and an integrated national ocean observation system. The system will include end-use products to support coastal and fishery management, data management and communication systems, and forecast models.		
H.R. 1584 (109th Cong.)	Ocean and Coastal Observation System Act of 2005	Weldon (R-PA)
Directs the Committee on Ocean Policy, acting through the National Ocean Research Leadership Council, to establish and maintain an integrated system of coastal and ocean observations, data communication and management, analysis, modeling, research and education, designed to provide for detection and prediction of ocean and coastal changes impacting the nation's social, economic, and ecological systems.		

State Activities

While Congress has begun to introduce federal legislation in response to the U.S. Commission on Ocean Policy's work, States around the U.S. have responded by initiating their own ocean policy activities. Some States have built on existing activities, some have begun new comprehensive ocean programs, and some have introduced State legislation to accomplish State goals for ocean governance. Table 4 summarizes these activities, highlighting the type of activity, how it has been established or proposed, and its timeframe. All of these actions demonstrate the desire of States to both mirror and support the ocean policy activities occurring at the federal level, through both the report of the U.S. Commission on Ocean Policy and resulting federal actions.

Table 4.—State Ocean Policy Activities*

State	Organization	Scope	Authority	Effective Date
California	California Ocean Protection Council	Coordination and improvement of the protection and management of California's ocean and coastal resources.	California Ocean Action Plan, California Public Resources Code, Division 26.5 §35500–35650	December 2004
Massachusetts	Comprehensive Ocean Resources Management Act	A bill to implement the recommendations of the Massachusetts Ocean Management Task Force to enable proactive planning for stewardship of these ocean resources held in trust for the public.	Senate Bill No. 529, 2005	January 2005
Oregon	Oregon Ocean Policy Advisory Council	Coordinated collaboration of State agencies involved in ocean and coastal management.	Oregon Revised Statute Title 19, 196.438	January 2004
Alaska	Alaska Ocean Policy Cabinet	Coordinated collaboration of State agencies involved in ocean and coastal management.	Governor Murkowski, Administrative Order No. 223	December 2004

* This table summarizes recent State Ocean Policy activities, as discussed above. See ns. 139–144 above.

Hawaii	Hawaii Ocean and Coastal Council	Gather information and provide advice and recommendations on direction and planning for addressing Hawaii's ocean and coastal matters to foster coordinated approaches that support local initiatives on ocean and coastal concerns.	Governor Lingle, Executive Order No. 5	January 2005
Washington	Washington State Ocean Policy Working Group	Identify recommendations of the U.S. Commission on Ocean Policy report appropriate for immediate implementation; provide comprehensive report on State ocean resource policies.	Washington ESSB 6090.PL § 116 (7)	April 2005
Florida	Florida Oceans and Coastal Council	Develop a research plan and performing a resource assessment, including patterns of use, natural resource features, location of research and monitoring infrastructure, commercial and recreational transit patterns, and socioeconomic trends of the state's oceans and coastal economy.	Florida Statutes, Part IV of Chapter 161, §§161.70–161.76	May 2005

Two new states, New York and New Jersey, have initiated state ocean policy activities since the original drafting of this manuscript. Also, the Washington State Ocean Policy Working Group has released its initial report, available online: <http://courses.washing.ecu/oceangov/OPWG_Docs/WashingtonOPWGReport.pdf>.

Of those coastal States that have responded to the Commission's findings, California has taken the lead on comprehensive ocean policy review.[139] As with many coastal issues, other States are once again looking to California as the leader in groundbreaking policy and management activities. After submitting his response to the draft Commission report, Governor Arnold Schwarzenegger released California's Ocean Action Plan,[140] outlining a comprehensive plan for ocean activities in the State. State legislation created the California Ocean Protection Council, with the charge of overseeing California's ocean policy activities and providing concentrated leadership for future State actions. The California Ocean Action Plan includes other aspects of ocean governance, such as education programs, ocean monitoring, science coordination, and financing. In a similar fashion, Massachusetts has built upon its existing ocean management programs through Governor Romney's Ocean Management Initiative,[141] which established an Ocean Management Task Force. This task force has worked a great deal on ocean management and policy issues on the State level, working to improve ocean and coastal management and to support federal activities affecting Massachusetts. Florida has recently passed its own legislation that will establish the Florida Oceans and Coastal Council, with the initial charge of developing an ocean research plan as well as a natural resource assessment.

Alaska has responded to the Commission's work by establishing its own Ocean Policy Cabinet, an agency that will spearhead ocean policy activities for the state.[142] The State of Hawaii created an Ocean and Coastal Council to oversee the State's ocean management activities, formed by executive order of Governor Linda Lingle in January 2005.[143] The State of Oregon has an Ocean Policy Advisory Council, formed before the Oceans Act and the U.S. Commission on Ocean Policy. This Council has recently been reconstituted, and is expected to begin a review of State ocean policies in the near future.[144] Washington State has begun an ocean policy review within the Governor's Office, designed to respond to the Commission's report, and recommend future State ocean policy activities. Thus, all western states have State ocean policy oversight activities taking place. The groundwork is laid institutionally for a State and federal dialogue about future ocean policies and activities.

139. California Ocean Resources Management Program, available online: <http://resources.ca.gov/ocean/>.

140. Available online: <http://resources.ca.gov/ocean/Cal_Ocean_Action_Strategy.pdf>.

141. Available online: <http://www.mass.gov/czm/oceanmgtinitiative.htm>.

142. Governor Murkowski, Administrative Order No. 223, December 17, 2004. Available online: <http://gov.state.ak.us/admin-orders/223.html>.

143. Governor Lingle, Executive Order No. 5, January 6, 2005.

144. Oregon Revised Statute, Title 19, 196.438.

CONCLUSION

Part I of this article illustrated how the Oceans Act of 2000 differed from the 1966 law establishing the Stratton Commission and changed it to suit the political climate of the late 1990s. The Stratton commissioners and the commission chair and vice chair were all chosen by the President. Further, the Stratton Commission worked closely with a National Marine Council composed of cabinet officials, and the law emphasized improving the nation's science and technology capabilities. The Oceans Act, on the other hand, reflected a concern by many Congressional leaders that constituency interests heavily invested in ocean resources and issues should be an integral part of the process. Thus we see an Oceans Act requiring extensive Congressional participation in Commissioner selection, geographic representation, requirements for hearings in many parts of the country, a mandatory review of a preliminary report by Governors, a requirement that environment and economic development be equally considered, and other provisions decentralizing and broadening the participation and factors to consider. Whereas the era in which the Stratton Commission was formed might be characterized as "top-down" and technocratic, with considerable faith in highly trained specialists and national leadership for change, the Oceans Act sought to elevate the role of the States and interested constituents to a level equaling that of the Executive and Congress.

Part II of this article presented the process of Commissioner selection that was highly political but resulted in a broadly representative and highly qualified Commission. Commissioners had a mix of marine-oriented specialties and leadership experience, and the four Commissioner choices by the Bush administration added diversity as well as extensive policy experience. More importantly, the choice of chairman, the preparation for the initial meeting, and Commission organizational procedures established a high standard that lasted throughout the three-year process. Much of the credit goes to Admiral James Watkins, the Commission chairman, who established a leadership style that insisted upon thoroughness, accuracy, and collegiality in all aspects of the Commission's work. In retrospect, the success of these organizational steps can be attributed to an "organic" process in which the marine science and policy community was given relative freedom to organize itself for this task with no apparent external policy agenda being forced upon them. The support of Congress, especially Senator Ernest Hollings, in providing the structure and the funding was essential.

Part III of this article provided an overview of the results of the Commission's labors, much of which is readily available in published and electronic forms. In addition to a comprehensive treatment of many topics, the report is a balance among capacity-building and problem-solving analysis and recommendations. As much attention is given to science, technology, educational development and governance reform as is given to matters of policy in fisheries, environment and other topics. The theme of "ecosystem-based management"[145] is a thread that runs throughout the report and is particularly evident in the recommendations for a regional approach to ocean management, including regional ocean councils. Ocean use and ocean protection are addressed, and a theme of sustainable multiple use of the seas is clear. Ultimately, the report represents a "blueprint" for the future—a guide to policy development and reform for many years to come.

Part IV of the article shows promising first steps already taken by the Executive Office of the President, Congress and the States in response to the final report that was released September 20, 2004. The Bush Administration issued an Executive Order and an Ocean Action Plan outlining a number of areas of interest and importance that they intend to pursue. Most importantly they established a cabinet-level Committee on Ocean Policy, including a number of sub-committees that reorganizes the structure for consideration of ocean policy by the Executive Office of the President. The Committee on Ocean Policy held its first meeting in April, 2005. Many bills have been introduced in the Congress in response to the Commission recommendations, only one of which has been enacted so far. A number of states have initiated ocean policy reform at their level, with California leading the way. It is too early to tell if a lasting trend of implementation steps is underway.

This article presented an overview of selected topics important to understanding and advancing U.S. ocean policy. Emphasis was placed on the legislative and administrative processes surrounding the work of the Commission on Ocean Policy. It acted as an introduction to a field that deserves further research in a number of areas.

First, the Commission report creates a policy baseline as well as a proposed blueprint for the future, and should lead to an explicit process to track changes in U.S. ocean policy as they occur. These changes could be specific policy outputs such as new laws, organizations, program activities and budget initiatives on various topics. It could also track outcomes that assess the status of ocean resources and activities, such as changes to fish resources, environmental quality, and marine economic development indicators.

Secondly, the review of legislative and administrative steps needs to be amplified with discussion of policy debate and reform for specific topics of

---

145. Ecosystem-based management is defined and described by the Commission at pages 63–67 of the final report (see n. 1 above). Its components include: defining new management boundaries; aligning decision making within ecosystem boundaries; precautionary and adaptive management; clear goals and objectives for ecosystem-based management plans; and the consideration of biodiversity.

marine policy. There is a rich history centering on the economic, social and political dimensions of such topics as fisheries policy, marine transportation, ocean research, marine protection, coastal management, ocean energy development, and many others that deserve careful review. Of particular interest will be the role of the U.S. Commission report and aftermath in policy change, should any occur.

Thirdly, policy researchers and analysts need to address how highly visible ocean issues of immediate concern might incorporate the longer range principles advanced in the report, especially those dealing with capacity building. At the time of this writing, the U.S. Congress is focused on tsunami detection, warning and emergency response; fisheries management and policy; and new offshore energy and aquaculture development. If these issues can be addressed in ways that advance the broader themes of the Commission report, then progress will have been made, even if in subtle and more hidden ways.

Fourthly, the success of efforts like those of the Commission often reflects the vision, leadership and management skills of particular individuals. The specific role of Senator Errnest Hollings, Senator Ted Stevens, Admiral James Watkins, and the Working Group chairs of the Commission (Bill Ruckelshaus, Paul Sandifer and James Coleman) deserve special recognition by those chronicling the Commission's work in the future.

Finally, the Commission operated within a public policy framework and a political and social environment that influenced the way it proceeded. Similarly, the successful Stratton Commission and the companion National Marine Council that existed between 1966 and 1971 operated in a different political context. Fortunately, Professor Edward Wenk, the Executive Secretary of the National Marine Council wrote an insightful book about that earlier era.[146] The time is ripe for a study of the politics of U.S. ocean policy at the dawn of the 21st century.

146. E. Wenk, *The Politics of the Ocean* (Seattle: University of Washington Press, 1972).

Collaborative Oceans Governance: Measuring Efficacy

Daniel B. Rubenstein*
Senior Research Associate, Canadian Comprehensive Auditing Foundation (CCAF–FCVI), Ottawa, Canada

INFINITY LOST—OCEANS UNDER STRESS

Introduction

For thousands of years there has been a myth that the oceans, which cover over 70 percent of the Earth's surface, are infinite in their extent and productive capacity. This myth is beginning to collapse as the world approaches real limits on the oceans' potential to absorb human waste and pollution. Effective governance of the human domestication and exploitation of the oceans is one treatment option for the "Pathology of the Limitless Ocean Sink." But how do we know when and where to apply a particular governance institution? How do we measure the efficacy of a given oceans governance regime?

There is a relative lacuna in the literature on how to measure the efficacy of the Collaborative/Ecosystem Oceans Governance Model (CEOGM), the new governance paradigm advocated by experts to control human exploitation of the oceans. An approach to measure the efficacy of the CEOGM is presented, based on the experience of the nation with the longest coastline in the world. This is the story of Canada's experience with the Oceans Act of 1997, an innovative piece of enabling legislation for oceans governance.[1]

A conceptual model maps oceans outcomes over time and space, linking governance with changes in human behavior and improvements in the health of oceans. A chain of oceans governance results is articulated.

---

* This article is written for my granddaughter Zoe Cecil Rubenstein Payne in the hope that she may inherit an infinite ocean, as did thousands of generations of her ancestors.

1. Oceans Act (1996, c. 31), available online: <http://laws.justice.gc.ca/en/O-2.4/text.html>.

Ocean Yearbook 20: 147–188.

The author demonstrates the importance of a chain of logic that explains the causal links between oceans policy and results. This chain of logic is predicated upon clear accountability for results. Accountability is then a "necessary" condition for the achievement of ocean governance results during the early years of implementation. Indicators of Accountability are proposed as proxy measures of the early efficacy of the CEOGM.

Detailed diagnostics, which are intended to provide an early warning of the ineffectiveness of an oceans governance regime, are developed, based on the Government of Canada's experience with the Oceans Act. The application of these Indicators of Accountability reveals a problem of "fit," or the extent to which the new oceans governance model is compatible with the traditional accountability conventions of the machinery of the Government of Canada.

The application of the Indicators of Accountability reveals four other important lessons learned from the Canadian experience. First, a collaborative process has a large "transaction" costs in terms of months and years of coordination and participation time required to achieve program coherence within a department, within government and between national, subnational governments and other users of a Large Ocean Management Area (LOMA).[2] Secondly, before a lead agency or department can effectively collaborate with oceans users outside the department or lead agency, there is a critical need to achieve strong internal collaboration and cooperation within the lead agency or department. These phenomena suggest a "Collaborative Accountability Paradox." The need for accountability increases with the number of internal and external "collaborators." Paradoxically, the ability to clearly define joint and several accountabilities is inversely related to the number of partners in a collaborative governance regime.

Thirdly, there is a critical need to provide a strong basis for accountability in the fundamental oceans policy or enabling legislation. There needs to be clarity around which department or agency is in the lead, as well as the obligations of the "follower" departments or agencies. Furthermore, there must be definitional clarity around the intended meaning of ambiguous terms such as an ecosystem approach, sustainable development, integrated management or the precautionary principle.

Fourthly, and perhaps most importantly, there may be a correlation between a lack of accountability and a lack of capacity, competence,

2. LOMAs are area-based management constructs of the Department of Fisheries and Oceans described in the 2002 *Policy and Operational Framework for Integrated Management of Estuarine, Coastal and Marine Environments in Canada.* Ecosystem-based management objectives will be established for LOMAs that may cover a large portion of one of Canada's three oceans or coastal zones, typically extending from the coast out to the limit of Canada's jurisdiction.

commitment to policy coherence and consequence. For example, a lack of a sense of accountability within a given department or agency to support a cross-cutting issue such as an ecosystem approach may undermine a department's capacity to re-assign the scientific resources "necessary" to develop measures of Marine Environmental Quality (MEQ).

This is the story of the Canadian experience with the Collaborative Accountability Paradox.

CANADA IS A "PERFECT" OCEANS GOVERNANCE LAB

As a legislative auditor and social scientist I have found in my work over the past twenty years that Canada is often the "perfect lab" to study social phenomena. It is "big enough to have all of the problems that beset the world, but small enough so as to be able to isolate the key variables."[3] Canada has the largest coastline in the world (243,789 kilometers) and as a result, the largest Exclusive Economic Zone (EEZ) in the world (78,000 million square kilometers of coastal, estuarine and marine environments). Canada has experience with ICZM. Canada is a Westminster model democracy with a federal government and strong provinces (or sub-national governments). Most importantly, Canada is one of the few jurisdictions that has embodied the CEOGM model into enabling legislation, the Oceans Act. The Canadian experience in implementing the Oceans Act provides researchers with eight years of experience to use in assessing the efficacy of the CEOGM, its limits and its strengths.

The Essence of the New Regime

Under the Oceans Act, the Government of Canada developed a new oceans policy based on two principles: an ecosystem-based approach and collaboration among the users of the ocean. The objective of the proposed new governance framework was to weave together an "adaptive" oceans governance institution at a geographic scale commensurate with the scale of the estuarine, coastal and marine environments to be "managed" for human use. This framework transcended existing political boundaries defined in constitutional arrangements between the Government of Canada

3. As a legislative auditor with the Auditor General of Canada, routinely one has to do benchmarking with other jurisdictions. In most cases the problems that confront other jurisdictions also confront Canada, yet the scale of their occurrence, and the more limited other variables, or *ceteris paribus* (all other things being equal) makes it somewhat easier to study them in a Canadian context.

and the Provinces. It was "adaptive" in the sense that it was largely based on trial and error rather than a traditional command-and-control model.

The governance approach in the Oceans Act was a radical departure from previous approaches to the governance of estuarine, coastal and marine environments.[4] The new regime is based on informal, largely regional institutions working within existing constitutional arrangements. The approach had many similarities with emerging theories articulated by leading academics such as Juda, Berkes, Folke, Colding, Ostrom, Holling, and others.[5]

The Canadian approach envisaged that "some management actions will still proceed to meet existing jurisdictional responsibilities. For example, actions necessary for conservation can proceed under the authority of the Minister of Fisheries and Oceans ... Participating program and regulatory authorities will remain chiefly responsible for implementation of the regulatory measures, policies and programs required to achieve the collective results."[6] It should be noted that Canada's Policy and Operational Framework for Integrated Management clearly distinguished between collaborative management systems and co-management:

> Collaboration: An approach to planning and decision-making aimed at improving relationships and seeking resolutions that meet the needs and interests of all parties to the greatest possible degree. Co-management: A management approach in which responsibility for resource management is shared between the government and resource user groups.[7]

4. S. Coffen-Smout, ed., *Annexes of the Canadian Ocean Assessment: A Review of Canadian Ocean Policy and Practice* (Halifax, Canada: International Ocean Institute, 1996).

5. F. Berkes, C. Folke and J. Colding, *Linking Social and Ecological Systems, Management Practices and Social Mechanisms for Building Resilience* (Cambridge, U.K.: Cambridge University Press, 1998); F. Berkes, J. Colding and C. Folke, *Navigating Social-Ecological Systems, Building Resilience for Complexity and Change* (Cambridge, U.K.: Cambridge University Press, 2003); C. S. Holling, *Panarchy: Understanding Transformations in Human and Natural Systems* (Washington, D.C.: Island Press, 2002); L. Juda, "Changing National Approaches to Ocean Governance: The United States, Canada and Australia," *Oceans Development and International Law* 34 (2003): 61–187; L. Juda, "Considerations in Developing a Functional Approach to the Governance of Large Marine Ecosystems," *Ocean Development and International Law* 30 (1999): 89–125; E. Ostrom, *Governing the Commons, the Evolution of Institutions for Collective Action* (Cambridge, U.K.: Cambridge University Press, 1990).

6. Fisheries and Oceans Canada, *Policy and Operational Framework for Integrated Management of Estuarine, Coastal and Marine Environments in Canada* (Ottawa: Fisheries and Oceans Canada, Oceans Directorate, 2002), s. 3.3, available online: <http://www.cos-soc.gc.ca/doc/publications_e.asp>.

7. Fisheries and Oceans Canada, n. 6 above, Appendix 2: Glossary of Terms.

Past oceans management in Canada had suffered from fragmentation, gaps and overlap in jurisdictions. Past attempts at oceans governance had primarily been concerned with more traditional ocean uses such as shipping and commercial fisheries. The new approach to oceans governance implicit in the Oceans Act is Integrated Management, an attempt to deal with these past failures.

Even though there was a commitment to the development of Integrated Management Plans for all estuarine, coastal and marine waters of Canada, the specifics for the process for implementation of these Integrated Management Plans was not clearly laid out. However, the Minister of the Department of Fisheries and Oceans was tasked with co-coordinating with other federal ministers, boards and agencies in the implementation of the Integrated Management Plans. This was necessary because the Minister of the Department of Fisheries and Oceans does not have sole jurisdiction over many of the activities and users of the oceans covered by the Integrated Management Plans. The Minister may establish or recognize existing advisory or management bodies, and may in consultation, establish MEQ guidelines.[8] The Minister is also responsible for leading and co-coordinating the development and implementation of Marine Protected Areas in Canadian waters.

The establishment of Integrated Management Bodies (see Figure 1) was expected to create and facilitate an environment conducive to collaboration. These Bodies consist of government representatives from all three levels of government and aboriginal organizations, marine users and non-governmental organizations. The Policy and Operational Framework was not definitive about the role of these Integrated Management Bodies; their role and makeup vary according to the circumstances. Some Integrated Management Bodies exist simply to share information and create an action plan for a LOMA. These Bodies provide advice to the decision makers and assume some responsibility for the implementation of Integrated Management Plans.[9] The nature of the required collaboration between each Integrated Management Body, the Minister of Fisheries and Oceans and Parliament was not addressed in the Strategy or Policy and Operational Framework.

The role of the Department of Fisheries and Oceans in this planning process is multi-dimensional: providing scientific knowledge, integrating technical knowledge with social and traditional knowledge, and facilitating the Integrated Management Process. The Policy and Operational Framework identified six steps in the Integrated Management Planning process: defining and assessing a management area, engaging affected interests,

8. *Oceans Act* 1997, n. 1 above, s. 35(2).
9. Fisheries and Oceans Canada, n. 6 above, s. 3.3.

FIG. 1.—Model for an Integrated Management Body

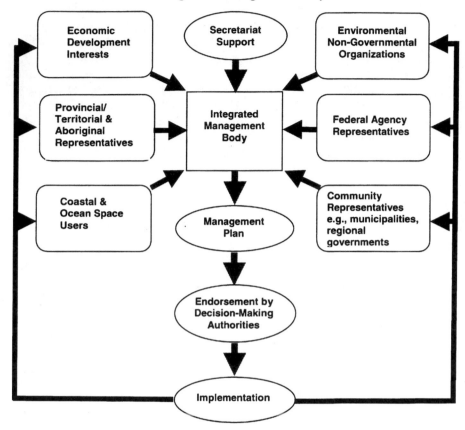

Source: Fisheries and Oceans Canada, 2002, n. 6 above.

developing an Integrated Management Plan, endorsing the Plan, implementing, monitoring and evaluating.

Canada now had a new approach to oceans governance that formally assumed that the principles of a collaborative and ecosystem-based approach can be reconciled with the principles of sound accountability, including ministerial responsibility.

Research Framework

The scope of this research is Canada's experience to date with the implementation of the Oceans Act. The scope of work included efforts at a national level to develop and implement an Accountability Process, a critical prerequisite to measuring the efficacy of the governance intervention. The regional case study used in the work was the Eastern Scotian Shelf Integrated Management (ESSIM) Initiative, which began in 1998. The ESSIM Initiative was the first Integrated Management Pilot with an offshore focus to be undertaken by the Department of Fisheries and Oceans. The research questions explored were:

- What did the peer-reviewed literature say about efforts to develop a methodology to evaluate the efficacy of the CEOGM?
- If there was not a comprehensive evaluation framework described in the literature, what did the literature say about the critical role of accountability, rendering an account and holding to account as a "necessary" condition for effective oceans governance?
- How might an evaluator or auditor go about developing a conceptual framework necessary to conduct an evaluation of the efficacy of the CEOGM and its "fit" with the accountability conventions of the machinery of the Government of Canada?

Within the foregoing context, a five-part research methodology was developed. The critical methodology piece was developing a conceptual model of how to measure the efficacy of the CEOGM, the "new" oceans governance approach. This conceptual model was developed based on interviews in Ottawa and the Maritimes Region of the Department of Fisheries and Oceans. Key elements of the resultant model were shared with senior program managers and knowledgeable external experts on oceans governance. Internal and external interviewees stated that the model was "relevant and useful" to those charged with implementation of the Oceans Act. There was universal agreement that clear accountability was a precondition for effective collaborative oceans governance. There was also universal agreement that establishing shared expectations, clear roles and responsibilities was a complex and daunting task.

HOW TO MEASURE THE EFFICACY OF OCEANS GOVERNANCE

The starting premise of the work was that while there is no accountability for the infinite ocean, there can and should be accountability for the use of finite portions of the oceans. If the purpose of governance is to influence and control the human use of the ever more finite oceans, then expected results or outcomes of oceans governance should be measurable changes in the individual and collective human use of the oceans. These measurable changes should be reasonably "attributed" to specific oceans governance interventions such as limiting oceans use and establishing voluntary protocols on ocean dumping, etc.

To identify oceans outcomes, it is critical to understand the broad concept of accountability for results, results measurement, attribution and the concept of social, economic and ecological outcomes.

The Search for Ocean Outcomes

As illustrated in Table 1, there are three broad categories of results. These are illustrated in the bottom right portion of the table. Relative to an anti-smoking program there are "outputs" such as anti-smoking advertisements and promotion. These are a means to an end. The end in this case is an "intermediate outcome" of compliance with the regulations and more importantly a reduced number of new smokers such as young people. But these "intermediate outcomes" are again a means to an end. The "end" is the reduced incidence of smoking-related health problems and deaths.

This public health example can be applied to the outcomes of oceans governance. The initial outputs of, for example, a Regional Seas Programme for a given sea could be Regional Action Plans. These Regional Action Plans are a means to an intermediate outcome such as changes in the individual and collective behavior of member states with regard to the use of the regional sea for fishing, oceans dumping or oceans transport, etc. The end outcome associated with these changes of behavior could be changes in MEQ and a measurable decline in sources of land-based pollution.

Important work on oceans governance outcomes has been done by Stephen Olsen and Charles Ehler. In a recent article, Stephen Olsen[10] takes the theoretical outcomes described in Table 1 and restates them in terms of an oceans governance context. Olsen identifies four orders of outcomes for oceans governance:

- First order outputs are societal actions that are required when a federal jurisdiction commits to a plan of action designed to modify the course of events in a coastal ecosystem;
- Second order (Intermediate outcomes in Table 1) outcomes are changes in the behavior of institutions and stakeholder groups;
- Third order (End outcomes in Table 1) outcomes are socio-economic and environmental outcomes that physically establish progress toward the ultimate goal of sustainable development; and
- Fourth order outcomes (End outcomes in Table 1) are ultimate goals like sustainable development that at present are simply undefined ideals.

10. S. Olsen, "Frameworks and Indicators for Assessing Progress in Integrated Coastal Management Initiatives," *Ocean and Coastal Management* 46 (2003): 347–361.

Table 1.—Terms and Concepts of Results and Performance

Terms and Concepts of Results and Performance

The concept of performance deals with how well things are done:

- Are the expected results accomplished?
- Are they accomplished within budget and in the most efficient manner?
- Are there undue, unintended consequences?

It also deals with whether the performance will continue or improve:

- Is the organization learning from past experience and adapting?

Performance, then, covers a number of ideas. Determining the specific aspect of performance to measure, and when, is not always straightforward. Government programs undertake a number of activities that produce a variety of results. Programs deliver two kinds of results: outputs, the direct products and services produced by government activities; and outcomes, the consequences of those outputs on Canadians and our society. Outputs are results that managers can largely control, while the outcomes are influenced by factors outside the programs of managers.

End outcomes (sometimes called long-term, final or ultimate outcomes) are the end results sought. In between the outputs and the end outcomes, a sequence of intermediate outcomes is expected to lead to a desired result but are not an end in themselves. Intermediate outcomes are more easily linked to the activities of a program than are end outcomes. The results chain is the sequence of outputs and outcomes that occurs as a result of the activities of the program.

The following illustrates how the various results of an anti-smoking program could be characterized.

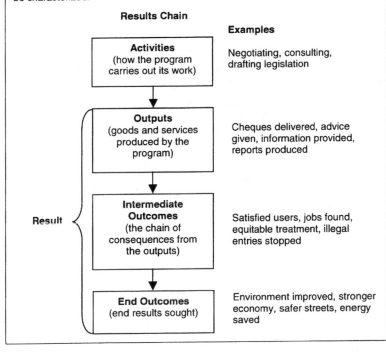

Results Chain

Examples

| Activities (how the program carries out its work) | Negotiating, consulting, drafting legislation |

| Outputs (goods and services produced by the program) | Cheques delivered, advice given, information provided, reports produced |

| Intermediate Outcomes (the chain of consequences from the outputs) | Satisfied users, jobs found, equitable treatment, illegal entries stopped |

| End Outcomes (end results sought) | Environment improved, stronger economy, safer streets, energy saved |

Result

Results

An Anti-Smoking Program

Outputs

- Anti-smoking advertisements and promotions
- Educational material distributed
- Enforcement of smoking regulations

Intermediate Outcomes

- Compliance with regulations
- Reduced number of smokers
- Reduced number of new smokers

End Outcomes

- Reduced incidence of smoke-related health problems and deaths
- Reduced costs of health care associated with smoking-related problems

---

Source: Auditor General of Canada. Report of the Auditor General of Canada–December Chapter 9–Modernizing Accountability in the Public Sector (Ottawa: Office of the Auditor General, 2002).

Charles Ehler provides further guidance on indicators to measure governance performance in ICZM. Ehler points out that broad high-level goals have to be transformed into measurable time-bound performance indicators. He states that general goals should be operationalized into quantifiable objectives for a meaningful analysis and assessment to be carried out. Ehler provides a tangible example of the difference between general goals vs. measurable objectives. An example of a general goal would be to protect, restore and enhance habitats.[11] A measurable time-bound objective would be to restore 25,000 acres of tidal and non-tidal wetlands by 2011 to a specified ecological condition.

This work provided a good starting point in developing a conceptual framework to measure oceans results. However, it was a largely incomplete one. The literature did not deal with two key issues: attribution and accountability. Attribution is the ability to explain a phenomenon by indicating a causal relationship between precursor policy and program interventions. In the case of an oceans governance intervention, attribution refers to the ability to link a specific governance intervention with measurable changes in the physical state of the oceans (i.e., MEQ) and the individual and collective behavior of oceans users that changed as a

---

11. C. Ehler, "Indicators to Measure Governance Performance in Integrated Coastal Management," *Ocean and Coastal Management* 46 (2003): 335–345.

reasonably direct result of the governance intervention. Attribution and accountability are interdependent concepts. Accountability is the foundation for attribution. Until an auditor or evaluator knows the results for which a steward charged with governance is accountable, it is difficult to establish a chain of attributed results, based on causal relationships. The focus of this article is on accountability, the glue that holds any governance regime together (a subsequent article will deal with this thorny issue of attribution in an oceans governance context). But what is accountability?

Accountability is a complex and chameleon-like term that is commonplace in the literature of public administration. In its most basic sense, accountability means answerability. Most would agree that accountability involves the process of being called to account to some authority for one's actions. This sense of duty is implicit in the core sense of accountability. Accountability has a number of features. The external dimension is critical in that the account is given to some other person or body outside the person or body being held accountable, but within the same jurisdiction. Accountability involves meaningful social interaction and exchange between one party who calls for the account, seeking answers and rectification, and the other party who is held accountable, responding and accepting sanctions. Accountability implies rights of authority; those calling for an account are assuming rights of superior authority over those who are accountable, including the right to demand answers and impose sanctions.

An accountability relationship is a relationship based on the medieval concept of stewardship. This involved two parties, the steward who offered a rendering of accounts and the lord who held the steward to account. In a more modern setting in government,[12] there will be three parties: the public servant, the elected legislative body and the electorate to whom the elected official is accountable.

Without accountability there can be no responsible collaborative oceans governance regime. A modern definition of accountability used by the Treasury Board Secretariat of Canada is:

> Accountability is a relationship based on the obligation to demonstrate and take responsibility for performance in light of agreed expectations.[13]

This modern definition makes explicit the obligation to answer for what has been accomplished or has not been accomplished that is of

---

12. D. B. Rubenstein, *Environmental Accounting for the Sustainable Corporation: Strategies and Techniques* (Westport, Conn.: Greenwood Publishing, 1994).

13. Treasury Board of Canada, *Modernizing Accountability Practices in the Public Sector* (Ottawa: Treasury Board of Canada, 1998), available online: <http://www.tbs-sct.gc.ca/rma/account/oagtbs_e.asp>.

significance and of value. This modern definition captures the essence of modern, collaborative and non-hierarchical relationships, without diluting the importance of the concept of accountability.

There are two other related terms that need to be defined. The first is accounting. The second term is audit, or more specifically, legislative audit. Accountability precedes an accounting and an audit. The traditional definition of accounting is the system or procedures of recording, sorting and analyzing economic data related to business and government transactions and preparing statements of the results to use in making decisions. The definition of accounting used in this article is a rendering of accounts for oceans stewardship. Stewards produce a credible reporting of their performance to those to whom they are accountable for performance. The definition of audit is a comparison of what is relative to what should be, based upon the norms agreed upon between the stewards of a governance enterprise and those to whom they are accountable for their stewardship.[14] The role of legislative auditors in a Supreme Audit Institution (SAI) is to provide elected officials with the objective, relevant and credible information they need to hold the government of the day to account.

Within the context of the Government of Canada, the concept of accountability is closely linked with the concept of ministerial responsibility. Ministers are individually accountable to Parliament for their own actions and all actions of their departments or agencies.

For any governance regime or unit of government there is an Accountability Process, as illustrated in Figure 2. There are two sides to the accountability coin, an accountability framework and an effective holding to account. The common currency between these elements is performance or results. A "chain of results" can only be evaluated against the expectations upon those charged with the accountability for a governance regime.

The research challenge was to bring these theoretical concepts of accountability and results down to a scale and level that they could be applicable to any given LOMA, such as the ESSIM Initiative of the Scotian Shelf off eastern Canada. In this endeavor the expert working group of the Oceans Management Research Network (OMRN) was invaluable.[15]

A Chain of LOMA Results

Under the auspices of the OMRN, an expert focus group was held in late 2003. The majority of participants were from the Department of Fisheries

---

14. Rubenstein, n. 12 above.
15. The Oceans Management Research Network is a leading research group interested in issues of oceans governance and ecosystem-based management, funded by Fisheries and Oceans Canada, available online: <http://www.omrn.ca>.

FIG. 2.—The Accountability Process

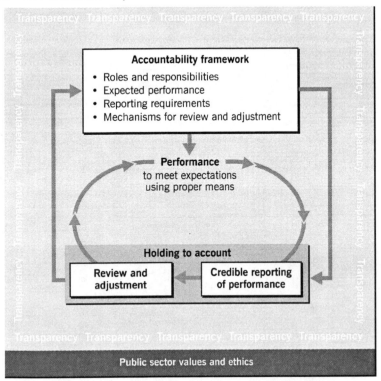

Source: Auditor General of Canada. *Report of the Auditor General of Canada—December Chapter 9—Modernizing Accountability in the Public Sector* (Ottawa: Office of the Auditor General, 2002).

and Oceans with direct experience with oceans governance issues. Membership of the expert focus group included: academic researchers with expertise in oceans issues and representatives from the Department of Fisheries and Oceans in Ottawa, the Central and Arctic, Maritimes and the Newfoundland and Labrador Regions.

The focus group looked at how to build accountability into collaborative arrangements for oceans governance and how to create a credible report on progress achieved and the information needed for a holding to account.

Figure 3, which was developed at the suggestion of the focus group, integrates most of the conceptual work covered so far. What the figure suggests is that during the early years of implementing the Oceans Act, it would be reasonable for an auditor or evaluator to concentrate on the design of an accountability framework. As illustrated in the shaded portion at the bottom of the figure, this accountability framework needs to be developed at three spatial scales—for the LOMA, at the regional scale and at

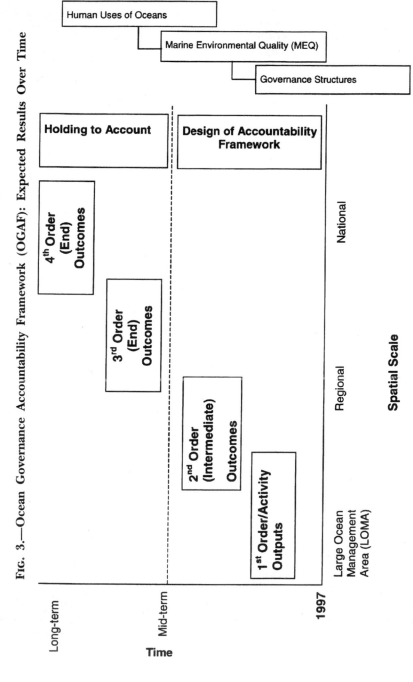

FIG. 3.—Ocean Governance Accountability Framework (OGAF): Expected Results Over Time

Source: Developed by the author, 2004.

the national scale. During the early years of implementation, as illustrated on the far right of the figure, the focus should be on governance structures—creating institutions and making sure that there is a proper fit between these institutions and the tasks at hand.

In the early years the focus should be on first order activity outcomes. There should be collaborative planning, engaging stakeholders, improving knowledge of the marine ecosystem and improving policies for marine pollution. The focus should be on a LOMA. However, there should be an overlap between first-order/activity outcomes and second-order outcomes.

The model is based on the pressure, state and response model for performance indicators. There is human pressure on the oceans; there is a measurable change in state, or MEQ; then there is a governance response to measurable changes in MEQ intended to modify the collective human use of the oceans. The focus for second order outcomes should be at the regional level. What is envisaged is that over time there should be a shift in approach from a fragmented approach to decisions on oceans use to integrated oceans management.

There should be development and implementation of Integrated Management Plans for LOMAs and for smaller coastal areas. Marine Protected Areas should be established. MEQ guidelines should be established, and a monitoring process should be created and put in place. As illustrated in the figure, the second order outcomes should become evident on a regional basis by the mid-term. The focus of this article is on first and second order outcomes.

Between the mid-term and the long-term, third-order (end) outcomes at the regional level should be expected. There should be tangible improvements in the state and health of the marine ecosystem. There should be some stabilization and possibly reductions in the human pressure on the oceans; less conflict among oceans users; some early institutional changes by oceans users such as changes in harvesting technology, oil and drilling or ferry technology; and fair and transparent planning for ocean and coastal development. As illustrated in the far right of the figure, the focus should be on changes in MEQ.

Fourth-order (end) outcomes should be expected in the long-term. Fourth order outcomes should include oceans and coastal development that is compatible with maintaining ecological integrity and healthy oceanic and coastal ecosystems. Fourth order outcomes should include viable communities that are based on harvesting and the human use of the oceans and coastal areas that can be sustained over time. There should be integrated oceans governance that would continually review and adjust governance interventions, based on changes in MEQ, relative to baseline data established during the initial period of creating LOMAs.

The underlying premise of Figure 3 is that there is an integral link between the sound design of an Accountability Process (Figure 2) and the achievement of third- and fourth-order outcomes. To fully test this premise will require further research work in, say, about five years when third-order outcomes could reasonably be expected. A key issue of attribution in the early days of the implementation of the CEOGM would be the causal links between the creation of accountable institutions and the relationship between these institutions and changes in MEQ and the collective usage patterns of a given LOMA.

Figure 3 represented the turning point in the development of a conceptual model. The litmus test for the author, a Legislative Auditor, was that the model provided a set of norms against which to hold those accountable for a governance regime to account. Figure 3 provided a vision of what should be in place, say, eight years after the promulgation of enabling legislation such as the Oceans Act. There should be governance structures in place for all major LOMAs and the design of a comprehensive accountability framework should have been complete. Figure 3 further suggests that the extent to which an Accountability Process (see Figure 2) was in place could be one proxy measure of results expected from the CEOGM, say, eight to ten years after any coastal state began to implement the model. This hypothesis is based on the concept of "necessary and sufficient" conditions for efficacy.

The concept of "necessary and sufficient" conditions can best be explained using a very simple example of a vehicle. The rear axle of a vehicle can be said to be "necessary" to move the vehicle forward. However necessary, the rear axle is not "sufficient" to move the car from destination A to destination B. To move the vehicle, other "necessary" conditions include an engine, a transmission, gasoline and a driver. These conditions are required to complete the journey. However, it would be fair to say that if there is not a rear axle, we can be very sure that the vehicle is going nowhere. The ultimate outcome of transportation will not be achieved. The lack of a "necessary" condition can be a good predictor of a potential failure to achieve desired results, such as travel from point A to B.

In the context of collaborative oceans governance, the author is then postulating that adequate accountability is like the rear axle. It is a "necessary" condition to move forward. But what conditions are "sufficient" to ensure the efficacy of collaborative oceans governance? There has to be capacity in terms of human and financial resources and accessible scientific knowledge. There has to be competence in terms of adequately trained and qualified professional and scientific staff. There has to be commitment, including political will, and the will to ensure a coherent government-wide and sectoral approach that transcends any given department or agency. And perhaps, most importantly, there has to be "consequence" with the electorate for not delivering the expected results.

As a minimum, these "sufficient" conditions will be required to ensure the efficacy of an oceans governance regime. Indicators of capacity, competence, commitment, coherence and consequence would also be useful in terms of predicting potential institutional failure. However, such indicators are beyond the scope of this research. This research focus is on indicators of whether the "necessary" precondition, that of accountability, is or is not in place.

Using the completeness of the design of an Accountability Process (see Figure 2) as a proxy measure for early results led the author to develop Indicators of Accountability.

Indicators of Accountability as a Proxy Measure

Indicators measure a condition or state. Indicators of Accountability measure the health of the Accountability Process articulated in Figure 2. They measure the extent to which a coherent and complete accountability framework has been established, communicated to others, and is used to ensure that institutional performance meets the expectations of participants in the governance regime. Indicators of Accountability measure the extent to which there is an effective holding to account by assessing the credibility of the reporting of performance, as well as the use of this information by elected officials to ensure that expected results are actually achieved.

The hypothesis was that these Indicators of Accountability would provide a good proxy measure, and in fact an early warning signal, of the potential ineffectiveness of any given CEOGM. To test this hypothesis, a conceptual framework was developed.

The Oceans Governance Accountability Framework (OGAF) (see Figure 4) is based on the Law of the Sea, which grants rights and obligations to coastal states for their EEZs. To discharge these obligations, coastal states must work within their existing national model of government. Any national government model is based on predefined constitutional arrangements that define the relative rights and obligations of the national state and the sub-national units of government. A national government model is based on a definition of accountability. To accommodate oceans governance, a modern definition of accountability is needed. Such a modern definition of accountability has to be further modified to adjust for oceans governance arrangements.

Within the national government model there are at least two main components, a legislative component (i.e., a Legislative Body) and an Executive Branch. In a Westminster model government, the Executive Branch is the Prime Minister's Office and Cabinet; the legislative body is Parliament.

The focus of the research is on measuring the robustness of the Accountability Process for the CEOGM. There are three dimensions of accountability that need to be measured using Indicators of Accountability.

FIG. 4.—Oceans Governance Accountability Framework (OGAF)

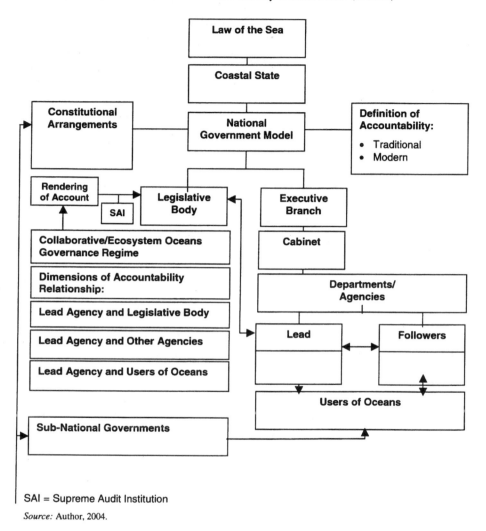

SAI = Supreme Audit Institution

Source: Author, 2004.

First, there is the accountability relationship between the lead agency or department and the legislative body. For example, in the Canadian context this is the relationship between the Minister of Fisheries and Oceans and Parliament. The next key relationship is the accountability relationship between the lead agency or department for the oceans and other agencies and departments that make decisions affecting the human use of the oceans. The final relationship of interest is the relationship between the lead agency or department and users of the oceans, including sub-national

Table 2.—Overview of Accountability Diagnostic Framework

Oceans Goverance Accountability Framework (OGAF)	The Accountability Process			
	Accountability Framework		Holding to Account	
Dimensions of Accountability Relationship:	Roles and Expectations	Reporting Requirements and Review	Credible Reporting	Review and Adjustment
Minister of Fisheries and Oceans and Parliament	Indicators of Vertical Accountability		Indicators of Credible Reporting	Indicators of Holding to Account
Minister of Fisheries and Oceans and Other Ministers	Indicators of Horizontal Accountability		N/A	N/A
Minister of Fisheries and Oceans and Users of Oceans	Indicators of Integrated Management		Indicators of Credible Reporting	N/A
Timing of Intended Use Diagnostic Tests	**Design Phase of Governance Institutions**		**5–10 Years After Promulgation of Enabling Legislation**	

governments. The scale of this relationship will generally be at the regional, or meso-level, commensurate with the characteristics of a LOMA.

Indicators of Accountability were developed to test whether the "necessary" condition of a sound Accountability Process had been put in place. Table 6 provides an overview of the diagnostic regime developed.

As illustrated on the left-hand columns of Table 2, the focus of the diagnostic framework is on three dimensions of the critical accountability relationships. The first dimension is between the Minister of Fisheries and Oceans and Parliament. As illustrated in the right-hand portion of Table 2, Indicators of Vertical Accountability were developed to test whether the Minister has established a robust accountability framework with clearly defined roles, expectations for performance, reporting requirements and some provision for review and oversight. Relative to the holding to account portion of the accountability relationship between the Minister of Fisheries and Oceans and Parliament, Indicators of Credible Reporting were developed. As well, an Indicator of an Effective Holding to Account was developed. Relative to the accountability relationship between the Minister of Fisheries and Oceans and other ministers, Indicators of Horizontal Accountability were developed.

Relative to the accountability relationship between the Minister of Fisheries and Oceans and oceans users, Indicators of Integrated Management were developed. Relative to the holding to account element of the accountability relationship, the Indicators of Credible Reporting that were developed to test the accountability of the Minister of Fisheries and Oceans to Parliament were also used to test accountability between the Minister of Fisheries and Oceans and users of the oceans.

Indicators of Vertical Accountability

To successfully implement the Oceans Act, the Department of Fisheries and Oceans has to merge the two accountability regimes, one based on traditional accountability for consequences (i.e., as a basis to assign blame) and one based on trust. Both regimes have to be in place. Indicators of Vertical Accountability were developed to assess the robustness of the traditional chain of vertical accountability between the Minister, the Deputy Minister (DM), the Associate Deputy Minister (ADM) Oceans, ADM Fisheries Management and the ADM Science. The span and complexity of this vertical chain of accountability is illustrated in Figure 5, Indicators of Vertical Accountability.

Figure 5 illustrates two types of accountability, each based on a different reporting relationship. There are "line" and "functional" reporting relationships. A "line" reporting relationship is a hierarchical relationship between a manager of higher rank and a subordinate of a lower rank. A "functional" reporting relationship, in contrast, may be between peers. It is not based on power, control or formal authority. Rather it is based on influence. One party is expected to provide leadership, advice and direction to the other party or parties in the relationship. These parties may or may not choose to follow this direction. Functional reporting relationships in the Department of Fisheries and Oceans are the basis of organizational management initiatives for cross-cutting issues such as ecosystem management.

The objective of vertical accountability is to ensure answerability for expected results, or outcomes, from the perspective of the Minister of Fisheries and Oceans. The Minister has overall accountability for the implementation of the Oceans Act. Responsibility for implementation of specific portions of the Act can be delegated, but ultimate responsibility rests with the Minister. The Minister is also accountable for ensuring the development of a strategy to implement the Act. The Minister is accountable for international leadership, understanding and protecting the marine environment and supporting sustainable economic opportunities. The Minister is accountable for credible reporting to Parliament on whether these results have been achieved.

As illustrated in the bottom left-hand portion of Figure 5, the ADM Oceans has functional responsibility to co-ordinate the implementation of

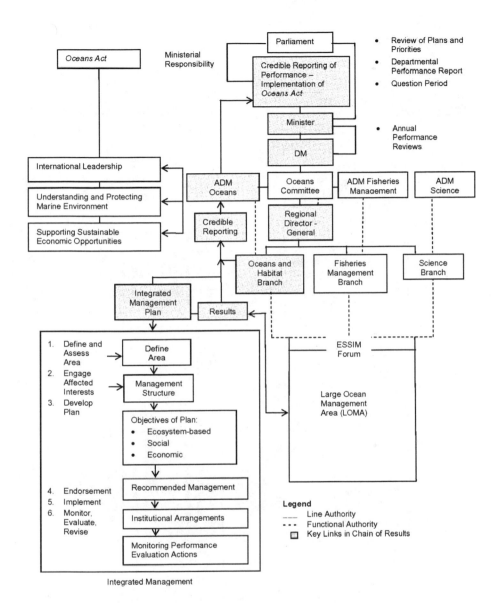

FIG. 5.—Indicators of Vertical Accountability

Table 3.—Line and Functional Accountability for Implementation of the Oceans Act

Framework / Branches	Accountability Framework			Holding to Account	
	Roles and Responsibilities What is the role of the individual in implementation of the Oceans Act and/or Integrated Management?	**Expected Performance** What are the expected measurable outputs, intermediate outcomes or results? When are they due?	**Reporting Requirements** Who is accountable for reporting progress implementing Integrated Management? When and how will results be reported and to whom?	**Credible Reporting of Performance** Who will use this reporting of results to exercise oversight, control and co-ordinate implementation of Integrated Management?	**Review and Adjustment** Who will ensure that mid-course corrections in direction are effectively carried out?
Minister	• Ensures framework developed, implemented and used.	• Strategy, vision and detailed workplan implemented.	• Establishes reporting regime.	• Tables state of oceans report in Parliament.	• Responds to concerns of Parliament.
Deputy Minister (DM)	• Ensures all ADMs and Regional Director Generals understand expected roles.	• Expected changes in management of oceans occur.	• Ensures state of oceans report produced.	• Ensures reporting is coherent, complete and accurate.	• Ensures ADMs change course, as required.
ADM Oceans	• Lead ADM for Oceans Act.	• Develops, implements strategy.	• Consolidates data, prepares state of oceans report.	• Accountable for state of oceans report.	• Monitors changes in all Branches to conform with Oceans Act.

ADM Fisheries Management	• Ensures fisheries managed with due regard for an ecosystem approach, the precautionary principle development.	• Fisheries management with due regard for an ecosystem approach, etc.	• Reports on progress following precautionary principle, an ecosystem approach and sustainable development for fisheries management.	• Accountable for reliability of data.	• Continuous pressure for changes in Branch.
ADM Science	• Ensures adequate scientific capacity applied to implementation of Oceans Act.	• Scientific capacity supports Integrated Management Process.	• Reports on progress developing/applying science to Integrated Management Process.	• Accountable for reliability of data.	• Continuous pressure for changes in Branch.
Regional Director-General	• Effective interface with oceans users for LOMA.	• Integrated Management for each LOMA.	• Reporting on regional progress implementing Integrated Management Process.	• Accountable for reliability of data.	• Continuous pressure for changes in Branch.

Source: Author, 2004.

the Integrated Management Process that involves a six-step process. However, a Regional Director-General, who reports directly to the DM, has line authority for co-coordinating and facilitating the Integrated Management Process for any given LOMA. What this means is that there has to be close co-ordination between the ADM Oceans and the Regional Director-General. Roles, responsibilities and expected results must be clearly defined. The Fisheries Management Branch needs to modify their strategy for fish harvesting to ensure the resilience of the LOMA. The Science Branch needs to provide information on MEQ to support the Integrated Management Plan. There must be clarity around roles and expected results in both Ottawa and the Region.

Table 3 provides an overview of the detailed methodology developed to test the robustness of the accountability framework in place in Ottawa and the Maritimes Region. The table is based on the basic principles of an accountability framework and an effective holding to account. As illustrated, the leaders of the implementation are the Minister, the DM, the ADM of Oceans, Fisheries Management and Science Branches and the Regional Director-General.

Indicators of Horizontal Accountability

In any collaborative governance regime, there must be institutions that transfer bureaucratic energy from vertical to a horizontal accountability regime. Figure 6, Nested Institutions, identifies the institutions that could be used to transfer accountability and power from the traditional power structure to support horizontal cooperation between government departments, within the DM community, within the various branches of the Department of Fisheries and Oceans, and between the Regional Director-General and other oceans users, including the Provinces. Starting at the top of Figure 6, a Ministers' Steering Committee on the Oceans, reporting directly to the Prime Minister, could ensure a coherent approach among and between the Department of Fisheries and Oceans and other government departments. A Privy Council Office Committee on the Oceans could facilitate cooperation between the DM community on oceans matters.

An Oceans Committee within the Department of Fisheries and Oceans could coordinate the efforts of the key Branches within the Department. At the level of a Regional Office, an Oceans Management Steering Committee could harmonize the work of the Branches under the control of the Regional Director-General. These Branches would all contribute to the Integrated Management Process for any given LOMA. A Regional Committee on Ocean Management could be the key mechanism for horizontal accountability and coordination between the Regional Directors-General of the Department of Fisheries and Oceans and other government depart-

FIG. 6.—Nested Institutions

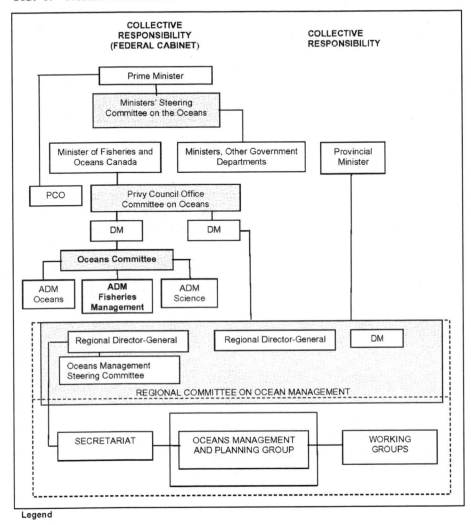

Legend

■ Key institutions for horizontal cross-scale interactions

Source: Adapted by author from the work of ESSIM Planning Office, Oceans and Coastal Management Division, Fisheries and Oceans Canada (Maritimes Region).

ments, such as Environment Canada, Natural Resources Canada, and provincial departments.

Indicators of Credible Reporting

The Minister of Fisheries and Oceans is accountable for credible reporting on the implementation of the Oceans Act. The basis of this reporting is in part based on the Minister's accountability under section 31 of the Oceans Act. This section states that "the Minister [of Fisheries and Oceans] in collaboration with other Ministers, Boards and Agencies of the Government of Canada, with Provincial and Territorial Governments and with affected aboriginal organizations, coastal communities and other persons and bodies, including those bodies established under land claims agreements, shall lead and facilitate the development and implementation of plans for the Integrated Management of all activities or measures in or affecting estuaries, coastal waters and marine waters that form part of Canada or in which Canada has sovereign rights under international law."[16] The information required to sustain an effective holding to account is illustrated in Table 4.

The expert focus group from the OMRN played a key role in developing the Indicators of Credible Reporting illustrated in Table 4. The focus group identified that there were three fundamental principles upon which the Oceans Act was based—integrated management, the precautionary principle and sustainable development. These principles were to be achieved through collaboration. This collaborative approach was a fundamental change relative to the way things had been done in the past at Fisheries and Oceans Canada. The focus group believed that Parliament wants information that would allow Members to assess whether this change in oceans governance had been a success.

Relative to Integrated Management, Parliament wants to know whether there has been adequate federal leadership resulting in a coherent inter-departmental oceans policy and program. The relevant standing committees want to know whether the Government of Canada and the Provinces have worked effectively to manage all sources of marine pollution and degradation, including land-based activity. More specifically, the relevant standing committees want to know whether federal decisions on fisheries and oil and gas were made in an integrated manner that was significantly different from the way decisions were made in the past when the Department of Fisheries and Oceans and Natural Resources Canada worked in relative isolation.

Relative to the precautionary principle, Members of Parliament want to know whether the number of collapses of species and habitats has been reduced and whether the Department of Fisheries and Oceans and Natural Resources Canada have erred on the side of caution in protecting sensitive

16. Oceans Act, n. 1 above, s. 31.

Table 4.—Information Needed by Parliament

Integrated Management/ Collaboration	Precautionary Principle	Sustainable Development
• Have the costs of collaboration been exceeded by the benefits? What are the benefits? • Have there been less conflicts over ocean use? • Is there adequate federal leadership that results in a coherent inter-departmental oceans policy and program? • Have the Federal Government and the Provinces worked effectively to manage all sources of marine pollution and degradation including land-based activities? • Are federal decisions on fisheries, oil and gas made in an integrated manner?	• Have there been collapses of species and habitats? • How do we know we have erred on side of caution in protecting sensitive marine habitat? • How do we know whether the Federal Government has erred on the side of caution on major oceans investment decisions (i.e., fisheries, oil and gas, aquaculture, ocean mining and marine transportation). • Have declines in Marine Environmental Quality been halted/arrested?	• Is there now a consistent, stable and coherent regulatory (and investment) climate across all Canada's ocean spaces? • Have there been any collapses of coastal communities? • Is Canada becoming a world leader in seizing ocean opportunities, creating innovation in marine industries? • Has "intelligent" investment occurred that has respected sensitive marine habitat, not resulted in further increases in Cumulative Environmental Effects?

Source: Expert Focus Group, Oceans Management Research Network Conference, 2003.

marine habitat. Parliament wants to know whether the Federal Government has erred on the side of caution on major oceans investment decisions, such as those taken for fisheries management, oil and gas exploration and development, aquaculture, oceans mining and marine transportation. Parliament wants to know whether declines in MEQ caused by increasing pressure and stress on coastal areas have been halted.

Relative to sustainable development, Members of Parliament are interested in changes in the investment climate and changes in economic opportunities in Canada's ocean spaces. Are oil and gas companies now more willing to invest? Has the decline in the economic and social well-being of coastal communities been arrested? As well, Members of Parliament want to know whether Canada has become a world leader in seizing ocean opportunities, creating innovation in marine industries. In summary, Members of Parliament want to know whether the expected benefits of the Oceans Act have been achieved.

Indicators of Accountability for Integrated Management

The focus of this research is on the relatively early stages of the implementation of the Oceans Act. As previously discussed, at this point in the implementation process, the expected outcomes include first and second order outcomes (see Figure 3). Table 5, Indicators of Integrated Management, matches the fundamental principles of accountability (i.e., the need for an accountability framework and an effective holding to account) with the principles of the Oceans Act—integrated management, the precautionary principle and sustainable development. Process measures are proposed because it is still too early to expect to see substantive changes in the human use of the oceans, and the resultant changes in cumulative environmental effects.

The text for each box in Table 5 defines the expected outcomes over time that could reasonably be expected during the first five to eight years of the implementation of the Act. For example, relative to the precautionary principle, the first step is to assign responsibility to develop guidelines that can be used in making resource development decisions for any given LOMA. The existence and approval of such guidelines is a tangible first-order activity or outcome. Relative to the precautionary principle, second-order outcomes, or early intermediate outcomes, include the use of these approved guidelines in major decisions on oceans use for a given LOMA.

What Table 5 has essentially done is provide detailed norms that could be used in an audit or an evaluation of whether the expected outputs and outcomes had in fact been achieved, eight years after the implementation of the Oceans Act. These detailed indicators could provide an early warning of institutional malaise. The validation of the Indicators of Accountability revealed a great deal about the nature of the CEOGM, based on the Canadian experience. The first major finding was a fundamental problem of "fit."

COLLABORATION PLAYS IN THE THEATRE OF FEDERAL POLITICS

The new oceans governance regime posed a fundamental dilemma for the Minister and the public servants charged with implementation of the Oceans Act. The dilemma was "how to reconcile the principles of a collaborative approach with the principles of sound accountability, including ministerial responsibility." There was a problem of "fit," not between the characteristics of a LOMA and a proposed governance regime, but between the proposed governance regime and the accountability conventions of the machinery of the Government of Canada.

Table 5.—Indicators of Integrated Management

Expected Outcomes	Timeframe (years)	Integrated Management	Precautionary Principle	Sustainable Development
1st Order Outcomes (Activities and Outcomes)				

- Roles and Responsibilities	5	• Collaborative institutions created.
		• Clear terms of reference, shared understanding among engaged oceans users.
			• Accountable decision-maker charged with developing plan for:
			  - Guidelines.
			  - Integrated Database.
			  - Due Diligence Process.
			  - Funding.
				• Shared understanding of responsibility to develop a timetable for action.
				• Development of practical definition of ocean development with due regard for:
				  Sensitive Marine Areas; and
				  Cumulative Environmental Effects, (MEQ).

- Performance Expectations	5	• Timetable, clear responsibility, a game plan for completion of Integrated Management Plan.	• Accountable decision-makers and Institutions approve guidelines for due diligence expectations.	• Ecosystem objectives established.
- Credible Reporting	5	• Clear responsibility, game plan, time table, resources to design, implement and operate credible Integrated Management Information System.		
- Review and Adjustment	5	• Explicit accountability for oversight established, guidelines/protocols established for monitoring Cumulative Environmental Effects, MEQ.		
2ND Order Outcomes (Early Intermediate Outcomes)				

- Roles and Responsibilities
- Expected Performance
	7
	7
		• Integrated Management Plan approved.
		• Explicit articulation of expected changes in behaviour:
		  - Department of Fisheries and Oceans (Fisheries Management, Marine Transportation).
		  - Natural Resources Canada (Oil & Gas Exploration & Development).
		  - Other Government Departments.
		  - Provincial Jurisdictions.
		  - Ocean users (oil and gas, fishing, transportation industries)
		• Strategy, Game Plan and Timetable developed to address sources of land-based pollution.
			• Due diligence process implemented, expected to be used in major resource use decisions.
			• Explicit accountability for oversight of due diligence process.
				• Marine Protected Areas created for Sensitive Areas.
				• Guidelines for MEQ established, implemented and monitoring process in place.
				• Economic and social objectives established, approved MEQ targets.

Expected Outcomes	Timeframe (years)	Integrated Management	Precautionary Principle	Sustainable Development
3rd Order Outcomes (Mature Intermediate Outcomes)				
- Credible Reporting	10	• Adherence to Integrated Management Process and Plan leads to Measurable Reduction in Human Pressure, Use/Exploitation of oceans by: - Fisheries. - Oil and Gas Exploration & Development. - Marine Transportation. - Other Users. • Measurable Reduction in Conflicts.	• Reduction/Stabilization in Cumulative Environments Effects. • Stabilization/Reductions in oceans use causes: • Measurable improvements in Marine Environmental Quality. • Exercise of due diligence, caution in major ocean use decision ensures that: - Sensitive Marine Areas preserved. - Thresholds of Cumulative Environment Effects not exceeded.	• Economic and Social Objectivity for Sustainable Livelihoods Achieved. • Measurable Improvement in Ocean Investment Opportunities.
- Credible Reporting	10-15	Timely, comprehensive, credible, reliable reporting of 3rd order outcomes.		
- Review and adjustment	10-15	Review of progress, results, and effective oversight leads to learning, changes in approach.		

Source: Expert Focus Group, Oceans Management Research Network, November 2003.

FIG. 7.—Traditional Governance Model: Fish

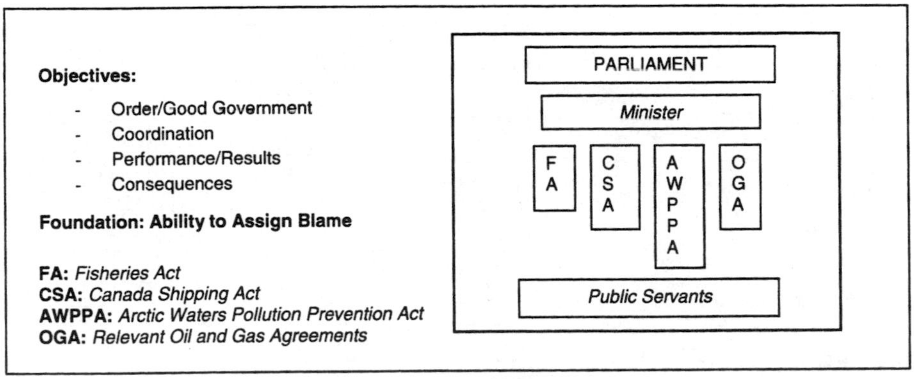

Objectives:

- Order/Good Government
- Coordination
- Performance/Results
- Consequences

Foundation: Ability to Assign Blame

FA: *Fisheries Act*
CSA: *Canada Shipping Act*
AWPPA: *Arctic Waters Pollution Prevention Act*
OGA: *Relevant Oil and Gas Agreements*

PARLIAMENT

Minister

| F A | C S A | A W P P A | O G A |

Public Servants

Source: Author, 2003.

Reconciling Regimes Based on Trust and Blame

Traditional vertical accountability is based on the ability to assign blame. As illustrated in Figure 7, the traditional governance model is based on a clear line of accountability between public servants, a minister and Parliament. This is the essence of the accountability relationship that holds together the many large, complex departments and agencies of the Government of Canada. A Minister is held to account for everything that happens in her or his department.

Figure 7 illustrates the vertical accountability of the Minister of Fisheries and Oceans Canada. Relative to the regulation of coastal, estuarine and marine environments, the Minister is responsible for the effective administration of over 30 acts, regulations and orders. Some of the major acts are listed in Figure 7. The Minister is responsible for the administration of sections of the Canada Shipping Act.[17] The proper regulation of ships will have a direct bearing on the marine environment—a failure of a hull can result in widespread contamination of a pristine marine environment.

The Fisheries Act is one of Canada's "strongest" pieces of environmental legislation.[18] Section 36(3) (administered by Environment Canada) states that "no person shall deposit or permit the deposit of a deleterious substance of any type in water frequented by fish..." The Fisheries Act grants the Minister of Fisheries and Oceans Canada the powers to establish fishing

17. Canada Shipping Act, R.S. 1985, c. S-9, available online: <http://laws.justice.gc.ca/en/S-9/text.html>.
18. Fisheries Act, R.S. 1985, c. F-14, available online: <http://laws.justice.gc.ca/en/F-14/text.html>.

FIG. 8.—New Governance Model: Oceans

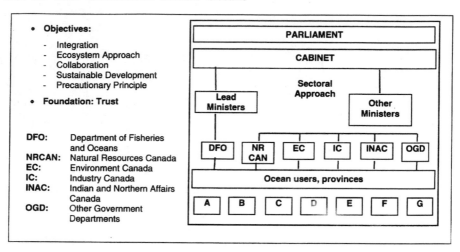

Source: Author, 2004

quotas. Section 7 states that "the Minister may, in his absolute discretion, wherever the exclusive right of fishing does not already exist by law, issue or authorize to be issued leases and licenses for fisheries or fishing, wherever situated or carried on." These powers of the Minister can be contrasted with the role of the Minister with regard to the Oceans Act.

The essence of the CEOGM is described in Figure 8, New Governance Model: Oceans. This Model is based on a "sectoral" approach where oceans users such as fishing companies, local communities, the oil and gas sector, the unions, the Provinces and the Federal Government would collaborate.

The new governance model is based on a "substantial ideological shift" in the management of ocean resources, the need for a more holistic approach, and the need to find ways to manage often competing and increasingly diverse oceans resource interests (including environmental, economic and social interests):

> Canada's oceans are governed by a complex web of laws and regulations managed by various Government organizations across several levels of Government. Over the past decades demands for oceans resources have changed dramatically, creating a need for a unified vision and an integrated approach to oceans management—

one that effectively considers the impact of individual sector activities on each other, and on the oceans as a whole.[19]

Figure 8 illustrates this sectoral approach and explores the accountability implications. The new governance model is largely based on trust. The lead minister is the Minister of Fisheries and Oceans. The model also implies that there will be other ministers that will make decisions on the use of the oceans such as the Ministers of Natural Resources Canada, Industry Canada, and Indian and Northern Affairs Canada. The model implies that there will be individual, joint and several accountabilities of the lead minister and the other ministers. The model introduces other problems from an accountability perspective, largely caused by the use of ambiguous terms, such as sustainable development, the precautionary principle, and an ecosystem approach.

The concept of sustainable development is an inclusive concept that implies new values, imprecise timeframes and definitional ambiguity. This definitional ambiguity makes it more difficult to reach a shared vision necessary to effectively implement a horizontal approach. This problem was clearly illustrated by another objective of the new governance regime—the use of the precautionary principle.

The precautionary principle is part of the operating philosophy of the Government of Canada. The precautionary principle is described by the Government of Canada as a "distinctive approach within risk management which primarily affects the development of management options and decisions. It is ultimately guided by judgment based on values and priorities. Guidance and assurance are particularly needed when there is a risk of serious or irreversible harm, the scientific uncertainty is significant and a decision must be made."[20] Section 30 of the Oceans Act stipulated that the foundation of Canada's Oceans Strategy be based on the precautionary principle.

Recent literature on the application of the precautionary principle to LOMAs has demonstrated the weakness of the principle. A leading researcher, David VanderZwaag, noted that the precautionary principle sounds good on paper but had yet to be convincingly implemented for LOMAs. In practice, VanderZwaag argued that its implementation has largely been ineffective due to definitional problems, confusion in terminology, definitional variations and generalities, and a lack of tangible

19. Fisheries and Oceans Canada, *Government Response to the Fourth Report of the Standing Committee on Fisheries and Oceans: Report on the Oceans Act, March 2002,* (Ottawa: Fisheries and Oceans Canada, 2003).

20. Fisheries and Oceans Canada, n. 6 above, s. 2.3.

guidelines to use in actually applying the principle.[21] As well, accountability for its implementation and the oversight of implementation has been weak.

An ecosystem approach is another ambiguous term that is used in the Oceans Act but not explicitly defined. It is unclear what a department implementing an ecosystem approach would be expected to do differently from traditional practice in terms of fisheries management, oil and gas exploration and development, and other ocean uses.

A Problem of Fit

There is one accountability model for the fish in the oceans, a second and profoundly different accountability model for the oceans in which the fish live. If there is a collapse in the harvest of a given species of fish, the Minister is deemed to be blamed for the collapse. Yet, if the health of the oceans deteriorates dramatically, the Minister may not be deemed accountable because of joint and several liabilities with other collaborators. The two accountability expectations do not meet.

The manifestations of this problem of fit are illustrated by the role of the Minister implicit in the new CEOGM. There are new accountabilities for the Minister of Fisheries and Oceans Canada, such as the responsibility to achieve sustainable development, establish an ecosystem approach and implement the precautionary principle. These new concepts pose problems of fit from an accountability perspective because there may not be shared expectations about intended outcomes or results. Without shared expectations about intended results, it is difficult to create a chain of results and attribute measurable changes in MEQ or behaviour with specific oceans governance interventions.

For a collaborative approach to work, it is critically important to define the accountabilities among and between a lead minister for the ocean and other ministers. It is critical to clarify the accountability among and between the various users of the oceans and the lead minister, the Minister of Fisheries and Oceans. What is the role of these "collaborators," relative to the levels of potential collaboration? Do they have decision-making power, or will they be advisory bodies? What, if any, is their collective accountability? For any decisions reached, who is accountable—the collaborators or the lead minister? Relative to decisions reached on an integrated sectoral approach, are these decisions binding on the other ministers? For example, when the Minister of Natural Resources Canada makes decisions that affect

21. D. VanderZwaag, "The Precautionary Principle and Marine Environmental Protection: Slippery Shores, Rough Seas and Rising Normative Tides," *Ocean Development and International Law* 33 (2002): 165–188.

offshore drilling, is that minister bound by the collaborative decisions made by the collaborators and affirmed by the lead minister?

Conclusions on the Indicators of Accountability

To merge a collaborative model with the traditional accountability model of the Government of Canada is a difficult and complex task. It is inherently difficult to establish an individual and collective accountability of national governments, sub-national governments and others involved in the collaborative process. Within this context, the author concluded that diagnostic Indicators of Accountability can help architects of oceans governance measure the extent to which accountability has successfully been built into an oceans governance regime. As well, such Indicators of Accountability can be useful to determine whether, five to ten years after the implementation of a governance regime, the intended accountability is in fact in place. This and the other research conclusions on the application of the Indicators of Accountability are summarized in Table 6.

Within the foregoing context of a problem of fit, it became clear to the author that the fundamental purpose of these Indicators was to measure the extent to which an irreconcilable difference in philosophy and approach had been reconciled. Failure to reconcile this problem of fit could result in a condition analogous to having a vehicle with an engine, a driver and no rear axle. Measuring the extent of fit between regimes based on blame and trust was deemed to be equivalent to determining whether the vehicle had a rear axle, a "necessary" precondition for achieving results. The researcher believed that failure to reconcile these regimes could be a good predictor that a governance model would not achieve the desired results in terms of first, second, third and ultimately fourth order outcomes. In short, these Indicators could be an early warning sign of the ineffectiveness of a given CEOGM.

Relationship Between "Necessary" and "Sufficient" Conditions

Based on the application of these Indicators of Accountability, the author began to see potential causal links, or some "attribution," between the "necessary" and "sufficient" conditions for effective collaborative oceans governance.

This is illustrated in Table 7. Looking at the left-hand column the "necessary" condition of accountability is analyzed from four different dimensions, or lenses. There is the perspective of Indicators of Vertical Accountability, Horizontal Accountability, Accountability for Integrated Management and a Credible Reporting and Holding to Account. Table 7

Table 6.—Summary of Research Conclusions

Oceans Governance Accountability Framework (OGAF)	The Accountability Process	
Dimensions of Accountability Relationship	**Accountability Framework**	**Holding To Account**
Minister of Fisheries and Oceans and Parliament	• Indicators are relevant and useful. • Complexities of developing comprehensive and coherent framework.	**Credible Reporting:** • Indicators are relevant and useful. • Need for comprehensive State of Oceans Report; need for timetable to create one. **Review and Adjustment:** • Need for questions on oceans in Parliament, not just questions on fish.
Minister of Fisheries and Oceans and Other Ministers	• Indicators are relevant and useful. • Complexities, constraints to developing mechanisms for horizontal management; complexities of defining accountability for horizontal co-operation.	**Credible Reporting:** • Need for transparent and comprehensive process in place; need for timetable to develop and use a credible reporting regime.
Minister of Fisheries and Oceans and Users of Oceans	• Indicators are relevant and useful. • Likelihood of confusion about roles of oceans users (i.e., collaborators) in regional Integrated Management Process	**Credible Reporting:** • Need for transparent and comprehensive process to be in place; need for timetable to develop and use a credible reporting regime.

Source: Author, 2004.

explores the potential causal relationships between these four Indicators and the "sufficient" conditions deemed to be required to implement the new collaborative oceans governance model.

For example, Vertical Accountability is critical to marshal the financial and human resources necessary to cover the transaction costs of coordination required by the CEOGM. Vertical Accountability is also required to ensure that sufficient knowledge is applied to tackling the difficult scientific

Table 7.—Early Warning Signs of Ineffectiveness

"Necessary" Condition	"Sufficient" Conditions			
	Capacity	Competence	Policy/ Coherence	Consequence
Vertical Accountability	Adequate resources for coordination.	Adequate scientific knowledge applied to government of LOMA.	No link identified.	Alignment of departmental priorities.
Horizontal Accountability	Adequate scientific resources applied to developing MEQ.	Adequate scientific knowledge applied.	Management of oceans rather than a focus on distribution of harvest of fish. Consistent, coherent government-wide policy implementation.	No link identified.
Accountability for Integrated Management	Adequate oversight of Integrated Management Process.	Science knowledge used to support implementation of precautionary principle.	Decisions made with a due regard for the precautionary principle.	No link identified.
Credible Reporting Holding to Account	Resources dedicated to creating necessary baseline data.	No link identified.	No link identified.	Political pressure necessary for adaptive governance.

Source: Author, 2004.

questions implicit in an ecosystem approach. Vertical Accountability is essential to ensure that there is an alignment of internal departmental priorities. For example, in a department such as Fisheries and Oceans, traditional vertical accountability is one lever that the DM can use to ensure that the requisite ADMs follow a sectoral approach to oceans governance.

Looking at the second row, Horizontal Accountability is critical to ensure that the adequate scientific resources are brought to bear on developing measures of MEQ and ecosystem objectives. The scientific capacity in Branches other than the Oceans Branch must be mobilized through Horizontal Accountability and cooperation within the Department. Horizontal Accountability is critical if there is to be a commitment to policy coherence and to ensure that there will be management of the oceans, rather than a pre-occupation with management of the harvest of fish. Of all the changes required to implement an ecosystem approach to oceans governance, this is one of the most pronounced changes. As well, Horizontal Accountability is critical to ensure that there is a consistent, coherent government-wide approach to policy implementation of the Oceans Act. For example, oil and gas leases should be awarded in a way that is consistent with the broad principles of the ecosystem approach and the precautionary principle. Coherence in a government context means that different policies and enabling statutes do not promote inconsistent end outcomes at odds with each other. Accountability for Integrated Management helps to ensure that there is proper oversight of the Integrated Management Process and that there is adequate scientific knowledge to support the implementation of the precautionary principle.

There is a critical link between Credible Reporting and consequence. The Oceans Act is based on adaptive governance, or enlightened trial and error. When a LOMA is under severe human pressure, there has to be adequate political pressure brought to bear on Members of Parliament, who then in turn put pressure on the Department of Fisheries and Oceans, to address the issue of a sick LOMA.

These potential relationships between "necessary" and "sufficient" conditions can be further explored when the Office of the Auditor General of Canada issues its report to Parliament on the Government of Canada's progress to date in implementing the Oceans Act. The Auditor General's work should be seen as an initial step in a journey to measure the results of Canada's experiment with a collaborative oceans governance regime. Citizens need to know if oceans governance interventions are effective. The Office of the Auditor General of Canada will be reporting its audit of the Oceans Act in the fall of 2005 to Parliament.[22] This report can be used by Parliamentary Committees to hold the Government of Canada to account for its stewardship of the longest coastline in the world.

A subsequent article by the author will analyze the implications of this important legislative audit. The focus of this forthcoming article will be on using the comprehensive, fact-based and insightful work of the Office of the Auditor General of Canada to develop a more robust predictive model of whether any given governance intervention built on the CEOGM will likely be effective in limiting the deleterious effects of the Pathology of the Limitless Oceans Sink.

22. See the web site of the Office of the Auditor General, <http://www.oag-bvg.gc.ca>.

THE US AROUND THE SEA

Reflecting on the Canadian Experience

The Canadian experience with the CEOGM suggests four areas of collective learning applicable to other coastal states considering adopting the CEOGM.

The first area of collective learning is that collaboration is a costly process in terms of the weeks and months of coordination and participation time required. Collaboration involves getting everyone needed at one table and getting them to agree on conventions, roadmaps and end points. Because much of this participation is essentially voluntary, the CEOGM requires three to five years at the outset just to create the necessary institutional infrastructure. During this period of infrastructure and capacity building there will be activity outputs, but few substantive intermediate outcomes. The CEOGM may well have a significant long-term payback. However, in the early years there are significant transaction costs. This would suggest that this model would be appropriate for LOMAs that are relatively healthy and pristine at the point of intervention. The model would likely be inappropriate for highly stressed, "sick" LOMAs that were close to the point of a major collapse.

The second lesson from the Canadian experience is that before any department or agency of the government can effectively collaborate with oceans users external to the government entity, the lead department or agency has to learn how to effectively cooperate internally. For example, Table 3 illustrates that to achieve a coherent approach within the Department of Fisheries and Oceans, the Minister and the DM had to effectively align the activities of three Branches. Given inevitable organizational inertia and the tendency of any Branch to continue pursuing its own initiatives, this is no small task. If a government entity works with external stakeholders prior to sorting out internal roles, responsibilities, expectations and accountabilities, these external stakeholders may be confused. The government may not be speaking with one voice.

Figure 9 illustrates the limitations of the new oceans governance model in terms of transaction costs and the relatively long timeframe required to achieve "end" outcomes. Figure 9 illustrates that significant transaction costs can be anticipated within a given government and within a federal and provincial context where there is a relatively homogenous bureaucratic and political culture. This suggests higher transaction costs can be anticipated in a multi-national context characterized by a non-homogeneous political and bureaucratic culture.

The third area of collective learning is the need for clarity in the accountability relationship between a lead minister for the oceans and other ministers. The rights and obligations of such a lead minister should be

FIG. 9.—"Transaction Costs" of Collaboration

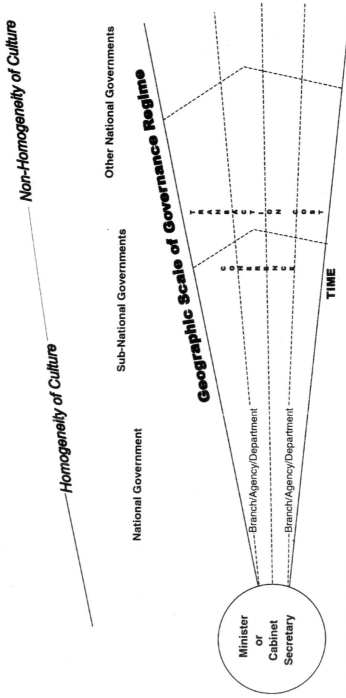

**Table 8.—Oceans Governance Accountability Framework (OGAF):
Foundation Questions**

• Is there a national oceans policy, act or other enabling statutes that: — Address issues of geographic, institutional and political fragmentation? — Establishes processes to improve co-ordination among and between levels of government institutions, users of oceans resources and the public? — Establishes a mechanism to ensure levels of funding commensurate with the objectives of the policy? — Clearly defines the role, expected results of the lead national agency/department and the other agencies/departments whose decisions on oceans use have a significant impact on coastal, estuarine and ocean ecosystems? — Establishes ultimate accountability for ocean outcomes (as well as defining the desired outcomes in terms of process and substantive changes in collective human behaviour and cumulative environmental effects), within the national government of a coastal state? — Explicitly defines terms such as ecosystem, biodiversity, sustainable development and the precautionary principle? • Is there a modern definition of accountability that accommodates collaborative arrangements? Has this definition been specifically modified/adapted to accommodate oceans governance application?

Source: Author, 2004.

articulated in a national oceans policy or enabling statute. In addition to this foundation issue, there are other issues that need to be addressed with considerable clarity in the oceans policy or enabling statute. These are illustrated in Table 8. There is need to explicitly define ambiguous terms such as ecosystem, biodiversity, sustainable development and the precautionary principle in the enabling statute.

Palliative or Curative Care?

The purpose of a governance intervention is to control the human use and misuse of the oceans. After three decades of experimentation with largely voluntary governance regimes, there is growing evidence of the increasing contamination of the oceans. A key question for those accountable, jointly and severally, for any oceans governance intervention is whether the intervention is "palliative" or "curative." A "palliative" oceans governance regime palliates, or alleviates, public concerns about declines in fish stocks and destruction of sensitive ocean habitat. A palliative regime allows federal governments to say that they are "adequately addressing the problem." A palliative regime may stabilize human pressures on the ocean but does not reduce the aggregate pressure. The focus is on equitable distribution of ocean resources and conflict avoidance. However, with the collective human pressure on the LOMA at a stable but high level, MEQ and biodiversity may continue to decline. The LOMA may approach the threshold of collapse. There is no "sabbatical" time for the LOMA to "lie fallow" to use an ancient biblical concept. More restrictive limits on human use would allow for sufficient time and space for regeneration.

A "curative" oceans governance regime creates a "no-use zone" at sufficiently large spatial and temporal scales for the ecosystem functions to begin the regenerate. The resiliency of the LOMA increases and the MEQ improves. Endangered species gradually move off the endangered list. Collective human use of the LOMA is dramatically reduced. The pressure of powerful lobby groups is focused on preserving the "supply" of ocean resources, rather than the equitable distribution of ocean resources.

What this research suggests is the need for good diagnostics to evaluate whether a given oceans governance regime is palliative or curative. This research has described one potential set of diagnostics, Indicators of Accountability. An emerging hypothesis is that weak accountability correlates with limited efficacy, or effectiveness. Limited efficacy correlates with a low probability that "sufficient" conditions will exist for a curative intervention.

For example, a decision to create a Marine Protected Area or a "no-use zone" will require the expenditure of significant financial and human resources and the expenditure of considerable political and bureaucratic capital. It is difficult to envisage a "curative" oceans governance intervention occurring without all the "necessary" and "sufficient" conditions for effective oceans governance being in place.

Perhaps if Rachel Carson published her seminal work[23] in 2005 she would have entitled it *The Us Around the Sea.* Infinity has been lost, yet humans still cling to the mythology of the limitless oceans sink. Clear accountability for the consequence of oceans exploitation and domestication is one way to close the ingenuity gap between oceans exploitation and oceans conservation. While there is no accountability for the infinite oceans, there can and should be clear accountability, a rendering of accounts and a holding to account for the human use of finite regional seas.

23. R. Carson, *The Sea Around Us* (Oxford, U.K.: Oxford University Press, 1989) first published 1951.

Low-Tide Elevations in International Law of the Sea: Selected Issues

Yoshifumi Tanaka*

Marine Law and Ocean Policy Centre, Martin Ryan Institute, National University of Ireland, Galway

INTRODUCTION

Currently low-tide elevations are increasingly important in international law of the sea in both theory and practice.[1] First, low-tide elevations have practical importance for the coastal State, since such elevations may have an impact on identifying the outer limits of the territorial sea. In this regard, Article 13(1) of the 1982 United Nations Convention on the Law of the Sea[2] (hereafter the LOSC) provides that:

> Where a low-tide elevation is situated wholly or partly at a distance not exceeding the breadth of the territorial sea from the mainland or an island, the low-water line on that elevation may be used as the baseline for measuring the breadth of the territorial sea.[3]

---

* The author would like to thank Dr. Anne Marie O'Hagan and Professor Clive Symmons for their useful comments on an earlier draft of this article.

1. With respect to low-tide elevations, the following are of particular interest. C. Symmons, "Some Problems Relating to the Definition of 'Insular Formations' in International Law: Islands and Low-Tide Elevations," *Maritime Briefing* 1 No. 5 (Durham: International Boundaries Research Unit, 1995): 1–32; P. Weil, "Les hauts-fonds découvrants dans la délimitation maritime: A propos des paragraphes 200–209 de l'arrêt de la Cour internationale de Justice du 16 mars 2001 en l'affaire de la Délimitation maritime et questions territoriales entre Qatar et Bahreïn," in N. Ando et al. eds., *Liber Amicorum Judge Shigeru Oda*, (The Hague: Kluwer, 2002): 307–321; G. Guillaume, "Les haute-fonds découvrants en droit international," in *La mer et son droit, Mélanges offerts à Laurent Lucchini et Jean-Pierre Quéneudec* (Paris: Pedone, 2003): 287–302; R. Lavalle, "Not Quite a Sure Thing: The Maritime Areas of Rocks and Low-Tide Elevations Under the UN Law of the Sea Convention," *International Journal of Marine and Coastal Law*, 19 (2004): 43–69; V. Prescott and C. Symmons, *Political Maritime Boundaries of the World*, 2nd ed. (The Hague: Brill, 2005).

2. Available online: <http://www.un.org/Depts/los/index.htm>.

3. That provision is identical to Article 11 of the 1958 Geneva Convention on the Territorial Sea and the Contiguous Zone. The origin of this provision could date

In connection with this, Judge Oda argued in the *Qatar/Bahrain* case (Merits) that "[i]n 1930 and 1958, low-tide elevations located in the rather narrow (three-mile) seabelt off the coast would not have had much effect on the extent or the boundary of the territorial sea, and these provisions might have reflected customary law prevailing at that time." Yet Judge Oda asked: "how could they have the same minor effect if the territorial sea were to be widened to 12 miles?"[4] Furthermore, the presence of low-tide elevations may produce an important question in maritime delimitations: whether low-tide elevations may be a relevant circumstance and, if this is the case, what is their effect on maritime delimitations? Considering that there are a number of areas where maritime delimitations are needed,[5] the impact of low-tide elevations upon this is worth examining.

Secondly, low-tide elevations provoke interesting theoretical questions relating to the concept of the "territoriality" in international law: Whether low-tide elevations could be regarded as part of land territory or as part of the seabed. If low-tide elevations are argued to be terrestrial territory, international law regarding the acquisition of territory is applicable to them. By contrast, if low-tide elevations are regarded as part of the seabed, such a feature should be subject to law of the sea. On this point, it is worth noting that the *Qatar/Bahrain* decision (Merits) of 2001 broke new ground.

It is against this background that this article seeks to examine low-tide elevations in international law focusing on three principal issues. Following an introduction, the identification of low-tide elevations will be addressed in Part Two. Part Three will examine the territoriality of low-tide elevations by analyzing the *Qatar/Bahrain* case (Merits). Furthermore, Part Four will consider the impact of low-tide elevations upon maritime delimitations on

---

back to the 1930 Hague Conference for the Codification of International Law. For a historical analysis regarding the effect to be given to low-tide elevations, see H. Dipla, *Le régime juridique des îles dans le droit international de la mer* (Paris: PUF, 1984): 57–74; M. S. McDougal and W. T. Burke, *The Public Order of the Oceans: A Contemporary International Law of the Sea* (New Haven: New Haven Press, 1987): 391–398.

4. Separate Opinion of Judge Oda in the *Qatar/Bahrain* Case (Merits), *ICJ Reports* (2001): 125, para. 7. Furthermore, with respect to Article 13 of the LOSC, Judge Oda pointed out that the latter simply copied the relevant 1930 and 1958 texts on those issues without any in-depth discussion at the Third United Nations Conference on the Law of the Sea on the effect which would follow from the broadening of the territorial sea from 3 miles to 12 miles. *Id.*

5. According to a study by the United States Department of State, the total number of potential maritime boundaries is 420. United States Department of State, Bureau of Oceans and International Environmental and Scientific Affairs, *Limits in the Seas, No. 108: 1st Revision, Maritime Boundaries of the World* (1990): 2. At the opening of the 21st century, maritime boundaries are settled by approximately 200 agreements, merely 48 percent of the total number of potential maritime delimitations. It is predictable from the above data that disputes over maritime delimitation will continue.

the basis of State practice as well as international decisions. Finally, a general conclusion will be added in Part Five.

IDENTIFICATION OF LOW-TIDE ELEVATIONS: ISLANDS OR LOW-TIDE ELEVATIONS?

Nature of the Problem

The first question that needs to be addressed concerns the identification of low-tide elevations. On this point, Article 13(1) of the LOSC defines low-tide elevations as follows:

> A low-tide elevation is a naturally formed area of land which is surrounded by and above water at low tide but submerged at high tide.[6]

On the other hand, island is defined as "a naturally formed area of land, surrounded by water, which is above water at high tide."[7] The distinction between islands and low-tide elevations is significant since islands may possess a continental shelf and an exclusive economic zone (EEZ), while low-tide elevations may have only a territorial sea (and, presumably, a contiguous zone) when these features are situated wholly or partly at a distance not exceeding the breadth of the territorial sea from the mainland or an island.[8] Thus it is not surprising that disputes may arise with respect to the legal status of a marine feature in national and international spheres.

The selection of the tidal datum is of central importance in determining whether a marine feature could be regarded as an island or a low-tide

---

6. The low-tide elevation may be a rock or a shoal, irrespective of its size. M. Nordquist, ed., *United Nations Convention on the Law of the Sea 1982: A Commentary,* Center for Oceans Law and Policy (Dordrecht: Nijhoff, 1993): 128. The United Nations Division for Ocean Affairs and Law of the Sea (UNDOALOS) defined the low-tide elevation as "a legal term for what are generally described as drying banks or rocks." UNDOALOS, *Baselines: an Examination of the Relevant Provisions of the United Nations Convention on the Law of the Sea* (New York: United Nations, 1989): 48. In this regard, Jayewardene categorized reefs, being awash at high tide, into the rubric of low-tide elevations. Yet, reef components permanently above water would qualify as islands. H. W. Jayewardene, *The Regime of Islands in International Law* (Dordrecht: Nijhoff, 1990): 95.

7. Article 121(1) of the LOSC.

8. Article 13(1) and Article 121(2) of the LOSC; C. Symmons, *The Maritime Zones of Islands in International Law* (The Hague: Nijhoff, 1979): 43; M. W. Reed, *Shore and Sea Boundaries,* Vol. Three (U.S. Department of Commerce, National Oceanic and Atmospheric Administration, 2000): 216–219; Lavalle, n. 1 above, at 68. See also the section on the impact of low-tide elevations on maritime delimitations, later in this article.

elevation.[9] In borderline cases, the legal status of marine features may be changeable depending on the tidal datum.[10] The problem is, however, that no tidal datum was given in Article 11 of the Geneva Convention on Territorial Sea and the Contiguous Zone,[11] as well as Article 13 of the LOSC.[12] In reality, there are several choices of tidal datum. In spite of attempts at international standardization of the tidal datum, currently there

9. A tidal datum may be defined as the reference plane (or surface) to which the height of the predicted tide is referred. N. S. M. Antunes, "The Importance of the Tidal Datum in the Definition of Maritime Limits and Boundaries," *Maritime Briefing*, 2, No. 7 (Durham: International Boundaries Research Unit, 2000): 5. The selection of tidal datum includes: (i) lowest low water (LLW)/highest high water (HHW); (ii) lowest astronomical tide (LAT)/highest astronomical tide (HAT); (iii) mean lower low water springs (MLLWS)/mean higher high water springs (MHHWS); (iv) mean low-water springs (MLWS)/mean high water springs (MHWS); (v) mean higher low water (MHLW)/mean higher high water (MHHW); (vi) mean low water (MLW)/mean high water (MHW); (vii) mean lower low water (MLLW)/mean lower high water (MLHW); (viii) mean low water neaps (MLWN)/ mean high water neaps (MHWN); (ix) mean sea-level (MSL) etc., *Id.*, pp. 28–29. See also UNDOALOS (n. 6 above), p. 43; D. P. O'Connell, "The Measurement of the Territorial Sea," in I. A. Shearer, ed., *The International Law of the Sea*, Vol. I (Oxford: Clarendon Press, 1982): Chapter 5, at 173–174; A. Shalowitz, *Shore and Sea Boundaries* (Washington: U.S. Government Printing Office, 1962): 82–104.

10. Antunes, *id.*, at 13; Symmons, n. 8 above, at 12.

11. For the text of the Convention, see M. D. Evans ed., *Blackstone's International Law Documents*, 4th ed., (London: Blackstone Press Limited, 1999): 71–77.

12. On this point, the United Kingdom's Court of Appeal, in the *Post Office v. Estuary Radio, Ltd.* case of 1967, had already stated that: "On these definitions [of Article 11 of the 1958 Geneva Convention on the Territorial Sea and the Contiguous Zone] interesting and difficult questions arise whether a "low-tide elevation must be above water at all low-tides, at mean low-water spring tides, at Admiralty datum, at the lowest tides experienced from time to time (and if so, how often?) in the course of a year, or at lowest astronomical tides. Some day some court, municipal or international, may have to decide this, aided, we hope, by evidence of international practice and the travaux preparatoires of the Convention." Yet that Court refrained from entering into this issue since the Court was not obliged to and it was better that it should not. J. T. Edgerley, ed., *The All England Law Reports 1967*, Vol. 3 (London: Butterworths, 1968): 685. On the other hand, in the *United States v. Alaska* case of 1997, the Special Master's Report indicated that 'high tide' has been understood as 'mean high water' under well-established United States practice. *Report of the Special Master*, J. K. Mann, March 1996, No. 84, Original, The Supreme Court of the United States, at 234–236. It appeared that the Supreme Court of the United States was also supportive of this view: 521 *United States Reports, Cases Adjudged in the Supreme Court at October Term 1996* (Washington 2000): 32. Even though the mean high tide is a well-established standard in the United States, this does not mean that that standard is an internationally accepted one. Concerning the analysis on this decision, see C. Symmons, "When is an 'Island' Not an 'Island' in International Law? The Riddle of Dinkum Sands in the Case of US v. Alaska," *Maritime Briefing* 2, No. 6 (Durham: International Boundaries Research Unit, 1999): 1–32. See also Reed, n. 8 above, at 133–140.

is no uniformity in State practice in this matter.[13] Furthermore, States have used more than one datum along their coasts. Thus the tidal datum used in one part of the coast does not necessarily have to be used in another stretch of the coast.[14] This practice may make the problem more complicated. Hence, one cannot but conclude that there are no customary rules regarding the use of tidal datum, and that States have discretion choosing an appropriate low-water line.[15] Yet a dispute can be raised where States concerned use different tidal datum, and the legal status of a marine feature differs depending on the datum. On this issue, two litigated cases concerning the *Anglo-French Continental Shelf* arbitration and *Qatar/Bahrain* (Merits) provide interesting examples of discussion on this issue.

Eddystone Rocks in the *Anglo-French Continental Shelf* Arbitration (1977)

In the 1977 *Anglo-French Continental Shelf* arbitration, a dispute arose between the Parties with respect to the use of Eddystone Rocks as a basepoint in the delimitation of the English Channel.[16] The United Kingdom maintained that the Rocks were to be regarded as islands and should accordingly be used as a basepoint for determining a median line in the English Channel west of the Channel Islands. According to counsel for the United Kingdom, the Eddystone Rocks were only totally covered at high water equinoctial springs. Thus he argued that they were uncovered at mean high water springs, which was the required definition of an island in the United Kingdom Territorial Waters Order in Council of 1964, and was surely also in accord with international practice.[17]

With respect to tidal datum, the United Kingdom maintained that, whether under customary law or under Article 10 of the 1958 Geneva Convention on the Territorial Sea, the relevant high-water line was the line of mean high-water spring tides, and it affirmed that this was also the practice of many other States. Moreover, the United Kingdom alleged that

13. On this point, O'Connell stated that, "It is evident then that an international low-water plane has not been established and that there is serious doubt respecting the possibility of establishing it." O'Connell, n. 9 above, at 177; Antunes, n. 9 above, at 8 and 11; R. R. Churchill and A. V. Lowe, *The Law of the Sea*, 3rd ed., (Manchester: Manchester University Press, 1999): 33.

14. Antunes, n. 9 above, at 8.

15. Guillaume indicated 17 different tidal datum in State practice. Guillaume, n. 1 above, at 291–293. On the other hand, UNDOALOS indicated that this will be close to the lowest tidal level. UNDOALOS, n. 6 above, at 3.

16. With respect to problems with Eddyston Rocks, see for instance, O'Connell, n. 9 above, pp. 184–185; Symmons, n. 8 above, pp. 44–45.

17. The *Anglo-French Continental Shelf* case, *Report of International Arbitral Awards*, Vol. 18 (New York, United Nations) p. 66, para. 122.

the high-water line shown on all British Admiralty charts was the line of mean high-water spring tides. In the view of the United Kingdom, the mean high-water spring tides was the only precise one.[18] Hence, the United Kingdom did not accept the use of equinoctial high-tide as sufficiently precise in this context.[19] According to the information presented by the United Kingdom, the height of the natural rock at the base of the stump of the old Smeanton lighthouse was approximately 2 feet above mean high-water spring tide and 0.2 feet above the highest astronomical tide. Consequently, the United Kingdom considered that the Eddystone Rocks were not to be ranked as low-tide elevation.[20]

By contrast, the French Government contested the use of the Eddy-stone Rocks as a basepoint because it was not an island but a low-tide elevation. Regarding the tidal datum, France contended that the British concept of "high-water" was very questionable and a large number of States, including France, took it as meaning the limit of the *highest tides*. Furthermore, France claimed that, as soon as a reef did not remain uncovered continuously throughout the year, it had to be ranked as a low-tide elevation, not as an island.[21] According to France, the Eddystone Rocks were described in French Sailing Directions as "ne couvrant complètement qu'aux pleines mers d'équinoxe."[22] Furthermore, France contended that the information given by the United Kingdom itself indicated that the highest part of the Rocks was only very slightly above the highest full-tides and may be covered by them. Thus, France considered the Eddystone Rocks a low-tide elevation.[23]

Regarding this difference of opinion, the Court of Arbitration made it clear that the question to be decided was not the legal status of the Eddystone Rocks as an island but its relevance in the delimitation of the median line in the Channel. It then found that France had previously acquiesced in the use of the Eddystone Rocks as a basepoint for the United Kingdom's fishery limits under the 1964 European Fisheries Convention,[24] as well as in the negotiations of 1971 regarding the continental shelf. Hence, the Court of Arbitration accepted the use of Eddystone Rocks as a

18. *Id.* at 68, para. 127.

19. *Id.* at 70, para. 130.

20. *Id.* at 68, para. 127. In another paragraph, the Court of Arbitration pointed to the fact that the present Admiralty Chart No. 1613 showed a drying height of 5.5 meters for the lower rock, exactly the same height as that of mean high-water spring tides above the lowest astronomical tide. *Id.* at 67, para. 124.

21. *Id.*, at 72, para. 138 and 67, para. 125.

22. *Id.* at 70, para. 130. Editors' translation.—"covered completely only with high tides at the equinox."

23. *Id.* at 72, para. 138.

24. Available online: <http://www.oceanlaw.net/texts/fish64.htm>.

basepoint.[25] Since there was no treaty or customary law with respect to the tidal datum, it appeared to be difficult for the Court of Arbitration to determine the status of the Eddystone Rocks in accordance with positive international law. In this sense, it was understandable that the Court of Arbitration took a pragmatic approach leaving the status of Eddystone Rocks unresolved. Thus, the question relating to tidal datum remained unsettled in this award.[26]

Qit'at Jaradah in the *Qatar/Bahrain* Case (Merits, 2001)

Later, a similar problem arose in the *Qatar/Bahrain* case (Merits) of 2001. In this case, the parties disputed whether Qit'at Jaradah, a maritime feature situated northeast of Fasht al Azm, was an island or a low-tide elevation. Bahrain contended that there were strong indications that Qit'at Jaradah was an island that remained dry at high tide. Furthermore, by referring to a number of eyewitness reports, Bahrain maintained that it was evident that part of its sandbank had not been covered by water for some time.[27] According to the data submitted by Bahrain, at high tide, its length and breadth were about 12 by 4 meters, and its altitude was approximately 0.4 meters.[28] By contrast, Qatar argued that Qit'at Jaradah was always indicated on nautical charts as a low-tide elevation.[29] Moreover, Qatar insisted that, even if there were periods when it was not completely submerged at high tide, its physical status was constantly changing and thus it should be considered no more than a shoal.[30]

Having carefully analyzed the evidence submitted by the Parties and the conclusions of experts, the International Court of Justice (ICJ) concluded that Qit'at Jaradah was an island which should be considered for the determination of the equidistance line.[31] At the same time, taking into account the smallness of the island, the Court ruled that the activities carried out by Bahrain on that island must be considered sufficient to support Bahrain's claim that it has sovereignty over it.[32] It appears, however,

---

25. The *Anglo–French Continental Shelf* case, n. 17 above, at 72–74, paras. 139–144.

26. O'Connell, n. 9 above, at 185.

27. *ICJ Reports* (2001): 98, para. 192; Argument by Professor Reisman, Counsel of Bahrain, Verbatim Record, CR 2000/14, paras. 26–31.

28. *ICJ Reports* (2001): 99, para. 197.

29. *Id.* at 99, para. 193; Argument by Professor Quéneudec, Counsel of Qatar, Verbatim Record, CR 2000/9, paras. 32–39.

30. *ICJ Reports* (2001): 99, para. 193.

31. *Id.* at 99, para. 195.

32. *Id.* at 99–100, para. 197.

that the Court failed to specify the reason why Qit'at Jaradah could be regarded an island, not a low-tide elevation. In fact, the Court did not stipulate which tidal datum was used in determining the status of Qit'at Jaradah.

In this respect, one should note that three Judges dissented with the majority opinion in respect to the legal status of Qit'at Jaradah for the following reasons: the inconsistency of the experts' opinions; the fact that it was not indicated as an island on British Admiralty charts; the removal of the upper surface of the feature in 1986; and the sedimentation which has taken place since then.[33] The three dissenters argued that the fact that the land was above the high-water line was not enough in itself for a feature to be classified as an island. Hence, three judges stressed, in particular, the element of *terra firma* as a condition of islands. In their words:

> The assimilation of islands to land territory is moreover explicable purely in terms of geomorphological considerations: in both cases, by contrast with atolls and cays, the stable underlying element is terra firma; thus they have a physically durable base which ensures their permanence.[34]

According to the three dissenters, however, Qit'at Jaradah did not have such *terra firma*. Thus, they concluded that Qit'at Jaradah was not an island for its geomorphological characteristics placed it in a category not provided for in the LOSC.[35]

Evaluation

The above survey shows that in reality the difference between tidal datums may produce disputes regarding the legal status of a marine feature. At present, however, there is no established treaty or customary law concerning choice of the type of tidal datum. Furthermore, it is inconceivable that there are "general principles of law recognized by civilized nations" on this issue. Accordingly, international courts and tribunals may face the risk of *non liquet* when a dispute arises with respect to the identification of low or high

---

33. Dissenting Opinion of Judges Bedjaoui, Ranjeva and Karoma, *Id.* at 207–208, para. 195. For the same reasons, Judge Vershchetin concluded that Qit'at Jaradah was a low-tide elevation. Declaration of Judge Vereshchetin, *Id.* at 220–221, para. 13.

34. Dissenting Opinion of Judges Bedjaoui, Ranjeva and Karoma, *Id.* at 209–210, para. 200.

35. *Id.* at 209, para. 199.

tides. In this regard, it may be possible to suggest three solutions when this question is raised before international courts and tribunals.

The first solution is that States involved establish a common tidal datum in a *compromis*. Thus the legal status of marine features could be judged on the basis of the common datum. Apparently, this solution will facilitate the work of international courts and tribunals. On the other hand, new hydrographic surveys may be needed if the legal status of these features is in dispute, which adds further costs.[36]

The second possibility is a pragmatic approach. As in the *Anglo-French Continental Shelf* dispute, international courts and tribunals may give judgments without determining the legal status of a marine feature. Yet this solution is not always possible in every dispute.

Thirdly, the concept of equity may be relevant in resolving the problem when this question arises in the context of maritime delimitations. In this regard, it might be arguable that only partial effect should be given to a disputed marine feature. In this respect, the 1990 Agreement between Belgium and France relating to a territorial sea boundary may offer an intriguing example regarding such a solution. The principal difficulty encountered in the negotiation resulted from different tidal datums being used by each party. Belgium did not recognize Banc Breedt, which was situated about 2.5 nautical miles (NM) off the French coast, as a low-tide elevation. Thus, Belgium argued that the basepoint should be placed on Trapegger, lying about 1.3 NM off the Belgian coast and Banc Smal, lying 1.6 NM off the French coast. On the other hand, France alleged that the delimitation should be based on Trapegger and Banc Breedt. For the purpose of a compromise, the parties divided into two equal parts the areas resulting from two different lines, i.e., the one based on Banc Smal and the other on Banc Breedt. This dividing line produced the agreed boundary between points 1 and 2.[37] In the context of maritime delimitation, the international courts and tribunals have applied the half-effect solution to

36. In connection with this, it may be recalled that in the *Gulf of Maine* case, the Special Agreement of 29 May 1979 between Canada and the United States provided that: "[n]otwithstanding the fact that the Parties utilize different vertical datums in the Gulf of Maine area, the two datums shall be deemed to be common" (Article IV(c)). *ICJ Reports* (1984): 254.

37. Report by Anderson, in J. I. Charney and L. M. Alexander, eds., *International Maritime Boundaries*, Vol. II, (Dordrecht: Nijhoff, 1993): 1893. In fact, Article 2 of the 1990 Agreement stipulates that: "The points defined above result from taking into account low-tide elevations close to the Belgian and French coasts. However, the application by Belgium and France of different methods for calculating heights has led to two distinct dividing lines. It was therefore agreed that the area lying between the two dividing lines should be divided into two equal parts." For the text of the Agreement, see *id.* at 1898–1899.

islands.[38] It appears that that solution might also be relevant to a marine feature whose legal status is disputed due to the use of different tidal datums.[39] It is predictable that disputes relating to the tidal datums may be raised particularly in maritime delimitation cases. Further considerations will thus be needed with respect to the tidal datum in international law.[40]

TERRITORIALITY OF LOW-TIDE ELEVATIONS: THE *QATAR/ BAHRAIN* CASE (MERITS, 2001)

The Nature of the Problem

The second question relates to the "territoriality" of low-tide elevations. While the concept of "territoriality" is of central importance in international law, the "territoriality" of low-tide elevations has been rarely discussed. Nevertheless, the ICJ had to wrestle with this question in the *Qatar/Bahrain* case (Merits) of 2001.[41] In that case, the sovereignty over Fasht ad Dibal was in issue. Both Qatar and Bahrain agreed that Fasht ad Dibal was a low-tide elevation. While Qatar argued that Fasht ad Dibal as a low-tide elevation could not be appropriated, Bahrain contended that low-tide elevations by their very nature were territory, and, thus, could be appropriated in accordance with the criteria which pertain to the acquisition of territory.[42] Arguments by the Parties can be summarized as follows.

Qatar's Arguments

Qatar argued that low-tide elevations were not part of the land territory of States and, thus, the law regarding the acquisition of territory could not be applicable to them. In this regard, Qatar asserted that:

---

38. The half-effect solution was adopted in the *Anglo-French Continental Shelf, Tunisia/Libya* and *Gulf of Maine* cases.

39. Guillaume, n. 1 above, at 295.

40. In this respect, the International Hydrographic Organisation (IHO) is particularly important. One of the objectives of the IHO is to bring about the greatest possible uniformity in nautical charts (Article II(b) of the Convention on the International Hydrographic Organization). Yet, the IHO is of a consultative nature, and the implementation of the IHO rules is voluntary.

41. With respect to a brief analysis on this issue, see Y. Tanaka, "Reflections on Maritime Delimitation in the *Qatar/Bahrain* Case," *International and Comparative Law Quarterly* 52 (2003): 69–73.

42. *ICJ Reports* (2001): 100, para. 200.

As a matter of fact, the possibility of a coastal State to use the low-tide mark on a low-tide elevation as the baseline for measuring the breadth of the territorial sea is strictly dependent on the distance of that low-tide elevation from the mainland or an island, that distance being determined by reference to the breadth of the territorial sea as adopted by the coastal State concerned in conformity with international law. In other words, in order to decide whether a low-tide elevation lying off the coast is under the sovereignty of the coastal State and may thus be used as a basepoint for the calculation of the external limits of the territorial sea, it is first necessary to make a projection of the territorial sea from the coast. And it is when, and only when, the low-tide elevation is situated wholly or partly within the projection of the territorial sea from the main coast that the coastal State has a title over that low-tide elevation and can use it as a basepoint for purposes of determining the outer limits of the territorial sea.[43]

In this respect, Professor Quéneudec, Counsel of Qatar, pointed out two essential points. First, from a strictly physical, practical point of view, a low-tide elevation was hardly something that can be appropriated, in the sense that an actual taking of possession is difficult to imagine. Secondly, in international law, a low-tide elevation cannot in principle be subject to sovereignty unless it is located wholly or partly within the territorial waters of a territory which is itself capable of appropriation. Quoting the precedents of the ICJ, Professor Quéneudec stated that:

> according to the Court's own jurisprudence, a low-tide elevation is not in itself "capable of appropriation." Therefore, if it is to be considered as falling under the territorial sovereignty of a State, this is solely as a consequence of its location within a maritime area already under that State's sovereignty, in other words, within that State's territorial sea.[44]

Furthermore, on the basis of the *Beagle Channel* arbitration in 1977, Professor Quéneudec argued that:

> When—as is the case here—one is dealing with tiny islets with regard to which the existence of territorial title is uncertain to say the least, it is the drawing of the maritime boundary, based on a number of other

---

43. Reply of Qatar, para. 7.40.
44. Argument by Professor Quéneudec, Verbatim Record, CR 2000/9, para. 45 (translation by the ICJ).

factors, that will determine the attribution of sovereignty over the islets in question.[45]

Hence he concluded that it was a maritime delimitation line that decided on a title over low-tide elevations and, consequently, a delimitation line should be drawn before determining title over those elevations.[46]

Bahrain's Arguments

By contrast, Bahrain alleged that low-tide elevations form part of the land territory and that their appropriation should be decided by the law regarding acquisition of territory. In its view, just as in the case of islands, it depends upon the *effectivités* which of them has a superior title to the low-tide elevation in question and is therefore entitled to exercise the right attributed by the relevant provisions of the law of the sea.[47] Hence Bahrain maintained that:

> [T]he fact that low-tide elevations may in some circumstances give rise to territorial sea entitlement demonstrates that they form part of the territory of the State in question and that they are subject to its territorial sovereignty. Territorial sea can only exist if territorial sovereignty exists to generate it. This brings to an end the old controversy as to whether low-tide elevations are capable of appropriation in sovereignty: it is accepted today that they are.[48]

Professor Weil, Counsel of Bahrain, elaborated on Bahrain's view in some detail. First, he argued that only territory could serve as a basepoint:

> ... seeing that straight baselines can only be drawn to and from "appropriate points"—in the words of the Convention itself—on the coast and certainly cannot be drawn to and from points in the water, aquatic points, out at sea, the principle laid down in this provision necessarily implies that by their nature low-tide elevations are land and not sea, and if they are land they form part of State territory. A straight baseline cannot be drawn to and from a point in the water.[49]

45. Argument by Professor Quéneudec, Verbatim Record, CR 2000/10, para. 63 (translation by the ICJ).

46. *Id.*, CR 2000/10, para. 64.

47. *ICJ Reports* (2001): 101, para. 203.

48. Counter-Memorial of Bahrain, para. 524.

49. Argument by Professor Weil, Verbatim Record, CR 2000/15, para. 76 (translation by the ICJ).

On the basis of the above reason, he questioned Qatar's view that low-tide elevations have the character of sea or *corps aquatique* since "[i]f they were not State territory by their nature, they could never generate maritime jurisdiction."[50] Furthermore, Professor Weil insisted that:

> Even though low-tide elevations, given that they are uncovered only at low tide, are *physically* only *part-time land*, they are nonetheless *legally full-time State territory*. If they were not full-time State territory, low-tide elevations would never generate territorial sea, and straight baselines could never be drawn to and from low-tide elevations, which is explicitly authorized under Article 7 of the 1982 Convention.[51]

Secondly, according to Professor Weil, the regime of low-tide elevations was historically built up from that of islands, shoals having originally been considered a special kind of island. Like islands, drying rocks and drying shoals, as they used to be called, were regarded as part of State territory. Hence, Professor Weil considered that, despite the differentiation between the regime of islands and that of low-tide elevations established by Articles 13 and 121 of the LOSC,

> the fundamental and original unity was nevertheless not to be called in question. State territory, natural elevations always were. State territory they remain, whether today they have island status within the meaning of Article 121 or the status of low-tide elevation within the meaning of Article 13.[52]

Thirdly, Professor Weil criticized Qatar's argument on the ground that it would reverse the fundamental principle of "the land dominates the sea" into "the sea dominates the land."[53] In summary, according to Bahrain, the Court should determine the sovereignty over low-tide elevations, if disputed between the Parties, and next should effect maritime delimitation.[54] In Bahrain's view, the appropriation of low-tide elevations should be determined by having recourse to the principle of effectiveness.[55] Thus, Bahrain

---

50. *Id.*, para. 77 (translation by the ICJ).
51. Argument by Professor Weil, Verbatim Record, CR 2000/25, para. 9 (translation by the ICJ).
52. *Id.*, para. 16 (translation by the ICJ).
53. Argument by Professor Weil, Verbatim Record, CR 2000/15, para. 54. It appears that Professor Weil maintained the same position in his article published in 2002. Weil, n. 1 above, at 307–321.
54. Counter-Memorial of Bahrain, para. 532; Reply of Bahrain, para. 302; Argument by Professor Weil, Verbatim Record, CR 2000/25, para. 31.
55. Reply of Bahrain, paras. 352–359.

submitted some evidence of Bahrain's sovereignty over Fasht ad Dibal, including surveys, the grant of oil concessions, and the construction of a cairn and an artesian well, etc.[56]

The Court's Solution

With respect to this divergence of opinions between the Parties, the ICJ made it clear that the decisive question is

> whether a State can acquire sovereignty by appropriation over a low-tide elevation situated within the breadth of its territorial sea when that same low-tide elevation lies also within the breadth of the territorial sea of another State.[57]

On this issue, however, the Court must have accepted that treaty law was silent on the question of whether low-tide elevations can be considered to be "territory" and that there is no uniform and widespread State practice on this matter. Nor was the Court aware of a uniform and widespread State practice which might have given rise to a customary rule which unequivocally permits or excludes appropriation of low-tide elevations. Hence, the Court concluded that it was only in the context of the law of the sea that a number of permissive rules have been established with regard to low-tide elevations which were situated a relatively short distance from the coast.[58]

In this regard, first, the Court noted that the few existing rules did not justify a general assumption that low-tide elevations were territory in the same sense as islands. Furthermore, the Court recalled that a low-tide elevation which was situated beyond the limits of territorial sea did not have a territorial sea of its own. A low-tide elevation as such does not generate the same rights as islands or other territory.[59] The Court therefore found that:

> It is thus not established that in the absence of other rules and legal principles, low-tide elevations can, from the viewpoint of the acquisition of sovereignty, be fully assimilated with islands or other land territory.[60]

In accordance with the Court, this view is supported by Article 4(3) of the 1958 Convention on the Territorial Sea and the Contiguous Zone and

56. *Id.,* para. 345.
57. *ICJ Reports* (2001): 101, para. 204.
58. *Id.* at 101–102, para. 205.
59. *Id.* at 102, para. 207.
60. *Id.,* para. 206.

Article 7(4) of the LOSC which provides straight baselines shall not be drawn to and from low-tide elevations unless lighthouses or similar installations which are permanently above sea level have been built on them.[61] If this is the case, how is it possible to decide on the sovereignty over low-tide elevations?

In this respect, the Court drew provisionally two equidistance lines. On the one hand, if no effect were given to Qit'al Jaradah and Fash al Azm was to be considered part of Sitrah island, the adjusted equidistance line would cut through Fasht ad Dibal, leaving the greater part of it on the Qatari side. On the other hand, if Fasht al Azm was seen as a low-tide elevation, the adjusted equidistance line would run west of Fasht ad Dibal. In either hypothesis, thus, Fasht ad Dibal is largely or totally on the Qatari side of the adjusted equidistance line. In conclusion, the Court held that:

> As Fasht ad Dibal is thus situated in the territorial sea of Qatar, it falls for that reason under the sovereignty of that State.[62]

Evaluation

The *Qatar/Bahrain* decision (Merits) was a landmark one in the sense that the ICJ determined the sovereignty over a low-tide elevation on the basis of a maritime delimitation line. It is inevitable to conclude that the ICJ in that case considered such elevations as part of the seabed, not terrestrial territory. Considering that neither the State practice nor the treaty made any general distinction on the basis of whether or not a low-tide elevation has been subject of an appropriation, some argued that this part of the decision concerned the "legislative" activity of the Court.[63]

On the other hand, it appears that to a certain extent, the conclusion of the Court in the *Qatar/Bahrain* case (Merits) is supported by the international jurisprudence. For instance, in the *Minquiers and Ecrehos* case, the Parties (France and the United Kingdom) had asked the ICJ, in the Compromis, to determine the question of sovereignty over the islets and rocks of the groups "in so far as they are capable of appropriation." In relation to this, the Court held that:

> These words must be considered as relating to islets and rocks which are physically capable of appropriation. The Court is requested to decide in general to which Party sovereignty over each group as a whole

---

61. *Id.*, para. 208.
62. *Id.* at 109, para. 220.
63. R. Kolb, *Case Law on Equitable Maritime Delimitation: Digest and Commentaries* (The Hague: Nijhoff, 2003): 544.

belongs, without determining in detail the facts relating to the particular units of which the groups consist.[64]

Sir Gerald Fitzmaurice commented on this phrase by saying that:

By this finding, the Court also implicitly endorsed the rule that certain kinds of territory are not capable of appropriation in sovereignty at all. The usual case is that of the island, rock, bank or shoal only uncovered at low tide.[65]

Sir Gerald further stated that:

It is a well-established rule of international law that territory, in order to be capable of appropriation in sovereignty, must be situated permanently above high-water mark, and not consist e.g., of a drying-rock, only uncovered at low tide, unless it is already within the territorial waters of appropriable territory.[66]

Furthermore, in the *El Salvador/Honduras* case concerning their *Land, Island and Maritime Frontier*, the Chamber of the ICJ ruled:

That Meanguerita is 'capable of appropriation,' to use the wording of the *dispositif* of the *Minquiers and Ecrehos* case, is undoubted; it is not a low-tide elevation, and is covered by vegetation, although it lacks fresh water.[67]

This phrase appears to suggest that if Meanguerita were a low-tide elevation, it would be incapable of appropriation.[68]

On the other hand, in the *Eritrea/Yemen* arbitration of 1999 (the first phase), the Court of Arbitration stated in its *dispositif* that "the islands, islet, rocks and low-tide elevations" forming certain islands are subject to "the territorial sovereignty" of Eritrea or Yemen.[69] In so stating, the Court of

64. *ICJ Reports* (1953): 53. Professor Quéneudec, Counsel of Qatar, referred to this judgment, see Verbatim Record, CR 2000/9, para. 44.

65. Sir Gerald Fitzmaurice, *The Law and Procedure of the International Court of Justice*, Vol. I (Cambridge: Cambridge University Press, 1993): 287.

66. *Id.* at 286–287.

67. *ICJ Reports* (1992): 570, para. 356.

68. Argument by Professor Quéneudec, Verbatim Record, CR 2000/9, para. 44. Judge Torres Bernárdez was supportive of this interpretation. Dissenting Opinion of Judge Torres Bernárdez, *ICJ Reports* (2001): 437–438, para. 526.

69. The *Eritrea/Yemen* Arbitration (Phase I: Territorial Sovereignty and Scope of Dispute), para. 527. The text is available online: <http://www.pca-cpa.org>.

Arbitration did not distinguish low-tide elevations and other marine features. Yet it appeared that this *dispositif* simply confirmed the territorial sovereignty over low-tide elevations forming a part of islands and no more. It was not suggested that low-tide elevations have the same nature of the terrestrial territory.[70]

In State practice, it is interesting to note that the 1978 Torres Strait Treaty between Australia and Papua New Guinea regarded low-tide elevations as a part of the seabed, by stipulating that:

"seabed jurisdiction" means sovereign rights over the continental shelf in accordance with international law, and includes jurisdiction over low-tide elevations, and the right to exercise such jurisdiction in respect of those elevations, in accordance with international law (Article 1(1)(i)).[71]

With respect to this issue, three tentative comments can be made. First, there is no doubt that a coastal State has sovereignty over low-tide elevations which are situated within its territorial sea.[72] This is because the coastal State has sovereignty over the territorial sea itself, including its seabed and subsoil. Accordingly, the fact that low-tide elevations are subject to territorial sovereignty does not directly mean that such features constitute the terrestrial territory. In relation to this, one may note with interest the opinion of three Judges, Bedjaoui, Ranjeva and Karoma. In discussing the legal status of Qit'at Jaradah, the three Judges stated that:

In law, this assimilation [of islands to land territory] must be understood in conjunction with the notion of effectiveness of sovereignty; sovereignty, in international law, implies a minimum stable terrestrial base, which is not to be found in maritime features above the waterline which are not islands.[73]

In accordance with this view, it appears to be arguable that low-tide elevations that are submerged at high tide lack a minimum terrestrial stability, and, thus, are not subject to *effectivité*.

---

70. Cf. Argument by Professor Quéneudec, Verbatim Record, CR 2000/9, para. 41.

71. For the text of the Treaty, see Charney et al., n. 37 above, at 937 *et seq.*

72. On the basis of this, Professor Weil considers that the *Qatar/Bahrain* judgment expressly indicates the possibility of the appropriation of low-tide elevations. Weil, n. 1 above, at 317. For the reason explained in the text, the statement of the Court did not justify that view.

73. Dissenting Opinion of Judges Bedjaoui, Ranjeva and Karoma, *ICJ Reports* (2001): 210, para. 200 (translated by the ICJ).

Secondly, it should be stressed that low-tide elevations can be used as basepoints only if situated within the breadth of the territorial sea. In other words, low-tide elevations generate territorial seas on the basis of the fact that they are already under the territorial sovereignty of coastal States. The power of low-tide elevations to generate a territorial sea depends on whether they are situated within the breadth of the territorial sea. In addition, one should note Article 7(4) of the LOSC, which provides that:

> Straight baselines shall not be drawn to and from low-tide elevations, unless lighthouses or similar installations which are permanently above sea level have been built on them or except in instances where the drawing of baselines to and from such elevations has received general international recognition.[74]

Arguably this provision also shows that low-tide elevations should be distinguished from islands.[75] Thus, the fact that low-tide elevations may be used as basepoints does not necessarily suggest that they enjoy the same status with islands.

Thirdly, it may be argued that, at least since the 1930 Hague Conference for the Codification of International law, low-tide elevations have been distinguished from islands.[76] In fact, Bases of Discussion No. 14 had stated that:

> In order that an island may have its own territorial waters, it is necessary that it should be permanently above the level of high tide. In order that an island lying within the territorial waters of another island or of the mainland may be taken into account in determining the belt of such territorial waters, it is sufficient for the island to be above water at low tide.[77]

74. By applying this provision, the Court of Arbitration in the *Eritrea/Yemen* dispute (Second Phase) ruled that Eritrea could not use "Negileh Rock" as a straight baseline of the territorial sea since the rock appeared not to be above water at any state of the tide. Paras. 141–146.

75. The 1958 Geneva Convention on the Territorial Sea and the Contiguous Zone contained a similar provision: "Baselines shall not be drawn to and from low-tide elevations, unless lighthouses or similar installations which are permanently above sea level have been built on them" (Article 4(3)). In this respect, Bowett indicates that, in relation to the drawing of baselines under the straight baselines method provided for in Article 4 of the 1958 Geneva Convention on the Territorial Sea, the assimilation of low-tide elevations to islands did not occur. D. W. Bowett, *The Legal Regime of Islands in International Law* (New York: Oceana, 1979): 12. With respect to the critical analysis on this provision, see Jayewardene, n. 6 above, 68–74.

76. Symmons, n. 1 above, at 14–15; Guillaume, n. 1 above, at 288.

77. Reproduced in S. Rosenne, ed., *League of Nations: Conference for the Codification of International Law 1930,* Vol. II (New York: Oceana, 1975): 272.

It is apparent that such a distinction has been succeeded in Article 11 of the 1958 Geneva Convention on the Territorial Sea and Contiguous Zone, as well as Article 13 of the LOSC. Thus, it is argued that the *legal* distinction between islands and low-tide elevations is currently well established in international law. In light of the above considerations, arguably the *Qatar/Bahrain* decision concerning low-tide elevations is persuasive, and will be an important precedent in this matter.

IMPACTS OF LOW-TIDE ELEVATIONS ON MARITIME DELIMITATIONS

Nature of the Problem

Finally, it is important to examine the impact of low-tide elevations on maritime delimitations. Where a maritime boundary is established on the basis of the equidistance method, the use of low-tide elevations as basepoints may affect the location of the boundary. Considering that international courts and tribunals tend to apply the equidistance method at the first stage of the delimitation, the impact of low-tide elevations is increasingly important.[78] In this respect, the distinction should be made between low-tide elevations integrated into the straight baseline system and such elevations *not* incorporated into the baseline. With respect to the former, in accordance with Article 7(4) of the LOSC, low-tide elevations may be the starting and terminal points of straight baselines, if lighthouses or similar installations permanently above sea level have been built on them or if their use as base points has received general international recognition.[79] Being

---

78. In the *Greenland/Jan Mayen, Qatar/Bahrain* and *Cameroon/Nigeria* cases, the ICJ has applied the equidistance method at the first stage of delimitation, and at the second stage, considered whether the provisional equidistance line should be shifted on the basis of relevant circumstances. This approach may be called corrective-equity. Furthermore, the Court of Arbitration in the *Eritrea/Yemen* dispute (the second phase) also took the corrective-equity approach. With respect to the overview of the courts' approach, see in particular, Y. Tanaka, *Predictability and Flexibility in the Law of Maritime Delimitation*, Thèse, (Geneva: I.U.H.E.I., 2002): 128–135; Y. Tanaka, "Reflections on the *Eritrea/Yemen* Arbitration of 17 December 1999 (Second Phase: Maritime Delimitation)," *Netherlands International Law Review*, 48 (2001): 209–212; Tanaka, n. 41 above, at 74–78.

79. In this connection, O'Connell argued that a low-tide elevation may be used as a basepoint on a straight baseline system, even when it lies beyond the territorial sea distance from any other basepoint, provided it qualifies as a basepoint by reference to the other criteria for drawing straight baselines, and provided that there is a permanently dry artificial construction upon it, but not otherwise. O'Connell, n. 9 above, at 210. The Virginia commentary is also supportive of that view. Nordquist, n. 6 above, 128.

integrated into the straight baseline system, low-tide elevations could be given full effect in determining the outer limits of marine spaces under national jurisdiction and of delimiting those spaces.[80]

On the other hand, the same may not be true of low-tide elevations *not* incorporated into the straight baselines. It is clear that such elevations may be used as the baseline for measuring the breadth of the territorial sea, pursuant to both Article 11(1) of the 1958 Convention on the Territorial Sea as well as Article 13(1) of the LOSC, where these features are not wholly situated at a distance from the mainland or an island that exceeds the breadth of the territorial sea. It follows that the presence of low-tide elevations in the delimitation area could affect the configuration of the delimitation line for the territorial seas.[81] It is debatable, however, that such low-tide elevations could affect the delimitation of the continental shelf and EEZ. On this issue, two hypotheses may be pointed out.

According to the first hypothesis, low-tide elevations should in no way affect the location of the outer limits of continental shelves or EEZs since these elevations have no continental shelf and EEZ for their own. It follows that these elevations should not affect the delimitation of the continental shelf and EEZ. This argument is reinforced by Article 121(3) of the LOSC, which provides that:

> Rocks which cannot sustain human habitation or economic life of their own shall have no exclusive economic zone or continental shelf.

If these marine spaces are refused to rocks, it is argued that they must be denied, *a fortiori*, to mere low-tide elevations.[82] If this is the case, in accordance with the first hypothesis, the presence of such elevations in the delimitation area should not influence the maritime delimitation line by virtue of the fact that low-tide elevations do not have continental shelves or EEZs.[83]

---

80. L. Caflisch, "The Delimitation of Marine Spaces between States with Opposite or Adjacent Coasts," in R-J. Dupuy and D. Vignes, eds., *A Handbook on the New Law of the Sea*, Vol. I (Dordrecht: Nijhoff, 1991): 487.

81. *Id.*

82. *Id.* at 488. Indeed, it is conceivable that low-tide elevations are neither suited to human habitation nor capable of supporting an economic base. Reed, n. 8 above, at 221. See also B. Kwiatkowska and A. H. A. Soons, "Entitlement to Maritime Areas of Rocks Which Cannot Sustain Human Habitation or Economic Life of Their Own," *Netherlands Yearbook of International Law* 21 (1990): 148.

83. Caflisch, n. 80 above, at 488. By contrast, Bowett insisted that while mere rocks cannot generate a shelf or economic zone, there was no reason why they cannot be used as basepoints. Bowett, "Islands, Rocks, Reefs, and Low-Tide Elevations in Maritime Boundary Delimitations," in Charney, n. 37 above, Vol. I, at 148.

By contrast, according to the second hypothesis, low-tide elevations *not* incorporated into the straight baseline system may serve as basepoints generating the continental shelf and EEZ if they are wholly or partly situated in the territorial sea. In this respect, Article 57 of the LOSC stipulates that:

> The exclusive economic zone shall not extend beyond 200 nautical miles from *the baselines from which the breadth of the territorial sea is measured.* [Emphasis added.]

Hence, in accordance with a literal interpretation, it may not be impossible to assert that low-tide elevation might generate an EEZ when such an elevation constitutes a part of the baseline measuring the breadth of the territorial sea. The same will be true of the continental shelf embodied in Article 76(1) of the LOSC.[84] In addition, Article 6 of the Geneva Convention on the Continental Shelf[85] also stipulates that the median or equidistance line is the line every point of which is equidistant from the nearest point of the baselines from which the breadth of the territorial sea of each State is measured.[86] On this point, Judge Oda had argued that Article 6 of the 1958 Convention on the Continental Shelf provided that the equidistance line should be measured from the baselines from which the breadth of the territorial sea was measured, that is to say, taking the existence of a low-tide elevation into account.[87] If this is the case, a low-tide elevation may affect the location of the continental shelf boundary. In light of divergence of opinions in this matter, the next subsection will address the legal effect of low-tide elevations *not* incorporated into the straight baseline system in both State practice and the case law.

84. Cf. R. Kolb, "L'interprétation de l'article 121, paragraphe 3, de la Convention de Montego Bay sur le droit de la mer: les <<rochers qui ne se prêtent pas à l'habitation humaine ou à une vie économique propre...>>," *Annuaire Français de Droit International,* 40 (1994), footnote 180, 899.

85. For the text of the Convention, see M. D. Evans, ed., *Blackstone's International Law Documents,* 4th ed. (London: Blackstone Press Limited, 1999): 88–91.

86. P. Weil, "A propos de la double fonction des lignes et points de base dans le droit de la mer," in P. Weil, *Écrits de droit international* (Paris: P.U.F, 2000): 283.

87. Dissenting Opinion of Judge Oda in the *Tunisia/Libya* case, *ICJ Reports* (1982): 267, para. 175. As will be discussed later, however, Judge Oda contended that in the *Tunisia/Libya* case, the presence of low-tide elevations should be ignored in continental shelf delimitations.

State Practice

Territorial Sea Delimitations

With respect to territorial sea delimitations, a low-tide elevation may serve as a legitimate basepoint. This point is supported by State practice. For instance, in the 1973 Agreement between Indonesia and Singapore, the turning points of the territorial sea boundary were equidistant between the low-tide elevations of both countries.[88] Furthermore, one may note with interest a Dutch low-tide elevation known as Rassen. This feature, 600 meters from east to west at low water, located approximately three kilometers (less than two nautical miles) off the westernmost point of the peninsula of Walcheren.[89] Rassen is a legitimate basepoint for measuring the breadth of the territorial sea of the Netherlands. In the Agreement between the Netherlands and Belgium relating to the delimitation of the territorial sea, Rassen was given full effect.[90]

Moreover, low-tide elevations were relevant in the 2000 Agreement between France and the United Kingdom (Jersey) relating to the territorial sea delimitation.[91] In the area to be delimited, there were low-tide elevations on both the Plateau de Barnouic and the Plateau des Roches Douvres belonging to France. The end point of the boundary is equidistant from three low-tide elevations, i.e., the Roches Douvres (France), Mouillière Rock (just off the northwest coast of Jersey) and Baleine Rock (Guernsey).[92] It is suggested, however, that slightly less than full weight was given to low-tide elevations which were located on the Plateau de Barnouic and the Plateau des Roches Douvres.[93] It is reported that certain low-tide elevations, which were rarely above the high tide and French sovereignty over them has been contested by the United Kingdom, were ignored.[94] A French low-tide

88. Report by Choon-ho Park, in Charney, n. 37 above, Vol. I, at 1,051. See also Jayewardene, n. 6 above, at 373.

89. Report by Anderson, in Charney, n. 37 above, Vol. IV, at 2,928.

90. Article 2 of the 1996 Agreement expressly mentioned Rassen as a basepoint. For the text of the agreement, *Id.*, pp. 2,938–2,939.

91. During much of the negotiations, the status of the area around Jersey concerned the continental shelf. Owing to the extension of the breadth of the territorial sea, however, the delimitation area became the territorial sea. Report by Anderson, in Charney, n. 37 above, Vol. IV, at 2,982.

92. *Id.* at 2986.

93. *Id.*

94. Such elevations were *Basse nord-ouest des Boefs* and *Basse de Taillepied.* Furthermore, French sovereignty over Bancs Fêlés was confirmed and half effect was given to the marine feature. See J-F. Dobelle, "Les accords franco-britanniques relatifs à la baie de Granville du 4 juillet 2000," *Annuaire du droit de la mer* 5 (2000): 18.

elevation was also disregarded in the 1974 Convention between France and Spain concerning the delimitation of the territorial sea and contiguous zone.[95] In addition, as pointed to earlier, the 1990 Agreement between Belgium and France relating to a territorial sea boundary gave only half effect to the French low-tide elevations, Banc Smal and Banc Breedt.[96] These examples show that only partial effects or even no effect may be given to low-tide elevations in establishing a territorial sea boundary if the parties so agreed.

Delimitations of the Continental Shelf and Single Maritime Boundaries

With respect to continental shelf delimitations, there were some agreements which gave a certain effect to low-tide elevations. A clear example may be furnished by the 1971 Agreement between Italy and Tunisia. Article I of the Agreement expressly accepted the use of low-tide elevations, by providing that:

> The boundary of the continental shelf between the two countries shall be the median line, every point of which is equidistant from the nearest points of the baselines from which the breadths of the Italian and Tunisian territorial seas are measured, taking into account islands, islets and low-tide elevations with exception of Lampione, Lampedusa, Linosa and Pantelleria.[97]

Furthermore, in the 1982 Agreement between France and the United Kingdom creating a continental shelf boundary, it is suggested that a French low-tide elevation, the Banc Breedt, and a British low-tide elevation, the Goodwin Sands as well as Long Sand Head, were taken into account when determining a simplified equidistance line.[98] Moreover, the presence of a low-tide elevation was at issue in the 1990 Agreement between Belgium and France establishing a continental shelf boundary. During negotiations, Belgium argued that low-tide elevations should not be used. By quoting the Franco-British Agreement of 1982 which had given full weight to the Banc Breedt vis-à-vis the Goodwin Sands, however, France maintained that low-

---

95. Report by Anderson, in Charney, n. 37 above, Vol. II, at 1,722.
96. Report by Anderson, *id.* at 1893.
97. For the text of the Agreement, Charney, n. 37 above, Vol. II, at 1,621–1,625.
98. Anderson indicated that from point 13 to point 14, the boundary was an equidistance line based on three low-tide elevations, that is to say, Banc Breedt, Goodwin Sands and Long Sand Head. Report by Anderson, in Charney, n. 37 above, Vol. II, at 1,743.

tide elevations could be used in the continental shelf delimitation. As a compromise, it is reported that Banc Breedt was given only one-fifth effect.[99]

Low-tide elevations were also discussed during negotiations between Belgium and the United Kingdom establishing a continental shelf boundary. As a result, the 1991 Agreement between the same parties used a Belgian sandbank known as Trapegger, lying 1.3 NM off the coast, in determining Point 1 (the Belgium/France/UK tri-point). On the English side, Long Sand Head, which is an extensive sandbank lying about 11.7 NM off the coast of Essex, was used in fixing the same tri-point.[100] On that point, thus, the two low-tide elevations were given full effect. Furthermore, point 3 of the 1991 continental shelf boundary was a tri-point based on equidistance between Wenduine on the Belgian coast, Orfordness on the Essex coast and a Dutch low-tide elevation, Rassen. Accordingly, a low-tide elevation belonging to a third State did affect the location of the continental shelf boundary.[101] Having fixed two tri-points, it has been suggested that the parties agreed to draw a continental shelf boundary giving one-third effect overall to Long Sand Head.[102]

In determining a continental shelf boundary between Belgium and the Netherlands, Rassen, a Dutch low-tide elevation, was discussed once again. It may be recalled that, in the negotiations with France, Belgium had taken the position that low-tide elevations were relevant to the territorial sea delimitation, but not to the continental shelf delimitation. In the end, the 1996 Agreement between Belgium and the Netherlands gave only one quarter weight to Rassen in establishing a continental shelf boundary.[103] In addition, in the 1965 Agreement between the Netherlands and the United Kingdom, it has been suggested that the United Kingdom used a low-tide elevation off Lowestoft within the breadth of the territorial sea of 3 NM in determining an equidistance line.[104] It is also suggested that the 1974 Agreement between Iran and Oman gave effect to low-tide elevations in determining an equidistance line for the continental shelf boundary.[105]

99. Report by Anderson, *id.* at 1,893.

100. Report by Anderson, *id.* at 1,903–1,904. On the other hand, it was found in the mid-1990s that a British low-tide elevation, Shipwash Sands, had been eroded and so no longer dried at low-water. Accordingly, the marine feature lost its value as a basepoint. *Id.* Yet, it is reported that surveys carried out between 1995 and 1997 show that the feature became a low-tide elevation again. Antunes, n. 9 above, at 19.

101. Report by Anderson, in Charney, n. 37 above, Vol. II, at 1,904.

102. *Id.*, at 1,905. See also C. Carleton and C. Schofield, "Developments in the Technical Determination of Maritime Space: Delimitation, Dispute Resolution, Geographical Information Systems and the Role of the Technical Expert," *Maritime Briefing* 3, No. 4 (2002): 59–61.

103. Report by Anderson, in Charney, n. 37 above, Vol. IV, at 2,928.

104. Report by Anderson, in *id.*, Vol. II, at 1,862.

105. Report by Pietrowski, Jr., in *id.* at 1,505.

In the context of delimitation of single maritime boundaries, some agreements used low-tide elevations as basepoints when determining an equidistance line. For instance, in the 1977 Agreement between the United States and Cuba, it is suggested that low-tide elevations associated with the Florida Keys were used in establishing an equidistance line as a single maritime boundary.[106] Another example may be provided by the 1982 Agreement between Australia and France (New Caledonia). It is reported that Australia's Middleton Reef, a mid-oceanic low-tide elevation situated 125 NM offshore, might have been given full effect in establishing an equidistance line.[107] Furthermore, in the 1980 Agreement between the Cook Islands and the United States (American Samoa), it is reported that all islands and any associated drying fringing reefs and low-tide elevations, regardless of size, location, and population, were given full effect in determining an equidistance line.[108] The same was true in the 1980 Agreement between New Zealand (Tokelau) and the United States (American Samoa).[109]

On the other hand, there are agreements where low-tide elevations were not taken into account. For instance, in the 1988 Agreement between the Republic of Ireland and the United Kingdom determining a continental shelf boundary, low-tide elevations were discounted on both sides.[110] Similarly, the 1969 Agreement between Iran and Qatar ignored islands, rocks, reefs and low-tide elevations in determining a continental shelf boundary on the basis of the equidistance method.[111] Moreover, it should be noted that, where a method other than the equidistance method is used, the relevance of low-tide elevations diminishes. In reality, there are a number of agreements which adopted the non-equidistance method, such as a parallel of latitude, particularly in delimitations between States with adjacent coasts. In such cases, the presence of low-tide elevations is not relevant.

106. Report by Smith, in *id.*, Vol. I, at 419.
107. Report by Choon-ho Park, in *id.*, Vol. I, at 907. On this point, Prescott appeared to be more prudent by saying that: "it is not beyond the realms of possibility that Middleton Reef was somehow involved in the calculation, even though it does not have any features which stand above high tide." V. Prescott, *The Maritime Political Boundaries of the World* (London: Methuen, 1985): 191.
108. Report by Smith and Colson, in Charney, n. 37 above, Vol. I, at 987.
109. Report by Smith, in *id.* at 1,127.
110. Report by Anderson, in *id.*, Vol. II, at 1,770.
111. Report by Pietrowski, Jr., in *id.* at 1513.

International Decisions

The Tunisia/Libya Case (1982)

Before the ICJ, the relevance of low-tide elevations in continental shelf delimitation was at issue in the *Tunisia/Libya* case. In this case, the Court examined legal effects given to the Kerkennah Islands, which were surrounded by low-tide elevations. In this respect, the Court stated that:

> the presence of the island of Jerba and of the Kerkennah Islands and the surrounding low-tide elevations is a circumstance which clearly calls for consideration.[112]

In drawing an illustrative continental shelf boundary, however, the Court disregarded the low-tide elevations surrounding the Kerkennah Islands without any reason. Moreover, the Court decided to attribute only "half effect" to the Kerkennah Islands. It did so by drawing a line bisecting the angle between the line of the Tunisian coast (42°) and the tangent of the seaward coast of the Kerkennah Islands (62°). Consequently, a line of 52° to the meridian was to be the boundary of the continental shelf in this area.[113]

At first sight, this is hard to reconcile with the view formerly expressed that the Kerkennah Islands *and* the surrounding low-tide elevations were circumstances clearly calling for consideration. On this point, Judge Evensen pointed out:

> If these low-tide elevations had been taken into account the line drawn from the westernmost point of the Gulf of Gabes to the Kerkennahs would run approximately in the direction of 66° to the meridian and not 62°. Even according to the Court's ruling of giving half effect to the Kerkennahs [...] the veering should in no event be a 52° line but a line running some 57.5° to the meridian.[114]

An explanation may be that the Court considered such elevations irrelevant in the continental shelf delimitation. In this regard, Judge Oda's view is worth noting. In accordance with Judge Oda, while it may be reasonable to provide that, in the case of the delimitation of the territorial sea, a low-tide elevation should be taken fully into account for determining the equidistance line (Article 12(1) of the 1958 Convention on the Territorial Sea), the situation might be quite different were this rule to be

112. *ICJ Reports* (1982): 63–64, para. 79.
113. *Id.* at 88–89, paras. 128–129.
114. Dissenting Opinion of Judge Evensen, *id.* at 304, para. 19.

applied in the case of delimitations of the continental shelf. The extent of the territorial sea will, in any case, be limited to a narrow belt from the coast, the effect of a low-tide elevation will probably not be very great. If the baseline used for measurement is extended seaward owing to the existence of a low-tide elevation, however, the effect will also be great. Judge Oda further maintained that a low-tide elevation could have been taken into account for measuring the territorial sea, or even the continental shelf, if it were located within so narrow a limit as three miles from the coast. However, it may be asked whether the same is true that the breadth of the territorial sea has been extended to 12 miles from the coasts. Undoubtedly this difference between the 3-mile limit and the 12-mile limit greatly affects the evaluation of the significance of a low-tide elevation within the limit. Hence, Judge Oda concluded that despite the provisions of the Convention on the Continental Shelf, it would be proper to ignore the existence of low-tide elevations in the case of a delimitation of the continental shelf.[115] It could be said at least that, where the presence of a low-tide elevation may produce an inequitable effect, such an elevation may be disregarded by international courts and tribunals. On this point, the *Tunisia/Libya* decision is a precedent where the Court gave no role to low-tide elevations in continental shelf delimitations.

The Qatar/Bahrain Case (2001)

Another important instance may be provided, once again, by the *Qatar/Bahrain* decision (Merits). In that case, a question was raised whether Fasht ad Dibal could be used as a basepoint. Both Parties agreed that Fasht ad Dibal was a low-tide elevation.[116] Fasht ad Dibal is situated in "the overlapping area" of the territorial seas of the parties.[117] Bahrain alleged that the Court should first determine to which State the low-tide elevation appertained on the basis of the *effectivités*.[118] As discussed above, however, the Court discarded Bahrain's argument by indicating that low-tide elevations could not be equated with islands. Thus, the Court ruled that:

115. Dissenting Opinion of Judge Oda in the *Tunisia/Libya* case, *ICJ Reports* (1982): 266–267, paras. 174–175.

116. Memorial submitted by Bahrain, at 270, para. 626; Argument by Professor Weil, Verbatim Record, CR 2000/15, para. 41; Memorial submitted by Qatar, at 238, para. 10.54, p. 239, para. 10.58. and 245, para. 10.73; Counter-Memorial submitted by Qatar, at 267, para. 8.43.

117. According to Qatar, Fasht ad Dibal is located 9.3 miles from the nearest point on the low-water line of Qatar and 13.7 miles from the nearest point on the low-water line of Bahrain. Memorial submitted by Qatar, at 212, para. 9.11.

118. *ICJ Reports* (2001): 101, para. 203. See also Weil, n. 1 above, at 320–321.

> When a low-tide elevation is situated in the *overlapping area of the territorial sea* of two States, whether with opposite or with adjacent coasts, both States in principle are entitled to use its low-water line for the measuring of the breadth of their territorial sea. The same low-tide elevation then forms part of the coastal configuration of the two States. That is so even if the low-tide elevation is nearer to the coast of one State than that of the other, or nearer to an island belonging to one party than to the mainland coast of the other. *For delimitation purposes the competing rights derived by both coastal States from the relevant provisions of the law of the sea would by necessity seem to neutralize each other.* [Emphasis added.][119]

It thus concluded that for the purposes of determining the equidistance line, such low-tide elevations must be disregarded.[120]

Nevertheless, the above solution is not free from problems. First, one may note that the idea of "overlapping territorial sea" is curious. Precisely speaking, it is the potential entitlement of territorial seas that could "overlap." Secondly, it is difficult to understand how *both* States could measure the breadth of the territorial sea from the *same* low-tide elevation. Thirdly, the fact that the low-tide elevation located in an overlapped area of the potential entitlement over the territorial sea does not immediately neutralize the rights of a State using such an elevation. Considering that Article 13(1) of the LOSC explicitly accepted the use of such an elevation which is wholly or partly situated in the territorial sea, it is questionable why a low-tide elevation could not be a basepoint if this feature is located in the overlapping area of potential entitlement over the territorial sea. As an alternative, it may be possible to ascertain, at the first stage, to which coast the low-tide elevation appertains and, at the second stage, to determine the legal effect given to this feature. As suggested earlier, the Court concluded that Fasht ad Dibal fell under the sovereignty of Qatar on the basis of the maritime delimitation line. Theoretically at least, it appears to be possible to give some partial effects to the low-tide elevation at the next step.

Evaluation

The above survey shows that there is a difference in opinion between States whether low-tide elevations could be used as basepoints in maritime delimitations. While some agreements gave full effect to low-tide elevations, other treaties gave only partial effects or even no effect to these features.

---

119. *ICJ Reports* (2001): 101, para. 202. See also para. 215.
120. *Id.* at 102–103, para. 209.

Owing to the uncertainty of State practice in this matter, it is still debatable whether treaty practice might provide sufficient evidence justifying the use of low-tide elevations in delimitations of the continental shelf and the single maritime boundary. On the other hand, it appears that the ICJ minimized the impact of low-tide elevations upon the location of maritime boundaries. In fact, the ICJ in the *Tunisia/Libya* case disregarded low-tide elevations in drawing an illustrative continental shelf boundary. Moreover, the *Qatar/Bahrain* decision (Merits) ignored such an elevation when located in the overlapping area of potential entitlement over the territorial sea.

In this regard, it must be noted that the concept of equity is of central importance in case law relating to maritime delimitations. Hence, it is possible that international courts and tribunals may disregard such elevations in order to avoid inequitable results. In relation to this, it may be relevant to recall that the ICJ in the *Libya/Malta* case found it equitable *not* to take Malta's islet of Filfla into account in drawing a provisional equidistance line. Thus, the Court held that:

> [T]he baselines as determined by coastal States are not *per se* identical with the points chosen on a coast to make it possible to calculate the area of the continental shelf appertaining to that State.[121]

In so holding, the Court explicitly accepted that the points used for constructing a continental shelf boundary might be different from those used for measuring the territorial sea.[122] Some members of the Court have been supportive of that view. For instance, in the *Tunisia/Libya* case of 1982, Judge Oda stated that:

> [I]t should be clear that the normal baseline for measuring the breadth of the territorial sea could not always be used for the equidistance method as applied to the delimitation of the continental shelf, despite the provisions of Article 6 of the 1958 Convention on the Continental Shelf.[123]

Recently, three Judges in the *Qatar/Bahrain* case (Merits) also expressed a similar opinion:

> International customary law does not stipulate that the lines and basepoints used for the delimitation of maritime areas must necessarily

---

121. *ICJ Reports* (1985): 48, para. 64.
122. However, the Court did not clarify why the use of Malta's straight baselines would produce an inequitable result. Kolb, n. 63 above, at 347.
123. Dissenting Opinion of Judge Oda, *ICJ Reports* (1982): 266, para. 174.

be the same as the lines and basepoints used to fix the external boundaries between maritime areas and the high seas.[124]

Following these views, even when a low-tide elevation serves as a basepoint for measuring the breadth of the territorial sea, this does not necessarily mean that such an elevation may be used in maritime delimitations before international courts.

CONCLUSION

The above considerations may be summarized in four points:

First, the difference between tidal datums may produce disputes regarding the legal status of marine features. Nevertheless, there is no uniformity regarding the selection of the tidal datum in State practice. Thus, in certain circumstances, international courts may face difficulties determining the legal status of marine features. In this respect, the Court of Arbitration in the *Anglo-French Continental Shelf* case as well as the ICJ in the *Qatar/Bahrain* case (Merits) avoided the problem by taking a pragmatic approach.

Secondly, low-tide elevations provide an important clue in considering a theoretical question relating to the concept of "territoriality" in international law. Significantly the ICJ, in the *Qatar/Bahrain* case (Merits), determined the sovereignty over a low-tide elevation on the basis of a maritime delimitation line. In so doing, the Court did not assimilate low-tide elevations to land territory or islands. The Court's view will have an enormous impact on the development of law of the sea in relation to this matter.[125]

Thirdly, with respect to the impact of low-tide elevations *not* incorporated into the straight baseline system upon continental shelf as well as single maritime boundaries, it appears that State practice is still inadequate to provide a decisive answer. On the other hand, the ICJ in the *Tunisia/Libya* and *Qatar/Bahrain* cases (Merits) was prudent to use low-tide elevations as basepoints in maritime delimitations.

Finally, low-tide elevations provide an interesting example for considering the interaction between law and nature. As the ocean is a dynamic natural system, law of the sea is inevitably affected by the dynamics of nature. Low-tide elevations, which are strongly affected by tidal levels,

124. Dissenting Opinion of Judges Bedjaoui, Ranjeva and Karoma, *ICJ Reports* (2001): 202, para. 183.

125. Separate Opinion of Judge Oda in the *Qatar/Bahrain* case (Merits), *id.* at 125, para. 9.

illustrate this fact. Thus, further clarification will be necessary with respect to technical aspects in the law, such as the selection of tidal datum.

International Law of the Sea, Access and Benefit Sharing Agreements, and the Use of Biotechnology in the Development, Patenting and Commercialization of Marine Natural Products as Therapeutic Agents

Montserrat Gorina-Ysern[1]
International Lawyer and Professorial Lecturer, School of International Service, American University, Washington, D.C.

Captain Joseph H. Jones
President, Captain Jones' Maritime Experts, Bethesda, Maryland

INTRODUCTION

Oceanographers specializing in biological and chemical research in their university laboratories play an important role in the collection of marine biota at sea and in the isolation of novel compounds for the biomedical and biotechnology industries.[2] This role is not very widely known.[3] To perform their role, biochemical oceanographers collect specimens of marine flora, fauna and microorganisms, describe their phenotype (i.e., observable characteristics), and identify and isolate their genotype (i.e., genetic functions). Oceanographic expeditions on board research vessels and submersibles obtain marine biota from a range of maritime areas around

---

1. Reproduced in part, with permission, from M. Gorina-Ysern, *An International Regime for Marine Scientific Research* (New York: Transnational Publishers, 2003).
2. Biota is a term used to describe the combined flora, fauna, and microorganisms of a given region. E. O. Wilson, *The Diversity of Life* (New York, London: W.W. Norton & Company, 1992). Glossary at p. 393.
3. For a concise overview see M. Gorina-Ysern, "Legal Issues Raised by Profitable Biotechnology Development Through Marine Scientific Research," *American Society of International Law Insights* (Sept. 2003), available online: <http://www.asil.org/insights/insigh116.htm>.

Ocean Yearbook 20: 221–281.

the globe.[4] If the biota attracting interest are located in the waters and submerged lands of another coastal nation of which the vessel's chief scientist (at the lead of the oceanographic project) is not a national, the chief scientist must obtain clearance for the oceanographic research vessel and submersible from the authorities of that coastal nation. Clearance for academic and not-for-profit research institutions is customarily negotiated through official channels that involve the diplomatic officials of the coastal nation and the nation of the flag under which the vessel sails.[5]

The conventional international law of the sea relating to Marine Scientific Research (MSR) activities comprises the 1958 Geneva Convention on the Continental Shelf (GCCS),[6] and the 1982 United Nations Convention on the Law of the Sea (hereinafter UNCLOS).[7] In addition to regulating most aspects of the marine habitat and ocean-related activities, the Law of the Sea regulates fundamental oceanographic research into the physical and biological characteristics of the continental shelf, the conduct of MSR activities, and other types of marine science activities by oceanographers in and around the world's oceans and seas. Coastal nations may withhold clearance for a foreign vessel requesting entry into areas under the maritime jurisdiction of the coastal nation if the chief scientist is not willing to comply with certain conditions relating both to entry into these areas and to the collection and use of certain information concerning the natural resources of the latter.[8] Part XIII of UNCLOS, deals with fundamental

4. Gorina-Ysern, n. 1 above, Part I, The Practice of States Regarding MSR Implementation. Chapter 1, International Implementation of the Marine Scientific Research Regime, 3–206, with the most comprehensive survey of State practice available to date. See book review by N. Matz, *Max Planck Yearbook of United Nations Law* 9 (2005): 697–704.

5. See U.S.-Flag Vessels Seeking Authorization to Conduct MSR in Foreign Waters, available online: <http://www.state.gov/g/oes/ocns/rvc/3504.htm>, which provides: "The United States recognizes that countries have jurisdiction over marine scientific research within their territorial seas (TS) and exclusive economic zones (EEZ). Consequently, should U.S. marine science research interests lie within the TS or EEZ of another country, written authorization from the respective country must be obtained prior to the start of the cruise. Once authorization is obtained, the Chief Scientist is obligated to submit a copy of the data collected during the cruise to each authorizing country. The Department of State, via 207 embassies worldwide, manages this application procedure and post-cruise data exchange for the U.S. research community. An average of 300 authorizations is obtained annually for an average of 130 cruises in foreign EEZs."

6. U.N. Doc. A/CONF.13/L.55, reprinted in 2 *UNCLOS Official Records* 142–43; and U.N.T.S. 311 (1964).

7. United Nations Convention on the Law of the Sea, Montego Bay, December 10, 1982, entered into force November 16, 1994, reprinted in *International Legal Materials* 21 (1982): 1245. See A. H. A. Soons, *Marine Scientific Research and the Law of the Sea* (The Hague: Kluwer Law and Taxation Publishers, 1982).

8. M. Gorina-Ysern, "Principles of International Law of the Sea Governing Coastal State Access to Marine Scientific Research Results," (Ph.D. Dissertation,

oceanographic research (MSR), but it allows the coastal State to exercise its discretion to grant or withhold permission for *bioprospecting* requests as well.[9] If the marine biota are collected "for the purpose of then exploring their biotechnology potential back in the laboratory," the term "marine bioprospecting applies to these activities, not the term MSR."[10] The conduct of MSR and bioprospecting activities for the collection of marine biota is regulated under the Law of the Sea as well as the Convention on Biological Diversity (CBD).[11] This highlights the importance of stating the "purpose" of the research as a main criterion for delimiting legal regulation. The bona fide statements of the chief scientist become critical. These are made by the chief scientist to the officials in his or her government who proceed, under the UNCLOS provisions, to submit a diplomatic request for clearance on behalf of the chief scientist and his or her entourage, so that the oceanographic research vessel and submersible can proceed into areas under the maritime control of the coastal nation and collect the marine biota of scientific interest. If the criterion that governments will use to separate pure science from commercially oriented marine biogenetic research (i.e., marine bioprospecting), relies on the stated purpose of the research, the official communications (i.e., negotiations) between foreign government departments will become more relevant and complex. To engage in integrated surveillance, monitoring and enforcement of MSR provisions, researching and coastal States require scientific infrastructure and seaborne capacity. In some regions, naval officers acting as observers on board foreign research vessels, pursuant to UNCLOS, hold the only oceanographic expertise in the nation and play an important, though limited, enforcement role regarding foreign entry conditions specified in the clearance negotiations.[12]

The very specialized subject matter (access to ocean biota), the codified nature of the rules on oceanographic research dating back to the 1950s, and their relatively smooth implementation in practice pursuant to the MSR provisions in force in UNCLOS, give MSR clearance the character of a

University of New South Wales Law School, Sydney, Australia. Submitted Sept. 1995; awarded Oct. 1996).

9. See D. Owen, *A Study into the Legal Framework for Marine Biotechnology Development in the United Kingdom* (Foresight Marine Panel. Marine Biotechnology Group, The Institute of Marine Engineering, Science and Technology, London, 2004). The issue is examined below in the section entitled International Regime for the Legal Regulation of Marine Scientific Research.

10. *Id.* at 11.

11. Reproduced in *International Legal Materials* 3 (1992): 882. Earth Summit, Convention on Biological Diversity, Final Text, United Nations Conference on Environment and Development (UNCED), Rio de Janeiro, Brazil 3–14 June 1992 (hereinafter CBD).

12. UNCLOS, n. 7 above, Article 248(f).

useful model for the much broader and complex field covered by the CBD. UNCLOS provides a neat regime for the regulation of access to marine biota.[13] However, its usefulness seems to have escaped the supporters, the opponents, and the Conference of the Parties to the CBD concerned with the implementation of Access and Benefit Sharing (ABS) Agreements for the protection of countries of origin, source or legal provenance of biodiversity.[14] The ABS debate ignores, to a great extent, the core provisions in the 1982 UNCLOS that could be useful in this debate.[15] The first goal of this article is to discuss in some detail UNCLOS Articles 241, 246.5, 249.2 and 250. Their implementation leads to results similar to those sought by Article 15 of the CBD. These UNCLOS articles protect a coastal State's economic interests over its natural resources, promote the conduct of MSR activities, and facilitate collaboration among coastal and researching States. Our first goal is relevant because, ultimately, the beneficiary of sound scientific inquiry in the marine biomedical research field is the general public across nations.

Our next aim is to document the rush to map, sequence and patent novel compounds and genetic functions of marine biota, an area not well covered by the international law of the sea. Our purpose is to highlight the increase in the use of biotechnology in the development of marine natural products into promising therapeutic agents for a range of applications.[16] The rush to patent is an important step in the protection of innovations.[17] It

13. Gorina-Ysern, n. 1 above; see also M. Gorina-Ysern, "Marine Scientific Research as the Legal Basis for Intellectual Property Claims?" *Marine Policy* 22, 4/5 (1998): 337–57.

14. See A. Seiler and G. Dutfield, *Regulating Access and Benefit Sharing. Basic Issues, Legal Instruments, Policy Proposals,* (BfN-Skripten 46, German Federal Agency for Nature Conservation, 2001).

15. Conference of the Parties to the Convention on Biological Diversity, Decision VII/119 on Access and Benefit Sharing as related to Genetic Resources (Article 15), available online: <http://biodiversity.org/decisions/defaiult.aspx?m=COP–07&id=7756> [hereinafter COP to the CBD].

16. Biotechnology, the field that combines molecular biology and genetic engineering, has yielded a range of new compounds that are traded in a lucrative and active international market for marine natural products. For a technical definition, see below.

17. Until the 1950s, U.S. courts tended to grant broad patents in the chemical field. In *Brenner, Commissioner of Patents v. Manson,* United States Supreme Court, 1966, 383 U.S. 519, 148 U.S.P.Q. 689, the Supreme Court was reluctant to grant patent protection to an applicant who had merely identified the functions of an organism without showing utility. The court did not decide the issue of whether policy changes in this field should belong to the courts or to Congress. We discuss this issue below. It is unclear whether patent examiners may in future recognize as innovative the synthesis of new compounds without specifying their precise use or the discovery of new gene functions, and grant a monopoly of use over identified genotype functions of an organism or microorganism extracted from a marine

serves to attract research and development (R&D) funding from private and public sources. A question of concern is the extent to which academic research is compromised by the rush to file for patent protection for inventions based on marine biota,[18] and whether under the pressure to compete and to protect sensitive information not yet patentable, marine researchers may choose a greater degree of secrecy about their knowledge, over the goals of collaborative research and capacity building.[19]

The contemporary Law of the Sea does not define key terms such as *sovereignty, sovereign rights, jurisdiction, marine environment, natural resources,* or *marine scientific research* (MSR). Interpreting these terms is complex and in recent years made more complex through the introduced distinction between the *genotype* and the *phenotype* of marine biota.[20] Genotype functions for patent procedure consist among others of isolated compounds or identified genetic functions protected by the patent. We suggest that these terms are useful for biotechnology and other industries using marine biota. However, UNCLOS and the CBD do not use these terms and, in our view,

environment under the control of a coastal State of which the researcher-inventor (physical person or institution) is not a national.

18. Academic research has produced 50% of new economic growth in industrial economies since 1945. This "second academic revolution" has occurred by transferring research, sometimes under pressure from government, to the private sector. See C. McSherry, *Who Owns Academic Work? Battling For Control of Intellectual Property* (Cambridge: Harvard University Press, 2001): 32–33; see also National Research Council, *Capitalizing on New Needs and New Opportunities: Government-Industry Partnerships in Biotechnology and Information Technologies* (Washington, D.C., 2001): 175, Fig. 14. In this process, most universities allocate royalties from copyrights to those employees who have produced books, textbooks and articles. Copyrightable works may include books, journals, articles, texts, glossaries, bibliographies, study guides, laboratory manuals, syllabi, tests and proposals, lectures, musical or dramatic compositions, and unpublished scripts, films, charts, transparencies, visual aids, video, audio tapes and cassettes, live-video audit broadcast, programmed instruction materials, and computer programs, see K. Chapman, "Intellectual Property Policies, Research Agreements, Consulting Agreements, and Conflicts of Interest," in *Understanding Biotechnology Law,* G. R. Peterson ed. (1993): 298. See also L. Nelsen, "Identifying, Evaluating, and Reporting Innovative Research Developments at the University," in *Understanding Biotechnology Law, id.* at 25–61; and R. G. Adler, "Choosing the Form of Legal Protection," in *Understanding Biotechnology Law, id.* at 64. Most U.S. universities and federal sponsors such as the National Science Foundation or the National Institutes of Health (through its Cancer Research Institute) discourage withdrawing information as trade secrets, do not undertake confidential research and promote, instead, open dissemination of research results.

19. For a discussion for capacity building in marine scientific and other marine research, see Gorina-Ysern, n. 1 above, at 527–98.

20. J. Straus, "Patents in Biomaterial—A New Colonialism or a Means for Technology Transfer and Benefit- Sharing?," in *Bioethics in a Small World,* F. Thiele and R. E. Ashcroft, eds. (Berlin, Heidelberg: Springer, 2005): 45–72 [hereinafter Straus 2005].

do not warrant their use as a means to weaken coastal nation's sovereign rights of control over genetic resources. Gaps in legal terminology and the inconsistent use of new terms not codified in the relevant international conventions are relevant and can lead to interpretations that could be considered not only inequitable and unjust, but also "manifestly absurd or unreasonable" in light of the criteria set out in the Vienna Convention on the Law of Treaties (VCLT).[21] For example, it would be unreasonable to argue that a new generation of roll-on/roll-off vessels escapes the jurisdiction of the coastal nation because UNCLOS does not specifically mention this type of vessel and, at the time of the drafting, delegates did not know that the technology was possible. It would seem unreasonable to suggest that after the entry into force of the CBD, any claims to collections of marine biota held *ex situ* have prescribed. If this argument had any validity, it would serve to legitimize a wholesale monopoly of use by juridical persons over the genotypes of species located within areas under coastal State maritime control (without a concomitant requirement to respect the proprietary rights of the coastal State over its marine biota and derivatives thereof). Coastal nations can oppose monopolies of use held by foreign patent holders pursuant to the 1994 Agreement on Trade Related Aspects of Intellectual Property (TRIPS).[22] We propose that the legitimacy of such acquisition without returns to the coastal State of origin, source or legal provenance, needs to be evaluated in light of critical dates for the entry into force of specific obligations arising under the 1958 GCCS, the 1973 Convention on International Trade in Endangered Species of Wild Flora and Fauna (CITES),[23] rules codified in the 1982 UNCLOS, and their subsequent customary implementation.[24] Failure to examine claims on a case-by-case basis could lead to unjust enrichment by physical and juridical persons. Such failure would be further unjustified pursuant to Article 22 of the CBD, according to which:

> 1. The provisions of this Convention [CBD] shall not affect the rights and obligations of any Contracting Party deriving from any existing

21. Article 31(2) and (3) Vienna Convention on the Law of Treaties, May 23, 1969, U.N. Doc. A/CONF.39/2, reproduced in *International Legal Materials* 8 (1969) p. 769 [entered into force on January 27, 1990].

22. The Agreement on Trade Related Aspects of Intellectual Property, Including Trade in Counterfeit Goods (TRIPS for short), constitutes Annex 1 C of the Final Act of the 1994 Uruguay Round under the General Agreement on Tariffs and Trade (GATT). Final Act signed at Marrakesh, Morocco, on April 15, 1994, by 109 States. Reproduced in *International Legal Materials* 33 (1994): 1,143–53, 1,224–47.

23. T.I.A.S. No. 8249 (1973).

24. UNCLOS, n. 7 above.

international agreement [i.e., GCCS, CITES, VCLT, UNCLOS], except where the exercise of those rights and obligations would cause a serious damage or threat to biological diversity. 2. Contracting Parties shall implement this Convention with respect to the marine environment consistently with the rights and obligations of States under the law of the sea [i.e., customary and conventional—1958–1982].

In this article we also discuss the assertion that "marine bacteria by themselves are of no [economic] value,"[25] and identify some leading patent cases that show the importance of bacteria in biotechnology development for therapeutic purposes. Finally, we briefly outline the need to coordinate the roles of enforcement agencies such as Customs and Coast Guards to ensure surveillance, monitoring and compliance of the international and national rules in force. It is suggested that patent offices must be privy to these enforcement mechanisms for greater compliance with international law.

First we describe in detail the rush to map and sequence the human genome, and its extension to all living organisms. We use the discussion of biogenetic research as a broader context of analysis that illustrates why ethical, economic and legal concerns have prevented States from reaching universal agreements on biogenetic research and proprietary claims to the inventions arising thereof. We then proceed to identify the increasing importance of the market in marine natural products as therapeutic agents. Next, we review the regime governing MSR activities pursuant to the international law of the sea, with an outline of the general jurisdictional powers that international law grants coastal States to prescribe conduct relating to MSR and other marine research activities. We provide only a brief summary of the regime of freedom of MSR on the high seas and in the Area beyond the limits of national jurisdiction, because our current focus is on the legal rules that apply to the conduct of MSR in areas of sovereignty, sovereign rights, and jurisdiction. We highlight the importance of the purpose stated when seeking clearance to undertake MSR in foreign waters, and highlight the relevance of negotiating clearance for the conduct of those activities under Article 250 of UNCLOS. We follow the discussion with an analysis of the provisions relating to the consent regime (Article 246 of UNCLOS) and Articles 241 and 249.2 of UNCLOS, relating to proprietary information and conditions on the publication of resource related research results. We discuss briefly the doctrine of unjust enrichment as the opposite

25. B. Cicin-Sain, R. W. Knecht, L. Denno-Bouman and G. W. Fisk, "Emerging Policy Issues in the Development of Marine Biotechnology," in *Ocean Yearbook* 12, E. Mann Borgese, N. Ginsburg and J. R. Morgan eds. (Chicago: University of Chicago Press, 1996): 179 at 204.

of an equitable outcome to negotiated access. Through our analysis of the indistinguishability between the marine natural resources regulated under the GCCS, UNCLOS, CITES and CBD, we identify critical dates of entry into force of these conventions and suggest that the CBD cannot override rights and obligations for coastal and researching States entered into under the earlier conventions. The CBD and TRIPS are briefly discussed in the next section, to highlight arguments that, in our view, have sought to trump obligations that in principle would be incurred by States under other international law instruments. A short discussion of enforcement measures concludes the article. We conclude with a call for more transparency in the field.

A RUSH TO MAP AND SEQUENCE ALL LIVING ORGANISMS

On April 26, 2005, George Mason University staged the play *Sequencing the Human Genome: Creating an Industry and a Workforce*, by Paul Mullin.[26] The play highlighted the socio-economic and labor implications inherent in every great scientific discovery, and underlined the dialectical nature of industrial progress. It focused on the moral and ethical responsibilities borne by individual scientists (whether funded with public or private R&D capital),[27] and by government officials with competence to make decisions on a large scale and with potentially irreversible effects.

Advancements in the mapping and sequencing of the human genome signify great leaps of contemporary science.[28] Human genome research has triggered a rush to map and sequence the genotype of every living organism on Earth.[29] Research on human DNA and research on the DNA of marine

26. Paul Mullin is an award-winning playwright. The staging of the play was made possible through a grant of the College of Arts and Sciences at George Mason University, and it was held at the Virginia Campus.

27. The two main characters of the play were Francis Collins (a medical doctor who was the Director of the National Human Genome Research Institute of the National Institutes of Health in the United States of America), and Craig Venter (a medical doctor and President of the Center for the Advancement of Genomics).

28. Gene Mapping is defined as a "low resolution method to assign gene locations (loci) to their position on the chromosome" in D. S. T. Nicholl, *An Introduction to Genetic Engineering* (Cambridge: Cambridge University Press 2d., 2002): 270 [hereinafter Nicholl]. See also J. D. Watson, *DNA. The Secret of Life* (New York: Alfred A. Knopf, 2005). The Human Genome Project was an initiative of the U.S. Department of Energy, officially launched in October, 1990 with James Watson as its director within the National Institutes of Health, and support of the U.S. National Academy of Sciences and the molecular biological community. The U.S. government pledged US$200 million annually over a 15-year period.

29. The genotype is the genetic constitution of an organism. A gene is described as a "unit of inheritance, located on a chromosome. In molecular terms, usually taken to mean a region of the DNA that encodes one function. Broadly,

biota share similar ethical, economic and legal (i.e., access and property-related) controversies.[30] These controversies affect the way the governments of different nations view the moral, ethical, and economic dimensions of international and domestic laws that protect proprietary claims over unique genotype characteristics—or isolated molecules thereof—of marine biota.[31]

The "rush to patent" inventions resulting from the use of molecular biology and genetic engineering (biotechnology) in recent years has been attributed to the conduct of Dr. Craig Venter. During Dr. Venter's tenure at the National Institutes of Health (NIH), more than 2,000 patent applications were filed with the U.S. Patent and Trademark Office.[32] Though the

therefore, one gene encodes one protein." Nicholl, n. 28 above. DNA is defined as a double stranded deoxyribonucleic acid, "a condensation heteropolymer composed of nucleotides. DNA is the primary genetic material in all organisms apart from some RNA [Ribonucleic Acid] viruses. Nicholl, *id.* at 273.

30. After the first preliminary draft of the entire sequence of the human genome was published in 2001, the Bioethics Committee of the United Nations Educational, Scientific and Cultural Organization (UNESCO), issued the Universal Declaration on the Human Genome and Human Rights, adopted in 1998 as the first international instrument dealing with the ethical, economic and legal issues posed by the Human Genome Project. Article 1 of the Declaration provides that the human genome is the heritage of humanity; Article 4 provides that the human genome in its natural state "shall not give rise to financial gain" in Justice M. Kirby, *Intellectual Property and the Human Genome* (Paris: UNESCO, 2001), available online: <http://lawgenecenter.org/fsru/1615/RTF/IP_Human-Genome_Kirby_En.rtf> [hereinafter Justice Kirby].

31. See ns. 189 and 195 below.

32. Justice Kirby, n. 30 above, at 7, comment by Mr. Jacques Warcoin (a French patent lawyer), to the effect that during Dr. Venter's work at the NIH, more than 2,200 genetic applications about "whose operation nothing was at the time known" were filed; see also comment by Professor Mireille Buydens (Catholic University of Louvain, Belgium), pointing out that after the momentous decision of the U.S. Supreme Court in *Diamond v. Chakrabarti* in 1980, Dr. Craig Venter contributed in the 1990s to a further rush to patent a very large number of applications for patents on gene sequences in the U.S., *id.* at 3; see also comment by Mr. Axel Kahn (Director of the Department of Genetics of Institut Coshin in Paris and chairperson of the high level group of experts for the life sciences within the European Commission), to the effect that under Dr. Venter's leadership of the NIH a new patent application policy was implemented that put pressure on the European Patent Office (EPO) to "provide a regime offering equivalent protections to European scientists and corporations. The result was the new draft European Directive which, after much debate, came into force in 1998 and required member States to amend their patent law to ensure compliance. As an outcome, the EPO almost immediately received thousands of relevant applications." *Id.* at 4. At the time of the writing (2001), Mr. Kahn observed that hundreds of patents had already been granted, in spite of the ethical dilemmas associated with the patenting of the living cells of plants and animals. Mr. Kahn further argued that although there was an "inventive step", as required by patent law, in "putting living materials to use", as new tests, new therapies, or for industrial purposes, "the result was a significant

NIH did not proceed with the applications, the news revealed an unprecedented move and "enlivened an urgent national and international debate" that triggered a rush to patent in Japan and Europe to protect intellectual property rights over health-related inventions.[33] In turn, the prospect of a new industrial bonanza generated an upsurge in stock market activity in pharmaceutical and biotechnology research.[34] New start-up companies with expertise in molecular biology and genetic engineering grew in significant numbers around the world.[35] In his play, *Sequencing the Human Genome: Creating an Industry and a Workforce,* Mullin airs two recorded messages from actual speeches made by the former U.S. President Bill Clinton. In the first message, Clinton has been advised that laying property claims to human genome sequences may be unethical and immoral, and his comments are to that effect.[36] However, in the second recorded message,

shift in economic power in favor of those who secured intellectual property protection." He went on to conclude that this shift in power was "against the public interest in developed countries. But could be even more devastating for developing countries" without specifying why.

33. In 2004, the University of California was granted 447 patents (becoming the lead institution with number 42 on the list). Among the top biotech contenders were Applera Corp., Degussa, U.S. Government Health and Human Services, and Millennium Pharmaceuticals. Biotechnology continues to spawn new patents from companies, government and academia. Since 1994, the total number of biotech patents has nearly doubled. See Patent Intelligence and Technology Report, available online: <http://www.ificlaims.com or http://www.wkhealth.com>.

34. According to a 2003 report by the Organization for Economic Cooperation and Development (OECD), biotechnology patents within the European Patent Office have been growing continuously in the last two decades. In 1999 alone, 5,838 patents were filed, with the US, Japan and Germany leading applications, followed by Canada, France, and the UK. Since 1993, the growth of biotech patents accounts for 14.3% a year, whereas overall patent applications amount to 8.3%. The U.S. leads the ratio of biotech patent applications within the EPO (45.3%), followed by the European Union (34.1% including Germany, United Kingdom, France, Netherlands, Belgium and Denmark), Japan (10.1%) and others (10.4% including Canada, Switzerland, Australia, Israel and Korea). *OECD Compendium of Patent Statistics* (Paris: OECD, 2003): 26–27.

35. *Genetic Inventions, Intellectual Property Rights and Licensing Practices. Evidence and Policies,* (Paris: Organization for Economic Co-operation and Development OECD, 2002). See also the web page of the Biotechnology Industry Organization (BIO), representing more than 1,000 biotechnology companies, academic institutions, state biotechnology centers and related institutions in the United States and in 33 other nations, available online: <http://www.bio.org>. BIO members are engaged in R&D of health-care, agricultural, industrial and environmental biotech products.

36. In 1999, President Clinton and British Prime Minister Tony Blair were negotiating an Anglo-American Agreement seeking to eliminate the patenting of human genes. According to J. Shreeve, *The Genome War. How Craig Venter Tried to Capture the Code of Life and Save the World* (New York: Alfred A. Knopf, 2004): 41–42

reacting to a "free fall" in biotech market shares, Clinton had been advised to remind the public that without property rights, researchers may keep their inventions secret and investors may not provide funds for much needed research and development (R&D) for new cures.[37]

The human genome was fully sequenced in June 2000, upon collaboration between Collins and Venter.[38] After the announcement, Dr. Venter literally embarked on the research vessel *Sorcerer II*, his private yacht with another important mission.[39] The R/V *Sorcerer II* is equipped with state-of-the-art research capabilities, and it has proceeded to circumnavigate the globe sampling, mapping and sequencing selected marine biota of the world's oceans and seas until the formal end of the expedition in December 2005.[40] The international law of the sea governs such expeditions and exploratory works.

In the United States, efforts to explore marine habitats to identify unknown biota are carried out on private and public research vessels under the aegis of prestigious international programs and institutions such as the

[hereinafter Shreeve], Celera Genomics, the company set up by Craig Venter, was the object of the agreement; on March 14, 2000, at a White House news conference, the President was reported to say that "the raw, fundamental data of the human genome, including the human DNA sequence and its variations, should be made freely available to scientists everywhere," implying that "the president and the prime minister were advocating a ban on intellectual property protection for *any* genetic discovery." The actual words used by President Clinton were: "This agreement says in the strongest possible terms our genome, the book in which all human life is written, belong to every member of the human race ... Already the Human Genome Project, funded by the United States and the United Kingdom, requires its grant recipients to make the sequences they discover publicly available within twenty-four hours. I urge all other nations, scientists, and corporations to adopt this policy and honor its spirit. We must ensure that the profits of human genome research are measured not in dollars but in the betterment of human life." *Id.* at 322.

37. *Id.* at 324. Shreeve observes that by the end of the day, the biotech sector had lost US$40 billion in withdrawals by panicked investors. It was the second-highest technology stocks loss in the history of the NASDAQ exchange.

38. The White House announced the completion of the first draft of the human genome on June 26, 2000. It covered 90% of the human genome and was subject to further refining. For details on the competition between the International Consortium responsible for the Human Genome Project and its competitor, Celera Genomics, see <http://www.genoscope.cns.fr/externe/English/Actualites/Presse/271202_1.html>.

39. K. Ruder, "Exploring the Sargasso Sea. Scientists Discover One Million New Genes in Ocean Microbes," in *Genome News Network*, available online: <http://www.genomenewsnetwork.org/articles/2004/03/04/sargasso.php> (posted March 4, 2004).

40. For the R/V *Sorcerer II* home page, see <http://www.sorcerer2expedition.org/version1/HTML/main.htm>.

Census of Marine Life,[41] the Ocean Drilling Program,[42] or Harbor Branch Oceanographic Institution.[43] Universities and research institutions, traditionally considered the ivory towers of fundamental research, have had to live up to governmental pressure to justify public funding by developing a hefty biotechnology patent portfolio,[44] thus blurring further the line between pure and applied marine research, but contributing to a lucrative biotech market in marine natural products of potential benefit to humanity.

THE INCREASING IMPORTANCE OF THE MARKET IN MARINE NATURAL PRODUCTS AS THERAPEUTIC AGENTS

Marine biotechnology is described as the science that "explores the capabilities of the 30,000 known species of marine microorganisms to develop new classes of human vaccines, medicines and other medical products, chemical products, enzymes and industrial processes."[45] Microorganisms include bacteria, viruses, fungi, plants and animals,[46] and are the

41. See <http://www.coml.org/>.

42. See <http://www-odp.tamu.edu/>.

43. Division of Biomedical Marine Research, available online: <http://www.hboi.edu/dbmr/dbmr_home.html>. In the United States, major federal sources of funding are the National Science Foundation, the National Oceanic and Atmospheric Administration, the Office of Naval Research, the National Institutes of Health and its Cancer Research Institute. In a PowerPoint presentation entitled "The NCI's Marine Biodiscovery Programs," D. J. Newman and G. M. Cragg observe that since the 1960s the National Cancer Institute of the U.S. National Institutes of Health had a collection program covering plants (via an interagency agreement with the USDA), microbes and marine invertebrates that until 1981, relied upon what could best be described as: "collections of opportunity and/or convenience." Collection for plant samples (amounting to some 35 kg) was carried out by scientists from government departments, during surveys or other specific tasks. Microbes were obtained from the excess microbial fermentations that companies in the antibiotic industry produced. Marine invertebrate samples were collected by marine biologists on a small scale, on occasion and whenever possible from specific geographic areas or phyla. Nearly 50,000 sample materials were shipped to NCI's contract laboratories, extracted, tested on mice and "active components" were isolated by academic contract chemists. NCI administered and developed any suitable agent, including three plant-derived drugs in clinical use, three marine-derived materials in clinical trials, with one, bryostatin 1, still under trials as a combination of therapies. Patents issued were retained by academic discoverers, not the NCI.

44. See Gorina-Ysern, n. 1 above, at 353.

45. J. K. Lu, "Marine Biotechnology, NTOU," PowerPoint presentation, available online: <http://ind.ntou.edu.tw/~jklu/Aquabiotech/lecture%20PDF%201/lecture%201%20marine%20%Biotech.pdf>.

46. Glossary of Terms, available online: <http://www.niaid.nih.gov/publications/pdf/microbesbook.pdf>.

sources of novel metabolites with the potential to be produced by fermentation in the laboratory. Fermentation is a valued property in biotechnology because a small sample amount suffices in the sustainable development of therapeutic agents, and minimizes the need to obtain large supplies from nature, a concern highlighted by conservation experts.[47] Marine microorganisms used to develop therapeutic agents include marine bacteria and fungi, algae, sponges, cnidaria, echinoderms, mollusks and tunicates.[48]

Microorganisms are important "raw materials" used extensively in genetic engineering methods and techniques to isolate molecules and create new compounds through "cutting tools."[49] Such a sophisticated "collage" of uses may pose difficulties in the determination of the origin, source or legal provenance of the raw material.[50] However, these difficulties have not affected the rush to patent or the granting of patents arising from inventions using marine biota. Since the 1980s, after the landmark case of *Diamond v. Chakrabarti*, the domestic laws of many industrialized countries

47. Farrier and Tucker consider the parallel aims of the CBD maybe irreconcilable because the CBD promotes the development of a biological resources "market" as well as sustainable use of the biodiversity that constitutes the "raw materials" for such a market. Thus, the CBD is offering "an incentive at an international level to biodiversity-rich countries to conserve their nature by facilitating bioprospecting as a profitable, low-impact, sustainable use of the environment." D. Farrier and L. Tucker, "Access to Marine Bioresources: Hitching the Conservation Cart to the Bioprospecting Horse," *Ocean Development and International Law* 32 (2001): 213–239, at 215–16 n. 20.

48. J. L. Frenz, A. C. Kohl and R. G. Kerr, "Marine Natural Products as Therapeutic Agents: Part II," *Expert Opinion Review* 14, 1 (2004): 17–33 [hereinafter Frenz et al.].

49. Genetic engineering consists of a technique, or series of techniques, used to alter the genetic material (DNA) of an organism by inserting genes from another organism. *The Human Body* (London: Dorling Kindersley Ltd. Tony Smith ed., 1995): 18–21. One important technique for modifying organisms involves the use of bacteria and viruses. Bacteria are microscopic single-celled organisms lacking nuclear membranes around the genes, with a single loop plasmid. See Wilson, n. 2 above. Plasmids direct bacteria to produce enzymes that can activate/inactivate drugs. Viruses are DNA or RNA molecules covered with a protein shell, but viruses cannot reproduce themselves. Bacteria are ideal in assisting viruses to reproduce. When the nucleic acid of a virus is injected into bacteria, its code instructs the bacteria to produce viral nucleic acid and protein coats. Then the bacteria ruptures the cell and disperses. As it is thus being "attacked" by the virus, the bacteria release enzymes that break up the viral DNA or RNA. Gorina-Ysern, n. 1 above, at 446–47. These enzymes can be used as "cutting tools," as for example to cut and paste different sections of the DNA to produce novel organisms. See S. D. Murphy, "Biotechnology and International Law," *Harvard International Law Journal* 42, 1 (2001): 47–139.

50. COP to the CBD, n. 15 above.

permit and encourage patents over live organisms.[51] As Professor Adelman observes, "Chakrabarti was a clear signal that patenting was broadly available in the biotechnology field, more a 'signal' than a 'result,' and this ruling opened the coffers of Wall Street to the biotechnology industry."[52]

To thrive, the industry needs the ability to retrieve a sustained and reliable harvest of marine biota so as to have sufficient quantities of material for study purposes. It needs to overcome difficulties with laboratory cultures,[53] and to attract funding for expensive instrumentation and equipment through public or private R&D sources. Funding is critical for holding and preserving house collections and storing cultures, for large scientific and technical databases and reference standards, and for human resources in the form of personnel with the training necessary to engage in multi-disciplinary research.[54] Strategic patenting is another important factor to secure future follow-on R&D investment by the private sector and by satisfied and hopeful shareholders, where the public sector provides limited funding.[55] Patents have been used as the ideal legal means to protect new compounds.[56] As Correa points out, biotechnology patents give the patentee

51. Patent rights are concerned with new products or new processes to encourage industrial development. The patentee is granted an exclusive right (i.e., monopoly) to exploit an invention for a limited time in return for the publication of the details of the invention. See M. J. Adelman, R. R. Rader, J. R. Thomas and H. C. Wegner, *Cases and Materials on Patent Law* (Saint Paul: West Group, 2d., 2003) [hereinafter Adelman]. Section 101 of the Patent Act (1952 US) provides that "a person who invents or discovers any new and useful process, machine, manufacture, or any composition of matter, or any new and useful improvement thereof, may obtain a patent therefore, subject to the conditions and requirements of this title." Clearly, the Act leaves room for discretion. In 1980, the U.S. Supreme Court found, in *Diamond v. Chakrabarti* [444 U.S. 303 (1980)], that a patent could be granted to protect the invention or discovery of a new and useful "manufacture" or "composition" of matter having a distinctive name, character and use, whose original source is a living microorganism.

52. Adelman et al., n. 51 above, at 107.

53. Lu, n. 45 above. See also D. J. Newman and G. M. Cragg, *The NCI's Marine Biodiscovery Programs* (Natural Products Branch, Developmental Therapeutics Program, NCI–Frederick, Maryland, 21702, USA).

54. Biotechnology Research Subcommittee, Committee on Fundamental Science, *Biotechnology for the 21st Century: New Horizons*, (National Science and Technology Council, July 1995), Chapter 6, Infrastructure Needs, available online: <http://www.nal.usda.gov/bic/bio21/> [hereinafter *Biotechnology in the 21st Century*]. Biotechnology may involve biochemistry, microbiology, structural biology, genetics, ecology, and engineering.

55. See OECD 2002, n. 35 above, at 53, discussing the policies of the National Institutes of Health in the U.S.

56. See Gorina-Ysern, n. 1 above, at 409, quoting S. Elias, *Patent, Copyright and Trademark* (Berkeley: Nolo Press 2d. ed., 1996): 2–3. An inventor seeking to obtain a patent must demonstrate that the invention is new and non-obvious. Novelty requires the invention to be different from any previous product, devise, method or

a monopoly over three types of claims: first, a gene or protein, standing alone, corresponding to that sequence; secondly, a vector or plasmid that incorporates the sequence; and thirdly, an organism transformed by the vector or plasmid. As a result of these claims, "the patent holder gains effective control over the use of the specified gene in genetic engineering."[57]

Bongiorno and Pietra report that between 1969 and 1995, 200 patents were issued for novel *compounds* for the pharmaceutical industry using marine natural products. These patents described novel therapeutic uses of known metabolites.[58] Frenz, Kohl and Kerr report that between 1996 and 1999, 68 patents were issued (an average of 20.4 patents per year), and between 1999 and May 2003, 67 patents were issued (an average of 15.8

---

written descriptive material. The novelty of an invention may be undermined for patent purposes if it is described in published form or put to public use one year prior to the inventor filing for patent protection. The concept of non-obviousness requires a patent examiner to certify that the inventor has produced "unexpected or surprising new results" not anticipated by the prior art and recognizable as such by a person with ordinary skill [35 U.S.C. 103]. The inventor must file a formal application for patent protection before his or her country's patent office, pay the required fee, and disclose or describe the invention adequately. The application must meet all the legal criteria and technical requirements, it must not interfere with pending or multiple applications by other inventors for the same subject matter, and the inventor must pay the required fees. The issued patent may be for a period ranging from 14 to 20 years. The owner of a patent can sue in court anyone who infringes it by using it without his or her permission. However, the validity of the patent can also be contested in court by the infringer on a number of grounds. If the patentee turns out to hold a valid patent, a court may order the infringer to refrain from using or selling the subject matter of the valid patent and pay damages to the patentee. The court may also call upon the parties to the dispute to reach agreement on the payment of royalties by the infringer for the use of the patent.

57. C. Correa, "Access to Plant Genetic Resources and Intellectual Property Rights," in *Perspectives on Intellectual Property*, P. Drahos and M. Blakeney eds. (2001).

58. Cited in Frenz et al., n. 48 above. Metabolites are small molecules produced by biological processes. The compounds cover various novel properties and include: the cytology of staurosporines (compounds: IB–97224 and IB–97225(1)), cytology of macrolides 3 and 4 and reference compounds (IB–96212(3), IB9612B(4), Cisplatin, Adriamicin, Pacilitaxol, Etopoxide). In addition, research has yielded the following compounds for which patents were issued: Bogorol A, SMP–2, Avrainvillamide, Halimide, Halovir A, Xestolactone A, Scytonemin, Asmarine B, Topsentin D, Nortopsentin-C, Manzamine A, Secobatzeline A, Discorhabin P, Halitulin, Wondorin A, Motuporamine C, Cribrostatin 5, Peloruside A, Laulimalide, Dicytostatin–1, Discalamide A and Discalamide A-methylester Chondropsin A, Rhadbasterol acetate, Adociasulfate 2, Eryloside F, Ornamide A, Mycalamide A and B, Lanosolide A, Discadermolide B, Ecteinsascidin 729, Subersic acid, Orostanal, Pelorol, Phakellistatin, Lotroridoside A, Cramescidin 816, Agelaglastatin, IK–8734, Rameswaralide, Eleutherobin, Desmethyleleutherobin, Jorumycin, Spisulosine 285, Shermilamine D, Coproverdine, as well as others extracted from marine bacteria, fungi, algae, sponges, cnidaria, echinoderms, molluscs and tunicates.

patents per year).[59] According to their phylogenetic group, the patent breakdown included sponges (52%), marine bacteria (16%), marine algae and fungi (respectively 6% each), tunicates, cnidarians, echinoderms and mollusks (5% each). The biological activity properties in the patents issued include anticancer (50%), antifungal and antibacterial (9% each), anti-inflammatory (5%), antiviral (4%) and other (23%).[60]

The survey provided by Frenz, Kohl and Kerr does not identify the geographical origin of the marine biota used to develop the novel products for which patents were issued in the period under study. Most patented inventions fail to provide exact details of the origin, source or legal provenance of the marine biota used in the inventions, even though the call for certificates of origin to be provided in such circumstances is already a decade old.[61] The failure to identify, clearly and consistently, the origin, source or legal provenance of the marine biota, coupled with the failure of the patent description to indicate whether marine biota from other nations used in the inventing process were obtained legitimately, adds to the arduous task of investigating the trail and tracing the marine biota back to the source country, and ascertaining whether the collection of specimens was officially authorized by the relevant coastal State government organ.

59. The patents were issued to the following institutions listed by patent volume: Harbor Branch Oceanographic Institution Inc. (13 patents); Instituto Biomar, S.A. (8 patents); The Regents of the University of California (7 patents); Pharma Mar S.A., (5 patents), University of British Columbia (3 patents); Guangzhou Institute of Chemistry, Sagami Chemical Research Institute, and Arizona Board of Regents (2 patents each respectively). The following institutions were granted one patent each: Marine Biotech Institute, Co. Ltd., Toyama Prefecture, Andersen et al., Ajimoto Co. Ltd., Okuya Keichi, Techno Network Shikoku, Co. Ltd., University of California, Zentaris AG, Toyama-Ken & Lead Chem. Co. Ltd., Braz. Pedido PI., National University of Singapore, University of Mississippi, Korea Marine Research Institute et al., Pharmacia Corp., Victoria Linn Ltd. et al., University of Hawaii et al., Arizona State University, the Government of the United States of America, Kyushu Teo, Co. Ltd., Military Medical University, Kirin Beer Kabu Shiki Kaisha, Sanyo Co. Ltd., Suntoz Ltd., National Institute of Advanced Industrial Science and Technology et al., Nagoya Industrial and Scientific Research Institute, Council of Science and Industry Research, Centre National de la Recherche Scientifique et al., and Board of Trustees of Illinois, in Frenz et al., n. 48 above, at 32–33.

60. *Id.* at 30–31.

61. United Nations University, *The Role of Certificates of Origin in ABS Governance,* available online: <http://ias.unu.edu/research/certificatesoforigin.cfm>. Brendan Tobin often cited as the originator of the concept as it applies to the CBD. In the multiple patent descriptions held by Harbor Branch Oceanographic Institution and in the U.S. Patent Office descriptions of these patents, the origin of marine biota involved is provided in maritime coordinates, not in legal or political boundary terms implying degrees of jurisdiction. See <http://hboi.edu/dbmr/dmbmr_patents.html>.

Clearly, this situation underscores the ethical, economic and legal, importance of the bona fide statements made by academic researchers through the clearance process.

The volume of issued patents suggests considerable R&D activity in the marine natural products field. As observed, a good patent portfolio is considered to be an indispensable strategic tool for business success,[62] an essential means to protect inventions,[63] a crucial way to reap commercial rewards for "sunk costs,"[64] and to attract further funding and private investment. Authors differ on whether the much heralded potential value of marine biotechnology has been realized.[65] A decade ago, it was anticipated that marine biotechnology would make a considerable contribution to the world economy.[66] However, others have argued that bioprospecting has received "disproportionate attention in the popular press as a means to finance habitat preservation."[67] In 2003, it was estimated that marine

62. See, for example, Mera Pharmaceuticals. Business Strategy, available online: <http://www.aquasearch.com/strategy.htm> (2004); See also Integrin Advanced Biosystems, available online: <http://www.integrin.co.uk/over.html>.

63. According to OECD 2002, n. 35 above, at 38, in the U.S. genomics field, pharmaceutical companies rated 52% of gene patent assignees, followed by universities (23%) and public or non-profit research organizations (19%).

64. R. S. Eisenberg, Patents and the Progress of Science: Exclusive Rights and Experimental Use *University of Chicago Law Review* 56 (1989): 1,017. Farrier and Tacker suggest that before a product moves to commercialization it may require a prior investment in the range of US$50–250 million over a ten-year period average.

65. Lu, n. 45 above, reports that compared to terrestrial biotechnology, marine biotechnology has yielded "minimal commercial success." The latter depends on the specific application that is sought through the use of marine biotechnology (i.e., aquaculture, seafood safety and human health, environmental remediation, biofilms and corrosion, or biomaterials and bioprocessing), and the specific areas of activity where biotechnology focuses. There are many pharmaceutical products derived from marine organisms in clinical trials, but only about a dozen drugs derived from marine organisms appear to be widely used.

66. It was announced that "Through the use of advanced tools such as genetic engineering, biotechnology is expected to have a dramatic effect on the world economy over the next decade," in *Biotechnology for the 21st Century*, n. 54 above. In the U.S., the $44 million invested by the federal government in marine biotech R&D in 1992 was expected to yield a $50 billion profit in sales and would generate considerable employment, in addition to promising to replace chemical pesticides to maximize crop yields and growth, thus saving the U.S. some $47 billion annually. *Id.*, n. 54 above, Chapter 5, Opportunities in Marine Biotechnology and Aquaculture, at 2 and 7.

67. J. H. Vogel, White Paper. Final Report. Commissioned by the Biodiversity Support Program on Behalf of the Inter-American Commission on Biodiversity and Sustainable Development, in preparation for the Summit of the Americas on Sustainable Development, Santa Cruz de la Sierra, Bolivia, December 6–8, 1996. *Case Study 6: Bioprospecting*, available online: <http://www.biodiv.org/doc/case-studies/abs/cs-abs-cartel.pdf>.

biotechnology was a logical follow-on from the US$22 billion in annual sales for terrestrial natural products.[68] Ultimately, the extent of the benefit provided by marine biotechnology is a matter for each nation to determine in light of its particular circumstances, taking into account the general health of its citizens as a measure of success, and in light of a wide range of development indicators such as marine scientific and technology infrastructure.

INTERNATIONAL REGIME FOR THE LEGAL REGULATION OF MARINE SCIENTIFIC RESEARCH ACTIVITIES

UNCLOS codifies principles for the regulation of fundamental oceanographic research into the biological characteristics of the continental shelf previously incorporated in the GCCS. UNCLOS also regulates official clearance communications through the provisions on MSR in its Part XIII. The conduct of MSR activities is subject to basic principles of maritime jurisdiction.

Jurisdiction to Prescribe and to Enforce

Coastal States' rights and obligations over foreign MSR activities vary according to where the activities are intended. International law distinguishes between different maritime zones for permitting or restricting coastal States to exercise full prescriptive and enforcement jurisdiction.[69] Jurisdiction is the broad capacity of a State to prescribe or to enforce a rule enacted under its municipal law.[70] Enforcement jurisdiction is the capacity to enforce by administrative or judicial action that legal rule. The exercise of national jurisdiction by a State may therefore be defined as its "capacity

---

68. Quoted in Integrin, n. 62 above. In Australia, with an estimated 20,000 marine macro- and micro-organisms surrounding its waters, the Australian government anticipates an excellent opportunity for pharmaceutical development in the field of cancer treatments from the sea. See *New Drug Development Deal for Cancer Treatments from the Sea* (Australian Institute of Marine Science. Media Release, September 14, 2004), available online: <http://www.aims.gov.au/news/pages/media-release–20040914.html>.

69. G. Marston, "Maritime Jurisdiction," *Encyclopedia of Public International Law*, 11: 221–224 [hereinafter Marston].

70. Jurisdiction has been defined as the power of a sovereign to affect the rights of persons, whether by legislation, by executive decree, or by the judgment of a court, see J. H. Beale, "The Jurisdiction of a Sovereign State," XXXVI, *Harvard Law Review* (1923), 241. See generally M. Akehurst, "Jurisdiction in International Law," *British Year Book of International Law* 46, (1972–1973): 145.

to exercise, in conformity with international law, legislative, executive and judicial functions over the sea and over persons and things on or under the sea.''[71]

These powers are complete with regard to the internal waters and the territorial sea of a State,[72] subject to a right of innocent passage of foreign ships through the territorial sea.[73] In the zone contiguous to the territorial sea (the Contiguous Zone), the coastal State has additional powers to prevent the infringement of its customs, fiscal, immigration and sanitary laws;[74] but 12–24 NM in the CZ partake of the regime of the Exclusive Economic Zone (EEZ). With regards to the continental shelf and the EEZ, international law allows coastal States to exercise prescriptive and enforcement jurisdiction for the purpose of protecting their sovereign rights to explore and exploit the natural resources of these zones.[75] They can also exercise prescriptive jurisdiction with respect to the conduct of MSR activities which, generally, are presumed to not relate to resources, unless otherwise such nature is declared, or revealed.[76]

The United States is the world's leading oceanographic State. It has not become a party to UNCLOS because Congress has other priorities.[77] In practice, the U.S. government already implements many of the provisions of UNCLOS as part of binding customary international law. This position provides the U.S. with consistency and certainty. The U.S. also adheres closely to the MSR regime of Part XIII of UNCLOS. Using a range of sources, Gorina-Ysern has documented that in the last 30 years, the U.S. has placed some 6,000 requests for clearance of U.S. research vessels in foreign waters. Of those, approximately only 104 were denied. In light of such apparently successful experience, she has concluded that the regime appears to be cumbersome, but has worked well in practice for the U.S. oceanographic research interests.[78] However, a review of the regime

---

71. Marston, n. 69 above, at 221. For a detailed analysis, see D. P. O'Connell, "The Theory of Maritime Jurisdiction," in *The International Law of the Sea*, I. A. Shearer ed. (Oxford: Clarendon Press, 2 vols., 1984): 733–746.

72. Marston, n. 69 above, at 222.

73. I. A. Shearer, "Problems of Jurisdiction and Law Enforcement Against Delinquent Vessels," *International and Comparative Law Quarterly* 35 (1986): 320–43.

74. *Id.* at 329–331.

75. *Id.* at 334–335 (referring to the EEZ); and Marston, n. 69 above, at 222.

76. T. Treves, "Principe du Consentement et Recherche Scientifique dans le Nouveau Droit de la Mer," *Revue General de Droit International* 84 (1980): 253–268, at 257–260 [hereinafter Treves 1980].

77. U.S. Commission on Ocean Policy, *An Ocean Blueprint for the 21st Century. Final Report* (Washington D.C., 2004), Part VIII, The Global Ocean: U.S. Participation in International Policy at 445–Recommendation 29–1: The United States should accede to the United Nations Convention on the Law of the Sea.

78. Gorina-Ysern, n. 1 above, at Chapter 1.

implementation around the world indicates that for many coastal States the MSR regime of UNCLOS remains nominal for lack of scientific and technological capacity. Most coastal States adhere to both the UNCLOS provisions as well as to the UN DOALOS Guide for its implementation.[79] However, in the absence of scientific and technological means, many coastal States have implemented legislation protecting their natural resource interests and remain suspicious of foreign MSR activities for lack of tangible benefits for the nation.[80] At the same time, many nations hope to engage in MSR collaboration with foreign researchers as a form of capacity building.[81] Good faith negotiations, transparency and compliance with international law are therefore critical.

The Importance of Negotiating Clearance (Article 250)

The failure of marine scientists, international lawyers and policy makers to agree on a definition of fundamental oceanographic research or MSR (as the preferred term used since 1972) underscores the relevance of Article 250 of UNCLOS: Communications concerning the MSR project shall be made through appropriate official channels, unless otherwise agreed.[82] It is generally accepted that MSR includes both pure and applied activities. Pure or fundamental MSR is not considered proprietary and its results are usually published openly (though they may still be subject to intellectual property claims). Applied marine science is characterized by its focus on exploration and exploitation of marine natural resources for economic gain. The results of this type of research are proprietary. The line between pure and applied marine research is hard to draw. As a result of this difficulty, the lack of a definition of MSR in the 1958 GCCS and the 1982 UNCLOS, reflects the inability of coastal and researching States to agree on criteria that would clearly identify what types of activities amount to pure or fundamental marine scientific research. States, however, agreed on a formula whereby, if

79. Office for Ocean Affairs and the Law of the Sea. *The Law of the Sea. Marine Scientific Research. A Guide to the Implementation of the Relevant Provisions of the United Nations Convention on the Law of the Sea* (New York: United Nations Publication, Sales No. E.91.V3, 1991) (now Division for Ocean Affairs and the Law of the Sea).

80. *Id.*

81. Intergovernmental Oceanographic Commission (IOC) of UNESCO, *Report of the Secretariat on the Results of the IOC Questionnaire 3 on the Practice of States in the Field of MAR and TMT, in Relation with Article 251 of UNCLOS* (Third Meeting of the Advisory Board of Experts on the Law of the Sea (IOC/ABE-LOS III) Lisbon, Portugal, May 12–15, 2003. Document IOC/ABE-LOS III/9, Paris, April 22, 2003.

82. For an extensive analysis of Article 250 as a *pactum de contrahendo/pactum de negotiando* and its function within international law, see Gorina-Ysern, n. 1 above, at 461–524.

certain conditions were met pursuant to Part XIII of UNCLOS, coastal State consent would be normally granted for the intended activities (not just mere notification by foreign researchers of a will to carry MSR activities in coastal State maritime areas). This formula, therefore, relies on effective communications between researching and coastal States of origin of marine biota. Since the adoption of UNCLOS, these communications are customarily pursued under its Article 250.[83]

83. For a thorough and systematic coverage of State practice, see Gorina-Ysern, n. 1 above, Part I: The Practice of States Regarding MSR Implementation 3–191. It reviews the practices of coastal nations in the Caribbean, Central America, South America, Asia-Pacific, Persian Gulf, East Mediterranean, Red Sea, Africa, and North America. It uses U.S. Department of State files from 1991 to 2001 and incorporates the following works: A. H. A. Soons, *Marine Scientific Research and the Law of the Sea*, n. 7 above; Treves, n. 76 above; T. Treves, "La notion d'utilization des espaces marins a fins pacifiques dans le nouveau droit de la mer," *Annuaire Française de Droit International* 698 (1980); and T. Treves, "Marine Research," *Encyclopedia of Public International Law*, 11: 207–10; A. Yankov, "A General Review of the New Convention on the Law of the Sea: Marine Science and Its Applications," in *Ocean Yearbook* 4, E. Mann Borgese and N. Ginsburg eds. (Chicago: University of Chicago Press, 1983): 150–75; A. J. Roach, "Marine Scientific Research and the New Law of the Sea," *Ocean Development and International Law* 27 (1996): 59–72; A. J Roach, "Research and Surveys in Coastal Waters," in Implementing the Provisions of the 1982 Law of the Sea Convention. Panel IV: Ocean Science and Technology under the 1982 Law of the Sea Convention (Newport, R.I.,: Center for Ocean Law and Policy, University of Virginia and U.S. Naval War College, March 15, 1996); and the following D. A. Ross and T. Landry, *Marine Scientific Research Boundaries and the Law of the Sea: Discussion and Inventory of National Claims* (Woods Hole: Woods Hole Oceanographic Institution, 1987); A. H. A. Soons, "Freedom of Scientific Research (The Developing Regime of Marine Scientific Research: Recent European Experience and State Practice," in *New Developments in Marine Science and Technology: Economic, Legal and Political Aspects of Change*, L. M. Alexander, S. Allen and L. C. Hanson eds. (Honolulu: The Law of the Sea Institute, 1988): 293; M. E. Brandon, *The 1982 United Nations Convention on the Law of the Sea Consent Regime for Marine Scientific Research: Caribbean Coastal State Responses to United States Clearance Requests* (unpublished Master of Marine Affairs paper, University of Rhode Island, 1997) (on file with author); J. A. Knauss and M. H. Katsourous, "Recent Experiences of the United States in Conducting Marine Scientific Research in Coastal State Exclusive Economic Zones," in *The Law of The Sea: What Lies Ahead?* T. A. Clingan, Jr. ed. (Honolulu: The Law of the Sea Institute, 1986): 297; D. Ross and J. Fenwick, "Marine Scientific Research: U.S. Perspective on Jurisdiction and International Cooperation," in *New Developments in Marine Science and Technology: Economic, Legal and Political Aspects of Change* (Honolulu: The Law of the Sea Institute, 1988): 308; J. Fenwick, *International Profiles On Marine Scientific Research* (Woods Hole: Woods Hole Oceanographic Institution, 1992): 181. For UN Reports, see *Oceans and the Law of the Sea. Report of the Secretary-General.* U.N.G.A. Doc A/56/58, 9 March 2001 at 82 (para. 465); *National Legislation 1989; The Law of the Sea. National Legislation on the Exclusive Economic Zone, The Economic Zone and the Exclusive Fishery Zone* (New York: UN Publication, Sales No. E.85.V.10, 1986); *The Law of the Sea. Current Developments in State Practice No. III* (New York: UN Publication, Sales No. E.92.V.13, 1992); *The Law of the Sea. Current*

Very few international law and ocean policy makers have remarked on the important role played by Article 250 of UNCLOS, as a homologue of Article 15 (1, 4 and 5) of the CBD,[84] (which does not have a similar Article 250 mechanism). Article 250 of UNCLOS serves as a substantive negotiation mechanism for seeking access by foreign vessels to maritime areas under the control of another nation, when access is requested with a view to collecting marine biota in the latter. Article 250 also serves as a procedural tool to negotiate and communicate changes in the conditions or circumstances surrounding access. The specific requirement that clearance for foreign research vessels and access to the marine biota of another coastal nation be

Developments in State Practice No. IV (New York: UN Publication, Sales No. E.95.V.10, 1995); and *Law of the Sea. Practice of States at the Time of Entry into Force of the United Nations Convention on the Law of the Sea* (New York: UN Publication, Sales No. E.94.V.13, 1994); and Office for Ocean Affairs and the Law of the Sea. The Law of the Sea, Marine Scientific Research. A Guide to the Implementation of the Relevant Provisions of the United Nations Convention on the Law of the Sea (New York: UN Publication, Sales No. E.91.V.3, 1991) [hereinafter OALOS Guide].

84. Article 15 provides:

1. Recognizing the sovereign rights of States over their natural resources, the authority to determine access to genetic resources rests with the national governments and is subject to national legislation.

2. Each Contracting Party shall endeavor to create conditions to facilitate access to genetic resources for environmentally sound uses by other Contracting Parties and not to impose restrictions that run counter to the objectives of this Convention.

3. For the purpose of this Convention, the genetic resources being provided by a Contracting Party, as referred to in this Article and Articles 16 and 19, are only those that are provided by Contracting Parties that are countries of origin of such resources or by the Parties that have acquired the genetic resources in accordance with this Convention.

4. Access, where granted, shall be on mutually agreed terms and subject to the provisions of this Article.

5. Access to genetic resources shall be subject to prior informed consent of the Contracting Party providing such resources, unless otherwise determined by that Party.

6. Each Contracting Party shall endeavor to develop and carry out scientific research based on genetic resources provided by other Contracting Parties with the full participation of, and where possible in, such Contracting Parties.

7. Each Contracting Party shall take legislative, administrative or policy measures, as appropriate, and in accordance with Articles 16 and 19 and, where necessary, through the financial mechanism established by Articles 20 and 21 with the aim of sharing in a fair and equitable way the results of research and development and the benefits arising from the commercial and other utilization of genetic resources with the Contracting Party providing such resources. Such sharing shall be upon mutually agreed terms.

negotiated through official channels is a welcome departure from the complex and rather unstructured ABS provisions of the CBD.

Part XIII of UNCLOS, establishing the MSR regime, sets out with the recognition that all States and competent international organizations have the right to conduct MSR activities,[85] and the duty to promote and facilitate the development and conduct of MSR in accordance with UNCLOS.[86] However, a research vessel hovering at the outer edge of another coastal nation's 200-nautical-mile Exclusive Economic Zone water-column boundary needs to have been cleared before it can undertake any MSR activities in the EEZ of that nation (200 NM to 12 NM),[87] or before it proceeds with research relating to the continental shelf (exceptionally to a distance of 350 NM and normally to 200 NM from the baseline from which the territorial sea is measured),[88] or with research on the inner section of the coastal nation's continental shelf (between 200 NM and the standard 12 NM outer edge of the territorial sea).[89]

If the vessel undertakes to carry MSR activities in conformity with the principles, criteria and conditions set out in UNCLOS Part XIII, exclusively for peaceful purposes, and in order to increase scientific knowledge of the marine environment for the benefit of all humankind, the coastal State is

85. UNCLOS, n. 7 above, Part XIII, Section 1, Article 238. The rights of neighboring land-locked and geographically disadvantaged States with respect to MSR are recognized in Section 3, Article 254.

86. *Id.* at Article 239.

87. UNCLOS, n. 7 above, Arts. 55 and 57. In the EEZ the coastal State enjoys jurisdiction with regard to marine scientific research (Article 56.1(b)(ii); and sovereign rights for the purpose of exploring, exploiting, conserving and managing the natural resources, whether living or non-living of the waters superjacent to the sea-bed and of the sea-bed and its subsoil, and with regard to other activities for the economic exploitation and exploration of the zone, such as the production of energy from the water, currents and winds.

88. UNCLOS, n. 7 above, Arts. 76.6 and Article 246.6 regulate claims to and MSR relating to the 350 NM exceptional outer limit of the continental shelf when the coastal State may have publicly designated these as areas in which exploitation or detailed exploratory operations are occurring or will occur within a reasonable period of time.

89. *Id.* at Art. 76. Access to the EEZ and the continental shelf of a foreign coastal State for the conduct of MSR activities requires the consent of the latter, as provided for in Art. 246.2: MSR in these zones "shall be conducted with the consent of the coastal State". State practice indicates that a majority of States implements Art. 50 by requiring that MSR clearances be negotiated through official channels. Most States require six month's lead time to process foreign clearance for MSR activities in their EEZs and continental shelves, pursuant to Art. 248. However, there is a significant number of coastal States which implements a more flexible three to six month lead time in the Caribbean, South Pacific (possibly expanded to 6 months under new regional guidelines), Asia and Europe.

bound to grant its consent without delay,[90] since these would be the defining characteristics (or the essence) of pure or fundamental marine scientific research. If, on the other hand, the vessel does not have any clearance, or deviates from the conditions provided for in the clearance granted, the coastal State may order the vessel to suspend the activities in progress, or to cease the MSR activities altogether, in the EEZ and the continental shelf areas.[91] For MSR purposes, the waters of the water column beyond 12 nautical miles territorial sea boundary do not partake of the regime of the high seas. The relevance of the clearance process pursuant to Article 250 of UNCLOS is clear. It consists of the communications through appropriate official channels between coastal State authorities and the authorities of the flag that the research vessel flies. Clearance must be sought at least six months prior to the intended start of MSR activities, unless the parties otherwise agree.[92]

The clearance process amounts to a procedural means toward legally binding ends, as the official involvement of a State seeking access to foreign waters on behalf of its nationals is not devoid of consequences at international law.[93] The agreements reached through meaningful, timely and effective communications pursuant to Article 250 are of the essence in the successful conduct of MSR activities worldwide. The clearance agreement will be politically binding, legally binding, or both, depending on the intention of the parties to it, and several other factors. The latter include the type of diplomatic correspondence used by the negotiating parties, the rank and capacity of the official negotiating on behalf of each State, the subject matter covered in the final clearance documents, and the detrimental reliance that may arise for both parties if either of them breaches the conditions placed by the other party and the obligations that bind both under Part XIII of UNCLOS, as well as under those provisions that have reached the status of customary international law relating to MSR.[94]

The limited involvement (or literature produced) by diplomatic embassy staff and government officials in the processing of clearance

90. *Id.* at Art. 246(3).

91. *Id.* at Art. 253.

92. Id. at Art. 248.

93. The consent regime of Part XIII, UNCLOS, n. 7 above, contains terms that postpone certain mutual obligations relating to the conduct of MSR in foreign waters. These mutual obligations cannot simply be communicated or notified. They must be negotiated because conditions may differ for access to different maritime zones and for access to the results arising from MSR activities undertaken in the different zones. The source of the general obligation to negotiate is clearly established because the criteria for access are indeterminate and need elaboration.

94. A majority of States implements Article 250 of UNCLOS by requiring that MSR clearance be negotiated through official channels. State practice compiled and reported in Gorina-Ysern, n. 1 above, Conclusions, at 603.

requests that straddle between UNCLOS, the CBD, CITES, and yield biotech patent activity is regrettable. There are also very few studies or literature on how ABS Agreements arising under the CBD are incorporated and integrated into clearance requests pursuant to UNCLOS for access by foreign researchers for the conduct of MSR activities, marine biogenetic research, or other forms of applied marine research for ulterior commercial gain in areas under coastal State maritime control. This is a great lacuna in our understanding of State practice that will require pressure on those with the relevant information to make it available for legal and policy research and public scrutiny.

The Consent Regime of Article 246

Research vessel access to areas under coastal State sovereign rights and jurisdiction is subject to four general principles,[95] one prohibition,[96] information criteria,[97] and to specific conditions relating to coastal State participation in the research activities, access to the research data, samples and results, and removal of installations and equipment after completing the research.[98] The function of Article 246 of UNCLOS is to safeguard the

95. UNCLOS, n. 7 above, at Art. 240. The principles also apply to MSR carried out on the high seas and in the Area: (a) the activities shall be carried out exclusively for peaceful purposes; (b) using appropriate scientific methods and means compatible with UNCLOS; (c) the activities shall not unjustifiably interfere with other legitimate uses of the sea compatible with UNCLOS and shall be duly respected in the course of such uses; and (d) the activities shall comply with all relevant regulations adopted under UNCLOS, including those for the protection and preservation of the marine environment.

96. *Id.* Article 241 provides that MSR activities shall not constitute the legal basis for any claim to any part of the marine environment or its resources.

97. *Id.* Article 248 requires the researching State or international organization to provide details about the nature and objectives of the project, the methods and means to be used, including a complete description of the vessel and its scientific equipment, the precise geographical areas where the research is intended, the dates of first appearance and final departure of the vessel, or deployment of the equipment, the name of the person and institution in charge of the project, and an estimate of whether the coastal State personnel should be able to participate or be represented in the project. Correlative to Article 248 is 252 providing for a regime of implied consent that it is very rarely applied in the practice of the majority of States worldwide. In essence, it would allow the research vessel to initiate the research if, having submitted all of the required information to the coastal State six months in advance of commencement of the MSR activities, it has not received any communication from the coastal State objecting to the research on given grounds that include insufficient or inaccurate information, and pre-existing post cruise obligations that have not been fulfilled.

98. *Id.* at Art. 249.

sovereign rights that the coastal State enjoys over the natural resources of the continental shelf and the EEZ.[99] UNCLOS achieved this aim with great difficulties,[100] through the requirement for prior coastal State consent for the conduct of any MSR in these zones.[101] The recognition that coastal States have discretion to withhold consent according to the above factors reinforces the need to negotiate the details for the exercise of such discretion, particularly in the absence of compulsory mechanisms for the settlement of disputes relating to the exercise of coastal State discretion to deny its consent to provide clearance for the foreign research vessel.[102]

99. As Treves observed [in translation]: "Marine scientific research, a technical matter and relatively marginal in appearance, became one of the most delicate problems in the formation of the new law of the sea." Treves, n. 76 above, at 253. Not having the means to assess whether proposed MSR activities were related to resources or to military research in areas under national jurisdiction, during UNCLOS III, the G–77 advocated for a consent regime as a safeguard for coastal State interests. As a result of this lack of means, G–77 rejected claims that a definition of MSR distinguishing between research of a purely scientific nature and research related to resources could be the basis for a regime of consent for the latter and mere notification for the former.

100. See U.N. G.A.O.R. (Doc. A/Conf. 62/C.3/L.17 of August 23, 1974, summarizing, the positions adopted by Brazil, Pakistan, Kenya, India, Tanzania, Ecuador, Peru, Colombia, Venezuela and Argentina for a regime of coastal State consent with respect to any MSR activities in zones under national jurisdiction, and requirements for coastal State participation, representation, and other conditions relating to access to and publication of research results. See also the position of U.S., Italy, LLGDS, FRG, Netherlands, Australia, Mexico and the USSR (later changing its position) with respect to freedom to conduct MSR activities beyond the territorial sea. The 1975 Summary Records show the divisions at UNCLOS III on the issue whether coastal States should have the right to a full consent regime for all research, a consent regime for research relating to resources, and a notification regime for MSR activities. 1975 Summary Records, Third Committee, 11 March–7 May 1975, reproduced in R. Platzoder, *Third United Nations Conference on the Law of the Sea: Documents, Vol. XI* (Dobbs Ferry, New York: Oceana Publications, Inc. 1987): 263–297. The consent regime divided delegations until the adoption of the Informal Composite Negotiating Text (ICNT) of 1977 A/Conf.62/C.3/L.13 Rev.2 (Iraq); A/Conf.62/C.3/L.19 (Austria and others); A/Conf.62/C.3/L.26 (Bulgaria and others) and A/Conf.62/C.3/L.28 (Netherlands); A/Conf.62/C.3/L.29 (Colombia, El Salvador, Mexico and Nigeria).

101. Pursuant to Article 246.5, UNCLOS, a coastal State may deny its consent for (a) research of direct significance for the exploration or exploitation of natural living or non-living resources, (b) research which involves drilling into the continental shelf, the use of explosives or the introduction of harmful substances into the marine environment, and (c) research requiring the construction, operation or use of artificial islands, installations and structures. Consent may also be denied if the information relating to the nature and objectives of the research provided under Article 248 is inaccurate, or where outstanding obligations exist from a prior research project by the same entity seeking consent.

102. Section 6 of Part XIII, Articles 264–265 regulates the settlement of disputes under Part XV, sections 2 and 3 of UNCLOS. It does not extend to disputes

While in appearance the power of the coastal State seems enhanced by Article 246, in practice, an oppressive exercise of the right to withhold consent may have extremely deleterious consequences for the coastal State, because researching States may not schedule their research vessels to conduct any MSR in areas under the control of the coastal State. The beneficial opportunities that might have derived from interaction between local scientists and foreign oceanographers may be lost if such opportunities for capacity building are dismissed on the grounds of excessive mistrust of foreign researchers' motives.[103]

Inversely, the discretion conferred to coastal States to evaluate through a series of "tests" the true nature of the activities intended by the foreign research vessel is the best means to safeguard their bargaining power with regards to the natural resources, whether living or non-living, located within the EEZ and on the continental shelf.[104] The consequences of losing the effective power to bargain were pointed out by Professor D.P. O'Connell in the *Aegean Sea Continental Shelf Case.*[105] This is the only international case bearing on the conduct of marine research activities, as distinct from exploration for resources, ever brought before the International Court of Justice. The claim dealt with unauthorized research activities carried out by Turkey and bearing directly on oil and gas resources located in the continental shelf claimed by Greece. In a classic passage Professor O'Connell observed:

questioning the exercise of coastal State discretion regarding consent and/or its decision to order the suspension or cessation of MSR activities underway in its EEZ or continental shelf pursuant to Article 253. In such cases, Section 6 provides, instead, for interim measures, during which MSR activities cannot be conducted or continued without express coastal State consent.

103. For a survey of regional State practices, see Gorina-Ysern, n. 1 above, at Chapter 1.

104. Some writers have forgotten that the *travaux préparatoires* leading to the adoption of UNCLOS matter a great deal, because the full records of UNCLOS III negotiations were never released as a result of the rules of procedure adopted by the participants. Decisions were not made strictly by a vote, but through general consensus that resulted in a "package deal." The Chairs of the committees also enforced the "gentlemen's agreement" rule according to which certain opinions expressed in some sessions would not be reported to the public or officially, so that delegations would express their interests freely. Therefore, only those that attended all of the sessions from 1974 to 1982 would be able to reveal what were the concerns of delegates regarding intellectual property rights and proprietary information in the context of marine science, other than those already mentioned above relating to Article 241 of UNCLOS ("*Marine scientific research activities shall not constitute the legal basis for any claim to any part of the marine environment or its resources*").

105. International Court of Justice, *Reports of Judgments, Advisory Opinions and Orders* (1976) (Greece v. Turkey) I.C.J. Pleadings, Oral Arguments, Documents, 624 (1980).

We all know that oil companies are highly secretive and jealous as to the knowledge they acquire of the fields which they are exploiting, and they have good reasons for cherishing their knowledge. These include the suppression of competition and the diversification of programs. Governments have the same motives as those whom they license to exploit. Their total discretion is impaired if someone else has access to the knowledge without their consent. If a foreign country has that knowledge, whether or not the claimant to the continental shelf has it in fact or not, it is shared knowledge available for economic and political exploitation. . . . It does not matter how one characterizes seismic activity, as exploration or research, the result is the same and that is what counts. Indeed, the distinction is a play upon words. The coastal State still has the exclusivity with respect to knowledge of the geophysics of the area of sovereign rights.[106]

The reference in the last sentence to "exclusivity with respect of knowledge of the geophysics of the area of sovereign rights" is critical. If the term "biochemistry" were used in place of the term "geophysics", a valid argument can be made: the coastal State, irrespective of whether a foreign nation or a foreign juridical person is requesting access into areas under coastal State sovereign rights for MSR or for bioprospecting purposes, "*still has the exclusivity with respect to the knowledge of the [biochemistry] of the area of sovereign rights*" [emphasis added]. This argument is particularly powerful when the coastal State: (a) grants access to its areas of sovereign rights (i.e., the continental shelf) so that a foreign research team can collect marine biota for declared non-commercial purposes; and (b) relies on foreign government official communications (pursuant to Article 250 of UNCLOS) attesting to the purely scientific nature of the activities on board a research vessel flying its flag. What remedy does the law offer to a coastal State whose trust in the foregoing statements has been breached? Would Professor O'Connell's observations about the "loss of bargaining power" by the coastal State resonate with current value? Would the "mutually beneficial terms" of the CBD's ABS Agreements apply here?

UNCLOS Article 246.5(a) permits the coastal State to deny its consent for "research of direct significance for the exploration or exploitation of natural living or non-living resources." A balanced implementation of this article helps the coastal State to guard against losing its bargaining power to negotiate with third parties for the development of its natural resources. In the Galapagos Case Study,[107] Gorina-Ysern has documented how a coastal

---

106. I.C.J. Pleadings, 1980 at 108.

107. Gorina-Ysern, n. 1 above, at 379–387. See the Case Study on the clearance of a U.S. Research Vessel seeking permission to undertake marine biomedical research in the Galapagos Islands. Although the U.S. Department of State was successful in arguing that it would experience a loss (detrimental reliance) if the

State can increase its bargaining power by withdrawing clearance, after having granted it. Such withdrawal may entitle the nation of the vessel's flag to raise an estoppel argument (i.e., detrimental reliance for the academic institution in incurring the expense of fitting the ship for the oceanographic research cruise). However, the coastal nation retains the discretion to refuse entry to a foreign research vessel when the chief scientist alleges the intent to conduct purely scientific research but, on balance, the evidence suggests the academic project has an underlying economic pursuit in collaboration with industry, and that royalties over potential benefits from the research have been negotiated but not disclosed to the coastal State of origin of the biogenetic resources. The coastal State is authorized to request a formal agreement to protect its resource interests prior to granting clearance. As the Galapagos Case Study shows, the estoppel argument is likely to prevail in the diplomatic arena.

The highly competitive and valuable nature of the activities described above, and the involvement of biotech and pharmaceutical industries, may foster a climate of secrecy among academic researchers until intellectual property rights are considered secured.[108] Although the purpose of the patent system is to maximize openness and release of information in exchange for a monopoly of use after the patent has been granted, secrecy and non-disclosure or delayed disclosure of information are legitimate tools within the intellectual property rights (IPR) system, as the latter is geared toward fostering competitive innovation.[109] It is therefore unclear whether confidential treatment of discoveries and inventions that use marine biota

clearance already granted were cancelled by the Ecuadorian government, the Charles Darwin Research Station and the Galapagos National Park Service succeeded in forcing the oceanographic institution to reveal a 2% financial interest in any bioactive compound that would be extracted from the collected microorganisms. This financial interest was not declared until the project was jeopardized on the Ecuadorian side.

108. Most Western universities in industrially developed researching States have established intellectual property rights (IPR) policies to deal with ownership of IPRs arising from inventions, patents, technology transfer and licensing. In the US, these policies are mandated under the 1980 Bayle-Dole Act (U.S.). See Public/ Private Partnerships in Science and Technology: An Overview (Organization for Economic Cooperation and Development (OEDC). 1–9 available online: <http:// www.oecd.org/EN/document/0,EN-document–54–1-no21–10044–54,00.html>.

109. This tension between regimes is best exemplified by "know-how." Valuable, proprietary information of a technical nature that may be licensed to industry despite its lack of patent protection. Know-how is factual knowledge not capable of precise, separate description, but that when used in an accumulated form, after being acquired as a result of trial and error, gives the one acquiring it an ability to produce something that he or she otherwise would not have known how to produce with the same accuracy or precision found necessary for commercial success. Chapman, n. 108 above, at 303–304.

may discourage marine scientists from engaging in direct forms of capacity building with colleagues from less industrialized coastal nations, as the latter participate as on-board observers from the coastal State in whose maritime areas of sovereign rights the research vessel operates. Coastal States make participation on board foreign research vessels in national waters mandatory and regard it as a low cost and effective means to bridge the gap between the haves and the have-nots. UNCLOS does not specifically mandate the transfer of know-how through two-way contacts between oceanographers and foreign participants or observers on board research vessels. However, this form of "capacity building" benefits marine science in general.[110]

Proprietary Information and Unjust Enrichment (Articles 241 and 249.2)

UNCLOS Articles 241 and 249.2 secure coastal State resource interests and protect its bargaining power. Article 241 provides that MSR activities "shall not be used as the legal basis for any claim to any part of the marine environment or its resources."[111] Curiously, this article has received virtually

---

110. See Gorina-Ysern, n. 1 above, Chapter 6. Mr. Elie Jarmache, Chair of the IOC Advisory Body of Experts on the Law of the Sea (IOC/ABE-LOS) opened the Fifth Meeting of IOC/ABE-LOS on Monday, 11 April 2005 in Buenos Aires, Argentina. Resolution EC XXVII–8 and paragraph 11 of the UNGA Resolution 59/24 instructed the IOC Secretariat to disseminate the "IOC Criteria and Guidelines on the Transfer of Marine Technology," considered at the 5th meeting. IOC/ABE-LOS V/3prov.

111. *Report of the Ad Hoc Committee to Study the Peaceful Uses of the Sea-Bed and the Ocean Floor Beyond the Limits of National Jurisdiction* (New York: United Nations, 1968). During the Ad Hoc Committee meetings concerns were expressed that scientific studies might create rights of exploitation of the seabed and the ocean floor. The UN Economic and Technical Committee (ECOTEC) gave assurances that research results would be published and made available to all countries. (*Id.* at 39.) The Report recommended to the UNGA the widest possible dissemination of scientific knowledge. In the *1969 Report of the Committee on the Peaceful Uses of the Sea-Bed and the Ocean Floor Beyond the Limits of National Jurisdiction* (SBC Report) (GAOR 24th Sess., Supp. No. 22, A/7622, 1969), further concerns were expressed about scientific research becoming the legal basis for claims to exploration and exploitation of ocean resources. See A/AC.138/SC.1/3 by the Informal Drafting Group. Its Report laid down the principle that: "(vi) no rights of sovereignty or exploitation are implied in the carrying out of scientific research," 1969 SBC Report at 33–43. However, this principle was not accepted by a number of delegations, including the UK and Japan, id. at 23. The 1970 SBC Report (Supp. No. 21, A/8021) United Nations, New York 1970, rejected a licencing system for the exploration of seabed resources and the conduct of scientific research. These activities, it was stressed, should not constitute the legal basis for claims. This principle was recognized in the *Declaration of Principles Governing the Seabed and the Subsoil Thereof Beyond the Limits of National Jurisdiction* (UNGA Res. 2749 (XXV) of 17 December 1970) receiving 108

no attention in international law literature, though its negotiating history identifies core concerns not yet resolved among developed and developing nations over the role of foreign science in the appraisal of natural resources located within the confines of national jurisdiction. At the core of these concerns was the issue of proprietary and non-proprietary research and the need to find a definition of MSR in the final Convention draft that would guarantee that commercially oriented marine research would not be disguised as pure science. There was no agreement on such a definition and the issue of intellectual property rights over data, samples and results was dropped, leaving lacunae in the UNCLOS. Although important, Articles 241 and 249.2 must be considered a fragile triumph for less industrialized coastal States. In combination with Articles 250 and 246.5, Articles 241 and 249.2 protect coastal State interests over foreign access to biogenetic resources located in areas under the sovereignty, sovereign rights, and jurisdiction of the coastal State, independently of whether the coastal State is a party to the CBD or not. Article 249.2 of UNCLOS, has a similar effect to Article 15 CBD. Article 249.2 entitles the coastal State "to require *prior agreement* for making internationally available the research results of a project of direct significance for the exploration and exploitation of natural resources."

Not very well-known or discussed, Article 249.2 of UNCLOS, entitles the coastal State to impose restrictions on the release of certain information by

---

votes in favor, none against, and 14 abstentions. The principle was formulated as follows: "Point 10. No such activity [scientific research] shall form the basis for any claim to any part of the ocean or its resources." The principle was restricted to the "Area" beyond national jurisdiction. Discussions and developments with respect to the prohibition to use MSR as the legal basis for claims continued to be discussed during 1972 and on 19 May 1972 an UNCTAD Conference issued Resolution 52 (III) relating to the right of the coastal State to dispose of the resources of its adjacent seas for the benefit of its population. See also SBC Report 1972, at 60–61, where the terms "Marine Scientific Research" were used for the first time as activities carried out for the benefit of humankind, executed with the participation by coastal States in planning programs and with availability of research results. MSR would not produce harmful effects on the marine environment; any samples of resources should not be taken in commercial quantities and the activities would not constitute the legal basis for claims to commercial, exploration or exploitation rights. See Canadian proposal A/AC.138.SCIII/L.18; the 1973 SBC Report acknowledged the Addis Ababa Declaration adopted on 24 May 1973 by the Organization of African Unity, recognizing the existence of an Exclusive Economic Zone beyond the territorial sea not exceeding 200 nautical miles from the baseline from which the territorial sea is measured over which coastal States enjoyed permanent sovereignty over all living and mineral resources, thus, excluding MSR as the legal basis for claims in these areas. During UNCLOS the issue of MSR as the legal basis for claims was raised in A/Conf.63/C.3/L.17 of 23 August 1974 summarizing delegations main positions with respect to dissemination and publication of MSR results and excluding the use of MSR activities as the legal basis for claims.

foreign researchers. If information with a direct bearing on the exploitation of the natural resources, living or non-living, of the coastal State were actually placed in the "public domain" or were appropriated by third parties with commercial rather than purely scientific aims, and no benefit accrued to the coastal State, there would ensue a loss for the coastal State and an unjust enrichment for those in the possession of the information. The similarity of purposes between the ABS requirements of Article 15 of CBD and UNCLOS Article 249.2 is quite outstanding.

In our view, the bona fide statements of the researcher become the key to the implementation of Part XIII of the UNCLOS regime. Conduct that refuses to reach prior agreement regarding research results directly significant for the exploration and exploitation of coastal State natural resources, or that seeks to underplay the resource-oriented significance of the intended research, would diminish the bargaining power of the coastal State. If not corrected by some measure, such conduct does not suggest the presence of bona fides. It could amount, instead, to an unjust enrichment by the party refusing to comply with the requirement of Article 249.2 of UNCLOS.[112] Samuel observes:

> There are some situations ... where the distinction between obligation wrongs and property rights is not so easy to determine; for example, if a defendant misuses another's property in order to make a profit for himself this can be seen either as a "wrong" vis-à-vis the owner of a "right" vis-à-vis the profit (*fructus*) in the defendant's patrimony. If, however, it is seen as a wrong there is something of a problem when it comes to assessing damages in that the plaintiff may well have suffered little or no damage. In these situations the role of the damages has to change; instead of compensation being measured in terms of the plaintiff's loss, they have to be assessed with reference to the defendant's profit or benefit, and this in effect turns a damages action into one that is closer to a debt in restitution. In fact, even if the defendant's profit could be turned into a plaintiff's *lucrum cessans*

---

112. B. Dickson, "Unjust Enrichment Claims: A Comparative Overview," *Commonwealth Law Reports*, 54 (1995): 100–126; see also R. Goff (now Lord Goff, H.L.) and Jones, *The Law of Restitution* (1993). A party receives a benefit at the expense of another party and the retention of the benefit does not arise from a legal entitlement. In common law countries such as Australia, Canada, England, Ireland, most States in the U.S. and New Zealand, the doctrine of unjust enrichment is applied by courts as a restitutory remedy recognized in the American Law Institute Restatement of the Law on Restitution (1937). In European civil law systems, it is recognized and applied in Austria, France and Germany, Greece, Italy, the Netherlands, Spain, and Switzerland. It is also applied in Japan. In mixed legal systems it is recognized in Scotland, South Africa, Quebec, and Israel.

(failure to gain) loss there may still be a reluctance to recognize this as a legally protected interest, at least in the absence of contract or fraud.[113]

A coastal State of origin of biogenetic resources wishing to raise a claim of unjust enrichment against foreign researchers will need to draw a factual time-line and resort to historical research and analysis. The task at hand will not be trivial and the advocates against the principle that unjust enrichment may have taken place may be mighty.

CRITICAL ENTRY INTO FORCE OF RELEVANT TREATIES (1964, 1975, 1990, and 1994)

There are at least three legal regimes prior to the entry into force of UNCLOS (1994) and the CBD (1993) which regulate the conduct of marine research activities on certain types of biological resources within certain areas of coastal State sovereign rights.[114] These regimes are by order of their entry into force: a) the 1958 GCCS (entered into force 1964), b) the 1973 CITES (entered into force 1975), and c) the 1969 VCLT (entered into force 1990). Our goal in this section is to illustrate how Article 22 of the CBD may be integrated with prior conventional law provisions and principles relating to MSR and bioprospecting.

The VCTL entered into force in 1990 and provides that a treaty "shall be interpreted in good faith in accordance with the ordinary meaning to be given to the terms of the treaty in their context and in the light of its object and purpose."[115] The context comprises the text, preamble and annexes, related prior agreements among the parties "in connection with the conclusion of the treaty," or any other similar instrument thereof, including those entered into subsequently.[116] The preparatory work of the treaty and the circumstances of its conclusion are considered a valid means of supplementary interpretation. These means should be used to avoid

---

113. G. Samuel, "Property Notions in the Law of Obligations," *Commonwealth Law Journal* 53 (1994): 524–545.

114. Few authors argue that under UNCLOS coastal States can regulate the conduct of MSR activities; the literature on the law of the sea has not developed sufficiently on the point of whether research on genetic resources is covered under UNCLOS. Our own view is that UNCLOS covers MSR and bioprospecting of genetic resources.

115. Article 31(1) Vienna Convention on the Law of Treaties, May 23, 1969, U.N. Doc. A/CONF.39/2 (entered into force Jan. 27, 1990), reproduced in *International Legal Materials* 8 (1969): 769. The U.S. has not ratified.

116. VCLT, Article 31(2–3).

ambiguous or obscure meanings as well as interpretations that are "manifestly absurd or unreasonable."[117]

The criteria of the VCLT allow us to interpret the provisions of the GCCS and UNCLOS to ascertain the meaning of key terms. For example, the "marine environment" (not defined in either convention) can be said to encompass the mass of water beyond the boundaries of a State's land domain, the submerged areas beneath that body of water, all the organic and inorganic substances found therein, and the boundary between the water and the air above it. Within the boundaries of the marine environment there are living and non-living resources.[118] A "resource" (not defined in the law of the sea conventions) is "a natural source of wealth or revenue."[119]

Marine resources are not defined either in the GCCS or in UNCLOS. Marine resources are in a constant state of discovery as technology and research improve.[120] They include geological resources, minerals of other origin, energy resources such as wind and currents, and living resources. The living resources found in a nation's EEZ include, but are not limited to, fish, anadromous stocks, catadromous species, marine mammals, and highly migratory species.[121] MSR activities, exploration and commercial exploitation of the EEZ may also target other activities such as the creation of energy from waters, currents and winds.[122] In the EEZ, coastal States enjoy sovereign rights "for the purpose of exploring, exploiting, conserving and managing the natural resources, whether living or non-living of the waters superjacent to the sea-bed and of the sea-bed and its subsoil."[123] The resources of the continental shelf (mineral and other non-living resources of the seabed and subsoil together with living organisms belonging to the sedentary species),[124] are dealt with in the next section. UNCLOS provides

117. *Id.* at Art. 32.

118. P. M. Fye, A. E. Maxwell, K. O. Emery and B. H. Ketchum, "Ocean Science and Marine Resources," in *Uses of the Seas,* E. A. Gullion ed. (Englewood Cliffs: Prentice-Hall, Inc., 1968): 17–68.

119. *Webster's Ninth New Collegiate Dictionary* (1984): 1,004.

120. Oceanographers are increasingly interested in the study of marine germplasm made up by organisms and microorganisms and species of marine flora and fauna found in hydrothermal vents, seamounts, deep-sea trenches, deep-water, reef-forming corals, cold seeps and pockmarks, gas hydrates, submarine canyons, and in seabirds, cetaceans, and transboundary fish stocks. The Southampton Oceanography Centre and Dr. A. C. de Fontaubert, *The Status of Natural Resources on the High-Seas* (Gland: WWF International, May 2001).

121. UNCLOS, n. 7 above, Arts. 66 (anadromous stocks), 67 (catadromous species), 65 (marine mammals) and 64 (highly migratory species).

122. Art. 56.

123. Art. 56.1(a).

124. Art. 77.4. Sedentary species are organism which, "at the harvestable stage, either are immobile on or under the sea-bed or are unable to move, except in constant physical contact with the sea-bed or the subsoil."

that the resources of The Area comprise all solid, liquid or gaseous resources *in situ,* at or beneath the seabed, including polymetallic nodules.[125] There are many new resources not specifically mentioned in UNCLOS, but the broad references to resources can be interpreted to include all the minerals, flora and fauna contained within the marine environment.

The Geneva Convention on the Continental Shelf

The GCCS entered into force on June 10, 1964. States parties to the GCCS were bound to comply with the provisions outlined below until the entry into force of UNCLOS in 1994, and beyond that date if they did not become parties to the latter. Disregard of the provisions of the GCCS would have amounted to a breach of international law among its parties.[126]

The GCCS does not define marine scientific research (a term that it does not use), but it introduces a distinction between "pure" and "applied" scientific research for the purpose of allowing coastal States to exercise a right to grant or to withdraw their consent with respect to the conduct of fundamental oceanographic or other scientific research concerning the continental shelf.[127] Coastal State consent is required for *any research concerning the continental shelf and undertaken there.* The coastal State shall not normally withhold its consent if the request is made by a qualified institution *with a view to purely scientific research into the physical or biological characteristics of the continental shelf,* provided certain conditions are complied with. First, the coastal State has the right, if it so desires, to participate or to be represented in the research. Second, research results should be published.[128]

Article 2.1 of the GCCS, recognizes the sovereign rights of the coastal State for the purpose of exploring and exploiting the natural resources of

125. UNCLOS, n. 7 above, Part V (Exclusive Economic Zone), Part VI (Continental Shelf) and Part XI (The Area).

126. GCCS, n. 6 above, at Art. 11; UNCLOS, n. 7 above, Art. 311.

127. Art. 5.1 and 5.8. The GCCS is one of the four Conventions adopted by the Geneva Conference on the Law of the Sea, called by General Assembly Resolution 1105 (XI) of 21 February 1957. The Conference began its work on 24 February 1958 and the final Drafts of the 1958 Geneva Conventions on the Law of the Sea were opened for signature on April 28, 1958. Article 5.1 of the GCCS refers to fundamental oceanographic research and other scientific research carried out with the intention of open publication. States are under a duty not to interfere with research to be undertaken in the waters covering the continental shelf. Arts. 5.1 and 5.8, GCCS constitute the first legal regime for marine scientific research.

128. CGCS, n. 6 above, at Art. 5.8.

the continental shelf. Article 2.4 of the GCCS defines the natural resources of the continental shelf as those including

> the mineral and other non-living resources of the sea-bed and subsoil *together with living organisms belonging to the sedentary species,* that is to say, organisms which, at the harvestable stage, either are immobile on or under the seabed or are unable to move except in constant physical contact with the seabed or the subsoil [italics added].

The definition is broad (i.e., living organisms) and can be considered broader (i.e., organisms belonging, *as in symbiosis,* to the sedentary species). The reference to "biological characteristics of the continental shelf" in the second paragraph of Article 5.8, would include studies of marine flora, coral reefs,[129] benthic species (such as shrimp),[130] and sedentary fisheries.[131] These resources refer to organisms virtually in constant physical contact with the seabed or subsoil, including a range of invertebrates such as sponges, most cnidarians (i.e., anemones, corals, hydroids), most parasite flatworms attached to rocky coasts and reefs, segmented worms and roundworms, the vast majority of mollusks, minor phyla living in seabed muds, marine arthropods, crustaceans (including ostracoda, maxillopoda and malacostraca),[132] echinoderms and invertebrate chordates.[133] It also includes microorganisms (i.e., bacteria, viruses, fungi, and other microscopic plants and animals). To argue otherwise would require a clear exclusion arising from the 1958 text itself or its preparatory work.[134] If the research

129. The Encyclopedia of Oceanography refers to the wide variety of benthic, demersal and other forms of life as natural resources of the nearshore zone. See also S. Schlee, *The Edge of an Unfamiliar World. A History of Oceanography* (1973). Chapter IV, Reefs, Rocks and Oozes: Geological Oceanography: 139–169.

130. Inter-American Council of Jurists, Final Act of the Third Meeting, Mexico City, January 17–February 4, 1956, Resolution XIII, pp. 36–37, reproduced in *Department of State Bulletin* 34 (1956): 298–299.

131. Sedentary fisheries are "natural resources permanently attached to the bed of the sea" as defined in U.N. Doc. A/CN.4/97 relating to the "Regime of the High Seas and Regime of the Territorial Sea". Report by J. P. François, Special Rapporteur. International Law Commission, *Yearbook of the International Law Commission* II (1956): 7. Sedentary fisheries reproduce in the shallow waters of the continental shelf and are seldom encountered at a depth greater that 200 meters.

132. Lobsters and crabs were not included, see n. 134 below.

133. D. Burnie and D. E. Wilson, eds., *Animal. The Definitive Visual Guide to the World's Wildlife* (Washington, D.C.: Smithsonian Institution, 2001): 522 et seq.

134. For example, F. M. Armas Pfirter reports that crustaceans (i.e., lobsters and crabs) were deleted from Article 2 as their status as sedentary species on account of the distance they traveled was left unresolved. F. M. Armas Pfirter, *Legal Implications Related to Management of Seabed Living Resources in "the Area" under UNCLOS* (Paper presented to the Legal and Technical Commission, International Seabed Authority, Tenth Session).

has such commercial aims, the coastal State reserves the right to negotiate the conditions of access by foreign researchers. This seems to be the plain meaning of Article 5.8 within its natural context.

The language of the GCCS, suggests that purely scientific research into the biological characteristics of continental shelf species can include studies ranging from taxonomy to identification of the biogenetic properties of the species targeted (biological characteristics). It would seem artificial or unreasonable to argue that purely scientific research into the biogenetic characteristics of coastal State continental shelf species is excluded because it is not mentioned or known, particularly as the science of genetics was given its name in 1909 by British biologist William Bateson.[135] What the GCCS excludes from its *regime of pure science* is the possibility that the species collected will be subsequently used in further studies leading to inventions subject to patents, and that those patents will be licensed to industry for profit, without any returns to the coastal State, under the guise that the research was not resource-oriented.[136] The entry into force of the CBD cannot override obligations incurred under the GCCS. However, in light of the few cross-disciplinary studies available, it may prove difficult (if not impossible) to ascertain the extent of those obligations, and only a case-by-case analysis can address the particular characteristics of each proprietary claim over the continental shelf resources of another State.

Convention on the International Trade in Endangered Species of Wild Flora and Fauna (CITES)

CITES operates through special government authorities in Member States charged with the implementation of an import/export control system that includes documentation from the export country where the species is located, monitoring of any imports of the species by the authority in the import country, and the setting of export quotas where appropriate.[137] A

---

135. Watson, n. 28 above, at 5.

136. Arts. 308.1 and 2 of UNCLOS dealing with entry into force of UNCLOS provisions. Legal complexities and the cost of raising legal claims, would postulate against raising claims against holders of patents over marine natural products issued after 1964 (date of entry into force of the 1958 GCCS); however, it is not implausible that the latter might owe obligations arising from duties relating to the exploration or commercial exploitation of coastal States natural resources on the basis of species collected for the purpose of conducting subsequent research into novel compounds for commercial gain. Without coastal State consent such collection would not have been permissible. If consent was granted upon request, it would be illustrative to know the details of the agreements reached and the conditions adopted between coastal State authorities and the foreign Chief Scientist (or his or her institution).

137. See <http://www.nmfs.noaa.gov/sfa/international/2001.int'lagrmts_up. htm> at 75. See also R. Ramsay and G. C. Rowe, *Environmental Law in Australia* (Sydney: Butterworths, 1995): 620.

permit for the importation of an Appendix I species requires the competent scientific authority in the importing State to certify, first, that importation is sought for purposes that are not "detrimental to the survival of the species"; and secondly, that the recipient of the specimen is "suitably equipped to house and care for it."[138] In addition, CITES requires the government authority in the importing State Member to certify that the imported specimen "is not to be used for primarily commercial purposes." Species listed in Appendix II require export permits only. In recent years, the Animals and Plants Committee of CITES and the Conference of the Parties have sought to protect marine species, including whales, dolphin, sharks, marine turtles, fish, queen conch and hard corals, and hawksbill turtle shells. It is considered that 34% of the recently reviewed species are marine species, whose listing has been the most controversial.[139]

In light of the reported volume of marine patent claims since the mid-1950s, the obscurity of the law in this area, and its being disregarded or ignored even by the experts, the question arises whether patents for inventions using marine biota issued prior to the entry into force of UNCLOS on 16 November, 1994, were, or were not, subject to conditions under the GCCS (for parties to the latter not yet parties to UNCLOS), or to export limitations under CITES (for endangered species).[140]

The question also arises regarding whether genetic resources are natural resources. Our discussion above sought to demonstrate that it is not "manifestly absurd or unreasonable" (interpreted pursuant to the 1969

138. CITES, Arts. III, IV and V.
139. See   <http://www.nmfs.noaa.gov/sfa/international/2001.int'lagrmts_up. htm>, at 76.
140. Convention on International Trade in Endangered Species of Wild Flora and Fauna, done at Washington DC, March 3, 1973. Entered into force on July 1, 1975, available online: <http://www.cites.org>. There are some 167 parties to CITES. The Convention establishes Appendices I, II and III listing selected species for particular degrees of protection. The Conference of the Parties is the organ entrusted with deciding through a vote and on the basis of a specific set of biological and trade criteria (under Resolution Conf. 9.24-Rev.CoP13), the species that will be listed in Appendices I and II. Appendix I covers species threatened with extinction. International trade in Appendix I species is prohibited or subject to exceptional conditions. Appendix II covers species whose trade must be controlled because if unchecked, they might become threatened with extinction. In Appendix III species that should be protected, at least in the country requesting their protection, are listed. The rules of procedure for listing species in Appendices I and II do not apply to Appendix III species, which is more flexible. Importation and export of listed species is allowed only if accompanied with the appropriate documentation. Documentation must be produced at the ports of exit (i.e., in the coastal State) or entry (i.e., researching State). CITES does not impede nations from establishing more stringent protections under domestic law than those conditions imposed under the Convention.

VCLT, in force 1990), to argue that there is an *indistinguishability* between the natural resources of the continental shelf regulated under the GCCS (in force in 1964), the natural resources of the continental shelf listed in the UNCLOS (in force 1994), and the *genetic* resources regulated under the CBD.[141] A coral colony attached to the continental shelf is a natural resource, it can be—or has been—a protected species,[142] and is also a genetic resource. To argue otherwise would mean that all the previous arguments must be rejected, as well as the power of the facts described above relating to the increasing importance of marine natural products and reported patent activity. Subject to convincing arguments to the contrary, Articles 2 and 5.8 of the GCCS, the relevant Appendices in CITES, and Articles 246.5 and 249.2 of UNCLOS, apply as between parties when determining whether continental shelf resources stored at *ex-situ* collections acquired from a coastal State provider after the entry into force of the GCCS in 1964, or of CITES in 1975, or of UNCLOS in 1994, enjoy total immunity from coastal State claims. If those resources were obtained by a party without consent from the former and in breach of rules in force for the conduct of alleged purely scientific studies under each treaty (GCCS, CITES, UNCLOS), jointly or separately, as the specific case under review might be, then the rules of interpretation of the VCLT (in force since 1990), would further strengthen the view that a breach took place by the party acting without coastal State consent.

The VCLT contains two further important rules of interpretation: *pacta sunt servanda* ("Every treaty in force is binding upon the parties to it and must be performed in good faith"),[143] and Article 27 providing that a Party "may not invoke the provisions of its internal law as justification for its failure to perform a treaty." These rules are important vis-à-vis the potential loss of bargaining power experienced by a coastal State whose natural resources might have been used, without its consent, in the development, patenting or other intellectual property claim by foreign researchers seeking to gain commercial advantage over the resources or the *fructus* (i.e., derivatives) under the sovereign rights of the coastal State.[144]

141. Some of these resources may also have been endangered species of flora and fauna of the continental shelf listed in the 1973 CITES (in force 1975).

142. As of February 2005, several continental shelf phyla are listed in Appendices I and II of CITES, including: sea cucumbers belonging to the Phylum Echinodermata; clams and mussels, snails and conches belonging to the Phylum Mollusca; corals and sea anemones, seaferns and fire corals belonging to the Phylum Cnidaria. It is beyond this paper to investigate the record of listing of these species. But the point is made that if these species had been listed between 1975 (entry into force of CITES) and 1993 (entry into force of the CBD), trade in such species would have been subject to the Permits and Certificates, and other restrictions.

143. VCLT, Art. 26.

144. The language of the International Law Commission is quite clear in the passage: "the text [of the 1958 GCCS] as now adopted leaves no doubt that the

The above considerations do not advocate in favor of litigation. Rather, they underline the existence of conventional and customary obligations in force at the different dates identified. The breach of these obligations would have generated international responsibility for the flags of the researching States parties to these conventions toward coastal State parties. Failure to comply with the relevant customary international law provisions could have incurred the responsibility of non-party States as well. If the organisms and microorganisms from the marine environment were collected "for the purpose of then exploring their biotechnology potential back in the laboratory," then the term "marine bioprospecting" as proposed earlier would apply to these activities, not the term MSR,[145] irrespective of whether the collection was obtained by "diving in coastal waters, trawling from the water column, grab-sampling of the seabed from a ship, or [the] use of a manned submersible."[146] The issue then becomes one of trust and of whether statements relating to marine biomedical research and other MSR focused on the biogenetics of marine biota in areas under the sovereignty, sovereign rights or jurisdiction of the coastal State have been made bona fide.

rights conferred upon the coastal State cover all rights necessary for and connected with the exploration and exploitation of the natural resources of the continental shelf." *Yearbook of the International Law Commission*, 1956, Vol. II at 297. The doctrine relating to sovereign rights as distinct from sovereignty has been elaborated as a qualification of the zone where States enjoy sovereign rights, not as a qualification of these rights themselves. It is accepted that the rights that the coastal State enjoys over the continental shelf are *ipso jure.* They imply the territoriality of coastal State rights over the seabed and submarine areas and also the existence of a "relationship back in time which would exclude the possible hypotheses of *res nullius* and *res communis.*" O'Connell, n. 71 above, Vol. 1, Chapter 13: *The Continental Shelf,* p. 467–509 at 478. Coastal State sovereign rights over the seabed have been recognized since the 1950s and have crystallized in 1969 with the decision of the International Court of Justice in the North Sea Continental Shelf Cases. However, some scholars have argued for a contrary view: Blakeney has argued that the language of the CBD is vague and that "sovereign rights" do not equate with, nor resolve the issue of, ownership over biogenetic resources. M. Blakeney, "Intellectual Property Aspects of Traditional Agricultural Knowledge," in *Perspectives on Intellectual Property*, P. Drahos and M. Blakeney eds. (2001): 40–42.

145. Owen, n. 9 above, at 11.

146. *Id.* The Executive Secretary of the CBD [in *Marine and Coastal Biodiversity: Review, Further Elaboration and Refinement of the Programme of Work* (UNEP/CBD/ SBSTA/8/INF/3/Rev.1 of Feb. 22, 2003 in preparation for the Subsidiary Body on Science, Technical and Technological Advice (SBSTTA), to meet at its Eighth Meeting in Montreal, March 10–14, 2003] also points out on p. 13 that "marine scientific research relating to genetic resources falls within that [UNCLOS 1982, Part XIII] regime."

Freedom of Marine Scientific Research on the High Seas and in the Area

There is freedom of scientific research on the high seas.[147] This freedom is not absolute as States must pay due regard to the interests of other States and comply with Part XII of UNCLOS, dealing with the conservation of the resources of the high seas and the preservation of the marine environment against environmental (particularly of rare and fragile ecosystems), and other forms of pollution; and with the rights under UNCLOS of other States with respect to activities in The Area beyond the limits of national jurisdiction. In the Area, MSR shall be conducted exclusively for peaceful purposes and for the benefit of humankind as a whole, in accordance with Part XIII of UNCLOS.[148] It is beyond the scope of this article to engage in a debate over MSR or bioprospecting activities in the Area, as this would serve as a distraction from the focus of this article.[149] A draft code for high seas and the Area's MSR and bioprospecting user communities has been advocated.[150] Its adoption, together with the disclosure of the origin of biogenetic materials in a systematically and accurate manner would contribute to it being reported properly in the literature on patents issued over inventions using such materials. This would minimize the likelihood that the patent system applied wholesale to high seas and Area discoveries over marine living resources could block coastal States from fulfilling their rights and aspirations under the GCCS, UNCLOS and the CBD with regard

---

147. UNCLOS, n. 7 above, Arts. 87 and 257.

148. *Id.*, Arts. 143 and 256. See United Nations University, *Bioprospecting of Genetic Resources in the Deep Seabed*, available online: <http://www.ias.unu.edu/publications/reports.cfm> (2005).

149. See T. Scovazzi, *Some Considerations on Future Directions for the International Seabed Authority* (Paper Presented at the Special Session of the Assembly to Mark the Tenth Anniversary of the Establishment of the International Seabed Authority, Kingston, May 25–26, 2004 (on file with the author); see also Pfirter, n. 134 above.

150. Statement of Ambassador Satya N. Nandan, Secretary-General of the International Seabed Authority. 5th Meeting of the United Nations Informal Consultative Process on the Law of the Sea, June 7–11 2004 (on file with the author). See also L. Glowka, "The Deepest of Ironies: Genetic Resources, Marine Scientific Research, and the Area," in *Ocean Yearbook* 12, Borgese, Ginsburg and Morgan eds., n. 25 above, at 96. Glowka relies on the premise that the CBD does not apply to biological diversity beyond the limits of national jurisdiction. In this way, he ignores the theory of the territoriality of ships as floating parts of a nation's territory linked to it by the flag of the vessel. Any vessel, including those registered under flags of convenience, will incur the international responsibility and liability of their flag for actions carried out on the high seas or in the Area beyond the limits of national jurisdiction. The issue is too complex to be dealt with in any depth here and our concern at this stage is with MSR and bioprospecting within areas of national jurisdiction.

to natural resources of the sedentary species type. A draft code may discourage high seas bioprospectors but may encourage foreign investors to re-consider coastal States of origin of biogenetic materials as partners for lucrative capacity building ventures involving R&D.

THE CONVENTION ON BIOLOGICAL DIVERSITY, ACCESS TO RAW MATERIALS AND COMMERCIAL SHARING OF BENEFITS

The Convention on Biological Diversity (CBD)[151] was adopted in 1992 in Rio de Janeiro, Brazil, by the United Nations Conference on Environment and Development (UNCED).[152] It recognizes sustainable development as a binding principle of international law and makes the protection of biological resources a matter of "common concern" for all States.[153] States have "sovereign rights" over their natural resources,[154] in accordance with the Charter of the United Nations and the principles of international law.[155] As discussed, the 1982 UNCLOS is an important source of those sovereign rights and principles.

The CBD aims to curb the destruction of biological species, habitats and ecosystems by encouraging their *in-situ* over *ex-situ* conservation, maintenance and recovery in natural surroundings.[156] It recognizes the intrinsic value of biological diversity and encourages States to cooperate in the promotion of sustainable development practices. Biological diversity has three elements: diversity of species, genetic diversity within species and diversity of ecosystems.[157] Sustainable use is defined as that where components of biological diversity are used "in a way and at a rate that does not lead to the long-term decline of biological diversity, thereby maintaining its potential to meet the needs and aspirations of present and future generations."[158]

151. Reproduced in *International Legal Materials* 31 (1992): 882.

152. Earth Summit, Convention on Biological Diversity, Final Text, United Nations Conference on Environment and Development (UNCED), Rio de Janeiro, Brazil 3–14 June 1992 (hereinafter CBD).

153. A. Boyle, "The Role of International Human Rights Law in the Protection of the Environment," in *Human Rights Approaches to Environmental Protection*, A. Boyle and M. Anderson eds. (Oxford: Clarendon Press, 1998 paperback): 55.

154. Preamble.

155. CBD, n. 11 above, Art/3.

156. *Id.*, Preamble and Art. 8.

157. *Id.* Article 2 defines biodiversity as "the variability among living organisms from all sources including, inter alia, terrestrial, marine and other aquatic ecosystems and the ecological complexes of which they are part; this includes diversity within species, between species and of ecosystems."

158. *Id.*

To achieve these aims, the CBD deals with four major issues. First, it provides the terms under which industrialized countries may have access to genetic resources in the countries of origin of these resources. Access, where granted, shall be on mutually agreed terms and subject to the provisions of the Convention.[159] Genetic resources means "genetic material of actual or potential value," that is, economic value. Genetic material includes plant, animal, microbial or other origin "containing functional units of heredity."[160] Secondly, the CBD deals with the terms under which countries of origin of biological resources may have access to environmentally sound technologies "that are relevant to the conservation and sustainable use of biological diversity..." and to new biotechnologies developed from materials and resources found in tropical forests and other natural habitats, such as marine habitats. Biotechnology is defined as any "technological application that uses biological systems, living organisms, or derivatives thereof, to make or modify products or processes for specific use."[161] Access to these technologies shall respect existing proprietary rights.[162] Thirdly, the CBD binds States to reach mutually agreed terms concerning the ownership and use of patent rights over the biotechnology produced from genetic material and biological resources.[163] And fourthly, it deals with the financial aid that is required by countries of origin of genetic material and biological resources to implement the terms of the CBD.[164]

The implementation of CBD provisions relating to the marine environment must be consistent with the rights and obligations of States under the law of the sea.[165] In 1995, the Conference of the Parties (COP) declared that the CBD applies to marine and coastal biodiversity by virtue of the Jakarta

159. *Id.*, Arts. 1, 15(4), 16 and 19.
160. *Id.*, Art. 2.
161. *Id.*, Preamble.
162. *Id.*, Art. 16 (2) (3) and (5).
163. *Id.* Article 1, 15(7) (States "shall take legislative, administrative or policy measures . . . with the aim of sharing in a fair and equitable way the results of research and development and the benefits arising from the commercial and other utilization of genetic resources with the Contracting Party providing such resources. Such sharing shall be upon mutually agreed terms"), 16 (5) (States, "recognizing that patents and other intellectual property rights may have an influence on the implementation of this Convention, shall cooperate in this regard subject to national legislation and international law in order to ensure that such rights are supportive of and do not run counter to its objectives"), and 19(2) (States "shall take all practicable measures to promote and advance priority access on a fair and equitable basis by Contracting Parties, especially developing countries, to the results and benefits arising from biotechnologies based upon genetic resources provided by those Contracting Parties. Such access shall be on mutually agreed terms").
164. *Id.*, Arts. 20–21.
165. *Id.*, Art. 22.2.

Mandate.[166] In contrast with UNCLOS, under the CBD coastal States are not obligated to grant access "in normal circumstances" to foreign research-ers.[167] Access for the conduct of MSR activities concerning biological and genetic marine resources may be granted when such access is beneficial *also* to the country of origin of the resources.

The CBD clearly rejects the application of "common heritage of humankind" principles to biogenetic resources within the limits of national jurisdiction.[168] Although this is not a new development, the literature on the CBD fails to take notice of the "sovereign rights" already enjoyed by coastal States pursuant to the GCCS and UNCLOS. As a result of this omission, ABS literature does not integrate the MSR clearance process as an important tool in the ABS debate relating to marine natural products.[169]

Under the CBD, ABS refers to agreements that include two elements: the prior informed consent (PIC) of the rightful owners of the genetic resources (i.e., local communities, indigenous peoples, state or federal authorities, as the case may be within the boundaries of the nation), regarding the utilization of genetic resources; and the mutually agreed terms (MAT) for the utilization of the biogenetic resources of the coastal nation. The goal of finding suitable and standard rules in the implementa-tion of these two fundamental ABS principles has generated a great deal of proposals within the COP of the CBD.[170] In our view, among the many ABS-CBD debate issues, three arguments deserve special consideration because they seek to erode coastal State sovereign rights over marine biota:

1. A few bacteria are worth nothing. Nothing is therefore owed to coastal States of origin of marine microorganisms (bacteria, viruses, fungi, etc.).

166. Available online: <http://www.biodiv.org/jm.html>.

167. See the consent regime of Article 246, n. 90 to 100 above and accompanying text.

168. G. Verhoosel, "Prospecting for Marine and Coastal Biodiversity: Interna-tional Law in Deep Water?," *International Journal of Marine and Coastal Law* 13 (1998): 91. Verhoosel has identified the "nationalization of genetic resources" as an equitable claim raised by developing countries, "who argued that it was unfair to make poor countries pay for expensive patented products resulting from free bioprospecting in those countries by the biotechnology industry from the developed world. If developing countries were to bear the economic opportunity cost of conserving, "their" genetic diversity, they also wanted to share in the benefits of its use."

169. Straus, n. 20 above; Keating, n. 173 below, COP to the CBD on ABS Agreements, n. 15 above.

170. CBD COP 7, Decision VII/19 Access and benefit-sharing as related to genetic resources (Art. 15), available online: <http://www.biodiv.org/decisions/default.aspx?m=COP–07&id=7756...>.

2. States do not enjoy ownership of the genotype of marine biota, though under the CBD they may exercise control over the phenotype of marine biota.

3. TRIPS trumps any other argument.

1. The argument that a few bacteria are worth nothing is widespread and rests on a double assumption: that renewable resources (i.e., biogenetic resources) that may require expensive processing (i.e., expensive vessel operations, years of laboratory testing and screening), are somewhat inherently less valuable than non-renewable resources (i.e., oil and gas), and that the loss of a few bacteria from a coastal State is not economically relevant for raising a claim against those deriving a commercial benefit from the application of biotechnology to the removed bacteria.[171] The first assumption seems to imply that marine bacteria are not resources. It would then follow that access is a non-issue for those who seek it and for those with the power to refuse it. In this light, any debate is idle talk, any law unnecessary. The second assumption disregards that CBD Article 2 refers to "genetic resources of actual or potential value," and that bacteria are key to genetic engineering and molecular biology development.

The potential value of a biogenetic compound is actualized through economic investment and further scientific and technological research at a university,[172] government, a not-for-profit institute, or at a private company

---

171. See for example, Cicin-Sain et al., n. 25 above, proposing that: "Clearly there is a significant difference between the extraction of hydrocarbons from a coastal nation's ocean zone or the taking of fish from its EEZ and the 'taking' of a few marine bacteria. In the former case, little processing, if any, is needed to make the resources immediately valuable in an economic and commercial sense. In the latter case, however, the *marine bacteria by themselves are of no value*" [emphasis added]. Straus, n. 20 above.

172. For example, research at the Division of Marine Biomedical Research, Harbor Branch Oceanographic Institution, includes several genus of marine sponges associated with a rich variety of bacteria and microbes in symbiotic relationship. The innovative aspect of this research is to ascertain the chemical and genetic nature of the interactions between the sponges and their hosts. Deep-sea sponges have a biomass that is 60 to 80 percent bacteria and microbes. The exact interaction of these bacteria and microbes is unknown. However, the bacteria within the sponges produce anti-microbial chemicals to inhibit the growth or settlement of potential competitors such as polyketides that have great promise for future pharmaceuticals. Erythromycin, a common antibiotic, and the cholesterol lowering drug lovastatin were derived from polyketides. Lasonolides are compounds isolated from the deep-sea sponge *Forcepia* sp., with potential pharmaceutical properties. Research continues on whether the lanosides are produced by the sponge or the microbes associated with it. Another interesting deep-sea sponge with microbial communities is the Theonellidae family of deep-sea sponges. Comparing DNA [deoxyribonucleic acid] gene sequences of microbes from two sponges of the same species harvested from different locations can shed light into the symbiotic relationships between sponges and microbes. Researchers aim to understand how

laboratory. Those called to ascertaining the economic value of samples of marine microorganisms include university researchers, lab technicians, biotech start-ups, pharmaceutical, drug and other industries, and other stakeholders. Several international bodies are developing guidelines on how to carry out the economic evaluation and the royalties arising from the commercialization of products derived from inventions on biogenetic resources.[173] The assessment is complex and may require a case-by-case analysis by the parties involved in the collection of marine microorganisms for the development, patenting and commercialization of marine natural products.[174] Over the last 20 years, guidelines have been adopted and implemented.[175] These guidelines require [marine] researchers to negotiate

the compounds excreted by the microbes protect the sponges from predators and whether this mechanism can be used as "self-defense" chemicals for drug discovery. Another sponge family with significant promise is the Spongosorite yielding the topsentin-class compounds with potential as an anti-inflammatory in cosmetics and pharmaceuticals. Research focuses on how the topsentin-class compounds are produced by the sponge and what is the relationship between and role played by the wide array of symbiotic, or beneficial, bacteria and microorganisms living with the sponge. Further, examples of potentially significant marine compounds include comparing the gene expression of organisms, such as in some species of soft coral (i.e., *Pseudopterogorgia elisabethae*), where the potency of the compounds produced varies between geographic locations, but can be applicable as anti-inflammatory medications. Research also focuses on sea squirts such as *Ecteinascidia turbinate*, leathery invertebrates that produce what is believed to be unique anti-cancer metabolites called ecteinascidians. However, synthesizing ecteinascidians in large quantities through cell cultures (as opposed to harvesting from nature) is extremely difficult. HBOI receives over 70% of its funding from competitively awarded outside grants and contracts. The remainder of the institution's annual operating budget is comprised of private donations from individuals, foundations, and various trust funds. See <https://secure.hboi.edu>.

173. D. Keating, "Access to Genetic Resources and Equitable Benefit Sharing Through a New Disclosure Requirement in the Patent System: An Issue in Search of Forum," *Journal of Patent and Trademark Office Society*, 87, 7 (2005): 525.

174. Gorina-Ysern, n. 3 above.

175. The National Cancer Institute of the National Institutes of Health has used collection contracts or Letters of Collection Agreement (LOCA) performed over 25 tropical and subtropical countries worldwide. Some 10,000 marine invertebrates and marine algae have been collected by Harbor Branch Oceanographic Institute, the Australian Institute of Marine Science, the University of Canterbury (New Zealand), and the Coral Reef Research Foundation, from areas mostly situated in the Indo-Pacific Region placed in the Natural Products Repository (Coral Reef Foundation). NCI retains ownership over the materials, but not necessarily IPRs over them. Recipients must respect the interests of Countries of Origin. NCI promotes policies of fair and equitable collaboration and compensation to Source Countries participating in the collection programs. The NCI extracts each organism in the Natural Products Extraction Laboratory using a 1 to 1 mixture of dichloromethane and methanol, and then using water. The extracts are stored at a temperature of −20 degrees Centigrade in the Natural Products Repository,

the following criteria with source countries of natural resources (i.e., microorganisms and other *raw materials*):

a. provider, recipient and collector;
b. informed consent of local and indigenous communities;
c. purpose of the agreement and its duration;
d. ownership of the biogenetic or other material to be transferred;
e. source of the biogenetic or other material collected;
f. identification of the material;
g. conditions of release;
h. consideration or compensation offered for the material;
i. any transfer of technology in this regard or capacity building measures;
j. export licenses under CITES;
k. conditions for the release to third parties;
l. confidentiality;
m. sustainability of supply and re-supply;
n. measures for the conservation of biodiversity;
o. experimental nature of the material;
p. disclaimers and liability clauses;
q. distribution of proprietary rights and duties over the material;
r. contributions made by each party, frequency of research reports;
s. publication of results, co-authorship and acknowledgment of contributions;
t. official institutional seal of approval; and
u. settlement of dispute mechanisms.[176]

The above negotiating criteria have been developed over the years through a series of more or less formal documents that include a range of

operated by SAIC at the Frederick Cancer Research and Development Center and tested in the cancer cell line screen held at NCI. The collections of marine microorganisms and invertebrates held at the NCI are legally considered a "national resource." Since the items deposited are the subject matter of LOCAs, only qualified institutions can gain access to the vials or to 96 well plates and access is subject to the signing of Material Transfer Agreements or MTAs that protect the rights of all the parties with an interest. See <http://dtp.nci.nih.gov/branches/npb/repository.html>; see also <http://ttb.nci.nih.gov/forms.htm>, reproducing a sample of an MTA to Academic/Not-for-Profit Organization; see also Traditional Knowledge: Contracts Database. Contract Summaries (MTA) at <http://www.wipo.int/tk/en/database/contracts/summaries/ncimta.html>.

176. List compiled using several documents used in the transfer of biological and other materials across international borders and among different institutions. See Gorina-Ysern, n. 1 above, Chapter Five: Agreements Complementing UNCLOS 1982 Marine Scientific Research Clearance Communications and Conclusions Chapter.

Memoranda of Understanding (MOUs), as well as standard collection and material transfer agreements among public and private institutions within a nation and across national boundaries. The latter include Letter of Collection Agreements (LOCAs), criteria for ABS Agreements in the Bonn Guidelines, Material Transfer Agreements (MTAs), Cooperative Research and Development Agreements (CRADAs), and MOUs. These agreements seek to protect the scientific and economic rights of the parties, to uphold proprietary rights of researchers, and to request that the parties treat the agreements with confidentiality. However, it is unclear whether efforts to integrate these standard procedures and the implementation of the Bonn Guidelines,[177] will result in greater information and transparency,[178] considering that the above agreements discourage the disclosure of proprietary information during the negotiations and exchanges and that the actual details of the contractual deals are not well-known outside the narrow circles of direct stakeholders and those with a proven interest.[179] The requirement advocated by Tobin, for an international certificate of legal provenance, origin or source of genetic resources would help in the implementation of ABS agreements and would provide a basis for equitable

177. CBD, n. 11 above, Article 1 seeks to ensure the "fair and equitable sharing of the benefits arising out of the utilization of genetic resources, including by appropriate access to genetic resources and by appropriate transfer of relevant technologies, taking into account all rights over those resources and to technologies, and by appropriate funding." The Bonn Guidelines on Access to Genetic Resources and Fair and Equitable Sharing of the Benefits Arising out of their Utilization were discussed by a Panel of Experts of the CBD Conference of the Parties at its 5th meeting held in Bonn, Germany, from 22–26 October 2001; and adopted at its 6th meeting (COP VI) in the Hague in April 2002 through decision VI/24. The Bonn Guidelines do not refer to the marine environment specifically. See <http://www.diodiv.org/programmes/socio-eco/benefit/default/asp>. The last meeting of the COP was held in February 2005 as COP VIII. It is to be hoped that the focal points for access and benefit sharing set up under the Bonn Guidelines will gather sufficient information and will coordinate and disseminate it with relevant agencies within the UN, so that concerned members of the public and professionals can gain access to the ensuing databases for study and analysis purposes. For a discussion of the Bonn Guidelines, see Owen, n. 9 above, p. 36.

178. *Bonn Guidelines on Access to Genetic Resources and Fair and Equitable Sharing of the Benefits Arising out of their Utilization,* UNEP and CBD (2002), available online: <http://www.biodiv.org/doc/publications/cbd-bonn-gdls-en.pdf>.

179. *Id.* Access to NCI's active repository containing over 3,000 active samples in the 60 cell line anti-tumor screen is restricted to U.S. based investigators who have undergone strict peer review; U.S. charted organizations by strictly reviewed request proposals; and organizations based in the Countries of Origin of the samples who have participated in the NCI collection programs, with regards to organisms originating in their country only. See also Standard Forms and Agreements at <http://ttb.nci.hih.gov/forms.html> providing samples of the main documents used from collection to clinical trial agreements for active compounds and bioassays.

outcomes.[180] However, others have documented the extent to which the new disclosure requirement is mired in disagreements regarding the proper international forum for its adoption,[181] or its difficulties in patent applications.[182]

The difficulty of putting a value tag, monetary and non-monetary, to a few marine bacteria, viruses and fungi, is exacerbated by the lack of disclosure of their commercial value in the development process,[183] or in the landmark patent case law represented by *Diamond v. Chakrabarti*,[184] *Funk Brothers* (biotechnology seeks to devise methods to synthesize useful quantities of proteins),[185] *Hybritech v Monoclonal Antibodies* (hybridomas help

180. D. Cunningham, B. Tobin and K. Watanabe, *Tracking Genetic Resources and International Access and Benefit Sharing Governance: The Role of Certificates of Origin*. Background paper for Smithsonian/UNU-IAS Roundtable on certificates of origin (Sept. 9, 2004), available online: <http://www.ias.unu.edu/research/certificatesoforigin.cfm#top>.

181. Keating, n. 173 above.

182. *Report on Disclosure of Origin in Patent Applications* (prepared by Queen Mary Intellectual Property Research Institute for the European Commission, DG-Trade, Oct. 2004), available online: <http://trade-info.cec.eu.int/doclib/docs/2005/june/tradoc_123533.pdf>.

183. The sources cited in this article do not disclose the economic value of marine biota traded through MSR or bioprospecting.

184. *Diamond, Commissioner of Patents and Trademarks v. Chakrabarti*, 447 U.S. 303 at 316 (1980) is the landmark case in the history of legal recognition of patents claims over living material that had been genetically engineered in the laboratory in 1972. Dr. Chakrabarti, a microbiologist, filed a patent application based on his invention concerning plasmids contained in a bacterium from the genus *Pseudomonas*. These plasmids could control the oil degradation abilities of certain bacteria and could break down multiple components of crude oil, particularly in oil spills. The novelty of Mr. Chakrabarti's invention was that naturally occurring bacteria do not possess the property to degrade crude oil. His bacterium had been genetically engineered by transferring it on to a single *Pseudomonas* bacterium. The patent claim was threefold: first, protection was sought for the method used in producing the new bacteria; second, he claimed protection for an inoculum comprised of a carrier material floating on water, such as straw, and the new bacteria; finally Mr. Chakrabarti claimed the bacteria themselves. Nowhere in the case is it stated how much value the bacteria had in monetary terms.

185. *In re Patrick H. O'Farrell, Barry A. Polisky and David H. Gelfaln (In re O'Farrell)* 853 F. 2d 894 (Fed. Cir. 1988) [No. 87-1486 U.S. Court of Appeals for the Federal Circuit, Decided August 10, 1988]. The appellants sought to control the expression of cloned heterologous genes inserted into bacteria through genetic engineering and molecular biology that created a hybrid vector method for regulating the translation of the heterologous DNA in the E-coli bacterial plasmid. U.S. Circuit Judge Ridge laid out the basic technology for DNA cloning in highly educational terms. The technology described herein explains the process used by laboratories in the creation and production of synthetic proteins that can be used for a number of purposes, including curative purposes (i.e., the production of synthetic insulin). The invention consists in two parts: the introduction of a gene into a selected

clinicians and scientists to isolate and cultivate single clones of lymphocytes for unlimited supply of antibodies specific to an epitope),[186] or the more controversial *Harvard College* case.[187]

bacterium and its expression as the sought protein that will be useful for the intended goal. The first part requires the isolation of a gene using recombinant DNA and to introduce it into host bacterium. First, it uses a bacteriophage virus to infect the bacteria using a cloning vector that ensures self-replicating DNA into the bacteria. Second, it uses a plasmid, a small circular loop of DNA found in the bacteria and different from the chromosome it replicates. The second part of the invention requires ensuring that the cloned heterologous gene that was inserted into the bacteria using a plasmid as a cloning vector will be expressed into a protein that can be used as intended. In summary, the information contained or coded in the body's nucleotides tell the cell how to go about living. DNA expression can be understood to involve the following. Living cells make proteins. Proteins are molecules with at least 50 amino-acids that are called peptide chains. Polypeptide chains display chemical properties determined by the shape and the sequence of the amino-acids that they contain. The bonds that bind smaller amino-acid chains (up to 20) are called peptide bonds. The sequence and shape of these chains determines the identity of the protein they contain and its chemical characteristics. There are some 100,000 proteins in nature. Deoxyribonucleic acid or DNA is a very long polymeric molecule wrapping around long strands called chromosomes. It stores information in the genes about the sequence in which the amino-acids must be assembled to make a particular protein molecule. A gene is therefore described as a region of the DNA long strand that contains the code for the sequence of a single polypeptide chain of a protein. Nucleotides are subunits of the DNA chain that include a nitrogen ring (a base), a five-carbon sugar (called deoxyribose) and a phosphate group. Nucleotides are bound by non-covalent bonds. There are 4 nucleotides: Adenine (A), Guanine (G), Cytosine (C), and Thymine (T). The sequence of these bases along the DNA molecule specifies which amino-acids will be inserted in sequence into the polypeptide chain of a protein. A combination of three nucleotides is called a codon and are represented by the combination of letters corresponding to the sequence: A or G, or C or T. Codons can combine 3 x 64 triplets. Some codons contain coded information for many amino-acids, whereas others are like sentence ends and are called stop codons. Codons are used in the transcription of messenger Reoxyribonucleic acid or mRNA and the translation into amino acid sequences in the protein. To "express" the information contained in the gene for replicating purposes, (crack the nut open), it is necessary to first make a copy of the DNA gene as RNA (using a different sugar and substituting U for T). The RNA moves where the proteins are synthesized as messenger RNA. Humans, mammals and plants are characterized as Eurocaryotic beings because their DNA is stored in the nucleus of the chromosomes. Bacteria are called Procaryotic because their DNA consists of a ring. Procaryotic bacteria are used as a factory to transform heterologous genes and translate them into proteins (cloned genes) that can be used to produce desired quantities for commercial distribution.

186. *Hybritech v. Monoclonal Antibodies*, 1986 USCA Fed. Cir. Since 1978 Hybritech was in the business of developing diagnostic kits using monoclonal antibodies to detect antigens for conditions such as pregnancy, cancer, growth hormone deficiencies, and hepatitis, for which it had a license that it defended with success in this case, as the U.S. Court of Appeal found the patent not obvious and

upheld the 29 claims it contained. In essence the technology at stake involved the following. Diseases that attack the body are called antigens. Antibodies are chemical substances within the human body that defend the organism against the invasion of microorganisms with foreign disease molecules or antigens. Antibodies are proteins and lymphocytes are B-cells that produce anti-bodies. The interesting trait of lymphocytes is that they recognize and respond to the epitopes contained within the antigens that attack the body, and reproduce or clone themselves to produce more antibodies with specific chemical properties to fight the specific epitopes within the antigen. This characteristic of antibodies is called to recognize and "complex with" antigens. The novelty of the invention consisted in trying to devise a method to obtain enormous synthetic (or cloned) amounts of antibodies needed without having to rely on mouse serum consisting of a mixture of antibodies from different clones of lymphocytes (i.e., polyclonal) antibody supplies (as was the current practice). Hybritech fused hybridomas (a mixture of myeloma or cancer cell) and spleen cells from a mouse (injected or immunized with an antigen) and used them in a fluid placed in a tube or well to produce antibodies to the antigen initially injected into the mouse. Each hybridoma was placed in one single tube and could be cloned in unlimited supply to combat one epitope. Hence, it was called monoclonal antibody. One characteristic of antibodies is their affinity to bond, detect or react with antigen. This is called the antibody-antigen complex. Immuno-assays are diagnostic methods for determining the present amount of an antigen in body fluids (blood or urine) with a radioactive substance or an enzyme (enzymes catalyze chemical reactions in the body). There are slow immunoassays and fast immunometric or sandwich assays. The latter involve the use of a labeled antibody with an unlabelled antibody reagent placed in a solid support surface inside the test tube. The antigen is placed between two antibodies. The competitive reaction between the two antibodies creates needed amounts of antibody reagents measured in moles per liter.

187. *Harvard College v. Canada (Commissioner of Patents)* 2002 SCC 76, available at http://www.lexum.umontreal.ca/csc-scc/en/rec/html/harvard.en.html [2002] 4. S.C.R. 45. The respondent (President and Fellows of Harvard College) filed for patent protection over an invention involving "transgenic animals." The invention consisted of injecting a cancer-promoting gene ("oncogene") into "fertilized mouse eggs as close as possible to the one-cell stage." The eggs were subsequently implanted into a female host mouse and monitored as they developed to term. The born mice were then tested for the presence of the oncogene. If they contained the oncogene they were called "founder" mice. Founder mice were mated non-genetically modified mice. A rate of 50% per cent of the born mice was expected to have "all of their cells affected by the oncogene." This meant that they could be further tested in animal carcinogenic studies. The respondent sought to protect the process for producing oncomice and the mice themselves (the "end product of the process, i.e., the founder mice and the offspring whose cells contain the onco-gene"). The controversy arose because the process and product claims extended to all non-human mammals. Whereas the process claims were allowed, the product claims were rejected by the Patent Examiner and by the appellant Commissioner. The Federal Court, Trial Division, dismissed the appeal against the appellant Commissioner, but allowed the appeal to the Federal Court of Appeal. The Supreme Court of Canada (McLachlin C.J. and Major, Binnie and Arbour JJ. dissenting) held: The appeal should be allowed. A higher life form is not patentable because it is not a "manufacture" or "composition of matter" within the meaning of "invention" in section 2 of the *Patent Act*.

The above cases do not involve marine bacteria, but show their relevance and value in genetic engineering and molecular biology. As indicated, the manipulation of the bacteria and other marine microorganisms has led to innovations yielding marine or other natural products for commercial use as therapeutic agents. Marine bacteria are worth a great deal in current and potential economic terms.

2. Professor Straus, a leading scholar in the patent field, has argued that States do not enjoy an "absolute right" to control access over genetic resources within areas under their sovereign rights, because genetic resources have a double nature: as phenotypes (individual plants and animals that may be considered tangible private goods), and as genotypes (storing information "embodied in the genetic constitution of microorganisms, plants or animal species, which may be considered public good"). In this light, the CBD is concerned with the phenotypic nature of biogenetic resources, whereas TRIPS is concerned with its genotypic nature.[188] This distinction has considerable legal implications. However, as documented in this article, there is nothing in the recorded preparatory work, or in the literature regarding this aspect of the international law of the sea (with which CBD has to be consistently applied), to support a narrowing of coastal State sovereign rights over biogenetic resources on the grounds of the difference between genotype and phenotype. Resources are not defined in such terms under the CGCS or UNCLOS. State practice indicates a trend to disregard the distinction[189] on at least three grounds:

188. Straus, n. 20 above, at 48–49.
189. See *Remarks by Hamdallah Zedan, Executive Secretary of the CBD to the Third Meeting of the Ad Hoc Open-Ended Working Group on Access and Benefit Sharing*, Bangkok, Thailand, Feb. 14–18, 2005. Professor Straus (2005) discusses with concern the legislation implementing CBD adopted by the Andean Community [Bolivia, Colombia, Ecuador, Peru and Venezuela] which, in Decision 391 (1996) it declares sovereign rights to the derivatives of genetic resources, which it defines as "molecule or composition or mixture of natural molecules, including raw extracts of living or dead organisms of biological origin, derived from the metabolism of living organisms" [Art. 5]. The Andean Community Decision goes on to withdraw recognition of any rights, including IPRs protected under TRIPS, to genetic resources, derivatives, synthesized products or related intangible components obtained or developed through non-compliance with the Common Access System. Professor Straus laments that bureaucratic obstacles in place in the Andean community make the granting of a patent an exceptionally difficult goal in the Andean Community system; by India's Biological Diversity Act, which requires foreign researchers to obtain prior permission from the National Authority for obtaining any biological resources originating in India or any associated knowledge for research, commercial utilization, or bio-survey and bio-utilization. In addition, anyone intending to apply for IPR protection anywhere in the world must obtain such prior consent for any invention based on any research or information on biological resources obtained from India. Similar legislation has been implemented by the Organization of African Unity (OAU, Model Legislation for the Recognition

first, reliance on the granting by international law of sovereign rights to coastal States over their natural resources, irrespective of the dual nature of genetic resources; secondly, "a deep distrust toward intellectual property rights,"[190] coupled with a profound mistrust of the good faith of foreign researchers alleging to conduct purely scientific research on those resources; and thirdly, the bargaining power retained by coastal States adopting a formal approach to negotiations for clearance pursuant to Article 250 of UNCLOS, and enhanced by Article 249.2 of UNCLOS. The distinction (phenotype vs. genotype) clearly seeks to erode coastal State control over genetic resources and has powerful supporters and advocates in industry.

3. Finally the remark that TRIPS,[191] trumps any other agreement rests on the double concern expressed by Professor Straus, that a world without

and Protection of the Rights of Local Communities, Farmers and Breeders, and for the Regulation of Access to Biological Measures); the Philippines (1995 Presidential Executive Order No. 247, Prescribing Guidelines and Establishing a Regulatory Framework for the Prospecting of Biological and Genetic Resources, their By-products and Derivatives, for Scientific and Commercial Purposes, and other Purposes); Costa Rica (1998 Biological Diversity Law 3388); Australia (1999 Environment Protection and Biodiversity Conservation Act; and the Environment Protection and Biotechnology Conservation Amendment Regulation 2001, still under discussion but covering access and benefit sharing issues), New Zealand; Brazil (1995 Draft Bill of law on access to Brazilian biodiversity and the 2001 Provisional Measure). Straus, n. 20 above, at 63.

190. Straus, *Id.*

191. The Agreement on Trade Related Aspects of Intellectual Property, Including Trade in Counterfeit Goods (TRIPS for short), constitutes Annex 1 C of the Final Act of the 1994 Uruguay Round under the General Agreement on Tariffs and Trade (GATT). Final Act signed at Marrakesh, Morocco, on April 15, 1994 by 109 States. Reproduced in *International Legal Materials* 33 (1994): 1143–53, 1224–47. The Uruguay Round was held at Punta del Este, Uruguay, in 1986, concluded in 1993, signed in 1994 and entered into force in 1995. The first GATT entered into force in 1948. Together with the International Monetary Fund (IMF) and the International Bank for Reconstruction and Development (World Bank), the GATT is the third pillar of the Bretton Woods global system of international monetary exchange. The GATT's main objective is to ensure free trade in commodities. The system was created in 1944, and implemented two core principles espoused by the UK and the U.S. in the 1941 Atlantic Charter: free access to raw materials and freedom of commercial transactions. The TRIPS agreement consists of 73 articles in Parts I to VII. It is the first international regime providing for the compulsory protection of intellectual property rights (IPRs) among member States of the World Trade Organization. Patents must be granted over inventions of products of processes that are new and involve an inventive step capable of industrial application (non-obviousness) (Art. 27.1). See <http://clea.wipo.int/clea/lpext.dll?f=templates &fn=main-h.htm&2.0> setting out the intellectual property legislation of these States. For a specific survey of Latin American States' implementation see M. Edelman, "TRIPS in Trouble: A Survey of Intellectual Property (Non) Compliance

technological innovation involving marketable discoveries and inventions, is a dangerous prospect;[192] and that different stages of economic development in different nations aggravate the solutions and exacerbate the problems regarding research in new technologies in general.

Economic theories are important analytical tools for evaluating whether patent protection provides the most suitable incentive for researchers to invent, a good defense against free riders (driving prices for products down through competition), and for investors to continue to fund innovation (because they can recover sunk costs and generate benefits from R&D).[193] The increasing number of patent applications for marine natural products suggests that in industrialized nations the patent law in force is considered adequate to protect biotechnology inventions for licensing purposes and as a stepping stone for the commercialization of marine natural products by the biotechnology and pharmaceutical industries.[194] However, in many countries, the patenting of life forms continues to be controversial and strongly opposed.[195]

in Latin America," available online: <http://www.adti.net/html_files/ip/TRIPS.htm>, December 1, 1999.

192. J. Straus, "Bargaining Around the TRIPS Agreement: The Case for Ongoing Public-Private Initiatives to Facilitate Worldwide Intellectual Property Transactions," (A Comment on the paper presented by Professors D. Lange, Duke University, and J. H. Reichman, Vanderbilt University), cited in *Duke Journal of Comparative and International Law* 9 (1996) at 91, available online: <http://www.law.duke.edu/journals/djcil/articles/djcil9p91.htm> [hereinafter Straus 1996].

193. Eisenberg, n. 64 above, reproduced in Adelman et al., n. 51 above, at 26–38.

194. The web site of Harbor Branch Oceanographic Institution, a leading holder of marine biomedical patents, lists patent protection provided over the last 15 years under the laws of the U.S., France, Germany, Great Britain, Italy, Spain, Switzerland, Canada and Japan. See <http://www.hboi.edu/dbmr/dbmr_patents?2.html>.

195. For a thorough analysis, see Gorina-Ysern, n. 1 above, at Part III: The New Marine Biogenetic Frontier, 353–524. Mexico, Argentina, the Andean Group, and Brazil exclude patentability of all genetic materials, or of all materials existing in nature. Patent protection in Brazil does not extend to living beings or biological materials found in nature, even if genetically engineered or isolated, including the genome or germplasm of any living being. C. Correa, "Access to Plant Genetic Resources and Intellectual Property Rights," in Drahos and Blakeney, n. 144 above. Brazil's position reflects the preferred approach generally adopted by many developing countries with regards to Article 27(3)(b) of the Agreement on Trade Related Aspects of Intellectual Property (TRIPS), and current disagreements with industrialized States over the scope of patent protection over isolated new biogenetic matter. Since genes are not whole organisms, World Trade Organization member States must afford patent protection to biogenetically engineered new life forms involving microorganisms where these inventions are capable of industrial development, since the commercialization of such products and processes consti-

For the supporters of TRIPS, industry requires IPRs, tax relief for R&D investment, and low bureaucracies for the establishment of new production sites. Without these key legal features, industry is unwilling or unprepared to proceed with Foreign Development Investment (FDI), which also requires finances, education, management and competition. States that disregard the triumph, the rationality and the pre-eminence of the free market system of economic development do so at their peril because, "Once a biological material has left the country, it is practically out of control of the original owner of the tangible good. Therefore, only IPRs can control the exploitation and secure a reward."[196]

To comprehend the complex terms used and the ramifications of the patent applications and litigation, policy-makers and the international public need to gain appropriate scientific and technological capacity.[197] Capacity is critical for informed decisions in view of the increasing privatization of university innovation and technology transfer. Informed and balanced decisions need to involve *both* the national legislature and the judicial organs in decisions relating to patents over controversial subject matter or leading to ethical and moral questions of relevant concern for the general public.[198] These important decisions cannot be left to narrow judicial margins. Leaving the courts with the sole institutional competence to regulate the extent of the patent system could lead to undemocratic decisions that could justify "libertarianism (or proprietarianism): protecting an individual's natural right to appropriate goods used in the expansion of proprietary regimes to such informational goods as indigenous knowledge

tutes an intrinsic and lucrative aspect of international trade. See S. D. Murphy, "Biotechnology and International Law," *Harvard International Law Journal* 42, 1 (2001): 47–139 at 69. While these exceptions are permitted under TRIPS, States are nevertheless compelled to protect patented genes belonging to other nations. In the U.S., Europe and Japan, the landmark case of *Diamond v. Chakrabarti* has lead to the convergence of legal and policy positions regarding the patentability of microorganisms, new plant and animal breeds and genetically modified plants and animals. Murphy, *id.* at 62, argues that in these jurisdictions protection extends to artificially isolated and purified forms of naturally-occurring DNA molecules, as long as the invention consists of a new and useful manufacture or composition of matter that has a distinctive name, character or use. The legal and policy approaches of the U.S., European Union States and Japan converge on the possibility of granting patent protection over biological materials and expanding the scope of protection over amino acid sequences and proteins encoded in gene isolates. EU patent policy differs slightly as it requires the inventor to reveal the structure, the process by which the new organism was obtained, or other criteria of novelty.

196. Straus 1996, n. 192 above, at 8.

197. Capacity building measures are extensively discussed in CBD COP 7, Decision VII/19.

198. E. R. Gold, "The Reach of Patent Law and Institutional Competence," *University of Ottawa Law and Technology Journal* 1 (2003–2004): 263.

and genetic resources."[199] Libertarian justice places overemphasis on the right of the inventor to be awarded a patent as a reward for thought and labor, regardless of whether the invention is socially beneficial.[200]

The preceding observations highlight the importance of IPRs in competition policy. Robert Pitofsky, former Chairperson of the U.S. Federal Trade Commission, has remarked that in the "New Economy" there is an increasing "dependence on products and services that are the embodiment of ideas,"[201] and that the major challenge ahead is to "identify policies that will allow a market economy to thrive in the context of this intellectual property revolution, and to evaluate the role of anti-trust laws upon the New Economy. In markets characterized by IPRs there is a "tendency to drift toward a single-firm dominance and even monopoly." The risk for competitors or challengers to the firm arising from this situation is that "the diversity of competing research and development programs and the pressure on the incumbent to innovate and stay ahead of competition are lost."[202]

The 2002 *OECD Report on Genetic Inventions, Intellectual Property Rights and Licencing Practices* suggests that inflexible attitudes on the part of biotech patent owners have resulted in abusive monopoly positions relating to health screening tests. However, the report also recognizes that though the solutions should involve changes in patent law, changing levels or degrees of protection would affect investment in therapeutic research.[203] The public ends up losing whether a strong system of IPR protection is, or is not, in place, because the price for medicines is high with an IPR system,[204] but needed medicines and other therapeutic agents may not be produced without one in place. In addition, "patent thickets" and "royalty stacking" proliferation in relation with gene patents, may contribute to inhibiting vaccines for diseases such as malaria, unless a newcomer into the market knows how to negotiate the narrowing of patents over relevant proteins for

199. *Id.* at 266. Professor Gold is concerned with courts that "hide beyond stealth libertarianism to avoid addressing fundamental issues that society faces with respect to knowledge and innovation." *Id.* at 267.

200. *Id.* at 266. Professor Gold identifies Professor Straus as a main exponent of this position.

201. R. Pitofsky, "Antitrust and Intellectual Property: Unresolved Issues at the Heart of the New Economy," *Berkeley Technology Law Journal* 16 (2001): 535, reproduced in *Intellectual Property Law Review* 34 (2002): 643.

202. *Id.* at 647.

203. OECD, n. 55 above, at 70.

204. Due also to factors that raise costs, including the "need for more and higher-quality epidemiological and genetic population data, increasing regulatory costs, including stricter quality assessment and quality control requirements, laboratory qualification costs, increased needs for counselling, and, potentially, liability costs. *Id.* at 71.

producing the vaccine (i.e., so that from 40 patents that need to be licensed only 5 core ones need to be negotiated for production).[205] Unless patient groups put pressure on the government, the field of therapeutic agents and pharmaceuticals is replete with examples of industrial and corporate practices that indicate a potentially systematic abuse of monopoly power,[206] because "systems designed to encourage and protect innovation such as patents and copyrights can be—and often are—used to barricade a market against entry by new rivals."[207] If the present system is "seriously flawed" because of the factors outlined as well as excessive increase in patent litigation, as suggested by Pitofsky, patent policy will need to be re-evaluated. In the meantime, marine natural products are governed and developed pursuant to the regimes identified above.

SOME COMMENTS ON ENFORCEMENT

Unlike MOUs and other ABS-type agreements, clearance agreements under UNCLOS do not provide for any enforcement measures against the breach of MSR provisions.[208] Article 253 of UNCLOS requires the coastal State to order the suspension or cessation of the MSR activities if the latter are not being conducted pursuant to the conditions imposed by the coastal State. Disputes concerning the interpretation of Part XIII of UNCLOS can be referred to compulsory procedures entailing binding decisions under Part XV (Article 287), which allows for a range of choice of procedures for the settlement of disputes, including submission to the International Tribunal for the Law of the Sea (Annex VI), the International Court of Justice, to conciliation (Annex V), to an arbitral tribunal (constituted under Annex VII governing Arbitration), or a special tribunal (constituted in accordance with Annex VIII).

Under the territoriality principle of jurisdiction, a nation may also proscribe conduct within its borders and over hovering vessels beyond its borders when the consequences of the vessel engaging in the conduct proscribed extend to its territory.[209] The CBD is silent on what action a

---

205. *Id.* at 15.

206. *Id.* at 17.

207. Pitofsky, n. 201 above, at 649.

208. Tidwell, n. 214 below, reports that in 1999 the Philippines fined Bristol-Meyers Squibb $600,000 in penalties for hunting for species of bioactive coral within the Philippines. Without the full details of the case it is unclear whether the oceanographer in charge of obtaining clearance for the vessel declared his connection with the giant pharmaceutical prior to or after the fine was imposed. The Philippine Government cancelled the permits that it had previously granted.

209. UNCLOS, n. 7 above, Art. 27(a).

coastal State may undertake against alleged delinquent vessels engaging in unauthorized MSR or other research activities in the areas under the sovereignty, sovereign rights or jurisdiction of the costal State. Any suggestions regarding the enforcement of international laws relating to the conduct of MSR activities and the equitable distribution of benefits arising from MSR results and other marine research activities need to be balanced.[210] The emphasis of the GCCS, UNCLOS and the CBD is on negotiation and compromise.[211] One action taken by the U.S. Department of State against delinquent scientists is to report them to the National Science Foundation (NSF) and other federal agencies. The latter have the discretion to withdraw funds for current or future projects in which the scientist is, or intends to be, engaged.[212]

Severe measures for the enforcement of MSR provisions, including boardings of foreign research vessels, fines, seizures, confiscations and even arrest of the personnel in charge on board the research vessel, have the potential to cause international incidents and to discourage building relationships of trust between nations.[213] These measures may be more or less suitable depending on the nature and extent of a potential breach of GCCS, CITES, UNCLOS and CBD provisions. Any action that would breach the fundamental rule that merchant vessels are immune from the criminal jurisdiction of any nation other than the flag State in the territorial sea (except in listed circumstances) or on the high seas, should be weighed. The consequences of creating an international incident must be also

210. There is no reported discussion in the literature in this field at this stage that marine biomedical research merits enforcement measures under UNCLOS or the CBD.

211. GCCS, n. 6 above, Art. 5.8; UNCLOS, n. 7 above, Arts. 250 and 249.2; CBD, n. 11 above, Art. 15.

212. The U.S. Department of State, Office of Oceans, Environmental and Scientific Affairs, penalizes the failure by the chief scientist to comply with post-cruise obligations of Part XIII of UNCLOS, Article 249, by inserting the following notice:

> Your failure to provide the above materials on the schedule you outlined in your preliminary cruise report has resulted in our canceling your ability to obtain foreign clearances through this office until they are delivered. Failure to inform this office of your rectification of this matter by ... will result in our notifying U.S. funding agencies. We have been advised by NSF, NOAA and ONR that they will not consider proposals for funding from scientists with delinquent post-cruise obligations to foreign coastal states. The consequence of non-compliance with post-cruise obligations is that coastal states have the right to reject further U.S. requests for clearances until all obligations have been met.

U.S. Department of State standard memorandum on *Upcoming Post Cruise Obligations for Cruise* . . . , obtained through the kind courtesy of OES.

213. A number of Latin American nations, China and the Russian Republic use their naval forces to monitor compliance with the provisions of UNCLOS.

carefully evaluated. In the hypothetical case that coastal States began to consider the possibility of implementing more stringent enforcement measures against foreign delinquent vessels than those provided for by Article 253 of UNCLOS, a procedure for coordinating governmental positions similar to the U.S. PD–27 is desirable.[214]

Breaches of international law that took place prior to the entry into force of the CBD in 1993 may never be punished and potential damages may never be recovered because the costs of discovery and litigation could be prohibitive and take many years. Breaches of international law of the sea and CBD provisions by individuals acting beyond the purview of government protection or sponsorship are beyond this study. However, some examples show that, under pressure, patent offices in the United States, and in Great Britain have been prepared to drop patents if is it blatantly obvious that the latter breach the rights of indigenous peoples.[215] This is an important form of enforcement that is being investigated and merits further consideration, as patent offices could collaborate with agencies in charge of

214. Although the PD 27 is mostly used in drug enforcement cases its consensual nature is valuable. The U.S. Coast Guard (USCG) enforces U.S. laws over all U.S. vessels anywhere in the world. Comity requires prior coastal State consent for U.S. enforcement actions over U.S. vessels in another nation's internal waters, territorial seas and archipelagic waters. Law enforcement in foreign waters may be undertaken only to the extent authorized by the coastal nation and the flag-State through "consensual boarding" under Presidential Directive 27 (PD27). Any Commander intending to board a foreign vessel must obtain a "statement of no objection" to board the foreign vessel with permission of the flag-State and in coordination between the USCG chain of Command and the U.S. Department of State. See *The Commander's Handbook on the Law of Naval Operations* (Norfolk: Department of the Navy, 1995).

215. Two examples illustrate the gravity of individuals operating outside the law. One is the theft by a British biochemist of sacred leaves to claim their neuromuscular properties in the Cunaniol patent, extracted from the leaves of the barbasco bush, sacred to the Wapishana of the border between Brazil and Guyana. The British patent office dropped the patent after a concerted NGO protest. In 1999, the U.S. Patent and Trademark Office revoked a patent granted to a U.S. pharmacology student who filed for patent protection over inventions arising from the use of Ayahuasca vine, a most sacred plant for Ecuadorian Indigenous Peoples for its healing and divination properties known for centuries. J. Tidwell, *Raiders of the Forest Cures*, (2002) available online: <http://nationalzoo.si.edu>. The misleading term of bio-piracy has been popularized to indicate a situation where certain types of property are appropriated without permission. For a discussion of bio-piracy and traditional knowledge in the context of Article 8(j) of the CBD, see N. S. Gopalakrishnan, "TRIPS and Protection of Traditional Knowledge of Genetic Resources: New Challenges to the Patent System," *European Intellectual Property Review* 27, 1 (2005): 11–18; see also D. Conforto, "Traditional and Modern-Day Biopiracy: Redefining the Biopiracy Debate," *Journal of Environmental Law and Litigation* 19 (2004): 357–396.

enforcing law of the sea, international law relating to TRIPS, and ABS Agreement provisions.

Under CITES, trade sanctions are a potentially effective measure against breaches of treaty obligations.[216] It is unclear whether nations would be willing to coordinate with Interpol to maintain records of offenders suspected, tried and convicted of violating wildlife trade laws, to develop international extradition agreement(s) to secure their prosecution, or to comply with orders of an international court or tribunal.[217]

CONCLUSION

In this article we have suggested that Part XIII of UNCLOS (Articles 241, 246.5, 249.2 and 250) has similar effects to those sought by Article 15, CBD, and concluded that UNCLOS is a much neater system of access when compared to the ABS mechanisms of the CBD. We have argued that the preparatory work of the GCCS and UNCLOS support the sovereign rights of coastal States over natural resources, and that the rules of interpretation of the VCLT support our conclusion that there is an indistinguishability between the marine biota covered in the law of the sea, the marine biogenetic resources of the CBD and, some marine species protected under CITES. We have documented the rush to claim patents over inventions derived from marine biota, and highlighted the growing market in marine natural products used as therapeutic agents. We have provided examples of the critical role of bacteria in the development of marine and other natural products and the importance of achieving balance within the patent system, so that patent monopolies do not result in bottlenecks that impede further

---

216. It has been used to protect rhinoceros, tiger, and other endangered species trade, including whales. In the latter case, it has worked quite effectively.

217. Such enforcement provision is envisaged in the 1976 Convention on the Protection of the Archaeological, Historical, and Artistic Heritage of the American Nations. It has been proposed that CITES parties could form international or regional tribunals in which civil and/or criminal charges can be brought against state and/or individual violators. See Yale Centre for Environmental Law and Policy, *Improving Enforcement and Compliance with the Convention on International Trade in Endangered Species* (prepared for the World Wildlife Fund by the Yale Environmental Protection Clinic), available online: <http://www.yale.edu/envirocenter/clinic/cities.html>. In the U.S., Customs, Fish and Wildlife Service and Coast Guard officers have extensive experience in the enforcement of CITES, environmental and fisheries provisions. Since the U.S. is the leading oceanographic State and also a leader in the development of marine natural products, the coordination of these services with changes in the Patent and Trademark Office policies on disclosure of the origin, source, and legal provenance of biogenetic materials in patent applications may merit further analysis. The Convention on the Recognition and Enforcement of Foreign Arbitral Awards would help reluctant nations.

scientific research for the benefit of populations around the world. As with any other area of legal regulation, good governance and political will should enhance the ability of States to reach mutually beneficial agreements on ABS through relationships of trust and effective clearance pursuant to negotiations through official channels within Article 250 of UNCLOS. The limited involvement (or literature produced) by diplomatic embassy staff and government officials in the processing of clearance requests that straddle between UNCLOS, the CBD, CITES, and biotech derived patent activity is regrettable. There are also very few studies or literature on how ABS Agreements arising under the CBD are incorporated and integrated into clearance requests pursuant to UNCLOS. More information is needed on how UNCLOS, CBD and CITES operate in the negotiation of access by foreign researchers for the conduct of MSR activities, marine biogenetic research, or other forms of applied marine research for ulterior commercial gain in areas under coastal State maritime control. These great lacunae in our understanding of State practice require exerting pressure on those with the relevant information to make it available for public scrutiny, and for legal and policy research that integrates different spheres of legal regulation for effective enforcement of international law.

In the Shoes of the Fisher: Commercial Fishers and the Tasmanian Marine Protected Area Policy Journey

Cheryle Hislop*

Ph.D. Candidate, School of Government, University of Tasmania, Australia

INTRODUCTION

Located south of the Australian mainland and separated by a stretch of water known as the Bass Strait, Tasmania is the nation's only island State. The vast majority of the State's population—approximately 475,000—reside on or very close to the 5,400 km of coastline, and Tasmania is renowned for production of high quality seafood—abalone, rock lobster, scallop, scalefish, kelp, giant crab, and a small commercial dive industry harvesting sea urchins and periwinkles.[1] Tasmania boasts unique physical and biologically diverse ocean and coastal environments; on any day one can encounter open sandy beaches, majestic sea cliffs, rocky reefs, small bays, extensive dune systems, and shallow estuaries, and discover species such as the endemic handfish, seadragons, basket stars, seafeathers, penguins, great white sharks, whales, and dolphins.[2]

The difficult, indeed wicked task besetting the Tasmanian Government (and indeed most if not all governments in industrialised coastal nations) is finding a balance between maintaining the lucrative commercial fishing industry and protecting the State's precious resources and habitats.[3] One

---

* EDITORS' NOTE: This article was the winning entry in the 2005 *Ocean Yearbook* Student Paper Competition.

1. For details of Tasmania's population, see Tasmanian Population online: <http://taspop.tasbis.com>. Details of Tasmania's commercial fishing industry can be found on the Department of Primary Industries, Water and Environment web site at: <http://www.dpiwe.tas.gov.au/inter.nsf/Topics/HMUY–67P23?open>.

2. Tasmania has the largest wild abalone fishery in the world. Department of Primary Industries, Water and Environment. Available online: <http://www.dpiwe.tas.gov.au/inter.nsf/Topics/HMUY–67P894?open>.

3. See H. Rittel and M. Webber, "Dilemmas in a General Theory of Planning," *Policy Sciences* 4 (1973): 155–169, for analysis of "wicked problems" in public policy.

Ocean Yearbook 20: 283–304.

tool in the suite of management instruments is the designation of regulated, spatially delimited areas known generically as marine protected areas (MPAs).[4]

Analysis of the Tasmanian MPA policy journey over the past two decades tells an interesting story, one replete with challenge, conflict, electioneering, and inertia. For over 20 years, successive state governments and opposition parties have committed publicly to the imminent designation of MPAs if elected, but dragged their heels once holding the reins of power, despite conclusive data indicating significant declines in commercial fish stocks and the need for expedient decisions regarding marine resource and habitat protection in State waters.

The identification, inclusion and ranking of stakeholders is one of the keys to the complex issue of resource protection, and as such there is much utility in analysing the Tasmanian MPA policy process through the lens of stakeholder theory in order to find out why the process has moved so slowly. There are particular elements of stakeholder theory that provide a valuable setting against which to tease out the political motivations of key participants in the marine management field, and the problems that come with expansion of the stakeholder arena in the contemporary policy milieu.[5] In socio-economic analyses of commercial fishers' attitudes to marine resource management it is also imperative that policy developers and decision makers be made aware of deeply rooted, socio-psychological elements such as history, tradition, and lifestyle, and the influence that these phenomena have on fishers' attitudes toward marine protected area proposals.

Interwoven with stakeholder status and attitudes are the *types* of policies that directly affect commercial fishers. In the context of the Tasmanian MPA policy experience, there is a body of evidence that supports Lowi's thesis that "policy causes politics."[6] The arguments involved in the

4. The preferred definition of "marine protected area" as intended in this article is: "any area of sea or ocean—where appropriate in combination with contiguous intertidal areas—together with associated natural and cultural features in the water column, within, or on top of the seabed, for which measures have been taken for the purpose of protecting part or all of the enclosed environment." H. Nijkamp and G. Peet, *Marine Protected Areas in Europe*. Report of a study within the BioMar Project commissioned by the LIFE program of the Commission of European Communities, AIDEnvironment, Amsterdam, March 1994, in J. C. Day and J. C. Roff, *Planning for Representative Protected Areas: A Framework for Canada's Oceans* (Canada: WWF, 2000). This definition reflects the generic nature of the term "marine protected area," and the multitude of similar terms with the same implications, for example, marine reserves, marine parks, marine management areas and habitat protection zones.

5. K. H. Mikalsen and S. Jentoft, "From User-Groups to Stakeholders? The Public Interest in Fisheries Management," *Marine Policy* 25 (2001): 281–292.

6. T. Lowi, "American Business, Public Policy, Case-Studies, and Political Theory," *World Politics* 16 (1964): 688.

Tasmanian context cannot be reduced to a comparative analysis of fixed pairs of binary opposites; there are many other actors, factors, and divergent interests involved in the contemporary, citizen-inclusive policy setting. Nevertheless, the most publicly vocal opposition to MPA policy proposals has been expressed by the commercial fishing industry, and to a lesser extent echoed by recreational fishers. On the other hand, those advocating or supporting the concept and establishment of MPAs have come from fields such as science, public environment agencies, environmental non-governmental organisations, citizens' groups, and academia. This situation is hardly unique to Australia's island State—the more inclusive approach to marine management generates a particular brand of politics that is reflected throughout the Antipodes and in other fishing and marine resource industry constituencies around the world. Therefore, the following analysis, conducted against the background of Lowi's policy typology and stakeholder theory, can be adapted to similar situations in other locales.

The broader lesson drawn from this research is the need to heighten awareness amongst decision makers, and the broader constituency, of deeply rooted socio-psychological elements that are shared amongst actors of the commercial fishing community, and to highlight the imperative of taking these phenomena into account *together with* the economic impact assessments of marine protected area proposals. There is no doubt that the undulating topography of the marine resource management arena is a challenge to public policy decision makers, to fishers who fear for their livelihoods and lifestyle, and to those whose values reflect the socio-ecological shifts of the past few decades and who believe that they also have a stake in conserving marine resources and habitats. Direct participation of *all* those who believe they have a legitimate place at the marine resource policy table is impossible; nonetheless, over the last two decades many more from the community-at-large have found themselves with an invitation and a chair. While governments may express publicly their joy that the wheels of deliberative democracy are turning, the ever-burgeoning body of those asserting a stake in marine resource policy-making must strike fear into the hearts of those bureaucrats hoping to make expedient decisions.

A final but important caveat is that this article is not intended to depict commercial fishers as ecologically or morally reprehensible, but as actors with a strong historical and cultural attachment to occupation and lifestyle, and with entitlements and certain rights that have co-evolved along with their roles as hunter-gatherers, as cogs in the treadmill of production, and as suppliers heeding the demands of the seafood consumption market.

IN THE SHOES OF THE FISHER

Policy Causes Politics

At the risk of stating the obvious, analysis of marine protected area policy proposals cannot be cleaved from the instrumental approach to fisheries management because: (i) MPAs continue to be presented as part of the fisheries management toolbox despite the rhetoric of ecosystem-based management; and (ii) managers operating within this particular public policy arena continue to identify marine resource harvesters as those most profoundly affected by resource management decisions. In the same vein, the fishing industry has traditionally turned to public sector managers to help resolve intra- and inter-sectoral conflict, settle distributive issues, and answer questions about restrictions and regulations. There are a number of phenomena that feed into this exclusive interaction, but which have been paid scant attention in socio-economic analyses of the impact of MPAs on the commercial fishing industry.

Firstly, one needs to consider the *type* of government policies and actions that contribute to fishers' attitudes, behaviour and perceptions of rights. Lowi describes three policy types—distributive, regulatory, and redistributive.[7] Although not mutually exclusive, each policy type generates a particular "brand" of politics because each can be distinguished by their typological characteristics, hence his "policy causes politics" dictum. Fisheries management in Tasmania is a constellation of distributive and regulatory policy types including, inter alia, individual transferable quotas (ITQs), total allowable catch (TAC) schemes, fishing seasons, fishing grounds, licences, and gear specifications. Indeed it has been argued that no other commercial sector has been subject to as much control and regulation as that of commercial fishing.[8] Thus it stands to reason that agency managers will communicate directly, and sometimes exclusively, with the sector that is most affected by resource appropriation policies of the distributive and regulatory mould.

Distributive and Regulatory Policies

Lowi derived the term "distributive" from the 19th century U.S. government practice of allocating public lands to private interests. In terms of costs

7. *Id.* at 690–711.
8. A. Scott, "Introducing Property in Fisheries Management," FAO Fisheries Technical Paper 404/1 (Rome: Food and Agricultural Organization of the United Nations, 2000a): 2.

and benefits, distributive policies are intended to operate to the distinct advantage of the recipient, or "indulged" as Lowi calls them.[9] The cost is displaced onto the broader revenue system and borne by all citizens, including those who have no access, no direct stake and often little or no interest in the resource itself.[10] The historical genesis of distributive policy, rooted as it is in the indulgence of some and not others, engenders a particular type of politics that nourishes a sense of ownership and perceptions of rights that are addressed in more detail below.

Traditionally, those seeking to gain or maintain political office have long seen distributive policy as an effective means of gaining political support and electoral reward from the indulged of their constituency. As the origin of distribution was that of "first come, first served" the connection between the disparate actors of the distributive policy arena was and continues to be that of privilege (indulgence). Nonetheless, despite the disparity of those actors in the distributive arena, the candidate recognizes the indulged as a group with significant political muscle, and thus the ability to pave a path to political glory or conversely, obscurity.[11]

While distributive decisions bestow benefits to the indulged, regulatory decisions impose costs and reduce the options of private individuals who occupy a sector of the economy.[12] In the context of fisheries management, the indulged of the distributive arena also find themselves affected by a multitude of regulations intended to temper individual self-interest. The sectoralism of regulation also has the effect of steering the regulated into a galvanized alliance in the face of state-sanctioned coercion and other challenges considered exogenous to their interests. Even though they are considered the nemesis of business,[13] regulations also endow the sector with a sense of "ownership," primarily because of the orientation and intent of rules, restrictions and enforcement. As Scott suggests, however, even though fishers argue about the means, they do understand the purpose of regulations, especially in light of evidence indicating significant declines in many commercial fish stocks.[14] Ownership is also a characteristic of distributive policy—not the distinctive form of ownership in terms of

9. Lowi, n. 6 above, at 692.

10. T. Lowi, "Decision Making vs. Policy Making; Toward an Antidote for Technocracy," *Public Administration Review*, 30 (1970): 320.

11. Lowi, n. 6 above, at 692–693.

12. *Id.* at 690.

13. See C. Lindblom, "The Market as Prison," *Journal of Politics*, 44 (1982): 324–336, for an elegant argument on the relationship between regulation and business.

14. A. Scott, "Moving Through the Narrows: From Open Access to ITQs and Self-Government," FAO Technical Paper 404/1 (Rome: Food and Agricultural Organization of the United Nations, 2000b): 105–117.

property rights, but a kind of "quasi-ownership" realized through the act of distributive indulgence. Distributive policies such as licenses and quota systems serve to reinforce fishers' perceptions of *rights* to harvest fish stocks.

Redistributive Policies

Redistributive issues cut a swathe across broad sections of society and are often presented as a battle being fought out on inhospitable terrain between two consistently distinctive and ideologically opposed sides, a fight between the "haves and have-nots, bigness and smallness, bourgeoisie and proletariat."[15] As Lowi argues, the impetus for the fight "is not use of property but property itself, not equal treatment but equal possession, not behavior but being."[16] Unlike the distributive arena where conflict remains internalized, the battles fought over redistributive issues are nourished by controversy and publicity in order to expand the support base and fortify the wall of opposition.[17] The nature of the redistributive beast is determined not by the eventual policy, but by expectations of what that policy *might* be.[18]

Schattschneider asserts that it is the displacement of conflict that is an integral component of the political game. In this regard he makes some salient points that can be drawn into this discussion concerning the MPA policy/redistributive arena. The nub of Schattschneider's argument is that "the definition of alternatives is the supreme instrument of power."[19] In Tasmania's contemporary, constituent-inclusive MPA policy arena the alternatives or redistributive issues include aquaculture, scientific research, environmentalism, indigenous people's claims, tourism, coastal community groups, recreational diving, marine mineral resources, and academia. This relatively new generation of stakeholders bring with them values that extend far beyond the economic. Examples include existence, health, option, ecological, and bequest values,[20] and such redistributive, value-laden "alternatives" are sometimes seen by traditional stakeholders in the fisheries policy arena as tantamount to the throwing down of the gauntlet, that is, as direct challenges to their own particular value sets.

15. Lowi, n. 6 above, at 691.
16. *Id.*
17. *Id.*
18. *Id.*
19. E. E. Schattschneider, *The Semisovereign People: A Realist's View of Democracy in America* (Illinois: Dryden Press, 1960): 62–71.
20. For an in-depth discussion on values, see R. de Groot, *Functions of Nature: Evaluation of nature in environmental planning, management and decision making* (Amsterdam: Wolters-Noordhoff, 1992).

The Fishers

As already argued, policy types and the behaviour they elicit have a profound influence on fishers' attitudes toward marine protected area proposals. Attitude is a socio-psychological phenomenon, related to, but also distinguishable from culture and personality. According to Powell, *attitude* involves three important and interconnected components: (i) the *cognitive*, which incorporates awareness, ideas, belief and knowledge; (ii) the *affective*, which encompasses fears, likes, and dislikes; and (iii) *behavior*, which is influenced by both the cognitive and the affective.[21] It is important that decision makers, managers and policy analysts keep in mind the historical, traditional and cultural underpinnings of fishers' attitudes and dispositions, especially in light of their expectations and interactions within the marine resource policy arena.

There exists a particularly significant socio-psychological component of fishers' attitude, one which was expressed most succinctly in the Imperial Economic Committee's 1927 report on the nascent Australian fishing industry, and which persists in the contemporary commercial fishery setting: "The fisherman stands out in an ordered world as the last representative, at any rate on a considerable scale, of the hunter," and as such, "tends to stand apart from the general life of a country."[22] The risks associated with the capture of fish stocks together with the loneliness and isolation that accompanies a life spent at sea mean that the lifestyle of the commercial fisher, although framed as it is by the romantic notion of the hunter-gatherer, appeals to only a relatively small minority. As such, it is a lifestyle that constitutes its own special form of exclusivity, but which also engenders a strong sense of camaraderie when the "going gets tough."

The Fish

Fisheries are a common pool resource (CPR), that is, "a natural ... resource system that is sufficiently large to make it costly (but not impossible) to exclude potential beneficiaries from obtaining benefits from its use."[23] By

21. J. M. Powell, *Environmental Management in Australia, 1788–1914* (Melbourne: Oxford University Press, 1976): 5.

22. Imperial Economic Committee, "Marketing and Preparing for Market of Foodstuffs Produced Within the Empire," 5th Report—Fish, (London: HSMO, 1927), pp. 9–10, in A. J. Harrison, *The Commonwealth Government in the Administration of Australian Fisheries: A Sort of Mongrel Socialism*, National Monograph Series 6, Royal Australian Institute of Public Administration (1991): 15.

23. E. Ostrom, *Governing the Commons: The evolution of institutions for collective action* (Cambridge: Cambridge University Press, 1990): 30.

sharing a CPR, either through voluntary, distributive and/or regulatory means, harvesters are "tied together in a lattice of interdependence,"[24] which may or may not lead to the creation of an organization. Organization can range from "a stage or degree of interaction" to a formalized institution,[25] but at a minimum it is a conduit through which those affected by decisions can channel their grievances to each other, and to the "outside" world. When confronted with government policy proposals that incite interaction, actors need organize only to the point where they can formulate and agree on strategies to enhance their joint benefits, reduce their joint costs, and protect and preserve their sectoral interests.[26]

The distinction between a CPR and a public good is also significant in the context of marine resource protection. As long as the cost of provision of a pure public good is shared around, those who contribute to its provision are not concerned with who uses it, or where or when it is used.[27] Those who contribute to the provision of a CPR, however, through, inter alia, license payments, royalties, taxes, and adhering to regulations, are deeply concerned about its usage irrespective of whether others contribute to its provision or not.[28] When one adds up contribution to CPR provision together with the politics generated by distributive and regulatory policy types and the hunter-gatherer/stand-apart lifestyle, it soon becomes clear why there exists a perception of "ownership" of marine resources among commercial fishers. It is imperative, however, to note the distinction between perceptions of ownership and the concept of property rights.

It is recognized through customary law that fish and marine habitats cannot be owned even though fishers will often refer to a fishery as "theirs" or to a territory being "reserved" for their use.[29] The 17th century Dutch jurist Hugo Grotius argued that claiming property rights on a "thing" was contingent upon two conditions being met. The first was that the individual had to have the power to appropriate the desired object and prevent others from gaining possession of it unless a transaction was involved. While commercial fishers (those empowered by distributive policies and restricted by regulations) have always had the capacity to appropriate fish stocks, they have themselves been relatively powerless to limit or prevent others from doing likewise. The second condition was that the desired object had to be relatively difficult to acquire and quantitatively limited so that efforts to

---

24. *Id.*, pp. 38–39.
25. D. Truman, *The Government Process* (New York, 1951): 50–51, in Schattschneider, n. 19 above, at 28.
26. Ostrom, n. 23 above, at 39.
27. Examples of "pure" public goods include clean air, seawater, the atmosphere, and lighthouses.
28. *Id.* at 221.
29. Scott, n. 8 above, at 4.

obtain it were warranted.[30] Grotius believed the fishes of the sea to be qualitatively unlimited: "For everyone admits that if a great many persons hunt on land or fish in a river, the forest is easily exhausted of wild animals and the river of fish, but such a contingency is impossible in the case of the sea."[31] The advent of the Industrial Revolution and mercurial developments in fish harvesting technologies have, however, led to serious quantitative limitations of fish stocks.

Despite quantitative limitations, however, the fish of the sea still cannot be claimed as property because property rights are further defined by three fundamental powers—the power of utility (or management of an object); the power of disposal (to sell it or cede it); and the power of capture. The fisher as vessel owner has all three powers, but as occupier of the fishery has only the third power—to capture and keep or sell the fish that are caught.[32] The absence of the first two powers deprived the fisher of any incentive to look after the fishery,[33] and as such Australian governments at both state and federal levels were motivated to introduce the individual transferable quota (ITQ) system, in addition to regulations. In essence, ITQs are a combination of government regulation with a somewhat ambiguous form of power defined by distributive-type "ownership," the latter being proportionate to allocation of quotas established through a total allowable catch (TAC) system.[34] The raft of fisheries-specific, legislatively imposed regulations in Tasmania, together with distributive policies that restrict access through mandatory limited licensing and quasi-property rights realized through the ITQ system have transformed lucrative fisheries into the legitimate, exclusive and "controlled preserve" of commercial harvesters.[35]

Nonetheless, the power of capture should not be underestimated in discussions of fishers' *rights*. At its core is the instrumentalist assumption made by both fishers and management that fish exist to be fished. Both regulatory and distributive decisions establish how much can be taken, who can take it, how it can be taken and when, but extraction itself remains a given.[36] A right to something is of course a perceptually and conceptually

30. *Id.*

31. Grotius, cited in E. A. Keen, "Common Property in Fisheries: Is Sole Ownership an Option?," *Marine Policy* 7, 3 (1983): 197–211, in R. Kearney, "Fisheries Property Rights and Recreational/Commercial Conflict: Implications of Policy Developments in Australia and New Zealand," *Marine Policy* 25 (2001): 49.

32. Scott, n. 8 above, at 4.

33. *Id.*

34. *Id.*

35. *Harper v. Minister for Sea Fisheries* (1989) 168 CLR 314, 325, in W. Palmer, "Legal Planning for Management of Fisheries Using Property Rights," "Use of property rights in fisheries management," FAO Technical Paper 404/2 (Rome: Food and Agricultural Organization of the United Nations, 2000): 66.

36. Scott, n. 8 above, at 4.

elastic term, a one-size-fits-all argument to counter any threats to the survival of one's self-interest. Managers, by virtue of their employment and position, have the right to manage using the primary tool provided by the state-legitimate coercion. Fishers talk of the right to fish, the right to make a living, and sometimes the right to compensation if these other rights are withdrawn.

As Schattschneider suggests, "nearly all theories about politics have something to do with who can get into the fight and who is to be excluded."[37] The triggers for fisheries-specific sectoral behavior—distributive and regulatory policies; the ambiguous legal status of *in situ* marine resources; a long history of unfettered appropriation; and perceptions of rights—are all important phenomena that nourish fishers' opinions, attitudes and patterns of behavior concerning marine protected area proposals. As the political and socio-psychological elements have now been examined, it is time to introduce some salient components from stakeholder theory in order to explore the ranking of policy actors in the contemporary Tasmanian MPA policy arena.

Stakeholders and the Firm

In the broadest possible sense, a *stakeholder* is defined as "any group or individual who can affect or is affected by the achievement of the firm's objectives."[38] Stakeholder theory is premised on two key issues. The first deals with stakeholder identification and thus addresses the question of who has a legitimate or rightful claim to managerial attention, while the second explores the salience of stakeholders, that is, those who are actually having their demands met at the management level.[39]

The distinction between *primary* and *secondary* stakeholders is also important. The survival of the firm is contingent on primary stakeholders—those actors located within the composite of interest groups that hold varying rights (be they real or perceived), expectations, responsibilities and objectives and who engage in direct transactions with the firm. Those stakeholders at the periphery of the firm's ambit—where no *direct* transactions are involved—are considered secondary even though the firm acknowledges their existence. Nonetheless secondary stakeholders can and

---

37. Schattschneider, n. 19 above, at 20.

38. R. E. Freeman, *Strategic Management: A Stakeholder Approach* (Boston: Pitman, 1984), in Mikalsen and Jentoft, n. 5 above, at 282.

39. R. K. Mitchell, B. R. Agle and D. J. Wood, "Toward a Theory of Stakeholder Identification and Salience: Defining the Principle of Who and What Really Counts," *Academy of Management Review* 22, 4 (1997), in Mikalsen and Jentoft, n. 5 above, at 282–284.

increasingly do exert a degree of influence, or conversely, are influenced by the firm even though they do not enjoy the full complement of rights extended to those identified in the primary category.[40]

Stakeholders are categorized or 'scored' by the firm according to their ability to meet each of the following attributes: *legitimacy* (legal, moral, or presumed); *power* (degree of influence); and *urgency* (claims demanding the firm's immediate attention). Each stakeholder's score posits them in one of the three following categories. The *definitive* stakeholder possesses all three attributes and thus has the undivided attention of the firm. The *expectant* stakeholder has two of the three attributes, and while enjoying an active relationship with the firm does not have its unequivocal attention. The *latent* stakeholder possesses only one of the above attributes, and as such the attention of the firm can be described as capricious at best.[41]

Stakeholder identification and categorization is a fluid and dynamic process: power, legitimacy, urgency, and expectations are subject to a barrage of exogenous dependent and independent variables that exert varying degrees of influence, not least those of economic fluctuations, citizen awareness, cultural shifts, and consumer demands and preferences. Nonetheless, it seems safe to conjecture that those who score highly have a tighter grip on their position than those with lower scores.

The *firm* itself is a network of private and public agents, a "political coalition" of interest groups operating within a matrix of inconsistent expectations and demands.[42] The role of management within the firm in the contemporary setting is a far more inclusive process than that of the traditional hierarchical model, and involves communication and transactions among predominantly autonomous agents rather than a top-down approach to organization.[43] Modern fisheries management systems, or to be more precise, the fisheries ministry and fisheries minister, fit comfortably within this model of the firm, "even though the role and legitimacy of government, including its claim of ownership to the resource, is not necessarily self-evident."[44]

As alluded to earlier, MPA policy proposals are often presented as fisheries management tools rather than as part of a broader approach to ecosystem management. Although identified as the primary definitive stakeholders in Tasmanian marine resource management, there has long

40. M. B. E. Clarkson, "A Stakeholder Framework for Analyzing and Evaluating Corporate Social Performance," *Academy of Management Review* 20, 1 (1995), in Mikalsen and Jentoft, n. 5 above, at 283.

41. Mitchell et al., n. 39 above.

42. R. M. Cyert and J. G. March, *A Behavioral Theory of the Firm* (Englewood Cliffs: Prentice Hall, 1963), in Mikalsen and Jentoft, n. 5 above, at 284.

43. Mikalsen and Jentoft, n. 5 above, at 284.

44. *Id.*

been an acrimonious relationship between firm and primary definitive stakeholders. For example, the now defunct Tasmanian Fisheries Development Authority (TFDA) was created in 1976 to forge a symbiotic relationship between the fishing industry and its regulators. Commercial fishers, however, remained suspicious and at arm's length from the TFDA advisory board. The latter was eventually dismantled and the Department of Sea Fisheries later arose from the ashes.[45] Australian governments, at state, territory, and federal levels, have a penchant for reshaping and renaming public agencies and departments, and "running the broom" over ministerial portfolios as testimony to their electoral victories and commitment to reorganization for the greater good. At the time of writing, the firm in the context of Tasmanian fisheries management operates under the title of Sea Fishing and Aquaculture, a designated statutory authority located within the Department of Primary Industries, Water and Environment. Commercial fisheries are the responsibility of the Minister for Primary Industries and Water, marine protected areas fall within the ambit of the Minister responsible for Resource Planning and Development, and enforcement of MPA legislation resides with the Minister of Police.[46]

The Tasmanian Marine Protected Area Policy Process 1980–2004

The following is a series of chronological snapshots of the Tasmanian MPA process from 1980 to 2004 with most of the data drawn from regional print media archives. It is imperative that it be viewed in light of the previous discussion concerning the socio-psychological roots of commercial fishers' attitudes to MPAs, the political inter-connectedness that is generated by policy types, and the relatively new approach of broader stakeholder inclusiveness that is part of the deliberatively democratic approach to marine management. Tables 1 and 2 depict the stakeholder "maps" for the Tasmanian MPA policy process in the 1980s and 1990s respectively.

The 1980s

1980: With the support and blessings of the National Parks and Wildlife Service (NPWS),[47] the Australian Heritage Commission provided a $16,000

45. M. Haward, "Institutions, Interest Groups and Marine Resource Policy: The development of fisheries and oil and gas policy in Bass Strait," (Unpublished Master of Arts Thesis, Department of Political Science, University of Tasmania, 1986).

46. Christian Bell, Tasmanian and South East Australia Co-ordinator, Marine and Coastal Community Network, pers. comm. March 2, 2005.

47. The National Parks and Wildlife Service (NPWS) is a federal, not state agency. See R. Herr and M. Haward, "Australia's Oceans Policy: Policy and

grant to marine biologist Graham Edgar to identify suitable marine park sites in Tasmanian waters.[48]

The issue of fishers' rights surfaced immediately following identification of a suitable site in the northwest of the State. In a letter to the Minister of the NPWS, the secretary of a local community group expressed the sentiments of members regarding the MPA proposal: "We feel it would be most unfair if we were denied the right to carry on fishing in this area."[49] While a tenuous agreement between the NPWS and TFDA to coordinate efforts for the MPA survey had been reached, inadequate funding limited the survey to areas adjacent to terrestrial parks and reserves.[50]

1981: The Joint Policy for the Establishment and Management of Marine Reserves in Tasmania recommended the establishment of three marine reserves in state waters. Even though the joint NPWS/TFDA proposal suggested all commercial and recreational activities be allowed to continue inside the reserve with the exception of netting, it was met with fierce and growing opposition.[51] There existed a palpable fear amongst commercial fishers, shack owners and local councillors that restrictions would soon be extended to all activities within the reserves. Two anti-MPA petitions were presented to the Tasmanian Parliament in late 1981, and in a complete *volte-face*, the TFDA renounced its joint policy coordinating role and rejected the MPA proposals.[52]

1984: Despite the backlash that the first survey and MPA policy proposals had generated, the NPWS funded a second marine survey and another four sites were recommended, including the Kent Group of Islands in Bass Strait.[53] In the same year, New Zealand MPA advocate Dr Bill Ballantine

---

Process," in M. Haward ed., *Integrated Oceans Management: Issues in Implementing Australia's Oceans Policy* (Hobart: Cooperative Research Centre for Antarctic and Souther Ocean, 2001) for details of Australia's federal system of government in the context of marine management.

48. "Coastline Study for Marine Parks," *Examiner* (April 29, 1980); L. K. Kriwoken, "Island of Management in a Sea of Mismanagement: Marine Reserves in Tasmania, in A. M. Ivanovici, D. Tarte and M. Olsen eds., *Protection of Marine and Estuarine Areas—A Challenge for All Australians.* Proceedings of the Fourth Fenner Conference on the Environment. Occasional Paper No. 4, Australian Committee for IUCN (1993): 67–72.

49. "Objections to Reserve," *Advocate* (July 1, 1980).

50. "Coastline Study for Marine Parks," *Examiner* (April 29, 1981); Kriwoken, n. 48 above, at 69; L. K. Kriwoken and M. Haward, "Marine and Estuarine Protected Areas in Tasmania, Australia: The Complexities of Policy Development, *Ocean and Shoreline Management* 15 (1991): 153.

51. Kriwoken and Haward, n. 50 above, at 151; "Marine Reserves Urged," *Mercury* (July 29, 1981); "Marine Park Bid Opposed," *Advocate* (August 25, 1981).

52. "Marine Life Area Study Rejected," *Examiner* (September 1, 1981).

53. "Six State Marine Parks Proposed," *Mercury* (September 25, 1984).

visited Tasmania for a series of seminars addressing spatially demarcated marine habitat protection, and support for the concept began gathering momentum among recreational divers, some local councils, and conservation groups.[54] Nonetheless, print media coverage of marine protection issues during this time was trained on the concept's most vocal opponents—commercial and recreational fishers. Advocates for marine resource and habitat conservation were also challenged by the strong developmentalist philosophy of the incumbent Liberal government (elected in 1982 and re-elected in 1986), which steadfastly opposed the concept of MPAs. These factors, along with a dearth of scientific research, lack of government-assigned agency responsibility for planning and management of marine reserves, and a draft policy devoid of any supporting legislation ensured that the second survey was never released for public comment.[55]

1986: With the endorsement and sponsorship of the Tasmanian Government, the Tasmanian Fishing Industry Council (TFIC) was formed to give a voice to fishers who believed their rights were best represented by a cohesive association capable of flexing "political muscle" in light of threats of increasing regulations concerning marine resources and habitats.[56] The mid-to-late 1980s marked a trend of declining catches in some of the State's most lucrative fisheries. Scallop beds were fished to the point of collapse following several decades of unregulated harvesting, and a 95 percent decrease in annual landings from 1982–87 eventuated in the closure of the fishery until the mid-1990s in an attempt to resuscitate stocks.[57] Rock lobster and abalone fishers also registered significant decreases in catches, triggering negotiations between these sectors and government over introduction of total allowable catch (TAC) and individual transferable quota (ITQ) systems. These were established in 1984 and 1985 respectively.[58]

While wild fish stock catches were plummeting, the inshore aquaculture industry began to flourish. Community and environmental groups, concerned about the effects of fish farm pollution on the marine environment, as well as ecological impacts of overfishing, point source sewage outfall, and dumping of industrial wastes at sea, embarked on a public awareness campaign to highlight these problems.[59] In light of the

---

54. "Marine Reserve Backed," *Mercury* (November 22, 1984).

55. Kriwoken, n. 48 above, at 70.

56. "Tasmanian Fishing Industry Faces Exciting Year," *Mercury* (April 28, 1986).

57. K. S. Edyvane, *Fisheries Production in Tasmanian Coastal Waters: Development of the Tasmanian Representative System of Marine Protected Areas,* Background Report No. 3 (Tasmania: Department of Primary Industries, Water and Environment, 2001): 12.

58. *Id.,* State of the Environment Report; "Coasts and Oceans," (Canberra: Department of Environment and Heritage, 2001).

59. Kriwoken and Haward, n. 50 above, at 156.

growing public profile of marine resource issues, the State opposition adopted a pre-election policy position on MPAs, declaring them beneficial to the fishing industry, necessary for scientific research, and long overdue.[60] Print media coverage of the MPA issue is relatively scant during this period. Nonetheless, the mood of the Tasmanian public, reflected in letters to the editors of various regional newspapers, indicates the redefinition of marine resource management as a broader social problem, that is, as a redistributive issue rather than the exclusive province of primary definitive stakeholders and the fisheries agency.

1989: A minority Labor government gained office with the support of five independent Greens and was promptly christened the "Tasmanian Parliamentary Accord," or more simply the "Accord." Amongst the fruits of this unusual coalition was a renewed commitment to establish MPAs in State waters. Immediately following the election the Tasmanian Conservation Trust (TCT) convened an informal working group to discuss issues of marine conservation.[61] The TCT, in collaboration with the IUCN and the Fund for Animals, lobbied the Tasmanian Government to expand the scope of debate beyond that of the interests and rights of fishers. The NGO coalition wanted the broader community to be involved in marine resource and habitat management issues and policy development, and a concerted media campaign to raise their profile resulted in a modicum of political leverage and a back seat in the policy arena.[62] At the same time, however, the Government also faced a rising tide of opposition to marine reserves from recreational and commercial fishers. Public meetings held in the south of the State drew over 700 anti-reservists angered by a fresh proposal to establish an MPA in the D'Entrecasteaux Channel. The TFIC and the Tasmanian Amateur Sea Fishermen's Association (TASFA) released a media statement condemning "the arbitrary and arrogant proposal" of the State government to establish an MPA in the area,[63] and describing the proposal as an exercise in "environmental embroidery."[64] Despite this wave of hostility, the Accord established a public sector marine reserves working group (MRWG) in November 1989. The Group's mandate was to provide

60. *Id.,* "ALP Bid to Calm Conflict Between Sea Users," *Mercury* (April 26, 1989); "Marine Park Plan Floated," *Examiner* (April 29, 1989).

61. The Tasmanian Conservation Trust is a not-for-profit local environmental non-government organization.

62. Kriwoken and Haward, n. 50 above, at 158.

63. "Channel Marine Park Unwanted," *Sunday Tasmanian,* (September 17, 1989); "Fishermen Slam Plan for Marine Park in Channel," *Mercury* (September 26, 1989).

64. "Plan for Marine Parks Cop Flak," *Mercury* (May 8, 1990).

Table 1.—Stakeholder Groups and Scores in the Tasmanian MPA
Policy Process during the 1980s.[88]

Stakeholders	Urgency	Power	Legitimacy
Definitive			
Commercial Fishers	High	High	High
Bureaucrats	High	High	High
Fish Workers	High	Medium	High
Local Communities	Medium–High	Medium	High
Expectant			
Scientists	Medium	Low	Medium
Media	Medium	Medium–High	Medium
Local Government	Increasing	Medium	Low
Recreational Fishers	Medium–High	Medium	Increasing
Enforcement Agencies	Medium	Medium	High
Latent			
Citizens	Increasing	Low	Increasing
Environmental Groups	Medium	Low	Low
Indigenous Peoples	High	Low	Low
Future Generations	Low	Low	Increasing
Consumers	Low	Low	Increasing
Tourist Industries	Low	Low	Low

advice to the Government on the creation, management and promotion of MPAs.[65]

The 1990s

1990: The State Labor Government's draft policy for the establishment and management of a number of marine reserves was formally launched in May 1990, which included, inter alia, another proposal for an MPA in waters around the Kent Group of Islands.[66] The Government also announced an intensive public consultation process. In response, fishers groups launched a fresh media campaign, denouncing the latest round of MPA proposals as "government policy without rationale" and declaring their intention to boycott the policy process.[67] However, despite the high media profile of the

65. Kriwoken, n. 48 above, at 71.
66. Tasmanian Government Media Release, Office of Michael Aird, MHA (May 7, 1990).
67. "Boycott on Marine Reserves," *Examiner* (May 7, 1990); "Plan for Marine Parks Cops Flak," *Mercury* (May 8, 1990).

fisher groups, the Government declared that the majority of public submissions received were supportive of the MPA draft policy.[68]

1991: The Tasmanian Government chose World Environment Day (June 5) to announce the *Marine Reserves Strategy* and designation of the State's first marine reserves in four locations. These were to be managed jointly by the Department of Parks, Wildlife and Heritage, and Sea Fisheries. While non-extractive recreational activities and scientific research would continue inside the reserves, they were off-limits to recreational and commercial fishing with the exception of a small section of the Maria Island Reserve (the largest of the four MPAs).[69] Angered by the implementation of the Strategy and annoyed at criticisms directed to them by a Green member of parliament, the Secretary of the Professional Fishermen's Association of Tasmania (PFAT) expressed the organization's sentiments in an emotional letter to the Editor of the State's major newspaper:

> Already the most over-taxed, over-(mis)managed [*sic*] and over-regulated industry in Australia, current policies are directly aimed at legislating the grass-roots Tasmanian multi-purpose fisherman out of existence to clear the way for the bigger, more "efficient" interstate and overseas interests whose money won't be coming back to Tasmania ... Grass-roots fishermen are the "workers" of the fishing industry. They are also gentlemen. They have no politically shrewd lobby group or advocate to act in their interests. It was callous of their managers to accuse them of being dinosaurs, when those same managers, with great determination and shortsightedness, are pursuing regimes to ensure that they become extinct.[70]

1995: Having ousted the Accord in the State election, the newly elected Liberal Government introduced the Living Marine Resources Management Act (LMRMA), following concerns among policy makers that a "tragedy of the commons" scenario appeared inevitable without State intervention. The Act's stated objectives were the protection of marine habitats and sustainable development of living marine resources via the ecosystem approach.[71] The Government declared the LMRMA the successor to the anachronistic Fisheries Act (1959) and the latter was repealed in the same year, thus opening the door for a new era of marine management.[72]

68. Joint media release for Office of Minister for Environment and Planning, and Office of Minister for Parks, Wildlife and Heritage (June 5, 1991).

69. *Id.*

70. H. Rowe, Letters to the Editor, *Mercury* (October 10, 1991).

71. Department of Primary Industries, Water and Environment, *Review of the Living Marine Resources Management Act 1995* (Tasmania, 2000).

72. Tasmanian House of Assembly, Hon. Robin Gray MHA, (Hansard, June 28 1995).

1996: As yet another State election loomed, both major parties and the Greens produced policies supporting the establishment of additional marine reserves. The Labor Opposition vowed to create a system of State representative MPAs by 2000 to honour Tasmania's commitment to contribute to a greater national representative system. Proposals again included, inter alia, sites in the Kent Group of Islands, the Port Davey/ Bathurst Harbour (an ecologically unique part of the marine environment in the State's southwest), and representative areas of the State's giant kelp forests.[73] Later that year at an MPA seminar conducted by the Marine and Coastal Community Network,[74] the Liberal party announced their pre-election policy to designate MPAs in the Kent Group of Islands and Port Davey/Bathurst Harbour.[75] Following re-election, the Liberal Government authorised a workshop for those interested in the future of marine reserves in State waters, and participants recommended that MPAs be established at both the Kent Group and Port Davey/Bathurst Harbour (PD/BH) within 12 months.[76]

1998: Draft discussion papers on the above proposals were prepared by the Parks and Wildlife Service and the Marine Resources Division and distributed to interested parties and stakeholders in 1997 and again in 1998. Labor was voted into Government in the same year. Nonetheless, despite the input of the 1996 stakeholder workshop, discussion paper responses and completion of draft policy for both the Kent Group and Port Davey/ Bathurst Harbour reserves, the State Government decided to suspend these specific proposals and attend instead to the development of an overarching State representative scheme. The Minister, who held both fisheries and environment portfolios, announced his concern "at the high level of objections coming from the fishing sector" and decided to consider carefully his course of action over MPAs. The discussion papers and stakeholders' responses were never released for public comment.[77]

73. Australian Labor Party media release, "Labor's Marine Reserves Plan," (January 14, 1996).

74. The Marine and Coastal Community Network is a non-government organization (NGO) funded by the Commonwealth to promote public education and awareness of marine resource and habitat issues. Half of the Network's participants represent other NGOs and as such there is a significant flow of information between the various organizations (State of the Environment Report 2001).

75. Resource Planning and Development Commission, *Inquiry into the establishment of a marine protected area within the Davey and Twofold Shelf Bioregions* (Tasmania 2002): 4.

76. *Id.*

77. *Id.*; Letter to MCCN from the Minister for Primary Industries, Water and Environment, Hon David Llewellyn MHA addressing the Kent Group and Port Davey/Bathurst Harbour draft marine reserve proposals (December 4, 1998).

1999: The Minister for Primary Industries, Water and Environment established the Marine and Marine Industries Council (MMIC) in August. Composed of a diverse range of representatives drawn from, inter alia, indigenous groups, coastal communities, tourism, aquaculture and environmental organizations as well as commercial and recreational fishers, the Council's initial brief was to develop an MPA policy framework for a State representative reserve system. The TFIC publicly declared that its representatives felt completely "outnumbered" by the groundswell of new stakeholders and an "out of control green bureaucracy" which, they believed, would shatter any opportunity for a "reasonable outcome."[78] The TFIC president argued that the overwhelming majority of those included in the MPA policy arena were there to ensure that a fundamental shift to the "anti-industry side of the environment debate" was underway.[79]

Into the New Millennium

2000–2004: The MMIC released the Tasmanian Marine Protected Areas Draft Strategy in July 2000. The Minister announced a 3-month public comment period to be facilitated through written submissions, standardized evaluation forms, and public consultation meetings in various venues around the State.[80] Most of the meetings were overwhelmed by hostile and vocal MPA opponents and members of the TFIC who declared for the public record their intention to wage a "long and hard" battle against any further increase in MPAs.[81] At open forums held around the State, and in written submissions to the architects of the Draft Strategy, fishers expressed their fears about job losses, deprivation of cultural heritage, erosion of ownership and rights, restricted access to fishing grounds, community and family breakdowns, lack of government action over exotic pests, marine pollution, declines in harvests due to the voracious appetite of seals, over-regulation of the industry, and the encroachment of "outsiders" into the traditional user-group dominated policy arena.[82]

78. S. Richey, "The President's Report," *Fishing Today* (October/November 1999).

79. *Id.*

80. Marine and Marine Industries Council (MMIC), *Draft Tasmanian Marine Protected Areas Strategy* (Hobart: Crown in Right of the State of Tasmania, 2000).

81. Department of Primary Industries, Water and Environment, *Draft Tasmanian Marine Protected Areas Strategy Public Consultation 18 July–13 October Summary Report* (2000); A. Barbeliuk, "A Plea for Calm Over Fisheries," *Mercury* (August 17, 2000).

82. Department of Primary Industries, Water and Environment, *Tasmanian Marine Protected Areas Strategy 2001*. Available online: <http://www.dpiwe.tas.gov.au/inter.nsf/Attachments/BHAN–5498CT/$FILE/mpa_strat egy.pdf>.

The Tasmanian Government received 4,166 responses to the Draft Strategy with 87 percent expressing support for its contents.[83] By September 2000, however, the Minister conceded to the demands of fishers' groups and announced a halt to any further plans to establish new MPAs in State waters, adding, however, that the Kent Group and Port Davey/Bathurst Harbour areas were still being considered for reserve status.[84] Both proposals were to remain in a protracted state of appraisal for a further four years. Acknowledging concerns from non-traditional stakeholders about the lack of progress in establishing MPA status for these areas and the body of scientific and technical work already completed, the Minister requested that the Resource Planning and Development Commission (RPDC) undertake a shortened assessment process to be finalized by 31 July 2002, although this was later extended to 30 May 2003. On 3 February 2004, the Tasmanian Government finally announced the designation of the Kent Group and Port Davey/Bathurst Harbour MPAs.[85] In the case of the former, the journey toward protection status had taken more than 20 years.

Table 2.—Stakeholder Groups and Scores in the Tasmanian MPA Policy Process from 1991–2004.[89]

Stakeholders	Urgency	Power	Legitimacy
Definitive			
Commercial Fishers	High	High	High
Bureaucrats	High	High	High
Enforcement Agencies	Medium	High	High
Scientists	High	Medium	High
Media	Medium	High	High
Expectant			
Local Government	High	Medium	Low
Recreational Fishers	Medium	Medium	Increasing
Environmental Groups	Medium	Medium	High
Indigenous Peoples	High	Low	High
Local Communities	Medium	Medium	High
Citizens	Increasing	Low	Increasing
Tourist Industries	Medium	Low	Medium
Latent			
Future Generations	Low	Low	Increasing
Consumers	Low	Low	Increasing

83. *Id.*

84. A. Haneveer, "Llewellyn Rules Out New Marine Zones," *Advocate* (September 15, 2000): 31.

85. Minister for the Environment, Hon Judy Jackson MHA, Media release (February 3, 2004).

89. Adapted from Mikalsen and Jentoft, n. 5 above, at 285.

SUMMARY AND CONCLUSIONS

The notion of fish stocks as a common pool resource, as described above, is important in the context of fisheries and issues of marine protection because it involves the identification and inclusion of potential new beneficiaries beyond the traditional occupants of Lowi's three policy arenas. Until a few decades ago, those identified as primary, definitive marine stakeholders had little to fear from "outsiders." With resource sustainability being swept up in the socio-ecological shifts of the past few decades, the primary stakeholders had found themselves confronted by challenges they perceived as coming out of the extrinsic "left field." Marine protected area policy proposals together with identification and inclusion of new stakeholders in a once relatively exclusive policy domain had mobilized fishers to interact, organize and vocalize their opposition in the highly contentious arena of marine resource management and habitat protection.

Analysis of the Tasmanian MPA policy process through these chronological snapshots supports the argument that fishers rally beneath the umbrella of camaraderie when confronted with challenges or threats to their economic security, fishing culture, "territory," and their socio-psychologically grounded and proud tradition of lifestyle and "difference." Likewise, those advocating a broader stakeholder-driven agenda in marine resource policy decisions also feel challenged by the tradition of near-exclusive exchange between primary, definitive stakeholders and firm, and insist that such exclusivity is both anachronistic and irrelevant. Burch offers a profound insight into the socio-psychological nexus between expectations of, and interactions between human groups, an insight that encapsulates the genesis and crystallization of attitudes and perceptions as demonstrated by the various stakeholder groups circulating in contemporary Tasmania's MPA/marine resource policy arena:

> [T]he habitats of human societies are not solely the function of ecosystem characteristics. Each human group develops its special collection of motives which designate the appropriate and inappropriate forms of conduct in regard to other men, other groups and the non-human environment, and these selective perceptions determine whether the unhuman environment will become a resource, a taboo, or remain unseen.[86]

86. W. R. Burch Jr., *Daydreams and Nightmares: A Sociological Essay on the American Environment* (New York, 1971), p. 51, in J. M. Powell, *Environmental Management in Australia 1788–1914: Guardians, Improvers and Profit; An Introductory Survey* (Melbourne: Oxford University Press, 1976), p. 3.

The seemingly endless search for consensus and common ground among an expanding constellation of stakeholders appears to have led to a position of almost chronic policy inertia in the Tasmanian MPA policy process, although it has been interceded with rare moments of policy implementation. It wasn't just that successive Tasmanian Governments had reached an impasse on the issue of MPA designation because of greater stakeholder participation and increasingly conflicting demands; rather it appears that as time went on, the "firm," or more precisely its manager, the Fisheries Minister, appeared to make use of such conflict as a constraint on policy implementation. The rhetoric of pre-election promises was not followed through with prompt action. As Mikalsen and Jentoft note:

> The fisheries ministry as "manager" should not be seen as the sole agent of the public interest, with the authority to decide the optimal use of the public resource. Rather, to be effective the ministry [needs] to employ its skills in manoeuvring within the turbulent waters of more or less legitimate, powerful, but conflicting stakeholder groups with more or less urgent needs and concerns.[87]

The traditional hunter-collector culture of marine resource harvesters—primary, definitive stakeholders—coupled with the instrumentalist approach taken by bureaucrats and ministers (the firm), exacerbates fishers' insistence on maintaining their position and primacy in the marine management domain. This has contributed to periods of policy inertia that are in danger of becoming behaviorally entrenched unless the government (the firm) and managers (Fisheries and Environment Ministries) acknowledge and act upon the need for expedient, apolitical decision-making (an ambitious but not necessarily naïve ambition) in marine protection, and indeed in environmental policies in general.

87. Mikalsen and Jentoft, n. 5 above, at 284.

The SEAFC Convention: A Comparative Analysis in a Developing Coastal State Perspective

Denzil G. M. Miller*
Commission for the Conservation of Antarctic Marine Living Resources, Hobart, Institute of Antarctic and Southern Ocean Studies, University of Tasmania

Erik Jaap Molenaar
Netherlands Institute for the Law of the Sea, Utrecht University

INTRODUCTION

The United Nations Fish Stocks Agreement[1] (hereafter the Fish Stocks Agreement) aims to strengthen relevant provisions of the United Nations Convention on the Law of the Sea[2] (hereafter the LOS Convention), particularly Articles 63, 64 and 116–119 addressing the management and conservation of straddling fish stocks and highly migratory fish stocks. Together with the FAO Code of Conduct,[3] the Fish Stocks Agreement provides a framework for the practical implementation of effective fisheries conservation and management. One of its main objectives is to progressively facilitate rational and long-term sustainable utilization of fisheries resources on both the high seas and in waters under national jurisdiction. It therefore

---

* The opinions expressed in this paper are those of the authors and do not represent the collective, or official, views or decisions of the Commission for the Conservation of Antarctic Marine Living Resources (CCAMLR).

1. Agreement for the Implementation of the Provisions of the United Nations Convention on the Law of the Sea of 10 December 1982 relating to the Conservation and Management of Straddling Fish Stocks and Highly Migratory Fish Stocks, New York, 4 August 1995. In force 11 December 2001, *International Legal Materials* 34 (1995): 1,542, available online: <http://www.un.org/Depts/los>.
2. United Nations Convention on the Law of the Sea, Montego Bay, 10 December 1982. In force 16 November 1994, 1833 *United Nations Treaty Series* 396, available online: <http://www.un.org/Depts/los>.
3. Code of Conduct for Responsible Fisheries (Rome: FAO, 31 October 1995), available online: <http://www.fao.org/fi>.

Ocean Yearbook 20: 305–375.

accords high priority to ensuring effective co-operation between coastal States and high seas fishing States on a range of fundamental and technical issues.

This article examines three international fisheries agreements whose negotiation processes began in the period between the Fish Stocks Agreement's adoption and entry into force (1995–2001). The rationale for selecting these three agreements and not others[4] is to a great extent the crucial role played by, and the overriding interests of, certain developing States in the negotiating processes which were largely attributable to their status as coastal States. Two of these agreements seek to implement the Fish Stocks Agreement; one in respect of straddling fish stocks in the South-East Atlantic Ocean (the SEAFC Convention),[5] the other in respect of highly migratory fish stocks in the Western and Central Pacific Ocean (the WCPFC Convention).[6] The third instrument is the Protocol on Fisheries,[7] developed by States Members of a regional economic/political alliance, the Southern African Development Community (SADC).[8] All of the current 14 Members of SADC are effectively developing States and about half are also coastal States.[9]

4. Other negotiation processes during that period (1995–2001) include those leading to the 2003 Antigua Convention, n. 70 below, and the Framework Agreement for the Conservation of Living Marine Resources on the High Seas of the Southeast Pacific (Galapagos Agreement), Santiago, 14 August 2000. Not in force, *Law of the Sea Bulletin* No. 45 (2001): 70–78, available online: <http://www.oceanlaw.net/texts/galapagos.htm>.

5. Convention on the Conservation and Management of the Fishery Resources in the South East Atlantic Ocean, Windhoek, 20 April 2001. In force 13 April 2003, *International Legal Materials* 41 (2002): 257, available online: <http://www.fao.org/Legal/treaties>. For the status of participation, see n. 17 below. For the purposes of this article, the SEAFC Convention is used to denote the 'Convention', the acronym SEAFO (South East Atlantic Fisheries Organisation) is used to denote the 'Organisation' (see Arts. 5, 6 and 9–11) and the acronym SEAFC (South East Atlantic Fisheries Commission) for the Convention's main regulatory body (see Arts. 5(2)(a), 6 and 8).

6. Convention on the Conservation and Management of Highly Migratory Fish Stocks in the Western and Central Pacific Ocean, Honolulu, 5 September 2000. In force 19 June 2004, *International Legal Materials* 40 (2001): 277, available online: <http://www.ocean-affairs.com>.

7. Protocol on Fisheries to the SADC Treaty, n. 8 below, Blantyre, 14 August 2001. In force 8 August 2003, available online: <http://www.sadc.int>.

8. Established under the Treaty establishing the Southern African Development Community (Windhoek, 17 August 1992. In force 30 September 1993), as amended. Available online: <http://www.sadc.int>.

9. At the time of writing, the following States were Members of SADC: Angola*, Botswana, Democratic Republic of the Congo (DRC)*, Lesotho, Malawi, Mauritius*, Mozambique*, Namibia*, Seychelles*, South Africa*, Swaziland, Tanzania*, Zambia and Zimbabwe (* = coastal States).

The sections below examine the SEAFC Convention, the WCPFC Convention and the SADC Fisheries Protocol. Subsections focus on objectives and general principles, areas of application, stocks covered, openness and transparency, institutional aspects, decision making, fishing opportunities, control measures, interests of developing States and the relationship with the Fish Stocks Agreement and other international instruments. Finally, conclusions and observations are provided.

SEAFC CONVENTION

Background

The regional fisheries management organization (RFMO) established under Article 5 of the SEAFC Convention effectively succeeds the International Commission for the Southeast Atlantic Fisheries (ICSEAF) put into place by the 1969 Convention of the same name.[10] The evolution of the 2001 SEAFC Convention was closely associated with the post-independence re-structuring of Namibia's fishing industry. Prior to Namibia's independence in 1990, ICSEAF strived to implement sustainable management of fisheries in the Southeast Atlantic in general, and in Namibian (then South-West African) waters in particular. However, in practice, many of ICSEAF's 17 Member States used it as a way of optimizing their own interests in exploiting the many target stocks concerned. Such exploitation was essentially unsustainable and endured despite South Africa's efforts to regulate fishing off the Namibian coast through the promulgation of an exclusive economic zone (EEZ) in 1981. This situation was also largely due to the refusal by many States, whose vessels were operating in Namibian waters, to recognize South Africa's administrative powers granted under the League of Nations' C-Class Mandate for the governance of South-West Africa in 1920, as formally overturned by United Nations General Assembly Resolution 2145 in 1961.

On independence, Namibia declared its own EEZ under the Territorial Sea and Exclusive Economic Zone of Namibia Act, 1990. Combined with the 1992 Namibian Sea Fisheries Act, this legislation was directed at improving the management of targeted stocks and at developing Namibia's own domestic fishing capacity. These actions were vindicated by a dramatic recovery in a large number of previously depleted fish stocks within the Namibian EEZ. As Namibia declined to become a Member of ICSEAF, it was

10. Convention on the Conservation of the Living Resources of the South-East Atlantic. Rome, 23 October 1969. In force 24 October 1971; information based on <http://www.fao.org/Legal/treaties>.

decided that ICSEAF should be terminated. Even though the 1990 Protocol of Termination[11] that was adopted for this purpose never formally entered into force,[12] ICSEAF effectively became defunct.

During the 1990s, Namibia attempted to consolidate the sustainable development of its fisheries. It therefore strived to implement fisheries management policies consistent with contemporary best practice through a systematic commitment to both national interest and obligations under various international fisheries agreements. A clear demonstration of this commitment is manifest in Namibia's signature and subsequent ratification of the Fish Stocks Agreement in 1998, and its accession to the ICCAT Convention[13] in 1999. However, Namibia continued to express concern that certain commercially valuable straddling stocks (such as Orange Roughy—*Hoplostethus atlanticus*) (Table 1) required better protection to avoid compromising their potential in Namibian waters as a result of unsustainable fishing practices on the adjacent high seas. Such concern was aggravated by uncertainty over the status of such stocks as well as over the precise fishing levels targeting them.

Taking heart from the successful Fish Stocks Agreement negotiations, Namibia approached three neighboring coastal States (Angola, South Africa and the United Kingdom, on behalf of its overseas territory of St. Helena and its dependencies Tristan da Cunha and Ascension Island) to establish an RFMO closely aligned to the Fish Stocks Agreement.[14] The main purpose of this RFMO would be to manage unregulated fisheries resources on the high seas adjacent to the four States' EEZs—an area roughly equivalent to FAO Statistical Area 47. During the four preliminary meetings in 1997 (Table 2) of what eventually became known as the "South East Atlantic

11. Madrid, 19 July 1990. Not in force, available online: <http://www.fao.org/Legal/treaties>.

12. At the time of writing only Angola, Cuba and Spain had deposited an instrument of acceptance of the Protocol (info based on <http://www.fao.org/Legal/treaties>).

13. International Convention for the Conservation of Atlantic Tunas, Rio de Janeiro, 14 May 1966. In force 21 March 1969, *United Nations Treaty Series* No. 9587 (1969), available online: <http://www.iccat.es>.

14. For a short overview of the negotiation process, see the "Final Minute of the Conference on the South East Atlantic Fisheries Organisation and of the Meetings of Coastal States and Other Interested Parties on a Regional Fisheries Management Organisation for the South East Atlantic" (Windhoek, 20 April 2001). For a more comprehensive overview, see A. Jackson, "The Convention on the Conservation and Management of Fishery Resources in the South East Atlantic Ocean 2001: An Introduction," *International Journal of Marine and Coastal Law* 17 (2002): 33–77.

Table 1.—Species Covered by SEAFC Convention (Based on FAO 3 ALFA Codes Listed in Section 2 of the Annex to the Convention)

ALFA CODE	SPECIES	LATIN NAME
ALF	Alfonsinos	Family Berycidae
HOM	Horse Mackerel	*Trachurus* spp.
MAC	Mackerel	*Scomber* spp.
ORY	Orange Roughy	*Hoplostethus* spp.
SKA	Skates	Family Rajidae
SKH	Sharks Armourhead Cardinal Fish Deepsea Red Crab Octopus & Squids Patagaonian Toothfish Hake	Order Selechomorpha *Pseudopentaceros* spp. *Epigonus* spp. *Chaecon maritae* Family Octopodidae/Loliginidae *Dissostichus eleginoides* *Merluccius* spp.
WRF	Wreckfish	*Polyprion americanus*
	Oreodories	Family Oreosomatidae

Fisheries Organisation (SEAFO) process,"[15] the coastal States developed a draft convention.

This draft was then presented to the European Community (EC), Japan, Norway, the Russian Federation and the United States. These parties were invited to participate in the SEAFO process as they had been identified as having an interest in fishing in the region. Iceland, the Republic of Korea, Poland and Ukraine later joined the negotiation process, which consisted of seven additional meetings and one technical consultation. The SEAFC Convention was adopted at the Conference on the South East Atlantic Fisheries Organisation, held at Windhoek, Namibia, on 20 April 2001. The four coastal States, the EC, Iceland, the Republic of Korea, Norway, and the United States signed the Convention on that date. Japan did not sign, but indicated its support for the Convention.[16] The SEAFC Convention entered into force on 13 April 2003 and had three parties at the time of writing.[17] The first meeting of the South East Atlantic Fisheries Commission (SEAFC) took place in March 2004.[18]

15. See n. 5 above.
16. Jackson, n. 14 above, at 37.
17. Namibia (7 June 2002), the EC (8 August 2002) and Norway (12 February 2003). Information based on <http://www.fao.org/Legal/treaties>.
18. Report of the First Session (Meeting) of the Commission of the SEAFO, available online: <http://www.intfish.plus.com/orgs/fisheries/seafo.htm>.

Table 2.—SEAFC Convention Negotiating Meetings

MEETING	LOCATION	DATE
Coastal States	Cape Town, South Africa	24–26 February 1997
	Otjiwarongo, Namibia	30 June–4 July 1997
	Cape Town, South Africa	9–10 September 1997
	Windhoek, Namibia	2 December 1997
First	Windhoek, Namibia	3–4 December 1997
Second	Cape Town, South Africa	19–22 May 1998
Third	Swakopmund, Namibia	22–25 September 1998
Fourth	Oxford, United Kingdom	8–11 March 1999
Fifth	Cape Town, South Africa	27 September–1 October 1999
Sixth	Midgard, Namibia	8–12 May 2000
Seventh	Windhoek, Namibia	9–11 November 2000
Eighth	Windhoek, Namibia	19 April 2001
Technical Consultation	Windhoek, Namibia	1–4 March 2000
Final Conference	Windhoek, Namibia	20 April 2001

The various drafts of the SEAFC Convention drew on existing instruments in an effort to provide for the highest possible, and most contemporary, standards of fisheries management. Particular cognizance was taken of relevant provisions of the LOS Convention, the Fish Stocks Agreement, the Code of Conduct and the 1982 Convention on the Conservation of Antarctic Marine Living Resources (CAMLR Convention).[19] Although the initial coastal State draft text was extensively modified during the negotiations, the core principles remain distinct in the final Convention text. These were strongly consistent with the Fish Stocks Agreement that provided a substantial basis for much of the SEAFC Convention text.

Objectives and General Principles

Articles 2 and 3 of the SEAFC Convention set out the "Objectives" and "General Principles" respectively. While these topics were included in a

---

19. Convention on the Conservation of Antarctic Marine Living Resources, Canberra, 20 May 1980. In force 7 April 1982, *International Legal Materials* 19 (1980): 837, available online: <http://www.ccamlr.org>.

single provision in the original coastal State draft, the Sixth Meeting decided to distinguish more clearly between the Convention's objective and the general principles associated with its effective implementation. Pursuant to Article 2 of the SEAFC Convention, its primary objective is:

> To ensure the long-term conservation and sustainable use of the fishery resources in the Convention Area through the effective implementation of this Convention.

During the negotiations, there was considerable debate about whether the term "fishery resources" should be applied instead of the much broader term "living marine resources." In this respect, it should be noted that the objective of the CAMLR Convention is related to "Antarctic marine living resources" which, in combination with its principles of conservation, thereby embraces an ecosystem approach.[20] For various reasons, the SEAFO process eventually opted for the narrower term, which was defined in Article 1(l) (see below). The EC strongly supported this option as it would ensure that SEAFO's mandate would fall largely or entirely within the scope of the EC's exclusive fisheries competence and thereby avoid a situation where EU Member States could participate alongside the EC. The CAMLR Convention is the only real example of an RFMO in which that situation occurs.[21] Other factors that could have played a role are the suitability of the SEAFC Convention Area for a genuine ecosystem approach, the fact that such an approach would be costly and ambitious and that ecological interests might appear to have been afforded priority at the cost of fishing interests.

In not opting for an ecosystem approach similar to that pursued by the Commission for the Conservation of Antarctic Marine Living Resources (CCAMLR), the SEAFC Convention nevertheless acknowledges the need for a broad approach to fisheries management. The term "living marine resources" is used throughout the SEAFC Convention and its Preamble and is defined in Article 1(n) as "all living components of marine ecosystems, including seabirds." Moreover, paragraphs (c)–(f) of Article 3 of the SEAFC Convention require that account be taken of various ecosystem considerations, as advocated by Article 5 of the Fish Stocks Agreement.[22]

Article 7 of the SEAFC Convention, entitled "Application of the Precautionary Approach," bears little resemblance to the way in which the initial coastal State draft addressed the precautionary approach. The latter

20. See CAMLR Convention Arts. I(2), II(1) and (3).
21. See the discussion in E. J. Molenaar, "CCAMLR and Southern Ocean Fisheries," *International Journal of Marine and Coastal Law* 16 (2001): 465, 490–497.
22. The substance of what are now paras. (a), (e) and (f) was also contained in the original coastal State draft.

drew heavily on Article 6 and Annex II to the Fish Stocks Agreement and the FAO Code of Conduct,[23] even to the point of producing two annexes detailing the approach's general implications and guidelines for the application of precautionary reference points. Article 7 consists of three paragraphs. While the first two are essentially similar to Article 6(1) and (2) of the Fish Stocks Agreement, the third requires the SEAFO to "take cognisance of best international practices," including the aforementioned Annex II and the FAO Code of Conduct. The significant modification of the original coastal State proposal was caused by the reluctance of certain participants in the SEAFO process (particularly Japan and the EC) to draw too heavily on the Fish Stocks Agreement, in absence of their formal adherence thereof.

Articles 18 and 19 of the SEAFC Convention deal with "Co-operation with Other Organisations" and "Compatibility of Conservation and Management Measures" (between straddling fish stocks in the Convention Area and in areas under national jurisdiction), respectively. The negotiation of both provisions was relatively uncontroversial. However, it should be noted that Article 19 does not closely follow the wording and complexities of Article 7 of the Fish Stocks Agreement but instead links the notion of compatibility to the need for consistency with measures established in accordance with Articles 61 and 119 of the LOS Convention. The reasons for this are probably similar to those mentioned above in relation to the precautionary approach.

Area of Application

As defined in Article 4, the SEAFC Convention Area encompasses waters beyond areas of national jurisdiction within an area that roughly corresponds to FAO Statistical Area 47 (see Figure 1). The Convention Area is bounded in the south (i.e., at 50° S) by the northern boundary of the CAMLR Convention Area and extends southeast of South Africa to 30° E in the Indian Ocean to account for hydrological/ecological linkages between the Benguela and Agulhas Currents in the Atlantic and Indian Oceans respectively, particularly in the vicinity of the Agulhas Bank to the east of South Africa. It deviates slightly from FAO Statistical Area 47 in the vicinity of Ascension Island to include the entire zone around the Island as well as the immediately adjacent high seas.

23. Especially Section 7.5 of the Code and Section 1.6 of the FAO Technical Guidelines for Responsible Fisheries No. 2, "Precautionary Approach to Capture Fisheries and Species Introductions," (Rome: FAO, 1996), available online: <http://www.fao.org/fi>.

FIG. 1.—The SEAFC Convention Area. SADC Member States (except Seychelles) are named.

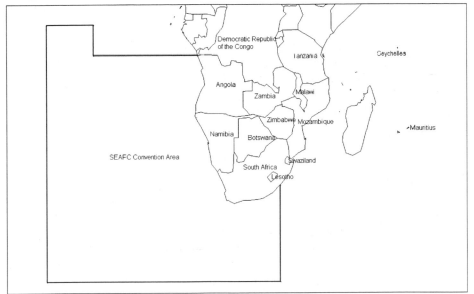

Source: Author.

In the Final Minute of 20 April 2001,[24] Angola insisted on the inclusion of Attachment II which contains a resolution by which the participants in the Conference of 20 April 2001 "agree to consider" to amend the SEAFC Convention for the northern boundary of the Convention Area to be extended further northwards in order to include the areas of high seas adjacent to the small Angolan province of Cabinda. This oil-rich enclave, which is cut off from the rest of Angola by a small stretch of Democratic Republic of the Congo (DRC) territory along the Congo River, has been the scene of a separatist struggle for a number of years.[25] Angola's insistence on including Attachment II does not seem to be directly motivated by particular fisheries interests. The resolution only determines that the amendment issue shall be considered by the first meeting of SEAFC. This did not happen.[26]

It should also be noted that Japan, in particular, was opposed to limiting the geographical application of the SEAFC Convention to areas outside national jurisdiction alone. This may have been motivated by a need

24. See n. 14 above.
25. "Country Reports on Human Rights Practices. Angola, 2003," available online: <http://www.state.gov>.
26. See the Statement by Angola at Annex 6 of the Report, n. 18 above. At the time of the meeting, Angola was not yet Party to the SEAFC Convention.

for consistency with their position in the "MHLC (Multilateral High Level Conference) process" that negotiated the WCPFC Convention. The need for such consistency is certainly not evident as the two processes dealt with different categories of stocks.[27] The Japanese position on geographical application was almost certainly linked to the allocation of fishing opportunities. While Article 20(1)(b) of the SEAFC Convention lists as one of the criteria for the allocation process "respective interests, past and present fishing patterns, including catches, and practices" this is linked to the "Convention Area," thereby excluding historic fishing performance in coastal maritime zones, most notably under ICSEAF.

Stocks Covered

As illustrated in Table 1 above, Article 1(l) of the SEAFC Convention defines "fishery resources" as "resources of fish, molluscs, crustaceans and other sedentary species within the Convention Area, excluding (i) sedentary species subject to the fishery jurisdiction of coastal States pursuant to [Article 77(4) of the LOS Convention]; and highly migratory species listed in Annex I of [the LOS Convention]." The exclusion of highly migratory fish species avoids a substantive overlap with the ICCAT Convention. In addition, Article 18(4) ensures that application of the SEAFC Convention's objectives and general principles to fishery resources requires co-operation with other relevant fisheries management organizations, such as the ICCAT Commission. This includes taking account of the latter's conservation and management measures for the region.

As, apart from the exclusions just mentioned, the term "fishery resources" is not further qualified, it includes by implication not just stocks that occur both within EEZs and on the high seas (straddling stocks), but also discrete high seas stocks (even though these may also occur on the high seas outside the SEAFC Convention Area). It should be pointed out that there are no generally accepted definitions of the terms "straddling stocks" and "discrete high seas stocks" and only Article 63(2) of the LOS Convention can offer some guidance.[28] The inclusion of discrete high seas stocks within the mandate of an RFMO is not unique as such.[29] Its significance lies in the fact that the SEAFC Convention does not explicitly distinguish between straddling and discrete high seas stocks while at the same time drawing on the Fish Stocks Agreement, which does not apply to

27. See the differences in wording between Arts. 63(2) and 64 of the LOS Convention in terms of spatial competence.
28. See also Jackson, n. 14 above, at 9.
29. For example, Arts. I and II of the CAMLR Convention.

discrete high seas stocks. The global legal framework for the latter stocks is mainly determined by Articles 116–119 of the LOS Convention. The implicit applicability of certain provisions of the Fish Stocks Agreement to discrete high seas stocks within the context of an RFMO is significant for the progressive development of international law relating to discrete high seas stocks. This matter is discussed further below.

Openness and Transparency

The openness of the SEAFO process is complemented by Articles 25 and 26 of the SEAFC Convention, which allow States and regional economic integration organizations to become parties to the Convention without having to meet onerous conditions or being dependent on the approval of existing members. Participation in the SEAFC Convention is not dependent on having a 'real interest,' as envisaged in Article 8(3) of the Fish Stocks Agreement. The SEAFO process went through considerable efforts to define the concept of real interest in relation to fishery resources falling under the Convention,[30] but was eventually unable to agree on a definition. The Preamble to the Convention nevertheless recognizes the importance of cooperation between coastal States and others with a real interest to ensure compatibility.

Further evidence of SEAFO's openness can be found in Article 22 on 'Non-Parties' to the SEAFC Convention. Paragraphs (1)–(3) of this article set out a two-tier approach encouraging cooperation with Non-Parties and the development of measures to deter fishing by such parties. This approach is modeled on the Fish Stocks Agreement[31] and is pursued by many other RFMOs. Article 22(4) of the SEAFC Convention specifically addresses co-operation with fishing entities and anticipates that such entities will enjoy benefits in terms of fishing opportunities "commensurate with their commitment to comply with management measures." Article 22(1) specifi-

---

30. The issue of "real interest" was discussed at length, particularly at the Second SEAFC Negotiating Meeting (Table 1). Considerable thought was given to the concept as it may relate to each of the negotiating parties and how it might be assessed. Discussions focused on a range of activities such as scientific interest, historic fishing performance, desire to fish, commitment to conservation and related matters in respect of both current and potential future participants. By way of example, Art. 1(h)(ii) of the SEAFC Convention linked scientific research directly to "fishing." For a full discussion of the concept of "real interest," see E. J. Molenaar, "The Concept of "Real Interest" and Other Aspects of Co-operation through Regional Fisheries Management Mechanisms," *International Journal of Marine and Coastal Law* 15 (2000): 475–531, with a discussion on the SEAFO process on pp. 508–509.

31. See Arts. 8(3) and (4), 17(1), (2) and (4) and 33 of the Agreement.

cally offers these conditional benefits to Non-Parties.[32] While the Fish Stocks Agreement did not envisage such considerations, a growing number of RFMOs are currently using the notion of 'Cooperating Non-Contracting Party' in the limited allocation of fishing opportunities to potential new members or Non-Parties.

How such participation could be assessed is not addressed and remains moot. Nevertheless, the encouragement of openness goes some way to avoiding complicated procedures to assess the rights of new participants following Article 11 of the Fish Stocks Agreement. In the case of the SEAFC Convention, account has also been taken of the potential conditions for allocation of fishing opportunities (see Article 20 of the Fish Stocks Agreement and the section on Fishing Opportunities below) along with consideration of developing State needs (Article 21 of the SEAFC Convention). To some extent, these considerations strengthen the SEAFC Convention's scope in relation to ensuring openness to involvement by any party.[33]

Complementing its efforts to promote openness, the SEAFC Convention expressly recognizes the need for transparency in SEAFO's activities. Article 8(9) is based on similar sentiments as Article 12 of the Fish Stocks Agreement, and urges SEAFC to urgently adopt procedures to promote transparency in SEAFO's activities. It further emphasizes that these rules should not be unduly restrictive and should provide for timely access to SEAFO's records and reports.

Institutional Aspects

Article 5 of the SEAFC Convention establishes the "Organisation" (i.e., SEAFO) responsible for carrying out institutional functions necessary for the Convention's successful implementation. SEAFO comprises the Commission, the Scientific and Compliance Committees, as subsidiary bodies, and the Secretariat. The Commission is empowered to establish any other subsidiary body as it deems necessary from time to time. The functions of the Commission and its subsidiary bodies are detailed in Articles 6 (Commission), 9 (Compliance Committee), 10 (Scientific Committee) and 11 (Secretariat) of the SEAFC Convention. In particular, the language of Articles 6, 10 and 11 draws heavily on similar provisions in the CAMLR Convention, namely Articles IX, XV and XVII respectively.

Budgetary considerations are addressed in Article 12 of the SEAFC Convention. Paragraph (1) clearly stresses that the Organization's budget

32. See also 20(2)(c) of the SEAFC Convention.
33. For further discussion of this point in relation to the allocation of fishing opportunities, see the subsection on fishing opportunities below.

should be cost-effective. As a matter of principle, each Contracting Party is required to contribute to the budget (Article 12(2)) with contributions being made up of an equal basic fee and a fee determined from the total catch of species covered by the Convention.

During negotiation Parties agreed that every effort should be made to activate SEAFO in order to anticipate, and ameliorate, potential problems likely to arise should fishing in the Convention Area suddenly increase. In budgetary terms, however, considerable uncertainty surrounds the economic value of both the current and any future fishery in the Area. The Parties thus anticipated that SEAFO's tasks would increase at a rate commensurate with development of the fisheries concerned.

To assess the urgency for SEAFO conservation measures and to provide a basis for budget estimates, the negotiating Parties attempted to share available catch data from the Convention Area. Initially, information was compiled by the South African Government up to 1999. The Fifth SEAFC Convention Negotiating Meeting (Table 2) agreed that, to ensure the veracity and consistency of collected and reported data, future attempts to monitor fishing in the Convention Area should await the SEAFC Convention's entry into force when obligations to that effect could be created. Therefore, the Technical Consultation held in February 2000 (Table 2) drafted interim measures to ensure collection of relevant data by Contracting Party flag States immediately upon the Convention's entry into force. These measures were annexed to the SEAFC Convention.

Following a similar approach to that in Article XIX(3) of the CAMLR Convention and its Financial Regulations,[34] Article 12(4) of the SEAFC Convention mandates an equal contribution from each Contracting Party for the first three years after the Convention's entry into force, or any shorter period as decided by the Commission. This was seen as a way to cover SEAFO's initial establishment costs. Thereafter, it was agreed that the assessed proportionate contributions alluded to in Article 12(2) would be applied so that the economic status of each Contracting Party is taken into account. The basis for assessing this status has not been made clear, although the final sentence of Article 12(3) indicates that it should be the economic status of any territory which adjoins the Convention Area as opposed to that of the Contracting Party governing such territory. This provision was inserted by the United Kingdom to account for the overseas territory (St. Helena and its dependencies) on whose behalf it was negotiating.

---

34. Available at <http://www.ccamlr.org>.

Decision Making

Contrary to many other RFMOs, the SEAFC Convention negotiators recognized the merit of ensuring that once a decision is reached on any matter of substance (e.g., a conservation measure) then every effort should be made to ensure that it is implemented by all the Contracting Parties so as to not require that it be revisited for any reason other than "exceptional circumstances."

Article 17 of the SEAFC Convention indicates that any SEAFO decisions on matters of substance will be taken by consensus. The wording of this particular article is similar to Article XII of the CAMLR Convention, which also provides for consensus-based decision making. Article 23 of the SEAFC Convention outlines how decisions will be implemented. As emphasized by Jackson,[35] and notwithstanding any compromises attached to attaining consensus, Article 17 provides for circumstances when a Contracting Party may register its non-acceptance of a decision(s) and therefore not be bound thereto. This is very similar to the non-acceptance procedures outlined in Article IX(6) of the CAMLR Convention and in Article XII of the NAFO Convention.[36]

Despite perceptions to the contrary, Article 23 attempts to make very clear the exceptional nature of any application of the SEAFC Convention's "non-acceptance" provisions. Consequently, this particular Article introduces a number of procedural checks to preserve the right of any SEAFC Convention Contracting Party not to comply with a SEAFO decision. These checks include written detail of any alternative measures to be implemented by the Party concerned, a clear explanation of why the Party is unable to be bound by the decision, the opportunity for all Contracting Parties to review the matter at a special meeting and, on request, the establishment of an ad hoc expert panel to make recommendations on the matter.[37] It is unclear how these provisions will work in practice. However, it should be stressed that in the CAMLR Convention's some 23-year existence, its "non-acceptance" provisions have been activated only once and then for purely technical reasons related to the data reporting requirements outlined in CCAMLR Conservation Measure 37/X.[38] The adoption of a new conserva-

---

35. Jackson, n. 14 above, at 41.

36. Convention on Future Multilateral Cooperation in the Northwest Atlantic Fisheries, Ottawa, 24 October 1978. In force 1 January 1979, 1135 *United Nations Treaty Series* 369, available online: <http://www.nafo.ca>.

37. The establishment of an ad hoc panel may be viewed as part of SEAFO's dispute resolution mechanism detailed in Art. 24 (particularly paragraph (3)), which was to be elaborated by the Commission's first meeting.

38. CCAMLR Commission Circular 91/84, of 23 December 1991.

tion measure (CCAMLR Conservation Measure 56/XI) the following year appeared to rectify the problem.

Finally, the SEAFC Convention does not provide any specific mechanism for resolving potential deadlocks in decision making. Consequently, it is implied that failure to resolve any deadlock would automatically result in a "dispute" being declared. The matter would then fall under the procedures outlined in Article 24 of the SEAFC Convention (see Dispute Settlement discussion below).

Fishing Opportunities

Not surprisingly, Article 20 of the SEAFC Convention dealing with allocation of fishing opportunities, was one of the last and most difficult to negotiate. Not only had equitable access to economic benefits to be addressed, consideration also had to be given to providing for a balance between the interests of distant-water fishing nations and those of developing coastal States eager to build their fishing industries. A key consideration was how historical fishing performance in the Convention Area should be weighted in providing access to resources for new entrants and in terms of providing equity of access to previously unregulated, or unexploited, resources. A clear illustration of the inherent complexity and difficulty of a similar debate was manifest during ICCAT's deliberations on quota allocation.[39]

In the first instance, all the SEAFC Convention negotiating Parties agreed that Article 116 of the LOS Convention should prevail. Consequently all States have a legitimate right to engage in fishing in the SEAFC Convention Area subject to their LOS Convention obligations and the rights and duties of coastal States provided for, inter alia, in Articles 63(2) and 64–67 of the LOS Convention. While the SEAFC Convention does not provide a precise recipe for fisheries or quota allocations, Article 20 gives extensive guidance. In this context, it is worthwhile noting that the term "fishing opportunities" was developed at the Third Meeting of the Coastal States (Table 2) in an attempt to detract from negative connotations attached to the use of such phraseology as "quota allocation" and "fishing rights."[40] It is also worth noting that an original coastal States' proposal to reserve a pre-determined, but unspecified, quota percentage for their use had fallen away by the Third Meeting.

39. See the ICCAT Criteria for the Allocation of Fishing Possibilities (Decision 01–25), available online: <http://www.iccat.es>.
40. The reports of early SEAFO negotiating meetings provide details of this discussion.

As previously indicated, Article 20 of the SEAFC Convention (Table 3) accounts for all the criteria set out in Article 11 of the Fish Stocks Agreement on fishing opportunities allocation. Noteworthy additions include the stage of fishery development (Article 20(1)(c)) and contributions to new and exploratory fisheries under Article 6(6) of the Fish Stocks Agreement (Article 20(1)(f) of the SEAFC Convention). However, Article 21(1) of the SEAFC Convention qualifies the application of the various criteria for allocation of fishing opportunities insofar that the Commission takes into account information, advice and recommendations on the implementation of, and compliance with, conservation and management measures by the Contracting Party concerned.

Table 3.—Factors To Be Taken Into Account by the SEAFO Commission When Determining Participatory Rights for Fishing Opportunities under Article 20(1) of the SEAFC Convention

(a)	The state of fishery resources including other marine living resources and existing levels of fishing effort, taking into account the advice and recommendations of the Scientific Committee;
(b)	Respective interests, past and present fishing patterns, including catches and practices in the Convention Area;
(c)	The stage of development of a fishery;
(d)	The interests of Developing States in whose areas of national jurisdiction the stocks also occur;
(e)	Contributions to conservation and management of fishery resources in the Convention Area, including the provision of information, the conduct of research and steps taken to establish co-operative mechanisms for effective monitoring, control, surveillance and enforcement;
(f)	Contributions to new and exploratory fisheries, taking account of the principles set out in Article 6.6 of the 1995 Agreement;*
(g)	The needs of coastal fishing communities which are dependent mainly on fishing for the stocks in the South-East Atlantic; and
(h)	The needs of coastal States whose economies are overwhelmingly dependent on the exploitation of fishery resources.

* Fish Stocks Agreement.

Pursuant to the above, Article 20 affords no priority weighting to any particular criteria nor indicates how they should be applied. However, it does attempt to recognize the diverse interests of SEAFO Parties in such a way that an element of transparency is introduced to the taking of decisions on the allocation of fishing opportunities. Also, while providing some guidance on allocation, possibly more than other regional conventions predating the Fish Stocks Agreement,[41] specific details have been left for the SEAFO Commission to develop at a later stage.

Control Measures

Understandably, the SEAFC Convention negotiations focused on developing a robust fisheries monitoring, control and surveillance (MCS) system. As emphasized by Jackson,[42] this system came to be based largely on flag State responsibilities on the one hand and complementary institutional measures on the other.

Flag State Measures

Article 14 of the SEAFC Convention sets out the flag State responsibilities of the Convention Parties. Article 14(1), (2) and (4) include the taking of necessary measures to ensure that the Convention is not undermined. The type of measures envisaged are outlined in Article 14(3) (Table 4). It is apparent that some of these measures (e.g., dealing with bilateral exchange of observers and deployment of vessel monitoring systems) are essentially similar to measures being applied by other RFMOs, and by CCAMLR in particular. In addition, Article 14(4) requires that SEAFO flag States ensure that their vessels operating in waters adjacent to the SEAFC Convention Area do not fish in such a way as to undermine the Organisation's agreed measures. As a whole, Article 14 of the SEAFC Convention draws heavily on Articles 18 and 19 of the Fish Stocks Agreement.

The generalities outlined in Article 14 of the SEAFC Convention are developed further in Article 16 in respect of observation, inspection, compliance and enforcement—the so-called MCS System. In particular, Article 16 establishes the principles underpinning the System (paragraph (2)) and introduces elements comprising control measures linked to flag State duties under Article 14 as well as at-sea and in-port inspection, at-sea observer programmes and procedures to follow-up on infringements (Article 16(2)). There was considerable debate on whether the System constituted an alternative mechanism for regional co-operation in enforcement, as per Article 21(15) of the Fish Stocks Agreement, or not. The EC in particular believed that it did, and therefore the detailed development of the SEAFC Convention's MCS procedures should await the Convention's entry into force, particularly in respect of reciprocal arrangements for

41. Jackson, n. 14 above, at 43.
42. *Id.*

Table 4.—Measures To Be Taken by SEAFC Convention Parties under Article 14(3) of the Convention to Ensure Flagged Vessels Give Effect to Measures Agreed by the SEAFO Commission

(a)	Ensure that flag States immediately investigate and report fully on actions taken in response to alleged violation(s) by a vessel flying their flag of measures adopted by the Commission;
(b)	Control such vessels in the Convention Area by means of fishing authorization;
(c)	Establish national records of fishing vessels authorized to fish in the Convention Area and provide for sharing this information with the Commission on a regular basis;
(d)	Require marking of fishing vessels and fishing gear for identification;
(e)	Require recording and timely reporting of vessel position, catch of target and non-target species, catch landed, catch transshipped, fishing effort and other relevant fisheries data;
(f)	Permit access by observers from other Contracting Parties to carry out functions agreed by the Commission; and
(g)	Require use of vessel monitoring system(s) as agreed by the Commission.

boarding and inspection as outlined in Article 22 of the Fish Stocks Agreement.

Consequently, Article 16 leaves it to the SEAFO Commission to establish its own observation, inspection, compliance and enforcement system (Article 16(1)). However, it also emphasizes that the "major purpose" of such a system is "to ensure that Contracting Parties effectively discharge their obligations under this Convention and, where applicable under the Fish Stocks Agreement, in order to ensure compliance with the conservation and management measures agreed by the Commission." Article 16(6) provides the additional caveat that after two years a special meeting may be convened (at the request of any Contracting Party) should the Commission not develop a satisfactory MCS system to strengthen the effective discharge of Contracting Party obligations under both the SEAFC Convention and the Fish Stocks Agreement. This compromise contrasts markedly with the mandatory institution of the procedures outlined in Articles 21–22 of the Fish Stocks Agreement in the event that consensus cannot be reached on a suitable MCS system within the first two years following the SEAFC Convention's entry into force. It also illustrates the difficulties faced by the SEAFC Convention negotiators in developing the Convention before the Fish Stocks Agreement's entry into force, particularly when extending the SEAFC Convention's mandate to include discrete stocks on the high seas in the absence of a clear international precedent.[43]

Article 16 of the SEAFC Convention anticipates that there is probably little point in applying specific MCS procedures in the absence of information on the form, extent, or direction of, as yet undeveloped, management measures. For this reason, Article 16(5) anticipates the setting up of the Convention's Annex (developed at the Technical Consultation in April 2000—Table 2) to provide interim arrangements for flag State reporting as a pre-cursor to the MCS System. These interim arrangements will remain in force until the System is adopted or until the SEAFO Commission decides otherwise.

Other Measures

Other key measures aimed at ensuring compliance in the absence of effective flag State control include attempts to outline Port State controls and to target individuals (i.e., "nationals") or national industries (i.e., "beneficial owners") as sources of non-compliance with SEAFO measures.

The SEAFC Convention Port State controls are relatively straightforward. Article 15 provides for in-port inspections and, where appropriate, prohibition of landings and transshipments. While the language of this particular Article is essentially similar to Article 23 of the Fish Stocks Agreement, a major difference is that it mandates Port State action.

In respect of nationals or national industries, the SEAFC Convention negotiations again experienced difficulties in the absence of any clear international precedent. For this reason, the wording of Article 13(6)(a) of the SEAFC Convention is complex, convoluted and highly qualified:

> Without prejudice to the primacy of the responsibility of the flag State, each Contracting Party shall, to the greatest extent possible, take measures, or co-operate, to ensure that its nationals fishing in the Convention area and its industries comply with the provisions of the Convention. Each Contracting Party shall, on a regular basis, inform the Commission of such measures taken.

The difficulties appeared to diverge as a matter of principle. Essentially, this depended on whether the negotiating Parties saw reference to nationals in Articles 116 to 118 of the LOS Convention as perfunctory, and/or salutary, as opposed to mandatory. Furthermore, the EC expressed some interpretational difficulties associated with the term "nationals," presumably based on

---

43. Jackson, n. 14 above, at 38.

the complimentary status of persons in respect of their sovereign birthright and their right to citizenship under the Treaty on European Union.[44]

In light of this divergence of opinion, and as for other parts of the SEAFC Convention, the compromise reached attempts to balance prevailing views. Therefore, as Jackson[45] has emphasized, according primacy to the flag State, along with recognition of exclusive jurisdiction of such States over their flagged vessels on the high seas,[46] limits the scope of Article 13(6)(a) of the SEAFC Convention to preventative measures before, or corrective measures after, nationals have fished in defiance of the SEAFC Convention measures. As a consequence, there is no suggestion that flag State jurisdiction aboard the vessel(s) concerned has been compromised in any way. Secondly, while the precise measures or type of co-operation are not spelt out, the obligation to act "to the greatest extent possible" is not insignificant.[47]

Despite their complexity, the SEAFC Convention provisions addressing control of nationals may be viewed as unique. While building on presumptive wording in Article 10(l) of the Fish Stocks Agreement, there is little doubt that they were developed against growing international concern over eliminating illegal, unreported and unregulated (IUU)[48] fishing, as well as a growing body of national practice aimed at addressing the problem[49] by denying vessel operators the economic benefits of this type of fishing.

44. Maastricht, 7 February 1992. In force 1 November 1993. Frequently amended. Consolidated version available online: <http://europe.eu.int/eur-lex/en>. See particularly Art. 2.

45. Jackson, n. 14 above, at 43–45.

46. Art. 30 of the SEAFC Convention is intended to ensure that nothing will affect the rights and obligations of States under the LOS Convention—a sentiment also implied in Art. 44 of the Fish Stocks Agreement. In addition, Art. 1(m) of the SEAFC Convention clearly indicates that a regional economic integration organisation (i.e., such as the EC) is considered as a flag State in respect of any vessel flying the flag of one of its Member States.

47. Jackson, n. 14 above, at 45, has indicated that this expression is open to interpretation and in practice may not exclude a situation where no measures are actually taken or co-operation is not forthcoming.

48. Para. 18 of the FAO International Plan of Action to Prevent, Deter and Eliminate Illegal, Unreported and Unregulated Fishing (IPOA on IUU Fishing; adopted by consensus by FAO's Committee on Fisheries on 2 March 2001 and endorsed by the FAO Council on 23 June 2001, available online: <http://www.fao.org/fi>) clearly duplicates the wording of Art. 13(6)(a) of the SEAFC Convention and indicates that: "In the light of the provisions of the [LOS Convention], and without prejudice to the primary responsibility of the flag State on the high seas, each State should, to the greatest extent possible, take measures or co-operate to ensure that nationals subject to their jurisdiction do not support or engage in IUU fishing. All States should co-operate to identify these nationals who are operators or beneficial owners of vessels involved in IUU fishing."

49. A number of States have introduced regulatory provisions to ensure that their nationals comply with international conservation and management measures

While it is recognized that effective action under Article 13(6)(a) of the SEAFC Convention may prove difficult for legal reasons (e.g., in terms of collecting evidence or attributing responsibility), its inclusion indicates recognition that action against nationals and/or national industries may be required. Obviously, this would only be in direct response to a detected violation of SEAFO measures.

Finally, Article 13(6)(b) requires States parties to exercise their fishing responsibilities over vessels flying their flags. This particular provision

inside or outside national waters. Notable examples include: Australia in application of the Fisheries Management Act, 1991 (Act No. 162 of 1991) (Section 8 of the Act applies the Act's provisions to specified areas outside the Australian Fishing Zone (AFZ) to Australian citizens, bodies corporate, vessels and persons aboard such vessels, including non-limitation of extra-territorial application of the Act; New Zealand subject to Part 6A of the New Zealand Fisheries Act, 1996 (Part 6A came into force on 1 May 2002 and prohibits New Zealand nationals [as defined in Section 2 of the Act] from using vessels not registered under the Ship Registration Act, 1992 to fish on the high seas unless specific authorization is provided in conformity with specified criteria); Norway in application of Article 6 of the 1977 Regulations Relating to Fishing and Hunting Operations by Foreign Nationals in the Economic Zone of Norway (this Article sets out conditions for issuing fishing licenses, or their withdrawal, in respect of: (a) fisheries within the Norwegian Economic Zone where a vessel owner or vessel has contravened national law; (b) where a vessel, or its owner, has taken part in fishing outside national quotas in international waters on stocks which are subject to Norwegian fisheries jurisdiction; and (c) where the vessel or vessel owner have taken part in fishing operations which contravene regulatory measures of regional or sub-regional fisheries management organizations or arrangements. The legislation was used in 2000 to comply a vessel "blacklist" for which the Norwegian authorities would not issue fishing licenses); South Africa in the application of its Marine Living Resources Act, 1998 (Act. No. 18 of 1988—South African Government Gazette Notice No. 189630 of 27 May 1998, (particularly provision 70(1)(b) which applies the jurisdiction of the courts under the Act to outside South African waters for citizens of the Republic or any person ordinarily resident in the Republic subject to the definition of a South African person contained in Section 1(liii) which includes trusts or close corporations); and Spain under Directive 1134/2001 of 31 October 2002 (this aims to establish a mechanism to deal with contraventions by legal and natural persons of Spanish fisheries regulations aboard vessels of other flags. It also establishes criteria to identify such flags and to provide for "aggravating circumstances" for non-compliance by Spanish nationals). A recent and interesting development of legal application of fisheries matters to state nationals has been the conviction by United States authorities of a number of South African citizens and joint South African-United States nationals under the United States Lacey Act. The conviction addressed offences concerning the illegal harvesting of South Coast Rock Lobster and Patagonian Toothfish, in defiance of South African statutes and CCAMLR measures. The individuals and companies concerned were heavily fined and prison sentences up to 46 months were handed down. Anon. "Three Seafood Industry Executives Sentenced to Federal Prison in Massive Seafood and Smuggling Regime," Press Release. (United States Attorney: Southern District Office of New York, 28 May 2004), p. 7.

attempts to deal with the chartering of vessels and is different from the Northwest Atlantic Fisheries Organization (NAFO) where one Contracting Party may charter a vessel from another without a change of flag.[50]

Interests of Developing States

Much of the impetus to negotiate the SEAFC Convention came from developing States. This was clearly reflected in various provisions, particularly the Articles dealing with fishing opportunities (Article 20) and the budget (Article 12). The balance of interests between distant-water fishing States and coastal developing States set out in Article 20 of the SEAFC Convention paved the way for a stand-alone provision (Article 21) that explicitly recognizes the special needs of developing States in the region. As such, Article 20 of the SEAFC Convention draws heavily on Articles 24 and 25 of the Fish Stocks Agreement. Emphasis is given to meeting the financial, technical and other needs of both present and future developing States in the region to provide for their improved conservation of, and sustainable access to, the resources covered by the Convention. Not only is recognition given to the general intent of Article 63(2) of the LOS Convention, the SEAFC Convention drafters clearly strived to ensure that SEAFO remain open to all States in the region, as well as other distant-water fishing States, whilst bearing in mind a common benefit to the region as a whole.

Other Provisions

Non-Parties

Like Article 33 of the Fish Stocks Agreement, Article 22 of the SEAFC Convention calls on Non-Parties to co-operate fully with SEAFO to ensure that its measures are not undermined (Article 22(1)) and that appropriate steps are taken by Contracting Parties under international law (Article 22(3)) to deter inappropriate fishing activities by Non-Contracting Parties when these undermine SEAFO conservation measures. However, Article 22 of the SEAFC Convention goes one step further than the Fish Stocks Agreement in specifically providing for the exchange of information on non-Party fishing activities (Article 22(2)) and in addressing the aspirations of fishing entities (Article 22(4)).

---

50. See Art. 14 of the NAFO Conservation and Enforcement Measures (NAFO FC Doc. 04/1), available online: <http://www.nafo.ca>.

Dispute Settlement

Article 24 of the SEAFC Convention outlines procedures for the settlement of disputes. To address issues likely to arise from both straddling and discrete stocks, the provision quite cleverly uses the dispute settlement procedure for the former contained in Part VIII of the Fish Stocks Agreement and for the latter in Part XV of the LOS Convention. As alluded to earlier, the SEAFC Convention provides for the establishment of an ad hoc expert panel to address technical disputes similar to that established under Article 29 of the Fish Stocks Agreement. Finally, the SEAFC Convention procedures apply to all Contracting Parties, whether or not they are Parties to the Fish Stocks Agreement and/or the LOS Convention.

Maritime Claims

Given the Angolan resolution attached to the Final Minute, a disclaimer on recognition, or otherwise, of claims, or positions, on the extent of waters or zones claimed by any Contracting Party was deemed necessary to avoid potential disputes in the future. Therefore, Article 31 specifically elaborates the attendant provisions necessary to protect SEAFO's position and those of all Contracting Parties.

Finally, it should be emphasized that all the SEAFC Convention negotiating Parties felt that it was not necessary to develop specific provisions, such as those in Articles 34 and 35 of the Fish Stocks Agreement, to address good faith and abuse of rights along with responsibility and liability respectively. In the case of the former, the sentiment was strongly expressed that finalization of the SEAFC Convention was in itself a clear indication of "good faith." However, the essential restatement of Article 34 of the Fish Stocks Agreement in Article 13(8) of the SEAFC Convention tends to counteract this interpretation even though the latter's standing and actual placing may still have some, but unclear, significance.

Relationship with the Fish Stocks Agreement and Other Instruments

Various links between the SEAFC Convention and the Fish Stocks Agreement have been identified. However, some of these are worth re-emphasizing, together with other considerations. Firstly, it is notable that the FAO was only an observer during the SEAFC Convention negotiation process and that no (international) non-governmental organizations (NGOs) attended any of the sessions. This prevailed despite the negotiators' obvious acceptance that SEAFO should be an "open" organization. Non-participation by such organizations was viewed by many of the negotiating Parties, particularly the coastal States, as a way of ensuring that these Parties' interests were not compromised by extraneous influences. A similar situation prevailed in the MHLC negotiations. Nevertheless, and despite limited involvement, FAO provided useful technical input into the SEAFC Convention negotiations.

Second, adopting the Fish Stocks Agreement as a basis for much of the SEAFC Convention negotiations resulted in some uncertainty since the former was not then in force. This was complicated by the fact that some participants in the SEAFO process (e.g., South Africa) had not yet signed the Fish Stocks Agreement and it was unclear whether all future parties of the SEAFC Convention would be bound by the Agreement. Some participants also appeared very wary of legitimizing the Fish Stocks Agreement through 'inappropriate' cross-referencing.

Together with the SEAFC Convention's application to discrete high seas stocks, such concerns raise a number of questions on the extent of the relationship between the SEAFC Convention and the Fish Stocks Agreement. One obvious question is whether the Convention's application to discrete stocks implies any extension of the Fish Stocks Agreement's mandate to all fishing on the high seas.

Prior to negotiating the SEAFC Convention, Articles 117–120 of the LOS Convention alone provided the general international legal framework outlining States' obligations to co-operate in the conservation of living resources on the high seas.[51] With the exception of the dispute settlement procedures in Article 24, the SEAFC Convention's provisions apply equally to *both* straddling stocks *and* discrete high seas stocks. It would therefore be reasonable to assume that at least the SEAFC Convention Parties have indicated their willingness to apply the Fish Stocks Agreement provisions to discrete high seas stocks. Based on the most recent draft of the Southern Indian Ocean Fisheries Agreement (SIOFA),[52] the SEAFC Convention is likely to have set an international legal precedent.

As illustrated by the preceding discussion, it was always intended that SEAFO should have a strong regional character. This was clearly catered for in the SEAFC Convention articles dealing with the budget (Article 12), MCS (Articles 14–16) and the special needs of developing States (Article 21). In all cases, cost-efficiency is emphasized.

51. Jackson, n. 14 above, at 38.
52. The most recent draft of the SIOFA is laid down in Annex G to the "Report of the Fourth Intergovernmental Consultation on the Establishment of a Southwest Indian Ocean Fisheries Commission, Mahe, Seychelles, 13–16 July 2004," *FAO Fisheries Report* No. 766 (2005). See, inter alia, the Preamble and Arts 1(j), 3(1) and 4. Particularly noteworthy is that this draft does not incorporate the notion of compatibility or another mechanism to ensure that account is taken of straddling stocks.

The negotiators of the SEAFC Convention allowed the SEAFO Commission to develop its own MCS System (Article 16(5) and the Convention Annex). In considering control measures, there was a lack of unanimity on how far, and to what extent, the Fish Stocks Agreement provisions could be transposed into the SEAFC Convention text. Obviously, such measures would depend on the MCS System that the SEAFO Commission eventually develops and only time will reveal the attached outcome.

Apart from addressing discrete high seas stocks, the extensive use of the Fish Stocks Agreement by the SEAFC Convention negotiators illustrates some of the Agreement's key strengths. The SEAFC Convention experience clearly shows that much of the Fish Stocks Agreement's language can be tailored to fit a rather more narrowly focused agreement of regional import. Contrary to Jackson's suggestion,[53] this may not necessarily mean that the Fish Stocks Agreement offers a rigid framework on which to base the drafting of such agreements, but at least it will facilitate negotiation. To further emphasize the point, both the SEAFC Convention and the WCPFC Convention processes clearly illustrate how easily the Fish Stocks Agreement lends itself to different regional contexts.

It can also be seen that the Fish Stocks Agreement remains flexible enough to make allowance for Parties that may not be parties to the Agreement. However, this may give rise to an apprehension that selective use of the Fish Stocks Agreement language may directly, and possibly prejudicially, affect the obligations to which particular SEAFC Convention Contracting Parties would become bound in a regional sense. As already highlighted, this could prejudice the interest(s) of such Parties elsewhere. However, as Rayfuse[54] has emphasized in re-iterating a quotation put forward in reference to the Antarctic Treaty, the Fish Stocks Agreement may have been "intended to create a regime which could become universally accepted. But there [was] no intention of imposing that regime; any attempt to do so would have been illegal." This is a situation that could also apply to the SEAFC Convention.

Jackson[55] has indicated that the situation where a SEAFC Convention Contracting Party is required to deal with similar subject matter in one agreement compared to another is not new, either to fisheries or international law. However, it could become more common, not only for SEAFO specifically but also for other fisheries agreements adopted after the

53. Jackson, n. 14 above, pp. 47–48.

54. R. Rayfuse, "The United Nations Agreement on Straddling and Highly Migratory Fish Stocks as an Objective Regime: A Case of Wishful Thinking?," *Australian Yearbook of International Law* 20 (1999): 253–278, 268.

55. Jackson, n. 14 above, at 48.

Fish Stocks Agreement's entry into force. To complicate matters further, it is worth pointing out that the Arbitral Tribunal in the *Southern Bluefin Tuna* case[56] accepted the notion of the 'parallelism of treaties' which means that although a dispute is 'centered' in a regional fisheries convention, certain provisions of the LOS Convention as well as its dispute settlement procedures may still be applicable.[57]

In the case of the SEAFC Convention, its application may be further convoluted by any "perceived" difference between the LOS Convention and the Fish Stocks Agreement dispute settlement procedures. Such perceptions are likely to assume particular prominence if not all the SEAFC Convention Parties are also parties to the Agreement. Article 30(5) of the Fish Stocks Agreement requires a court or tribunal to apply specific provisions of the LOS Convention and the Agreement in addition to those of any relevant regional, or global, fisheries arrangement "as well as generally accepted standards for the conservation and management of living marine resources and other rules of international law not incompatible with the LOS Convention." Article 24 of the SEAFC Convention applies to all Contracting Parties whether or not they are parties to the Fish Stocks Agreement. The situation may be complicated further in the SEAFC Convention's case when applied to discrete high seas stocks (see above) to which the Fish Stocks Agreement clearly does not specifically apply. The question of potential conflicts between the dispute resolution procedures of other regional fisheries arrangements and those under the LOS Convention are discussed further below in respect of the SADC Fisheries Protocol.

Finally, it is notable that the SEAFC Convention drew on the experiences of other RFMOs. In particular, its provisions on the functions of the Commission and Scientific Committee (Articles 8 and 10 respectively), decision making (Article 17) and implementation (Article 23) have much in common with similar provisions of the CAMLR Convention.[58] However, and despite considerable agreement between the coastal States, certain provisions of the CAMLR Convention outlining application of the precautionary approach or addressing ecosystem management (Article II) did not find favor in the final SEAFC Convention text. The exact reasons for this are not clear. However, one explanation might be that international debate on these specific topics remains protracted and inconclusive, particularly in

---

56. (Australia and New Zealand v. Japan), Arbitral Tribunal constituted under Annex VII of the United Nations Convention on the Law of the Sea, Award on Jurisdiction and Admissibility of 4 August 2000, available online: <http://www.worldbank.org/icsid>.

57. See paras. 52 and 64 of the Award.

58. Arts. IX, XV, XII and IX(6) of the CAMLR Convention.

elaborating the "burden of proof" in the context of the precautionary approach.[59] As has been submitted:

> While the conceptual soundness of the precautionary approach is difficult to contest, considerable difficulties remain in its practical implementation.[60]

Similarly, while various national laws (e.g., by Australia, New Zealand, South Africa and the United States) address elements of ecosystem management, they fall short of setting an international standard for consistent application of ecosystem-based fisheries management.[61] Such considerations suggest that the complexity of the principles to be addressed, along with concern for setting unreasonable precedents, were probably the primary reasons for the SEAFC Convention negotiators' reluctance to fully subsume specific CAMLR Convention provisions into the final text rather than intransigence per se (see also the section on Objectives and General Principles above).

Finally, as already emphasized, Article 30 of the SEAFC Convention does not release any Contracting Party from its obligations under the LOS Convention, or any other compatible agreement, nor erodes its rights under any such agreement. While the question of compatibility of subsequent agreements with the LOS Convention remains open to interpretation, given the precedents of international law to date, this is unlikely to constitute a major shortcoming in Article 30's effective application.

WCPFC CONVENTION

Background

The Western Central Pacific is the source of between 50 percent and 60 percent of the world's total tuna catch and far exceeds catches taken in the Indian, Atlantic and Eastern Pacific Oceans.[62] Annual catches are valued at

---

59. D. Freestone, *The Burden of Proof in Natural Resources Legislation*, FAO Legislative Study, No. 63. (Rome: FAO, 1998), 27 p. at p. 1–6.

60. E. J. Molenaar, "Ecosystem-Based Fisheries Management, Commercial Fisheries, Marine Mammals and the 2001 Reykjavik Declaration in the Context of International Law," *International Journal of Marine and Coastal Law* 17 (2002): 561–595, at p. 590–591.

61. Molenaar, n. 58 above, at 581.

62. Cf. *The State of World Fisheries and Aquaculture, 2002* (SOFIA 2002; FAO, Rome; <http://www.fao.org/fi>), at 15 and 51–52; T. Aqorau, "Tuna Fisheries Management in the Western and Central Pacific Ocean: A Critical Analysis of the Convention for the Conservation and Management of Highly Migratory Fish Stocks in the Western and Central Pacific Ocean and Its Implications for the Pacific Island States," *International Journal of Marine and Coastal Law* 16 (2001): 379–431, 382; A.

between US$1.5 and 2.0 billion and represent the single most important element in the economies of the Pacific Island States.[63] While stocks were not generally under threat in the late 1980s, growing distant-water fishing capacity, coupled with an increased likelihood of over-fishing and possible detrimental consequences to the economies of the Pacific Island States, raised considerable concern on the future sustainability of such stocks. As a consequence, steps were initiated to protect these very valuable economic resources and to ensure that a sound institutional framework was in place prior to the need for management measures[64] to regulate catch levels or fishing effort.

Negotiation of an international cooperative arrangement for the management of highly migratory fish stocks in the Western Central Pacific persisted for well over a decade. One early initiative for the southern albacore fishery broke down in 1991, due to a dispute between the major protagonists—the Pacific Island States on the one hand and the distant-water fishing States on the other—over the proposed arrangement's scope.[65] In 1993, this initiative was revived[66] and spurred on by the Fish Stocks Agreement negotiations, as well as by the fact that the Western and Central Pacific Ocean was the only area without an international agreement for conserving and managing highly migratory fish species, the South Pacific Forum Fisheries Agency (FFA) convened the first Multilateral High Level Conference (MHLC) in 1994 to commence negotiation of a comprehensive agreement for the region.

Subsequently, the Conference met on seven occasions over the next three years. Its sessions became increasingly discordant with the Conference Chair in particular being criticized for favoring Pacific Island States at the expense of other fishing States' interests. Amongst other criticisms, fair or not, the Chair was accused of refusing to admit the EC as a participant

Langley, J. Hampton and P. Williams, "The Western and Central Pacific Fishery, 2002: Overview and Status of Stocks," *Tuna Fisheries Assessment Report No. 5* (Oceanic Fisheries Programme: 2002), available online: <http://www.spc.int/OceanFish/Docs/Research>, at iv–v.

63. S. D. Murphy, "Conservation of Fish in the Western and Central Pacific Ocean," *American Journal of International Law* 95 (2001): 152–155, 153.

64. Welcome address by President Imata Kabua, President of the Marshall Islands (MHLC, Report of the Second Multilateral High Level Conference," 1997). Annex. 4, at 26.

65. R. G. Rayfuse, *Non-Flag State Enforcement in High Seas Fisheries* (Leiden/Boston: Martinus Nijhoff Publishers: 2004): p. 299.

66. D. Doulman, *A Preliminary Review of Some Aspects of the Processes in the Western and Central Pacific Ocean and the South-East Atlantic Ocean to Implement the UN Fish Stocks Agreement,* paper presented to Conference on the Management of Straddling Fish Stocks and Highly Migratory Fish Stocks and the UN Agreement (Bergen, Norway 1999): 4.

relying too heavily on the Fish Stocks Agreement text, and trying to influence the negotiations' outcome by confining discussion to his own draft negotiating text.[67] In the end, the final WCPFC text was adopted by vote on 5 September 2000. Nineteen States voted in favor of the text with two (Japan and Korea) voting against it. China, France and Tonga abstained.[68] A resolution was also adopted to set up a Preparatory Conference (PrepCon) to establish the WCPFC Convention Commission. The PrepCon has met six times since the Convention's adoption and has completed work on a number of issues. The EC and Russia were admitted as participants at PrepCon II in early 2002 and Japan returned to participate later that year in PrepCon III.

Being finalized slightly prior to the SEAFC Convention, the WCPFC Convention was technically the first agreement concluded after the Fish Stocks Agreement. However, the latter entered into force sooner. The WCPFC Convention's entry into force required ratification by three States north of 20° N and seven states south of 20° N. Alternatively, it would enter into force if ratified by 13 States after September 2003 (Article 36). As of 19 December 2003, thirteen instruments of ratification had been filed by states south of 20° N. Under Article 36, the Convention will enter into force after the deposit of instruments of ratification, acceptance, approval or accession by three States north of 20° N or on 19 June 2004—six months after the deposit of the thirteenth instrument of ratification—or whichever is earlier. The WCPFC Convention entered into force under the latter condition on 19 June 2004. At the time of writing, the number of Contracting Parties had risen to sixteen, while Chinese Taipei had agreed to be bound pursuant to Article 9(2) and Annex I of the WCPFC Convention.[69]

Objective and General Principles

The Convention's objective is to ensure effective management, long-term conservation and sustainable use of highly migratory stocks in the Western and Central Pacific Ocean, in a manner compatible with both the LOS Convention and the Fish Stocks Agreement (Article 2 of the WCPFC Convention). Upon the Convention's entry into force, a Commission will be

67. Cf. Rayfuse, n. 65 above, at 299. Ambassador Satya Nandan also chaired the Fish Stocks Agreement negotiations.

68. The Final Act of the Multilateral High Level Conference on the Conservation and Management of Highly Migratory Fish Stocks in the Western and Central Pacific was signed by representatives from 21 States and New Caledonia and Chinese Taipei. The WCPFC Convention was signed by 19 States. Information available online: <http://www.wcpfc.org>.

69. Information available online: <http://www.wcpfc.org>.

established and charged with various functions (Article 9 of the WCPFC Convention). The modalities of the Commission and its functions dominated the PrepCon agendas with the Commission being charged with: (a) determining total allowable catches (TACs) or total level of fishing effort, (b) adopting conservation and management measures for target and non-target species, (c) compiling and analyzing statistical and scientific data, (d) adopting generally recommended international minimum standards for the responsible conduct of fishing operations, and (e) establishing cooperative mechanisms for effective MCS and enforcement (Articles 9 and 10). The Commission relies on advice from a Scientific Committee as well as a Technical and Compliance Committee (Articles 11–14). The latter is responsible for reviewing compliance and making recommendations to the Commission. It is also charged with reviewing MCS implementation and developing enforcement measures. In respect of all these particular provisions, there are obviously many similarities between the WCPFC and SEAFC Conventions.

Articles 5 and 6 of the WCPFC Convention deal with principles for conservation and management as well as application of the precautionary approach respectively. These particular provisions follow those of the Fish Stocks Agreement more closely than the comparable provisions of the SEAFC Convention.

Worth noting is that Article 6(1)(a) of the WCPFC Convention specifically outlines the requirement for Contracting Parties to apply stock-specific reference points of Annex II to the Fish Stocks Agreement. It also clearly states that Annex II to the Fish Stocks Agreement forms an integral part of the WCPFC Convention—a far more specific cross-reference than any in the SEAFC Convention. It seems to be that this goes in fact beyond a mere cross-reference but effectively incorporates Annex II into the WCFPC Convention.

Article 7 of the WCPFC Convention mandates that the conservation and management principles in Article 5 should be applied to areas under national jurisdiction within the Convention Area where highly migratory fish stocks may be found. Similar consideration is manifest in Article 8, where a call is made for compatibility of measures on the high seas with those in areas under national jurisdiction.

Area of Application

Pursuant to Article 3, the WCPFC Convention applies to all waters of the Western and Central Pacific from the south coast of Australia to the north of Japan (Figure 2). The regulatory area of the WCPFC abuts that of CCAMLR in the south and that of the Inter-American Tropical Tuna Commission

(IATTC)[70] in the north-east, while overlapping in part with IATTC's regulatory area in the south-east. Apart from a small section in the south, the negotiations were unable to agree on a western and northern boundary. While there is a small overlap with the regulatory area of the Indian Ocean Tuna Commission (IOTC)[71] in the southwest, the intention of the WCPFC Convention to comprise all waters of the "Pacific Ocean," implies that the remainder of the western boundary abuts the regulatory area of the IOTC. The absence of a north-end point to the eastern boundary is not necessarily problematic as the competence will in practice be limited by the geographical distribution of the regulated species (approximately 4° S). Scientific evidence on such distribution will then determine if States like the Russian Federation should be treated as coastal States.

It should also be pointed out that the use of "all waters" is intended to encompass all the maritime zones that form part of the Pacific Ocean, including not only the high seas and EEZs but also the (marine) internal waters, territorial seas and archipelagic waters. The inclusion of archipelagic waters also proved contentious during the negotiations, if only for their cumulative size. The linkage between "areas under national jurisdiction" and "sovereign rights" in Article 7 of the WCPFC Convention could be interpreted as excluding areas in which a coastal State has sovereignty. Moreover, during the negotiations the Chairman made assurances that archipelagic waters would be excluded for the purpose of the assessment of financial contributions.[72]

Stocks Covered

Subject to the species listed in Annex I to the LOS Convention, but excluding sauries, and such other species as the Commission may determine, the WCPFC Convention applies to all highly migratory fish stocks found in the Convention Area (Articles 1 and 3(3)). Conservation and management measures to be adopted by the Commission apply either

70. Set up under the Convention for the Establishment of an Inter-American Tropical Tuna Commission (Washington D.C., 31 May 1949. In force 3 March 1950, 80 *United Nations Treaty Series* 4, available online: <http://www.iattc.org>). The 1949 IATTC Convention is to be replaced by the Convention for the Strengthening of the Inter-American Tropical Tuna Commission Established by the 1949 Convention between the United States of America and the Republic of Costa Rica (Antigua Convention) (Washington D.C., 14 November 2003. Not in force, available online: <http://www.iattc.org>).

71. Set up under the Agreement for the Establishment of the Indian Ocean Tuna Commission (Rome, 25 November 1993 (105th Session FAO Council). In force 27 March 1996, available online: <http://www.iotc.org>.)

72. See Molenaar, n. 30 above, at 480–481.

FIG. 2.—The WCPFC Convention Area.

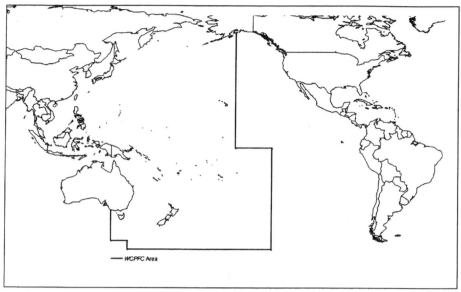

Source: Author.

throughout the entire migratory range of the stocks, or to specific areas, as determined by the Commission (Article 3). This is significantly different from the SEAFO Commission, which cannot adopt measures for waters under national jurisdiction. However, akin to Article 19 of the SEAFC Convention, measures for high seas and those for areas under national jurisdiction should be compatible, so ensuring that all measures adopted by the WCPFC Convention Commission and the coastal States are in firm accordance with the Fish Stocks Agreement principles. Consequently, Articles 5–8 of the WCPFC Convention repeat many similar Fish Stocks Agreement provisions. These include use of the best scientific advice available taking into account the precautionary approach and ecosystem concerns (Articles 5 and 6 of the Fish Stocks Agreement).

Openness and Transparency

Articles 21 and 22 of the WCPFC Convention clearly recognize the need for openness and transparency in the Commission's work. The attached elements are similar to those in the SEAFC Convention (Articles 8, 18 and 22). However, in marked contrast to the SEAFC Convention, the WCPFC Convention's conditions for accession (Article 35(2)) are far more restrictive and require a specific invitation (based on consensus of all the WCPFC

Convention Commission Members) for any Party to join the Commission after the Convention's entry into force.

Institutional Aspects

Articles 9–16 of the WCPFC Convention address institutional matters attached to the work of the Commission and its subsidiary bodies, including the Secretariat. Financial arrangements are detailed in Articles 17–19. Like SEAFO (see Article 12(1) of the SEAFC Convention), the principle of cost-efficiency is applied (Article 9(5) of the WCPFC Convention). However, unlike SEAFO, any arrears of more than two years in a Party's financial contributions automatically attracts interest on outstanding monies and disqualifies the Party concerned from partaking in decision making until all outstanding contributions are paid (Article 18(3)). The latter provision is remarkably similar to that set out in Article XIX(6) of the CAMLR Convention. While similar conditions concerning non-payment were raised during the SEAFC Convention negotiations, there was general agreement that they were discriminatory and not appropriate. It was also felt that they ran contrary to the strong recognition by the SEAFC Convention negotiators that SEAFO be an 'open' organization.

Decision Making

Like the SEAFC Convention, and as a general principle, all WCPFC Convention decisions are taken by consensus (Article 20(1)), particularly when in relation to the setting of TACs or total fishing effort levels. Consensus-based decision making thus applies to all measures in the absence of any formal objection at the time the decision was taken. Except where the Convention requires a decision to be taken by consensus and in the event of failure to secure consensus, decisions may be taken by following the voting procedures set out in Articles 20(2) and (3). Under these circumstances, substantive decisions require a double three-fourths majority.[73] However, under Article 20(4), the Chairman of the Commission has the power to appoint a conciliator to reconcile any differences blocking consensus when the Commission requires that any decision should be consensus-based.

73. Three-fourths of the South Pacific Forum Fishery Agency (FFA) Member States and three-fourths of the other Contracting Parties to the WCPFC Convention (Art. 20(2)).

Again, as in Article 23 of the SEAFC Convention, Article 20(6)–(9) of the WCPFC Convention provides for an objection procedure to decisions as well as the institution of a review procedure (including the appointment of a review panel in accordance with conditions set out in Annex II). This complicated decision-making mechanism, while not dissimilar to that under the SEAFC Convention, is designed to ensure that no one party, or block of parties, unduly influences the WCPFC Commission's work. Whether this will be feasible, or whether it will simply result in deadlock and endless submission to the review procedures, remains to be seen. At least, and unlike the SEAFC Convention, any attendant review constitutes an intermediary step between deadlock and dispute. This is likely to be simpler to apply than a full dispute resolution process.

Contracting Party Obligations

Commission Members (i.e., "Contracting Parties") are obligated to enforce the WCPFC Convention provisions and any related conservation or management measures adopted by the Commission under Articles 23 and 25. Similar to Article 6 of the SEAFC Convention, Article 23 of the WCPFC Convention prescribes the provision of specific information (Article 23(2)), some control over nationals and for the gathering of information attached to fishing activities (Article 23(5)). Under the latter provision, and at the request of any Contracting Party, or when supplied with relevant information, Contracting Parties must fully investigate any alleged violation and report on the conduct of such investigation, including any action taken or proposed to be taken. Reports are to be made to both the requesting Contracting Party and the Commission within two months of the date of request. The outcome(s) of any investigation must also be reported when completed.

Under Article 25 of the WCPFC Convention, and if satisfied that there is sufficient evidence for an alleged violation by one of its vessels, a flag State is required to refer the case to its authorities so as to institute legal proceedings and, where appropriate, detain the vessel. Where a serious violation of the WCPFC Convention conservation and/or management measures has occurred, the flag State must also ensure that the vessel involved ceases its activities (Article 25(4)) and does not resume fishing in the Convention Area until such time that there is compliance with any outstanding sanctions imposed by that State (under Article 25(7)).

To facilitate domestic legal proceedings, all the WCPFC Convention Parties are obligated, to the extent permitted by their national laws, to establish arrangements for making evidence available to the prosecuting authorities of other WCPFC Convention Contracting Parties (Article 25(5)). Investigations and judicial proceedings are to be carried out expeditiously and the sanctions imposed should be sufficiently severe to secure compliance and to discourage future violations (Article 25(7)). Furthermore, such sanctions aim to deprive offenders of the benefits accruing from their illegal activities. Action may also be taken against offending fishing vessel Masters or Officers. The latter may result in withdrawal of fishing permits and/or suspension of service authorization. Annual reports to the WCPFC Convention Commission on compliance and imposition of sanctions for any violation are to be provided (Article 25(8)).

Other WCPFC Convention provisions (Article 25(11)) urge Contracting Parties to take action, consistent with international law, to deter fishing vessels from fishing in the Convention Area when such vessels have violated WCPFC Convention measures and until such time as action is taken by the flag State concerned. They also provide (Article 25(12)) for the development of non-discriminatory trade measures to be applied to parties, or entities, when the latter's fishing vessels undermine conservation and management measures adopted by the Commission.

A major difference between the WCPFC Convention and the SEAFC Convention is that the latter is less specific on the details of compliance measures (Article 16 of the SEAFC Convention) and does not mix these with Contracting Party obligations (Article 13 of the SEAFC Convention). Furthermore, Article 6 of the SEAFC Convention clearly indicates that all Contracting Parties are Commission Members. A similar qualification is absent in Article 9 of the WCPFC Convention, and the inter-changeable use of the terms "Contracting Parties" and "Commission Members" in the operative paragraphs of the various Articles discussed in this Section could lead to confusion.

Fishing Opportunities

Unlike Article 20 of the SEAFC Convention, the WCPFC Convention does not provide a single article dedicated to detailing consideration to be taken into account when allocating fishing opportunities or catches. However, Article 10(1)(g) tasks the WCPFC Commission with "developing, where necessary, criteria for the allocation of the total allowable catch or the total level of fishing effort for highly migratory fish stocks in the Convention Area." Article 10(3) also addresses many of the considerations found in Article 20 of the SEAFC Convention in relation to the kinds of criteria which might be applied.

Control Measures

Flag State Measures

The WCPFC Convention outlines very detailed flag State duties (Article 24), and procedures to ensure compliance and enforcement (Article 25). In contrast to the comparatively minimalist approach adopted by the SEAFC Convention, the WCPFC Convention provides considerably more detail on matters such as a regional observer program (Article 28), the conduct of transshipment operations (Article 29) and at-sea boarding/inspection procedures (Article 25). Indeed, a primary objection by Japan, Korea and others to the WCPFC Draft Convention was that it "contained too many words"[74] and over-specified Contracting Party obligations better left to the discretion of the WCFPC Commission once established. By implication, it would appear that the SEAFC Convention negotiators were more open to such views and so developed the rather less detailed enforcement and compliance regime discussed earlier.

It is interesting to note that much of the substance of the WCPFC Convention's provisions highlighted in the previous paragraph deal with enforcement-related matters and often simply repeat, or otherwise incorporate, Fish Stocks Agreement provisions. With many Japanese proposals for revision being all but ignored, tensions were heightened. This probably resulted in Japan refusing to participate in a number of key small drafting groups, ultimately voting against the text and not signing the Final Act of the negotiation process.[75]

Under the WCPFC Convention, flag States are obliged to ensure that their vessels comply with Commission measures and do not engage in any activities to the contrary. The details set out in Article 24 largely mimic those of Article 14 of the SEAFC Convention, explicitly in respect of the need for vessels only being authorized to fish when the flag State is able to control the vessel effectively. National registers of authorized vessels are to be compiled and provided to the WCFPC Commission. They should be updated expeditiously as, and when, necessary (Article 24(4) and (5) of the WCPFC Convention).

When operating on the high seas, vessels are required to follow terms and conditions for fishing laid out in Annex III to the WCPFC Convention. These address conditions attached to compliance with national laws, obligations with respect to observers, regulation of transshipments, report-

---

74. Statement of Japanese delegation at MHLC 3 as reflected in Newsletter No. 269 (24 July 1998) from the Japanese Ministry of Agriculture, Forestry and Fisheries, available online: <http://www.maff.go.jp/mud/269.html>.

75. See Final Act, n. 68 above. See also Rayfuse, n. 65 above, at 301.

ing requirements and enforcement measures (e.g., marking of vessels). In the latter regard, flag States are required to ensure deployment of satellite-based vessel monitoring systems (VMS) on all their vessels fishing in the WCPFC Convention Area (Article 24(8)). These systems should simultaneously transmit positional information to the Commission and the flag State. This requirement is one step beyond the dual VMS reporting system currently operating in the North-East Atlantic Fisheries Commission (NEAFC)[76] or NAFO and is essentially a centralized system like that recently developed by CCAMLR.[77] As far as possible, and under Article 29, transshipments by WCPFC Convention Contracting Party vessels are to be conducted in port. Transshipments at sea (Article 29(4)) are only sanctioned in strict accordance with Article 4 of Annex III to the WCPFC Convention. Transshipment from purse-seine vessels is prohibited (Article 29(5)). Again, such details go well beyond any SEAFC Convention provisions.

Finally, the terms and conditions for fishing set out in Annex III to the WCPFC Convention include compliance with national laws (Article 3), obligations with respect to observers (Article 4), regulation of transshipment (Article 4), reporting requirements as per Annex I to the Fish Stocks Agreement and other general, enforcement-related matters (such as complying with lawful instructions from an identified Commission Member, identification of the vessel, communication procedures and stowing/securing of gear when passing through areas under national jurisdiction) (Article 6). As such, Annex I to the Fish Stocks Agreement gives effect to the various considerations associated with establishing a "probable cause" by WCPFC Parties when initiating and pursuing enforcement action.

At-Sea Boarding and Inspection

Article 26 of the WCPFC Convention specifically requires the Commission to establish procedures for boarding and inspecting fishing vessels in the Convention Area, including on the high seas. All vessels used for such boarding and inspection are to be clearly marked and identifiable as being authorized to undertake the necessary actions (Article 26(1)). In early drafting, the negotiating text simply subsumed the Fish Stocks Agreement's boarding and inspection provisions (Article 22) into the WCPFC Conven-

---

76. Established by the Convention on Future Multilateral Cooperation in the North-East Atlantic Fisheries, London, 18 November 1980. In force 17 March 1982, 1285 *United Nations Treaty Series* 129, available online: <http://www.neafc.org>.

77. Cf. Report of the Twenty-Third Meeting of the Commission. CCAMLR, Hobart 2004, available online: <http://www.ccamlr.org>.

tion.[78] As for the SEAFO process, such cross-referencing was considered unacceptable by some parties, most notably Japan and Korea. In the end, the WCPFC Convention wording was modified to provide a specific cross-reference to Articles 21 and 22 of the Fish Stocks Agreement as a fallback provision. In the event that the WCPFC Commission is unable to agree on boarding and inspection procedures or on suitable, equally effective, alternative measures, within two years of the Convention's entry into force, Articles 21 and 22 of the Fish Stocks Agreement will be applied.

Under the above circumstances, boarding and inspection, and any subsequent enforcement action, will be conducted in accordance with Fish Stocks Agreement procedures and/or any such additional procedures that the WCPFC Commission may agree. Whichever scheme is applied, the WCPFC Convention Contracting Parties are required to ensure that their vessels accept boarding by duly authorized inspectors according to WCPFC Convention procedures and that these inspectors comply with such procedures. Put simply, the WCPFC Commission is obligated to adopt a non-flag based boarding and inspection scheme. Should it fail in this task, the Fish Stocks Agreement provisions will apply.

The PrepCon Meetings were used to elaborate the boarding and inspection scheme further. PrepCon I established a Working Group to deal with MCS issues in general.[79] During PrepCon III, the Working Group adopted a list of principles to be included in the WCPFC Convention boarding and inspection scheme. These provided details such as the scheme's definition, scope and objectives, vessels and personnel authorized to conduct boarding and inspection activities on the high seas in the Convention Area, standardized training for enforcement personnel, guidelines governing boarding and inspection procedures and guidelines governing the use of force. Mechanisms have also been developed to co-ordinate Secretariat actions with those of Contracting Party and flag State enforcement authorities, particularly between the latter.[80]

Undoubtedly, the WCPFC Convention inspection and boarding scheme outlined here has to be linked to the Convention's broader enforcement and compliance provisions. As the scheme is only part of a more comprehensive compliance and enforcement regime, this has tended to down-weight its priority.

78. See Chairman's Draft Convention Texts in Documents MHLC/WP.1 (22 June 1998); MHLC/WP.1/Rev. 1 (26 June 1998); MHLC/WP.1/Rev. 2 (19 February 1999); MHLC/WP.2 (20 July 1999); MHLC/WP.1/Rev.3 (9 September 1999); MHLC/WP.1/Rev. 4 (16 September 1999).

79. Working Group III: Monitoring, Control and Surveillance, Summary Report by the Chairman of the Working Group to the third session of the Preparatory Conference, the WCPFC Convention/PrepCon/21, 22 November 2002.

80. For example complementary to NEAFC.

During the WCPFC Convention negotiations, there appeared to be a general feeling that the use of force should be limited to situations when the safety of life (e.g., of the members of a boarding/inspection party) and/or property (e.g., the vessels involved) is threatened. In addition, Article 21(18) of the Fish Stocks Agreement needed to be taken into account since this liability is extended to States for damage or loss attributable to unlawful, or unreasonably excessive, actions during boarding and inspection. Such consideration reflect developments in NAFO where Canadian inspectors are being, or have been, charged or sued in Spanish courts over events occurring during at-sea inspections.[81] Despite these contentious issues, the negotiating Parties went a long way in elaborating the WCPFC Convention boarding and inspection scheme at PrepCons IV and V. By contrast, no such considerations were addressed during the SEAFO process.

Port State Measures

Whereas much of Article 23 of the Fish Stocks Agreement ("Measures taken by a port State") has been incorporated into Article 15 of the SEAFC Convention and Article 27 of the WCPFC Convention, there are some significant differences. The latter essentially repeats verbatim the wording and heading of Article 23 of the Fish Stocks Agreement apart from some small differences most likely attributable to the transformation of a global instrument into a regional one. The arguments by Japan, Korea and others during the MHLC negotiations that exercising port State jurisdiction in relation to high seas fisheries is not consistent with the LOS Convention, were therefore not accepted.

On the other hand, Article 15 of the SEAFC Convention is not only entitled 'Port State Duties and Measures Taken by a Port State' but the repeated use of "shall" in its paragraphs also arguably bolsters the mandatory nature of port State jurisdiction under the SEAFC Convention in contrast to Article 23 of the Fish Stocks Agreement and Article 27 of the WCPFC Convention. Accordingly, the inspection of, inter alia, documents, fishing gear and catch on board fishing vessels that voluntarily enter ports is mandatory under the SEAFC Convention but voluntary under the WCPFC Convention.

---

81. T. McDorman, "Canada's Aggressive Fisheries Action: Will They Improve the Climate for International Agreements?," *Canadian Foreign Policy* 2 (1994): 5–28; B. M. Caldwell, "United Nations Fishing Agreement in Force 11 December 2001: An Incremental Step Towards Enforcement on the High Seas," 2002. Revised version of a paper published in the March 2002 issue of *Fisherman Life Magazine,* available online: <http://www.admiraltylaw.com/fisheries/Papers/unclos.htm>.

Also noteworthy is that Article 15(1) of the SEAFC Convention does not include the condition that port State jurisdiction "shall not discriminate in form or in fact against the vessels and any State" which appears in Article 23(1) of the Fish Stocks Agreement as well as in Article 27(1) of the WCPFC Convention. The need to avoid non-discrimination is nevertheless explicitly covered by Articles 16(2)(b) and 23(1)(d)(iii) and implicitly by Article 13(8) of the LOS Convention.

Finally, the requirement that flag States must be informed of action taken by port States set out in Article 15(4) of the SEAFC Convention, does not appear in the other two treaties. This requirement was obviously inserted on behalf of the interests of flag States, particularly in view of the mandatory nature of port State jurisdiction.

All the provisions discussed above conclude with a non-prejudicial clause that nothing in them affects the exercise by States of their sovereignty over ports in their territory in accordance with international law. This reflects the ongoing controversy on the scope and extent of port State jurisdiction under international law and can be invoked by States that take the view that they have broader port State rights than provided by the three treaties.

Regional Observer Program

While responsibility for enforcement under the WCPFC Convention clearly rests with the flag State, the Convention provides other mechanisms to augment its practical execution. The most interesting, and revolutionary, of these establishes a regional observer program (Article 28) and outlines its various elements. Unlike other RFMO observer programs (e.g., in NAFO and CCAMLR), the WCPFC Convention program is coordinated (Article 28(2)) by the Secretariat (established under Article 15). In addition, it is envisioned (Article 28(3)) that observers are independent and impartial (i.e., not appointed by, or answerable to, a particular flag State), although the nationals of each Contracting Party are entitled to be included in the program (Article 28(6)(a)). Observers are authorized, trained and certified in accordance with procedures agreed by the Commission (Article 28(6)(c)), which may enter into contracts for the provision of observer services (Article 28(2)).

Essentially, WCPFC Convention observers are to be truly international and impartial, much along the lines of the on-board observer program under the International Dolphin Conservation Programme (IDCP).[82] In

---

82. See Annex II to the Agreement on the International Dolphin Conservation Program (Washington D.C., 21 May 1998. In force 15 February 1999, as amended, available online: <http://www.iattc.org>). See also Rayfuse, n. 65 above, at 269.

fact, the WCPFC Convention may potentially go farther than that program as it does not limit the number of observers supplied by the Secretariat to only 50 percent of the total (Article 28(2)). Nevertheless, the WCPFC Convention observer program remains subject to later decision(s) by the Commission on applicability and extent (Article 15(7)).

Unlike the CCAMLR Scheme of International Scientific Observation,[83] which expressly avoids any enforcement role for observers, the WCPFC Convention program empowers observers to monitor implementation of conservation and management measures, including the reporting of any findings to the Commission in this regard (Article 28(6)(e)). The WCPFC Convention Contracting Parties (Article 28(4) of the WCPFC Convention) are therefore required to ensure that fishing vessels flying their flag carry an observer from the WCPFC Convention programme, as required by the Commission, except when such vessels are operating exclusively within waters under that Party's national jurisdiction. This provision also applies when a vessel is fishing in waters under the jurisdiction of one or more coastal States or where the jurisdiction of two or more coastal States may apply (Article 28(5)).

In addition to monitoring implementation of conservation and management measures, WCPFC Convention Observers are mandated to monitor catch and scientific data as well as report the results of such observations (Article 28(6)(e)). However, they should not unduly interfere with the lawful operations of the vessel on which they serve and should carry out their activities with due regard to the vessel's operational requirements, communicating regularly with the Master to this end (Article 28(6)(d)). Obviously, this raises some questions as to what an Observer is expected to do when an operation is deemed to be "unlawful." To avoid potential conflict, a WCPFC Convention Observer is not allowed to undertake any of the observations or actions specified above when a vessel is within the EEZ of its flag State, unless the flag State agrees (Article 28(5)).

Other WCPFC Convention non-flag State-based measures include joint actions taken by Contracting Parties (e.g., under Article 23(5)) or those against Non-Contracting Parties (Article 32). In terms of the latter, the WCPFC Convention allows Contracting Parties to take measures to deter the activities of Non-Contracting Party vessels deemed to have undermined the effectiveness of, or otherwise violated, Commission measures.

---

83. Information available online: <http://www.ccamlr.org/pu/e/pubs/bd/pt10.htm>.

Other Measures

WCPFC Convention Contracting Parties are mandated to exchange information on activities of Non-Contracting Party vessels fishing in the Convention Area (Article 32(1)). In addition, the Commission can draw the attention of any flag State whose vessels, or nationals, are (in the Commission's opinion) affecting the WCPFC Convention's implementation (Article 32(3)). Commission Members, either individually or jointly, may request Non-Parties to ensure that their vessels cooperate fully in implementing the Commission's agreed measures. As in Article 19 of the SEAFC Convention, Co-operating Non-Contracting Parties are seen to be eligible to enjoy the benefits of participating in a fishery commensurate with their commitment to comply with, along with their record of compliance with, Commission measures for relevant stocks (Article 32(4)). However, like the SEAFC Convention, this particular provision remains silent on how such commitment would be assessed and by whom. Nevertheless, and to a large extent, Article 32 of the WCPFC Convention has much in common with Article 17 of the Fish Stocks Agreement.

As already highlighted, Article 25(10) of the WCPFC Convention provides for any Contracting Party to draw the attention of the flag State concerned and, as appropriate, the Commission as well, to situations when there are reasonable grounds to believe that a fishing vessel flying the flag of any (presumably Contracting or Non-Contracting Party) State has undermined the effectiveness of Commission measures. To the extent permissible under national law, the reporting Contracting Party may then supply the flag State with full supporting evidence. It may also provide a summary of such evidence to the Commission. The Commission cannot circulate the attached information until the flag State has had reasonable time to comment on the allegation and has submitted, or objected to, evidence, as the case may be. Contracting Parties are also able to take action in accordance with the Fish Stocks Agreement and international law to deter fishing vessels from fishing in the Convention Area, until such time as appropriate action is taken by the flag State (Article 25(11)), when such vessels have engaged in activities that undermine the effectiveness of, or which otherwise violate, Commission measures.

Interests of Developing States

Other provisions of the WCPFC Convention expressly recognize the special requirements of developing States (Article 30), procedures for dispute settlement (Article 31) and allude to the recognition of good faith (Article 33). In respect of Article 31, the provisions set out in Fish Stocks Agreement Part VIII are applied *mutatis mutandis*. Both Articles 30 and 33 replicate much of what is contained in Articles 24–26 and 34 of the Fish Stocks Agreement respectively. In the former case there are obvious similarities with Article 21 of the SEAFC Convention with the major exception being that Article 30(3) of the WPCFC Convention makes provision for the establishment of a special fund to facilitate effective participation by developing States, especially small island developing States.

Relationship with the Fish Stocks Agreement and Other Instruments

From the preceding discussion, it can be seen that like the SEAFC Convention, the WCPFC Convention has much in common with the Fish Stocks Agreement. However, a number of attendant details are worth highlighting. First, in both the SEAFC Convention and the WCPFC Convention, the issue of detailed cross-referencing to the Fish Stocks Agreement appeared to offer a barrier to negotiation. However, despite objection by the same party (Japan) in both fora, it would appear that cross-referencing to the Fish Stocks Agreement in the WCPFC Convention text is far more extensive, detailed and specific than in the SEAFC Convention— particularly in respect of compliance and enforcement (Article 26 of the WCPFC Convention). The reasons for this difference are not readily apparent. However, a contributory factor could be that there were more Pacific Island States signatories of the Fish Stocks Agreement than there were SEAFC Convention coastal States. While both categories of participants probably had most to lose by not applying the Fish Stocks Agreement provisions in detail, in the former case the weight of numbers was sufficient to counter the interests of distant-water fishing States in part at least. Despite this, cross-referencing to the Fish Stocks Agreement remains patchy in both the WCPFC Convention and the SEAFC Convention texts.

A particular difference between the SEAFC and WCPFC Conventions is apparent in the way that they deal with dispute resolution. As already highlighted, the SEAFC Convention's dispute resolution provisions attempt to address *both* straddling and discrete high seas stocks. This requires explicit cross-referencing to *both* the LOS Convention and the Fish Stocks Agreement. It also intimates that Fish Stocks Agreement provisions apply whether SEAFC Convention Parties are party to the Agreement or not. On the other hand, such complications do not prevail for the WCPFC Convention and consequently the dispute resolution provisions are applied only in respect of Part VIII of the Fish Stocks Agreement, although express application to Non-Agreement Parties is also applied.

Unlike the SEAFC Convention, and in deference to the nature of the stocks concerned (migratory as opposed to straddling/discrete), the WCPFC Convention Area includes areas under national jurisdiction. This difference may have as much to do with history and politics (see discussion in the Conclusions and Observations) as with geography, or the biology of the stocks concerned. In the former context, it is notable that the SEAFC Convention, the WCPFC Convention and the Fish Stocks Agreement all detail the special needs of developing States.

However, a marked difference between the SEAFC and WCPFC Conventions is the way that the latter has addressed the question of fishing opportunities. As a consequence, Article 20 of the SEAFC Convention goes a long way to giving explicit effect to Articles 10–12 of the Fish Stocks Agreement. In contrast, Article 10(3) of the WCPFC Convention is a little less prescriptive. There is little doubt that the WCPFC Convention negotiations on allocation became entangled in essentially contradictory needs associated with the balance of economic power between the negotiating parties. These included differences in expectation and influence between the coastal States and the distant-water fishing fleets with the latter possessing the means *and* historic precedent to fish in the region.

The arguments during both the SEAFC and WCPFC Convention negotiations concerning allocation were essentially similar. On the one hand, coastal States maintained that the respective Commissions should only allocate high seas quotas (i.e., fishing opportunities), leaving coastal States with the right to set national quotas and determine EEZ access. Most distant-water fishing States, notably Japan, appeared to favor both in-zone and high seas allocation procedures based on historic fishing levels (a factor favoring distant-water fleets). The situation is mirrored by heated debate on the similar issues in relation to quota allocations within ICCAT over the past few years.[84] By removing coastal State EEZs from the equation, and by exhibiting some political accommodation, the SEAFC Convention negotiators were able to finalize the allocation of the fishing opportunities issue and lay down some attached guiding principles.

Two other factors appear to have contributed to the SEAFC Convention's comparatively rapid negotiation and entry into force. First, the ICSEAF experiences of the three African coastal States involved undoubtedly increased their political resolve to counter distant-water fleet interests. Second, the perceived value of the straddling stocks being considered was essentially unknown and seen as probably not very high. This could have served to reduce distant-water fishing States' perceptions of what they had to "lose."

Therefore, being less politically or economically-charged, the SEAFO process could be cynically viewed as having been of such low intensity that specific provision for abuse of rights was played down and essentially incorporated into an article (Article 13(8) of the SEAFC Convention) dealing with Contracting Party obligations in general. We do not agree with

84. Jackson, n. 14 above, at 42.

this in view of Article 13(8). This was obviously not the case in the WCPFC negotiations where all Parties supported a clear and stand-alone restatement of Article 34 of the Fish Stocks Agreement as being in their collective interest. A final similarity is that both Article 30 of the SEAFC Convention and Article 4 of the WCPFC Convention specifically reinforce their non-prejudicial relationships with the LOS Convention.

SADC FISHERIES PROTOCOL

Background

In the South-East Atlantic, the Southern African fisheries sector is predominantly industrially based with some 90 percent of the total catches being landed in Angola, Namibia and South Africa. Artisanal and recreational fisheries are more common on the Western Indian Ocean coast where they have both social and economic importance. The annual mean catch for the entire SADC region is about 1.9 million tonnes, roughly equivalent to 25 percent of sub-Saharan marine protein production. In Namibia the fisheries sector contributes more than 35 percent of GDP and employs more than 12,000 people. In South Africa, the annual revenue from coastal resources (fisheries, infrastructure and tourism) has been estimated at more than US$17,500 million (approximately 37 percent of the country's GDP) while the total value of SADC fishery exports in 2002 was just under US$900 million.[85]

Depletion of fish stocks through unsustainable harvesting has been a major concern to many SADC countries for over a decade, and for longer in countries such as Namibia. Most of the region's coastal and marine resources have suffered from unsustainable levels of exploitation, combined with increasingly efficient harvesting methods. This was caused by an ever-growing need for edible protein driven by socio-political considerations such as population increase (including urban migration to coastal areas), rising economic demand from the developed world, lucrative export markets and the need to support expanding tourism demands.[86] These factors affect the SADC coastal States as well as land-locked countries in the region and distant-water fishing fleets.[87] Furthermore, the incidence of

---

85. SOFIA 2002, n. 62 above, at 46.

86. R. Sherman, *Briefing on National, Regional and International Fisheries and Marine-Related Agreements* (GLOBE Southern Africa: March 2003; on file with authors).

87. *African Environment Outlook, Past, Present and Future Perspectives* (United Nations Environment Programme: 2002, available online: <http://www.unep.org/aeo/113.htm> and <http://www.unep.org/aeo/034.htm>).

88. See n. 9 above, for the list of SADC Members.

marine pollution from land-based activities and degradation of coastal areas in the SADC region are on the rise as is extensive utilization of coastal areas. The potentially negative effects of these and other factors remain undetermined. In particular, it is anticipated that there will be severe consequences arising from sea-level rise due to global warming. This could cause inundation of major coastal settlements and coastal infrastructure leading to population displacement as well as associated ecosystem damage.

The SADC Fisheries Protocol was initiated to address such concerns at a workshop for inland and marine fisheries held in Windhoek, Namibia, in February 1997. This workshop produced a Draft Protocol in December 1999 that was forwarded to all SADC Member States for comment. The Draft was discussed domestically and at a regional workshop in Lusaka, Zambia, in April 2000. On 21 May 2001, the final version of the Protocol was approved by the SADC Fisheries Ministers[88] in Maputo, Mozambique. It was signed by all SADC Heads of State in Blantyre, Malawi on 14 August 2001. It entered into force on 8 August 2003. At the time of writing, all SADC Members except for the Democratic Republic of the Congo, the Seychelles, Swaziland and Zimbabwe had ratified.[89]

Objectives and General Principles

Article 1 of the Protocol provides some key definitions (Table 5) while Article 2 applies the Protocol to living aquatic (both freshwater and marine) resources and aquatic ecosystems within the waters (marine and inland) of SADC Members. The latter Article attempts to preserve the rights and obligations of the Parties in respect of such resources where their ranges extend outside areas under national jurisdiction, or onto the high seas. A major impact of Article 2 is that the rights and obligations under the Fish Stocks Agreement are explicitly recognized, as are those under Articles 116–119 of the LOS Convention. Finally, the provision also focuses on fishing and related activities by State Party nationals as well as on international activities outside SADC that are in conformity with the Protocol's objectives.

The Protocol's primary objective (Article 3) is to promote the responsible and sustainable use of living aquatic resources and aquatic ecosystems consistent with the interests of SADC Parties as a whole. The five key considerations identified aim to:

(a) promote and enhance food security and human health;
(b) safeguard the livelihood of fishing communities;

89. Information available online: <http://www.sadc.int>.

Table 5.—Some key definitions from Article 1 of the SADC Fisheries Protocol

"Aquaculture": All activities aimed at producing in restricted areas, processing and marketing aquatic plants and animals from fresh, brackish or salt waters;

"Critical Habitat": A habitat that is essential for maintaining the integrity of an ecosystem, species or assemblage of species;

"Exotic Species": Those species that are not indigenous or endemic to a specific area;

"Fish": Any aquatic plant or animal, and includes eggs, larvae and all juvenile stages;

"Fishing": All activities directly related to the exploitation of living aquatic resources and includes transshipment;

"Fish Stock": A population of fish, including migratory species, which constitutes a coherent reproductive unit;

"Highly Migratory Species": Species of fish which move seasonally from one ecological area to another;

"Related Activities": All activities associated with exploitation of fish, including processing, marketing, transportation and trade of fish and fish products;

"Resources": All aquatic ecosystems, fish and fish stocks to which this Protocol applies;

"Shared Resources": Shared aquatic ecosystem, shared fishery and shared fish stock;

"Subsistence Fisheries": Fishing activities where fishers regularly catch fish for personal and household consumption and engage from time to time in the local sale or barter of excess catch;

"Transboundary": Populations, natural systems, activities, measures and effects, which extend beyond the effective jurisdiction of a State Party; and

"Transshipment": Unloading of all or any of the aquatic resources on board a fishing vessel to another fishing vessel either at sea or in port without the products having been recorded by a port State as landed.

(c) generate economic opportunities for nationals in the Region;
(d) ensure that future generations benefit from these renewable resources; and
(e) alleviate poverty with the ultimate objective of its eradication.

From these considerations, it is obvious that the Protocol enjoys a high level of socio-economic support in SADC, a situation that probably reflects the detailed consultations held with various stakeholders in each of the Member States. It is also worth noting that the Protocol is closely aligned with Articles 10–11 of the FAO Code of Conduct: particularly Article 10(2)(2) which highlights the need to account for economic, social and cultural factors when assessing the potential value of coastal resources.

Article 4 outlines the five key principles on which the Protocol is based. It is implemented nationally, with responsibility for trans-boundary resources being shared by, and being dependent on good co-operation between, the Parties concerned. The other principles are largely socio-economic and endeavor to:

- Ensure participation of all stakeholders in promoting the Protocol's objective;
- Take appropriate measures to regulate use of living aquatic resources and protect such resources against over-exploitation, whilst developing environmental expertise and building capacity for sustainable utilization of resources; and
- Promote gender equality and address any potential inequalities attached thereto.

Article 14 of the Protocol urges Parties to conserve aquatic ecosystems, including their biodiversity and unique habitats, insofar as these contribute to the livelihood and aesthetic values of the people and the Region. Parties are called on to apply the precautionary approach to ensure that activities within their jurisdiction and control do not cause excessive trans-boundary and/or adverse impacts. As such, they are required to co-operate with appropriate SADC institutions and other relevant international agencies to take concerted action to protect endangered living aquatic species and their habitats. Steps in this regard include compiling lists of endangered species, introducing measures to progressively replace fishing gear and other technologies which are hazardous to the environment, promoting broad awareness by all stakeholders of the need for protection of the species and their habitats, and seeking alternative economic activities for those whose livelihoods impact upon the survival of endangered species. Other than a reference to the precautionary approach, Article 14 is in keeping with the other provisions of the Protocol already discussed. Again, it exhibits a substantial degree of socio-economic bias.

In Article 11, the Protocol expressly accounts for the rights and obligations set up under Articles 116–119 of the LOS Convention in relation to management of high seas fishing. Specifically, the Protocol urges Parties to:

(a) recognize that all States have the right for their nationals to engage in fishing on the high seas;
(b) work towards effective management of the high seas living aquatic resources;
(c) collaborate in the establishment of common positions and policies with regard to the effective management of the high seas living aquatic resources; and

(d) support the activities of international organizations that conserve and manage living aquatic resources on the high seas, and which act in non-discriminatory manner in relation to State Parties.

Article 5 urges SADC Parties to take measures, at both the national and international level, to harmonize their fisheries legislation, policies, plans and programs to promote the Protocol's objectives. It calls for adoption of measures to ensure that nationals and judicial persons act in a responsible manner when utilizing living aquatic resources in, within and beyond national jurisdictional limits.

The Protocol mandates due authorization to fish for vessels flying SADC Party flags in the regions' waters. It is foreseen that such authorization should only be granted where a Party is able to effectively exercise its responsibilities.[90] Parties are requested to ensure that vessels, or nationals, fishing in waters covered by the Protocol, take appropriate steps to comply with measures adopted under it, and that they do not engage in any activity that undermines the effectiveness of such measures. Finally, Parties are requested to ensure that living aquatic resources in areas under their national jurisdiction are not endangered by over-exploitation or unsustainable harvesting practices.

International Relations

Article 5 urges Protocol Parties to establish common positions in order to undertake coordinated and complementary actions in various relevant international organizations and fora identified in Protocol Appendices 1 and 2 (Table 6) with special emphasis being given to the LOS Convention, the Fish Stocks Agreement and the Compliance Agreement.[91] Such action is envisaged to include facilitation of trans-boundary activities and movements pursuant to the Protocol's objectives.

Management of Shared Resources

Article 7 of the Protocol provides considerable detail aimed at resolving potential disputes on the status of shared resources under that article. The

---

90. This refers to the key designation associated with the primacy of flag State responsibility detailed in Art. III of the FAO Compliance Agreement (Agreement to Promote Compliance with International Conservation and Management Measures by Fishing Vessels on the High Seas, Rome, 24 November 1993). In force 24 April 2003, *International Legal Materials* 33 (1994): 969, available online: <http://www.fao.org/legal>.

91. *Id.*

Table 6.—Key Marine, Fisheries and Other Conventions/Agreements of Significance to the Southern African Marine Environment*

Biodiversity-Related Conventions	
Convention on Biological Diversity (*CBD*)	1992
Convention on International Trade in Endangered Species (*CITES*)	1973
Convention on Migratory Species (*CMS*)	1979
International Coral Reef Initiative (*ICRI*)	1995
Regional Seas Programmes & Agreements	
Global Programme of Action for the Protection of the Marine Environment from Land-based Activities	1995
Convention for Cooperation in the Protection and Development of the Marine and Coastal Environment of the West and Central African Region (Abidjan)	1981
Convention for the Protection, Management and Development of the Marine and Coastal Environment of the Eastern African Region (Nairobi)	1985
Marine-Related Conventions	
International Convention for the Prevention of Pollution of the Sea by Oil (amended in 1962 and 1969)	1954
International Convention on Civil Liability for Oil Pollution Damage (amended 1976, 1981, 1984)	1969
International Convention Relating to Intervention in the High Seas in Cases of Oil Pollution Casualties	1969
Amendments to the International Convention for the Prevention of Pollution of the Sea by Oil, 1954, Concerning Tank Arrangements and Limitation of Tank Size	1971
International Convention on the Establishment of an International Fund for Compensation for Oil Pollution Damage (amended 1976, 1984, 1994)	1971
Convention Relating to Civil Liability in the Field of Maritime Carriage of Nuclear Material	1971
Convention for the Prevention of Marine Pollution by Dumping from Ships and Aircraft (amended 1983, 1989 and again in 1989)	1972
Convention on the Prevention of Marine Pollution by Dumping of Wastes and Other Matter (amended)	1972
Protocol Relating to Intervention in the High Seas in Cases of Marine Pollution by Substances Other than Oil	1973
International Convention for the Prevention of Pollution from Ships (MARPOL)	1973
Convention on Limitation of Liability for Maritime Claims	1976
Protocol to the International Convention on Civil Liability for Oil Pollution Damage	1976
Protocol of 1978 Relating to the International Convention for the Prevention of Pollution from Ships (MARPOL), 1973	1978
Amendments to Annexes to the Convention on the Prevention of Marine Pollution by Dumping of Wastes and Other Matter Concerning Incineration at Sea	1978
Protocol to Amend the International Convention on Civil Liability for Oil Pollution Damage	1984

Marine-Related Conventions (continued)

International Convention on Salvage	1989
International Convention on Oil Pollution Preparedness, Response and Cooperation	1990
Protocol of 1992 to Amend the International Convention on Civil Liability for Oil Pollution Damage, 1969	1992
Protocol of 1992 to Amend the International Convention on the Establishment of an International Fund for Compensation for Oil Pollution Damage	1992
1996 Protocol to the Convention on the Prevention of Marine Pollution by Dumping of Wastes and Other Matter, 1972	1996
Protocol of 1996 to amend the Convention on Limitation of Liability for Maritime Claims, 1976	1996
International Convention on Liability and Compensation for Damage in Connection with the Carriage of Hazardous and Noxious Substances by Sea	1996
Protocol to the Convention on the Prevention of Marine Pollution by Dumping of Wastes and Other Matter, 1972	1996

Oceans-Related Conventions

Convention on the Territorial Sea and the Contiguous Zone	1958
Convention on the High Seas	1958
Convention for the International Council for the Exploration of the Sea (amended 1970 and 1975)	1964
LOS Convention	1982
Agreement Relating to Implementation of Part XI of the United Nations Convention on the Law of the Sea	1994

Fisheries Conventions

International Convention for the Regulation of Whaling (IWC)	1946
Protocol to the International Convention on the Regulation of Whaling	1956
Convention on Fishing and Conservation of the Living Resources of the High Seas	1958
Agreement concerning Co-operation in Marine Fishing	1962
ICCAT (amended 1984 and 1992)	1966
CAMLR Convention	1980
Protocol Relating to Modification of ICCAT	1984
Convention on Fisheries Cooperation among African States bordering the Atlantic Ocean	1991
Convention for the Conservation of Southern Bluefin Tuna (CCSBT)	1993
Agreement for the Establishment of the Indian Ocean Tuna Commission (IOTC)	1993
FAO Compliance Agreement	1993
FAO Code of Conduct	1995
United Nations Fish Stocks Agreement	1995
SEAFC Convention	2001

* Adapted from "International Environmental Governance: Multilateral Environmental Agreements (MEAs)," United Nations Environment Programme (UNEP/IGM/1/INF/3) (2001).

resolution of such disputes can be referred to the SADC Integrated Committee of Ministers for determination.[92] While the latter could easily be applied to disputes concerning inland waters, Article 7(2) clearly ensures that due consideration is given to the rights and obligations of State Parties under the LOS Convention, and other compatible agreements. Consequently, the enjoyment of a LOS Convention Contracting State's rights, or the discharge of their obligations, under the Protocol should not be affected. In simple terms, it is envisaged that Protocol Parties are able to assume the LOS Convention dispute resolution mechanism. This issue is discussed further below.

Article 7 of the Protocol goes on to outline conditions for any exchange of information on shared resources (Article 7(3)), coordination of shared resource management (Article 7(4)), including development of management plans (Article 7(5)), and a variety of other actions. For example, the latter includes promotion of wide stakeholder participation (Article 7(7)), elimination of over-fishing and reduction of fishing capacity (Articles 7(8) and (9)), and legislation enabling rapid response to issues associated with utilization of shared resources (Article 7(10)).

Area of Application

In conformity with the SADC Treaty itself, the Protocol's Preamble calls on SADC Member States to co-operate in all *areas* necessary in order to foster regional development and integration. By implication such areas would be limited to topics as well as geographic regions in which SADC parties may have vested, and Protocol-relevant, interests. Other than this general manifestation, the Protocol is not geographically bound in its application.

Stocks Covered

Article 1 applies the Protocol to all aquatic ecosystems, fish and fish stocks. It defines the terms: "exotic species," "fish," "fish stocks," "highly migratory species," "resources" and "shared resources" as well as various activities associated with fishing including the term "trans-boundary" (Table 5). Together, the definitions imply that the Protocol is primarily concerned with fishing and related activities; the latter comprising "all activities associated with the exploitation of fish, including processing, marketing, transportation, and trade of fish and fish products." Both

---

92. Set up under Art. 12 of the SADC Treaty, n. 8 above.

"illegal fishing"[93] and "nationals"[94] are also addressed. Similarly, "stake-holders" (Article 1 of the SADC Protocol) are seen as "all persons whose interests are materially affected, either directly or indirectly, by fishing and fishing related activities under this Protocol." In other words, broad substance is given to the Protocol's applicability to fisheries-related activities, ecosystem protection and socio-economic issues.

Institutional Arrangements

SADC is required to establish an oversight committee to ensure the Protocol's effective implementation (Article 19).[95] This committee is not yet in existence, although Parties are called on to allocate the necessary funds to ensure results (Article 20).

Fishing Opportunities

Article 10 of the Protocol calls for harmonization between Parties on the terms and conditions for fishery access by non-SADC Parties to resources. Article 10(2) indicates that such agreements should be non-discriminatory (i.e., similar provisions are applied in all SADC States waters), while Article 10(3) allows for joint negotiation by SADC Parties of foreign fishing access agreements with a regional or sub-regional dimension, especially for highly migratory species. This final clause appears directed at forming a SADC negotiating "power-block" within various tuna commissions (most notably ICCAT).

Dispute Settlement

Article 23 binds the Protocol Parties to referring any dispute on the Protocol's interpretation or application to the SADC Tribunal. As drafted,

93. "Illegal fishing" is defined in Art. 1 as "any fishing or related activity carried out in contravention of the laws of a State Party or the measures of an international fisheries management organisation accepted by a State Party and subject to the jurisdiction of that State Party."

94. "Nationals" are defined in Art. 1 as "persons who are citizens of a State Party and includes any body corporate, society or other association of persons established under the laws of a State Party."

95. For more information on the SADC Protocol, its implementation and attached Sector Coordinating Unit, see <http://www.sadcfisheries.com/scu.asp?id=1>.

the relationship between this particular provision and Article 7 is not entirely clear. During the Protocol's negotiation, South Africa queried whether Article 23 might not draw into question the SADC Tribunal's competence to deal with disputes of the kind likely to arise in connection with the Protocol on matters customarily assumed to fall under the LOS Convention. For political reasons, particularly in the interests of presenting a united faith in SADC's efficacy, the matter was taken no further. However, on the Protocol's signing by the SADC Heads of State, South Africa went on record as emphasizing that Article 23 should in no way be seen to compromise the rights of the LOS Convention Parties in relation to matters covered by that Convention.[96]

Control Measures

Article 8 stipulates that Protocol Parties should take measures to harmonize national legislation on relevant matters. This provision is aimed at ensuring that all illegal fishing and related activities by nationals and legal persons of a SADC State Party are deemed as offences under the national law of the Party concerned. Article 8 also notes that Parties should establish appropriate arrangements to facilitate co-operation in respect of "hot pursuit" of vessels which violate the laws of one Party and enter, or try and escape to, the jurisdiction of another. In practical terms, the Protocol urges Parties to co-operate in enforcing effective legislation through adopting measures such as:

(a) procedures for the extradition to another Party of persons charged with offences against the fisheries laws of one Party and/or serving a sentence under the laws of that Party;

(b) establishment of region-wide comparable levels of penalties imposed for illegal fishing by non-SADC flag vessels;

(c) consultation over joint actions to be taken when there are reasonable grounds for believing that a vessel has been used for a purpose that undermines the Protocol's effectiveness; and

(d) establishing mechanisms for the registration of international and national fishing vessels to serve as a compliance instrument and as a means of sharing information on fishing and related activities.

Article 9 of the Protocol sets out conditions (summarized in Table 7) for effective enforcement under national responsibilities outlined in Article 5.

96. Similar to the point already made in relation to dispute resolution above.

**Table 7.—Law Enforcement Components Addressed by
Article 9 of the SADC Fisheries Protocol**

(a)	States Parties to take adequate measures to optimize existing fisheries law-enforcement resources;
(b)	States Parties to co-operate in use of surveillance resources to increase cost-effectiveness of surveillance activities and reduce surveillance costs to the Region;
(c)	Two or more States Parties may arrange to co-operate in provision of personnel and use of vessels, aircraft, communications, databases and information, or other assets, for fisheries surveillance and law enforcement;
(d)	States Parties may designate competent persons to act as fisheries enforcement officers or on-board observers to carry out activities on behalf of two or more States Parties;
(e)	State Party may permit another State Party to extend its fisheries surveillance and law enforcement activities to the former's inland waters and the exclusive economic zone. In such circumstances, the conditions and method of stopping, inspecting, detaining, directing to port and seizing vessels will be governed by the national laws and regulations applicable to the waters where the fisheries surveillance or law enforcement activity is carried out;
(f)	States Parties to harmonize technical specifications for vessel monitoring systems and emerging technologies of interest to fisheries surveillance activities; and
(g)	In applying Protocol provisions, States Parties are called on to co-operate, either directly or through international fisheries organizations or arrangements, to ensure compliance with, and enforcement of, applicable international management measures.

Other Provisions

Various other provisions of the Protocol deal, inter alia, with (a) establishing common SADC positions on subsistence, artisanal and small-scale commercial fisheries (Article 12), (b) a rudimentary code of conduct for aquaculture (Article 13), (c) human resources development (Article 15), (d) trade and investment (Article 16) (Table 8), (e) science and technology (Article 17) and (f) exchange of information (Article 18). As a whole, these provisions strive to give effect to specific issues, both regionally and internationally, in respect of the special needs of SADC (developing) States (e.g., as per Articles 25 to 26 of the Fish Stocks Agreement and Article 5 of the FAO Code of Conduct). Other articles address collection and sharing of data (e.g., as per Annex I to the Fish Stocks Agreement), responsible aquaculture development (as per Article 9 of the Code of Conduct), post-harvest practices and trade (as per Article 11 of the FAO Code of Conduct) and fisheries research (Article 12 of the FAO Code of Conduct). In these terms, the Protocol clearly aims to codify and harmonize many of the Code's provisions at a regional level.

**Table 8.—Trade and Investment Provisions of Article 16
of the SADC Fisheries Protocol**

(a) The Protocol calls on Parties to promote sustainable trade and investment in fisheries and related goods and services by: (i)   Reducing barriers to trade and investment; (ii) Facilitating business contacts and exchange of information; and (iii) Establishing basic infrastructure for the fisheries sector.
(b) It also calls on Parties to create favourable economic conditions to support sustainable fishing and processing activities to promote regional food security and fisheries development.
(c) In establishing joint ventures, the Protocol urges Parties to give special consideration to: (i)   Ensuring sustainability of living aquatic resources; (ii)   Preventing over-fishing and excess fishing capacity; (iii) Promoting regional food security; (iv) Promoting trade in fish products in the Region; (v)   Promoting value-added processing; (vi) Establishing a favourable cross-border investment regime; and (vii) Ensuring that nationals and their vessels comply with applicable domestic and international laws.

Relationship with the Fish Stocks Agreement and Other Instruments

Pursuant to the various considerations highlighted above, a comparative analysis of the Protocol's intended impact clearly indicates a strong regional push to urge SADC Members to review their relevant national legislation and to establish whether these:

- Contain clear statements on the scope of application and the authority responsible for fisheries management;
- Facilitate broad participation in fisheries management including co-management;
- Support and implement policies and set out the ability to use a wide range of fisheries management mechanisms and measures, including the use of fishing rights or quotas and management planning;
- Facilitate implementation of the FAO Compliance Agreement, FAO Code of Conduct and the Fish Stocks Agreement;

- Enable implementation of a full range of monitoring, control and surveillance[97] (MCS) and enforcement action, and in this context:
  - Consider possible adoption of administrative processes and penalties to enforce fisheries laws;
  - Adjust penalty levels with the view to increasing them;
  - Enhance Port State enforcement so as to address any lack of essential capacity and resources to undertake enforcement and other MCS activities, introduce long-arm enforcement, protect confidentiality of information, particularly where it concerns fishing operations and where the use of vessel monitoring systems (VMS) for vessel position and catch reports is anticipated.

Taking such considerations into account, there is little doubt that the Protocol is the first major attempt to regionally codify many of the Fish Stocks Agreement's broader legal obligations, particularly those in the FAO Code of Conduct, in terms of the collective interests of a specific group of States. It is anticipated that one of its key impacts will be to focus regional action by the SADC community on key operational aspects such as harmonizing legislative provisions, ensuring effective implementation of relevant fisheries agreements such as the SEAFC Convention, developing common management and enforcement measures, and promoting sustainable utilization of aquatic resources in the face of socio-economic needs/demands. In these terms, the Protocol is clearly a political manifesto as well as a fisheries management instrument—both qualities likely to affect its eventual implementation and success.

CONCLUSIONS AND OBSERVATIONS

Growing concern over the finite nature of many natural resources and widening recognition of developing State aspirations preoccupied the postcolonial world of the late 1970s and early 1980s. Rooted in the "common heritage of mankind" debates of the United Nations General Assembly in 1967, these concerns culminated in the LOS Convention being opened for signature on 10 December 1982 in Montego Bay, Jamaica. As emphasized in its Preamble, the LOS Convention attempts to establish true universality in global efforts to achieve "a just and equitable international economic order" governing ocean space. An equally profound principle is that

97. Protocol Art. 1 defines "surveillance" as "the monitoring and supervision of fishing and related activities to ensure compliance with control measures."

effective governance of the oceans is important in terms of contributing to the maintenance of peace, justice and progress for all peoples of the world.

The LOS Convention is a 'package' product of the circumstances prevailing at the time of its negotiation.[98] This means that each individual provision is accordingly weighted throughout the text to produce intricate impartiality as a basis for universality. These strengths have rendered the LOS Convention provisions difficult to apply effectively at an operational level; a consideration compounded by geography and economic disparity. As a result, paragraph 17.49 of Agenda 21 adopted at the 1992 UN Conference on Environment and Development urged States to take effective and appropriate action, both bilaterally and multilaterally, at subregional, regional and global levels to ensure that high seas fisheries are managed in accordance with LOS Convention provisions. This particular injunction culminated in the setting up of the 1992 UN Conference on Straddling Fish Stocks and Highly Migratory Fish Stocks pursuant to paragraph 1 of UNGA Resolution 47/192. The subsequent negotiating process resulted in the Fish Stocks Agreement.

This article has clarified that during, and following, the Fish Stocks Agreement negotiations, the South-East Atlantic and Western Central Pacific regions, in particular, recognized that there were gaps in the available fisheries agreements. Such gaps directly affected the potential sustainability of straddling and highly migratory fish stocks in the two regions in question. They also highlighted many imponderables associated with practical implementation of Articles 116–119 of the LOS Convention in respect of discrete high seas stocks.

There was growing appreciation attached to the above that affected States had a responsibility, as well as the right, to institute steps to empower themselves to compete with other States, particularly with distant-water fishing fleets which had exercised almost exclusive access to such resources in the past and in many cases carried out fishing in the EEZs of the Pacific Island States.

In the above context four key considerations, amongst others, are identifiable. These are the need to

- Develop fairer ways to allocate fishing opportunities. The aim is to "level the playing field" for fishing rights based on historic performance in relation to developing State aspirations where for

---

98. Such circumstances included the large number of negotiating States, the often conflicting interests cutting across traditional lines of negotiation by region, the strong need for the Convention to be flexible in practice so as to be durable over time and the need not to encroach on the sovereignty of States.

political or economic reasons such States had been excluded from the potential benefits of fisheries in their particular regions;

- Provide fair and equitable access to fishing opportunities for States with limited, or no, previous access;
- Fairly and equitably reduce fishing opportunities for, or access to, stocks exploited beyond sustainable levels; and
- Manage fishing capacity to provide a more even distribution between developing and developed States, but not at the expense of target stock sustainability.

In 1999, Lugten[99] reviewed 22 FAO and non-FAO regional fisheries organizations and arrangements. She focused on the various measures taken by these bodies to address contemporary fisheries issues. A key finding was that very few such arrangements had, up to that time, made efforts to implement the conservation and management measures provided for in post–1982 (i.e., post LOS Convention) fishery instruments. At a global level, such efforts largely depend on effective co-operation between RFMOs;[100] a key feature illustrated in Appendix I.

Appendix I also illustrates the high level of commonality between the SEAFC and WCPFC Conventions, in spite of the differences highlighted earlier. This observation suggests that, for at least two regions, substantive and essentially independent efforts to develop workable policies have achieved a remarkably similar result in facilitating implementation of conservation and management measures following the Fish Stocks Agreement. Therefore, the clear identification of objectives by both the SEAFC and WCPFC Conventions are likely to contribute significantly to improving international standards of ocean governance, particularly application of the precautionary approach, harmonization of measures, elaboration of flag and port State duties, and the setting up of workable compliance and enforcement regimes. The SADC Protocol takes matters a step further by providing a political and socio-economic framework to mobilize the political will necessary to enhance regional co-operation on, and to co-ordinate application of, agreements like the SEAFC Convention.

In these terms, the SEAFC Convention and SADC Fisheries Protocol in particular are effectively the first and, until now, only fruits of contemporary efforts aimed at integrating equity, equality and sustainability for the commercial exploitation of fish stocks on a regional basis. If effective, they

99. G. L. Lugten, "A Review of Measures Taken by Regional Fishery Bodies to Address Contemporary Fishery Issues," *FAO Fisheries Circular* No. 940 (Rome: FAO, 1999).

100. G. L. Lugten, "Cooperation and Regional Fisheries Management," *Environmental Policy and Law* 30 (2000): 251, 255–256.

should contribute greatly to sustainable fisheries as a key element in securing global food security, the primary aim of the Kyoto Declaration and Plan of Action.[101] Together with the WCPFC Convention, they also go some way to addressing many developing State aspirations and needs identified in Articles 24–26 of the Fish Stocks Agreement. Most notably this would serve to:

- Enhance regional opportunities for developing States to gain access to geographically proximal and harvestable fish stocks;
- Improve the ability of developing States to sustainably manage such stocks; and
- Ensure that developing States are not economically or socially prejudiced by unsustainable harvesting of relevant stocks and/or through being disproportionately responsible for the burden of their conservation.

As emphasized earlier, the Fish Stocks Agreement constitutes a blueprint for regional arrangements aimed at ensuring sustainable utilization of straddling and highly migratory fish stocks. While such agreements can be tailored for specific regional application, their general objectives and underlying principles remain the same. It is therefore anticipated that the impact of post-Fish Stocks Agreement agreements, such as the SEAFC and WCPFC Conventions, will contribute greatly to ensuring responsible and improved governance of the oceans' fishery resources in the future.

Rayfuse[102] has stressed that there is little doubt that eventual State practice in relation to regional instruments such as the SEAFC and WCPFC Conventions will serve to clarify their interrelationships with the Fish Stocks Agreement. This is not only self-evident from some of the Fish Stocks Agreement's strengths highlighted here, but applies specifically in the SEAFC Convention's case to regulation of discrete high seas stocks. Therefore, the SEAFC Convention process is likely to test whether any useful precedent has been set and whether such innovative developments are in fact workable when combined with other new measures (e.g., control of individual nationals and industries).

Despite the close similarities between the SEAFC Convention and Fish Stocks Agreement texts, it remains to be seen how these will affect the practical allocation of fishing opportunities. Furthermore, although the Preamble to the SEAFC Convention expressly links the two instruments, a number of SEAFC Convention negotiating parties were obviously apprehen-

101. Kyoto Declaration and Plan of Action on the Sustainable Contribution of Fisheries to Food Security, 1995, available online: <http://www.fao.org/fi>.
102. Rayfuse, n. 54 above, at 277–278.

sive concerning the perceived commonality with the Fish Stocks Agreement text.

For the WCPFC Convention, the most distinctive feature is its attempt to provide essential detail for a compliance and enforcement regime compatible with the Fish Stocks Agreement. The SEAFC Convention on the other hand is not as prescriptive and again it may be concluded that only State and institutional practices will eventually give some indication of how effective these two approaches compare with each other.

The SADC Protocol undoubtedly constitutes a model for how essential regulatory provisions may be put into practice to address political and socio-economic needs in a regionally integrated way. The Protocol is thus the "sharp-end," as it were, of potential outputs likely to arise from fisheries agreements such as the SEAFC and the WCPFC Conventions. There is much to be gained from SADC States making sure that the Protocol is effective so that the entire RFMO "process" is seen to benefit distant-water and developing States alike. All the SADC States should be seen to participate in this process, while other States should be encouraged to develop similar arrangements to identify their own particular regional and/or political needs.

The SEAFC Convention lays the ground for the next developmental phase in orderly ocean governance—the consideration of discrete stocks on the high seas. Consequently, the SEAFC Convention's future success is obviously crucial, especially in light of growing global concern over the ecologically damaging and economically unfair practice of IUU fishing which indiscriminately targets high seas stocks in particular.

In such terms, Table 9 makes it clear that the effects of the SEAFC Convention, the WCPFC Convention and the SADC Protocol are likely to be profound and should hold great significance for the future, legitimate, impartial and orderly governance of the oceans, including the high seas. These effects are as much a result of the need to address the essential balance between the issues highlighted above, as they are to ensuring a more equitable approach to deal with the inalienable "freedom to fish on the high seas." It is therefore concluded that the three recent instruments considered in this article represent the dawn of a "new age" in fisheries management; an age which will be consistent with the direction set by both the LOS Convention and the Fish Stocks Agreement.

Finally, we wish to make a final point concerning the etiology of the various agreements on which this article has focused. There is little doubt that Articles 24 and 25 of the Fish Stocks Agreement served as strong motivation for essentially disenfranchised, developing, and small island States to institute collective action to counter previous imbalances in gaining access to economic opportunities arising from living marine resource exploitation in their respective "neighborhoods." For developing States, it therefore follows that the eventual successes of the SEAFC

Table 9.—Some Anticipated Outcomes from SEAFC Convention, WCPFC Convention and the SADC Fisheries Protocol

Proof of Effectiveness with Future Experience
Fairer and More Equitable Allocation of Fishing Opportunities
"Level Playing Field" to Balance Fishing Rights Based on Historic Performance with Developing State Aspirations (Especially when Prevalence of Historic/Political Exclusion in Region)
Allow Fair & Equitable Access to Fishing Opportunities by States Denied, or Without, Previous Access
Equitably Reduce Access to Stocks Exploited Beyond Sustainable Levels
More Even Distribution of Fishing Capacity Between Developing & Developed States
Precedent for Managing Discrete High Seas Stocks (SEAFC Convention's Future Application)
Combat Ecologically Damaging/Economically Unfair *IUU* Fishing

Convention, WCPFC Convention and SADC Fisheries Protocol will only become apparent to the extent that tangible benefits are seen to arise from effective implementation of Article 25.1(a) of the Fish Stocks Agreement in particular.[103] We suggest that such benefits will be perceived to rest on effective promotion of the conservation, management and fisheries development of relevant straddling, migratory and discrete high seas fish stocks.

103. This provides: "States shall cooperate, either directly or through subregional, regional or global organizations to enhance the ability of developing States, in particular the least-developed among them and small island developing States, to conserve and manage straddling fish stocks and highly migratory fish stocks and to develop their own fisheries for such stocks."

Appendix I.—Summary of Fish Stocks Agreement (UNFSA), SEAFC Convention (SEAFC), WCPFC Convention (WCPFC) and SADC Fisheries Protocol (Protocol) Provisions*

TOPIC	UNFSA	SEAFC	WCPFC	PROTOCOL
Origin	UN Conference on Straddling Fish Stocks & Highly Migratory Fish Stocks (1992–1995) Manage high seas fisheries consistent with LOSC (especially Articles 63–64)	Namibia & Coastal States post-UNFSA (1996) Replace ICSEAF to promote sustainable utilization of high seas resources in interests of region's fishing industries	FFA & USA at UNFSA time in context of USA/South Pacific Fisheries Treaty 1993/94 reviews Pacific Island States concern on sustainability & equitable economic benefit from region's migratory stocks	SADC Workshop (1997) Need for consistent regional promotion responsible and sustainable use of living aquatic resources subject to international agreements
Process Name	UN Conference on Straddling Fish Stocks & Highly Migratory Fish Stocks	Meeting of Coastal States & Other Interested Parties on a Regional Fisheries Management Organisation for the South-East Atlantic Ocean	Multilateral High-Level Conference on the Conservation and Management of Highly Migratory Fish Stocks in the Western & Central Pacific Ocean	SADC Fisheries Protocol Negotiations
Organization Name	Co-ordination of RFMOs (New & to be formed)	Southeast Atlantic Fisheries Organisation (SEAFO)	Commission for the Conservation and Management of Highly Migratory Fish Stocks in the Western & Central Pacific Ocean	SADC Fisheries Protocol Oversight Committee

TOPIC	UNFSA	SEAFC	WCPFC	PROTOCOL
Convention Name	*Agreement for the Implementation of the United Nations Law of the Sea of 10 December 1982 relating to Straddling Fish Stocks & Highly Migratory Fish Stocks*	*Convention on the Conservation and Management of Fishery Resources in the South-East Atlantic Ocean*	*Convention on the Conservation and Management of Highly Migratory Fish Stocks in the Western & Central Pacific Ocean*	*SADC Fisheries Protocol*
Convention Area	Global (i.e., not defined)	High seas areas outside national jurisdiction—approximately FAO Statistical Area 47 bounded at 6° S, 20° W, 18° E & 50° S (Fig. 1) (Article 3)	Roughly to boundaries of IOTC in west, IATTC in east, CCAMLR in south and 4° S in north. EEZs included (Fig. 2) (Article 3)	SADC Region (Fig. 1) Waters under national jurisdiction (freshwater & marine) & high seas
Species Covered	Straddling Fish Stocks & Highly Migratory Fish Stocks excluding sedentary species under LOSC Article 77	Straddling/discrete stocks on high seas. Excludes sedentary species under LOSC Article 77 & highly migratory species in LOSC Annex I. Limited assessment past/potential catches	Highly migratory stocks of species in LOSC Annex I Mainly skipjack, yellowfin, bigeye & albacore tuna. Good historic catch data record maintained by FFA	All aquatic ecosystems, fish and fish stocks to which Protocol applies
Signature Entry into Force	**4/12/1995 11/12/2001**	**20/4/2001 13/4/2003**	**5/9/2000 19/6/2004**	**14/8/2001 8/8/2003**

TOPIC	UNFSA	SEAFC	WCPFC	PROTOCOL
Objective	Ensure long-term conservation & sustainable use of straddling and highly migratory fish stocks through effective implementation of *LOSC* (Article 2)	Long-term conservation & sustainable use of fishery resources (straddling & discrete stocks) in *Convention Area* (Article 2)	Long-term conservation & sustainable use of highly migratory fish stocks in *Convention Area* under *LOSC* & *UNFSA* (Article 2)	Promote responsible & sustainable use of living aquatic resources for various socio-economic benefits (Article 3)
General Principles	Give effect to management of straddling & highly migratory fish stocks by adopting scientifically-based measures, applying precautionary approach, environmental protection, etc., including data gathering & conservation measure enforcement (Article 5)	Give effect to management of *Convention Area*'s fishery resources by adopting scientifically-based measures, applying of precautionary approach, environmental protection, etc., (Article 5)	Give effect to management of *Convention Area*'s fishery resources by adopting scientifically-based measures, applying of precautionary approach, environmental protection, etc., including data gathering & conservation measure enforcement (Article 5)	National responsibility, protect resources against over-exploitation accounting for various socio-economic needs (Article 4)
Precautionary Approach	Details approach & guidelines on application of reference points. Special mention of new & exploratory fisheries (Article 6 & Annex II)	Caution in the face of uncertainty & cross-reference to reference points in *UNFSA* Annex II & *Code of Conduct* (Article 7)	Identical to *UNFSA* Article 6, including direct reference *UNFSA* reference points (Article 6)	Protect aquatic environment applying "precautionary principle" through co-operation & common standards for protecting areas & habitats (Article 14)

TOPIC	UNFSA	SEAFC	WCPFC	PROTOCOL
Compatibility of Measures	Compatibility of national & international measures. Co-operation on high seas (Article 7)	Compatibility of national & international measures. Avoid undermining *LOSC* Articles 61 & 119 (Article 19)	Compatibility with national & international measures. Largely duplicates *UNFSA* Article 7 and reinforces need to implement *Convention*'s principles in national areas (Article 8 & 7 respectively)	Contracting Party legislation to be harmonized, including commonality of sanctions (Article 8)
Contracting Party Obligations	Not specifically identified. Some details provided on State obligations in ensuring co-operation under *RFMO* or other relevant arrangement(s) (Article 10)	Detailed provisions on, inter alia, data collection/exchange/submission, ensuring effective measures. Co-operation to ensure compliance by flagged vessels & nationals & limitation of access to Party flagged vessels (Article 14)	Outlines obligations. Detailed provisions include prompt implementation of measures, data submission, etc., taking measures to ensure compliance by flagged vessels & nationals (including procedures to be followed on alleged violations) (Article 23)	Co-ordinate cross-SADC action in accordance with principles, national responsibilities, international relations & shared resources (Articles 4 to 7)

TOPIC	UNFSA	SEAFC	WCPFC	PROTOCOL
Flag State Duties	States only to authorize fishing vessels in manner not undermining RFMO measures & when able to assume responsibility for flagged vessels. Details measures to be applied & entreats States to ensure MCS measures are compatible with any regional system in force (Article 18) Also outlines Flag State compliance & enforcement provisions (Article 19)	Ensure flagged vessels comply with SEAFO measures, possess authorization to fish, details measures to give effect to control of flagged vessels & urges need to ensure that vessels do not undermine measures by unauthorized fishing in Convention & adjacent areas (Article 14)	Ensure flagged vessels comply with measure, possess authorization to fish in all Convention Area, details measures to give effect to control of flagged vessels & urges need to ensure such vessels do not undermine measures by unauthorized fishing in Convention & adjacent areas & mandates VMS deployment (Article 24)	No specific reference to Flag State responsibilities although implicit in respect of references to application of national jurisdiction, especially in direct/indirect cross-reference to LOSC & UNFSA (Articles 6(2) & 11)
Port State Duties	Empowers Port States to take measures consistent with international law & RFMO provisions (Article 23)	Similar to UNFSA Article 23 – Port State measures consistent with international law (Article 15)	Similar to UNFSA Article 23 – Port State measures consistent with international law (Article 27)	Implied in law enforcement provisions (Article 9)

TOPIC	UNFSA	SEAFC	WCPFC	PROTOCOL
Compliance & Enforcement	Details co-operation in enforcement, sub-regional enforcement co-operation & basic boarding/inspection procedures (Articles 20–22 respectively)	Establishes *MCS* framework as alternative system under *UNFSA* Article 20(15). Details for first Commission meeting, but interim guidelines provided (Article 16 & *SEAFC* Annex)	Details *MCS* framework, including schemes for boarding/inspection, observers & regulating transshipment (per *UNFSA* Articles 20–25). Also outlines terms & conditions for fishing & information requirements (Articles 25, 26, 28, 29, Annexes. III & IV)	Calls for pooling of *MCS* & enforcement capabilities, human resource development & transfer science/ technology (Articles 9, 15 & 17)
Control of Nationals	No specific mention. Implied in ensuring national "industries" co-operation (Article 10(c))	Specific reference to nationals & industries (no prejudice to Flag State Responsibility) (Article 13(3))	Similar to *SAEAFC* but with some elaboration (Article 23(5))	Specific application to nationals (Article 2(a))
Fishing Opportunities	Limits resource access to *RFMO* participants/ members. Indicates considerations to be taken into account in determining nature/ extent of participatory rights for new entrants (Articles 8(4) & 11 respectively)	Details considerations for determining fishing opportunities with caveat that Commission may agree rules. (Article 20)	No single consideration of fishing opportunity allocation, but some direction provided (Articles 10.1(g) & 10(3))	No direct consideration of allocation. Recognizes economic equity in application of sustainable resource use, providing access to third parties & promoting trade/ investment (Articles 3, 10 & 16)

TOPIC	UNFSA	SEAFC	WCPFC	PROTOCOL
Good Faith & Abuse of Rights	Specific provisions (Article 34)	Subsumed into Contracting Party obligations (Article 13(8))	Specific provision (Article 33)	Builds on *SADC* principles of regional co-operation uncer Articles 4 & 5 of the *1992 SADC Treaty* but not specifically mentioned in *Protocol*
Non-Contracting Parties (*NCPs*)	Specific provisions emphasizing duty not to undermine *RFMO* measures & need to adopt regulations consistent with *UNFSA* (Articles 17 & 33)	Call for co-operation, exchange of information, taking of internationally acceptable steps to deter *NCP* activities undermining measures. *NCPs* to enjoy benefits commensurate with commitment to comply with measures (Article 22)	Call for co-operation, information exchange, taking internationally acceptable steps to deter *NCP* activities undermining measures. *NCPs* enjoy benefits commensurate with commitment to comply, & compliance record for measures (Article 32)	Not expressly mentioned but subsumed in cross-reference to *LOSC* & *UNFSA* (Article 1(2))
Decision-Making	Not specified	Consensus with opt out on exceptional circumstances. No provision for breaking deadlock. Immediate resort to dispute resolution provisions (Articles 17 & 23)	Generally consensus, opt out provided in case of voting against decision & capacity to appoint review panel to break deadlock (Article 20)	Not specifically mentioned, but subsumed as under *SADC Treaty* (i.e., consensus unless decided otherwise)

TOPIC	UNFSA	SEAFC	WCPFC	PROTOCOL
Budget	Not specified	Budget adopted by consensus. Equal for first three years then part equal & part calculated from catch levels. Some recognition of capacity to pay & cost-efficiency (Article 12)	Budget by consensus. Based on assessed contributions as adopted (taking into account equal basic fee & other criteria for remaining portion). Recognize ability to pay. No voting on arrears for two years. Interest payable on arrears. Special fund for developing States	(Articles 17, 18 & 30(3))
Dispute Resolution	Resolution by peaceful means, including prevention of disputes & definition of technical disputes. (Articles 27 to 29)	Procedures for settlement under, *mutatis mutandis* provisions of *LOSC* Part XV, other *LOSC* & *UNFSA* provisions & provisional measures pending settlement (Articles 30 & 31)	As per *LOSC* Part XV & *UNFSA* Part VIII. By implication former applies to discrete stocks & latter to straddling stocks. Also applies to *SEAFC* Parties not party to *LOSC* &/or *UNFSA* (Article 24)	Direct application of *UNFSA* Part VIII (Article 31)

TOPIC	UNFSA	SEAFC	WCPFC	PROTOCOL
Developing States	Specific considerations, including recognition of needs, forms of co-operation & provision of assistance (Articles 24 to 26)	Recognition of special needs subsuming provisions of *UNFSA* Articles 24 to 26 (Article 21)	Recognize qualified special needs of Small Island Developing States. Establish special fund for Developing States (Articles 30 & 30(3))	Preamble & various provisions recognize need to uplift *SADC* Parties (all Developing States) by promoting *Protocol* as a whole
Real Interest	Real interest in fisheries leading to support for RFMO (Article 8(3))	Perfunctory promotion of co-operation for "real interest" (Preamble) Implicit condition in allocating fishing opportunities (Article 20)	No direct referenced, but implicit in pre-negotiation[104]	No direct reference

104. See Molenaar, n. 30 above.

Globalization, Sea Farming and Flexibility in Norwegian Coastal Zone Planning

Roger G. Bennett
Centre for Studies of Environment and Resources, University of Bergen, Norway

Ole Martin Lund
County Planning Office, Rogaland County, Norway

INTRODUCTION

Regional and local change is increasingly contingent upon and fuelled by global economic processes. As Hudson states, "The strategies of capital are undoubtedly of great significance in shaping the landscapes of capitalism," but "... whilst companies seek to shape space to meet their requirements for profitable production, other social forces seek to shape space according to other values and criteria."[1] The state and its bureaucracies, regional and local government, private organizations, social groups and individuals, may constitute these forces. The convergence of different values and interests on particular spaces and places is the cause of numerous debates and conflicts that in European contexts usually involve public planning. Thus local planning, although limited in its scope and jurisdiction, often "takes place in the context of a global-scale web of relationships," to which it must adapt.[2] This applies equally as much to zoning for sea farming in coastal peripheries as it does to the planning of contested spaces in our major cities.

This article is broadly concerned, then, with how Norwegian coastal zone planning at the local level is being influenced by the sea farming industry in its continuous search for competitive advantage in the global market for farmed fish. More specifically it is concerned with flexibility as

---

1. R. Hudson, *Production, Places and Environment: Changing Perspectives in Economic Geography* (Harlow: Prentice Hall, 2000).
2. J. A. Throgmorton, "Planning as Persuasive Storytelling in a Global-Scale Web of Relationships," *Planning Theory* 2, no. 2 (2003): 125–151.

Ocean Yearbook 20: 377–392.

Table 1.—Key Figures in Norwegian sea farming, 31 December 2003

	Salmon and rainbow trout	Other fish species	Shellfish and crustaceans
Quantity sold (tonnes)	578,475	4,112	1,800
First-hand value (millions €)	1,171	14	1
Licences in operation (number)	870	308	593
Direct employment (persons)	2,317	406	717

Source: Directorate of Fisheries, 2004, http://www.fiskeridirektoratet.no.

applied to spatial planning, and to the zoning of Norwegian coastal waters in particular. The justification for this is that the Norwegian fisheries authorities, whose responsibility it is both to regulate and promote the interests of the sea farming industry, contend that coastal zone plans produced by local authorities are not flexible enough to cater for the changing requirements of sea farming—a statement often repeated, but largely unsubstantiated. This raises two questions, one theoretical and the other of a more practical nature: 1) How is the concept of flexibility in planning to be understood? and 2) In what ways may local coastal zone planning in Norway be said to lack flexibility? The article attempts to throw light on these questions and it discusses what implications flexible planning for sea farming might have for integrated coastal management. In order to answer these questions adequately, it is necessary first to sketch briefly the main trends in sea farming and then to outline the planning regime on the Norwegian coast.

SEA FARMING

In Norway the farming of salmon and rainbow trout is an industry of particular national, regional and local significance, in terms of exports, up-stream and down-stream activities, local employment and incomes. The country is the world's largest single producer of farmed Atlantic salmon, supplying approximately 50 percent of the world market. In 2003, sales of salmon and rainbow trout totalled c. 578,000 tonnes, at a first-hand value of over €1 billion (Table 1). As yet, the cultivation of marine fish species and shellfish is comparatively modest, but future expansion is expected.

In order to meet international market competition, both the sea farming industry itself and the fisheries authorities are particularly con-cerned with the exploitation of comparative advantages, such as ideal ecological conditions for growth, clean water and healthy fish. Such concerns and visions of future expansion place local planning authorities under constant pressure to provide better farming localities and more space.

NORWEGIAN COASTAL PLANNING

In 1985, the new Planning and Building Act empowered local authorities to produce spatial plans for coastal waters as far out to sea as the baseline. By far the most important driving force behind this legislation was sea farming, particularly the farming of Atlantic salmon and rainbow trout. In the late 1980s and early 1990s, therefore, many peripheral coastal municipalities, realizing the economic and social significance of the sea farming industry, began to produce spatial plans for their coastal waters, even communes with little or no previous experience or competency in spatial planning. In 1989–1990, planning was in many cases hastened on by a major epidemic of infectious salmon anemia (ISA), which necessitated the establishment of new spatial arrangements designed to hinder the spread of disease. The introduction of hygienic buffer zones of 1 to 5 km in width between farming localities, and the practice of rotation between 2 or 3 different approved localities, have meant increased demands for space—in some area even a shortage of space—and thus increasing pressure on public planning.[3] A further motive for planning, reported by the municipalities, is the necessity to resolve conflicts between different user interests.[4]

By the term coastal zone plan, we usually mean a spatial plan (often with guidelines) for the use and protection of coastal waters, passed in accordance with the Planning and Building Act. Approved plans have legal status and are required by law to be reviewed every 4 years. By the end of 2003, 193 of 280 coastal municipalities had first or second generation coastal plans and 19 were in the process of planning.[5]

Planning according to the PBA is intended to integrate national, regional and local interests. Although the municipality itself has the right to decide on what and how much to plan, it is required to consult all stakeholders, and the relevant sector authorities are required to assist the commune with its plan. On paper this would appear to ensure integration of all interests. Experiences during the 1990s, however, show that theory and practice can be two different things. In some cases local authorities failed to consult stakeholders, sector authorities failed to provide sufficient input,

3. For a fuller account of early developments in coastal planning, see R. G. Bennett, "Norwegian Coastal Zone Planning," *Norsk geografisk Tidsskrift*, 50 (1996): 201–213: R. G. Bennett, "Challenges in Norwegian Coastal Zone Planning," *GeoJournal*, 39, no. 2 (1996): 153–165; R. G. Bennett, "Coastal Planning on the Atlantic Fringe, North Norway: The Power Game," *Ocean and Coastal Management*, 43 (2000): 879–904.

4. J. H. Sandberg, *Kartlegging av arealbrukskonflikter i kystsonen* (Report to the Norwegian Ministry of Fisheries, Oslo, 2002).

5. Directorate of Fisheries, *Nøkkeltall fra norsk havbruk* (2004), available online: <http://www.fiskeridirektoratet.no>.

and conflicts of interest between sector authorities created a difficult planning climate. Of particular significance were the frequent conflicts between municipalities and the fisheries authorities over spatial provision for aquaculture.[6] More recently the atmosphere of confrontation of the mid-1990s has been superseded by one of greater mutual understanding and collaboration, as both municipalities and sector authorities have come to realize the benefits to be gained from good planning.

Some of the friction over zoning arrangements has been due to overlapping jurisdictions, between on the one hand, the fisheries authorities, whose duty it is to effectuate national policy on sea farming, and local planning, which per definition must integrate all interests on the other. The fisheries authorities have generally been opposed to spatial restrictions on sea farming, except in areas that are obviously unsuitable or where conflicts are obvious. They have therefore raised frequent objections to plans that exclude aquaculture (A) from areas where there is no demonstrable conflict with other interests, and to plans that they consider to allocate insufficient space for sea farming.

FLEXIBILITY IN PLANNING—A CONCEPTUAL FRAMEWORK

Internationalization and demands for harmonization of the conditions for economic activity across national boundaries have brought flexibility to the forefront of economic politics.[7] Lack of flexibility is considered to be a hindrance to international competition and change. Translated to the political agenda of the coastal zone, flexibility is said to be necessary in order to enable Norwegian sea farming to compete in a global market for farmed salmon. The Norwegian Planning Commission states that flexible planning tools are necessary in order to maintain the legitimacy of planning in the public domain. Planning must be relevant to the needs and challenges facing society at any particular time.[8] Obviously these two understandings of flexibility are related.

In the somewhat sparse literature on flexibility in public planning, it is usual to define the term in the context of planning understood as instrumentally rational action.[9] However, principles of public participation

6. Bennett (2000), n. 3 above.

7. K. Nielsen, "Towards a Flexible Future—Theories and Politics," in *The Politics of Flexibility, Restructuring State and Industry in Britain, Germany and Scandinavia*, ed. B. Jessop (Aldershot: Edward Elgar, 1991).

8. *NOU 2001:7. Bedre kommunal og regional planlegging etter plan- og bygningsloven. Planutvalgets forste delutredning* (Oslo: Ministry of Environment, 2001).

9. A. Faludi, *A Decision-Centred View of Environmental Planning* (Oxford: Pergamon, 1987); T. Sager, "Notions of Flexibility in Planning-Related Literature," *Meddelande, Nordiska Institutet för Samhällsplanerande*, no. 5 (1990).

and deliberation embodied in the planning laws of many democratic countries today imply that social and communicative rationalities must also play an important part in planning.[10] Between these rationalities conflicts may arise concerning the realization of policies, goals and individual interests.[11] Although the Habermasian concept of communicative rationality has been one of the more important contributions to the notion of planning as something more than instrumentally rational action, the concept of flexibility as it might apply to communicative planning has not been explored specifically, although many writings on communicative planning subsume flexibility in planning processes.[12]

Instrumental Flexibility

The paradigm of planning and management as rational instrumental action is well-known and well-established in the Western world today. Its rationality lies in its search for optimal solutions to goals and its analytical approach, in which each step follows logically from the previous one. Its efficiency can be evaluated by the extent to which results match goals. Predictability is therefore a central concern. On the other hand, the desire for predictability is matched by an equal and opposite desire to hold options open in order to meet unexpected events and accommodate new developments, i.e., flexibility. This is a well-known planning dilemma.[13] The coastal plan for Rogaland County recognizes the problem when it states, "It is a challenge to find a good balance between predictability and flexibility with regard to future sea farming activity."[14]

Planning systems tackle the predictability-flexibility dilemma in different ways. In the Norwegian system, the spatial part of the municipal plan [*arealdelen*] ensures predictability since it is legally binding. The PBA allows for flexibility in two ways: 1) by law the plan must be reviewed and if

10. J. Friedmann, *Planning in the Public Domain: From Knowledge to Action* (Princeton: Princeton University Press, 1987); T. Sager, *Communicative Planning Theory* (Aldershot: Avebury, 1994).

11. Bennett (2000), n. 3 above.

12. See, for example, A. Faludi and W. Korthals Altes, "Evaluating Communicative Planning: A Revised Design for Performance Research," *European Planning Studies*, 2 (1994): 403–417; P. Healey, *Collaborative Planning: Shaping Places in Fragmented Societies* (London: Macmillan, 1997); J. Amdam and R. Amdam, *Kommunikativ Planlegging: Regional Planlegging som Reiskap for Organisasjons- og Samfunnsutvikling* (Oslo: Samlaget, 2000).

13. P. Booth, *Controlling Development: Certainty and Discretion in Europe, the USA and Hong Kong* (UCL Press, 1996): 10.

14. Rogaland County Council, *Fylkesdelplan for kysten av Rogaland* (Stavanger, 2001). Authors' translation.

necessary revised every four years, and 2) the local authority may grant dispensations from the plan if there are good reasons to do so. In practice, however, local authorities tend not to review plans as often as the law requires, and the Ministry discourages liberal practice in the granting of dispensations, since this tends to undermine the purpose of planning and may also run contrary to various national policies.

Sager defines flexibility in plans with reference to three types of reaction to uncertainty:[15]

- Robustness: a measure of how little a plan binds the future. The plan does not unconditionally recommend an action when the desirability of it only becomes known at a later date. The plan does not recommend actions that limit future choice in a detrimental way.
- Corrigibility: a measure of how easy it is to change a plan when undesirable effects and mistakes arise. It must not be difficult to adjust the plan if it becomes unsatisfactory in its original form.
- Stability: a measure of flexibility indicating the extent to which a plan is effective under variable conditions. A stable plan seldom needs correction and does not recommend actions that are only effective under a particular narrow set of circumstances.

This set of concepts provides us with the means to evaluate actual plans.

However, we need also to be aware that, "Flexibility is an empty concept if unrelated to a set of specific rigidities. . . . Flexibility in one area requires rigidities (or stability) in many other areas."[16] Applied to the coastal zone, this means that flexibility with regard to one set of stakeholder interests, such as sea farming, implies restrictions on others, and that flexibility with regard to all interests would generate a situation of extreme uncertainty, both as regards the terms of competition between actors and future conditions for operation.

Sector planning and regulation by the fisheries authorities, for example, is predominantly instrumental in character, and can be ascribed to the fact that the legitimacy of an agency depends upon the technical and economical efficiency of its regulatory activity in the eyes of the industry affected by it.[17] The Ministry of Fisheries justifies its demand for flexibility in coastal planning as a means to ensure growth in the sea farming industry in the face of future uncertainty. "By flexibility, we mean plans that are

15. Sager, n. 9 above.
16. Nielsen, n. 7 above.
17. Bennett (2000), n. 3 above; R. Amdam, "Sectoral Versus Territorial Regional Planning and Development in Norway," *European Planning Studies,* 10, no. 1 (2002): 99–111.

adapted to different needs and situations in individual communes and regions. In some places flexibility will mean detailed planning in the form of sub-categories [in zoning], single categories, and ordnances/guidelines. In other places where there is less need for planning, zones of multiple use may be appropriate or the area can be left unplanned."[18] The Ministry's arguments reflect an understanding of flexibility as both stability and robustness. The demand that the municipalities designate sufficient space for the expansion of sea farming and impose few limitations implies stability. And assuming that the plan does not narrow options for future location of sea farming implies robustness.

The instrumentally rational demand for flexibility by the Ministry has of course other consequences; it places limitations on the municipalities' coastal planning by restricting local political choice, and, if we are to follow Nielsen's line of argument, it implies at least on a theoretical level, a corresponding degree of restriction with regard to other user interests.

Communicative Flexibility

Jürgen Habermas's alternative to instrumental rationality is communicative rationality.[19] This form of logic is linked to argumentative dialogue, which is deemed to be rational if it is orientated towards mutual understanding based on the strength of argument alone. It presupposes that the parties involved are willing to accept the better argument and adapt their actions accordingly. According to Eriksen, deliberative democracy, such as the Norwegian one, is based on the principle that it is possible to reach agreement through debate.[20] This implies that there are no objective standards that guarantee a rational solution to conflicts. Accordingly, flexibility cannot be justified by reference to a particular planning objective alone; what is normatively valid cannot be determined on the basis of individual preferences or choice, but must be established communally. This is particularly true in the coastal zone where there are a great number of conflicting interests and policies. Validity of an argument is not a matter of demonstrating that something is indisputably true, but of being able to gain acceptance for a particular point of view. Political decisions must therefore satisfy the requirement that they are justifiable to those who are affected by them. This forms a yardstick against which political decisions can be

18. Ministry of Fisheries in a letter to the Planning Commission (July 6, 2001).
19. J. Habermas, *The Theory of Communicative Action*, vol. 2. *Life World and System: A Critique of Functionalist Reason* (Boston: Beacon Press, 1987).
20. E. O. Eriksen, "Den Politiske Diskurs-fra Konsensus til Modus Vivendi?," in *Den Politiske Orden*, ed. E. O. Eriksen (Trondheim: Tano, 1994).

evaluated. Evaluation according to goal achievement is the opposite standard.

On this basis a second understanding of flexibility can be established— flexibility achieved and justified by the process through which the planning decision was arrived at. Flexibility in communicative terms refers therefore to the degree to which the planning process has contributed to rational agreement between the various interests involved.

Provision for stakeholder participation in the Planning and Building Act institutionalizes the communicative principle in coastal planning by local authorities, thus embodying ideals of social mobilization and inclusive democracy.[21] When balancing interests in the coastal zone, communes are allowed some discretionary freedom. By comparison with sector planning, in which decisions are usually based on scientific and professional knowledge, the knowledge for local spatial planning is not specialized, stable, standardized or scientific. The knowledge for this type of planning is contextually dependent and may lead to different results in time and space.[22] This in itself can be regarded as a flexible attribute of planning. Though it may not be justified by its effectiveness in goal achievement, it may achieve legitimacy for itself in so far as it is able to establish some form of agreement between the parties concerned. This does not necessarily mean consensus, but that the parties are able to come to an acceptable arrangement. Eriksen coins the term *modus vivendi*—a decision that the interested parties find fair and acceptable under the particular circumstances. *Modus vivendi* derives its legitimacy primarily from procedures ensuring that the process of planning is conducted in a fair and proper way, but the agreement must also be justifiable in public debate, and the compromise must be workable for each and every stakeholder if the flexibility achieved in the process is to be maintained.[23]

FLEXIBILITY IN PRACTICE

Armed with two concepts of flexibility we now turn to two examples of planning in the coastal zone, drawing on case studies made by Lund and Teige at the Department of Geography, University of Bergen.[24]

21. R. Amdam, "Sectoral versus territorial regional planning and development in Norway," *European Planning Studies*, 10, no. 1 (2002): 99–111.

22. Id.

23. See Eriksen, n. 20 above.

24. O. M. Lund, "Fleksibilitet i kystsonen. En studie av fleksibilitet i kommunal kystsoneplanlegging og fiskeriemyndighetenes regulering av havbruksnæringens arealtilgang," (M.A. diss., Dept. Geography, University of Bergen, 2004); S. Teige, "Kystsoneplanlegging i et maktperspektiv," (M.A. diss., Dept. Geography, University of Bergen, 2000).

The Sandnes Plan

Sandnes is a suburban municipality close to the city of Stavanger in southwest Norway. It has a broad mix of economic activities and a population of c. 54,000. Being part of the recreation fringe of Stavanger, it has over 2,500 holiday cottages, most of which are located in the coastal zone. Of its three fjords, two are unsuited for sea farming for various reasons, whereas the third, Högsfjord (Figure 1), is suitable. Sandnes is one of the more important sea farming municipalities in the county with 7 licences to farm salmon and 2 licences for shellfish farming in 2003.

Sandnes started on its first coastal plan in 1995, but it was never completed. Work was resumed in 2000 in connection with review of the municipal development plan. The council finally approved it in November 2002. An executive group consisting of the municipal planning officer, planning advisor and environmental officer was given executive responsibility for the planning process. The group reported to the municipal planning committee. Its duties entailed the making of maps, drafting the plan, preparing the agenda of the planning committee, and contact with stakeholders and regional sector authorities. The main planning objectives were as follows:

> To ensure responsible and holistic management of coastal waters and beaches based on local and national [political] signals ...[To] produce a steering tool with which to take care of different user interests and counteract and resolve conflicts.

The plan also aimed to ensure: "Good conditions for sea farming, ... flexible coastal management being a necessity to ensure further development." At the same time, it opened for more holiday cottages.

In interviews, members of the executive group expressed the view that neither the regional fisheries office nor the sea farming industry itself had in the past shown sufficient regard for conflicts with other users or for professional considerations necessary in planning the coastal zone. Consequently, the group decided to keep a tight hold on the future location of sea farming. Furthermore, it felt that there was no political understanding in Sandnes of the necessity to decide on priorities and to balance interests in the coastal zone, the political aim for more sea farms being incompatible with the aim for more holiday cottages. (In fact, the planning committee showed only a superficial interest in zoning arrangements in the coastal zone.) Thus, in a situation where the fisheries office and sea farmers took little heed of conflicts and local politicians were unaware of the need to decide on priorities, there was in the opinion of the group the need for an "authority" able to integrate the various interests in a master plan, i.e., the need for professional planning—rational planning independent of politics.

FIG. 1.—Simplified excerpt of the current coastal plan for Sandnes municipality, South-West Norway, showing existing and planned localities for sea farming, holiday cabins, marine recreation areas and multiple use.

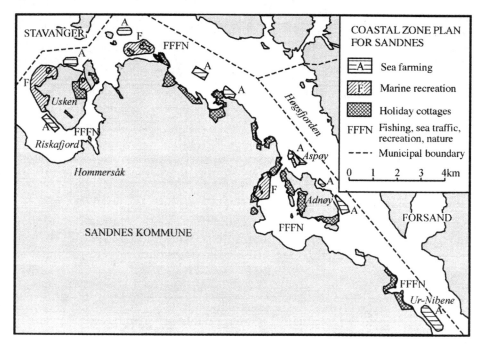

Source: Author.

Consequently, the executive group drew up a plan in which the areas allocated to sea farming were so small that "localities" would be a more appropriate description. All of them were placed at least 100 meters from the shore, which meant that fish cages would have to be placed 200 meters away in order to accommodate mandatory prohibition zones. In so doing, Sandnes made a problem for itself from the point of view of instrumental flexibility. Applications for sea farming usually necessitate adjustments to locations dependent upon the type of organism farmed, size of facility, form of production, environmental considerations, etc. But in this case even small adjustments would require dispensation from the coastal plan—a time-consuming and costly process, which may encourage other stakeholders to demand a replay. In this sense the plan lacks flexibility, since it is difficult to correct. According to the executive group, however, a rigid plan was necessary in order to achieve the professional objective of avoiding conflicts with other interests.

However, the predictability that the Sandnes plan attempted to achieve (through its rigidity) was dependent upon whether the 6 new areas designated for sea farming were in fact suitable for such a purpose. To be certain of this, qualified, rational evaluation of suitability (currents, salinity, temperature, and depth) for the farmed organisms in question would have been necessary. This would have entailed consultation with the fisheries authorities, but they were not invited to join in the new round of planning in 2000–2002. The executive group defended the plan as a compromise. However, in order to qualify as such, it would have to be realizable for sea farming, which is doubtful due both to the small size and location of the areas allotted. (It is worth noting that the 1997 draft designated much larger areas for aquaculture.) The compromise therefore has questionable legitimacy.

The Rogaland Fisheries Office did not enter the planning process before the plan was sent for hearing. Even then, it omitted to use its authority to further national policy and secure larger and more suitable areas for sea farming. Overlooking the fact that several of the localities would interfere with sea traffic and that they were too small to accommodate current applications for licenses, it took the plan *ad notam* stating that it would form the basis for further growth of sea farming. This apparent lapse on the part of the fisheries office is the more surprising considering that fisheries authorities in other regions pursue national sea farming policy very vigorously, as we shall see in the case of Gildeskaal below.[25]

There are no grounds to suggest that the Sandnes plan was the result of communicative flexibility. There was no stakeholder involvement apart from the mandatory hearing and there was no political debate or negotiation in the planning committee. Nevertheless, the planners presented it as a compromise to the committee. The protests of the sea farmers were dismissed on the same basis. The planners justify the so-called compromise on the grounds of professional considerations, implying the existence of objective standards that guarantee the rational solution of conflicts, without recourse to politics. But the test of a rational compromise—*modus vivendi*— is that it is viable for all parties, i.e., it can be realised for all stakeholders. This, however, is in serious doubt as far as sea farming is concerned.

The Gildeskaal Plan

Gildeskaal municipality is located in northern Norway just north of the Arctic Circle. It has long traditions in fishery and agriculture. Its total area is approximately 1,500 km², of which 840 km² is sea. It is thinly populated, having only c. 2,450 inhabitants. Sea farming is an important industry, there being five licenses to farm salmon, two licenses to farm scallop, one research station for fisheries and sea farming, and a combined fish slaughtering plant

25. See Bennett (2000), n. 3 above.

and landing station. The coastal zone contains trawling areas for prawns, fish spawning areas, important bird sanctuaries (Fuglöy, Fleinvaer and others), as well as a fjord-river system of national importance for wild salmon (Beiarfjorden—not shown on Figure 2). Recreational fishing is popular and there is a growing number of holiday cabins owned locally or by people from the nearby town of Bodö, but recreational interests are very modest by comparison with Sandnes.

Planning began in 1994 in connection with a regional project in which 18 coastal communes joined forces to plan their coastal zones concurrently.[26] A draft plan was sent for hearing in 1996, after which there followed a two-year period of conflict and negotiation between the municipality and the regional fisheries office. Space allows only brief mention of the main issues here. Even though the municipality had allocated 47 km^2 to sea farming, the fisheries office objected to its exclusion from multiple use areas (FFFN areas in Figure 2), which in its opinion should have been left unplanned. Secondly, it objected to the nature area (N) at Fuglöyvaer, which at that time was included in the proposed Coastal Conservation Plan for Nordland, over which there was hot controversy. Sea farming would have been excluded from this area had it been established as a nature reserve. Later however, when the area was taken out of the Conservation Plan, the municipality allocated it to nature (N) and sea farming (A) in the final version of the municipal plan. Thirdly, the fisheries office objected to the inclusion of a temporary wild salmon protection area in the fjord district to the east (not shown on Figure 2), as this would have entailed a change in the area's legal status. In early 1998, the municipal council approved a modified plan, from which the remaining areas of conflict were removed. These were sent to the Ministry of the Environment for adjudication. The Ministry decided in favor of the municipality in 2000. The plan will be reviewed in the course of 2005 in connection with revision of the municipal development plan.

The need for coastal zoning was typically precipitated by the necessity to sort out potential conflicts between various interests, particularly between fishing and salmon farming, and also to secure viable conditions for future development in sea farming. As in Sandnes, a planning committee was formed under the municipal council and an executive group was established in the administration, but in contrast to Sandnes the planning process was characterized by extensive consultation with all the major stakeholders, including the fish farmers, fishermen, the Fisheries Office in Nordland, the county governor's Environmental Department, and District Veterinary Officer. The fishermen and fish farmers also worked together to provide information on fishing grounds and areas suitable for fish farming,

26. *Id.*

FIG. 2.—Simplified excerpt of the current coastal zone plan for Gildeskaal municipality, North Norway, showing localities for sea farming, nature conservation and multiple use.

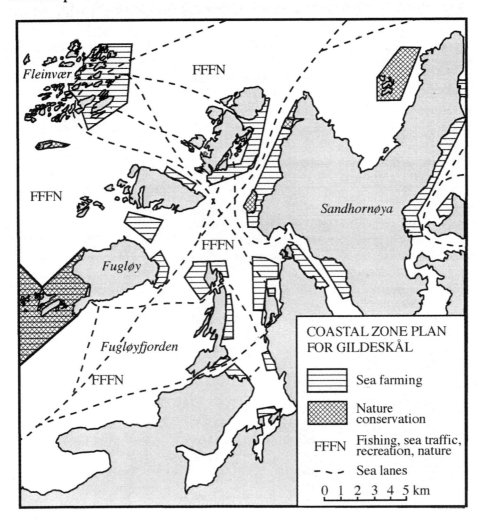

Source: Author.

and in so doing sorted out their differences and developed mutual understanding. And the general public was invited to discuss the first draft in an open meeting.

The plan, which was sent for hearing in March 1998, bore all the characteristics of communicative flexibility and was justified as such by the municipality when the fisheries office raised objections to it. At the local level at least a broad agreement (*modus vivendi*) had been reached among stakeholders on the zoning of coastal waters. The plan was also accepted with minor adjustments by Nordland County and all regional sector authorities except the fisheries office, indicating a large degree of compatibility with national and regional policies.

Figure 2 shows a simplified version of the plan. Noticeable features are the extensive areas reserved for sea farming (A), designated nature conservation areas (N) in compliance with the proposed Coastal Conservation Plan for Nordland, and the fact that most of the remaining sea areas were designated as multipurpose areas (FFFN) for fishing, traffic, recreation and nature. In these spatial arrangements the commune achieved a very large degree of predictability. Since areas for sea farming were clearly delimited and sea farming was expressly excluded from multipurpose areas, there was no doubt as to the future location of sea farming, thus facilitating licensing. A very large degree of instrumental flexibility was also achieved, not least for sea farming. The areas designated for it were numerous enough and large enough to enable adjustments to locations of farms, and provided sufficient room for rotation between farming localities as well as room for future expansion of the industry. The areas were also sufficiently large and far enough apart to enable mandatory three-kilometer hygienic buffer zones between fish farms (designed to hinder the spread of disease). In this sense the plan was both predictable and robust. The municipal planner reports that the plan still has adequate room for sea farming and that no major changes to zoning arrangements are envisaged when the municipal plan is revised later in 2005.

Some Reflections

Of course it is impossible to draw conclusions as to the flexibility of Norwegian coastal planning on the basis of two case studies. To our knowledge, however, a few municipalities such as Sandnes and some of its neighbors in Rogaland have attempted to determine the location of sea farming in great detail, but most municipalities tend to use a broad-brush approach to zoning similar to that of Gildeskaal, thereby achieving some degree of instrumental flexibility. Of course conditions vary from municipality to municipality. Available space and intensity of use of the coastal zone place real restrictions on how flexible a coastal plan can be with respect to sea farming. Many peripheral, fisheries dependent municipalities in northern Norway contain huge sea areas and few user interests, whereas municipalities in the southwest are smaller and have a greater variety of interests to take into account. In suburban municipalities like Sandnes it is difficult to find room for expansion of sea farming without coming into conflict with other strong interests.

As far as we know, there are no comprehensive studies of the extent to which Norwegian municipalities have used a communicative approach in their coastal planning. Since the Planning and Building Act was passed in 1985, however, the Ministry of the Environment has placed great emphasis on stakeholder participation and consultation in municipal planning. In consequence, many local authorities have attempted some form of communicative approach (although it may have been far from perfect), using working groups, workbooks, local discussion meetings and informal hearings. Few seem to have chosen an expert approach in the manner of Sandnes. The examples that we do know of, which have chosen both a communicative approach and broad-brush zoning, seem to have produced robust coastal plans.

The question that remains to be answered is whether the fisheries authorities' contention that coastal zone planning lacks flexibility is justified or not. In the case of Sandnes it is true both in an instrumental and communicative sense, but Sandnes is probably not representative. In Gildeskaal it was not true. To the extent to which Gildeskaal is representative, coastal planning achieves a fair mix of predictability and flexibility in both meanings of the concept. We close the discussion then as is customary, with a call for more research: can the fisheries authorities' accusation of inflexibility in coastal planning be corroborated with reference to either or both concepts of flexibility, or is it part of a strategy to reinforce its own position of power in coastal management?[27] The many conflicts between the fisheries authorities and municipalities over zoning arrangements suggest that this may indeed be the case.[28]

FLEXIBILITY AND INTEGRATED COASTAL MANAGEMENT

Finally it is desirable to say some words on flexibility in the context of integrated coastal zone management. In most academic literature on the subject questions of rationality and flexibility are not raised. It is usual to assume that rationality refers to the objective handling of ends and means, and that flexibility refers to the same concept of rationality. Although many authors pay attention to stakeholder involvement, it is usually within the general framework of the paradigm of ends and means—stakeholders need to be introduced to the rationality of management in order to ensure the achievement of rational goals. This overlooks one essential characteristic of planning and management, namely that they are essentially political activities. Just as there can be no objectively rational standard of flexibility,

27. Lund, n. 24 above.
28. Bennett (2000), n. 3 above.

there can be no corresponding standard of integration. Most coastal management has to deal with a multiplicity of conflicting interests and considerations. And in many countries a number of conflicting policies apply in the coastal zone. It would be a serious underestimation of the conflicting and contradictory nature of politics to suggest that integration concerns the coordination of management activities within the framework of one holistic national policy for the coastal zone, even if one existed.

What then is integration? And how can we relate it to notions of flexibility? This article indicates that full instrumental flexibility in practice is probably a chimera. It may be attainable for particular sector interests, but this implies restrictions on others that may not be acceptable or viable. It may also be short-lived, as the underlying assumptions of plans rapidly become out of date in a changing world. If rationality in planning and management concern what is achievable under a particular set of circumstances, then they concern rational compromise in communicative terms (i.e., *modus vivendi*). The achievement of communicative flexibility is essential if plans and management regimes are to work. Public authorities today possess neither the adequate reach nor the resources to control all developments in the coastal zone. Flexibility in the communicative sense of the concept is therefore essential to the achievement of integrated policies and management. A means of balancing interests operating at different geographical scales, it should not be regarded as an addendum to rational management, but as a prerequisite—the very vehicle of integration, however fragile and short-lived that may be.

Environment and Coastal Management

Is the Opening of the Bystroe Shipping Channel Compatible with the Danube Delta Biosphere Reserve and the Adjacent Black Sea Ecosystem?

Alexandru S. Bologa*
National Institute for Marine Research and Development "Grigore Antipa," Constanta, Romania

> It can be hoped that the Danube Delta will not be further channelized for shipping, and that the restoration measures may increase its nutrient retention capacity for the benefit of the Black Sea.[1]

THE DANUBE AND ITS WATERSHED

The Danube River, the second largest European river after the Volga, has its source in the Black Forest Mountains of Germany and flows into the Black Sea through three branches—Chilia, Sulina, and Saint George. It is 2,840 km long, has 817,000 km² of watershed, crosses ten countries[2] from 17 tributary countries, and bathes four capitals—Vienna, Bratislava, Budapest, and Belgrade. The water discharge distribution of the main branches is Chilia (58 percent), Sulina (19 percent), and Saint George (23 percent). The significance of the Danube River, its hydrographic basin (Fig. 1), and related matters are common knowledge and the details have been the topic of several recent publications.[3]

* The author expresses his sincere gratitude to Drs. J. Bloesch and G. Baboianu for the thorough review of this paper.

1. J. Bloesch and U. Sieber, "The Morphological Destruction and Subsequent Restoration Programmes of Large Rivers in Europe," *Archiv für Hydrobiologie, Supplementband* 147, 3–4 (*Large Rivers* 14, 3–4) (2003): 363–385.

2. Germany, Austria, Slovak Republic, Croatia, Serbia and Montenegro, Hungary, Romania, Moldova, Bulgaria, and Ukraine.

3. D. G. Le Marquand, *International Rivers: The Politics of Cooperation* (Vancouver, Canada: Wastewater Research Centre, University of British Columbia, 1977); J. Bloesch, "Integral Water Protection Along the Danube—Trite or Concept—And How Is IAD Engaged," *Archiv für Hydrobiologie, Supplementband* 141, 1–2 (*Large Rivers* 13, 1–2), (2002): 123–128; B. Meinier, "Prospects for Institutional Change in the Black Sea Catchment to Address Water Quality Problems," Report No. 304 (Simon Fraser University, Canada, 2002): 93 pp.; B. Meinier, "The Quest for Integration:

FIG. 1.—The contribution of the Danube River Basin to the Black Sea catchment area

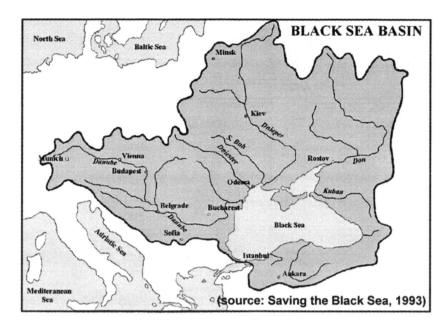

(source: Saving the Black Sea, 1993)

Pollution constitutes the main focus in the Danube, where some progress in improving water quality has been observed, particularly in the Upper Danube.[4] In 1992, the European Union started its Danube activities

Prospects for Institutional Changes in the Black Sea Basin," *Cercetari marine— Recherches marines* 34 (2002): 321–329; A. S. Bologa, "Regional Research and Management Developments in the Black Sea," *Ocean Yearbook* 14, eds. E. Mann Borgese, A. Chircop, M. McConnell and J. R. Morgan (Chicago: University of Chicago Press, 2000): 515–519; A. S. Bologa, "Recent Changes in the Black Sea Ecosystem," *Ocean Yearbook* 15, eds. E. Mann Borgese, A. Chircop, and M. McConnell (Chicago: University of Chicago Press, 2001): 463–474; A. S. Bologa, "The Danube Drainage Basin—The State of the Black Sea Ecosystem: Need for Continuing Co-operation and Partnership," *13th Stockholm Water Symposium*, Abstracts Volume, 11–14 August 2003 (Stockholm, Sweden: Stockholm International Water Institute, 2003): 149–152; H. Kroiss, M. Zessner and C. Lampert, "Nutrient Management in the Danube Basin and Its Impact in the Black Sea," Proceedings of IOI–BSOC Leadership Seminar, Mamaia, Romania, 27–29 September 2002, *Journal of Coastal Research* 19, 4 (2003): 898–906; P. Moisi, "Danube Environmental Forum (DEF)—A Successful Example of a River Basin Non-Governmental Organization," *13th Stockholm Water Symposium*, Abstracts Volume, 11–14 August 2003, (Stockholm, Sweden: Stockholm International Water Institute, 2003): 145–148; S. Cinca, "Dunarea vie—un parteneriat cu natura," *Romania libera*, Opinii in aldine, (27 February 2004): 2.

4. J. Bloesch, "The International Association for Danube Research (IAD): Its Future Role in Danube Research," *Archiv für Hydrobiologie, Supplementband* 115, 3 (*Large Rivers* 11, 3) (1999): 239–259.

FIG. 2.—The Danube Delta shared by Romania (82%) and Ukraine (18%).

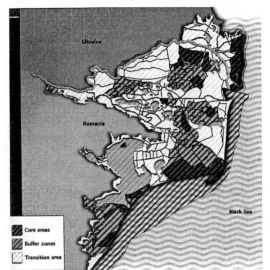

Source: UNESCO.

with the Danube Programme Co-ordination Unit, which was linked with and assisted by the European Commission's Phare Programme and the Global Environment Facility (GEF-United Nations Development Programme, United Nations Environment Programme, and the World Bank), among others. Further international efforts resulted in the founding of the International Commission for the Protection of the Danube River (ICPDR) in 1998.[5] According to J. Bloesch, President of the International Association for Danube Research from 1998 to 2004, the three most important topics in need of international co-operation in the Danube River Basin are the Danube Delta, the wetlands and flood plains, and the sturgeons.

THE DANUBE DELTA AND DANUBE DELTA BIOSPHERE RESERVE

During the last 16,000 years the Danube River has built the Danube Delta (Fig. 2) at its three Black Sea mouths. Hence, the Delta plays a key role as the interface between the river (freshwater) and the sea (brackish water).

5. J. Bloesch, "Flood Plain Conservation in the Danube River Basin: The Link Between Hydrobiology and Limnology." Summary report on the 34th IAD Conference, 27–30 August 2002, in Tulcea, Romania and the 21st IHP/UNESCO Hydrological Conference, 2–6 September 2002, in Bucharest, Romania," *Archiv für Hydrobiologie, Supplementband* 147, 3–4 (*Large Rivers* 14, 3–4) (2003): 347–362.

The Danube Delta is one of Europe's largest natural wetlands.[6] Its main ecosystems consist of tributaries, lakes, reed beds, sand dunes, wetland forests, and dryland forests. Much of it has been developed for agriculture, but its varied habitats still support a wide range of plant and animal life, especially bird life in terms of breeding pairs, winter residents, and migratory visitors.

Along Ukraine's Black Sea coast, 15,000 hectares are protected as a National Reserve. On the Romanian side of the Delta, the reserve covers 564,000 hectares and a wide variety of ecosystems. In 1990, the Government of Romania recognized the ecological importance of the Danube Delta, which by then had become a UNESCO Biosphere Reserve and a World Heritage site, and established the Danube Delta Biosphere Reserve Authority.[7] The government stopped all future reclamation works, banned sand mining, and initiated a policy to give priority to the conservation of nature and natural resources. Hence, large parts of the Delta meet the requirements of international organizations to be recognized as a Biosphere Reserve.[8] The Delta has 18 strictly protected areas of 506 km², economic zones of 3,061 km², and buffer zones of 2,233 km², comprised of Delta buffer zones of 1,203 km² and a marine buffer zone of 1,030 km².

At 5,800 km², the Danube Delta is 2.5 percent of the total Romanian territory. It is the 22nd largest delta in the world, the third largest delta in Europe after the Volga and Kuban, and includes 30 types of ecosystems and represents the greatest reed bed expanses worldwide at 1,560 km².

The Danube Delta is important as a natural physical and chemical filter for Danube water and as a natural control of erosion and floods. It supports more than half of the European population of the common pelican *Pelecanus onocrotalus* (8,000 individuals) and a large share of the world's population of the Dalmatian pelican *Pelecanus philippensis* (sin. *P. crispus*) (200 individuals). It is home to 60 percent of the world's population of two endangered species, the pigmy cormorant *Phalacrocorax pygmeus* (6,000 individuals) and 50 percent of the entire population of red-breasted goose *Branta ruficollis* (40,000 individuals). The Delta is a potentially significant economic resource for natural products (e.g., reeds, timber, and fish) and tourism.

The Delta shelters about 90 species of fish and 300 species of birds, some of which are very rare, and most are endangered. It plays a key role in the Danube River Basin and is the interface to the Black Sea.[9] Its complex

6. *Saving the Black Sea,* "Programme for the Environmental Management and Protection of the Black Sea," (New York, Nairobi, Washington D.C.: UNDP, UNEP, The World Bank, June 1993): 28 pp.

7. See <http://www.ddbra.ro/>.

8. Danube Delta Biosphere Reserve, Eco-tourism map 1:175,000 (1995).

9. UNESCO, "Biosphere Reserves: The Sevilla Strategy and the Statutory Framework of the World Network," (Paris: UNESCO, 1996); G. Baboianu, "The Role of the Biosphere Reserve for Biodiversity Protection and Sustainable Develop-

role for biodiversity protection and sustainable development in the Danube Delta, as well as the need for ecological restoration in the Danube Delta have been discussed in detail.[10] Certainly the most important issue for the Danube Delta concerns restoration measures, which may increase its nutrient retention capacity with respect to sustainable development and protection.[11] Overviews about the inventories, the management plans, and ecological restoration programmes have also been published.[12] The importance of the Danube Delta was proven once again by the Danube Delta Biodiversity Project, launched in 1992 by the GEF, covering both Delta countries. As to the management strategy,[13] J. Bloesch resumed the conservation, development and logistic functions, taking into consideration the inventories of biodiversity (5,492 species, Figs. 3 and 4), education and public awareness, and the legal framework.

THE BYSTROE SHIPPING CHANNEL: DANUBE–BLACK SEA

The first information on the Ukrainian Bystroe Shipping Channel Project, linking the Danube and the Black Sea (Fig. 5), appeared in April 2003.[14] In 2004, despite strong Romanian and international criticism,[15] Ukraine's Ministry of Transportation contracted the German company, Josef Moebius Baugesellschaft GmbH of Hamburg, to start building the deep-water Bystroe shipping channel after Ukraine's request had been rejected by several Dutch companies.

The Bystroe channel, connected with the Chilia branch of the Danube—a natural border between Ukraine and Romania—is to cross the

ment in the Danube Delta," *International Association for Danube Research* 34, (2002): 633–641; R. Suciu, A. Constantinescu and C. David, "The Danube Delta: Filter or Bypass for the Nutrient Input into the Black Sea," *Archiv für Hydrobiologie, Supplementband* 141, 1–2 (*Large Rivers* 13, 1–2), (2002): 165–173; See Bologa (2000) and Bologa (2001), n. 3 above, and Bloesch, n. 5 above.

10. Baboianu, n. 9 above; R. Stiuca, M. Staras and M. Tudor, "The Ecological Restoration in the Danube Delta. An Alternative for Sustainable Management of Degraded Wetlands," *International Association for Danube Research* 34, (2002): 633–641.

11. Suciu, n. 9 above; M. C. Trifu, J. Garnier, G. Billen and R. Drobot, "Nutrient Fluxes in the Danube Delta: Modelling Approaches," in IHP/UNESCO: *21st Conference on the Danube Countries on the Hydrobiological Forecasting and Hydrological Bases of Water Management*, 2–6 September 2002, Bucharest, Romania, Conference Proceedings (CD-ROM, ISBN 973–0–02759–5) (2002).

12. Baboianu, n. 9 above; Stiuca et al., n. 10 above.

13. Bloesch, n. 5 above.

14. D. Padurean, "Canalul Bastroe—scandalul anului," *Romania libera*, Dobrogea (23 October 2004): 19.

15. *Marea Noastra*, "Bastroe—un canal al dezastrului ecologic," LNR, Redactia, 14, 3 (52) (July–September 2004): 6–8.

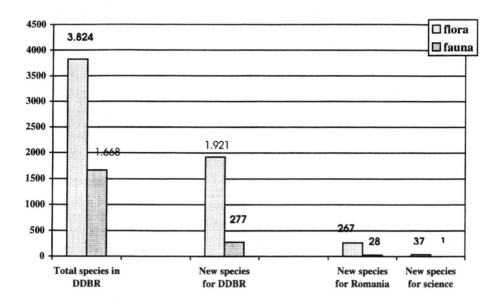

FIG. 3.—Identified species in the Danube Delta Biosphere Reserve (cf. Danube Delta Biosphere Reserve—Ecotourism map, 1995)

protected Ukrainian Danube Delta Reserve, the most recent reserve and among the most ecologically precious regions of Europe. The construction of the Bystroe channel aims to ensure navigation and trade from the Black Sea to the Danube harbors of Izmail, Reni and Ust-Dunaisk. Approximately 4.2 million tons per year of merchandise, mainly iron ore, oil and wheat, are to be shipped through the channel. The present navigation fees and the dependence on Romanian transit approvals are frustrating for Ukraine. The 170-km long channel is expected to cost US$200 million. The navigation route originates in the Chilia branch, passes through the Bystroe passage, through the Danube plain for many kilometers, and ends, protected by dams, 3 km into the Black Sea where it is 120 meters wide and 8 meters deep.

It is understandable how important shipping activities are to Ukraine. Apart from the economic reasons, the geo-strategic/geo-political control of the Danube mouths is vital as it guarantees control of the whole river and hence the Black Sea.[16] But shipping activities should not harm the environment, especially Europe's largest biosphere reserve. Furthermore, the nature of the Romanian-Ukrainian border will change in the future

16. See Padurean, n. 14 above; *Ziua,* "Stop destroying the Danube Delta!," Special issue, XI, 3101, (24 August 2004).

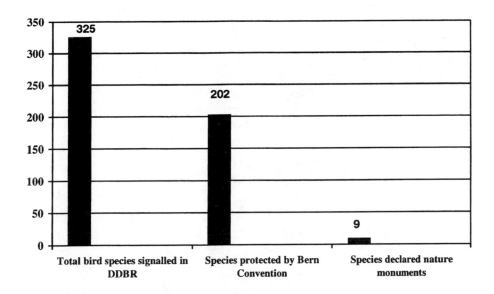

FIG. 4.—Bird species in the Danube Delta Biosphere Reserve (cf. Danube Delta Biosphere Reserve—Ecotourism map, 1995)

when Romania joins the European Union (EU). At that time the now natural border will become the east-west border between the EU and Ukraine, which is non-EU, and virtually Russia.

ECOLOGICAL CONSEQUENCES AND THE NEED FOR AN ENVIRONMENTAL IMPACT ASSESSMENT

The main negative ecological impacts foreseen after the opening and exploitation of the Bystroe channel consist of increased Danube water flow and velocity in the Chilia branch, the drying up of vast deltaic territories, destruction of rare and threatened flora and fauna, especially ichthyofauna and avifauna species, and the loss of about 100 million tons of fish per year.[17]

According to V. Ciochia, founder of the Society of Ornithology, Bird and Nature Protection in Romania, the Bystroe channel will lead to future radical changes in the northern part of the present Danube Delta, with effects on the whole Danube Delta Biosphere Reserve, including the "bird

17. *Ziua,* "Autocratul Kucima vrea sa castige alegerile calcand peste pelicani," Eveniment, (24 August 2004): 4.

FIG. 5.—Location of the Bystroe Danube–Black Sea shipping channel

paradise" with the unique common pelican (*Pelecanus onocrotalus*) colony in Europe together with various other bird species.[18] As of the end of July 2004, the first victims of the Bystroe shipping channel were observed.[19] About 1,380 sea terns (*Sterna sandvicensis*) had already left their colonies because the noise generated by the dredging fleet can be heard from a distance of 7 km, which shows the potential impact for small birds.[20] Furthermore, several hundreds of sea tern and sea swallow (*S. hirundo*) chicks died.[21]

The ICPDR is deeply concerned about possible transboundary environmental impacts resulting from the construction of the Bystroe Danube–

18. P. M. Bacanu, "Staro-Stambulskoe Garlo, Musura si ambitiile ucrainiene," *Romania libera*, Eveniment (24 August 2004): 3.

19. E. Chirita, "Canalul Bastroe distruge ecosistemul," *Romania libera*, (24 November 2004): 3; G. Coman, "Ucraina a trecut la cucerirea gurilor Dunarii," *Ziua*, Externe (13 May 2004): 8.

20. European Foundation for Nature—EURONATUR, 2004.

21. Centre for Ecological Analysis, Galati, Romania, 2004; Society for Bird Research and Nature Protection from Slovenia, 2004.

Black Sea deep navigation channel at the Danube River mouth.[22] ICPDR President, Catherine Day, called upon the Government of Ukraine "to halt the future stages of the construction until a proper international evaluation of environmental consequences of the project can be undertaken." The ICPDR had initially expressed concern about the possible impacts of the project during the December 2003 Ordinary meeting. The ICPDR has also begun an assessment of a limited number of documents made available about the project and came to the conclusion that the information provided to date is clearly insufficient to assess the possibility of adverse transboundary environmental impacts. The ICPDR has requested full disclosure of all relevant documents and studies evaluating the environmental impacts of the channel to ensure that measures can be taken to minimize or eliminate negative consequences. "To continue to proceed further with the project without completing a proper assessment and discussion of potential transboundary impacts is contrary to the spirit and requirements of the Danube River Protection Convention," said Ms. Day, "However, both Romanian and Ukrainian delegations signalized willingness to jointly debate and negotiate the issue."

Under Agenda Item 4.9 "Trans-European Transport Networks,"[23] Resolution 2 concluded: "The ICPDR a) takes note with concern of the plans for construction of the Bystroe Canal in the Danube Delta of Ukraine, b) mandates the ICPDR President to write a letter to the Government of Ukraine asking for information about the Canal Project expressing concerns related to possible environmental impacts of the Canal and stressing the necessity for a comprehensive environmental assessment of those impacts (together with other international bodies on Danube and Black Sea water quality—BSC, Ramsar Secretariat, UNESCO MAB and EC)."

An environmental impact assessment (EIA) under international expertise and supervision, supported by, among others, German Chancellor Gerhard Schroeder after his meeting with the Romanian Prime Minister,[24] should be carried out to evaluate the short-, medium- and long-term effects of the Bystroe channel on the Danube Delta and Black Sea coastal ecosystems, in order to stop or allow the continuation of the initiated dredging works. According to Chancellor Schroeder, "the channel that is

22. International Commission for the Protection of the Danube River (ICPDR), "ICPDR Statement of the Opening of the Danube Black Sea—Deep Navigation Canal (Bystroe area) in Ukraine," Ref. 04915 (25 August 2004).

23. See ICPDR, n. 22 above.

24. C. Damian, Schroeder on Bystroe: "Stop This Irresponsible Operation. The Chancellor's Immediate Reaction to Protests of Romanian and International Civic Society," in *Ziua*, Special issue, XI, 3101, (24 August 2004), special issue, pages not numbered.

being built in the Danube Delta, one of the most important and sensitive systems in Europe, only seems to be a Romanian and Ukrainian topic. It is clear that such a project can only be achieved after international analysis of environmental impact and any other action is irresponsible." Schroeder also said that the Executive he was in charge of could not prevent a private building company from getting involved in this project, but he specified that he had not given support to this company. The German magazine *Umwelt Journal* published an article called "German Company that Leaves Bird Corpses Behind."[25] The EU and the U.S. State Department have protested in vain in this respect. The Ukrainian Academy of Sciences[26] has contested a Bystroe channel-related study/report produced by 21 Ukrainian scientists instead of an EIA. Although the Romanian authorities requested the report, it was received incompletely.[27]

REPORTS OF EXPERT ORGANIZATIONS

Reactions have followed the development in the endangered areas. Critical reports on the construction of the Bystroe shipping channel, alternative proposals for a waterway through the Ukrainian part of the Danube Delta (Ocheakovskyi Rukav branch and Prorva channel, sluiced channel from Solomonov branch to Zhebranskaya Bay of the Black Sea), and the need for an impartial EIA have been issued by UNESCO's Man and Biosphere Programme and the Ramsar Convention Secretariat,[28] the Convention on the Conservation of European Wildlife and Natural Habitats,[29] and a call was issued for an immediate halt to plans for building this channel by the WWF International Danube-Carpathian Programme.[30]

25. Id.

26. V. Grigore, "Nu au existat considerente ecologice pentru construirea canalului Bastroe: Speciile rare pot fi distruse, pentru ca mai exista si in alte zone," *Romania libera*, Eveniment (27 August 2004): 3.

27. *Romania libera*, "Raportul ucrainian-praf in ochi," Eveniment (28 August 2004): 4.

28. J. Kvet and T. Salathé, UNESCO (Man and Biosphere Programme) and Ramsar Convention, Mission Report, Danube Biosphere Reserve /Kyliiske Mouth Ramsar Site, Ukraine, 27–31 October 2003.

29. H. Léthier, Council of Europe, "Convention on the Conservation of European Wildlife and Natural Habitats, Standing Committee 24th Meeting, Strasbourg, 29 November–3 December 2004, Possible New File, Shipping Canal in the Bystroe Estuary (Danube Delta, Ukraine)," Report of the on-the-spot appraisal, 22–24 July 2004. 17 pp.

30. B. Hajdu and M. Baltzer, "WWF Press Release: Ukraine Breaches International Agreements and Puts Europe's Second Largest Wetland Under Threat," (10 May 2004).

REACTIONS AND WARNINGS OF CIVIL SOCIETY

Civil society associations promoting respect for international law have asked the President of Ukraine to stop the building of the Bystroe Channel. They warned of several major impacts on the Danube Delta, and were supported by notable organizations such as World Wildlife Fund International, Wetlands International, Bird Life International, and the International Association for Danube Research, among others. Their concerns relate to the following aspects:

- Large quantities of the Delta's land will be severely damaged. More than 1,500 hectares will be lost and several unique habitats and nearly extinct bird and fish species will disappear;
- The Delta's natural capacity to provide water resources for fish survival, drinkable water and irrigation water will be damaged; and
- The lack of best solutions for economic and social matters in the Danube Delta. According to UNESCO and the Ramsar Convention Secretariat, the building of the Bystroe channel is the least fit and most destructive option for a Ukrainian shipping channel in the Danube Delta.

With almost 20,000 signatures, 140 organizations and institutions from Romania, Ukraine and numerous other countries have reminded Ukraine that by building this channel, Ukraine is breaking various international assignments and agreements to which it has subscribed:[31]

- Ramsar Convention on Wet Lands of International Importance especially as Waterfowl Habitat (1991);
- Paris Convention on the Protection of the World's Cultural and Natural Heritage (1975);
- Bern Convention on the European Wildlife and Natural Habitats Protection (1979);
- Rio de Janeiro Convention on Biological Diversity (1992);
- Helsinki Convention on the Protection and Use of Transborder Waters and International Lakes (1992);
- Sofia Convention on the Co-operation, Protection and Durable Use of the Danube River (Danube Convention, 1994); and
- Agreement between the Romanian Government and the Ukrainian Government on Co-operation in Management of Boundary Waters (Galati, 1997).

31. See *Ziua*, n. 16 above.

It is alleged that Ukraine violated other conventions during the process of Bystroe channel construction, including the following:

- Bonn Convention on Conservation of Migratory Species;
- African-Eurasian Migratory Waterfowl Agreement;
- Espoo Convention on Environmental Impact Assessment in a Transboundary Context; and
- Aarhus Convention on Access to Information, Public Participation in Decision-making and Access to Justice in Environmental Issues.

Non-governmental organizations' strong concerns for and protests of the construction of the Bystroe channel have been expressed by, among many others, the Ecological Group Pechenegi,[32] the Forum of the NGOs from the Danube River Basin,[33] and the Oceanic Club.[34] The online petition,[35] launched in August 2004 by the Romanian daily newspaper *Ziua* and Romanians World Wide (RWW), was second worldwide according to the number of signatures and access frequency. On 26 August 2004, an event celebrating the finish of the first segment of the Bystroe channel, intended to be linked with Ukraine's Independence Day on August 24, was followed by an ample protest march in Bucharest on the same day.[36]

Ukrainian authorities obviously failed to adequately inform neighboring countries and the ICPDR about the technical details and ecological implications of the Bystroe channel on the Danube Delta Biosphere Reserve ecosystem and the adjacent Black Sea coastal area, both already stressed by anthropogenic impacts and facing a fragile ecological equilibrium in the last few decades. Due to the lack of Romanian-Ukrainian bilateral understanding through the usual diplomatic means, Romania is going to undertake all necessary actions and measures in order that international commitments and obligations are respected. Consequently, after the inauguration of the first segment of the Bystroe channel, Romania initiated its protest against Ukraine at the International Court of Justice in The Hague concerning both the channel issue and the older litigation on the status of Serpent Island and the delimitation of the continental shelf and the Economic Exclusive Zones of both countries in the Black Sea.[37] Furthermore, a possible

32. Ukrainian coalition "For Wild Nature" (pecheneg@ic.kharkov.ua), Campaign News: Save the Danube National Reserve (2 August 2004).

33. Resolution, Odessa, Ukraine, 6 October 2004.

34. R. Popescu Mirceni, B. Nita, Oceanic Club, Comunicat de presa (2004).

35. See <http://www.petitiononline.com/RomDelta and savedelta@europe.com>.

36. *Ziua*, "Veniti la marsul pentru salvarea Deltei," Eveniment, (24 August 2004): 4.

37. D. Hadareanu, "Ucraina, reclamata la Haga si pentru Bastroe si pentru platforma continentala," *Romania libera*, Eveniment (28 August 2004): 4; C. Manea, "Diferendul romano-ucrainian privind impartirea zonelor maritime din Marea

Romanian action against the German entrepreneur Josef Moebius is being considered with the help of a German law firm.[38]

Due to the expected ecological effects of the Bystroe shipping channel, Romanian environmental protection-related authorities ordered studies of the ecological reconstruction of about 40,000 hectares for agriculture and pisciculture in the Danube Delta.[39] Numerous national and international news agencies such as France Press, Reuters, Truth News, Turkish Press, and Voice of America, among others, published serious warnings against the construction of the Bystroe channel, contrary to the Ukrainian and Russian pro-channel campaign. Various other Danube Delta and Bystroe channel-related commentaries are listed in the Annex of Statements in this article.

RECENT DEVELOPMENTS

During a Ramsar Convention meeting held in Erevean, Armenia in late 2004 on the protection of wetlands of international importance, Wetlands International submitted an evaluation of wetlands for the whole of Europe. Its conclusions are alarming considering the ecological degradation of such protected areas. Of the 798 Ramsar sites, 62 percent are continuously degrading. Only 2 percent are ecologically improving. The Danube Delta Biosphere Reserve belongs to this latter category, together with other improving zones in Italy, Greece and Iceland. According to V. Munteanu, Governor of the Danube Delta Biosphere Reserve, halting ecological degradation of the Danube Delta depends on the ecological restoration programme that enabled the improvement of the deltaic biotope and led to a significant amelioration of related environmental factors.[40]

Notwithstanding the withdrawal of dredging equipment in the Bystroe delta at the end of 2004, Ukrainian authorities pursued further the completion of the project they initiated. This undertaking entails serious consequences for the Danube Delta biotope. A semblance of public debate has been organized in Izmail, Ukraine. Invitations made to the Romanian Ministry of Foreign Affairs in Bucharest, several hours before the start, could not be honored. The same attitude prevailed towards Ukrainian non-

Neagra trece intr-o noua faza—cea a justitiei internationale," *Marea Neagra* 14, 4 (53) (2004): 15; G. Petre, "Jurnalul confruntarilor romano-ucrainiene (I)," *Marea Noastra* 14, 4 (53) (2004): 17–19.

38. See *Ziua*, n. 36 above, at 4.

39. N. Amihulesei, "Pentru combaterea efectelor produse de canalul Bastroe: Mii de hectare destinate pisciculturii vor fi reconstruite ecologic in Delta," *Romania libera*, Eveniment (11 September 2004): 4.

40. N. Amihulesei, "Biotopul din Delta Dunarii se imbunatateste prin reconstructii ecologice," *Romania libera*, Economie (18 December 2004): 5.

governmental organizations (NGOs) opposed to the project: the "Pechene-gi" and "Ecopravo" organizations joined the "debate." Both have cited former Ukrainian President L. Kuchma and the Ukrainian Ministry of Transportation in court because they promoted the ad hoc investment without consultation with the Ukrainian citizenry, ignoring national and international agreements on environmental protection. Yet Ukraine has signed various international agreements regarding environmental protection, but in the Bystroe case they have not been respected.[41] Furthermore, during December 2004 no information could be secured about Aleksandr Voloskievich, Governor of the Ukrainian Danube Delta Reserve, or his family.

Many environmental NGOs oppose the situation between Romania and Ukraine with respect to this project. The recent election of the new President of Ukraine, Viktor Iushchenko, has been understandably lauded by Romania's Minister of Foreign Affairs, M.R. Ungureanu, who expressed hopes for the acceptance of previously proposed European solutions that recognize the need for an independent, international environmental impact assessment of the Bystroe shipping channel, and for solving the Romanian-Ukrainian dispute on the delimitation of the respective share of the Black Sea continental shelf. Since it is considered as a genuine transboundary problem, it is recommended to solve it within the framework of the International Commission for the Protection of the Danube River.

CONCLUSION

The Danube Delta is one of Europe's largest natural wetlands, with large parts under national and international protection (e.g., UNESCO Biosphere Reserve, at least 11 bilateral and international agreements/conventions), and it is shared between Romania and Ukraine. The Man and Biosphere (MAB) Programme of UNESCO recognized the universal value of the Danube Delta Biosphere Reserve in August 1990 through its inclusion in the international network of biosphere reserves. Since September 1990 when Romania became Party to the Ramsar Convention, the Danube Delta Biosphere Reserve has been an internationally recognized wetland zone, mostly in its capacity as habitat for aquatic birds. The importance of the Biosphere Reserve was also recognized in December 1990 when it became Party of the Cultural and Natural World Patrimony. The Ukrainian side of the Danube Delta was declared a biosphere reserve under the UNESCO/

41. N. Amihulesei, "Scandalul Bastroe a ajuns la Geneva: Reprezentantul Ucrainei catre romani: "Va ucidem," *Romania libera* (16 December 2004): 5.

MAB Programme in 1998. In 1999, UNESCO recognized the Transboundary Biosphere Reserve Danube Delta of Romania/Ukraine.

The unilateral decision of Ukraine to make use of the Bystroe shipping channel represents a major impact on the Danube Delta ecosystem, mainly on the Danube Delta Biosphere Reserve area. Navigation in general, and the newly constructed first segment of the Bystroe shipping channel in particular, are threatening the unique plant and animal life and hence biodiversity in the Danube Delta through direct or indirect impacts (i.e., hydrological and physical alterations).

Despite the lack of a sound environmental impact assessment, several major ecological interactions have been predicted, such as: higher water flow on the Chilia branch and lower flow on the Sulina and Saint George branches; a decrease of water resource and implicitly of drinkable and irrigation resources in the Danube Delta, with increased pollutant input into the Black Sea; less oxygenated water input on the Sulina and Saint George branches with ecological consequences; diminished Danube Delta natural biofiltering capacity; degradation of the Letea tropical forest ecosystem (oldest Romanian natural reserve since 1938) only 15 km away from the Bystroe channel; declines of fish catch with about 100 tons per year for 300 Romanian fishermen from Sulina, Periprava, Chilia Veche (20 tons of freshwater fish, 80 tons of marine fish); degradation of reproduction and conservation grounds of fish and bird species (9 species on the European Red List and 42 on the Ukrainian Red List); degradation of the ecologically protected zone, Rosca Buhaiova, the biggest European colony of common pelican; eventual changes of Mediterranean and African ecosystems due to modified bird migration routes; acceleration of sanding of the Sulina barrier bar, with related geomorphological changes of the Romanian Black Sea littoral zone; and aggravation of the socio-economic situation of Romanian Danube Delta communities.

A bilateral solution to the Bystroe shipping channel should consist of negotiating better economic conditions and regulations for Ukrainian (and other) ships, in order to concentrate shipping impacts and stress in the already built Sulina channel, inaugurated in 1861 for navigation, and to conserve the other channels of the Danube Delta. The transboundary aspect of the Bystroe shipping channel and its related ecological problems should be considered by the International Commission for the Protection of the Danube River. The Commission should take the lead responsibility for solving it as an international body recognized by both Romania and Ukraine.

ANNEX OF STATEMENTS

I.V. Stalin: *In order to assure the USSR's security, the territory occupied by the Danube's manholes with all its three channels to be transferred to the USSR—*

Talks protocol between Stalin and A. Eden, 9th point of the "confidential" agreement.[42]

Konstantin Grishenko, Ministry of Foreign Affairs, Ukraine: *The construction of such a channel does not affect the ecological balance of the Danube Delta.*[43]

Valeriy Panteleev, First Secretary, Embassy of Ukraine in Austria: *We do construct on our territory, not on the Romanian one.*[44]

Sergey Shaparenko, President of Council, Environmental Group "Pechenegy": *Leads to the destruction of natural area, part of World Heritage and unique in its global aspect. Hampers the renewal of shipping on the Ukrainian part of the Danube Delta. Passes the threat of possible international isolation of Ukraine. If our Ministry of Transportation and Ministry of Environment, instead of lobbying the interests of close circle of businessmen and politicians, had been really concerned about the renewal of shipping, economic prosperity of that region and about the welfare of its population, preservation of national complexes of the Danube Delta, they would have considered ecologically and economically sounded alternatives of shipping channel in the Danube Delta.*[45]

Dimitri Skrilnikov, lawyer, ecological company: "Ecopravo Lvov": *Ukrainian officials have broken all environmental protection regulations.*[46]

Bogdan Aurescu, Secretary of State, Ministry of Foreign Affairs of Romania: *Ukraine refuses to cooperate and to inform the riparians about the project.*[47]

George Cristian Maior, Secretary of State, Chief of Department for Euro-Atlantic Integration and Defense Politics, Ministry of National Defense of Romania: *We are confronted in this case with an important ecological risk.*[48]

Dan Hulea, Executive Director, Romanian Ornithological Society: *This construction has terrible impact on the whole biosphere and on bird migration. The channel concerns one of the most important nesting zone in Eastern Europe. Also, the migration process of birds from Russia to South Africa and back, as well as the wintering process of birds in the Delta. The situation will awfully affect the Danube Delta while the economic pressure in Romania is also increasing.*[49]

42. C. Damian, "The Danube Delta from Stalin to Kuchma and Putin," *Ziua*, Special issue, XI, 3101, (24 August 2004), n. 24 above.

43. G. Coman, "Romanian, Slovenian and Ukrainian ecologist NGOs are very concerned: The Bystroe Channel kills," *Ziua*, Special issue, XI, 3101, (24 August 2004), 4.

44. See *Ziua*, n. 17 above.

45. S. Shaparenko, "Ukraine misinforms other countries and the international community," *Ziua*, Special issue, XI, 3101, (24 August 2004), ns. 24 and 42 above.

46. See Damian, n. 24 above.

47. See *Ziua*, n. 17 above.

48. C. Sava, "Comportamentul Ucrainei, ca in perioada razboiului rece," *Romania libera*, Investigatii (7 September 2004): 5.

49. See Coman, n. 19 above.

Calin Cotoi, sociologist, Geopolitics Centre of Bucharest University: *The building of the Bystroe channel actually transfers the control of the Danube mouths to Ukraine and is the most severe incident that has taken place lately.*[50]

Jürg Boeschl, President, International Association for Danube Research: *Deltas are known to be depositional areas with braided branches and floodplains as hot spots of biodiversity. Therefore, straightening and deepening channels and establishing bank construction have a great negative impact on the functioning of the ecosystem.*[51]

Jean-Christophe Filori, spokesman, European Commission: *We do not want to threaten ... but the construction of this channel does not represent an acceptable evolution and will not help our relationships with Ukraine.*[52]

Jamie Pittock, Director, WWF's Living Waters Programme: *The building of this canal flouts several international agreements and goes against the concept of international management of shared rivers; WWF is calling on the Ukrainian government to hold up its end of the bargain.*[53]

Michael Baltzer, Conservation Director, WWF's Danube Carpathian Programme: *Ukraine has failed to honor commitments made at a head of state summit organized three years ago in Romania.*[54]

Ulrich Eichelmann, WWF: *There have been several variants of the project, the chosen one is the worst of all.*[55]

Martin Schneider, Project co-ordinator, EURONATUR: *The so-called respect for the environment is a joke.*[56]

Adam Ereli, deputy spokesman, U.S. Department of State: *We are deeply concerned about the achievement of this project.*[57]

50. C. Cotoi, "The Danube—Orientation of Romania, A Key Position Undermined by Ukraine," *Ziua*, Special issue, XI, 3101 (24 August 2004), 3 pp.

51. Statement of the International Association for Danube Research (IAD), "With Regard to the Ongoing Reopening of the Bystroe Canal for Shipping in the Chilia Branch of the Danube Delta, Ukraine" (23 August 2004): 3.

52. *Romania libera*, "Bruxelles-ul se infurie: UE cere din nou oprirea lucrarilor si avertizeaza cu posibile sanctiuni," Eveniment (26 August 2004): 3.

53. World Wildlife Fund Press Release, "Ukraine Breaches International Agreements and Puts Europe's Second Largest Wetland Under Threat" (10 May 2004).

54. Id.

55. See *Ziua*, n. 17 above.

56. See Damian, n. 24 above.

57. D. Hadareanu, "O 'profunda preocupare': Statele Unite critica dur Ucraina," *Romania libera*, Eveniment, (25 August 2004): 3.

Environment and Coastal Management

The Economic Valuation of Coastal Areas: The Case of Uruguay

Denise Gorfinkiel
Multidisciplinary Unit, Faculty of Social Science, University of Uruguay, Uruguay

INTRODUCTION

Coastal areas are among the most diverse and productive ecosystems on the planet. They lie between the land and the sea, and their complex systems and interrelations make them very vulnerable.[1] They are valuable resources for the economic and social development of countries, and some societies have achieved high levels of development through exploiting their coasts for agricultural production, and the sea for transportation and commerce. This helps to explain why coastal areas tend to be quite densely populated: the activities that take place in them cannot be undertaken anywhere else.

The coastal areas of Uruguay are home to a wide variety of goods and services, some of which provide basic necessities for human life. These goods and services include tangible resources such as commercial fishing, sport fishing, and also less tangible advantages like recreational activities, clean beaches, marine and coastal habitats and attractive areas for housing. In Uruguay, as in most countries with coastal areas, some of these goods and services are increasingly scarce, and this has led to different types of conflicts. These difficulties are hard to resolve because there is free access to these areas and many of the services in them are public.

One of these spheres of conflict has to do with the fast growth of urban areas, a phenomenon that has caused problems between the demand for and the supply of coastal goods and services. One example is eutrophication or water contamination, which results from harbor, agricultural, and urban activities, and which conflicts with the need for good quality clean water for recreational activities and tourism, and also with scenic beauty and clean

1. GESAMP, IMO/FAO/UNESCO-IOC/WMO/WHO/IAEA/UN/UNEP Joint Group of Experts on the Scientific Aspects of Marine Environmental Protection, "Protecting the Oceans from Land-based Activities," Rep. Stud. GESAMP, (71): The Hague, 2001. 162 p.

Ocean Yearbook 20: 411–434.

beaches.[2] Resolving such conflicts generally involves a trade-off between different interests. What criteria can be applied when seeking reasonable trade-offs? From an economic perspective, analyses about which changes in society entail a gain and which entail a loss should take account of the economic value of the environment. This means that one of the criteria for resolving trade-offs between conflicting interests should be the economic valuation of coastal resources and environmental change.

Economic and social factors are essential to an understanding of many of the problems and questions that arise when it comes to managing coastal resources.[3] The interconnection between the natural environment and socio-economic factors is now acknowledged, and this has resulted in efforts to more fully integrate environmental considerations into economic analyses and to more fully integrate socio-economic considerations into environmental decisions.

In this article we present a summary of the key findings of various studies of the socio-economic factors that influence the Uruguayan coastal economy,[4] studies that were aimed at gauging the contribution coastal activities and resources make to the Uruguayan economy. Although the focus was mainly on economic activities with a market value, the studies established the scope, methodology and usefulness of this type of research. They produced results that were important in terms of finding and analyzing the information that was available, and these data could be used as a baseline for estimating the real extent of the economic and social impact of these activities. The studies were designed to help establish the economic importance of coastal areas and give it more weight as a factor in the decision-making process. The results presented here reflect the first steps

2. J. M. Barragán, *Medio Ambiente y Desarrollo en Areas Litorales: Introducción a la planificación y gestión integradas* (Puerto Real, España: Universidad de Cádiz, 2003).

3. L. Hildebrand, "Integrated Coastal Management: Lessons Learned and Challenges Ahead," Discussion Document for Managing Shared Water/Coastal Zone Canada 2002, International Conference, Hamilton, Ontario, Canada, June 2002.

4. These studies were initiated by Ecoplata (this is a multidisciplinary and inter-institutional Urguayan project on Integrated Coastal Management, which is financed by the Canadian International Development and Research Centre) to determine the feasibility of a project on the economic valuation of coastal and marine resources and to determine what experience was available in the country. These studies are compiled in D. Gorfinkiel (comp.), G. Bittencourt, P. Ceiter, S. Garibotto and G. Sención, *La Zona Costera del Uruguay y su Valoración Económica. Compilación de Investigaciones Económicas en las Costas del Uruguay*, available online: <http://www.ecoplata.org/estudios/Ecoplata_Compila-Invest-Econo-Costas-Uruguay.pdf>. A summary of these was presented at the conference "Encuentro Regional: Cooperación en el Espacio Costero," 28–30 September 2004, Montevideo, Uruguay.

towards a larger effort in the economic valuation of coastal and marine resources, and there is still much work to be done.

This article is organized as follows: in the first section we give a brief background of the need for economic valuation and describe the challenges to be faced in the context of integrated coastal management. In the second section we discuss the need for homogenous socio-economic information to help institutions with responsibilities for coastal areas to manage those areas. The third section provides an overview of the methodology used in generating the values obtained. A fourth section discusses the key results from the economic valuation of the coastal areas of Uruguay. Lastly, we examine the implications of these findings for coastal policy and make some final comments.

ECONOMIC VALUATION IN THE CONTEXT OF INTEGRATED COASTAL MANAGEMENT

The attempt to pursue the dual objectives of environmental protection and economic development creates big challenges for policy makers in the sphere of conservation and management of coastal resources. It means recognizing the many different interests of the various sectors involved in the use of these resources in the context of long-term development and prevailing socio-economic conditions, and also taking account of biological limitations and the equilibrium of the ecosystem.[5]

According to GESAMP,[6] Integrated Coastal Management (ICM) is "a process that unites government and the community, science and management, sectoral and public interests in preparing and implementing an integrated plan for the protection and development of coastal ecosystems and resources. The overall goal of ICM is to improve the quality of life of human communities who depend on coastal resources while maintaining the biological diversity and productivity of coastal ecosystems."

The problem in Uruguay is that people are damaging and over-exploiting the coastal ecosystems, and this means that in the future these resources will shrink, their productivity will be lower, or perhaps there will be nothing left at all. ICM is crucial to ensuring the continued productive flow of the net benefits of coastal ecosystems. Fish can be harvested, and wetlands, clean water, beaches and estuaries can be used so long as these

5. B. Cicin-Sain and R. W. Knecht, *Integrated Coastal and Ocean Management: Concepts and Practices* (Covelo: Island Press, 1998).

6. GESAMP, (IMO/FAO/UNESCO-IOC/WMO/WHO/IAEA/UN/UNEP Joint Group of Experts on the Scientific Aspects of Marine Environmental Protection), "The Contribution of Science to Coastal Zone Management," Rep. Stud. GESAMP, (61): Rome, 1996. 66 p.

activities do not damage the ecosystem or over-exploit the natural production levels of each ecosystem.

One way to encourage improvement in the management, protection and support for these coastal ecosystems is to place economic values on them and on their products and uses.[7] Society tends to value money and to understand costs and benefits in monetary terms, so the information we present here is an attempt to give an approximation of the economic values of coastal resources so that people will place more importance on the management and long-term protection of them. Hopefully this will lead to an improvement in the management of these resources and help justify the investment required to control the ways in which they are used.

The economic valuation of coastal resources involves assigning a measurable value, which is generally monetary, to a particular resource, product or activity. This covers more than just the valuation of ordinary goods and services. Although coastal resources are valued according to the price of the market goods they produce (where their value is the price determined by the market), this only reflects part of their real value since these resources include other values that are often more significant, on top of those already priced in the market.

There are more components in the coastal ecosystem than just those that can be measured in market terms.[8] These components can be used directly as products (fish, biodiversity, fauna and marine flora), or indirect benefits can be derived from their interactions, functions or attributes.[9] Besides this, people may also appreciate their mere existence even though they do not use them. Valuing coastal resources means assigning a value to all of their components, functions and attributes. These values will play an important role as we work to protect the future of the coastal environment.

The formulation of policies for coastal resources should be based on the objectives of sustainability, development and conservation. This means that conflicts between different possible alternative uses have to be resolved, and so, there is a need for clear criteria for making these decisions. In this context, if the objective is to satisfy the demands of economic growth and sustainable development at the same time and in an efficient way, the economic valuation of coastal resources should be prior to the formulation of any policy.

7. J. R. Clark, *Coastal Zone Management Handbook* (New York: Lewis Publishers, 1992).

8. R. Costanza, R. d'Arge, R. de Groot, S. Farber, M. Grasso, B. Hannon, K. Limburg, S. Naeem, R. V. O'Neill, J. Paruelo, R. G. Raskin, P. Sutton and M. van den Belt, "The Value of the World's Ecosystem Services and Natural Capital," *Nature* 387 (1997): 253–260.

9. R. S. De Groot, *Functions of Nature* (Amsterdam: Wolters-Noordhoff, 1992).

The aim of this article is to illustrate some of the market values of Uruguay's coastal resources, and to describe, albeit through only two cases, how the environmental economic valuation approach can help in judging what decisions are reasonable to take from an economic perspective.

INTEGRATED COASTAL MANAGEMENT AND THE NEED FOR HOMOGENEOUS INFORMATION

The integrated management of coastal areas involves understanding the coastal area through gathering socio-economic and biological information in order to make an integrated management plan.[10] As regards the socio-economic information, what is sought is to synthesize demographic, sociological and economic data to contribute to the integrated management decision-making process. Socio-economic information is not only needed because people are the primary actors in economic development and their activities have an impact on the health and quality of the natural coastal environment, but also because people will ultimately be a determining factor in any integrated management strategy that is implemented. We still know much less about our coasts than about other natural resources such as the agriculture or forestry sectors.

An understanding of the demands human beings make of their natural resources base (upon which the natural ecosystem also depends) allows the decision maker to identify who would benefit from different policies and also who would bear the social and economic costs. Generating this type of information is of fundamental importance if decision makers want to behave in a proactive way. This information helps them to define and evaluate options for sustainable economic growth employing strategies that promote economic and social equity and that preserve environmental goods and services.

An understanding of the changes taking place in the coastal economy is also essential to understand the changing nature of the social demands for this scarce but very sought after resource, and to predicting environmental changes that might be negative for the welfare of society. These activities are mainly reflected in the economic uses of the coast and the ocean.

The need for this information is clear. It will help the institutions with responsibility for coastal areas to manage those areas. It will also help civil

---

10. J. T. Kildow (University of Southern California), B. Baird (State of California), C. S. Colgan (University of Southern Maine), H. Kite-Powell (Woods Hole Oceanographic Institution), R. Weiher (NOAA, Department of Commerce), "Developing Better Economic Information about Coastal Resources as a Tool for Integrated Ocean and Coastal Management," available online: <http://noep.csum.edu>.

society organizations to adopt more solid and defensible positions. Today, certain sectors of civil society are asking for specific coastal areas to be protected, but there is not much information about what the economic consequences of implementing these schemes would be.

Even in situations where we do have economic information, it is not organized to answer specific questions about the ocean and the coast. The systematization of data series about these activities will provide information on trends, and this will make it easier to predict economic growth in specific sectors and the rate of consumption of natural resources, and thus make it possible to identify potential environmental problems.

The aim of generating and systematizing this type of information is to seek to answer the following questions: Where are we? Is the coast important? Why? Who does what and how? Do we need to change the situation? How can we harmonize the different uses of these areas? Also, if several economic activities compete for the same area, in this case the coast, decision makers will need to consider the possible economic and social trade-offs: How much employment will be generated or lost? How will taxes be affected? What will be the multiplier effect on the local economy?

THE CHARACTERISTICS OF URUGUAY'S COASTAL AREAS

The Rio de la Plata and Atlantic coastal area of Uruguay has 680 km of shoreline and comprises six departments.[11] Uruguay's coastal resources and environments constitute strategic assets for the development of the country. A good example of this is the government policy to attract private investment to coastal tourism, port infrastructure and maritime transport as a means of offering opportunities for diversifying and strengthening the Uruguayan economy.

The importance of Uruguay's coastal areas can be seen in the high percentage of the Gross Domestic Product (GDP) that is derived from the six coastal departments (approximately 70 percent). Nearly 69 percent of Uruguayans live within 50 km of the coast, and coastal areas support economic activity, provide spaces for recreation, are home to a wide variety of plants and wildlife, and are an important part of the culture and history of the country.

The presence of key industries or attractions in some coastal areas forms a centerpiece for an array of other economic opportunities. The coast is essential not only for a large number of economic activities such as fishing and maritime transportation, but it also enhances or attracts other activities

---

11. We use the term "departments" since Uruguay is divided into 19 administrative units or jurisdictions called *departamentos.*

Fig. 1.—Latin America and Uruguay

www.cmalliance.org/ im/maps/latin/

such as tourism and recreation, coastal construction, coastal real estate and mineral extraction.

Most of the main cities in the country, including five commercial ports, are located in this area, and 82 percent of the industrial sector is located in coastal areas. Tourism along the ocean coast is one of the most important industries in the country, and over the past decade it has grown considerably both as regards the number of visitors and in terms of income from tourism.

This illustrates how much the economy of Uruguay is linked in complex and diverse ways to the Rio de la Plata and the South Atlantic Ocean. The studies mentioned above were the first step towards gathering and analyzing socio-economic information to yield a better understanding of the coastal economy of Uruguay. Here we present some of the more important results on the economic valuation of these areas.

FIG. 2.—Map of Uruguay

METHODOLOGY OVERVIEW

In this article we give a summary of the results of different research papers that investigate the economic importance of Uruguay's coastal areas. In this section we present an overview of the different methodologies adopted in the studies. Two basic approaches were used: one approach operates at the macroeconomic level and the other operates at the microeconomic level and recognizes the need to take the total economic value of these resources into account.

First, it is important to define what we understand by "coast" and "coastal" in our study since the coastal economy and the ocean economy are not the same thing.[12] These two concepts are generally used as if they were synonymous but in fact they are not. The ocean sector is that part of the economy that depends on the ocean as an input for the production process or that takes place on or under the ocean. The coastal sector is that part of the economy that functions on or near the coast. In this article, we adopt a broad definition: the economic activities we include are those for which the ocean or the coast is an input (in the production function sense), and those for which proximity to the ocean is of economic significance. These activities have value added because of the ocean or their proximity to it. To estimate the economic impact of these activities, to compare them with other non-coastal activities and to measure the changes through time is a first step to understanding the contribution coastal and ocean areas make to the national economy.

Two basic steps in the research are data collection and impact analysis. A key part of the effort to estimate the economic value of the coast is to make estimates of the values of their goods and services that are traded in the market economy. These estimates should include the output of industries associated with the ocean and other measures of economic activity, including income generated and employment, etc. This information allows the coastal economy to be compared to other areas in the context of other economic activities.

The economic importance of coastal sectors can be shown in several ways such as their direct and indirect contributions to GDP, how many people are employed, how much these people earn in wages and salaries, and how much output these sectors generate. Input-output analysis extends the direct impact to capture so-called indirect and induced effects. Indirect effects are those involving the purchase of inputs by an industry to assist in its own operations. Induced effects are those that accumulate as incomes are earned in an industry and are spent and re-spent throughout the economy. Because of lack of data, only direct and indirect impacts were modeled.

The ocean and coastal sector is defined as any industry or industrial sector that derives its resources directly from the ocean and coast and/or uses the ocean as a medium of operation, and/or provides its products for use in the ocean environment.[13] This economic sector also includes

---

12. C. S. Colgan, "The Changing Ocean and Coastal Economy of the United States: A Briefing Paper for Governors," University of Southern Maine, National Ocean Economics Project, Prepared for National Governors Association, March 25, 2004, available online: <http://noep.csumb.edu/Download/govns_brief.pdf>. See also M. I. Luger, "The Economic Value of the Coastal Zone," *Journal of Environmental Systems* 21, 4 (1991–92): 279–301.

13. Mandale Consulting, Canmac Economics Ltd., and North American Policy Group, "Estimating the Economic Value of Coastal and Ocean Resources: The Case of Nova Scotia," (Prepared for the Oceans Institute of Canada and the Atlantic Coastal Zone Information Steering Committee, Halifax, Canada, 1998).

government agencies that have mandates and responsibilities, wholly or partly, for activities related to the ocean or to ocean and coastal resources. The impact of this sector is measured in relation to the total economy.

Estimating the value of the ocean sector in Uruguay will contribute to the development of coastal and ocean policy and to the management of coastal and ocean resources. This is the first study to attempt this estimation in Uruguay. We have employed a methodology that was first developed and used in a study in Nova Scotia, Canada,[14] and then applied to the Canadian provinces of New Brunswick[15] and Newfoundland and Labrador.[16] The coast-related sectors that were identified as relevant to the valuation of coastal resources are:

1. Traditional fishing

2. Fish processing

3. Coastal tourism

4. Coastal mineral extraction

5. Marine transportation

6. Port activities

7. Shipbuilding and boat building

8. Coast-related commercial activities

9. Coast-related services

10. Government agencies with coastal responsibility

It is worth mentioning that activities 1 to 4 are sensitive to the deterioration of coastal resources, and 5 and 6 are possible sources of pollution.

Although the aim of this study was to include as many relevant activities as possible, lack of data for some activities precluded their use in the analyses. For this reason, the estimates of economic impact should be considered as conservative. The analyses of the direct and indirect impact of activities such as 4, 7, and 10 could not be included due to lack of information.

14. See *id.*

15. See Mandale Consulting, Canmac Economics and P.Y. Chiasson & Associates, "The Economic Value of Marine Related Resources in New Brunswick," (Prepared for the New Brunswick Department of Fisheries and Aquaculture and Fisheries and Oceans Canada, Fredericton, 2000).

16. See "Estimating the Value of the Marine, Coastal and Ocean Resources of Newfoundland and Labrador," prepared by Economics and Statistics Branch, Department of Finance for Fisheries and Oceans Canada—Science, Oceans and Environment Branch and the Department of Fisheries and Aquaculture, Canada, 2002, available online: <http://www.economics.gov.nf.ca/oceans.asp>.

Coastal areas are not only economic resources but also ecological systems.[17] Combining economics and environment involves economic and management challenges because the value of this area goes far beyond what is measured in market terms. For example, coastal ecosystems are valuable in that they perform ecological functions that should be taken into account, such as the fact that mangroves trap sediment that would otherwise remain suspended and contribute to low water quality, or the fact that the aesthetic value of coastal systems contributes to the growth of tourism. By internalizing the worth of these non-marketable functions we can make better estimations of the economic value of environmentally derived goods and services, and we can more correctly evaluate options for development that may protect or destroy parts of the environment. At present, research into these questions has not gone very far: it includes the identification of appropriate tools for the economic valuation of non-market environmental services and functions, and the application of these tools in two case studies. In Uruguay there is still a lot to do in this area.

SUMMARY OF KEY FINDINGS

1. The coast is not just one single place.

Socio-economic information suggests that people's relationships with different parts of the coastal land are highly varied. There are at least three different regions. To the west of the capital city of Montevideo the prevailing activities are cattle raising and intensive agriculture, mainly the highly technological production of dairy products. To the east of Montevideo there is some agriculture, mostly fruit farming and horticulture, and some cattle raising and forestation, but the main activity is tourism, and this is mostly focused along the Atlantic coast. And there is Montevideo itself, a city port where more than half the total population of Uruguay lives and where the majority of the infrastructure and services of the country are located.[18]

17. G. C. Daily, ed., *Nature's Services: Societal Dependence on Natural Ecosystems* (Washington, D.C.: Island Press, 1997).

18. Ecoplata, "Recursos Naturales y Actividades Económicas en la Zona Costera del Río de la Plata," published under the auspices of the Programa de Apoyo a la Gestión Integrada de la Zona Costera (Ecoplata), Report: D. Gorfinkiel and S. Garibotto; maps by V. Fernández, C. Peña and Y. Resnichenko. 2002.

2.   There is considerable pressure from population growth in the coastal areas.

For the last 30 years around 70 percent of the population of Uruguay has been located in coastal regions. From 1985 to 1996, the rate of growth of the population living in these areas grew more than the average rate of growth in the country as a whole. In the eastern part of the coast, the population has doubled over a 30-year period.[19]

Inland migratory flows towards the coast are centered on the city of Montevideo and the surrounding area. This region absorbs 57.8 percent of the people who come from the rest of the country. Figure 3 shows the rate of immigration into the six coastal departments. From 1991 to 1996, two regions, Maldonado and Canelones, had high immigration rates (almost 140 percent and 133 percent respectively). In the former, this immigration was due to the growth of the tourist industry, and in the latter to the fact that people began to move from the urban area of Montevideo to more suburban areas in search of less congestion and better environmental conditions, while still remaining within commuting distance of the capital city.

This information shows what was happening ten or more years ago. Population projections for 2005 (Table 1) were used, which show that by 2005 the coastal population area would have grown 14 percent according to a linear projection and 16 percent using an exponential projection. The numbers for the urban coastal areas are higher: 19 percent by the linear projection and 24 percent by the exponential one.

Therefore we can conclude that the pressure of population growth in coastal regions is due to the increasing size of the population in the same set areas on the coast, and from a "move to the coast."

3.   A substantial proportion of the Gross National Product (GNP) depends on the coastal areas.

This is one of the findings of a study done as a pilot project whose principal aim was to estimate how important the coastal- and ocean-related economic sectors are to the Uruguayan economy.[20] Coastal areas are an essential part

19. D. Gorfinkiel (Comp.), G. Bittencourt, P. Ceiter, S. Garibotto and G. Sención, *La Zona Costera del Uruguay y su Valoración Económica. Compilación de Investigaciones Económicas en las Costas del Uruguay,* available online: <http://www.ecoplata.org/estudios/Ecoplata_Compila-Invest-Econo-Costas-Uruguay.pdf>. A summary of these was presented at the conference "Encuentro Regional: Cooperación en el Espacio Costero," 28–30 September 2004, Montevideo, Uruguay.

20. G. Bittencourt, D. Gorfinkiel and S. Gustavo, "Avances en la Valoración de los Recursos Costeros," Ecoplata: Integrated Coastal Zone Management Project (University of Uruguay, Dalhousie University, IDRC, and Environmental Ministry of Uruguay, November 2003).

Fig. 3.—Domestic Immigration Rate (1991–1996)

Domestic Immigration Rate (1991 - 1996)

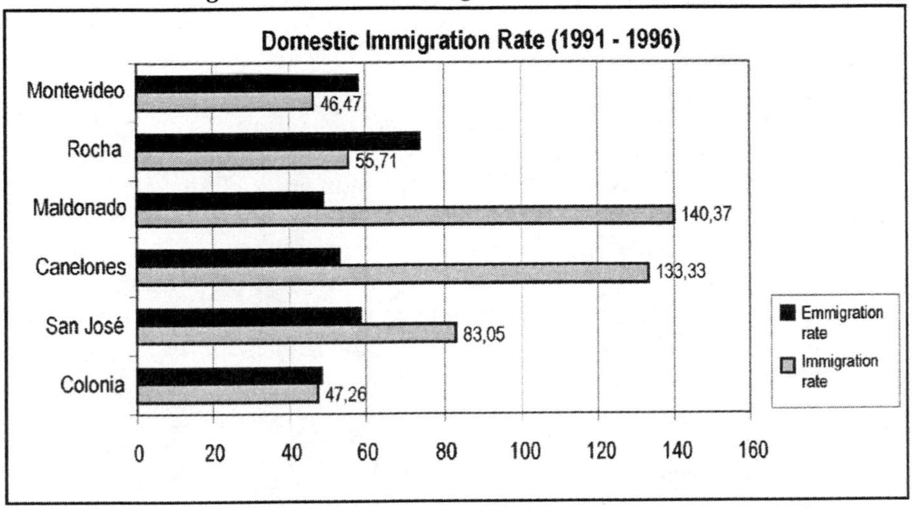

Source: Ecoplata 2004 (n. 2 above).

Table 1.—Population Projections in Coastal Departments and Coastal Areas

Projections 2005–Coastal Departments

	Coast %	Montevideo %	Rest of the country %	Total %
Linear	13.88	2.22	4.33	6.00
Exponential	15.95	2.27	4.51	6.63

Projection 2005–Urban Coastal areas

	Coast %	Montevideo %	Rest of the country %	Total %
Linear	19.25	1.95	10.92	8.93
Exponential	23.47	1.98	12.17	10.39

Source: Ecoplata 2004, n. 2 above.

of that economy. The coastal departments account for 67 percent of the total value added, which means that more than two-thirds of the country's economic activity and income generation has a direct or indirect link to coastal areas.

Table 2 shows that most of the economic activity included in the coastal sectors definition are located in the coastal departments. The whole fishing extraction sector and 72 percent of fish processing occurs in that area, 82 percent of port activity is concentrated in the coastal area, and more than three-quarters of the activity of the tourist industry takes place on the Rio de la Plata and South Atlantic Ocean coasts.

At the regional level, most of the economic activity included in the sectors mentioned above takes place in the coastal departments. The value added generated by these activities in these departments amounts to 44 percent of total coastal GDP, which shows how important these activities are in the economic life of the coastal region.

Table 3 shows how some of these coastal activities impact on the coastal sector itself. Data were only available for the activities included in Table 3. It can be seen that marine transportation plays an important role in the coastal sector: it outranks the fishing industry even though it employs fewer people than fishing does. This may suggest that there are competitive pressures on the transportation industry and improved technologies, and these are tending to bring down the demand for labor even when the overall economic importance of the industry is growing.

4. The Fishing Industry

The overall performance of traditional and industrial fishing in Uruguay has improved in terms of volume, and economic performance has grown strongly. Over the period 1990–2001, the total catch ranged from 90,000 metric tons in 1990 to 104,272 tons in 2001. Over the same period, export values increased from just under US$60 million in 1975 to US$120 million in 2000—an increase of 100 percent.

However, the growth that has characterized this sector in recent decades is jeopardized in the long term because of a biomass decline in some species, including hake: the catch of this fish fell from 61 percent in 1991 to 26 percent in 2001.

Table 2.—Coastal Departments—Value Added by Economic Sectors, 1998. (Millions US dollars)

	Montevideo	Canelones	Colonia	Maldonado	San José	Rocha	Total Coastal Departments	Total Uruguay	Coastal Departments/Total %
Coastal Sectors									
Fish Extraction	36.1	0.0	0.0	0.2	0.0	8.7	44.9	44.9	100.0
Fishing Industry	32.4	0.0	0.0	0.0	0.0	0.0	32.5	45.3	71.6
Restaurants and Hotels	357.9	58.2	27.2	60.7	15.1	14.2	533.4	710.1	75.1
Transport and storage	732.7	72.3	29.9	24.2	14.5	15.3	888.8	1,083.3	82.0
Real Estate	2,826.7	121.2	59.0	148.8	37.0	44.1	3,236.8	3,594.1	90.1
Other Services	1,470.3	198.0	73.4	66.3	62.5	0.0	1,870.5	2,459.1	76.1
Subtotal	5,456.1	449.6	189.5	300.2	129.1	82.3	6,606.8	7,936.9	83.2
Non-Coastal Sectors									
Oil refinery	504.7	0.0	0.0	0.0	0.0	0.0	504.7	504.7	100.0
Other primaries	45.6	203.0	89.4	40.8	107.9	71.3	558.0	1,598.8	34.9
Other industries	2,509.2	378.8	205.3	50.6	99.2	35.0	3,278.1	3,761.4	87.2
Construction	483.5	141.2	40.1	275.6	26.9	54.0	1,021.3	1,323.1	77.2
Other Services	2,271.3	354.0	156.7	163.8	92.8	90.0	3,128.6	4,328.5	72.3
Government & Import rights								3,106.8	
Total Departmemts	11,270	1,527	681	831	456	333	15,098	22,560	66.9
Departments/Uruguay %	50.0	6.8	3.0	3.7	2.0	1.5	66.9	100.0	

Source: Bittencourt et al. (n. 20 above).

Table 3.—Key Variables For Key Coastal Activities

Economic Activity	Gross Output %	Gross Value Added %	Salaries %	Employment %	Intermediate Consumption %
Fishing Industry	28	35	49	72	26
Ship and Boat Building	5	8	12	9	4
Marine Transportation	66	57	39	19	70
Total Coastal Economic Activities	100	100	100	100	100

Source: Ecoplata 2004, n. 2 above.

5.   Ports and Harbors

According to a 1998 study,[21] the port of Montevideo contributed to the Uruguayan economy through the handling of 5 million tons of commodities. Marine commerce reached a value of US$2.9 billion, which amounts to an average value of US$580 per ton.

It is worth commenting on what the data collected show: 98 percent of wood production is exported by marine transportation, and this amounts to 16.4 percent of the total cargo handled by the port of Montevideo. Besides this, 99 percent of minerals and fertilizers are exported by sea, which accounts for 34 percent of total cargo movement. Almost two decades ago the Uruguayan government decided to develop the forestry industry so land was sold to forestry developers, and Montevideo is the main port for exporting these products. It is also important to note that, because of its strategically advantageous location, Uruguay has enormous potential as a possible distribution center for the whole Mercosur (Common Market of the Southern Cone) region.

6.   Tourism

The natural characteristics of the Uruguayan coast provide a strong basis for intense tourist activities. The tourist industry has been growing steadily throughout the last decade, and tourism stands alongside fishing and port activity as one of the most important industries in the coastal area. Values

21. Unidad de Transporte–Comisión Económica Para América Latina—Naciones Unidas, "Perfil Marítimo de América Latina," Chile, 1998, available online: <http://www.eclac.cl/transporte/perfil/index.htm>.

Table 4.—Income, Visitors and Expenditure from Tourism

Year	Income USD millions	Number of Visitors	Expenditures USD millions
1989	227.8	1,240,431	183.6
1990	238.2	1,167,040	204.1
1991	332.5	1,509,962	220.2
1992	381.3	1,801,672	211.6
1993	446.8	2,002,541	223.1
1994	632.2	2,175,457	290.6
1995	611.0	2,176,930	280.7
1996	716.8	2,258,616	317.4
1997	759.3	2,462,532	308.3
1998	694.8	2,323,993	299.0
1999	652.8	2,273,164	287.2
2000	651.8	2,235,887	291.5

Source: Ecoplata 2004, n. 2 above.

Table 5.—Foreign Income Generated by Tourism. Millions US Dollars, 1998–2000

	Total	Coastal Tourism	Total Coastal Tourism*/Total Tourism %	Coastal tourism where recreation was explicit reason	Coastal Tourism where recreation was explicit/Total Tourism %
1998	694.8	638.7	91.9	448.9	64.6
1999	652.8	592.7	90.8	405.6	62.1
2000	651.8	583.4	89.5	404.3	62.0

* Refers not only to those that visit the country for recreation but also because of work or to see family members, etc.
Source: Ecoplata 2004 (n. 2 above).

for annual sales (output) show that this industry has undergone considerable growth as regards the number of visitors, visitor expenditures and income generated.

The overall economic performance of the tourist industry shows considerable growth over the period 1990–2000. Tourism as a percentage of exports grew from 14.2 percent in 1989 to 24.3 percent in 1998, when it accounted for 25 percent of foreign earnings.

In this study, the approach we used to measure the economic value of the coast for tourism in Uruguay was conservative. A coast-related tourist was defined as that subset of the total tourist population for which accessibility of the coast and its facilities for recreation was a significant component of the decision to visit the Uruguayan coast. Table 5 shows the percentages of income generation derived from coast-related tourism to the total tourist sector. Of the total income generated by tourism, 62 percent was directly linked to the South Atlantic Ocean and the Rio de la Plata coasts.

**Table 6.—Direct and Indirect Effects of Coastal Economic Activities 1998
(Millions US Dollars)**

	Direct Net Value Added	Indirect Net Value Added	Total Net Value Added	Direct GDP	Indirect GDP	Total GDP
Fish and sea products	90	33	123	135	50	185
Restaurants and hotels	275	123	398	531	238	769
Transport	250	65	315	423	110	533
Property	373	47	420	374	48	422
Other services	300	65	365	271	58	329
Total coast related activities	1,288	334	1,622	1,734	504	2,238
% Coast related activities /Total Uruguay	5.97%		7.52%	8.04%		10.38%

Source: Bittencourt et al., n. 20 above.

7.   Direct and Indirect Effects of the Coastal Sector

Operating at a national and regional level (the macro level), an input-output model for Uruguay was modified to show the direct and indirect impact of the coastal and marine sectors on Uruguay's economy and income.[22] Initial results estimating the direct and indirect impact, calculated by means of multipliers built into the input-output model, showed that coastal and ocean sectors accounted for a direct impact amounting to 8.4 percent of GDP. When indirect impact was included, this rose to 10.7 percent of GDP (Table 6). This is comparable to levels in more developed countries (Table 7). As Table 6 shows, the largest contributor to total coastal GDP was the tourist industry (34 percent), followed by marine transportation (24 percent) and coastal real estate (19 percent).

It can be seen in Table 7 that the weight in the Uruguayan economy of coastal economic activities is similar to the weight estimated for Australia in 1994, and higher than that in the United Kingdom and Canadian economies. When compared to the coastal economies of the different Canadian provinces, where economic and technological development levels and also population density are higher, the information available shows that the impact on the Uruguayan economy is slightly less than the impact on the Nova Scotia and Prince Edward Island economies,[23] higher than the

22. This model was produced in 1990 for projecting electric power demand, and modified in 1999 to project water demand. A number of adjustments were made to the 1999 model to achieve the aims of this small coastal project. It is recognized that a more sophisticated application of input output modeling is needed.

23. Canmac Economics Ltd., Dalhousie University, Enterprise Management Consultants, ACZISC, "The Value of the Ocean Sector to the Economy of Prince Edward Island," Prepared for the PEI Departments of Fisheries, Aquaculture and

Table 7.—Coastal Sector Values for Some Countries

Country or Province	Year	Estimation (% of the total economy)
Uruguay	1998	8.0 (Direct GDP) 10.4 (Direct and Indirect GDP)
United Kingdom	1994–95	
Australia	1994	8.0 (GDP)
Canada	1988	1.6 (GDP)
	1996	1.4 (GDP)
Nova Scotia (Canada)	1994	9.6 (Direct GDP) 17.5 (Total GDP)
New Brunswick (Canada)	1995–1997	4.3 (Direct GDP) 7.2 (Total GDP)
Newfoundland and Labrador (Canada)	1997–1999	14.1 (Direct GDP) 26.5 (Total GDP)
Prince Edward Island (Canada)	1997–1999	10 (Direct GDP) 17.1 (Total GDP)

Sources: Bittencourt et al., n. 20 above; Mandale et al. (1998), n. 13 above; Mandale et al. (2000), n. 15 above; D. Pugh and L. Skinner, "An Analysis of Marine-Related Activities in the UK Economy and Supporting Science and Technology," Inter-Agency Committee on Marine Science and Technology (IACMST) Information Document No. 5, (December 1996); Australian Marine Industries and Science Council (1997) Marine Industry Development Strategy, Australian Development of Industry, Science and Tourism; Newfoundland and Labrador Department of Finance (2002), n. 16 above.

impact in New Brunswick, but lower than the impact on the economy of Newfoundland and Labrador.

When the indirect economic effects are included, the numbers are higher for the Canadian provinces than for the Uruguayan coastal economy. This may be due to the more intensive impact these coastal activities have on the rest of the provincial economies or to the fact that induced effects have an important weight in those cases, an effect that was not possible to estimate for Uruguay because of lack of data. Another explanation might be that the fishing industry generates a greater impact in the rest of the economy than the tourist sector, which is mainly based on services.

Environment; Development and Technology; and Tourism, and Fisheries and Oceans Canada, Environment Canada and the Atlantic Canada Opportunities Agency, Charlottetown, 2002.

8.   The Economic Value of Non-Market Goods and Services

Since ecosystem services are not totally captured in commercial markets they are often given too little attention in policy decision. To evaluate the options for coastal management, the decision maker needs to be provided with complete information on the potential impact of these decisions. One of the main reasons for valuing coastal resources is that once it is possible to quantify the costs involved and the benefits derived from them, a benefit-cost analysis of the policy being proposed to manage or protect the resource can be done. The trade-off between protecting and managing coastal resources as against the alternative of not managing them and allowing them to be destroyed or to deteriorate can also be evaluated using benefit-cost analysis.

A number of methods are available for making this kind of economic valuation, and each has its advantages and disadvantages.[24] It is often difficult to apply these methods, partly because they tend to be complex in themselves, and partly because they need quite detailed information on how people are affected by changes in nature. These techniques are aimed at arriving at what is called the total economic value, which consists of use and non-use values. Use value measures the consumption value (direct use values) of tangible natural resources such as fish, timber, and also of non-consumption (indirect use values), the ecological and recreational uses of natural resources such as diving, swimming, and boating. Non-use values may be derived even if individuals do not use the resource directly. Existence value, also known as preservation value, means the value to a person of knowing that a resource that he or she never intends to consume is protected. Existence value is also frequently defined as option value (the value of natural resources for future generations). Option value is the willingness to pay (WTP) for the option of using/consuming the resource, including undiscovered qualities such as the potential medicinal use of a plant or marine organism in the future. Valuation efforts should attempt to aggregate both the use and non-use values of natural resource systems when assessing total economic value.

---

24. We do not present the different valuation methods and techniques for conducting environmental economic valuation here. Some of the classics on this subject are E. Barbier, M. Acreman and D. Knowler, "Valoración Económica de los Humedales: Guía para Decisores y Planificadores," available online: <http://www.ramsar.org/lib_val_s_intro.htm>. R. S. De Groot, n. 9 above; S. Georgiou, D. Whittington, D. Pearce and D. Moran, *Economic Values and the Environment in the Developing World* (U.K.: Edward Elgar Publishing Limited, 1997); N. Hanley, J. F. Shogren and B. White, *Environmental Economics in Theory and Practice* (Oxford, U.K.: Oxford University Press, 1997).

Although Uruguay is a long way from including this type of economic valuation of goods, functions and services in the decision-making process, the latest studies done in the context of the economic valuation of the coastal zone have begun to take account of the importance of the environment in the economy. These studies constitute efforts towards valuing all ecosystem components, incorporating non-market values.

Working at ecosystem levels, a simplified methodology was applied to value the Santa Lucía wetlands that are to the west of Montevideo. The methodology used to obtain a first estimation of the economic value of the Santa Lucía wetlands was based on different wetland valuation studies. The idea was to present a range of values (a minimum, a mean and a maximum value)[25] for this area taking the results of different studies and analyzing the values that were found for different ecosystem functions, such as water quality, habitat protection, fishing, and hunting. This methodology was used to obtain an indication of the order of magnitude of the total economic value of the wetland and to help determine whether its value was significant, i.e., when estimates have a high monetary value and deserve further research with a new study. This study suggested a mean value for environmental services at US$800 per hectare per year, or US$16 million per year for the whole Santa Lucía area.

The other study done to value the coastal ecosystem focused on the valuation of a change in the environmental quality of a beach located in Punta del Este, Maldonado, the main tourist resort in Uruguay. After a high-speed road was built, difficulties with the drainage of water from inland to the ocean began to occur, and these were reflected in problems such as the fact that the sand was always wet. When a beach loses its high environmental quality due to the impact of development projects, many people may be affected in one way or another: the people who want to go to that beach, the beach vendors and the owners of the restaurants close to that beach, the employees and the suppliers of those stores, the suppliers own employees and suppliers, and the city government that obtains revenues from concessions at the beach.

25. R. F. Kazmierczak, Jr., "Economic Linkages Between Coastal Wetlands and Water Quality: A Review of Value Estimates Reported in the Published Literature," Staff Paper 2001–02, Department of Agricultural Economics and Agribusiness, Louisiana State University, Baton Rouge, May 2001; "Economic Linkages Between Coastal Wetlands and Hunting and Fishing: A Review of Value Estimates Reported in the Published Literature," Staff Paper 2001–03, Department of Agricultural Economics and Agribusiness, Louisiana State University, Baton Rouge, May 2001; "Economic Linkages Between Coastal Wetlands and Habitat/Species Protection: A Review of Value Estimates Reported in the Published Literature," Staff Paper 2001-04, Department of Agricultural Economics and Agribusiness, Louisiana State University, Baton Rouge, May 2001.

Although a complete assessment of the economic impact of a negative environmental change in the quality of the beach needs to take all of these different effects into consideration, the objective of the study was to find out how willing beach visitors were to pay for the sand to be dry. One approach, known as contingent valuation, involved interviewing beach users and finding out what their maximum willingness to pay would be, for example, by asking them if they would be willing to pay so that the city government could implement measures to improve the quality of the sand. Non-parametric methods were employed,[26] and the result was that people were willing to make a one-off payment of an average of US$96. The study showed that people living in the area and who would in fact benefit from a cleaner beach accepted an increase in their property tax.[27]

IMPLICATIONS FOR COASTAL POLICY

The increase in tourism, fishery activities and marine traffic in recent decades, and also the growth of housing areas and industrial activities, and the plans to build infrastructure in the basin area, are all factors that have and will have a significant impact on the coastal areas of the Rio de la Plata and South Atlantic Ocean. These findings suggest a number of important implications for State policy in several different areas, including coastal resource management, transportation, land use planning, economic development, and State economic data collection and management.

For Coastal Resource Management and Land Use Planning

Population growth is an issue in all coastal areas in Uruguay. Population growth pressures are more likely to occur in the departments on the coast and close to the immediate shoreline. Population growth on the coasts will also be caused by people who come to the coast for short periods of time: tourists and visitors seeking recreation who cause the population of coastal areas to double or triple in the summer. Economic growth in coastal areas is pushing up the demand for land to be converted from open space or wildlife habitat to residential and commercial uses. This suggests that

26. Non-parametric methods were applied because, due to the lack of data, it was not possible to use the econometric methods that underlie the contingent valuation technique.

27. These people are the ones who benefit from tourism: owners of the stores and restaurants, people who rent their houses to tourists or they mostly use the beach.

problems that have to do with non-point source pollution and storm water runoff will increase.

For Transportation

Coastal departments and communities must plan for and build transportation infrastructure to serve a much larger population than that currently living in the coastal areas, while still maintaining the character of the environment. Investments in marine transportation (facilities for the transportation of freight and passengers) are providing increasingly valuable services to the economy as a whole, and particularly to the economies of coastal departments. Marine transportation investment will become more and more critical to the competitiveness of departmental economies, and also to the competitiveness of the national economy, as port facilities come to play a greater role in moving the increasing volume of imports and exports. This suggests a possible conflict between uses for tourism on the one hand and port activities on the other.

For Economic Development and Economic Data and Information

Changes in the coastal economy are creating major economic development challenges. Tourism and recreation are growing robustly, and coastal departments will be competing with one another for that market. The transition in fishing communities away from dependence on declining fisheries will be an issue in the future. Aquaculture may partially replace the employment and economic activity that are linked to traditional fisheries, and recently there has been some development in aquaculture.

Knowledge of the coastal economy is very imprecise because little has been invested in developing the needed data, especially when compared to the investment made in understanding other natural resource industries. Coastal departments need to work closely with the national government to provide the basic data to measure the coastal and ocean economies.

FINAL COMMENTS

The different studies of the economic value of the coastal areas of Uruguay were the first step to gathering and analyzing coastal socio-economic information so as to better understand the country's coastal economy. The studies have made a big contribution to estimating the value of coastal areas. First, they offer decision makers homogeneous information about the social and economic importance coastal areas have for the welfare of society and its economic development. Secondly, this information gives decision makers a tool for evaluating different options for sustainable coastal development through strategies promoting policy coordination around the objectives of economic growth and the preservation of the coastal area. And thirdly, they provide information that makes it possible to compare the costs and benefits of different development options and so promote the rational use and the sustainable management of coastal resources.

The general conclusion is that coastal areas are important for the Uruguayan economy. Not only are they where numerous and varied activities take place and where more than half of the population lives, but also they are where some of the more important economic sectors in the domestic economy such as tourism and port activities are located. Both of these activities have a great potential for growth, but they are in conflict since port activities may have a negative impact on the tourist industry.

This study has used economic assessment techniques taken from Canadian studies to estimate the importance of the ocean sector in the Uruguayan economy. However, data to achieve a more realistic assessment of the value of the coastal sector were lacking. This means that it will be necessary to refine data collection to include activities that are currently left out because of difficulties in obtaining data.

The value of coastal and ocean environments far exceeds what is measured in economic or market terms. But these studies only took account of products derived from, or uses of, coast-related environments that could be exchanged for money, and not all activities could be measured. Therefore, further studies ought to acknowledge the important 'non-market' values of natural functions of coasts and oceans, such as their contribution to the hydrological cycle or the aesthetics of coastal scenery, so as to take the principles of environmental economics into account.

Any future work should bear in mind the analysis of the environmental and economic costs of development, such as those related to the exhaustion of resources, pollution, and the deterioration of the coastal and marine environment. An integrated coastal management strategy should seek equilibrium between the environmental and the economic aspects of using these resources. Reaching equilibrium among the social, economic, and environmental aspects requires an integrated effort and perspective from the various public and private actors involved in the use of coastal resources so that a sustainable development path can be achieved.

Environment and Coastal Management

Marine Invasive Species in North America: Impacts, Pathways and Management

Lesley A. MacDougall, Robin McCall, Kenneth A. Douglas,
Trisha A. Cheney, Melanie Oetelaar, Kevin Squires, Citlalli V.
Alvarez Saules, Hussein Alidina, Esther Nagtegaal-Cunningham,
Sean C. Weseloh McKeane, Jeffrey Joseph Y. Araula,
Nasiruddin Md. Humayun, Shaun Lawson, Nancy C. Chiasson,
Gloria C. Diaz, Talia A. Choy, Kofi E. Ankamah, Boaz O.
Ohowa, Allen T. Toribio, Juan J. del Toro
*Marine Affairs Program Students 2003–2004, Dalhousie University,
Halifax, Canada*

Robert O. Fournier and Christopher T. Taggart
Oceanography Department and *Marine Affairs Program, Dalhousie
University, Halifax, Canada*

INTRODUCTION

Species invasions into marine habitats, including range expansions and propagation in non-native ecosystems, occur naturally and as a result of human activities and are documented for five continents.[1] The introduction of invasive species is considered a major threat to marine and coastal environments as the rapid reproduction and competitive advantage of invasives allows them to dominate local ecosystems to the detriment of native species, thereby resulting in environmental alterations, human health impacts and economic losses worldwide.[2] Preventative measures, along with

* Our sincere thanks to two anonymous reviewers for providing insightful comments that have greatly improved this article.

1. N. Bax, A. Williamson, M. Aguero, E. Gonzales, and W. Geeves, "Marine Invasive Alien Species: A Threat to Global Biodiversity," *Marine Policy* 27, 4 (2003): 313–323.

2. M. L. Reaka-Kudla, D. E. Wilson and E. D. Wilson, eds., *Biodiversity II: Understanding and Protecting our Biological Resources* (Washington: Joseph Henry Press, 1997); C. A. De Fontaubert, D. R. Downes and T. S. Agardy, *Biodiversity in the Seas: Implementing the Convention on Biological Diversity in Marine and Coastal Habitats*

Ocean Yearbook 20: 435–469.

management and control methods, have been developed using science and technology[3] where efficacy should be balanced against potential impact on native species and damage to local ecosystems.[4]

Contemporary international attention is primarily focused on the shipping industry due to the economic importance and extent of world shipping and the number of species that can be and are being transported via ballast water, tank sediments and hull fouling. Marine invasive species are also transported along other vectors, including aquaculture, canals, aquarium trade, recreational boating, hydrocarbon exploration and transportation activities and floating debris.[5] In general, these latter vectors receive less attention than shipping with the consequence that their contribution to the invasive species problem is not as well-known or recognized. Regulations and management initiatives reflect this claim, i.e., the development of marine transport treatment technologies, standards and evaluation and risk assessment procedures to control invasives is greatly advanced relative to that for the less prevalent vectors.[6]

A recent draft framework released in Canada, *Addressing the Threat of Invasive Alien Species: A Strategy for Canada*,[7] claims to seek the incorporation of principles related to a coordinated effort, setting priorities, assessing risk, and including environmental, social and economic considerations. The draft framework, while striving for breadth and inclusiveness, outlines the need for scientific information in shaping management decisions while the

(Cambridge: IUCN, 1996); D. Beach, *Coastal Sprawl: The Effects of Urban Design on Aquatic Ecosystems in the United States* (Arlington: Pew Oceans Commission, 2002); Global Ballast Water Management, 2000, "The Problem," available online: <http://globallast.imo.org/index.asp?page=problem.htm>.

3. National Invasive Species Council (NISC), 2001. Management Plan, Meeting the Invasive Species Challenge, available online: <http://www.invasivespecies.gov/council/nmp.shtml>.

4. M. B. Thomas and A. J. Willis, "Biocontrol—Risky But Necessary?," *Trends in Ecology and Evolution* 13, 8 (1998): 325–329; K. D. Lafferty and A. M. Kuris, "Biological Control of Marine Pests," *Ecology* 77, 7 (1996): 1989–2000.

5. J. T. Carlton, "Dispersal of Living Organisms into Aquatic Ecosystems as Mediated by Aquaculture and Fishing Activities," in A. Rosenfield and R. Mann eds., *Dispersal of Living Organisms into Aquatic Ecosystems* (Maryland Sea Grant College, University of Maryland, College Park, 1992): 13–46; D. Reid and M. Orlova, "Geological and Evolutionary Underpinnings for the Success of Ponto-Caspian Species Invasions in the Baltic Sea and North American Great Lakes," *Canadian Journal of Fisheries and Aquatic Sciences* 59 (2002): 1144–1158; D. K. A. Barnes, "Invasions by Marine Life on Plastic Debris," *Nature* 416 (2002): 808–809; J. T. Carlton, *Introduced Species in U.S. Coastal Waters: Environmental Impacts and Management Priorities* (Arlington: Pew Oceans Commission, 2001).

6. Barnes, n. 5 above, at 808–809.

7. Environment Canada, Biodiversity Convention Office, 2004. Draft: *Addressing the Threat of Invasive Alien Species: A Strategy for Canada*. Available online: <http://www.bco.ec.gc.ca/en/activities/addressing.cfm>.

underlying data and evidence, particularly for marine invasive species, remains demonstrably inadequate. For example, while known invasive vascular plants, birds, insects, mammals, reptiles, amphibians, and freshwater fish are enumerated within the draft, marine invasives appear only in reference to "several molluscs" and with no distinction drawn between marine and freshwater species. Likewise, a discussion of economic threats includes detailed examples from the forestry and agriculture sectors, but warrants only two sentences addressing marine threats: the European green crab (*Carcinas maenas*) and the alga *Codium fragile*.

Knowledge of land-based species invasions and their potential impacts is typically more advanced than marine-based knowledge, perhaps in part because of the relative ease of studying land-based activities. This article, compiled prior to the release of *Addressing the Threat of Invasive Alien Species,*[8] concentrates on examples from the marine environment with an emphasis on Canada and the United States, except where examples from elsewhere provide additional comparative insights.

For the scope of this article, we define "exotic" species as those found outside of their normal range and "invasive" species as those that establish themselves and have a measurable impact once established. We define "established" species as organisms that are consistently reported to occur outside of their normal range, consequently they are considered to be noteworthy. We assume that once established, "invasive" organisms have an actual or potential effect (positive or negative) on any or all of native organisms, habitats, and encompassing environments.

We describe the potential ecological impacts of invasives and include a discussion of the importance of shipping as a force in the world's economy and as a pathway for invasives. In recognition of the disparate effort that has been directed at shipping in general, we also illustrate the diversity of vectors and potential risks associated with poorly monitored pathways. A discussion of the economic impacts of invasive species follows, illustrating that while some general information exists on the cost of aquatic invasions, those estimates are usually limited to direct damage or control expense and do not include indirect effects such as loss of biodiversity or compromised ecosystem services.[9] In spite of the limitations, managers are expected to make decisions regarding the control of invasives. Thus, we highlight some of the international and national policy tools that provide guidance to decision makers. Management actions for assessment and control of pathways and invasives are described and we address risk assessment

8. *Id.*

9. D. Pimentel, R. Zuniga and D. Morrison, "Update on the environmental and economic costs associated with alien-invader species in the United States," *Ecological Economics* 52 (2005): 273–288.

methodologies that help set priorities. Contemporary initiatives for international collaboration and regional partnerships are explored and in the end we submit that the effective employment of the various tools and methods reviewed can provide the support necessary for managers to make informed decisions in addressing aquatic invasive concerns without full scientific certainty.

ECOLOGICAL CONCERNS

A growing number of exotic aquatic species are being introduced via an increasingly diverse group of vectors that have emerged out of increasingly complex transportation systems and widespread human activities.[10] For example, the rate of species introduction in the United States' coastal zone has grown exponentially since the 18th century (Figure 1),[11] with San Francisco Bay as a prime example. Invasion rates in this area have increased from an average of one species every nine months during the period from 1850 to 1970, to one species every six months since 1970 (Figure 2).[12]

One estimate suggests that 85 percent of all exotic plants and animals do not pose a problem to native species.[13] The remainder, however, may threaten existing ecosystems with varying magnitude and severity, depending on the species involved and the complexity of the affected ecosystem.[14] Manifest impacts of marine invasive species include rapid reproduction rates that give rise to large dominant populations, local native extinctions due to population outbreaks, alteration of physical environments, transfer of pathogens and modifications to food webs.[15] For example, many planktonic species have long-lived reproductive stages (spores, cysts or eggs) that remain viable in unfavourable conditions.[16] Toxic dinoflagellates, along

10. Bax et al., n. 1 above, at 313–323; Union of Concerned Scientists, *The Science of Invasive Species* (California, 2001) 12 pp.; Carlton, 1992, n. 5 above, at 13–46.

11. Carlton, 2001, n. 5 above.

12. A. N. Cohen and J. T. Carlton, "Accelerating Invasion Rate in a Highly Invaded Estuary," *Science* 279 (1998): 555–558.

13. N. Kassulke, "Tales from the Exotics Battlefront," *Wisconsin Natural Resources Magazine*, 2001, available online: <http:// www.wnrmag.com/supps/2001/jun01>.

14. IMO (International Maritime Organization), *International Convention for the Control and Management of Ships Ballast Water and Sediments*, adopted 13 February 2004; J. T. Carlton, "Patterns of Transoceanic Marine Biological Invasions in the Pacific Ocean," *Bulletin of Marine Science* 41, 2 (1987): 452–465.

15. *Id.*

16. J. P. Hamer, T. A. McCollin and I. N. Lucas, "Dinoflagellate Cysts in Ballast Tank Sediments: Between Tank Variability," *Marine Pollution Bulletin* 40 (2000): 731–733.

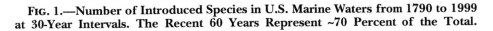

FIG. 1.—Number of Introduced Species in U.S. Marine Waters from 1790 to 1999 at 30-Year Intervals. The Recent 60 Years Represent ~70 Percent of the Total.

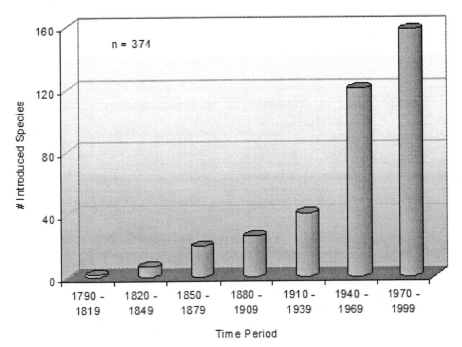

Source: Carlton, n. 5 above.

with other algal species, can cause the death of fish or shellfish and pose a serious risk to human health.[17] Rapidly expanding invasive populations can deplete oxygen, thereby resulting in fish deaths, altered habitats and community assemblages, fouled stabilizing structures and water intakes and reduced primary productivity so essential for marine food chains.[18] As all ecosystems appear to show some vulnerability to invasive species, and as the consequences of a successful invasion are often irreversible,[19] greater awareness by policy makers is essential if they are to devise appropriate

17. G. M. Hallegraeff and C. J. Bolch, "Transport of Toxic Dinoflagellate Cysts Via Ships Ballast Water," *Marine Pollution Bulletin,* 22 (1991): 27–30.
18. E. Grosholz, "Ecological and Evolutionary Consequences of Coastal Invasions," *Trends in Ecology and Evolution* 17, 1 (2002): 22–27; J. Cloren, "Phytoplankton Bloom Dynamics in Coastal Ecosystems: A Review with Some General Lessons from Sustained Investigations of San Francisco Bay, California," *Review of Geophysics* 34 (1996): 127–168.
19. M. Doelle, "The Quiet Invasion: Legal and Policy Responses to Aquatic Invasive Species in North America," *International Journal of Marine Coastal Law* 18, 2 (2003): 261–294.

FIG. 2.—San Francisco Bay has long been a known recipient of invasive species in United States. From 1850 to 1909 the number of new introductions in San Francisco Bay represented more than 50 percent of the total known species introductions in U.S. Since 1910 San Francisco Bay has been responsible for approximately 30 percent of the total species introduced.

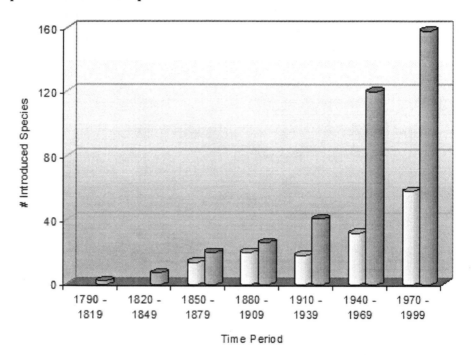

Sources: Carlton, n. above; A. N. Cohen and J. T. Carlton, Nonindigenous Aquatic Species in a United States Estuary: A Case Study of the Biological Invasions of the San Francisco Bay and Delta (Berkeley: University of California, Williams College—Mystic Seaport, 1995)

responses for possible impacts. The necessity of a coordinated and focussed management response becomes readily apparent with increasing awareness of the many and diverse ways that species may be introduced.[20] In general, contemporary and historical regulations have proven ineffective in mitigating the harmful effects of invasions.[21]

20. Carlton 1992, n. 5 above, at 13–46.
21. O. Endresen, H. L. Behrens, S. Brynestad, A. B. Andersen and R. Skjong, "Challenges in Global Ballast Water Management," *Marine Pollution Bulletin* 48 (2004): 615–623; Bax et al., n. 1 above, at 313–323; Doelle, n. 19 above, at 261–294.

Marine Transport

Marine transportation has long been suspect as an important vector of species transfer,[22] though ballast-tank inspections did not confirm its role until the 1970s. Attempts to prevent ballast water dispersal of invasive species have been underway since the early 1990s.[23] Ballast water, tank sediments and hull fouling are now widely accepted as important vectors for the introduction of exotic marine species around the world.[24]

Accounting for 80 percent of world trade, shipping is the dominant mode of transport accounting for 10,429 million tonnes (M mt) of cargo transported each year.[25] The transport of cargo by shipping is facilitated by the corresponding transfer of 3,500 M mt of ballast water used to maintain vessel balance, stability and structural integrity (Table 1).[26] Ballast water can contain unwanted marine organisms that can be carried around the world and discharged into new environments.[27] Contemporary estimates provide for 2,800 M mt of ballast water discharged annually worldwide,[28] and while most species die without becoming established, some species do survive to form viable populations. The development of steel-hulled vessels, increased ballast volume and reduced trip duration increase the probability of successful establishment by exotic species.[29] While ballast water has received

22. C. J. Ostenfeld, "On the Immigration of Biddulphia Sinesis Grev. and Its Occurrence in the North Sea During 1903–1907," *Medd. Komm. Havunders., Ser. Plankton* 1 (1908): 44 pp., as cited in Hallegraeff et al., n. 17 above.

23. R. J. Williams, F. B. Griffiths, E. J. Van der Wal and J. Kelly, "Cargo Vessel Ballast Water as a Vector for the Transport of Non-Indigenous Marine Species," *Estuarine, Coastal and Shelf Science* 26 (1988): 409–420; GloBallast (Global Water Management Programme), 2003a, Ballast Water Treatment R&D Directory, International Maritime Organization, 75 pp.

24. J. T. Carlton and T. B. Geller, "Ecological roulette: The Global Transport of Nonindigenous Marine Organisms," *Science* 261 (1993): 78–82; P. N. Lewis, C. L. Hewitt, M. Riddle and A. McMinn, "Marine Introductions in the Southern Ocean: An Unrecognized Hazard to Biodiversity," *Marine Pollution Bulletin* 46 (2003): 213–223; Endresen et al., n. 21 above, at 615–623.

25. UNCTAD (United Nations Conference on Trade and Development), 2003, *Review of Maritime Transport, 2003: Report by the UNCTAD Secretariat* (Geneva: United Nations Conference on Trade and Development, UN 387.5 P3), 140 pp.; J. Hoffmann and S. Kumar, "Globalization: The Maritime Nexus," In: C. Grammenos, ed., *Handbook of Maritime Economics and Business* (London: London Press, 2002): 35–62.

26. D. Pughuic, "Ballast Water Management and Control: An Overview," *Tropical Coasts,* 7 (2001): 42–49; Endresen et al., n. 21 above, at 615–623; Hoffman et al., n. 25 above, at 35–62.

27. Endresen et al., n. 21 above, at 615–623.

28. *Id.*

29. J. G. Field, G. Hempel and C. P. Summerhayes, *Oceans 2020: Science, Trends, and the Challenge of Sustainability* (Washington: Island Press, 2002), 177 pp.

the majority of attention directed at ship-mediated biological invasions, "no ballast on board" (NOBOB) vessels do in fact contain some ballast and tank sediment though they are effectively unregulated.[30] Once released, invasives can disrupt the natural ecological balance of the receiving ecosystem by out-competing native species for resources and upsetting predator-prey relation-ships.[31]

Table 1.—World Ship Cargo Trade (M mt) among Regions in 2000

Region	Exports	Imports	Total
Asia Pacific	1,395	2,106.1	3,501.1
Europe	673.4	1,421.8	2,095.2
North America	536.2	910.7	1,446.9
Latin America / Caribbean	948.3	313	1,261.3
Persian Gulf	832.3	76.2	908.5
Other	829.2	386.6	1,215.8
Total	5,214.5	5,214.5	

Source: Hoffmann et al., n. 25 above.

In addition to ballast water and tank sediment, hull fouling is a mechanism for species conveyance worldwide. The impact of methods used to reduce hull fouling offers a note of caution for potential management. Effective antifouling hull coatings (e.g., containing tributyl tin, TBT) offer some environmental benefits that include decreased fuel consumption, reduced fuel combustion emission and the reduction of invasive species via hull fouling. However, the environmental cost associated with such treatments can be considerable,[32] a subject further addressed below. As the size and number of vessels in the world shipping fleet continues to grow,[33] the problems associated with marine transportation will escalate in parallel, with possible intensification resulting from increasing coastal eutrophica-

30. L. A. Drake, P. T. Jenkins and F. C. Dobbs, "Domestic and International Arrivals of NOBOB (No Ballast on Board) Vessels to Lower Chesapeake Bay," *Marine Pollution Bulletin* 50 (2005): 560–565.

31. GloBallast 2003a, n. 23 above.

32. S. M. Evans, A. C. Birchenough and M. S. Brancato, "The TBT Ban: Out of the Frying Pan into the Fire?," *Marine Pollution Bulletin* 40, 3 (2000): 204–211; A. O. Valkirs, P. F. Seligman, E. Haslbeck and J. Caso, "Measurement of Copper Release Rates from Antifouling Paint Under Laboratory and In Situ Conditions: Implications for Loading Estimation to Marine Water Bodies," *Marine Pollution Bulletin* 46 (2003): 763–779.

33. UNCTAD, n. 25 above.

tion.[34] Shipping is clearly important to world trade and simultaneously to the spread of invasive species. Consequently, shipping receives an inordinate amount of attention directed to regulatory activities and control mechanisms,[35] often overshadowing the considerable risks posed by many other transport vectors.

Other Vectors

Vectors recognized for their potential to spread exotic species include aquaculture, canal development, aquarium trade, floating marine debris, and oil and gas development activities. The magnitude and extent of invasive impact from vectors other than shipping have been described on occasion, but much work remains before sufficient information will be available for reliable decision making purposes. As much as 60 percent of marine invasive plants can be transferred by means distinct from shipping (Table 2).[36] Illustrating this point, 56 exotic species have been identified in an estuary receiving no international shipping.[37] Bax et al. suggest that mariculture could be responsible for up to 25 percent of exotic species establishments,[38] through deliberate and/or accidental releases of target organisms, along with their "hitchhiking" pathogens or parasites.[39] In a similar vein, intentional or accidental releases of aquarium species into coastal ecosystems have the potential to create ecosystem instability. A well-known example is that of *Caulerpa taxifolia,* an alga native to the tropics that was accidentally released in 1984 from the Oceanographic Museum of Monaco. It has flourished and contemporary estimates have it covering 30,000 hectares of coastal sea floor adjacent to six Mediterranean countries. The same alga was discovered in Agua Hedionda Lagoon in California,[40]

34. F. Zhang and M. Dickman, "Mid-Ocean Exchange of Container Vessel Ballast Water. 1: Seasonal Factors Affecting the Transport of Harmful Diatoms and Dinoflagellates," *Marine Ecology Progress Series* 176 (1999): 243–251.

35. A. Ricciardi, "Facilitative Interactions among Aquatic Invaders: Is an 'Invasional Meltdown' Occurring in the Great Lakes?," *Canadian Journal of Fisheries and Aquatic Sciences* 58 (2001): 2513–2525; Endrescn ct al., n. 21 above, at 615–623.

36. M. A. Ribera Siguan, "Review of Non-Native Marine Plants in the Mediterranean Sea," in E. Leppakoski, S. Gollasch and S. Olenin, eds., *Invasive Aquatic Species of Europe-Distribution Impacts and Management* (London: Kluwer Academic Publishers, 2002), 291–310.

37. K. Wasson, C. J. Zaban, L. Bedinger, M. C. Diaz and J. S. Pearce, "Biological Invasions of Estuaries Without International Shipping: The Importance of Intraregional Transport," *Biological Conservation* 102 (2001): 143–153.

38. Bax et al., n. 1 above, at 313–323.

39. Carlton, n. 5 above, at 513–546.

40. C. Wabnitz, M. Taylor, E. Green and T. Razak, *From Ocean to Aquarium* (Cambridge: UNEP-World Conservation Monitoring Centre, 2003).

where chlorine was used in an eradication attempt at a cost of US$1.5 million.[41]

Table 2.—Relative Magnitude of Vectors Responsible for
Transfer of Exotic Marine Plants

Vector	No. of Exotics	Percent
Shellfish Transport	49	30
Ship Fouling	39	24
Ballast	25	16
Suez Canal	24	15
Import for Aquaculture	15	9
Other Vectors (Research, Fishing, Aquaria)	10	6

Source: Ribera Siguan, n. 36 above.

The construction of canals to improve shipping removes natural barriers and facilitates the active or passive dispersal of invasive species such as zebra mussels (*Dreissena polymorpha*), cladocerans and jellyfish across broad biogeographic regions.[42] Such species have profoundly modified ecosystems ranging from the Black Sea to the Great Lakes and have severely reduced or altered important commercial fish catches in such regions.[43]

Commercial fishing provides a transport vector for invasives through fouling of boat wells, hulls and equipment,[44] while transient boaters are suspect as a major vector for overland dispersal.[45] There is evidence that

41. J. Withgott, "California tries to rub out the monster of the lagoon," *Science* 295 (2002): 2201–2202.

42. Reid et al., "Geological and Evolutionary Underpinnings for the Success of Ponto-Caspian Species Invasions in the Baltic Sea and North American Great Lakes," *Canadian Journal of Fisheries and Aquatic Sciences* 59 (2002): 1144–1158; E. Leppakoski, S. Gollasch, P. Gruszka, H. Ojaveer, S. Olenin and V. Panov, "The Baltic—A Sea of Invaders," *Canadian Journal of Fisheries and Aquatic Sciences* 59 (2002): 1175–1188; S. Gollasch, D. Minchin, H. Rosenthal and M. Voigt, eds., *Exotics across the Ocean: Case Histories on Introduced Species* (Kiel: Department of Fishery Biology, Institute of Marine Science, University of Kiel, 1999).

43. A. Ricciardi, n. 34 above, at 2513–2525; Reid et al., n. 42 above, at 1144–1158.

44. Anonymous, *Marine Pest Information Sheet: Vessel and Gear Fouling,* Centre for Research on Marine Invasive Pests, 2004, available online: <http://crimp.marine.csiro.au>.

45. D. K. Padilla and L. E. Johnson, "Geographic Spread of Exotic Species: Ecological Lessons and Opportunities from the Invasion of the Zebra Mussel," *Biological Conservation* 78 (1996): 23–33.

invasion rates in enclosed marinas can be 3- to 19-fold greater than in adjacent coastal areas.[46] In 2000, inspections conducted in Maine (U.S.) showed that 4 percent of recreational boats carried water milfoil (exotic freshwater vascular plant) at a time when an outbreak was occurring in the State.[47] The estimated 50,000 boats that cross the State borders each year represent considerable potential for the import and export of invasive species.

Floating marine debris (FMD) poses two significant environmental threats. First, as foreign and polluting objects, and second, through passive wind and current transport it can carry invasive hitchhikers over long distances.[48] Before Annex V of the International Convention for the Prevention of Pollution from Ships (MARPOL) came into force in 1988 it was estimated that the shipping industry discarded 639,000 plastic containers into the marine environment each day—over 233 billion containers annually.[49] One study in the South Pacific, subsequent to the adoption of Annex V, revealed a significant increase in marine littering coincident with a decrease in publications on the activity and suggested that Annex V might not have been as responsible for reducing marine litter as previously assumed by the scientific community.[50] Studies have shown bryozoans and barnacles to have crossed the Tasman and Caribbean Seas and the North Atlantic Ocean while attached to FMD.[51] Generally, invasions facilitated by FMD occur in mid-latitudes (<60°), possibly excluded from the higher latitudes by rough seas, cold temperature and increased intensity of ultraviolet light.[52] The potential effects of global warming on the future transport and survival of organisms to higher latitudes are virtually unknown.[53]

Oil and gas maintenance and replacement activities also act as invasive vectors. In 1991, the corals *Tubastraea coccinea* and *Mycetophyllia rees* were identified growing on 11 oil platforms off the coasts of Texas and Louisi-

46. National Institute of Water and Atmospheric Research, "Biosecurity and Human Health: What's on the Bottom of Your Boat?" *Biodiversity Update* 2 (2001): 1.

47. Land and Water Resources Council, "Action Plan for Managing Invasive Aquatic Species," Maine, 2002, available online: <http://www.state.me.us/>.

48. Barnesk, n. 5 above, at 808–809.

49. International Convention for the Prevention of Pollution from Ships, (MARPOL), UN Legislative Series ST/LEG/SER.B/18 of 2 November, 1973, *International Legal Materials*, 12 (1993): 1319; J. G. B. Derraik, 2002, "The Pollution of the Marine Environment by Plastic Debris: A Review," *Marine Pollution Bulletin* 44 (2002): 842–852.

50. P. G. Ryan and C. L. Moloney, "Biodiversity Invasions by Marine Life on Plastic Debris," *Nature* 416 (April 25, 2002): 808–809.

51. Derraik, n. 49 above, at 842–852.

52. *Id.*

53. Barnes, n. 5 above, at 808–809.

ana.[54] Prior to that discovery, they had only been observed in the Gulf of Mexico on oil platforms off the coasts of Campeche and Veracruz. The logical connection is that they appeared off Texas and Louisiana through the movement of oil rigs.[55]

ECONOMIC ASPECTS

Biodiversity protection is difficult to incorporate in policy, and little incentive exists for vector-control initiatives unless there are obvious and measurable impacts to human health or the economy.[56] Despite the availability of data on ecological impacts of invasive species and the methods of their transport, few efforts to quantify realized costs and benefits associated with an invasion have reached specific and complete assessment. Difficulties remain in communicating the economic risks associated with invasive species, as contemporary economic models may be inadequate to gauge indirect effects.

Effects resulting from the presence of invasive species are difficult to separate from those caused by climate change and other forms of habitat alteration and pollution, and assessing attributes like aesthetic value or human well-being presents an even greater challenge. There are no "standard methods" to collect and/or analyse invasive-related economic data and no central databases or collaborative bodies of knowledge to illustrate the consequences of past decisions or to inform future decisions. The inter-connected nature of the marine environment makes it difficult to attach costs to specific sectors—some invasives have the potential to damage many industries simultaneously, but only a broad overall cost is determined. A damage estimate exceeding $1 billion resulting from invasions into the United States of the European green crab (*Carcinus maenus*), the Asian clam (*Corbicula fluminea*) and the shipworm (*Teredo navalis*) is expected to range across several industries, including aquaculture, fisheries, marine infrastructure and shipping.[57] Beyond such specific examples, precise economic costs for marine invasive species are not readily available. If estimates have been attempted they often include only damage or control costs; indirect costs such as biodiversity loss, aesthetic impacts or degraded ecosystem services are seldom, if ever, approximated.[58] In general, control or eradication of

54. D. Fenner, "Biogeography of Three Caribbean Corals (Scleractinia) and the Invasion of Tubastraea Coccinea into the Gulf of Mexico," *Bulletin of Marine Science* 69, 3 (2001): 1175–1189.

55. *Id.*

56. Doelle, n. 19 above, at 261–294.

57. Pimentel et al., n. 9 above, at 273–288.

58. *Id.*

invasive species is expensive and an accurate assessment of costs with the goal of determining how best to spend mitigative effort is difficult.

The world economy is heavily dependent on maritime shipping and shipping is a major vector for invasive species. To curtail invasives, new treatment methods are necessary that will require equipment installations, especially on older vessels. Onboard ballast water treatment systems and deep water ballast exchange are two methods that result in increased operating costs. The International Maritime Organization (IMO) has suggested that ballast water exchange could add US$160 million to annual shipping costs and in some cases could increase the potential for capsizing.[59] The IMO currently sponsors ballast water management research programs, each costing nearly $70,000,[60] and has partnered with the Global Environment Facility (GEF) and the United Nations Development Programme (UNDP) to assist developing countries to implement IMO ballast water guidelines through Globallast—the Global Water Management Program. Globallast demonstration sites are established in six countries at a cost of US$10.2 million.[61] As fouling from ballast water does not create a direct negative economic impact for the shipping industry, the costs associated with improvement of ballast exchange methods to prevent fouling may not seem to be a worthwile investment for the shipping industry. This is not the case with hull fouling. A fouled hull increases drag resulting in increased fuel consumption and cost. Thus, reduced hull fouling has the incentive of reduced cost.[62]

Marine invertebrates can damage coastal infrastructure or obstruct waterways. For example, the Asian clam and the shipworm can threaten native species, damage coastal piers and structures, block intake pipes, and destabilize banks.[63] Freshwater species such as the Asian clam and the zebra mussel (*Dreissena polymorpha*) are tolerant of estuarine conditions.[64] Damage

59. G. R. Rigby and G. M. Hallegraeff, "The Transfer and Control of Harmful Marine Organisms in Shipping Ballast Water: Behaviour of Marine Plankton and Ballast Water Exchange on the MV 'Iron Whyalla,'" *Journal of Marine Environmental Engineering* 1 (1994): 91–110.

60. D. Oemeke, "Ballast Water Treatment Technology," *Port Corporation of Queensland Research and Development on Ballast Water Technology*, 1998 as cited in IMO-Globallast, 2004, n. 14 above.

61. IMO (International Maritime Organization), 2004, n. 14 above; Global Water Management Program website: <http://globallast.imo.org/index.asp?page=gef_interw_project.htm&menu=true>.

62. Evans et al., n. 32 above, at 204–211; Valkirs et al., n. 32 above, at 763–779; Lewis et al., n. 24 above, at 213–223; Bax et al., n. 1 above.

63. Pimentel et al., 2005, n. 9 above, at 273–288; D. Pimentel, ed., *Biological Invasions: Economic and Environmental Costs of Alien Plant, Animal, and Microbe Species* (Boca Raton: CRC Press, 2002), 369 p.

64. P. W. Fofonoff and G. M. Ruiz, "Biological Invasions in the Cheasapeake and Delaware Bays: Patterns and Impacts," *Proceedings of the Aquatic Invaders of the*

from the zebra mussel has received much more comprehensive documentation than many other marine invasive species and consequently it can be used as a surrogate in attempts to predict potential impacts arising from similar marine invertebrates. Annual North American expenditures for the control of the zebra mussel increased 70 fold from $234,140 in 1989 to $17,751,000 in 1995, perhaps a glimpse of the potential economic impact associated with the invasive saltwater mussel *Perna viridis*.[65] Impacts can encompass damage to infrastructure, reductions in tourism, altered recreational activities, algal clogging of waterways and threats to human health.[66] The impacts of some are easily quantified while others, such as the loss of human life are more appropriately moral or ethical issues.[67]

Aquaculture practices introduce a unique set of concerns. The propagation of native and non-native species can be equally problematic, however, we preferentially address the latter, recognizing that the control of invasive species within aquaculture may not be a complete solution. From an aquaculture perspective, the non-native (otherwise invasive) species are of economic benefit—in fact a necessity. Nearly 10 percent of the 22 M mt of worldwide aquaculture production (marine and freshwater) is founded on the culture of non-native species (Figure 3).[68] Regionally, up to 50 percent of aquaculture production is derived from non-native species.[69] For example, 90 percent of global seaweed production occurs in China,[70] where the introduced kelp *Laminaria japonica* is responsible for about 50 percent of total production.[71] The commercial cultivation of non-native species poses serious threats to the local ecosystem and its native species, e.g., the release of parasites and disease from cultured organisms to the environment.[72] On occasion, the economic benefits of aquaculture using non-indigenous species have been balanced by the reporting of negative economic impacts, such as an outbreak of *Haplosporidium nelsoni* MSX

Delaware Estuary Symposium, Malvern, Pennsylvania, May 20, 2003. 5–8, available online: <http://www.signis.org/publicat/proceed/aide/foforuiz.htm>.

65. C. R. O'Neill, Jr., "Economic Impact of Zebra Mussels—Results of the 1995 National Zebra Mussel Information Clearinghouse Study," *Great Lakes Research Review* 3, 1 (April 1997): 33–44.

66. Bax et al., n. 1 above.

67. *Id.*

68. L. Garibaldi, "List of Animal Species Used In Aquaculture," FAO Fisheries Circular No. 914 FIRI/C914 (Rome: FAO, 1996).

69. *Id.*

70. FAO, *The State of World Fisheries and Aqaculture 2002* (Rome: FAO FisheriesDepartment, 2002).

71. K. Lüning and S. Pang, "Mass Cultivation of Seaweeds: Current Aspects and Approaches," *Journal of Applied Phycology* 15 (2003): 115–119.

72. N. L. Naylor, J. Eagle, and W. L. Smith, "Salmon Aquaculture in the Pacific Northwest: A Global Industry with Local Impacts," *Environment* 45, 8 (2003): 18–39.

(Multinucleate Sphere X) disease in oyster populations that destroyed an estimated 75 percent of cage-cultured oysters at Cape Breton's (Canada) largest oyster producer in spring 2003, and spread to local ecosystems.[73] In other instances, the escape of cultured organisms has been reported, but the consequential economic impacts have not. Contemporary estimates suggest over one million Atlantic salmon (*Salmo salar*) have escaped from farms in British Columbia and Washington State since 1991 and the non-native species has subsequently been reported in the wild in at least 80 rivers ranging from British Columbia to the Bering Sea.[74] Escapes occur as a result of storms, human error and predatory attacks on aquaculture facilities by marine mammals. Escaped animals can transmit disease and parasites to wild stock, feed on native species, and compete with native species for habitat and food requirements.[75] In short, the culturing of non-indigenous species can provide strong economic benefit (subsidized or not) in concert with equally subsidized negative ecological impact; the benefit accrues to private interests while the costs become externalized (Figure 3).[76]

Invasive species can negatively impact the wild-harvest fishery through predation or competition with commercially exploited species,[77] damage to fish-protection devices on intakes,[78] damage to fishing gear,[79] and export barriers for fish products because of disease concerns.[80] However, there is a paucity of data accurately describing the economic consequences of damage caused by invasive species on wild fishery resources (Table 3).[81]

In Canada, damage from identified aquatic nuisance species has been estimated at $343 million annually, mostly to commercial and sport

73. A. MacIssac, pers. comm., 24 March 2004; Fofonoff et al., 2003, n. 64 above, at 5–8.

74. Atlantic Salmon Watch Program statistics, available online: <http://www.pac.dfo-mpo.gc.ca/sci/aqua/ASWP/Asl_escapes.pdf>; Naylor, et al., n. 72 above, at 18–39.

75. Naylor, et al., n. 72 above, at 18–39.

76. J. E. Bardach, "Aquaculture, Pollution and Biodiversity," in *Sustainable Aquaculture* ed., J. E. Bardach, (New York: John Wiley and Sons, Inc., 1997); C. Perrings, "Biological Invasions in Aquatic Systems: The Economic Problem," *Bulletin of Marine Science* 70, 2 (2002): 541–552.

77. R. Mann and J. M. Harding, "Invasion of the North American Atlantic coast by a large predatory Asian mollusc," *Biological Invasions* 2, 1 (2000): 7–22.

78. Lafferty et al., n. 4 above, at 1989–2000.

79. W. M. Graham, D. L. Martin, D. L. Felder, V. L. Asper and H. M. Perry, "Ecological and Economic Impacts of a Tropical Jellyfish Invader in the Gulf of Mexico," *Biological Invasions* 5, 1–2 (2003): 53–69.

80. R. Claudi, "Environmental and Economic Costs of Alien Invasive Species in Canada," *Report for the Canadian Information System for the Environment* (Ottawa: RNT Consulting, Inc. March 26, 2002).

81. *Id.*

FIG. 3.—Percentage of total aquaculture production of introduced species by country.

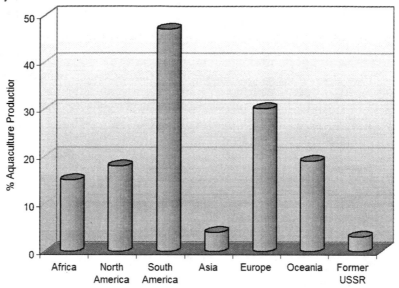

Source: Garibaldi, n. 68 above.

Table 3.—Contemporary Knowledge Base for Invasive Impacts on Canadian Economy and Environment

Species	Number of References	References with Dollar Value
Fourspine Stickleback *Apeltes quadracus*	2	0
Salmonid disease *Piscirickettsia salmonis*	2	0
Round goby *Neoglobus melanostormus*	11	0
Whirling disease *Myxobolus cerebalus*	20	0

Source: Claudi, n. 80 above.

fisheries.[82] The wide confidence interval ($298 to $776 million) around such an estimate illustrates the high degree of uncertainty, largely associated with sparse data, in determining the economic impacts of invasives. Attempts to quantify the economic impacts of nuisance species rarely extend to the marine environment (Table 4).[83] In North America, economic studies that address the impacts of invasive species are rare, often localized to a particular industry or area, and typically describe only direct cost or current worth associated with a threatened industry (Table 4). For example, the European green crab is an invasive species currently considered to threaten some of Canada's most lucrative shellfish fisheries on both coasts (Table 4). In the United States, attempts have been made to quantify direct damage by invasive species on specific fisheries or localities (Table 4), but indirect impacts (e.g., increases in predation by jellyfish on some fish) have not been quantified.[84] The difficulty involved in identifying marine invasions, let alone evaluating them, is a problem partially attributable to limited public awareness of the problem.[85] A global invasion tracking system may facilitate early response, help set priorities, supply information needed for management actions, and allow consideration of low-risk and beneficial introductions.[86]

MANAGEMENT ACTIONS

Following the establishment of an invasive species within a given ecosystem, the invader can exert a devastating influence and be very difficult and costly to eradicate or even control. Adequate legal authority and administrative support, paired with early assessment and control activities, significantly increases the potential to effectively reduce the impact of invasive species on natural systems.[87] Globally, at least 45 binding and non-binding internation-

82. R. I. Colautti, S. A. Bailey, C. D. A. van Overdijk, K. Amundsen and H. J. MacIssac, "Characterised and Projected Costs of Nonindigenous Species in Canada," *Biological Invasions* (in press).

83. *Id.*

84. Graham et al., n. 79 above, at 53–69.

85. Bax et al., n. 1 above, at 313–323.

86. A. Ricciardi, W. Steiner, R. Mack and D. Simberloff, "Toward a Global Information System for Invasive Species," *Bioscience* 50, 3 (2000): 239–244; B. Morton, "The Nature of the Aquatic Nuisance Species Problem: A Global Perspective," In *Sixth International Zebra Mussel and Other Aquatic Nuisance Species Conference, Dearborn, Michigan, March 1996* Unpublished document; C. R. Townsend, "Individual, Population, Community, and Ecosystem Consequences of a Fish Invader in New Zealand Streams," *Conservation Biology* 17, 1 (2003): 38–47.

87. J. A. McNeely, L. E. Neville and M. Rajmanek, "When Is Eradication a Sound Investment?," *Conservation in Practice* 4, 1 (2003): 30–31.

Table 4.—Available Invasives-Related Economic Data from Canada and the United States

Invasive	Sector	Impact	Cost	Reference
European Green Crab	Fisheries	Predator of invertebrates and seaweeds. Threatens recreational and commercial shellfish fisheries.	Threat to fisheries: $200 million/yr shellfish, $25 million crab fishery. (BC and Washington) $57 million clam, mussel and oyster, $500 million lobster (Canadian Atlantic).	Standing Committee Report 2003
Chinese Mitten Crab	Fisheries	Fouls fish bypass structures on power plants: 51,000 crabs/day on fish bypass structures in 1999.	98–99 percent fish mortality at the Federal facility through the summer of 1999: over $1 million in losses.	Chinese Mitten Crab Task Force 2002
Jellyfish *Phyllorhiza punctata*	Fisheries	Clogs shrimp nets and preys on eggs and larvae of commercially important species. Gulf of Mexico, abund. in the summer of 2000 = 5.37 x 10^6/150km^2	Shrimp net damage estimated at millions of dollars. No attempt to quantify the damage to fish stocks caused by increased egg and juvenile mortality.	Graham et al. 2003

Sources: Standing Committee on Fisheries and Oceans, T. Wappel, Chair, *Aquatic Invasive Species: Uninvited Guests.* Fourth Report of the Standing Committee on Fisheries and Oceans (Ottawa: Communication Canada Publishing, Ottawa, 2003), 38 p.; Chinese Mitten Crab Task Force, *A Draft National Management Plan for the Genus Eriochheir*, Submitted to the Aquatic Nuisance Species Task Force, US, 2002, available online: <http://anstaskforce.gov/chinese-mitten-crab-plan2-02.pdf>; W. M. Graham, D. L. Martin, D. L. Felder, V. L. Asper and H. M. Perry, "Ecological and Economic Impacts of a Tropical Jellyfish Invader in the Gulf of Mexico," *Biological Invasions* 5, 1–2 (2003): 53–69.

al conventions and agreements address aquatic invasive species—many that concentrate on marine invasions.[88] About half of these instruments have implications for aquatic invasive species in North America.[89]

A number of means exist to manage and control invasive species and they require a combination of scientific and management techniques for success to accrue. Risk assessment can be useful as a tool to assess proposed (or potential) introductions, but it represents only one of many devices and should not be the sole basis for decision-making.[90] Often, information needed to produce a rapid response is unavailable or unattainable, and controlling the invader becomes increasingly difficult if the response is delayed by the time required to secure the necessary information.[91] We offer a simple illustration. Much of the available literature addresses terrestrial problems and examples, however, the marine environment is very different from its terrestrial counterpart. Despite this, the precautionary approach is explicitly described in Canadian policy and legislation, and work is proceeding to standardize its implementation in science-based decision making across federal departments, suggesting a commitment to the principle. Conversely, the need for more research is not an excuse for inaction, especially with new invasions occurring at an exponential rate.[92] Thus, managers must be guided by clear, proactive policies, must employ risk assessment tools, and must secure useful and credible information and commit to institutional sharing of insights as a means of dealing with uncertainty.

Legal and Administrative Support

Contemporary concerns regarding invasive species are being addressed by governments, institutions, policy and planning interest groups and individuals. Internationally, the United Nations Convention on the Law of the Sea (UNCLOS, 1982) refers to invasive species in a general manner.[93] Article 196 states:

88. J. A. McNeely and F. Schutyser, "Invasive Species: A Global Concern Bubbling to the Surface," Presented at the International Conference on the Impact of Global Environment Problems on Continental and Coastal Marine Waters, Geneva, Switzerland, 16–18 July 2003.

89. Doelle, n. 19 above, at 261–294.

90. D. Simberloff, "How Much Information on Population Biology Is Needed to Manage Introduced Species?," *Conservation Biology* 17, 1 (2003): 83–92.

91. *Id.*

92. *Id.*

93. M. L. McConnell, "Ballast and Biosecurity: The Legal, Economic and Safety Implications of the Developing International Regime to Prevent the Spread of Harmful Aquatic Organisms and Pathogens in Ships' Ballast Water," *Ocean Yearbook* 17, eds. E. Mann Borgese, A. Chircop and M. McConnell (Chicago: University of Chicago Press, 2003): 213–255.

States shall take all measures necessary to prevent, reduce and control pollution of the marine environment resulting from the use of technologies under their jurisdiction or control, or the intentional or accidental introduction of species, alien or new, to a particular part of the marine environment, that may cause significant and harmful changes thereto.[94]

UNCLOS is the precursor to many more recent conventions and guidelines. The most recent is the IMO International Convention for the Control and Management of Ship's Ballast Water and Sediments (the Ballast Water Convention). Adopted in February 2004, it is based on guidelines created in 1997 that seek to minimize the transfer of harmful invasives.[95] The Ballast Water Convention defines the general rights and responsibilities of States along with treatment standards and sediment management.[96] The Convention on Biological Diversity (CBD), adopted in 1992,[97] includes a set of provisions that define conservation of biological diversity at the genetic, taxonomic and ecosystem levels.[98] This latter Convention is actually a treaty, a binding agreement that establishes goals rather than obligations,[99] e.g., Article 8(h), the Interim Guiding Principle for the Prevention, Introduction and Mitigation of Impacts of Alien Species.[100]

The United States currently has several federal acts that deal with non-indigenous species,[101] and four are briefly discussed here. The Lacey Act addresses intentional introductions and regulates species such as wild mammals, birds, fish and some invertebrates, including eggs and offspring that could be considered injurious to humans or important resources, such as agriculture, horticulture, forestry or wildlife. The Act prohibits the importation of species identified on its "blacklist" that currently includes a

---

94. United Nations Convention on the Law of the Sea (UNCLOS) 1982.

95. M. L. McConnell, "GloBallast Legislative Review—Final Report," *GloBallast Monograph Series No. 1,* (London: IMO, 2002).

96. McConnell, n. 93 above, at 213–255.

97. Bax et al., n. 1 above, at 313–323.

98. L. Glowka and C. de Klemm, "International Instruments, Processes, Organization and Non-Indigenous Introductions: Is a Protocol to the Convention on Biological Diversity Necessary?," in *Invasive Species and Biodiversity Management,* O. T. Sandlund, P. J. Schei and Å. Viken, eds., (Dordrecht: Kluwer Academic Publishers, 1999): 389–405.

99. *Id.*

100. L. Glowka, "Bioprospecting, Alien Invasive Species, and Hydrothermal Vents: Three Emerging Legal Issues in the Conservation and Sustainable Use of Biodiversity," *Tulane Environmental Law Journal* 13 (2000): 329–360.

101. V. Nadol, "Aquatic Invasive Species in the Coastal West: An Analysis of State Regulation within a Federal Framework," *Environmental Law* 29, 2 (1999): 339–375.

mollusc and a crustacean.[102] The National Invasive Species Act (NISA) is an amendment to certain provisions of the Non-Indigenous Aquatic Nuisance Prevention and Control Act (NANPCA), which broadens policy beyond the Great Lakes focus of NANPCA to include national considerations. NISA established rules and policies for ballast water exchange by ships prior to their entry into the Great Lakes. In addition, it required ballast water management programs to employ technologies and practices that prevent introductions, it made new funding available through a new clearinghouse for national ballast water data and authorized research on the prevention and control of aquatic invasive species in Chesapeake Bay, the Gulf of Mexico and along the Atlantic coast. Unfortunately, NISA failed to overcome some important problems associated with the NANPCA. The ballast exchange process is mandatory only in the Great Lakes, and there are no voluntary ballast water guidelines for other national regions.[103] Further, NISA has insufficient funding to implement the requirements and it lacks enforcement mechanisms for non-compliance.[104]

Arguably, the contemporary benchmark policy for the control of invasive species in the United States is President Clinton's 1999 Executive Order 11312.[105] The Order attempts to correct shortcomings in earlier legislation by establishing a comprehensive co-ordination to prevent the introduction of invasive species via the National Invasive Species Council that in 2001 developed the National Invasive Species Management Plan, designed to coordinate federal efforts in the prevention, detection and rapid response to any introductions.[106]

Invasive species policy in the United States appears to fall short of adequately regulating the introduction of alien species because regulation is based on voluntary compliance, it is focused on activities instead of environment, and federal policy effectively ignores all vectors other than ballast water.[107] The United States is presently reviewing the National Aquatic Invasive Species Bill 2003, designed to amend and improve the NANPCA and the NISA. The Bill seeks to regulate issues that include vectors other than ballast water; regions other than the Great Lakes; and treatment methods for ballast water. The National Aquatic Species Bill 2003 was at the

102. Doelle, n. 19 above, at 261–294.

103. S. B. Zellmer, "The virtues of 'Command and Control' Regulation: Barring Exotic Species from Aquatic Ecosystems," *University of Illinois Law Review* 2000, 4 (2000): 1233–1285.

104. Nadol, n. 101 above, at 339–375.

105. Available online: <http://ceq.eh.doe.gov/nepa/regs/eos/eo13112.html>; Doelle, n. 19 above, at 261–294.

106. *Id.*

107. Nadol, n. 101 above, at 339–375.

hearing stage during the preparation of this article; its final provisions and enactment remain to be determined.[108]

State legislation in the United States can be enacted to provide regulatory alternatives to omissions in federal legislation, but regardless of such efforts, no truly effective regulatory structure for invasive species management can exist without a comprehensive federal role. California provides a comprehensive state response to invasive species,[109] though functional difficulties exist, including a lack of coordination with neighbouring states in the event of species introduction and spread, a lack of provisions to address pathogens or viral invasions, and a lack of direction regarding eradication or mitigation measures in the event of an invasive establishment.[110]

The Canadian approach to the aquatic invasives problem can be viewed as inconsistent, piecemeal, uncoordinated, delayed and devoid of a comprehensive regulatory structure.[111] The jurisdiction for aquatic invasive species lies with the federal government and its constitutional authority over fisheries, shipping and its obligation to maintain "peace, order and good government."[112] No less than five laws under various jurisdictional agencies pertain to aquatic invasive species:

(1) the Fisheries Act (1985);

(2) the Canada Shipping Act (1985);

(3) the Canadian Environmental Protection Act (CEPA, 1999);

(4) the Canadian Environmental Assessment Act (1992); and

(5) the Wildlife Animal and Plant Protection and Regulation of International and Interprovincial Trade Act (1992).[113]

Additionally, there are two policies that address invasives:

(1) Guidelines for the Control of Ballast Water Discharge from Ships in Waters under Canadian Jurisdiction (2000); and

(2) Biodiversity Strategy (1995).

The Fisheries Act is the legislation with the greatest capacity to address threats from aquatic invasives,[114] where Fisheries and Oceans Canada (DFO)

---

108. Senate Committee on Environment and Public Works, Subcommittee on Fisheries, Wildlife and Water, *U.S. Senate Committee on Environment and Public Works Hearing Statements* S. 525 (2003).

109. Nadol, n. 101 above, at 339–375.

110. *Id.*

111. Doelle, n. 19 above, at 261–294; Nadol, n. 101 above, at 339–375.

112. *Id.* at 273.

113. *Id.* at 261–294.

114. *Id.*

has jurisdictional responsibility for licensing and controlling intentional introductions, as well as sanctioning unintentional introductions where they are deemed to be deleterious to fish or fish habitats.[115]

The overarching policy for invasives in Canada rests with the Canadian Biodiversity Strategy.[116] The Canadian Biodiversity Strategy requires database development for identification, monitoring, risk assessment, eradication and research measures relating to invasive species.[117] In September 2001, the federal government identified invasive species as a priority under the Strategy whenever a multi-layered collaborative effort on the part of government has been adopted to tackle the issue. The aim is to develop a National Action Plan on Invasive Species with DFO as the agency responsible for addressing the aquatic invasive species portion of the plan. DFO's mandate is thus to determine the primary routes of entry and spread of aquatic invasive species in Canadian waters, highlight fragile ecosystems, conduct risk assessments, and recommend specific actions that can be taken by the various jurisdictions. At time of writing this article, the plan remains a draft.[118]

In 2000, Canada developed Guidelines for the Control of Ballast Water Discharge from Ships in Waters under Canadian Jurisdiction.[119] These voluntary guidelines were proposed to implement the International Maritime Organization's resolution A.868(20), "Guidelines for the Control and Management of Ships' Ballast Water to Minimize the Transfer of Harmful Aquatic Organisms and Pathogens" in waters under Canadian jurisdiction.[120]

As with contemporary international policy, these Guidelines do not address the potential risks of NOBOB vessels.[121] In addition, the Guidelines for the Control of Ballast Water Discharge and the Canadian Biodiversity Strategy are policy-based initiatives and may lack the effectiveness of legislated regulatory measures with respect to compliance and enforcement.[122]

Canadian environmental policy does recognise the need to take action in situations where there is a paucity of data. The precautionary principle is

115. Fisheries Act, R.S., c. F-14, ss. 34–43, 1985.

116. Doelle, n. 19 above, at 261–294.

117. *Id.*

118. DFO (Fisheries and Oceans Canada) *Government Response to the 4th Report of the Standing Committee on Fisheries and Oceans—Aquatic Invasive Species: Uninvited Guests,* (Ottawa: Fisheries and Oceans, 2003).

119. Transport Canada, The Guidelines for the Control of Ballast Water Discharge from Ships in Waters Under Canadian Jurisdiction, (Ottawa: Transport Canada, 2001).

120. *Id.,* section 5.1.

121. Drake et al., n. 30 above, at 560–565.

122. Doelle, n. 19 above, at 261–294.

explicitly identified in both the Oceans Act and in the Canadian Environmental Protection Act.[123] In an adaptation of Principle 15 of the Rio Declaration, the Canadian Environmental Protection Act asserts that the Government of Canada will

> exercise its powers in a manner that . . . applies precautionary principle where there are threats of serious or irreversible damage, lack of full scientific certainty shall not be used as a reason for postponing cost-effective measures to prevent environmental degradation. . . . [124]

The keyword here may be "cost-effective," perhaps suggesting an imperative for accurate accounting in terms of expected cost of treatment and the cost of no action. In 2000, Canada initiated the consistent application of the precautionary approach in all federal science-based regulatory programs to strengthen risk management practices. A discussion paper with guiding principles has been finalized and mechanisms are being implemented in various federal departments to adopt the new principles.[125] A precautionary approach, coupled with contemporary assessments and management techniques, should help to bridge gaps and lead to more effective identification of invasive species and their control.

Assessment and Control

Management actions for invasive species include prevention, early detection, control management and restoration, research and monitoring, and partnership efforts (National Invasive Species Council 2001).[126] Science can provide information on:

(1) the nature and extent of threats;

(2) the patterns of invasive distribution;

(3) methods of dispersal;

123. Oceans Act, R.S., c. 31 preamble and section 30, 1996; Canadian Environmental Assessment Act, R.S., c. 33, section 2(1)(a) and section 6 (1)(1), 1999.
124. United Nations Conference on Environment and Development, *Agenda 21: Programme of Action for Sustainable Development; Rio Declaration on Environment and Development, United Nations Conference on Environment and Development (UNCED), 3–14 June 1992, Rio de Janeiro, Brazil* (New York, UN Dept. of Public Information) 1993. 294 p; Canadian Environmental Assessment Act, n. 123 above.
125. Environment Canada, "A Canadian Perspective on the Precautionary Approach/Principle," available online: <http://www.ec.gc.ca/econom/pp_e.htm>.
126. National Invasive Species Council, n. 3 above.

(4) economic costs;

(5) management methods; and

(6) enumeration of contemporary "hot" spots.[127]

All can contribute to informed management decisions and to reduced risk of aquatic invasions.

As noted above, much attention has been concentrated on the management of invasive species transported through shipping activities. At present, the only internationally approved ballast water management practice is that of ballast water exchange (BWE),[128] as recommended by the IMO Ballast Water Convention. Open ocean BWE involves replacing coastal water with oceanic water during a voyage,[129] either by emptying and refilling ballast tanks (sequential exchange) or by continuous or sequential flow-through dilution (three-fold tank volume).[130] Both methods can achieve 95 percent water exchange.[131] Oceanic BWE is not always biologically effective and can compromise ship safety (stability).[132] Continuous dilution helps circumvent safety problems though there can be an increase in time and cost to the shipper.[133] Safety and operational concerns about BWE and uncertainties in biological effectiveness have compelled the consideration of other ballast water treatment and management methods that complement or replace BWE and are more effective (Table 5).

We know of no internationally sanctioned evaluation standards for the formal acceptance of emerging techniques.[134] Prototype ballast water treatment technologies surveyed and certified by IMO are required to be

127. A. Ricciardi and J. B. Rasmussen, "Predicting the Identity and Impact of Future Biological Invaders: A Priority for Aquatic Resource Management," *Canadian Journal of Fisheries and Aquatic Sciences* 55 (1998): 1759–1765.

128. International Maritime Organization (IMO). The IMO Guidelines, Resolution A.868 (20), Guidelines for the Control and Management of Ships' Ballast Water to Minimize the Transfer of Harmful Aquatic Organisms and Pathogens, 1997, 17 p.

129. International Maritime Organization, 2004, n. 14 above.

130. Endresen et al., n. 21 above, at 615–623; M. A. Champ, "Economic and Environmental Impacts on Ports and Harbours from the Convention to Ban Harmful Marine Anti-Fouling Systems," *Marine Pollution Bulletin* 46 (2003): 935–940.

131. G. Rigby and A. H. Taylor, "Suggested Designs to Facilitate Improved Management and Treatment of Ballast Water on New and Existing Ships," Discussion Paper prepared for the Australian Quarantine and Inspection Service, Research Advisory Group Ballast Water Research Programme—Australia. Report Series No. 12. 2000.

132. Endresen et al., n. 21 above, at 615–623; Champ, n. 130 above, at 935–940; Rigby et al., n. 131 above.

133. Endresen et al., n. 21 above, at 615–623.

134. International Maritime Organization, 2004, n. 14 above.

Table 5.—Internationally Proposed Ballast Water Management Methods and Preliminary Evaluation, State Water Resources Control Board and U.S. Environmental Protection Agengy

Treatment/Management Technology			Safety	Biological Effective-ness	Environmental Acceptability
Exchange		Empty and refill exchange	A	N	N
		Flow-through exchange	A	N	N
Treatment	Mechanical	Filtration	A	P	A
		Cyclonic separation	U	U	U
	Physical	Thermal	U	U	U
		Ultraviolet	U	U	U
		Ultrasound	U	U	U
		Magnetic fields	U	U	U
		Ozone	U	U	U
		Pulse Plasma	U	U	U
		Deoxygenation	U	U	U
	Chemical	Oxidizing biocide	U	U	U
		Antifouling coating	A	P	P
Isolation		Onshore treatment	A	A	A
		Return to origin	U	U	U

A—Acceptable   P—Partially acceptable   N—Not acceptable   U—Unknown

Source: State Water Resources Control Board/California Environmental Protection Agency (SWRCB/CEPA), Evaluation of Ballast Water Treatment Technology for Control of Nonindigenous Aquatic Organisms, 2002. 76 pp.

safe to ship and crew, environmentally friendly, biologically effective, compatible with ship design and operation, and cost-effective.[135]

Most national and regional ballast water management regulations are modeled on IMO (voluntary adherence) guidelines.[136] If ballast water is "clean" (e.g., free of oil pollution), legislation does not exist to prevent species introductions unless nations adopt the guidelines.[137] A variety of

135. *Id.*
136. International Maritime Organization, 1997, n. 128 above.
137. G. M. Hallegraeff, C. Bolch, B. Koerbin and J. Bryan, "Ballast water: a danger to aquaculture," *Australian Fisheries* 47, 7 (1988): 32–34.

methods are available to address fouling of the outer structure of a vessel, including chemical treatments and mechanical harvesting. Chemical agents such as organo-mercury compounds, lead, arsenic and DDT were used as antifouling treatments on vessel hulls and marine infrastructure until they were shown to pose severe environmental and human health risks and were subsequently withdrawn in the early 1960s.[138] The first use of organotin (TBT) antifouling paints began in the early 1970s and by the mid-1980s they were found to adversely effect non-target organisms such as oysters and snails. Environmental regulations ensued that limited the usage and release rate of antifouling paints containing TBT. In 2001, the IMO Convention on Control of Harmful Anti-fouling Systems on Ships banned the use of TBT in antifouling paints. The convention enters into force 12 months subsequent to ratification by 25 nation states representing 25 percent of the world's merchant fleet tonnage. The convention will require that ships not apply, or re-apply, organotins, shall not bear such compounds on their hulls or external parts or surfaces, or shall bear a coating that forms a barrier to such compounds leaching from the underlying non-compliant anti-fouling systems.[139] Chemical treatment of recreational vessels is less common; strategies to control the spread of invasives via recreational boating include mechanical hull cleaning and anti-fouling programs along with educational programs for boat owners and operators to prevent the spread of invasives from one ecosystem to another.[140] Likewise, mechanical harvesting is most frequently used to address the threat of invasives in ballast tank sediments.[141] However, this process does necessarily kill the organisms and if discarded offshore, currents can conceivably carry them back to coastal waters.

Establishing policies and regulations on shipping-related vectors is necessary though arguably insufficient for addressing all invasives as few studies address other vectors. A generalized policy to control marine invasives would include exclusion, eradication, containment, mitigation and adaptation.[142] Early detection (monitoring) and eradication (using biological control, chemical agents, traps, mechanical harvesting etc.) should prove to be the optimum methods for mitigation. However, some methods and

138. Evans et al., n. 32 above, at 204–211.

139. IMO press release, "IMO adopts Convention on Control of Harmful Anti-Fouling Systems on Ships," available online: <http://www.imo.org/Newsroom/mainframe.asp?topic_id=67%doc_id=1486>.

140. Land and Water Resource Council (LWRC), n. 47 above.

141. J. M. Kelly, "Ballast Water and Sediments as Mechanisms for Unwanted Species Introductions into Washington State," *Journal of Shellfish Research*, 12, 2 (1993): 405–410.

142. C. Perrings, "Biological Invasions in Aquatic Systems: The Economic Problem," *Bulletin of Marine Science* 70, 2 (2002): 541–552.

agents have the capacity to impact native ecosystems in unpredictable and deleterious ways.[143] Unexpected outcomes, including poisoning non-target species, bioaccumulation of chemicals in the food chain, ineffective control of the target species, and habitat alteration or destruction become increasingly likely as the variety of methods and agents and variety of interacting invaders (and complexity of the ecosystem) increases.

Biological control introduces natural enemies to control invasive species and can include parasitoids, predators, pathogens, antagonists or competitor populations. While extensive research on biocontrol in terrestrial agro-ecosystems has been done, little is known about its application to the marine environment. Although biological control has been successful in eradicating invasive species in terrestrial agro ecosystems resulting in economic benefits, numerous establishments have not had the desired effect on pest organisms and may have caused adverse effects on non-target native species.[144] In recent years, biological control has also come to include genetic alteration of populations to interrupt reproductive cycles. The effectiveness of biological control is widely debated; it is difficult to predict the effects of biological agents before their introduction and host-specificity tests are not necessarily designed to quantitatively predict impacts on non-target species or to predict outcomes alternate to the one desired. In addition, biological agents can evolve (adapt) and move to alternative and native hosts.[145] While several principles apply to both terrestrial and marine environments, marine systems differ with respect to the types of control agents available, the spatial scale for which biocontrol must operate effectively, the degree of pest-population reduction required for effective control, the practicality of implementation, and the nature and degree of

143. R. E. Thresher, M. Werner, J. T. Hoeg, I. Svane, H. Glenner, N. E. Murphy and C. Wittwer, "Developing the Options for Marine Pests: Specificity Trials on the Parasitic Castrator, *Sacculina Carcini*, against the European Crab, *Carcinus Maenus*, and Related Species," *Journal of Experimental Marine Biology and Ecology* 254 (1) (2000): 37–51; S. M. Louda and P. Stiling "The Double-Edged Sword of Biological Control in Conservation and Restoration," *Conservation Biology* 18, 1 (2004): 50–53; E. S. Zavaleta, R. J. Hobbs and H. A. Mooney, "Viewing Invasive Species Removal in a Whole-Ecosystem Context," *Trends in Ecology and Evolution* 16, 8 (2001): 454–459; Thomas et al., n. 4 above, at 325–329; Evans et al., n. 32 above, at 204–211.

144. D. J. Greathead, "Benefits and Risks of Classical Biological Control," in H. M. T. Hokkanen and J. M. Lynch, eds., *Biological Control: Benefits and Risks* (Cambridge: Cambridge University Press, 1995), 53–60; D. Simberloff and P. Stiling, "Risks of Species Introduced for Biological Control," *Biological Conservation* 78, 1–2 (1999): 185–192.

145. Thresher et al., n. 143 above, at 37–51; Thomas et al., n. 4 above, at 325–329; Louda et al., n. 121 above, at 50–53; D. E. Pearson and R. M. Callaway, "Indirect Effects of Host-Specific Biological Control Agents," *Trends in Ecology and Evolution* 18, 9 (2003): 456–461; M. S. Hoddle, "Restoring Balance: Using Exotic Species to Control Invasive Exotic Species," *Conservation Biology* 18, 1 (2004): 38–49.

concern for safety.[146] Implementation of biological control agents in marine environments has had varying levels of success. For example, parasitic castration has been identified as a possible control agent for the European green crab,[147] but little is known of its efficacy. Aquaculture industry experiments to induce infertility in Pacific oyster (*Crassostrea gigas*) report 20 percent of the individuals rendered triploid (thus infertile) reverted to diploid, thus there is considerable doubt about the effectiveness of such a treatment.[148]

Risk Analysis

Management priorities, ordered in the face of an analysis of risk, can help determine the most effective use of funds and effort in addressing invasive species issues. Management must be prepared to establish priorities "under conditions of incomplete information about the set of possible invaders, the likelihood of their introduction, establishment and spread, and the potential damages if they do."[149] As previously noted, invasive-control management is challenging in part due to uncertainty,[150] but modeling to parameterize uncertainties and gauge their relative influence on the outcome can help to choose the most promising courses of action.[151] Risk assessment can facilitate the consideration of alternative treatments, open dialogue, and broaden public understanding of the issues.[152]

Compiling pre-invasion data can be a costly and unreliable exercise for predictive purposes,[153] and thus risk assessment may have to rely on flexible valuation techniques to define the specific value of vulnerable areas or the assessment of potential damage. A technique similar to the "contingent

146. Lafferty et al., n. 4 above, at 1989–2000.

147. Thresher et al., n. 143 above, at 37–51.

148. G. Shatkin, S. Shumway and R. Hawes, "Considerations Regarding the Possible Introduction of the Pacific Oyster (*Crassostrea Gigas*) to the Gulf of Maine: A Review of Global Experience," *Journal of Shellfish Research* 6, 2 (1997): 463–477.

149. R. D. Horan, C. Perrings, F. Lupi and E. H. Bulte, "Biological Pollution Prevention Strategies under Ignorance: The Case of Invasive Species," *American Journal of Agricultural Economics* 84, 5 (2002): p. 1303.

150. D. Simberloff and P. Stiling, "Risks of Species Introduced for Biological Control," *Biological Conservation* 78(1–2) (1996): 185–192.

151. E. Slooten, D. Fletcher and B. L. Taylor, "Accounting for Uncertainty in Risk Assessment: Case Study of Hector's Dolphin Mortality Due To Gillnet Entanglement," *Conservation Biology* 14, 5 (2000): 1264–1270.

152. Laffery et al., n. 4 above, at 1989–2000.

153. M. H. Thomas and A. Randall, "Intentional Introductions of Nonindigenous Species: A Principal-Agent Model and Protocol for Revokable Decisions," *Ecological Economics* 34 (2000): 333–345.

valuation" survey-based process currently used for environmental valuation in economic terms may be adapted for informed decision-making regarding invasives.[154] A quantitative ecological risk assessment, similar to those used in the nuclear and chemical process industries, has been proposed to evaluate the effectiveness of new technologies such as ballast water management strategies.[155] With a cadre of such tools in hand, managers can develop priorities for those situations where they have determined a high probability for success, where they can choose the response most likely to provide the greatest success, and where the funds and effort required can be known. The consequences of the management decision(s) must be routinely documented if the decision-making process is to successfully evolve toward one that is functional, efficient and timely.

Partnerships and Cooperation

The problems posed by invasive species often involve two or more parties (countries, regions, agencies etc.), often with uncertain consequences. Non-existent, delayed or ineffective coordination among parties serves only to undermine the efficiency of assessment and management.[156] Formal partnerships improve cooperation and provide a mechanism to organize efforts. The recent Ballast Water Convention highlights the effectiveness of establishing partnerships and cooperation among countries.[157] Such arrangements can lead to:

(1) proposition of additional regulations for a more effective prevention of invasions;

(2) the assignment of priorities and responsibilities to avoid the duplication of measures and resources; and

(3) enhanced funding availability to help build capacity.[158]

154. J. van den Bergh, P. Nunes, H. M. Dotinga, W. Kooistra, E.G. Vrieling and L. Peperzak, "Exotic Harmful Algae in Marine Eco-Systems: An Integrated Biological-Economical-Legal Analysis of Impacts and Policies," *Marine Policy* 26 (2001): 59–74.

155. K. R. Hayes, "Ecological Risk Assessment for Ballast Water Introductions: A Suggested Approach," *ICES Journal of Marine Science*, 55 (1998): 201–212.

156. A. M. Perrault and W. C. Muffett, "Turning off the tap: A strategy to address international aspects of invasive alien species," *Review of European Community and International Law* 11, 2 (2002): 211–224.

157. IMO (International Maritime Organization), *International Convention for the Control and Management of Ships Ballast Water and Sediments*, adopted 13 February 2004, available online: <http://www.imo.org/home.asp>.

158. A. Dextrase, "Preventing the Introduction and Spread of Alien Aquatic Species in the Great Lakes," in *Alien Invaders in Canada's Waters, Wetlands and Forests*, Claudi et al., eds. (Ottawa: Natural Resources Canada and Canadian Forest Service, 2002): 219–231.

International organizations do exist that provide more comprehensive response to global concerns. Such organizations can be enlisted to foster collaborative efforts regarding invasive species. Organizations such as the United Nations Environment Programme (UNEP), IMO, the Food and Agriculture Organization (FAO), the Secretariat for the Convention on Biological Diversity (CBD) and the World Conservation Union (IUCN) have varying nation-state memberships, although they all appear to encourage cooperation and collaboration in many domains. An independent but international body could coordinate information collection across many aspects of invasive species including taxonomy, ecological interrelationships, resource contacts, and methods of control, etc.[159]

The Global Invasive Species Program (GISP) is an international program dedicated solely to invasive species issues, and has the IUCN and CBD as member-partners. The GISP strives to improve the scientific bases for decision making, to develop capacity for early warning and rapid assessment and response, to enhance invasive management capability, to reduce economic impacts of invasives and to develop better risk assessment, and strengthen international agreements.[160] GISP provides the ways and means for achieving high-level discussions on the sharing of information and the adoption of best practices, but additional direction is required to translate the work done by GISP into effective regional management techniques. Developing functional links between local cooperating institutions along with national and international planners is necessary for cross-border invasive species management.[161] The North American Commission for Environmental Cooperation (CEC), composed of the senior governmental officials responsible for the environment in Canada, Mexico and the United States, is an example of international collaboration to address environmental concerns, including invasive study and response.[162] The CEC is currently involved in a project to develop prevention and control measures to eliminate pathways in coastal and fresh waters of North America, and has created a comprehensive overview of available scientific and policy information for the North American region.[163] The CEC aims to

159. The World Conservation Union (IUCN), Position Statement on Translocation of Living Organisms: Introductions, Reintroductions and Re-Stocking, approved by the 22nd Meeting of the IUCN Council, Switzerland, 4th September 1987.

160. Global Invasive Species Programme, available online: <http:www.gisp.org/>.

161. A. Grosse and B. Gregg, "Invasive Species as a Trilateral Challenge," *Report on the Plenary Session at VIII Trilateral Committee Meeting, Albuquerque, New Mexico* (2003).

162. The Commission for Environmental Cooperation (CEC), available online: <http://www.cec.org/who_we_are/index.cfm?varlan=english>.

163. The Commission for Environmental Cooperation (CEC), available online: <http://www.cec.org/programs_projects/conserv_biodiv/project/index.cfm?projectID=20&varlan=english>.

identify common aquatic invasive issues and pathways, develop a North American Invasive Species Information Network and a directory of legal institutions, and identify and develop tools for raising awareness and capacity in decision makers, as well as compliance incentives for the industrial and economic sectors.[164] Although created in 1993 under the North American Agreement on Environmental Cooperation (NAAEC), the CEC only began to address invasive aquatic species in 2001 and has to date held three meetings to address invasive aquatics. Thus, this partnership is in the early stages of developing collaborations to address invasive concerns.[165] As summarized above, a cohesive action plan for Canada is still under development, although according to its Biodiversity Office, Environment Canada has become the lead agency for an inter-departmental Canadian effort to address invasive species.[166] Functional implementation among the various federal agencies is not complete and so the utility of the initiative remains to be seen.

At the regional level, awareness programmes such as the one coordinated by the Ontario Federation of Anglers and Hunters, in partnership with the Oshawa Creek Watershed Committee and the Ontario Ministry of Natural Resources represents a cooperative example of defining the problem for the resource users and policy makers alike.[167] Similarly, the partnership created between the State of Washington (United States) and Province of British Columbia (Canada) has been instrumental in the sharing of information and the initiation of activities focussed on the prevention of invasions.[168] Partnerships between government and community groups can help to adapt comparatively ambiguous policy to very specific practices appropriate to the location or invasive concern.

CONCLUSIONS AND RECOMMENDATIONS

Management decisions must provide realistic goals and objectives that balance available resources with the plausibility of obtaining effective control over the target problem, on a case-by-case basis. This requires a proactive ideology and a capacity to predict, with uncertainty, the outcome of a decision along with a determination of which potential consequences are most desirable for a given situation. Recent arguments introduced in

164. The Commission for Environmental Cooperation (CEC), available online: <http://www.cec.org/files/pdf/BIODIVERSITY/225–03–05_en.pdf>.

165. *Id.*

166. Environment Canada, Biodiversity Convention Office, 2004, n. 7 above.

167. Central Lake Ontario Conservation Agency, available online: <http://www.cloca.com/news/news2004/alien%20workshop.pdf>.

168. Doelle, n. 19 above, at 261–294.

Addressing the Threat of Invasive Alien Species: A Strategy for Canada (March 2004)[169] suggest that Canada will concentrate on setting response priorities and will attempt to balance costs and benefits against the probability for success. Judicious priority setting will require the ability to predict likely outcomes of decisions, and the ability to modify decisions as more information is received. These are elements that are recognized by the authors of the strategy as they petition for the evolution of invasives management "from a reactive to a predictive discipline,"[170] and we would add from reactive to proactive.

Contemporary management of invasives has low capability and poor predictive skill regarding the species that pose the greatest threat, which environments are most vulnerable, and what the economic or environmental impacts of an invasion will be. We offer suggestions in two principal areas that should lead to increased capability and predictability:

(1) Improve the technology and scientific knowledge relevant to the problem.

    (a) Advance the scientific data and modeling techniques required to assess impacts of invasives. Begin with what limited data there are to determine where the lacunas lie and monitor the evolution of known invasives and any/all mitigation measures.

    (b) Use the existing scientific literature and ancillary information to anticipate particularly vulnerable communities where effort might be concentrated.

(2) Improve the coordination of effort, information sharing and standardizations (where warranted).

    (a) Achieve internationally accepted, scientifically sanctioned and functional protocols for detection, assessment, control implementation, or evaluation of control efficacy where perfection is not the primary goal.

    (b) Achieve effective coordination of effort and information sharing across all engaged institutions (including industry) at the national and international level.

    (c) Achieve legislated regulations that go beyond the strictly voluntary and are designed with the motivational bases commensurate with predictably high levels of compliance.

It is generally accepted that managers will rarely have the luxury of making decisions regarding invasives with complete information and high

169. Environment Canada, Biodiversity Convention Office, 2004, n. 7 above.
170. *Id.* at 26.

predictive skill. In the absence of complete information, the choice of an appropriate management response will require the guidance provided by a clear, proactive policy, well constructed risk assessment procedures, sound documentation and the support of effective and fully functional collaborative efforts.

International initiatives including the IMO Ballast Water Convention,[171] the Convention on Biological Diversity,[172] and Agenda 21[173] represent important keys to guiding an effective response to a global concern. In the case of ballast water, an overall strategy based on a range of management and treatment options is the generally accepted approach, at least for now. International guidelines are needed for the regulation and safe use of invasive control measures, similar to the Biocontrol Code of Conduct.[174] International endorsement of practices can have significant influence on acceptance of those practices at the national level, and can expedite adoption into domestic policy. This has been shown in the recognition of the precautionary principle in some national policies in Canada, as well as in ballast water regulations in Canada and the United States, though comprehensiveness, clarity and enforceability regarding aquatic invasive law and policy in either country has yet to be achieved.

As the precautionary principle gains prominence in national policy at the rhetorical level and more desirably at the practical level, managers will rightfully and increasingly be called upon to make decisions in conditions of incomplete knowledge. Risk analysis practices, coupled with efficient and timely information sharing structures, including consequences recorded from previous or ongoing responses, can help to inform the decision bases, particularly if uncertainties are integral to the process. Techniques that model cost-accounting for assessment of potential ecological damages can place expected costs of control into context with the estimated costs of no response, where the latter also demands assessment.

The Canadian strategy for addressing invasive species addresses the necessary partnerships and the integration of data sharing and informed decision making,[175] but the ensuing action plans will determine the functionality of the concepts as they will in many respects in the United States. International, local and regional partnerships and collaborative efforts can provide the impetus *and* the support necessary to transform

---

171. McConnell, n. 95 above.

172. Bax et al., n. 1 above, at 313–323.

173. United Nations Conference on Environment and Development, n. 124 above, at 294.

174. A. Gassman, ed., *Profile: The IOBC Newsletter*, Issue 73 (Darmstadt, Germany: International Organization for Biological and Integrated Control of Noxious Animals and Plants Publication Commission, 2001).

175. Environment Canada, Biodiversity Convention Office, 2004, n. 7 above.

policy into practice. The work of the CEC, while still in its infancy, may prove to be invaluable to the environmental agencies of Mexico, the United States and Canada. Functional cooperation among local, regional, national and international institutions and planners also encourages the establishment and impetus for cross-border invasive species management.[176] Governmental priority and sustained fiscal resources will provide the level of motivation that is conducive for such initiatives and their cooperating agencies to realize the broader corporate objectives.

176. A. Grosse and B. Gregg, ''Invasive Species as a Trilateral Challenge,'' *Report on the Plenary Session at VIII Trilateral Committee Meeting. Albuquerque, New Mexico,* 2003.

Environment and Coastal Management

Evaluation of New Zealand's National Coastal Policy Statement: Has It Been Effective?

Johanna Rosier
School of People, Environment and Planning, Massey University, Palmerston North, New Zealand

INTRODUCTION

New Zealand's Coastal Policy Statement (NZCPS) was gazetted in 1994.[1] Section 57 of the Resource Management Act requires that there shall be at least one NZCPS in place at all times, containing matters of national importance.[2] It was the first national policy statement prepared in New Zealand as part of resource management legislative reforms carried out in the late 1980s and early 1990s, aimed at ensuring sustainable management of New Zealand's natural and physical resources. It is the only mandatory national policy statement and it is still the only policy statement translated into Maori (New Zealand's second official language).[3] This article reports on the findings of an independent review of the NZCPS.[4] It also outlines changes in New Zealand's coastal management regime at the national level and the effect of those changes on the role and content of the NZCPS. The evaluation was difficult because this is the first review carried out on a national policy statement in New Zealand, so the meaning of the term "effectiveness" has various interpretations.

---

1. Department of Conservation, *New Zealand Coastal Policy Statement*, Department of Conservation, Wellington, New Zealand, 1994.
2. Sections 6, 7, 8 and Section 58 of the Resource Management Act 1991 (and amendments to 2004).
3. Department of Conservation, *Te Kupu Kaupapahere Takutai Mo Aotearoa* (Maori Language Version of the NZCPS). Department of Conservation, New Zealand, 1994, pp. 26.
4. J. Rosier, *Independent Review of the New Zealand Coastal Policy Statement*, A report prepared for the Minister of Conservation (Palmerston North, New Zealand: School of People, Environment and Planning. Massey University, 2004), 135.

Ocean Yearbook 20: 471–504.

A Board of Inquiry[5] was appointed by the Minister of Conservation to inquire into the draft NZCPS,[6] hear submissions and make recommendations about the wording of the final NZCPS. The Board of Inquiry played an important role in determining the content of the NZCPS, the prescriptiveness of policies and the interpretation of key terms associated with the NZCPS, such as *Kaitiakitanga* (stewardship by Maori) and "significant." The NZCPS has no direct influence on use, subdivision or development, apart from Ministerial decisions about restricted coastal activities and the need for councils to "have regard" to the NZCPS in the preparation of plans and policy statements and in consideration of resource consents. Therefore, there have been considerable difficulties in attributing successful environmental outcomes to individual NZCPS policies or methods used in subnational plans and policy statements.

Resource Management Act: Context for the New Zealand Coastal Policy Statement

The Resource Management Act identifies the coastal environment[7] as an area of national priority in planning for sustainable management. Estuarine environments at the mouth of streams and rivers are also included in the Coastal Marine Area, an area seaward of Mean High Water Springs (MHWS) out to the 12-nautical mile limit. Particular coastal matters of national importance to be provided for include the preservation of the natural character of the coastal environment, maintenance and enhancement of public access to and along the coastal marine area, and the relationship of Maori and their culture and traditions with ancestral lands, water, sites of particular cultural and historic significance, *waahi tapu* (sacred places) and other *taonga* (gifts). However, Maori generally feel that there remain a number of barriers that prevent effective participation by Maori in resource management planning processes, particularly in relation to coastal planning.[8]

5. Board of Inquiry, *Report and Recommendations of the Board of Enquiry into the New Zealand Coastal Policy Statement.* A Report to the Minister of Conservation, Department of Conservation, Wellington, New Zealand, 1994.

6. Department of Conservation, *Draft New Zealand Coastal Policy 1992,* Department of Conservation, Wellington, New Zealand, 1992.

7. Although it varies considerably around the country, the coastal environment is generally an area that includes land-based coastal features such as dune systems, coastal cliffs and rocky features out to the 12 nautical mile limit of New Zealand's territorial sea.

8. M. Mutu, "Barriers to *Tangata Whenua* participation in resource management," in *Whenua* ed., M. Kawharu (Auckland: Reed Press, 2003), 75–95. Barriers discussed by Mutu include Councils overriding legal rights of local *hapu,* difficulties in communicating indigenous knowledge appropriately in the planning system and attitudes of planners.

By the time the Resource Management Act was enacted in 1991, it was generally agreed that a national coastal policy statement was needed to deal with important coastal matters and to provide a clear definition of the 'coastal environment.' Reasons for special coastal provisions include the sensitivity of the coastal environment, complexity of the interface between land and sea, and fluctuations in long-term cycles of environmental change.[9] The coastal environment is seen as a finite resource that would be subject to increased competing demands for conservation.[10]

There are a series of plans and policy statements through which the coastal provisions of the Resource Management Act are implemented as demonstrated in Figure 1. Berkes et al.[11] have detailed the character of the New Zealand planning system, which is a cooperative rather than hierarchical planning system. All policy statements and plans have a particular role in achieving the purpose of the Act—sustainable management. All are required to achieve integrated management and all have individual roles in the resource management system.[12]

The Minister of Conservation's current roles under the Resource Management Act provisions include approval of the NZCPS, approval of regional coastal plans (management of the Coastal Marine Area) and as the consent authority for Restricted Coastal Activities which are processed at the regional level of planning. The Minister is also responsible for deciding how land reclaimed from the sea under the Resource Management Act is to be vested in the Crown or converted to private property, and how space is tendered in the Coastal Marine Area for extraction of sand, gravels and shell.

Regional councils are responsible for catchment-level planning considered crucial for achieving an integrated approach to sustainable management of natural and physical resources. Regional policy statements prepared by regional councils provide for sustainable management of privately owned land and activities by individuals. Regions are based on river catchments, facilitating management of land-based pollution and sediment discharges from river systems to the Coastal Marine Area. Regional coastal plans are

9. Minister of Works and Development, *Coastal Planning and Development,* A Statement by the Minister of Works and Development (August 1974), Wellington, New Zealand, at 10; Ministry of Transport 1980. *Proceedings Coastal Zone Management Seminar 1980,* Wellington, New Zealand.

10. Department of Conservation, *Draft New Zealand Coastal Policy 1992,* Department of Conservation, Wellington, New Zealand, 1992.

11. P. Berkes and J. Crawford, "Do cooperative environmental planning mandates produce good plans? Empirical results from the New Zealand experience," *Environment and Planning B: Planning and Design* 26 (1999): 643–664.

12. For example, the functions of regional councils and territorial authorities are outlined in Sections 30 and 31 of the Resource Management Act 1991.

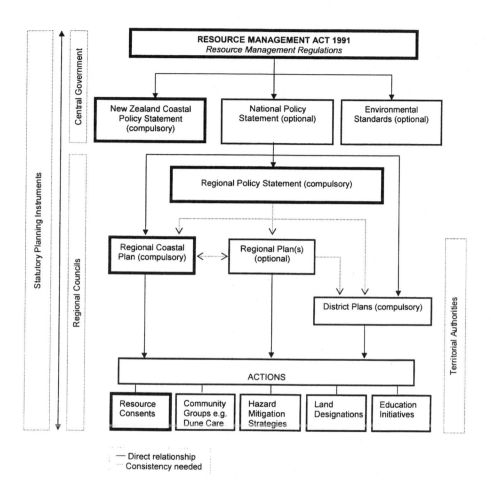

FIG. 1.—Relationship between Levels of Planning under New Zealand's Resource Management Act

prepared to achieve sustainable management of coastal resources in the coastal marine area out to the 12-nautical mile limit.

Territorial Authorities are responsible for preparing the district plan—most important for protecting natural character on land in the coastal environment at a local level and providing for public access to and along the Coastal Marine Area.

THE 1994 NEW ZEALAND COASTAL POLICY STATEMENT AND THE REVIEW

The purpose of the NZCPS as outlined in section 56 of the Resource Management Act is "to state policies in order to achieve the purpose of this Act in relation to the coastal environment of New Zealand." Section 58 contains the matters that were required to be considered and provided for in the NZCPS when it was prepared. These are all concerns of national importance to New Zealanders:

- National priorities for the preservation of the natural character of the coastal environment of New Zealand, including protection from inappropriate subdivision, use, and development;
- The protection of the characteristics of the coastal environment of special value to the *tangata whenua* including *waahi tapu*, *tauranga waka* (canoe landing sites), *mahinga maataitai* (food), and *taonga raranga* (weaving materials);
- Activities involving the subdivision, use, or development of areas of the coastal environment;
- The Crown's interests in land in the coastal marine area;
- The matters to be included in any or all regional coastal plans in regard to the preservation of the natural character of the coastal environment, types of activities which have or are likely to have a significant or irreversible adverse effect on the coastal marine area; and areas in the coastal marine area that have significant conservation value;
- The implementation of New Zealand's international obligations affecting the coastal environment;
- The procedures and methods to be used to review the policies and to monitor their effectiveness; and
- Any other matter relating to the purpose of a New Zealand Coastal Policy Statement.

The preparation of the NZCPS took several years and after the section 32 analysis was completed in 1992,[13] an interdepartmental committee again reviewed the draft before it was publicly released and put to the Board of Inquiry in 1992. After two years of extensive public consultation, the current NZCPS was gazetted in May 1994.

---

13. Department of Conservation, *Options and Implications Assessment: The Application of Section 32 of the Resource Management Act to the Preparation of the Draft New Zealand Coastal Policy Statement*, Department of Conservation, Wellington, New Zealand, 1992.

The Board of Inquiry noted that the NZCPS is mainly given effect through the approval of regional coastal plans and via the approval of Restricted Coastal Activities.[14] However, this independent review[15] focuses on the following range of methods that have been used by the Department and local authorities to implement the NZCPS:

- The Department of Conservation's submissions to regional policy statements, regional coastal plans and district plans.
- The Minister's approval of sixteen regional coastal plans.
- The role of the Minister's appointee on hearing committees for consideration of Restricted Coastal Activities.
- The Minister's role as a consent authority for Restricted Coastal Activities.
- Plans and policy statements prepared under the provisions of the Resource Management Act, which prior to 2003 could not be inconsistent with the NZCPS.
- The consideration that local authorities give to the NZCPS when assessing resource consents (the NZCPS is one of the matters to which a consent authority shall have regard when processing resource consents in the coastal environment).
- State of the Environment monitoring by local authorities.
- Other non-statutory methods used to achieve an integrated approach to sustainable management of the coastal environment.

NZCPS Policy 7.1.1 requires that the *effectiveness* of the NZCPS be reviewed within nine years of its gazettal. The general aims were to determine the extent to which the NZCPS has guided the preparation of plans and policy statements at the regional and territory authority levels of planning, and how much it has influenced the resource consent process in the "coastal environment" and resulted in desired environmental outcomes. At the time of implementation, plans and policy statements could not be "not inconsistent" with the NZCPS. The effectiveness of the Minister of Conservation's involvement in preparing Regional Coastal Plans and in approving Restricted Coastal Activities also needed to be assessed to determine the extent to which it achieved the purpose of the Resource Management Act in relation to the coastal environment—sustainable management of natural and physical resources. Therefore, in this review, effectiveness was pragmatically assessed by:

14. Board of Inquiry, *Report and Recommendations of the Board of Enquiry into the New Zealand Coastal Policy Statement*, A Report to the Minister of Conservation, Department of Conservation, Wellington, New Zealand, 1994.
    15. Rosier, n. 4 above.

- Summarizing the emerging issues in coastal management and the assessment of the adequacy of the NZCPS policies in addressing these issues;
- Examining how the NZCPS policies have been implemented through plans, policy statements and resource consents;
- Consulting with NZCPS users from central and local government, industry and other organizations about the implementation of the NZCPS; and
- Making recommendations to the Minister of Conservation for the need, if any, to review, change, and revoke any policies in the NZCPS.

REVIEW METHODOLOGY

Various authors have carried out evaluations or assessments of plans or policies for a variety of reasons, including the need to understand the degree to which those plans or policies are effective. For example, there are several authors who have focused on assessing the effectiveness of urban plans.[16] These studies focus on the process of preparing and implementing plans and the nature and applicability of information used as a basis for urban plans. They are concerned with the interpretation of legislative requirements by government and local planners, appropriate use of analytical methodologies, and the effective use of planning resources.

There have also been several studies about the effectiveness of national coastal and ocean policy programmes that inform the development of a methodology for assessing the effectiveness of the NZCPS. These studies may seek to assess the degree to which a program achieves specific objectives such as "integration"[17] "public access"[18] or protection of natural beaches,

16. Land Use Consultants, *Good Practice on the Evaluation of Environmental Information for Planning Projects Research Report* (Department of the Environment Planning Research Programme, HMSO, London, U.K. 1994), at 1985; J. Steel and V. Nadin, *The Efficiency and Effectiveness of Local Plan Enquiries* (Department of Environment, Planning Research Programme, HMSO, London, U.K. 1994), at 161; Queensland Treasury, *Guidelines for the Development of Performance Indicators*, (Queensland Treasury, Brisbane, Australia, 1990), at 34; Queensland Department of Local Government, *Plan and Deliver: Effective Process in Corporate Planning for Queensland Local Government* (Department of Local Government and Planning Incorporating Rural Communities, Brisbane, Australia, 1999), at 43.

17. R. Knecht and J. Archer, "Integration in the US Coastal Zone Management Program," *Ocean and Coastal Management* 21 (1993): 183–199.

18. P. Pogue and V. Lee, "Providing Public Access to the Shoreline: The Role of Coastal Zone Management Programs," *Coastal Management* 27 (1999): 219–237.

dunes, bluffs and rocky shores.[19] Some studies provide a useful guide because they seek to determine the degree to which specific environmental outcomes are achieved "on the ground." For example, Hershman et al.[20] focus on assessing the degree to which individual state coastal management programs implemented the objectives of the U.S. Coastal Zone Management Act. It was determined, that, although the U.S. states did implement the national objectives, it was difficult to measure environmental outcomes. A similar finding resulted from the assessment of the review of the implementation of Australia's Oceans Policy.[21]

Most of the plan evaluation authors acknowledge the need for a pragmatic, balanced approach between scientific rigor and comprehensiveness and the need to provide timely information to improve the preparation of policy. Most also comment on the difficulty of implementing national policy across a hierarchy of management systems and the lack of templates for designing the assessment process. For example, Hoch[22] reinforces the benefits of a pragmatic approach to evaluation of plans, arguing the importance of abandoning the separation of theory and practice and examining whether a plan has improved the practice of planning in relation to a specific topic area. The template for the assessment process should be flexible, recognize the complex interrelationships involved in implementing a plan, and focus on the shared consequences of the plan, rather than shared assumptions in preparing the plan. Hoch argues that an emphasis on a more rational approach requires precise information and expertise that might not always be available.

The New Zealand planning system presents additional challenges when assessing effectiveness or quality of plans and policy statements. Under the "cooperative mandate,"[23] sub-national planning agencies are given considerable flexibility in implementing national priorities and goals.[24] Berkes et

19. T. Brand-Cohen and M. Gordan, "State Coastal Program Effectiveness in Protecting Natural Beaches, Dunes, Bluffs and Rocky Shores," *Coastal Management* 27 (1999): 187–217.

20. M. J. Hershman, J. W. Good, T. Bernd-Cohen, R. F. Goodwin, V. Lee and P. Pogue, "The Effectiveness of Coastal Zone Management in the United States," *Coastal Management* 27 (1999): 113–138.

21. TFG International 2002. Review of the Implementation of the Oceans Policy: Final Report, TFG International, 25 October 2002, National Oceans Office, Commonwealth of Australia, Canberra, Australia.

22. C. Hoch, "Evaluating plans pragmatically," *Planning Theory* 1, 1 (2002): 53–73.

23. P. R. Berkes and J. Crawford, "Do Cooperative Environmental Planning Mandates Produce Good Plans? Empirical Results from the New Zealand Experience," *Environment and Planning B: Planning and Design*, 26 (1999): 643–664.

24. New Zealand methods of implementation may include rules in plans, provision of a service, provision of information or education, charges and incentives, monitoring and finally the option of "doing nothing."

al. describe New Zealand intergovernmental arrangements as "consensus building," "co-joint" or "collaborative." However, the flexibility inherent in sub-national planning results in problems for assessing effectiveness or quality of plans interpreting national priorities and goals, and in assessing the degree to which environmental change actually results from planning actions.

Several authors suggest that plan content analysis supported by analysis of the outcomes of development applications and interviews with plan users are appropriate methods to measure plan quality in relation to specified criteria.[25] The major strength of plan analysis is that the researcher is not reliant simply on the opinion of plan users as to whether higher level planning goals and priorities are met.

The methodology for the NZCPS review was debated by members of the Department of Conservation's expert panel guiding the Minister's brief to the reviewer. A number of matters were considered. For example, many of the regions do not have final versions of the first generation Resource Management Act plans and policy statements. In some cases, councils are poorly resourced and have had difficulties carrying out the studies needed to inform plan preparation. It was finally determined that for this review a variety of methods were needed to assess effectiveness of the NZCPS. Firstly, quantitative analysis was carried out to understand the geomorphological implications of district plan provisions about coastal erosion.[26] This analysis provided evidence about the implementation of NZCPS policies concerning the protection of coastal environments from coastal hazards and the degree to which climate change issues have been incorporated into sub-national planning about management of coastal hazards.

Secondly, the results of two reviews about restricted coastal activity decision making were used to understand the degree to which Ministerial involvement in those processes has been effective.[27] This information also

25. P. R. Berkes, D. J. Roenigk, E. J. Kaiser and R. Burby, "Enhancing Plan Quality: Evaluating the Role of the State Planning Mandates for Natural Hazard Mitigation," *Journal of Environmental Planning and Management*, 39 (1996): 79–96; Berkes et al., n. 23 above; L. C. Dalton and R. J. Burby, "Mandates, Plans and Planners," *Journal of the American Planning Association*, 60 (1994): 444–462; R. Hedrick, "Evaluating Comprehensive Plans: Evaluation Criteria," Paper presented to the American Planning Association Conference, New Orleans 2001; A. Khakee, "Reading Plans as an Exercise in Evaluation," *Evaluation* 6 (2000): 119–136.

26. M. Jacobsen, *Review of the NZCPS 1994—Coastal Hazards*, Report prepared for the Minister of Conservation, January 2004, Volumes I and II, Wellington, New Zealand, at 260.

27. T. Yeboah, *A Review of Restricted Coastal Activities*. Conservation Policy Division, Department of Conservation, Wellington, New Zealand, 1 March 1999); Woodward-Clyde, 1998, *Restricted Coastal Activities and Regional Coastal Plans*, A report prepared for the Minister of Conservation June 1998, Wellington, New Zealand.

provided valuable understanding about the degree of consensus among participants in both studies about the effectiveness of the NZCPS in guiding sub-national plans and policy statements and achieving environmental outcomes consistent with sustainable management of New Zealand's coastal and marine resources.

Thirdly, a literature review of research and various assessments regarding consultation with *Tangata whenua* (indigenous people of particular areas in the country) was undertaken to determine the extent to which the NZCPS has been effective in dealing with issues of importance to Maori. Fourthly, key stakeholders with an interest in the coastal environment were interviewed, including representatives of government departments concerned with matters in the coastal and marine environment (i.e., the oceans policy group), industry (ports, utilities and infrastructure, developers, fishers, aquaculture), coastal researchers, the regional coastal planners group, the Department of Conservation regional coastal planners group, surf life savers (lifeguards), national conservation groups, national boating clubs/organizations and professional organizations.

Fifthly, the review was advertised calling for public submissions and submissions from various professional organizations whose members work with coastal plans and policy statements in their work. For example, invitations were posted on the Quality Planning web site,[28] and notices were placed in key environmental journals of interest to coastal and professional local government practitioners. A brochure prepared by the Department of Conservation in 2003 was sent to people who submitted in relation to other reviews on coastal interest (i.e., submitters to the Oceans Policy Review process and the review of the Marine Reserves Act), calling on them to participate in this review.

Most importantly, content analysis of sub-national plans and policy statements was carried out to determine the degree to which the provisions are "not inconsistent with" the NZCPS. Planning documents analyzed include regional policy statements, regional coastal plans and district plans along with the outcomes of resource consents and non-statutory plans and strategies dealing with aspects of the coastal environment (i.e., growth strategies, coastal management strategies), and State of the Environment Monitoring Strategies.

Three regions including Auckland, Bay of Plenty and Southland (see Figure 2) were selected for the review of plans, policy statements and other methods. Their selection was based on the need to be representative of the geographical diversity of the regions around the country. The assessment also needed to be based on relatively complete resource management planning documents.

28. See <http://www.qualityplanning.org.nz/>.

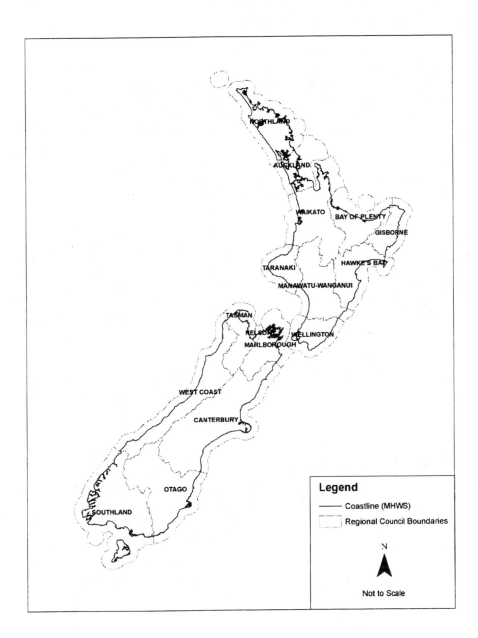

FIG. 2.—New Zealand's Regional Coastal Boundaries

Auckland Region is New Zealand's largest metropolitan region with a highly developed coastal environment because over 90 percent of the region's residential and commercial development is occurring in the area defined by the regional council as the "coastal environment." The coastal environment in the Auckland Region contains extensive harbors, estuaries and embayments and a myriad of islands.[29] The coastal environment of Auckland is under some of the most intense development pressure in New Zealand. Auckland Regional Council's regional policy statement and regional coastal plan were assessed along with the district plans for Rodney District (strong emphasis on non-statutory methods) and Waitakere City (an Agenda 21 city). Both districts are under considerable development pressure.

The Bay of Plenty Region borders Auckland Region and is experiencing rapid growth because of its popularity as a retirement centre. Coastal erosion is a natural feature of the region's coastline, while other hazards include tsunamis and storm surges. The region is growing rapidly, and there is considerable pressure on coastal areas, particularly for agricultural production, assimilation of waste and use of land for development. Much of the growth is focused on the coastal plains and the City of Tauranga. The Port of Tauranga is the largest export port in New Zealand. The Environment Bay of Plenty Regional Council has developed a strong coast-care program and also manages a significant rural hinterland. The district plans for two districts were assessed—Tauranga (a city of 90,906 people) and the Western Bay of Plenty, a rural district with small beach settlements which experiences significant population increases in the summer.

The Southland Region is a sparsely developed region dominated by agricultural industries, mainly pastoral farming. The region adjoins the Fiordland World Heritage Site. The Coastal Marine Area of the Southland Region covers over 3,000 km of coastline, which is approximately one seventh of New Zealand's coastline. There are few development pressures outside the principle towns of Invercargill and Bluff. However, any development has the potential to cause significant adverse effects on nationally important natural coastal landscapes and ecological values. Both Invercargill and Southland District Councils manage coasts with a strong rural character and are councils with a limited rating base, which affects their operational budgets for carrying out resource management functions.

The keyword search of plans and policy statements was used to assess the extent to which the documents "had regard" to the NZCPS policies. Although the aim was to use a qualitative technique (i.e., applying the Nudist[30] computer program) to carry out this analysis, a pilot analysis of the

29. Auckland Regional Council (ARC), 1999, *Auckland Regional Policy Statement*, Auckland Regional Council, Auckland, New Zealand, 1999, (ARPS operational 31 August 1999), at 71.

30. See <http://minnow.cc.gatech.edu:8080/hci/191> regarding the applicability of NUDIST Computer Program, a flexible structured coding system that enables the researcher to analyze recorded human behavior and analyze large amounts of information.

Rodney District Plan indicated that this technique was not precise enough to analyze documentation because districts have not always used the keywords contained in NZCPS policies, or in some cases the words themselves. So the keyword search was carried out manually and subjective judgments were made about the extent to which plan provisions did reflect the content and intent of the NZCPS.

Appendix 1 contains the keywords used in the search. Keywords are derived from the wording of individual NZCPS policies or the expected outcomes listed in the section 32 analysis carried out in the preparation of the NZCPS. The entire planning documents were searched for references to NZCPS policy wording and intent. The number of times the NZCPS is referred to in the document is an indication of the importance placed on it. Searching for 'coast' also picked up coastal environment, coastal marine area, coastal zone and coastline. Many of the requirements to protect the coastal environment are treated by councils in an integrated way with managing land, water and air as required in Part II of the Resource Management Act. As such, the coastal environment is provided for, but is not placed as a higher priority in Resource Management Act decision-making as required by the NZCPS.

If a planning document contained references to the actual wording of NZCPS policies in policies and reasons for policies, and provided more detailed policies and methods to address the intent of NZCPS policies, it was judged to be "excellent." If the NZCPS was not referred to specifically in policies and methods, but the general wording of NZCPS policies was reflected in the wording of policies, the planning document was judged to be "fair." This type of document sometimes contained words that were similar to NZCPS wording, but did not provide specifically for implementation of NZCPS policies. "Poor" planning documents simply referred generally to the NZCPS as a policy document influencing the preparation of the planning document without specific reference to NZCPS policies or words. A number of additional matters also needed to be addressed in analyzing the planning documents and resource consents.

Other Matters of Importance in the Review of the NZCPS

In reviewing policies and methods used in planning documents and the reports about resource consent applications, it was also necessary to consider a number of additional points that were identified by the group of coastal experts advising Department of Conservation officers. These points included the:

- Degree to which Resource Management Act section 6, 7 and 8 matters of national importance are acknowledged in the policy details, where councils have provided more detail in interpreting those Resource Management Act provisions, referring to specific NZCPS policies, with more background information provided and techniques/actions used by councils to deal with any coastal issue and implement the NZCPS policies, are articulated.

• Degree to which councils have used rules in the district plans to protect the "environmental bottom line" in managing coastal land. The environmental bottom line in the Coastal Marine Area is protected by Resource Management Act section 12. Where regional coastal plans facilitate activities, adverse effects on important Coastal Marine Area values are avoided, remedied or mitigated.

Regional councils and territorial authorities were asked to provide information about the review of regional coastal plans and environmental monitoring strategies. Monitoring plan outcomes also required the analysis of resource consent outcomes resulting from use and development on land and in the Coastal Marine Area. Where possible, a mix of restricted coastal activities, coastal permits, joint coastal permits (matters dealt with by regional councils and territorial authorities using joint hearings), and non-notified/notified consents were used. Resource consents were chosen by agreement between the reviewer, the Department of Conservation's Conservancy staff and council officers, and in the case of significant development applications, implementation of the NZCPS was a relevant issue. Applications below MHWS dealt with different aspects of management—discharge to water, occupation, erection of a structure, and reclamation. It was important to see evidence of reference to the NZCPS in reviewing officer reports and hearing committee decisions for the resource consents, for outcomes to be considered as not being inconsistent with NZCPS policies.

One problem, given the scale of the review, was the difficulty of dealing with hundreds of permitted activities in each region, given the potential for cumulative effects of many small actions. It was impractical to carry out detailed surveys regarding this matter. There seem to be two main issues for further study. Have permitted activities been monitored for compliance once structures/activities are in place or carried out? Are permitted activities meeting the permitted activity test in the relevant district or regional plan? If so, they have minor effects and do not need resource consents.

The effectiveness of the Minister of Conservation's involvement in sub-national planning was measured by the number of times the Department of Conservation case was successful in Environment Court proceedings, or provided guidance to the Court about matters of importance in the coastal environment. The case law was analyzed in a separate report by Department of Conservation.[31]

RESULTS AND DISCUSSION

The results are presented across all three regions by category of policy statement or plan, including regional policy statements, regional coastal plans, and district plans, with additional reference to resource consent outcomes where applicable. Reference is also made to the material collated from interviews and the analysis of Environment Court decisions.

Regional Policy Statements

All three Regional Councils have acknowledged the need to implement New Zealand's international obligations and have initiated monitoring programmes in cooperation with other agencies. Auckland Regional Council and Environment Bay of Plenty have initiated a variety of community environmental care programmes, whereas Environment Southland has initiated a variety of economic tools to offset possible adverse environmental effects resulting from development in the coastal environment.

Both the Auckland (1999) and Environment Bay of Plenty (1999) Regional Policy Statements are not inconsistent with the NZCPS and are considered "fair" planning documents. Both include frequent references to NZCPS policies in setting the scene for management of the coastal environment. However, there is minimal reference to NZCPS policies and principles in justifying the provisions of both regional policy statements. The Auckland Regional Policy Statement satisfies NZCPS Chapter 1 requiring the preservation of the natural character of the coastal environment, but the Environment Bay of Plenty Regional Policy Statement does not provide for avoidance of adverse effects on natural character of the coastal environment. The Environment Southland Regional Policy Statement (1997) is an "excellent" document because it is thorough in terms of referring to NZCPS policies, in justifying the objectives, policies and methods outlined in the Southland Regional Policy Statement, and the wording of regional policy statement policies reflects the wording and intent of the NZCPS.

---

31. S. McRae, *The NZCPS Caselaw: A Summary of Court Interpretation of the New Zealand Coastal Policy Statement,* Department of Conservation, Wellington, New Zealand, 2004.

Both the Auckland and Environment Bay of Plenty Regional Policy Statements contain policy and objectives on the Treaty of Waitangi, Maori culture and traditions, consultation, partnership and plan making. These general regional policy statement policies do not directly satisfy the relevant NZCPS policies. The regional policy statements contain general objectives, policies and methods with regard to the Treaty of Waitangi, Maori culture and traditions, consultation and partnership, which do not completely satisfy NZCPS policies.

In the Auckland region, the regional policy statement provides no provision to ensure access to the coast is available for people with disabilities. The Auckland Regional Policy Statement policies about the adoption of a precautionary approach, and the sharing of knowledge are partially satisfied by the establishment of shared inventories managed across the various local authorities and agencies in the Auckland region (e.g., Sites of Natural Significance).

The Environment Bay of Plenty Regional Policy Statement provides objectives, policies and methods with regard to the preservation of the natural character of the coastal environment, including the Coastal Management Area. The Environment Bay of Plenty Regional Policy Statement policies provide for recognition of significant ecosystems and habitats. However, provision is not made for the *avoidance* of adverse effects of subdivision use and development. The Environment Bay of Plenty Regional Policy Statement also contains policies to protect heritage areas and other values against the adverse effects of subdivision, use and development, including consideration of habitat, cumulative effects, water quality, access, and land management.

Although the topic is of high priority in the NZCPS, disposal of human sewage is not an issue explicitly provided for in the Bay of Plenty Regional Policy Statement. Sewerage reticulation is only referred to in the Air chapter in relation to sources of odors, which is interesting given the pressure of urban growth in the region.

The Southland Regional Policy Statement is thorough in that most principles and policies of the NZCPS are referred to throughout the document, particularly in its introductory sections and in some of the explanations for policies and objectives. In places where the NZCPS has not been directly acknowledged, the wording of the policies is true to the intent of the NZCPS statement and thus considered to be an "excellent" planning document.

NZCPS policies concerning matters of interest to *tangata whenua* and Maori resource management are well provided for. Reference is also made throughout the regional policy statement for the identification and joint-management of resources important to Maori, and the possible transfer/ delegation of power under Sections 33 and 34 of the Resource Management Act, enabling Maori to manage natural and physical resources important to each tribe. The Southland Regional Policy Statement makes a superficial reference to the fact that the foreshore and seabed is of interest to all New Zealanders and that public access to the coast is to be protected. The Regional Policy Statement does satisfy the NZCPS policy in addressing important questions regarding the relationship between the Crown and *tangata whenua* as established by the Treaty of Waitangi.

Financial contributions are considered as a method to offset the cost of restricting public interest in the coastal marine area. Water quality standards are managed by several policies in the Southland Regional Policy Statement, including provisions in NZCPS, which state that water quality will be maintained and enhanced wherever practicable. Non-point source discharges need to comply with water quality standards in the various plans to be prepared by the regional council.

The Southland Regional Policy Statement contains excellent provisions to satisfy the monitoring requirements of the NZCPS policy. The NZCPS requires those managing the coast to identify the procedures and methods that will be used to monitor the coastal environment. Those monitoring requirements identified in the Southland Regional Policy Statement include the number and type of coastal permits issued, coastal protection works and their effects, background water quality levels, the background condition of areas of the coast, and the impacts of marine farming.

Regional Coastal Plans

Generally speaking, all Regional Coastal Plans were judged to be "excellent" in terms of consistency with NZCPS policies because Regional Coastal Plans are approved by the Minister of Conservation. All have included additional areas requiring special management to achieve conservation objectives. All contained innovative methods to deal with issues that are difficult to manage through a regulatory approach.

The Auckland Regional Coastal Plan is only partially operative, and is in the final stages of gaining approval from the Minister of Conservation. The results of many of the challenges to the Plan were not surveyed as part of this analysis. Overall, NZCPS policies have been incorporated into the Auckland Regional Coastal Plan, with individual NZCPS policies and the Schedule of Restricted Coastal Activities is referred to explicitly.

The Auckland Regional Coastal Plan has used "Conservation Protection Areas (CPAs) One (areas requiring preservation) and Two (areas requiring protection)" as a method to protect the natural character elements provided for in Chapter One of the NZCPS. Conservation Protection Area One areas have higher protection and the imperative to avoid adverse effects, because of their significant value and higher vulnerability to adverse effects.

NZCPS policies about *kaitiakitanga*, Section 33 transfers and participation in decision making have been satisfactorily provided for in Auckland Regional Coastal Plan policies about *tangata whenua* management areas (traditional harvesting areas). Although these matters have also been referred to in general discussions about the potential adverse effects of various activities, provisions relating to the transfer of power or delegations have not been comprehensively included in policies, rules and standards related to management of activities.

Discharges of sewage and other pollutants, and maintenance/enhancement of water quality are comprehensively provided for, with discharge of human sewage a restricted coastal activity as required in the NZCPS. NZCPS policy regarding rubbish collection and sewage connections is not provided for in the rules about marina development.

That part of the Environment Bay of Plenty Regional Coastal Environment Plan referring to land in the coastal environment was approved by the regional council on 12 December 2002. The part of the regional coastal plan referring to the Coastal Management Area is currently awaiting approval from the Minister of Conservation.

Quite often wording of NZCPS policies are altered in the Regional Coastal Environment Plan to suit different issues and activities, and this means that the objectives, policies and methods rarely quote the NZCPS, or use its words. This gives the impression that the Regional Coastal Environment Plan has changed the intent of the NZCPS in some parts. Few NZCPS policies are ignored in this Regional Coastal Environment Plan and it includes a summary of the issues covered in the NZCPS. It is not obvious that including the whole of the coastal environment in the Regional Coastal Environment Plan has improved the potential for an integrated approach to coastal management in the region.

The Southland Regional Coastal Plan was notified as a proposed plan in November 2000. There are a number of references in the Plan and these can be viewed in the amended version of the Plan dated November 2001. In several sections of the Southland Regional Coastal Plan, an entire chapter of the NZCPS is quoted word for word, followed by discussion on how this is relevant to the Southland coastal marine environment. Furthermore, the explanation/reasons for the adoption of the various policies and objectives often refer directly to the specific NZCPS policy/principle that it is aiming to satisfy and be consistent with. There are also specific instances in the Southland Regional Coastal Plan where it can be said that the Southland Regional Council has not only satisfied the intent of the NZCPS principles and policies but has in fact also gone beyond it. Environment Southland, the Regional Council has entered a "Coastal Marine Area Agreement" with the Minister of Conservation, Invercargill City Council and Southland District Council, so that management is more effective.

The Southland Regional Coastal Plan is satisfactorily consistent with the NZCPS requirement to protect characteristics of special value to *tangata whenua*. A reasonable amount of background to the values and beliefs of local Maori is provided in the Plan, including the mythology which is central to the perspective of *Kai Tahu* (local *tangata whenua*), and an abridged version of the Treaty of Waitangi is provided in Maori and English. Particularly important issues identified by *Kai Tahu* are listed in the Southland Regional Coastal Plan. NZCPS policy is also provided for through an outline of Southland Regional Council intentions to consult with *Kai Tahu*. The Council not only recognises that the coast is important to the people of the Southland region, but that "the coast and access to the coast is rated very highly by all New Zealanders"—unusual in most of the other coastal planning documents.

District Plans

All the district plans analyzed contain only general provisions about matters of importance to *tangata whenua*. The Western Bay of Plenty District Plan is the only district plan examined which identifies land required for esplanade reserves and alternative provisions under Sections 338 or 440 of the Maori Land (*Te Ture Whenua Maori*) Act 1993 to ensure that reserves are not alienated from Maori ownership when Maori traditional land is subdivided, fulfilling the requirements of NZCPS policies.

The Waitakere District Plan was made operative on 23 March 2003.[32] While there are some issues yet to be resolved through appeals, these do not substantially affect the provisions about the coastal environment. The NZCPS is only explicitly referred to in the general introduction to the District Plan along with other statutory plans and policy statements. Some of the NZCPS policies are reflected in policies without explicit rules and standards (e.g., cumulative effects and precautionary approach) being included. It could be argued that the impact of this on the quality of decisions about development can only be measured over time.

The NZCPS policies concerning preservation of natural character are explicitly provided for in policies that define natural character of the coastal environment, acknowledge the need to protect natural character, and manage the adverse effects of activities, including removal of shell, sand and soils from beaches and estuaries.

The Waitakere District Plan has rules and standards relating to effects of land-based activities on the natural character of coastal and freshwater.

32. Waitakere City Council (WCC), 2003, *Waitakere District Plan* (WDP), Waitakere City, New Zealand (Operative 27 March 2003).

Emphasis is placed on minimizing effects at the source of pollution targeting bush and other land clearance, storm water discharges and adverse effects on spiritual values, riparian values and amenity. The major concern with the plan is that there is so much flexibility in the rules, only monitoring over time can provide information about the ability of the plan to protect "bottom-line" values in the coastal environment.

The Waitakere District Plan is an "excellent" plan in generally providing for ecological matters, so that many of the NZCPS policies are implemented because overall catchment management in urban areas is better. The city also has a number of other initiatives that reinforce the "eco-city" image and also contribute to implementation of NZCPS policies, including the Green Network Pamphlet series about living in various parts of the city. One example—"Living by the Waitemata Harbour"[33]—provides advice to residents about managing pets, pollution, protecting important environmental features, joining environmental groups in the area, and good plants for residential gardens at the harbor's edge!

The proposed Rodney District Plan is rated as a "fair" plan. Rodney District Council adopted a different philosophy when preparing its district plan. The coast is not considered separately except in terms of hazard management. Instead, the Council has been guided by Section 6 of the Resource Management Act believing it has a "clear duty to protect and maintain natural resources and landscapes" and focuses on "Highly Valued Natural Resources." The council has not referred explicitly to NZCPS policies in establishing highly valued landscapes, or used the NZCPS to explain or justify policies, rules and standards about use and development of natural resources in the coastal environment. Therefore, although NZCPS policies about preservation of natural character have generally been implemented, it is difficult to assess whether the intent of the individual NZCPS policies has been retained. For example, the plan does not provide for adverse effects to be avoided in habitats important to endangered species or areas containing nationally valuable species or nationally outstanding examples of indigenous community type.

The proposed Rodney District Plan provides for places of significance as discussed in NZCPS policies by establishing protection zones with rules and standards about subdivision use and development. Subdivision development on "Greenfield" sites needs to include infrastructure appropriate to avoid adverse effects on the coastal environment and to provide financial contributions—but it is not clear that the contribution will offset unavoidable environmental damage. The Rodney District Plan has also used bylaws effectively to deal with matters in the Gulf Harbour marina (navigation,

---

33. See <http://www.waitakere.govt.nz/AbtCit/ec/livsus/pdf/livwstcst.pdf>.

fires, protection of structures and personal conduct) and urban streams (storm water).

The Tauranga District Plan prepared by the Tauranga District Council only considers the NZCPS superficially and is a "fair" plan.[34] Reference is made to the NZCPS in the Tauranga District Plan introduction as one of a number of guiding documents to be taken into account. The Tauranga District Plan includes general policies and methods related to protection of the natural character of the Coastal Management Area that partially satisfy NZCPS policies. There is a Special Ecological Site Register that describes significant ecological habitats and sites. However, there are very few rules outside those relating to conservation zones to provide protection of outstanding values and avoid, remedy or mitigate adverse effects of subdivision use and development, especially in a district undergoing urban expansion.

The Tauranga District Plan subdivision rules and the rules with relation to adverse effects of subdivision development, partially satisfy the requirements of NZCPS policy. However, rules have clauses that are subject to interpretation and standards may be relaxed. The TDP identifies financial contributions under section 108 of the Act as a tool to offset general "adverse effects," but there is no imperative to offset environmental effects because financial contributions "may" be used in the coastal environment.

The Western Bay of Plenty District Plan was operative from 4 July 2002 and is currently subject to proposed plan changes. Overall the Western Bay of Plenty District Plan is a "fair" plan, although there is little direct reference to the NZCPS or individual NZCPS policies.

The Western Bay of Plenty District Plan includes objectives, policies and methods related to protection of the natural character of the Coastal Management Area and includes schedules describing "identified significant ecological features," "identified significant landscape features," and "identified significant heritage features," as well as rules and performance standards that partially satisfy NZCPS policies about natural character.

The Invercargill District Plan was notified by the Invercargill District Council on 11 May 2002. Overall, the Plan is "fair," and partially satisfies the policies of the New Zealand Coastal Policy Statement (NZCPS). The Invercargill District Plan is partially consistent with the natural character policies in the NZCPS. The Plan provides a degree of protection to the significant indigenous vegetation and significant habitats of indigenous fauna. The Council outlines what are permitted activities (i.e., maintenance, restoration or amenity planting is a permitted activity), and discretionary activities for the area such as the removal of any live indigenous vegetation.

34. Tauranga District Council (TDC), 2003, *Tauranga District Plan*, Tauranga, New Zealand (operative 1 July 2003).

The Southland District Plan was made operative by the Southland District Council on 27 June 2001. The council identifies the district by way of "landscape character areas," and the "coast" landscape is defined as "the area in which coastal factors are dominant." The Southland District Plan is "fair" in being generally consistent with the NZCPS by classifying any subdivision in the "coastal resource area" as a discretionary activity. The reason provided in the plan for this rule is that the "discretionary activity" status allows the council to refuse a subdivision resource consent with potential cumulative effects that are not compatible with the natural character of the coast. However, there are few standards in the Southland District Plan to guide development density or character, and each application is judged on its individual merits, with the potential for significant cumulative effects on the adjoining World Heritage Area.

The Southland District Plan states that any adverse effects, particularly on remaining significant indigenous vegetations and wildlife habitats of the coastal environment, should be avoided or remedied, partially satisfying NZCPS policy. The Southland District Plan also classifies the clearance, removal, etc., of indigenous flora and fauna as a discretionary activity. Geological sites and landforms are provided for and protection is provided to such sites by classifying any activity with likely adverse effects on landforms as a discretionary activity.

Financial contributions are considered as a method to offset environmental damage in Coastal Resource Areas where land is required alongside rivers, streams and lakes for riparian protection. The Council may give preference to the acquisition of land over financial contributions. This partially satisfies NZCPS policy. The District Council will maintain and enhance access to *Mahinga Kai* (coastal resources), where possible, through esplanade reserve provisions.

Sustainable land management practices are promoted in the Southland District Plan, with planning maps identifying those areas in the District that are at risk from actual or potential hazards—including "coastal sites susceptible to erosion and the effects of sea level rise" as required by NZCPS policy.

Feedback from the various workshops and interviews about the NZCPS review demonstrate there is general support for the existence and retention of the NZCPS as a comprehensive tool in achieving the purpose of the Resource Management Act in relation to New Zealand's coastal environment, and in guiding the second generation sub-national policy statements and plans about the coastal environment. The brevity of the NZCPS is praised, and many believe it is a straightforward document that is easy to read—commendable attributes of any national policy statement. Most submitters acknowledge the need to protect public interests. However, many believe that a cautious approach should be taken in any planning document reviews so that a balance of public and private interests in the coastal environment is preserved, and any required changes to sub-national plans and policy statements do not result in further costs, delays and confusion.

Those submitters who expressed qualitative support for the NZCPS suggested a number of changes such as including a vision statement in the NZCPS. Many believe that NZCPS should focus on matters that need to be considered in preparing local plans and policy statements, without determining local outcomes as experienced in the regional coastal plan process. Local government is seen as being the level of planning to control all decision making and day-to-day management activities in the coastal environment, with national input limited to guidance in the NZCPS about plan preparation, submissions to resource consents, and approval of the regional coastal plans. Many industry NZCPS users believe that more proactive NZCPS policies are needed to guide the balancing act between social, economic, cultural and environmental factors in coastal management.

Those in opposition to the NZCPS as a policy document generally believe that the NZCPS is redundant now that regional coastal plans are in place. Many complain about the lack of environmental monitoring and the loss of natural character in the coastal environment around the country. The Department of Conservation is criticized for not advocating or promoting the NZCPS in a general sense and some people were not sure that the NZCPS exists. Some local politicians believe that only the Minister of Conservation is responsible for the implementation of the NZCPS. Many groups argued that the NZCPS is ineffective as it is not being applied or referred to in some policy statements, particularly at the district level. In fact, several submitters referred to the reluctance of local authorities to implement anything coming from the Ministry of the Environment or the Department of Conservation if there is no funding support for implementation. There is also some concern about the lack of national environmental standards that should have been written to support national priorities.

The analysis of Environment Court Decisions between 1994 and 2003 demonstrates that the NZCPS is only generally referred to in applications and officer reports about resource consents applications.[35] Judges make more detailed reference to NZCPS policies in relation to appeals of individual applications for resource consent, than in appeal decisions about aspects of sub-national plans and policy statements.

THE FUTURE: OTHER NATIONAL REVIEWS

Change in New Zealand central government policy means that some coastal issues may be dealt with in other national policy initiatives at a national level

35. See McRae, n. 31 above.

in addition to NZCPS policies. Important policy programs include the completion of the New Zealand Biodiversity Strategy, the development of National Environmental Performance Indicators, and the ongoing preparation of an Oceans Policy for New Zealand. Other reports that provide information and ideas about how New Zealand may improve the management of the coastal and marine environment include: "Coastal Management: Preserving the Natural Character of the Coastal Environment" (April 1996) and "Setting Course for a Sustainable Future: The Management of New Zealand's Marine Environment" (1999), both of which were prepared by the Office of the Parliamentary Commissioner for the Environment.

The "Proposed Indigenous Biodiversity National Policy Statement" is about to be publicly notified with implications for NZCPS policies concerning natural character and amenity. New Resource Management Act provisions for regional coastal plans ensure that aquaculture projects will be better managed and further progress will be made in relation to implementing a system of charging users who occupy space in the coastal marine area. Changes to other related legislation, including the Marine Pollution Regulations mean that some parts of the current NZCPS are redundant.

Since 1994, government has placed significant emphasis on integrating marine protection into the wider contexts of managing production activities such as fisheries management. The 2000 Hauraki Gulf Marine Park Act provides for integrated planning for the coastal marine area and land catchments on the mainland and Hauraki Gulf Islands as part of a multi-agency approach to achieving integrated coastal management.[36] Also, the draft Marine Protected Area Policy Statement and Implementation Plan was advertised in 2004.[37]

The most important central government review affecting the future role and content of the NZCPS is the gazettal of the Foreshore and Seabed Act 2004 and associated changes to the Resource Management Act.[38] Ownership of the foreshore and seabed is formally vested in the Crown, integrating all rights and interests within existing systems for regulating

36. The Hauraki Marine Park Act planning model provided for in the Hauraki Gulf Marine Park Act 2000 requires that local authorities, community interest groups, *iwi* and government departments responsible for the various aspects of marine and land management have a place on the Hauraki Gulf Marine Park Forum. Officers from the various agencies also participate in a technical group to deal with issues affecting the marine park and its land catchments. There is some confusion about the roles of various agencies and the Department of Conservation in terms of implementation.

37. Department of Conservation 2004, Draft Marine Protected Area Policy Statement and Implementation Plan, Ministry of Fisheries and Department of Conservation, Wellington, New Zealand.

38. Office of the Deputy Prime Minister, 2004, *The Resource Management Amendment (Foreshore and Seabed) Act* 2004.

activities in those areas. Maori customary rights and interests would be protected through their right to participate—not through ownership rights but through being allocated Customary Territorial Authority over areas contiguous with land which has been continuously occupied by a tribe or *iwi.*

The Oceans Policy Review initiative has been delayed by the foreshore and seabed debate. It is not clear whether a proposed Oceans Plan/Strategy would be a statutory document.[39] Given that most of the conflict between people's activities occurs within the limits of the territorial sea, it is difficult to see how a non-statutory oceans plan or strategy could deliver more effective national guidance than a statutory Resource Management Act national policy statement in local political environments where there is so little support for national level input to planning.

The NZCPS and the Marine Reserves Act (1972) do not guide policy beyond the territorial sea where other marine management problems exist. The lack of protection for important marine environments beyond the territorial sea is one of the constraints of existing policy systems that could be amended through the Oceans Policy review. The major strength of the Oceans Policy review is its interdepartmental character. For example, an Oceans Plan/Strategy could provide an overall vision for all management in New Zealand's coastal waters, information and data management principles or standards to ensure compatibilities between databases about marine resources, environmental indicators and monitoring requirements. Part of each participating department's budget could be allocated to an Oceans Office for distribution satisfying coordinating requirements and improving accountability in achieving a national oceans vision and research priorities. In addition, the Oceans Policy Review needs to deal with the current confusion about responsibility for monitoring and implementing international obligations.

39. Oceans Policy Secretariat, 2003, *Draft Oceans Policy Options,* draft working paper—not government policy, 25 June 2003, Ministry of the Environment, Wellington, New Zealand; Oceans Policy Secretariat, 2003, *Draft Outline—Ocean Policy Options, Working Paper Five, Oceans Policy,* draft working paper, 2 May 2003—not government policy, Ministry of the Environment, Wellington, New Zealand; Oceans Policy Secretariat, 2003, *Adapting to Future Changes, Working Paper Nine, Oceans Policy,* Draft working paper only 28 February 2003—not government policy, Ministry of the Environment, Wellington, New Zealand; Oceans Policy Secretariat, 2003. *Ocean Use Rights, Working Paper Two, Oceans Policy,* draft working paper only, 28 February 2003—not government policy, Ministry of the Environment, Wellington, New Zealand; Oceans Policy Secretariat, 2003, *The Land-Sea Interface, Working Paper Five, Oceans Policy,* draft working paper only, 28 February 2003—not government policy, Ministry of the Environment, Wellington, New Zealand.

Public walking access along water margins was also reviewed in 2003.[40] Issues examined include access to the foreshore of coasts, lakes and rivers across private land, clarification of the legal issues associated with land access and the considerable number of misconceptions about people's rights. The conclusions call for increased national leadership, improved certainty of public walking access, and changes to those legal provisions that hinder walking access.

Non-statutory methods have also changed the implementation of NZCPS policies. Since 1994, regional councils and some territorial authorities have initiated coast-care groups and other community environmental programmes to engage communities, increase people's awareness of environmental problems and achieve landscape restoration.

Some methods incorporate survey and analysis, enabling property owners and community groups to improve environmental practices. Other initiatives provide information about the sensitivity of environmental values or the effects of peoples' activities. For example, the National Institute of Water and Atmospheric Research stream monitoring kits for farmers is a catchment tool that indirectly results in improved water quality in the Coastal Management Area.[41]

The Otaraua Hapu guidelines for *hapu* and *iwi* prepared in partnership with Shell Petroleum Mining Ltd., are an excellent example of the statutory initiatives to improve the capacity of Maori to manage *kaimoana* (food from the sea).[42] Given the pressures these marine resources are under, common understanding of good management practice, monitoring and standards enable Maori communities to adapt *tikanga Maori* (traditional practice) and management techniques to meet changing needs and expectations of Maori and the general community.[43]

40. B. E. Hayes, *The Law on Public Access along Water Margins,* (MAF Policy, Ministry of Agriculture and Policy, Wellington, New Zealand, 2003), at 118; Land Access Ministerial Reference Group, 2003, *Walking Access in the New Zealand Outdoors,* MAF Policy, Ministry of Agriculture and Policy, Wellington, New Zealand, at 121.

41. B. Biggs, C. Mulcock, B. Stuart, S. Washington, J. van Rossem, M. Scarsbrook and C. Kilroy, 2002, *Stream Health Monitoring and Assessment Kit—Stream Monitoring Kit,* NIWA Technical Report Number NTR111, at 190.

42. Otaraua Hapu, 2003, *Kaimona Survey—Guidelines for Hapu and Iwi* (Ministry for the Environment, Wellington, New Zealand, October 2003).

43. Concerns were expressed at the Gisborne *hui* or meeting about the definition of Maori in regulations at a national level of government, and that Maori should be able to define what terms mean in each area or "*rohe.*" For example, the Maori practice of *kaitiakitanga* or environmental guardianship is often limited by government regulations, such as the case for customary fishing, where regulations impose limits on when and how harvesting can occur. This takes away the decision-making power of any local *hapu.* Individual *hapu* have not been able to exercise their roles as *kaitaki* of the fishery and other coastal resources, or protect the local decision-making processes related to the practice of *kaitiakitanga.*

The Auckland and Environment Bay of Plenty regions have well resourced Coast Care Environmental Programmes that involve local communities in coastal management. Environment Bay of Plenty has also prepared a series of Beach Care Information Brochures that provide guidance about dune usage, fore-dune vegetation, planting guides, vehicle damage, backyard care, and beach care codes. Environment Bay of Plenty also has a number of sand dune revegetation schemes.

National environmental education efforts in NZ are coordinated through the Ministry for the Environment's Sustainable Environmental Management Programme to ensure consistency of good quality advice, and avoid the potential for duplication of efforts. The preparation of some local guidelines about good practice may need funding towards research and publication—already offered by the Ministry.

CONCLUSIONS

Consideration of NZCPS effectiveness is difficult because the purpose of the Resource Management Act is achieved though a series of plans and policy statements and a variety of other methods at national, regional and district levels of planning. All levels are required to achieve integrated sustainable management of natural and physical resources and to avoid, remedy or mitigate adverse effects of people's activities. Therefore, the assessment of the effectiveness of NZCPS policies in achieving environmental outcomes in the coastal environment is dependent not only on the actions of the Department of Conservation, but also on the philosophy and actions of local government planners and the effectiveness of their policy statements and plans. In addition, the purpose of district planning on land is to allow people to carry out activities unless they are *restricted* by a rule in a district plan. Whereas, the purpose of planning, in the Coastal Marine Area, is to prohibit activities unless they are *facilitated* by a rule in a regional coastal plan or a resource consent.

The first NZCPS has been effective in generating debate about New Zealand's national priorities for coastal management. Along with the Resource Management Act provisions, implementation of the NZCPS has also required local government to change the way in which coastal issues are considered in local planning frameworks.

NZCPS policies have generally been effectively implemented through the regional policy statements and regional coastal plans analyzed in this review. Most regional coastal plans are operative—nine are mostly operative and only seven need to be approved by the Minister.

The NZCPS is an important national method in the Resource Management Act regulatory regime about coastal management that is necessary even if an Oceans Policy is implemented. Given the 2003 amendments to the Resource Management Act, councils are now required to "give effect to" NZCPS policies and other national policy statements in the preparation of their plans and policy statements—ensuring that some implementation difficulties experienced in the previous nine years since 1994 may be overcome. More specific provisions are needed regarding the requirements for coastal occupation charges.

The NZCPS has been effective in guiding the preparation of sub-national plans and policy statements. Although coastal planning capacity in local authorities has developed since 1994, particularly in regional councils, feedback from the local government workshops[44] and the review analysis indicate that there is considerable variation in planning capacity between councils, a concern that may be addressed if Local Government NZ coordinates discussion and analysis of coastal planning topics in its online forums.[45] Further analysis is needed to determine if plans, with content that vary considerably from the Resource Management Act and other policy documents, are less effective if challenged in the Environment Court.

The NZCPS has been effective in changing current practice concerning direct discharges of sewage effluent in the coastal marine area. Restricted Coastal Activities have been implemented where appropriate in regional coastal plans. As a result of Environment Court decisions, areas that have been set aside as conservation areas protecting significant marine resources, are not all designated as Areas of Significant Conservation Value as provided for in section 68(4)(b) of the Resource Management Act.

The NZCPS has not been changed or a new or additional NZCPS prepared since 1994. One of the most significant issues to emerge since then is the occupation of space in the Coastal Marine Area for aquaculture purposes. The analysis of case law demonstrates that although the NZCPS policies about natural character and the precautionary approach were effectively applied in the decisions, there appears to be little analysis about whether new NZCPS policies are required to guide the designation of Aquaculture Management Areas.

The NZCPS has only been partially effective in influencing district plans. The analysis of plans and policy statements in this review highlights the fact that, although the NZCPS is only briefly acknowledged in most of the six district plans analyzed, the wording of NZCPS policies is generally reflected in many District Plan phrases, especially in the policy sections of the plans. The Department of Conservation has not provided the same level

---

44. D. Young, *Monitoring the Effectiveness of the New Zealand Coastal Policy Statement: Views of Local Government Staff* (Conservation Policy Division, Department of Conservation, Wellington, New Zealand, 2003), at 53.

45. See <http://www.localgovt.co.nz/>.

of input to district plans as was provided for regional coastal plans.[46] The Department of Conservation could advocate and make submissions that argue for implementation of NZCPS policies, but it would be impractical to fight all District Plans through to the Environment Court.

The poorest area of NZCPS implementation has been in monitoring environmental outcomes and assessing the degree to which plans and policy statements have influenced environmental results. This has prevented analysis of NZCPS effectiveness in achieving desired environmental outcomes. Only the Taranaki Regional Council[47] has assessed the efficiency and effectiveness of the Taranaki Regional Coastal Plan (with a brief mention of the NZCPS), concluding that the Regional Coastal Plan has been effective in summarizing key achievements, including health of coastal waters and community attitudes about council service. It is still difficult to link environmental outcomes to specific objectives policies and rules in the plan except in the management of discharges. One Taranaki Regional Council assumption seems to be that the Taranaki Regional Coastal Plan is effective because there has never been a successful appeal against plan provisions.

Environment Southland and other regional councils are preparing their approaches to carry out plan monitoring.[48] Indicators generally refer to the contribution of Resource Management Act plans and policy statements in achieving environmental results by analyzing consistency of interpretation, tracking difficulties in implementation, and identifying the degree to which activities comply with provisions or resource consent conditions. However, it would be useful to provide national guidance to ensure increased consistency between local authority approaches to implementation so that review of national policy statements is more effective. District councils have also been developing monitoring strategies.[49]

There is often a reluctance to implement national requirements at the local government level because of funding implications.[50] This is one area where responsibilities are blurred at all levels. The national level of policy-making needs to clarify responsibilities at all levels for environmental and

46. N. Bradly, "An Evaluation of Coastal Management by the Department of Conservation under the Resource Management Act 1991 in New Zealand," (University of Delaware, U.S.: Unpublished Ph.D. Thesis, 2000).

47. Taranaki Regional Council, 2002. *Efficiency and effectiveness of the Regional Coastal Plan for Taranaki*, an interim review report on the Regional Coastal Plan for Taranaki, TRC, Stratford, New Zealand.

48. Environment Southland, 2001, *Environment Southland Approach—Plan Suitability/Effectiveness Monitoring*, Southland Regional Council, Invercargill, New Zealand.

49. Western Bay of Plenty District Council, 2002, *Environmental Monitoring Strategy*. Tauranga, New Zealand.

50. This concern was commonly raised at the Local Government Workshops reported by Young, see n. 44 above.

plan monitoring as discussed in both the NZCPS review and the Oceans Policy Review. A similar situation exists in relation to the management of natural hazards. More clarity is needed at the national level of planning, especially in regard to the influence of climate change data on location and design of public infrastructure around the country.

The next generation of NZCPS policies may need to be more prescriptive. However, a balance is needed between increasing policy prescriptiveness and improving guidance about implementation of more general policies, an option that provides more flexibility for local government. Most local authority planners believe that NZCPS policies relating to natural character of the coastal environment need to be strengthened.

Other matters that should be addressed in the preparation of the second generation NZCPS include:

- In what circumstances should a NZCPS be prepared? In other words, what criteria need to be met to trigger the process to review an existing NZCPS or prepare a new NZCPS? Many submitters believe that a new NZCPS was required to guide local government analysis to define the location of Aquaculture Management Areas in regional coastal plans—a management method that evolved with Environment Court guidance in a national policy vacuum.
- Could the Hauraki Gulf Marine Park Act model guide the development of a "place based" NZCPS? The model could assist in dealing with problems associated with achieving integrated coastal management in nationally significant coastal marine/land seascapes/landscapes—with community and industry involvement. For example, the Fiordland Integrated Management Strategy[51] could be formalized using this model. This could be a process driven by regional communities to meet national objectives. The process may also be important to manage inland catchments behind Aquaculture Management Areas.

Although the Department of Conservation's implementation strategy for the NZCPS has not been explicitly provided for, the Department has carried out important activities to implement the NZCPS. Action is ad hoc and although the reasons for various activities and guidelines have been implicitly understood within Head Office, they are difficult to trace through Department of Conservation outputs programmes[52] and it is not always clear

51. Guardians of Fiordland's Fisheries and Marine Environment, 2003, Fiordland Draft Conservation Strategy. Ministry for the Environment, Wellington, New Zealand.
52. Bradly, n. 46 above.

how Department of Conservation coastal management outputs relate back to implementation of the NZCPS.

Once the new NZCPS is approved, the Department of Conservation needs to implement a transparent implementation strategy and be more accountable for implementation actions and analysis. The strategy should include regular updating of information for planners concerned with coastal matters in local authorities. The information should include timely interpretation of recent case law regarding the coastal environment, examples of good practice and regional updates. Central government policy should focus on cost-effective research about issues of national interest to improve the quality of coastal planning in local government. These matters are all being considered along with other recommendations in this review in the preparation of the second generation NZCPS.

Appendix 1.—Keywords Reflecting NZCPS Policies and Outcomes

Natural Character	Keywords
Policy 1.1.1 Protection from inappropriate subdivision	Natural character / Sustainable management Effects of subdivision / Headlands / [actual locations specified]
Policy 1.1.2 Preserve natural character of coastal environment	Indigenous species / Community types / Ecological (includes corridors) / Ecosystems Endangered / Rare / Migratory / Wetlands / Estuaries / Mangroves / Dunes / [actual locations specified]
Policy 1.1.3 Preserve features of coast	Landscapes / Seascapes / Landforms / Wild and scenic / Historic / Cultural / [actual locations specified]
Policy 1.1.4 Preserve natural processes	Landscapes / Seascapes / Landforms / Wild and scenic / Historic / Cultural / [actual locations specified]
Policy 1.1.5 Restore and rehabilitate natural character	Rehabilitate / Restore/ [actual locations specified]
Maori	
Policy 2.1.1/2.1.2 Characteristics special to Maori	Tikanga / Tangata whenua / Maori
Policy 2.1.3 Transfer of power	Transfer / Iwi authorities / Delegation
Maintenance and Enhancement of Amenity Values	
Policy 3.1.1 Public use	Adverse effects / Amenity value / Safety / Enjoyment
Policy 3.1.2 Identify special significance in coastal environment	Scenic / Historic / Recreational / Spiritual / Cultural / Scientific / Special significance
Policy 3.1.3 Protection and recognition of importance open space in coastal environment	Open space
Policy 3.2.1 Appropriate subdivision, use and development defined in plans	Subdivision / Appropriate
Policy 3.2.2 Where unavoidable adverse effects should be mitigated or remedied	Mitigate / remedy adverse effects

Policy 3.2.3 Where un-avoidable adverse effects compensate	Section 108 / Financial contributions
Policy 3.2.4 Cumulative effects not adverse	Cumulative
Policy 3.2.5 Adequate services	Waste disposal
Policy 3.2.6 Appropriate development but adverse effects a consideration	*Papakainga / marae*
Policy 3.2.7 Improve water quality	Land management
Policy 3.2.8 Protection for commercial, recreational, traditional, cultural species	Habitats
Policy 3.2.9 New structures	Marine Safety Authority / Navy
Policy 3.2.10 Restoration	Indigenous species / Local genetic stock
Policy 3.3.1 Unknown effects	Precautionary
Policy 3.3.2 Share information	Knowledge / Information
Policy 3.4.1 Plans identify	Coastal hazards
Policy 3.4.2 Sea level rise	Sea level / Global warming / Natural defence / Erosion / Inundation
Policy 3.4.3 Protect subdivision use and development	Beaches / Sand dunes / Mangroves / Wetlands Barrier islands
Policy 3.4.4 Natural features migrate inland	Dynamic coastal processes / Migrate
Policy 3.4.5 New subdivisions avoid hazard protection works	Hazard protection
Policy 3.4.6 Existing use-coastal protection work only where best option	Coastal protection works limited

Maintenance and Enhancement of Public Access to and along the Coastal Marine Area	
Policy 3.5.1 Public Access Restrictions only imposed	Significant indigenous vegetation / Cultural Health / Security (consistent with Resource C)
Policy 3.5.2 Enhance public access	Disability
Policy 3.5.3 Enhance public access with	Esplanade reserves / Esplanade strips / Access strips
Policy 3.5.4 Access to cultural sites	*Tikanga / Maori*
Maintenance and Enhancement of Water Quality	
Policy 5.1.1 Rules required to enhance water quality	Public interest / *Tangata whenua* / Human sewage
Policy 5.1.2 Discharge of human waste	Land disposal / *Tangata whenua* / Consultation
Policy 5.1.3 No discharge cause significant adverse effects	Significant adverse effects / Habitats / Feeding grounds / Ecosystems
Policy 5.1.4 Review permits to make sure rules being met	Review / Monitor / Permits
Policy 5.1.5 Contamination	Trade wastes
Policy 5.1.6 Contamination	Non-point sources
Policy 5.1.7 Warnings be given	Unsafe swimming / Unsafe shellfish gathering
Limiting Adverse Effects from Vessel Waste Disposal or Maintenance	
Policy 5.2.1 Facilities in ports, marinas, busy areas	Rubbish disposal / Residues (from vessel maintenance)
Policy 5.2.2 New ports and marinas	Sewage disposal
Policy 5.2.3 Encourage use of sewage and rubbish facilities	Education
Policy 5.3 Restricted coastal activities	Schedule 1 criteria

The Growing Significance of Coast Guards in the Asia-Pacific: A Quiet Development in Regional Maritime Security

Sam Bateman
Centre for Maritime Policy, University of Wollongong, Australia
Institute of Defence and Strategic Studies, Singapore

INTRODUCTION

The maritime security scene in the Asia-Pacific region is currently volatile. By 2009, regional countries may be spending a combined US$14 billion on new naval ships or almost double the figure for 2003.[1] New naval acquisitions include "state of the art" submarines, larger surface warships and even aircraft carriers, although some other name, such as large amphibious ship, might be used to describe them. This activity is not just a consequence of concerns about the threat of maritime terrorism and ongoing problems of law and order at sea, particularly piracy and armed attacks against ships, but is also due to lingering bilateral tensions that occasionally re-surface, especially in the context of disputed claims to sovereignty over islands or offshore areas.[2] These developments all serve to add to maritime insecurity in the region.

It is all too easy to say that economic growth and a desire to assert greater control over adjacent waters, particularly exclusive economic zones (EEZs), are driving naval developments in the region. While this may have been true in the 1990s and earlier, these developments now appear to be driven much more by direct perceptions of threats and maritime insecurity. Some regional navies, which previously had only limited coast guard-type functions, are building up enhanced offshore capabilities—not only highly

---

1. "Naval Ship Spending to Increase in Asia Pacific, Defense Experts Say," *The China Post* (11 November 2003), available online: <http://www.chinapost.com.tw/p_detail.asp?id=43042&GRP=A&onNews=>.
2. The first few months of 2005 have seen disputes flare up between South Korea and Japan over their separate claims to sovereignty over the Takeshima/Tokdo islands, and between Indonesia and Malaysia over hydrocarbon rights off Sipidan and Ligitan islands East of Borneo.

Ocean Yearbook 20: 505–531.

capable surface combatants and submarines, but also significant numbers of aircraft for both maritime strike and surveillance. In the light of pessimistic threat assessments and general regional insecurity, regional navies are focusing more on their capabilities for war-fighting and are becoming reluctant to be too heavily involved in tasks that could be assigned to a separate coast guard. The latter tasks divert navies from the complex and expensive business of preparing for modern naval warfare. Employing high technology warships and maritime aircraft on policing tasks may be an "over-kill" and a misemployment of highly trained naval personnel. They may be better left to a separate coast guard, especially equipped and trained for maritime policing.

At one time it was thought that the extension of maritime jurisdiction and sovereign rights allowed under the 1982 United Nations Convention on the Law of the Sea (UNCLOS)[3] would provide justification for established navies to acquire more vessels, and for smaller nations to establish a navy.[4] However, the extension of coastal State jurisdiction under UNCLOS has not had quite as much impact on naval force planning as was anticipated initially. In fact we are now seeing a different trend with most regional navies concentrating on their primary war-fighting role. Nations that had not previously had coast guards are establishing them, and those that already had coast guards are building them up. There are a number of reasons for this development. Navies are high-profile symbols of sovereignty whose employment in disputed maritime areas may be provocative. Cooperation between regional coast guards offers advantages for maritime cooperation and confidence building by overcoming some of the sensitivities that might inhibit the employment of navies.

The main geographical focus of this article is the Western Pacific and the seas of East Asia. This area has complex maritime geography with many islands and archipelagos, narrow straits and shipping channels with numerous overlapping claims to maritime jurisdiction and few agreed maritime boundaries. Shipping traffic is heavy and is increasing year by year, as economic growth in the region proceeds. Growing resource scarcities drive increased research for offshore oil and gas reserves and the over-exploitation of marine living resources. Southeast Asia, in particular, has

3. United Nations Convention on the Law of the Sea, 1982, entered into force November 1994, available online: <http://www.un.org/Depts/los>.

4. A. Hu Nien-Tsu and J. K. Oliver, "A Framework for Small Navy Theory: The 1982 U.N. Law of the Sea Convention," *Naval War College Review* (Spring 1988): 37–48; M. A. Morris, "Comparing Third World Navies," in *Ocean Yearbook* 8, eds. E. Mann Borgese, N. Ginsburg and J. R. Morgan (Chicago: University of Chicago Press, 1991): 307–325; J. R. Morgan, "Constabulary Navies in the Pacific and Indian Oceans," in *Ocean Yearbook* 11, eds. E. Mann Borgese, N. Ginsburg and J. R. Morgan (Chicago: University of Chicago Press, 1994): 368–383.

become notorious for piracy and other problems of law and order at sea, including drug trafficking, illegal fishing and people smuggling. These geo-strategic factors provide the context in which this article reviews the reasons why regional coast guards are growing in significance and the implications that might flow from this.

THE ROLES OF MARITIME SECURITY FORCES

The maritime security forces of a country may comprise a navy and a separate paramilitary force, such as marine police or a coast guard, to undertake constabulary tasks, particularly those of a civil policing nature. This article uses the term "coast guard" to refer to these latter forces, although they may have different names in different countries, e.g., the Malaysian Maritime Enforcement Agency or the Korean National Maritime Police.

The war-fighting role of a navy may be fairly distinct but the roles of a coast guard may be rather less so.[5] Based on a categorization originally provided by Ken Booth, maritime security forces are required to fulfill three main functions or roles.[6] These are:

- A military or war-fighting role to defend the nation against threats, primarily of a military nature. This role requires capabilities for combat operations either at sea (e.g., surface warfare, anti-air warfare, submarine warfare, maritime strike, mine warfare, protection of shipping or coastal defense), or from the sea (e.g., amphibious operations, naval gunfire support, or land strike using cruise missiles). These may be either sea assertion operations to assert the ability to use the sea for one's own purposes, including for power projection, or sea denial operations to deny the use of the sea to an adversary. Sea denial and sea assertion are the basic dimensions of *sea control.*
- A constabulary or policing role concerned with sovereignty protection and the enforcement of national laws at sea. Specific tasks might include maritime surveillance and enforcement, sea patrol, fisheries protection, search and rescue (SAR), combating drug smuggling and piracy, and controlling illegal immigration. The importance of this role has increased for most countries in recent years due to higher

5. J. Kelly, "Coast Guards and Regional Security Cooperation," *Maritime Studies* 127 (November–December 2002): 13.
6. K. Booth, *Navies and Foreign Policy* (London: Croom Helm, 1977): especially 15–16.

levels of offshore resource exploitation, greater marine environmental awareness and increased illegal activity at sea.[7]

- A diplomatic role involving the use of security forces as instruments of foreign policy. This may range from straightforward, rarely controversial activities to support foreign policy objectives, such as civil assistance and regional security cooperation (e.g., port visits, personnel exchanges, passage exercises, etc.), through to manipulative/coercive naval presence missions to influence the political calculations of other states in situations short of actual conflict. These latter missions are in line with Sir James Cable's "gunboat diplomacy," or what Edward Luttwak has called "naval suasion."[8]

In the past, the diplomatic role has been very much the prerogative of navies, while coast guards, to the extent that they existed, were only employed in home waters. This situation is changing. Coast guards are being used increasingly as instruments of foreign policy in waters well beyond the limits of national jurisdiction. Some regional countries are also demonstrating a preference for deploying coast guard ships and personnel in sensitive situations at sea rather than naval ships and personnel. Coast guards are thus emerging as more important national institutions with the potential to make a major contribution to regional oceans governance and security cooperation.

The military role is fundamental to the other two roles of maritime security forces. The ability of a navy to undertake constabulary and diplomatic roles depends on its demonstrable capability to deploy maximum force and to fight and win a conflict at sea. This war-fighting capability becomes more important as the level of tension associated with diplomatic and constabulary activities increases. The level of force (or war-fighting capability) required may vary inversely with the probability of the task being required.[9]

At the end of the Cold War, some questioned the priority of the war-fighting role suggesting that diplomatic and constabulary roles were becoming more significant. Booth, for example, spoke about "New Times for Old Navies," concluding that, "Turning warships into lawships is a

7. The UN Secretary-General noted that in the 20 years since the adoption of UNCLOS, crimes at sea have become more prevalent and are increasing. UN General Assembly, *Oceans and the Law of the Sea—Annual Report of the Secretary-General,* UN Doc. A/57/57, 7 March 2002, para. 134, p. 26.

8. Sir J. Cable, *Gunboat Diplomacy 1919-1979* (London: Macmillan, 1981); E. N. Luttwak, *The Political Uses of Sea Power* (Baltimore: John Hopkins Press, 1974): especially Ch. 1.

9. G. Till, "Maritime Power and the Twenty-First Century," *Seapower: Theory and Practice,* ed. G. Till (Newbury Park: Frank Cass, 1994): 176–199.

rational way ahead for future international society in which the costs of war are dramatically increasing and the benefits clearly decreasing."[10] At that time, UNCLOS had been opened for signature for several years and all indications were that it would soon enter into force bringing with it extended coastal State jurisdiction (Table 1 shows the size of maritime zones in the Western Pacific and East Asia). Countries were becoming more aware of the need to build institutions for the exercise of state power at sea, to establish national arrangements for policing offshore areas and to acquire capabilities (ships, aircraft and systems) for maritime surveillance and enforcement. Navies already had these capabilities. Thus the new law of the sea and the extension of maritime jurisdiction under UNCLOS were expected to provide additional justification for maintaining a navy, particularly for the constabulary role.

Extended maritime jurisdiction was seen as the basic rationale for small navies.[11] Many of the world's navies "are not blue-water, power-projection, sea-control navies—rather regional navies that also enforce laws, protect resources, conduct search and rescue, prevent environmental damage, and maintain aids to navigation."[12] However, as the years have gone by, some navies, particularly Southeast Asian ones, which previously were focused on constabulary tasks, have shaken off those tasks and are concentrating on their war-fighting/national defense mission. Rather than providing a rationale for naval expansion, it now seems that extended maritime jurisdiction has provided more of a rationale for establishing and developing coast guards.

UNCLOS and its extended jurisdiction has also created a new dimension to the diplomatic role of navies, and potentially also for coast guards. This involves demonstrating presence within the EEZ and the resolve to protect sovereign rights. Many of the sovereignty assertion (or naval presence) activities undertaken by navies of the East Asian countries, which have conflicting claims to islands and offshore jurisdiction, are more in the nature of the diplomatic role of navies rather than constabulary activities. Similarly, some of the initiatives for coordinated or joint patrols to combat piracy between neighboring countries may be more diplomatic (i.e., for presentational purposes), rather than constabulary in the sense of actually being able to do something jointly to enforce law and order at sea.

While coastal States have greater rights in their littoral waters under UNCLOS, they also have increased responsibilities. A coastal State has to

10. K. Booth, "The Role of Navies in Peacetime," *Naval Power in the Pacific: Toward the Year 2000*, eds. H. Smith and A. Bergin (Boulder: Lynne Reimer, 1993): 161.

11. See Hu and Oliver, Morris and Morgan, n. 4 above.

12. Vice Admiral J. Loy, USCG, and Captain B. Stubbs, USCG, "Exporting Coast Guard Expertise," *USN Institute Proceedings* (May 1997): 56.

Table 1.—Maritime Zones of the Western Pacific and East Asia

Country	Land Area (km²)	Maritime Zones (km²)	Maritime/Land Area Ratio
Japan	370,370	3,861,000	10.4
North Korea	121,730	129,650	1.1
South Korea	98,400	348,478	3.5
China	9,600,000	1,355,800	0.1
Taiwan	32,360	392,381	12.1
Philippines	300,000	1,891,247	6.3
Vietnam	332,556	722,337	2.2
Thailand	414,001	324,812	0.6
Malaysia	332,649	475,727	1.4
Singapore	588	343	0.6
Indonesia	1,904,342	5,409,981	2.8
Brunei	5,765	24,352	4.2
Cambodia	181,041	55,564	0.3
Papua New Guinea	462,243	2,367,000	5.1
Palau	508	629,000	1238.0
Solomon Islands	28,520	1,340,000	47.0
FSM	701	2,900,000	4137.0
Kiribati	684	3,540,000	5175.0
Vanuatu	11,880	680,000	57.2
Marshall Islands	181	2,131,000	11773.0
Australia	7,692,300	8,148,250	1.1

Source: Based on H. J. Buchholz, *Law of the Sea Zones in the Pacific Ocean* (Singapore: Institute of Southeast Asian Studies, 1987), Table 6, p. 100.

maintain safety in its waters, protect the marine environment, and generally maintain good order at sea. Surveillance and enforcement operations to protect rights and fulfill obligations at sea require capabilities to monitor activities ("surveillance"); and intercept, board, inspect, and if necessary, detain or arrest vessels or individuals believed to be acting illegally ("enforcement"). Surveillance may be undertaken by aircraft, satellite or land-based radar, but enforcement invariably requires a surface vessel to intercept, and if necessary, board, search and arrest a suspect vessel.

In the "new" world order following the Cold War major Western navies, in particular, faced the prospect of "peace dividends" and downsizing. They were forced to re-think much of their basic rationale. The response was a new focus in naval doctrine on the projection of power from the sea rather than on the traditional concern with oceanic sea control that prevailed during the Cold War years. This is evident in the USN's *Forward ... From the Sea* doctrine, and *The Fundamentals of British Maritime Doctrine* published by the Royal Navy.[13] The new focus on power projection has since been justified with naval operations associated with Kosovo and more recently by the invasion of Iraq and the "War on Terrorism."

THE EMERGENCE OF COAST GUARDS

Trends towards the establishment or further development of coast guards are a clear consequence of the recognition by regional countries of the significance of national rights and obligations under the new law of the sea. Table 2 shows how countries in the Asia-Pacific region are approaching the allocation of responsibility for maritime policing tasks between navies and separate paramilitary forces. A preference for a separate service is evident with 17 of the 22 countries in the survey opting for a paramilitary service to undertake maritime surveillance and enforcement separate from the navy. It is also apparent that only the smaller countries have not established a separate service. Some of these new paramilitary services are very recent and are still in the process of being established (e.g., in Indonesia and Malaysia).

There are several reasons for establishing a separate coast guard. Legal considerations are important. A coast guard should be a paramilitary organization. Its officers must have the ability to enforce national maritime laws with wide powers of arrest over both foreigners and national citizens, but in many countries, there are constitutional and political reasons why military forces should not be involved in policing duties against national citizens.[14] In the U.S., for example, the military is constrained by the principle of *posse comitatus*, with the Posse Comitatus Act embodying the traditional American principle of separating civilian and military authority and prohibiting the use of the military in civilian law enforcement.

Coast guard units are more suitable than warships for employment in sensitive areas where there are conflicting claims to maritime jurisdiction and/or political tensions between parties. Warships are high-profile symbols of sovereignty whose employment in disputed maritime areas may be

13. *Forward ... From the Sea* (Washington, D.C.: U.S. Department of the Navy, 1994); *BR1806—The Fundamentals of British Maritime Doctrine* (London: HMSO, 1995 and 1999).

14. H. Smith, "The Use of Armed Forces in Law Enforcement," *Policing Australia's Offshore Zones—Problems and Prospects*, eds., D. MacKinnon and D. Sherwood (Wollongong Papers on Maritime Policy No. 9, Centre for Maritime Policy, University of Wollongong, 1997): 74–97.

Table 2.—Regional Approaches to Paramilitary Maritime Tasks

Country	Paramilitary Service(s)	Name of Service(s)
Australia	Yes	Australian Customs Service
Bangladesh	Yes	Coast Guard
Brunei	Inshore	Royal Brunei Police Force
Cambodia	No	
Canada	Yes	Coast Guard
China	Yes	Customs & Public Security Bureau & Border Defence
India	Yes	Coast Guard
Indonesia	Yes	Sea Security Coordination Agency
Japan	Yes	Coast Guard
Malaysia	Yes	Maritime Enforcement Agency
Myanmar	Yes	People's Pearl and Fishery Ministry
New Zealand	No	
North Korea	Inshore	Coastal & Port Security Police Force
Papua New Guinea	No	
Philippines	Yes	Coast Guard
Singapore	Yes	Police Coast Guard
South Korea	Yes	National Maritime Police Agency
Sri Lanka	No	
Taiwan	Yes	Coast Guard Administration
Thailand	Yes	Marine Police
United States	Yes	Coast Guard
Vietnam	Yes	Coast Guard

Main Sources: Jane's Fighting Ships and *The Military Balance 2003–2004.*

provocative. In sensitive areas, the arrest of a foreign vessel by a warship may provoke tension, whereas arrest by a coast guard vessel may be accepted as legitimate law enforcement signaling that the arresting party views the incident as relatively minor. A basic clash also exists between the military ethos of applying maximum available force and that of law enforcement, which is more circumspect and usually involves minimum force.

Maritime safety is often a task assumed by coast guards. This task involves issuing certificates for seafarers, ship inspections, vessel traffic management and accident investigations. It does not sit easily with conventional naval activities. Lastly, there is the issue of costs with coast guard vessels and aircraft generally being less expensive than naval units. Furthermore, in developing countries the civil nature of the coast guard's role may support access to funding from international aid agencies to acquire new vessels.[15]

NATIONAL ARRANGEMENTS AND DEVELOPMENTS

Australia

Australia's arrangements for the enforcement of national legislation and the protection of national interests at sea are currently quite complex, not least of all because Australia has a federal system of government and the states and territories have jurisdiction over internal waters and the first 3 nautical miles of territorial sea. There are 12 Commonwealth agencies with an ongoing role in maritime enforcement and compliance, whilst others may request assistance on an ad hoc basis.

The principle civil maritime surveillance and enforcement agency is Coastwatch, a division of the Australian Customs Service (ACS) with a two-star officer from the Royal Australian Navy (RAN) seconded as Director-General Coastwatch. It manages the aerial surveillance program and coordinates surface response operations when required by its "client" agencies, and develops intelligence systems for maritime surveillance and enforcement. Much of the surface response is provided by RAN patrol boats, but there is also a National Marine Unit (NMU) of Australian Customs Vessels (ACVs) under the ACS. The NMU has eight seagoing patrol vessels, the *Bay* Class, based mainly in northern Australia and routinely deployed in the constabulary role. As from November 2004, the NMU also includes the ice strengthened, 105-m vessel, *Oceanic Viking*, for patrolling Australia's maritime zones in the Southern Ocean, and maintained under a 2-year lease by P&O Maritime Services.

The NMU and Coastwatch are becoming de facto the Australian Coast Guard. Seagoing Australian Customs personnel are now armed, well trained and uniformed. They exhibit all the characteristics of members of a paramilitary constabulary force. The ACS and/or Coastwatch also routinely represent Australia in regional coast guard meetings.

15. An example of this process is the acquisition by the Philippines Coast Guard of two large (56 m length overall) "search and rescue vessels" that are clearly patrol vessels in every respect other than name. B. Beecham, "'San Juan' and 'Don Emilio'," *Asia Pacific Shipping* 1, 4 (January 2001): 18.

Bangladesh

Bangladesh formed a coast guard in December 1995 under the Department of Home Security to strengthen the nation's capacity in the areas of anti-smuggling, anti-piracy and protection of offshore resources. Two ships were initially made available on loan from the Bangladesh Navy, but additional vessels have since been acquired, including decommissioned cutters from the U.S. Coast Guard. The roles of the Bangladesh Coast Guard include "participation in rescue and salvage operations in times of natural catastrophes and salvage of vessels, human beings and goods met with an accident."[16] Since its establishment, the Coast Guard has had a major role in dealing with maritime natural disasters (e.g., storm surge, floods, and cyclones) and ferry accidents to which Bangladesh is prone.

Canada

The Canadian Coast Guard (CCG) is regarded as one of the major coast guards in the world.[17] As of April 2005 it is a special operating agency under the Department of Fisheries and Oceans and operates a fleet of nearly one hundred vessels ranging from large icebreakers and offshore patrol and research vessels through to navigational aid tenders of various sizes, small inshore patrol craft and lifeboats. It has five basic roles: maritime safety, protection of the marine environment, facilitation of maritime trade, support to marine science, and support to Canada's federal maritime policies.[18] Much of its fleet are employed on duties such as ice breaking, the maintenance of navigational aids, search and rescue, and marine scientific research, which are not directly law enforcement related. However, this situation is changing as the CCG comes to play a more important role in the increased levels of Canadian maritime readiness and response post 9/11.

Like most other national coast guards, the CCG has been given a major role in enhanced security against the risks of maritime terrorist attack. The new National Security Policy of Canada released in April 2004 strengthens coordination and accountability between the various portfolios involved in maritime security, including the establishment of Maritime Security Operations Centres, increased on-water patrols by the Coast Guard and other agencies and enhanced security of ports and shipping.[19] The threats of

16. Bangladesh Parliament, *The Coast Guard Act, 1994*, Act No. 26 of 1994, Article 7—Functions of the Armed Force.

17. See Kelly, n. 5 above, at 10.

18. Canadian Coast Guard homepage, <http://www.ccg-gcc.gc.ca/overview-apercu/roles>.

19. Privy Council Office, *Securing an Open Society: Canada's National Security Policy* (Ottawa: Government of Canada, April 2004).

maritime terrorism (e.g., the hijacking or destruction of ships or oil and gas installations or the sabotage of port facilities or undersea cables and pipelines), or of terrorists and their weapons (including possibly weapons of mass destruction) entering a country by sea seem likely to be with us for a long time. These threats have introduced a whole new dimension to the role of a coast guard in national security.

The CCG has an extensive international program and is a key player in Canada's overseas aid and assistance programs. It has had numerous bilateral relationships over the years with coast guard administrations and maritime authorities in the Asia-Pacific region, including in the Philippines and Vietnam.[20] At the invitation of the International Maritime Organization (IMO), the CCG has participated in discussions with Malaysia, Indonesia and Singapore on the development of the Marine Electronic Highway project in the Malacca Straits. With all these activities, including a leading role in relevant international forums, the CCG provides a fine example of how coast guards can contribute to ocean governance and regional security cooperation.

China

The situation in China is rather complex with numerous and diverse agencies involved under the control of either the Central or Provincial Governments and with overlapping functions. Since 1999, the Headquarters of the China Oceans Supervision Contingent and regional corps have been set up for the South China Sea, the East China Sea and the Beihai regions with significant law enforcement responsibilities.[21] In the meanwhile, the coastal provinces, municipalities and autonomous regions also have their own maritime law enforcement bodies.

Four main paramilitary forces can be identified in China with functions akin to those of a national coast guard.[22] These are the Customs Service *(Hai Guan)*, the Maritime Section of the Public Security Bureau *(Hai Gong)*, the Maritime Command of the Border Security Force *(Gong Bian)* and Border Defence *(Bian Jian)*. All these forces operate patrol craft of various types and sizes. The *Hai Guan* tends to operate the larger and newer vessels and appears to have the main responsibility for EEZ patrols. The *Hai Gong* is under the People's Armed Police and its missions include maintaining

20. For more details on the CCG's overseas activities, see Kelly, n. 5 above, at 10–16.

21. D. Gang, "China Has Built Up a Complete Ocean Supervision Contingent," *People's Daily*, available online: <http://english.peopledaily.com.cn/>.

22. Commodore S. Saunders ed., *Jane's Fighting Ships 2001-2002* (Coulsdon: Jane's Information Group, 2001): 142.

maritime public security and combating human smuggling, drug trafficking and piracy.[23] The *Gong Bian* has a large number of coastal patrol craft, some of which were suspected in the early 1990s of having been involved in piracy and other illegal activities.[24]

China established a "South Sea Marine Surveillance Force" in 2000 to safeguard its claims and identify marine and aquatic resources in the South China Sea.[25] It was reported in September 2001 that China was "discreetly" expanding its naval patrols in the South China Sea with the commissioning of 20–24 Qui-M-Class patrol craft.[26] These vessels are about 100 m long, a displacement of about 3,500 tons, and fitted with a twin main gun of around 30 mm. They have a uniformed crew and the markings of the Customs Service (*Hai Guan*), although the crews are believed to be all People's Liberation Army/Navy regulars. The first of these vessels was reported to have entered service in March 2005.[27]

In recent years, China has been markedly increasing its military expenditure from year-to-year with real increases above 10 percent each year. Much of this increased expenditure is going towards maritime capabilities (ships, submarines and aircraft), and it may be expected that these will include ones of a coast guard nature.

India

The Indian Coast Guard (ICG) is the principal agency for the enforcement of national laws in the maritime zones of India.[28] The ICG was established in 1978 as an independent paramilitary service to function under the Ministry of Defense but with its budget met by the Department of Revenue. However, the ICG was brought into the Defense budget in 2001, although the Director-General of the ICG will report to the Defense Secretary rather than

23. Dr. You Ji, University of New South Wales, pers. comm. (27 July 2002).
24. See Saunders, n. 22 above.
25. "China Sets Up South Sea Patrol Force," *People's Daily* (16 July 2002), available online: <http://english.peopledaily.com.cn/english/200006/08/print20000608_42493.html>. The China Marine Surveillance Force (CMSF), of which the South Sea Marine Surveillance Force is part, may previously have been the China Oceans Supervision Contingent.
26. R. Sae-Liu, "South China Sea Patrols Boosted," *Jane's Defence Weekly* (26 September 2001): 11
27. "China's Most Advanced Maritime Patrol Boat Hits Water," *People's Daily*, available online: <http://english.peopledaily.com.cn/200502/23/print200500223_174393.html>.
28. Captain V. Chaudhari IN, "Management of the Maritime Zones of India," in MacKinnon and Sherwood, n. 14 above, at 187–192.

to the Chief of Naval Staff.[29] There have been calls that it should now be brought fully under the Navy on the grounds that the "line between war and peacetime has blurred" with increased ship hijacking, gun running and drug smuggling giving "a new dimension to security threats at sea."[30]

The functions of the ICG include the safety and protection of offshore installations, search and rescue, marine environmental protection, anti-smuggling operations and enforcing national laws in the maritime zones. Surveillance and patrol of these zones is the primary *raison d'être* of the service.[31] The force levels of the ICG have been gradually increased over the years and it currently operates about 55 vessels, including 13 large offshore patrol vessels, and 20 aircraft. Of these vessels, about 30 are capable of sustained operations offshore while the others are for inshore operations. It would function in support of the Navy during wartime on tasks such as the defense of offshore installations, local naval defense, examination services, control of merchant shipping, maritime surveillance and support in amphibious operations and logistic support.[32] Following the success of the Indian Coast Guard in retaking the pirated Japanese vessel *Alondra Rainbow* in November 1999,[33] India has also been advocating joint action on Asian sea piracy.

Indonesia

As one of the major archipelagic States in the world, Indonesia is very much aware of the extent of its maritime interests and of the need to protect its maritime sovereignty and to maintain law and order at sea. However, its efforts in this regard have been thwarted by the lack both of capacity and of coordination between the various government agencies that have responsibility for some aspect of maritime enforcement. At least 10 agencies have been identified as being involved in maritime security management with 9

29. Government of India, *Reforming the National Security System*, Recommendations of the Group of Ministers, (February 2001): 71.

30. P. Das, "Coast Guard Needs Sea Change," *The Indian Express* (11 July 2002), available online: <http://www.indian-express.com/print.php?content_id=5760>.

31. R. Roy-Chaudhury, *India's Maritime Security* (Delhi: Knowledge World, 2000): 68.

32. P. Sen, "India's Coast Guard Comes of Age," *Maritime International* 1, 2 (February 1995): 8.

33. In October 1999, the cargo ship *Alondra Rainbow* was taken by pirates after leaving an Indonesian port for Japan. On 16 November 1999, the Indian Coast Guard and Indian Navy intercepted the vessel under another name off Goa and was successful in boarding the ship and arresting the pirates. IMO, "Piracy and Armed Robbery at Sea," *Focus on IMO* (January 2000): 1, 7.

authorized to conduct law enforcement operations at sea.[34] The situation has been further complicated since the collapse of the Suharto Government by government reforms, including the enactment of autonomy laws that involve devolution of authority to provincial governments, including possibly some responsibility for law enforcement at sea.[35] Other reforms include the separation of the Indonesian National Police from the Armed Forces.

The current reform agenda includes the establishment of an Indonesian Coast Guard-the *Kesatan Penjaga Laut dan Pantai*—(KPLP) (literally the Indonesian Beach and Coast Guard Unit), under the Ministry of Transportation.[36] A Sea Security Coordination Agency, referred to as BAKORKAM-LA, has also been established to have oversight of sea security and relevant policy. Hitherto the responsibility for law enforcement at sea has largely rested with the Indonesian Navy, which has had the ships and aircraft but not the legal powers to deal with the range of illegal activities at sea.[37] The Japan Coast Guard (JCG) is playing a key role in the establishment of the KPLP with the stationing of three JCG officials in the Indonesian Ministry of National Development Planning (BAPPENAS) to assist in planning the new service.[38]

Japan

The Japanese Maritime Safety Agency (JMSA) was renamed the Japan Coast Guard (JCG) on 1 April 2000.[39] It is an excellent example of a paramilitary, marine constabulary force established by a major power with extensive maritime interests and a reluctance to involve conventional military forces in routine maritime enforcement activities. This reluctance is due both to the limitations of the Japanese constitution and fears of provoking concerns in other countries about a possible resurgence of Japanese militarism.

34. RADM (Ret) R. Mangindaan, "The Indonesian Coast Guard: Guarding Coast and Territorial Waters," (paper presented at the First Meeting of the CSCAP Study Group on Capacity Building for Maritime Security Cooperation, Kunming, 6–7 December 2004).

35. D. Dirhamsyah, "Maritime Law Enforcement and Compliance in Indonesia: Problems and Recommendations," *Maritime Studies*, 144 (September/October): 9.

36. See Mangindaan, n. 33 above.

37. D. Urquhart, "Japan Helping Indonesia to Set Up Coast Guard," *The Business Times* (25 March), available online: <http://business-times.asia1.com.sg/sub/shippingtimes/story/0,4574,76347,00.ht ml?>.

38. *Id.*

39. See Saunders, n. 22 above, at 392.

The JCG is an external organization of the Japanese Ministry of Transport that carries out patrol and rescue duties (through its Guard and Rescue Department), as well as hydrographic and navigation aids services.[40] It is a very considerable organization with a fleet of over 400 patrol vessels, patrol craft, surveying ships, navigational aid tenders and special service craft. Some JCG vessels are very large (up to 6,500 tonnes in the case of the *Shikishima* Class and 4,900 tonnes with the *Mizuho* Class) and equipped to carry helicopters. JCG vessels effectively have a global capability having been involved as escorts for the ships carrying radioactive waste from Europe to Japan.

Japan attaches high importance to international cooperation to deal with crimes such as the smuggling of people, arms and drugs, and piracy and armed robbery against ships. The JCG is the principal means by which Japan fosters this cooperation and assists in building the capacity of Southeast Asian nations to deal with piracy and maritime terrorism. Since 2000, Japan has been actively exploring the scope for JCG vessels to participate in anti-piracy activities in Southeast Asian waters.[41] In November 2000, a JCG vessel visited Southeast and South Asia for exercises with the Indian Coast Guard and Malaysian authorities.[42] In July 2002, the JCG sent a large patrol ship, the 5,300-ton *Mizuho*, and a Falcon 900 maritime surveillance aircraft to help combat piracy in Southeast Asian waters.[43] The *Mizuho* previously participated in joint exercises with the Philippine Coast Guard in October 2001, and later with the Marine Police, Royal Brunei Police Force.[44] In a further diplomatic initiative, the JCG has sponsored meetings of the Indian Ocean (Bangladesh, India, Pakistan and Sri Lanka) Maritime Safety Practitioners' Conference. Most recently, Japan has proposed selling 1,000- and 2,000-ton decommissioned vessels from the Japan

40. Commander T. Inami JMSA, "Japanese Maritime Safety Agency and the United Nations Convention on the Law of the Sea: From the View Point of Legislation and Enforcement," in MacKinnon and Sherwood, n. 14 above, at 193.

41. N. Chanda, "Foot in the Water," *Far Eastern Economic Review* (9 March 2000): 28–29; M. J. Valencia, "Joining Up With Japan to Patrol Asian Waters," *International Herald Tribune* (28 April 2000).

42. Embassy of Japan in India, "Japanese Coast Guard Vessel to Visit India," *Press Release No. 34*, available online: <http://www.japan-emb.org.in/PressReleases/Embassy_Of_Japan/press-embassy34.htm>.

43. The *Mizuho* was to be initially based in Brunei to engage in drills mainly in cooperation with the local "coast guard" while the aircraft was to fly to Malaysia, Singapore and Indonesia to carry out drills and patrol. "Japan to Send Boat, Jet to Southeast Asia to Fight Piracy," *The Japan Times* (July 17, 2002), available online: <http://www.japantimes.co.jp>.

44. "Coast Guard Heads to Manila for Antipiracy Drill," *Japantoday* (October 24, 2001), available online: <http://www.japantoday.com/e/tools/print.asp?content+news&id=147618>.

Maritime Self Defence Force (JMSDF) and JCG to Indonesia, Malaysia or Singapore to assist in the fight against piracy and maritime terrorism.[45]

Malaysia

Malaysia provides a good example of the general trend towards navies concentrating on their war-fighting role and separate coast guards being established. Over a decade ago, Mak Joon Num described how the Royal Malaysian Navy (RMN), like virtually all the navies of maritime Southeast Asia, was caught on the horns of a dilemma in terms of finding a proper balance between the coast guard function and the war-fighting mission.[46] During the years when the USN provided the overall maritime security umbrella for the Asia-Pacific region and the main threats to national security were perceived as land-based, the RMN was able to concentrate its attention on constabulary missions. But times have changed and Mak identified a need for the RMN to get back to basics and concentrate on its primary war-fighting mission and, if need be, hand over its lesser patrol vessels to another agency responsible for coast guard roles.[47]

In line with this approach, Malaysia has moved in recent years to establish a separate coast guard. The legislation to establish this service, the Malaysian Maritime Enforcement Agency (MMEA), was ratified by the Malaysian Senate in June 2004.[48] It became operational in March 2005 and has taken over law enforcement in Malaysia's territorial sea and EEZ.[49] Its responsibilities also include search and rescue, pollution control, and counter piracy and drug trafficking on the high seas.[50] The impetus to establish the new agency largely came from the RMN whose officers "thought it was a waste of resources to use large, sophisticated warships for maritime enforcement given the wear and tear on extended operations, as well as the time taken up in court appearances by officers aboard ships that made arrests."[51] The Agency will operate at least six helicopters and fixed-

45. D. Mahadzir, "New Maritime Agency Steps Up," *Asia-Pacific Defence Reporter* (February 2005): 27.

46. J. N. Mak, "Malaysia's Naval and Strategic Priorities: Charting a New Course," in *Maritime Change—Issues for Asia*, eds., R. Babbage and S. Bateman (North Sydney: Allen & Unwin, 1993): 117–125.

47. *Id.* at 123.

48. Captain Mat Taib Yassin RMN (Rtd), "The Malaysian Maritime Enforcement Agency (MMEA)" (paper presented at First Meeting of the CSCAP Study Group on Capacity Building for Maritime Security Cooperation in the Asia-Pacific, Kunming, 7–8 December 2004).

49. See Mahadzir, n. 45 above, at 26.

50. See Yasin, n. 48 above.

51. See Mahadzir, n. 45 above, at 26.

wing aircraft and about 80 small and medium-sized vessels. These assets are drawn from diverse maritime agencies, such as the Marine Police, Navy, and the Fisheries and Customs Departments.

Philippines

The Philippines is another major archipelagic State in the Asia-Pacific region. The Philippine archipelago is geographically complex, crisscrossed by a network of international and domestic ship routes, relatively rich in marine living resources, with numerous environmentally sensitive sea areas and a relatively high incidence of marine disasters. The attack by Abu Sayyaf terrorist group on the passenger ferry *Superferry 14* in Manila Bay in February 2004, resulting in a death toll of about 116, is the worst act of maritime terrorism around the world in recent years. The risks of terrorist attacks in the Philippines are still relatively high due to the presence in the country of several major terrorist groups that could have the capabilities to launch attacks on shipping. Maintaining security and safety in the archipelago is a task mainly for the Philippine Coast Guard (PCG), although it suffers poorly in the competition for resources with the other elements of the Philippine Armed Forces. It has suffered budget cuts in recent years that have adversely affected its ability to perform its mandated roles.

The PCG has a long history having celebrated its 100th anniversary in 2001. Plans for the organization to devolve to the Department of Transportation have not yet eventuated and it remains a command of the Philippine Navy.[52] In recent years the PCG has acquired new vessels from Australia and Spain. It has close ties with the JCG and the Korean National Maritime Police Agency with which it has a Memorandum of Understanding to permit closer cooperation between the two agencies, including personnel training exchanges.[53] In the South China Sea, where the Philippines has claim to several islands, the PCG is the main service used for sovereignty protection tasks.

Singapore

Formerly known as the Marine Police, the Singapore Police Coast Guard operates a large fleet of more than 80 port security and fast interceptor craft

52. See Saunders, n. 22 above, at 524.
53. CDR L. M Tuason Jr. PCG, "Maritime Security—The Philippine Experience," (paper presented at APEC High Level Meeting on Maritime Security, Manila, 8–9 September 2003).

for combating piracy, drug smuggling and illegal entry.[54] The Coast Guard works closely with the Republic of Singapore Navy (RSN) and the Indonesian Navy (TNI-AL) to provide coordinated patrols to counter acts of piracy and armed robbery against ships in the Singapore Straits. In December 2003, the Coast Guard conducted a counter terrorism and piracy exercise with units of the JCG.[55]

South Korea

The Korean National Maritime Police Agency (KNMPA) fulfils the functions of a coast guard in the Republic of Korea (ROK). It operates four offshore patrol vessels of over 1,000 tonnes and numerous other smaller vessels and patrol craft, including tugs and rescue craft. The responsibilities of the NMPA are listed as:[56]

- Maritime guard, including fishery protection with a specific reference to cooperation with China and North Korea;
- Maritime law enforcement to combat crimes at sea, including illegal fishing, people smuggling and other forms of smuggling;
- Maritime Safety Control to reduce risks of shipping accidents and provide rescue services; and
- Marine Pollution to protect and preserve the marine environment from a diversity of pollution sources, including ships, dumping and scrapped vessels.

The KNMPA plays a leading role in maritime cooperative activities between South Korea and other regional countries. Its personnel are also stationed on the disputed islands of Tokdo/Takeshima as a symbol of Korean sovereignty.[57]

54. See Saunders, n. 22 above, at 622; "Background," Police Coast Guard homepage, available online: <http://www.spf.gov.sg/aboutspf/pcg2/pcgback.htm>.

55. "Singapore and Japanese Coast Guards Conduct Largest Counter Terrorism and Piracy Exercise," *Channel News Asia* (4 December 2003), available online: <http://channelsnewsasia.com/stories/eastasia/print/60479/1/.html>.

56. National Maritime Police Agency web site, <http://www.nmpa.go.kr/>.

57. "S. Korea Reclaims Sovereignty Over Small Islet Dokdo," *Xinhua* (23 February 2005), available online: <http://xinhuanet.com/english/2005–02/23/content_2609613.htm>.

Taiwan

The Coast Guard Administration (CGA) was formally the Maritime Security Police until a change of name on 1 January 2000.[58] It comes under the Ministry of the Interior but its numerous patrol boats are integrated into the Navy for operational purposes. The service has several large patrol craft and in a rationalization of roles, the larger vessels of the Customs fleet were transferred to the CGA in 2000. It now has a total of about 124 ships, including smaller patrol craft, and is a "unique combination of the former coast guard command of the military, marine police and parts of the customs office's personnel and equipment."[59]

The CGA is responsible for maritime law enforcement and the security of fishing vessels within the EEZ. Its operations extend to the Pratas and Spratly Islands in the South China Sea where CGA personnel now garrison islands rather than the military.[60] Press reports point to some expansion of the role and influence of the CGA with the upgrading of the coastal radar network,[61] and a leading role in the formation of maritime policy in Taiwan.[62]

Thailand

The Royal Thai Marine Police is part of the Thai Police Bureau. The service acts as a coast guard in inshore waters with about 65 armed patrol craft (the largest of which is about 600 tonnes) and over 65 smaller vessels equipped only with small arms.[63] It has increased commitments to fight terrorism and counter piracy, particularly in the northern part of the Malacca Strait and has been seeking additional funds to upgrade its fleet.[64]

---

58. See Saunders, n. 22 above, at 680.

59. B. Hsu, "Coast Guard Holds Small Drill for Press in Kinmen," *Taipei Times* (31 August, 2002), available online: <http://www.taipeitimes.com/news/2002/08/31/print/0000166264>; B. Hsu, "Coast Guard Planning to Upgrade Radar Systems," *Taipei Times* (22 December 2001), available online: <http://www.taipeitimes.com/news/2001/12/22>.

60. Ming-hsien Wong and Tung-lin Wu, "Taiwan's Maritime Strategy in New Security Environment," (paper presented to International Conference on Taiwan's Security and Sea Power, Taipei, 11 January 2002): 18.

61. See Wong and Wu, n. 60 above.

62. B. Hsu, "Coast Guard to Take Lead in Maritime Policy," *Taipei Times* (19 April 2002), available online: <http://www.taipeitimes.com/news/2002/04/19/story/00001132454>.

63. See Saunders, n. 22 above, at 694.

64. K. Sookpradist, "Thai Police Plan to Spend More in FY2004," *Bangkok Post* (25 April 2003), as reported online: <http://strategis.ic.ca/epic/internet/inimr-ri.nsf/en/gr115943e.html>.

United States

The U.S. Coast Guard (USCG) has a long history. It traces its origins to 1790 and the establishment of the U.S. Revenue Cutter Service. Progressively over the years there were mergers with the Lifesaving Service, the Lighthouse Service and the Bureau of Marine Inspection and Navigation to form the USCG as it is today.[65] The American response to events of September 11, 2001, is having a large impact on the USCG and its mission priorities with service moving to the Department of Homeland Security where its primary mission is the "defense of our homeland."[66] Working closely with other agencies in this department, the USCG is implementing its new Maritime Strategy for Homeland Security to support the broader national strategy for protecting the U.S. homeland.[67]

The USCG is the most well known example of a modern coast guard. It has five maritime security roles: maritime safety, maritime mobility (primarily the facilitation of maritime transportation, including navigational aids and vessel traffic services), maritime law enforcement, marine environmental protection and a national defense (political-military) role in support of foreign policy and defence objectives.[68] The latter role has received more attention over the last decade due to the higher probability of low-level regional conflict post the Cold War and the suitability of USCG forces for many associated tasks rather than conventional naval forces. These include crisis response through less threatening military presence, peacekeeping, humanitarian aid, the initial handling of maritime terrorist incidents, and military assistance abroad to assist navies of developing countries in developing their capability to handle constabulary tasks. All these tasks could be considered examples of the *diplomatic* role of coast guards.

In many ways, the USCG is the most *complete* coast guard, although the JCG is very much its clone. As well as law enforcement, lifesaving and marine environmental protection tasks, the USCG is also a safety and regulatory agency with responsibilities for matters such as recreational boating safety, ship classification and Port State Control, and a navigation agency with responsibility for navigational aids, ship communications and vessel traffic

---

65. Lieutenant R. Canty USCG, "The Coast Guard and Environmental Protection—Recent Changes and Potential Impacts," *Naval War College Review*, LII, no. 4 (Autumn 1999): 80.

66. The White House, Office of the Press Secretary, "Presidential Policy on CG's Primary Mission," *Briefing by Ari Fleischer* (July 16, 2002).

67. Admiral T. H. Collins USCG, "Change and Continuity—The U.S. Coast Guard Today," *Naval Review*, LVII, no. 2 (Spring 2004): 15.

68. Captain B. Stubbs USCG and S. C. Truver, *America's Coast Guard—Safeguarding U.S. Maritime Safety and Security in the 21st Century* (Arlington: Center for Security Strategies and Operations, 2000): 1.

services. In other countries, regulatory activities in particular are likely to be the responsibility of another agency.

The USCG attaches considerable importance to what has been termed "exporting Coast Guard expertise."[69] The tasks involved are both operational and training. Operational activities include joint law enforcement activities (particularly against drug trafficking and people smuggling), sanctions enforcement (either through the deployment of USCG vessels or the use of Coast Guard Law Enforcement detachments (LEDets) onboard USN ships), the deployment of Port Security Units (PSUs), disaster relief and search and rescue exercises.[70] Training activities are mainly conducted under the International Military and Education Training Program (IMET) and include the use of Mobile Training Teams (MTTs) that travel to a range of host countries throughout the world to conduct a variety of technical training using host nation facilities (such as firefighting, marine safety and law enforcement). The resident training program involving foreign students training at USCG specialty schools in the U.S. is the other half of IMET. Lastly, USCG vessels making port calls overseas also conduct onboard training and familiarization on an ad hoc basis.

Vietnam

The Vietnamese Coast Guard was formed in 1998 "to strengthen maritime management and to maintain order and security at sea in order to create good premises for marine exploration, exploitation to build a powerful marine economy of the country."[71] It is set up to meet the demands of socio-economic development, security and defense of Vietnam.[72] The Coast Guard is an integral part of the military, subordinate to the Navy and may take on customs duties. It has a specific role to cooperate with "Coast Guards or concerned forces of other countries in order to contribute to maintaining security, order, peace and stability in regional and international maritime zones."[73]

Vietnam has two forces responsible for managing and ensuring security and order at sea. The Border Guard is a specialized force responsible for managing defense of sovereignty, territorial integrity, security and order of

69. See Loy, n. 12 above, at 55–57.

70. S. C. Truver, "The World is Our Coastline," *USN Institute Proceedings* (June 1998): 46.

71. H. T. Nguyen, "The Ordinance of the Vietnamese Coast Guard," *Vietnamese Law Journal,* no. 4 (1998): 37.

72. H. T. Nguyen, "Establishment of the Vietnamese Coast Guard," *Maritime Studies* 103 (November–December 1998): 14.

73. See Nguyen, n. 71 above, at 39.

state boundaries on land, on islands and in maritime zones. The main sphere of action of the Border Guard is internal waters and ports.

REGIONAL MARITIME COOPERATION

The importance of regional maritime cooperation flows from the complexity of the maritime environment, overlapping maritime jurisdiction and the risks of tensions and disputes at sea. As well as being essential for the effective management of regional seas, maritime cooperation is an important maritime confidence and security building measure (MCSBM) and a "building block" for greater regional stability. *Maritime cooperation* encompasses any cooperative activity associated with an interest in the sea, the protection of the marine environment or a use of the sea or its resources. *Naval cooperation* between regional navies is a subset of the broader concept of *maritime cooperation* and an important MCSBM in its own right.

Concerns have been expressed about increased naval expenditure in the region and the risks of increased tension at sea unless there is a new focus on MCSBMs and "building blocks" for regional stability.[74] Maritime cooperation, including cooperation between regional navies, should be a major component of this process, but naval cooperation is subject to some limitations and countries may prefer to use coast guards for operational cooperation rather than their navy.

Operational cooperation involves problems with common doctrine, language and interoperability of equipment. These may be more acute with navies than with coast guards. Regional navies acquire their ships, submarines and aircraft from a wide range of sources. The problems involved become even more acute as the technological levels of navies increase. Regional navies are at different stages of technological development. Technical deficiencies in some navies may significantly inhibit cooperation with the less advanced navies being reluctant to engage in operational cooperation for fear that their deficiencies will be too apparent.

Another problem is that naval cooperation may be used to gain intelligence on the capabilities of a potential adversary. It is well known that even innocuous naval port visits provide an opportunity to gather intelligence both by the host nation collecting information about the visiting ship and by the visiting ship about the host nation. This might include signals intelligence gained by listening in on the host nation's naval communications while the foreign warship is in port. Normally it is standard practice for

74. S. Bateman, "Dangerous Waters Ahead," *Jane's Defence Weekly*, 35, 13 (28 March 2001): 24–27; A. Bergin, "East Asian Naval Developments—Sailing Into Rough Seas," *Marine Policy* 26 (2002): 121–131.

a host nation to close down sensitive transmissions while a "potential intelligence collector" (PIC) is in port. Expert intelligence collectors can obtain much vital information on another navy, particularly data on weapons, sensors and communications systems during operations with ships of another navy. In the current environment of maritime insecurity and strategic competition, regional navies are cautious about proceeding too far with joint exercises, particularly those that involve more than basic seamanship drills.

COAST GUARD COOPERATION

Cooperation between coast guards may offer benefits not available with naval cooperation. Warships from major maritime powers may overwhelm vessels from small navies by their sheer size, technology and firepower. On the other hand, coast guard vessels may appear less intimidating and in periods of tension they may be less provocative.[75] They are "less threatening than larger, more heavily armed haze-gray warships," and are able to carry out exercises and training with other nations that might not be possible on a navy-to-navy basis.[76] It has been observed, for example, that the Chinese have been "wary" of working closely with the U.S. military for fear that might reveal their weaknesses, and that while planned USN-Mexican Navy exercises in 1996 met with outrage and political controversy in Mexico, cooperation between the USCG and the Mexican Navy was able to proceed routinely and quietly.[77]

Cooperation between regional coast guards is expanding rapidly. At a multilateral level there is the Northern Pacific Heads of Coast Guard Agencies forum,[78] and the Heads of Asian Coast Guards meetings. Some working groups of APEC (e.g., on maritime transportation), as well as the Asia-Pacific Heads of Maritime Safety Agencies meetings, involve cooperation between coast guards. Bilateral activities are becoming more common, including between China and Vietnam, South Korea and China, China and Japan, and Russia and Japan. As has been noted, both the Vietnamese Coast Guard and the South Korean National Maritime Police Agency include regional and international cooperation in their specific functions.

75. Captain B. B. Stubbs USCG, "The U.S. Coast Guard—A Unique Instrument of U.S. National Security," *Marine Policy*, 18, 6 (1994): 518.
76. See Truver, n. 70 above, at 45.
77. *Id.* at 45–46.
78. This North Pacific coast guard summit was launched in 2000 as an initiative of Japan. Participating countries are Canada, China, South Korea, Russia and the USA.

Under the leadership mainly of the JCG, the Heads of Asian Coast Guards meetings now have some significant achievements. The Asia Maritime Security Initiative 2004 (AMARSECTIVE 2004) was agreed at the meeting in Tokyo in June 2004, and the more recent Regional Cooperation Agreement on Combating Piracy and Armed Robbery against Ships in Asia (ReCAAP)[79] was agreed in November 2004. All ASEAN nations, Japan, China, Korea, India, Bangladesh and Sri Lanka are working under ReCAAP to set up an information network and a cooperation regime to prevent piracy and armed robbery against ships in the regional waters. ReCAAP is a very significant achievement for the region that provides the basis for regional cooperation to counter piracy and armed robbery against ships. It includes an authoritative definition of "armed robbery against ships," and provides for the establishment of an Information Sharing Center (ISC) to be located in Singapore.

LOOKING TO THE FUTURE

The Independent World Commission on the Oceans delivered its highly critical review of the current state of the oceans during the International Year of the Ocean in 1998.[80] It noted that the oceans are the setting of major problems. Territorial disputes that threaten peace and security, global climate change, illegal fishing, habitat destruction, species extinction, pollution, drug smuggling, congested shipping lanes, sub-standard ships, illegal migration, piracy and the disruption of coastal communities are among these problems. Dealing with them has become a major objective of global governance requiring a high level of international and regional cooperation that subordinates national interests to a greater common good.

The Commission believed that navies must assist in meeting this challenge of international oceans management. Its report noted that: "The role of navies and, where appropriate, other maritime security forces, [should] be reoriented, in conformity with present international law, to enable them to enforce legislation concerning non-military threats that affect security in the oceans, including their ecological aspects."[81] However, for the reasons discussed in this article, it is unlikely that navies will accept this role and it is more likely to be assumed by coast guards.

There is more and more distance opening up between warships optimized for war-fighting and coast guard-type vessels designed for

---

79. Regional Cooperation Agreement on Combating Piracy and Armed Robbery against Ships in Asia (signed April 28, 2005).

80. *The Ocean Our Future—The Report of the Independent World Commission on the Oceans* (Cambridge: Cambridge University Press, 1998).

81. *Id.* at 17.

maritime policing. As Colin Gray has suggested, navies and coast guards are "driven by the beats of different drummers."[82] This is increasingly so with navies being consumed by high technology weapon systems and the concepts of network-centric warfare (NCW) and the revolution in military affairs (RMA). Navies are attracted to larger vessels that can carry more weapons and sensors and are less vulnerable. Even smaller navies such as those of Singapore, Malaysia and Brunei are building larger vessels. Maritime strategists opine that due primarily to the benefits of networking, "big is beautiful" and smaller numbers of larger vessels have advantages over larger numbers of smaller vessels.[83] By 2020, the USN may well have no frigates left and all its destroyers will be relatively large, expensive and very much an "over-kill" for policing tasks.[84] On the other hand, the U.S. nationally may well lack a sufficient number of "hulls in the water" to undertake the full range of maritime policing and overseas engagement tasks. It may well fall to the Coast Guard to provide the additional hulls under the concept of a National Fleet.[85]

The type of expertise that navies have is becoming more different than that possessed by coast guards, which in turn have expertise that is not the same as naval expertise. Coast guard personnel have to be "lifesavers, guardians and warriors."[86] Greater use of the sea, increased illegal activity at sea, and concern for the marine environment have increased the number of international regimes that are applicable and made the business of maritime policing more complex. As Gray has described it, "The guesswork involved in naval planning is nearly absent from forecasts bearing upon the Coast Guard—because the primary focus of the service is not the national defense duties legally laid upon it but marine safety, maritime law enforcement, and marine environmental protection."[87] The trends with these activities are known but the same cannot be said about what war-fighting tasks might confront a navy in the future, except that hopefully these tasks might never eventuate! There is much uncertainty with naval futures and "so high-end naval power—in general and specifically—can quite easily be dismissed as

82. C. S. Gray, "The Coast Guard and Navy—It's Time for a "National Fleet," *Naval War College Review*, LIV, no. 3 (Summer 2001): 116.

83. N. Friedman, *Seapower as Strategy—Navies and National Interests* (Annapolis: Naval Institute Press, 2001): 242.

84. C. S. Gray, "Keeping the Coast Guard Afloat," *The National Interest*, no. 60 (Summer 2000): 86.

85. See Collins, n. 67 above, at 21.

86. B. Stubbs, "We Are Lifesavers, Guardians, and Warriors," *USN Institute Proceedings* (April 2002): 50–53.

87. See Gray, n. 82 above, at 127.

yesterday's unaffordable and irrelevant answer to the bold novelties of tomorrow."[88]

Part of this conundrum is associated with changing concepts of security. Navies and warships are designed to fight wars and combat military threats while coast guards and coast guard patrol vessels are primarily concerned with social, resources and environmental threats to national well-being and a comprehensive view of security. Some authors talk about "threats without enemies," and the scope for an "Oceanguard" to protect the oceans and their living resources from environmental stress and the loss of biodiversity.[89] While the constabulary or policing role at sea has been seen in the past as a national one, it is possible that in the future it will involve international policing on the high seas beyond the limits of national jurisdiction. As Gwyn Prins has described it, an "Oceanguard would be a high seas equivalent of a coast guard, performing similar missions but in defense of the global commons and in the enforcement of international, not specific, national laws in those areas stated to be, and accepted as being, free of the exercise of sovereign rights."[90]

As well as a global Oceanguard under the auspices of the UN or a UN agency, regional arrangements might be possible. An ASEAN Coast Guard has been suggested, as well as well as a Pacific Islands Ocean Guard that would bring together the scarce resources of the Pacific island countries (PICs) into a cooperative maritime surveillance and enforcement regime.[91] A basic framework of legal regimes and cooperation already exists in the PICs, primarily through the Pacific Islands Forum, that might be used as a basis for a regional Ocean Guard. The Ocean Guard would police the region not only for fisheries protection but also for economic, environmental protection, humanitarian and constabulary purposes.

CONCLUSIONS

There are encouraging aspects of the developments discussed in this article. The emergence of coast guards as significant forces in regional maritime

---

88. *Id.* at 114.
89. G. Prins, ed., *Threats Without Enemies: Facing Environmental Insecurity* (London: Earthscan, 1993); G. Prins, "Oceanguard: The Need, the Possibility, and the Concept," *Ocean Yearbook* 14, eds. E. Mann Borgese, A. Chircop, M. McConnell and J. R. Morgan (Chicago: Chicago University Press, 2000): 398–419.
90. *Id.* at 411.
91. Captain G. I. Dela Cruz PN, "Time for a NEW Coast Guard," *USN Institute Proceedings* (March 1994): 58–60; S. Bateman, "Developing a Pacific Island Ocean Guard: The Need, the Possibility and the Concept," in *The Eye of the Cyclone: Issues in Pacific Security*, ed. I. Molloy (Sippy Downs: Pacific Islands Political Science Association and University of the Sunshine Coast Press, 2004): 208–224.

security cooperation is not occurring as part of any grand plan of national defense or power projection, but rather as a basic response to national needs and a sense of responsibility with regard to fulfilling a shared responsibility and interest in good order at sea. While much naval planning and thinking is a reaction to the past, the development of coast guards is in many ways a response to future needs.

A coast guard offers a cost-effective alternative to a navy. Navies with their drive to modernize and introduce the highest level of war-fighting technology and capability that their budget can afford are in effect pricing themselves out of the maritime policing market. Even with the concern in the region for the threat of maritime terrorism, in many countries the role of countering this threat has fallen more to the coast guard than to the navy, although the latter might still provide the "muscle" to deal with higher level threat scenarios. And as we have seen with the efforts of the Japanese Coast Guard, and the Canadian Coast Guard in particular, for developed countries a coast guard may offer a more politically acceptable alternative than a navy for assisting developing countries with building their capacity to maintain law and order in their adjacent waters.

Current trends in globalization are supporting the importance of sea power in general and, at least in the Asia-Pacific region, both navies and coast guards are expanding. The roles of maritime security forces do not necessarily involve a "zero-sum" game, and thus the relative importance of the war-fighting and constabulary roles may not be changing. Both might be growing. Maritime policing is a growth industry and while the same might be said of navies in the current regional environment, the latter trend might eventually be reversed. As navies go on focusing on the war-fighting mission, they will eventually become targets for naval arms control measures, and to the extent that they themselves are involved in processes of maritime confidence building, they may in time work themselves "out of a job." If current trends are any indication, coast guards appear to have a much more certain future in the Asia-Pacific region.

International Regulation and Maritime Safety Mechanisms after the *Prestige* Catastrophe on the Galician Coast

Fernando González-Laxe
University Institute of Maritime Studies, Universidade da Coruña, Spain

INTRODUCTION

Maritime accidents and catastrophes have reflected a terrible trend during recent years. They are common in all regions of the planet and have had enormous impacts at all levels. They emphasize the fact that some areas are more vulnerable to such risks than others and that these risks have a negative effect on the living conditions of the affected populations and territories.[1] The consequences of these risks go beyond the short-term, and in some cases these accidents bring about irreversible changes in both the socio-economic structure and the environment.

The increase of maritime traffic of hazardous goods means that some areas are more exposed to risk, and therefore they reach a higher level of vulnerability. In this sense, the vulnerability is the tendency to suffer from significant transformations as a consequence of the interaction between external or internal processes. We interpret transformation as a structural change, or at least a permanent and deep modification. Consequently, vulnerability considered as a trend, is not an absolute property, but is related to both a system in a specific context and a type of change or concrete threat.

As noted above, it is clear that a system can be either vulnerable or strong depending on diverse circumstances. A rigorous analysis of the risks should consider the following elements: a) sensitivity, or to what extent the system can be changed or affected by an alteration; b) the capacity to answer which has to be scheduled to face or resist the alteration, as well as to moderate the potential damages and to take advantage of the opportunities—among other things, questions about resistance, availability of stocks,

---

1. V. Beck, *La sociedad del riesgo* (Barcelona: Editorial Paidos, 1986).

Ocean Yearbook 20: 533–560.

regulatory mechanism, and cooperative links; c) to what extent the system is exposed to this alteration, that is, the time and the effects related to the system; and d) the impacts on the system, where the calculation of vulnerability, exposition, possibility of new occurrences, magnitude, intensity and persistence, are included.

In this article a detailed analysis of some relevant questions for maritime safety in the European context is carried out using relevant information obtained from the *Prestige* accident on the Galician coast of Spain in November 2002. The first section describes the impact on the Galician coast. Then the costs and damages caused by the *Prestige* are evaluated and the European Union (EU) regulations are analyzed. The article concludes by considering the mechanisms to compensate affected parties, and defining their scope and degree of coverage. The last section details a qualitative analysis of the institutional and social capacity to respond during the "crisis."

THE COMPLEX MARITIME SYSTEM

Globalization has encouraged the growing integration of different economic areas, the development of international trade, the elimination of obstacles that facilitate the easier transit and flow of goods and services, and a greater mobility of direct foreign investment. This integration of national economies contributes to both the acceleration of competitiveness and a new repositioning of companies in world trade. The maritime world has not been left out of those powerful forces of change, and the economic environment related to the international transport of hydrocarbons and dangerous products has become extremely complex, as the following characteristics highlight:

a) The global industrial development and the growing interchanges have meant that the oil-based societies have eliminated their fleets and small independent ship owners of tankers have appeared in the market. As a consequence, oil-based societies control less than one-quarter of the global tanker fleet, whereas the majority belongs to independent owners.

b) The widespread appearance of vessels with flags of convenience from "free registration" countries is a challenge. About half of the tonnage that is carried by the world fleet of tankers is registered with flags of convenience and there are "second registers" in many developed countries where the aforementioned vessels have similar characteristics to the ones registered with a flag of convenience.

c) There is evidence of quality problems in a significant number of vessels carrying potentially polluting substances. About 70 percent of the vessels are single-hull tankers and 39 percent of the tonnage carried in tankers is in vessels greater than 20 years old.

d) Large difficulties exist to exert efficient controls over the maritime transport of dangerous goods. There is no international legislation adopted by affected countries to establish risk prevention criteria on traffic of this kind. It is only when an accident takes place that the interest in speeding up the implementation of more strict legislation becomes stronger. The recommendations of the Erika I and Erika II (discussed later) and the subsequent declarations of the *Prestige* incident are telling examples of this after-the-fact approach.

e) Another issue is the existence of economic limitations on civil liability due to hydrocarbon spills. This means that, as there is no regulation on who pollutes, it allows the free riders to act with high "benevolence" on the part of public authorities and international organizations.

Thus, the framework for maritime safety has to be reconsidered. The international civil society is more exigent regarding information, control, and sanctioning capacity. This society demands greater safety levels and lower risk. As some actions related to socio-economic and environmental damages are not penalized, some economic actors and operators have been acting as free riders, without being afraid of the additional cost of repairing damages or paying sanctions. That means there are no anticipatory or preventive measures to reduce their negative impacts, and at the same time the permissiveness is evident when it comes to sanctioning.

The oil freight market is unregulated and therefore subject to intense competition. The aim is to look for cheaper oil transports, and since market volatility is assumed, there are no long-term contracts among the operators. Finally, it is difficult to determine who the owners of both the vessels and the cargoes are at any moment, and this situation increases the margin of vulnerability and lack of safety if preventive measures are adopted so that civil liabilities could be assumed.

The experience of the *Prestige* incident has made clear the existence of two important focal points of performance and behavior on the part of some operators. On the one hand, there has been a significant increase in small companies in charge of the transport of dangerous goods.[2] These are companies registered in tax havens, with an organization of accountability that is difficult to follow. They are created and disappear very quickly in

---

2. F. González-Laxe, *El impacto del Prestige. Análisis y evaluación de los daños causados por el accidente del Prestige y dispositivos para la regeneración medio-ambiental y recuperación económica de Galicia* (Coruña: Fundación Pedro Barrié de la Maza, 2003).

order to avoid controls, and are acquired in an open market at very low prices without having total or strict safety conditions for both the vessels and crews. On the other hand, the international institutional framework has not managed to design a regulation system that avoids, mitigates, or reduces the negative impacts that these maritime business situations may potentially cause. That is because there are no restrictions or strong rules to promote good sectoral performance.

The performance of the International Maritime Organization (IMO) proves to be a key factor in this field. The IMO has presented itself as having a good and proper attitude, but its achievements regarding the implementation of resolutions are slow given the continuous pressures by States and oil companies. The current divergence of interests among the European countries, the difficulties to implement certain rules related to the renewal of vessels, and the particular self-interests of both the oil and maritime transport industries are the reasons for the present delay to harmonize these rules on a worldwide scale.

THE IMPACT OF THE *PRESTIGE* ON THE GALICIAN COASTS

The Importance of Fishing in Galicia

Galicia is located very close to one of the main European maritime corridors. Around 45,000 merchant ships transit waters opposite Galicia, and 13,000 of them transport some kind of dangerous product. That is, 122 vessels cross the Galician coasts every day, and 36 of them entail some measure of risk. The *Prestige* incident was not the first maritime accident in Galicia, an area that is the most affected by maritime tragedies in the last 25 years. Some catastrophes, such as the *Polycommander*, the *Erkowitz*, the *Urquiola*, the *Aegean Sea*, the *Andros Patria*, and the *Casson*, characterise Galician history (Table 1).

Table 1.—Maritime Accidents in Galicia

VESSEL	QUANTITY (TONS)	YEAR	CARGO
Urquiola	101,000	1976	Oil
Aegean Sea	80,000	1992	Oil
Prestige	64,000	2002	Fuel oil
Andros Patria	16,000	1978	Oil
Polycommander	15,000	1970	Oil
Erkowitz	286 (2,000 barrels)	1970	Pesticides
Casson	1,100	1987	Chemical products

Galicia, with about 2.7 million inhabitants, represents 6.5 percent of the total Spanish population. About 60 percent of this population is concentrated in the coastal area and this figure has increased in recent years because of the processes of deruralization and deagrarization on the part of the population located in the inner areas. The aforementioned 60 percent of the coastal population, which lives in one-fifth of the Galician territory, shows a population density of 224 inhabitants/km^2, much higher than the Galician average (92 inhabitants/km^2) and the Spanish average (81 inhabitants/km^2). Of the 53 regions in Galicia, 20 are on the coast, which shows how important the questions related to the coastal area are.

The Galician Gross Domestic Product (GDP) is around €16,700 per capita, lower than the Spanish average (€18,900) and that of the EU–15 (€23,000). For this reason, Galicia is considered an Objective 1 region when it comes to implementing the EU Structural Funds to mitigate the existing regional inequalities. Likewise, the rates of employment and activity are lower than the Spanish average and the ageing processes are greater.

Galicia is characterized by significant population dispersion, small town councils, and limited managerial capacity in its economic establishments. This highlights that the main Galician features are homes with few inhabitants, companies without employees, and a predominance of micro-companies that supply their own products and services to the local and regional market. The economic specialization in this region is characterized by those activities linked to the availability of natural resources, namely, milk, meat, wood, fish, shellfish, granite, slate, and electric energy. The highest specialization coefficients show high ratios in those industries related to both the transport (shipbuilding and automobile industries) and textile sectors.

By contextualizing our analysis, it can be said that Galicia is the premier Spanish fishing region in terms of fleet, employment, and production. In terms of Gross Value Added (GVA), the fishing sector represents 2.54 percent of the total in Galicia with the canning industry at 0.82 percent and the rest of the fishing activities at 1.79 percent. Altogether, it represents 5.15 percent of the total Galician GVA (0.2 percent in the EU–15). Employment accounts for more than 30,000 direct jobs, which represents 2.7 percent of the active population. And finally, the unloaded cargo in the Galician ports is equivalent to 10 percent of the total European Community production, and the agricultural production represents 18 percent of the total European Community production.

Fishing activities in Galicia are very heterogeneous because the harvesting, processing, and organizational sectors are very diverse. For their importance, we can highlight artisanal fishing, deep-sea fishing, fleets fishing in international waters, marine farming, mollusk fishing, and the processing and marketing industries. Artisanal fishing accounts for 87 percent of the vessels and the tonnage per vessel is between 2 and 12 tons. Small, usually family-owned ships operate near coastal areas catching fish that are commercialized as fresh products. Their operational capacity depends on the official authorizations and licenses to fish. The industrial and coastal fleet includes those vessels less than 200 tons that operate in domestic fishing grounds or in those grounds managed by the EU, as well as in the Moroccan Exclusive Economic Zone. Fishing is directed for some specific species, the markets are national or European in some cases, and the companies are medium-sized, which demands a significant capitalization. The fleet that fishes in the deep sea is comprised of larger and more autonomous vessels with high technological advances. This fleet has the equipment necessary to freeze and process fish onboard. The markets are international and they require a high degree of capitalization.

Regarding shellfish production and marine farming, three production systems exist. Shellfish gathering (mainly clams and cockles) extends all over the Galician coast due to the high productivity of the existing natural sites. It employs mainly women, and they operate in shellfish gathering seasons regulated by the Autonomic Institution (Regional Galician Government). Secondly, the development of miticulture, which has its basis on 330 floating platforms (so-called *bateas*), anchored in the Galician *rias* where primarily mussels, but also oysters and scallops, are produced. Galicia is the top European producer of mussels. And thirdly, aquaculture with the already existing farming plants specialized in turbot farming (first national producer), and the short-term implementation to farm red sea bream, croaker, and octopus. This third system of production can also be considered as an emerging and expanding activity.

As far as the processing and marketing industries are concerned, they include the canning industry (the top Spanish companies are located in Galicia), cold stores, fish wholesalers, and retailers that account for a total of more than 25,000 people, with an increasing trend. In short, the important dimension of the fishing sector in Galicia reveals a high diversity of activities and processes. The total annual production stands at around 400,000 tons, with an equivalent value of €500 million. Therefore, we are witnessing an enormous sea-industrial complex.[3]

3. Consello Económico Social de Galicia, *Situación e perspectivas do sector do marisqueo a pé en Galici* (Santiago de Compostela, 2001); Consello Económico Social de Galicia, *O sector pesqueiro en Galicia* (Santiago de Compostela, 2002); F. González Laxe, *Estrategia y desarrollo de la pesca en Europa* (A Coruña: Ed Netbiblo, 2002); M. C. García Negro, *Táboas input-output pesca-conserva galega 1999* (Santiago de Compostela, 2003).

The Impact of the *Prestige* on the Galician Coasts

The experience accumulated from previous analyses has allowed us to undertake an analysis of the *Prestige* catastrophe in accordance with several considerations. The first conclusions to be highlighted are: a) it is the first time that a maritime accident affected several countries (Figure 1); b) Galicia received several "floods" of fuel from the *Prestige* with different intensities, and at the same time it was observed that the fuel split into a large number of black slicks of different sizes; c) the *Prestige* spillage has affected a long and heterogeneous coastal area with different ecosystem components; d) with reference to the fauna associated with intertidal and subtidal substrates, the affected area is very important from a biological perspective (Table 2); e) the basis and specialization of the economic activities in the affected territories depends on fishing and marine farming; and f) finally, this accident set a precedent in the history of oil slicks because of its duration, the means used (tugboats, containment barriers), and the recovered quantities.

Table 2.—Short- and Long-Term Effects of the *Prestige* Accident

Affected Areas	Ecological imbalance	Consequences for natural patrimony	Ruined maritime richness	Effects on economic activities
140 beaches and 4 natural parks	Alteration of ecosystems. Species displacement. Changes in production.	Marshes, natural areas, dunes, habitats, and intertidal complexes were all affected.	Surface area: clams, mussels, goose barnacles; Inter-tidal area: razor clams; Infra-littoral area: octopus, spider crab, sole, squid, etc.	It affected production, trade and industrialization processes, e.g., fishery, shellfish gathering, marine farming, and fish canning.

Source: González-Laxe, n. 2 above.

The Galician coastal area is one of the richest fishing and shell fishing areas in Europe. Thus, the high level of concern that these maritime accidents cause around the coast is hardly surprising. Firstly, it is clear that oil slicks generate an immediate impact upon the flora and fauna of these coastal areas. Hay and Théboud claim that one ton of fuel can cover a surface area of 12 square kilometers.[4] In the *Prestige* case, with more than

4. J. Hay and O. Théboud, "Marée noires: quel coût économique," *Problèmes économiques*, n. 2800, La Documentation Francaise, 2003.

FIG. 1.—Areas Affected by the *Prestige* Catastrophe

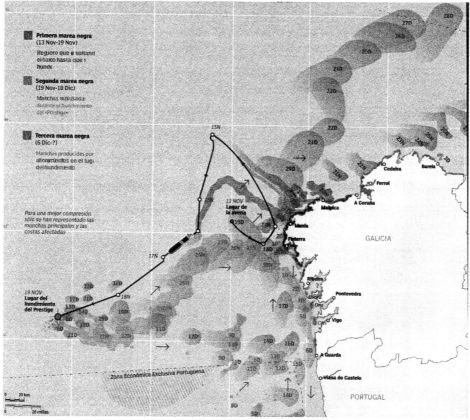

Source: La Voz Gallicia. Special Issue. January 2003, reprinted with permission.

60,000 tons spilled, the affected area would exceed 700,000 square kilometers, an area larger than France.

The total oil spilled after accidents often exceeds the capacity of the environment to absorb them, which results in high species mortality. Therefore, a first consequence is that both the exploited and non-commercial species are altered. It is easy to establish a causal relationship between the oil slick and the immediate mortality of fish, mollusks, and crustaceans. It is also obvious to prove the appearance of certain pathologies, such as changes in growth, emergence of colonizing species, and mutations in the ecosystems.

The estimates to determine the consequences of the pollution derived from maritime accidents and catastrophes are not easy because of several reasons: a) not all species are affected by the impacts in the same way; b) the mobility of some species from one area to another makes it difficult to analyze the consequences; c) the estimates are carried out on the basis of drawing a comparison with catch data from previous years, but it is obvious that the exploitation conditions are not identical; and d) there are new intergenerational externalities of species that makes it difficult to carry out exact comparisons.

As far as the biological dimension is concerned, the growth rates of a resource depend on its size and structure, which for their part depend on the previous years' stocks. The biological parameters are exogenous because the total catch is determined by the total fishing effort. The producers' behavior becomes evident individually, although there is interdependence between the production functions of the whole fleet that exploits the resource in a specific area. That is, every single producer can determine the total of his investments in the selected fishing equipment and in the number of days fished, but he has no direct control over his production. This point makes sense and becomes important in the case of damages caused by oil slicks as they show an externality derived from the loss of extractive chances for the producers as a whole. This externality will be greater or smaller according to both the stocks and the influence of the damage on the fishing areas, natural sites, or farms. That is, there will be fishing and farming areas that will not be able to be open for exploitation and/or their accesses will be temporally limited.

We also have to mention the non-commercial biomass, that is, those species that are not commercially exploited, and therefore without a destination in a specific market. It is very difficult to estimate the extent of damage, as it is not easy to have previous reference points to follow their evolution.

In order to analyze the impacts of the *Prestige* incident we can isolate those that are evaluative because they can be quantified with the purpose to estimate the lost benefits both in the market and outside of it. On the other hand, we have to distinguish those impacts whose estimates will only be quantified several years later, because in some cases they include immaterial assets.

Likewise, two mechanisms can be used. The mechanism related to production, that is, the losses are calculated by carrying out comparisons between the production of the current year with the production of previous years. And the second mechanism could be carried out according to the market losses, estimating the product quantities that have been deviated—temporary or definitively—to new competitors in the national and international markets. In both assumptions, the difficulties are numerous and the results have to wait for several years in order to obtain coherent and reliable results.

As the people affected by oil slicks receive an economic compensation, usually managed by public administrations based on a commitment that ranges from the political public liability to the juridical considerations derived from the actions aimed at mitigating the direct and immediate effects of the catastrophes, the scope of the damages could be obtained from the total compensation paid by the public administration.

Economics distinguishes between three concepts: the option value,[5] existence values,[6] and the value of nature and the ecosystems. The use values are associated with an option value, therefore, only comparable losses are discussed in the catastrophes, taking no notice of other considerations such as the ones related to species biomass or the value of ecosystems. Thus, the inherent value linked to the existence of an ecosystem has to be considered as a question apart from the value that is attributed to the use of this area, which, in this case, is transmissible to subsequent generations. It can become a very high potential value and it also takes into account the optional value generated by the current production.

Therefore, the ecological damages generate two losses of value: the option value and the existence value. For this reason, the methods used to estimate the damages vary considerably, from estimates based on the contingent assessment to estimates obtained by means of technical coefficients derived from the tables of social accounts.[7]

Our research tried to aggregate the impacts and repercussions of the whole affected society.[8] The work directed towards cleaning and restoration programmes, as well as the direct effects that could potentially impact the economic activities in Galicia, were included.

By way of synthesis, the negative and direct effects of an economic nature were focused on those activities related to fishing, aquaculture-related activities, and tourism. It is necessary to emphasize that these activities are the economic basis of the total productive structure. They are the activities that the affected area specializes in; the specialization index is notorious and significant. They are branches of production and services that have a comparative advantage with respect to other areas. They are those most competitive activities included in international markets and they constitute the pillar of the *milieux territoriaux* on the Galician coasts.

The main economic repercussions affected a total of about 34,000 people distributed as follows: ship owners (6,652), crewmembers (11,149), shellfish gatherers (5,729), traders (2,019), related industries (4,500), related services (3,900), which accounts for a total of 33,849 affected people (Table 4).

5. B. Weisbrod, "Collective-Consumption Services of Individual-Consumption Goods," *Quarterly Journal of Economics* 78 (1964): 471–477.

6. J. A. Kutrilla, "Conservation Reconsidered," *American Economic Review* 57 (1967): 777–786.

7. P. Riera, *Manual de valoración contingente* (Madrid: Instituto de Estudios Fiscales, 1994).

8. González-Laxe, n. 2 above.

FIG. 2.—Cleaning and Biological Regeneration Process on the Galician Coast (2003–2015)

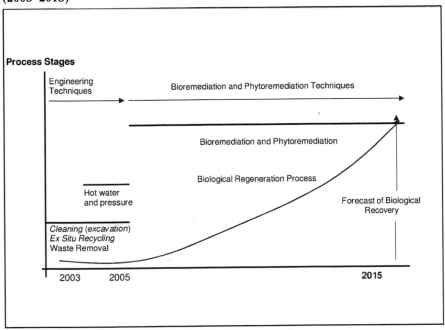

Source: Author.

Likewise, another direct consequence of the impact of this catastrophe is the effect on the population displacements, since the inland migratory movements are accelerated as many of the affected areas have very low birth rates and very high ageing indices. This has brought about a process of depopulation in some areas and an acceleration of change in activity.

With regard to those activities related to tourism, the repercussions were focused on the "dissuasion effect," caused by the "potential inconveniences" that could be accumulated in the affected area, and the possible loss of visitors could be accompanied by both lower investments and modernisations in the already existing facilities in Galicia.

These economic and assessed impacts are aggregated to the estimated costs related to cleaning and recycling, cleaning and waste disposal, the application of hot water on the affected areas, and techniques of bioremediation and phyto-remediation (Figure 2). All of these costs would give a first estimate of the costs of the processes of cleaning and biological recovery of the coast (Table 3). Our research was carried out by estimating the affected area and adjusting the proportion of the costs of the aforementioned tasks in Galicia to the costs of the tasks carried out in Alaska after the *Exxon Valdez* catastrophe (Table 5).

**Table 3.—Estimated Costs (Euros) of the Short-Term Processes
of Cleaning and Biological Recovery**

PROCESS PHASES	ESTIMATION €/m³	TOTAL € (Thousands)
Cleaning and recycling	620	620
Cleaning and disposal of waste products	662	993
Pressurized hot water	450	562
Bioremediation	179	223
Phytoremediation	58.5	73
Total	1,965.50	2,471

Source: Author's estimates.

**Table 4.—Estimated Costs to Maintain the Incomes of the
Affected Groups (Non-Recoverable Financial Assistance
in the Period December 2002–May 2003)**

	Potential number of affected people	Payment to affected people per inactive day (€)	Total monthly and six-monthly non-refundable amounts paid by Public Administrations (Millions €)
Ship owners	6,652	31.3	6.15/36.9
Crewmembers	11,149	40	13.4/80.2
Shellfish gatherers	5,729	40	6.9/41.2
Traders	2,019	35	2.1/12.6
Related industries	4,500	40	5.4/32.4
Related services	3,900	40	4.7/28.1
TOTAL	33,849	-	38.65/231.5

Source: Author's estimates.

These estimates reveal that the *Prestige* catastrophe can be considered the worst maritime and ecological disaster on record in terms of both the spillages and the affected areas if data are compared with other accidents (Table 6).

Table 5.—Basic Data of Economic Boost Derived from the
Prestige **Spillage in Galicia (First Estimates)**

CONCEPT	ESTIMATES
Kilometers of affected coastline (fishing forbidden)	1,000 km
People unemployed (fishing and shellfish gathering only)	30,000 people
People affected directly or indirectly (only fishing sector and related ones)	120,000 people
Added gross value lost (fishery and fish-canning sectors and sectoral interrelations)	1,000 million €/year
Cleaning costs and other technical aspects (mid-January 2003)	€950/1,000 million
Investment necessary for recovery and economic boost of the affected areas (Plan Galicia of the Spanish Government)	€12,459 million

Source: Author's estimates.

It is even more difficult to evaluate the damages on the non-trading resources. These are the impacts on both the active uses of natural heritage such as tourism and recreation, and the impacts on the passive uses, for example, biodiversity, patrimonial legacy related to wetlands, sandy areas, and different ecological areas, which are considered unique spaces for birds and marine mammals.

The fact that these losses are not incorporated into the institutional framework evaluating the economic compensation or liabilities means that these estimates only have an academic effect. That is why the estimation of the *Exxon Valdez* damages included an analysis of "loss of collective values," and it was the oil company Exxon who agreed to compensate these effects by financing assessment studies and restoration programmes aimed at recovery of the damaged ecosystems until they had reached the same condition as they were in before the accident. And when it came to assessing the damages caused by the *Erika* accident, the methods used were carried out by means of a "contingent assessment," that is not accepted by the International Fund for Compensation for Oil Pollution Damage (IOPC Fund).

Table 6.—Basic Characteristics of Major Maritime Accidents that Have Occurred in Europe (1978–2002)

	AMOCCO CADIZ	TANIO	AEGEAN SEA	BRAER	SEA EMPRESS	ERIKA	PRESTIGE
Currency	Millions French francs	Millions French francs	Millions Spanish ptas	Millions British pounds	Millions British pounds	Millions French francs	Millions euros
Date	1/3/1978	7/3/1980	1/12/1992	1/1/1993	1/2/1996	12/12/1999	17/11/2002
Spillage (Tons)	220,000	13,500	80,000	86,500	72,000	19,800	64,000
Km Affected Coastline	350	200	100	40 km^2	150–200	400	1,000
Compensation process length	13 years	8 years	9 years	8 years	>5 years	>3 years	?
Number of claims	n.a.	100	4,600	2,270	1,200	5,600	At present 27,000 claims presented by fishermen
Total estimated cost	4,543-5,215	n.a.	n.a.	n.a.	68–129	5552-6447	€895 million according to the Government
Compensation claims	4,959	1,168	62,396	154	56	877	
Compensation paid	965	362	2,952	57	34	159	

Notes: n.a.—Not available.
Source: O. Thébaud, except for the *Prestige* incident (Author's estimates).

In short, four main categories of costs are associated with oil slicks: a) the cost of cleaning and restoration operations; b) the economic losses suffered by the producers (estimated by the effects of pollution and the value losses of associated assets, as well as the impacts on the ecosystem); c) the impacts derived from pollution on consumers, the effects on the coastal population and the visitors; and d) the ecological damages, linked to the immediate, and medium- and long-term impacts.

THE EUROPEAN INSTITUTIONAL FRAMEWORK

The European institutional framework related to oil slicks had been quite limited and vague until the *Prestige* and *Erika* accidents. It was limited to the extent that the existing instruments for the regulation of maritime activities displayed a very narrow scope. The control of maritime traffic, the inspection of the characteristics of vessels carrying dangerous goods, the conditions to enter into European ports, the knowledge of operators, or the responsibilities regarding compensations, are examples of this secondary and vague role that the European institutions adopted.

The European Union reacted positively after the *Erika* accident in 1999 and started to elaborate new sets of regulations to improve maritime safety, the so-called Erika I and Erika II sets of measures. They included new inspections and controls for both vessels and classification societies, and they verified the conditions of maritime traffic. But this European reaction was less exigent and decisive than the U.S. procedures after the *Exxon Valdez* accident in 1989. The enactment of the Oil Pollution Act (1990) meant a change in trend.

The unilateral North American intervention included very important aspects such as: a) the liability is unlimited in case of accidents, so ship owners have to provide a €1,000 million guarantee, as well as to appoint a representative in the affected territory with whom to demand civil liabilities in case of an accident; b) a list was drawn up of ports to give refuge to those vessels with lower safety conditions and have the suitable infrastructures and means to act if necessary; and c) the safety measures for vessels were increased and strengthened. A subsequent analysis of the enactment of this regulation shows that there have not been more oil spills of the first magnitude since the implementation of this legislation.

The analysis of the implementation process for the proposals considered in the Erika I and II sets of measures highlights the need to continue pursuing those methods undertaken so as to reach the following aims:

a)   The clarification of liabilities through the reinforcement of the flag-state link. This will exert greater control of vessel activity, avoid "flags of convenience," and eliminate distorted business practices due to competition, which means a greater exposure to risky situations. In short, a better identification of those to be held responsible.

b)   The existence of safety measures that guarantee the efficient control of vessels, which aims to increase both the physical (tugs, radars, etc.) and the human means (inspectors, technicians, etc.).

c)   The safety of port facilities so that ports have the suitable means and infrastructures to give refuge to vessels at risk.

d)   The harmonization of European regulations, with the aim to avoid both national and international unilateral measures, which can distort competitiveness.

e)   The precise definition of a network of refuge ports or reference ports that act as points of control and inspection in the European coastal areas.

Table 7.—Erika I Packages (21 March 2000)

MEASURES	AIMS
To strengthen vessel control on the part of the Port State	Survey of vessels with risk that want to call at a European port; the European Commission publishes a black list of those vessels; greater information of movements and inspections.
Control of Classification Societies	More severe control on Classification Societies so as to standardize the evaluation systems, applying of sanctions or determining of liabilities in cases of negligence.
Prohibition of mono-hull oil tankers	It aims to substitute double-hull oil tankers for mono-hull ones.

Table 8.—Erika II Packages (6 December 2000)

MEASURES	AIMS
Community system of monitoring, control of maritime traffics information	It aims to conciliate the principle of free traffic along the seas by strengthening controls; and it is desired vessels carrying dangerous goods to European ports be known, and, consequently, controlled. It is evident control in the port is not sufficient.
Improvement of regimes of liability and damage compensation	The European Commission wants to complete the compensation system in a wider sense and to accelerate compensation payment.
Creation of the European Agency of Maritime Safety	The aim is to act by means of: technical assistance, inspection, organization of training actions, monitoring of traffic information, evaluation of the Classification Societies, etc.

All these things considered, the implementation of the Erika I and Erika II Packages helped to mitigate, though not definitively, the "bad practices" that still persist when the market fails or there is no regulation (Tables 7 and 8).

The continuance of the European Union in the IMO has sometimes limited the European agreements. In fact, not all the business groups related to maritime transport agree to incorporate into their regulations and guidelines those articles that have to determine the environmental liabilities and increase the number of inspections. Ecology groups and the areas that were affected by the different catastrophes demand that the IMO strengthen its role regarding both maritime safety and the prevention of pollution.

In view of the present limitations to widen the scope in the European context, it is not surprising that in the unfinished performances the following difficulties are underlined: the absence of agreements to apply "penal sanctions against those that spill their cargo in the sea"; the question related to the definition of "refuge places," or "reference locations," if necessary, constitutes the evidence of the belated reaction before the urgent need that civil society demands against the increase of risks and vulnerabilities that the most sensitive territories are exposed to; and the insufficient legal framework when it comes to determining the reparation of the damages caused by the contamination.

Our study on how the intervention framework evolved after the *Prestige* incident let us highlight the initiatives carried out, as well as re-examine the institutional European framework from the point of view of maritime safety, with special attention to the following points:

a) New and more exigent rules to transport hydrocarbons. The acceptance to limit this kind of transport to double-hulled vessels under 15 years constituted one of the first successful European initiatives.

b) Greater numbers of missions by the European Maritime Safety Agency (EMSA), which should expand its functions to fight against pollution (through greater technical and scientific assistance to the Member States), and the possibility to acquire special material and vessels; to increase the training of crews; and to improve maritime and port safety against terrorist attacks by means of greater controls and inspections.

c) The publication and diffusion of the "blacklist," by virtue of the Directive 95/21/EC[9] on port state control, which includes those vessels with refused access to EU ports, since they do not satisfy the current regulation on maritime safety.

d) Agreements to put into practice European regulations to sanction those vessels that commit voluntary polluting actions, such as the cleaning of their holds.

e) Notifications to the Member States to speed the preparation of plans to let vessels with problems enter refuge places.

Nevertheless, the implementation of these instruments depends on the European Members passing the necessary initiatives, since these Members often differ on both the application of inspections and the control of vessels. Therefore, since 21 October 2003, when the European Community

---

9. Council Directive 95/21/EC of 19 June 1995 concerning the enforcement, in respect of shipping using Community ports and sailing in the waters under the jurisdiction of the Member States, of international standards for ship safety, pollution prevention and shipboard living and working conditions (port State control).

regulation came into effect, no double-hull tankers carrying heavy oil have been allowed to enter or leave a European port. The EU-15 asked the IMO to change the International Convention for the Prevention of Pollution from Ships (MARPOL),[10] so that this regulation could be applied on a worldwide scale, as all international operators are required to follow more severe rules concerning maritime safety.

This change was passed during the 50th session of the Marine Environment Protection Committee (4 October 2003); therefore, on 5 April 2005 the following restrictions, which will positively affect maritime safety, came into effect: a) highly dangerous oil products have to be carried exclusively in double-hull vessels; b) all the coastal States will be authorized to forbid single-hull vessels that do not comply with the age limits, or with the technical controls planned in the MARPOL Convention, to call at their ports or sail in their territorial waters; c) the programme to phase-out single-hull vessels extends until 2010, which means that after this date there will no longer exist these types of vessels, except for foreseeable exceptions; d) the special regime to inspect tankers and assess their structural state is extended to those single-hulled units more than 15 years old and an imposed supplementary regime of inspections strengthens the controls; e) the diplomatic functions are strengthened in the countries closest to the EU, especially Russia, which is exporting heavy oil by sea, and whose transports sail off the European coast, which exposes the coastal areas to an increased risk of maritime catastrophes.

The acceleration of the process to phase out single-hulled tankers became one of the EU goals. The change of the Regulation 417/2002[11] established the limits to phase out the aforementioned tankers that can enter ports under the jurisdiction of the Member States and fly the flags of Member States. The stipulated period was 2010–2015 according to some characteristics of vessels. Subsequently, the number of vessels to be destroyed was reduced and the new Regulation 1726/2003[12] forbids the transport of hydrocarbons or dangerous goods in single-hulled tankers as of 2005. That means 40 percent of the single-hull tanker fleet will have to be renewed at least in 2005, and 80 percent of this fleet in 2010, with reference

10. International Convention for the Prevention of Pollution from Ships, 1973, as modified by the Protocol of 1978 (MARPOL 73/78).

11. Regulation (EC) No. 417/2002 of the European Parliament and of the Council of 18 February 2002 on the accelerated phasing-in of double hull or equivalent design requirements for single hull oil tankers and repealing Council Regulation (EC) No. 2978/94.

12. Regulation (EC) No. 1726/2003 of the European Parliament and of the Council of 22 July 2003 amending Regulation (EC) No. 417/2002 on the accelerated phasing-in of double-hull or equivalent design requirements for single-hull oil tankers.

**Table 9.—Regulations on Safety and Maritime Traffic
Enacted in Spain After the *Prestige* Catastrophe**

REGULATIONS	AIMS
Royal Decree Law 9/2002	On measures for single-hull tankers under any flag carrying hazardous or polluting cargoes, which are banned from entering Spanish ports.
Royal Decree 1381/2002	On measures to protect the marine environment and the use of port facilities where ship waste and cargo residues are discharged.
Royal Decree 90/2003 (It enacts the provisions of Directive 2001/105/EC)	On the recognition of organizations that were authorized to inspect ships and issue the relevant safety certificates on behalf of the Member States.
Royal Decree 91/203 (It enacts the provisions of Directive 2001/106/EC)	On the enforcement of international standards for ship safety, pollution prevention and shipboard living and working conditions.
Royal Decree 1249/2003 (It enacts the provisions of the Directives 2002/6/EC and 2002/84/EC)	On reporting formalities for ships arriving in and/or departing from Spanish ports, to increase transparency, trying to forbid those vessels from sailing that do not comply with this regulation.
Royal Decree 210/2004 (It enacts the provisions of the Directive 2002/59/EC)	On the measures provided for tracking the movement of ships and carriage of dangerous substances through Spanish waters, so as to mitigate the environmental consequences in case of maritime accidents, by strengthening the collaboration between the Member States.

Source: Self-elaboration from official publications of Spanish Central and Autonomous Public Administrations, several years.

to the existing fleet in 2000. Furthermore, the IMO itself will intensify the controls to reach the goal of absolutely no single-hull tankers by 2015.

Another line of performance that has been modified after the *Prestige* incident is those decisions referring to sanctions for maritime pollution (Table 9). The institutional actions have been strengthened and, therefore, the European Directive considers maritime pollution as a criminal infraction. The ship owner, the cargo owner, the classification society, or anyone who makes severe negligent actions can be sanctioned to stop the thousands of present deliberate discharges of waste materials that some vessels cause. The 390 oil spots discovered in the Baltic Sea and the 596 in the North Sea show the need to end the thousands of deliberate vessel disposals of waste materials.

Likewise, the changes carried out on matters of control of vessels in ports, the liabilities of States, and of greater transparency are clear. The aim is to have greater control of vessels, in both their inspections and immobilizations, and the notification of their schedules. The masters, ship owners, those in charge of the vessel exploitation, Port Authorities, and the Member States are obliged to communicate information fully in order to improve maritime safety. The Council Directive 98/25/EC[13] also tries to update the incorporations to the international conventions on the prevention of pollution (MARPOL), the safety of life at sea (SOLAS), and the standards of training, certification and watch keeping for seafarers (STCW).[14]

The IMO promotes vigilance so that States apply those measures on safety and defend the legislation on shipbuilding from an environmental and technical point of view. By strengthening cooperation, the IMO insists on finding a "link" between the vessel and the State where it is registered. Some mechanisms of European harmonization are also under way in the field of sanctions in case of pollution.

THE REGIMES OF CIVIL LIABILITY AND THE COMPENSATORY PROCESS OF MARITIME CATASTROPHES

Increasing the safety of maritime transport of oil products is one of the essential questions the affected people put forward. Among the measures that contribute to achieving this greater safety, it is important to highlight the implementation of a new European system of liabilities of the different agents involved in maritime transport. Firstly, that means establishing the liabilities for both the carrier and the cargo owner, and, secondly, to increase the collective compensation regimes.

The two agreements that were established in the IMO (after the *Torrey Canyon* accident in 1967), i.e., the Civil Liability Convention (CLC), and the International Fund for Compensation for Oil Pollution Damage (IOPC Fund), have established some economic limits for each spill, which amounts to 59,700,000 SDR in the case of the CLC, and 135,000,000 SDR in the case of the IOPC. Those limits were increased to 89,770,000 SDR and 203,000,000 SDR, respectively, in November 2003 (see Figure 3). The first

13. Council Directive 98/25/EC of 27 April 1998 amending Directive 95/21/EC concerning the enforcement, in respect of shipping using Community ports and sailing in the waters under the jurisdiction of the Member States, of international standards for ship safety, pollution prevention and shipboard living and working conditions (port State control).

14. International Convention for the Prevention of Pollution from Ships, 1973, as modified by the Protocol of 1978 (MARPOL 73/78), n. 10 above; International Convention for the Safety of Life at Sea (SOLAS), 1974; International Convention on Standard of Training, Certification and Watchkeeping (STCW).

FIG. 3.—Evolution of the Compensation Limits Under the CLC and the IOPC

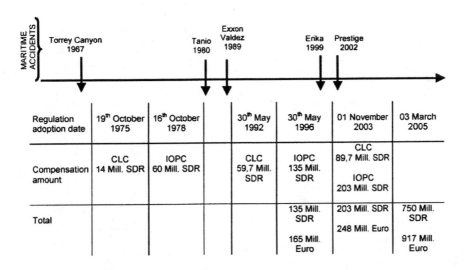

	Torrey Canyon 1967	Tanio 1980	Exxon Valdez 1989		Enka 1999	Prestige 2002
Regulation adoption date	19th October 1975	16th October 1978	30th May 1992	30th May 1996	01 November 2003	03 March 2005
Compensation amount	CLC 14 Mill. SDR	IOPC 60 Mill. SDR	CLC 59,7 Mill. SDR	IOPC 135 Mill. SDR	CLC 89,7 Mill. SDR IOPC 203 Mill. SDR	
Total				135 Mill. SDR 165 Mill. Euro	203 Mill. SDR 248 Mill. Euro	750 Mill. SDR 917 Mill. Euro

Source: Author.

one regulates the ship owner liability, whereas the second completes the compensations of those damages originated by pollution.

In some cases, it is evident that the limits established in these international agreements, as in the *Prestige* catastrophe, are not enough to compensate the ecological disasters caused by maritime accidents. Hence the need to complete the performance principles, the funds, and the limits of the aforementioned compensations. The *Prestige* incident has brought about the need to update the limits of liability regarding compensation, and the first answer is the implementation of a Supplementary Fund with a limit of 750 million SDR, i.e., €917 million. Those successive increases of the compensation limits corroborate the imbalances between the impacts of the catastrophes and the systems of reparation and compensation for the damages. In the case of important accidents these funds do not cover all the repercussions and they do not address the global impacts.

The present performance procedures are creating intense fights between the public administrations and the affected people. On the one hand, the total compensation funds for the damages (at present advances are being paid instead of not lodging appeals) are not enough for most affected people, and on the other hand, there are no compensations for many activities carried out to clean and regenerate or for some negative impacts affecting both trade and non-trade activities. Therefore, it is necessary to clarify that some damages have to be compensable with regard

FIG. 4.—Total Economic Value

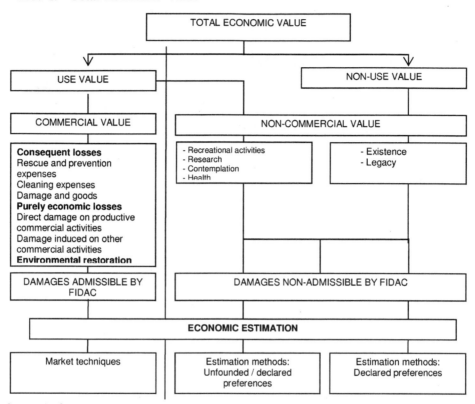

Source: Author.

to the IOPC, whereas other repercussions and negative effects are not taken under consideration by the IOPC.

Private damages are subject to IOPC liabilities. This means direct damages on natural and environmental resources by oil slicks are excluded from the assessment and reparation by civil authorities, which is a clear transgression of the concept of sustainable development underscored by EU texts. The main conclusions of this analysis are: a) the present regime does not guarantee a quick compensation for those people affected, since the judicial procedures are long and complicated; b) the largest amount of compensation has to be established so that it is high enough to face the demands of the greatest maritime catastrophes, as in the case of the *Prestige*; and c) the liability and compensation regime is to guarantee that the carriers and the owners of the cargoes of dangerous and polluting products use high quality vessels.

The Spanish public administrations' performance was limited to "pay the affected groups in advance on account of the compensations." At the end of 2003, a year after the accident, a total of 27,000 people have opted for the regulation that gives the economic compensations in advance, with an average compensation of €10,570. This would mean the damage to be repaired amounts to €215 million. There is still a group of affected people that are against this procedure and have lodged individual appeals before the IOPC.

In May 2003, the IMO Diplomatic Conference adopted a new Protocol that establishes a Supplementary Fund to compensate over the available quantities by virtue of the Oil Pollution Compensation Fund, known as the 1992 Fund for damages caused by pollution to all those States parties to the protocol. The adoption of this Protocol has improved the available amount to 750 million SDR (c. €917 million) for compensation in all catastrophes. It was supposed to come into effect on 3 May 2005, once Germany, Denmark, Spain, Finland, France, Ireland, Japan and Norway had ratified it.

This Supplementary Fund will not substitute the current Fund, but it will contribute with an additional compensation that will be offered to the victims of those States that ratify the Protocol. In short, the Supplementary Fund will have $845 million, as well as $314 million that comes from the 1992 Fund, which totals $1,159 million.

The new conditions of the compensation system are: a) in practically all cases it would be possible to pay 100 percent compensation of the total damages agreed upon between the Fund and those affected; and b) it would not be necessary to establish an amount lower than 100 percent of the damages that are suffered during the first phases in the most important catastrophes.

The analysis of the activities carried out due to the *Prestige* incident leads us to make the following statements: a) the official estimate of the catastrophe (€1,100 million) was much higher than the available amount for compensation (€171 million), and that is why in May 2003 the Fund decided to limit the payments to 15 percent of the losses and damages; b) Spain demanded to be paid, in case of exceptional circumstances, an amount higher than the "official amounts"; and, after this demand, in October 2003 the Fund paid to the Spanish Government, on some conditions and after assessing the total damages, 15 percent of the €895 million Spain had justified as impact, i.e., €57,555,000 as payment on account and in advance; c) in the meeting that took place in June 2004, the IOPC, on the basis of a provisional assessment, stated that the Spanish government had been paid €57,555 million to pay the claimants; and d) in the meeting that took place in October 2004, the Spanish Administration claimed €513.8 million and made public a second claim for €120 million, since this amount corresponds to the costs of the operations to remove hydrocarbons inside the vessel.

HOW TO MANAGE THE CRISIS: AN ANALYSIS OF THE CAPACITY TO RESPOND TO THE *PRESTIGE* CATASTROPHE

After the first tank broke, the *Prestige*, which carried 77,000 tons of heavy fuel oil, 40–50,000 of which spilled when the accident took place and 22,000 tons in the course of the following weeks, began an erratic journey (in six days it had three different directions), leaving a trail of hydrocarbons whose extent is still now very difficult to quantify. Therefore, only 13,800 tons remained in the tanks and were extracted in the course of 2004. This erratic journey extended and generalized the contamination, worsened the effects and threatened a wide set of coastal areas in different countries. What was the reaction and what lessons have been learned?

a) There have been advances made on the control of traffic with mechanisms to separate and remove vessels from the Galician coast. Four routes were established, two to the North (for vessels with conventional goods) and two to the South (for vessels with hazardous goods). Vessels are to be taken away from the coast and placed 29 miles to the North and 42 miles to the South.

b) Likewise, it is positive that the IMO admits in some sensitive areas, that is, the most exposed areas to the risks derived from maritime accidents, that there must be controls on transshipment vessels that carry crude and heavy oil, tar, and other highly dangerous products and that these vessels must announce their transshipment 48 hours before entering these areas. The area considered as especially sensitive extends to 80 miles to the North and 130 miles to the West.

c) In the European institutions discussions have stressed the extent of liability. It is an important advance to try to place the liability on ship owners, but it should also be extended to those economic operators that are part of the "maritime business." Likewise, this issue should be applied immediately, without waiting for the regulation to come into effect in the short-term, otherwise the free riders are still encouraged to act with impunity.

d) Two other questions have assumed a greater political importance, but have been slow to be taken up. The first one refers to performance protocols, and the second one refers to the need to take under consideration a network of shelter ports. Regarding the first question, the performance protocols in case of accidents have not yet been updated or revised, both from the physical point of view (they have not been increased), and in human means (they are still pending training more technicians and increasing their technical capacity). With regard to shelter ports, the discussion is in progress, although there are already different controversies on

Table 10.—Proposed and Under Development Regulations and Aims on Maritime Safety and Pollution Prevention

REGULATIONS	AIMS
Regulations on exploitation	Establishment of methods concerning safety; appointment of territorial representatives in the country where the accident takes place; and existence of safety certificates for vessels and cargo.
Control by the State of port state of the port	Control of regulation as regards to maritime safety; pollution prevention; and respect to social rules on board.
Information about improvements on safety	Improvement of information exchange among States to obtain more efficient cooperation; use of EDI; warning of traffic of dangerous and pollutant goods; regulation on arrival and departure of vessels; appointment of refuge ports or reference ports.
Conditions of vessel load and unload	Harmonized procedures on load and unload, existence of quality regulation, and appointment of representatives in terminals and vessels.
Pollution prevention	Existence of port facilities to store waste products.
Control of certification organisms	Strengthening of control, regulation and rules on organisms entitled to make controls of vessels and definition of State liability.
Sanctions	Introduction of sanctions, fines, prohibitions and definition of penal liabilities in the case of infringement.
Vessel equipment	Introduction of IBC codes for chemical vessels and ICG for tankers.

different questions, namely, if masters are obliged to obey instructions of the affected country, how to assess the consequences for the safety of the people in the areas closer to shelter ports, and how to estimate the effects on the industrial, urban and natural environments.

One of the main challenges is the adaptation of the principle of free movement in the seas concerning a framework of a more regulated activity. This brings about the demand for a set of measures as regards safety, as well as the efficiency of the mechanisms implemented that guarantee coherence in the actions adopted in all fields of activity. A way to explain this would be to specify the main aims and highlight the main recommendations (Table 10).

The main conclusions that can be obtained as a result of the Galician events after the *Prestige* incident are shown in Table 11, where the favorable and unfavorable criteria with regards to the behaviors and the capacities to respond are shown. They are defined according to those aspects that the

**Table 11.—Capacity to Answer on the Part of the
Galician Society**

FAVORABLE	UNFAVORABLE
Positive reaction on part of citizens: positive, quick and constructive reaction.	The Contingency Plan that was found to be dysfunctional and presented a degree of lack of co-ordination all through the catastrophe remains unreviewed.
Increase of levels of environmental awareness and liability.	There is no new acting plan that permits acting in a simultaneous and differentiated way, both at land and sea.
Increase of levels of citizens' active participation.	The mechanism to take decisions attending to the different Public Administrations and for administrative sub-levels has not been reviewed.
Strengthening of degrees of worry and demands to public policies, concerning risk increase.	The means available have not been increased enough to reduce the consequences: tugs, barriers, rescue equipment. Corrections have not been carried through in "rescue patterns."
Greater awareness that certain risks are to be assumed under international environments.	Corrections and performances on ports to provide space to vessels with problems have not been carried out.
Relevant budget actions to palliate the catastrophe effects and to face investment on infrastructures.	The Compensation system for those affected has not been modified.
The sensitive maritime areas have been catalogued and it has been carried out with a greater control on vessels with problems.	There is no Scientific-Technical Advisory Council that can provide solutions, at least in a consultative way.

Galician population considered as being the most sensitive, and on which there should have been immediate response with medium- and long-term programmes.

CONCLUSIONS

Maritime regulation and safety have become one of the main challenges for international, regional and local public institutions since a catastrophe can happen anywhere. It is not just a question of "getting away from danger," but is necessary to apply instruments to guarantee the safety of vessels and goods carried by sea. There are two basic issues when it comes to analyzing this matter, namely, to prevent natural risks and those risks emerging from maritime navigation. On both assumptions, maritime safety concentrates on prevention in order to avoid such vulnerability of the means of transport.

It is absolutely necessary to have a new international institutional framework that allows governments, public organizations, local and regional administrations, and social and economic sectors to apply those codes and measures proposed by experts. The advances in the field of maritime safety as a result of the *Prestige* catastrophe meant the emergence of an action-reaction effect, that is, each big catastrophe brings about the instrumentalization of sets of measures, rules and instruments to improve environmental protection, but not to mitigate natural risks or those risks coming from maritime navigation. These advances also meant a wide institutional deployment from a unilateral perspective, that is, regulatory advances implemented by those organizations and public institutions closer to the catastrophic locations, which were not followed by other countries or organizations. Examples of this are the processes to strengthen EU maritime safety policy (i.e., Erika I and Erika II Packages, European Maritime Safety Agency).

The limits to the international regimes on maritime safety and the difficulties to implement some measures aimed at establishing internationally accepted methodologies on risk management and liabilities, as well as compensation measures, underline the challenges that remain after the *Prestige* catastrophe on the Galician coast.

In fact, this article shows two clearly defined action axes. On the one hand, market failures cause the proliferation of small companies that carry dangerous goods under conditions of an "informal economy," which usually avoids safety controls for the vessel and crew, with vessels acquired at low prices in an open market. On the other hand, the present institutional framework has still not been able to offer a complete regulatory system that avoids, mitigates, and reduces the negative impacts in catastrophic or risky situations. In short, in this case we are talking about public policy failures.

Finally, the lack of anticipatory measures, together with the insufficient exploitation of the sanctioning capacity, shows certain laxity with regard to interventions. In the light of the *Prestige* catastrophe, a "pressure game" or a "divergence of opinions" can be observed among the different countries, which can be considered the main reason for the delay when it comes to implementing rules or regulations related to the renewal of vessels or safety conditions. In this sense, in a previous paper[15] a model with financial compensatory mechanisms is proposed so that polluting companies cannot have incentives, nor can they avoid the implementation of prevention measures in an attempt to reverse the legal order by means of prolonged legal strategies to reduce the costs generated by the damage.

This article emphasizes that the recommendations on maritime safety carried out after the *Prestige* catastrophe can be summarized in the following points:

---

15. González-Laxe, n. 2 above, at 5.

a) Greater control of the vessel in the European ports, according to the different types of vessels (age, structure of the hull, safety rules, etc.), and establishment of rules for the traffic of those vessels that carry hydrocarbons or hazardous goods are needed.

b) Greater control, on the part of the States, on the classification societies and the adoption of liabilities in cases of accidents or catastrophes; improvement of traffic information, navigation conditions, and inspections by the States and the international organizations.

c) Adaptation of compensation funds to cover the damages in all fields, with the aim to repair these damages and establish sanctions. In short, to change the "polluter pays" principle to the "polluter is sanctioned and pays" principle.

d) Stronger measures to promote the withdrawal of obsolete and old vessels, by introducing severe quality and safety measures; introduction of social rules that guarantee more suitable working conditions under special circumstances.

e) Establishment of mechanisms that introduce legal sanctions to the offenders. In the shortest time possible, the European Maritime Safety Agency will have to constitute a Technical and Advisory Council composed of technicians and experts from the area most sensitive to accidents.

f) Port modernization; ports with better infrastructure and means to answer to the challenges of the new industrial maritime development, and establishment of contingency plans and models to immediately intervene, mitigate and repair in the case of accidents.

Straits Used in International Navigation, User Fees and Article 43 of the 1982 Law of the Sea Convention

Nilüfer Oral
Marine Law Research Center, Istanbul Bilgi University, Turkey

INTRODUCTION

Navigational aids used by the coastal State to provide safety of navigation and protection of the marine environment are becoming increasingly reliant on sophisticated technology such as satellite-based services. Navigational aids include a wide variety of means to manage vessel traffic in a safe and efficient manner. Anything from the millennium-old system of lighthouses and buoys to the modern-day, satellite-based vessel traffic monitoring systems, all fall within the category of navigational aids. Current international rules and regulations require that ships engaged in international voyages be fitted with automatic identification systems (AIS),[1] voyage data recorder systems (VDRs)[2] and eventually long distance range tracking systems (LDRTS). However, in order for these devices to provide optimal performance the coastal State must have the requisite shore-based infrastructure. Other navigational aids include traffic separation schemes, ship reporting systems, pilotage, and towage, etc. In 2001, a multi-million dollar state-of-the-art experimental Marine Electronic Highway (MEH) for the Malacca Straits was initiated. Although these aids contribute greatly to safety of navigation, it is not without significant cost to the providing State.

---

1. Regulation 19 of Chapter V of the International Convention for the Safety of Life at Sea (SOLAS) requires AIS to be fitted aboard all ships of 300 gross tonnage, and upwards, engaged on international voyages, cargo ships of 500 gross tonnage, and upwards, not engaged in international voyages, and passenger ships, irrespective of size constructed on or after 1 July 2002. Ships constructed before 1 July 2002 were required to be fitted beginning 1 July 2003 but not later than 1 July 2008. Available online: <http://www.imo.org>.

2. Regulation 20 of Chapter V of the International Convention for the Safety of Life at Sea (SOLAS) requires VDRs to be fitted aboard all ships of 3,000 gross tonnage, and engaged on international voyages, constructed on or after 1 July 2002. Available online: <http://www.imo.org>.

Ocean Yearbook 20: 561–594.

International law, as codified by the 1958 Geneva Convention on the Territorial Sea and Contiguous Zone (Territorial Sea Convention)[3] and the 1982 Law of the Sea Convention (LOSC)[4] prohibit the levying of tolls and duties upon foreign ships during their innocent passage through the territorial sea.[5] However, an exception was recognized allowing the coastal State to levy fees for specific services rendered to the ship.[6] An important question is whether the same right to charge such fees exists for States bordering straits used in international navigation under Part III (straits used for international navigation) of the LOSC. Straits used in international navigation are by definition narrower passageways and for this reason present greater risks both to the vessel plying its waters and to the coastal State, and for these reasons are in greater need of navigational aids.

Over the past years the significant increase in the amount of oil being transported through critical "chokepoint" straits has brought greater pressure on the coastal States to invest in sophisticated and expensive navigational aids. The Malacca and Singapore Straits are an example of such chokepoint straits faced, with large numbers of tankers and volumes of oil plying their waters and having to expend millions of dollars to protect these waterways. The problem is one of both equity and economics as to how to recover the cost when other States are deriving significant benefits.

Article 43 of the LOSC is considered to be the mechanism by which straits used in international navigation are regulated by the transit passage regime provisions of Part III (Part III straits). Article 43 exhorts the "user" States of Part III straits to cooperate in establishing and maintaining navigational and safety aids and in the prevention, reduction and control of pollution. Despite being in force for over 10 years, to date no such agreement has been concluded. This is surprising to some degree given that the negotiation of the "transit passage" regime adopted by the LOSC was one of the most hotly debated issues at the Third United Nations Conference on the Law of the Sea (UNCLOS III). And central to the debate was the strong concern expressed by straits States of the dangers associated with high volumes of maritime traffic and in particular the transport of dangerous and hazardous cargoes. In response to these concerns the maritime States offered Article 43 as a consolation provision for the loss of non-suspendable innocent passage right in straits used for international navigation.

3. 516 *United Nations Treaty Series* 205 (1958).

4. Adopted at Montego Bay, 10 December 1982, in force 16 November 1994, reprinted in *International Legal Materials* 21 (1982): 1261–1354.

5. Article 18(1) of the 1958 Territorial Sea Convention and Article 26(1) of the LOSC.

6. Article 18(2) of the 1958 Territorial Sea Convention and Article 26(2) of the LOSC.

The development of the legal regime of straits under international law has been the subject of many scholarly debates and little new can be added to the impressive body of scholarly writings on the subject. The subject matter of this article is not an historical analysis of the developments of the various Straits' regimes adopted and codified by the LOSC, but rather an effort to better understand the importance of Article 43, an underused and almost forgotten provision of the LOSC. This article will examine the development of Article 43 of the LOSC, the pressures on major straits including energy chokepoint straits, followed by a detailed legal analysis of Article 43, the possible role of the polluter pays principle, a mechanism for sustainable financing of straits and a conclusion.

THE DEVELOPMENT OF THE TRANSIT PASSAGE REGIME

The Legal Regime of Straits before UNCLOS III

The "transit passage" regime applicable to straits used in international navigation, not otherwise subject to an exception, was the creation of UNCLOS III.[7] Until that time both customary international law and later the 1958 Territorial Sea Convention adopted the regime of non-suspendable "innocent passage" for that part of a strait that fell within the territorial sea of the coastal State. The only difference between the right of innocent passage through the territorial sea and through a strait that formed part of the territorial sea of a coastal State was the restriction against suspending passage in the latter case. Until UNCLOS III the debate on the passage regime for straits used in international navigation was related to the broader issue of defining the breadth of the territorial sea and the meaning of "innocence."[8]

The discussion on straits during the 1930 League of Nations Conference for the Codification of International Law (Hague Conference) was narrowly framed within a single question that asked Governments the

---

7. B. Bing Jia, *The Regime of Straits in International Law* (Oxford: Clarendon, 1998); J. A. de Yturriaga, *Straits Used for International Navigation: A Spanish Perspective* (Boston: Martinus Nijhoff, 1990); S. N. Nandan and D. H. Anderson, "Straits Used for International Navigation: A Commentary on Part III of the United Nations Convention on the Law of the Sea 1982," *British Yearbook of International Law* 60 (1989): 159–204.

8. Jia, n. 7 above; de Yturriaga, n. 7 above; Nandan et al., n. 7 above; W. G. Grandison and V. J. Meyer, "International Straits, Global Communications, and the Evolving Law of the Sea," *Vanderbilt Journal of Transnational Law* 8 (1975): 393–449; E. Bruel, *International Straits: A Treatise on International Law*, 2 Vols. (Copenhagen: Nyt nordisk Forlag, 1947), vol. 2.

"[c]onditions determining what [were] the territorial waters within a strait connecting two areas of open sea or the open sea and an inland sea: (a) when the coasts belong to a single State; (b) when they belong to two or more States.[9] Among the Governments that responded, the U.S. Government was the only one that raised the issue of tolls or passage fees making specific reference to the Danish Straits in its response.[10] There was no debate on the nature of the passage regime itself, the innocent passage regime being generally accepted for straits used in international navigation connecting one part of the high seas to another. This was later confirmed by the International Court of Justice (ICJ) in the landmark Corfu Channel case.[11] According to the ICJ the legal regime of passage through a strait used in international navigation and connecting one part of the high seas to another was non-suspendable innocent passage. This was subsequently codified in the 1958 Territorial Sea Convention.[12] Prior to the adoption of the transit passage regime for straits under the LOSC, according to generally accepted principles of international law the regime for innocent passage prohibited the coastal State from imposing any conditions that would result in impeding navigation, such as the levying of passage fees, requiring prior notification or authorization, mandatory pilotage, or towage. However, fees could be charged for specific services such as towage or pilotage, if requested.

The issue of creating a separate straits passage regime did not enter the discussion either during the 1930 Hague Conference or the First Law of the Sea Conference (UNCLOS I) held in 1958. Instead, the debates centered on issues such as the meaning of innocent passage, whether a coastal State had the right to require prior authorization from war vessels seeking passage, and breadth of the territorial sea. The question of granting a broader freedom of passage, such as a high seas freedom, did not enter into the debate among nations until the emergence of two superpowers during the cold war.

9. S. Rosenne, ed., *The League of Nations Conference for the Codification of International Law* (1930), 4 vols. (New York: Oceana Publications, 1975), vol. 2, pp. 55–60.

10. The U.S. reply made reference to the note sent by the then Secretary of State, Mr. Buchanan, to the Danish Minister referring to the prohibition under the "law of nations" against the Danish right to levy duties on vessels engaged in passage through straits connecting two seas. Bruel, n. 8 above, at 56.

11. Corfu Channel Case (Merits) *International Court Justice Reports* 4 (1949).

12. Article 14(2).

UNCLOS III

The regime of passage for straits used in international navigation was one of the most debated issues during UNCLOS III. The United States had made it a *sine qua non* condition that it would accept an extension of the breadth of the territorial sea up to 12 nautical miles (NM) only if high seas freedoms would be preserved for straits used in international navigation that would otherwise be transformed into part of the territorial sea of a coastal State that exercised its 12 NM extension right.[13] The United States' demand included rights of overflight and submerged transit for submarines.[14] The former USSR, having become a world naval power, joined the US in seeking to maintain freedom of passage rights through straits used in international navigation.[15] Yet, equally staunch in its position was a small group of strait States, including Spain, who fought rigorously to maintain the customary law of innocent passage rights.[16] Malaysia, Indonesia, Philippines, Cyprus, Egypt, Morocco and Yemen formed what became known as the strait States group.

In support of the continued application of the innocent passage regime for straits used in international navigation Spain and Malaysia argued that

13. On 23 May 1970, President Nixon made a statement on U.S. policy for oceans law. The statement included territorial sea in return for free transit rights through straits. Letter containing statement reproduced in *International Legal Materials* 9 (1970): 806–09. However, the U.S. had already expressed its interest in exchanging recognition of a 12 NM territorial sea in exchange for free passage (versus innocent passage) rights through straits in 1967, de Yturriaga, n. 7 above, at 42. For an analysis of the U.S. view of the extension of the territorial sea to 12 NM, see Cmdr. K. D. Lawrence, "Military-Legal Considerations in the Extension of Territorial Seas," *Military Law Review* 29 (1965): 47–96. See also, W. R. Slomanson, "Free Transit in Territorial Straits: Jurisdiction on an Even Keel?," *California Western International Law Journal* 3 (1973): 375–396; G. Knight, "The 1971 United States Proposals on the Breadth of the Territorial Sea and Passage Through International Straits," *Oregon Law Review* 51 (1972): 759–787; M. Reissman, "The Regime of Straits and National Security: An Appraisal of International Lawmaking," *American Journal of International Law* 74 (1980): 48–76.

14. J. N. Moore, "The Regime of Straits and the Third United Nations Conference on the Law of the Sea," *American Journal of International Law* 74 (1980): 77–121, 81.

15. The former USSR had declared a 12 NM territorial sea since 1909 that was not recognized by the United States. However, in 1968 the USSR and the U.S. agreed upon a 3-article draft for a 12-mile territorial sea in return for free passage through international straits. It was subsequent to this that President Nixon issued the U.S. oceans policy statement in 1970, de Yturriaga, n. 7 above, at 46–57.

16. Explaining the concerns of the smaller States, including Straits States in relation to the demands of the U.S. and USSR for free transit, see R. P. Anand, "Freedom of Navigation Through Territorial Waters and International Straits," *Italian Journal of International Law* 14 (1974): 169.

the dangers of modern shipping, such as oil tankers, and the extraordinary technological development in shipping created a potential pollution menace to every coastal State.[17] The Malaysian delegate went so far as to characterize the mere passage of oil tankers as non-innocent requiring the coastal State to adopt regulatory and management powers as self-protection measures. The delegate expressed concern over any diminution of national sovereignty efforts to control pollution.[18] The representative from Indonesia echoed the same concerns that the coastal State needed to maintain its authority in order to be able to take the necessary protective measures against the dangers of pollution, particularly from supertankers.[19] Singapore joined the concerns of these States, although appeared more amenable to the transit passage regime.[20]

In response, the compromise offered to these States by the two super naval powers, the United States and USSR, was to allow the strait State to establish compulsory traffic separation schemes as developed by IMO (previously IMCO),[21] as well as requiring all vessels engaged in transit passage rights through the straits to comply with the International Regulations for Preventing Collisions at Sea (COLREG).[22] However, the

17. The Law of the Sea Straits Used for International Navigation, Legislative History of Part III of the United Nations Convention on the Law of the Sea/Office of Oceans Affairs and the Law of the Sea, 2 Volumes (New York: United Nations, 1992), vol. 1, p. 30 (hereinafter referred to as "Legislative History").

18. *Id.* at 36. [Statement by Lal Vohrah, 12 August 1971, Doc. A/AC.138/SC.II/ SR.11.].

19. *Id.* at 37 and 54; Knight, n. 13 above, at 774; Grandison and Meyer, n. 8 above, at 404, n. 45. The authors relate how pollution concerns for the Malacca Straits prompted Indonesia to announce a ban against supertankers that was never carried through, and outline the discussions by Malaysia and Indonesia to collect fees from transiting vessels for navigational aids.

20. See Legislative History, n. 17 above, at 44.

21. The International Maritime Consultative Organization (IMCO) officially changed its name to the International Maritime Organization (IMO) on May 22, 1982.

22. See "Draft articles on straits used for international navigation submitted by the Union of the Soviet Socialist Republics," which provided, inter alia, provisions requiring strict compliance with the international rules concerning the prevention of collisions between ships or other accidents [para. 2(b)], taking precautionary measures to avoid causing pollution [para. 2(c)] and provided for flag State liability for any damage caused by a ship in transit passage [para. 2 (d)]. See n. 18 above, at 48. The United States representative also expressed the U.S. agreement that ships when exercising transit passage right through straits observe "reasonable traffic safety and marine pollution regulations" and that any such safety standards applied in international straits be internationally developed through IMCO, such as international traffic schemes and further supported that such traffic schemes be made compulsory with enforcement rights accorded to the coastal States. See n. 18 above, at 61.

proposed compromise was not well-received by the strait States who in turn introduced their own set of draft articles that included a provision to allow the strait State to be compensated for works undertaken to facilitate passage.[23] The United States, not surprisingly, rejected these draft articles expressing its particular disapproval with the provision on compensation.[24]

Similarly, a joint paper containing a set of draft articles submitted by Ecuador, Panama and Peru, during the second session of the Seabed Committee (2 July–4 August 1973), included a provision allowing for an "equitable charge" to be established in favor of a strait State by "international oceans space institutes."[25] The charge was to be collected by the coastal State and then paid into a fund that was to be administered by the "international ocean space institutions." The resources of such a fund were to be used to maintain and facilitate safe passage of the straits and to compensate the coastal State(s) for any damage resulting from passage of vessels.[26] Another proposal was submitted by Norway, recognizing that, despite efforts to ensure safety of navigation in straits, accidents would continue to occur, and suggested the inclusion of a clause providing for the creation of a mandatory "insurance pool" as a guarantee of compensation to the strait riparian State in the case of an accident.[27]

Ultimately, the compromise regime that had initially been introduced by the United Kingdom would become the new *transit passage* regime adopted as Part III of the LOSC. The set of draft articles introduced by the United Kingdom during the second session of the meeting of the Second Committee had for the first time introduced the concept of the "transit passage" regime.[28] The transit passage regime as drafted by the U.K. offered the coastal State fewer regulatory rights than did the traditional regime of non-suspendable innocent passage but, on the other hand, more coastal

23. See Legislative History, n. 17 above, at 75, Draft Article 11(3).

24. See Legislative History, n. 17 above, at 85.

25. Specifically, the draft provision read: "Nevertheless, when a strait used for international navigation the breadth of which is less than 24 nautical miles (a) requires dredging, the installation and maintenance of aids to navigation or the adoption of other measures to maintain or facilitate safe passage, or (b) when passage of certain types or classes of vessels, in the event of accident, could cause considerable loss of human life or substantial injury to economic activities or to the marine environment in the area, the coastal State or States may request the international ocean space institutes to establish an equitable charge payable without discrimination by all vessels or by all vessels of the relevant class or type, as the case may be, using the strait." Article 40(2). See n. 17 above, at 102.

26. Article 40(3). *Id.*

27. Legislative History, n. 17 above), vol. 2, p. 3. Norway's suggestion was supported by Turkey. *Id.* at 12.

28. No reference was made to the 1921 Convention and Statute on Freedom of Transit, Barcelona, 20 April 1921. In force 31 October, 1922. *League of Nations Treaty Series 7* (1921–22): 13–33.

State rights than were permitted under the high seas passage regime.[29] Moreover, Article 5 of the United Kingdom draft articles was adopted verbatim and became subparagraph (a) of Article 43 of the LOSC. The British draft Article 5 provided that:

> User States and straits States should by agreement cooperate in the establishment and maintenance in a strait of necessary navigation and safety aids or other improvements in aid of international navigation or for the prevention and control of pollution from ships.[30]

Interestingly, a set of draft articles submitted jointly by Malaysia, Morocco, Oman and Yemen included a provision similar to the U.K. draft Article 5 but employed the permissive "may" instead of "should." But this was rejected and the British draft accepted.[31]

More than 30 years have passed since these debates took place and time has proven the concerns of the strait States to be valid. The increase in commercial shipping and the increase in maritime transport of dangerous and hazardous cargoes have resulted in the very dangers articulated by the small group of strait States at UNCLOS III. In addition to the omnipresent threat of pollution, the threat of piracy and of terror attacks, especially targeted against oil tankers navigating major "chokepoint" straits further exacerbates the associated risk of navigation in these narrow waterways. One year before the September 11, 2001 terrorist attacks in the United States, an explosives-loaded zodiac boat rammed into a French-flagged VLCC *Limberg* in Yemeni waters demonstrating both the vulnerability of tankers to such attacks and what relatively easy targets they could be.[32] The vulnerability of tankers was also demonstrated in a lesser known incident that took place in the Turkish Straits in 2003, when as a result of a grounding incident, officials discovered that a foreign-flagged vessel was carrying 16 tonnes of unreported explosives.[33]

---

29. Doc. A/CONF.62/C.2/L.3, 3 July 1974, Legislative History, n. 17 above, at 16.

30. Draft Article 5. Legislative History, n. 17 above, at 14.

31. The coastal State *may* require the cooperation of interested States and appropriate international organizations for the establishment and maintenance of navigational facilities and aids in a strait. Draft Article 23 "Special rights of coastal States," *id.* at 22.

32. In addition there have been other "unsuccessful" attempts. For further details, see G. Luft and A. Korin "Terrorism Goes to Sea," *Foreign Affairs* 83, 6 (2004): 61–71. According to the authors, in June 2002 the Moroccan government arrested a group of al Qaeda operatives suspected of plotting raids on British and U.S. tankers passing through the Strait of Gibraltar.

33. On 3 March 2004, as a result of a grounding on the Strait of Çanakkale, the *Delfin I* was discovered to be transporting 16 tonnes of explosives. See F. Uğur and M. Altunay, "Bogazlardan cephane gecmistir," Zaman Gazetesi, (4 March 2004).

CHOKEPOINTS, STRAITS AND THE TRANSPORT OF OIL

A "chokepoint" has been described as a narrow waterway with heavy maritime traffic susceptible to being blocked due to accidents or pirate/terror attacks.[34] As described by one author:

> Chokepoints are a common concept in transport geography as they refer to locations that limit the capacity of circulation and cannot be easily bypassed, if at all. This implies that any alternative to the chokepoint involves a level of detour or the use of an alternative that amounts to substantial financial costs and time delays. They can also be perceived as a resource which usefulness varies with the ebb and flows of the geography of circulation. Considering the characteristics of maritime transportation, maritime chokepoints are particularly prevalent.[35]

According to the United States Energy Information Agency (EIA), there are eight major chokepoints for the transport of energy: the Strait of Hormuz (linking the Persian Gulf to the Arabian Sea), the Strait of Gibraltar (linking the Mediterranean Sea to the Atlantic Ocean), the Straits of Malacca and Singapore (linking the Indian Ocean with the Pacific Ocean), the Turkish Straits (linking the Black Sea to the Mediterranean Sea), Strait of Bab-el Mandab (linking the Arabian Sea to the Red Sea), the Panama Canal (linking the Pacific and Atlantic Oceans) and the Suez Canal (linking the Mediterranean Sea and the Red Sea). The latter two are man-made passageways and consequently are subject to different rules under international law than are natural straits.

Once again, according to the EIA, as of March 2004, over 45 million barrels/day of crude oil, amounting to two-thirds of the world supply, are shipped by tankers across the oceans and seas of the world. And of this volume 35 million barrels/day navigate through these narrow waterways.[36] In total, nearly 2 billion tons of petroleum is shipped every year by sea, and of this 50 percent is transported to the U.S. and 25 percent to Japan.[37] The remaining is shipped by alternative routes, primarily through pipelines. Consequently, the world is dependent on the oceans and on these narrow

---

34. Available online: <http://www.iea.gov>.

35. J-P. Rodrigue, "Straits, Passages and Chokepoints: A Maritime Geostrategy of Petroleum Circulation," *Les Cahiers de Geographie du Quebec*, 48, 135 (2004): 357–374. The author lists three criteria: (1) limited physical capacity to handle maritime transportation, (2) limited usage of it, and (3) control over the chokepoint as a resource.

36. Available online: <http://www.eia.doe.gov/emeu/cabs/choke.html>.

37. Rodrigue, n. 35 above.

waterways for the transport of vital oil supplies. Paradoxically, most of the oil is found in areas farthest from the major oil consuming countries. The Persian Gulf basin by far contains the greatest amount of proven reserves of 715 billion barrels.[38] On the other hand, the biggest oil consumers, such as the United States (20 million barrels/day (mb/d)), import over 50 percent of its oil,[39] the People's Republic of China (6.9 mb/d) imports nearly 50 percent,[40] and Japan (5.4 mb/d)[41] imports nearly 100 percent of its crude oil supplies,[42] are all dependent on the seas for transport of this vital resource. Germany, which ranked fourth in global consumption of crude oil (2.6 mb/d) also ranked fourth as importer of nearly 100 percent of its oil needs.[43] And, most of the oil that is transported by sea must pass through at least one of these chokepoints.

Specific amounts of oil that are shipped through these natural waterways are as follows:

- Bab-el Mandab (3.2–3.3 bbl/day)[44]
- Turkish Straits (3.0 bbl/day)
- Strait of Hormuz (15–15.5 bbl/day)
- Strait of Malacca (11 bbl/day)
- Suez Canal (3.8 bbl/day)
- Panama Canal (0.4 bbl/day)

The export of oil is mostly transported in tankers. According to figures provided for vessel transit in the Straits of Malacca and Singapore for 1997, a total of approximately 104,000 vessel transits occurred in these Straits.[45] In 2001, approximately 146,265 vessels visited the Port of Singapore.[46] More than an estimated 32,000 of these vessels were tankers. These numbers will

---

38. Available online: <http://www.eia.doe.gov/emeu/cabs/pgulf.html>.

39. As of April 22, 2005 the United States DOE reported that the U.S. had imported 10,863 mb/d of crude oil. Available online: <http://tonto.eia.doe.gov/oog/info/twip.asp>. The average amount imported in 2003 was 11.1 mb/d. See <http://www.eia.doe.gov/emeu/cabs/topworldtables3_4.html>. China produced 3.54 mb/d in the same year, of which it consumed the entire amount. Available online: <http://www.eia.doe.gov/emeu/cabs/topworldtables1_2.html>.

40. 2.0 mb/d in 2003. Available online: <http://www.eia.doe.gov/emeu/cabs/topworldtables3_4.html>.

41. Statistics reflect oil consumption for 2003 as reported by the DOE. Available online: <http://www.eia.doe.gov/emeu/cabs/topworldtables3_4.html>.

42. 5.3 mb/d. *Id.*

43. 2.5 mb/d. *Id.*

44. 1 bbl/day = 50 million tonnes annually (MTA).

45. C. C. Capon, "The Threat of Pollution in the Malacca Strait: Arguing for a Broad Interpretation of the United Nations Law of the Sea Convention on the Law of the Sea," *Pacific Rim Law and Policy Journal* 7, 1 (1998): 117–141.

46. *Id.*

continue to increase as the demand for oil by China grows at record pace. The tanker traffic in the Turkish Straits has also increased significantly in a period of less than a decade. The number of tankers transporting hazardous cargoes, crude oil in particular, through the Turkish Straits has increased from approximately 4,500 in 1996 to 9,399 in 2004.[47] Similarly, the Danish Straits have also witnessed a large increase in both the volume of oil and the number of tankers in the past few years.[48] Considering that 90 percent of the Persian Gulf oil is transported in tankers through the Strait of Hormuz, safety and protection of the marine environment presents even greater challenges. The Strait of Hormuz, in terms of the amount of oil that is transported through it, is a veritable "golden" horn. Approximately 15.5 mb/d is shipped through it.[49] Moreover, 88 percent of this amount is transported to Japan, Europe and the United States. Seventy-five percent of Japan's oil supplies is transported through the Strait of Hormuz.[50]

The Suez Canal has the capacity to handle up to 25,000 ships per year, but averages 14,000 or about 38 per day, which equals 14 percent of world trade. The Panama Canal has the capacity to handle 50 ships per day, but usually operates at 35 ships per day (13,000 per year). The toll is US$2.57 per net ton, an average of US$45,000 per transit.[51]

These waterways are not only important for the transport of oil. An estimated 90 percent of world trade is transported by sea. In 2004, the world fleet grew to a total tonnage of 857 million dead-weight tonnage and transported 6.2 billion tons of cargo.[52] The Straits of Malacca alone handle 30 percent of the world's trade. The Black Sea region, including its neighbors in the south Caucasus and Balkan Peninsula, are all countries in economic transition. As the economies of these countries grow, the amount of commerce carried by ships to and from Black Sea ports increases.

The primary responsibility of the strait States is as critical passageways for energy supplies, upon which most of the world depends, providing for the safe, secure and reliable transport of oil supplies. But the dilemma is that this is a costly duty for a benefit derived by others. Without the service provided by these waterways the expense of transporting oil would be higher, and subject to greater hazards of navigation, in some cases.

47. Information provided by the Turkish Administration of Coastal Safety and Salvage in Istanbul.
48. See n. 97 below, at 12.
49. Available online: <http://www.eia.doe.gov/emeu/cabs/pgulf.html>.
50. Rodrigue, n. 35 above.
51. *Id.*
52. UNCTAD Transport Letter No. 27, First Quarter (2005).

FIG. 1.—Major Oil Transportation Chokepoints and Daily Flow of Oil

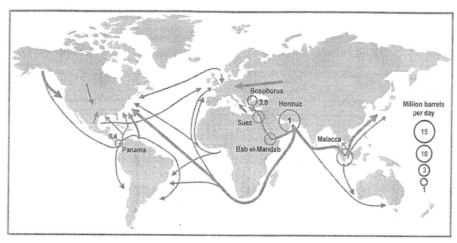

Source: J-P. Rodrigue, "Straits, Passages and Chokepoints: A Maritime Geostrategy of Petroleum Circulation," *Les Cahiers de Geographie du Quebec,* 48, 135 (2004): 357–374. Reprinted with the permission of the author.

THE COST OF BEING A STRAIT

There are over 100 important straits used in international navigation. In addition to the above-mentioned straits, other straits that are of particular importance to international shipping and military uses include the Strait of Dover, the Straits of Magellan, the Torres Strait, the Danish Straits, the Korean Straits and the Strait of Gibraltar.[53] These waterways handle a high volume of maritime traffic and as a result are exposed daily to the risk of accidents and pollution. In order to abate these risks the coastal States must take some sort of preventative action. These measures include establishing traffic separation schemes (TSS), vessel traffic monitoring systems that are increasingly radar and satellite-based,[54] towage and tug services, pilotage, oil prevention equipment, monitoring and surveillance devices, enforcement infrastructure, buoys, lighthouses, ship reporting systems and others.[55]

53. This list is not intended to be exhaustive, but merely illustrative.
54. M. Heikkila, "Ship-Shore and Ship-ship Data Transfer," *Journal of Navigation* 49, 3 (1996): 309–16; C. W. Koburger, *Vessel Traffic Systems* (Maryland: Cornell Maritime Press, 1986).
55. In general, see G. Plant, "The Relationship between International Navigation Rights and Environmental Protection: A Legal Analysis of Mandatory Ship Traffic Systems," in H. Ringbom, *Competing Norms in the Law of Marine Environmental Protection* (London; Boston: Kluwer Law International, 1997): 11–30; G. Plant,

However, such measures are also expensive, both in their establishment, and their maintenance. The following is a brief survey of some of the important straits used in international navigation and the navigational and safety measures adopted.[56]

The Strait of Dover

The Strait of Dover handles approximately 100,000 vessel transits a year, of which over one-third carry dangerous, harmful or polluting goods.[57] It serves as an important transport artery between the U.K. and the rest of the world. It has also been the location of many maritime accidents. Until a traffic separation scheme (TSS) was established in 1972 there was an average of 30 accidents each year.[58] The TSS was a consequence of a series of tragic accidents in 1971 that resulted in the loss of 55 lives and pollution.[59] The Dover TSS is the first traffic separation scheme established by IMCO and the first to be under radar surveillance. The TSS is jointly administered by the United Kingdom and France. In 1999, the ship reporting system was made mandatory in accordance with SOLAS Reg. 8–1, Chapter V, for all vessels over 300 gross tons (CALDOVREP).[60] The system relies heavily on communications and electronic infrastructure. Accident results have shown the effectiveness with an average of four accidents per year between 1980 and 2000.[61]

"International Legal Aspects of Vessel Traffic Services," *Marine Policy* 14, 1 (1990): 71–81.

56. See also J. Van Dyke, "Legal and Practical Problems Governing International Straits," in B. A. Hamzah, ed., *The Straits of Malacca: International Cooperation, Trade, Funding and Navigational Safety* (Kuala Lumpur: MIMA, 1997): 305–26; T. Scovazzi, "Management Regimes and Responsibility for International Straits," *id.* at 327–55.

57. In 2000, a total of 93,509 vessels transited the Dover Strait, of which 36,531 transported dangerous, harmful or polluting goods. Information kindly provided by the MRCC of Dover, 6 April 2001.

58. *Id.*

59. On 11 January 1971, the *MV Paracas* and the *MT Texaco Caribbean* collided in the Strait of Dover. The tanker exploded and broke in half killing eight crewmembers and sunk. However, the next day another vessel struck the submerged wreck of *Texaco Caribbean* and capsized resulting in the death of 21 crewmembers. The following day, disaster struck again, when another vessel also struck the submerged wreck and sank taking 22 more lives with her. See <http://www.mcga.gov.uk/c4mca/mcga-hm_coastguard/channel_navigation_information_service_(cnis)/how_cnis_works.htm>.

60. The corollary system in France is the MANCHEREP.

61. *Id.*

The Turkish Straits

The Turkish government recently invested in a sophisticated radar-based Vessel Traffic Management and Information System (VTMIS) at an initial cost of some US$20 million, excluding operating and maintenance costs.[62] The system was adopted as a result of more than 500 accidents in the Turkish Straits over a period of 50 years. Two of the more serious accidents were the 1979 *Independenta* tanker collision that resulted in an oil spill of 95,000 tonnes (ranked 11th worst in world)[63] and the loss of 43 crewmembers, and the 1994 *Nassia* tanker collision that resulted in an oil spill of 24,000 tonnes and the loss of 29 crewmembers. These figures may have greater meaning if compared to the *Exxon Valdez* incident in 1989 that resulted in a 20,000-tonne oil spill, with no loss of human life.

In response to the increase in maritime traffic and accidents in the straits, Turkey adopted several navigational and safety measures. These included the establishment of a TSS that was approved and adopted by the IMO[64] and the enactment of the 1994 Turkish Straits Maritime Regulations.[65] In 2004, a state-of-the-art, sophisticated VTMIS was installed at a cost of over US$20 million.[66]

The Turkish Straits present a unique—*sui generis*—regime quite different from the Part III Straits. Although not yet a party to the LOSC, as straits falling within the exception created by Article 35(c) of the LOSC the Turkish Straits would be excluded from the regime of transit passage.[67] Since 1936 the legal regime of the Turkish Straits has been regulated by the 1936 Montreux Convention regarding the Regime of the Straits (Montreux Convention).[68] In contrast to the prevailing norms of international law at the time (and now), the Montreux Convention included provisions that

---

62. The VTMIS for the Turkish Straits began operation after 30 December 2003. Available online: <http://www.coastalsafety.gov.tr/default.asp?id=2&sid=4&lng=en>.

63. Based on International Tanker Owner Pollution Fund (ITOPF) ranking. Available online: <http://www.itopf.com/stats.html>.

64. IMO Resolution A.19/827 (24 November 1994).

65. Türk Boğazlari Trafik Düzeni Tüzüğü [Turkish Straits Maritime Traffic Scheme Regulations] adopted in 1994, amended in 1998. Official Gazette 6/11/1998 No. 23515. See G. Aybay and N. Oral, *Turkish Straits Maritime Traffic Scheme Regulations*, English translation (Istanbul: Aybay & Aybay, 1998).

66. It includes eight radar towers along the shore of the Istanbul Strait and five on the Çanakkale Straits. There is a separate VTMIS Center for each Strait. Available online: <http://www.coastalsafety.gov.tr/default.asp?id=2&sid=4&lng=en>.

67. Article 35(c) excludes from the provisions of Part III straits that are regulated in whole or in part by a long-standing international convention in force.

68. Concluded in Montreux, July 20, 1936. *Great Britain Treaty Series* no. 30 (1937).

allows Turkey to charge foreign-flagged ships engaged in transit passage a set tax or charge based on ship tonnage.[69] These fees are to cover the cost of providing general navigational aids such as a lighthouse, light and channel buoys, and life-saving services. Whereas, under international law and practice, coastal States cannot charge for these types of navigational aids as they are "general" aids not subject to charge.

The Straits of Malacca and Singapore

The Straits of Malacca and Singapore are also among the world's busiest straits having a high volume of ships, including many tankers transporting dangerous and polluting cargo.[70] These two straits have also witnessed a substantial number of serious accidents resulting in marine pollution. Between 1975 and 1995 a total of 496 casualties, including oil spills, occurred in the Straits.[71] The Malacca Strait is also vulnerable to piracy attacks resulting in commercial losses amounting to billions of dollars, but also millions of dollars to the bordering States for policing and protecting shipping in such dangerous waters. Not surprisingly the Straits of Malacca and Singapore are also very vulnerable targets for international terrorism.[72]

69. Article 2 and Annex I of the Montreux Convention. For a detailed examination of the negotiations and the provisions of the Montreux Convention, see N. Ünlü, *The Legal Regime of the Turkish Straits* (The Hague, New York: Martinus Nijhoff, 2002); N. Oral and G. Aybay, "The Meaning of Freedom of Passage and Navigation Under the 1936 Montreux Convention on the Regime of the Turkish Straits," *Turkish Review of Balkan Studies* 4 (1998–99): 179–90; S. Toluner, "Rights and Duties of Turkey Regarding Merchant Vessels Passing the Straits," in I. Soysal ed., *Turkish Straits: New Problems New Solution* (Istanbul: OBIV, 1995), pp. 27–33; C. L. Rozakis and P. N. Stagos, *The Turkish Straits* (The Hague, London: Martinus Nijhoff, 1987); A. R. DeLuca, *Great Power Rivalry at the Turkish Straits: The Montreux Conference and Convention of 1936*, East European Monograph Series, no. 77 (New York: Columbia University Press, 1981).
70. R. M. Kamaruzaman, "Navigational Safety in the Strait of Malacca," 2 *Singapore Journal of International and Comparative Law* 2 (1998): 468–485; H. Djalal, "Pointers on the Safety of Navigation in the Straits of Malacca and Singapore," *Singapore Journal of International and Comparative Law* 2 (1998): 436–41; E. E. Mitropolous, "Enhancing Navigational Safety in the Malacca and Singapore Straits," *Singapore Journal of International and Comparative Law*, 3 (1999): 305–15; H. Djalal, "Funding and Managing International Partnerships for the Malacca and Singapore Straits Consonant with Article 43 of the UNCLOS, 1982," *Singapore Journal of International and Comparative Law* 3 (1999): 457–69.
71. Kamaruzaman, n. 71 above, at 473. In general, see Malacca Straits Research and Development Center website. Available online: <http://www.fsas.upm.edu.my/~masdec/web/straits.html>.
72. C. S. Kuppuswamy, "Straits of Malacca: Security Implications," Paper no. 1033 (South Asia Analysis Group) Available online: <http://www.saag.org/papers11/paper1033.html>.

In 1977, as a measure to control the increase in shipping traffic, a TSS was established and adopted for the Strait of Malacca. It was later amended in 1981 and 1998. Dredging is another important service provided for these shallow straits.[73] Further, in 1998 a mandatory ship reporting system, known as STRAITREP, was adopted by the IMO in accordance with SOLAS Regulation 8–1, Chapter V. The Malaysian Government reports that it has invested RM52 million[74] to install 256 navigational aids and RM100 million for a VTMIS.[75]

The natural resources of the Straits of Malacca and Singapore have been valued at US$5 billion.[76] Each year an estimated RM 3.1 trillion worth of goods is transported through them.[77] The Straits of Malacca and Singapore have garnered significant international attention dating back to the debates at UNCLOS III in the early 1970s. For nearly four decades, however, the coastal States have continued to express their concerns over increased maritime traffic, and risks of pollution, as well as increases in costs of maintenance of the Strait. On the latter aspect the Strait of Malacca is unique as being the only strait where a cost-sharing mechanism was created. In 1981, a revolving fund was established with a 400-million yen contribution by Japan, one of the major user States of the Straits. It is administered by a Tripartite Commission made up of Japan, Malaysia and Singapore. The fund was primarily intended to provide funds in case of an oil spill. However, other than Japan, no other user States have contributed to the fund.[78] In addition, the Malacca Straits Commission created by a group of Japanese businesses also provided the funds for the installation of 40 navigational aids between 1968 and 1988.[79]

More recently, the Strait of Malacca has taken the lead in innovative measures to meet ship management challenges. In 2001, the IMO and the

---

73. There is a required under-keel clearance of 3.50 meters that must be maintained at all times.

74. Calculated on current exchange rates (US$1.00 = 3.8 MR) this would amount to approximately US$14 million. However, keeping in mind inflation and changing rates the "real" value could be much greater.

75. Available online: <http://www.fsas.upm.edu.my/~masdec/web/straits.html>.

76. *East Asia and Pacific 4E-Marine Electronic Highway, GEF Project Brief.* Available on-line: http://www.gefweb.org/Documents/Work_Programs/wp_Jul03/Executive_Summary10.pdf.

77. Available online: <http://www.fsas.upm.edu.my/~masdec/web/straits.html>.

78. Japan is estimated to save RM1.3 billion annually by use of the Malacca Strait. Available online: <http://www.fsas.upm.edu.my/~masdec/web/straits.html>.

79. T. A. Grigalunas, Y-T. Chang and J. Opaluch, "Sustainable Financing for Controlling Transboundary Pollution by Shipping in the Malacca Straits—Options and Implications," *International Journal of Maritime Economics*, 2 (2000): 331–51, 337.

coastal States of the Malacca Straits embarked upon a project for establishing a Marine Electronic Highway (MEH).[80] The MEH is intended to both increase the efficiency of traffic through the Strait while increasing safety and protection of the marine environment by use of digital technology.[81] Relying on an integrated and coordinated system of electronic navigational charts (ENC), Electronic Chart Display and Information System (ECDIS) fitted on ships and onshore, radar, real-time ship-to-shore communication, large-scale resolution environmental forecasting, and many other features, so that when fully operational, the MEH will allow ships to transit even in dangerous fog conditions.[82] The goal is to eventually create a regional system of such MEHs.

However, it is a costly investment. An initial amount of US$15 million has been allocated for the demonstration project that will cover a 100-km area of the Strait of Malacca.[83] The project implementation period is from 1 April 2004 until 31 March 2008. One of the criteria for project sustainability will be "the feasibility of a MEH fund to co-finance the system and to support coastal and marine resource conservation and management in the Straits area."[84] The project is relying on Article 26(b) of the LOSC as

---

80. "First phase of East Asia's Marine Electronic Highway takes off," at <http://www.imo.org/Newsroom/mainframe.asp?topic_id=67&doc_id=526>. However, discussions for such a project were begun between the IMO-UNDP and GEF in 1996. See K. Sekimizu, J-C. Sainlos and J. N. Paw, "The Marine Electronic Highway in the Straits of Malacca and Singapore: An Innovative Project for the Management of Highly Congested and Confined Waters," (July 2001), Available online: <http://www.imo.org/includes/blastDataOnly.asp/data_id%3D3668/marineelectronic highwayarticle.pdf>; C. Thia-Eng and S. A. Ross, "Marine Electronic Highway: Concepts and Challenges, The Part III: Framework for Cooperation in Preventing and Managing Marine Pollution," *Singapore Journal of International and Comparative Law* 3 (1999): 388–401.

81. According to the GEF Project Brief, the "potential full-scale MEH program's development objectives are to increase the efficiency of marine transport through the Straits, reduce its negative environmental impacts, and strengthen the conservation and management of neighboring marine and coastal environments. The MEH would achieve these objectives by: (a) reducing the frequency of ship collisions in the Strait's congested sea lanes and ports; (b) making marine navigation in the Straits safer and therefore more often feasible in poor weather; (c) tracking and monitoring vessel operations, such as illegal bilge water releases, in the Straits, with benefits for the management and protection of marine and coastal resources; and (d) testing the feasibility of a MEH fund to co-finance the system and to support coastal and marine resource conservation and management in the Straits area. *East Asia and Pacific 4E-Marine Electronic Highway, GEF Project Brief.* See n. 76 above.

82. Sekimizu et al., n. 80 above.

83. The GEF has provided US$8 million and the remaining amount has been provided by foreign banks and the participating governments.

84. *Id.* at 19.

providing the legal grounds to charge voluntary users of the MEH as specific services rendered to ships.[85] However, as discussed later in this article, Article 26(b) may not be applicable to straits falling under the transit passage regime, such as the Malacca and Singapore Straits. Nonetheless, if successful, the MEH Malacca Project will be a model for other straits and particularly chokepoints.

Korea/Tsushima Straits

The Tsushima Straits serve as an important route between the Sea of Japan/ East Sea and the East China Sea.[86] In 1997, an estimated 7,387 vessels of all types completed 75,293 voyages through the Strait. Of these, 1,069 tankers made 9,597 voyages.[87] Similar to other Straits, in addition to providing a transit route for international shipping, the Strait is an important ecosystem for fish and other marine living resources. The threat of pollution, particularly from an oil spill, would have serious economic and ecological consequences. In the past such accidents did occur. For example, on 25 January 1997 a 25-year-old Russian tanker broke apart in heavy storms and spilled more that 30,000 barrels of heavy fuel oil in an area near 15 nuclear power plants and coastal fisheries. Within two weeks an oil slick had spread along 450 km of coastline. Just a few months later, on 2 July 1997 a 259,000 dead-weight tonne supertanker transporting 1.9 million barrels of crude ran aground on a reef in Tokyo Bay. Luckily, the spill was minor.

In response to these incidents a feasibility study of the Korea/Tsushima Straits was undertaken in 1997. After a detailed analysis, including a comparative one of other similar straits and possible measures to be taken, the study recommended against an active VTS system based on its cost and complexity.[88] Since then, no VTS system has been established.

The Torres Strait

The Torres Strait stretches 150 miles between Australia and Papua New Guinea. Measuring 90 miles in width, navigation is made dangerous by the

85. GEF Project Brief, n. 76 above, at 11–12.
86. For Korean Straits, C. Young Pak, *The Korean Straits* (Dordrecht, Boston: Martinus Nijhoff, 1988).
87. L. M. B. Paul, "A Vessel Traffic System Analysis for the Korea/Tsushima Strait," paper presented at the ESENA Workshop: Energy-Related Marine Issues in the Regional Seas of Northeast Asia, Berkeley, California, 8–10 December 1997, at 21. Available online: <http://www.nautilus.org/archives/papers/energy/PaulESENAY2.pdf>.
88. Paul, *id.* at 21.

many narrow channels. It is a natural extension of the Great Barrier Reef and falls within areas of EEZ, territorial sea and internal waters. The Strait is rich in biodiversity, providing a habitat to many rare and unique marine living resources. In economic terms the Great Barrier Reef and Torres Strait provide sea access for AU$17 billion of export trade each year thus serving as an important trade route.[89]

In 2003, Australia and Papua New Guinea jointly applied to the IMO to have the Torres Strait declared a particularly sensitive sea area (PSSA).[90] The two governments also requested adoption of additional measures in association with the Strait being designated a PSSA. The additional measures involved amending existing routing measures into a two-way route and extending the mandatory pilotage scheme already adopted for the Great Barrier Reef into the Torres Strait.[91] Although, in contrast to other straits used in international navigation, the volume of shipping traffic in the Torres Strait is less intense with approximately 3,136 voyages in a 12-month period in 2002.[92] Nevertheless, these include cargo of all types. Over the years there have been numerous accidents, groundings and near misses in the Strait. One of the main concerns expressed by the two governments in their application was the increase in the volume of maritime traffic and the size of ships navigating the Strait in recent years. On the other hand, they pointed out that statistics showed a significant decrease in the number of ships voluntarily employing pilotage through these sensitive and risky waters.

The requested PSSA designation and two-way route was approved. The two-way route also included new navigation aids: two lights and a day mark, complete differential GPS (DGPS) coverage of the area by the Australian Maritime Safety Authority's DGPS station and two Ship Reporting System (SRS) reporting points allowing communications with REEFCENTRE via VHF radio; an AIS base station in the Prince of Wales Channel providing complete radar coverage for the entire southern and central section of the Strait; automated position reporting via INMARSAT C and reliable tidal height predictions at eight locations along the route. Again, each of these navigational and safety aids presents a significant cost to the bordering State.

89. IMO doc. MEPC 49/8 (Submitted by Australia and Papua New Guinea).
90. *Id.*
91. *Id.*
92. *Id.* at 13.

Danish Straits

The Danish Straits consist of three different bodies of waters: the Sound, the Great Belt and the Little Belt.[93] The Straits are a link between the Baltic Sea and the North Sea, serving as the only connection to other seas of the world for some of the coastal States. The Great Belt and Sound handle the heaviest volume of maritime traffic. Indeed, over the past years traffic has doubled in the Sound.[94] In 1997, a total daily volume of 24,000 tonnes of goods was transported through the Great Belt.[95] In 2003, approximately 55,000 vessels navigated the straits.[96] In 1997, approximately 56 MTA of oil was transported through the Danish Straits. However, the amount of oil being transported from the Baltic Sea in 2003 reached 160 MTA and is expected to increase 40 percent by 2015.[97] Most if not all of this oil must traverse the Great Belt or the Sound.

In order to provide safety of navigation and protection of the marine environment, Denmark, through the IMO, adopted a traffic management measure known as a "T route." It includes a TSS and a deep-water route. In 2002, because of an increase in traffic in the Straits, the IMO amended the existing TSS to include a recommendation for the use of pilotage when transiting the Sound and Great Belt.[98] Furthermore, in 1991, a VTS system was established for the Great Belt that was made mandatory in some parts, and voluntary in others. However, as a result of accidents and numerous violations of the TSS by foreign ships, in 1996 a mandatory ship reporting system was established in the Great Belt in accordance with SOLAS Regulation 8, Chapter V.[99]

Moreover, the increase in the volume of Russian oil being shipped from Baltic ports in recent years has resulted in a significant increase in both the

---

93. E. Brüel, *Les Detroits Danois au Point de Vue du Droit International* Recueil des Cours 1936 (Tome 55), 610; K. Bangert, "Denmark and the Law of the Sea," in L. Pineschi and T. Treves, eds., *The Law of the Sea, the European Union and Its Members* (The Hague: Martinus Nijhoff, 1997): 97–126, 106.

94. *Statistical Analyses of the Baltic Maritime Traffic* (24 September 2002), available online: <http://www.vtt.fi/tuo/projects/seastat/balticstatfinal20021.pdf>.

95. *Passage through the Great Belt* [1991] *CCJ Rep.* 11, 109–10; see "Written Observations by Denmark," at 3.

96. Amendment of IMO resolutions A. 620 and A. 579, HELCOM SEA 4/2001, Fourth Meeting 2/11/Rev.1, (30 November 2001).

97. IMO Doc. MEPC 51/8/1 "Designation of the Baltic Sea area as a Particularly Sensitive Sea Area," (submitted by Denmark, Estonia, Finland, Germany, Latvia, Lithuania, Poland and Sweden), at 13.

98. IMO Doc. Resolution A.579 (14) and A.620 (15) adopted in 1985 and 1987 respectively.

99. A. G. Oude Elferink, "The Regime of Passage through the Danish Straits," *International Journal of Marine and Coastal Law* 15, 4 (2000): 555–66, 563.

volume of dangerous cargo passing through the Danish Straits, as well as in the number of tankers. This rise in oil exports has raised regional concerns and prompted all of the Baltic Sea States, with the exception of the Russian Federation, to apply to the IMO to have the Baltic Sea declared as a PSSA.[100] The IMO, in 2004, approved the designation in principle, however, without any associated protective measures (APMs). Such measures, if any, were left to a future date for decision.

A LEGAL ANALYSIS OF ARTICLE 43

Article 43, under the heading "Navigational and safety aids and other improvements and the preventions, reduction and control of pollution" provides that:

> User States and States bordering a strait should by agreement cooperate:
>
> (a) in the establishment and maintenance in a strait of necessary navigational and safety aids or other ·improvements in aid of international navigation; and
>
> (b) for the prevention, reduction and control of pollution from ships.

Article 43 of the LOSC was adopted in response to the concerns expressed by the straits States about the dangers and risks of vessel-source pollution and maritime accidents. It aimed to provide Part III States (straits subject to the transit passage regime) with international support, primarily financial, by encouraging cooperative agreement arrangements between the "strait" States and the "user" States who were deriving an important benefit from the use of the strait. However, since coming into effect in 1994, Article 43 has remained in a somewhat dormant state. To date, no such "cooperative agreement" has been concluded, although there has been some academic interest in the issue, prompted mostly by the Malacca and Singapore Straits.

Why an Article 43?

Why was there a need to include a provision that "exhorted" user States to cooperate with strait States "by agreement" for the establishment of "necessary" navigational and safety aids? Why was not a similar provision included for the innocent passage regime? Professor Bernard Oxman raised this issue in response to the view by some authors that Article 26(b) of the LOSC would serve as a legal basis to justify imposing fees on foreign-flagged

---

100. IMO Doc. MEPC 51/8/1.

vessels engaged in transit passage for the use of navigational aids in Part III straits.[101] While Article 26(a) prohibits coastal States from charging vessels passage dues, Article 26(b) allows a coastal State to charge vessels engaged in innocent passage a fee for *specific* services rendered during passage such as towage or pilotage,[102] whereas no similar provision was included in Part III for straits. According to Oxman this absence was not unintentional.[103] Consequently, Oxman is of the view that States bordering Part III straits are not permitted to charge for specific services absent an Article 43 agreement. In other words, without an agreement made between the strait State and the user State, there is no legal basis upon which the State can charge a ship for specific services rendered during transit passage. Furthermore, a strict reading of Article 43(a) limits the scope of such an agreement to navigational and safety aids or other improvements in aid of international navigation that are *necessary*. While Article 43 cannot prevent States concluding an agreement for "non-necessary" aids this was clearly not deemed part of the obligation of "user" States. Furthermore, even if Article 26(b) were to apply to Part III straits, not all navigational aids would qualify for charging under the rubric of a *specific service.*

If the proper interpretation of Article 43(a) is as Oxman argues, the financial burden on the State bordering Part III straits has been made all the more cumbersome, having been deprived of the right to charge for specific services rendered. Moreover, such limitation on the ability of the coastal State to charge ships engaged in transit passage for specific services could have a negative impact on safety of navigation and protection of the environment. Poorer coastal States will not be able to sustain the costs of maintaining such navigational aids and other infrastructure necessary for providing for safety of navigation and protection of the environment, as well

101. B. H. Oxman, "Observations on the Interpretation and Application of Article 43 of the United Nations Convention of the Law of the Sea with Particular Reference to the Straits of Malacca and Singapore," *Singapore Yearbook of International Law* 3 (1999): 408–26.

102. Article 26(b) would also apply to other straits that are not subject to Part III of the LOSC.

103. Oxman, n. 101 above, at 410. The author cautions against placing too much emphasis on the use of the word "should" rather than "shall" in light of the "clear duty of States to co-operate to protect and preserve the marine environment from pollution of all sources, including accidents" under the 1982 LOS Convention. See also, M. L. Pal and G. Gottsche-Wanli, "Proposed Usage and Management of the Fund Part IV: Funding and Managing International Partnerships," *Singapore Yearbook of International Law* 3 (1999): 475–94. The authors also express the view that "too much emphasis should not be put on the hortatory nature of the language of Article 43 as reflected in the use of the word 'should' because the Convention on various occasions uses various words as expressions which, at the most pragmatic level, highlights the urgent needs for cooperative endeavors—cooperation, agreement and action." *Id.* at 479–80.

as security against the threat of terrorist attacks against shipping. Even for those States that do have the economic ability to establish and maintain state-of-the-art safety and navigational aids, there could be a significant economic disincentive for improving the infrastructure of navigational aids if there is no ability to recover the costs of such investments. According to certain maritime economists the inability to charge for navigational aids that are deemed to be a free public good is a classic case of market failure as there is less incentive for the coastal State to invest in aids, the cost of which they cannot recover.[104]

In this light, promoting the application of Article 43 becomes critical. The question then becomes, what is the nature of the legal mandate to do so?

"Should," "Shall" or Does It Matter?

A strict textual analysis of the LOSC demonstrates the reluctance of the drafters to commit user States to providing financial compensation for transit passage rights. Article 43 does not mandate cooperation by the "user" States as reflected by the employment of the hortatory "should" and not the mandating "shall." The hortatory "should" employed in Article 43 fell short of rendering co-operation between States, a required State duty under international law. How much importance should be given to the choice of "should" over "shall" by the drafters of the LOSC? If the corollary right to charge for specific services was intentionally excluded in regard to Part III straits, then likewise it can be concluded that the employment of "should" rather than "shall" was also intentional on the part of the authors of the Convention. Contrary to the position of some eminent experts in the law of the sea, the employment of the hortatory "should" and not the imperative "shall" does have some significance.

The LOSC is replete with language mandating State cooperation. A close review of these provisions reveals that the great majority of these provisions employed the mandatory "shall" language in contrast to the very few employing "should" or "may" (See Table 1). However, whether this

---

104. For a detailed economic discussion of straits financing, see T. A. Grigalunas, Y-T. Chang and J. Opaluch, "Sustainable Financing for Controlling Transboundary Pollution from Shipping in the Malacca Straits—Options and Implications," *International Journal of Maritime Economics* 2, 4(2000): 331–351. In analyzing the Strait of Malacca the authors explain that because navigational aids are "public goods" that must be provided free of charge there is little incentive for users to voluntarily pay for such services creating the "free rider" problem. Likewise, this also results in the coastal State not providing more navigational aids which provides a classic example of market failure. *Id.* at 5.

amounts to a generalized State obligation to cooperate, even when not expressly provided for by the Convention, is debatable. A closer examination of the provisions that have employed some sort of inter-State "cooperation" language reveal that these are quite issue-specific and, with one exception, not subject to generalized application. The only invocation of general duty for States to cooperate is found in Article 192, requiring that "States have the obligation to protect and preserve the marine environment." This, however, does not *ipso facto* include the requirement that States *pay* for specific services rendered during passage through straits used for international navigation. Although, subparagraph (b) of Article 43, which exhorts States to cooperate for the "prevention, reduction and control of vessel source pollution," may fit under the broader umbrella of Article 192 it does not necessarily impose any obligation to provide some sort of financial contribution. How does one interpret Article 43(b) in relation to Article 192? Would the "should" language in Article 43(b) be negated by the mandatory "shall" of Article 192. Then why was Article 43(b) included? If the primary purpose of Article 43 was to provide some legal support for user States to contribute financially to Part III straits, then it would make sense that the drafters very specifically chose "should" over "shall." And, for this reason the "should" in Article 43 is of interpretative significance (see Table 2).

In the numerous provisions of the Convention establishing some duty between States to cooperate, the vast majority make it mandatory employing the imperative "shall." By contrast, Article 43 stands out as one of the very few articles where cooperation was not made mandatory. Indeed, it is one of two provisions that used the hortatory "should". This, coupled with the omission of the corollary to Article 26 in the section regulating transit passage through straits used in international navigation, weakens the argument that there is any obligation of user States, specifically the Flag States, from paying for any service rendered, leaving the matter entirely to negotiation between the States. Indeed, SOLAS ChapterV/8–1(k) prohibits a State from charging a fee for mandatory Ship Reporting Services established under SOLAS. This would support the view expressed by Pal and Gottsche-Wanli that by making reference to States bordering Straits, Article 43 was to be applied on a strait-by-strait basis and not one single model of cooperation applicable to straits falling within the transit passage regime.[105]

In light of the attention given in the drafting of the provisions on transit passage the employment of "should" rather than "shall" was clearly intentional. The question remains whether there is another source outside of Article 43 that would provide a legal mandate for user States to *financially* cooperate with Part III straits?

---

105. Pal and Gottsche-Wanli, n. 103 above.

Table 1.—Provisions that Mandate State Cooperation with "shall"

Article 130(2)	Duty of States to cooperate to eliminate delays or difficulties between transit States and land-locked States
143(3)	Duty of States to promote cooperation in marine scientific research
144(2)	Duty of States and the Authority to promote transfer of technology and scientific knowledge relating to activities in the Area
197	Duty of State to cooperate on a global basis or regional basis for elaborating and formulating international standards, rules and practices and procedures for the protection and preservation of the marine environment
199	Duty of States to cooperate to eliminate the effects of pollution and preventing or minimizing damage
200	Duty of States to cooperate to promote studies, undertaking of programmes of scientific research and exchange of information
201	Duty of States to cooperate to establish scientific criteria for the elaboration of rules, standards and recommended practices and procedures for the prevention, reduction and control of pollution in the marine environment
242	Duty of States to promote marine scientific research for peaceful purposes
268	Duty of States to promote international cooperation at all levels [for development and transfer of marine technology]
270–274	Section II devoted to international cooperation for development and transfer of marine technology
278	Duty to cooperate among international organizations related to Marine Scientific Research
61(2)	States required to cooperate for determining allowable catch of living resource
64(2)	States required to cooperate for conserving highly migratory fish and promoting optimum utilization
65	States required to cooperate for conservation of marine mammals
66(3)(b-4)	Cooperation for conservation of anadromous stock
70(4)	States required to cooperate in establishing equitable division of fish stock when State can harvest TAC limit
94(7)	Requires cooperation between Flag State and other State in investigation of a marine casualty
100	Duty of States to cooperate in repression of piracy on the high seas or other areas outside their jurisdiction

108(1)	Duty of States to cooperate in the repression of illicit narcotic/psychotropic drugs on the high seas
109(1)	Duty of States to cooperate in the repression of unauthorized broadcasting from the high seas
117	Duty of States to cooperate for taking measures with respect to their nationals in the conservation of living resources of the high seas
118	Duty of States to cooperate in management and cooperation of living resources in the areas of the high seas
120–	Duty of States to cooperate in the management and cooperation of mammals in areas of the high seas
270–274	Section II devoted to international cooperation for development and transfer of marine technology
278	Duty to cooperate among international organizations related to Marine Scientific Research

Table 2.—Provisions Employ Permissive "May" or Hortatory "Should"

108(2) (permissive)	Flag State may request cooperation of coastal State to suppress illicit trafficking of narcotic drugs or psychotropic substances
123 (hortatory)	Exhorts States bordering enclosed or semi-enclosed seas to cooperate in exercising their rights and performing their duties under that section
129 (permissive)	Transit State and land-locked Sate may cooperate in constructing or improving means of transit,
217(5) (permissive)	Flag State may request assistance of any other State when investigating a violation of a rule relating to dumping established by the competent international organization (IMO)

THE POLLUTER PAYS PRINCIPLE

While Article 43 may not have established a legal obligation rising to the level of a State duty under international law for user States (and other interests) to cooperate "in the establishment and maintenance of necessary navigation and safety aids or other improvements in aid of international navigation, or for the prevention and control of pollution from ships," including paying for specific services provided by the strait States, another norm of international environmental law that merits examination is the "polluter pays" principle (PPP). Not a new concept, the PPP was first introduced in 1972 as part of the OECD Council Recommendations

"Guiding Principles."[106] The OECD Guiding Principles defined the PPP as follows:

> The principle to be used for allocating costs of pollution *prevention* and *control* measures to encourage rational use of scarce environmental resources and to avoid distortions in international trade and investment is the so-called "Polluter-Pays Principle." This principle means that the polluter should bear the expenses of carrying out the above mentioned measures decided by public authorities to ensure that the environment is in an acceptable state. In other words, the cost of these measures should be reflected in the cost of goods and services which cause pollution in production and/or consumption. Such measures should not be accompanied by subsidies that would create significant distortions in international trade and investment [emphasis added].[107]

However, this was not meant to be passed on to the consumer, but included in production costs.[108]

Of course, these were "guidelines" and not legal obligations. As a legal principle the PPP was enshrined in Principle 16 of the 1992 Rio Declaration.[109] However, the PPP has become an accepted norm of international law and not simply a "soft" law ideal. Since the 1992 Rio Summit the PPP has been included in international environmental instruments, where it is relevant. However, even before the Rio Declaration, the PPP had become official policy of the EC in 1987.[110] And, more recently the European

---

106. "Environment and Economics Guiding Principles Concerning International Economic Aspects of Environmental Policies," (OECD Recommendation adopted on 26th May, 1972), C(72)128. The concept, however, was first introduced in 1971 by the Commission on International Trade and Investment Policy. See C. S. Pearson, "Testing the System: GATT + PPP = ?," *Cornell International Law Journal* 27 (1994): 553–75, 554.

107. Principle 4, *id.*

108. Pearson, n. 106 above, at 555.

109. The Rio Declaration on Environment and Development was adopted during the 1992 United Nations Conference on Environment and Development held in Rio de Janeiro, 1992. U.N. Doc. A/CONF. 151/5/Rev.1 (1992), reprinted in *International Legal Materials* 31 (1992): 874–80, 878.

110. Treaty Establishing the European Community, 25 March 1957 [Treaty of Rome]; 1986 Single European Act, the 1992 Treaty on European Union, OJ C 224 (entered into force 1 November 1993); and Treaty of Amsterdam amending the Treaty on European Union, the Treaties establishing the European Communities and related acts, 2 October 1997, 1997 O.J C340 (entered into force 1 January 1999), available online: <http://europa.eu.int/eur-lex/en/index.html>. Article 174(2) states in part: "Community policy on the environment shall be . . . based on the precautionary principle and on the principles that preventive action should be taken, that environmental damage should as a priority be rectified at source and that the polluter should pay."

Commission adopted what has popularly been referred to as the "Polluter Pays Directive,"[111] further emphasizing the importance of shifting the cost of pollution away onto the actual polluters and not the public. However, the EC Directive is limited to application of imposing a strict legal liability regime on the parties responsible for the pollution in a *post-pollution* situation versus in preventing polluting activities.[112] Whereas, the OECD Guidelines included application of the PPP to prevention and *control* measures, which would be extremely relevant for purposes of Article 43. However, as noted by some authors the precise meaning of the PPP under EC law remains varied.[113] Despite a seemingly broad acceptance of the PPP, as one author observes, the definition of the PPP as a legal norm remains unclear:

> The PPP is a normative doctrine of environmental law. Although its precise legal definition remains elusive, the core of this principle stems from the fundamental, logical, and fair proposition that those who generate pollution, not the government, should bear pollution costs. The principle underlies much of modern environmental law, and in recent years, has become increasingly important in guiding environmental policy, especially at the international level.[114]

The basic goal of the PPP is cost allocation by shifting the cost of pollution from the governments to the private sector. It is meant to prevent governments from subsidizing the polluters through internalization of these costs. The cost of "pollution" should be reflected in the price of goods and services instead of being borne by the taxpayer.[115]

---

111. Directive 2004/36/CE on environmental liability with regard to the prevention and remedying of environmental damage (21 April 2004) O J L/2004/143/56. See E. T. Larson, "Why Environmental Liability Regimes in the United States, the European Community, and Japan Have Grown Synonymous with the Polluter Pays Principle," *Vanderbilt Journal of Transnational Law* 38, 2 (2005): 541–75.

112. For a detailed explanation of the Directive, see the "European Commission White Paper on environmental liability," COM (2000) 66 final.

113. "Both the OECD and the EC recognized that by allocating abatement costs to the private sector, market prices would more closely reflect the social costs of production. This would tend to encourage pollution abatement by reducing consumption of pollution-intensive products. International adoption of the PPP would avoid distortions to international trade and investment arising from differential." Pearson, n. 106 above, at 555.

114. J. R. Nash, "Too Much Market?: Conflict between Tradable Pollution Allowances and the "Polluter Pays" Principle," *Harvard Environmental Law Review 24* (2000): 465–535, 466.

115. *Id.* at 469; Pearson, n. 106 above, at 555. See also, E. Hey, T. Ijistra and A. Nolkaemper, "The 1992 Paris Convention for the Protection of the Marine Environment of the North-East Atlantic: A Critical Analysis," *International Journal of Marine and Coastal Law* 8 (1993): 1–76, pp. 13–14; C. Stevens, "Trade and the

Related to the PPP is the User Pays Principle (UPP) which has been described as "the natural resources analogue to the PPP."[116] The difference is that the UPP attempts to assess the value of the use, depletion and possible damage to the natural resource (forest, water and land) and charge this to the users by a "users fee." However, unlike the PPP there is no international mandate for State adoption of the UPP. Nevertheless, the ultimate objective of these two principles is closely inter-related: that is to ensure that the "user"—who is obtaining a commercial benefit from the resource—be financially responsible for the damage, depletion and mainte-nance of it, and not the public.

Another important issue is the implementation of the PPP or even the UPP in shared environments. As noted by one author the problem with implementation of the PPP for shared environmental problems is adopting the international agreement, which takes time and, even if successfully adopted, the actual enforcement of it poses other challenges.[117] Article 43 would bear out this observation as to date there has been no international agreement negotiated. For this reason, enforcement remains a theoretical issue, nonetheless an important one.

Does the PPP or UPP provide the requisite legal foundation to mandate "user" State cooperation under Article 43? In answering this question, it must be recalled that the PPP began as an economic approach to environmental protection. The underlying concept was that if the polluter had to pay the "real" cost of polluting it would seek to take measures to *prevent* polluting activities. Governments should not subsidize polluters. The economic concept has become a legal norm of international environmental law, although the application and definition of the PPP remains unclear.

Should vessels be financially responsible for the pollution caused as a result of passage through a strait? According to the PPP and the UPP, the answer would be in the affirmative. In this regard, straits used in international navigation can even be viewed as scarce or limited natural resources, particularly those that constitute "chokepoints." They are limited or scarce in the sense that they can be exhausted, in either physical capacity, or more importantly, their existence as healthy viable ecological systems. Consequently, the use of straits should not be subsidized by governments, but rather the actual users should be charged based on cost recovery for

Environment: The OECD Guiding Principles Revisited," *Environmental Law* 23A (1993): 607–19; C. Stevens, Interpreting the Polluter Pays Principle in the Trade and Environment Context," *Cornell International Law Journal* 27 (1994): 577–90; S. E. Gaines, "The Polluter-Pays Principle: From Economic Equity to Environmental Ethos," *Texas International Law Journal* 26 (1991): 463–96.

116. Pearson, n. 106 above, at 562.

117. Stevens, n. 115 above, at 587. The author addresses the issue within the context of a "free trade" perspective.

those measures necessary to ensure safety of navigation and protection and preservation of the marine environment. This would be consistent, if not mandated, by current legal norms applicable to international environmental law.

Who Are the "User" States?

The term "user" is somewhat vague and could include a wide range of entities from the flag State of ships plying the straits to other direct and indirect beneficiaries of the convenience and savings afforded by the strait. This could include a wide array of beneficiaries from cargo interests to the ultimate consumer.[118] For example, transportation costs are said to amount to only 10 percent of the price of oil as charged at the pump.[119] The imposition of an additional charge for safety and anti-pollution measures could be added to the pump price. If limited only to "cost recovery" the added amount would barely be noticed, but would contribute significantly to preserving the marine environment. Furthermore, this additional charge would not constitute an unfair charge on the consumer in contravention of the PPP goal because the consumer of oil carries a responsibility to protect the environment.

A more readily available source is the petroleum industry which has always been an easy "user" to identify and one that has the financial resources to provide the amount of financial investment that would be necessary for the navigational and safety aids necessary for straits. But oil tankers constitute only a fraction of the "users" of straits. Other users include dry bulk carriers, liquid bulk carriers, Ro-Ro ships, passenger ships and fishing vessels.[120] Furthermore, even if all ship types were made to participate in an Article 43 agreement, the next question would be determining who? Would it be the State of the owner, operator, charterer, cargo interest? After all, each is benefiting from the strait in question. In

118. For a discussion on defining the "user" under Article 43, see S. Tiwari, "Funding and Managing International Partnerships: Legal Mechanisms for Establishing a Fund," *Singapore Journal of International and Comparative Law* 3, 2 (1999): 470–74; A. T. Khee-Jin, "Control of Pollution in the Straits of Malacca and Singapore: Modalities of Co-operation—Rapporteur's Report," *Singapore Journal of International and Comparative Law* 2, 2 (1998): 269–283.

119. Rodrigue, n. 35 above.

120. S. Nandan provides a detailed analysis of the users of the Malacca and Singapore Straits, including transits by vessel types. According to this analysis dry bulk cargo and general cargo constitute the lion's share of users of the Straits in terms of "type" of vessel. S. Nandan, "The Management of Straits used for International Navigation: International Cooperation in Malacca Singapore Straits," *Singapore Yearbook of International Law* 3 (1999): 429–43.

practical terms the more likely candidate will be the flag State of the vessel. Identification of other interests would be difficult and involve inquiries possibly in violation of transit passage rights.

ENFORCEMENT

Even if the user and straits States succeed in concluding an Article 43 agreement, another issue raised is enforcement of the agreements. Would this be a flag State implementation problem? Keeping in mind that Article 43 is restricted to user States, and not private interests, the user State would ultimately be the responsible party. Therefore, the user State would have two choices: either participate directly, i.e., provide direct financial contribution to the strait State, or enter into an agreement on behalf of vessels registered under its flag. In the latter option vessels registered under the flag of the user State party to the Article 43 agreement would be obligated to "cooperate."

Although emphasis has been given to cooperation by some sort of pecuniary participation, the language of Article 43 is broad enough to be interpreted to include participation in non-pecuniary aspects as well. In addition to financial cooperation, i.e., paying for specific services, a broader cooperation could include an agreement by the user States that vessels flying its flag will, for example, employ pilotage or towage services. In other words, creating by agreement what international law otherwise would not allow in a Part III strait. However, enforcement of either of these types of agreement would fall squarely on the user State. In either case, an interesting question is whether enforcement of an Article 43 agreement is a flag State obligation under Article 217(1) of the LOSC?

SUSTAINABLE FINANCING OF STRAITS

A detailed "economic" model for a possible financing mechanism of an Article 43 arrangement is beyond the scope and the competence of this article. However, available options that have been suggested for Article 43 include:[121]

---

121. For a detailed analysis of funding and cost-sharing options for the Malacca Straits, see B. A. Hamzah, "Funding partnerships for safer navigation and a cleaner environment in the Straits of Malacca," paper presented at the *Regional Conference on Sustainable Financing Mechanism for the Prevention and Management of Marine Pollution*: Public Sector-Private Sector Partnerships, Manila Philippines on 14–16 November 1996. Available online: <http://www.mima.gov.my/mima/htmls/papers/pdf/MNB/funding%20partnership%20safer%20navig.pdf>.

(1) Cooperative arrangements between user States and littoral States for the imposition of uniform dues.[122] These could be bilateral or multilateral. The revolving fund established for the Malacca Strait is an example of such a cooperative agreement.

(2) Establishing a Fund.[123] A Fund could be established either directly between the parties to an Article 43 agreement, such is the case with the Malacca and Singapore Straits, or through an international organization such as the IMO. In 1997, the United Kingdom introduced a paper at the Maritime Safety Committee of the IMO entitled "Developing principles for charging users the cost of maritime infrastructure."[124] However, the reaction was "cautious" and the U.K. did not pursue the matter. As mentioned earlier, one of the draft proposals introduced during UNCLOS III included the creation of a fund managed by an "Oceans Space Institute."[125]

(3) Sliding scale charge based on actual frequency of use.[126] Under this model, the cost recovery would be apportioned based on actual frequency of use of the Strait. However, this first requires defining the "user" or the "beneficiary." Second, what should the criteria for cost allocation be based on: number of transits? Size of vessel? Nature of cargo (dangerous versus non-dangerous)?

(4) The Donaldson Report, titled "Paying for Pollution Prevention" that was prepared following the *Braer* accident suggested that "anti-pollution" measures be paid for through a series of port state control charges—and not by the taxpayer. This would be consistent with the PPP.[127] This approach would not require an Article 43 agreement, as the coastal State is entitled to impose port fees. However, such fees could be specifically designated by the strait State for straits maintenance. Would this, however, amount to an unlawful user charge for straits passage? If so, an Article 43 agreement would be advisable. However, if the charge is imposed upon ships that have called at port, such vessels would not have engaged in transit passage as defined by Article 38 of the LOSC.

---

122. *Id.* at 10. Grigalunas gives the example of the agreement between the United Kingdom and Ireland, with dues to cover expenses for lighthouses, buoys, beacons, tenders etc., and the Gulf Area of the Middle East, the Middle East Navigation Service (MENAS). See Grigalunas, n. 104 above.

123. Pal and Gottsche-Wanli, n. 103 above.

124. IMO Doc. LEG 76/Inf.2, September 2, 1997. See also, Nandan and Anderson, n. 7 above.

125. See n. 26 above.

126. Grigalunas, n. 104 above, at 12.

127. Nandan and Anderson, n. 7 above.

CONCLUSION

The transit passage regime adopted by the LOSC was a compromise regime created to satisfy the navigational interests of the two superpowers at the time. In return for recognizing the right of the coastal State to extend its territorial sea up to 12 NM the coastal State had to forfeit non-suspendable passage rights in straits used in international navigation that would be regulated under Part III of the LOSC. Furthermore, to address some of the concerns voiced by the strait States over the many problems associated with modern shipping, particularly the transport of dangerous and hazardous cargoes, Article 43 was adopted, which exhorted the user States of Part III straits to cooperate with the straits State.

Over the past three decades the increase in overall shipping and the substantial increase in the transport of dangerous/hazardous cargoes through narrow "chokepoint" straits have demonstrated the concerns of the straits States to be well-founded. In order to respond to increased dangers of accidents and pollution the straits States must invest in navigational aids, which are becoming increasingly expensive. State-of-the-art navigational aids such as radar-based satellites contribute greatly to safety of navigation but are also very expensive. The question is how strait States can recover the cost of these navigational aids and what legal means permit them to do so? Article 43 becomes critical in this regard.

The language of Article 43 did not make cooperation mandatory as reflected by the employment of the exhortatory "should," nor did it restrict its ambit solely to financial cooperation. However, a strict textual analysis does indicate that, unlike the innocent passage regime where the coastal State is authorized under Article 26(2) to charge ships fees for specific services rendered during passage, the same right was not included in Part III. Consequently, in order for a Part III strait State to charge a fee to ships engaged in transit passage an agreement between the flag State of the vessel (as a user State) and the straits State would be a pre-condition.

In examining whether there are other legal norms that would compel users of straits to contribute to the costs of maintaining such straits the PPP would appear to provide, at least in theory, legal grounds. However, the meaning of the PPP remains unclear and actual implementation of it has focused on post-pollution liability rather than using it as a method to prevent pollution as originally intended as an economic model. Whereas, the importance of the PPP should serve to dissuade polluting activities by making the polluter pay the "true" cost of polluting through fees. Navigational and safety aids are important pollution prevention measures for which the "users," who are the cause of the polluting activity, should pay under norms of modern international law.

However, defining who the "user" is for purposes of Article 43, is not clear, although more likely than not it will be based on the flag State of the vessel, as this is certainly more readily identified over other potential "user States," such as the cargo interest. Furthermore, Article 43 is not restricted solely to financial cooperation but could be employed in a broad fashion to include agreements for the flag State vessel to use navigational aids, such as pilotage, the employment of which it could not otherwise make mandatory under international law.

In conclusion, Article 43 provides an important legal mechanism for strait States to use to recuperate expenses for maintaining navigational aids. Indeed, it may be the only way in which they can impose fees to recover the cost of navigational and safety aids necessary to ensure the safety and the protection of the marine environment. However, to date it has remained in a somewhat dormant state with the exception of attempts being made by Malaysia and Singapore for the Malacca Straits to activate it. Yet, clearly there is a need for most of the strait States to invigorate this unused provision of the LOSC. As oil prices surge and the oil transport sector reaps significant profits the strait States are losing the opportunity to obtain the much needed financing to both maintain and improve upon the navigational aid infrastructure critical to the protection of the straits. The Malacca Strait electronic highway project will provide a valuable opportunity to test the workability of Article 43. However, other strait States should also assume a more active role in examining practical and sustainable methods by which to employ Article 43 and ensure the future safety, security and protection of the environment in straits used in international navigation.

Dealing with Risk and Uncertainty: How to Improve the Basis for Decisions about Granting Refuge to Ships in Need of Assistance

Jens-Uwe Schröder*
World Maritime University, Malmö, Sweden

INTRODUCTION

Even before the debates about places of refuge following the most recent tanker accidents in Western Europe, i.e., *Prestige, Erika* or *Castor,*[1] the issue of granting refuge to ships in need of assistance was discussed. One could say that the history of shipping was always also a history of granting refuge to ships in need of assistance. Chircop argues that granting refuge is an old customary law.[2] In a very recent publication he presents evidence that granting refuge to ships in distress has been included in international treaties since ancient times.[3] Not only does granting refuge to ships in distress or in need of assistance have a long history, there are a number of

---

* The views expressed in this article are those of the author and not necessarily of the World Maritime University.

1. The *Prestige* was a 26-year old single-hull tanker that sprang a leak in the Bay of Biscay in November 2002. After the Spanish Government refused to grant refuge to the ship, the ship finally sank and subsequently caused massive environmental damage to the French, Spanish and Portuguese coasts. In December 1999, the tanker *Erika* broke in two in the Bay of Biscay after it was refused to enter a French place of refuge for potential repairs and/or unloading the cargo. In December 2000, the tanker *Castor* experienced severe weather damage off the coast of Spain. The ship was unable to find a place of refuge for 35 days and was finally towed to Tunisia where the cargo of unleaded gasoline was unloaded.

2. A. Chircop, "Living with Ships in Distress—A New IMO Decision-Making Framework for the Requesting and Granting of Refuge," *WMU Journal of Maritime Affairs* 3, no. 1 (2004): 31–49.

3. A. Chircop, "The Customary Law of Refuge for Ships in Distress," *Places of Refuge for Ships: Emerging Environmental Concerns of a Maritime Custom*, eds., A. Chircop and O. Lindén (Leiden: Martinus Nijhoff Publishers, an imprint of Koninklijke Brill N.V., 2005), pp. 163–230.

Ocean Yearbook 20: 595–621.

examples where refuge was granted under remarkable circumstances.[4] If authors like Browne or van Hooydonk strongly believe that granting refuge applies to ships in need of assistance, and if these authors argue that granting refuge should not be given up or limited by maritime administrations, one could raise the question, why do we have to discuss the matter?[5]

In the previous paragraph, three cases were mentioned where granting refuge to these ships was not considered as an option to limit potential environmental implications at a very early stage of a serious accident. However, one has not always to make reference to these exceptional serious examples. Özçayir lists examples of less severe cases that have occurred within the last 30 years.[6] However, the above-mentioned cases have promoted a thorough discussion about the current practice of granting refuge to ships in need of assistance. This discussion focused, among many other important issues, specifically on the question of whether there is a tendency to give up granting refuge to ships in need of assistance in order to protect certain coastlines against potential environmental pollution. The increased interest in this topic by politicians and other stakeholders of the maritime policy framework could in fact be interpreted to mean that more and more coastal States tend to refuse refuge to ships.[7] There are a number of refused requests for refuge that are interpreted by Chircop in a way that humanitarian assistance as such is not refused. What is refused, in his opinion, is more and more the entry of the ship to a place of refuge when

4. In 1746, during the English-Spanish War the Governor of Havana allowed the English warship *Elisabeth* to enter the port of Havana as a place of refuge after a hurricane in the Gulf of Mexico.

5. B. Browne, "Places of Refuge—The IUMI Solution," (paper presented at the IUMI Conference 2003, Seville, 14–18 September 2003), available online: <http://www.iumi.com/Conferences/2003_sevilla/1609/BBrowne.pdf>; E. van Hooydonk, "Some Remarks on Financial Securities Imposed by Public Authorities on Casualty Ships as a Condition for Entry into Ports," in *Marine Insurance at the Turn of the Millennium*, ed. M. Huybrechts Marc (Antwerpen: Intersentia, 2000) Vol. 2, at 117–136.

6. Z. O. Özçayir, "Ports of Refuge," *Journal of International Maritime Law* 9, no. 5 (2003): 486–495.

7. Apart from increased publications in recent years by, e.g., Chircop, ns. 2 and 3; Browne, n. 5 above; van Hooydonk, see n. 5 above; Özçayir, see n. 6 above; R. Shaw, "Places of Refuge: 'International Law in the Making,'" *Journal of International Maritime Law* 9, no. 2 (2003): 159–180; "'Sink or Shelter?—A Question of Collective Responsibility'—The Fourth Cadwallander Annual Memorial Lecture," *International Maritime Law* 8, no. 2/3 (2002): 47–58; international associations (such as the International Union of Marine Insurance, or the Comité Maritime International) discussed the issue intensively. The increased attention on this topic is also reflected in a number of dedicated workshops and meetings organized to debate the issue, such as the International Workshop on Places of Refuge (11 December 2003) hosted by the University of Antwerp, Belgium.

the resulting risks are considered to be high. He calls this the "not-in-my-backyard syndrome."[8] However, if one considers the published lists of requests of recent years it seems that this is questionable. Özçayir lists a number of countries that have refused and denied entry to a place of refuge at different occasions. It seems that the recent cases of *Castor, Erika* and *Prestige* have generated a perception that refuge is denied more and more. This cannot be supported by statistical evidence. However, what can be concluded is that coastal States have a general difficulty of assessing the overall threat resulting from a request for refuge and have therefore to be very careful in decision-making.

One reason for this carefulness is certainly the changed risk profile of maritime casualties in a historical context. When the ancient Greek and Roman treaties about granting refuge were negotiated, ships did not really pose a threat to the coastal community in terms of pollution and resulting economic hardship. Until the middle of the last century, the risk of spreading diseases was considered the biggest threat caused by shipping. Cholera was the most feared disease in this respect. In order to limit the potential impact from shipping on the public health of coastal communities, the Risk Control Option (RCO) quarantine was established. In 1348, to name one example, Venice provided a council of three persons with decision-making powers to detain ships, cargoes and individuals, for up to 40 days in the lagoon in order to observe if infectious diseases could spread from the ship or through an individual.[9] Earlier arrangements targeting travelers from plague or leprosy areas are known. Specific maritime arrangements were made in many other countries at that time, and some of them are still followed today. In more recent history the immigration movement to the United States has often been overshadowed by cholera outbreaks or other diseases.[10] Despite the fear of granting refuge, it was never suspended. A remarkable example in this respect is the case of the *England* in 1866.[11] This ship was on its way to New York with 1,200 passengers when an outbreak of cholera occurred. The ship was granted refuge on a small island close to Halifax in order to treat the infected passengers and to limit further spreading among those on the ship that had not suffered so far.

Nowadays, the risk profile of shipping has changed. Disastrous diseases are no longer the main threat. The nature of the cargo and related environmental consequences, in case of accidental pollution, are the driving

---

8. Chircop, n. 2 above, at 33–36.
9. For more information refer to: *History of Quarantine*, available online: <http://www.pbs.org/wgbh/nova/typhoid/quarantine.html>.
10. *Id.*
11. For more information refer to: *McNabs History*, available online: <http://www.mcnabsisland.ca/history/hist-s6.html>.

forces in a system where granting refuge to ships in need of assistance becomes an RCO, which is less and less considered as an option at all. In times of mass media where any events are covered online in great detail, maritime disasters can be exploited by different stakeholders for different purposes. The introduction of the double hull is one of the disputed outcomes of such developments.[12] It is often not practicably feasible to distinguish between a ship in need of assistance and a ship in distress. Where does an emergency situation begin? What is the likelihood that a ship in need of assistance will turn into a maritime disaster with far-reaching environmental implications? These are questions that maritime administrations have to answer when they are approached to grant refuge. Decisions will surely be influenced by considerations about the eventual coverage in the mass media when a disaster occurs.

The complexity of the subject is also reflected in the scientific literature. There are no simple answers regarding perfect RCOs or risk assessment verification. The already mentioned double hull requirement, the introduction of Particularly Sensitive Sea Areas (PSSAs), transit routes for tankers etc., are RCOs aimed at achieving a higher safety level. However, every new RCO influences a complex system of technical and human interaction in a very specific way. The risk profile of the whole system will be changed in an unexpected way resulting in a greater difficulty to carry out a thorough risk assessment.[13] As a result, many decisions are made on a subjective basis, including a number of speculations and assumptions that are not always verified in practice. A typical example is the discussion about the impact of accidental oil pollution. Where some authors concerned about potential impacts of oil pollution try to identify and discuss the consequences of pollution,[14] others provide evidence about the overestimation of the environmental impact of previous acts of pollution.[15] This does not always support the decision-makers when they are forced to react to

12. After the collision of the *Tern* with the double-hull tanker *Baltic Carrier* in the Baltic in March 2001 Greenpeace started several awareness campaigns. One of the objectives was to create political pressure for an earlier introduction of double-hull tankers. Although this had no relation to the accident, the topic was taken up by some local politicians.

13. An example is the double hull. The double hull increases the capability of a ship to cope with groundings and contact damage. It involves, however, a greater risk of corrosion, which could lead, in combination with bad management, to severe consequences. Inappropriate management has contributed to the accidents of *Prestige* and *Erika* significantly.

14. B. Forsman, *Socioekonomiska Effecter av Store Oljepåslag, Förstudie med Scenario, Rapport till Räddningsverket*, SSPA Rapport No. 2003 3294 (Göteborg: SSPA, 2003).

15. W. Ritchie, "The *Braer* Oil Spill: Ten Years Later, Was It Really a Disaster?," (paper presented at the Safety at Sea: Safer Ships, Safer Lives Conference, Greenwich London, 23–24 March 2004).

catastrophes under the glare of mass media. The perceived risk of unjustified mass media coverage in case of a serious accident resulting from unsuccessful granting of refuge to a ship in need of assistance could therefore also have an influence on the decision-making process in such instances.

One objective of this article is therefore to support objective risk assessment for granting refuge to ships in distress. Since the dilemma of providing a solid basis for such risk assessment is acknowledged, this article is also intended to contribute to the discussion of how to obtain such a basis. To this end, in the first part the current practice of granting refuge is summarized. Resulting from this summary, conclusions regarding strengths and weaknesses of the current practice are formulated. Based on the conclusions suitable risk assessment methodologies, which are either already in use or which could be used for granting refuge purposes, will be identified and discussed. The discussion will then focus specifically on the necessary preconditions for the implementation of the risk assessment methodologies and advantages and disadvantages linked to individual methodologies.

CURRENT PRACTICE OF RISK ASSESSMENT FOR GRANTING REFUGE TO SHIPS IN NEED OF ASSISSTANCE

Before risk assessment methodologies for granting refuge to ships in need of assistance can be discussed, the current practice should be analyzed. As already mentioned, especially after the recent casualties of the tankers *Erika, Prestige* and *Castor*, more focused discussions about the issue of granting refuge were started, resulting in a number of legal instruments. The most prominent on the international level is the International Maritime Organization (IMO) Resolution A.949(23),[16] which aims at providing a globally accepted standard on how to deal with granting refuge to ships in need of assistance. However, not only IMO has been dealing with this issue. Granting refuge has been introduced as a measure to limit accidental consequences in a number of regional legal instruments, such as in the European Union (EU) Directive 2002/59/EC,[17] the Protocol concerning Cooperation in Preventing Pollution from Ships and, in Cases of Emergen-

16. Guidelines on Places of Refuge for Ships in Need of Assistance, IMO Assembly Resolution A.949(23), adopted on 5 December 2003, IMO Doc. A 23/Res. 949, 5 March 2004.

17. Directive 2002/59/EC of the European Parliament and of the Council of the 27 June 2002 Establishing a Community Vessel Traffic Monitoring and Information System and Repealing Council Directive 93/75/EEC, Official Journal L 208, 5.08.2002, p. 10, refer in particular to article 20.

cy, Combating Pollution of the Mediterranean Sea,[18] or the Copenhagen Declaration of the Baltic Marine Environment Protection Commission (HELCOM).[19]

Apart from the pure introduction of the measures of granting refuge to ships in need of assistance the discussion was supported through studies, mainly from the Comité Maritime International (CMI), during 2002 and 2003.[20] The CMI approached national member associations and asked for information about the legal framework (i.e., ratification of international legal instruments) and past experience on granting refuge (primarily by focusing on casualties that occurred in the territorial waters, EEZ, etc.); 24 member associations participated in the survey. The results were summarized as input for IMO stimulating further discussions about the practice of granting refuge. The disadvantage, as far as the topic of this article is concerned was that the CMI survey did not gather any data about the practical aspects of granting refuge.

In addition to the CMI surveys, another survey was carried out recently by the World Maritime University (WMU).[21] Unlike the CMI survey, the WMU survey approached maritime administrations directly and specifically focused on the practices of granting refuge. Representatives from 27 different maritime administrations responded to the WMU survey that focused on five areas:[22]

18. Protocol Concerning Cooperation in Preventing Pollution from Ships and, in Cases of Emergency, Combating Pollution of the Mediterranean Sea, UNEP Doc. UNEP(OCA)/MED IG.14 Protocol, 25 January 2002, available online: <http://www.unepmap.gr/Archivio/All_Languages/WebDocs/BC&Protocols/Emergency02_eng.pdf>, refer in particular to article 16.

19. Declaration on the Safety of Navigation and Emergency Capacity in the Baltic Sea Area (HELCOM Copenhagen Declaration), 10 September 2001, available online: <http://www.helcom.fi/ministerial_declarations/en_GB/declarations/>, refer in particular to measure XII.

20. CMI, "Places of Refuge—Report of the CMI to the IMO," in *CMI Yearbook 2002* (Antwerp: CMI, 2003), pp. 117–146. The CMI carried out another survey in 2003 (refer to: *Places of Refuge, Summary of Responses to the CMI's Second Questionnaire*, IMO Doc. LEG 87/7/2, 16 September 2003) that focused entirely on liability issues. The 2003 CMI survey can therefore not be considered for comparative purposes in this article.

21 J.-U. Schröder, "Review of Decision-Making by Maritime Administrations for Ships in Need of Assistance—Lessons for Risk Assessment," in *Places of Refuge for Ships: Emerging Environmental Concerns of a Maritime Custom*, ed. A. Chircop and O. Lindén (Leiden: Martinus Nijhoff Publishers, an imprint of Koninklijke Brill N.V., 2005), pp. 93–118.

22. Australia, Bolivia, Cambodia, Canada, Chile, China, Denmark, Finland, Germany, Haiti, Iceland, Iran, Ireland, Jamaica, Lebanon, Myanmar, Netherlands, New Zealand, Philippines, Romania, Singapore, Slovenia, South Africa, Sweden, Turkey, United Kingdom, and the United States.

FIG. 1.—Overview of the Administrations Responsible for Granting Refuge

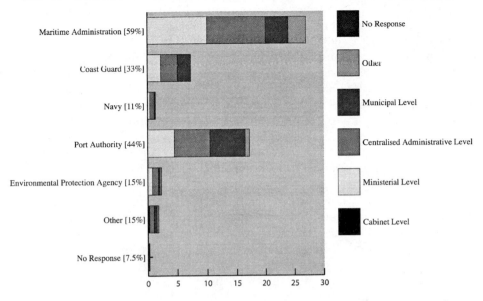

The survey participants were allowed to tick more than one answer. The percentage figures displayed in the graphs relate to the number of 27 countries surveyed and not to the overall number of ticked options in the answers.

- General information;
- Past practice on granting refuge;
- Legal framework for granting refuge;
- Guidelines for granting refuge; and
- Follow-up to IMO Res. A.949(23).

The results of this survey are summarized in the following paragraphs.

General Information about Granting Refuge

The first section of the survey focused on the question of responsibilities for granting refuge and the level of decision-making. The summary of the answers of the survey participants is shown in Figure 1. The findings can be summarized as follows. In a majority of the countries surveyed (14 countries—52%) one single administration is responsible for granting refuge to ships in need of assistance. This will most likely be the maritime administration on a centralized administrative level. However, there are a variety of existing options for dealing with granting refuge. Refuge may also be granted by the coast guard, port authority, the navy, or even the environmental protection agency, in some countries. In 13 (48%) countries surveyed more than one administration is involved in the decision-making about granting refuge to a ship in need of assistance. Similar statements can be made about the level of decision-making. Typical scenarios in the past were that either the maritime administration (and/or coast guard) or the port authority functioned as the lead authority. In addition, depending on the severity of the case, other administrations were involved and decisions were made on different levels. One trend can be summarized from the answers. More severe potential consequences from an unsuccessful attempt to support a ship in need of assistance usually require a higher level of decision-making and a larger number of administrations involved. This result as such was probably predictable. However, it could also be interpreted in a way that high-level decision-making and coordination with a number of administrations has an influence on the efficiency of the response to the request for refuge.[23] A number of countries have therefore introduced centralized response centers in recent years in order to enhance cooperation between the different authorities involved.

Past Practice on Granting Refuge

This section was introduced into the survey in order to find out if past experience with this matter had an impact on the decision-making about subsequent requests. The questions in this section focused on past experience, occasions when refuge was granted, and the results and consequences of granting refuge to ships in need of assistance.

Twenty survey participants (74%) indicated that the responsible administrations in their countries were asked to grant refuge. Refuge was

23. Such coordination difficulties were mentioned, e.g., in an investigation report (*Unabhängige Expertenkommission Havarie Pallas,* available online: <http://cdl.niedersachsen.de/blob/images/C793204_L20.pdf>) following the response to the fire on board the *Pallas,* an accident which occurred in October 1998 at the Danish/German North Sea Coast and resulted into the total loss of the ship and subsequent pollution. The investigation report identifies among other also insufficient coordination and competition of different involved administrations. One suggestion (Recommendation No. 2, at 77) to overcome such problems in future was to create one central response command that has the overruling authority in response activities to disasters at the German coast.

granted in all countries that were covered in the survey. However, this does not mean that refuge was also never refused on specific occasions. When asked to specify occasions when refuge was granted, it seemed to be difficult or impracticable to distinguish between a distress situation where the Search and Rescue (SAR) Convention applies,[24] where countries are obliged to provide assistance to the crew, and "normal" incidents where the ship is so far only in need of assistance and not in imminent danger. The results of granting refuge are diverse. Nine survey participants indicated that cases in their countries resulted in minor damage; two indicated that major damage occurred at some time. Only participants from countries that faced environmental damage resulting from granting refuge were asked to comment on changes of regulations as a result of such an incident. Remarkably enough, 16 survey participants replied. Rules and procedures, however, were only changed in two countries, where the system in these countries was not completely changed but amended in order to incorporate lessons learned. It is not quite clear if a thorough evaluation of individual cases is made in different countries in order to learn lessons for the future. In this respect no evidence is given that granting refuge is not considered as an option any longer and that support to a ship in need of assistance is only given in terms of the evacuation of the crew.

Another indicator that dealing with granting refuge is a delicate issue is confirmed by two other questions in this section. Eight survey participants indicated that they would not grant refuge if the level of risk is unclear or cannot be confidently estimated. Ten survey participants also indicated that special conditions can be posed on ships in question, e.g., maintaining a minimum distance from the coastline, thus reducing the risk.

Legal Framework for Places of Refuge

The section on the legal framework of the questionnaire was inserted in order to find out if there are obligations in domestic law to deal with granting refuge and if this would have an impact on the overall system of a coastal State to grant or refuse refuge.

A majority of survey participants (17 of 27–63%) indicated that there are policies for granting refuge in their countries. Other participants did not specifically mention current policies, but comments made allow for the conclusion that policies are under development in a number of countries. Results of this question showed that in those 17 countries that have a policy,

---

24. *International Convention on Maritime Search and Rescue*, IMO Convention, adopted on 27 April 1979.

the objective is to avoid damage to persons, the ship, the cargo and the environment.[25]

Guidelines for Granting Refuge

The most interesting section, as far as this article is concerned, is certainly the section about guidelines assisting the decision-making process for granting refuge. Fifteen survey participants (56%) confirmed that guidelines are available in their countries and two more participants pointed out specifically that guidelines were currently under development. The questions in the guideline section were aimed at obtaining information about the contents of the guidelines in order to draw conclusions about the nature of risk assessment carried out prior to making a decision about the granting or refusal of refuge.

An important question in this respect is the question about preconditions to be met by ships to be considered for refuge. The majority of survey participants from administrations with guidelines (8 of 15–53%) stated that no specific preconditions have to be met. The criteria to be observed by the remaining 7 survey participants were specific cargoes that would not qualify for refuge and specific flags (because of Port State Control (PSC) statistics) that would not qualify. In addition, appropriate insurance coverage was mentioned and in one case, criteria that were defined by individual port committees. These port committees are part of the decision-making framework in the United States. As such they can outline the criteria that a port captain needs to take into consideration when asked to grant refuge to a ship in need of assistance.

The following questions in this section focused on additional information having an influence on the decision-making process, such as surveys on the ship in question, review of relevant documents, involvement of experts and other useful information to be considered in the decision-making process. In summary, most survey participants (14 of the 15 with guidelines—86%) considered surveys on the ship in question as essential. Seven participants explained they would prefer to carry out as many surveys as possible. This attitude does not fully apply to document review. Only seven participants indicated that any kind of document review is carried out, most likely documentation from classification societies and insurance companies. Expert opinion in the decision-making process is viewed as very essential. All 15 participants from administrations having guidelines confirmed that they would rely on expert opinion, and 14 of them (93%) would also include

25. This was confirmed by 11 (64%) out of 17 survey participants from countries with a policy for granting refuge that commented on this question.

external experts, such as salvors, class experts, etc. Other information is regarded as valuable, too. Twelve participants (81%) underlined that additional information about the ship and the shipping company (e.g., history of the ship, the company, etc.) would be taken into consideration during the decision-making process on the granting or the refusing of refuge to a ship in need of assistance. Apart from the uniformity with which some questions were answered, there was an indication that a number of national specific characteristics in the decision-making process must be taken into account. One participant pointed out that in addition to the assessment of the ship, an assessment of the impact of the cargo on the local population would be carried out. Hazardous cargo polluting the environment of a small country can create significant problems for such a country. Similar observations were made in comments provided by other participants.

Follow-up to IMO Res. A.949(23)

The last section of the survey focused on the follow-up to IMO Res. A.949(23)[26] in order to find out if, due to this resolution, changes were stimulated in the systems of countries to decide about requests for refuge for ships in need of assistance. In addition, survey participants from countries with no current guidelines for granting refuge were asked about how such guidelines would look in their countries.

The first question in this section focused on the general approach followed in granting refuge. The results are shown in Figure 2 below. Countries are usually following one of the three main philosophies of including places of refuge in contingency plans. A ship can either be directed to a pre-allocated place of refuge on a coastline, which has been specifically designated and assessed for these purposes, or a suitable place of refuge assigned according to the specific situation (having cargo, status of the ship and environmental suitability in mind). This can be done either based on a previous assessment of the coastline, as suggested by IMO, or on a spontaneous basis due to a high degree of practical knowledge of the coastline. The third option is that a combined approach of fixed places of refuge and potential places of refuge is chosen.

At least in the countries of the survey participants, no general trend could be identified as to which approach is applied when refuge is granted. Based on some comments and discussions, it seems that a high degree of flexibility is appreciated by the participants. This was pointed out by the five participants who ticked the category "Others." The next question in this

26. IMO Res. A.949(23), n. 17 above.

FIG. 2.—**Overview of the Different Philosophies to Grant Refuge Applied in the Survey Countries**

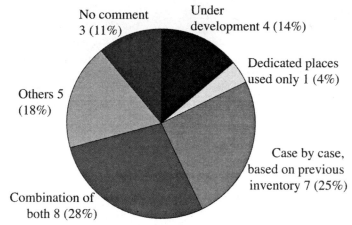

Source: J.-U. Schröder, "Review of Decision-Making by Maritime Administrations for Ships in Need of Assistance—Lessons for Risk Assessment," in *Places of Refuge for Ships: Emerging Environmental Concerns of a Maritime Custom,* ed. A. Chircop and O. Lindén (Leiden: Martinus Nijhoff Publishers, an imprint of Koniklijke Brill N.V., 2005): 110.

section was intended to find out if IMO Res. 949(23) would stimulate some changes in the current systems. Twelve participants (44%) do not want to change their systems. Other participants indicated that they do not have a system or have just started to prepare appropriate systems to deal with granting refuge for ships in need of assistance. Only three participants (11%) indicated that their systems were amended according to IMO Res. 949(23). It is, however, too early for general statements about the implications of IMO Res. 949(23) on the practice of granting refuge. In this respect it has to be noted that the EC has made the IMO requirements mandatory for the EU coastal member States.[27] There is no indication yet if this will lead to major changes of the existing procedures about granting refuge in the member countries of the EU.

The remaining questions focused on the potential content of guidelines in those countries that currently do not have guidelines for granting refuge to ships in need of assistance. The questions in this section were identical to the questions in the previous section when participants from countries with guidelines were asked about the requirements in their countries. The answers provided in this section were compared to the

27. Directive 2002/59/EC, n. 17 above, refer in particular to article 20.

answers provided by survey participants from countries with guidelines. The comparison seems to allow for two conclusions:

- Guidelines have been developed as a reactive measure to limit future impact of failed attempts to mitigate accidents through providing a place of refuge for a ship in need of assistance.
- The more affected a certain region was in the past with the issue of places of refuge, the more detailed the guidelines are.

Supporting evidence for the conclusion can be drawn from the following comparisons. Ten (84%) of 12 survey participants from administrations without guidelines did not specify preconditions to be met for granting refuge. Only 48% of administrations surveyed with guidelines have not identified specific preconditions to be met. Seven participants (58%) indicated that surveys should be carried out in order to support the decision-making process to grant refuge (compared to 86% of participants from administrations with guidelines opting for multiple surveys). Ten participants (83%) opted for the involvement of expert judgment, compared to 100% from administrations with guidelines about the involvement of technical experts in the decision-making process.

Conclusions about Risk Assessment in Connection with Granting Refuge to Ships in Need of Assistance

The WMU survey provides data for a number of previous assumptions about granting refuge. Although a number of participants from coastal States that have been subject to a number of requests for refuge in the past supplied information in the survey, participants from countries that most recently have been affected negatively by granting refuge, like France, Spain, and Portugal, chose not to participate in the survey. This had an effect on the results of the survey. Another factor, which should not be underestimated, is the issue that only administrations in charge of granting refuge were approached in this survey. It was greatly appreciated that they reacted positively to this survey. However, the level of detail in the responses was quite diverse and does not always allow for detailed general conclusions. This, most likely, applies to questions with regard to the follow-up of unsuccessful attempts to support ships in need of assistance.

In general, the approaches to grant refuge described by the survey participants vary significantly. As shown in Figure 1, there is no "typical" system of dealing with requests for refuge. Interpreting the answers freely, it seems that in general elaborate response systems to deal with requests for refuge were established in countries that have been approached more frequently. This is supported through the level of detail in the answers and the additional documentation provided in the survey from countries like Australia, South Africa, the United Kingdom and the United States. It seems that in those countries negative experience was one of the driving forces to establish administrative structures for efficient response.[28] Although not previously affected by large oil pollution, Finland has opted for a similar way by delegating all responsibilities to the Finnish Environmental Institute. However, two neighboring countries, Denmark and Sweden, still maintain a system of shared responsibilities between different ministries. Least formalized structures for the response have been reported from countries that so far have not been affected by large pollution and where granting refuge is still largely under the authority of the harbormaster. Decision-making is influenced by the severity of the incident and the experience of the person in charge. This seems to be an area of concern.

A similar situation was identified regarding guidelines for granting refuge. The spectrum of information provided to questions related to this issue varied from elaborate procedures to personnel experience and capabilities only. It also seems here that negative experience and/or public sensitivity are driving forces behind elaborate risk assessment procedures.

Although the answers provided to this survey vary in detail and depth, the following conclusions can be carefully drawn:

- Quantification of instances concerning granting refuge for ships in need of assistance is difficult. This has an impact on the perceived relevance of the subject. It also affects efficient handling of the rare instances when refuge is requested.
- Guidelines have been developed as a follow-up to a number of requests to grant refuge in certain countries. As a result, a number of different approaches, varying in detail and methodology used have been developed worldwide.
- As a consequence of the previous two observations, risk assessment methodologies were included in guidelines in a very diverse manner ranging from very simple to quite elaborate scientific methodologies. The question remains: What are suitable approaches to risk assessment in connection with granting refuge to ships in need of assistance?
- Apart from IMO Res. 949(23), no detailed global standards are available on risk assessment for places of refuge. One question to be

---

28. Prior to the already mentioned accident of the *Pallas* in 1998 at the German coast leading to the demand for a single response centre, a similar request was made in the United Kingdom during the follow-up to the *Sea Empress* disaster in 1996 subsequently resulting in the establishment of the Secretary of States Representative (SOSREP).

asked is, if such standards should be further developed? Would more detailed global standards help or shall global standards remain on a more general level? Should regional approaches be expedited in addition to the IMO standards in order to allow for a more specific consideration of regional and national particularities?

These conclusions will be further discussed in the following sections of this article.

QUANTIFICATION OF THE ISSUE GRANTING OF REFUGE

Every risk assessment methodology, no matter for which purposes, and no matter in which industry or in which other field, has to deal with the issue of quantification of a hazard or threat. This naturally applies to risk assessment for places of refuge too. Quantification is necessary in order to estimate the significance of an issue in the whole risk assessment process. The objective of risk assessment is to determine the level of risk based on frequency/ likelihood of an event to occur and the severity of consequences resulting from such an event. The risk is usually displayed in a risk matrix and can be accepted if it is in the so-called "as low as reasonably practicable" (ALARP) area.[29] Based on the likelihood-consequence relationship for hazardous events, appropriate RCOs are identified and implemented. The higher the risk the more extensive and the more expensive RCOs can be. This general methodology certainly applies when a decision has to be made whether refuge can be granted or not. The question therefore is, how can risk involved in granting refuge to a ship in need of assistance be quantified?

As already mentioned in the introduction, there are a number of prominent cases that vaulted to the title pages of newspapers in recent years causing some subjective speculation about maritime safety in general. These prominent examples, however, only represent the tip of the iceberg—the worst-case scenario. They are not typical. If decision-makers focus only on these well-known and well-documented cases, then unjustified and unbalanced decisions will result.[30] What we know at the least from Heinrich's studies out of the 1930s,[31] is that before a major catastrophe occurs at least

---

29. Guidelines for Formal Safety Assessment (FSA) for Use in the IMO Rule-Making Process, IMO Doc. MSC/Circ. 1023, MEPC/Circ. 392, 5 April 2002.

30. See n. 13 above.

31. H. W. Heinrich, *Industrial Accident Prevention—a Scientific Approach* (New York, London: McGraw-Hill Insurance Series, 1931). Although not the most recent findings, Heinrich's figures are still referred to in a number of safety assessment related publications (refer, e.g., to S. Kristiansen, *Maritime Transportation—Safety Management and Risk Analysis* (Burlington: Elsevier Butterworth-Heinemann, 2005): 417; S. Sagen, *The ISM Code—in Practice* (Oslo: Tano Aschehoug, 1999): 127. Other authors suggest different figures, which is not critical as long as the principle of

30 minor accidents, 300 near accidents and 3,000 unsafe acts and conditions are pointing towards the likelihood of a major catastrophe occurring for the same causes. It is only an unfortunate combination of circumstances that enables the major catastrophe, but the basic causes are the same. A single major catastrophe is therefore not a representative case. The number of minor accidents is much more significant and those incidents should be analyzed much more carefully in order to allow for a more objective RCO determination. But how can data about such accidents be gathered? Some administrations are able to quantify requests for places of refuge,[32] but this is unfortunately an exception. There are no large-scale statistics available about requests, nature of damage, follow-up activities and results of support given. In addition, another problem exists. There is no international legal obligation to inform a coastal State about repairs carried out by a ship in its territorial waters.[33] Non-critical damage occurs in every technical system and has to be repaired. If it affects the engine, ships often stop and drift while undergoing the repair work. If the ship is in territorial waters it interrupts the innocent passage, but from a legal point of view, this is considered as *force majeure.* In most of the cases nothing will happen and the ship finishes repairs and continues its voyage. However, by a certain combination of circumstances a severe development is possible. There have been cases where coastal States were eventually asked for support when it was already too late.[34] There are certainly many good reasons why not every individual repair should be announced to the coastal State in whose waters the repair is carried out. But as a result these coastal States lose preparation time in case the damage to be repaired is more serious than expected and affects vital systems of the ship. Another set of interesting data for risk assessment is therefore not available. While the number of minor accidents happening at places of refuge can still be estimated, the number of near accidents (when ships carry out repairs) is simply unknown. This does of course not help when the overall risk of granting refuge is focused on.

occurrence of incidents relative to accidents is not questioned. The individual estimates of the different frequencies of incidents relative to accidents are influenced by definitions, transportation modes, and other conditions.

32. National Plan Management Committee, *National Maritime Places of Refuge Guidelines* (Canberra: National Plan Management Committee, 2002).

33. However, some countries have regulations that require a notification in case of an accident that affects the seaworthiness in their territorial waters. In the United States such a notification is due via the agency of the ship in question, when a marine casualty or incident occurs according to: Code of Federal Regulations, Title 46 Shipping, Part 4 Marine Casualties and Investigations, Para. 4.05–1 (2004).

34. Tanker accidents like the grounding of the *Amoco Cadiz* in 1978 or the grounding of the *Braer* in 1993 (both accidents involved the loss of steering or propulsion prior to the grounding) can be referred to when underestimation of potential consequences of the loss of key technical systems in ships is concerned.

How could such a situation be overcome? The Automatic Identification System (AIS) technology offers a variety of opportunities including improved chances to determine the number of "near-refuge" cases. AIS data are currently stored by a number of maritime administrations for evaluation purposes.[35] So far no attempt has been made to identify the number of anchoring ships (outside roads of ports and not waiting for orders) or drifting ships (not waiting for orders). This number would not automatically mean that all ships identified are automatically in need of assistance. Further studies would be necessary in order to find out exactly how many of these ships are undergoing repairs, etc. For a first indication in risk assessment, however, this number might be used. (With precaution, but better than only relying on pure expert opinion—a combination of both could be helpful in a first instance.) Recent requests to some parties storing AIS data unfortunately did not provide the desired data.[36] Further lobbying is necessary in order to allow for more detailed studies on the available data. More technical issues to facilitate risk assessment are discussed later in this article.

GUIDELINES FOR PLACES OF REFUGE

Like many other areas linked to maritime safety, accidents have been a driving force behind guidelines for risk assessment involved in granting refuge to ships in need of assistance. The IMO has dealt with these issues since the 1980s, but began more thorough discussions about places of refuge following the already mentioned accidents mentioned at the beginning of this article. As a result of these discussions, the IMO has adopted the Resolutions R.949(23)[37] and R.950(23)[38] in order to support maritime administrations charged with reviewing a request for refuge from ships in need of assistance. While the first resolution deals with guidelines of how refuge should be granted, the second resolution attempts to streamline the process of providing assistance to ships in danger by establishing a single point of contact in coastal States for these ships to call. The IMO guidelines

---

35. As an example the Danish Maritime Administration stores these data on behalf of HELCOM for the entire Baltic Sea area.

36. For the purpose of this article only HELCOM and the United Kingdom Secretary of States Representative (SOSREP) were approached. Both confirmed that they do not have these specific data yet. The responsible HELCOM party expressed an interest to look further into this matter.

37. IMO Res. A.949(23), n. 17 above.

38. Maritime Assistance Services (MAS), IMO Assembly Resolution A.950(23), Adopted on 5 December 2003, IMO Doc. A 23/Res. 949, 26 February 2004.

dedicate a whole section of Res. 949(23) to risk assessment. A twofold approach is suggested in the guidelines:

- Generic assessment and preparatory measures regardless of whether requests for refuge are expected or not; and
- Event-specific assessment when a ship calls for refuge.

Whereas the first step can be seen as contingency planning, in order to ensure an effective response to a request for refuge by a ship in need of assistance, the second step deals with a concrete request that can then be handled on the basis of the results of the first step.

IMO Res. A. 949(23) is an achievement insofar as it is the first international document recognizing the need to provide guidance on risk assessment for places of refuge, especially to those administrations that were not confronted with requests for refuge by ships in need of assistance or administrations that preferred not to deal with this matter in the past. As with all IMO documents, it represents the least common denominator. The guidelines therefore remain at a general level.

Thus, in a number of countries, detailed guidelines are missing. In addition, existing guidelines usually only list a number of issues to be considered without priorities to be observed. Is this efficient? The argument that is raised against stricter and more detailed guidelines is the argument of flexibility. Practitioners in countries with a solid knowledge base and expertise with granting refuge argue that decisions about the granting or the refusing of refuge sometimes have to be made within 30 minutes. In other words, complicated and formalized risk assessment would slow down such a process. The argument against this is certainly that, although it is acceptable in countries that have a long and successful record of dealing with requests to grant refuge, administrations with no or less expertise could be supported in decision-making through more elaborate guidelines. Both surveys mentioned before have not specifically addressed this issue. However, as mentioned earlier in this article, 8 out of 27 (30%) respondents of the WMU survey pointed out that they would not grant refuge if they could not clearly identify the level of risk involved. More formal guidelines for risk assessment, allowing for a more transparent risk evaluation, could help in this respect to increase the willingness of dealing with requests for a place of refuge.

RISK ASSESSMENT METHODOLOGIES

In the previous two sections of the article a number of issues influencing the complexity of risk assessment in connection with granting refuge were highlighted. The most important factors in this respect are:

- Requests for a place of refuge for a ship in need of assistance can be considered as relatively rare events. Because of this it is stochastically very likely that all cases are different. Therefore (with a few exemptions only) most administrations confronted with such a request will not house an extensive knowledge base of how to deal with such a request.
- The complexity of individual cases may require close (interdisciplinary) cooperation between different administrations in order to assess potential effects when efforts to provide assistance to a ship fail.
- Many decisions need to be made in a very short time. Practitioners therefore prefer to have a high degree of flexibility in the whole decision-making process. Formal guidelines are sometimes seen as a measure limiting flexibility and subsequently chances of success for effective support to a ship in need of assistance.

The question therefore is how established risk assessment methodologies can support the decision-making process for granting refuge to a ship in need of assistance without creating additional burdens and formalities leading to the loss of valuable time when a fast decision is needed. Proper risk assessment has advantages that should not be underestimated:

- Formalized risk assessment can provide guidance to less experienced groups that have to make a decision, which is a likely case for many maritime administrations.
- Formal risk assessment allows for transparency, which is important especially when measures to support a vessel in need of assistance fail and cause environmental pollution.
- Due to the transparency involved, an improvement of the whole system as a follow-up to individual instances is much easier than without a formal system.[39]

In the next section a very brief overview about current risk assessment methodologies is given aiming at a wider discussion in the context of places of refuge.

---

39. Quality Assurance Systems whose benefits are widely recognized follow similar principles.

Currently Practiced Risk Assessment Methodologies for Places of Refuge

Risk assessment in general aims at identifying the individual level of risk involved in, or resulting from, a certain operation, in order to allow for a decision about whether this operation should be carried out or not. Risk assessment methodologies can be subdivided into quantitative and qualitative risk assessment. Qualitative risk assessment methodologies are often also called subjective risk assessment methodologies because the basis of all these approaches is expert judgment. Quantitative risk assessment, contrary to qualitative risk assessment, aims at providing statistically or stochastically based calculations on the probability and/or consequences of an incident. They have been primarily developed for highly sensitive technical applications, such as nuclear power plants, medical applications or aviation. Referring to previous parts of this article it can be concluded that given the nature of spontaneous decisions involved in any request for a place of refuge qualitative risk assessment will, in most cases, be the tool that is used for evaluating whether the request can be met or has to be refused. Unless an administration in charge of the risk assessment process is willing to build up a comprehensive data pool, in most cases expert judgment is the only source for reasoning under uncertainty. This was reflected in the answers of the WMU survey. In most countries surveyed, expert judgment (partly supported by checklists and other decision supporting material, i.e., contingency plans, etc.) is used in order to come to a decision whether refuge can be granted or not.

A more elaborate formal risk assessment methodology for refuge is suggested by the Spanish administration in charge of places of refuge.[40] This is the only formal risk assessment methodology involving quantitative techniques, worldwide, that the author is aware of. The Spanish approach is hereby following a simple safety matrix assessment, which is also used in other IMO documents,[41] as a suggestion for comprehensive safety assessment. Based on statistics about certain incidents and consequences, with the objective to distinguish between dangerous and less dangerous events, a step-by-step assessment approach is suggested. In order to facilitate the methodology, a matrix and an event tree approach are followed. The matrix approach aims at establishing a standard risk matrix showing the individual level of risk for a certain event. The tree approach is followed to have a

---

40. G. Gomez Barquin, "Methodology for Risk Assessment in Coastal Zones in Spain," (paper presented at the International Workshop on Places of Refuge, University of Antwerp, Antwerp, 11 December 2003), available online: <http://www.espo.be/news/2003/events/Gonzalo%20Gómez%20Barquín.pdf>.
41. IMO FSA Guidelines, n. 29 above.

better understanding of the potential development of an incident (e.g., different types of maritime casualties and their consequences, such as focusing on which developments may result from a blackout—the ship could start drifting, run aground and with a certain impact of waves, break into two parts and cause an oil spill, etc.). This approach needs some preconditions for the implementation. The first precondition is a detailed database about maritime incidents—their origins, developments and consequences. The second precondition is a very detailed stocktaking of the coastline in order to assess the suitability of places along the coastline for different refuge scenarios (i.e., maximum draft of ships in need of assistance, types of cargo that can be accepted at this place in terms of potential danger to the environment, etc.), and the location of pollution-combating equipment to be used at this place. Reliable risk assessment can be carried out only if both preconditions are taken into consideration. This is the Achilles' heel of this methodology. Insufficient accident data will have an impact on the accuracy of risk estimated. This very formal approach certainly goes beyond most other published risk assessment methodologies for places of refuge. However, it is in contrast to the requirement of flexibility that many administrations prefer when facing a request for refuge by a ship in need of assistance.

Looking at the above, the resulting question is, how elaborate and strict does risk assessment for granting refuge have to be? According to the survey participants risk assessment should allow for flexibility. A detailed risk assessment protocol may therefore be too restrictive, especially considering the lacking data support from historical incidents. At the same time some guidance should be given. So what is needed can be characterized as a decision support tool. This tool could consist of a database containing details about requests for refuge in terms of:

- Ship particulars;
- Reasons for the request of assistance;
- Circumstances under which refuge was granted or refused;
- Particulars of the coastline where the ship was given refuge;
- Response activities to support the ship; and
- Outcome of the support activities.

An extensive and sufficiently detailed database could help administrations that have to react to a request for refuge to see how other administrations reacted and moreover, if such a data pool is maintained by more than one country, provide for the opportunity to contact another administration that had to deal with a similar request for advice.

This database should be embedded in a loose framework of procedures, which in line with the IMO requirements, provides for efficient response in terms of risk acceptance criteria, coordination with other parties involved in the response to a request for refuge, dealing with oil combating equipment, etc.

Data to Support Risk Assessment for Places of Refuge

How can a database as outlined above be established? Basic accident data can be gathered on a regional or international basis. There are more and more efforts to obtain more detailed standardized accident and incident data. The IMO maintains its Global Integrated Shipping Information System (GISIS).[42] The information about accidents and incidents could be filtered in order to allow for a display of accidents following requests for refuge. In this respect the IMO should develop a data scheme for reporting on such accidents and incidents. This could help to build up a worldwide database on places of refuge. In order to allow for better regional cooperation databases at a lower level are imaginable. HELCOM is collecting basic data for the Baltic Sea. The European Maritime Safety Agency (EMSA) has recently started to build up a database on maritime accidents and casualties as well. Since EMSA is expected to play a leading role in oil pollution response in European waters it would be quite natural if this database would support risk assessment for places for refuge.

Concrete decision support, apart from basic factual descriptions of previous accidents, could be given through Bayesian network calculations. Bayesian networks have a long tradition of use in risk assessment.[43] Their strength is that they can combine data retrieved from studies and expert opinion and show levels of the risk involved in different approaches to a particular problem. The problem here, of course, is that the accuracy of the calculations relies on the quality of the data.

Technology Use in Support of Data Gathering for Risk Assessment

Apart from focusing on accident and incident reports one should consider improved opportunities from recent technologies. A number of interesting technologies exist that are used for maritime safety purposes (e.g., the above-mentioned AIS), but not in relation to places of refuge. Besides AIS, Geographic Information Systems (GIS) provides further opportunities to

42. Available online: <http://gisis.imo.org/Public/>.

43. A. Friis-Hansen, "Bayesian Networks as a Decision Support Tool in Marine Applications," (Ph.D. diss., Technical University of Denmark, 2000), available online: <http://www.mt.mek.dtu.dk/reports/PHDthesis/pdf/afh.pdf>.

gather and organize data for risk assessment purposes related to places of refuge.

AIS is primarily a technical system used in shipping in order to increase maritime safety by providing a set of data (e.g., ships' name, gross tonnage, speed, destination, etc.) available to Vessel Traffic Service (VTS) centers and ships. AIS data can also be used for risk assessment purposes. This is currently done through the identification of high-risk areas in maritime traffic.[44] The data can be used to identify current high-risk areas or for traffic simulation purposes.[45] The results of such surveys can be displayed on navigational charts. However, first of all they can be used for contingency planning; HELCOM has established an expert working group on tanker transit routes through the Baltic. A transit route concept could include fixed places of refuge and related to this, response forces and materials could be located accordingly.[46] Denmark has considered contingency planning where places of refuge were identified in Danish waters.[47] Twenty-two places of refuge have been preliminarily established in Danish waters, located in a way that ships in need of assistance in Danish waters do not have to cross unnecessarily long distances to a particular place of refuge. Oil pollution response vessels and shore-based equipment have been allocated accordingly. However, the authorities in Denmark have not only focused on the preliminarily designated places of refuge. Support, if necessary, can also be given outside these areas. As the report about the allocation of places of refuge in Denmark points out, the current designated places of refuge reflect the present risk situation. A review is to be carried out from time-to-time in order to reassess the suitability of arrangements in Danish waters with AIS data being a vital part of these considerations.

Another tool that can be used in combination with AIS data is GIS. The GIS covers a wide range of systems, e.g., hardware, software, data that are

44. An application example in the Baltic Sea is described in: R. Mueller, A. Zoelder and F. Hartmann, "Historical AIS Data Use for Navigational Aids," *Hansa International Maritime Journal* 142, no. 1 (2005): 14–21.

45. T. Rosqvist, T. Nyman, S. Sonninen and R. Tuominen, "The Implementation of the VTMIS System for the Gulf of Finland—A FSA Study," in *Royal Institution of Naval Architects (RINA) International Conference on Formal Safety Assessment, London 18–19 September 2002* (London: RINA, 2002): 151–164. Although no AIS data were used for this particular project, AIS data would certainly improve the accuracy of such simulations. The traffic simulation in this project was carried out by GRACAT, a software tool developed at the Technical University of Denmark <http://www.mt.mek.dtu.dk/gracat/>.

46. Such a wide scope of a transit route is unfortunately currently not considered by the expert working group. So far routing measures have been suggested only.

47. Miljostyrelsen: "*Redegorelse om udpegning af nodområder i de danske farvande,*" available online: <http://www.mst.dk/default.asp?Sub=http://www.mst.dk/udgiv/publikationer/2004/8 7–7614–145–4/html/>.

used to gather, administer, analyze and show spatial data. GIS is used in a number of industries in order to combine geographical data with other information relevant for the specific application in focus. GIS is, for instance, used for maritime environmental protection services and traffic risk analysis.[48] Examples are HELCOM's Maritime Accident Response Information System (MARIS)[49] and the Canadian software tool Maritime Activity and Risk Investigation System (MARIS).[50] The HELCOM MARIS is a web-based software tool used to combine geographical data, such as accidents that have occurred in the past or results of traffic flow simulations, in order to visualize risk areas in the Baltic. In addition, ports and terminals are shown as well as the allocation of oil spill combating forces and tools.

This tool can be considered as a decision support tool in line with the requirements of this article. It should be extended in order to include information about previous requests for refuge and related data. This could further support administrations in the Baltic region. This might, however, not be necessary, as there is a very close cooperation within HELCOM and involved administrations are informed about incidents in the Baltic. The Canadian MARIS software aims at achieving the same objective, although the main scope is not so much the response to oil spills, but Search and Rescue (SAR). However, both software tools demonstrate how risk analysis can be combined with geographical data in order to provide enhanced visualized decision support tools that could also be used for places of refuge. Other countries, like the United Kingdom or countries in the North Sea region, have similar services in place. Such a development is in contrast with a number of countries surveyed in the WMU survey that allocates places of refuge in a flexible way without having such a formal data basis for the coastline.

Stakeholder Participation in Risk Assessment for Places of Refuge

One important issue in the process of granting refuge is certainly the issue of risk acceptance criteria. Who defines what is considered an acceptable risk? The key problem here is the divided view of different stakeholders of the wider coastal and ocean zone framework on the issue of granting refuge.

---

48. J. Shahrabi and R. P. Pelot, "Geographic Information Services in Coastal Management, with Applications of Spatial Analysis to Marine Traffic in Canada," (paper presented at the 1st International Management Conference, Tehran, Sharif University, 29–31 December 2003).

49. For further information refer to the HELCOM MARIS webpage: <http://62.236.121.188/website/maris/viewer.htm>.

50. For further information refer to the MARIS webpage: <http://www.marin-research.ca/english/maris_software/index.html>.

According to Cicin-Sain and Knecht, there still exist separate views on the coastal and on the ocean zone.[51] Whereas the ocean zone is very much dominated by maritime administration issues, the coastal zone is dominated by coastal use issues, such as fisheries, environmental conservation, tourism and others. The borderline between ocean and coast has unfortunately also created a borderline for responsibilities. It is therefore quite complicated to deal with issues like places of refuge within such a framework where granting refuge clearly goes beyond traditional ocean use. This was also reflected in the answers to the WMU survey. Whereas maritime administrations, on a central level, still dominate decision making for places of refuge, more and more countries have acknowledged the advantages of bringing together all stakeholders involved in ocean and coastal zone use. The frameworks, methodologies and approaches suggested within Integrated Coastal Zone Management are intended to allow for such an integrated approach. In this respect, one way to overcome potential local opposition, e.g., by the Agreement for Cooperation in Dealing with Pollution of the North Sea by Oil and Other Harmful Substances (Bonn Agreement) in its counter pollution manual,[52] would be to invite local stakeholders to join for the pre-selection of potential places of refuge. The selection of Danish places of refuge was carried out as a joint effort of various ministries (e.g., defense, transport, environment, and economic affairs).

An approach for the involvement of stakeholders in order to evaluate environmental consequences is Environmental Assessment, which was developed in the United States in the 1960s.[53] It has been further developed under the name Environmental Impact Assessment (EIA) for project influence evaluation.[54] Most recently, assessment of strategic decisions such as policies or plans, was suggested under the name Strategic Environmental Assessment (SEA).[55] Environmental assessment is not only mandatory in a number of countries, to a certain extent it can be compared to Formal Safety Assessment (FSA),[56] as it also only provides a framework of different

51. B. Cicin-Sain and R. W. Knecht, *Integrated Coastal and Ocean Management* (Washington, Covelo: Island Press, 1998).

52. Bonn Agreement, *Bonn Agreement Counter Pollution Manual,* available online: <http://www.bonnagreement.org/eng/html/counter-pollution_manual/welcome. html>. In Chapter 26 under point 26.1.4 the Manual acknowledges that "the designation and use of places of refuge could encounter local opposition and involve political decisions."

53. National Environmental Policy Act of 1969, as amended.

54. D. A. Tiwi, *Improving Environmental Impact Assessment for better Integrated Coastal Zone Management* (Lisse: A. A. Balkema Publishers, 2004).

55. M. A. Nilsson and H. Dalkmann, "Decision Making and Strategic Environmental Assessment," *Journal of Environmental Assessment Policy and Management* 3, no. 3 (September 2001): 305–327.

56. IMO FSA Guidelines, n. 29 above.

phases to be considered during the risk assessment. However, there is a consultation process involved that enables all stakeholders to raise their concerns. The application of EIA or SEA therefore seems to be more desirable when the pre-selection of potential places of refuge is carried out.

GLOBAL STANDARDS VERSUS REGIONAL AND NATIONAL APPROACHES

Regional aspects should, however, not only be considered when data collection is concerned. A general question to be asked is if there is a need for global standards and how could regional or national approaches contribute to the efficient granting of refuge to ships in need of assistance. As mentioned in earlier parts of this article, IMO set the global standards for places of refuge through its Res. A.949(23).[57] It was mentioned that a number of regional agreements exist in order to deal with granting refuge. The strength of regional and national approaches is that local specifics can be taken into account in a significantly better way than on a global level. This applies especially to risk perception or geographic areas of protection. This is where the author believes that regional and national approaches could support the IMO initiatives best. As mentioned in earlier parts of this article, regional agreements within the EU or HELCOM can provide for mandatory consideration of the IMO guidelines. In addition, they can support risk assessment in a larger context through regional cooperation. The previously mentioned HELCOM MARIS software is a good example. Together with other HELCOM arrangements, like enhanced cooperation during combating oil spills, for instance, a powerful set of risk barriers exist in order to limit potential severe consequences at a place of refuge in the Baltic. The Baltic is not the only example of regional cooperation; similar arrangements exist in other parts of the world. These regional arrangements should be intensified and extended.

SUMMARY AND CONCLUSIONS

This article is intended to contribute to the discussion concerning the risk and uncertainty involved in decisions related to requests for refuge by ships in need of assistance. Based on a review of the current practice of granting refuge, some principle remarks about risk assessment have been introduced. In addition, a review of risk assessment, as currently practiced, has been carried out and areas for improvement identified. The issues addressed in

---

57. IMO Res. A.949(23), n. 16 above.

this article with regard to risk assessment have focused mainly on the quantification aspects of granting refuge, the development of guidelines, and new technologies supporting enhanced risk assessment.

The challenge in risk assessment for places of refuge is that it seems, on the one hand, to be desirable to have a more formal guidance framework for risk assessment. This could support especially inexperienced administrations in charge of dealing with requests for refuge. On the other hand, practitioners point out that most cases are different from each other, requiring quick decisions to be made that necessitates a high degree of flexibility. For these reasons strict and formal rules for risk assessment could slow down the decision-making process. Taking this into account a loose procedural framework is suggested. This framework should contain a decision support tool in the form of a database about outcomes of previous requests for refuge in similar situations. Such a tool could, if sufficient data are available, provide guidance for less experienced administrations without limiting flexibility. The key issue is, how to develop such a detailed database? In this respect IMO should take a leading role and extend its present GISIS. Additional regional arrangements can facilitate these efforts.

It is suggested that dealing with places of refuge should be a proactive process. This means that prior to any request for refuge, general preparations should have been made by the administrations in charge of these matters. In other words, proactive allocation of potential places of refuge can save time and help to balance coastal community interests against the potential damage to be expected from unsuccessful support to a ship in need of assistance at a place of refuge. For these reasons all stakeholders should be invited to provide input for such a balanced and transparent decision about the pre-selection of potential places of refuge along a certain coastline. There is a significant need in many countries for all the stakeholders of the coastal community to be better integrated. Modern technology, such as AIS and GIS can facilitate risk assessment in coastal communities.

In this respect the issue of places of refuge should not be understood as a threat but rather an opportunity for the better integration of stakeholders in a coastal community so as to provide enhanced, transparent and subsequently (hopefully), more acceptable risk assessment at places of refuge.

Education and Training

Public Education: Seeking to Engender Marine Stewardship at the U.K. National Maritime Museum

David E. Johnson*
Southampton Solent University, Southampton, United Kingdom

Jonathan S. Potts
National Maritime Museum, Greenwich, United Kingdom

INTRODUCTION

The aim of this article is to report on research undertaken to inform and underpin the U.K. National Maritime Museum's (NMM's) *Planet Ocean* initiative. *Planet Ocean* themes include the oceans and environmental change; biodiversity and sustainable development; and deep-sea exploration, navigation and discovery, media and the environment, and public citizenship and community stewardship. This initiative reflects the Museum's aim to not be bound to a narrow historic focus but to portray contemporary issues in increasingly innovative, inclusive and inspiring ways. The research has provided an opportunity to analyse and evaluate public awareness of the marine environment and to clarify the public's concerns regarding its sustainable future. This has been achieved through a literature review, structured interviews with acknowledged experts and a programme of visits to maritime museums around the world.

Traditionally ethnographic research has been used extensively to assess interpretative frameworks.[1] Analyses of visitor surveys and observation of on-site behaviour highlight the need to better explain the context of exhibits and fully illuminate milestones and events. Thus, much of the academic research into what is most effective in terms of interpretation lies within the

* Research support for this article was provided by a short-term Caird Research Fellowship from the National Maritime Museum. Elements of the research were presented at Littoral Conferences held in Porto, Portugal (2002) and Aberdeen, Scotland (2004).

1. C. Goulding, "Interpretation and Presentation," in *Heritage Visitor Attractions: An Operations Management Perspective*, eds. A. Leask and I. Yeoman (London: Cassell, 1999): 54–68.

Ocean Yearbook 20: 623–642

realm of environmental psychology. Museum visits are perceived as planned events within which the primary mode of activity is exploration.[2] Early studies recognised "attraction gradients," the pull of one exhibit over another, created by different exhibits and a consequent need to orient the visitor.[3] Attraction gradients are perceived to increase when sensory experiences are stimulated, with better lighting and by adding interactive features.[4] For the purposes of this research, a critical evaluation of the Monterey Bay Aquarium (MBA) and the latest U.K. marine attraction, *The Deep*, in Hull, is presented. The latter incorporates observational analysis of visitors, and structured interviews with management, visitors and locals, in order to provide further insight.

In addition, in order to assess interpretation effectiveness within the NMM *Planet Ocean* initiative, both visitors and exhibition displays have been evaluated on the basis of an analysis of learning styles and learning provision. This draws on a body of work by educational psychologists that has explored the linkages between personality and learning style.[5] Neil Flemming of Lincoln University, New Zealand has used work on neuro-linguistic programming,[6] to produce a VARK (visual, aural, read and write, kinesthetic [learning by doing]) questionnaire now regularly used in U.K. higher education.[7] The objective of the questionnaire is to determine individual preferences for taking in and communicating ideas and information. A survey of the learning preferences for 230 visitor groups to the NMM was undertaken during the summer of 2002. Subsequently, visitor priorities gathered from public reaction to the latest environmental gallery within the NMM have also been analysed.

INTERPRETATION AND THE WAY WE LEARN

Interpretation has been defined as "an activity, which aims to reveal meanings and relationships as an art, and revelations based upon informa-

2. P. A. Bell, T. C. Greene, J. D. Fisher and A. Baum, *Environmental Psychology*, 5th ed. (USA: Harcourt College Publishers, 2001).

3. E. S. Robinson, "The Behaviour of the Museum Visitor," *American Association of Museums New Series*, no. 5 (1928).

4. S. C. Bitgood and D. D. Patterson, "The Effects of Gallery Changes on Visitor Reading Time and Object Viewing Time," *Environment and Behaviour* 25 (1993): 761–781; M. L. Harvey, R. J. Loomis, P. A. Bell and M. Marino, "The Influence of Museum Exhibit Design on Immersion and Psychological Flow," *Environment and Behaviour* 30 (1998): 601–627.

5. G. Lawrence, *People Types and Tiger Stripes: A Practical Guide to Learning Styles* 2d ed. (Gainsville, Florida: Center for the Application of Psychological Type, 1982).

6. J. O'Connor and J. Seymour, *Introducing NLP* (London: Thorsons, 1995).

7. Available online: <http://www.vark-learn.com>.

tion whose aim is not instruction but provocation.''[8] Subsequent commentators have continued to emphasise the importance of the story (constructing images and conveying information), its context and continuity, combined with an understanding of visitor expectations.[9]

Within visitor attractions, audiences are perceived as active consumers. The product is a visitor experience based on learning in an informal environment achieved using exhibitions supported by relevant artefacts. Learning theory suggests interpretative material uses relatively advanced "learning steps," and that creators of exhibits should pay attention to the continual and dynamic nature of the learning process and learning behaviour.[10] Research into the development of learning objectives for visitor attractions has highlighted the importance of individuality of the interpretative experience[11] and the need to link learning concepts and principles (for a summary, see Table 1).[12] A clear distinction has been made between environmental education and environmental interpretation.[13]

Table 1.—Summary of Learning Concepts and Principles

LEARNING CONCEPTS	LEARNING PRINCIPLES
We all bring our pasts to the present	People learn better when they're actively involved in learning processes
Categories can blind us	People learn better when they're using as many senses as appropriate

8. F. Tilden, *Interpreting Our Heritage,* 3d ed. (Chapel Hill: University of North Carolina Press, 1977): 7. Tilden also maintained that any interpretation should connect its topic to something within the personality or experience of the visitors.

9. D. Uzzell, "The Hot Interpretation of War and Conflict," in *Heritage Interpretation Volume 1: The Natural and Built Environment,* ed. D. Uzzell (London: Belhaven Press, 1989), pp. 33–47; T. Stevens, "The Visitor—Who Cares? Interpretation and Consumer Relations," in *Heritage Interpretation Volume 2: The Visitor Experience,* ed. D. Uzzell (London: Belhaven Press, 1989): 103–107; G. Moscardo, "Mindful Visitors: Heritage and Tourism," *Annals of Tourism Research* 23, 2 (1996): 376–397; L. K. Zimmerman, "Knowledge, Affect and the Environment," *Journal of Environmental Education* 27, 3 (1996): 41–44; Goulding, n. 1 above, at 54–68.

10. A. L. Grinder and E. S. McCoy. *The Good Guide—A Source Book for Interpreters, Docents and Tour Guides* (Scottsdale Arizona: Ironwood Publishing, 1985).

11. J. H. Falk and L. D. Dierking, *The Museum Experience* (Washington D.C.: Whaleback Books, 1992).

12. J. A. Ververka, *Interpretive Master Planning* (Helena Montana: Falcon Press Publishing, 1994).

13. R. Ballantyne and D. Uzzell, "A Checklist for the Critical Evaluation of Informal Environmental Learning Experiences," in *A Sourcebook for Environmental Education: A Practical Review based on the Belgrade Charter,* eds. W. D. S. Leal Fiho, Z. Murphy and K. O'Loan (Carnforth: Parthenon/ERTCEE University of Bradford, 1995): 166–181.

LEARNING CONCEPTS	LEARNING PRINCIPLES
First impressions are especially important	People prefer to learn what has most relevance to them
Unless helped, we often fail to find, see or comprehend	Personal discovery produces excitement and satisfaction
To understand the parts, we must first see the whole	Learning requires activity on the part of the learner (cognitive and mindfulness)
Discovery makes learning fun	Friendly competition stimulates learning (most visitors attend in groups)
Meanings are in people not words	Knowing the usefulness of the knowledge makes learning effective
Information overload causes distortion and fatigue	People learn best from hands-on experience (or do they simply play for longer-research is inconclusive)
Simplicity and organisation clarify messages	Questions can help people derive meanings
A picture can paint a thousand words	Providing visitors with expectations focuses attention and improves learning. The ways in which people are responded to affects their learning

Source: Wallis, 1996 (adapted from Ververka, 1994).

An analysis of interpretation as a social experience argues that, above all, an interpretive visit must be an enjoyable leisure experience.[14] More recently the following trends in international interpretation have been identified:[15]

- Growing concern with theory in interpretive practice;
- Changes in environmental interpretation associated with the rise of ecotourism;
- Tension between homogeneity and uniqueness (as a reaction to globalisation);
- The need to interpret more contested issues and emotive heritage; and
- Adoption of a grassroots approach to interpretive planning.

14. L. Dierking, "Interpretation as a Social Experience," in *Contemporary Issues in Heritage & Environmental Interpretation*, eds. D. Uzzell and R. Ballantyne (London: The Stationary Office, 1998): 56–76.
15. R. Ballantyne and D. Uzzell, "International Trends in Heritage and Environmental Interpretation: Future Directions for Australian Research and Practice," *Journal of Environmental Research* 4, 1 (1999): 59–75.

Generally, however, the following fundamentals are accepted:[16]

- The importance of the story;
- The need to engage visitors in an emotional experience; and
- The creation of opportunities whereby visitors can question their prejudices.

Past Descriptions

Throughout history the marine environment has inspired literature and poetry, cinema and television, music, painting and photography. Our relationship with the sea is complex, one that has informed the public consciousness and associated values. The following explanatory text board introduced an exhibition of works in the U.K. by artists influenced by the beauty and power of the sea:

> The sea has been presented as a living entity, a higher and more powerful being, which at the same time supports its own life system. The sea has been personified as numerous gods and mythical characters and is frequently used as a means of expression through metaphor. Its changing tides, its unpredictability and its ability to nurture as well as destroy all add to its mysteriousness. These are just some of the aspects of the sea that have been absorbed into art forms, including visual arts, literature and music.[17]

On this basis we expect to find the sea represented in a variety of guises based on how it has been experienced by others. Key elements of association, drawn from both fiction and non-fiction, that illustrate such expectation, are identified in Table 2. Equally many representations focus on the way in which the sea has been used. An historical compilation of songs and poems of the sea asserted that "awakening of 'sea-magic' is a nineteenth century characteristic. Before Byron and Shelley not much was said or sung about the ocean [although]... of old it was ever the way of adventure, discovery, of conquest; the girdle of safety; an unfathomable mystery, a terror, a desolation. Swinburne, Buchanan, Arnold and Tennyson depict the sensations and emotions to which the sea gives birth."[18] Some

16. J. Swarbrooke, "Museums: Theme Parks of the Third Millennium?," in *Tourism and Heritage Relationships: Global, National and Local Perspectives*, eds. M. Robinson, N. Evans, P. Long, R. Sharpley and J. Swarbrooke (Sunderland: Business Education, 2000): 417–431.

17. Wolverhampton Art Gallery, U.K., 9 February–13 April 2002

18. W. Sharp, ed., *Songs and Poems of the Sea (Sea Music)* (London: Walter Scott, 1888), prefactory note.

Table 2.—Key Elements of Association with the
Marine Environment

ELEMENT	DESCRIPTION	EXAMPLE
Sea state (combined with meteorological phenomenon)	Wild, frightening, savage, choppy, tossing, chaotic Calm, placid, tranquil, glassy-smooth	Descriptions in novels such as C. S. Forester's *Midshipman Hornblower* Nautical photography exemplified by the Mystic Seaport Rosenfeld Collection
Colour	Blue, emerald, green, grey, inky-black, silver	Paintings by Stanhope-Forbes and the Newlyn School
Remoteness	Hidden depths, creatures, vast expanse	Thrilling adventure stories such as Jules Verne's *Twenty Thousand Leagues under the Sea*
Challenge	Man against the elements	Account of Grace Darling's rescue of survivors of the steamer *Forfarshire* in 1838
Mystery	Myths and legends	Tales of mermaids
Place	Landmarks, character, memories	Atlantic rollers, seaside postcards
Habitat	Seascapes, species	Whale and dolphin music
Diversity (created by constant movement and change)	Tides, currents, erosion, deposition	Landscape photography by Joe Cornish

more recent images are geographically very specific. Benjamin Britten's evocative opera score *Peter Grimes,* for example, depicts the wild and desolate Suffolk coast from Dunwich to Walberswick.

Rachel Carson's *Silent Spring,*[19] first published in 1962, remains perhaps the single-most influential 20th century document in terms of raising public awareness of the vulnerability of the environment. Like other classic texts in environmental studies,[20] the emphasis is towards the need for joint responsibility and joint action to avoid the scenario being described or explained. Fundamental concerns now include the concept of ecological

19. R. Carson, *Silent Spring* (Boston: Houghton Mifflin Co., 1987).

20. N. Nelissen, J. Vander Straaten and L. Klinkers eds., *Classics in Environmental Studies: An Overview of Classic Texts in Environmental Studies* (Utrecht: International Books, 1997).

footprints and the need to consider each individual's relationship with the natural world.[21] In this respect the marine environment has tended to be a poor relation to its terrestrial equivalent and "the perception of oceans as being infinitely vast has tended to undermine concern over their increasing exploitation by human society, despite their economic and ecological importance."[22]

Non-governmental organisations including Greenpeace, Worldwide Fund for Nature, and the U.K. Marine Conservation Society have been influential in raising public awareness. Seminal television documentaries, such as the BBC's *Blue Planet*, have further stimulated public interest and concern for the oceans. Key contemporary marine environmental stories to be expounded and interpreted include:

- Sustainable development (including pollution prevention and control);
- Fisheries (oceans as a natural life-support system);
- Coral reefs (threats to natural habitats);
- Whaling (biodiversity and endangered species);
- Discovering hidden depths and unknown worlds (sub-sea exploration);
- Coastal flooding (relative sea-level rise and climatic change); and
- Marine recreation (oceans as playgrounds).

Such a list includes threats and opportunities. Ignorance of the way marine ecosystems function is a fundamental challenge to the consideration of resource conservation and pollution prevention. For example, an explanation of overfishing involves linking climatic and ocean circulation, nutrient availability, limited population sizes of commercial species, and technological fishing capability to human greed and ignorance. In this respect, a geographical focus is a useful storyline as shown, for example, when highlighting the threat that deep-sea trawling poses to the unique ecology of the Rockall Trough.[23] Similarly, the Southern Ocean surrounding Antarctica provides the setting to consider a history of unsustainable practices including 19th century exploitation of seals, subsequent pursuit of great whales, finfish stocks and Antarctic krill. In this way sustainable development of the oceans can be shown to be an intensely political process involving continual trade-offs. Such environmental issues have been classi-

21. N. Chambers, C. Simmons and M. Wackernagel, *Sharing Nature's Interest: Ecological Footprints as an Indicator of Sustainability* (London: Earthscan, 2000).

22. N. Middleton, *The Global Casino: An Introduction to Environmental Issues* (London: Arnold, 1995): 127.

23. M. Linklater, "A Graveyard at the Bottom of the Sea," *The London Times* (February 26, 2002).

fied as "hot" or controversial interpretation topics,[24] for which interpreters should play a positive role in leading and shaping public opinion.

Contemporary Issues

There are few quantitative evaluations of the level of public awareness concerning contemporary maritime environmental issues. The exception is a national survey of the American public that suggested Americans' knowledge of the oceans was superficial and ocean environments were not perceived to be in immediate danger.[25] The need for action to protect the oceans was deemed to be less of a priority than tackling other environmental problems such as air emissions. At a more detailed level this survey revealed five attitudinal groups—young beach lovers; zoo, aquarium, and museum goers; older beach lovers; unconnected and unconcerned; and landlocked and unconcerned. Categorisation of this type is important in order to establish target markets, common preferences and priorities. It is also important because museums and aquaria are currently not fulfilling their potential to convince the public about the urgent need to take action to conserve our oceans. Such information can therefore inform a communication strategy and, in this case, it demonstrated a dichotomy between the need to reinforce personal connections to the ocean for some groups and for others the need for basic explanations about the interconnectedness of natural systems. A summary of the survey's recommendations for communications is presented in Table 3. They link closely with interpretation theory and perhaps reflect the responsibility placed on those producing interpretive displays.

24. D. Uzzell and R. Ballantyne, "Heritage that Hurts: Interpretation in a Post-Modern World," in *Contemporary Issues in Heritage and Environmental Interpretation: Problems and Prospects*, eds. D. Uzzell and R. Ballantyne (London: The Stationary Office, 1998): 152–171.

25. Belden, Russonello & Stewart and American Viewpoint, *Communicating about Oceans: Results of a National Survey* (unpublished research report for The Ocean Project, 1999).

Table 3.—Communication Recommendations

Recommendations for communication action to increase the urgency of ocean protection:
Combine emotion and information
Start with values
Appeal to individual responsibility
Connect values to messages of recreation and healthy futures
Further education: especially concerning destructive fishing practices and coastal development
Generally persuadable targets include those who live close to the ocean
Specific messages are needed for different attitudinal groups

Source: Adapted from Belden, Russonello & Stewart and American Viewpoint, *Communicating about Oceans: Results of a National Survey* (unpublished research report for The Ocean Project, 1999).

Throughout the world attempts are in hand to try to engage people more deeply with these and other marine environmental issues. Common elements are present in many of the world's maritime museums. Often these museums exploit their waterfront location using dramatic modern architecture in combination with varied indoor and floating exhibitions (e.g., the New Zealand National Maritime Museum, Auckland). Several world-class attractions focus on the presentation of a single spectacular vessel (e.g., the Vasa Museum, Stockholm; the Fram Museum, Oslo). However, interactive approaches to displays are increasingly being adapted by maritime museums, serving both to portray a country's socio-cultural history and as marine tourist attractions.[26] Nevertheless, in general, maritime museums fail to focus sufficiently on environmental issues when compared to aquaria and sea life centres.

Contemporary research classifying maritime heritage-related visitor attractions broadly divided them into either intrinsic (based around an authentic artefact collection) or ersatz (relying on replicas, reproductions, and simulations of historical subject matter).[27] This work proposed that intrinsic sites should accentuate the uniqueness of their collections, rather than compete on the ersatz attraction territory, which can be emotively laden but inauthentic. Evidence drawn from visits to a selection of international maritime museums suggests that this is a common approach. However, the results are often exhibitions that remain too static, too historical and largely passive. It is often difficult using obsolete artefacts to

26. M. Orams, *Marine Tourism: Development, Impacts and Management* (London: Routledge, 1999).

27. K. J. Wallis, "Contrived Authenticity: Visitor attractions and the Maritime Heritage of Great Britain," (Ph.D. diss., University of Wales Cardiff, 1996).

trigger visitors' imagination relating to contemporary and future issues. Furthermore, intrinsic sites face difficult decisions in terms of how they adapt to increasingly technological interpretative media.

The Powerhouse Museum in Sydney, Australia is an example of a non-maritime museum, where a balance between intrinsic and ersatz has been successfully achieved. Exhibitions use cutting-edge technology and design without devaluing artefacts. Juxtaposed video screens, piped music, artefacts in bottom-lit glass tubes, interactive touch screens, exhibits set in sinuous glass plate floor panels and ingenious use of mirrors create an ultra modern display environment. The environmental message is delivered by an exhibition entitled "EcoLogic: creating a sustainable future." The message is a positive one. A series of interactive games examine environmental indicators, planning decisions, ecological footprints and biodiversity. Fish in the sea features eight species of fish commonly found off the Australian coast. A touch screen activates each fish, which then delivers a series of facts in a humorous way. Messages relate to personal lifestyles and to different age groups; they challenge visitors to examine their attitudes and impacts.

In November 2003, the Global Conference on Oceans, Coasts and Islands, with the aim of catalysing action on implementation of the World Summit on Sustainable Development (WSSD), included a significant emphasis on public information, education and awareness. This was in response to the WSSD call for "education at all levels, providing communities with educational opportunities and adopting a decade of education for sustainable development starting in January 2005." The World Ocean Network, comprising aquariums, zoos, National Park authorities, maritime museums, education centres, non-governmental organisations and other institutions dealing with the public at large, claims annual contact with over 200 million people. An example of good practice is the Centre for Environmental Education, India—with awareness-raising initiatives throughout India, including interpretative material for the Andaman and Nicobar Islands, the Chilika Lagoon Ramsar site, and a nation-wide schools program. However, whilst such efforts are important, the political will to support them and fully engage the public in the short timeframe required is singularly lacking. It can be supposed that decision-makers remain unwilling to face ocean problems because their constituencies are not empowering them to do so.

EXAMPLES OF CURRENT PRACTICE

The mission statement of one of the world's leading aquaria, located in Monterey Bay California, is "to inspire conservation of the oceans." An amazing location, 200 award winning galleries and live exhibits deliver this message. The facility is open to the ocean, so wild animals, especially sea otters, regularly visit. Within the aquarium the signature kelp forest exhibit presents an "overwhelming, diver's-eye view of a living kelp forest community." Monterey Bay National Marine Sanctuary provides inspirational material—expansive kelp forests, a massive underwater canyon and proximity to shore of the deep ocean environment including features such as the Davidson Seamount. Particularly impressive is the current exhibit "Vanishing Wildlife," a new view into the million-gallon Outer Bay exhibit, focusing on human threats to sharks, tuna and turtles—and what visitors can do to help protect them. A philosophy to underpin the attraction with scientific endeavour has brought collaboration between Monterey Bay Aquarium (MBA), Monterey Bay Aquarium Research Institute (MBARI) and the National Oceanic and Atmospheric Administration (NOAA). David Packard, the philanthropic founder of MBA/MBARI, urged his research team to "Go deep. Stay long. Take risks. Ask big questions."[28] The Education and Research Testing Hypothesis (EARTH) project links scientists and educators.

A key feature of the MBA, however, is the use of information technology (IT) and interactive media to involve an audience beyond its confines. To this end six live cams focus on major exhibits and "sea notes," and an e-mail newsletter engages people worldwide. MBARI research, both oceanographic data and images, is accessible remotely via microwave links to vessels and through data visualisation software. An extensive video annotation and reference system provides a comprehensive video archive based on annual remote operated vehicle (ROV) dives (in excess of 300 per annum). This material informs MBA exhibits such as "Mysteries of the Deep" and "Jellies—Living Art." In 2002, MBARI hosted the production of "The Abyss—LIVE," a live awareness raising broadcast seen around the world.

The latest U.K. marine-related attraction is marketed as the world's only "submarium"—a dramatic fusion of aquaria and state-of-the-art interactives telling the story of the world's oceans through time, latitude and depth. This £40 million investment is called *The Deep*. Dramatic architectural design and technological innovation has resulted in impressive initial visitor numbers. *The Deep* is a good example of a purpose-built attraction, creating interest rather than capitalising on heritage. It relies on capturing the thrill of the unknown ocean, transporting visitors in an "underwater lift" and allowing them to investigate the story of the oceans. First and foremost the attraction is an aquarium, relying on the pull of unusual live exhibits and high-resolution screens.

28. MBARI (Monterey Bay Research Institute)'s First Decade: A Retrospective 1987–1997, available online: <http://www.mbari.org>

However, a key issue at *The Deep* is an apparent marginalisation of important environmental conservation messages in favour of high impact global marine life images. There is no debate, for example, about overfishing, its consequences and any possible solutions. Association with the local environment, based on an investigation of the Humber estuary, is limited to a single exhibit, a periscope linked to a remote camera, explaining how an estuary receives inputs and outputs. This is interesting in itself but misses the opportunity to tell the story of the demise of the local Hull-based fishing industry, using traditional objects and oral histories. Some local people regard this as a fundamental omission. Similarly, no connection is made with associated developments such as the local windfarm at Easington, the dynamic coastal environment of Spurn Head, North Sea gas platforms (the closest is only 20 miles offshore), or the local marine-based economy (850 people in Hull work for BP Chemicals). Local people would also like to see a tangible connection to their environment, perhaps the reinstatement of the ferry to Grimsby and Cleethorpes as a means of integrating the wider region. Placement of exhibits along the visitor trail is also very important. Some of the most instructive stations, such as "cod lottery" are towards the end of the trail, by which time visitors are experiencing a degree of exhibit fatigue.

Visitors interviewed as part of this analysis had enjoyed their experience at *The Deep*. For many the state-of-the-art interactives are novel and have a high attraction gradient. Observation of school groups confirmed the attraction of hands-on exhibits but also demonstrated that many of the exhibits are not substantive enough for older learners. The better interactive screens allow visitors to drill down to more detailed information, but more structure to the experience, with additional staffed teaching stations at key areas, would make a real difference. Where these are in place, such as the touch tank, visitor interest is held for a significant extra time. Several exhibits also have an "audio umbrella," but these have limited range and cater for an optimal group size of about six. For larger groups the sound can be missing and any message lost. In many instances younger visitors, eager to work the computer screens, failed to associate interactives with associated information. The positioning of interactives currently creates "pinch points" and there is a danger that the predominance of hi-tech exhibits overwhelms less computer literate, older visitors. Furthermore, the noise and excitement generated by school groups leaves little opportunity for private meditation or reflective thought.

Overall, *The Deep* has very few intrinsic or original artefact exhibits. Those present are undersold. For example, "Deep Flight," Dr Sylvia Earle's redundant remotely operated vehicle (ROV), lacks appropriate lighting or explanation. A problem with dependency on ersatz or wholly manufactured exhibits is that to retain learning people need to be intellectually engaged in addition to "enjoying the ride." Historical objects have an aura and a tangible connection to their previous purpose. Ersatz exhibits, such as *The Deep's* "Nautilus Pilot Training Pods"—akin to a modern arcade game—are excellent and wholly absorbing for younger children, but are unlikely to make an impact on other visitor segments. The approach taken raises an interesting debate as to the effectiveness of marine attractions for wider audiences. The city of Hull has a complicated social mix, including relatively deprived areas whose residents are unlikely to visit without an incentive. Non-English speakers, physically handicapped and visually impaired visitors are not best served by the existing set-up, given that the concept relies heavily on dim lighting and fixed position interactive screens. A £6.5 million extension featuring the "Twighlight Zone," an enhanced learning centre facility and cutting-edge research, aims to lengthen visitor stay. In the opinion of the authors, however, additional resource must be combined with an enhanced learning experience to both justify significant public investment and to ensure long-term survival of the attraction.

PLANET OCEAN AT THE NATIONAL MARITIME MUSEUM

Since its opening in 1937 the NMM has been responsible for collecting, interpreting and celebrating the U.K.'s and international maritime heritage. With over two million maritime-related artefacts the NMM is the largest repository of its kind in the world. The Museum receives over 1.4 million visitors a year and holds pre-eminent collections reflecting humankind's relationship with the sea across centuries, cultures and continents. Its mission is to illustrate the ongoing importance of this relationship.

Over the past 60 years, however, the relationship of humankind with the marine environment has changed markedly. Fundamental shifts in attitudes toward, and involvement with, the sea have occurred within institutional, academic, commercial and, importantly, public spheres. The Museum recognised these changes and when it "re-opened" in 1999 it offered both revised interpretations of its existing collections and new approaches to meeting the diversity and complexity inherent in marine issues. Within its 16 new galleries a central display called *Future of the Sea* covered a range of contemporary themes and issues directly related to the marine environment. Significant emphasis has been placed on the use of a range of Information Communication Technologies (ICTs) to complement more traditional methods in the display and communication of the various collections, archives, galleries and new themes.[29]

29. J. S. Potts, "Recent developments at the National Maritime Museum, U.K., and their potential for capacity building," *Marine Policy* 24 (2000): 79–81.

In 2002, the NMM launched *Planet Ocean*, a further development that has allowed the Museum to bring together and showcase the past, present and future of the oceans. In the U.K. the NMM is working towards becoming a hub for translating marine science, policy and management issues into accessible, inspirational and balanced end products: displays, research and educational programmes. This innovative and long-term initiative covers a number of key themes:

- Oceans and environmental change;
- Biodiversity and resources;
- Pollution and conservation;
- Citizenship, communities and sustainable development; and
- Media and the environment.

The initiative is now well established and has a strong sector profile and growing reputation with the U.K.'s marine environment community. Phase I (2002–2004) of the strategy was concerned with raising the profile of the NMM in this subject area, establishing the necessary partnerships and other resources to drive the initiative forward. Other key achievements have included the:

- Registering of the NMM's seriousness and commitment to this subject area;
- Development of a robust research and publication portfolio for the NMM (including conferences, seminars, fellowships and journals);
- Installation of an initial trilogy of high profile marine environment related galleries and displays;
- Creation of a distinct *Planet Ocean* education base as well as informal education programmes and other life-long learning packages;
- Hosting of several high profile "industry-based" events; and
- Securing significant sponsorship monies for a range of *Planet Ocean* projects.

Internal appraisal and feedback from both key stakeholders and the public identified, however, a number of weaknesses in the provision of this first stage. In particular, it was noted that there was a relatively limited development of public interpretation and outreach projects. Further weaknesses included:

- Limited public participation and involvement in the initiative and delivery of its programmes;
- Limited collection base (i.e., a lack of objects and other resources to illustrate the subject); and
- No clear link up with aquaria and wider maritime heritage partners.

Market research at the NMM has revealed that less than 10 percent of visitors stay over 4 hours. Consequently, learning provision (displays and information) needs to be unambiguous, with direct exposure of visitors to accessible objects and experiences. The most recent Market & Opinion Research International (MORI) visitor research survey was published in November/December 2001. The survey confirms a visitor profile skewed towards older age ranges and better educated/higher class (ABC1) visitors (87 percent). However, 22 percent of group parties visit with children. An analysis of the learning profiles of a sample of these visitors, using an adapted version of VARK, confirms a preference for visual and read/write material in the most prominent age group (45–54 year olds), but strong preferences for kinesthetic material shown by younger visitors and school groups. Thus, two distinct learning profiles have been identified, which the Museum must cater for and to whom the importance of the marine environment should be conveyed.

An analysis of the three *Planet Ocean* exhibitions was undertaken within this research, by classifying their constituent elements according to the VARK categories. Although this is a somewhat crude tool, it highlights that the learning provision broadly corresponds with the older age group learning profile. Observations of visitor behaviour reflect this, with particular interest being shown in plasma screen interactives devoted to tides and surges, weather and waves and latitude and longitude. However, there are mismatches between the learning preference profile and museum provision for younger visitors. In this respect *Making Waves* scores well. The hands-on paddle that powers the 3-meter wave flume represents a strenuous physical activity available for children and young adults. NMM education officers can climb into the wave tank and demonstrate how boats move through water, but the sound and dramatic effect of waves are largely missing. *Oceans of Discovery* is a more traditional, object-rich gallery with an emphasis on read and write learning. *Future of the Sea* featured visual learning strengths, but clearly needed additional material to actively engage younger visitors.

Phase II of *Planet Ocean* (2004–2007) seeks, therefore, not only to address these challenges but more importantly to build on the achievements and to become a market leader in this field—both nationally and internationally. The focus of this second stage is to improve public interpretation and outreach via:

- Developing an integrated, inclusive and inspiring approach for the public;
- Leading on environmental learning and citizenship;
- Collecting and integrating a marine environment object and resource base;
- Sustaining and extending partnerships; and

- Identifying and exploiting commercial opportunities to benefit the wider marine environment community.

The NMM is breaking new ground in trying to encompass multi-disciplinary contemporary issues. The partnership approach has been adopted with key stakeholders, including, The Crown Estate, the Worldwide Fund for Nature, the National Oceanography Centre, The Institute of Marine Engineering, Science and Technology, the Marine Conservation Society and the Maritime and Coastguard Agency, aimed at helping to better understand, protect and celebrate, the oceans.

The flagship project for Phase II will be the installation of a new, permanent gallery titled *Your Ocean*. This gallery replaces the previous *Future of the Sea* display. Opening in late 2005, the gallery will offer a unique and innovative approach to engaging the Museum's diverse range of audiences. The gallery will focus on the broad idea that each and every one of us is connected to the sea by our lifestyles, actions and choices. The main aim is to raise awareness of current issues and present them didactically in the context of local, national and international situations. The core target audiences are family, teenage and school groups that will help promote an inclusive, debate driven approach to the subject issues. The gallery will consist of five zones, each dealing with a specific topic. Each zone will include a mix of graphics, text, case studies, objects and interactives to stimulate debate and raise awareness.

Importantly, to help develop "ownership and citizenship," visitors' opinions have already been sought on how they think current issues should be addressed. Feedback has been displayed for other visitors to share and respond to and will be used to encourage debate and inclusion beyond the Museum. This has been achieved using a temporary *Your Ocean* display, in place during spring and summer of 2005, piloting a citizenship approach. An "opinion wall," soliciting individual responses in favour of conservation action, written and displayed on luggage tag type labels, was popular generating some 500–1,000 responses/week over a 7-month period. Part way through this pilot a series of more specific questions were introduced including:

- Pollution—who is responsible?
- Are wind farms at sea a good idea?
- Global warming—how will it affect your life?
- What should we be doing to help fish stocks recover?
- The oceans' resources—how much is my fair share?

A preliminary qualitative analysis of the 70 percent of responses that were not flippant or facile revealed a variety of individual expression from a very international audience with both political and religious dimensions. NMM has no control over the maturity, prior knowledge or motivation of respondents. Indeed, observation of visitors' behaviour revealed that people commonly want to read what others have written before adding their own views or perhaps copying an opinion with which they have empathy. Nevertheless, the exhibit engages interest and provides an outlet for individual expression that is age and gender inclusive. Responses indicate pollution awareness, fondness and respect for the oceans, concern about declining fish stocks, an understanding of universal responsibilities, worries about future uncertainties and the need to share resources. Responses were broadly classified as:

- Self-agenda forming—for example, a personal commitment not to litter;
- Issue prioritising—such as the need to conserve water resources;
- Confirmation of intentions—advocacy and pledges to give money to marine conservation; and
- Support for the work of the NMM in general.

As interesting were the subject areas not mentioned, for example, the environmental impact of shipping; and an abdication of responsibility by many of the replies, with some responses suggesting that these are issues for scientists to address; and an element of denial that issues raised are a problem for the current generation. A clear role for *Your Ocean* will be to provoke and galvanise individuals not yet convinced about the scale of potential problems for the marine environment and the urgency needed to tackle them.

The most significant challenge, however, for *Your Ocean* is how the NMM will be able to ensure topicality and highlight the inter-related nature of the subject area, whilst at the same time being inspirational, reflective and credible. To this end, the NMM is working with key stakeholders active across the subject area to provide information, which is both topical and scientifically credible. From here the Museum will "translate" the science into accessible and responsible resources with direct links back to the stakeholders and their work. The gallery will also seek to promote a genuine sense of participation and inclusion for all the different types of visitors. Extensive audience evaluation has shown that visitors to this gallery want to participate in a proactive manner. As such, the gallery will facilitate this by enabling visitors to see the impact of their actions and to state their opinions via information communication technologies installed in the space.

Your Ocean will also be designed to accommodate both structured formal educational programmes and general visitor "drop-in" activities. This will enable the Museum to meet stipulated targets for education provision, as well as promoting repeat visits so that members of the public can keep themselves informed and check on their "environmental citizenship performance." By targeting teenagers the Museum will be diversifying and developing an audience base that is currently under-represented in both the NMM's and other national museum visitor profiles. Further visitor research is being conducted into how best to attract and retain this market and how teenagers interpret, respond to and debate such issues.

An important factor in approaching the physical development of the gallery space will be how the NMM can install a gallery that is "environmentally sound" and reflects the practices of marine stewardship. To this end the Museum is looking at its own practices and processes in relation to sustainability, as well as more widely into products and designs that are socially, ethically and environmentally feasible and appropriate.

Finally, the development of both *Planet Ocean* and in particular *Your Ocean* is providing the Museum with a unique opportunity to further its understanding of the relationship between itself, the key stakeholders and the public. The work undertaken for this project will contribute to clarifying the role the NMM and the wider U.K. maritime heritage resource will play in developing public understanding and participation. Both installing the *Your Ocean* gallery and incorporating a dynamic, topical and inclusive approach to its ongoing development will help not only enhance the NMM's existing resources but also answer several key questions, including:

- What are the stakeholders' needs in raising awareness and brokering public involvement?
- What is the public interest in understanding and engaging with these issues—now and in the future?
- What is the role of the Museum in addressing these needs and developing creative solutions?

The findings will also benefit the NMM's partner organisations as well as having a broader national and international relevance to the marine environment community and the public.

CONCLUSIONS

Historically the marine environment has been explained through many media, all of which can be used as prompts to achieve the level of engagement desired to promote conservation. Perceptions are drawn from a combination of such media, personal experience, and admiration of the feats of others. A review of relevant literature suggests successful interpretation should focus on engaging the visitor. Raising awareness involves marrying factual information with people's personal experience, values and everyday lives. A problem with evolving issues is that explanations quickly become dated: visitors need immediacy. One in three Americans visit museums and aquaria on an annual basis.[30] Awareness researchers have therefore concluded that these institutions have a unique opportunity to inform the public about the marine environment and the need to contribute towards its conservation. But whilst an emotional connection to the oceans can be established, public awareness and concern about the oceans' health remain low.

It is therefore incumbent upon the managers of these attractions worldwide to engage and educate the public in a way that engenders individual responsibility. Stimulating, engaging and involving visitors requires interpretation with appropriate context and continuity. Experts confirm that explaining current and future scenarios demands the truth. We must link conservation values to cultural realities. We must also find a way of seeing beyond short-term and compartmentalised thinking. The public expects something tangible. Most are not interested in abstract notions.

In the meantime, international advocates of integrated ocean management remain frustrated at the overall lack of political will and public awareness. Current practice reflects divisions between the interpretation of science, natural history and socio-cultural history. Such tensions are unhelpful when addressing multidisciplinary problems and concepts. Key contemporary marine environmental issues include the plight of endangered species, unknown depths, and the oceans as an economic resource. The linkages between these issues remain largely "uninterpreted," although the MBA in California provides an example of exemplary public outreach on a global scale. *The Deep*, a much smaller purpose-built regional attraction located in Hull U.K., a former focal point for the fishing industry, has the potential to integrate biology, history, culture and economic challenges. As this attraction matures the opportunity to further connect visitors with ocean problems should be grasped. In particular attention needs to be given to the translation of core terminology (i.e., scientific terms) into appropriate and accessible language; increasing the potential for interactive and IT-based interpretation; and the balance of "intrinsic" and "ersatz" exhibits and objects. Maritime attraction-based learning materials are also important in the context of widening participation.

The NMM approach is an example of good practice, where interpreters have recognised the need to focus on core issues, been open to new ideas, and embraced new technologies. However, a mismatch identified between visitor learning styles and learning provision suggests that further detailed "experience engineering" work is possible. Although confined to a very limited physical space, the *Your Ocean* gallery within the NMM intends to stimulate debate from the outset. The future of our oceans depends on our

30. Belden, Russonello & Stewart and American Viewpoint, n. 25 above.

decisions and choices. It requires collective remedial action and active participation. In the opinion of the authors, this can only be achieved by a balanced presentation of the facts in ways that touch hearts and minds.

Annual Report of the International Ocean Institute

Report of the International Ocean Institute, 2004*

This report covers the progress and exciting developments of the International Ocean Institute (IOI) in 2004. Over the year there has been a spirit of change and movement forward. This year has seen an acceleration of the IOI activities in all areas of its competence and this report provides readers with an overview of the achievements, challenges, problems met and solutions found. There are examples of research and capacity-building highlights that present the IOI as an international asset.

The structure of the report is similar to the one published in 2003 and corresponds to the IOI goals and functions that are presented in the IOI Statutes, adopted by the Governing Board in October 2003. The structure and content of the report takes into account comments made by the participants of the Governing Board and Committee of Directors' meetings in 2004. It is based on the contributions received from the IOI Operational Centres and the Secretariat.

LETTER FROM THE PRESIDENT

The ocean community of the International Ocean Institute should be proud of its achievement in 2004, which is a tribute to the founder and a testimony to her legacy. The contribution of the Secretariat at Headquarters, the Committee of Directors and members of the Governing Board has been remarkable due to their commitment and dedication to complete the reform measures that began two years ago and the implementation of the IOI mission in its many manifestations.

The IOI extended its family network by welcoming Egypt as the latest country to establish an IOI Operational Centre in Suez. The meeting of the Board and Committee of Directors in Slovenia was a milestone in

---

* EDITORS' NOTE.—This report has been extracted from the "Report of the International Ocean Institute (IOI) for 2004," March 2005, provided by IOI Headquarters in Malta. It has been edited for publication in the *Ocean Yearbook* and the section on "Institute Management and Budget: Network Development" and six annexes have been omitted.

determining the priorities and future challenges to the IOI through a memorable brainstorming session, reflecting the new spirit of transparency and frank dialogue that is the basis of policy-making in IOI. Consolidated efforts were made to strengthen and modernize the training capacity of the Institute through the establishment of OceanLearn as the umbrella and coordinating mechanism for IOI human resource development efforts.

Regrettably, 2004 ended with the tragic event of the Asian tsunami which sadly reminded us all that we need not only to live off the ocean, but also to live with it. The IOI, which reacted immediately to that tragic event, is determined to play its role in the future in awareness, preparedness and mitigation of ocean hazards through its partnerships and capacity-building programs. We look ahead to another year of activities with the vision and mission of our dear founder, Elisabeth Mann Borgese, and invite you through this report to discover the many activities of IOI in the sustainable management of the ocean—the source of all life.

Dr. Awni Behnam
President of IOI

HIGHLIGHTS OF THE YEAR[1]

The IOI and its partners have an undeniable duty and responsibility to fulfill: to contribute to stopping the deterioration of the ocean and to preserve its outstanding natural, cultural and human heritage. In fact, we are implementing comprehensive ocean security, *Pacem in Maribus*, of which ocean governance and sustainable management of the oceans and coastal zones are integral parts.

As it is presented in the "Tokyo Declaration on Securing the Oceans" proposed by the Institute of Ocean Policy, Ship and Ocean Foundation of Japan in December 2004, it means that "aspects of ocean management, including military activities, the peaceful use of oceans, resource extraction, environmental management, and scientific research should be addressed in an integrated manner." Achieving sustainable management requires resolving many intertwined environmental, social and economic issues, from developing practical methods for ecosystem conservation to ensuring participation of stakeholders in decision making and establishing legal and economic frameworks.

The IOI Governing Board at its 42nd Session in October 2004 reconfirmed the importance of three main areas of activities of the Institute: ocean governance and research; capacity building through training and education; and awareness, partnership and cooperation.

The implementation of IOI's Strategic Plan, defined in 2002, continues to be a priority for the IOI. In this respect, the IOI Network is actively pursuing the priorities and thematic issues, where each Operational Centre tends to align and emphasize these according to its expertise, whether it is awareness-raising at the community level, training, or whether it is based on research. One of the most significant decisions taken in 2004 was the rationalization of the IOI's capacity-building programme, recognized as one of the three "pillars" of the IOI.

Among the routine activities such as training and education, research and awareness raising that are part of the activities of most Operational Centres, IOI wishes to orient its network towards more innovation and entrepreneurship. In the area of education and training, a great deal of innovation is occurring in the IOI Network, especially in the realm of multimode course delivery. Such innovation is seen as having great potential to generate new funding opportunities and the formation of new partnerships.

During 2004, IOI continued to advance in meeting its objectives, particularly in the areas of capacity building and establishing new partner-

---

1. This section gives a short overview of the most important IOI activities implemented in 2004. Detailed information on the work of IOI and its Centres is given in the sections that follow.

ships with a commitment to the IOI mission and vision. The sustained work of the IOI Operational Centres and the Secretariat in a multi-year, capacity-building programme has helped IOI to achieve a few important results.

In 2004, IOI Centres developed many thematic, hands-on courses focused to meet local and regional needs and challenges. The range of capacity-building opportunities that IOI provided allowed participants to gain knowledge and develop intellectual and practical skills. The B Training Course on Ocean Governance at Dalhousie University continued to be an IOI flagship activity. The development of a new B Training Course on Ocean Governance for Mediterranean and Eastern European Countries to be held at the University of Malta has come to a final phase with a target to the first regional course in November-December 2005.

A key element of the IOI training programme is to link each training action to fieldwork, so as to immediately apply knowledge and skills through concrete experience. IOI continued to develop and refine a set of tools necessary for effective capacity building that included new technologies in active learning and training (OceanLearn), project development and information sharing. IOI devoted a special effort in helping to build the capacity of civil society, with a strong focus on grassroots and local environmental groups.

The IOI capacity-building programme has helped to create a critical mass of ocean governance experts and marine environmental protection practitioners throughout the globe. These individuals may become partners, adding value to each other's actions, and building their own set of alliances within their areas of interest. The decision of the IOI Board to create the alumni association will facilitate the interaction.

In the coming years IOI will strive to reach the younger generation and youth organizations who are engaged in ocean research and protection, and offer them well-tested capacity-building opportunities. In 2004, new steps were taken in this direction through organizing summer schools (IOI-Russia, IOI-Caspian Sea) and supporting a joint IOC/IOI Floating University Project in the Caspian Sea.

The year 2004 was one of consolidating existing partnerships and ensuring that the impact of organizations and individuals was multiplied. Much was done to promote coordination with marine-related agencies in the UN system. The role that IOI played in the past working for enhanced collaboration across the UN on ocean governance has gained new momentum through fostering cooperation with the UN (DOALOS), UNESCO, IOC, IMO and WMO. MOUs on cooperation were signed with IOC and CRFM and the preparation of the MOU on joint activities with IMO and the UNESCO Marine Heritage Programme was in process. IOI has supported a host of initiatives targeted at developing partnerships in a number of ways.

Inputs were submitted to the reports of DOALOS, DPI and DESA on the IOI contribution to the implementation of different conventions and agreements and on the IOI information exchange policy, including a contribution to the UN Secretary-General comprehensive annual report on oceans and the law of the sea (A/59/62). This contribution was especially acknowledged by UN/DOALOS. The IOI experts presented the Institute's work at various conferences and meetings using the opportunities for promoting the IOI objectives and activities and establishing new partnerships.

In compliance with the decision of the 41st meeting of the Governing Board, held in October 2003 in Kiev, there was no PIM Conference in 2004 as the frequency of the Conferences was changed from annual to biennial events. However, preparation for the PIM-31 Conference in Townsville, Australia in October 2005 titled "Building Bridges towards Integrated Oceans Governance: Linking Ocean Science, Engineering, Technology and Policy" was on the agendas of all IOI meetings. Discussions covered a wide range of topics, including the formulation of the programme, selection of themes and speakers, identification of side events, local arrangements and funding. The Conference is expected to prompt the development of new approaches involving NGOs and public participation, reinforcing the legal instruments and increasing financing of IOI activities.

The discussion of problems facing the Arafura and Timor Seas will be a focus of one of the conference themes. These semi-enclosed seas are an important shared resource for the bordering countries and the coastal communities that depend on them. Research cooperation, knowledge sharing and integrated coastal management are increasingly important and the ways will be discussed as to how many stakeholders and disciplines engaged in the Seas issues might work together towards better management of the social, economic and environmental impacts of human activities.

The task of the IOI Executive Committee, Governing Board and Committee of Directors is to help IOI live up to the promises of the IOI mission. In July 2004, the 3rd Session of the Executive Committee took place in Malta with the objective of reviewing the progress achieved by IOI in the first half of 2004. The meeting brainstormed on the further strengthening and development of IOI. Special attention was given to the adoption of the Rules of Procedure and plan of actions on marketing, the improvements in communication and reporting procedures, the development of the training programme in Malta and the formulation of the training strategy, and the proposal for a coordinating mechanism of training activities. Out of this came several suggestions that were later brought to the attention of the Governing Board. Included among them were the "OceanLearn" programme, a proposal for the second phase of the Women/Youth and the Sea Programme, the approval of the 2003 Audit Report, and a request for the publication of the IOI Rules of Procedure and

Statutes prior to the meetings of the Board and Committee of Directors in October 2004. The meeting also gave the opportunity to reflect and assess the development of IOI. Operational Centres were established in Canada, Egypt and Fiji. The establishment of Centres in Cuba, USA and Philippines were under negotiation. The establishment of these Centres permitted and will permit to close gaps in the Network of Operational Centres in the eastern Mediterranean, Caribbean Basin and North America.

The Board and Committee of Directors' meetings were held in October 2004 in Slovenia. These were the first meetings after the adoption of the new IOI Statutes and Rules of Procedure. These basic documents helped to streamline discussions and increased the effectiveness of adopted decisions. The attention of the participants was focused on the assessment of the Network activities, on the extension of the Network, programme implementation, fund raising, cooperation with the UN and other international organizations, and IOI management, among other topics. With widespread discussion on the ways of increasing Network effectiveness, the Board agreed on the need for regular assessments of the Centres' activities and recommended ways to implement it. It was also recognized that the limited resources of the IOI do not permit an uncontrolled extension of the Network. It was recommended that new Centres be approved only after, as a result of the assessment, non-functional Centres are closed.

The Committee of Directors and the Board reviewed the progress achieved by the IOI Network and decided to organize an in-depth discussion during 2005 on the evolving role of the IOI. It was also decided to consider the need to widen thematic areas of system-wide projects. Four areas were proposed: coral reef research and protection, integrated coastal area management, marine hazards management, including risk assessment and insurance, and the participation in the International Polar Year. The interest of the IOI Operational Centres in participating and contributing to these areas should be further explored. Women/Youth and the Sea and Training and Education Programmes continued to be at the spearhead of the IOI system-wide activities. It is expected that the adoption of the OceanLearn programme and the decision of having PIM-32 in 2007 dedicated to the Youth and the Sea will give a new boost to these programmes.

In the ongoing efforts to increase the effectiveness of its programmes and to strengthen relationships between the UN system and IOI, a brainstorming meeting was organized on 13 October, 2004 with the participation of Board and Committee members and invited experts. Dr. V. Golitsyn, head of DOALOS, and Dr. E. Saruchanian from WMO informed the Board of the main responsibilities of DOALOS that relate to the discharge of the functions in the field of oceans and the law of the sea, and of the WMO participation in the International Polar Year planned for 2007–2008. The participants underscored the importance of brainstorming meetings and expressed a desire to increase collaboration between the organizations, especially in such areas as education and training, research and promotion.

The Board adopted the workplans and budget of the Institute for 2005–2006 and agreed that starting from 2005 the Institute will operate based on a biennial budget with adjustments and updates made every year. The Board recommended that in the coming years the focus within training and education be on increasing the quality of courses based on the OceanLearn approach. In research, the focus will be the organization of the PIM Conference in 2005 in Townsville, Australia, the implementation of the Women/Youth and the Sea Programme, and the development of new system-wide projects. In awareness and promotion, the focus will include partnerships with other organizations, strengthening relationships with appropriate research communities and the private sector, determination of the relevance, efficiency, effectiveness and impact of the Institute activities in improvement to its objectives, organizing outreach campaigns, improvement of the Institute visibility, communication and transparency.

TRAINING AND EDUCATION

The IOI has supported capacity building for ocean affairs and provided opportunities for training and education since its very inception. Its activities emerged out of necessity created by both the process and outcomes of the United Nations Convention on the Law of the Sea (UNCLOS) and are responding to the needs of different groups of society from coastal communities to those involved in decision-making and diplomacy. The strengths of the Institute in the areas of capacity building have led to regional and global activities that have consequences more far-reaching than just the policy development itself.

Training Courses

Annual reports provided by the Directors of the Operational Centres at the end of the year show that during 2003, more than 6,000 persons were impacted by some 46 training activities. These can be classified accordingly: 87 percent women, youth and the general public; 11.5 percent managers, government and NGO personnel, and 1.5 percent school and university students.

IOI Canada offered in 2004 for the 24th time the class B Training Programme on Ocean Governance, held annually at Dalhousie University. This Programme continues to be the IOI flagship training programme and is widely recognized as the longest standing and most reputed, comprehensive capacity-building program in ocean governance in the world.

According to the Course Director, the Class of 2004 was perhaps the most active and engaging. A number of interesting observations and recommendations resulted from the training course. Coming on the eve of the 25th anniversary of the training programme, all participants displayed a strong interest in this important event offering many excellent ideas, which they believe would make for a meaningful and significant observance.

Overall, the existing modules remained a strong core for the programme covering a range of issues that are essential to achieving effective ocean governance. However, there was a clear sense that this needed revision and updating to address emerging issues and relevant concerns that had very definite policy implications. Issues pertinent to (1) the governance of island states; (2) global warming and climate change as related to ocean governance planning and policy development; (3) new challenges to maritime transport, port and harbour facilities, as well as maritime trade, and (4) widening of the geographical scope of the training programme, were considered as highly topical.

One important aspect was the involvement of the course participants as a primary training resource. This has managed to help participants focus on local issues within the broader global context. A new aspect was the inclusion of IOI alumni as members of the teaching faculty. Another aspect was a felt need to include a hands-on training module in coastal resources mapping in the training course, in view of its effectiveness as a management tool for coastal management.

An important recommendation was made by the participants to establish an alumni association and network that could become one of the pillars of the IOI in its future developments. Alumni could be especially important in identifying candidates for future classes as well as fundraising.

As in the previous 4 years, IOI awarded its 2004 Danielle de St. Jorre Scholarship of 10,000 Swiss Francs to a young female researcher from a small island developing state. By means of this award, Ms. Marlene Isidore from Seychelles was able to participate in the 2004 IOI Training Programme on Ocean Governance.

IOI Pacific Islands ran a course on Responsible Fisheries in the Pacific Islands with a view on the implementation of post-UNCED international instruments. The course content addressed aspects of fisheries management polices and legal issues, as well as the monitoring, control and surveillance of fishing activity.

Another capacity-building training course dealt with the Economics for Community-based Project Management in the Pacific region. This event addressed important project management aspects and was targeted for middle management officials from the Pacific region.

IOI Germany organized a 1-month long course on the Sustainable Use of Coastal Living Resources in collaboration with Bogor University, Indonesia. This training course was targeted at university students and young scientists and covered important aspects of fisheries science.

IOI Indonesia ran a 3-day training course (9–12 September 2004) at the University of Indonesia on Coral Reef Ecosystem and Management. This course was addressed to undergraduate students of the University and emphasized the importance of raising awareness of coral reefs from an ecosystem point of view. It was organized in collaboration with the Indonesian Coral Reef Foundation and the University of Indonesia.

In June 2004, IOI Indonesia organized a training course on Geographic Information Systems for the Management of Coastal and Marine Areas. This training course was done in collaboration with the Laboratory of Geographic Information Systems of the Geography Department of the University of Indonesia. The objective of the training course was to support human resources engaged in coastal and marine management, with the capability of applying the knowledge of GIS to manage these habitats in a sustainable manner. A model was applied that provided guidance for the management of coastal and marine areas. A total of 20 participants attended this course.

During the same year, this Operational Centre organized another training course on scuba diving. The purpose of such training was to teach scuba diving techniques to academic students involved in marine biology and coastal conservation. A total of 39 participants, coming from several universities and colleges, attended this course.

IOI Malta continued to support the Mediterranean Institute of the University of Malta in the preparation of its MA course in Maritime Studies. Participating students are expected to be in a position to specialise either in maritime archaeology, history or oceanography for their thesis. During 2004, various marketing tools were planned, including logistical course details. It is envisaged that the first students for this MA course will be welcomed in October 2005.

During 2004, the IOI continued the development of a regional course on Ocean Governance for Mediterranean and Eastern European Countries. Similar to the one held by IOI Canada, this course will uphold the principles enshrined in UNCLOS and on application of its concepts, with an emphasis on the governance of the Mediterranean Sea, and on the Black, Baltic and Caspian Seas. This IOI training course, coordinated by IOI Malta, is being created to help ensure that governments of Eastern Europe and of developing countries in the Mediterranean have access to trained staff who are able to use UNCLOS and other agreements for the benefit of national polices and their economies. It is also expected that they will play the role of trainers and share their gained knowledge with their colleagues at home.

The course is specifically designed to benefit mid-career professionals, educators, researchers and civil society members that have coastal/marine-related responsibilities, functions or interests. The first course is to be held in Malta at the end of 2005. Further information about this training course is available online from http://capemalta.net/ioimoc/course.

IOI Russia focused on marine education for children. It organized a marine festival for children in Soransk (Mordovia region) and a special summer camp "Smena." The Centre took part in the Second Underwater Festival held in February 2004, in Moscow. Activities on the instruction of underwater diving for children were also carried out in May 2004 in Lake Bezdonnoe and the Black Sea. The Centre was engaged in the formulation of university courses on risk assessment and management of the marine coastal zone.

IOI Southern Africa continued to implement its Education through Technology Programme. This programme develops and delivers training courses to support governance of oceans and coasts, and conducts research into the appropriate use of technology in teaching and learning. Courses were prepared for a wide range of audiences from community groups to university students to professionals in ocean and coastal management. Such training courses ranged from being fully computer-based to fully classroom-based, dependent on the nature of the course, the nature of the learners and the resources and technology that were available in each circumstance.

As part of its ongoing efforts at rationalization and increasing work efficiency, IOI-SA was in the process of constructing a more formalized training programme to replace the existing ad-hoc system of course delivery. This was a strategic move aimed at increasing the efficiency of use of training courses, allowing more efficient planning with IOI-SA, including the sourcing of funding in order to run courses and allowing for more timely and predictable delivery of courses within the training programme. This training programme will coordinate with that of the greater IOI and will be incorporated into the IOI OceanLearn.

A course on integrated coastal management was delivered by IOI Southern Africa by means of distance e-learning. This course was targeted towards mid-career decision-makers, students of environmental management, coastal engineering, and environmental law. Another training course dealing with the improvement of municipal wastewater management was organized during 2–5 August 2004 at the University of Western Cape. This capacity-building course was targeted to municipal wastewater managers, health officials, and NGOs involved in the improvement of water and sanitation services. Other institutions collaborated in this event, which included the UNESCO-IHE Institute of Water Education and the UNEP/GPA Coordination Office.

In collaboration with Kalmar University, IOI Baltic Sea organized three intensive academic courses dealing with marine ecology, integrated management of tropical coastal environments, and introduction to marine systems.

These three courses were aimed at undergraduate students from the University of Kalmar.

IOI Ukraine organized a set of lectures on the marine environment, aimed at young and postgraduate students.

IOI OceanLearn

The mission of IOI OceanLearn is to deliver education, training and capacity-building products so as to promote understanding and sustainable management of ocean spaces and resources that will meet the needs of developing nations while addressing the issues as a whole.

During 2004, the IOI has worked on an initiative to rationalize its education, training and capacity-building programs, so as to benefit from its current standing as a teaching establishment and to be able to forge partnerships with leading agencies engaged in similar activities.

During 24–28 May 2004, the IOI, in collaboration with the Center for Tropical Marine Ecology (ZMT) and the Hanse-Wissenschaftskolleg (HWK), organized a workshop on Global Learning in Ocean Science in Delmenhorst, Germany, attended by 23 experts from 20 institutions worldwide. This workshop was convened to address the critical need to build ocean capacity and knowledge, particularly in developing and small island states, as recognized by the United Nations Secretary General's reports to international, regional and national fora. Participants of this workshop included the Directors of IOI Operational Centres from the Baltic Sea, Southern Africa, Costa Rica and Brazil, as well as senior representatives of UN agencies, European universities, and the private sector.

During this workshop, IOI introduced the IOI-OceanLearn initiative as its coordination, training and capacity-building programme. IOI-Ocean-Learn is intended to tackle the diverse and complex capacity-building needs of marine environmental organisations. Following this workshop, a draft of the IOI-OceanLearn business plan has been produced that spelled out clearly the aim of this initiative, namely, (1) the coordination, consolidation and quality assurance of the IOI's education, training and capacity-building activities through a branded training and capacity-building program, and (2) the delivery of IOI products to markets in an effective manner and in such a way the brand will become recognised with quality and delivery. The Governing Board of the IOI approved this initiative in 2004, with a launching date in 2005.

DEVELOPMENT THROUGH RESEARCH

Development through research activities was a major focus of some of the Operational Centres. There was a wide range of research carried out by Operational Centres. Much of it had long-term practical relevance, or was concerned with monitoring and surveying coastal marine resources. Coordination of major research projects was also the purview of some of the most active Operational Centres.

Between 2003 and 2004, a total expenditure of more than US$800,000 was made to support research. A number of Centres carried out activities that were supported entirely by their host institutions, while others supported research activities from the Centre resources. Much of the research was in the field of marine science, but also in the areas of social science and ocean governance. Some Centres supported (at least in part) post-graduate student research, which is considered to be an important contribution to capacity building and in which the IOI is a key player.

The range of community-related activities was large, impacting many participants at workshops and training courses. The focus of some Centres on improving the livelihoods of coastal villagers was well planned and successful, and for this reason it has attracted regional and global attention and funding. Awareness-raising and training in the sustainable use of coastal resources was also a significant activity where community-based coastal management and conservation of resources such as mangroves and coral reef ecosystems have been given high priority.

IOI Eastern Africa continued with its activities related to the development of seaweed farming and community aquaculture as a means of broadening and sustaining the livelihoods of poor coastal communities. Seaweed farming is a simple but very laborious industry that produces dried seaweed and/or extracts for domestic and export markets. During 2004, the Operational Center implemented a study on community-based seaweed farming in which prototype seaweed drying beds were devised for use by farmers. This study was based on the commercial potential of seaweed farming in the region and also addressed preliminary regional marketing strategies for such products.

IOI Malta worked on several capacity-building activities related to marine and coastal management. One was on the management of marine data and information, with the main aim of identifying state-of-the-art and future marine data and information management for the Mediterranean. In January 2004, IOI Malta overviewed the national key issues and trends concerning marine research and related developments in marine affairs. In this exercise, IOI Malta urged national authorities to establish its marine environmental monitoring programme that would include a coastal and sea operational observing system to fully comply with the Malta environmental obligations as a new EU member. Assisting in this is the Malta Blue Pages

Directory, which is an Internet-based distributed directory system for ocean and marine data and information that IOI Malta started to construct in 2004. This online directory aims at establishing a single-point online reference for a number of marine data sources and descriptions in the field of oceanography and marine coastal environment in Malta.

IOI Southern Africa continued to be active in the use of seaweed for sustainable livelihoods. Thus in 2004, the Centre carried out the maintenance of the Seaweed Africa Database, intended to be used by researchers and coastal managers and seaweed users including the mariculture industry. Seaweed Africa is an Internet-based project providing free access to information on commercial or potentially commercial seaweeds. Another important project was maintaining the Seawaste Network with the objective of developing a communication network for integrated waste management professionals from 13 southern and eastern African countries. This Network is assisted by a dedicated web site, e-mail and newsletter to enhance the information distribution. IOI Southern Africa organized a workshop to train the St. Helena Bay community in the construction of a seaweed farming raft.

The Global Invasive Species Programme that was established in 1997 to address global threats caused by invasive alien species and to provide support to the implementation of the Convention on Biological Diversity was continued in 2004. The deliverables of this programme include a web portal on the subject linked to a public/private information interface. As far as public awareness on sustainable livelihoods is concerned, IOI Southern Africa has disseminated brochures on this subject aimed at the general public, tourists and visitors as well as to coastal communities.

All these activities were being done in collaboration with external agencies, including the International Maritime Organization, the Directorate of Marine and Coastal Management, the Department of Environmental Affairs and Tourism of South Africa, the Conservation Planning Unit, and the Cape Nature Conservation Board of South Africa.

IOI Sweden participated in the organisation of an International Conference on Global Waters Assessment and Integrated Waters Management (22–25 August 2004, Kalmar, Sweden). The main objectives of this event were to assess the methodologies for identification of root causes and policy options of water management, to create a dialogue among stakeholders, scientists and decision-makers, to raise awareness and achieve integrated solutions. This event was done in collaboration with GIWA, the University of Kalmar, HELP and VASTRA.

IOI China and the State Oceanic Administration (SOA) of China organized a two-day training course on the work of the International Tribunal for the Law of the Sea and on the process of settling disputes (1–2 July 2004, Beijing, P. R. China). In view of its success, IOI China planned another meeting in November dealing with the role of UNCLOS in connection with the 10th anniversary of the entry into force of the Convention.

The Centre initiated three new research projects: research on the laws and regulations in the International Seabed Area; research on the countermeasures for sustainable utilization of marine resources in the China Sea; establishment and maintenance of a database for examination and approval of science and technology projects.

IOI Indonesia was involved in the development of a seawater quality monitoring programme and in the research on the occurrences of Harmful Algal Bloom (HAB) microorganisms in Hurun Bay, Lampung Bay, South Lampung in Indonesia, in cooperation with the University of Tokyo.

IOI Pacific Islands contributed to the development of the locally managed marine area network on Vanuaso Tikina coastal habitat restoration, as well as to the International Waters Program. The workshop on gender and population aspects was organized within the national integrated coastal management programme.

IOI Slovenia supported the activities of the observatory of the northern Adriatic that is a joint venture of the municipalities from Slovenian, Croatian and Italian coastal regions and northern Adriatic marine research centres. The Centre was the host of the international meeting "Biodiversity Research and Monitoring in the Mediterranean and the Black Sea," held in Piran from 23–27 October 2004.

IOI Canada continued at a strong pace the cooperation with the Korean Ocean Research and Development Institute (KORDI). This cooperation was exemplified by two activities: the contribution of an IOI expert at the International Symposium on New Deep Seabed Mineral Resources Development Policy, organized by KORDI at Ausan, South Korea, during 29–30 January 2004, and the execution of a research study on Comparative Analysis of Deep-sea and Land-based Mineral Resource Development. The research study constituted the third phase of a KORDI-IOI project, the first phase of which, completed in 2002, dealt with the legal aspects of deep-sea mineral resource development, the second phase, completed in 2003, dealt with the economic aspects. The 2004 phase concentrated on the exercises of estimating costs of production in land-based and deep-sea mining and comparison of important factors that influence such costs.

IOI Australia continued to work its research activities in the field of marine biodiversity, with the focus on Samoa and Indonesia. It resulted in the publications and reports to funding agencies, as well as reporting the progress to the 10th International Coral Reef Symposium in Okinawa, Japan. The Centre was working with the International Coral Reef Initiative to promote policy development by countries in coral reef areas of the world through leadership seminars to be held in the sides of the Barbados+10 meetings in Mauritius in 2005. The Director of the Centre was successful in a peer review of his achievements in research, resulting in the Award of

Fellow of the Institute of Marine Engineering, Science and Technology, and as a Chartered Marine Scientist within IMarEST.

IOI Caspian Sea carried out a few research activities and among them the participation in the public ecological monitoring of the Volga River Delta, implementation of Phase 1 of the GRAND project, participation in the meetings of UNESCO on the second phase of the Demonstration Project for Volga-Caspian Region, and of NATO on the Design of the Caspian Basin Observing System to form the basis for environmental forecasting.

The Centre initiated actions for the development of the GOOS (Global Ocean Observing System) regional alliances network. Successful realization of this project jointly with IOC, WMO and other partners will give the possibility to establish an integrated Caspian observing system, transfer new technology and share experience in operational oceanography between partners and will be complementary to the CAPAS project.

IOI Ukraine completed the publication of reports, proceedings, a CD and other PIM-30 materials. The Centre supported the publication of a book on the Black Sea harmful algae developed in cooperation with the NGO Women-Ecologists of Ukraine. Jointly with the Junior Academy of Sciences of Ukraine the competition for the best ecological expert among students was organized. Lectures were delivered on marine ecology and coastal zone management. The book entitled *Ecology: Problems and Solutions—The Vision of the Youth* was prepared and published, containing the results of students' research. The book was dedicated to the international Oceans Day.

The work continued on the development of a set of bioindicators for the coastal zone and bays of estuarine type of Ukraine. It is a contribution to the work implemented in Ukraine for the indication of the environmental status of different coastal areas.

IOI Western Africa organized a three-day interactive forum with stakeholders (traditional rulers, women and youth groups), with the objective to further promote mutual trust, confidence, cooperation and the participatory approach in subsequent activities of IOI in the area. A one-day mini-workshop on the various options and opportunities in local entrepreneurship was conducted in collaboration with Double-M, an NGO dedicated to poverty alleviation among others.

An inventory of natural resources of the Nigerian coastal area was being compiled. Subsequently, similar inventories will be compiled for Cameroon, Benin, Togo, Ghana and Cote d'Ivoire. When the exercise is over there will be a publication of the natural resources in the coastal area of the Gulf of Guinea LME as an IOI product. Such a publication would bring to the fore the imperative sustainable development in the Gulf of Guinea LME coastal area.

With technical assistance from the fish technology unit of the Nigerian Institute for Oceanography and Marine Research (NIOMR), a contemporary smoking kiln was constructed for use by women fish processors in the Orimedu community. In this contemporary kiln, the drudgery and other limitations associated with the traditional kilns have either been minimized or eliminated altogether. The kiln will promote the socio-economic upliftment of the women beneficiaries in this community where fish processing (by dry curing) is the predominant activity of the women.

Women/Youth and the Sea Programme

The Women and the Sea Programme is intended to enhance the capacity and participation of women in poor developing countries in ocean and coastal affairs. Rejuvenation of the IOI is vital and is being done through the Youth Programme by raising awareness and the participation of youth in marine and coastal science. To implement the programme, a total of US$150,000 was distributed to 8 IOI Operational Centres in Canada, Brazil, Costa Rica, India, Nigeria, Iran, Senegal and Caspian Sea. Within the Programme, funding was provided to IOI Canada to support the participation of women in the annual training programme on ocean governance.

The improvement of coastal community infrastructure formed part of ongoing projects that are being run by the Operational Centres in Costa Rica and Brazil. These projects were designed to give continuity to the development programs of coastal communities on Venado Island in the Gulf of Nicoya and on the coast of Parana State in Brazil. At the same they intend to generate a process of community management and development that allows an improvement of life and quality of the inhabitants by strengthening the community's organizations and the development of social infrastructure. The projects aim at enabling the community to progress and generate productive projects that improve conditions of women and their families.

The activities of the eco-villages project, coordinated by IOI India since 1997, formed part of a wider eco-villages project that is being implemented in 40 coastal villages in Southern India. IOI India focused on the improvement of the livelihood of women since they are under greater pressure compared to other members of the community. Women from these communities have to bear the double burden of home care and income generation, besides making huge daily efforts to collect water and firewood.

IOI Iran was engaged in the enhancement of the technical and vocational skills of women living in coastal areas. Its Women/Youth and the Sea Project was aimed at developing marine-related handicrafts by women living in coastal areas and by developing their technical and vocational skills.

In doing so the role of women in society is enhanced and further sustained. The target groups for this project were girls and women living in coastal areas of the Northern and Southern parts of the country, which total to 7 provinces. The activities addressing these objectives included the organization of training courses, publication of audio-visual material, exhibition of marine-related handicrafts made by women, as well as awareness raising and networking activities.

The empowerment of women on aspects of marine ecology, conservation and safety at sea was a project that was coordinated by IOI Nigeria. The activities falling under this project took place in Orimedu and its environment in Ibeju Lekki local government area of Lagos State. The project assisted women and youth to form viable cooperative groups with enough credibility to attract credit facilities, support and patronage. It was linked to many governmental and non-governmental agencies and programmes with similar goals and objectives.

IOI Caspian Sea region actively collaborated with IOI Iran in the organization of summer camps, workshops and youth diving festivals for children. Educational topics were wide ranging and included marine ecology, taxonomy, pollution, sea level change and socio-economic development of the region. Another important activity that was tied with youth education was the involvement of teachers on aspects of developing interactive educational methods in schools.

IOI Senegal coordinated a project that was designed to target 250 women from one of the main fishing villages in Fass Boye. The main objectives of the Project included: minimisation of the losses from fish processing; securing and marketing fish products; training of the female fish processors; financing equipment; and the setting up of a credit line for the processing and commercialization of fish products.

COOPERATION AND PARTNERSHIP

The long-term success of the activities undertaken by IOI would not be guaranteed without the active participation and the empowerment of local communities, groups and organizations. IOI gathers together individuals, organizations and communities working for effective and sustainable ocean governance. IOI has been instrumental in forging many new partnerships for ocean governance. It was part of the effort to strengthen dialogue and win public support for economic and social development. New concepts and new mechanisms of cooperation were emerging and were tested. Within the IOI Network there were four types of cooperation:

1.   *With external partners including governmental and non-governmental organizations, industries, foundations, etc.*

IOI supported the ideas presented in the GMA policy report prepared by the Group of Experts and expressed interest and readiness to contribute to the World Water Assessment Programme in several areas, namely, through training and capacity building, through consultations with stakeholders, and on advising on the implications of coastal and habitat degradation for human health, well-being and safety.

The IOI aligned itself with the statement of the major groups to the Commission on Sustainable Development of April 30, 2004, which contained a call to raise awareness of the importance of the Johannesburg Plan of Implementation, including the Millennium Development Goals (MDGs), and to mobilize the political will to give the Johannesburg Plan the highest priority on the political agenda, as well as to mobilize the financial resources required. IOI input to meeting MDGs in 2004 is outlined in the table. IOI has begun to re-evaluate its activities in the light of MDGs and to realign policies in order to maximize the chances of meeting them. IOI continued to cooperate extensively with other organizations. First and foremost was the cooperation and linkages with the agencies and programmes of the UN System.

IOI demonstrated its identity and potential for beneficial cooperation through participation in the 5th Meeting of the Informal Consultative Process on Ocean Affairs and the Law of the Sea (June 2004, New York) where recent developments on international and national ocean issues have been discussed, through the contribution to the international meetings to review implementation of the Barbados PA for sustainable development of SIDS (January 2004, Bahamas), and to White Water to Blue Water Conferences in Miami and Cairns, Australia. IOI was represented at the governing meetings of IMO, IOC and WMO and used opportunities to advocate the IOI mission and objectives and increase awareness in the IOI activities. The result was signing the MOU on cooperation and joint actions with IOC and the preparation of the MOU with IMO.

The MOU between the Caribbean Regional Fisheries Mechanism (CRFM) and IOI was signed for the joint provision of capacity building in ocean governance in support of the Caribbean Region. The IOI contribution to the work of the UNESCO World Heritage Marine Programme (PSSA) laid the basis for the formalization of the relationship between WHMP and IOI and the possibility of having an MOU on cooperation was discussed.

The IOI President participated as a key speaker in the side-event on "The Mediterranean Response to the WSSD Commitments," held during the 12th Session of the UN Commission for Sustainable Development (April 2004, New York) where he informed the participants of the IOI initiatives in

Millennium Development Goals and the IOI Response	
1. Eradicate Extreme Poverty and Hunger	• Eco-villages programme in Southern India and Africa. • Facilitation of South-South cooperation (IOI/UNDP Projects)
2. Achieve Universal Primary Education	• Training programmes in skills, development issues, vocations and ecology for children in Asian Centres and Fiji • Development and Publication of educational materials for schools • Training and education activities for school children in Russia and European Centre (ecology camps, summer schools, and diving clubs).
3. Promote Gender Equality and Empower Women	• Women and the Sea Programme • Studies of the social role and condition of women in small-scale fishing communities in Brazil and Costa Rica • Reinforcing feminine understanding in the sector of skilled fish processing in Fass Baye, Senegal • Improvement of the quality of life of a group of women living in a poverty stricken island community in the Gulf of Nicoya • Educating mid-career female professionals on Ocean Governance: Policy Law and Management • Training on marine-related handicrafts for women living in the coasts of Bandar Abbas, Iran
4. Ensure Environmental Sustainability	• Organization and delivery of workshops and training courses on law and the environment in the Pacific, integrated coastal zone management in various regions, community leadership, sustainable use of coastal resources including coral reefs, and application of mapping technologies for marine and coastal management (Australia, Malta, Indonesia, Thailand, South Africa)
5. Develop a Global Partnership for Development	• Launching of an initiative towards global learning in ocean sciences (OceanLearn Project) • PIM Conferences • Establishment of MOUs on co-operation

the Mediterranean, the IOI priority actions and obstacles in implementing them.

In the ongoing efforts to strengthen relationships that matter between the UN System and IOI, a new Director of UN DOALOS Office, Dr. V. Golitsyn, and Dr. Ed Sarukhanian, Special Adviser to the WMO Secretary-General on the International Polar Year, were invited to take part in the work of the Board and Committee of Directors. Dr. Golitsyn invited IOI to collaborate with UN DOALOS in the identification and formulation of a five-year plan to be submitted to GEF for its next funding cycle, focusing on an improved delivery of the TRAIN-SEA-COAST programme. In this proposal, emphasis should be given to move the various training approaches so far developed to the field. He also invited IOI to consider potential contributions to the work of UN oceans-targeted task forces that may be established within the mechanism of inter-agency cooperation that will be dealing with emerging issues or issues that require joint action and integrating outside the UN System.

2. *With host institutions under the auspices of which the Operational Centres fulfill functions.*

IOI acknowledged the importance of broadly based advice that the IOI Centres receive from the host institutions. The health of the IOI Network depends on these outstanding institutions. The high level administrations of the host institutions should be included in the Centre Advisory Committees (or Boards) to provide guidance to the Centre Director. Every opportunity should be used to have the heads of the host institutions invited to the Committee of Directors meetings and PIM Conferences.

3. *Among the Operational Centres through joint projects and improved communication.*

The coordination of large research projects and monitoring programmes, or participation in global programmes such as TRAIN-SEA-COAST, GMA and GIWA, GOOS and the UN consultative process provides many opportunities for cooperation and networking among IOI Centres and several Operational Centres were engaged in such activities. The IOI's strengths in the areas of oceans policy have led to regional and global activities that have consequences that are more far-reaching than just the policy development itself. But there is a much greater scope for entrepreneurship and innovation within the IOI Network than at present; time and resource constraints are the main hindrances. Wherever possible such activities should be encouraged as they enhance the reputation of IOI and conform to its mission and goals.

Themes on ocean governance, on gender equity, on regional security and capacity building have made a strategic impact towards strengthening the institute and fostering bonds of cooperation between the Centres. New thematic areas for system-wide projects were proposed in 2004 where the networking of Centres will be crucial. They included coral reef research and protection, integrated coastal area management, marine hazards management and the participation in the International Polar Year.

For the success of the cooperative actions of Operational Centres it is critical to have reliable and operational communication arrangements. In 2004, considerable progress has been achieved by the IOI that is presented in the following section.

4. *Cooperation with IOI Alumni*

The rough estimate shows that in 2004 about 6,000 persons were impacted by some 46 training activities. These young professionals have a big potential to become future leaders. Since 2003 steps have been taken to make alumni active partners and supporters of IOI. In 2004, the alumni database was established which by the end of the year contained more than 1,000 names, half of which were validated and interfaced with the IOI web page and are online. This data will be enriched and used both to assist in the improvement and marketing of the IOI products, as well as an information source to reach and mobilize the IOI alumni. The template was developed to help each Centre to update its alumni database. National/ regional lists of alumni will be relayed to the IOI Headquarters for final compilation in the global database.

An ad hoc working group was established to define the role of alumni; develop further the role of the alumni database; plan an alumni survey taking into account optional outreach strategies; and setting up an alumni association. When the alumni association is established, it may also serve as a public forum and will be an important instrument for promoting cooperation and partnership.

COMMUNICATION AND AWARENESS

The IOI can be considered as a virtual organization relying on appropriate communication tools to manage its interdependent processes, including the creation and sharing of ideas and information and the integration of ideas and information with existing knowledge to construct new knowledge. IOI is conscious of the need to make the public aware of its work and importance. Efforts are being made to achieve public recognition of the IOI activities.

Limited international links and difficulties in establishing effective communication processes have for many years been great restraints on the effectiveness of the Network. In parallel with the ever-increasing global network, the IOI had to develop special mechanisms, which act as a platform for dialogue between the Centres and the outside world. This dialogue was established through the IOI web site, IOI*nforma* and the alumni database.

In 2004, efforts were continued to enhance communication within the IOI. These initiatives were aimed at overcoming fragmentation of communication and to establish a suitable communication process. An internal exercise was carried out by IOI to identify appropriate communication elements that depend on the type of information flow between Headquarters and the Operational Centres, as well as among the Operational Centres themselves. Through this exercise, it was found that for IOI, virtual discussion boards may be harder to use than electronic mail since the latter is more direct and return-receipts ensure that messages are being read. Communication by telephone is much better, but is costly, the same as with teleconferencing. Alternative VoIP can result in much cheaper communication with the network. In all cases, good leadership and clear objectives are needed when communication is initiated.

During 2004, an initiative to enhance the Network communication was launched. This approach was based on the "knowledge ecology" concept, and intended to open up new possibilities for better communication. During this initial stage, proposals were presented as guiding decisions regarding tools, process and people that must be the basis of a sound IOI communications system.

IOI*nforma*—an electronic newsletter of the IOI—continued to be the medium through which operational news was delivered to the IOI Network and members. A total of 18 issues were disseminated in 2004, and more recipients have been included in the mailing list. IOI*nforma* is intended to cover IOI-related work in progress, including missions, debate and implementation, new research and partnerships that will hopefully be of general interest.

The following are actions taken during 2004 to enhance the information content of the IOI web site:

- The homepage was augmented with information about the organizational structure of IOI, web links were enhanced to *The IOI Story* published by IOI some years ago, direct hyperlinks to all Operational Centres, and a link to the training and education activities organized by the IOI Network. Links to IOI news and outside events were being relayed to Headquarters. These mainly relate to conferences, workshops and symposia and training courses. IOI also worked on the linkage of IOI web sites with those of host Institutes aimed at strengthening networking and knowledge sharing between the Centres and host Institutes.
- The e-library, which serves as a source of online information about the IOI activities, continued to be updated. In 2004, online additions included the Proceedings of the Leadership Seminar on Sustainable Development and Regional Security of the Caspian Sea and its Deltas region, and the 2003 Activities Report, the Statutes and Rules of Procedure of IOI and archives of the IOI*nforma* publications.

- In 2004, Headquarters developed an online, password protected site that can be accessed by registered IOI members, including Centre Directors and Board Members. Registered members were given permission to access restricted sites that contained documents of an administrative nature. This facility has worked well in making available documents for the Governing Board and Committee of Directors meetings held in Slovenia, in October 2004.

PROMOTION AND MARKETING

The need to promote and market the IOI is considered to be multifaceted, and mainly focuses on concept, such as generation of awareness of the role and mission of IOI, on its deliverables and relevance, fund-raising from donor agencies, and promoting a greater share of IOI in relevant initiatives at global-regional-local scales. Focusing on a suitable marketing strategy is deemed as vital to keep the IOI very competent in delivering capacity-building programs and to be able to attract external sources of funding.

Such a primary emphasis on building a marketing strategy is seen as being part of an "institutional reform" that puts IOI in a better position to continue implementing its mission and goals in a dynamic and effective manner. This reform can be supported by a three-way approach, namely (i) for IOI to continue promoting itself as a global institution through high-profile projects in which all the network is involved; (ii) Operational Centres need to do their own profiling and marketing to increase the visibility of IOI in their region, and (iii) for the IOI Network to channel its promotional activities through the marketing opportunities offered by their host institutions. The development of unique IOI products could further promote its effectiveness. This will be further supported in the coming years by compartmentalizing and branding the major activity pillars defining the IOI, namely *IOI-Outreach* (consisting of all IOI publications, Conferences (PIM) and communication and marketing initiatives), *IOI-OceanLearn*, and *IOI-Ocean Governance* (by regrouping all of the IOI Network's Ocean Governance research, advocacy and consultancy activities).

On these lines, the Headquarters embarked in 2004 with the production of promotional material such as IOI pins, an IOI medal, together with a full colour IOI brochure and flyer depicting the mission, goals and activities of IOI. The IOI medal, dedicated to the memory of the IOI Founder, Professor Elisabeth Mann Borgese, is to be awarded to people who, according to IOI, have distinguished themselves in the field of the ocean sustainability and the peaceful use of the oceans. Development of promotional materials will remain core activities of IOI, as they are fundamental to the Institute's ability to promote itself and develop partnerships and funding opportunities.

On the same lines, IOI started to plan a promotional exercise for its Women/Youth and the Sea Programme as to be able to attract external funding to support its system-wide programme, as well as to attract external partners to participate in this IOI Programme. This initiative includes the production of a promotional brochure that will be finalized in 2005.

A number of IOI Operational Centres continued to promote their activities and in doing so, IOI's mission goals and objectives. This was done in various ways, including creation and updating of Centres' web pages, dissemination of annual reports, brochures and promotional flyers, as well as dissemination of educational material bearing the mission and goals of the IOI.

In 2004, the proceedings of the 30th international conference *Pacem in Maribus*, held in Kiev in October were published and widely disseminated. This 800-page publication contains all the presentations delivered during the conference, which were also published in CD-ROM format. Another important publication that resulted from the 30th *Pacem in Maribus* Conference will be the publication of an album containing the artworks of Ukrainian children depicting the beauty, bounty and wonders of the sea. This publication is planned for 2005.

Operational Centres produced a number of deliverables resulting from their initiatives that include books, technical reports, conference papers and posters, refereed papers, course reports, and audio-visuals. IOI continued to cooperate in the publication of the *Ocean Yearbook*. Some interesting products were the CD of the Malawai Youth Choir from the Island of Gau, Fiji, and the award-winning *West Coast Cookbook* conceived by IOI Southern Africa. IOI Costa Rica finalized translation into Spanish of the *Oceanic Circle* by the late Elisabeth Mann Borgese. This translation was done to commemorate and preserve her life-long achievements towards the peaceful usage of the ocean and to the implementation of the concept of oceans as a common heritage of mankind. During the same year, IOI Pacific Islands translated the FAO Code of Conduct booklet into seven Pacific Island languages.

Selected Documents and Proceedings

Oceans and the Law of the Sea Report of the Secretary-General, 2005*

SUMMARY

The present report has been prepared in response to the request of the General Assembly, in paragraph 101 of its resolution 59/24 of 17 November 2004, for the Secretary-General to present at its sixtieth session his annual comprehensive report on developments and issues relating to oceans and the law of the sea. It is also presented to States parties to the United Nations Convention on the Law of the Sea, pursuant to article 319 of the Convention, to be considered by the meeting of States parties under the agenda item: "Report of the Secretary-General under article 319 for information of States Parties on issues of a general nature relevant to States Parties that have arisen with respect to the Convention." It will be presented as a basis for discussion at the sixth meeting of the United Nations Open-ended Informal Consultative Process on Oceans and the Law of the Sea and contains information on fisheries and their contribution to sustainable development and marine debris, the areas of focus chosen for the sixth meeting of the Consultative Process, as recommended by the General Assembly. The report also contains information on the status of the Convention and its implementing Agreements, on declarations and statements made by States under articles 287, 298 and 310 of the Convention, and on recent submissions to the Commission on the Limits of the Continental Shelf. The report includes a special section on the Indian Ocean tsunami disaster and a section on capacity-building activities and elaborates on recent developments regarding the safety and security of navigation and protection of the marine environment. Finally, it covers the activities of the Oceans and Coastal Areas Network, a mechanism for inter-agency coordination and cooperation.

    * EDITORS' NOTE.—This document was provided by the United Nations Division for Ocean Affairs and the Law of the Sea (DOALOS) and is extracted from the United Nations General Assembly, Sixtieth Session, Item 76(a) of the preliminary list (A/60/50), UN Document A/60/63, 4 March 2005, available at the DOALOS Web site: http://www.un.org/Depts/los. The document has been edited for publication in the *Ocean Yearbook*.

CONTENTS

ABBREVIATIONS

FAO	Food and Agriculture Organization of the United Nations
GEF	Global Environment Facility
GPA	Global Programme of Action for the Protection of the Marine Environment from Land-based Activities
IAEA	International Atomic Energy Agency
ILO	International Labour Organization
IMO	International Maritime Organization
IOC	Intergovernmental Oceanographic Commission of UNESCO
MARPOL	International Convention for the Prevention of Pollution from Ships, 1973, as modified by the Protocol of 1978 relating thereto
MEPC	IMO Marine Environment Protection Committee
MSC	IMO Maritime Safety Committee
SOLAS	International Convention for the Safety of Life at Sea
SPREP	South Pacific Regional Environment Programme
STCW Convention	International Convention on Standards of Training, Certification and Watchkeeping for Seafarers
SUA Convention	Convention for the Suppression of Unlawful Acts against the Safety of Maritime Navigation
SUA Protocol	Protocol for the Suppression of Unlawful Acts against the Safety of Fixed Platforms Located on the Continental Shelf
TSC	TRAIN-SEA-COAST
UNCLOS	United Nations Convention on the Law of the Sea
UNCTAD	United Nations Conference on Trade and Development
UNDP	United Nations Development Programme
UNEP	United Nations Environment Programme
UNESCO	United Nations Educational, Scientific and Cultural Organization
WHO	World Health Organization

I. INTRODUCTION

1. The world was appalled by the tragic loss of life caused by the devastating tsunami that struck countries along the rim of the Indian Ocean on 26 December 2004. The earthquake-generated waves caused extensive damage to the environment, destroyed the fishing industries of several countries and severely damaged homes and infrastructure. The present report contains a special chapter on the tsunami and its aftermath. As the tsunami disaster made clear, more scientific research is required in order to understand and to be able to predict ocean-related natural disasters. Indeed, a major theme underlying developments throughout the year is the importance of marine scientific research.

2. The future of the planet and our security depend upon increased understanding of oceans processes and their interaction. Oceans-related issues should be addressed in a comprehensive manner, taking an integrated approach. To fully understand the value of the oceans, it is necessary to undertake worldwide oceanic research to acquire scientific knowledge about the state of the marine environment in its different aspects and phenomena. Improving scientific knowledge and applying it to management and decision-making can make a major contribution to eliminating poverty, ensuring food security, supporting human economic activity, conserving the world's marine environment, predicting and mitigating the effects of and responding to natural events and disasters, and, generally, promoting the use of the oceans and their resources for the objective of sustainable development.

II. THE UNITED NATIONS CONVENTION ON THE LAW OF THE SEA AND ITS IMPLEMENTING AGREEMENTS

A. Status of the Convention and its Implementing Agreements

3. As at 31 January 2005, following ratification by Denmark on 16 November 2004, accession by Latvia on 23 December 2004 and ratification by Burkina Faso on 25 January 2005, the number of States parties to the United Nations Convention on the Law of the Sea (UNCLOS or "the Convention"), including the European Community, has risen to 148 (129 coastal States from among the total of 153 and 18 landlocked States from among the total of 42). Burkina Faso, Denmark and Latvia have expressed their consent to be bound by the Agreement relating to the implementation of Part XI. In addition, Botswana acceded to this Agreement on 31 January 2005, bringing the number of parties to 121.

4. Since the issuance of the addendum to the previous report of the Secretary-General (A/59/62/Add.1), there have been no changes in the

status of the 1995 United Nations Fish Stocks Agreement. The number of parties to the Agreement remains at 52, including the European Community.

B.   Declarations and Statements under Articles 287, 298 and 310 of the Convention

5. Denmark made a declaration upon ratification of UNCLOS, stating that the exception from the transit passage regime provided for in article 35 (c) of UNCLOS applies to the specific regime in the Danish straits (the Great Belt, the Little Belt and the Danish part of the Sound), which has developed on the basis of the Copenhagen Treaty of 1857, and that the present legal regime of the Danish straits therefore remains unchanged.

6. Denmark declared that, pursuant to article 287 of UNCLOS, it had chosen the International Court of Justice for the settlement of disputes concerning the interpretation or application of the Convention and that, pursuant to article 298 of UNCLOS, it did not accept an arbitral tribunal constituted in accordance with annex VII for any of the categories of disputes in article 298.

7. Denmark further declared, in accordance with article 310 of UNCLOS, its objection to any declaration or position excluding or amending the legal scope of the provisions of UNCLOS, and stated that "passivity with respect to such declarations or positions shall be interpreted neither as acceptance nor rejection of such declarations or positions".

8. Finally, Denmark recalled that it had transferred competence to the European Community in respect of certain matters governed by UNCLOS and referred to the detailed declaration made by the European Community, upon deposit of its instrument of formal confirmation, on the nature and extent of the transfer of competence. Denmark also stated that the transfer of competence did not extend to the Faroe Islands and Greenland.

III.   MARITIME SPACE

A.   Overview of Recent Developments Regarding State Practice, Maritime Claims and the Delimitation of Maritime Zones

9. *Continental shelf of Trinidad and Tobago.* In October 2004, Trinidad and Tobago informed the Secretary-General that the Parliament of Trinidad and Tobago had enacted the Continental Shelf (Amendment) Act, 1986 (Act No. 23 of 1986), which amended the definition of the continental shelf of Trinidad and Tobago as contained in the Continental Shelf Act,

Chapter 1:52 of the Laws of Trinidad and Tobago, in order to bring it into conformity with article 76 of UNCLOS.

10. *Exclusive economic zone of Greenland.* In November 2004, Denmark informed the Secretariat that, as of 1 November 2004, Act No. 411 of 22 May 1996 on the exclusive economic zones would apply to Greenland, as provided by Royal Decree No. 1005 of 15 October 2004. Denmark also stated that Royal Decree No. 1004 of 15 October 2004, on the amendment of the royal decree on delimitation of the territorial waters of Greenland, in force from 1 November 2004, adjusted the baselines from which the territorial sea and the EEZ are measured, in accordance with recent surveys. In pursuance of Decree No. 1005, the Minister for Foreign Affairs of Denmark issued an Executive Order on 20 October 2004 on the exclusive economic zone of Greenland, which provides that "the exclusive economic zone of Greenland shall comprise waters outside and abutting the territorial waters up to a distance of 200 nautical miles from the baselines in force from time to time" and specifies delimitation of that zone in relation to foreign States. Denmark also indicated its intention to deposit the corresponding information in conformity with UNCLOS, upon the entry into force of UNCLOS for Denmark.

11. *Statement of position by Cyprus.* On 30 December 2004, the Secretary-General received a statement of position from the Government of Cyprus with respect to the information note by Turkey concerning the objection of Turkey to the Agreement between the Republic of Cyprus and the Arab Republic of Egypt on the Delimitation of the Exclusive Economic Zone, signed on 17 February 2003 (see A/59/62, para. 32, and A/59/62/Add.1, para. 51). In this statement, Cyprus refuted the arguments put forth by Turkey as "vague and unfounded, both in law and in substance." Cyprus stated, inter alia, that the Agreement on the Delimitation of the Exclusive Economic Zone was signed between the Governments of two sovereign States, one of them being the Republic of Cyprus, and referred in this regard to General Assembly resolution 3212 (XXIX) and Security Council resolutions 541 (1983) and 550 (1984) on Cyprus. Regarding technical aspects of Turkey's objection to the delimitation of the exclusive economic zone between Cyprus and Egypt, the statement of position declared that Cyprus and Egypt had exercised their legitimate sovereign rights to delimit the exclusive economic zone lying between their respective coasts in a distance less than 400 nautical miles and that, when doing so, they had followed strictly the internationally accepted technical methods and specifications. Furthermore, when deciding on the extent of the delimitation line, the two countries had agreed to avoid extending that line into areas where the rights of third coastal States could be affected. The full text of the statement of position has been circulated to States parties to the Convention and will be published in the *Law of the Sea Bulletin*, No. 57.

12. *Adriatic Sea: communications by Slovenia and Croatia.* In a note verbale dated 30 August 2004 addressed to the Secretary-General, Slovenia provided an explanation with reference to a note of Croatia dated 8 July 2004 (see A/ 59/62/Add.1, paras. 42–44). The full text of the communication from Slovenia was circulated to States parties to UNCLOS and published in the *Law of the Sea Bulletin*, No. 56. On 13 January 2005, the Secretary-General received a communication from Croatia dated 11 January, which contains a response to the note of Slovenia dated 30 August 2004. The communication was circulated to States parties to UNCLOS and will be published in the *Law of the Sea Bulletin*, No. 57.

13. *Exclusive economic zone of Finland.* In a communication dated 11 January 2005, Finland informed the Secretary-General of the entry into force on 1 February 2005 of the Act on the Exclusive Economic Zone of Finland (1058/2004). According to the Act, Finland establishes an exclusive economic zone comprising the part of the sea immediately adjacent to its territorial waters. The outer limits of the zone are determined by the agreements concluded by Finland with other States and the outer limit of the zone is given by a Government decree that also entered into force on 1 February 2005.

B.   Deposit and Due Publicity

14. Between August 2004 and January 2005, several coastal States deposited charts or lists of geographical coordinates of points with the Secretary-General, as required by UNCLOS. On 27 August 2004, Brazil deposited with the Secretary-General, in accordance with article 75, paragraph 2 of UNCLOS, the list of geographical coordinates of points defining the outer limit of the Brazilian Exclusive Economic Zone. On 16 September 2004, China deposited with the Secretary-General, in accordance with article 16, paragraph 2, article 75, paragraph 2 and article 84, paragraph 2 of UNCLOS, the list of geographical coordinates of points specified in the Agreement between the People's Republic of China and the Socialist Republic of Viet Nam on the Delimitation of the Territorial Sea, the Exclusive Economic Zone and Continental Shelf in Beibu Bay/Gulf of Tonkin, which was signed by the two countries on 25 December 2000, and officially took effect on 30 June 2004. Finally, on 30 November 2004, Viet Nam deposited with the Secretary-General, in accordance with article 16, paragraph 2, article 75, paragraph 2 and article 84, paragraph 2 of the Convention, the same list of geographical coordinates as referred to above.

C. Access to and from the Sea and Freedom of Transit

15. The General Assembly, in its resolution 59/245 on specific actions related to the particular needs and problems of landlocked developing countries, reaffirmed the right of access of landlocked countries to and from the sea and freedom of transit through the territory of transit countries by all means of transport, as set forth in article 125 of UNCLOS. The Assembly stressed the need for the implementation of the Sao Paulo Consensus adopted at the eleventh session of the United Nations Conference on Trade and Development, held in Sao Paulo, Brazil, from 13 to 18 June 2004, by the relevant international organizations and donors in a multi-stakeholder approach (see also A/59/62/Add.1, para. 54). It also urged the 2005 high-level event of the General Assembly on the review of the United Nations Millennium Declaration to address the special needs of landlocked developing countries, within a new global framework for transit transport cooperation for landlocked and transit developing countries.

IV. INSTITUTIONS ESTABLISHED BY THE UNITED NATIONS CONVENTION ON THE LAW OF THE SEA

A. International Seabed Authority

16. The International Seabed Authority held its tenth session from 24 May to 4 June 2004. For information on the work of that session and on the commemoration of the Authority's tenth anniversary, see paragraphs 21 to 30 of document A/59/62/Add.1.

17. The Authority held a workshop in Kingston from 6 to 10 September 2004 for the establishment of environmental baselines at deep seafloor cobalt-rich crusts and deep seabed polymetallic sulphides mine sites in the Area for the purpose of evaluating the likely effects of exploration and exploitation on the marine environment. The workshop was organized to assist the Legal and Technical Commission of the Authority in preparing guidelines for use by potential contractors in the establishment of environmental baselines. The Workshop decided to use the recommendations adopted by the Legal and Technical Commission for the guidance of contractors in assessing the possible environmental impacts arising from exploration for polymetallic nodules (ISBA/7/LTC/1/Rev.1) as the basis for the new guidelines, amending them to take account of the specific characteristics of polymetallic sulphides and cobalt crusts. The full report and recommendations of the workshop will be available to the Legal and Technical Commission for consideration during the Authority's eleventh session, to be held from 15 to 26 August 2005. At that session, the Council of the Authority will begin consideration of the draft regulations for prospect-

ing and exploration for polymetallic sulphides and cobalt crusts prepared by the Legal and Technical Commission.

B.   International Tribunal for the Law of the Sea

18. The International Tribunal for the Law of the Sea held its seventeenth session from 22 March to 2 April and its eighteenth session from 20 September to 1 October 2004. The sessions were devoted essentially to legal matters having a bearing on the judicial work of the Tribunal and other administrative and organizational issues. The Tribunal, inter alia, undertook a review of its rules and judicial procedures and prepared budget proposals for 2005–2006.

19. On 14 December 2004, the Tribunal and Germany signed the headquarters agreement. The agreement defines the legal status of the Tribunal in Germany and regulates the relations between the Tribunal and the host country. It will enter into force on the first day of the month following the date of receipt of the last of the notifications by which the Tribunal and Germany inform each other of the completion of their respective formal requirements for the entry into force of the agreement.

20. On 1 September 2004, Horst Köhler, President of the Federal Republic of Germany, visited the Tribunal, accompanied by approximately 140 members of the diplomatic corps accredited to Germany. In commemoration of the tenth anniversary of the entry into force of the Convention, a symposium on maritime delimitation was held at the Tribunal on 25 and 26 September 2004. It was attended by more than 150 participants, including a large number of representatives of States.

21. In 2004, the Korea International Cooperation Agency provided a grant to fund the participation of interns from developing countries in the internship programme of the Tribunal. To date, 11 interns coming from 11 countries have benefited from the grant.

C.   Commission on the Limits of the Continental Shelf

22. The Commission on the Limits of the Continental Shelf held its fourteenth session from 30 August to 3 September 2004.[1] The Commission considered, inter alia, the submission made by Brazil;[2] the training manual

---

1. For more information regarding the fourteenth session, see CLCS/42. For an overview of the first six years of work of the Commission, see A/59/62, paras. 83–109.

2. Brazil delivered its submission on 17 May 2004; see A/59/62/Add.1, para. 19.

to assist States in preparing a submission to the Commission; the projected workload of the Commission and its need for appropriate facilities; the consolidation of the rules of procedure; the election of officers; and vacancies in the subcommission established to consider the submission made by the Russian Federation.

Consideration of the Submission Made by Brazil

23. The head of the Brazilian delegation, Lúcio Franco de Sá Fernandes, Director of Hydrography and Navigation, Ministry of Defence of Brazil, who was accompanied by a delegation of experts, made a presentation of the submission. He provided an overview of its content including the information required by section II, of annex III to the rules of procedure. Members of the Brazilian delegation answered questions posed by members of the Commission in regard to various technical and scientific issues related to the submission (see CLCS/42, para. 11).

24. The Secretariat informed the Commission that on 30 August 2004, the Legal Counsel of the United Nations had received a letter from the Deputy Permanent Representative of the United States of America to the United Nations, with a request that it be circulated to the members of the Commission and to all Member States. In the letter, the Government of the United States commented on the executive summary of the Brazilian submission, which had been circulated to all Member States, and suggested that the Commission might wish to pay attention to certain issues related to sediment thickness and the Vitoria-Trindade feature.[3]

25. The Commission decided that the Brazilian submission would be examined by way of a subcommission, and appointed the following to serve

3. With reference to the letter from the Deputy Permanent Representative of the United States of America, the Commission noted that, in accordance with annex II to the Convention and the rules of procedure, the Commission is required to consider communications from States other than the submitting one only in the case of disputes between States with opposite or adjacent coasts or in other cases of unresolved land or maritime disputes. Consequently, the Commission concluded that the content of the letter should not be taken into consideration by the subcommission. After the fourteenth session, the Deputy Permanent Representative of the United States conveyed to the Legal Counsel the disappointment of her Government at the decision of the Commission. In particular, the United States asked the Commission to reconsider its conclusions, arguing that the rules of procedure require the Commission and subcommission to consider comments from other States regarding the data reflected in the executive summary, not only comments related to disputes between States with opposite or adjacent coasts or other disputes. This correspondence is available on the website maintained by the Division for Ocean Affairs and the Law of the Sea, at www.un.org/Depts/los/clcs_new/submissions_files/submission_bra.htm.

as its members: Osvaldo Pedro Astiz, Lawrence Folajimi Awosika, Galo Carrera Hurtado, Mladen Juraèiæ, Wenzheng Lu, Yong-Ahn Park and Philip Alexander Symonds. The subcommission elected Mr. Carrera as its chairman and Messrs. Juraèiæ and Symonds as vice-chairmen.

26. The chairman of the subcommission informed the Commission that the subcommission had carried out a preliminary examination of the submission and accompanying data and, in view of their nature, had decided to seek the advice of another member of the Commission, Harald Brekke.

27. The chairman of the subcommission outlined the general timetable for its work, stating that the subcommission had concluded that the examination of the voluminous and complex data received could not be completed during the two-week period allocated following the fourteenth session. Consequently, the subcommission would resume its meetings at the fifteenth session to review the work carried out intersessionally and to prepare a draft of the first working document related to the submission. That meant that two subcommissions would work simultaneously at the fifteenth session, if the Commission decided to examine a new submission by way of a subcommission.

Consequences of the Projected Workload of the Commission

28. In response to two notes verbales (dated 16 January and 9 July 2004) that the Division for Ocean Affairs and the Law of the Sea of the Office of Legal Affairs circulated to ascertain the timing of potential submissions to the Commission, 13 coastal States have informed the Division of their intention to make submissions before the end of 2009: Nigeria, before August 2005; Ireland, in 2005; Tonga, between January 2005 and December 2006; New Zealand, in 2006; Norway, not before 2006; the United Kingdom of Great Britain and Northern Ireland, before 2007; Namibia and Sri Lanka, in 2007; Uruguay, not before 2007; Pakistan, in 2007 or 2008; and Japan, Myanmar and Guyana, in 2009. Several other States have replied, indicating that the preparation of their submission was under way but that they were not yet in a position to specify a date for its completion.

29. Given the projected workload of the Commission, and the likelihood that multiple subcommissions would be working simultaneously in the future, concerns were expressed with regard to the functioning of the Commission. In response to a letter from the Chairman of the Commission, dated 2 July 2004, the Director of the Division for Ocean Affairs and the Law of the Sea informed the Commission that steps had already been taken to expand the facilities at the Division designed for the use of the Commission. A second geographical information system laboratory is under construction at the Division; the storage space has been expanded; and the conference room is being enlarged to meet the needs of the Commission. The

upgraded facilities should be available in time for the fifteenth session of the Commission, so that two subcommissions will be able to work simultaneously.[4]

Submission made by Australia

30. On 15 November 2004, Australia delivered its submission to the Commission through the Secretary-General. In accordance with rule 50 of the Commission's rules of procedure, the Secretary-General circulated a Continental Shelf Notification, containing the executive summary of that submission, including all charts and coordinates indicating the proposed outer limits of the Australian continental shelf and the relevant territorial sea baselines, to all Member States of the United Nations, including the States parties to the Convention.

31. The United States, the Russian Federation, Japan and Timor-Leste transmitted to the Secretary-General written comments on the executive summary of the Australian submission through notes verbales dated, respectively, 3 and 9 December 2004, 19 January 2005 and 11 February 2005. The United States and the Russian Federation indicated that they did not recognize any claims in relation to territories located in the area covered by the Antarctic Treaty nor any State's rights over the seabed and subsoil of the submarine areas beyond and adjacent to the continent of Antarctica, and that they supported Australia's request to the Commission that it not take any action on the portion of the submission relating to areas of the seabed and subsoil adjacent to Antarctica. Japan made similar comments and stressed that the balance of rights and obligations in the Antarctic Treaty should not be affected. Timor-Leste observed that, in its view, the Australian submission was without prejudice to the question of delimitation of any maritime boundaries between Timor-Leste and Australia and requested that this point be made by the Commission during its examination of the submission.[5]

Programme of Work for 2005

32. In 2005, the Commission will hold two sessions: the fifteenth session, from 4 to 22 April, and the sixteenth session, from 29 August to 16

---

4. In paragraph 31 of its resolution 59/24, the General Assembly requested the Secretary-General to submit to it at its sixtieth session proposals on how to ensure that the Commission could fulfil its functions under the Convention, taking into account the need for expanded facilities adequate to the projected workload of the Commission.

5. The correspondence by the United States, the Russian Federation, Japan and Timor-Leste is available on the Division's website, at www.un.org/Depts/los/clcs_new/submissions_files/submission_aus.htm.

September. The Commission will begin consideration of the Australian submission at the fifteenth session.

Training Manual

33. The training manual to assist States in preparing a submission in accordance with article 76 of the Convention, the preparation of which was requested by the Commission (see CLCS/21, para. 21), has been finalized by the Division for Ocean Affairs and the Law of the Sea with the assistance of two members of the Commission (for further details, see para. 47 below).

V.   SETTLEMENT OF DISPUTES: CASE LAW SUMMARIES

34. UNCLOS provides for four alternative forums for the settlement of disputes: the International Tribunal for the Law of the Sea, the International Court of Justice, an arbitral tribunal constituted in accordance with annex VII to UNCLOS or a special arbitral tribunal constituted in accordance with annex VIII to UNCLOS. States parties may choose one or more of those forums by written declaration made under article 287 of UNCLOS and deposited with the Secretary-General of the United Nations.

35. *International Court of Justice.* Cases still pending before the Court and of relevance to law of the sea matters are: *Territorial and Maritime Dispute (Nicaragua v. Colombia); Maritime Delimitation between Nicaragua and Honduras in the Caribbean Sea (Nicaragua v. Honduras)* and *Case concerning Maritime Delimitation in the Black Sea (Romania v. Ukraine).* In the only new oceans-related case since the previous report of the Secretary-General, on 16 September 2004, Romania instituted proceedings against Ukraine in a dispute described in its application as "concern[ing] the establishment of a single maritime boundary between the two States in the Black Sea, thereby delimiting the continental shelf and the exclusive economic zones apper-taining to them". In its order of 19 November 2004, the Court fixed 19 August 2005 as the time limit for the filing of Romania's memorial and 19 May 2006 as the time limit for the filing of Ukraine's counter-memorial. Information on cases before the International Court of Justice is available on its website at www.icj-cij.org, as well as in its reports to the General Assembly, which contain summaries of cases.

36. *International Tribunal for the Law of the Sea.* On 18 December 2004, the Tribunal delivered its judgment in the case *St. Vincent and the Grenadines v. Guinea-Bissau,* ordering the prompt release of the St. Vincent vessel *Juno Trader* and its crew being detained by Guinea-Bissau. The full text of the judgment is available at the Tribunal's website at www.itlos.org.

37. *Annex VII arbitration:* Case concerning Land Reclamation by Singapore in and around the Straits of Johor (Malaysia v. Singapore). In

2003, the Tribunal considered a request for provisional measures by Malaysia against Singapore in respect of their land reclamation dispute in the Straits of Johor (see A/59/62/Add.1, para. 141). Subsequently, the parties constituted an arbitral tribunal under annex VII to UNCLOS to hear the case on the merits. In early January 2005, Singapore and Malaysia reached a negotiated agreement to settle their dispute on the basis of the recommendations of an independent group of experts appointed by both Governments to study the impact of land reclamation. The parties intend to submit their signed settlement agreement to the arbitral tribunal to form the basis of its award.

VI. CAPACITY-BUILDING

A. Overview

38. The Convention acknowledges the needs of developing States for capacity-building and technical assistance in areas such as marine scientific research, the transfer of technology, activities in the Area and the protection and preservation of the marine environment. The need for capacity-building has also been emphasized in successive General Assembly resolutions on oceans and the law of the sea. As underscored in paragraph 37.1 of Agenda 21, the programme of action adopted at the United Nations Conference on Environment and Development:[6] "The ability of a country to follow sustainable development paths is determined to a large extent by the capacity of its people and its institutions as well as by its ecological and geographical conditions. Specifically, capacity-building encompasses the country's human, scientific, technological, organizational, institutional and resource capabilities."

39. The term "capacity-building" is often incorrectly used as a synonym of technical assistance. However, capacity-building has characteristics differentiating it from other forms of assistance and cooperation: it focuses on sustainability and on the development of national competencies (see TD/B/WP/155). Capacity-building activities have the direct effect of enabling the beneficiaries to perform and sustain the targeted functions.[7]

40. The Division for Ocean Affairs and the Law of the Sea carries out a diverse range of activities relevant to capacity-building: provision of advisory

6. *Report of the United Nations Conference on Environment and Development, Rio de Janeiro, 3–14 June 1992* (United Nations publication, Sales No. E.93.I.8 and corrigenda), vol. I: *Resolutions adopted by the Conference*, resolution 1, annex II.

7. UNCTAD/GDS/DMFAS/2003/1, p. 4, available at www.unctad.org/en/docs/gdsdmfas2003/_en.pdf.

services; administration of trust funds; organization of briefings and training programmes; preparation of studies, handbooks and publications; maintenance of databases; and dissemination of information through the Internet. To meet the requirements of various international instruments and in the light of the evolution of priorities, the Division is moving from the provision of technical assistance upon request, to proactive initiatives to better equip States to face the challenges of implementing the Convention and deriving benefits from it. The following section provides an overview of both the traditional and the new capacity-building activities carried out by the Division.

B.   Specific Programmes

1.   *United Nations Institute for Training and Research*

41. From 12 to 14 October 2004, the Division for Ocean Affairs and the Law of the Sea, in conjunction with the United Nations Institute for Training and Research, organized a briefing on developments in ocean affairs and the law of the sea, 10 years after the entry into force of the United Nations Convention on the Law of the Sea. The briefing focused on both overviews and key developments with regard to the Commission on the Limits of the Continental Shelf, the International Seabed Authority and the International Tribunal for the Law of the Sea; navigation; assistance to developing States; maritime zones; marine scientific research; conservation and management of marine living resources; and vulnerable and threatened marine ecosystems and biodiversity. The response of the approximately 60 participants in the briefing was very positive. The next briefing will be held on 4 and 5 October 2005, and will be organized with a view to facilitating the negotiations on the draft resolutions related to the item entitled "Oceans and the law of the sea" on the agenda of the sixtieth session of the General Assembly.

2.   *Hamilton Shirley Amerasinghe Memorial Fellowship Programme*

42. Established in 1981 in memory of Hamilton Shirley Amerasinghe, the first President of the United Nations Conference on the Law of the Sea, the Fellowship provides participants with in-depth knowledge and additional skills related to ocean affairs and the law of the sea, in order to foster a wider appreciation and application of the Convention and to benefit their countries. Fellows spend six months carrying out supervised research and study at a participating university of their choice, followed by three months of practical training at the Division for Ocean Affairs and the Law of the Sea or at other United Nations entities, depending on their choice of topic. In 2004, the award was given to Milinda Gunetilleke, of Sri Lanka, the

nineteenth recipient, who intends to carry out his research on legal issues relating to the continental margin.

43. The General Assembly has repeatedly called upon Member States, interested organizations, foundations and individuals to continue to make voluntary contributions towards the financing of the fellowship. In 2004, contributions to the fellowship fund were received from Monaco, Namibia and Sri Lanka. Information on the Amerasinghe Fellowship may be found on the website of the Division for Ocean Affairs and the Law of the Sea, at www.un.org/Depts/los.

3.   United Nations-Nippon Foundation Fellowship Programme

44. In April 2004, the United Nations and the Nippon Foundation of Japan concluded a technical cooperation agreement to provide capacity-building and human resource development opportunities to developing coastal States, both parties and non-parties to UNCLOS, through a nine-month academic fellowship programme on maritime affairs. This programme is being administered by the Division for Ocean Affairs and the Law of the Sea, with certain support services provided by the Department of Economic and Social Affairs. The fellowship programme is currently being implemented in partnership with 24 academic institutions, international agencies and international organizations in 16 countries.

45. The selection committee, established in accordance with the technical cooperation agreement between the United Nations and the Nippon Foundation, held its first meeting on 6 and 7 December 2004 and selected the first 10 fellows on the basis of their qualifications and in accordance with the relevant provisions of the technical cooperation agreement. They come from the following countries: Bahamas, Bangladesh, Bulgaria, Cambodia, Libyan Arab Jamahiriya, Mauritius, Peru, Philippines, Saint Lucia and Viet Nam. Fellows were selected from nearly 30 candidates nominated by their respective Governments. Invitations for the second round of nominations will be sent in April 2005. Detailed information is available at www.un.org/Depts/los.

4.   TRAIN-SEA-COAST Programme

46. The TRAIN-SEA-COAST (TSC) programme provides capacity-building at the local and regional levels with an emphasis on (a) building up permanent national capabilities; (b) training targeted to the specific needs of countries; and (c) cost-effectiveness. It is administered by the Division for Ocean Affairs and the Law of the Sea and funded by the Global Environment Facility (GEF) of the United Nations Development Programme (UNDP) through its project GLO/98/G35, expected to end in the first half of 2005. TSC has continued to strengthen its cooperation with other United Nations bodies and programmes (see A/59/62/Add.1, para.

150). In this regard, the TSC course development unit established within the UNEP GPA Coordination Office has added new deliveries of its course on improving wastewater management in coastal cities, in Bangladesh, Kenya, Maldives, Mozambique, Pakistan, Philippines, Sri Lanka, Turkey and the United Republic of Tanzania. In addition, the TSC/IMO course on ballast water management (see A/58/65/Add.1, para. 135) was delivered at the regional level in Cape Town, South Africa in March 2004 and at the national level in China in June 2004. As an attempt to utilize GEF funding for the new course on submissions to the Commission on the Limits of the Continental Shelf was unsuccessful, the delivery of this course by the Division for Ocean Affairs and the Law of the Sea was funded from other sources (see next section).

5. Training Courses to Promote Compliance with Article 76 of the Convention

47. As noted in paragraph 33 above, the Division for Ocean Affairs and the Law of the Sea finalized the training material for its training course for delineation of the outer limits of the continental shelf beyond 200 nautical miles and for preparation of a submission of a coastal State to the Commission on the Limits of the Continental Shelf, based on the outline for a five-day course prepared by the Commission (CLCS/24) in order to facilitate the preparation of submissions in accordance with its scientific and technical guidelines (CLCS/11 and Add.1). The training material consists of a trainer's manual, including a set of slides accompanied by instructions for delivery of the modules, and a trainee's manual that contains nine modules as well as a set of relevant exercises.

48. In cooperation with intergovernmental bodies and host Governments, the Division for Ocean Affairs and the Law of the Sea has begun organizing workshops for developing States, at the regional and subregional levels, using the aforementioned training material. The purpose of the workshops is to train technical staff of wide-continental-margin States intending to establish the outer limits of their continental shelf, with a view to (a) enhancing their knowledge and skills for the preparation of submissions to the Commission on the Limits of the Continental Shelf in conformity with the technical and scientific requirements of article 76 of UNCLOS and in accordance with the guidelines prepared by the Commission; and (b) helping them to develop an in-depth understanding of the full procedure for the preparation of the submission, of the required technical and scientific data, and of how different fields of expertise have to be combined for the purposes of the submission.

49. The first regional workshop was organized by the Division for Ocean Affairs and the Law of the Sea, in cooperation with the South Pacific Applied Geoscience Commission and the Commonwealth secretariat, in Suva, Fiji, from 28 February to 4 March 2005. The workshop was attended by

technical personnel of the following developing countries: Fiji, Indonesia, Malaysia, Micronesia, Palau, Papua New Guinea, Philippines, Solomon Islands, Tonga, Vanuatu and Viet Nam. The second regional workshop is tentatively planned to take place in Sri Lanka in May 2005. It is organized for Indian Ocean developing countries by the Division for Ocean Affairs and the Law of the Sea in cooperation with the Government of Sri Lanka. At least three more workshops are planned by the Division in Africa and in Latin America and the Caribbean.

6.   *Publications*

50. At the tenth anniversary of the entry into force of the Convention, the Division for Ocean Affairs and the Law of the Sea and the International Seabed Authority jointly issued a commemorative publication on marine mineral resources. This publication provides an overview of the existing legal framework for marine mineral resources, the scientific aspects of these resources, and the economic and technological perspectives. To provide assistance to States parties in fulfilling all their obligations under UNCLOS, in 2004 the Division also published a compendium of obligations of States parties under the Convention and complementary instruments. The compendium identifies obligations of States under UNCLOS as well as instruments establishing the international standards, rules, regulations, practices and procedures referred to therein.

C.   **Trust Funds**[8]

51. *Trust fund for assistance to States participating in the Conference on Maritime Delimitation in the Caribbean.* During the reporting period, there was no activity with regard to this trust fund. As at 31 December 2004, there was $116,773 in the fund.

52. *Trust fund for the purpose of facilitating the preparation of submissions to the commission on the limits of the continental shelf.* This trust fund was established by the General Assembly in its resolution 55/7; its terms of reference were subsequently amended by resolution 58/240. The goal of the fund is to provide assistance to countries, in particular the least developed countries and small island developing States, to enable them to prepare submissions to the Commission. The fund covers the training of technical and administrative staff, desk-top studies and advisory assistance or consultancies. Applications to the fund are considered by the Division for Ocean Affairs and the Law of the Sea with the assistance of an independent

---

8. Further information on the trust funds is available at www.un.org/Depts/los.

panel of experts. In December 2004, the panel of experts recommended and the Division agreed that assistance from the fund be provided for up to two applicants each from Indonesia, Malaysia, the Philippines and Viet Nam, to attend the training course in Fiji described in paragraph 49 above. As at 31 December 2004, there was $1,148,000 in the fund. Norway contributed $1 million in 2000 and Ireland contributed 90,000 euros in three instalments, the last one in 2004.

53. *Trust fund for the purpose of defraying the cost of participation of the members of the Commission on the Limits of the Continental Shelf from developing States.* This trust fund was established pursuant to paragraph 20 of General Assembly resolution 55/7 to enable members of the Commission from developing countries to participate fully in the work of the Commission. As at 31 December 2004, there was $93,500 in the fund. No contributions were made to the fund in 2004. Four members of the Commission received financial support from the fund for the purpose of defraying the cost of their participation in the fourteenth session of the Commission.

54. *Assistance fund under part VII of the 1995 United Nations Fish Stocks Agreement.* The assistance fund became operational in the second half of 2004. Administered by the Food and Agriculture Organization of the United Nations (FAO) in collaboration with the Division for Ocean Affairs and the Law of the Sea, the fund has received $200,000 from the United States of America.

55. *Trust fund to assist States in their settlement of disputes through the International Tribunal for the Law of the Sea.* This fund was established pursuant to General Assembly resolution 55/7; its terms of reference are set out in annex I to resolution 55/7. As at 31 December 2004, there was $69,153 in the fund. No contributions were received in 2004. The first application to the fund was made in 2004 by Guinea-Bissau, which requested financial assistance to defray its expenses in the case of *St. Vincent and the Grenadines v. Guinea-Bissau* for the release of the arrested vessel *Juno Trader* and its crew (see para. 36 above). In January 2005, the Secretary-General approved the recommendation of the panel of experts, established pursuant to the terms of reference of the fund (China, Russian Federation and United Kingdom), to provide financial assistance of $20,000 to Guinea-Bissau in response to its request.

56. *Voluntary trust fund for the purpose of assisting developing countries in attending meetings of the United Nations Open-ended Informal Consultative Process on Oceans and the Law of the Sea.* This trust fund was established by General Assembly resolution 55/7. As at 31 December 2004, there was $157,097 in the fund. No contributions were made in 2004. Representatives from the following 11 countries received assistance to attend the fifth meeting of the Consultative Process: Bahamas, Cape Verde, Fiji, Guinea, Madagascar, Marshall Islands, Mozambique, Myanmar, Peru, Samoa and Zimbabwe.

VII. DEVELOPMENTS RELATING TO INTERNATIONAL SHIPPING ACTIVITIES

57. International shipping makes a significant contribution to international trade and the world economy as an efficient, safe and environmentally friendly method of transporting goods around the globe. The primary responsibility for ensuring that ships are safe and adequately manned, the crew adequately trained and provided with decent working conditions, the cargo properly stowed and the ship safely navigated, and that no pollution occurs, rests with the flag State. Articles 94, 211 and 217 of UNCLOS set out the measures a flag State is required to take to fulfil those objectives, although other articles are also relevant. The measures the flag State is required to implement and enforce to ensure safety at sea must conform to the international rules, regulations, standards, procedures and practices contained in instruments developed by international organizations such as IMO and the International Labour Organization (ILO).

A. Ship Construction and Equipment

58. Comprehensive revisions to the technical regulations of the Protocol of 1988 relating to the International Convention on Load Lines, adopted by the IMO Maritime Safety Committee (MSC) at its seventy-seventh session (resolution MSC.142(77)), entered into force on 1 January 2005. New amendments to annex B to the Protocol were adopted at the seventy-ninth session of MSC (resolution MSC.172(79)). Amendments to the guidelines on the enhanced programme of inspections during surveys of bulk carriers and oil tankers (resolution MSC.144(77)) also entered into force on 1 January 2005.

59. In 2004, contracting parties to the International Convention for the Safety of Life at Sea (SOLAS) adopted amendments to chapters II-1, III, V, VII, XI-1, XII, and the annex to SOLAS, and to the 1988 Protocol relating to SOLAS (resolutions MSC.170(79) and MSC.171(79)). Chapter XII of SOLAS was amended to introduce restrictions on sailing with any hold empty and new provisions relating to double-side skin construction for new bulk carriers of 150 m in length and over as an alternative to single-side skin construction. The IMO Codes mandatory under SOLAS[9] and a number of non-mandatory Codes[10] were also amended.

---

9. Amendments were adopted to the International Code for the Application of Fire Test Procedures (resolution MSC.173(79)), the International Codes of Safety for High Speed Craft of 1994 and 2000 (resolutions MSC.174(79) and MSC.175(79)), the International Code for the Construction and Equipment of Ships Carrying Dangerous Chemicals in Bulk (resolution MSC.176(79)), the International Code for the Construction and Equipment of Ships Carrying

60. Other relevant developments during the period under review include the decision of IMO not to restrict its future work on passenger ship safety to large ships;[11] and its development of goal-based new ship construction standards in order to introduce a system whereby the standards would be a measure against which the safety of the ship could be assessed during its design and construction stages, as well as during its operation. In a related, but separate project, the International Association of Classification Societies is developing common structural rules for ships, initially for bulk carriers and tankers.[12]

B.   Training of Seafarers and Fishers and Labour Conditions

Training

61. MSC adopted amendments to part A of the Seafarers' Training, Certification and Watchkeeping Code by resolution MSC.180(79), which will enter into force on 1 July 2006. The list of parties to the International Convention on Standards of Training, Certification and Watchkeeping for Seafarers, confirmed by MSC to have communicated information demonstrating that they have given full and complete effect to the relevant provisions of the Convention, as amended (the so-called "white list"), now includes 114 parties.

62. IMO member States have been urged to become parties to the 1995 International Convention on Standards of Training, Certification and Watchkeeping for Fishing Vessel Personnel, in order to bring it into force and enhance training standards for fishing vessel personnel. The new Code of Safety for Fishermen and Fishing Vessels, 2005, which is a revised version of the original Code approved in the 1970s, has been developed for use primarily by competent authorities, training institutions, fishing vessel owners, fishers' representative organizations and non-governmental organizations having a recognized role in fishers' safety and health and training. Part A of the Code provides guidance on the development of national codes

Liquefied Gases in Bulk (resolution MSC.177(79)), the International Code for the Safe Carriage of Packaged Irradiated Nuclear Fuel, Plutonium and High-Level Radioactive Wastes on Board Ships (resolution MSC.178(79)) and the International Management Code for the Safe Operation of Ships and for Pollution Prevention (resolution MSC.179(79)).

10. See resolutions MSC.181(79), MSC.182(79), MSC.183(79), MSC.184(79), MSC.185(79), MSC.186(79) and MSC.187(79).

11. IMO document MSC 79/23, para. 4.12.

12. International Chamber of Shipping/International Shipping Federation, *Mariscene* 31, Winter 2005.

and fishers' education and training manuals and guidance on the safety and health of fishers.

Labour Conditions

63. The nature of seafaring has made seafarers a politically, legally and economically weak group in society.[13] Increasingly, seafarers have been charged with criminal offences and detained for long periods following a maritime accident, in some cases without wages and without the benefit of due process. The prospect of a prolonged detention acts as a disincentive to those considering joining the profession. The revision and consolidation by ILO of the maritime labour conventions, the revision of the Convention concerning Seafarers' National Identity Documents (see para. 87 below), and the joint work by IMO and ILO on liability and compensation regarding claims for death, personal injury and abandonment of seafarers, and more recently also on the fair treatment of seafarers in the event of a maritime accident, represent important initiatives in addressing some of the problems facing seafarers.

64. A new consolidated maritime labour convention is being designed by ILO to replace almost all the maritime labour conventions adopted since 1920. It will emphasize compliance and enforcement measures in order to ensure decent working conditions for seafarers and will contain a simplified amendment procedure allowing technical details to be rapidly updated. The new convention is expected to be adopted at the ninety-fourth maritime session of the International Labour Conference in February 2006. In September 2004, the Preparatory Technical Maritime Conference was able to resolve a very large number of difficult and important issues, but did not have time to consider amendments to provisions on which consensus had been reached in the High-Level Tripartite Working Group on Maritime Labour Standards. In order to provide an opportunity to discuss these amendments and the remaining bracketed text, the Governing Body of ILO decided to convene tripartite intersessional meetings from 21 to 27 April 2005.

65. The Preparatory Conference also adopted a resolution in which it urged members (a) to agree among themselves on measures of cooperation which would develop national institutions and capacity for the inspection and certification of maritime labour conditions; (b) to provide training and to exchange knowledge and experience with respect to national policies, laws and regulations and procedures in this area; and (c) to strengthen

---

13. See United States submission to the first session of the Joint IMO/ILO Ad Hoc Expert Working Group on the Fair Treatment of Seafarers in the Event of a Maritime Accident, IMO document IMO/ILO/WGFTS 1/6/3.

measures to develop cooperation, the exchange of information and the provision of material assistance at the international, regional and bilateral levels in support of the ratification and implementation of the future convention.[14]

66. Complementing the consolidation of standards for seafarers, ILO is working on the development of a comprehensive standard (a convention supplemented by a recommendation) concerning work in the fishing sector (see A/59/62/Add.1, para. 59). At the ninety-third session of the International Labour Conference, in May 2005, the Committee on the Fishing Sector will consider the text of the proposed instruments, which has already been sent to all member States for comments,[15] a summary of the comments received thereon, the report of the tripartite meeting of experts on the fishing sector held in December 2004, a commentary by the International Labour Office explaining changes made to the text based on the comments received, and the texts of a proposed convention and recommendation on work in the fishing sector.

67. The development of guidelines on the fair treatment of seafarers in the event of a maritime accident was considered in January 2005 at the first session of the joint IMO/ILO working group established for this purpose (see A/59/62/Add.1, para. 61). The concept of "fair treatment" is assumed to include not only a legal right to due process, but other aspects of fairness such as a right to adequate access to provisions to meet basic physical needs and a right to be treated in a non-discriminatory manner (see IMO document IMO/ILO/WGFTS 1/7). Several international instruments, including UNCLOS, in particular articles 292 and 230, contain provisions supporting this objective. The Working Group prepared a draft resolution for adoption by the IMO Assembly and the ILO Governing Body that would stress the concern of the entire maritime industry on the matter, recall the relevant international instruments and urge all States to respect the basic human rights of seafarers, expeditiously investigate maritime accidents to avoid any unfair treatment, and adopt procedures to allow for the prompt repatriation or re-embarkation of seafarers. The draft resolution will be considered by the Governing Body of ILO in March and by the IMO Legal Committee in April 2005.[16]

---

14. Reports of the Conference can be consulted on the ILO website at www.ilo.org/public/english/standards/relm/maritime/.

15. Report V(1) is on the ILO website at www.ilo.org/public/english/standards/relm/ilc/ilc93/pdf/rep-v-1.pdf.

16. Report of the Joint IMO/ILO Working Group on Fair Treatment of Seafarers, IMO document IMO/ILO/WGFTS 1/11.

C.   Transport of Goods

68. MSC, at its seventy-ninth session, adopted the Code of Safe Practice for Solid Bulk Cargoes, 2004 (resolution MSC.193(79)) and intends to provide for the mandatory application of some parts of the Code in the future through the adoption of amendments to chapters VI and VII of SOLAS.

69. With respect to the transport of radioactive materials, recent developments include the shipment by the United States of weapons-grade plutonium to France for fabrication into civilian power reactor fuel for test irradiation in the United States.

70. Ships engaged in the carriage of irradiated nuclear fuel, plutonium and high-level radioactive wastes must comply with the International Code for the Safe Carriage of Packaged Irradiated Nuclear Fuel, Plutonium and High-Level Radioactive Wastes on Board Ships. Carriage requirements for highly radioactive cargo (for example, design, fabrication, maintenance of packaging, handling, storage and receipt), which are applicable to all modes of transport, are contained in the International Atomic Energy Agency (IAEA) Regulations for the Safe Transport of Radioactive Material.[17] Missions of the IAEA Transport Safety Appraisal Service help countries to assess and enhance their implementation of the Agency's transport safety standards. In 2004, IAEA published reports on missions to Turkey, Panama and France. A mission to Japan is scheduled for late 2005. Maritime transport of radioactive material is addressed in all missions.

71. The General Assembly in its resolution 59/24, welcomed the adoption by the General Conference of IAEA of resolution GC(48)/RES/10 and the approval by the Board of Governors of IAEA of the Action Plan for the Safety of Transport of Radioactive Material (see A/59/62/Add.1, paras. 64–66). The IAEA International Action Plan for Strengthening the International Preparedness and Response System for Nuclear and Radiological Emergencies was approved by the Board of Governors in June 2004. In its resolution GC(48)/RES/10, as in past years, the IAEA General Conference reaffirmed maritime rights and freedoms, as provided for in international law. It welcomed the practice of some shipping States and operators of providing in a timely manner information and responses to relevant coastal States in advance of shipments for the purpose of addressing concerns regarding safety and security, including emergency preparedness, and

---

17. The 1996 edition of the Transport Regulations (as amended in 2003) was published in 2004. Further review of these regulations resulted in approval by the Board of Governors for publication of the 2005 edition. Changes approved for this 2005 edition will be included in the 2005 edition of the United Nations Model Regulations and will then be incorporated in the 2007 editions of international air, sea, road and rail regulations, to become effective 1 January 2007.

invited others to do so in order to improve mutual understanding and confidence regarding shipments of radioactive materials. Shipping States and relevant coastal States were encouraged to continue informal discussions on communication, with IAEA involvement, as recommended by the President of the 2003 International Conference on the Safety of Transport of Radioactive Material (see A/58/65/Add.1, paras. 37–40) and included in the Action Plan.[18]

72. The resolution also stressed the importance of having effective liability mechanisms in place to insure against harm to human health and the environment, as well as actual economic loss due to an accident or incident during the maritime transport of radioactive materials. In order to aid the understanding and authoritative interpretation of the IAEA nuclear liability instruments, an explanatory text has been developed by the IAEA International Expert Group on Nuclear Liability.[19] Future work of the Group includes an examination of any serious gaps in the regime.

73. In June 2004, Pacific Islands Forum members continued their technical-level dialogue with France, Japan and the United Kingdom on issues related to the shipment of radioactive materials through the Pacific, including prevention, emergency response preparedness and liability and compensation. Forum members were assured that best-practice prevention and response mechanisms are in place and that the regional interest in timely prior notification, information exchange and media coordination is built into planning and procedures. Forum members were also given a full explanation of claims procedures under the revised liability conventions.[20] In August 2004, Forum leaders reiterated their concerns about possible economic loss in a non-release situation and sought assurances from shipping States that, where there is a demonstrable link between the incident and economic loss, Forum countries would not be left to carry such a loss unsupported by the shipping States.[21]

74. In the Mauritius Strategy for the further implementation of the Programme of Action for the Sustainable Development of Small Island

---

18. The text of the action plans and the IAEA resolution can be found on the IAEA website at www.iaea.org.

19. An overview of the modernized IAEA nuclear liability regime, i.e., the 1997 Protocol to Amend the Vienna Convention on Civil Liability for Nuclear Damage and the Convention on Supplementary Compensation for Nuclear Damage, is provided in IAEA document GOV/INF/2004/9-GC(48)/INF/5, available at www.iaea.org/About/Policy/GC/GC48/Documents/gc48inf-5.pdf. The explanatory texts are available at www.iaea.org/About/Policy/GC/GC48/Documents/gc48inf-5explanatorytexts.pdf.

20. Information provided by the secretariat of the Pacific Community.

21. Communiqué of the thirty-fifth Pacific Islands Forum, Apia, Samoa, 5–7 August 2004. See press statement 56–04 of the Pacific Islands Forum secretariat at www.forumsec.org.fj/docs/Communique/2004%20Communique.pdf.

Developing States,[22] the international community notes that cessation of transport of radioactive materials through small island developing States' regions is an ultimate desired goal of small island developing States and some other countries, and recognizes the right of freedom of navigation in accordance with international law. States are encouraged to maintain dialogue and consultation, in particular under the aegis of IAEA and IMO, with the aim of improving mutual understanding, confidence-building and enhanced communications in relation to safe maritime transport of radioactive materials. States involved in the transport of such materials are urged to continue to engage in dialogue with small island developing States and other States to address their concerns, including the further development and strengthening, within the appropriate forums, of international regulatory regimes to enhance safety, disclosure, liability, security and compensation in relation to such transport (A/CONF.207/CRP.7, para. 20 quater).

D. Safety of Navigation

Hydrographic Surveys

75. MSC, at its seventy-eighth session, approved circular 1118 on the implementation of SOLAS regulation V/9—hydrographic services (IMO document MSC/Circ.1118), in order to remind Governments of their obligations under SOLAS regulation V/9, which entered into force on 1 July 2002 (see A/58/65, para. 71), and to inform them that the International Hydrographic Bureau could assist in examining their needs for developing or improving their hydrographic capabilities.

Ship Routing and Reporting Measures

76. At its seventy-ninth session, MSC adopted new and amended existing traffic separation schemes, including associated routing measures, which will take effect on 1 July 2005 (IMO document COLREG.2/Circ.55). The Committee also adopted a new area to be avoided and a mandatory no anchoring area in the West Cameron Area of the Gulf of Mexico and a new area to be avoided in the region of the Berlengas Islands (Portugal), that will also take effect on 1 July 2005 (IMO document SN/Circ.240).

22. The Mauritius Strategy was adopted on 14 January 2005 at the International Meeting to Review the Implementation of the Programme of Action for the Sustainable Development of Small Island Developing States and is contained in draft form in document A/CONF.207/CRP.7.

77. The guidelines and criteria for ship reporting systems were amended by resolution MSC.189(79) to require the use of geographical coordinates in World Geodetic System 1984 (WGS 84) datum or in the same datum as the nautical chart if this chart is based on a datum other than WGS 84 (see IMO document MSC 79/23, annex 31). A similar amendment has been proposed to the General Provisions on Ships' Routing for adoption by the Assembly of IMO. The Committee also adopted the proposed mandatory ship reporting system in the Western European Particularly Sensitive Sea Area (resolution MSC.190(79)), to take effect on 1 July 2005.

Straits of Malacca and Singapore

78. The IMO Council, at its ninety-third session, held in November 2004, decided that the Organization had played and could play a role in the protection of shipping lanes of strategic importance and significance. It decided that IMO and its Secretary-General should, in cooperation with the littoral States concerned, continue efforts to enhance safety, security and environmental protection in the Strait of Malacca through assisting the littoral States, user States and other stakeholders to take appropriate action to ensure that the Strait remains safe, secure and open to international navigation, including through awareness raising, information-sharing, personnel training, capacity-building and technical cooperation. To that end, IMO and its Secretariat are to seek to promote the marine electronic highway project specifically designed for the Straits of Malacca and Singapore. The GEF/World Bank/IMO marine electronic highway project demonstrates the use of digital technology in navigation to, inter alia, reduce the frequency of ship collisions in the Straits' congested sea lanes and deter bilge water and other ship waste releases. The Council decided to convene an IMO-sponsored meeting in 2005 to consider ways and means to enhance safety, security and environmental protection in the Straits of Malacca and Singapore. Past conferences on navigational safety and the control of pollution in the Straits were convened by IMO and the Institute of Policy Studies, Singapore in 1996 and 1999 (see A/55/61, para. 81).

E.   Implementation and Enforcement

79. In its resolutions 59/24 and 59/25, the General Assembly recommended actions aimed at strengthening flag States' implementation of their responsibilities under international law. Language similar to that contained in paragraph 38 of resolution 59/24 was included in the Mauritius Strategy (see A/CONF.207/CRP.7, para. 23(f)). As regards operative paragraph 40 of resolution 59/24, it can be noted that the Joint MSC/IMO Marine Environment Protection Committee (MEPC)/Technical Cooperation Com-

mittee Working Group on the Voluntary IMO Member State Audit Scheme
has agreed, in principle, that the draft code for the implementation of IMO
instruments[23] should be the basis for the audit standard; that further work
was needed to ensure that the code met the requirements of the audit
standard; and that the draft code should be evaluated against the draft
audit. The IMO Council acknowledged at its twenty-second extraordinary
session that the obligations and responsibilities of member States should be
auditable in accordance with the code.

80. With respect to the issue of the genuine link, the IMO Council, at its
ninety-third session, noted that the Secretary-General of IMO had consulted
the executive heads of other competent international organizations on how
best to implement the invitation made by the General Assembly in its
resolutions 58/240 and 58/14. It agreed that an inter-agency meeting
should be convened by the Secretary-General of IMO and requested him to
report on its outcome at the next session of the Council for consideration
and action as appropriate, before a relevant submission is conveyed to the
United Nations for consideration by the General Assembly at its sixty-first
session in 2006 (IMO document C 93/D, para. 17(a)). The inter-agency
meeting will take place on 7 and 8 July 2005.

81. MSC, at its seventy-ninth session, approved a joint MSC/MEPC
circular on transfer of ships between States, providing a procedure whereby
the transfer of ships between flag States should be conducted so that the
"gaining" flag State could seek safety-related information from the "losing"
flag State.

F.   Jurisdictional Immunities

82. Article 16 of the United Nations Convention on Jurisdictional
Immunities of States and Their Property, adopted by the General Assembly
by its resolution 59/38, restates the principle in UNCLOS that ships owned
or operated by a State and used, for the time being, only on government
non-commercial service, have sovereign immunity. According to article 16,
State immunity is also maintained in respect of any cargo on board a ship
owned or operated by a State, as well as any cargo belonging to a State and
used or intended for use exclusively for government non-commercial
purposes. However, if a State owns or operates a ship which, at the time the
cause of action arose, was used for other than government non-commercial
purposes, it cannot invoke immunity from jurisdiction before a court of
another State that is otherwise competent in a proceeding which relates to

23. It has not been decided yet whether the code will cover only mandatory
instruments.

the operation of the ship or to the carriage of cargo on board the ship. In such case, irrespective of the type of proceeding, whether *in rem* or *in personam*, States may plead all measures of defence, prescription and limitation of liability which are available to private ships and cargoes and their owners. If required, the Government and non-commercial character of the ship or cargo, may be proven by a certificate signed by a diplomatic representative or other competent authority of the State.

VIII. MARITIME SECURITY AND CRIMES AT SEA

83. Most of the major threats to international peace and security identified in the report of the High-level Panel on Threats, Challenges and Change (A/59/565) have a maritime component. For example, resource security, food security and human health can be threatened by over-exploitation of living marine resources and degradation of the marine environment. Competing demands over dwindling resources can lead to inter-State conflict. Ships can be used for illicit purposes, for example, to transport nuclear, radiological, chemical and biological weapons or small arms and light weapons. They can also be the object of a terrorist attack or used for terrorist purposes. Transnational organized criminals misuse maritime transport for illicit traffic in narcotic drugs and psychotropic substances, smuggling of migrants and other criminal activities. Recent actions taken by the international community to prevent and suppress acts of terrorism against shipping and illicit traffic in weapons of mass destruction, their means of delivery and related materials, as well as piracy and armed robbery at sea, smuggling of migrants and illicit traffic in narcotic drugs and psychotropic substances are set out below.

A.   Maritime Security

International Ship and Port Facility Security Code

84. In its resolution 59/24, the General Assembly welcomed the entry into force of the International Ship and Port Facility Security Code and related amendments to SOLAS on 1 July 2004, and encouraged States to ratify or accede to international agreements addressing the security of navigation and to adopt the necessary measures, consistent with UNCLOS, to implement and enforce the rules contained in those agreements. Data gathered by the IMO secretariat and the port and shipping industries shows that compliance with the Code is now close to 100 per cent, as compared to some 86 per cent of ships and 69 per cent of port facilities immediately prior to its entry into force. Reports on control and compliance measures

taken against ships in the aftermath of the entry into force of the Code are relatively small in number. However, there is concern over information that some Governments and port authorities in certain regions have not yet taken all of the actions necessary to implement the Code fully in their port facilities. It has also been suggested that the security regime needs further improvement.[24]

85. In order to facilitate the consistent, uniform and harmonized implementation of the security measures in SOLAS and the Code, in 2004 MSC adopted interim guidance on control and compliance measures to enhance maritime security (resolution MSC.159(78)) and also approved a number of circulars,[25] including guidance to masters, companies and duly authorized officers on the requirements relating to the submission of security-related information prior to the entry of a ship into port (MSC/Circ.1130). The latter circular includes a standardized data-set of security-related information that ships could be expected to provide in advance of their arrival in port. It recommends that unless a coastal State has established a different time period for the submission of the required information prior to the expected entry of the ship into port, the default minimum period should be not less than 24 hours. Australia has announced its proposal to establish a maritime identification system up to 1,000 nautical miles from the coast, based on cooperative international arrangements, including with neighbouring countries, in accordance with international and domestic law, to be implemented during 2005. Australia will require ships intending to call at its ports to provide advance arrival information up to 1,000 nautical miles from its coast. Ships intending to come within 200 nautical miles of the coast will be asked to provide information on a voluntary basis up to 500 nautical miles from the coast. Some neighbouring States were reported to have raised concerns regarding the proposed establishment of what has been perceived as a new maritime zone.[26]

24. Opening address by the Secretary-General of IMO at the seventy-ninth session of MSC, IMO document MSC 79/23, p. 9.

25. Guidance relating to the implementation of SOLAS Chapter XI-2 and the ISPS Code (MSC/Circ.1132); Interim guidance on voluntary self-assessment by SOLAS Contracting Governments and by port facilities (MSC/Circ.1131), which includes a self-assessment questionnaire to assist SOLAS Contracting Governments in the implementation of, and the maintenance of compliance with, the requirements of SOLAS Chapter XI-2 and the ISPS Code; Reminder of the obligation to notify flag States when exercising control and compliance measures (MSC/Circ.1133); and a revised circular on false security alters and distress/security double alerts (MSC/Circ.1109/Rev.1).

26. See Special press summary: Australia's maritime identification zone, 21 December 2004, prepared by the Pacific Virtual Information Center, at www.vic-info.org. The summary includes the press release of the Australian Prime Minister's announcement of the zone.

86. Other actions taken by IMO to assist States in the implementation of the amendments to SOLAS and the International Ship and Port Facility Security Code include technical assistance activities in the two global programmes under the IMO Integrated Technical Cooperation Programme. The global programme on maritime and port security will now focus on specific operational measures that need to be taken to safeguard the security of passengers and crews; and a "train-the-trainer" programme will help Governments to strengthen their maritime security implementation through the provision of trained instructors capable of delivering quality training using the relevant IMO model courses.

87. IMO has underlined the need for a proper balance between the needs of security, the requirement to maintain the safety and working efficiency of the ship, and the protection of the human rights of seafarers and port workers (see IMO document MSC/Circ.1112). The ILO Seafarers' Identity Documents Convention (Revised), 2003 (No. 185), which entered into force on 9 February 2005, is expected to strengthen international port security while also facilitating the transit, transfer and shore leave of seafarers in the normal conduct of their profession. The Convention requires the issuance of a new seafarers' identity document. Its biometric feature, the fingerprint, is based upon "global interoperability," so that it is possible for the fingerprint information on the identity document issued in one country to be read correctly by equipment used in another. To enable this, the ILO Governing Board adopted in March 2004 a single standard (ILO SID-0002, Finger minutiae-based biometric profile for seafarers' identity documents, with specifications to be followed in national systems and products for generating the biometric representation of fingerprints on the identity document, and for verifying that the seafarer's fingerprint corresponds to the fingerprint on the identity document. ILO has since tested products from potential suppliers and, as at 15 January 2005, had identified two products that meet the requirements of Convention No. 185 and the ILO SID-0002 standards.

Revision of the SUA Convention

88. The Legal Committee of IMO and its working group on the revision of the Convention for the Suppressing of Unlawful Acts against the Safety of Maritime Navigation (SUA Convention) and the Protocol for the Suppression of Unlawful Acts against the Safety of Fixed Platforms Located on the Continental Shelf (SUA Protocol) have continued their consideration of the draft protocol to the SUA Convention, focusing primarily on the non-

proliferation offences and the boarding provisions.[27] The terrorist offence provisions have received general support. The Committee decided to expand the definition of "death or serious injury or damage" to include substantial damage to the environment. The working group agreed to include a general reference to UNCLOS in the preamble.

89. At its meeting early in 2005, the working group reached agreement on the inclusion of a definition of transport for the purposes of the Convention. A substantial majority in the working group agreed on the wording of the offence consisting of the transport of nuclear materials and the offence for the transport of dual use equipment, materials or software or related technology (see IMO document LEG/SUA/WG.2/4).

90. New boarding provisions have been included in the draft protocol which: (a) require express flag State authorization before a boarding may take place; (b) require the requesting party to consider warning other States if a flag State does not comply with its obligation to respond to a request; (c) require States to take into account the dangers and difficulties involved in boarding a ship at sea and searching its cargo and to consider whether other appropriate measures agreed between the States concerned could be more safely taken in the next port of call or elsewhere; and (d) specify that the flag State may consent to the exercise of jurisdiction by another State having concurrent jurisdiction. It was agreed that any use of force during boarding must not exceed the minimum degree of force necessary and reasonable in the circumstances and to include provisions concerning compensation for unjustified boarding or if the measures are unlawful or exceed that reasonably required. The authorization to board by a flag State will not per se entail its liability. It was furthermore agreed that it was not necessary to exclude specific offences from the boarding provisions, since the flag State's consent already determined which offences would trigger boarding provisions.

91. The working group also reviewed the proposed amendments to the Protocol for the Suppression of Unlawful Acts against the Safety of Fixed Platforms Located on the Continental Shelf (SUA Protocol) (see LEG/SUA/WG.2/4, paras. 93–104) and agreed that some provisions of the draft protocol to the SUA Convention would also apply mutatis mutandis to the offences in the SUA Protocol. The IMO Legal Committee will devote one week of its two-week session in April 2005 to consideration of the draft protocols to the SUA Convention and the SUA Protocol. A diplomatic conference is scheduled to adopt the draft protocols in October 2005.

92. The High-level Panel on Threats, Challenges and Change has recommended that ongoing negotiations at IMO to amend the SUA

27. See IMO document LEG 89/16, and the report of the working group in LEG/SUA/WG.2/4.

Convention should be completed in a timely manner in order to reinforce international legal provisions against illicit trafficking of nuclear, biological and chemical weapons and materials. The Panel states in its report (A/59/565) that if progress in the negotiations is not satisfactory, the Security Council may need to be prepared to consider mandatory action. The Panel also recommends that all States be encouraged to join the Proliferation Security Initiative (described in A/59/62, para. 162).

93. Pursuant to the Statement of Interdiction Principles adopted by States participating in the Proliferation Security Initiative, the United States and the United Kingdom are pursuing cooperation in the prevention of the flow of weapons of mass destruction, their delivery systems, and related materials to and from States and non-State actors of proliferation concern on a bilateral basis by concluding boarding agreements with individual flag States.

B.   Piracy and Armed Robbery Against Ships

94. Whether an attack can be qualified as an act of piracy or armed robbery depends on the location and the nature of the offence. Piracy is defined in article 101 of UNCLOS and armed robbery in the IMO Code of Practice for the Investigation of the Crimes of Piracy and Armed Robbery against Ships.

95. The International Maritime Bureau of the International Chamber of Commerce received reports of 325 actual and attempted acts of piracy and armed robbery during 2004.[28] The number of incidents of piracy and armed robbery against ships reported to IMO during the first nine months of 2004 was 252. While this figure represents a decrease of 28 per cent compared with the corresponding period in 2003, the level of violence has escalated. During the period, 30 crew members and passengers were reportedly killed, 94 were injured and 113 were taken hostage. The areas most affected by acts of piracy and armed robbery against ships were the Far East, in particular the South China Sea and the Malacca Strait; South America and the Caribbean; the Indian Ocean; and West and East Africa. Most of the attacks worldwide were reported to have occurred or been attempted in territorial seas while ships were at anchor or berthed.

96. Seafarers consider that the international community and the international shipping industry have failed to provide effective responses to the growing threats posed by piracy and armed robbery attacks on merchant ships. They believe that the absence of any concerted and coordinated

28. International Maritime Bureau, *Annual report of incidents of piracy and armed robbery against ships* (2004).

international action to tackle the problem means that merchant shipping is becoming an increasingly attractive target not only to traditional "pirates" and armed robbers, but also to terrorists. They consider it essential for the international community to urgently demonstrate a "zero tolerance" approach to piracy and armed attacks on shipping.[29]

97. MSC, at its seventy-ninth session (see IMO document MSC 79/23, sect. 16), urged all Governments and the industry to intensify and coordinate their efforts to eradicate these unlawful acts. Governments were urged to provide information to IMO on the action they took with regard to incidents reported to have occurred in their territorial waters. The Committee furthermore noted the activities of the IMO secretariat in conducting workshops and seminars on combating piracy and armed robbery; the plan to hold a regional seminar on piracy and armed robbery against ships and maritime security in Yemen in March or April 2005; and the actions taken pursuant to the Secretary-General's initiative on the protection of vital shipping lanes (see para. 78 above).

98. General Assembly resolution 59/24 underlined the need for States to give urgent attention to the promotion, adoption and implementation of cooperation agreements, in particular at the regional level in high-risk areas. The Regional Cooperation Agreement on Combating Piracy and Armed Robbery against Ships in Asia, adopted on 11 November 2004 in Tokyo, is expected to strengthen regional cooperation in preventing and combating piracy and armed robbery against ships in Asia.[30] It will establish a network of cooperation and information sharing among the maritime safety and coastguard institutions of 16 Asian States. Singapore will host an information-sharing centre to collect, analyse and prepare reports on information transmitted by the contracting parties concerning piracy and armed robbery against ships, including other relevant information, if any, relating to individuals and transnational organized criminal groups committing such acts. The reports will be disseminated to the parties, the shipping community and IMO. The centre will also alert contracting parties if there is a reasonable ground to believe that a threat of an incident of piracy or armed robbery against ships is imminent.

29. Report by the National Union of Marine, Aviation and Shipping Transport Officers (NUMAST), providing the seafarers' perspective of the unacceptable threat to merchant shipping and how seafarers perceive the problem could be best addressed, available on NUMAST website at www.numast.org.

30. The Government of Japan expects that this agreement will strengthen the anti-piracy activities in Asia, especially in the Malacca and Singapore Straits, and become a leading model of regional cooperation in Asia (Ministry of Foreign Affairs of Japan, press conference 12 November 2004, at www.mofa.go.jp/announce/press/2004/11/1112.html).

C.   Illicit Traffic in Narcotic Drugs and Psychotropic Substances

99. It is estimated that criminal organizations gain $300 billion to $500 billion annually from illicit traffic in narcotic drugs and psychotropic substances (A/59/565, para. 166). Many drugs are transported illicitly by sea. Containers facilitate the trafficking of large quantities of heroin and cocaine. For example, in 1999, 64 per cent of the global seizure volume of cocaine reported to the World Customs Organization was intercepted in maritime containers. In response to the projected doubling of the container trade by 2012, the United Nations Office on Drugs and Crime has launched a Container Control Pilot Programme in partnership with the World Customs Organization to support port State control measures in developing countries by providing them with training and equipment to target illicit trafficking via maritime freight containers. Activities will start with the ports of Guayaquil (Ecuador) and Dakar.[31]

100. Article 108 of UNCLOS and article 17 of the 1988 United Nations Convention against Illicit Traffic in Narcotic Drugs and Psychotropic Substances provide the legal framework for cooperation among States in the suppression and combating of illicit traffic of narcotic drugs and psychotropic substances by sea. In order to further enhance cooperation, the United Nations Office on Drugs and Crime has issued two guides: a maritime drug law enforcement training guide and a practical guide for competent national authorities under article 17 of the 1988 Convention. However, as noted by the Executive Director of the Office in his third biennial report on the world drug problem (see E/CN.7/2005/2/Add.3, sect. VII), much remains to be done in the area of combating illicit traffic in drugs by sea, as only a few States reported that they were using the available tools. Since the twentieth special session of the General Assembly in 1998, 43 States reported that they had reviewed, simplified or otherwise strengthened procedures for executing requests in connection with countering illicit traffic by sea. From June 2002 to June 2004, only a few States reported that they had received, sent or executed requests for assistance in relation to illicit traffic by sea. Some States reported that statistics were not available. Difficulties encountered included staff limitations and the time-consuming nature of the requests, lack of resources, requests received from an unrecognized competent authority, lack of reliable information and failure by requesting Governments to verify information.

31. See "United Nations launch container control programme against illicit trafficking," press release UNIS/NAR/863 of 21 October 2004, at www.unis.unvienna.org/unis/pressrels/2004/unisnar863.html. An electronic link is provided to a PowerPoint presentation on the Container Control Programme.

101. In October 2004, the Government of Japan, in cooperation with the United Nations Office on Drugs and Crime, hosted a maritime drug law enforcement seminar for enforcement agencies from nine countries of the Asian region (Cambodia, China, Indonesia, Japan, Malaysia, Republic of Korea, Thailand, Philippines, Viet Nam) to further international cooperation in combating illicit drug trafficking by sea through training on the Office's practical guide for competent national authorities. In addition, the Japanese coastguard demonstrated a secure, fast e-mail system that enables the exchange of information on suspect vessels, including photographs of such vessels. The authorities in Japan and China tested the system between them and found it to be very efficient and inexpensive. The Japanese coastguard offered to make the system available to other law enforcement agencies in the region.

102. IMO has decided to revise its guidelines for the prevention and suppression of the smuggling of drugs, psychotropic substances and precursor chemicals on ships engaged in international maritime traffic (contained in IMO Assembly resolution A.872(20)) on an urgent basis in order to align them with the International Ship and Port Facility Security Code. A considerable number of aspects addressed in the IMO guidelines relating to security matters are now dealt with in the Code. However, it has been emphasized that security measures should not inhibit interdiction activities and that the maintenance of the security measures and procedures in place on board a ship have to be appropriately balanced with the need to allow searches of a ship for illicit drugs, psychotropic substances and precursor chemicals. The IMO Facilitation Committee intends to submit draft amendments to the guidelines to the twenty-fourth session of the IMO Assembly for adoption in late 2005.

D.   Smuggling of Migrants

103. The total number of incidents related to unsafe practices associated with the trafficking or transport of migrants by sea reported to IMO from 1999 to 30 July 2004 was 597, involving 20,175 migrants (IMO document MSC.3/Circ.7). But the actual number of incidents is estimated to be much higher. General Assembly resolution 59/24 welcomed the entry into force of the Protocol against the Smuggling of Migrants by Land, Air and Sea and the Protocol to Prevent, Suppress and Punish Trafficking in Persons, Especially Women and Children, supplementing the United Nations Convention against Transnational Organized Crime. As of 4 February 2005, 67 States had become parties to the smuggling protocol and 79 to the trafficking protocol. In order to assist States in the ratification and implementation process, the United Nations Office on Drugs and Crime has developed and published legislative guides for the implementation of the

Convention against Transnational Organized Crime and its protocols. The Conference of the Parties to the Convention, at its second session, in October 2005, will consider, among other matters, difficulties encountered by States parties in the implementation of the smuggling protocol and technical assistance possibilities.

IX. THE MARINE ENVIRONMENT, MARINE RESOURCES AND SUSTAINABLE DEVELOPMENT

A. Protection and Preservation of the Marine Environment

1. Pollution from Land-based Activities

104. Marine pollution from land-based activities has significant negative implications of global magnitude for human health, poverty alleviation, food security and safety, and for affected industries. It amounts to about 80 per cent of marine pollution. While sewage remains the largest source of contamination, other serious land-based threats include persistent organic pollutants, many of which are transported globally via the atmosphere, non-biodegradable litter, and changes to natural sediment loads in rivers. Groundwater, storm water, rivers, sewage systems and the wind all transfer terrestrially derived pollutants to the oceans, where the pollutants accumulate in both biological and geophysical resources, thus reducing the economic, social and environmental value of coastal and oceanic systems.[32]

(a) Legal and Policy Framework

105. UNCLOS, in articles 194, 207 and 213, provides the legal framework for States to protect the marine environment from land-based pollution. This framework is complemented by the Global Programme of Action for the Protection of the Marine Environment from Land-based Activities (GPA),[33] which provides guidance to national and regional authorities for devising and implementing sustained action to prevent, reduce and control or eliminate marine degradation from land-based activities. GPA addresses the impacts of land-based activities on the marine and coastal environment, including contaminants, physical alteration, point and non-point sources of pollution and such areas of concern as critical

---

32. United Nations Environment Programme, *Global Environment Outlook 3* (Earthscan Publications, 2002).
33. The Global Programme of Action was adopted by an intergovernmental conference held in Washington, D.C., in October and November 1995. The text is contained in document A/51/116, annex II.

habitats, habitats of endangered species and protection of ecosystem components such as breeding and feeding grounds. It is the only global programme addressing the interface between freshwater and saltwater environments. In 2001, GPA underwent its first intergovernmental review, during which the Montreal Declaration (E/CN.17/2002/PC.2/15, annex, sect. 1) and a programme of work for the GPA Coordination Office of UNEP were adopted. The second intergovernmental review meeting will be held in 2006. In preparation, UNEP has initiated a process of consulting a cross section of stakeholders on organizational matters and possible themes.

106. Issues relating to pollution from land-based activities were discussed, in particular, at the first meeting of the United Nations Open-ended Informal Consultative Process on Oceans and the Law of the Sea in 2000. The General Assembly, at its fifty-fifth and subsequent sessions, has stressed the importance of ensuring full implementation of GPA, calling upon States to prioritize action on marine pollution from land-based activities. The Johannesburg Plan of Implementation[34] adopted at the World Summit on Sustainable Development called on Governments to advance implementation of GPA and the Montreal Declaration, with particular emphasis, during the period from 2002 to 2006, on municipal waste water, the physical alteration and destruction of habitats, and nutrients.

(b) Municipal Waste Water Management

107. Municipal waste-water discharges are considered one of the most significant threats to coastal environments worldwide. Associated effects include the spreading of pathogens, suspended solids, nutrients, plastics and other debris, and toxic substances like heavy metals and persistent organic pollutants in cases where industrial effluents are mixed with municipal waste water.[35]

108. The importance of addressing the environmental aspects of the Johannesburg Plan of Implementation targets on water and sanitation was reiterated in the Jeju Initiative,[36] which noted that an ecosystem approach to

---

34. *Report of the World Summit on Sustainable Development, Johannesburg, South Africa, 26 August–4 September 2002* (United Nations publication, Sales No. E.03.II.A.1 and corrigendum), chap. I, resolution 2, annex.

35. See GPA website at www.gpa.unep.org/pollute/sewage.htm.

36. Proceedings of the UNEP Governing Council/Global Ministerial Environment Forum at its eighth special session, held in Jeju, Republic of Korea, from 29 to 31 March 2004, UNEP document UNEP/GCSS.VIII/8, annex II. The Jeju initiative, prepared by the Chair and moderators of the UNEP Governing Council/Global Ministerial Environment Forum at its Eighth Special Session, is a summary of the rich and interactive discussion on the part of the ministers and other heads of delegations attending the meeting, rather than a consensus view on all points.

sanitation should incorporate the demands and effects of sanitation services on water catchments, downstream countries and communities and the coastal environment. Issues relating to water, sanitation and human settlements were addressed by the twenty-third session of the UNEP Governing Council, held in Nairobi from 21 to 25 February 2005, which considered the "Ten Keys for Local and National Action on Municipal Wastewater Management" developed by the GPA Coordination Office in the context of the Strategic Action Plan on Municipal Wastewater.[37] The Ten Keys were already recommended as best practice principles in the Jeju Initiative. Water, sanitation and human settlements are also the focus of the 2004–2005 cycle of the Commission on Sustainable Development.

(c) Nutrients

109. Eutrophication can result from the augmentation of nutrient inputs to coastal and marine areas as a consequence of human activities. Usually, eutrophication is confined to the vicinity of coastal discharges but, because of both the multiplicity of such discharges and regional atmospheric transport of nutrients, the affected area can be extensive. The effects of the enhanced mobilization of nutrients are enhanced productivity, as well as changes in species diversity, excessive algal growth, dissolved oxygen reductions and associated fish kills and, it is suspected, the increased prevalence or frequency of toxic algal blooms. The GPA Coordinating Office is identifying marine areas where nutrient inputs are causing or are likely to cause pollution, directly or indirectly. The goal is to reduce nutrient inputs into the areas identified; to reduce the number of marine areas where eutrophication is evident; and to protect and, where appropriate, to restore areas of natural denitrification.[38]

(d) Physical Alterations and Destruction of Habitats

110. The increase of population and economic activities in coastal areas is leading to an expansion of construction, which in turn leads to alterations to coastal ecosystems, including of coral reefs, coastlines, beachfronts, and the sea floor. Affected ecosystems include spawning grounds, nurseries and feeding grounds for already depleted fish stocks of crucial importance to

37. The Strategic Action Plan on Municipal Wastewater was developed by UNEP, the World Health Organization, the United Nations Human Settlements Programme and the Water Supply and Sanitation Collaborative Council; text at www.gpa.unep.org/pollute/documents/SAP/SAP%20Wastewater.pdf.

38. Suggested actions to be undertaken at the national, regional and global levels can be found on the GPA Coordination Office website at www.fao.org/gpa/nutrients/nutintro.htm.

world food security. Their destruction is an increasing threat to the food security of coastal populations, in particular in developing countries. In the framework of its project on physical alterations destruction of habitats programme, the GPA Coordination Office has developed sectoral key principles and checklists for improving existing institutional and legal frameworks. The economic sectors identified as having the most significant impact on physical alterations and destruction of habitats are tourism, aquaculture, mining and ports and harbours.[39]

111. Other problems identified by the Coordination Office include pollution by persistent organic pollutants, radioactive substances, heavy metals, oils (hydrocarbons), litter and sediment mobilization.

(e) Activities at the National Level

112. As the primary responsibility to implement GPA rests with national Governments, the GPA Coordination Office, with the support of donors, takes an active role in the development and implementation of national programmes of action for the protection of the marine environment from land-based activities. A target of 40 national programmes of action by 2006 was set in the framework for action on water and sanitation tabled at the World Summit on Sustainable Development. This target will likely be exceeded. The GPA Coordination Office, in partnership with national Governments and institutions, as well as with relevant GEF projects, has launched a project aimed at developing guidance on legislative provisions to support the implementation of national programmes of action.

(f) Activities at the Regional Level

113. Cooperation with the UNEP Regional Seas Programme provides an important platform for regional implementation of GPA. In collaboration with the Programme, the GPA Coordination Office conducted an inventory of regional-specific data on water supply, sanitation and wastewater treatment coverage in the UNEP regional seas. The GPA Coordination Office has also explored the possible use of regional waste-water emission targets,[40] as discussed extensively during the Global H2O: Hilltops-2-Oceans Partnership Conference, held in Cairns, Australia, from 10 to 14 May 2004 (see A/59/62/Add.1, paras. 102 and 103).

39. The key principles developed under the project for each of these sectors are presented on the GPA Coordination Office website at http://padh. gpa.unep.org.
40. A GPA report on this subject can be found at http://www.gpa.unep.org/ pollute/documents/SAP/WET/UNEP%20WS%20Targets%20RS%20section3.doc.

(g) Conclusions

114. The primary responsibility to reduce marine degradation from land-based activities rests with individual States. Regional cooperation is of great importance in achieving this goal. GPA is a very important guide to action and should be implemented at all levels. The work of the GPA Coordination Office in this regard should be supported and enhanced. In the development of national, regional and international policies, freshwater and saltwater issues should be considered jointly and the connection to the health and productivity of coastal and marine waters must be taken into account. Global efforts to implement the Johannesburg Plan of Implementation, the internationally agreed goals contained in the United Nations Millennium Declaration and the Monterrey Consensus on Financing for Development should emphasize the link between freshwater, the coastal zone and marine resources.

2. Pollution from Ships

115. Although shipping is responsible for a comparatively small percentage of the pollution entering the world's oceans, pollution incidents generally receive a lot of publicity and are met with increasing public intolerance. However, threats to the marine environment from shipping can arise not only from polluting accidents, but also from operational discharges; physical damage to marine habitats; the use of toxic anti-fouling paints on ships' hulls; ballast water discharge; and intense underwater anthropogenic noise. UNCLOS regulates pollution from ships by requiring States, acting through the competent international organization or general diplomatic conference, to establish international rules and standards to prevent, reduce and control pollution of the marine environment from vessels, and to re-examine these from time to time as necessary. Apart from the IMO safety-related conventions, which are vital for the prevention of accidents, the international rules and standards for the prevention and control of pollution from vessels are mainly contained in MARPOL and its six annexes, which regulate the discharge of oil (annex I), noxious liquid substances (annex II), harmful substances carried by sea in packaged form (annex III); sewage (annex IV); garbage or marine debris (annex V; see also paras. 254–256 below) and air pollution (annex VI). The use of harmful anti-fouling systems is regulated by the International Convention on the Control of Harmful Anti-Fouling Systems on Ships, which is not yet in force. The need to bring this Convention into force was underlined by MEPC at its fifty-second session (see IMO documents MEPC 52/15 and MEPC 52/24, sect. 15) and by the General Assembly in its resolution 59/24. Developments relating to ballast water discharge and anthropogenic noise pollution are reported in paragraphs 131 and 157 of the present report.

(a) Developments relating to Annex I to MARPOL

116. A revised version of annex I to MARPOL, containing regulations for the prevention of pollution by oil, was adopted by MEPC in 2004 (resolution MEPC.117(52)) and under the tacit amendment procedure is expected to enter into force on 1 January 2007. It incorporates in a user-friendly and simplified annex the various amendments adopted since MARPOL entered into force in 1983, including the amended regulations on the phasing-in of double hull requirements for oil tankers. It separates the construction and equipment provisions from the operational requirements and makes clear the distinctions between the requirements for new and existing ships.

117. The revised annex I includes new requirements relating to the provision of double bottoms for the pump rooms of oil tankers (regulation 22), and relating to the construction of oil tankers delivered on or after 1 January 2010 so as to provide adequate protection against oil pollution in the event of stranding or collision (regulation 23). MEPC adopted a resolution giving explanatory notes on matters related to the accidental oil outflow performance required under regulation 23. It approved unified interpretations to the revised annex I and a circular containing cross-reference lists between the "old" and "new" regulations, intended to facilitate familiarization with the new numbering system of the revised annex I. Guidelines for the application of the revised annex I requirements to floating production, storage and offloading units and floating storage units are expected to be finalized for adoption by MEPC in 2005 (see IMO document MEPC.52/24).

(b) Developments relating to Annex II

118. The revised annex II, containing regulations for the control of pollution by noxious liquid substances in bulk, was also adopted by MEPC in 2004 (resolution MEPC.118(52)) and is expected to enter into force on 1 January 2007. It includes a new four-category classification system for noxious and liquid substances determined according to the level of harm caused to either marine resources or human health as a result of the discharge of such substances into the marine environment from tank cleaning or de-ballasting operations. If the discharge presents a major hazard, then the substances fall within category X and justify a prohibition of the discharge into the sea. If the discharge is deemed to present a hazard to either marine resources or human health or cause harm to amenities or other legitimate uses of the sea, then the substances fall within category Y and justify a limitation on the quality and quantity of the discharge into the sea. If the discharge is deemed to present a minor hazard to either marine resources or human health, then the substances fall within category Z and

less stringent restrictions on the quality and quantity of the discharge into the sea are justified. Substances that are evaluated and found to fall outside categories X, Y or Z, because they are considered to present no harm to marine resources, human health, amenities or other legitimate uses of the sea when discharged into the sea from tank cleaning or de-ballasting operations, are categorized as other substances. The discharge of bilge, ballast water, or other residues or mixtures containing these substances is not subject to any requirements of annex II.

119. The revised annex incorporates improvements in ship technology, such as efficient stripping techniques, that have made possible significantly lower permitted discharge levels for certain products. Thus, for ships constructed on or after 1 January 2007, the maximum permitted residue in the tank and its associated piping after discharge will be set at 75 litres for products in categories X, Y and Z, as compared with previous limits of 100 or 300 litres, depending on the product category.

120. In order to revise annex II, the marine pollution hazards of thousands of chemicals were evaluated by the Joint Group of Experts on the Scientific Aspects of Marine Environmental Protection. The Group's hazard profile indexes the substance according to its bioaccumulation, biodegradation, acute toxicity, chronic toxicity, long-term health effects and effects on marine wildlife and benthic habitats. As a result of this hazard evaluation process and the new categorization system, vegetable oils previously categorized as unrestricted are now required to be carried in chemical tankers. The revised annex permits the exemption of ships certified to carry individually identified vegetable oils, subject to certain provisions relating to the location of the cargo tanks carrying the oil. MEPC also developed guidelines to allow general dry cargo ships that are currently certified to carry vegetable oil in bulk to continue to carry these vegetable oils on specific trades.[41]

121. The Committee adopted consequential amendments to the International Code for the Construction and Equipment of Ships Carrying Dangerous Chemicals in Bulk reflecting the changes to MARPOL annex II. The amendments include revisions to the categorization of certain products relating to their properties as potential marine pollutants, as well as revisions to ship type and carriage requirements.

(c) MARPOL Special Areas

122. The Committee adopted stricter controls on discharge of oily wastes for the Oman Sea area of the Arabian Sea as a result of its designation

---

41. The guidelines, contained in resolution MEPC.120(52), will take effect on 1 January 2007.

as a MARPOL Special Area under annex I. The designation is included in the revised annex I.

(d) Reception Facilities

123. In recognition of the fact that the provision of reception facilities is crucial for effective MARPOL implementation, in particular in Special Areas, MEPC at its fifty-second session strongly encouraged member States, particularly port States that are parties to MARPOL, to fulfil their treaty obligations relating to the provision of adequate reception facilities. Since the incentives to improve reception facilities are dependent, at least partly, on the receipt of adequate information about alleged inadequacies, Governments were also urged to respond to a questionnaire on alleged inadequacy of port reception facilities (IMO document MEPC/Circ.417) and to report their experiences to the Committee at its fifty-third session with the aim of identifying problem areas and developing a future action plan. The responses received by the IMO secretariat indicate that the overall awareness of ships' masters of the reporting procedures to be followed in case of alleged inadequacy of port reception facilities appears to be very low; the contact details of the national authorities responsible for handling reports are not widely available; the format for reporting alleged inadequacies could be further improved; not all port States have ensured the provision of proper arrangements to consider, investigate and respond appropriately and effectively to reports of inadequacy of port reception facilities; the obligation of the port State to report the outcome of its investigation to IMO and the flag State is not clearly stated in the reporting procedures; the existing reporting procedures do not seem to offer appropriate incentives for ships to report alleged inadequacies and for port States to respond appropriately to such reports; and fear of retaliation for reporting alleged inadequacies of port reception facilities seems to be one of the main causes of the low reporting rate by ships (see IMO document FSI 13/19). In order to promote the implementation of the waste reception facility reporting requirements, the IMO secretariat has developed a draft outline for a port reception facility database to form an integral part of the IMO global integrated shipping information system (see IMO document FSI 13/19/2).

(e) Particularly Sensitive Sea Areas

124. The Western European Waters is the seventh area to have been designated by MEPC as a Particularly Sensitive Sea Area (resolution

MEPC.121(52)).[42] The area covers the western coasts of the United Kingdom, Ireland, Belgium, France, Spain and Portugal, from the Shetland Islands in the north to Cape Vicente in the south, and the English Channel and its approaches. The mandatory ship reporting system adopted by the Committee as an associated protective measure will take effect on 1 July 2005. The use of the reporting system for ships entering the area will be free of charge (IMO document MEPC 52/54, para. 8.4).

125. Four other marine areas have also been approved in principle as Particularly Sensitive Sea Areas, but have not yet been designated by the Committee, pending the adoption of associated protective measures. One of these areas is the Torres Strait region, which was designated a Particularly Sensitive Sea Area in principle at the Committee's forty-ninth session. Australia's proposed associated protective measure to introduce a compulsory pilotage arrangement in the Torres Strait region was discussed in 2004 by the IMO Subcommittee on Safety of Navigation, MEPC, the IMO Legal Committee and MSC. The Protection Committee had agreed to refer the legal aspects of compulsory pilotage in straits used for international navigation to the Legal Committee, in order to enable the seventy-ninth session of MSC to consider the proposal with the issue of the legal basis resolved. However, the Legal Committee was unable to reach agreement at its eighty-ninth session on the legality of compulsory pilotage in a strait used for international navigation. Among other things, views differed on whether the absence of a specific provision in UNCLOS could be interpreted as permitting the introduction of a compulsory pilotage system in a strait used for international navigation (see IMO document LEG 89/16, sect. O).

126. At the seventy-ninth session of MSC, Australia made a new proposal to extend the current associated protective measure of a system of non-compulsory pilotage within the Great Barrier Reef, in resolution MEPC.45(30), to include the Torres Strait. MSC agreed that the proposal should be adopted and that a new paragraph, which would recommend that flag States inform their ships that they should act in accordance with Australia's system of pilotage when transiting the Torres Strait, be incorporated in a revised resolution MEPC.45(30) (IMO document MSC 79/23, paras. 10.11–10.16). In July 2005, MEPC will give further consideration to the extension of the Great Barrier Reef Particularly Sensitive Sea Area to include the Torres Strait, taking into account the decision of MSC. At that

---

42. Other areas designated as Particularly Sensitive Sea Areas are the Great Barrier Reef, Australia (1990); the Sabana-Camagüey Archipelago, Cuba (1997); Malpelo Island, Colombia (2002); around the Florida Keys, United States (2002); the Wadden Sea, Denmark, Germany, Netherlands (2002); and Paracas National Reserve, Peru (2003). MEPC has approved in principle the Torres Strait (Australia and Papua New Guinea), the Baltic Sea (except Russian waters), waters of the Canary Isles (Spain) and the Galapagos Archipelago (Ecuador).

session, the Committee will also consider the outcome of the work of the correspondence group which has been established to review the IMO guidelines for the identification and designation of Particularly Sensitive Sea Areas.[43] The group is preparing a draft IMO Assembly resolution and a proposed revised text of the guidelines.

(f) Liability and Compensation for Oil Pollution Damage

127. The 2003 Protocol establishing an International Oil Pollution Compensation Supplementary Fund, whose adoption was welcomed by the General Assembly in its resolution 59/24, entered into force on 3 March 2005. It has been ratified by eight States, which have received a combined total of 450 million tons of contributing oil. Participation in the Fund is optional, although open to all States parties to the International Convention on the Establishment of an International Fund for Compensation for Oil Pollution Damage, 1992 (Fund Convention). The 2003 Fund will supplement the compensation available under the International Convention on Civil Liability for Oil Pollution Damage, 1992 and the Fund Convention with an additional, third tier of compensation available to victims in the States which accede to the Protocol. The Supplementary Fund will have available approximately $835 million, in addition to the $315 million which is available in the 1992 Fund. As noted by the Fund secretariat, the Fund acts within the objective of article 235 of UNCLOS, namely to ensure that prompt and adequate compensation is available to victims of oil pollution, and is an example of cooperation between States to achieve this objective.

(g) Air Pollution

128. The regulations for the prevention of air pollution from ships, contained in annex VI to MARPOL, will enter into force on 19 May 2005. They set limits on sulphur oxide and nitrogen oxide emissions from ship exhausts and prohibit deliberate emissions of ozone depleting substances. At its fifty-second session, MEPC reviewed the draft amendments to annex VI that had been approved at previous sessions of the Committee, with a view to their adoption at the fifty-third session. These amendments relate to the designation of the North Sea area as a sulphur oxide emission control area and to the introduction of the harmonized system of survey and certification into annex VI.

43. The review of the Guidelines is based on a proposal by the United States (MEPC 52/8). Other submissions contained in documents MEPC 52/8/1, MEPC 52/8/2, MEPC 52/8/3 and MEPC 52/8/4 are taken into account, as well as the discussions and direction given in MEPC 52/24, paras. 8.14–8.34 and annex 15.

129. MEPC also made progress in developing draft guidelines on the carbon dioxide indexing scheme and urged members to carry out trials using the scheme and to report to the next session. One purpose of developing guidelines on carbon dioxide emission indexing is to develop a simple system that could be used voluntarily by ship operators during a trial period. The Committee agreed that a carbon dioxide indexing scheme should be simple and easy to apply and take into consideration matters related to construction and operation of ships and market-based incentives. As for the IMO guidelines on greenhouse gas emissions, the fifty-second session of MEPC recognized that they should address all six greenhouse gases covered by the Kyoto Protocol, which calls for the reduction of emissions from ships of carbon dioxide, methane, nitrous oxide, hydrofluorocarbons, perfluorocarbons and sulphur hexafluoride.

European Union

130. A 2002 communication from the Commission of the European Union to the European Parliament and to the Council sets out a strategy to reduce atmospheric emissions from seagoing ships. The basic objective of the strategy is to take stock of the environmental and health problems caused by atmospheric emissions from seagoing ships and to define objectives, actions and recommendations to help reduce such emissions over the next 10 years. The strategy includes a proposal for a directive on the sulphur content of marine fuels. The communication also outlines a number of actions to achieve its objectives, including coordinating the positions of member States of the European Union within IMO to press for tougher measures to reduce ship emissions. The entry into force of MARPOL annex VI is a fundamental aspect of the strategy; if IMO has not proposed tighter international standards by 2007, the European Union will bring forward a proposal to reduce nitrogen oxide emissions from seagoing vessels.

3. *Control of Harmful Organisms and Pathogens in Ballast Water*

131. The main source of introductions of alien invasive species is considered to be ballast water from ships. Significant advances have been made in management of ballast water in recent years, and the rapid entry into force and effective implementation of the International Convention on the Control and Management of Ships' Ballast Water and Sediments[44] by IMO member States will further assist in dealing with the problem. At its fifty-second session, MEPC finalized guidelines for the approval of ballast

---

44. For information on the Convention see A/59/62, paras. 179–181.

water management systems and approved the procedure for approval of active substances, with a view to their adoption at the fifty-third session. The development of other guidelines will continue in the Subcommittee on Bulk Liquids and Gases and at future sessions of MEPC.

4. *Waste Management*

132. The twenty-sixth consultative meeting of contracting parties to the Convention on the Prevention of Marine Pollution by Dumping of Wastes and Other Matter, 1972 (London Convention) examined the scope of article III(1)(b)(i) of the Convention, which states that "dumping" does not include normal operations of vessels. The consultative meeting noted that the Scientific Group, at its twenty-seventh session, had expressed concern with regard to the broad interpretation of the "cargo-associated wastes" which could be discharged by ships under MARPOL annex V (garbage). The consultative meeting agreed to approach the Marine Environment Protection Committee of IMO to clarify the boundaries between MARPOL and the London Convention and the 1996 Protocol. It also reviewed the wide range of possible relations with other organizations, where there could be a strong cross-sectoral linkage. Monitoring of the marine environment, coastal management and technical cooperation and assistance were considered to be the main cross-sectoral issues.

133. The consultative meeting considered the challenge of stabilizing greenhouse gas concentrations in the atmosphere and recognized that carbon dioxide capture and storage in geological structures under the sea might offer important possibilities for making fossil fuel use more compatible with climate change mitigation policies. In this context, it was agreed that the issue of carbon dioxide sequestration should be included in the work programme of the London Convention and to initially focus on sequestration of carbon dioxide in geological structures. Legal, scientific and technical issues involved are to be examined in the intersessional period so that the next consultative meeting can review the progress and give guidance on what further work should be done to establish a clear position.

134. In preparation for the entry into force of the 1996 Protocol, possibly in 2005, the consultative meeting embarked on the review of an initial text containing options for compliance procedures and mechanisms under article 11 of the Protocol. Once the Protocol is in force, its most significant effect will be to move away from a list of materials which may not be dumped at sea (as under the London Convention itself) to a reverse listing approach, prohibiting all dumping except for a restricted list of non-

hazardous materials that may be considered for disposal at sea, only after an environmental assessment.[45]

5.   *Shipbreaking/Recycling/Dismantling*

135. Ships sold for scrapping may contain environmentally hazardous substances such as asbestos, heavy metals, waste oils, ozone depleting substances and others, which need to be disposed of safely. Concerns have also been raised about the working and environmental conditions at many of the world's ship scrapping facilities, generally located in developing countries. Currently, only a few scrapping facilities can perform ship recycling in an acceptable way in relation to the environment and workers' health and safety. A recent report by the European Commission predicts that, even with a planned increase in "green" recycling facilities, they will be able to handle only around 30 per cent of the expected total scrapping demand in most years, and much less in the peak demand years.[46] Demand will increase after April 2005, due to the accelerated phase-out scheme for single hulled oil tankers adopted by IMO in 2003 (see A/59/62, paras. 172 and 173).

136. *International Labour Organization.* At its two hundred eighty-ninth session, the ILO Governing Body adopted guidelines on safety and health in shipbreaking for Asian countries and Turkey, which provide a coherent framework under which Governments, employers and workers can improve occupational safety and health in the shipbreaking yards. These guidelines will complement those already adopted by IMO in 2003 and the Conference of the Parties to the Basel Convention in 2002 (see para. 138 below). In addition, ILO has embarked upon a three-year UNDP-funded technical cooperation project in Bangladesh on safe and environmentally friendly ship recycling.

137. *International Maritime Organization.* In its resolution 59/24, the General Assembly welcomed the adoption of the IMO guidelines on ship recycling (resolution A.962(23)) and called upon States to follow these guidelines in order to minimize marine pollution. At its fifty-second session, MEPC agreed that certain parts of the guidelines might be given mandatory effect (IMO document MEPC 52/24, sect. 3). It also decided to develop a reporting system for ships destined for recycling that is transparent and effective, ensures uniform application, respects commercially sensitive

---

45. See report of the twenty-sixth consultative meeting of Contracting Parties to the London Convention, IMO document LC 26/15.

46. European Commission, Directorate-General Energy and Transport, *Oil Tanker Phase Out and the Ship Scrapping Industry: A study on the implications of the accelerated phase out scheme of single hull tankers proposed by the EU for the world ship scrapping and recycling industry,* June 2004, p. 11.

information and facilitates the control and enforcement of any mandatory provisions that might be developed. A draft outline of the system has been developed in order to identify, in a schematic way, what should be reported, to whom and by whom (IMO document MEPC 52/WP.8). MEPC further agreed to replace the existing appendices 1, 2 and 3 to the guidelines with a "single list" that provides guidance on the identification of potentially hazardous materials on board ships and the preparation of the relevant inventories. The Committee also approved guidelines for the development of a ship recycling plan (IMO document MEPC/Circ.419). In order to assist developing countries improve environmental and safety levels in ship recycling operations, the Committee agreed that ship recycling should be included in the future thematic priorities of the IMO Integrated Technical Cooperation Programme and invited the Technical Cooperation Committee to consider further the arrangements for establishing a dedicated ship recycling fund.

138. *Basel Convention.* The seventh Conference of the Parties to the Basel Convention on the Control of Transboundary Movements of Hazardous Wastes and their Disposal[47] adopted decision VII/26 on environmentally sound management of ship dismantling. In its decision, the Conference of the Parties noted that a ship may become waste as defined in article 2 of the Basel Convention and that at the same time it may be defined as a ship under other international rules. In this connection, the Conference of the Parties realized that States may have distinct obligations as parties to UNCLOS and relevant IMO conventions, including their obligations as flag States, and as Parties to the Basel Convention, including their obligations as States of export, and noted that States should be able to meet these obligations in a consistent manner. In this regard, the Conference of the Parties invited the IMO/ILO/Basel Convention Joint Working Group to discuss the responsibility of flag States in the context of environmentally sound management of ship dismantling. Finally, the Conference reminded the Parties to fulfil their obligations under the Basel Convention, in particular their obligations with respect to prior informed consent, minimization of transboundary movements of hazardous wastes and the principles of environmentally sound management, and invited developed States in particular to encourage the establishment of domestic recycling facilities. These decisions, which were adopted despite the disagreement of some States and part of the shipping industry, arrived at a time when a large number of single hull oil tankers are due to be recycled.[48]

47. United Nations, *Treaty Series*, vol. 1673, p. 57.
48. It is estimated that approximately 2,000 single-hull oil tankers will be scrapped in the next five years. European Commission, Directorate-General Energy and Transport, supra note 46.

139. *Abandonment of ships.* The Conference of the Parties to the Basel Convention adopted, for the first time, a decision on abandonment of ships (decision VII/27). Concerned that the abandonment of ships on land or in ports could have effects on human health and the environment, the Conference invited parties to submit information in this regard to the secretariat of the Basel Convention for consideration and action by the Open-ended Working Group. The secretariat of the Basel Convention was also requested to consult IMO on this issue.

140. *Joint ILO/IMO/Basel Convention Working Group on Ship Scrapping.* The Joint Working Group on Ship Scrapping held its first meeting in February 2005 to consider the respective work programmes of the pertinent bodies of ILO, IMO and the Conference of the Parties to the Basel Convention on the issue of ship scrapping, with the aim of avoiding duplication of work and overlapping of roles, responsibilities and competencies among the three organizations, as well as identifying further needs. It also undertook an initial examination of the relevant guidelines produced by each of the organizations and considered mechanisms to jointly promote their implementation.

141. The Group agreed that the three organizations should ensure that the issue of abandonment of ships on land or in ports would be adequately covered by an international legally binding instrument. It also decided that the three organizations should be asked to consider a global technical cooperation programme on ship scrapping. Regarding the establishment of a ship recycling fund, the Group was of the opinion that all efforts should be focused on the further consideration by IMO of the proposal agreed to in principle by MEPC at its fifty-second session.

6. Regional Cooperation

(a) UNEP Regional Seas Programme

142. The Regional Seas Programme continues to provide a comprehensive institutional framework for regional and global cooperation on issues pertaining to the coasts, oceans and seas. Currently, the Programme covers 17 regions, supported through either a regional convention or a regional action plan. The strategic directions for the conventions and action plans and for the Regional Seas Programme Coordination Office were further addressed at the sixth Global Meeting of the Regional Seas Conventions and Action Plans, held in Istanbul, Turkey, from 30 November to 2 December 2004. The Global Meeting identified actions to be implemented during 2004–2007 to strengthen the Regional Seas Programme at the global level, while continuing to implement the action programmes of the individual regional seas programmes as agreed by their governing bodies. Some actions taken by the Coordination Office in Nairobi include the development of a database that identifies existing actors and potential partners in

the regional seas programmes, in order to share best practices in the field of conservation and management of the marine and coastal environment among the various programmes; the forging of new partnerships (e.g., the White Water to Blue Water partnership in the Caribbean); and the establishment of a new Web-based information centre. In addition, a memorandum of understanding between the International Oceanographic Commission (IOC) of the United Nations Educational, Scientific and Cultural Organization (UNESCO) and UNEP was signed, which will provide a framework for collaboration between the Global Ocean Observing System and the Regional Seas Programme.

143. On the regional level, the Northwest Pacific Action Plan celebrated its tenth anniversary with the opening of a co-hosted Regional Coordinating Unit in Toyama, Japan and Busan, Republic of Korea. The States members of the Action Plan signed the memorandum of understanding for the regional oil spill contingency plan, which is a benchmark for the protection of a shared marine environment in the region and will serve as the basis for cooperation between the affected country and its neighbours in the case of major oil spill emergencies. In the Mediterranean Sea region, the amended Barcelona Convention entered into force in June 2004, widening its scope to address sustainable development and biodiversity conservation. The Regional Organization for the Conservation of the Environment of the Red Sea and Gulf of Aden, with the assistance of the Marine Environmental Studies Laboratory of IAEA, has reviewed the ongoing monitoring and assessment activities in the region. Based on this review, PERSGA developed its regional environmental monitoring programme. In order to implement this programme and using a phased approach, PERSGA began a one-year capacity-building programme in July 2004.

(b) Arctic

144. According to the report entitled "Impacts of a Warming Arctic,"[49] the Arctic climate is warming rapidly, at almost twice the rate as the rest of the world in the past two decades. This is evidenced by widespread melting of glaciers and sea ice, thawing permafrost and the shortening of the snow season. The report, published in November 2004, synthesized the key findings of the Arctic Climate Impact Assessment, an evaluation commissioned by the Arctic Council and the International Arctic Science Committee (an international scientific organization appointed by 18 national academies of science). The culmination of an unprecedented four-year scientific study of the region conducted by an international team of 300

---

49. *Impacts of a Warming Arctic: Arctic Climate Impact Assessment,* Cambridge University Press, November 2004.

scientists, the report states that at least half the summer sea ice in the Arctic is projected to melt by the end of this century, along with a significant portion of the Greenland Ice Sheet, as the region is projected to warm an additional 4 to 7 degrees centigrade by 2100.

145. The effects of a warmer Arctic for natural systems and society in the area are reported to be manifold. Since more than half of the Arctic region consists of oceans, climatic variations will have a large impact on marine environments and marine-related activities. These impacts would include rising sea levels; changes in ocean salinity, which could strongly affect regional climate; the decline or extinction of marine species due to habitat loss; expanding marine shipping; and the enhancement of some major Arctic fisheries together with the decline of others. Climate change is also projected to have effects outside the Arctic, such as global sea-level rise and intensifying global warming. The Arctic provides natural resources to the rest of the world, which are likely to be affected by climate change. The Arctic Climate Impact Assessment report and other studies[50] agree that, in addition to climate change, many other stresses caused by human activities are affecting Arctic life, including pollution, overfishing, increasing levels of ultraviolet radiation due to ozone depletion and habitat alteration.

146. At the fourth ministerial meeting of the Arctic Council, held in Reykjavik in November 2004, the ministers issued a declaration[51] noting with concern the findings and impacts documented by the Arctic Climate Impact Assessment. The ministers acknowledged that such findings, as well as the underlying scientific assessment, would help inform Governments as they implemented and considered future policies on global climate change. They emphasized the importance of circumpolar and international cooperation in addressing circumpolar challenges; requested the Working Group on the Protection of the Arctic Marine Environment to conduct a comprehensive Arctic marine shipping assessment; recognized the evidence that many global environmental changes were having significant effects on the Arctic's living resources, the Arctic environment and Arctic residents; and noted that conservation of biodiversity was necessary for achieving sustainable development in the region.

50. European Environment Agency, *Arctic environment: European perspectives*, 2nd edition, 2004; G. Matishov and others, *Barents Sea, Global International Waters Assessment Regional Assessment 11*, University of Kalmar, Kalmar, Sweden, August 2004; UNEP, Global Environmental Outlook–3, Fact sheet: the Polar regions, available from www.unep.org/GEO/.

51. Reykjavik Declaration, available at www.arctic-council.org/en/main/messageslistpage/1.

(c) Antarctic

147. The unique Antarctic environment continues to be under threat from a rapidly warming atmosphere, the thinning of the ozone layer, and increasing levels of fishing and tourism. According to recent studies, the Antarctic Peninsula is among the fastest-warming places on earth, with annual temperatures that have risen around 2.5 degrees centigrade in the past 50 years. These warmer conditions have reportedly led to increased colonization by plants in certain areas and to a decline in sea ice, which could be responsible for a considerable drop in Antarctic krill. Since krill is at the heart of the food web, Antarctic whales, seals, fish and penguins could be threatened by food shortages in the Southern Ocean, as a consequence of this decline in krill stock.[52] Disintegration of ice shelves and melting of glaciers[53] due to regional warming may also cause sea levels to rise.[54]

148. The twenty-seventh consultative meeting of parties to the Antarctic Treaty endorsed the guidelines for ships operating in Arctic and Antarctic ice-covered waters (decision 4 (2004)) for transmission to IMO, with a request to consider them at the earliest opportunity. The Guidelines include provisions on construction, equipment and operational issues, as well as provisions regarding environmental protection and damage control. The meeting also adopted measure 4 (2004) and resolution 4 (2004), which recommend that Governments require those under their jurisdiction organizing or conducting tourist or other non-governmental activities in Antarctica to have appropriate contingency plans and sufficient arrangements for health and safety, search and rescue and medical care, as well as adequate insurance, before undertaking any such activities; and resolution 1 (2004) on enhancing prevention of marine pollution by fishing activities.

B.   Marine Biological Diversity

149. In recent years the issue of the conservation and sustainable use of marine ecosystems and biodiversity has been considered in a number of forums. In 2003, the General Assembly focused on the protection of vulnerable marine ecosystems generally, while in 2004 the focus was on the

52. See A. Atkinson and others, "Long term decline in krill stock and increase in salps within the Southern Ocean," *Nature*, vol. 432, 4 November 2004, pp. 100–103.

53. On the Antarctic Peninsula, the speeds at which several glaciers are surging into the sea have increased eight-fold between 2000 and 2003. See "Antarctica, warming, looks ever more vulnerable," *The New York Times*, 25 January 2005.

54. "Grass flourishes in warmer Antarctic," *The Sunday Times* (London), 26 December 2004.

conservation and management of biodiversity in areas beyond national jurisdiction. In paragraph 73 of resolution 59/24, the Assembly decided to establish an ad hoc open-ended informal working group to study issues relating to the conservation and sustainable use of marine biological diversity beyond areas of national jurisdiction. In order to assist in the preparation of the agenda of the working group, the Assembly also requested the Secretary-General to prepare a report on a number of issues identified in paragraph 73. The report for the working group will be issued as an addendum to the present report.

Convention on Biological Diversity

150. At its seventh meeting, held in Kuala Lumpur in February 2004, the Conference of the Parties to the Convention on Biological Diversity adopted an Elaborated Programme of Work on Marine and Coastal Biological Diversity, including programme elements on the implementation of integrated marine and coastal area management; marine and coastal living resources; marine and coastal protected areas; mariculture; and invasive alien species.[55]

151. At its tenth meeting, held in Bangkok in February 2005, the Subsidiary Body on Scientific, Technical and Technological Advice of the Convention considered draft global outcome-oriented targets for the Programme of Work on Marine and Coastal Biological Diversity. The draft targets, as requested by the Conference of the Parties in decision VII/30, outline how the Convention's goal of achieving a significant reduction of the current rate of biodiversity loss by 2010 can be reached for oceans and coasts.[56] The Subsidiary Body recommended that the Conference of the Parties at its eighth meeting, to be held in 2006, endorse the integration of these targets into the Programme of Work (recommendation X/4) and that it adopt a new work programme on island biological diversity, developed with the assistance of an ad hoc technical expert group. The new programme of work contains goals, global targets, time frames and island-specific priority actions, and is available in the annex to recommendation X/1.[57]

152. The Ad Hoc Open-ended Working Group on Protected Areas, established by decision VII/28 to, inter alia, explore options for cooperation for the establishment of marine protected areas in marine areas beyond

---

55. See UNEP/CBD/COP/7/21, annex, decision VII/5. For a summary of the Elaborated Programme of Work on Marine and Coastal Biological Diversity, see A/59/62, para. 228.

56. See UNEP/CBD/SBSTTA/10/8 and Add.1 and UNEP/CBD/SBSTTA/10/INF/6.

57. Report of the meeting not yet available.

national jurisdiction, will hold its first meeting in Montecatini, Italy, in June 2005. Two background documents will be presented to the Working Group: a scientific analysis of high seas biodiversity and a legal analysis of existing international and regional legal instruments, including options for cooperation for the establishment of marine protected areas beyond national jurisdiction.

Convention on International Trade in Endangered Species of Wild Fauna and Flora

153. The thirteenth Conference of the Parties to the Convention on International Trade in Endangered Species of Wild Fauna and Flora, held in Bangkok in October 2004, decided to list the great white shark and the humphead wrasse, two fish species of great commercial value, in appendix II to the Convention. This means that they can now only be traded between parties to the Convention with permits. Another marine species, the Irrawaddy dolphin, was transferred from appendix II to appendix I, which forbids all commercial trade.[58] A proposal to downlist minke whales was rejected. The Conference of the Parties also adopted a decision on trade in alien invasive species (resolution Conf.13.10). At the conclusion of the meeting, the Secretary-General of the Convention noted that in recent years the Convention had started to list commercially valuable fish species, suggesting that Governments believe the Convention can contribute to the goal agreed at the World Summit on Sustainable Development, of restoring fishery stocks to sustainable levels by 2015.[59]

Corals

154. Coral reefs and associated ecosystems are invaluable human treasures. They support the most diverse marine communities and beautiful seascapes on the planet, and provide wave-resistant structures and resources for local communities, fisheries and tourism. However, coral reefs and associated ecosystems are now under serious threat of collapse because overfishing, development of the coastal zone, including dredging and landfill, and terrestrial run-off, as well as climate change, act synergistically to stress coral reefs leading to severe bleaching and extensive coral mortality.[60] The report "Status of Coral Reefs of the World: 2004"

58. Notification to the Parties No. 2004/073, Geneva, 19 November 2004.
59. See press release at http://www.cites.org/eng/news/press/2004/041014_cop13final.shtml.
60. Okinawa Declaration on Conservation and Restoration of Endangered Coral Reefs of the World, Tenth International Coral Reef Symposium (28 June to 2 July 2004, Okinawa, Japan). The Declaration recommends four key strategies: (a) achieve sustainable fishery on coral reefs; (b) increase effective marine protected

highlights the main threats to coral reefs and puts forward a number of conservation and governance recommendations.[61]

155. The vulnerability of cold-water coral ecosystems is becoming an important component of the work on coral reefs. The UNEP Coral Reef Unit, in partnership with Ireland, Norway, the United Kingdom and WWF (formerly the World Wildlife Fund), prepared a comprehensive and up-to-date report entitled "Cold-water coral reefs, out of sight—no longer out of mind."[62]

156. The United Kingdom/Seychelles secretariat of the International Coral Reef Initiative decided at its second general meeting to include cold-water coral reef issues within the remit of the Initiative. A draft programme of work on cold-water corals will be presented for adoption at the next general meeting. The meeting will also celebrate the 10-year anniversary of the International Coral Reef Initiative. Starting in July 2005, the Governments of Japan and Palau will co-host the next secretariat of the Initiative.

Anthropogenic Noise Pollution

157. Human-produced underwater ocean noise pollution has received increasing attention in international forums, including the International Whaling Commission,[63] the European Parliament[64] and the third World Conservation Congress of the International Union for the Conservation of Nature and Natural Resources.[65] In the report on the fifth meeting of the United Nations Open-ended Consultative Process on Oceans and the Law of the Sea (A/59/122, para. 97) undersea noise pollution was included among the issues that could benefit from attention in future work of the General Assembly.

C.   Climate Change

158. *United Nations Framework Convention on Climate Change.* The tenth anniversary session of the Conference of Parties to the United Nations Framework Convention on Climate Change, held in December 2004,

---

areas on coral reefs; (c) ameliorate land-use change impacts; and (d) develop technology for coral reef restoration.

61. *Status of Coral Reefs of the World: 2004*, vols. 1 and 2, edited by Clive Wilkinson.

62. A. Freiwald and others, *Cold-water coral reefs, out of sight—no longer out of mind*, UNEP-World Conservation Monitoring Centre, Cambridge, United Kingdom, 2004.

63. www.iwcoffice.org/_documents/sci_com/SCRepFiles2004/56SCrep.pdf.

64. Bulletin of the European Union 10–2004, Environment (14/17).

65. Resolution 3.53 of the third World Conservation Congress.

adopted the Buenos Aires programme of work on adaptation and response measures (decision 1/CP.10). The programme includes further scientific assessments of vulnerabilities and options for adaptation, support to the national action plans on adaptation of least developed countries, new workshops and technical papers on various aspects of climate change risk and adaptation and support for mainstreaming adaptation into sustainable development planning. The Conference of Parties requested the Convention secretariat to convene a seminar of governmental experts in May 2005, to promote an informal exchange on (a) actions relating to mitigation and adaptation to assist parties to continue to develop effective and appropriate responses to climate change; and (b) policies and measures adopted by their respective Governments that support the implementation of their existing commitments under the United Nations Framework Convention on Climate Change and the Kyoto Protocol. Other key decisions related to the rapidly evolving carbon market where allowances and credits from projects that reduce emissions can be purchased and sold. As of 1 January 2005, emissions trading has become a reality for 12,000 companies in the European Union.

159. *The 1997 Kyoto Protocol to the United Nations Framework Convention on Climate Change.* On 18 November 2004, the Russian Federation ratified the Protocol, enabling it to come into force on 16 February 2005. The Kyoto Protocol adds detailed requirements to the general principles established in the Framework Convention by committing annex I parties to individual, legally binding targets to limit or reduce their greenhouse gas emissions. The individual targets for annex I parties listed in annex B to the Kyoto Protocol add up to a total cut in greenhouse gas emissions for those countries of at least 5 per cent from 1990 levels in the commitment period 2008–2012.

D.   Small Island Developing States

160. Small island developing States are among the most vulnerable in the world in relation to the intensity and frequency of natural and environmental disasters, and face disproportionately high economic, social and environmental consequences. The tragic impacts of the 26 December 2004 Indian Ocean earthquake and tsunami and the recent hurricane/cyclone/typhoon seasons in the Caribbean and Pacific highlight their vulnerability. Small island developing States have undertaken to strengthen their respective national frameworks for more effective disaster management and are committed, with the necessary support of the international community, to achieve sustainable development and to improve the lives of

their inhabitants.[66] This context highlighted the importance of the International Meeting to Review the Implementation of the Programme of Action for the Sustainable Development of Small Island Developing States, held in Port Louis, Mauritius from 10 to 14 January 2005, essentially to review the 1994 Barbados Programme of Action and to seek innovative ways to improve the situation of approximately 51 small island developing States located throughout the world. The Meeting unanimously adopted both a proactive strategy to further implement the programme of action, called the Mauritius Strategy, and a political declaration, the Mauritius Declaration.

161. The major document to come out of the Meeting, the Mauritius Strategy for the Further Implementation of the Barbados Programme of Action, states that small island developing States are already experiencing major adverse effects of climate change, that climate change may even threaten their very existence and that adaptation to adverse impacts of climate change and sea-level rise remains a major priority for them.

162. The Strategy notes that small island developing States are defined by their historic, cultural and economic links to the oceans and seas. They continue to be heavily dependent on their marine resources, particularly for the sustainable livelihoods of coastal communities. While small island developing States have integrated the management of coastal and marine resources into broader ocean management strategies since the entry into force of UNCLOS, implementation of the Convention continues to be impeded by financial constraints and lack of capacity. The Strategy recognizes the importance for small island developing States of giving priority at all levels to oceans issues, including fisheries. It declares that further action is required, with the necessary support of the international community, to enable small island developing States to complete the delimitation of their maritime boundaries, submit any claims to the Commission on the Limits of the Continental Shelf, and assess seabed living and non-living resources within their national jurisdiction.

163. The Strategy further recognizes that action is required to build small island developing States' technical and financial capacities to (a) establish effective monitoring, reporting and enforcement and control of fishing vessels, including by small island developing States as flag States, so as to further implement international plans of action to prevent, deter and eliminate illegal, unreported and unregulated fishing and to manage capacity; (b) strengthen or develop national and regional sustainable and responsible fisheries management mechanisms, consistent with the FAO Code of Conduct for Responsible Fisheries; (c) fully implement surveillance and monitoring systems; (d) analyse and assess the status of stocks; (e) consider becoming parties, if they have not yet done so, to the United

66. Mauritius Strategy, supra note 22, para. 19.

Nations Fish Stocks Agreement and the FAO High Seas Fishing Compliance Agreement, as well as to relevant regional fisheries agreements; and (f) establish or enhance the necessary infrastructure and legislative and enforcement capabilities to ensure effective compliance with, and implementation and enforcement of, their responsibilities under international law. Until action is taken on the last point, small island developing States that are flag States are encouraged to consider declining the granting of the right to fly their flag to new vessels, suspending their registry or not opening a registry.

164. The Strategy also states that small island developing States will work to put in place integrated policies and sound management approaches, such as marine protected areas, consistent with relevant international agreements, and develop national capacity to monitor, conserve and sustainably manage coral reefs and associated ecosystems, taking into account the Elaborated Programme of Work on Marine and Coastal Biological Diversity (see para. 150 above). Small island developing States should address as a priority the impacts of coastal development, coastal tourism, intensive and destructive fishing practices, pollution and the unreported and illegal trade in corals on the future health of coral reefs. To facilitate these initiatives, the international community should provide support for IOC marine science programmes of interest to small island developing States. Small island developing States and development partners should fully implement the GPA, taking initiatives with UNEP to address their specific vulnerabilities.

165. The Strategy acknowledges the progress made by some small island developing States in planning and implementation of waste management policies, programmes and strategies, but recognizes that most of them have serious difficulties in terms of financial and technical capacity in dealing with waste management issues. It states that marine debris, ballast water, shipwrecks with potential to cause environmental hazard due to leaks, and other forms of waste threaten small island developing States' ecological integrity.

Food and Agriculture Organization of the United Nations

166. As a follow-up to the Mauritius International Meeting, FAO will convene a special conference of ministers of agriculture of small island developing States to review the Mauritius Strategy during its Governing Conference, to be held in Rome from 19 to 26 November 2005. The Strategy urges the FAO special conference to consider endorsing priority actions for an enhanced contribution of agriculture, forestry and fisheries to small island developing States' sustainable development policies.

UNEP Regional Seas Programme

167. The Regional Seas Programme and the GPA Coordination Office prepared a policy publication on UNEP and small island developing States, entitled *UNEP and Small Island Developing States: 1994–2004 and future perspectives*, as part of the preparatory process for the Mauritius International Meeting. Within the context of UNEP support to small island developing States, to the South Pacific Region Environment Programme and to the secretariat of the Basel Convention, the Regional Seas Programme assisted the Basel Convention secretariat in the preparation of a paper on the preliminary elements for the development of an integrated waste management strategy for the Pacific island States, which was presented to the Mauritius International Meeting.

X.   AREAS OF FOCUS AT THE SIXTH MEETING OF THE CONSULTATIVE PROCESS

A.   Fisheries and Their Contribution to Sustainable Development[67]

1.   *Role of Fisheries in Sustainable Development*

(a) General

168. The 1987 report of the World Commission on Environment and Development (the Bruntland Commission) defines sustainable development as "development that meets the needs of the present without compromising the ability of future generations to meet their own needs."[68] FAO indicates that "Sustainable development is the management and conservation of the natural resource base, and the orientation of technological and institutional change in such a manner as to ensure the attainment and continued satisfaction of human needs for present and future generations. Such development conserves land, water, plant and genetic resources, is environmentally non-degrading, technologically appropriate, economically viable and socially acceptable."[69]

---

67. This section makes use of contributions from FAO, GEF, UNEP, the Baltic Marine Environment Protection Commission, the United Nations University, the Northwest Atlantic Fisheries Organization, the Pacific Community, the Committee for the Eastern Central Atlantic Fisheries and the Commonwealth secretariat.
68. *Our Common Future: The World Commission on Environment and Development* (Oxford University Press, 1987), p. 43.
69. FAO Committee on Fisheries, cited in FAO Fisheries Technical Paper 353, *Living marine resources and their sustainable development—Some environmental and institutional perspectives* (FAO, Rome, 1995), p. 3.

169. Sustainable development is usually divided into four primary dimensions: economic, environmental, social and institutional. Application of the concept requires the integration of economic, social and environmental issues in decision and policymaking at all levels, including those that address traditional economic sectors and government activities, such as economic planning, agriculture, health, energy, water, natural resources, industry, education and the environment. As a people-centred concept, sustainable development must include as its main objectives progress (improving quality of life), justice, durability, stability and resilience.[70]

170. In setting the internationally agreed goals contained in the United Nations Millennium Declaration, the international community has committed itself to making a sustained effort to combat poverty. While confirming that eradicating poverty is the greatest global challenge facing the world today, the World Summit on Sustainable Development also acknowledged that oceans and coastal areas are critical for global food security and agreed on ambitious new targets for resources management and fisheries. Fisheries, including aquaculture, play an important economic role and contribute to sustainable development in many countries, as they are capable of providing current generations with access to food, employment, recreation and trade without compromising the ability of future generations to meet their own needs.

171. For the fisheries sector to contribute to sustainable development, it has itself to be managed in a sustainable way. Fisheries management should promote the maintenance of the quality, diversity and availability of fishery resources in sufficient quantities for present and future generations in the context of food security, poverty alleviation and sustainable development. Management measures should ensure the conservation not only of target species but also of species belonging to the same ecosystem or associated with or dependent upon the target species. Fisheries management should also take account of the economic, social and cultural needs of fisheries-dependent communities, as well as the requirement of developing countries to maintain revenues from trade that are necessary for their development.

172. In 1984, the FAO World Conference on Fisheries Management agreed on a Strategy for Fisheries Management and Development,[71] recommending the adoption of fishery development plans, including all aspects of the fisheries sector, not only harvesting, processing, marketing, servicing and material supply, but also the development of the infrastruc-

---

70. See Department for International Development (DFID), Background Briefing, *Socially Sustainable Development: Concepts and Uses*, August 2002, available at www.dfid.gov.uk/pubs/files/wssd-brief-sdd-concepts.pdf.

71. See *Report of the FAO World Conference on Fisheries Management and Development, Rome, 27 June–6 July 1984* (FAO, Rome, 1984).

ture, technology and human resources to enable developing countries to better exploit their fishery resources, to increase added value to the economy and to improve employment opportunities. The Strategy stressed the importance for all those involved in the fishing sector to understand the social value of fisheries as a source of food, employment and profit, and thus to use fishing methods and processes that do not exhaust resources or threaten ecosystems. The Strategy recognized the special role and needs of small-scale fisheries, rural fishing and fish-farming communities and recommended that they be given priority in fisheries development policies.

(b) Contribution of Fisheries to Poverty Alleviation and Food Security[72]

173. In 2000, employment in the capture fisheries and aquaculture sectors was estimated at 35 million people, while the number of those dependent on fisheries as a source of income has been estimated at 200 million worldwide. The number of fishers has been growing at an average rate of 2.2 per cent per annum since 1990, whereas aquaculture workers have increased by an annual average of 7 per cent. Around 97 per cent of all fishery workers live and work in developing countries. The majority of them live in Asia (85 per cent) and Africa (7 per cent), with far fewer employed in Europe, North America and South and Central America (around 2 per cent each).[73]

174. Aside from trade benefits, the more considerable and substantial contribution of the fisheries sector, particularly small-scale fisheries and aquaculture, to sustainable development is its contribution to poverty alleviation and food security, especially in remote coastal areas. Small-scale fisheries can be broadly characterized as employing labour-intensive harvesting, processing and distribution technologies to exploit fishery resources. They may operate at widely different organizational levels ranging from self-employed single operators through informal microenterprises to formal sector businesses, but they all provide employment opportunities and income generation to many people in coastal and rural communities, most of whom are poor.

175. Most fishers in developing countries depend on small-scale, artisanal or subsistence fishing and fish farming for livelihood and income. Typically men are engaged in fishing and women in fish processing and marketing. Women are also known to engage in near-shore harvesting

---

72. Much of this section is drawn from *Strategies for increasing the contribution of small-scale capture fisheries to food security and poverty alleviation*, FAO Committee on Fisheries, twenty-fifth session, Rome, 24–28 February 2003, document COFI/2003/9.

73. FAO, Fisheries Department, *The State of World Fisheries and Aquaculture, 2002* (FAO, Rome, 2002), pp. 13 and 16.

activities and men are known to be involved in fish marketing and distribution. Fishing or fish farming is often undertaken next to other economic household activities including farming and small-scale trading. These multiple economic activities not only help to bridge the great seasonality in the abundance of fishery resources, but also insure against risks of failing production in any single activity. The socio-economic importance of these activities is often difficult to measure, but it is undeniable, not only in terms of their contribution to production and income but also of food security for the communities concerned.

176. Ancillary activities are also created by fishing in coastal communities. Fisheries often generate significant indirect multiplier effects through intrasectoral interactions (e.g., between capture fisheries and other activities, such as net-making and repair, or between capture fisheries and aquaculture through the supply of fishmeal), as well as intersectoral interactions (e.g., between forestry and fisheries through the supply of timber for boat-building, or between agriculture and aquaculture through the supply of feed). Moreover, the infrastructure developed for fisheries (feeder roads, landing sites and coastal havens, water-retaining ponds) tend to trigger further economic developments in other sectors, such as tourism or agriculture.

177. In addition to providing employment, fisheries are considered to be critical to food security in many countries, particularly in low-income food-deficit countries. As the FAO World Food Summit indicated in 1996, "Food security exists when all people, at all times, have physical and economic access to sufficient, safe and nutritious food to meet their dietary needs and food preferences for an active and healthy life."[74] Fisheries contribute to such food security by increasing available food supply and consumption (fish as food); by doing so at times when other foods are in scarce supply (continuity of supply); and by generating income for the purchase of food (fish as source of income).

178. Small-scale fisheries exploit a renewable source of food that provides animal protein, fish oils and essential micronutrients such as calcium, iodine and certain vitamins. Globally, some 17 per cent of the animal protein supply for human consumption comes from fisheries, and in many developing countries, especially in the Asian region, this share is above 50 per cent.[75] Fish has become the primary source of protein for 950

---

74. *Rome Declaration on World Food Security and World Food Summit Plan of Action* (FAO, 1998), para. 1.

75. FAO, *Fisheries and economic development* at www.oceansatlas.com/worldfisheriesandaquaculture/html/issues/sustain/fiecond.

million people and is an important part of the diet of many more; worldwide, people eat more fish than any other type of animal protein.[76]

179. Due to the perishable nature of fishery products, production from many small-scale fisheries is consumed locally as well as processed into forms that do not perish easily. Whether conducted full-time or part-time, or just seasonally, activities of small-scale fisheries are often targeted on supplying fish and fishery products to local and domestic markets, and for subsistence consumption. Export-oriented production, however, has increased during the last decade thanks to greater market integration and globalization.

180. With particular reference to low-income food-deficit countries, aquaculture has integrated naturally with agriculture and constituted a realistic strategy to increase food security at small cost, by providing the means for fishers and farmers to bridge the food gap they confront between planting and harvesting. In those countries, fish is a well-known and frequently consumed and traded food product, even in the poorest communities, and is an important source of income.

181. Through local trading, fishers and fish farmers in developing countries contribute to better food security not only for their own households but also for households where members neither capture fish in the wild nor raise it in captivity.[77] Moreover, the poor agro-ecological characteristics of much coastal land means that fishing can play an important role as a safety valve when agricultural production or livelihood strategies in non-fishing communities are under threat. Consequently, it is important for those fishing communities to have secure access to fishery resources and to manage such resources at sustainable levels.

(c) Contribution of Fisheries to World Trade

182. The role of the fisheries sector in international trade is significant. Fish products are valuable commodity exports for both developed and developing countries. In 2000, total world trade of fish and fishery products was estimated to have an export value of $55.2 billion. In some countries fish exports are a major contributor to foreign exchange earnings, often ranking far higher than other agricultural commodities. In many countries, fishery exports are essential to the economy. Fishery trade is particularly valuable for developing countries. It accounts for more than two thirds of the total value of traded commodities in countries such as the Seychelles,

76. International Centre for Trade and Sustainable Development, Natural Resources, International Trade and Sustainable Development Series No. 1, *Fish for thought—fisheries, international trade and sustainable development.*
77. FAO, *Contribution of fisheries to food security*, at www.oceansatlas.com/ worldfisheriesandaquaculture.html/.

and the trade surplus in fishery commodities is significant in South America, Africa, China and Oceania. Net export trade from developing countries increased from $10 billion in 1990 to $18 billion in 2000.[78] Licensing fees from foreign fishing fleets and access agreements with foreign nations have also provided a source of foreign exchange revenue for many developing coastal States. Another important aspect of international fish trade is the increasing share of products derived from aquaculture.

183. Developed countries account for more than 80 per cent of the value of fishery product imports. Japan is the largest importer of fishery products, accounting for some 26 per cent of the global total, while fish makes up 4 per cent of its total merchandise trade. The United States of America, in addition to being the fourth largest exporting country, is the second largest importer of fish and fish products. European Union member States are also dependent upon imports for their fish supply, with Spain being the third largest importer of fish products in the world.[79] However, while revenues from the international fish trade can generate significant benefits for the countries involved, such trade can also generate social and environmental problems. Increased foreign demand for fish products can, for instance, exacerbate pressure to harvest fish unsustainably or lead to excessive investment in fishing capacity, which in turn may lead to overfishing and depletion of fishery resources.

2. Legal and Policy Framework Enhancing the Contribution of Fisheries to Sustainable Development

184. In recognition of the importance of fisheries to world food security, to the attainment of national economic and social goals and to the well-being and livelihoods of individuals and families involved in fisheries, the international community has adopted over the years a number of international instruments to ensure sustainability of the world's fisheries. Some of these instruments establish rights and obligations generally applicable in respect of fishery resources in marine areas within national jurisdiction and on the high seas, while others establish regimes for the conservation and management of specific fisheries. Whether legally binding or not, these instruments are aimed at ensuring the conservation and long-term sustainability of marine living resources, including fishery resources.

185. In recent years the concept of the precautionary approach[80] and an ecosystem approach aimed at improving governance of oceans and their

---

78. *The State of World Fisheries and Aquaculture, 2002*, supra note 73, p. 34.
79. Ibid., pp. 34 and 39.
80. The precautionary approach is a recognition of the fact that because uncertainty affects all elements of the fishery management system in varying degrees, the use of precaution is required at all levels of the system, including development planning, conservation measures, management decisions, research,

resources have received wide recognition. Increasingly, the adoption of marine protected areas is advocated as an important tool for fishery conservation and management. Recent instruments recommend the strengthening of flag States' responsibilities in respect of vessels flying their flag fishing on the high seas, and in some instances, they introduce non-flag State enforcement on the high seas as a means to address the weakness of flag State jurisdiction, as well as port State measures to ensure compliance with international conservation and management measures. In addition, many conservation and management measures implementing global fishery instruments have been agreed among interested parties through regional fisheries management organizations to ensure conservation and management of specific species or stocks at the subregional and regional levels. National policies emphasizing the importance of fisheries for sustainable development have also been adopted in several countries.

(a) Global Instruments Promoting the Conservation and Sustainable Use of Fishery Resources

186. *United Nations Convention on the Law of the Sea.* Part V and Part VII, section 2, of UNCLOS provide the legal framework for the conservation, management and sustainable utilization of marine fishery resources in the exclusive economic zone and on the high seas. In the exclusive economic zone, the coastal State has the obligation to ensure that living resources, including fishery resources, are not endangered by overexploitation, taking into account the best scientific evidence available to it, with a view to promoting the optimum utilization of such resources. To this end, it is entitled to enforce its fisheries laws and regulations in the exclusive economic zone against foreign fishing vessels, by taking such measures as boarding and inspection, arrest and judicial proceedings, to ensure compliance with its laws and regulations. On the high seas, fishing States are required to adopt conservation measures for fishery resources in respect of vessels flying their flag on the basis of the best scientific evidence available to them and to cooperate with each other in the conservation and management of such resources.

187. In areas both within and beyond national jurisdiction, UNCLOS provides that conservation measures are aimed at maintaining or restoring populations of harvested species at levels which can produce the maximum sustainable yield, as qualified by relevant environmental and economic factors. With particular reference to the exclusive economic zone, UNCLOS (article 61.3) requires specific consideration of the economic needs of

technology development as well as legal and institutional frameworks (Contribution of the Northwest Atlantic Fisheries Organization).

coastal fishing communities, as one of the relevant environmental and economic factors that needs to be addressed.

188. *The 1995 United Nations Fish Stocks Agreement.* The Agreement's stated objective is to ensure the long-term conservation and sustainable use of straddling fish stocks and highly migratory fish stocks through effective implementation of the relevant provisions of UNCLOS. In order to further this goal, the Agreement requires application of the precautionary approach and the ecosystem approach in the conservation and management of the two types of stocks. It also gives full consideration to the interests of artisanal and subsistence fishers as well as the special requirements of developing States in respect of the conservation and management of straddling fish stocks and highly migratory fish stocks. It further incorporates strong compliance control provisions that encompass subregional and regional cooperation in enforcement and port State control, in addition to flag States' enforcement duties.

189. *The 1993 FAO High Seas Fishing Compliance Agreement.* The Agreement sets out the responsibilities of the flag State to ensure compliance with international conservation and management measures by fishing vessels flying its flag. Under the Agreement, a vessel requires an authorization from the flag State in order to conduct fishing activities on the high seas. The flag State must grant such authorization only if it can exercise effectively its responsibilities vis-à-vis such a vessel. Restrictions are also put on the reflagging of fishing vessels, which had previously undermined international conservation and management measures. The Agreement requires flag States to maintain a record of fishing vessels entitled to fly their flag and authorized by them to fish on the high seas. All States parties are required to cooperate in the exchange of information on activities of fishing vessels reported to have engaged in activities undermining international conservation and management measures, in order to assist the flag State in fulfilling its responsibilities.

190. *The 1995 FAO Code of Conduct for Responsible Fisheries.* The Code is a voluntary instrument that, inter alia, establishes principles for responsible fishing and fisheries activities, taking into account all their relevant biological, technological, economic, social, environmental and commercial aspects, and promotes the contribution of fisheries to food security and food quality, giving priority to the nutritional needs of local communities. The Code also seeks to promote and facilitate structural adjustment in the fisheries sector so that fisheries are utilized in a long-term sustainable and responsible manner for the benefit of present and future generations. The Code is complemented by four international plans of action: the plan to prevent, deter and eliminate illegal, unreported and unregulated fishing; the plan for reducing incidental catch of seabirds in longline fisheries; the plan for the conservation and management of sharks; and the plan for the management of fishing capacity.

191. *Kyoto Declaration.* The Declaration and Plan of Action adopted by the International Conference on the Sustainable Contribution of Fisheries to Food Security in 1995 recognized the significant role played by marine fisheries, inland fisheries and aquaculture in providing food security for the world, both through food supplies and through economic and social well-being, and declared that the international community should base policies, strategies and resource management and utilization for sustainable development of the fisheries sector on specific requirements such as the maintenance of ecological systems, use of the best scientific evidence available, improvement in economic and social well-being, and inter- and intra-generational equity. To this end, the Declaration requested States, among other immediate actions, to assess and monitor the present and future levels of global and regional production and supply and demand of fish and fishery products and their effects on food security, employment, consumption, income, trade and sustainability of production, and to provide technical and financial assistance to developing countries, in particular low-income food-deficit countries and small island developing States, in order to achieve the contribution of fisheries to food security.

192. *Convention on Biological Diversity.* The Convention provides the international legal framework for the conservation of biological diversity, the sustainable use of its components and the fair and equitable sharing of benefits arising from the utilization of genetic resources. In promoting the protection of ecosystems and natural habitats and the maintenance of viable populations of species in natural surroundings, the Convention also has a role in promoting sustainable fisheries. The Elaborated Programme of Work on Marine and Coastal Biological Diversity adopted by the Conference of the Parties to the Convention (see para. 150 above) contains several elements relevant to the achievement of sustainable fisheries.

(b) Regional Conservation and Management Measures Promoting the Sustainable Use of Fishery Resources

193. The international community places great importance on cooperation within regional fisheries management organizations and other arrangements for the regional conservation and management of fisheries resources. Since 1945, over 30 regional fisheries management organizations have been established in many regions of the world's oceans and seas to oversee governance of capture fisheries. Some organizations have only advisory capacity, while others have competency to regulate fishery resources. Nonetheless, all regional fisheries management organizations play a pivotal role in conserving and managing fisheries resources and in generally promoting responsible and sustainable behaviour in the fisheries sector.

194. Many regional fisheries management organizations have taken measures to enhance the contribution of fisheries under their management

to sustainable development. A number of them consider that the new approaches to fisheries conservation and management, in particular the precautionary approach and ecosystem approach, are important in the management of fisheries resources, habitat protection and restoration (see also A/57/57, paras. 188 and 189).

195. Recognition of the importance of interactions between fishing activities and ecosystems, particularly the long-term impacts of fishing activities on ecosystems, including the adverse effects of removing large quantities of species from the marine environment, as target species or by-catch, as well as the physical impact of fishing gear on critical habitats, has convinced a number of regional fisheries management organizations to apply an ecosystem approach to the management of fishery resources under their competency. However, concerns may arise as to how immediate social and economic factors can be taken into account in applying the precautionary approach and an ecosystem approach without undermining their effectiveness.[81]

196. In their reports to the Secretary-General, a number of organizations have provided information on their activities aimed at enhancing the contribution of fisheries to sustainable development. The secretariat of the Pacific Community has engaged over the reporting period in stock assessment, scientific monitoring and biological research on the regional tuna and billfish fisheries and in support to coastal fisheries. Its activities in support of oceanic fisheries include the monitoring of the exploitation levels of stocks of commercially important tuna and billfish species; assessing the status of these stocks; providing information on the biology and ecology of tunas, billfish and bait species; and assessing the interaction between different fisheries for oceanic species through the study of population dynamics. In addition, its support to coastal fisheries concentrates on support and advisory services towards the development of commercial fisheries and export opportunities for Pacific islanders, as well as on assessment and management of subsistence and artisanal fisheries and community-based management of fisheries. The Forum Fishery Agency has concentrated its activities during the reporting period in assisting member countries in the management and development of their tuna resources, including their interests in maximizing domestic benefits from sustainable use of their tuna resources. The Agency has also helped in the negotiation and implementation of regional agreements among its members and with distant-water nations. Furthermore, the newly established Commission for the Conservation and Management of Highly Migratory Fish Stocks in the

---

81. FAO Fisheries Circular No. 985, *Summary information on the role of international fishery organizations or arrangements and other bodies concerned with the conservation and management of living aquatic resources* (FAO, Rome, 2003), pp. 6–7.

Western and Central Pacific Ocean, which is to promote sustainable management over short-term maximization of exploitation, will integrate the management of tuna fisheries in the exclusive economic zones of Pacific Island Forum countries with the currently unregulated high seas areas and other parts of the waters of western and central Pacific rim countries that are part of the geographical range of the Pacific highly migratory fish stocks.

(c) National Policies Promoting the Contribution of Fisheries to Sustainable Development[82]

197. The Johannesburg Plan of Implementation adopted at the World Summit on Sustainable Development has stressed that States have the primary responsibility for achieving sustainable development. They are responsible for the identification of sustainable development priorities, orientation policies, implementation of national strategies, and measures to strengthen national institutions and legal frameworks. Thus, in relation to fisheries, States are urged to adopt measures that are conducive to improving governance of fisheries both on the high seas and in areas under national jurisdiction, so that the sector may contribute to global food security, economic prosperity and the well-being of national economies, including those in developing countries.

198. However, the weakness of the surveillance systems of some developing coastal States constitutes a major constraint. Indeed, limited resources and the large size of the ocean space over which they exercise jurisdiction have hampered these countries' ability to enforce conservation and management measures against unauthorized fishing. Unauthorized fishing activities have been carried out through the use of flags of convenience, illegal fishing in the exclusive economic zone and on the high seas, and misreporting of catch. Developing coastal States dependent on access fees for their economic development are particularly vulnerable because of the effects of fee levels that are proportionate to the volume of catch.[83]

199. Consequently, coastal States in some regions have established a regional register of foreign vessels with a common database of all relevant information about vessels, updated annually, containing information about their owners, operators and masters, call sign and port of registry. The regional register is used not only as a source of information on fishing vessels, but also as a tool to ensure compliance with coastal States' laws and

82. This section is drawn in part from *Strategies for increasing the contribution of small-scale capture fisheries to food security and poverty alleviation,* supra note 72.

83. Information provided by the South Pacific Applied Geoscience Commission.

regulations. Coastal States have also taken additional measures, such as harmonization of the terms and conditions of access and adoption of agreements permitting a party to extend its fisheries surveillance and law enforcement activities to the territorial sea and archipelagic waters of another party (see A/57/57, para. 184).

200. In addition, many developing coastal States have now taken measures to improve the national legal and policy frameworks within which small-scale fisheries operate in view of the importance of this subsector for their economies, in order to enhance its contribution to food security and poverty alleviation. A number of strategies are being pursued to achieve these goals. Some strategies lie within the fisheries sector, and can be tackled by fisheries-specific initiatives, while others require action by planners, policymakers and practitioners in other sectors.

201. Strategies within fisheries include activities relating to: (a) data collection and research for strategy development; (b) reduction of vulnerability and ways to increase the added value of small-scale fishing activities; (c) resource allocation and management; (d) addressing trade-offs between short-term and long-term objectives and the impacts of different policies and strategies; and (e) measures aimed at improving governance. However, it should be borne in mind that the small-scale fisheries subsector is not homogenous within and across countries and regions and attention to this fact is warranted when formulating strategies and policies for enhancing its contribution to food security and poverty alleviation.

(i)   Data Collection and Research for Strategy Development

202. In order to develop effective fisheries-specific strategies, there is a need to better measure and understand the causal factors of poverty in small-scale fishing communities. Such measures would demonstrate the validity of assistance to small-scale fisheries, not only because of levels of poverty in the sector, but also because of its current and potential contribution to food security and poverty alleviation at the local, regional and national levels as well as its contribution to the country's export revenues. It is also necessary to identify how many people are actually involved in small-scale fisheries as, without such knowledge, it is clearly impossible to measure the fisheries' real contribution to food security and poverty alleviation. Moreover, better data and information provide a better understanding of (a) the process by which people in small-scale fishing communities move in and out of poverty; (b) corresponding solutions in terms of *ex ante* risk management and *ex post* support; (c) the strategies required to increase the contribution of small-scale fisheries to local and national food security and to poverty alleviation; and (d) how such strategies could be put into action.

(ii)   Reducing Vulnerability and Increasing Value

203. A number of actions can be taken to address vulnerability in small-scale fishing communities. Actions ought to be tailored to the source of such vulnerability; for example, vulnerability to natural disasters such as hurricanes can be reduced through preparedness programmes and early warning systems, while vulnerability to occupational hazards such as accidents at sea or health problems caused by food processing can be addressed through sea safety programmes and programmes aimed at reducing the health effects of fish smoking (e.g., improved ovens). Another strategy to reduce vulnerability in small-scale fishing communities is to officially recognize and enforce their rights to the fishery resources facilities and land they live on or use, whether they are sedentary or migratory. Other actions include the development of fishers' organizational capacity and the introduction of methods that facilitate their effective participation at local and national levels in decisions affecting the fisheries sector, their livelihoods and work conditions, in order to create a sense of ownership and accountability in the decision-making process.

204. Value added can be increased in small-scale fisheries through, inter alia, improved infrastructure and management of landing sites, storage facilities and market buildings; better information about markets; and enhanced processing and reduced post-harvest waste, including improved handling, processing and distribution of both by-catch and target species.

(iii)   Resource Allocation and Management

205. Resource allocation and management may also be used to increase the contribution of small-scale fisheries to food security and poverty alleviation, particularly in overexploited stocks, by (a) improving the resource base through better resource management (e.g., reduction in destructive fishing practices) and stock rebuilding strategies (protected areas, restoration, stock and habitat enhancements); (b) allocating a greater share of resources to small-scale fisheries as opposed to industrial fisheries, including more explicit quota allocations to small-scale fisheries and the setting up of wider areas reserved for their exclusive use; (c) promoting the use of fish aggregation devices, where appropriate, to increase stock aggregation and accessibility in coastal areas; and (d) providing alternative livelihoods under effective governance structures so as to reduce pressure on overfished resources. Provision of alternative livelihoods can reduce poverty in fishing communities and allow stocks to recover. Stock recovery can then generate possibilities for increased supplies of fish for human consumption; enhanced earnings in small-scale fisheries; income and

employment multipliers in fishing communities; and increased national export revenues from small-scale fisheries.

(iv) Addressing Trade-offs and Impacts of Different Strategies

206. Trade-offs, which imply consideration of the impacts of each strategy in terms of costs and benefits, need to be addressed when adopting improved policies, institutions and processes in the fisheries sector. Implicit in policy decisions designed to combat food insecurity and poverty, trade-offs must be based on information from data collection and research.

207. Several types of trade-offs are frequently encountered. For example, what are the costs and benefits of reducing industrial fishing activity (with corresponding decreases in foreign exchange earnings) in favour of small-scale fisheries catches with increases in small-scale fishing profitability and multiplier effects? In other words, what are the effects of trading an increase in equity for a decrease in efficiency, which means changing the balance in the factors of production in favour of labour over capital inputs and may result in greater employment, but can reduce profitability? What are the costs and benefits of supporting export versus production for the national market? This means increased revenues for small-scale fisheries and enhanced foreign exchange earnings for the Government, but may lead to a decrease in the availability of fish for sale in local markets and may have important effects on the distribution of poverty and food security. What are the costs and benefits of supporting foreign or local fisheries for enhanced national income? This may bring increased licensing revenues and royalty payments from foreign fishing fleets, or increased export earnings from national semi-industrial or industrial fleets, but may result in lesser fish catches for small-scale fisheries, with implications for food security and poverty alleviation. What are the costs and benefits of adopting short-term initiatives to reduce poverty and improve food security, such as credits or subsidies to small-scale fisheries, which could have an adverse impact on long-term sustainability of the fisheries sector (e.g., overexploitation, falling catches and declining profitability)?

(v) Improved Governance

208. Improved governance is critical to the success and effectiveness of any strategy to enhance the contribution of small-scale fisheries to food security and poverty alleviation. It requires inclusiveness (empowerment and decentralization); lawfulness (enforcement of fisheries laws and regulations, elimination of legislation and practices considered to be detrimental to small-scale fisheries and conflict resolution between resource

users); and transparency and accountability (accountability of all fishery governing structures, anti-corruption measures, access to information, and participatory monitoring and evaluation of initiatives aimed at supporting small-scale fisheries).

3.   *Factors Limiting the Contribution of Fisheries to Sustainable Development*

209. The United Nations Conference on Environment and Development identified a number of factors considered to be major hindrances to the contribution of fisheries to sustainable development. These factors reduce the ability of fisheries to contribute to economic development, poverty alleviation and food security, while increasing the risk of ecosystem degradation.

High Seas Fisheries

210. The Conference indicated that the management of high seas fisheries is inadequate in many areas and some resources are overutilized. Agenda 21 pointed out that the main problems affecting high seas fisheries are unregulated fishing, overcapitalization, and excessive fleet size, vessel reflagging to escape controls, insufficiently selective gear, excessive by-catch, lack of enforcement of conservation measures, unreliable databases and lack of sufficient cooperation between States.[84] Most of these issues arise from the open access nature of high seas fisheries, which encourages "free riders" and "bad actors" in ocean fisheries, does not favour meaningful cooperation among States, and prevents an effective management of high seas fisheries. Yet, without effective management, fisheries resources tend towards overexploitation and depletion, inhibiting possibilities for sustainable development.

211. A broader issue undermining the sustainability of high seas fisheries is the absence of a consensus on the nature of the duty to cooperate under international law for the conservation and management of high seas fisheries. Limits on harvesting agreed upon within regional fisheries management organizations can be easily undermined by non-contracting parties, whose vessels fish without restraint because the flag States are not parties to the organizations or arrangements which imposed the limits. By ignoring the regional organization's regulations, these States not only undermine the objective pursued by the parties, namely conservation and sustainable use of the managed fisheries, but also derive an indirect

---

84. Agenda 21, *supra* note 6, para. 17.45.

benefit from the reduction in the general fishing effort in the areas concerned.[85]

Fishing in Areas under National Jurisdiction

212. Many fisheries conducted in areas under national jurisdiction, including small-scale fisheries, are facing difficulties relating to local excess fishing capacity, unauthorized incursions by foreign fleets in violation of the sovereign rights of the coastal State under articles 56, 61 and 62 of UNCLOS, ecosystem degradation, undervaluation of catch, excessive by-catches and discards, and increasing competition between artisanal and large-scale fishing and between fishing and other types of activities.[86] The absence of controls on the overall fishing effort and the fishing practices of local fishers and foreign fishing vessels, prompted by the inadequacy of monitoring, control and surveillance, is the root cause of such unsustainable fishing practices. These practices have adverse effects on the sustainable development and conservation of fishery resources and the economies and food security of coastal States, particularly developing coastal States.

213. In addition, concerns have been expressed over the last one or two decades about fisheries' role in sustainable development owing to the prevalence of unsustainable fishing practices and human-induced changes in the ecosystem. Some fishery bodies advising developing coastal States in the conservation and management of resources under national jurisdiction have expressed concern over the increase and globalization of fish trade and the possible negative effects of foreign access agreements on conservation, local supplies and equity. These organizations have advised their member States to take progressive management measures in access regulation rather than wait for the fisheries to be overexploited. They also stress the need for consultations with all stakeholders in the sector to regulate access and manage fishing capacity through protocols and consultation mechanisms.

Overfishing

214. The FAO report on the state of world fisheries and aquaculture in 2002 indicated that the number of underexploited and moderated exploited fisheries resources, represent 25 per cent of the major fish stocks and

---

85. E. Franckx, *Pacta Tertiis and the Agreement for the Implementation of the Provisions of the United Nations Convention on the Law of the Sea of 10 December 1982 relating to Conservation and Management of Straddling Fish Stocks & Highly Migratory Fish Stocks*, FAO Legal Papers on Line No. 8, June 2000, p. 7.

86. Agenda 21, *supra* note 6, para. 17.72.

continue to decline slightly; 47 per cent were fully exploited and thus had reached their maximum sustainable limits; 18 per cent were reported as being overexploited without any prospect for expansion or increased production; and the remaining 10 per cent were considered to be significantly depleted.[87] An earlier report stated that the global shortfall of fish caused by the depletion of fisheries, expected to increase considerably over the next decades, would pose a major threat to the food supply of millions of people (see A/53/456, paras. 261–263).

Illegal, Unreported and Unregulated Fishing

215. Illegal, unreported and unregulated fishing has been reported in various regions of the world, either on the °high seas or in areas under the national jurisdiction of coastal States. This type of fishing has adverse effects on the conservation of fishery resources, economies and food security of coastal States, particularly developing coastal States, and is routinely associated with unsustainable fishing practices on the high seas (see A/54/429, paras. 249–257).

Constraints on Small-scale Fisheries

216. Small-scale fishing communities are vulnerable to many external factors contributing to poverty, including economic factors such as market price fluctuations and variable access to markets, as well as climatic and natural events such as yearly seasonal fluctuations in stock abundance, poor catches, bad weather, natural disasters including cyclones and hurricanes, and the dangers of working at sea.[88] The severe impact of the recent tsunami disaster in South-East Asian coastal communities, which caused loss of income generation and livelihood for many fishing communities of several States in the Indian Ocean, is a harsh reminder of the catastrophic consequences of such natural events.

217. Governance and policy issues associated with access to and control over aquatic environment and resources may also constrain small-scale fisheries. Access control and distribution issues are often linked with competition from industrial and foreign interests. Additional constraints include lack of access to capital, limited alternative employment opportunities and a lack of appropriate technology. Such constraints can reduce the ability of those fisheries to contribute to food security and poverty alleviation.[89]

87. *The State of World Fisheries and Aquaculture, 2002*, supra note 73, pp. 22–23.
88. Ibid.
89. *Strategies for increasing the contribution of small-scale capture fisheries to food security and poverty alleviation*, supra note 72, para. 20.

218. Conflicts between small-scale and industrial fishing activity may originate from governance and policy issues, such as inadequate enforcement capability or a lack of will for enforcement, or preferential treatment given to industrial fisheries. Examples of such preferences include long delays in processing complaints about incursions of industrial vessels into small-scale fishing areas, exclusion of small-scale fishers from fishing grounds, subsidies to industrial fisheries, and the payment by industrial fishing interests of arbitrary, informal incentives to obtain access to resources or markets.[90] In some regions, inshore fishing by industrial vessels, especially trawlers, besides competing with artisanal fisheries, has had an adverse impact on nearshore marine environment, by forcing artisanal fishers to work in ever-shrinking areas of shallow water and to fish for juveniles in coastal nursery areas.[91] The two fisheries may also be in conflict in the market to the extent that they catch the same species of fish. Mass landings of large-scale fisheries may depress fish prices and make small-scale fishers increasingly uncompetitive. While this may seem to be an economically efficient process, in that the more efficient (low-cost) industrial producers displace the marginal (high cost) small-scale producers, the outcome may be neither efficient nor equitable because (a) it creates distortions and imperfections in the capital market; (b) it is a socially unacceptable distribution of income; and (c) it ignores the lack of alternative employment opportunities for displaced fishers.[92]

219. These conflicts show the importance of improving policies, institutions and processes and orienting them towards the reduction of the vulnerability of small-scale fishers and defending their rights. They also demonstrate the need for the appropriate authorities to make explicit choices between trade-offs in policy decisions when, for instance, they decide to maximize food security and poverty alleviation.

220. Additional constraints on small-scale fishers are their lack of geographical and occupational mobility. A limited fishing range due to lack of technological development prevents them from fishing seaward while the lack of alternative employment, already referred to above, limits their exit from fisheries, making them particularly vulnerable to encroachment from both land and sea. Thus, small-scale fishers are often faced with a "mouse-trap" constraint: entry is relatively easy and not very costly, but exit is difficult for a variety of reasons ranging from chronic indebtedness to lack of alternative employment outside the fishery.[93] In many developing

90. Ibid., para. 21.
91. FAO Fisheries Technical Paper 353, supra note 69, p. 16.
92. FAO Fisheries Technical Paper 228, *Management concepts for small-scale fisheries: economic and social aspects* (FAO, Rome, 1982), p. 25.
93. Ibid., p. 22.

countries, fishing is viewed as the employment of last resort: people fish when farming is not feasible.[94]

221. Moreover, many fishing techniques used by small-scale and artisanal fishers on reefs, such as dynamite fishing, drive netting and poison fishing, have adverse impacts on the abundance of fishery resources and the health of related ecosystems in tropical environments. They may result in overfishing of coastal fish species and invertebrates as well as an irreversible depletion of reef species, in view of the crucial role of coral reefs as spawning grounds and habitats for invertebrates and fish.[95] Although these practices are officially banned, they often persist because the people involved have little, if any, alternative livelihood.[96]

Environmental Issues linked to Aquaculture

222. Experts believe that although aquaculture may appear to be more sustainable than capture fishing, the industry needs to address the adverse ecological effects of methods used in the production of farmed fish on the marine environment, wild fisheries and human health.[97]

4. *Capacity-building Activities of International Organizations Promoting Sustainable Fisheries*

223. In recognition of the importance of fisheries in the sustainable development of developing countries, a number of competent international organizations have extended technical and financial assistance to these countries in the form of capacity-building activities designed to enhance the role of fisheries, particularly small-scale fisheries, in combating poverty and improving food security.

224. FAO, as the United Nations agency competent in fishery issues, is engaged in many activities promoting the contribution of fisheries to

---

94. R. B. Pollnac and J. Sutinen, "Economic, social, and cultural aspects of stock assessment for tropical small-scale fisheries" in *Stock Assessment for Tropical Small-scale Fisheries*, ed. by S. B. Saila and P. M. Roedel (University of Rhode Island, International Center for Marine Research and Development, Kingston, Rhode Island), pp. 48–50; see also FAO Fisheries Technical Paper 228, supra note 92, p. 30.

95. M. J. Kaiser and others, "Impacts of fishing gear on marine benthic habitats" in *Responsible Fisheries in the Marine Ecosystem*, ed. by M. Sinclair (FAO, Rome, 2003), p. 201.

96. FAO Fisheries Technical Paper 443, *The ecosystem approach to fisheries—issues, terminology, principles, institutional foundations, implementation and outlook*, (FAO, Rome, 2003), p. 11.

97. *The State of World Fisheries and Aquaculture, 2002*, supra note 73, pp. 74–83; see also FAO Fisheries Circular 989 (FIRI/C989), *Genetically modified organisms and aquaculture* (FAO, Rome, 2003), pp. 19–22; and *Financial Times*, 13 January 2004.

sustainable development. Most of these activities are undertaken through the implementation of the Code of Conduct for Responsible Fisheries and related international plans of action. FAO has provided technical assistance to developing countries in the field of participative approaches to fisheries management, complemented by the development of appropriate institutional frameworks. It also established guidelines of key indicators for socio-economic and demographic issues, problems and opportunities in fishery resource management, and for monitoring the impact of management measures on the socio-economic well-being of coastal and fishing communities. FAO has identified and disseminated information on available tools for effective management of small-scale fisheries, and has addressed the issue of access rights to fisheries resources in small-scale fisheries.

225. Since 1999, FAO has implemented the United Kingdom-funded Sustainable Fisheries Livelihood Programme to assist 25 West African countries in reducing poverty in coastal and inland fisheries communities through the improvement of their livelihoods. The Programme intends to reach its objectives through (a) the development of social and human capital in fisheries-dependent communities; (b) the enhancement of the natural assets of these communities; and (c) the development of appropriate policy and institutional environments. The Programme expects to achieve a lasting impact on governance at the central and local levels, and on policy formulation and execution at the national level.

226. Other activities to enhance the contribution of fisheries to sustainable development include assistance to Nigeria and Malawi to improve the access of their fisheries institutions to information and documentation on the management of fisheries and aquaculture; training of personnel in Viet Nam and the Islamic Republic of Iran in the collection of marketing information and preparation of market reports; preparation and dissemination of fisheries manuals on the Atlantic coast of Nicaragua; workshop on the development of a national strategy for fisheries management and development in Viet Nam; workshops and seminars on fish and fish products safety and quality, in Bremen (Germany), in Spain for the Mediterranean countries, in Pakistan, Viet Nam, the Islamic Republic of Iran, Bulgaria and China and in Bangladesh for South and South-East Asian countries; expert consultation on the role of small-scale fisheries in poverty alleviation and food security; programmes to enhance capacity-building to combat illegal, unreported and unregulated fishing, including assistance in the development and implementation of national plans of action; and assistance to countries such as Senegal and Thailand, and organizations such as the West African Subregional Fisheries Commission and the Latin American Organization for the Development of Fisheries in addressing the implementation of the international plan of action for the management of fishing capacity (see para. 190 above).

227. The United Nations Development Programme Global Environment Facility (GEF) in cooperation with other donors has provided financial assistance to projects addressing sustainable management of marine fisheries in developing countries and in countries with transition economies. One of these projects, relating to the implementation of the strategic action programme of the Pacific small island developing States, supported the negotiations leading to the conclusion of the Convention on the Conservation and Management of Highly Migratory Fish Stocks in the Western and Central Pacific Ocean, which entered into force in 2004. A project on the reduction of environmental impact from tropical shrimp trawling through the introduction of by-catch reduction technologies and change of management, with the participation of countries in Africa, Latin America, the Caribbean and South Asia, addresses destructive fishing techniques. Other initiatives address the issue of overfishing, and promote the development of an ecosystem approach to fisheries management, using large marine ecosystems as management units. They include the project for combating living resource depletion and coastal degradation in the Guinea Current large marine ecosystem through ecosystem-based regional actions, with the participation of 16 West African countries and several organizations and donors; the strategic partnership for sustainable fisheries in the large marine ecosystems of sub-Saharan Africa; the strategic partnership for the Mediterranean large marine ecosystem; and the preparation of a transboundary diagnostic analysis and preliminary framework for the Bay of Bengal large marine ecosystem.

228. The Commonwealth secretariat has implemented a work programme focusing on the development of coastal fisheries conducted as small to medium enterprises. The programme has been motivated by the fact that an increasing number of Commonwealth developing coastal States experience serious overexploitation of their coastal fisheries resources due to a rapid shift from subsistence to commercial fishing. Projects aim to assist in the development of institutional capacity in member countries and to train fisheries business owners to adapt and incorporate the profit motive of business in national strategies on sustainable management and development of coastal fisheries resources.

229. The United Nations University has been involved in capacity-building activities in the fisheries sector. The University's Fisheries Training Programme, in cooperation with several Icelandic research institutions, has conducted postgraduate training courses for developing countries in Iceland in the following fisheries-related fields: fishery policy and planning, marine and inland water resource assessment and monitoring, quality management of fish handling and processing, fishing technology, management of fisheries companies and marketing, and environmental assessment and monitoring.

5. Conclusions

230. Fisheries can play an important role in the world economy and contribute to sustainable development if they are managed responsibly, so as to provide current generations with food, employment, recreation and trade without compromising the ability of future generations to meet their own needs. The contribution of small-scale fisheries to poverty alleviation and food security in many countries, particularly developing countries, should be fully acknowledged. However, for fisheries to contribute to sustainable development, Governments have to develop innovative measures to address a number of issues that stand in the way of achieving this goal. These are the problems of overfishing, illegal, unreported and unregulated fishing and unsustainable fishing practices, which are linked to larger issues of oceans governance on the high seas and in areas under national jurisdiction, as well as flag States' responsibilities and coastal States' capabilities.

231. It is of particular importance to provide financial and technical assistance to developing countries to improve management of the living marine resources in areas under their national jurisdiction. Measures should include efforts to reduce the many sources of vulnerability in small-scale fishing communities. Among these, particular attention should be given to the improvement of the legal and policy framework within which small-scale fisheries operate, in order to enhance their contribution to food security and poverty alleviation.

B. Marine Debris

232. The information in this chapter is to a large extent extracted from the feasibility study on sustainable management of marine litter[98] that was prepared by UNEP in consultation with a number of United Nations and other intergovernmental organizations, as well as non-governmental organizations, who have experience in issues related to marine litter. The study was submitted to the sixth Global Meeting of the Regional Seas Conventions and Action Plans, held in Istanbul from 30 November to 2 December 2004.

1. General

233. Marine debris, also referred to as marine litter, is any persistent, manufactured or processed solid material discarded, disposed of or abandoned in the marine and coastal environment. Marine debris may be

---

98. UNEP(DEC)/RS.6.1.INF.9, available at www1.unep.org/dec/RegionalSeas /INF.9MarineLitterFeasibilityStudy.doc.

found near the source of input, but can also be transported over long distances by ocean currents and winds. As a result, marine debris is found in all sea areas of the world—not only in densely populated regions, but also in remote places far away from any obvious sources. Generally speaking, urban debris is predominant in the vicinity of large cities, while ship-generated debris is a major contributor on remote coastlines.[99]

234. There are no recent and reliable figures on the amount of marine debris worldwide. Furthermore, comparisons of the accumulation of marine debris among locations is complicated by differences in the intensities and periods of study and the methods of classifying debris and beach substrate.[100] Some calculations estimate that eight million items of marine debris enter oceans and seas every day.

235. Marine debris has become an increasing problem in recent times. Most marine litter consists of material that degrades slowly, if at all, so that a continuous input of large quantities of these items results in a gradual build-up in the coastal and marine environment. In the last few years, the issue of marine debris has been mentioned in a number of General Assembly resolutions, evincing the growing concern of the international community about this problem.[101]

2. Sources of Marine Debris

236. A variety of land-based and marine activities result in the introduction of debris into the marine environment. It is generally acknowledged that land-based sources account for 60 to 80 per cent of marine debris. But the main source of marine debris may differ from region to region and from country to country.

237. *Main land-based sources of marine debris.* Land-based sources are extremely widespread, and include recreational beach-goers and fishers; materials manufacturers, processors and transporters; shore-based solid waste disposal and processing facilities; sewage treatment and sewer overflows; inappropriate or illegal dumping on land; and public littering.[102] Debris can be blown, washed, or discharged into the water from land areas. A major source is sewer overflows and sewage treatment plants. When run-off from seasonal precipitation exceeds the handling capacity of the sewage

---

99. Joint Group of Experts on the Scientific Aspects of Marine Environmental Protection (GESAMP) Reports and Studies 71, *Protecting the oceans from land-based activities* (available at http://gesamp.imo.org/no71/index.htm), pp. 15–26.

100. Ibid.

101. See General Assembly resolutions 59/24, para. 92; 59/25, para. 60; 58/14, para. 44; 57/142, para. 23; and 55/8, para. 20.

102. Seba B. Sheavly, "Marine debris—an overview of a critical issue for our oceans", paper presented at the 2004 International Coastal Cleanup Conference, 14–18 May 2004, San Juan, Puerto Rico, available from www.coastsweep.umb.edu.

treatment facility, materials can bypass treatment systems and enter waterways. Legal and illegal shore-based solid waste management practices, both in coastal areas and along inland waterways, also contribute to the problem of marine debris.

238. Natural phenomena can also have a role in the creation of marine debris. In addition to causing tremendous loss to human life and property, the Indian Ocean tsunami created enormous amounts of debris that ended up in the marine environment. Debris can provoke further physical damage to already damaged vulnerable ecosystems.[103]

239. *Main sea-based sources of marine litter.* Accidental, deliberate or routine discharges or dumping from ships, pleasure craft, fishing vessels and offshore oil and gas platforms are among the main sea-based sources of marine debris. It is estimated that shipping contributes 10 to 20 per cent of the world's marine debris. Larger vessels with many people on board typically generate considerable amounts of waste. It is estimated that from 1.4 to 2.5 kg of wet garbage and 0.5 to 1.5 kg of dry garbage is produced per person, per day on medium-sized ships.[104] Similarly, offshore oil and gas platforms and offshore supply vessels can generate debris both from daily operations and from the crew. In the absence of appropriate treatment facilities on board and reception facilities on land, waste may be dumped intentionally. Cargo washed overboard can also constitute marine debris.

240. *Fishing gear and related marine debris.* Commercial fishing activities introduce marine debris into the ocean through accidental loss of fishing gear or through intentional disposal of worn-out gear.[105] It is estimated that 30 per cent of all marine debris originates from the fishing industry. Debris items originating in fisheries activities include nets, monofilament lines and ropes, salt treatment bags, bait boxes and bags, fish baskets or totes, fish and lobster tags and trawl floats. Due to the resistance of modern synthetics to degradation, it is believed that some derelict fishing gear continues to circulate with the currents for years or decades, until it ends up on shallow reefs, banks or beaches, eventually degrading.[106] This type of marine debris has been identified as the most biologically threatening of the debris categories.[107]

---

103. www.noaanews.noaa.gov/stories2005/s2362.htm.

104. www.ukmarinesac.org.uk.

105. The lack of on-shore storing and disposal facilities has been cited as one of the reasons why fishers purposefully discard damaged gear. See Proceedings of the Fourth International Marine Debris Conference on Derelict Fishing Gear and the Marine Environment, Honolulu, Hawaii, 2000 (available through http:// hawaiihumpbackwhale.noaa.gov), p. 27.

106. Ibid., p. 31.

107. Ibid., p. 21.

3.   *Effects of Marine Debris*

241. Marine debris is a visible sign of human impact on the marine environment and a source of public concern, as it causes environmental, economic, health and aesthetic problems.

242. *Human health and safety.* Items such as broken glass, medical waste, ropes and fishing lines pose a threat to human safety. The presence of litter can also indicate more serious water quality concerns that affect human health. Swimmers, divers and snorkelers can become entangled in submerged or floating debris. Medical and personal hygiene debris that enters the waste stream through direct sewage outflows or inadequate sewage treatment systems can indicate the presence of invisible pathogenic pollutants and other bacterial contamination that could cause serious illnesses.[108]

243. *Effects on tourism and other economic activities.* Marine debris has repercussions on coastal economic activities, particularly tourism. Whether deposited on beaches, on the seabed or floating in coastal waters, stranded materials can pose risks to human health and cause aesthetic deterioration of beaches and coastal waters, thus affecting tourism with resulting loss in revenues. It is also expensive to clean up. New Jersey spends $1.5 million annually to clean up its beaches and $40,000 to remove debris from the New York/New Jersey harbour.[109]

244. *Navigation.* Marine debris can also be a navigational hazard. For example, derelict fishing gear in the form of nets and ropes, invisibly floating just below the water's surface, can entangle vessel propellers and rudders. One of the most common causes of burned-out water pumps in recreational boats is plastic bags clogging and blocking water intake valves. Repairs can be costly and result in a significant loss of operational time. It has been estimated that the Japanese fishing industry spent $4.1 billion on boat repairs in 1992.[110]

245. *Effects on marine species.* A review of the effects of marine debris on marine wildlife indicates that at least 267 species of marine wildlife are affected by debris.[111] Entanglement and ingestion are the primary kinds of direct damage to wildlife caused by marine litter. Species affected by entanglement and ingestion mostly include sea turtles, seabirds and marine mammals. Debris can cause amputations or increased vulnerability to predators due to impeded movements. Heavy, large plastic sheets and other large debris smother or trap benthic-dwelling animals and drown those that

108. Sheavly (n. 102 above).
109. *Marine Debris Abatement* on website of United States Environmental Protection Agency at www.epa.gov/owow/oceans/debris.
110. Ibid.
111. Information from www.oceansatlas.org.

must rise to the surface to breathe. Ingestion incidents may lead to suffocation or digestive problems. Ingestion of solid waste can bring about irritation and damage to the digestive tract as well as disruption of normal feeding patterns, causing some animals to stop eating and slowly starve to death. Even at low levels, ingestion can interfere with gut function and metabolism, and may have toxic effects.

246. *Habitat destruction and alien species introduction.* Other threats to wildlife and the environment from marine litter include physical damage, such as covering of coral reefs, smothering of seagrass beds and other seabed ecosystems, and disturbance of habitats from mechanical beach cleaning. Marine litter is also increasingly believed to be a source of accumulation of toxic substances in the marine environment, and environmental changes due to the transfer and introduction of invasive species. In fact, marine debris drifting on ocean currents may eventually become home to entire communities of potentially harmful, non-native organisms which can be carried to the far corners of the oceans.

247. *Fisheries.* Marine debris may put additional pressure on already stressed commercial fish stocks. Marine debris, including debris originated from fishing activities, is an important cause of by-catch. Problems associated with marine debris include "ghost fishing" (the entanglement of fish and marine mammals in lost fishing gear) by lost gill nets, bottom longlines and other passive gear such as traps and pots. Studies conducted in the Atlantic Ocean suggest that discarded gear may be responsible for significant losses of some commercially valuable fish and crab species (see A/59/298, para. 81). Marine debris may also have a considerable impact on coral reefs and seagrass beds,[112] which have been recognized as important spawning and nursery grounds for fish. Furthermore, plastics and sewage-related debris have been identified as the two major types of litter interfering with fishing gear. Inconvenience and economic loss can be caused by the need to clean debris entangled in nets, reduction in the effectiveness of gear, the impairment of static fishing gear and the blockage of trawls by dense litter.[113]

4.   *Measures to Prevent and Reduce Marine Debris*

248. Because marine debris comes from both land- and sea-based sources, measures to prevent or reduce marine debris in the marine and coastal environment have to be taken in many areas, within many activities and by many actors. A distinction can be made between measures that are aimed at preventing and reducing marine debris at source and those that

112. Sheavly (n. 102 above).
113. T. Fanshawe and M. Everard, *The Impacts of Marine Litter*, Marine Pollution Monitoring Management Group, 2002, p. 13.

are taken to deal with debris once it is found in the marine and coastal environment.

249. Measures to prevent and reduce marine debris include (a) better waste management on land and at sea, including through improved recycling of materials and the development of more degradable packaging materials; (b) effective implementation and enforcement of international instruments; (c) improvement of port reception facilities; and (d) improvement of education and awareness-raising activities to influence behaviours.

(a)   Waste Management

250. The most effective way of reducing marine debris is by diminishing the generation of waste on land and from ships, fishing vessels, pleasure craft and offshore platforms, for example by reusing and recycling materials. Once generated, waste must be collected and taken care of in an environmentally sound manner, either for reuse, recycling or safe disposal. The development of degradable materials might help decrease the total amount of persistent plastics in the marine and coastal (and terrestrial) environment. However, developing more "litter-friendly" materials should not send the signal that contaminating the environment with "litter-friendly" waste is considered acceptable. Efforts to enhance land-based waste management should include the proper management by municipalities of landfills and sewage treatment facilities. Moreover, recreational areas such as beaches and camping grounds should be sufficiently equipped with waste bins to cater for the needs of visitors. Education, information and training are vital components in such efforts towards more effective waste management.

251. Large vessels and offshore platforms should have waste management plans, and preparations for proper waste management should be made in advance by those on-board smaller vessels and pleasure craft. For example, in 2001, members of the International Council of Cruise Lines adopted cruise industry waste management practices and procedures and committed themselves to: implementing a policy goal of zero discharges of MARPOL annex V solid waste products (garbage) by use of more comprehensive waste minimization procedures to significantly reduce shipboard generated waste, and to expanding waste reduction strategies to include reuse and recycling to the maximum extent possible so as to land ashore even smaller quantities of waste products. Waste generated at sea should be stored on-board and discharged ashore in a proper reception facility, unless the discharge of the material in question into the marine environment is permitted under MARPOL (see para. 254 below).

(b)   Legal Instruments

252. Marine debris is not always specifically mentioned in international legal instruments. However, when these instruments include, for example,

requirements to decrease or eliminate the discharge of ship-generated waste, or measures to stop the discharge of solid waste from land-based sources, or action to reduce the loss of fishing gear from fishing vessels, the issue of marine debris is implicitly covered. For example, the conventions on the protection and conservation of the marine and coastal environment adopted under the UNEP Regional Seas Programme and partner programmes regulate various sources of pollution and thus generally support the prevention and reduction of marine debris, even when the issue is not specifically addressed. Some regions have gone a step further and adopted specific protocols on the protection of the marine environment against pollution by land-based sources or by dumping, providing a more targeted approach to the problem of marine debris.

(i)   UNCLOS

253. Part XII of the Convention sets out the duties of States to protect and preserve the marine environment. UNCLOS requires States to take, individually or jointly as appropriate, all measures necessary to prevent, reduce and control pollution of the marine environment from any source, using for this purpose the best practicable means at their disposal and in accordance with their capabilities. States have a duty not to transform one form of pollution into another and not to introduce alien or new species which may cause harm to the marine environment. States are required to develop international rules and standards for the prevention of pollution from land-based sources and take these into account when adopting national laws and regulations. They are also required to develop international rules and standards for the prevention of pollution by dumping and from vessels, and to implement and enforce them at the national level. These international rules and standards represent the minimum standards for flag States. They can be enforced against a foreign vessel by a coastal State and also by a port State where there has been a discharge violation. Coastal States may adopt and enforce stricter rules and standards for the prevention, reduction and control of pollution from vessels in accordance with article 211. UNCLOS also requires coastal States to develop, implement and enforce international rules and standards for the prevention, reduction and control pollution of the marine environment from artificial islands, installations and structures.[114]

114. A determination as to whether the legal regime for vessels or that relating to artificial islands, installations or structures applies to mobile offshore craft such as floating production, storage and offloading units, is dependent on a number of factors: the type of unit involved, (whether it is self-propelled or not); its mode of operation (whether or not it is on station and whether it is engaged in exploration and exploitation of the seabed); and the kind of activity being regulated.

(ii) MARPOL

254. The international rules and standards for the prevention, reduction and control of pollution from vessels referred to in UNCLOS are mainly contained in MARPOL, which regulates discharges from ships in six annexes (see para. 115 above). The discharge of garbage is regulated by annex V, which applies to all ships, including fishing vessels and pleasure craft, unless expressly provided otherwise. The disposal of plastics (including fishing nets and gear) anywhere into the sea is prohibited, and discharges of other garbage from ships into coastal waters and MARPOL Special Areas is severely restricted. Foreign ships may be inspected in ports in cases where there are clear grounds for believing that the master or crew are not familiar with the essential shipboard procedures relating to the prevention of pollution by garbage, and to inspect the garbage record book. All parties to MARPOL are obliged to provide adequate reception facilities for ships calling at their ports. This requirement is especially necessary in the Special Areas where, because of the vulnerability of these areas to pollution, more stringent discharge restrictions have been imposed. The Special Area requirements have not taken effect in the Black Sea, Gulfs, Mediterranean Sea, Red Sea and the wider Caribbean areas, as defined in MARPOL, because of a lack of adequate reception facilities.

255. The disposal of garbage is prohibited from fixed or floating platforms engaged in the exploration, exploitation and associated offshore processing of seabed mineral resources, and from all other ships when alongside or within 500 metres of such platforms.

256. In order to assist States in the implementation of annex V, IMO has adopted guidelines for the implementation of annex V (resolution MEPC.59(33) as amended by resolution MEPC.92(45)), a standard specification for shipboard incinerators and guidelines for the development of garbage management plans (MEPC/Circ.317). An appendix to annex V provides a standard form for a garbage record book.

(iii) London Convention

257. The Convention on the Prevention of Marine Pollution by Dumping of Wastes and Other Matter, 1972, governs worldwide any dumping at sea of wastes and other matter from vessels, aircraft, platforms, etc. and, from this perspective, prohibits the disposal at sea of, inter alia, persistent plastics and other persistent synthetic materials. The London Convention adopts a "black and grey list" approach, by which dumping of black-listed materials is prohibited and dumping of grey-listed materials is allowed provided a special authorization from a designated national authority is given. All other material or substances may be dumped after a

general permit has been issued. It will soon be replaced by the 1996 Protocol, which prohibits all dumping except for a list of non-hazardous materials that may be dumped only if they pass an environmental assessment. Neither the London Convention nor its 1996 Protocol cover the disposal at sea of wastes derived from the normal operation of vessels.

(iv) Basel Convention

258. The Basel Convention establishes a notification and consent system among parties for transboundary shipments of "hazardous" and "other" wastes (as defined in article 1 of the Convention) and prohibits trading in covered wastes with non-parties. Parties are also required to minimize waste volumes and to ensure the availability of disposal facilities for the environmentally sound management of hazardous and other wastes. The Basel Convention could therefore be applicable to land-based marine debris. Some non-hazardous land-based marine litter would also fall under the scope of the Basel Convention under the categories of wastes requiring special consideration (e.g., wastes collected from households). Solid plastic waste would not generally be considered as a covered waste, unless it exhibits any hazardous characteristics as identified in annex III to the Convention and is listed under annex IX, list B.

(v) Convention on Biological Diversity

259. One of the main goals of the Convention on Biological Diversity is the conservation of biological diversity. Some of its provisions are therefore relevant to the problem of marine debris and its impacts on marine biological diversity.[115] In the context of the Jakarta Mandate on Marine and Coastal Biodiversity, the issue of marine litter is considered within the activities dealing with land-based and marine pollution. This issue is particularly relevant for the thematic areas on marine and coastal living resources (smothering of the seabed, and the effects of entanglement and ingestion of litter on fish, marine mammals and seabirds), and alien species (litter as a vector for transport of species).[116]

115. For example, article 8, on in situ conservation, calls for States to promote the protection of ecosystems and natural habitats and the maintenance of viable populations of species in natural surroundings; to rehabilitate and restore degraded ecosystems and promote the recovery of threatened species; and to prevent the introduction of, control or eradicate those alien species which threaten ecosystems, habitats or species.

116. For relevant decisions of the Conference of the Parties to the Convention at its seventh meeting, see UNEP/CBD/COP/7/21, annex.

(vi) Agreement on the Conservation of Albatrosses and Petrels

260. Under the Agreement, an instrument negotiated under the Convention on the Conservation of Migratory Species of Wild Animals, the problem of marine debris is specifically referred to in the action plan contained in annex II. Section 3.3 of the action plan, on pollutants and marine debris, provides that the parties shall take appropriate measures, within environmental conventions and by other means, to minimize the discharge from land-based sources and from vessels of pollutants that may have an adverse effect on albatrosses and petrels either on land or at sea.

(vii) FAO Code of Conduct for Responsible Fisheries

261. The 1995 Code is a voluntary instrument aimed at everyone working in and involved with fisheries and aquaculture, irrespective of whether they are located in inland areas or in the oceans.[117] It generally requires that fishing be conducted with due regard to the protection of the marine environment. Therefore, the Code contains a number of provisions related to marine debris. It requires States to take appropriate measures to minimize waste, discards and catch by lost or abandoned gear. In this regard, the Code says that States should cooperate to develop and apply technologies, materials and operational methods that minimize the loss of fishing gear and the ghost fishing effects of lost or abandoned fishing gear (article 8.4.6). The Code also includes provisions on the minimization and treatment of garbage on fishing vessels (articles 8.7.2–8.7.4).

(viii) Global Programme of Action for the Protection of the Marine
       Environment from Land-based Activities

262. The Global Programme of Action (GPA) provides guidance to national and regional authorities for devising and implementing sustained action to prevent, reduce, control or eliminate marine degradation from land-based activities. Litter is one of the nine pollution source categories identified in GPA. Sewage is also identified as a pollution source, and at present the issue of municipal wastewater management is a priority in the implementation of GPA.

263. GPA sets a number of objectives in relation to marine litter, including (a) establishing controlled and environmentally sound facilities for receiving, collecting, handling and disposing of litter from coastal area

---

117. See www.fao.org/fi/agreem/codecond/codecon.asp.

communities; and (b) significantly reducing the amount of litter reaching the marine and coastal environment by preventing or reducing the generation of solid waste and improving its management, including through the collection and recycling of litter.

264. In order to achieve these objectives, national actions, policies and measures should focus on reducing the generation of solid wastes; installing garbage containers for citizens in public areas for the purposes of appropriate collection and recycling; establishing and properly operating solid waste management facilities onshore; launching awareness and education campaigns for all stakeholders on the need to reduce waste generation and to dispose of and reuse waste in environmentally sound ways; improving local planning and management capacity to avoid location of waste-dump sites near coastlines or waterways and to avoid litter escape to the marine and coastal environment; improving management programmes in small rural communities to prevent the escape of litter into rivers and the marine and coastal environment; and establishing campaigns and permanent services for collecting solid wastes that pollute coastal and marine areas.

265. Regional actions should include the promotion of regional cooperation for the exchange of information on practices and experiences regarding waste management, recycling and reuse and cleaner production, as well as regional arrangements for solid-waste management. International actions should include participation in a clearing house on waste management, recycling and reuse and waste-minimization technologies, and cooperation with countries in need of assistance, through financial, scientific and technological support, in developing and establishing environmentally sound waste-disposal methods and alternatives to disposal.

(ix) Agenda 21 and the Johannesburg Plan of Implementation

266. Chapter 21 of Agenda 21 addresses the issue of solid waste, underlining that environmentally sound waste management encompasses safe disposal or recovery but also the root cause of the problem, such as unsustainable production and consumption patterns. Chapter 17, in paragraphs 17.24 to 17.27, focuses on actions to address the problem of pollution from land-based activities. Paragraph 17.30 (d) calls upon States to facilitate the establishment of port reception facilities for the collection of oily and chemical residues and garbage from ships, especially in MARPOL Special Areas, and to promote the establishment of smaller scale facilities in marinas and fishing harbours.

267. Paragraph 22 of the Johannesburg Plan of Implementation deals with the prevention and minimization of waste and the maximization of reuse and recycling and the use of environmentally friendly alternative

materials. Paragraph 32 deals with land-based sources, emphasizing the importance of the implementation of GPA, and paragraph 33 deals with marine pollution from shipping, stating that relevant international conventions should be ratified and implemented.

(c) Reception Facilities

268. The provision of adequate reception facilities in all ports, including marinas and fishing harbours, for the mandatory discharge of wastes is of central importance for achieving a reduction in ship-generated waste. Indeed, the major obstacle to the better implementation and enforcement of MARPOL is the lack of or insufficient number of reception facilities in many ports worldwide. It is a particularly acute problem for small island developing States, whose ports are frequently visited by cruise ships.

269. It is necessary to address the economic, as well as the technical aspects of this issue if the problem relating to reception facilities is to be satisfactorily resolved. What is required are major investments in infrastructure in ports in many parts of the world, as well as sound management of the waste once it has been delivered ashore. IMO has developed a comprehensive manual on port reception facilities and guidelines for ensuring the adequacy of reception facilities. It has also provided technical assistance to a number of countries, with a view to bringing into effect the Special Area status under MARPOL.

270. Where adequate port waste reception facilities exist, ships should not be deterred from discharging waste to port reception facilities by high costs, complicated procedures, undue delays in ports, unnecessary paperwork, excessive sanitary regulations, customs regulations or other impediments. For example, members of the Baltic Marine Environment Protection Commission do not charge a special fee for the reception of ship-generated waste. The cost of receiving waste is included in the overall port or harbour fee.[118]

(d) Raising Awareness

271. Marine debris is not only an environmental problem that can be solved solely by means of legislation, law enforcement and technical solutions; it is also a cultural problem and has to be addressed as such, by efforts to change attitudes, behaviours and management approaches, education and the involvement of all sectors and interests, including the

---

118. See the Baltic Strategy for Port Reception Facilities for Ship-generated Wastes and Associated Issues, at www.helcom.fi/stc/files/Publications/Proceedings/bsep62.pdf.

public at large. Initiatives such as the convening of international conferences on marine debris and the study prepared by UNEP with other organizations (see para. 232 above) help to raise awareness at the global and regional levels.

272. In order to educate and inform people and make them feel that they can be part of the solution and not only part of the problem, regular clean-up operations are carried out in many countries throughout the world. These activities should be encouraged and supported.

5.   Measures to Deal with Existing Marine Debris

273. Measures to deal with existing marine debris include clean-up operations on beaches and the sea-bed and projects to allow fishing vessels to leave marine debris caught in fishing gear ashore without having to pay a garbage fee. Regular clean-up operations are carried out in many countries throughout the world. In most cases, the work is done by local authorities, volunteers or non-governmental organizations. Examples of global clean-up operations include the International Coastal Clean-up and Clean Up the World. The costs of clean-ups can be significant. In 1998, 64 local communities in the North Sea region reported that they had to spend about $6 million annually on cleaning their beaches in order to maintain their recreational and aesthetic values and keep them safe for beach-goers.

6.   Conclusions

274. Despite efforts made at the global, regional and national levels, there are indications that the marine debris problem continues to intensify. Inadequate waste management and deficiencies in the implementation and enforcement of existing international, regional and national regulations and standards that could improve the situation, combined with a lack of awareness among the main stakeholders and the general public, are the major reasons why the marine debris problem not only persists, but appears to be increasing worldwide.

275. Environmentally sound waste management practices are essential to the prevention and reduction of marine debris. Once generated, marine debris should be collected and disposed of appropriately. Costs can be reduced through the organization of joint clean-up operations among States in the same region. But it is also important to involve all stakeholders. Collection programmes could provide incentives. For example, Governments could create a subsidized buy-back scheme for old fishing nets to provide a financial incentive for the fishers to collect these nets.[119]

119. Fact sheet on marine debris of the Humane Society International, Australia, at www.hsi.org.au/news_library_events/fact_sheets/F0053.htm.

276. The aforementioned legal instruments provide a legal framework for the prevention and reduction of marine debris. More effective implementation and enforcement of the existing international instruments are needed. Effective implementation can be further facilitated through the issuance of guidelines, for example, for tourism, boating and other sectors, as well as the publication of information on good waste management practices.

277. To address the problem of marine debris from land-based sources, the ongoing activities to address waste management in the context of GPA should be enhanced at the national and regional levels. At the regional level, the regional protocols on land-based sources should be fully and effectively implemented with respect to marine debris. Moreover, land-based sources of debris should be adequately taken into account when such protocols are being developed. At the national level, action should focus on the effective implementation of the GPA provisions relating to waste management. To ensure better implementation of GPA, cooperation with countries in need of assistance should be enhanced through financial, scientific and technological support, in developing and establishing environmentally sound waste-disposal methods and alternatives to disposal.

278. As regards the effects of marine debris on marine biodiversity, States should take into account this specific threat in implementing relevant instruments, such as the Convention on Biological Diversity, and in adopting policy decisions in that regard. The International Coral Reef Initiative (see para. 156 above) could also offer a forum for discussion of the issue.

279. Marine debris from all ships can not be effectively prevented or reduced without adequate port reception facilities. The fact that reception facilities for ship-generated waste, including solid waste and garbage, are lacking or inadequate in many ports and marinas worldwide is the major obstacle to the effective implementation and enforcement of MARPOL annex V and the entry into force of the Special Area requirements in several regions. States require technical assistance in order to be able to ensure the availability of adequate waste reception facilities in ports, including in marinas and fishing harbours. IMO has requested Governments to report their experiences with the aim of identifying problem areas and developing a future action plan (see para. 123). Where adequate facilities exist, it is important to ensure that fees do not act as a deterrent to the use of the facilities.

280. Measures to improve the enforcement of the relevant international instruments for the prevention and reduction of marine debris from sea-based activities include increasing surveillance of ships, in particular fishing boats and tourist and recreational vessels, imposing fines for illegal discharges or disposal which are high enough to act as a deterrent, and strengthening port State control.

281. Regarding fishing-generated marine debris, a number of measures have been proposed to minimize loss or abandonment of fishing gear and to facilitate its retrieval, including the use of global positioning systems in fishing gear to locate its position, mandatory marking of all fishing gear and mandatory reporting of lost fishing gear.[120] It has also been suggested that regional fisheries management organizations and arrangements should incorporate into their mandate and conservation measures a prohibition on discarding fishing gear and related debris and a requirement to maximize recovery of lost gear.[121]

282. To address the significant gaps in our knowledge about the global marine debris situation and the uneven geographical coverage of the available information, it is necessary to improve and consolidate the knowledge base on marine debris through further research and monitoring activities. To this end, strategies for identifying the types, sources, amounts, interactions and key user groups need to be established, as well as strategies for assessment of the socio-economic aspects of marine debris. Monitoring mechanisms should be established where none exist and a limited number of basic marine indicators should be developed for use in all monitoring activities so that data and information about quantities and trends in marine debris are more coherent and compatible and enable the building of a common global basis for action. Global and regional assessments of the state of the coastal and marine environments should include marine debris as an issue of concern. The GPA Clearing-house node (Global Marine Litter Information Gateway), which was established to provide a global mechanism for the sharing of information about marine litter from land-based sources, could also be utilized to share information on all sources of marine debris based on information provided by relevant organizations.

283. Given its potential for causing transboundary pollution, marine debris is a global problem as well as a national one. There is no single solution to the problem and it must be addressed through a wide range of carefully targeted integrated measures. Therefore, the entities that are addressing the problem of marine debris in a variety of contexts should cooperate in order to ensure that the battle against marine debris is waged in a comprehensive and effective manner at the national, regional and global levels.

---

120. See *Recommendations for the marking of fishing gear*, Supplement to the Report of the Expert Consultation on the Marking of Fishing Gear; Victoria, British Colombia, Canada, 14–19 July 1991, ISBN: 92–5-103330–7.

121. Proceedings of the Fourth International Marine Debris Conference, supra note 105, p. 216.

XI. THE INDIAN OCEAN TSUNAMI DISASTER

284. On 26 December 2004, an earthquake of magnitude 9.3 on the Richter scale[122] off the island of Sumatra (Indonesia) generated a devastating tsunami, flooding vast expanses of coastal areas in countries all around the Indian Ocean rim from Indonesia to Somalia, including Sri Lanka, India, the Maldives, Thailand, Myanmar, Malaysia, Kenya, Madagascar, Seychelles and the United Republic of Tanzania. A tsunami ("wave in the port" in Japanese) is a series of large waves, which can reach vertical heights of 10 to 30 metres or more at the shoreline. It can be generated when the sea floor abruptly deforms and vertically displaces the overlying water as a result of an earthquake, submarine landslide or volcanic eruption. Subduction earthquakes (or tectonic earthquakes) are particularly effective in generating tsunamis and occur where denser oceanic plates slip under continental plates in a process known as subduction. These events generally occur around the crustal plate subduction zone known as the "ring of fire" in the Pacific Ocean. The devastating megathrust earthquake of 26 December 2004 was caused by the release of stresses that developed as the India plate subducted beneath the overriding Burma plate. Preliminary locations of larger aftershocks following the megathrust earthquake show that approximately 1200 km of the plate boundary slipped as a result of the earthquake.[123] This was confirmed in a recent survey by the *HMS Scott* conducted in the exclusive economic zone of Indonesia under the marine scientific research provisions of UNCLOS.[124]

A. Impact of the Tsunami

285. It is estimated that the Indian Ocean tsunami took the lives of 273,770 people, displaced over 1.6 million and rendered over half a million homeless.[125] It eroded coastlines and caused extensive flooding. The affected countries suffered several billion dollars worth of damage to property, infrastructure, coastal environments and essential ecosystems. Vital ocean-related economic sectors, such as the fisheries and tourism, were

---

122. "Dr. Seth Stein on tsunami earthquake" at www.northwestern.edu/univ-relations/broadcast/2005/02/tsunami.html; *The New York Times*, 8 February 2005.

123. United States Geological Survey website http://earthquake.usgs.gov/.

124. As reported in *Landslides seen on Indian Ocean seafloor near earthquake*, Environment News Service, 11 February 2005. *HMS Scott* is a UK deep-water hydrographic survey vessel which started collecting images of the Indian Ocean seafloor near the epicentre of the earthquake in January 2005.

125. International Federation of Red Cross and Red Crescent Societies at www.ifrc.org/cgi/pdfappeals.pl?04/280449.pdf.

severely impacted. Exports from these sectors alone represented over $30 billion of the annual earnings of the States concerned.[126]

286. The tsunami destroyed or seriously damaged fishing harbours and tens of thousands of fishing boats; resulted in the loss or damage of hundred thousands of fishing gear; the destruction of thousands of fish cages and fish ponds; and caused serious damage to aquaculture and fish processing plants. As a result, exports of fish and fish products from affected countries are expected to decline in the short term and local fish production is expected to be reduced by as much as 90 per cent, with implications for the food security of local populations.[127] For many people in coastal communities, fisheries are the only source of income and livelihood.

287. Maritime infrastructure, such as ports, navigational aids and global positioning system ground stations, was also damaged by the tsunami. For example, in the Strait of Malacca thousands of navigational aids, such as buoys held in place by mushroom-shaped anchors, were carried off to new locations by waves, thereby possibly sending out false positions.[128] The International Association of Marine Aids to Navigation and Lighthouse Authorities (IALA) and the International Hydrographic Organization (IHO) have begun the process of assessing in detail the extent of damage to ports and their approaches, navigational channels and navigational aids in the areas affected by the tsunami.

288. The high intensity of the tsunami and the wave of deposits and the debris it generated damaged coral reefs, seagrass beds, mangroves and associated ecosystems. In the case of coral reefs, some areas appear to have been severely damaged, while others were spared or should recover in the next 5 to 10 years.[129] Generally, most of the affected countries suffered varying degrees of similar tsunami-induced environmental problems. Tsunami-generated waste poses a risk to human health as well as to ecological functions. Coastal waters have been contaminated as a result of damage to sewage collection and treatment systems, as well as to industrial installations.

289. Post-tsunami environmental assessments revealed that coastal ecosystems, including coral reefs, mangrove forests and seagrass beds, acted as a natural buffer, at least partially protecting the coastline of some countries from destruction. Both in Thailand and in the Maldives the extensive reefs reduced the impact of the tsunami and losses were thus smaller compared to other areas. Unfortunately, the protective reefs, sand

126. United Nations press release IHA/995-TAD/2006, 18 January 2005.
127. Information provided by FAO, at www.fao.org/newsroom/en/news/2005/88321/index.html.
128. The National Maritime portal at portsworld.com.
129. "Powerful tsunami's impact on coral reefs was hit and miss," *Science*, vol. 307, 4 February 2005.

dunes and mangroves in many areas of the Indian Ocean have been destroyed by economic development, in particular tourism and aquaculture. As a result, many coastal communities found themselves with no such shields against the tsunami. Protection of the environment is essential for the protection of human life.

B.   Responses to the Tsunami Disaster

290. In response to the huge loss of life and massive destruction caused by the Indian Ocean tsunami, the international community acted quickly to address the immediate humanitarian crisis, to establish an early warning system, and to initiate rehabilitation and reconstruction. Many States, international organizations, non-governmental organizations and private entities contributed or pledged their resources for humanitarian and disaster relief.[130]

1.   Early Warning Systems

291. Early warning and preparedness play a critical role in preventing hazardous events from turning into disasters. Clear warnings received in time, coupled with the knowledge of how to react, can mean the difference between life and death, or between economic survival and ruin, for individuals and communities. In the case of the Indian Ocean tsunami, the initial underestimation of the magnitude of the earthquake prevented the issuance of a timely warning. The urgent need to establish early warning systems at the global and regional levels was emphasized in a number of global and regional forums, including the General Assembly.[131]

292. The special meeting of the Association of Southeast Asian Nations held in Indonesia on 6 January 2005, inter alia, called for the establishment of a regional tsunami early warning system for the Indian Ocean and the South-East Asia region. At the subsequent ministerial meeting on regional cooperation on tsunami early warning arrangements held in Bangkok on 29

---

130. The United Nations Indian Ocean Tsunami/Earthquake Flash Appeal was launched on 6 January 2005. The appeal focuses on supporting people in Indonesia, Maldives, Myanmar, Seychelles, Somalia and Sri Lanka from January to the end of June 2005. As of 22 February 2005, $6.3 billion was pledged by States, regional organizations including development banks, non-governmental organizations and other private entities.

131. In its resolution 59/279, the General Assembly recognized the pressing need to develop and promote national and regional capacity and access to technology and knowledge in building and managing a regional early warning system and in disaster management, through national and regional efforts as well as through international cooperation and partnership.

January 2005, it was decided to take immediate and practical steps to enhance early warning capabilities in the Indian Ocean and South-East Asia and to cooperate towards the establishment of interim early warning arrangements and strengthening and upgrading of national systems, while moving towards a coordinated regional system. The ministerial meeting agreed that a regional early warning system should be developed, if possible by June 2006, within a United Nations international strategy coordinated by IOC.

293. The World Conference on Disaster Reduction, held in Kobe, Japan from 19 to 22 January 2005, adopted a common statement on the Indian Ocean disaster (A/CONF.206/6, annex II) that recognized the need to use the experience of the existing Pacific Ocean tsunami early warning systems, making use of the existing coordination mechanisms of IOC and other relevant international and regional organizations. However, the establishment of an interim Indian Ocean early warning system was also considered at the Conference. It would involve the Japanese Meteorological Agency and the IOC Pacific Tsunami Warning Centre[132] providing national authorities in the Indian Ocean region with information and warning arising from their monitoring activities.

294. It was also decided during the Conference to create an international early warning programme, if possible by June 2007, to cover not just the tsunami but all other threats such as storm surges and cyclones. In order to coordinate the many initiatives advanced by organizations and countries, IOC will host the international coordination meeting for the development of a tsunami warning and mitigation system for the Indian Ocean within a global framework in Paris from 3 to 8 March 2005. This meeting is expected to produce a draft work plan and timetable for a tsunami warning and mitigation system for the Indian Ocean and a draft design plan for a global tsunami warning system.

295. The need for early warning systems for natural hazards was also underscored at the meeting of small island developing States held in

---

132. The Pacific Tsunami Warning Center provides warnings for Pacific basin teletsunamis (tsunamis that can cause damage far away from their source) to almost every country around the Pacific rim and to most of the Pacific island States. This function is carried out under the guidance of the UNESCO/IOC International Coordination Group for the Tsunami Warning System in the Pacific (ICG/ITSU). The ICG/ITSU was formed in 1968 and is a subsidiary body of the IOC/UNESCO. Its purpose is to recommend and coordinate programmes most beneficial to countries belonging to the IOC, whose coastal areas are threatened by tsunamis. The IOC also maintains the International Tsunami Information Centre (ITIC) to assist in the work of the ICG/ITSU, and the identification of improvements to the international tsunami warning system currently operated by the Pacific Tsunami Warning Center. For information about the Deep-ocean Assessment and Reporting of Tsunamis project, see http://www.pmel.noaa.gov/tsunami/Dart.

Mauritius in January 2005. Delegates agreed that early warning systems were vital and that reducing vulnerability required not only technology, such as telecommunications and sea-based buoys, but community-based initiatives involving education and training.

296. The establishment of a Caribbean tsunami early warning system was considered at an expert group meeting held in Barbados in February 2005. The group reviewed the existing monitoring networks within the region, examined data-sharing arrangements and devised a future programme of action. Working groups will determine the risk to coastal communities through tsunami flood mapping and design medium to long-term education and outreach programmes.

297. The vital importance of effective telecommunications systems for early warning systems and prevention of loss of life, and for the support of rescue and relief operations, has been underlined by the international community. IMO has proposed, inter alia, that the satellite and radio-based communications infrastructure that it established for the promulgation of maritime safety information could be used for the dissemination of tsunami warnings particularly to ships and fishing vessels. WMO will provide the use of its global telecommunication system for data collection and dissemination.

298. In order to ensure a better response to disasters, prevent the loss of life and help survivors, regulatory barriers that impeded the use of telecommunications resources for disasters have been waived with the entry into force on 8 January 2005 of the Tampere Convention on the Provision of Telecommunication Resources for Disaster Mitigation and Relief Operations.[133] Victims of disasters will now be able to benefit from faster and more effective rescue operations, since telecommunication is at the basis of the coordination of complicated rescue and relief operations.

299. Assistance that States have offered in support of early warning systems includes (a) help in building a United Nations database on disasters; (b) contributing new tsunami detecting buoys through the Global Earth Observation System of Systems; and (c) training disaster experts in developing countries. For example, a seminar launched by the International Strategy for Disaster Reduction was held in Japan from 22 to 24 February 2005 to provide to high-level administrative policy makers operational and technical information on how an early warning system can operate at the national level.[134]

2.   Reconstruction and Rehabilitation

300. While natural disasters affect all countries, they have a disproportionately greater impact on developing countries, including small island

---

133. See United Nations press release IHA/983 of 7 January 2005.
134. See United Nations press release IHA/1017 of 18 February 2005.

developing States. The crippling damage to the coastal zone and the various economic sectors and the environment caused by the Indian Ocean tsunami resulted in the loss by millions of people in the region not only of their homes and possessions, but also of the means to support their families. Therefore, economic revival and the generation of employment are among the pressing priorities once the need for emergency relief starts to ebb. Many States and organizations are supporting reconstruction and rehabilitation efforts in the affected areas.

Coastal Zone Planning and Development

301. The important role of natural features such as coral reefs and mangroves in defending small islands and low-lying coastal areas from aggressive and destructive seas was underlined at the meeting of small island developing States held in Mauritius in January 2005. Governments agreed that more action should be taken to conserve these vital ecosystems by, for example, better assessing the impact of coastal developments. UNEP has underlined that the destruction caused by the tsunami to the environment offers an opportunity to rebuild in a manner that preserves natural resources for the benefit of the local communities that were hardest hit by the disaster.[135] A meeting on coastal zone rehabilitation management for the tsunami-affected region was held in Egypt in February 2005 to discuss basic principles for coastal reconstruction and rehabilitation within the broader framework of integrated coastal zone management and to provide information on related policy tools and mechanisms aiming to reduce the impacts of possible future disasters. A document containing key principles to guide the reconstruction of coastlines affected by the tsunami was introduced at the meeting.[136]

302. In Thailand, environmentalists and some tourist industry professionals are cautioning against unfettered construction on tsunami-hit beaches, advising instead strictly regulated construction so as to ease pressure on the environment and preserve the islands' environment. Officials and local authorities have indicated they would regulate beachfront development more stringently.[137]

Tourism

303. In the Maldives, whose economy largely depends on the tourism industry, the Government has established an "Adopt an Island" programme

---

135. See UNEP report "After the tsunami: rapid environmental assessment," available at www.unep.org.

136. See www.gpa.unep.org/documents/Key_PrinciplesFINAL.doc.

137. Amy Kazmin, "Disaster brings chance to regain paradise," *The Financial Times*, 25 January 2005.

to try to persuade businesses to participate in the cost of rehabilitating and rehousing the 12,000 people displaced by the disaster.[138]

304. The World Tourism Organization has adopted the Phuket Action Plan to encourage tourists back to Thailand, Sri Lanka, the Maldives and Indonesia. The Plan focuses on saving jobs in the tourism industry, relaunching tourism-related businesses and increasing visitors' numbers. UNCTAD has pointed out that since the tsunami negatively affected employment and sustainable livelihoods, immediate trade measures should be focused on socio-economic recovery and include special measures to revive the tourism industry and infrastructure.[139]

Fisheries Sector

305. FAO produced and intends to distribute an atlas on tsunami-damaged areas in Asia. It established a Special Fund for Emergency and Rehabilitation Activities which was instrumental in its being able to rapidly assist Governments and international financing institutions in assessing the damage and losses to agriculture and fisheries. Following its first assessment of the extensive damage to the fisheries sector of the riparian States of the Indian Ocean, FAO made a concerted effort to assist the marine capture fisheries and aquaculture of the affected countries through relief and rehabilitation measures. FAO intends to assist Indonesia, Maldives, Myanmar, Seychelles, Somalia, Sri Lanka and Thailand, according to their needs, in the repair and reconstruction of fishing infrastructure such as harbours and fish ponds, the repair and replacement of fishing vessels and gear, and the relief and rehabilitation of affected fishing communities through activities like the provision of financial aid and training.

Maritime Infrastructure

306. IMO has underlined the strategic importance of ensuring that ports, navigational aids and other key elements of the maritime infrastructure are in working order as soon as possible, both to facilitate the medium- and long-term recovery of the affected areas and to ensure that short-term aid can arrive by sea efficiently and in safety. It has developed a joint plan for future actions to be undertaken together with IALA and IHO. The three organizations, together with the World Meteorological Organization, will be focusing their attention principally on ensuring the integrity of the

---

138. Edward Luce, "Tsunami disaster: Maldives up for adoption," *The Financial Times*, 8 February 2005.
    139. Ibid.

maritime navigational infrastructure to ensure the safe navigation of ships, including those carrying urgently needed relief supplies.[140]

Environment

307. The central role of a healthy environment in long-term disaster risk reduction was discussed at the World Conference on Disaster Reduction. The Hyogo Framework for Action 2005–2015 (A/CONF.206/L.2/Rev.1*) notes that disaster risk increases when hazards interact with, inter alia, environmental vulnerabilities. Consequently, in order to reduce the underlying risk factors, the environment and natural resources should be used and managed in a sustainable manner and fragile ecosystems (e.g., coral reefs) should be managed appropriately.

308. In the immediate aftermath of the tsunami, UNEP established the Asian Tsunami Disaster Task Force, which supports the national authorities of the affected countries and the United Nations in assessing and addressing the environmental impacts from the disaster, providing environmental expertise and mobilizing and coordinating international efforts in the environmental sector. The Task Force, inter alia, mobilizes immediate environmental assistance by integrating short-term environmental needs into the humanitarian flash appeal. It also aims at integrating environmental assessment and recovery in the reconstruction of affected areas. UNEP has also responded to requests from most of the affected countries for assistance in assessing the environmental damage, for example on coral reefs, and devising action plans to address the environmental issues identified and develop early warning capacity.

309. The UNEP World Conservation Monitoring Centre will provide remote sensing and geographic information system support in assessing impacts on biodiversity, in particular on coral reefs, shorelines and protected areas. UNEP will also facilitate and support the development of a waste management strategy and guidance materials, in particular to immediately address debris management.

310. Other organizations that are currently active in providing assistance to the affected countries include the International Union for the Conservation of Nature and Natural Resources. It established a high-level task force to develop responses to the devastating effects of the Indian Ocean tsunami, with an emphasis on damage assessment and rehabilitation of coastal environments.

140. IMO document COMSAR 9/3/1; IMO, IHO and IALA meet to coordinate tsunami responses, IMO press briefing, 12 January 2005, and IMO to help coordinate restoration of key maritime infrastructure in tsunami aftermath, IMO press briefing, 5 January 2005, at www.imo.org.

XII. INTERNATIONAL COOPERATION AND COORDINATION

A.   United Nations Open-ended Informal Consultative Process on Oceans and the Law of the Sea

311. By its resolution 54/33, the General Assembly decided to establish an open-ended informal consultative process to facilitate the annual review by the Assembly, in an effective and constructive manner, of overall developments in ocean affairs and the law of the sea. By its resolution 57/141, the Assembly decided to continue the Consultative Process for a further period of three years. At its sixtieth session, the Assembly will review the effectiveness and utility of the Consultative Process. Pursuant to paragraph 3(e) of resolution 54/33 and after consultations with Member States, by letter dated 10 December 2004, the President of the General Assembly reappointed Felipe H. Paolillo (Uruguay) and Philip Burgess (Australia) as co-chairpersons of the sixth meeting of the Consultative Process, to be held from 6 to 10 June 2005.

312. In accordance with General Assembly resolution 59/24, the sixth meeting of the Consultative Process will focus its discussions on fisheries and their contribution to sustainable development and on marine debris, as well as issues discussed at previous meetings.

B.   Regular Process for the Global Reporting and Assessment of the State of the Marine Environment, including Socio-economic Aspects

313. The World Summit on Sustainable Development agreed in paragraph 36(b) of the Johannesburg Plan of Implementation[141] to establish by 2004 a regular process under the United Nations for global reporting and assessment of the state of the marine environment, including socio-economic aspects, both current and foreseeable, building on existing regional assessments (the regular process). The General Assembly endorsed this proposal in resolution 57/141 and in resolution 58/240 requested the Secretary-General to organize a group of experts, an international workshop on the regular process and an intergovernmental meeting to formally establish the regular process. The international workshop held in June 2004 concluded that it appeared premature to hold the intergovernmental meeting in 2004 as mandated by the General Assembly (see A/59/126, para. 16).

141. (n. 34 above).

314. During the debate on oceans and the law of the sea at the fifty-ninth session of the General Assembly, States reaffirmed the importance of establishing the regular process as a significant mechanism for increased research and collection of information for the protection of the marine environment and biodiversity. Although there was agreement on the need to focus on the start-up phase, and in particular the "assessment of assessments" (see A/AC.271/WP.1, paras. 8–11), it was also concluded that there was no consensus upon which to launch the preparatory phase of the process. Consequently, in paragraph 86 of its resolution 59/24, the General Assembly decided to convene a second international workshop to continue considering issues relating to the establishment of the process. This workshop will be held from 13 to 15 June 2005.

C. Oceans and Coastal Areas Network

315. The first meeting of the Oceans and Coastal Areas Network (UN-Oceans) was held in Paris at the headquarters of IOC from 25 to 26 January 2005. It was attended by representatives from the secretariat of the Convention on Biological Diversity, FAO, the International Atomic Energy Agency, IMO, IOC, the International Seabed Authority, the Department of Economic and Social Affairs and the Division for Ocean Affairs and the Law of the Sea, UNDP, the GPA Coordination Office, the World Meteorological Organization and the World Bank. Patricio Bernal of IOC was elected Coordinator of UN-Oceans and Anne Rogers, of the Department of Economic and Social Affairs, was elected Deputy Coordinator, both for two-year terms.

316. The objective of UN-Oceans is to enhance cooperation and coordination among the secretariats of the international organizations and bodies concerned with ocean-related activities, in particular by (a) coordinating and harmonizing the agencies' activities related to oceans; (b) reviewing programmes and activities and identifying issues needing to be addressed, with a view to updating and enriching the relationship between UNCLOS and Agenda 21; (c) ensuring integrated ocean management at the international level; and (d) undertaking joint activities to address emerging challenges and issues like global marine environmental assessment, regional ocean governance and the development of guidelines for the application of the ecosystem approach.

317. UN-Oceans is to operate as a flexible mechanism to review joint and overlapping ongoing activities and to support related deliberations at the Consultative Process. UN-Oceans plans to meet once a year in conjunction with Consultative Process meetings, and may hold special meetings when required. In order to minimize financial and human resource requirements, UN-Oceans will have a "distributed secretariat,"

with the Division for Ocean Affairs and the Law of the Sea as the "organizing secretariat" and IOC as the "implementing secretariat."

318. UN-Oceans will pursue time-bound initiatives, with well-defined terms of reference, through ad hoc task forces open to the participation of non-governmental organizations and other international stakeholders, as required. The task forces, coordinated by a lead institution with a mandate and major activities in the specific issues being considered, will foster collaboration around existing and future joint activities. The following four task forces were established: Task Force on Post-Tsunami Response (chaired by IOC), Task Force on the Regular Process (Division for Ocean Affairs and the Law of the Sea), Task Force on Biodiversity in Marine Areas beyond National Jurisdiction (secretariat of the Convention on Biological Diversity), and Task Force on the Second Intergovernmental Review of GPA (GPA Coordination Office). The next meeting of UN-Oceans will take place in conjunction with the Consultative Process, from 2 to 3 June 2005.

XIII. CONCLUSIONS

319. The future of the oceans depends on enhanced scientific research into ocean processes, effective implementation of the international instruments that regulate various ocean activities and a comprehensive and integrated approach to ocean management. Yet, as the present report indicates, our oceans and seas are threatened by climate change, natural disasters, environmental degradation, depletion of fisheries, loss of biodiversity and ineffective flag State control. To address these threats and thereby achieve security and sustainability of the oceans, including the internationally agreed goals contained in the Millennium Declaration, it is suggested that a number of concerted actions be taken by the international community:

(a) As security depends on respect for and compliance with the rule of law, States should ratify and fully implement UNCLOS and other ocean-related instruments and strictly apply and enforce their provisions.

(b) As the lack of effective flag State control can pose a threat to the security and safety of navigation and the marine environment and lead to overexploitation of marine resources, States should be called upon to exercise effective control over their vessels and should not register vessels if they cannot exercise such control.

(c) States should be encouraged to take further measures to address the threat of climate change and associated effects, such as sea level rise and coral bleaching.

(d) To address continued degradation of the marine environment from land-based activities, States should increase their efforts to implement GPA.

(e) To deal with the persistent problem of marine debris, in addition to effectively implementing the relevant international instruments, States should foster environmentally sound waste management practices, ensure the availability of adequate reception facilities and take firm measures to deal with fisheries-related marine debris.

(f) To address the very serious issue of the depletion of fisheries, States should:

(i) Take urgent action and adopt innovative measures to eliminate overfishing and illegal, unregulated and unreported fishing;

(ii) Improve the legal and policy framework within which small-scale fisheries operate;

(iii) Provide financial and technical assistance to developing countries to improve governance of marine natural resources under their national jurisdiction.

(g) With respect to marine biodiversity, States should support work in various forums to prevent further destruction of marine ecosystems and associated losses of biodiversity, and be prepared to engage in discussions of the conservation and sustainable use of marine biodiversity in the ad hoc open-ended working group established by the General Assembly (see para. 149 above).

(h) To increase understanding of ocean processes and the marine environment, States should make a concerted effort to launch the initial phase of the regular process for global reporting and assessment of the state of the marine environment, including socio-economic aspects.

Selected Documents and Proceedings

Report on the Work of the United Nations Open-Ended Informal Consultative Process on Oceans and the Law of the Sea at its Sixth Meeting*

Letter dated 7 July 2005 from the Co-Chairpersons of the Consultative Process addressed to the President of the General Assembly

Pursuant to General Assembly resolutions 54/33 of 24 November 1999 and 57/141 of 12 December 2002, we were appointed as the Co-Chairpersons of the sixth meeting of the United Nations Open-ended Informal Consultative Process on Oceans and the Law of the Sea. We now have the honour to submit to you the attached report on the work of the Consultative Process at its sixth meeting, which was held at United Nations Headquarters from 6 to 10 June 2005.

In accordance with paragraph 3(h) of General Assembly resolution 54/33, and bearing in mind General Assembly resolution 59/24 on oceans and the law of the sea, the sixth meeting agreed to a number of elements relating to fisheries and their contribution to sustainable development to be suggested to the General Assembly for consideration under its agenda item "Oceans and the law of the sea," as set out in section 1 of part A of the present report. However, it was not possible to finalize all elements under consideration by the Consultative Process, and we were requested by the meeting to forward to the General Assembly our proposed elements relating to marine debris and cooperation and coordination. These elements are set out in section 2 of part A. A summary of the discussions held during the sixth meeting is presented in part B of the report. Part C contains information on additional issues that have been proposed for inclusion in the list of issues that could benefit from attention in the future work of the General Assembly on oceans and the law of the sea (see A/58/95 and A/59/122).

We kindly request that the present letter and the report of the Consultative Process be circulated as a document of the sixtieth session of

* EDITORS' NOTE.—This document was provided by the United Nations Division for Ocean Affairs and the Law of the Sea (DOALOS) and is extracted from United Nations General Assembly, Sixtieth Session, Item 76(a) of the preliminary list (A/60/50 and Corr.1.), UN document A/60/99, 7 July 2005. Available online at the DOALOS Web site: http://www.un.org/Depts/los. The document has been edited for publication in the *Ocean Yearbook*.

the General Assembly under the agenda item "Oceans and the law of the sea."

(*Signed*) Cristián Maquieira and Philip D. Burgess
Co-Chairpersons

PART A

Elements to be Suggested to the General Assembly for Consideration under its Agenda item entitled "Oceans and the Law of the Sea"

1. The sixth meeting of the United Nations Open-ended Informal Consultative Process on Oceans and the Law of the Sea ("the Consultative Process") met from 6 to 10 June 2005 and, pursuant to General Assembly resolution 59/24, organized its discussions around the following areas: fisheries and their contribution to sustainable development; and marine debris.

2. On Friday, 10 June 2005, the meeting commenced its consideration of the elements proposed by the Co-Chairpersons. The meeting was able to reach agreement on most of the elements relating to fisheries and their contribution to sustainable development presented in section 1 below. However, as it was not possible to finalize the elements relating to marine debris and cooperation and coordination, it was agreed that the Co-Chairpersons' proposed elements would be forwarded to the General Assembly. These elements are presented in section 2 below.

1.   Agreed Elements

3. Fisheries, both commercial and artisanal, are a major contributor in many States to economic development, food security and the cultural and social well-being of their people. The importance of fisheries to many local communities in developing States was brought into stark focus by the devastating Indian Ocean tsunami in December 2004.

4. The contribution of fisheries to sustainable development relies on the continuing health of functioning, productive ecosystems. However, the report of the Food and Agriculture Organization of the United Nations on the state of world fisheries and aquaculture in 2004 confirms a trend already observed at the end of the 1990s, of growing concerns with regard to the livelihoods of fishers and the sustainability of commercial catches and the aquatic ecosystems from which they are extracted. While this is a general trend, it is important to note that there is a broad range of differences in the status of fisheries resources, the management of fisheries by States and

regional arrangements, and the ability to respond to the need for effective and adaptive management.

5. In many instances, conventional approaches to fisheries management need to improve. The need for an integrated ecosystem-based approach to fisheries and oceans governance, based on the best available science, is widely and increasingly considered the key to maintaining fishery productivity and its continuing contribution to sustainable development.

6. It was proposed that the General Assembly:

(a) Recall its previous resolutions related to oceans and the law of the sea and sustainable fisheries;

(b) Note with concern the increasingly urgent need to address the problems afflicting many of the world's fisheries, both within and beyond national jurisdiction;

(c) Welcome and encourage the work of the Food and Agriculture Organization of the United Nations (FAO) and its Committee on Fisheries, in particular the recent call to effectively implement the various instruments already developed to ensure responsible fisheries;

(d) Welcome also the outcome of the Conference on the Governance of High Seas Fisheries and the United Nations Fish Agreement—Moving from Words to Action, held in St. John's, Canada, from 1 to 5 May 2005, particularly its Ministerial Declaration, and ongoing work on illegal, unreported and unregulated fishing;

(e) Welcome the fourth round of informal consultations of States Parties to the Agreement for the Implementation of the Provisions of the United Nations Convention on the Law of the Sea of 10 December 1982 relating to the Conservation and Management of Straddling Fish Stocks and Highly Migratory Fish Stocks (the Agreement); encourage wide participation in accordance with article 36 of the Agreement in the Review Conference, to be held in May 2006, and in its preparatory process; and encourage those States that are able to do so to become parties to the Agreement prior to the Review Conference;

(f) Encourage States, as appropriate, to recognize that the general principles of the Agreement should also apply to discrete fish stocks in the high seas;

(g) Urge States to eliminate subsidies that contribute to illegal, unreported and unregulated fishing and to overcapacity, while completing the efforts undertaken at the World Trade Organization to clarify and improve its disciplines on fishery subsidies, taking into account the importance of this sector for developing countries;

(h) Urge States to eliminate obstacles that are not consistent with their obligations to the World Trade Organization, taking into account the importance of the trade of fishery products, particularly for developing countries.

7. Noting the key and evolving role that subregional and regional fisheries management organizations and arrangements can play in ensuring effective and sustainable fisheries and ocean conservation and management, it was proposed that the General Assembly:

(a) Call upon all States and entities referred to in the United Nations Convention on the Law of the Sea ("the Convention") and in article 1, paragraph 2(b), of the Agreement and fishing in areas of competence of these organizations and arrangements to become members or to agree to apply their conservation and management measures;

(b) Welcome and urge efforts by regional fisheries management organizations and arrangements to:

(i) Fill gaps in their mandates to include ecosystem and biodiversity considerations, the precautionary approach, based on the best available scientific information;

(ii) Develop criteria for allocations;

(iii) Strengthen integration, coordination and cooperation with regional fisheries organizations, regional seas arrangements and other relevant organizations;

(c) Encourage States through their participation in regional fisheries management organizations and arrangements to initiate processes for their review, and welcome the involvement of FAO in the development of general objective criteria for such reviews.

8. Fisheries, including artisanal, or small-scale fisheries, contribute significantly to poverty alleviation, food security and economic growth. In the case of small-scale fisheries, it was proposed that the General Assembly:

(a) Welcome the work of FAO in developing guidance on the strategies and measures required for the creation of an enabling environment for small-scale fisheries, including the development of a code of conduct and guidelines for enhancing the contribution of small-scale fisheries to poverty alleviation and food security that include adequate provisions with regard to financial measures, transfer of technology and capacity-building; and encourage studies for creating possible alternative livelihoods for coastal communities;

(b) Urge States and relevant international and national organizations to provide for participation of small-scale fishery stakeholders in related policy development and fisheries management strategies, consistent with the duty to ensure the proper conservation and management of those fisheries resources;

(c) Encourage increased capacity-building and technical assistance by States, international financial institutions and relevant intergovernmental organizations and bodies for fishers, in particular small-scale fishers, in developing countries, and in particular small island developing States, consistent with environmental sustainability.

9. The lack of effective implementation and enforcement of flag State responsibilities is still a critical shortcoming in the effectiveness of overall oceans governance and a serious impediment to the contribution of responsible fisheries to sustainable development. It was proposed that the General Assembly:

(a) Note the ongoing work of the International Maritime Organization (IMO) in cooperation with other competent international organizations, following the invitation extended to it by the General Assembly in its resolutions 58/14 and 58/240 to study, examine and clarify the role of the "genuine link" in relation to the duty of flag States to exercise effective controls over vessels flying their flag;

(b) Recall the appeal made by the Ministers of Fisheries of FAO in their Declaration on Illegal, Unreported and Unregulated Fishing, adopted at the FAO Ministerial Meeting on Fisheries, held on 12 March 2005, to take international action to eliminate illegal, unreported and unregulated fishing by vessels flying flags of convenience, as well as to require that a genuine link be established between States and fishing vessels flying their flag;

(c) Encourage work by competent international organizations to develop guidelines on flag State performance in relation to fishing vessels;

(d) Emphasize the obligations of States to apply flag State responsibilities in accordance with the Convention and the Agreement with respect to conservation measures for fisheries resources on the high seas;

(e) Encourage States to apply the FAO Port State Model Scheme at the national and regional levels, promote its application through regional fisheries management organizations and consider the possibility of adopting a legally binding instrument;

(f) Call upon States to promote, consistent with national law, the establishment of positive and negative lists of vessels fishing within areas covered by regional fisheries management organizations and arrangements to assist in the determination of compliance with conservation and management measures and encourage improved coordination among all parties to share and use this information;

(g) Request States and relevant international bodies, in consultation with the World Trade Organization and FAO, to develop more effective measures to trace fish and fishery products to enable importing States to identify fish or fisheries products caught in a manner that undermines agreed international conservation and management measures in accordance with international law, and at the same time to recognize the importance of effective market access for fish and fisheries products caught in a manner that is in conformity with such international measures;

(h) Call upon all flag States to ensure that vessels flying their flag do not engage in trans-shipments of fish caught by fishing vessels engaged in illegal, unreported and unregulated fishing; and upon States, individually or through regional fisheries management organizations, to develop more effective enforcement and compliance measures to prevent and suppress such trans-shipments in accordance with international law;

(i) Encourage the work of the International Labour Organization, in particular in relation to the convention and recommendation concerning work in the fishing sector;

(j) Welcome the adoption of the revised Code of Safety for Fishermen and Fishing Vessels and encourage its effective application, and urge States to become parties to the 1993 Protocol to the Torremolinos International Convention for the Safety of Fishing Vessels.

10. Illegal, unreported and unregulated fishing continues to seriously undermine the contribution of responsible fisheries to sustainable development. It was proposed that the General Assembly:

(a) Welcome and support the Rome Declaration on Illegal, Unreported and Unregulated Fishing adopted at the FAO Ministerial Meeting on Fisheries, held on 12 March 2005, as well as the Ministerial Declaration adopted at the 2005 Conference on the Governance of High Seas Fisheries and the United Nations Fish Agreement—Moving from Words to Action;

(b) Urge States, individually and through relevant regional fisheries management organizations and arrangements, to establish mandatory vessel monitoring, control and surveillance systems for fishing vessels, including the sharing of information on fisheries enforcement matters, and to give consideration to transforming the existing voluntary monitoring, control and surveillance network into an international unit with dedicated resources that can assist fisheries enforcement agencies;

(c) Encourage and support the development of a comprehensive global record of fishing vessels within FAO, including refrigerated transport vessels and supply vessels, that incorporates available information on beneficial ownership, subject to confidentiality requirements in accordance with national law, and ensure that all large-scale fishing vessels operating on the high seas be required by their flag State to be fitted with vessel monitoring systems no later than December 2008, or earlier if so decided by their flag State or any relevant regional fisheries management organization;

(d) Urge States and relevant organizations to expand the use of negative vessel lists to identify products from illegal, unreported and unregulated catches, and where possible to establish tracking and verification mechanisms to do so;

(e) Encourage the establishment of regional guidelines for States to use in establishing sanctions, for non-compliance by vessels flying their flag and by nationals, that are adequate in severity to effectively secure compliance, deter further violations and deprive offenders of the benefits deriving from their illegal activities;

(f) Urge States to implement multilaterally agreed trade measures in accordance with the International Plan of Action to Prevent, Deter and Eliminate Illegal, Unreported and Unregulated Fishing.

11. It was proposed that the General Assembly:

(a) Reaffirm the importance it attaches to resolution 59/25, paragraphs 66 to 71, and urge accelerated progress on implementing these elements of the resolution;

(b) Welcome progress made in the implementation of paragraphs 68 and 69 of resolution 59/25 calling for the expansion of the competence of existing regional fisheries management organizations or for the establishment of new regional fisheries management organizations to cover areas of the high seas where no such organization or arrangement currently exists;

(c) Request regional fisheries management organizations and arrangements with existing competency to implement spatial and temporal measures to protect vulnerable marine ecosystems to do so as a matter of urgency;

(d) Request States and regional fisheries management organizations and arrangements to be in a position to report on actions pursuant to paragraphs 66 to 69 of General Assembly resolution 59/25 when the Assembly reviews progress in 2006 and consider further recommendations for action;

(e) Encourage progress to establish criteria on the objectives and management of marine protected areas for fisheries purposes and welcome the proposed work of FAO to develop technical guidelines in accordance with the Convention on the design, implementation and testing of marine protected areas, and urge close coordination and cooperation with relevant international organizations, including the Convention on Biological Diversity;

(f) Call upon States to urgently accelerate their cooperation in establishing interim targeted protection mechanisms for vulnerable marine ecosystems in regions where they have an interest in the conservation and management of marine living resources;

(g) Request States and regional fisheries management organizations and arrangements to urgently implement all measures recommended in the FAO Guidelines to Reduce Sea Turtle Mortality in Fishing Operations to help prevent the decline of all species of sea turtles;

(h) Acknowledge the role of certification and ecolabelling schemes, which should be consistent with the requirements of the World Trade Organization and guidelines adopted by FAO.

12. It was proposed that the General Assembly:

(a) Call for more timely and comprehensive reporting of catch and effort data, including for straddling fish stocks within and outside exclusive economic zones and for discrete high seas stocks, including by-catch and discards;

(b) Encourage States [individually or through] regional fisheries management organizations and arrangements and regional seas programmes to work to ensure that fisheries and other ecosystem data can be consolidated and incorporated into the Global Earth Observation System of Systems for coordination at an ecosystem level;]

(c) Encourage enhanced science for conservation and management measures that incorporate and strengthen ecosystem considerations, including through implementation of the Strategy for Improving Information on Status and Trends in Capture Fisheries and a greater reliance on scientific advice in adopting such measures;

(d) Request further studies and consideration of the impacts of ocean noise on marine living resources;

(e) Commend the Advisory Group of Experts on the Law of the Sea of the Intergovernmental Oceanographic Commission of the United

Nations Educational, Scientific and Cultural Organization (UNES-CO) for its work on the legal aspects of marine scientific research and the transfer of marine technology in conformity with the Convention and in cooperation with the Division for Ocean Affairs and the Law of the Sea of the Office of Legal Affairs of the Secretariat, and encourage the Group to continue such work.

13. Access and capacity constraints continue to be serious impediments to many developing countries, in particular the least developed countries, small island developing States and coastal African States, in benefiting from fisheries and their contribution to sustainable development. It was proposed that the General Assembly:

(a) Encourage the international community to enhance the opportunities for sustainable development in developing countries, in particular the least developed countries, small island developing States and coastal African States, by encouraging greater participation of those States in fisheries activities being undertaken by distant-water fishing nations within their exclusive economic zones in order to achieve better economic returns from their fisheries resources and an enhanced role in regional fisheries management;

(b) Request distant-water fishing nations, when negotiating access agreements and arrangements with developing coastal States, to do so on an equitable and sustainable basis, including by giving greater attention to catch processing within the jurisdiction of the developing coastal State to assist the realization of the benefits from the development of fisheries resources;

(c) Encourage greater assistance for developing States in designing, establishing and implementing relevant agreements, instruments and tools for the conservation and sustainable management of fish stocks, including the enhancement of research and scientific capabilities through existing funds, such as the Assistance Fund under Part VII of the Agreement, bilateral assistance, regional fisheries management organizations and arrangements assistance funds, the FAO FishCode Programme, the World Bank's global programme on fisheries and the Global Environment Facility.

2.   Proposed Elements not Discussed at the Meeting

Marine Debris

14. Marine debris is a global transboundary pollution problem that constitutes a serious threat to human health and safety, endangers fish stocks, marine biodiversity and marine habitats and has significant costs to local and national economies. There are many different types of marine

debris; different approaches to their prevention and removal are therefore required.

15. It was proposed that the General Assembly:

(a) Note the lack of information and data on marine debris and encourage relevant national, regional and international organizations to undertake further studies on the extent and nature of the problem;

(b) Encourage States to develop partnerships with industry and civil society to raise awareness of the extent of the impact of marine debris on the health and productivity of the marine environment and consequent economic loss;

(c) Urge States to integrate the issue of marine debris into national strategies dealing with recycling, reuse and reduction and promote the development of appropriate economic incentives to address this issue;

(d) Encourage States to cooperate regionally and subregionally to develop and implement joint prevention and recovery programmes;

(e) Recognize the need to build capacity in developing States to raise awareness and implement improved waste management practices, noting the particular vulnerability of small island developing States to the impact of marine debris;

(f) Invite IMO, in consultation with FAO, the United Nations Environment Programme (UNEP) and the Division for Ocean Affairs and the Law of the Sea, to review Annex V of the International Convention for the Prevention of Pollution from Ships, 1973, as modified by the Protocol of 1978 relating thereto, and to assess its effectiveness in addressing sea-based sources of marine debris;

(g) Welcome the continuing work of IMO relating to port waste reception facilities and encourage the work of its Marine Environment Protection Committee in identifying problem areas and developing a comprehensive action plan;

(h) Welcome the convening of the Second Intergovernmental Review of the Global Programme of Action for the Protection of the Marine Environment from Land-based Activities as an opportunity to discuss marine debris in relation to the source categories of the Global Programme of Action and urge broad high-level participation.

16. It was proposed that the General Assembly encourage close cooperation and coordination among relevant organizations, United Nations programmes and other bodies, such as FAO, IMO, UNEP, the Global

Programme of Action, regional seas arrangements, regional and subregional fisheries management organizations and relevant stakeholders, to address the issue of lost and discarded fishing gear and related marine debris through initiatives such as:

(a) Analysis of the implementation and effectiveness of the existing measures relevant to the control and management of derelict fishing gear and related marine debris;

(b) The establishment and maintenance of national inventories of net types and other gear used by fisheries within national jurisdictions;

(c) The establishment of a clearing-house mechanism to facilitate the sharing of information between States on fishing net types and other gear used by fisheries around the world;

(d) Regular, long-term collection, collation and dissemination of information on derelict fishing gear found within national jurisdictions;

(e) Development and implementation of targeted studies to determine the socio-economic, technical and other factors that influence the accidental loss and deliberate disposal of fishing gear at sea;

(f) Assessment of preventive measures, incentives and disincentives relating to the loss and disposal of fishing gear at sea;

(g) Consideration of the outcomes of the Asia-Pacific Economic Cooperation (APEC) Education and Outreach Seminar on Derelict Fishing Gear and Related Marine Debris, held in January 2004, by the Global Programme of Action, the FAO Committee on Fisheries and other relevant intergovernmental and regional organizations;

(h) Awareness-raising within regional fisheries management organizations of the issue of derelict fishing gear and related marine debris and identification of options for action;

(i) Consideration by the FAO Committee on Fisheries of the issue of derelict fishing gear and related marine debris at its next meeting, and in particular the implementation of the FAO Code of Conduct for Responsible Fisheries.

17. It was proposed that the General Assembly request the United Nations Open-ended Informal Consultative Process on Oceans and the Law of the Sea to undertake another review of marine debris within five years, including the question of effective implementation of relevant international instruments.

Cooperation and Coordination

18. Under the item coordination and cooperation, a report was provided by the Executive Secretary of the Intergovernmental Oceanographic Commission of UNESCO, Coordinator of UN-Oceans, outlining progress to date on the establishment and the work of UN-Oceans.

19. It was proposed that the General Assembly:

(a) Welcome the work that the secretariats of agencies, programmes and funds of the United Nations system as well as secretariats of relevant international conventions have done to enhance inter-agency coordination and cooperation on oceans issues;

(b) Encourage States to work closely with and through international organizations, funds and programmes as well as the specialized agencies of the United Nations system and relevant international conventions to identify emerging areas of focus for improved coordination and cooperation and how best to address these issues.

PART B

Co-Chairpersons' Summary of Discussions

Agenda items 1 and 2: Opening of the Meeting and Adoption of the Agenda

20. The sixth meeting of the Consultative Process had before it the annual report of the Secretary-General on oceans and the law of the sea (A/60/63) as well as submissions by Costa Rica (A/AC.259/13), Pakistan (A/AC.259/15) and UNEP (A/AC.259/14).

21. The meeting was opened by the two Co-Chairpersons, Cristián Maquieira (Chile) and Philip Burgess (Australia), who in their introductory statements outlined the programme of work of the sixth meeting and briefly reflected on the functions of the Consultative Process and the format for the discussions, in particular with regard to the discussions of the elements for consideration by the General Assembly.

22. They presented the proposals of the Co-Chairpersons for the format and the annotated provisional agenda of the sixth meeting (A/AC.259/L.6). One delegation proposed to replace in the format and provisional annotated agenda the word "recommendations" to be suggested to the General Assembly with "elements" to make it consistent with the language of General Assembly resolution 54/33. The meeting supported this proposal and the format and the annotated agenda were subsequently adopted, as orally amended.

Agenda item 3: General Exchange of Views on Areas of Concern and Actions Needed, including on Issues Discussed at Previous Meetings

23. A number of delegations expressed their appreciation to the Secretary-General and the staff of the Division for Ocean Affairs and the Law of the Sea for the Secretary-General's report "Oceans and the law of the sea" (A/60/63). They highlighted the comprehensive nature of the report and its importance for the discussions at the Consultative Process. In addition to the material on the two areas of focus before the sixth meeting of the Consultative Process, the part of the report devoted to the Indian Ocean tsunami was highlighted as being of particular importance. With respect to the chapter in the Secretary-General's report relating to maritime security, one delegation expressed its dissatisfaction with the inclusion of a reference to the Proliferation Security Initiative.

The Consultative Process

24. Since the sixth meeting of the Consultative Process marked the end of the second three-year cycle and the General Assembly would be reviewing the effectiveness and utility of the Consultative Process at its sixtieth session, a number of delegations considered it useful to evaluate its achievements and to reflect on its future. Delegations expressed strong support for the Consultative Process and underlined its contribution to the work of the United Nations and, in particular, to an open exchange of views on topical issues relating to oceans and the law of the sea. They stated that, in general, the Consultative Process had achieved its goals and facilitated the annual review by the General Assembly of developments in ocean affairs and the law of the sea. Its inclusiveness and open-ended nature were highlighted by many delegations as indicators of its relevance and success. They noted that it had made a crucial contribution towards achieving a more integrated approach to the solution of issues of global oceans governance and strengthened coordination and cooperation among all relevant actors. For these reasons, delegations called for a renewal of the mandate of the Consultative Process, indicating, at the same time, that its format needed to be improved.

25. One delegation stressed the importance of the principles contained in resolution 54/33 to guide the Consultative Process, and underlined that the discussions in the Consultative Process should, inter alia, proceed within the framework established by the Convention and other relevant international instruments, focus on international coordination and cooperation in ocean affairs and deal with issues of common concern to all States and refrain from considering specific issues of interest only to some coastal States. The delegation also stressed that recommendations and suggestions from the Consultative Process should be made by consensus.

26. A number of delegations put forward their views on how the Consultative Process could be improved. Several delegations noted that the issues on the agenda had not been sufficiently focused to enable a fruitful

interdisciplinary discussion and proposed making available prior to the meeting information on the precise nature and focus of the presentations; having more experts; and more active participation by and clear input from competent international organizations in the debate. One delegation underlined the need to receive more information from non-United Nations organizations. Several delegations underlined that the European Community was a party to the Convention and the Fish Stocks Agreement and expressed the hope that the discrepancy between the observer status of the European Community and its competencies—whether exclusive or mixed— with respect to many issues discussed at the Consultative Process could be resolved.

27. A number of delegations expressed their dissatisfaction with the limited amount of time available for the consideration of the elements that are forwarded to the General Assembly. Some delegations pointed out that time constraints prevented them from consulting officials in their capitals. One delegation stated that its Government would be unable to agree to the text under such conditions. Some delegations expressed the view that rather than negotiating a text word for word, the meeting should focus on putting forward elements to the Assembly that reflected the different points of view. Other delegations considered that the General Assembly was best served by a negotiated text, but that more time was needed for the discussions of the elements. One delegation suggested convening meetings of the Consultative Process later in the year, shortly before the consideration by the General Assembly of the agenda item "Oceans and the law of the sea," so that the Consultative Process could facilitate the preparation of the draft resolution.

Indian Ocean Tsunami

28. Margareta Wahlstrom, Assistant Secretary-General for Humanitarian Affairs and United Nations Special Coordinator for the tsunami response, presented an overview of the United Nations response to the Indian Ocean tsunami disaster and progress achieved in providing emergency relief as well as assistance with the rehabilitation and reconstruction of the affected regions. She, inter alia, highlighted the need for new mechanisms and improved international coordination with a view to preventing loss of life and substantial material damage in the future.

29. A number of delegations provided details about their response to the Indian Ocean tsunami disaster, including financial support. They elaborated on reconstruction and rehabilitation strategies. Sustainable development of fisheries in line with the FAO Code of Conduct for Responsible Fisheries was mentioned as being one of the core elements of such rehabilitation. The delegations of Indonesia and Thailand expressed their gratitude for the unprecedented response of the international community to the Indian Ocean tsunami. One delegation highlighted the

vulnerabilities of small island developing States to such natural disasters and referred to the Mauritius Strategy for the Further Implementation of the Programme of Action for the Sustainable Development of Small Island Developing States.

30. Several delegations informed the meeting about the European Union tsunami action plan, which included the establishment of an early-warning system for the Mediterranean Sea, the Atlantic Ocean and the Indian Ocean. One delegation informed the meeting about its commitment, in partnership with the international community, to expand and enhance the existing Pacific Ocean tsunami warning system into a global system. Another delegation pointed to the link between marine scientific research and early warning systems.

31. The representative of the Intergovernmental Oceanographic Commission of UNESCO informed the meeting about the status of the Indian Ocean tsunami warning system. A network of 19 national tsunami focal points had been established to receive advisory information from the Pacific Tsunami Warning Centre and the Japan Meteorological Agency and existing observational networks had been upgraded to enable them to transmit real-time information regarding tsunamis.

Advisory Body of Experts on the Law of the Sea of the Intergovernmental Oceanographic Commission

32. The representative of the Intergovernmental Oceanographic Commission of UNESCO informed the meeting that a copy of the Criteria and Guidelines on the Transfer of Marine Technology, which the advisory body of experts on the law of the sea of the Commission had prepared and which were subsequently adopted by the Commission Assembly in 2003, had been distributed at the meeting of the Consultative Process, in accordance with the request of the General Assembly in resolution 59/24 to disseminate the criteria and guidelines. He also informed the meeting that the advisory body had finished drafting an internal procedure to apply article 247 of the Convention in the work of the Commission, which is scheduled for adoption at the twenty-third session of the Commission Assembly. Support was expressed for the work of the advisory body by some delegations.

Safety and Security of Navigation, and Labour Conditions

33. The representative of IMO provided information on recent activities, including the adoption of new instruments and progress in the development of a voluntary member State audit scheme for IMO. He also informed the meeting that, in response to the invitation contained in General Assembly resolution 58/240, the Secretary-General of IMO would convene an ad hoc inter-agency consultative meeting from 7 to 8 July 2005

comprising representatives of the Division for Ocean Affairs and the Law of the Sea, FAO, the International Labour Organization (ILO), the United Nations Conference on Trade and Development, the Organization for Economic Cooperation and Development and IMO to study, examine and clarify the role of the "genuine link" in relation to the duty of flag States to exercise effective control over ships flying their flags, including fishing vessels. As requested by the General Assembly in resolution 59/24, the outcome of the study undertaken by IMO and the other competent organizations would be communicated to the Secretary-General of the United Nations for him to report to the sixty-first session of the General Assembly.

34. A group of non-governmental organizations suggested that the Consultative Process discuss the issue of the genuine link at its next meeting and that the Division for Ocean Affairs and the Law of the Sea should develop an implementing agreement for the Convention on the full and effective implementation and enforcement of flag State responsibilities.

35. The representative of ILO informed the meeting about progress in the development of the consolidated maritime labour convention and a convention and recommendation concerning work in the fishing sector. He requested the assistance of the Consultative Process in promoting widespread ratification and implementation of ILO instruments, including the Seafarers' Identity Documents Convention (Revised).

36. Some delegations underlined the need to strengthen labour laws and ensure the protection of human rights of crew on-board vessels. A group of non-governmental organizations recommended that the Consultative Process consider the human and labour rights of those employed in the fishing and maritime sectors (see also paras. 68 and 69 below).

37. The need to strengthen capacity-building for the production of nautical charts, especially electronic charts, with the participation of the International Hydrographic Organization and funding institutions, was raised by one delegation.

38. Some delegations emphasized the need to cooperate with the International Atomic Energy Agency to ensure that sensitive sea areas are protected from the transport of radioactive materials by sea.

39. One delegation provided information about various initiatives to improve safety and security of navigation and environmental protection in the Straits of Malacca and Singapore, including an IMO-sponsored meeting to be held in Jakarta in 2005, and the marine electronic highway project. The delegation pointed out that, in order to maintain maritime security, States had to act strictly in accordance with international law, avoiding the application of any unilateral policies in contravention of existing legal norms derived from the Convention.

40. One delegation called for strengthened efforts to prevent and eliminate impacts on coral reefs as a result of collisions by ships; the

promotion of exchange of information between States and organizations in case of accidental damage to corals; the establishment of a list of experts to assess damage to vulnerable marine ecosystems; and the development of liability and compensation mechanisms for such damage.

Conservation and Management of Marine Biodiversity

41. A number of delegations commented on the issue of high seas biodiversity. Some delegations emphasized the need for a coherent approach to the conservation and management of marine biodiversity both within zones under national jurisdiction and on the high seas.

42. Several delegations welcomed the establishment of the ad hoc open-ended informal working group to study issues relating to the conservation and sustainable use of marine biodiversity beyond areas of national jurisdiction. Some pointed out that the agenda of the group needed to be broad and that fisheries should be seen as a key component.

43. Several delegations said that General Assembly resolution 59/25 provided short-term measures to address adverse impacts on high seas biodiversity, but that in the medium term, measures should be aimed at developing an implementing agreement to the Convention. They recalled their statement at the fifth meeting of the Consultative Process that, in principle, they would support the development of an instrument within the framework of the Convention that would provide for the conservation and management of biological diversity in areas beyond national jurisdiction, including the establishment and regulation on an integrated basis of marine protected areas where there is a scientific basis for establishing them. Those delegations stated that the UNEP Regional Seas Programme and other regional seas conventions should have a role in the assessment of areas in urgent need of protection from certain damaging activities.

44. Some delegations referred to the call in the Johannesburg Plan of Implementation to establish a representative network of high seas protected areas and expressed their support for exploring the potential for them, stating that they were a flexible tool that could be constructed to achieve a wide range of outcomes. During the discussions, there were diverging views as to the use and effectiveness of marine protected areas. Some delegations pointed out that since measures such as marine protected areas could restrict the freedoms of the high seas, their implementation should be subject to the consent of States concerned. Restrictions should be based on binding instruments negotiated in conformity with international law, taking into account the interests of transparency, legitimacy and effectiveness. One delegation noted that where marine protected areas were related to the resources of the deep seabed, the participation of the International Seabed Authority with regard to scientific research, the protection and conservation of the natural resources of the Area and the prevention of damage to the

flora and fauna of the marine environment in the Area should be respected as well. Another delegation expressed the view that if marine protected areas were established on the high seas, it should be done on a case-by-case basis and on the basis of scientific information, and even then it should be a last resort. Yet others referred to the difficulties regarding the enforcement of such protected areas in the high seas.

Anthropogenic Underwater Noise Pollution

45. A group of non-governmental organizations drew attention to anthropogenic underwater noise as a largely unregulated form of pollution. They suggested using the Convention as a legal basis for action to regulate this form of pollution; organizing a multinational task force to develop international agreements regulating noise levels; and applying the precautionary principle to significantly reduce, mitigate or cease activities resulting in the production of intense underwater noise until effective guidelines were developed. One delegation underlined the need for the international community to address underwater noise pollution.

Areas of Focus

46. The two areas of focus—fisheries and their contribution to sustainable development, and marine debris—were discussed in depth by panels A and B, as well as in the plenary during the consideration of agenda item 3. The discussions in each panel were launched by a number of panellists. (Due to page constraints, the panel presentations are not included in the present report. Available panel presentations have been posted on the website of the Division for Ocean Affairs and the Law of the Sea at www.un.org/Depts/los.)

47. It was emphasized by some delegations that, when examining the two areas of focus, the connection between them, as well as the need for an integrated, interdisciplinary and intersectoral approach, had to be borne in mind. One delegation highlighted the relationship between current and past areas of focus, such as protection and preservation of the marine environment and vulnerable marine ecosystems.

1. Fisheries and their Contribution to Sustainable Development

(a) Panel Presentations

48. The first segment of the panel presentations was devoted to recent developments and was launched by Serge Garcia, Director of the Fisheries Resources Division, FAO Fisheries Department, who provided an overview

of the state of the world's fisheries and reported on the outcome of the twenty-sixth session of the FAO Committee on Fisheries, held from 7 to 11 March 2005. David Balton, Chairman of the fourth round of informal consultations of States Parties to the Fish Stocks Agreement and Deputy Assistant Secretary for Oceans, Bureau of Oceans, International Environmental and Scientific Affairs, Department of State, United States of America, then reported on the outcome of the fourth round of informal consultations, which were held from 31 May to 3 June 2005. The third panellist, Lori Ridgeway, Director-General, International Coordination and Policy Analysis, Fisheries and Oceans, Canada, presented a summary of the results of the Conference on the Governance of High Seas Fisheries and the United Nations Fish Agreement—Moving from Words to Action, held in St. John's, Canada, from 1 to 5 May 2005. The fourth panellist, Kjartan Hoydal, Secretary of the North-East Atlantic Fisheries Commission, provided a report on the outcome of the fourth meeting of Regional Fishery Bodies, which was held on 14 and 15 March 2005. Evelyne Meltzer, adviser to the delegation of Canada, introduced her research work entitled "Global Overview of Straddling and Highly Migratory Fish Stocks," which she prepared for the St. John's Conference at the request of the Government of Canada.

49. The second panel segment, on commercial/large-scale fishing, was launched by Patrick McGuiness, President of the International Coalition of Fisheries Association, and Javier Garat, Secretary-General, Federación Española de Organizaciones Pesqueras, Spain, who provided an industry perspective. The third panellist, Matthew Gianni, international fisheries consultant, proposed measures to address bottom trawling and illegal, unreported and unregulated fishing.

50. The third panel segment was devoted to small-scale and artisanal fishing and was launched by Fabio Hazin, Director of the Fisheries and Aquaculture Department, Universidade Federal Rural de Pernambuco, Brazil, and Sidi El Moctar Ould Mohamed Abdallahi, Head of Coastal Fisheries Development, Ministry of Fisheries and Maritime Economy, Mauritania. Both provided information on the contribution of this fisheries sub-sector to food security and poverty alleviation as well as the difficulties faced by small-scale fisheries, and suggested possible measures.

51. A scientific and civil society perspective was provided during the fourth panel segment. Boris Worm, Assistant Professor in Marine Conservation Biology, Biology Department, Dalhousie University, Halifax, Canada, made a presentation on the causes and consequences of and solutions to the global decline in large pelagic fish. Callum Roberts, Professor in Marine Conservation Biology, Environment Department, University of York, United Kingdom, explained how marine reserves could benefit fisheries and ecosystem recovery and stability. Sebastian Mathew, Programme Adviser, International Collective in Support of Fishworkers, Chennai, India, focused,

inter alia, on the role of fisheries, including aquaculture, as a major source of employment. Karen Sack, Oceans Policy Advisor, Greenpeace International, called for action to address deep sea bottom trawling.

(b) Summary of Discussions in Panel A and the Plenary

52. Many delegations underlined the positive contribution of sustainable fisheries to food security, poverty alleviation, economic development and social stability, such as through the reduction of unemployment, especially in the case of developing countries, in particular small island developing States.

53. The need to increase developing States' capacity in the field of sustainable management of fisheries was recognized by a number of delegations, which underlined the need for subsistence assistance, capacity-building and transfer of technology for developing countries, in particular small island developing States. In that regard, some delegations referred to the possibility of assistance being provided through the United Nations University Fisheries Training Programme, the Assistance Fund under Part VII of the Agreement, the World Bank PROFISH programme and official development assistance. One delegation acknowledged the importance of both developing an integrated system of assistance that would focus on sustainable and responsible fisheries and ensuring that developing States maximize the use of the assistance they receive.

54. Another delegation suggested that the General Assembly urge the international community to encourage greater participation of developing countries, particularly small island developing States, in fishing activities undertaken by distant-water fishing nations within their exclusive economic zones (EEZs), to enhance the opportunities for sustainable development for those States. The same delegation furthermore suggested that the Assembly urge distant-water fishing nations to negotiate access agreements with developing countries on an equitable and sustainable basis, and encourage those nations to process catch taken from the EEZs of developing countries within the territory of those States, thereby creating employment and contributing further to the sustainable development of developing coastal States.

55. Some delegations suggested that there was a need to abolish protectionist measures (subsidies in particular), which hinder access to markets by developing countries. An urgent review of subsidies at the World Trade Organization in the light of the Doha Declaration was suggested.

56. Several delegations highlighted the difficulties in the use of the terminology of small-scale and artisanal fisheries. While some highlighted the need for standard terminology, others considered this impractical. Several delegations highlighted the difficulties experienced by small-scale

fishers in gaining access to high seas fishing grounds. Some delegations stressed the need for the involvement of small-scale and artisanal fishers in decision-making. In order to improve understanding of the contribution of small-scale fisheries to food security, it was suggested by one delegation that, inter alia, small-scale fisheries be made a priority subsector in national development plans and in regional development programmes, and that information on the potential of small-scale fishing to meet household and national food-security targets be broadcast. The need for increased activities in the areas of resource management and assessment, monitoring, control and surveillance and capacity-building at the national and regional levels was underlined by some delegations. One delegation identified the need to address activities that could contribute to a reduction in coastal pollution and strategies to attract a new generation of small-scale fishermen and fisherwomen to the subsector. The same delegation emphasized that there was an urgent need in many developing countries for long-term partnerships between public and private organizations geared towards upgrading the secondary sector to develop high-quality traditional fishery products for national and regional consumption.

57. One delegation noted that small-scale fisheries were at times in conflict with industrial fishing and aquaculture. Another delegation underlined that both small- and large-scale fishing had to be conducted in a sustainable manner. Yet another delegation noted that if small-scale fisheries were unsustainable, there was a need to assist countries in finding alternative livelihoods for fishers.

58. Some delegations pointed out that the sustainable development of fisheries was another aspect of the contribution of fisheries to sustainable development. In that regard, one delegation noted that the issue was directly linked to the protection of the marine environment, the balancing of the needs of present and future generations, the equitable access of all States to fishing resources and the relations between coastal and high seas fisheries.

59. Another delegation underlined the need for States to examine in depth the issue of resource access and allocation in order to prevent over-exploitation of available resources. Some suggested involving the industry and fishers, including those involved in small-scale fisheries, in decision-making processes. One delegation proposed co-management and shared resource stewardship by industry, including through innovative codes of conduct. A representative from a non-governmental organization suggested that industry be provided with secure rights of access in return for compliance incentives based on user rights.

60. From the institutional point of view, several delegations were of the view that ocean resources were best managed at the national and regional levels. They underlined the important role of regional fisheries management organizations and arrangements. Some advocated a strengthening of

their role and a modernization of their operation. In this regard, one delegation indicated that the said organizations should have the responsibility of determining how the assessment of their performance was to be conducted. Some delegations underlined the need for a stronger ecosystem-based focus. Others suggested that active linkages among regional fisheries management organizations be promoted as well as between those organizations and regional seas programmes and other relevant regional organizations.

61. The need to establish regional fisheries management organizations in areas where they are not yet in place was also underlined by several delegations. In this connection, reference was made by some delegations to a new initiative to establish a fisheries management organization for non-tuna species in the South Pacific. Some delegations expressed the view that where no regional fisheries management organization exists, coastal States should have the right and duty to adopt conservation measures.

62. One delegation noted that there was an increased need for coordination and cooperation, not only among States, but among an increasing number of organizations active in this field, including the World Trade Organization. That delegation also underlined the important role played by non-governmental organizations, as well as by the fishing industry.

63. Many delegations underlined the importance of States becoming parties to and effectively implementing the existing legal instruments, including the Convention, the Agreement and the 1993 High Seas Fishing Compliance Agreement, as well as implementing the FAO Code of Conduct for Responsible Fisheries and the FAO international plans of action. The need for improved governance and management of high seas resources was also underlined by some delegations, as well as the need to address any gaps in the conservation and management of discrete fish stocks in the high seas.

64. Several delegations expressed support for the outcome of the FAO Committee on Fisheries, the 2005 Rome Declaration on Illegal, unreported and unregulated Fishing and the Conference on the Governance of High Seas Fisheries and the United Nations Fish Agreement—Moving from Words to Action, held in St. John's, Canada. They also welcomed the outcome of the fourth round of informal consultations of States parties to the Agreement. One delegation indicated that it disagreed with the inclusion of a reference to the St. John's Conference in the elements relating to illegal, unreported and unregulated fishing to be suggested to the General Assembly, but that it would not stand in the way of consensus on that point.

65. Effective flag State implementation and enforcement of flag State responsibilities were regarded by a number of delegations as fundamental to the proper implementation of the existing rules and standards. It was suggested by one delegation that vessel registers and vessel-marking standards be used to identify fishing vessels authorized to fish.

66. It was observed that failure to implement conservation and management frameworks offered an opportunity for fishing operations to reflag and move to lower-cost operations, a phenomenon directly linked to illegal, unreported and unregulated fishing. Some delegations and non-governmental organizations underlined the need to ensure that there was a genuine link between the fishing vessel and the owner and emphasized the need to define the genuine link.

67. Some delegations suggested strengthening the role of port State control by requiring States to implement the FAO Model Scheme on Port State Measures directly, and through regional fisheries management organizations. Several delegations highlighted the need to harmonize custom codes for fishing products.

68. The need to ensure respect for human rights in the fisheries and shipping sectors was underlined by some delegations. A group of non-governmental organizations called attention to the link between the practice of illegal, unreported and unregulated fishing and poor social and safety conditions for crews on-board fishing vessels. They pointed out that labour conditions on-board fishing vessels were in some cases analogous to slavery. Vessel reflagging and the lack of any widely accepted global convention on safety and personnel requirements for fishing vessels, as well as the lack of enforcement of ILO instruments on labour conditions, were identified among the root causes. However, it was noted that sub-standard treatment of seafarers was not confined to vessels flying flags of convenience. The representative of IMO underlined the need to encourage States to become parties to the International Convention on Standards of Training, Certification and Watchkeeping for Fishing Vessel Personnel. He informed the meeting that a revised code of safety for fishermen and fishing vessels had been adopted this year and also suggested that States should be asked to explain why they had not become parties to the Protocol to the Torremolinos International Convention for the Safety of Fishing Vessels.

69. One delegation and a representative of a non-governmental organization emphasized the need to consider ethics and human rights in fisheries, as well as bioethics and animal welfare.

70. Many delegations and representatives of international organizations and non-governmental organizations underlined that illegal, unreported and unregulated fishing constituted a major threat to the sustainable development of fisheries. Other delegations called for a wider application of the FAO Code of Conduct for Responsible Fisheries and the International Plan of Action to Prevent Illegal, Unreported and Unregulated Fishing. Some delegations referred to the ongoing work of the Organization for Economic Cooperation and Development (OECD) on illegal, unreported and unregulated fishing. However, one delegation could not accept the reference to OECD in the agreed elements.

71. A number of delegations emphasized the need for additional measures, such as the reduction of subsidies that lead to overexploitation and overcapacity. Many underlined the need to reduce excess fishing capacity and to maintain capacity at levels commensurate with the sustainability of target fish stocks. One delegation stated that there was a need to control construction of new vessels that contribute to overcapacity. The same delegation suggested the adoption of capacity controls by regional fisheries management organizations, by using, for example, white lists. Another delegation stated that since fishing was directly linked to the livelihood of many communities, it was necessary to generate new sources of income for fishermen that would enable them to reduce the levels of their fishing activity.

72. Also suggested by some delegations was the establishment of a list of fishing vessels engaged in illegal, unreported and unregulated fishing by regional fisheries management organizations and enhanced port State control. The need to prevent and suppress transhipment of fish caught by fishing vessels engaged in illegal, unreported and unregulated fishing was also highlighted.

73. Many delegations underlined the need for enhanced monitoring, control and surveillance. The vital role of regional fisheries management organizations and arrangements in this regard was highlighted by one delegation. The need to improve the sharing of information on fisheries enforcement matters was also underlined. Some delegations suggested strengthening the international monitoring, control and surveillance network and urging States to consider participating in it. Others suggested the development of a comprehensive global record of fishing vessels authorized to fish. One delegation proposed expanding the use of negative vessels lists, particularly in conjunction with statistical document programmes to identify products from illegal, unreported and unregulated catches. Several delegations highlighted the need to harmonize customs codes for fishing products. One delegation proposed using multilateral trade measures, including tracking mechanisms by regional fisheries management organizations, preferably in electronic format, and in accordance with international law. Another delegation suggested developing regional guidelines for States to use in establishing sanctions in cases of noncompliance. A third delegation stated that it had required the mandatory installation of vessel monitoring and surveillance systems and planned to set up special tribunals to deal with the issue of illegal, unreported and unregulated fishing.

74. Some delegations referred to the adoption by FAO of international guidelines for the ecolabelling of fish and fishery products from marine capture fisheries, and the recommendation by the FAO Committee on Fisheries to prepare international guidelines on the ecolabelling of fish and fishery products from inland fisheries.

75. Some delegations stressed the importance of the application of the ecosystem and precautionary approaches in the conservation and management of marine living resources. They underlined that it was necessary to consider the specific needs of rare and vulnerable marine ecosystems and habitats, as well as marine species, such as sea turtles, sharks and sea birds.

76. A number of delegations referred to the problems of by-catches as well as to the issue of destructive fishing practices, in particular bottom trawling. A representative of a non-governmental organization underlined the near-extinction of the leatherback turtle as a result of long-line fishing in the Pacific and called for a moratorium on that practice. This call was supported by only some delegations. One delegation noted that not all species of turtles were in danger of extinction, and that some species were in fact increasing.

77. The continued use of destructive fishing practices, such as bottom trawling, whether conducted within an EEZ or on the high seas, was deplored by several delegations and non-governmental organizations. They advocated the adoption of a moratorium on high seas bottom trawling as an interim measure until a lasting solution could be devised by the international community. Other delegations opposed the adoption of a global moratorium, which they considered would be ineffective. Others drew attention to the need to distinguish between moratoriums imposed at the national, regional or global level.

78. Several delegations referred to the call for action set out in paragraphs 66 to 71 of General Assembly resolution 59/25. Some delegations called upon States to cooperate to give effect to this call. One delegation emphasized that the review of progress on actions taken in response to the call by the General Assembly had to be rigorous and take place well within the agreed time frame.

79. During the consideration of the elements to be suggested to the General Assembly, some delegations proposed to include a subparagraph that called upon States to immediately establish interim targeted protection measures, including interim bans on bottom trawling in vulnerable marine ecosystems, until such time as regional agreements or arrangements had been established. Other delegations proposed to call upon States to urgently agree on an open mechanism to cooperate in the protection of vulnerable marine ecosystems.

80. Some delegations held the view that since bottom trawling affected the resources on the seabed, including sedentary species, the competency of the International Seabed Authority should be respected. One delegation noted with regard to paragraph 11(f) of the agreed elements that a reference to the International Seabed Authority should have been included.

81. Some delegations underlined the need to adopt measures, including marine protected areas, to limit the effects of destructive fishing practices on vulnerable marine ecosystems and habitats. During the

discussions, diverging views were expressed as to the use and effectiveness of marine protected areas (see also para. 44 above). It was noted by the representative of FAO and a non-governmental organization that it was necessary to differentiate between zones for protecting biodiversity and those for fisheries management. The representative of the International Union for the Conservation of Nature and Natural Resources suggested that the work by FAO on the elaboration of technical guidelines on the design, implementation and testing of marine protected areas be expedited in consultation with relevant international bodies.

82. During the consideration of the elements for the General Assembly, it was proposed by one delegation that the Assembly encourage progress to establish globally agreed criteria on the objective, location, and management of marine protected areas and study the role of competent entities and institutions set up by treaties, including regional fisheries management organizations, in identifying and managing the said zones. That delegation also proposed the inclusion in the elements of a paragraph requesting that management regimes, as well as conservation and management measures, be supported by the best scientific evidence available, transparent and not applied in a discriminatory manner. However, due to time constraints, it was not possible to discuss this proposal.

83. Several delegations underlined that an improved understanding of the oceans was crucial to the improvement of the sustainable management of fisheries and highlighted the importance of sound scientific information for decision-making. Reference was made to the need for scientific data on fish stocks and for data on discards. The representative of the International Union for the Conservation of Nature and Natural Resources called for a global mechanism for providing scientific advice to regional fisheries management organizations. She also underlined the need for scientific information and assessment on the effects of fisheries on deep water fish stocks and their ecosystems, in order to establish a baseline for future research and assessment, identify what is at stake for the international community and expedite an agreement on appropriate measures. One delegation indicated its willingness to share the data and information it had compiled at the national level about fish stocks, pollution, salinity and temperature. Another delegation suggested that the precautionary approach to fisheries management be applied in the absence of conclusive scientific information.

84. At the end of the panel discussions, some delegations expressed their disappointment that the discussions had focused primarily on constraints to the sustainable development of fisheries rather than on how fisheries could contribute to sustainable development.

2.   Marine Debris

(a)   *Panel Presentations*

85. Seba Sheavly (Director, Office of Pollution Prevention and Monitoring, the Ocean Conservancy) and Cees van de Guchte (Senior Programme Officer, UNEP/Global Programme of Action Coordinating Office) launched the panel presentations with an overview of the problem of marine debris, its characteristics, distribution, sources, threats it posed to marine life and other damage it caused, as well as the measures that the International Coastal Clean-up and UNEP had taken in response. Thomas Cowan (Director, Northwest Straits Commission) explained how the derelict fishing gear removal project of the Northwest Straits Marine Conservation Initiative addressed the location and removal of such gear. Ilse Kiessling (National Oceans Office of Australia) highlighted the importance of addressing root causes for lost fishing gear and described how her country was dealing with the problem of derelict fishing gear at the national and regional levels. Laleta Davis-Mattis (Senior Legal Adviser, National Environment and Planning Agency, Jamaica) described the sources of marine debris in her country, the measures that had been taken in response and the priority areas for action.

(b)   *Summary of Discussions in Panel B and in the Plenary*

86. The representative of IMO pointed out that neither Annex V of the International Convention for the Prevention of Pollution from Ships, 1973, as modified by the Protocol of 1978 relating thereto (MARPOL 73/78), nor the Convention on the Prevention of Marine Pollution by Dumping of Wastes and Other Matter, 1972 (London Convention) cover the unintentional loss of fishing gear. He stated that Annex V was not in effect in some regions because of an insufficient number of port waste reception facilities. IMO was developing a text for reporting inadequacies of port waste reception facilities, a comprehensive plan of action for reception facilities, and a port waste reception facility database, which aimed at facilitating global access to information on reception facilities around the world and promoting exchange and accuracy of data. IMO also contributes to, and funds, an array of activities through its technical cooperation programme, including capacity-building activities with small island developing states, with special emphasis on the wider Caribbean region. It was expected that IMO would review Annex V with a view to introducing stricter requirements for on-board waste management and stringent discharge regulations. IMO would need to work with FAO to address the issue of marine debris from fishing vessels.

87. The representative of the Permanent South Pacific Commission said that its plan of action to protect the marine environment, including vulnerable marine ecosystems, and the Convention for the Protection of the Marine Environment and Coastal Area of the South-East Pacific and its Protocols provided the basis for action with respect to marine debris. The Commission focused its efforts on promoting integrated management and the development of national plans of action for the protection of the marine environment. He pointed out that the Commission attached great importance to educational campaigns.

88. The representative of the United Kingdom of Great Britain and Northern Ireland, speaking on behalf of the Commission for the Protection of the Marine Environment of the North-East Atlantic, referred to the need to further develop ecological quality objectives and measures, as in the case of the North Sea, which would enable the effective measuring of ecosystem health and the effectiveness of mitigation programmes. Preliminary results from the North Sea projects had led to the adoption of European Community directives to address the impacts from ships. Much of the debris was the result of carelessness by beach-goers and represented an important challenge for local communities. He noted that the fishing industry was being encouraged to bring back to port, and dispose of, their material free of charge. He pointed out that there was a need for a multifaceted approach to marine debris. Speaking on behalf of the Joint Secretariat of the International Coral Reef Initiative, he drew attention to the destructive effects of marine debris on coral reefs.

89. The representative of the Helsinki Commission described the Baltic Strategy for Port Reception Facilities for Ship-generated Wastes and Associated Issues as an effective tool for addressing ship-generated wastes, which had led to a reduction in detected illegal oil discharges. The strategy was based on: adequate port reception facilities, not only in commercial ports but also in marinas and fishing harbours; a mandatory requirement for all ships to deliver wastes that could not be discharged legally in the Baltic Sea; the imposition of a "no special fee," i.e., the cost for receiving wastes from ships was payable by all ships, irrespective of whether the wastes were delivered; and efficient law enforcement and awareness raising.

90. During the plenary and panel discussions, many delegations pointed to inadequate waste management, deficiencies in the implementation of existing standards and lack of awareness of the issue as the main reasons for the increase in marine debris. They identified the main sources of debris in the ocean and in coastal areas as poorly managed landfills, waste carried by wind from urban areas and by sewage systems and rivers into the ocean, as well as shipping. Derelict fishing gear was identified as the most harmful debris to ocean life. One delegation noted that, as different types of marine debris have various effects on the marine environment, it would be inappropriate for the international community to declare a comprehensive

ban on the discharge of marine debris. Instead, priority should be given to the prevention of discharges generally recognized as the most harmful to the marine environment.

91. Several delegations expressed the view that solutions to the problem of marine debris not only needed to be implemented within the marine environment, but should also be linked to recycling, waste-reduction and packaging strategies. The need for awareness-raising programmes and education campaigns for all stakeholders was highlighted by many delegations. One delegation said that it was important to encourage the wide dissemination of information on marine debris through international meetings. In the opinion of some delegations, marine debris was not only an environmental problem that could be solved by legislation, law enforcement and technical solutions; it was also a cultural problem requiring the deployment of policies and efforts to change attitudes, behaviours and management approaches. Some delegations provided examples of national policies and actions they had taken in that regard. Some suggested that States be encouraged to participate in data collection and beach clean-up activities. One delegation suggested that the International Coastal Cleanup Campaign programme be replicated in other countries.

92. Many delegations underlined the importance of compliance with and enforcement of existing instruments. Some noted that although emphasis should be placed on implementation and enforcement, it was nonetheless also important to review the efficiency of existing instruments, including Annex V to MARPOL 73/78, and to address the wide scope of issues raised by marine debris.

93. It was noted that although discharge of plastics at sea was prohibited under Annex V to MARPOL 73/78, in some parts of the world the levels of marine debris had been reported to be increasing. Several delegations underlined the need to take urgent steps to improve the availability of port waste reception facilities. Some delegations expressed their support for the establishment of regional port waste reception facilities rather than requiring States to establish these on an individual basis. One delegation suggested that States should give effect to Annex V to MARPOL 73/78 through implementation of both flag State enforcement and port control measures and seek the introduction of compulsory reporting requirements for lost fishing gear.

94. The view was expressed by some delegations that there was a need for States to support targeted studies to determine the factors that motivate the loss and disposal of fishing gear at sea. There was also a need for States to implement the FAO Code of Conduct. It was proposed that the fishing industry develop codes of conduct. Some delegations emphasized that economic incentives formed part of the solution to the problem of marine debris. Others reported on the measures they had taken at the national level, including the adoption of national codes of conduct for responsible

fisheries pursuant to the FAO Code of Conduct and the implementation of a fishing-net name-tag system (for punitive measures in the case of recovery of derelict fishing gear); and incentive policies, such as buy-back programmes of fishing gear and other wastes and free disposal of used gear. Some delegations suggested that FAO address the issue of lost fishing gear and review the implementation of the Code of Conduct and explore possible cooperation with IMO.

95. Some delegations indicated the need for a coordinated set of measures, which they said could be better achieved at the regional level. It was suggested that the issue of derelict fishing gear be discussed within regional fisheries management organizations in order to raise awareness; that regional fisheries management organizations, FAO and other appropriate intergovernmental organizations be encouraged to undertake initiatives to collect information on associated economic costs incurred as a result of derelict fishing gear; and that best management practices be developed with respect to derelict fishing gear and related marine debris. One delegation suggested the establishment of inventories of net types and other gear used in fishing within national jurisdictions or a clearing-house mechanism to facilitate the sharing of information on fishing net types and other gear used in fisheries around the world.

96. It was suggested that States and regional organizations be encouraged to review the outcome of the APEC Education and Outreach Seminar on Derelict Fishing Gear and related Marine Debris. Attention was also drawn to joint agreements as a way to address the issue of marine debris in an integrated manner, taking into account land-based sources and to establish effective and compulsory systems of reporting and registration of fishing gear. The Northwest Pacific Action Plan was cited by one delegation as a regional cooperative model that States could use in their efforts to reduce marine debris.

97. The importance of implementing the Global Programme of Action was underlined by several delegations, as well as the need to assist countries in that regard. In this connection, one delegation recalled paragraph 65 of General Assembly resolution 59/24. Some delegations highlighted the importance of taking a variety of measures at the national level, such as the building of solid waste-collection centres or the adoption and promotion of recycling policies.

98. Delegations noted with appreciation the offer by the Government of China to host the second intergovernmental review meeting of the Global Programme of Action in 2006. It was proposed that to ensure the success of the review meeting, a broad participation of ministers and high-level officials would be essential.

99. In the marine debris section of the report of the Secretary-General, one delegation pointed out the absence of a reference to explosives and oil pollution from shipwrecks dating from the Second World War, and

expressed the view that this subject should be included under the present area of focus, although substantively a bilateral approach to finding a solution was preferable.

100. It was noted by several delegations that special attention ought to be paid to the need for capacity-building by developing countries in respect of better waste management on land and at sea, including through the improved recycling of materials, and that assistance to developing countries should be provided, especially in the field of research, transfer of technology, training of personnel and financing.

Agenda Item 4: Cooperation and Coordination on Ocean Issues

101. Patricio A. Bernal, Executive Secretary of the Intergovernmental Oceanographic Commission of UNESCO and Coordinator of UN-Oceans, informed the meeting that the latter body had held two meetings since it was established in 2004 by the United Nations System Chief Executives Board for Coordination. UN-Oceans was pursuing its coordination work through: task forces on post-tsunami response; the regular process for global reporting and assessment of the state of the marine environment, including socio-economic aspects; biodiversity in marine areas beyond national jurisdiction; and the second intergovernmental review of the Global Programme of Action. The UN-Oceans website was operational and could be accessed at www.un-oceans.org. Lastly, he also stated that UN-Oceans continued to manage the work of the United Nations Atlas of the Oceans under the auspices of FAO.

102. In this connection, the Director of the Fisheries Resources Division of FAO, Serge Garcia, made an electronic presentation of the United Nations Atlas of the Oceans and explained that it was an integrated source of knowledge and policy advice, developed collaboratively by funds, programmes and agencies of the United Nations system dealing with oceans issues. However, he underscored that the Atlas was having financial difficulties and needed funds to continue its work. The Atlas website can be accessed at www.oceansatlas.org.

103. Delegations underlined the need for cooperation and coordination. One delegation emphasized that voices of non-United Nations agencies should be heard more systematically. However, some delegations questioned the core functions of UN-Oceans in relationship to its proposed inclusion of organizations outside the United Nations system for certain activities.

104. Some delegations expressed the view that in deciding on which activities to engage in UN-Oceans should consider the views of member States. One delegation suggested that UN-Oceans play a greater role in reporting on specific issues under discussion in the Consultative Process.

Agenda Item 5: Identification of Issues for Further Consideration

105. The Co-Chairpersons noted that an extensive list of issues for the future work of the General Assembly on oceans and the law of the sea had been proposed by delegations over the past five meetings of the Consultative Process, as reflected in the reports of the fourth and fifth meetings (A/58/95, part C and A/59/122, part C). Delegations were invited to submit proposals for additional issues in writing to the Secretariat. Additional issues proposed by delegations during the sixth meeting are set out in paragraph 106 below.

PART C

Issues that could benefit from attention in the future work of the General Assembly on Oceans and the Law of the Sea

106. There was agreement that the list of issues identified at the five previous meetings of the Consultative Process remained valid, thus meriting attention from the General Assembly. Additional issues suggested at the sixth meeting were:

(a) The application of an ecosystem approach to oceans management;

(b) Integrated management approaches to address marine pollution;

(c) Human and labour rights of those employed in the fishing and maritime sectors;

(d) Short-, medium- and long-term ecosystem management mechanisms to address and prevent the decline and extinction of associated species, including fish, billfish, sea turtles, seabirds and marine mammals;

(e) Promotion of marine scientific research, as well as capacity-building for the development of scientific information;

(f) Legal and institutional frameworks at the international level for the protection of marine mammals;

(g) Naturally occurring meso-scale marine ecosystems;

(h) Coastal hazard preparedness.

Selected Documents and Proceedings

United Nations Convention on the Law of the Sea Report of the Fifteenth Meeting of States Parties New York, 16–24 June 2005*

CONTENTS

* EDITORS' NOTE.—This document was provided by the United Nations Division for Ocean Affairs and the Law of the Sea (DOALOS) and is extracted from the Report of the Fifteenth Meeting of States Parties, New York, 16–24 June 2005, SPLOS/135, 25 July 2005, available at the DOALOS Web site: http://www.un.org/ Depts/los. The document has been edited for publication in the *Ocean Yearbook.*

I.   INTRODUCTION

1. The fifteenth Meeting of States Parties to the United Nations Convention on the Law of the Sea[1] was convened in New York from 16 to 24 June 2005, in accordance with article 319, paragraph 2(e), of the Convention and the decision taken by the General Assembly at its fifty-ninth session (resolution 59/24, para. 17).

2. Pursuant to that decision and in accordance with rule 5 of the Rules of Procedure for Meetings of States Parties (SPLOS/2/Rev.4), invitations to participate in the Meeting were addressed by the Secretary-General of the United Nations to all States parties to the Convention. Invitations were also addressed to observers in conformity with rule 18 of the Rules of Procedure, including to the President and the Registrar of the International Tribunal for the Law of the Sea, the Secretary-General of the International Seabed Authority and the Chairman of the Commission on the Limits of the Continental Shelf.

---

1. See The Law of the Sea: Official Texts of the United Nations Convention on the Law of the Sea of 10 December 1982 and of the Agreement relating to the Implementation of Part XI of the United Nations Convention on the Law of the Sea of 10 December 1982 with Index and Excerpts from the Final Act of the Third United Nations Conference on the Law of the Sea (United Nations publication, Sales No. E.97.V.10).

II. ORGANIZATION OF WORK

A. Opening of the Fifteenth Meeting of States Parties and Election of Officers

3. Norma Elaine Taylor Roberts, Deputy Permanent Representative of Jamaica to the United Nations and Vice-President of the fourteenth Meeting of States Parties, opened the fifteenth Meeting on behalf of Ambassador Allieu Kanu (Sierra Leone), President of the fourteenth Meeting of States Parties, who was unable to attend due to exigencies of service.

4. The Meeting elected by acclamation Ambassador Andreas D. Mavroyiannis (Cyprus) President of the fifteenth Meeting.

5. Krassimira T. Beshkova (Bulgaria), Ali Hafrad (Algeria), Isabelle F. Picco (Monaco) and Gaile Ann Ramoutar (Trinidad and Tobago) were elected Vice-Presidents.

6. Nicolas Michel, the Under-Secretary-General for Legal Affairs and Legal Counsel, welcomed delegations to the fifteenth Meeting. In his introductory statement, the Legal Counsel stated that States parties should remain united in implementing the goals of the Convention, in particular its goal of the promotion of the peaceful uses of the seas and oceans. He urged States parties to deploy all their efforts with a view to the effective implementation of this important instrument.

B. Introductory Statement by the President

7. In his opening statement, the President welcomed all States parties, in particular Burkina Faso, Denmark and Latvia, which had become parties to the Convention since the fourteenth Meeting, bringing the total number of parties to 148. The President announced with regret the recent passing away of Ambassador Kenneth Rattray (Jamaica), Rapporteur-General of the Third United Nations Conference on the Law of the Sea. The President recounted the contribution of Ambassador Rattray to the development of the law of the sea, including the position he held as Rapporteur-General of the conference, and requested the delegation of Jamaica to convey the sympathy of the Meeting to the family of Ambassador Rattray and to the Government of Jamaica. A minute of silence was observed in honour of Ambassador Rattray.

8. The President welcomed the President and Registrar of the Tribunal, the Secretary-General of the Authority and the Chairman of the Commission, emphasizing the important achievements of those bodies since the fourteenth Meeting.

9. In his introductory remarks, the President stated that the Convention should be fully implemented and that its integrity should be maintained, as

underlined by many delegations at the sixth meeting of the United Nations Open-ended Informal Consultative Process on Oceans and the Law of the Sea, which took place from 6 to 10 June 2005.

C.   Adoption of the Agenda and Organization of Work

10. Referring to the provisional agenda (SPLOS/L.43), the President noted that, following the decision taken at the fourteenth Meeting, the report of the Secretary-General on oceans and the law of the sea to the General Assembly (A/60/63) is also presented to the Meeting of States Parties pursuant to article 319 of the Convention, to be considered under the agenda item entitled "Report of the Secretary-General under article 319 for the information of States parties on issues of a general nature, relevant to States parties that have arisen with respect to the United Nations Convention on the Law of the Sea." The President completed the overview of the provisional agenda referring to the items relating to the information concerning the Authority and the Commission, as well as procedural aspects such as the adoption of the agenda, the organization of work, the election of the Vice-Presidents and the appointment of the Credentials Committee.

11. After a general overview of the provisional agenda by the President, the Meeting adopted the agenda (SPLOS/130) with some amendments suggested by the President. Subsequently, the President outlined the organization of work, drawing particular attention to the election of the seven members of the Tribunal to fill the vacancies that will occur on 1 October 2005 and informing the delegations that the Secretariat had consolidated all the amendments to the Rules of Procedure for Meetings of States parties in a new document (SPLOS/2/Rev.4). The Meeting approved the organization of work as outlined by the President.

III.   REPORT OF THE CREDENTIALS COMMITTEE

12. On 20 June 2005, the Meeting appointed a Credentials Committee consisting of the following nine members: Bahamas, Canada, Czech Republic, Greece, Grenada, Indonesia, Malaysia, South Africa and Uganda. The Credentials Committee held two meetings, on 21 and 22 June. It elected Rosette Katungye Nyirinkindi (Uganda) Chairperson. At its meetings, the Committee examined and accepted the credentials of representatives to the fifteenth Meeting from 147 States parties to the Convention and the European Community. On 22 June, the Meeting approved the first and second reports of the Committee (SPLOS/131 and 134).

IV. MATTERS RELATED TO THE INTERNATIONAL TRIBUNAL FOR THE LAW OF THE SEA

A. Annual Report of the Tribunal

13. The annual report of the International Tribunal for the Law of the Sea for 2004 (SPLOS/122) was submitted to the Meeting in accordance with rule 6, paragraph 3(d), of the Rules of Procedure.

14. The President of the Tribunal, Judge Dolliver Nelson, in introducing the document, drew attention to the election of seven judges of the Tribunal to be held during the Meeting. He then proceeded with the description of the work carried out by the Tribunal during the two sessions held in 2004, the seventeenth, from 22 March to 2 April, and the eighteenth, from 20 September to 1 October.

15. With regard to legal and judicial matters, he informed the Meeting that the Committee on Rules and Judicial Practice and the plenary had reviewed the rules and judicial procedures of the Tribunal, discussing, in particular, the procedure for revision or interpretation of a judgement or order with respect to urgent proceedings before the Tribunal, a code of conduct for counsel, amicus curiae before international courts and tribunals, contributions towards the expenses of the Tribunal, bonds and other financial security under article 292 of the Convention, rules regarding evidence and the implementation of the decisions of the Tribunal. With regard to administrative and organizational matters, the President mentioned that the Tribunal had dealt with the draft budget proposals for 2005–2006, draft financial rules, the annual report, the appointment of staff, amendments to the Staff Regulations and Rules, maintenance of the premises and electronic systems, library facilities and publications.

16. The President continued with the description of the judicial work carried out by the Tribunal in relation to the *"Juno Trader" Case (Saint Vincent and the Grenadines* v. *Guinea-Bissau), Prompt Release.* The case, the thirteenth on the Tribunal's list of cases, involved the prompt release of the vessel *Juno Trader* and its crew under article 292 of the Convention. Proceedings were instituted on 18 November 2004 by an application filed on behalf of Saint Vincent and the Grenadines against Guinea-Bissau. The Tribunal met from 30 November to 18 December and adopted unanimously its judgement, which was delivered on 18 December (see SPLOS/122, paras. 23–29). The President also recalled the *Case concerning the Conservation and Sustainable Exploitation of Swordfish Stocks in the South-Eastern Pacific Ocean (Chile/European Community),* which was still pending on the docket. That case was submitted to a special chamber of the Tribunal, and by an order dated 16 December 2003 the time limit for making preliminary objections with respect to the case was extended at the request of the parties until 1 January 2006 to enable them to reach a settlement.

17. The President went on to note that jurisprudence created by the Tribunal had already made a significant contribution to the development of international law. In that regard, he underlined that the existence of the Tribunal was conducive to the peaceful settlement of disputes, as noted by the General Assembly in its resolution 59/24. From another perspective, the President noted that on several occasions, the Registry had received requests for information regarding the institution of prompt release proceedings, and on more than one occasion cases had not been instituted because negotiations between the parties proved successful. The President noted in that regard that it was a function of the Tribunal to be easily available to parties, a factor that could facilitate the negotiation process between the parties to a dispute.

18. He noted that currently only 35 States parties to the Convention had filed declarations under article 287 of the Convention, and 21 States parties had chosen the Tribunal as the means or one of the means for the settlement of disputes concerning the interpretation or application of the Convention. He also reminded the delegations that in the absence of declarations under article 287 of the Convention, or if the parties had not selected the same forum, the dispute could only be submitted to arbitration, unless the parties otherwise agreed. In that connection, he noted that the parties could submit their disputes to a special chamber of the Tribunal, in accordance with article 15, paragraph 2, of its Statute, a procedure that represented an alternative to arbitration. He highlighted other features, namely the availability of advisory proceedings of the Tribunal and of a trust fund that would assist States parties in the settlement of disputes through the Tribunal.

19. The President also drew attention to the recommendation contained in General Assembly resolution 59/24 (para. 26), in which the Assembly called upon States that had not done so to consider ratifying or acceding to the Agreement on the Privileges and Immunities of the Tribunal.[2] Only 16 States parties had so far ratified or acceded to the Agreement.

20. He reiterated the appeal contained in the same resolution (para. 25) to all States parties to pay their assessed contributions to the Tribunal in full and on time, underlining that, in view of the significant amount of outstanding contributions (€1,595,915 for the period 1996 to 2004 and €2,779,905 for the 2005 period, as at 31 May 2005), the Tribunal would face short-term liquidity problems and might have to resort to the Working Capital Fund. In that regard he made reference to the notes verbales by the Registrar reminding all States parties concerned of the amount of the

2. SPLOS/25.

arrears in the payment of their contributions to the Tribunal's budgets for the financial periods from 1996–1997 to 2005.

21. The President informed the Meeting that on 14 December 2004 the headquarters agreement between the Tribunal and Germany was signed. He expressed gratitude to the host country for the cooperation extended to the Tribunal in this matter and recalled that earlier in the year (1 September 2004) the Tribunal had had the honour of receiving Horst Köhler, President of Germany, accompanied by 140 members of the diplomatic corps.

22. The President reported that a symposium on maritime delimitation organized in commemoration of the tenth anniversary of the entry into force of the Convention had taken place on the premises of the Tribunal on 25 and 26 September 2004. He reminded delegations of the internship programme of the Tribunal and the grant provided by the Korea International Cooperation Agency for funding participation in the programme. A total of nine interns from developing countries benefited from the grant in 2004. He expressed the Tribunal's gratitude to the Korea International Cooperation Agency.

23. After the statement by the President of the Tribunal, the delegation of Germany expressed its satisfaction for the conclusion of the headquarters agreement with the Tribunal and informed the Meeting that the internal requirements necessary for the entry into force of the agreement would be completed as soon as possible.

24. Some delegations noted that the report showed that the Tribunal was fully equipped to carry out its mandate expeditiously.

25. The Meeting took note with appreciation of the report of the Tribunal.

B. Financial Statements of the Tribunal and Report of the External Auditors for 2003

26. The President of the Tribunal introduced the report of the external auditors for 2003. The report also contained the financial statements of the Tribunal as at 31 December 2003 (SPLOS/121). He stated that the annual financial statements gave a true and fair view of the net assets, financial position and results of the operations of the Tribunal in accordance with principles of proper accounting and the Financial Regulations and Rules of the United Nations, which were applied *mutatis mutandis*.

27. The President also informed the Meeting that the external audit of the accounts for 2004 had been completed and that the report would be officially transmitted to the next Meeting after its consideration by the Tribunal.

28. Some delegations enquired as to whether the external auditor's report for 2004 could be made available to the current Meeting of the States Parties. If that was not possible because of the existing rules, one delegation asked whether it would be possible to change the Financial Rules in order to enable the Meeting to discuss the external auditor's report on the same financial year. The Registrar clarified this issue noting that, due to the Financial Regulations of the Tribunal, as adopted by the Meeting, the auditor's report had to be transmitted to the Meeting through the Tribunal. The Tribunal therefore had to consider the document prior to its transmission, attaching comments as appropriate. Since the external audit was completed two weeks prior to the Meeting of States Parties, the Tribunal could examine the report only at its next meeting, in September 2005. In addition, the Registrar explained, there would be practical difficulties in transmitting the external auditor's report in the same year, as reports were released only in May/June, thus leaving an insufficient amount of time to produce it in all official languages in time for the Meeting.

29. Some delegations reiterated the importance of sound financial management of the Tribunal.

30. The Meeting took note with appreciation of the report of the external auditors for 2003.

C.   Appointment of the auditor for the Tribunal for the financial periods 2005–2006 and 2007–2008

31. The President of the Tribunal introduced a note by the Tribunal on the appointment of an auditor for the financial periods from 2005 to 2008 (SPLOS/123). He explained that the note had been prepared pursuant to regulation 12.1 of the Financial Regulations of the Tribunal in order to provide the Meeting with information in the event that the Meeting decided to appoint as auditor an internationally recognized firm.

32. An open-ended working group was established to deal with the agenda item. The President of the Meeting indicated that the choice before the Meeting was either to choose an internationally recognized firm of auditors, an Auditor-General or an official of a State party with an equivalent title. It was decided to continue to resort to international firms, since they had proved to be reliable and cost-effective and since there were no established procedures for electing a State official as auditor. Three international firms had been proposed by the Tribunal in document SPLOS/123.

33. It was proposed by one delegation that, in order to ensure continuity in the auditing of the Tribunal, the firm of auditors used by the Tribunal be accorded the opportunity once more to carry out the auditing.

After careful consideration of the proposal, the Meeting decided to select the lowest bidder, the BDO Deutsche Warentreuhand firm of auditors.

D.   Election of Seven Members of the Tribunal

34. On 22 June 2005, the Meeting elected seven members of the Tribunal to replace those members whose terms of office would expire on 30 September 2005 (SPLOS/125 and 126) in accordance with article 4, paragraph 4, of the Statute of the Tribunal and document SPLOS/L.3/Rev.1.

35. An invitation calling for nominations was addressed to all States parties in accordance with article 4 of the Statute of the Tribunal. Fifteen candidates were nominated (SPLOS/124). By a note verbale dated 6 April 2005, the Permanent Mission of Greece to the United Nations informed the Registrar of the Tribunal of the decision of the Government of Greece to withdraw the nomination of Haritini Dipla (SPLOS/124/Add.1). By a note verbale dated 11 May 2005, the Permanent Mission of Oman to the United Nations informed the Registrar of the Tribunal of the decision of the Government of Oman to withdraw the nomination of Mohammed Al-Sameen (SPLOS/124/Add.2).

36. Before the voting began, the President outlined the procedure for voting. He stated, inter alia, that the procedure for the first election, approved by consensus by the fifth Meeting and followed for elections in subsequent years, was contained in documents SPLOS/L.3/Rev.1. He further stated that, during the last elections, it had been announced that ballots would be deemed invalid if votes were cast for more candidates than the number of seats allocated to each region.

37. The election required five rounds of balloting during which the representatives of Canada, China, Mexico, Nigeria and Slovakia acted as tellers.

38. At the first round, out of 147 ballots cast, with 27 invalid ballots and no abstentions, a majority of 80 was required for the election. The following candidates were elected: L. Dolliver M. Nelson (Grenada) (113 votes), Shunji Yanai (Japan) (113 votes), Choon-Ho Park (Republic of Korea) (101 votes) and Helmut Tuerk (Austria) (85 votes).

39. At the second round there were no invalid ballots and no abstentions. Out of 147 ballots cast, a majority of 98 was required for the election. No candidates were elected.

40. At the third round there were no invalid ballots and no abstentions. Out of 146 ballots cast, a majority of 98 was required for the election. No candidates were elected.

41. At the fourth round, out of 145 ballots cast, with no invalid ballots and no abstentions, a majority of 97 was required for the election. The

following candidates were elected: James L. Kateka (United Republic of Tanzania) (111 votes) and Albertus Jacobus Hoffmann (South Africa) (108 votes).

42. Following the fourth round, the representative of Croatia withdrew the candidature of Budislav Vukas.

43. A fifth ballot was carried out for the remaining seat. A total of 133 ballots were cast. There were five abstentions and no invalid ballots. With a required majority of 86, Stanislaw Pawlak (Poland) (128 votes) was elected.

44. On behalf of the Meeting, the President announced the election of Albertus Jacobus Hoffmann, James L. Kateka, L. Dolliver M. Nelson, Choon-Ho Park, Stanislaw Pawlak, Helmut Tuerk and Shunji Yanai and congratulated them on their election.

E.   Consideration of budgetary matters of the International Tribunal for the Law of the Sea

Adjustment of the remuneration of members of the Tribunal

45. The President introduced the report on conditions of service and compensation for members of the Tribunal. On the adjustment of the remuneration of members of the Tribunal (SPLOS/2005/WP.1), the President recalled that the fourth Meeting of States Parties had decided to use the emoluments of the members of the International Court of Justice as the comparator to determine the remuneration of the members of the Tribunal. The General Assembly, in its resolution 59/282 of 13 April 2005, increased the annual salary of the members of the Court by 6.3 per cent to $170,080, effective 1 January 2005. As a consequence, it was proposed that the annual maximum remuneration of the members of the Tribunal also be increased to $170,080, effective 1 January 2005. The President explained that the financial impact of the increase would amount to only €200 for 2005–2006 thanks to the favourable fluctuations in the exchange rate. He further explained that the adjustment of the level of remuneration would automatically affect the pensions of former judges by virtue of the pension scheme regulations and that that would represent an additional appropriation of €6,500.

46. He underlined that the daily subsistence allowance for the members of the Tribunal, based on the rate determined for Hamburg by the United Nations, had increased from €211 in March 2004 to €233 in March 2005, requiring an additional appropriation of €108,800 for 2005–2006.

47. To cover the aforementioned increases, a total of €115,500 was required. The President proposed that the Tribunal be authorized to finance the additional increase by transfers, as far as possible, between

appropriations and by using part of the savings from the financial period 2002.

48. One delegation stated that although it understood the reasons for the request for adjustment of the annual remuneration of judges of the Tribunal, it could not support the proposal contained in document SPLOS/ 2005/WP.1 because of its retroactive applicability. The delegation also noted that when a higher remuneration was adopted at the ninth Meeting, it was not applied retroactively.

49. An open-ended working group was established to discuss this agenda item in detail. After its deliberations, and on the recommendation of the open-ended working group, the Meeting adopted the adjustment of the remuneration of members of the Tribunal set out in document SPLOS/ 132.

Effects of Fluctuations in Exchange Rate on the Remuneration of the Members of the International Tribunal for the Law of the Sea

50. In response to a request by the Meeting in 2004, the Registrar prepared a proposal for an appropriate mechanism for addressing the effects of fluctuations in the exchange rate on the remuneration of the members of the Tribunal (SPLOS/2005/WP.2). That document examined the floor/ceiling mechanism applicable to the emoluments of the members of the International Court of Justice since 1988, which had provided protection against the exchange rate fluctuations in respect of the emoluments of the members of the Court.

51. The President of the Tribunal, in introducing the document, drew attention to the report of the Secretary-General on conditions of service and compensation for officials other than the Secretariat officials (A/C.5/59/2), in which it was noted that the United States dollar had lost, on average, 26.8 per cent against the euro since January 2002. As a result, the annual and special allowances of the members of the Tribunal had been adversely affected. The Tribunal proposed to apply the floor/ceiling mechanism adopted for the members of the International Court of Justice to the members of the Tribunal as from 1 July 2005.

52. The President explained that should the floor/ceiling mechanism be adopted, an additional appropriation amounting to €764,889 would be required for the period from July 2005 to December 2006. The figures take into account the adjusted level of the annual remuneration of the members of the Tribunal. In order to finance this amount, the Tribunal proposed to use part of the savings from the financial year 2002 and the savings from the financial year 2004. In addition, the Tribunal sought a supplementary budget amounting to €351,889 for 2005–2006. The document was discussed in the open-ended working group, and on the recommendation of the

working group, the Meeting adopted a floor/ceiling mechanism to regulate the remuneration of the members of the Tribunal (see SPLOS/133).

Report on Common Staff Costs

53. The President of the Tribunal introduced a report on common staff costs (SPLOS/127), which had been prepared in response to a request made at the fourteenth Meeting. He recalled that, in preparing the budget proposal for the biennium 2005–2006, the Tribunal had expressed its preference for the method of budgeting common staff costs on the basis of a percentage of the net salary used by the United Nations. He stated that in order to determine whether the amount of €896,400 approved for 2005 would be sufficient to cover actual costs in 2005, the Tribunal was proposing a new estimate of €903,894, taking into account the performance in 2004. The amount was slightly higher than the one approved for 2005. He also stated that, as the difference was minimal, there was no need to make adjustments to the common staff costs for 2005 but added that, if necessary, the matter could be further reviewed in 2006.

54. The Meeting took note with appreciation of the report on common staff costs.

Budget Performance for 2004

55. The President of the Tribunal introduced the report on action pursuant to the decision on budgetary matters for 2004 taken by the fourteenth Meeting (SPLOS/128). He stated that the performance remained within the approved budget. He explained that several budget lines were overrun in 2004 mostly as a result of the weakening of the United States dollar against the euro. He referred to a decision of the fourteenth Meeting (SPLOS/118) authorizing the Tribunal to finance overexpenditures by transfers, insofar as possible, between appropriation sections. He also indicated that the overexpenditures were offset against savings under other appropriation sections. He further underlined that the performance report contained two additional items, namely, the investment of funds of the Tribunal and the Korea International Cooperation Agency trust fund, created in March 2004.

56. The Meeting took note with appreciation of the report.

V.   INFORMATION ON THE ACTIVITIES OF THE INTERNATIONAL SEABED AUTHORITY

57. The Secretary-General of the International Seabed Authority, Ambassador Satya N. Nandan, informed the Meeting of the activities carried

out in 2004 by the International Seabed Authority. He referred to the draft regulations for the exploration and prospecting of polymetallic sulphides and cobalt rich crusts, which, when adopted, would complement the existing ones on polymetallic nodules. He stated, that whereas polymetallic nodules were widely dispersed on the surface of the seabed, polymetallic sulphides, found along the oceanic ridges, and cobalt-rich crusts, located on back arcs and seamounts, were three-dimensional and more localized. Consequently, they had to be regulated differently because the size of their deposit would not be easy to determine before extensive exploration. This affected block sizes and the number of blocks that should be assigned to enable a contractor to have a reasonable and viable area to explore without allocating unduly large areas to any one contractor. In addition, this affected the nature of participation by the Authority. Since it might not be practical to apply the existing parallel system of exploitation for polymetallic nodules, the draft regulations provide for equity participation by the Authority as an option. The draft regulations, developed by the Legal and Technical Commission, are being reviewed by the Council.

58. The Secretary-General of the Authority also recalled the workshop on polymetallic sulphides and cobalt crusts—their environment and considerations for the establishment of environmental baselines and an associated monitoring programme for exploration, which was held from 6 to 10 September 2004. The workshop was the seventh in a series aimed at increasing the understanding of the potential impact of the exploration of those resources on the marine environment, determining what is required for baseline studies, ascertaining the relevance of current or past research programmes to that effort and suggesting guidelines to be submitted to the Legal and Technical Commission for establishing environmental baselines and for subsequent environmental monitoring. The workshop was attended by 40 participants from 18 countries, but it ended prematurely owing to the threats posed by hurricane Ivan. As a consequence, the three working groups were unable to complete their work. The Secretary-General of the Authority stated, however, that a meeting between the chairs of the working Groups and a representative of the mining industry had just taken place in New York to finalize the recommendations to be presented to the Legal and Technical Commission at its eleventh session and that the recommendations of the working groups and the proceedings of the workshop would be published by the Authority.

59. The Secretary-General of the Authority informed the Meeting of the development of a geological model for polymetallic nodule deposits in the Clarion-Clipperton Fracture Zone, which he had announced at the thirteenth Meeting and which was aimed at assisting the Authority in its administration of the Area as well as contractors and prospectors working in the Clarion-Clipperton Fracture Zone by improving the resource assessment for the Area. He drew attention to a meeting of technical experts convened

by the Authority in Kingston from 6 to 10 December 2004 to outline the scope of the work required to develop the geological model, ascertain the availability of data on selected proxies, schedule the work required to gather, evaluate and incorporate suitable data sets into the model through mathematical algorithms and produce the first iterations of the geological model and draft of the prospector's guide. The group of technical experts identified the approach it would use to create the mode, and specified the proxy data that would be tested for use in predicting nodule grade and abundance. A follow-up meeting was convened by the Authority from 25 to 27 May 2005 at its headquarters in Jamaica. That meeting was attended by representatives of the technical experts involved in the model and contractors with the Authority for polymetallic nodule exploration in the Clarion-Clipperton Fracture Zone. The aims of the meeting were for the technical experts to describe the specific data that the Secretariat was requesting from contractors and how the data provided would support the development of the model, to determine specific descriptions of the data that would be supplied by the contractors and to identify potential ways in which the technical staff from the contractors could participate in the project. A full description of the progress made to date and future goals will be presented to the Legal and Technical Commission and the Council at its eleventh session.

60. The Secretary-General of the Authority also gave an update on the Kaplan project, which was being carried out by scientists from the University of Hawaii, the British Natural History Museum, the Southampton Oceanography Centre, Shizuoka University and the French Research Institute for Exploitation of the Sea (IFREMER), with the potential for participation by some of the contractors. The project aims at acquiring information on biodiversity, species ranges and gene flow in the abyssal Pacific nodule-bearing province with a view to predicting and managing the impact of deep seabed mining in order to facilitate future regulations for polymetallic nodule exploitation. Since the previous Meeting, a third research cruise to the Clarion-Clipperton Fracture Zone was conducted, under the auspices of IFREMER. It collected additional animal samples that are currently being analysed and investigated mining tracks produced by IFREMER 26 years before in order to monitor recovery and decolonization of the disturbed areas. The Kaplan project is expected to be completed in July 2006, and the Authority will receive the data that have been accumulated as well as recommendations regarding the recovery of the deep abyssal plain communities likely to have been disturbed by a test mining system.

61. He further informed the Meeting that the Authority may receive an application for the approval of a plan of work in the form of a contract from Germany in respect of a mine site in the Clarion-Clipperton Fracture Zone before the eleventh session (15–26 August 2005). That would be the first new application since the entry into force of the Convention. The existing

seven contractors had made their applications as pioneer investors to the Preparatory Commission.

62. The Secretary-General of the Authority urged all States parties who were members of the Authority to participate in the meetings of the Authority. The Authority, he noted, can conduct its business effectively only in the presence of a majority of its members. From a procedural point of view, the Convention requires for the meetings of the Assembly a quorum of at least one half of the member States, a threshold that has not always been met.

63. He made an appeal also to the countries that were not yet parties to the 1994 Agreement relating to the implementation of Part XI of the Convention (General Assembly resolution 48/263, annex), as well as to the Protocol on the Privileges and Immunities of the International Seabed Authority (ISBA/4/A/8), to become parties to those instruments

64. The Meeting took note with appreciation of the statement by the Secretary-General of the Authority.

VI. INFORMATION ON THE ACTIVITIES OF THE COMMISSION ON THE LIMITS OF THE CONTINENTAL SHELF

65. The Chairman of the Commission, Peter Croker, informed the Meeting of States Parties of the activities of the Commission. Besides conveying the information reflected in his letter dated 5 May 2005 addressed to the President of the fifteenth Meeting of States Parties (SPLOS/129), he informed the Meeting that Norway intended to proceed with its submission by 2006, Namibia and Sri Lanka in 2007 and Pakistan in 2007/08. He further stated that, since the issuance of his statement on the progress of the work of the fifteenth session (CLCS/44) and the issuance of his letter dated 5 May 2005, Ireland had made its submission.

66. The Chairman gave a PowerPoint presentation on the projected workload of the Commission. He emphasized that the presentation was based on several assumptions and his own estimates of the time required to complete the examination of each submission, and did not constitute the view of the Commission or the subcommissions. In that connection, he informed the Meeting that the chairmen of the current subcommissions were not able to give an estimate as to the projected completion of the work under their examination. On the assumption that there would be 10 sessions by the end of 2009, with an average of 19 members attending each session, the Chairman outlined three scenarios, characterized by different numbers of States making submissions. He also explained that an average of two to three subcommissions could be established to work in parallel at any given time.

67. The first scenario was based on the number of responses to the notes verbales addressed by the Division for Ocean Affairs and the Law of the Sea of the Office of Legal Affairs to certain coastal States requesting them to indicate the projected timing of their submissions to the Commission. According to that scenario, the Commission would receive 16 submissions by the end of 2009. Those include submissions from Oman and Tonga, States potentially having continental shelves. Since the Commission could support only up to three subcommissions, members of the Commission would be overallocated and there would be a need to extend the duration of the meetings of the subcommissions or the intersessional periods. Problems would become particularly severe by the eighteenth session when there would be eight members allocated at 200 per cent of capacity. From the twentieth to the twenty-fifth session, the Commission would have an average of five submissions for simultaneous consideration. That would require each member of the Commission to spend an average of three and a half months per year in New York.

68. The second scenario was based on a calculation made in 1978 during the Third United Nations Conference on the Law of the Sea, according to which 33 States may have an extended continental shelf and 28 of them would have a deadline expiring by the end of 2009. As in the previous scenario, the problems would intensify by the eighteenth session, and from the eighteenth to the twentieth session, members would be required to be in New York for three and a half months per year dealing with an average of eight submissions. From the twenty-first to the twenty-fifth session, the average would rise to nine submissions. He stated that that level of work would be unsustainable under the present system and that it would be necessary either to change the working method of the Commission or to queue the submissions.

69. According to the third scenario, based on a wider list of States that may have an extended continental shelf, there would be 59 States, 50 of which may have a deadline by the end of 2009. The Chairman did not go into the details of that scenario, since the second one had made clear already the scale of the difficulties the Commission was bound to face.

70. One delegation expressed the hope that the Commission would have the financial and material resources needed to carry out its mandate properly in view of the immense volume of work that lay ahead for its members. It underlined the increasing importance of cooperation between the Division and the Commission, referring, in particular, to the training manual and courses developed by the Division, which were of extreme importance to developing countries.

71. The delegation of Sri Lanka expressed its gratitude to the Division and the Commission for the training course held in Colombo in May 2005. The course had been supported by the Commonwealth Secretariat and the Government of Sri Lanka. It was attended by representatives of South Asian

and African developing countries in the Indian Ocean region. The course, which had proved to be a very articulate and intensive example of capacity-building, received a very positive response from the participants.

72. In response to a request by one delegation, the Chairman of the Commission stated that the projected schedule would be given to the Commission for discussion at its next session and, if all the members were in agreement, it would be published as a Commission document.

73. The Meeting took note of the information provided by the Chairman of the Commission.

74. During the debates that took place under the agenda item entitled "Other matters," several delegations, in particular those whose submissions were being examined by the Commission, expressed their concern regarding the consistency of rule 52 of the Rules of Procedure of the Commission (CLCS/40) with the provisions of article 5 of annex II to the Convention. In their view, those provisions of the Convention did not empower the Commission alone to determine to which of its proceedings a coastal State may send its representatives. One representative of a State whose submission is under consideration by the Commission noted with appreciation the interaction between the Commission and his delegation, emphasizing that his statement was of a legal and technical nature and did not address an immediate practical concern. Another delegation added that in its experience, the Commission had applied its Rules of Procedure in a way which did not reflect the provisions of the Convention, stating that the Commission should not depart from the provisions of article 5 of annex II to the Convention.

75. Following a discussion on how to best proceed in that regard, it was agreed that the concerns of States parties expressed at the Meeting would be reflected in the present report and brought to the attention of the Commission, on the understanding that individual States were free to address separate communications on the issue to the Commission. It was further agreed that the sixteenth Meeting might revisit the matter if necessary.

76. The delegation of Cuba informed the Meeting that, in compliance with the relevant deadline, its Government was carrying out the scientific and technical work necessary to prepare a submission to the Commission under the oversight of a ministerial working group. The representative of Portugal announced that his country intended to make a submission to the Commission in 2009.

VII. Matters related to Article 319 of the United Nations Convention on the Law of the Sea

77. Under this agenda item, the fifteenth Meeting had before it the report of the Secretary-General on oceans and the law of the sea (A/60/63).

78. General statements were made on the report. Several delegations welcomed the accession of new States parties to the Convention as an indication of its universal acceptance. A number of issues addressed in the report were noted and commented upon. These included effects of and developments, on the Indian Ocean tsunami; the genuine link and the exercise of flag States responsibilities; reflagging and illegal, unregulated and unreported fishing; fishing subsidies; destructive fishing practices, including the issue of a moratorium on bottom trawling; the United Nations Fish Stocks Agreement Review Conference in 2006; the role of the port State; illegal migrants; marine scientific research and the work of the Advisory Body of Experts on the Law of the Sea of the Intergovernmental Oceanographic Commission of the United Nations Educational, Scientific and Cultural Organization; marine biological diversity, bioprospecting and the ad hoc working group to be convened in 2006; the Proliferation Security Initiative as a means of ensuring safety of navigation and its effects on innocent or transit passage; the Conference on Maritime Delimitation in the Caribbean and capacity-building.

79. Concerns were expressed regarding the continued deterioration of the conditions of seafarers and possible means for improvement; the vulnerability of small island developing States; and environmental risks associated with the maritime transport of radioactive material, which are being addressed through a new instrument adopted by the International Atomic Energy Agency. The important role of the institutions established under the Convention was also noted, as was the work of the Division and two members of the Commission in preparing the training manual to assist States with their submissions in accordance with article 76 of the Convention as well as the organization of training workshops in that regard by the Division. The issues of the future workload of the Commission and the fast-approaching deadline for submissions were also highlighted by some delegations.

80. However, at the fifteenth Meeting, divergent views continued to be expressed with regard to this agenda item.

81. The view that the Meeting of States Parties should not be limited to discussing administrative and budgetary matters, but that it should also consider substantive issues relating to the implementation of the Convention was reiterated by several delegations. According to those delegations, article 319, paragraph 3(a), of the Convention constituted the legal basis for the consideration of issues relating to the implementation of the Convention by the Meeting. The Meeting of States Parties represented the logical forum for discussions on all issues pertaining to the implementation of the Convention and could contribute to finding consensus on emerging issues. Such a role would increase the effectiveness and usefulness of the Meeting. It was suggested that discussions at the Meeting of States Parties would complement the work of the Consultative Process and the General Assembly

by providing a forum for exchange of information on State practice, promote cooperation and further debates on relevant issues of interest to States parties. One delegation pointed out that by assuming this role, States parties would be giving effect to their duty to cooperate under the Convention. Another delegation, however, stated that that should lead to the opening of the agenda item to a broader political discussion of substantive issues.

82. The view that the Meeting of States Parties did not have the competence to consider issues relating to the implementation of the Convention was also reiterated by some delegations. The relevant parts of the Convention that referred to the Meeting of States Parties were annexes II and VI, which required the Meeting to elect the members of the Commission on the Limits of the Continental Shelf and the judges of the International Tribunal for the Law of the Sea, as well as to determine the budget of the Tribunal. In the view of those delegations, article 319, therefore, should be interpreted as giving the Meeting of States Parties only an administrative and budgetary role. Furthermore, treaties that contained a mechanism to oversee their implementation explicitly provided for it, which was not the case in respect of the Convention. Furthermore, the negotiating history of the Convention had showed that a proposal to establish a mechanism to review common problems and address new uses of the sea had failed to attract the necessary support. It was also underlined that the General Assembly was the only inclusive forum in which to discuss substantive issues raised in the reports of the Secretary-General as well as the implementation of the Convention. The Consultative Process, on the other hand, had been established by the Assembly to facilitate its annual review of developments in ocean affairs. It was noted by one delegation that since the report of the Secretary-General was presented to the Meeting of States Parties for information on the practice of States and on issues of general nature with respect to the Convention, only the first five chapters of the report (A/60/63) qualified under that description.

83. The Meeting decided to retain the agenda item "Report of the Secretary-General under article 319 for the information of States parties on issues of a general nature, relevant to States parties that have arisen with respect to the United Nations Convention on the Law of the Sea" to be included on its agenda for the next Meeting of States Parties.

VIII. OTHER MATTERS

A. Statement by a Representative of a Non-Governmental Organization Regarding Seafarers

84. In accordance with rule 18, paragraph 4, of the Rules of Procedure, a representative of the Seamen's Church Institute was invited to address the

Meeting as an observer. In his statement, he recalled that the drafters of the Convention had recognized that preserving and protecting an orderly environment for the men and women who worked on the seas was crucial to protecting all of the other interests addressed in the Convention.

85. Noting the entry into force of the International Ship and Port Facility Security Code, he stated that restrictions on merchant mariners' access to shore leave and welfare activities had improved but that much remained to be done, referring, as an example, to the ratification of the 2003 International Labour Organization (ILO) Seafarers' Identity Documents Convention (No. 185), which would strengthen maritime security and improve seafarer's access to shore leave. He recalled that pirates continued to threaten merchant mariners and that they were becoming increasingly brazen and violent. He also raised concerns regarding the erosion of the rights of seafarers attempted by maritime employers and also to the growing exposure of seafarers to criminal sanctions for non-criminal activities.

86. He further noted that fishing activities continued to be one of the most dangerous occupations, with high casualty rates and few regulatory safety protections. He also voiced disappointment that the annual ILO conference had not adopted the new convention on fishers, which would have improved safety and working conditions for the people working in the global fishing sector.

87. In conclusion, he reiterated an earlier appeal to the Meeting of States Parties to place on its agenda, as a matter of priority, the protection of seafarers and a review of how States parties implemented the relevant provisions of the Convention.

B.   Duration of Meetings

88. Several delegations stated that, despite the need to elect seven members of the Tribunal, the fifteenth Meeting had lasted longer than necessary. They suggested that future meetings be limited to four or a maximum of five working days, even when elections were scheduled. Other delegations stated that, in the light of the discussions carried out under article 319, the sixteenth Meeting should be scheduled for a minimum of five working days.

C.   Small Island Developing States

89. Some delegations from small island developing States highlighted the importance of capacity-building, in particular for those States, and requested further assistance in that regard. They reiterated the importance

of the sustainable use of the marine environment and stated that they were encouraged by the Secretary-General's recognition of the central role of the oceans and seas in the historical, cultural and economic development of small island developing States. In that connection, they stated that they would like to see more attention paid to the need to avoid environmental destruction caused by deep-sea bottom trawling.

90. One delegation welcomed the fact that the Secretary-General's report contained proactive initiatives to better equip States to face the challenges of implementing the Convention and requested that part to be expanded. Appreciation was expressed for the fellowship programmes of the Division for Ocean Affairs and the Law of the Sea, such as the Hamilton Shirley Amerasinghe Memorial Fellowship on the Law of the Sea and the United Nations-Nippon Foundation Fellowship Programme, which facilitate capacity-building and human resources development. Member States that were in a position to do so were encouraged to contribute to the voluntary trust funds of the Division.

91. One delegation underlined the value of the Secretary-General's report to small island developing States that have limited capacity to gather, assess and act on the vast but scattered materials of interest in this area that are generated each year. It was further stated that the discussions at the Meeting provided a unique opportunity to understand, assist and cooperate in the special concerns of States parties relating to the implementation of the Convention and that States parties had special obligations to cooperate in good faith in the face of common and special difficulties. The forum could be used to build coalitions and plan strategies among States parties relevant to the work of the General Assembly meetings later in the year. Therefore, discussions on the substance of the report of the Secretary-General were necessary.

D. Statement by the President at the closure of the Fifteenth Meeting of States Parties

92. The President opened his statement by noting that 148 States parties had participated in the Meeting, as reported by the Credentials Committee. He then recalled agenda items and the programme of work adopted by the Meeting.

93. On behalf of the Meeting, he expressed appreciation to the President of the Tribunal, the Secretary-General of the International Seabed Authority and the Chairman of the Commission on the Limits of the Continental Shelf for the information they had provided on the work of their respective institutions. He also expressed appreciation to the members of the Bureau, the Credentials Committee and the tellers for various roles performed during the Meeting.

94. He drew the attention of States parties to the need to ensure that the assessed contributions to the Tribunal were paid in full and on time. Similarly, he recalled that the Secretary-General of the International Seabed Authority had also underlined the need to pay contributions to the Authority in full and on time. He also urged States whose experts served on the Commission on the Limits of the Continental Shelf to facilitate their participation in meetings of the Commission and invited all States parties to consider how to provide further support to the Commission, taking into account the information contained in the statement of its Chairman.

95. The President recalled that the election of seven members of the International Tribunal for the Law of the Sea had been held in accordance with article 4, paragraph 4, of the Statute of the Tribunal.

96. He noted that the observer for the Seamen's Church Institute had brought to the attention of the Meeting important issues concerning maritime security and the well-being of crews of ships. He expressed his confidence that representatives of States parties had taken note of the statement as appropriate and would report the concerns of the workers at sea to their Governments.

E.   Dates and Programme of Work for the Sixteenth Meeting of States Parties

97. The sixteenth Meeting of States Parties will take place in New York, probably in June 2006.

98. The sixteenth Meeting will have on its agenda, inter alia, the following items:

(a) Report of the International Tribunal for the Law of the Sea to the Meeting of States Parties for 2005 (rule 6 of the Rules of Procedure for Meetings of States Parties);

(b) Information reported by the Secretary-General of the International Seabed Authority;

(c) Information reported by the Chairman of the Commission on the Limits of the Continental Shelf;

(d) Financial statement of the International Tribunal for the Law of the Sea and report of the external auditors for the financial year 2004;

(e) Draft budget of the International Tribunal for the Law of the Sea for the biennium 2007–2008;

(f) Report of the Secretary-General under article 319 for the information of States parties on issues of a general nature, relevant to States parties, that have arisen with respect to the United Nations Convention on the Law of the Sea;

(g) Other matters.

It should be noted that the items may not necessarily follow the above sequence.

Directory of Ocean-Related Organizations

This directory was updated in September 2005. Additions and amendments are welcomed and should be sent by e-mail to ocean.yearbook@dal.ca.

1. GLOBAL INTERGOVERNMENTAL ORGANIZATIONS

Alliance of Small Island States (AOSIS)
Permanent Representative of the Republic
   of Mauritius to the United Nations
211 East 43rd Street, 15th floor
New York, NY, 10017, USA
Contact: Chairman
Tel: 1 212 949–0190
Fax: 1 212 697–3829
E-mail: mauritius@un.int
http://www.sidsnet.org/aosis/

Basel Convention on the Control of
   Transboundary Movements of Hazardous
   Wastes and Their Disposal (Basel
   Convention)
International Environment House
13–15, chemin des Anémones
CH-1219 Châtelaine, Geneva, Switzerland
Contact: Secretariat
Tel: 41 22 917 8218
Fax: 41 22 797 3454
E-mail: sbc@unep.ch
http://www.basel.int/

Commission on Science and Technology
   for Development
United Nations Conference on Trade and
   Development (UNCTAD)
8–14, avenue de la Paix
Palais des Nations, Building E
CH-1211 Geneva 10, Switzerland
Contact: Chief, Technology for
   Development Section
Tel: 41 22 917 5069
Fax: 41 22 907 0197
E-mail: stdev@unctad.org
http://www.unctad.org/stdev/

Commission on the Limits of the
   Continental Shelf
Division for Ocean Affairs and the Law of
   the Sea
Office of Legal Affairs
Room DC2–0450, United Nations
New York, NY, 10017, USA
Contact: Secretary
Tel: 1 212 963–3966
Fax: 1 212 963–5847
E-mail: doalos@un.org

http://www.un.org/Depts/los/clcs_new/
   clcs_home.htm

Convention on Biological Diversity
413 Saint Jacques Street, 8th floor, Office
   800
Montréal, QC, H2Y 1N9, Canada
Contact: Secretariat
Tel: 1 514 288–2220
Fax: 1 514 288–6588
E-mail: secretariat@biodiv.org
http://www.biodiv.org/

Convention on International Trade in
   Endangered Species of Wild Fauna and
   Flora (CITES)
International Environment House
13–15, chemin des Anémones
CH-1219 Châtelaine, Geneva, Switzerland
Contact: Secretariat
Tel: 41 22 917 8139/40
Fax: 41 22 797 3417
E-mail: cites@unep.ch
http://www.cites.org/

Convention on Migratory Species
United Nations Premises
Martin-Luther-King-Str. 8
D-53175 Bonn, Germany
Contact: UNEP/CMS Secretariat
Tel: 49 228 815 2401/02
Fax: 49 228 815 2449
E-mail: secretariat@cms.int
http://www.cms.int/

Division for Ocean Affairs and the Law of
   the Sea (DOALOS)
Office of Legal Affairs
United Nations
Room DC2–0450
New York, NY, 10017, USA
Contact: Director
Tel: 1 212 963–3962
Fax: 1 212 963–5847
E-mail: doalos@un.org
http://www.un.org/Depts/los/

Division for Sustainable Development
Department of Economic and Social Affairs
Two United Nations Plaza, Room
   DC2–2220
New York, NY, 10017, USA
Contact: Secretariat
Tel: 1 212 963–8102

Fax: 1 212 963–4260
http://www.un.org/esa/sustdev/

Food and Agriculture Organisation of the
    United Nations (FAO)
Viale delle Terme di Caracalla
I-00100 Rome, Italy
Contact: Director General
Tel: 39 06 5705 1
Fax: 39 06 5705 3152
E-mail: FAO-HQ@fao.org
http://www.fao.org/

Global Biodiversity Information Facility
    (GBIF)
Universitetsparken 15
DK-2100 Copenhagen, Denmark
Contact: Secretariat
Tel: 45 35 32 14 70
Fax: 45 35 32 14 80
E-mail: gbif@gbif.org
http://www.gbif.org/

Global Environment Facility (GEF)
1818 H Street NW
Washington, DC, 20433, USA
Contact: Secretariat
Tel: 1 202 473–0508
Fax: 1 202 522–3240 or 522–3245
E-mail: secretariat@TheGEF.org
http://www.gefweb.org/

Global International Waters Assessment
    (GIWA)
Kalmarsund Laboratory
Barlastgatan 1
SE- 391 82 Kalmar, Sweden
Tel: 46 480 44 73 53
Fax: 46 480 44 73 55
E-mail: info@giwa.net
http://www.giwa.net/

Global Programme of Action for the
    Protection of the Marine Environment
    from Land-based Activities (GPA)
GPA Coordinating Office, UNEP
PO Box 16227
NL-2500 BE, The Hague, The Netherlands
Contact: Coordinator
Tel: 31 70 311 4460
Fax: 31 70 345 6648
E-mail: gpa@unep.nl
http://www.gpa.unep.org/

GLOBEFISH
FAO, Fishery Industries Division
Viale delle Terme di Caracalla
I-00100 Rome, Italy
Contact: Coordinator
Tel: 39 06 5705 6244
Fax: 39 06 5705 5188
E-mail: globefish@fao.org
http://www.globefish.org/

Intergovernmental Oceanographic
    Commission (IOC)
UNESCO
1, rue Miollis
F-75015 Paris, France
Contact: Secretariat
Tel: 33 1 4568 3984
Fax: 33 1 4568 5812
E-mail: ioc.secretariat@unesco.org
http://ioc.unesco.org/

Intergovernmental Panel on Climate
    Change (IPCC)
c/o World Meteorological Organization
7 bis, avenue de la Paix
CP 2300
CH-1211 Geneva 2, Switzerland
Contact: Secretariat
Tel: 41 22 730 8208
Fax: 41 22 730 8025
E-mail: ipcc-sec@wmo.int
http://www.ipcc.ch/

International Continental Scientific Drilling
    Program
GeoForschungsZentrum Potsdam
ICDP-OSG
Telegrafenberg
D-14473 Potsdam, Germany
Contact: Research Coordinator
Tel: 49 331 288 1020
Fax: 49 331 288 1002
E-mail: ossing@gfz-potsdam.de
http://www.icdp-online.org/

International Coordination Group for the
    Tsunami Warning System in the Pacific
    (ICG/ITSU)
IOC
1, rue Miollis
F-75732 Paris Cedex 15, France
Contact: Secretariat
Tel: 33 1 4568 4046
Fax: 33 1 4568 5812

E-mail: p.pissierssens@unesco.org
http://ioc.unesco.org/itsu

International Court of Justice (ICJ)
Peace Palace
NL-2517 KJ, The Hague, The Netherlands
Tel: 31 70 302 2323
Fax: 31 70 364 9928
E-mail: information@icj-cij.org
http://www.icj-cij.org/

International Hydrographic Organisation
    (IHO)
4, Quai Antoine 1er
BP 445
MC-98011 Monaco Cedex, Principality of
    Monaco
Contact: IH Bureau
Tel: 377 93 10 81 00
Fax: 377 93 10 81 40
E-mail: info@ihb.mc
http://www.iho.shom.fr/

International Labour Organization (ILO)
4, route des Morillons
CH-1211, Geneva 22, Switzerland
Contact: Communications and Files Section
Tel: 41 22 799 6111
Fax: 41 22 798 8685
E-mail: ilo@ilo.org
http://www.ilo.org/

International Maritime Organisation (IMO)
4 Albert Embankment
London, SE1 7SR, United Kingdom
Contact: Secretary General
Tel: 44 207 735 7611
Fax: 44 207 587 3210
E-mail: info@imo.org
http://www.imo.org/

International Mobile Satellite Organisation
    (IMSO)
99 City Road
London, EC1Y 1AX, United Kingdom
Tel: 44 207 728 1249
Fax: 44 207 728 1172
http://www.imso.org/

International Oil Pollution Compensation
    Funds (IOPC)
Portland House, Stag Place, 23rd floor
London, SW1E 5PN, United Kingdom
Tel: 44 207 592 7100

Fax: 44 207 592 7111
E-mail: info@iopcfund.org
http://www.iopcfund.org/

International Satellite System for Search
    and Rescue (COSPAS/SARSAT)
700 de la Gauchetière West, Suite 2450
Montreal, QC, Canada H3B 5M2
Contact: Secretariat
Tel: 1 514 954–6713
E-mail: cospas_sarsat@imso.org
http://www.cospas-sarsat.org/

International Seabed Authority (ISA)
14–20 Port Royal Street
Kingston, Jamaica, West Indies
Contact: Secretary General
Tel: 1 876 922–9105
Fax. 1 876 922–0195
E-mail: postmaster2@isa.org.jm
http://www.isa.org.jm/

International Tribunal for the Law of the
    Sea
Am Internationalen Seegerichtshof #1
D-22609 Hamburg, Germany
Contact: President
Tel: 49 40 3560 70
Fax: 49 40 3560 7245
E-mail: itlos@itlos.org
http://www.itlos.org/

International Tsunami Information Center
    (ITIC)
National Weather Service
737 Bishop Street, Suite 2200
Honolulu, HI, 96813, USA
Contact: Director
Tel: 1 808 532–6422
Fax: 1 808 532–5576
E-mail: itic.tsunami@noaa.gov
http://www.prh.noaa.gov/itic/

International Whaling Commission
The Red House
135 Station Road, Impington
Cambridge, CB4 9NP, United Kingdom
Contact: Secretary
Tel: 44 1223 23 3971
Fax: 44 1223 23 2876
E-mail: secretariat@iwcoffice.org
http://www.iwcoffice.org/

IOC Science and Communication Centre
on Harmful Algae
University of Copenhagen
Oster Farimagsgade 2 D
DK-1353 Copenhagen K, Denmark
Contact: IOC Project Coordinator
Tel: 45 33 13 44 46
Fax: 45 33 13 44 47
E-mail: hab.ioc@unesco.org;
henrike@bot.ku.dk
http://ioc.unesco.org/hab/act5.htm

IOC-WMO-UNEP Committee for Global
Ocean Observing System (I-GOOS)
c/o Directeur Délégué pour l'Outre-Mer
Météo France
1, quai Branly
F-75340 Paris Cedex 07, France
Contact: Chair
Tel: 33 1 4556 7011
Fax: 33 1 4556 7005
E-mail: francois.gerard@meteo.fr
http://ioc.unesco.org/goos/i-goos.htm

Joint Group of Experts on the Scientific
Aspects of Marine Environmental
Protection (GESAMP)
c/o International Maritime Organisation
4 Albert Embankment
London, SE1 7SR, United Kingdom
Contact: Administrative Secretary
Tel: 44 207 587 3119
Fax: 44 207 587 3210
E-mail: ksekimizu@imo.org
http://gesamp.imo.org/

Joint IOC/IHO Guiding Committee for the
General Bathymetric Chart of the
Oceans (GEBCO)
National Oceanography Centre
Empress Dock
Southampton, SO14 3ZH, United Kingdom
Contact: Permanent Secretary
Tel: 44 23 8059 6564
Fax: 44 23 8059 3052
E-mail: bob.whitmarsh@noc.soton.ac.uk
http://www.ngdc.noaa.gov/mgg/gebco/

Joint WMO/IOC Technical Commission for
Oceanography and Marine Meteorology
(JCOMM)
Ocean Affairs Division
Applications Programme Department
WMO

7 bis, avenue de la Paix
CP 2300
CH-1211 Geneva 2, Switzerland
Tel: 41 22 730 8449
Fax: 41 22 730 8128
E-mail: oca@wmo.int
http://www.wmo.ch/

Office of the High Representative for the
Least Developed Countries, Landlocked
Developing Countries and Small Island
Developing States
United Nations
Room UH-900
New York, NY, 10017, USA
Tel: 1 212 963–7778
Fax: 1 917 367–3415
E-mail: ohrlls-unhq@un.org
http://www.un.org/special-rep/ohrlls/sid/
default.htm

Paris Memorandum of Understanding on
Port State Control
Ministry of Transport, Public Works and
Water Management
Transport and Water Management
Inspectorate
PO Box 20904
NL-2500 EX, The Hague, The Netherlands
Contact: Secretariat
Tel: 31 70 351 1508
Fax: 31 70 351 1599
http://www.parismou.org/

Ramsar Convention on Wetlands
28, rue Mauverney
CH-1196 Gland, Switzerland
Contact: Secretariat
Tel: 41 22 999 0170
Fax: 41 22 999 0169
E-mail: ramsar@ramsar.org
http://www.ramsar.org/

Stockholm Convention on Persistent
Organic Pollutants (POPs)
11–13, chemin des Anémones
CH-1219 Châtelaine, Geneva, Switzerland
Contact: Secretariat
Tel: 41 22 917 8191
Fax: 41 22 797 3460
E-mail: ssc@pops.int
http://www.pops.int/

Tokyo Memorandum of Understanding on
  Port State Control
Tomoecho Annex Building 6F, 3–8–26,
Toranomon Minato-ku
Tokyo 105–0001, Japan
Contact: Secretariat
Tel: 81 3 3433 0621
Fax: 81 3 3433 0624
E-mail: secretariat@tokyo-mou.org
http://www.tokyo-mou.org/

United Nations Commission on
  International Trade Law (UNCITRAL)
Vienna International Centre
PO Box 500
A-1400 Vienna, Austria
Contact: Secretariat
Tel: 43 1 26060 4060
Fax: 43 1 26060 5813
E-mail: uncitral@uncitral.org
http://www.uncitral.org/

United Nations Conference on Trade and
  Development (UNCTAD)
Palais des Nations
8–14, avenue de la Paix
CH-1211 Geneva 10, Switzerland
Contact: Office of the Secretary-General
Tel: 41 22 917 5809
Fax: 41 22 917 0051
E-mail: info@unctad.org
http://www.unctad.org/

United Nations Development Programme
  (UNDP)
One United Nations Plaza
New York, NY, 10017, USA
Tel: 1 212 906–5295
Fax: 1 212 906–5364
http://www.undp.org/

United Nations Environment Programme
  (UNEP)
UN Avenue, Gigiri
PO Box 30552, 00100
Nairobi, Kenya
Contact: Executive Director
Tel: 254 20 621234
Fax: 254 20 624489/90
E-mail: eisinfo@unep.org
http://www.unep.org/

United Nations Framework Convention on
  Climate Change (UNFCCC)
PO Box 260124
D-53153 Bonn, Germany
Contact: Secretariat
Tel: 49 228 815 1000
Fax: 49 228 815 1999
E-mail: secretariat@unfccc.int
http://unfccc.int/

United Nations Industrial Development
  Organization (UNIDO)
Vienna International Centre
PO Box 300
A-1400 Vienna, Austria
Tel: 43 1 26026 0
Fax: 43 1 26926 69
E-mail: unido@unido.org
http://www.unido.org/

World Meteorology Organisation (WMO)
WMO Building
7 bis, avenue de la Paix
CP 2300
CH-1211 Geneva 2, Switzerland
Tel: 41 22 730 8111
Fax: 41 22 733 8181
E-mail: wmo@wmo.int
http://www.wmo.int/

World Tourism Organization
Capitán Haya, 42
E-28020 Madrid, Spain
Tel: 34 91 5678 100
Fax: 34 91 5713 733
E-mail: omt@world-tourism.org
http://www.world-tourism.org/

World Trade Organization (WTO)
Centre William Rappard
154, rue de Lausanne
CH-1211 Geneva 21, Switzerland
Contact: Committee on Trade and
  Environment
Tel: 41 22 739 5111
Fax: 41 22 731 4206
E-mail: enquiries@wto.org
http://www.wto.org/

2. GLOBAL NONGOVERNMENTAL ORGANIZATIONS

Advisory Committee on Protection of the
Sea (ACOPS)
11 Dartmouth Street
London, SW1H 9BN, United Kingdom
Contact: Director
Tel: 44 207 799 3033
Fax: 44 207 799 2933
E-mail: terry.jones@acops.org
http://www.acops.org/

Association Internationale Villes et Ports
(International Association Cities and Ports -
AVIP/IACP)
45, rue Lord Kitchener
F-76600 Le Havre, France
Tel: 33 2 3542 7884
Fax: 33 2 3542 2194
http://www.aivp.com/

Baltic and International Maritime Council
(BIMCO)
Bagsvaerdvej 161
DK-2880 Bagsvaerd, Denmark
Contact: Secretary General
Tel: 45 44 36 68 00
Fax: 45 44 36 68 68
E-mail: mailbox@bimco.org
http://www.bimco.org/

Baltic Marine Biologists
c/o Department of Evolutionary Biology-
Plant Ecology
Uppsala University
Villavägen 14
SE-75236 Uppsala, Sweden
Contact: General Secretary
Tel: 46 18 471 28 85
Fax: 46 18 55 34 19
E-mail: pauli.snoeijs@cbc.uu.se
http://www.smf.su.se/bmb/

BirdLife International
Wellbrook Court
Girton Road
Cambridge CB3 0NA, United Kingdom
Tel: 44 1223 277 318
Fax: 44 1223 277 200
E-mail: birdlife@birdlife.org
http://www.birdlife.net/

Charles Darwin Foundation for the
Galapagos Islands
Av. 6 de Diciembre N 36–109 y Pasaje
California
PO Box 17–01–3891
Quito, Ecuador
Tel: 593 2224 4803
Fax: 593 2224 3935
E-mail: cdrs@fcdarwin.org.ec
http://www.darwinfoundation.org/

Comité International Radio-Maritime
(CIRM)
(International Association for Marine
Electronics Companies)
Southbank House
Black Prince Road
London, SE1 7SJ, United Kingdom
Contact: Secretary General
Tel: 44 207 587 1245
Fax: 44 207 587 1436
E-mail: secgen@cirm.org
http://www.cirm.org/

Comité Maritime International (CMI)
(International Maritime Committee)
Mechelsesteenweg, 196
B-2018 Antwerp, Belgium
Tel: 32 3 227 3526
Fax: 32 3 227 3528
E-mail: admini@cmi-imc.org
http://www.comitemaritime.org/

Commission for the Geological Map of the
World (CGMW)
77, rue Claude-Bernard
F-75005 Paris, France
Contact: Secretary General
Tel: 33 1 4707 2284
Fax: 33 1 4336 9518
http://www.ccgm.org/

Conservation International
1919 M Street, NW Suite 600
Washington, DC, 20036, USA
Tel: 1 202 912–1000
http://www.conservation.org/

Coral Cay Conservation
The Tower, 13th Floor
125 High Street, Colliers Wood
London, SW19 2JG, United Kingdom
Tel: 44 870 750 0668
Fax: 44 870 750 0667

E-mail: info@coralcay.org
http://www.coralcay.org/

Coral Reef Alliance (CORAL)
417 Montgomery Street, Suite 205
San Francisco, CA, 94105, USA
Tel: 1 415 834–0900
Fax: 1 415 834–0999
E-mail: info@coral.org
http://www.coral.org/

Det Norske Veritas
Veritasveien 1
N-1322 Hovik, Norway
Contact Head Office
Tel: 47 67 57 99 00
Fax: 47 57 67 99 11
E-mail: DNV.corporate@dnv.com
http://www.dnv.no/

Engineering Committee on Oceanic
  Resources (ECOR)
c/o Royal Institution of Naval Architects
10 Upper Belgrave Street
London SW1X 8BQ, United Kingdom
Contact: Executive Secretary
Tel: 44 20 7235 4622
Fax: 44 20 7259 5912
E-mail: hq@rina.org.uk
http://www.rina.org.uk/showarticle.pl?id=
  7634&n=

Federation of National Associations of Ship
  Brokers and Agents (FONASBA)
Ground Floor North
85 Gracechurch Street
London, EC3V 0AA, United Kingdom
Contact: Secretariat
Tel/Fax: 44 207 623 3113
E-mail: generalmanger@fonasba.com
http://www.fonasba.com/

Fish for All
PO Box 500, GPO
10670 Penang, Malaysia
Tel: 60 4 626 1606
Fax: 60 4 626 5530
E-mail: fishforall@cgiar.org
http://www.fishforall.org/

Global Aquaculture Alliance
5661 Telegraph Road, Suite 3A
St. Louis, MO, 63129, USA
Tel: 1 314 293–5500

Fax: 1 314 293–5525
E-mail: homeoffice@gaalliance.org
http://www.gaalliance.org/

Global Ocean Ecosystem Dynamics
  (GLOBEC)
Plymouth Marine Laboratory
Prospect Place
Plymouth, PL1 3DH, United Kingdom
Contact: International Project Office
Tel: 44 1752 63 3160
Fax: 44 1752 63 3101
E-mail: globec@pml.ac.uk
http://www.pml.ac.uk/globec/

Greenpeace International
Ottho Heldringstraat 5
NL-1066 AZ, Amsterdam, The Netherlands
Contact: Executive Director
Tel: 31 20 718 2000
Fax: 31 20 514 8151
E-mail:
supporter.services@int.greenpeace.org
http://www.greenpeace.org/

ICC Committee on Maritime Transport
c/o International Chamber of Commerce
38 cours Albert 1er
F-75008 Paris, France
Contact: Senior Policy Manager
Tel: 33 1 4953 2895
Fax: 33 1 4953 2859
E-mail: viviane.schiavi@iccwbo.org
http://www.iccwbo.org/home/transport/
  maritime_transport_committee.asp

ICC International Court of Arbitration
38 cours Albert 1er
F-75008 Paris, France
Contact: Secretariat
Tel: 33 1 4953 2905
Fax: 33 1 4953 2933
E-mail: arb@iccwbo.org
http://www.iccarbitration.org/

ICHCA International Limited (IIL)
85 Western Road, Suite 2
Romford, Essex, RM1 3LS, United
  Kingdom
Contact: International Secretariat
Tel: 44 1708 73 5295
Fax: 44 1708 73 5225
E-mail: info@ichcainternational.co.uk
http://www.ichcainternational.co.uk/

Institute for Fisheries Management and
Coastal Communities Development
(IFM)
North Sea Center
Willernoesvej 2
PO Box 104
DK-9850 Hirtshals, Denmark
Tel: 45 98 94 28 55
Fax: 45 98 94 42 68
E-mail: ifm@ifm.dk
http://www.ifm.dk/

Institute of Chartered Shipbrokers (ICS)
85 Gracechurch Street
London, EC3V 0AA, United Kingdom
Tel: 44 207 623 1111
Fax: 44 207 623 8118
E-mail: info@ics.org.uk
http://www.ics.org.uk/

Institute of International Container Lessors
(IICL)
555 Pleasantville Road, Suite 140 South
Briarcliff Manor, NY, 10510, USA
Tel: 1 914 747–9100
Fax: 1 914 747–4600
E-mail: info@iicl.org
http://www.iicl.org/

International Arctic Social Sciences
Association (IASSA)
Ilisimatusarfik
The University of Greenland
Postboks 279
DK-3900 Nuuk, Greenland
Contact: Secretariat
Tel: 299 324 566
Fax: 299 324 711
E-mail: iassa@Ilisimatusarfik.gl
http://www.iassa.gl/

International Association for Biological
Oceanography (IABO)
c/o Scottish Association for Marine Science
Dunstaffnage Marine Laboratory
Oban, Argyll, PA37 1QA, United Kingdom
Contact: President
Tel: 44 1631 559000
Fax: 44 1631 559001
E-mail: info@sams.ac.uk

International Association for the Physical
Sciences of the Ocean (IAPSO)
PO Box 820440

Vicksburg, MS, 39182–0440, USA
Contact: Secretary General
Tel: 1 601 636–1363
Fax: 1 601 629–9640
E-mail: camfield@vicksburg.com
http://www.olympus.net/IAPSO/

International Association for the Study of
Common Property (IASCP)
PO Box 2355
Gary, IN, 47409, USA
Contact: Executive Director
Tel: 1 219 980–1433
Fax: 1 219 980–2801
E-mail: iascp@indiana.edu
http://www.iascp.org/

International Association for the Study of
Maritime Mission (IASMM)
School of Education and Theology
York St. John College
Lord Mayor's Walk
York, YO31 7EX, United Kingdom
Contact: Secretariat
Tel: 44 1904 716861
Fax: 44 1904 612512
E-mail: s.friend@yorksj.ac.uk
http://www.freewebz.com/iasmm/

International Association of Aquaculture
Economics and Management (IAAEM)
Aquaculture Fisheries Centre
University of Arkansas at Pine Bluff
Mail Stop 4912
1200 N University Drive
Pine Bluff, AS, 71601, USA
Contact: President
E-mail: iaaem@uaex.edu
http://www.uaex.edu/cengle/IAAEM/

International Association of Aquatic and
Marine Science Libraries and
Information Centers (IAMSLIC)
c/o Harbor Branch Oceanographic
Institution Library
5600 US 1 North
Fort Pierce, FL, 34946, USA
Contact: Librarian
Tel: 1 772 465–2400 ext. 201
Fax: 1 772 465–2446
E-mail: metzger@hboi.edu
http://www.iamslic.org/

International Association of Classification
  Societies (IACS)
36 Broadway, 6th floor
London, SW1H 0BH, United Kingdom
Contact: Permanent Secretariat
Tel: 44 207 976 0660
Fax: 44 207 808 1100
E-mail: permsec@iacs.org.uk
http://www.iacs.org.uk/

International Association of Dredging
  Companies (IADC)
PO Box 80521
NL-2508 GM, The Hague, The Netherlands
Contact: Secretary General
Tel: 31 70 352 3334
Fax: 31 70 351 2654
E-mail: info@iadc-dredging.com
http://www.iadc-dredging.com/

International Association of Dry Cargo
  Shipowners (INTERCARGO)
9th floor, St. Clare House
30–33 Minories
London, EC3N 1DD, United Kingdom
Contact: Secretary General
Tel: 44 207 977 7030
Fax: 44 207 977 7031
E-mail: info@intercargo.org
http://www.intercargo.org/

International Association of Hydrogeologists
  (IAH)
PO Box 9
Kenilworth, CV8 1JG, United Kingdom
Contact: Secretary General
Tel: 44 1926 450677
Fax: 44 1926 856561
E-mail: iah@iah.org
http://www.iah.org/

International Association of Hydrological
  Sciences
c/o Ecole des Mines de Paris
35, rue Saint Honoré
F-77305 Fontainebleau, France
Contact: Secretary-General
Tel: 33 1 6469 4740
Fax: 33 1 6469 4703
E-mail: iahs@ensmp.fr
http://www.iahs.info/

International Association of Independent
  Tanker Owners (INTERTANKO)
Bogstadveien 27B
PO Box 5804
Majorstua
N-0308 Oslo, Norway
Tel: 47 22 12 26 40
Fax: 47 22 12 26 41
E-mail: oslo@intertanko.com
http://www.intertanko.com/

International Association of Institutes of
  Navigation (IAIN)
The Royal Institute of Navigation
1 Kensington Gore
London, SW7 2AT, United Kingdom
Contact: Secretary General
E-mail: ra.ed.smith@blueyonder.co.uk
http://www.iainav.org/

International Association of Marine Aids to
  Navigation and Lighthouse Authorities
  (IALA/AISM)
20 ter rue Schnapper
F-78100 St. Germain-en-Laye, France
Contact: Secretary General
Tel: 33 1 3451 7001
Fax: 33 1 3451 8205
E-mail: iala-aism@wanadoo.fr
http://www.iala-aism.org/

International Association of Maritime
  Economists (IAME)
Integrated Freight Systems Research Unit
Faculty of Science, Engineering and
  Technology
Victoria University
Melbourne, Australia
Contact: Permanent Secretariat
Tel: 61 03 9919 8097
Fax: 61 03 9919 8074
E-mail: secretariat@iame.info
http://www.staff.vu.edu.au/iame/

International Association of Maritime
  Universities
Kaiyo Senpaku Building, 6th floor
1–15–16, Toranomon
Minatu-ku, Tokyo 105–0001, Japan
Contact: Secretariat
Tel: 81 3 5251 4131
Fax: 81 3 5251 4134
E-mail: info@iamu-edu.org
http://www.iamu-edu.org/

International Association of
  Meiobenthologists
Department of Marine Science
Coastal Carolina University
PO Box 261954
Conway, SC 29528–6054, USA
Contact: Chair
http://www.meiofauna.org/

International Association of Ports and
  Harbours (IAPH)
7th floor, South Tower, New Pier
  Takeshiba
1–16–1 Kaigan
Minato-Ku, Tokyo, 105–0022, Japan
Contact: Secretary General
Tel: 81 3 5403 2770
Fax: 81 3 5403 7651
E-mail: info@iaphworldports.org
http://www.iaphworldports.org/

International Cable Protection Committee
  (ICPC)
PO Box 150
Lymington, SO41 6WA, United Kingdom
Contact: Secretary
Tel: 44 15 9068 1673
Fax: 44 87 0052 6049
E-mail: secretary@iscpc.org
http://www.iscpc.org/

International Cartographic Association
  (ICA)
c/o Faculty of GeoSciences
Utrecht University
PO Box 80115
NL-3508TC Utrecht, The Netherlands
Contact: Secretary General
Tel: 31 30 253 1373
Fax: 31 30 254 0604
E-mail: f.ormeling@geog.uu.nl
http://www.icaci.org/

International Centre for Coastal and Ocean
  Policy Studies (ICCOPS)
Via Piacenza 54
I-161138 Genova, Italy
Contact: Technical Secretariat
Tel: 39 10 846 8526
Fax: 39 10 835 7190
E-mail: info@iccops.it
http://www.iccops.it/

International Centre for Earth Tides
  (ICET)
Observatoire Royal de Belgique
Avenue Circulaire 3
B-1180 Brussels, Belgium
Contact: Executive Officer
Tel: 32 2 373 0248
Fax: 32 2 374 9822
E-mail: b.ducarme@oma.be
http://www.astro.oma.be/ICET/index.html

International Chamber of Shipping (ICS)
12 Carthusian Street
London, EC1M 6EZ, United Kingdom
Contact: Secretary General
Tel: 44 207 417 8844
Fax: 44 207 417 8877
E-mail: post@marisec.org
http://www.marisec.org/

International Christian Maritime Association
  (ICMA)
s-Gravendijkwal 64
NL-3014 EG, Rotterdam, The Netherlands
Contact: Secretariat
Tel: 31 10 225 1799
Fax: 31 10 225 0692
E-mail: icma@wanadoo.nl
http://www.icma.as/

International Collective in Support of
  Fishworkers (ICSF)
27 College Road
600 006 Chennai, India
Contact: Executive Secretary
Tel: 91 44 2827 5303
Fax: 91 44 2825 4457
E-mail: icsf@vsnl.com
http://www.icsf.net/

International Commission on Polar
  Meteorology (ICPM)
Ohio State University
1090 Carmack Road
Columbus, Ohio, 43210–1002, USA
Contact: President
E-mail: bromwich@polarmet1.mps.ohio-
  state.edu
http://www.antarctica.ac.uk/met/ICPM/

International Committee on Seafarers'
  Welfare (ICSW)
Forsyth House, 2nd floor
77 Claredon Road

Watford, Hertfordshire, WD17 1DS, United
Kingdom
Contact: Executive Secretary
Tel: 44 1923 22 2653
Fax: 44 1923 22 2663
E-mail: icsw@icsw.org.uk
http://www.seafarerswelfare.org/

International Congress of Maritime
Museums (ICMM)
PO 326
Mystic, CT, 06355, USA
Contact: Secretary General
E-mail: thomas@marinpro.com
http://www.icmmonline.org/

International Cooperative Fisheries
Organization (ICFO)
c/o National Federation of Fisheries
Co-operative Association (ZENGYOREN)
Co-operative building, 7th floor
1–1–12 Uchikanda, Chiyoda-ku
Tokyo 101 8503, Japan
Contact: Chairman
Tel: 81 3 3294 9617
Fax: 81 3 3294 9602
E-mail: icfo@zengyoren.jf-net.ne.jp
http://www.coop.org/icfo/

International Coral Reef Action Network
(ICRAN)
c/o UNEP-World Conservation Monitoring
Centre
219 Huntingdon Road
Cambridge, CB3 0DL, United Kingdom
Contact: ICRAN Director
Tel: 44 1223 27 7314, Ext. 287
Fax: 44 1223 27 7136
E-mail: icran@icran.org
http://www.icran.org/

International Coral Reef Initiative (ICRI)
c/o UNEP-World Conservation Monitoring
Centre
219 Huntingdon Road
Cambridge, CB3 0DL, United Kingdom
Contact: ICRI Secretariat
Tel: 44 1223 27 7314, Ext. 289
Fax: 44 1223 27 7136
E-mail: icri@unep-wcmc.org
http://www.icriforum.org/

International Council of Cruise Lines
(ICCL)
2111 Wilson Boulevard, 8th Floor
Arlington, VA, 22201, USA
Contact: President
Tel: 1 703 522–8463
Fax: 1 703 522–3811
E-mail: info@iccl.org
http://www.iccl.org/

International Council of Marine Industry
Associations (ICOMIA)
Marine House
Thorpe Lea Road
Egham, Surrey, TW20 8BF, United
Kingdom
Contact: Secretariat
Tel: 44 1784 22 3700
Fax: 44 1784 22 3705
http://www.icomia.com/

International Council of Scientific Unions
(ICSU)
51, boulevard de Montmorency
F-75016 Paris, France
Contact: Secretariat
Tel: 33 1 4525 0329
Fax: 33 1 4288 9431
E-mail: secretariat@icsu.org
http://www.icsu.org/

International Council on Monuments and
Sites (ICOMOS)
49–51, rue de la Fédération
F-75015 Paris, France
Contact: International Secretariat
Tel: 33 1 4567 6770
Fax: 33 1 4566 0622
E-mail: secretariat@icomos.org
http://www.international.icomos.org/

International Desalination Association
PO Box 387
Topsfield, MA, 01983, USA
Contact: Secretary General
Tel: 1 978 887–0410
Fax: 1 978 887–0411
E-mail: info@idadesal.org
http://www.idadesal.org/

International Dolphin Watch (IDW)
10 Melton Road
North Ferriby

East Yorkshire, HU14 3ET, United
   Kingdom
Contact: Secretary
Tel: 44 1482 63 2650
Fax: 44 1482 63 4914
E-mail: idw@talk21.com
http://www.idw.org/

International Ecotourism Society
733 15th Street NW, Suite 1000
Washington, DC, 20005, USA
Tel: 1 202 347–9203
Fax: 1 202 387–7915
E-mail: ecomail@ecotourism.org
http://www.ecotourism.org/

International Federation of Hydrographic
   Societies
PO Box 103
Plymouth, PL4 7YP, United Kingdom
Contact: Manager
Tel/Fax: 44 1752 22 3512
E-mail: helen@hydrographicsociety.org
http://www.hydrographicsociety.org/

International Federation of Shipmasters'
   Associations (IFSMA)
202 Lambeth Road
London, SE1 7JY, United Kingdom
Contact: General Secretary
Tel: 44 207 261 0450
Fax: 44 207 928 9030
E-mail: hq@ifsma.org
http://www.ifsma.org/

International Fishmeal and Fish Oil
   Organization (IFFO)
2 College Yard
Lower Dagnall Street
St. Albans, Hertfordshire, AL3 4PA, United
   Kingdom
Contact: Director General
Tel: 44 1727 84 2844
Fax: 44 1727 84 2866
E-mail: secretariat@iffo.org.uk
http://www.iffo.net/

International Game Fish Association (IGFA)
300 Gulf Stream Way
Dania Beach, FL, 33004, USA
Contact: President
Tel: 1 954 927–2628
Fax: 1 954 924–4299

E-mail: hq@igfa.org
http://www.igfa.org/

International Geographical Union (IGU)
c/o National Academy of Sciences
1710 Sixteenth Street W
Washington, DC, 20009, USA
Contact: Secretary-General
Tel: 1 202 352–6222
Fax: 1 202 234–2744
E-mail: rabler@aag.org
http://www.igu-net.org/uk/igu.html

International Glaciological Society
Scott Polar Research Institute
Lensfield Road
Cambridge, CB2 1ER, United Kingdom
Tel: 44 1223 355974
Fax: 44 1223 354 931
E-mail: igsoc@igsoc.org
http://www.igsoc.org/

International Hydrofoil Society
PO Box 51
Cabin John, MD, 20818, USA
Contact: President
E-mail: president@foils.org
http://www.foils.org/

International Institute for Sustainable
   Development (IISD)
161 Portage Avenue East, 6th Floor
Winnipeg, MB, R3B 0Y4, Canada
Contact: President & CEO
Tel: 1 204 958–7700
Fax: 1 204 958–7710
E-mail: info@iisd.ca
http://www.iisd.org/

International Institute of Fisheries
   Economics and Trade (IIFET)
Department of Agricultural and Resource
   Economics
Oregon State University
Corvallis, OR, 97331–3601, USA
Contact: Executive Director
Tel: 1 54137–1414
Fax: 1 54137–2563
E-mail: iifet@oregonstate.edu
http://www.orst.edu/Dept/IIFET/

International Loran Association
ILA Operations Center
741 Cathedral Pointe Lane

Santa Barbara, CA, 93111, USA
Tel: 1 805 967–8649
Fax: 1 805 967–8471
E-mail: ila@loran.org
http://www.loran.org/

International Marine Contractors
    Association (IMCA)
5 Lower Belgrave Street
London, SW1W 0NR, United Kingdom
Contact: Secretary
Tel: 44 207 824 5520
Fax: 44 207 824 5521
E-mail: imca@imca-int.com
http://www.imca-int.com/

International Marine Minerals Society
    (IMMS)
c/o Marine Minerals Technology Center
University of Hawaii
1000 Pope Road, MSB 303
Honolulu, HI, 96822, USA
Contact: Administrative Office
Tel: 1 808 956–6036
Fax: 1 808 956–9772
E-mail: imms@soest.hawaii.edu
http://www.soest.hawaii.edu/HURL/IMMS/

International Marinelife Alliance
PO Box 12648 Ortigas
Center Pasig City
Metro Manila 1600, The Philippines
Contact: International Headquarters
Tel: 632 637 8860
E-mail: vpratt@marine.org
http://www.marine.org/

International Maritime Bureau (IMB)
Maritime House
1 Linton Road
Barking, Essex, 1G11 8HG, United
    Kingdom
Contact: Director
Tel: 44 208 591 3000
Fax: 44 208 594 2833
E-mail: imb@icc-ccs.org.uk
http://www.icc-ccs.org/imb/overview.php

International Maritime Economic History
    Association
Maritime History Publications
Memorial University of Newfoundland
St. John's, NL, A1C 5S7, Canada

Contact: President
Tel: 1 709 737–2602
Fax: 1 709 737–8427
E-mail: zeles@otenet.gr
http://www.mun.ca/mhp/imeha.htm

International Maritime Pilots' Association
    (IMPA)
HQS Wellington
Temple Stairs
Victoria Embankment
London, WC2R 2PN, United Kingdom
Contact: Secretary General
Tel: 44 207 240 3973
Fax: 44 207 240 3518
E-mail: secgen@impahq.org
http://www.impahq.org/

International Navigation Association
    (PIANC/AICPN)
Graaf de Ferraris Building, 11th Floor
Boulevard du Roi Albert II, 20 - Box 3
B-1000 Brussels, Belgium
Contact: General Secretariat
Tel: 32 2 553 7161
Fax: 32 2 553 7155
E-mail: info@pianc-aipcn.org
http://www.pianc-aipcn.org/

International Network of Basin
    Organisations
21, rue de Madrid
F-75008 Paris, France
Contact: Permanent Technical Secretariat
Tel: 33 1 4490 8860
Fax: 33 1 4008 0145
E-mail: riob2@wanadoo.fr
http://www.inbo-news.org/

International Ocean Institute (IOI)
PO Box 3
Gzira, GZR 01, Malta
Contact: Executive Director
Tel: 356 21 346529
Fax: 356 21 346502
E-mail: ioihq@ioihq.org.mt
http://www.ioinst.org/

International Organization for
    Standardization (ISO)
1, rue de Varembé, Case postale 56
CH-1211 Geneva 20, Switzerland
Contact: Secretariat
Tel: 41 22 749 0111

Fax: 41 22 733 3430
http://www.iso.org/

International Organization of Masters,
    Mates and Pilots (IOMMP)
700 Maritime Boulevard
Linthicum Heights, MD, 21090–1941, USA
Contact: International Headquarters
Tel: 1 410 850–8700
Fax: 1 410 850–0973
E-mail: info@bridgedeck.org
http://www.iommp.org/

International Petroleum Industry
    Environmental Conservation Association
    (IPIECA)
209–215 Blackfriars Road, 5th floor
London, SE1 8NL, United Kingdom
Contact: Executive Secretary
Tel: 44 207 633 2388
Fax: 44 207 233 2389
E-mail: info@ipieca.org
http://www.ipieca.org/

International Salvage Union (ISU)
PO Box 32293
London, W5 1WZ, United Kingdom
Contact: Secretary General
Tel: 44 207 345 5122
Fax: 44 207 345 5722
E-mail: isu@randell.fsnet.co.uk
http://www.marine-salvage.com/

International Seaweed Association
Instituto de Biociências
Universidade de Sao Paulo
CP 11461
Sao Paulo, SP 05422–970, Brazil
Contact: Secretary
Tel: 55 11 3091 7630
Fax: 55 11 3091 7547
E-mail: pbixler@isinc.to
http://www.isaseaweed.org/

International Ship Managers' Association
    (ISMA)
PO Box 156
Horsham, RH13 9ZH, United Kingdom
Tel: 44 1403 733070
Fax: 44 1403 733165
E-mail: secretary@isma-london.org
http://www.isma-london.org/

International Ship Suppliers Association
    (ISSA)
The Baltic Exchange
St. Mary Avenue
London, EC3A 8BH, United Kingdom
Contact: Secretariat
Tel: 44 207 626 6236
Fax: 44 207 626 6234
E-mail: issa@dial.pipex.com
http://www.shipsupply.org/

International Shipping Federation (ISF)
12 Carthusian Street
London, EC1M 6EZ, United Kingdom
Contact: Secretary General
Tel: 44 207 417 8844
Fax: 44 207 417 8877
E-mail: isf@marisec.org
http://www.marisec.org/

International Society for Mangrove
    Ecosystems (ISME)
c/o Faculty of Agriculture
University of Ryukyus
Okinawa 903–0129, Japan
Contact: Secretariat
Tel: 81 98 895 6601
Fax: 81 98 895 6602
E-mail: isme@mangrove.or.jp
http://www.mangrove.or.jp/

International Society for Microbial Ecology
    (ISME)
c/o Kenes International
17, rue du Cendrier
PO Box 1726
CH-1211 Geneva, Switzerland
Tel: 41 22 908 0488
Fax: 41 22 732 2852
E-mail: info@microbes.org
http://www.microbes.org/

International Society for Reef Studies
    (ISRS)
School for Marine Sciences and
    Technology
University of Newcastle Upon Tyne
Newcastle Upon Tyne, NE1 7RU, United
    Kingdom
Contact: President
E-mail: n.polunin@ncl.ac.uk
http://www.fit.edu/isrs/

International Society of Acoustic Remote
Sensing of the Atmosphere and Oceans
(ISARS)
British Antarctic Survey
PSD Meteorology
High Cross, Madingley Road
Cambridge, CB3 0ET, United Kingdom
Contact: Chairperson
Tel: 44 1223 221489
E-mail: philip.s.anderson@bas.ac.uk
http://www.boku.ac.at/imp/isars/

International Society of Offshore and Polar
Engineers (ISOPE)
PO Box 189
Cupertino, CA, 95015–0189, USA
Tel: 1 650 254–1871
Fax: 1 650 254–2038
Contact: Executive Director
E-mail: info@isope.org
http://www.isope.org/

International Support Vessel Owners'
Association (ISOA)
12 Carthusian Street
London, EC1M 6EZ, United Kingdom
Tel: 44 207 417 8844
Fax: 44 207 417 8877
E-mail: isoa@marisec.org
http://www.marisec.org/marisec/marisec.htm

International Tanker Owners Pollution
Federation (ITOPF)
1 Oliver's Yard
55 City Road
London, EC1Y 1HQ, United Kingdom
Contact: Managing Director
Tel: 44 207 566 6999
Fax: 44 207 566 6950
E-mail: central@itopf.com
http://www.itopf.com/

International Transport Workers'
Federation (ITF)
ITF House
49–60 Borough Road
London, SE1 1DR, United Kingdom
Tel: 44 207 403 2733
Fax: 44 207 357 7871
E-mail: mail@itf.org.uk
http://www.itf.org.uk/

International Union of Biological Sciences
(IUBS)
51, boulevard de Montmorency
F-75016 Paris, France
Contact: Executive Director
Tel: 33 1 4525 0009
Fax: 33 1 4525 2029
E-mail: secretariat@iubs.org
http://www.iubs.org/

International Union of Geodesy and
Geophysics (IUGG)
c/o CIRES
Campus Box 216
University of Colorado
Boulder, CO, 80309, USA
Contact: Secretary General
Tel: 1 303 497–5147
Fax: 1 303 497–3645
E-mail: jjoselyn@cires.colorado.edu
http://www.iugg.org/

International Union of Geological Sciences
(IUGS)
Geological Survey of Canada
601 Booth Street
Ottawa, ON, K1A 0E8, Canada
Contact: Secretary General
Tel: 1 613 947–0333
Fax: 1 613 992–0190
E-mail: pbobrows@nrcan.gc.ca
http://www.iugs.org/

International Union of Marine Insurance
(IUMI)
C.F. Meyer-Strasse 14
PO Box 4288
CH-8022 Zurich, Switzerland
Contact: Secretary General
Tel: 41 44 208 2870
Fax: 41 44 208 2838
E-mail: mail@iumi.com
http://www.iumi.com/

International Water Association
Alliance House
12 Caxton Street
London, SW1H 0QS, United Kingdom
Contact: Executive Director
Tel: 44 207 654 5500
Fax: 44 207 654 5555
E-mail: water@iwahq.org.uk
http://www.iawhq.org.uk/

IUCN - The World Conservation Union
28, rue Mauverney
CH-1196 Gland, Switzerland
Contact: Director General
Tel: 41 22 999 0000
Fax: 41 22 999 0002
E-mail: achim.steiner@iucn.org
http://www.iucn.org/

IUGG Commission on Geophysical Risk
   and Sustainability
c/o Institute of Meteorology
University of Leipzig
Stephanstrasse 3
D-04103 Liepzig, Germany
Contact: Secretary General
Tel: 49 341 97 32 850
Fax: 49 341 97 32899
E-mail: tetzlaff@uni-leipzig.de
http://www.mitp.ru/georisk/

IWMC World Conservation Trust
3, Passage Montriond
CH-1006 Lausanne, Switzerland
Contact: Head Office
Tel/Fax: 41 21 616 5000
E-mail: iwmc@iwmc.org
http://www.iwmc.org/

Lloyd's Register of Shipping
71 Fenchurch Street
London, EC3M 4BS, United Kingdom
Contact: Enquiries
Tel: 44 207 709 9166
Fax: 44 207 488 4796
E-mail: lloydsreg@lr.org
http://www.lr.org/

Marine Aquarium Council
923 Nu'uanu Avenue
Honolulu, HI, 96817, USA
Contact: Executive Director
Tel: 1 808 550-8217
Fax: 1 808 550-8317
E-mail: info@aquariumcouncil.org
http://www.aquariumcouncil.org/

Marine Technology Society
5565 Sterrett Place, Suite 108
Columbia, MD, 21044, USA
Contact: Executive Director
Tel: 1 410 884-5330
Fax: 1 410 884-9060

E-mail: mtsdir@erols.com
http://www.mtsociety.org/

Multiport Ship Agencies Network
14 Greenwich Quay, 2nd Floor
Clarence Road
London, SE8 3EY, United Kingdom
Contact: Secretary General
Tel: 44 208 469 9188
Fax: 44 208 469 9189
E-mail: multiport@dial.pipex.com
http://www.multiport.org/

Ocean, Offshore and Arctic Engineering
   Division (OOAE)
American Society of Mechanical Engineers
c/o ASME International
Three Park Avenue
New York, NY, 10016-5990, USA
Contact: Chair
Tel: 1 973 882-1170
Fax: 1 212 591-7674
E-mail: chair@ooae.org
http://www.ooae.org/

Oceana
2501 M Street, NW
Washington, DC, 20037-1311, USA
Contact: Executive Director
Tel: 1 202 833-3900
Fax: 1 202 833-2070
E-mail: info@oceana.org
http://www.oceana.org/

Oil Companies International Marine Forum
   (OCIMF)
27 Queen Anne's Gate
London, SW1H 9BU, United Kingdom
Tel: 44 207 654 1200
Fax: 44 207 654 1205
E-mail: enquiries@ocimf.com
http://www.ocimf.com/

Organization of Islamic Shipowners (OISA)
PO Box 14900
Jeddah 21434, Saudi Arabia
Contact: Secretary General
Tel: 966 2 665 3379
Fax: 966 2 660 4920
E-mail: mail@oisaonline.com
http://www.oisaonline.com/

Ornamental Fish International
Fazantenkamp 5

NL-3607 CA, Maarssen, The Netherlands
Contact: Secretariat
Tel: 31 346 240141
Fax: 31 346 240161
E-mail: secretariat@ornamental-fish-int.org
http://www.ofish.org/

Partnership for Observation of the Global
    Oceans (POGO)
Bedford Institute of Oceanography
1 Challenger Drive
Dartmouth, NS, B2Y 4A2, Canada
Contact: Executive Director
Tel: 1 902 426–8044
Fax: 1 902 426–9388
E-mail: pogo@sio.ucsd.edu
http://www.ocean-partners.org/

Permanent Service for Mean Sea Level
Proudman Oceanographic Laboratory
Joseph Proudman Building
6 Brownlow Street
Liverpool, L3 5DA, United Kingdom
Contact: Director
Tel: 44 151 795 4800
Fax: 44 151 795 4801
E-mail: psmsl@pol.ac.uk
http://www.nbi.ac.uk/psmsl/

Pew Center on Global Climate Change
2101 Wilson Boulevard, Suite 550
Arlington, VA, 22201, USA
Tel: 1 703 516–4146
Fax: 1 703 841–1422
http://www.pewclimate.org/

Reef Ball Foundation
890 Hill Street
Athens, GA, 30606, USA
Contact: Executive Director
Tel: 1 770 752–0202
Fax: 1 770 360–1328
E-mail: kathy@reefball.com
http://www.reefball.org/

Reef Check
PO Box 1057
17575 Pacific Coast Highway
Pacific Palisades, CA, 90272–1057, USA
Tel: 1 310 272–1057
Fax: 1 310 230–2376
E-mail: rcinfo@reefcheck.org
http://www.reefcheck.org/

Scientific Committee on Antarctic Research
    (SCAR)
Scott Polar Research Institute
Lensfield Road
Cambridge, CB2 1ER, United Kingdom
Contact: Executive Secretary
Tel/Fax: 44 1223 33 6550
E-mail: info@scar.org
http://www.scar.org/

Scientific Committee on Oceanic Research
    (SCOR)
Department of Earth and Planetary
    Sciences
The Johns Hopkins University
Baltimore, MD, 21218, USA
Contact: Executive Director
Tel: 1 410 516–4070
Fax: 1 410 516–4019
E-mail: scor@jhu.edu
http://www.jhu.edu/scor/

Scientific Committee on Problems of the
    Environment (SCOPE)
51, boulevard de Montmorency
F-75016 Paris, France
Contact: Executive Director
Tel: 33 1 4525 0498
Fax: 33 1 4288 1466
E-mail: secretariat@icsu-scope.org
http://www.icsu-scope.org/

Seacology
2009 Hopkins Street
Berkeley, CA, 94707, USA
Tel: 1 510 599–3505
Fax: 1 510 599–3506
E-mail: islands@seacology.org
http://www.seacology.org/

Society for Underwater Technology (SUT)
80 Coleman Street
London, EC2R 5BJ, United Kingdom
Contact: Executive Secretary
Tel: 44 207 382 2601
Fax: 44 207 382 2684
E-mail: info@sut.org
http://www.sut.org.uk/

Society of Environmental Toxicology and
    Chemistry
1010 North 12th Avenue
Pensacola, FL, 32501–3370, USA

Contact: SETAC North America
Tel: 1 850 469–1500
Fax: 1 850 469–9778
E-mail: setac@setac.org
http://www.setac.org/

Society of International Gas Tanker and
Terminal Operators (SIGTTO)
17 St. Helen's Place
London, EC3A 6DG, United Kingdom
Contact: Secretariat
Tel: 44 207 628 1124
Fax: 44 207 628 3163
E-mail: secretariat@sigtto.org
http://www.sigtto.org/

Society of Naval Architects and Marine
Engineers (SNAME)
601 Pavonia Avenue
Jersey City, NJ, 07306, USA
Contact: Executive Director
Tel: 1 201 798–4800
Fax: 1 201 798–4975
E-mail: ccali-poutre@sname.org
http://www.sname.org/

The Nature Conservancy
4245 North Fairfax Drive, Suite 100
Arlington, VA, 22203–1606, USA
Tel: 1 703 841–5300
E-mail: comment@tnc.org
http://www.nature.org /

The Nautical Institute
202 Lambeth Road
London, SE1 7LQ, United Kingdom
Contact: Secretary
Tel: 44 207 928 1351
Fax: 44 207 401 2817
E-mail: sec@nautinst.org
http://www.nautinst.org/

UNEP World Conservation Monitoring
Centre
219 Huntingdon Road
Cambridge, CB3 0DL, United Kingdom
Tel: 44 1223 27 7722
Fax: 44 1223 27 7136
E-mail: info@unep-wcmc.org
http://www.unep-wcmc.org/

Wetlands International
International Coordination Unit
PO Box 471

NL-6700 AL, Wageningen, The Netherlands
Tel: 31 31 747 8854
Fax: 31 31 747 8850
E-mail: jane.madgwick@wetlands.org
http://www.wetlands.org/

World Aquaculture Society (WAS)
Louisiana State University
143 J.M. Parker Coliseum
Baton Rouge, LA, 70803, USA
Contact: Secretary
Tel: 1 225 388–3137
Fax: 1 225 388–3493
E-mail: wasmas@aol.com
http://www.was.org/

World Fish Center
PO Box 500, GPO 10670
Penang, Malaysia
Contact: Director General
Tel: 60 4 626 1606
Fax: 60 4 626 5530
E-mail: worldfishcenter@cgiar.org
http://www.worldfishcenter.org/

World Fisheries Trust
#204 1208 Wharf Street
Victoria, BC, V8W 3B9, Canada
Contact: President
Tel: 1 250 380–7585
Fax: 1 250 380–2621
E-mail: bharvey@worldfish.org
http://www.worldfish.org/

World Glacier Monitoring Service (WGMS)
Department of Geography
University of Zurich
Winterthurerstrasse 190
CH-8057 Zurich, Switzerland
Contact: Director
Tel: 41 44 635 5120
Fax: 41 44 635 6848
E-mail: wgms@geo.unizh.ch
http://www.geo.unizh.ch/wgms/

World Resources Institute
10 G Street, NE, Suite 800
Washington, DC, 20002, USA
Tel: 1 202 729–7600
Fax: 1 202 729–7610
E-mail: swilson@wri.org
http://www.wri.org/

World Ship Trust
3 the Green, Ketton
Stamford, Lincshire PE 3RA, United
Kingdom
Contact: Executive Secretary
Tel: 44 1780 721628
E-mail: worldship@lynnmallet.demon.co.uk
http://www.worldshiptrust.org/

World Travel and Tourism Council
1–2 Queen Victoria Terrace
Sovereign Court
London, E1W 3HA, United Kingdom
Tel: 44 207 481 8007
Fax: 44 207 488 1008
E-mail: enquiries@wttc.org
http://www.wttc.org/

World Watch Institute
1776 Massachusetts Avenue, NW
Washington, DC, 20036–1904, USA
Tel: 1 202 452–1999
Fax: 1 202 296–7365
E-mail: worldwatch@worldwatch.org
http://www.worldwatch.org/

World Wide Fund for Nature International
(WWF)
Avenue du Mont-Blanc
CH-1196, Gland, Switzerland
Contact: Director General
Tel: 41 22 364 9111
Fax: 41 22 364 8836
http://www.panda.org/

3. GLOBAL ACADEMIC ORGANIZATIONS

Chartered Institute of Logistics and
Transport (CILT)
11/12 Buckingham Gate
London, SW1 6LB, United Kingdom
Contact: Director General
E-mail: cyril@railnews.co.uk
http://www.cilt-international.com/

Circumpolar Universities Association
The Roald Amundsen Centre of Arctic
Research
University of Tromso
N-9037 Tromso, Norway

Contact: Secretariat
Tel: 47 77 64 52 40
Fax: 47 77 67 66 72
E-mail: frits.jensen@arctic.uit.no
http://www.arctic.uit.no/cua.html

Dangerous Goods Advisory Council
1100 H Street, NW, Suite 740
Washington, DC, 20005, USA
Tel: 1 202 289–4550
Fax: 1 202 289–4074
E-mail: info@dgac.org
http://www.dgac.org/

Institute of Marine Engineering, Science
and Technology (IMarEst)
80 Coleman Street
London, EC2R 5BJ, United Kingdom
Contact: Secretariat
Tel: 44 207 382 2600
Fax: 44 207 382 2670
E-mail: info@imarest.org
http://www.imarest.org/

InterMARGINS
Independent Administration Institution
Japan Agency for Marine-Earth Science and
Technology (JAMSTEC)
2–15 Natsushima-cho, Yokosuka
Kanagawa, 237–0061, Japan
E-mail: im-office@jamstec.org.jp
http://www.intermargins.org/

International Marine Simulator Forum
(IMSF)
c/o Tokyo University of Mercantile Marine
Etchujima 2–1–6 Koto-Ku
Tokyo 135, Japan
Contact: Chairman
Tel/Fax: 81 3 5245 7392
E-mail: kobayashi@e.kaiyodai.ac.jp
http://www.imsf.org/

International Maritime Law Institute
(IMLI)
PO Box 31
Msida MSD 01, Malta
Contact: Director
Tel: 356 21 319343
Fax: 356 21 343092
E-mail: info@imli.org
http://www.imli.org/

International Maritime Lecturers'
Association (IMLA)
PO Box 500
SE-201 24 Malmö, Sweden
Contact: President
Tel: 46 40 35 63 67
Fax: 46 40 12 48 27
E-mail: rajendra.prasad@wmu.se
http://www.wmu.se/imla/

InterRidge
Leibniz-Institut für Meereswissenschaften
Wischhofstrasse 1–3
D-24148 Kiel, Germany
Contact: Coordinator
Tel: 49 431 600 2133
Fax: 49 431 600 2924
E-mail: coordinator@interridge.org
http://interridge.org/

United Nations University (UNU)
53–70 Jingumae 5-chome Shibuya-ku
Tokyo 150 8925, Japan
Tel: 81 3 3499 2811
Fax: 81 3 3499 2828
E-mail: mbox@hq.unu.edu
http://www.unu.edu/

World Maritime University (WMU)
PO Box 500
SE-201 24 Malmö, Sweden
Tel: 46 40 35 63 00
Fax: 46 40 12 84 42
E-mail: info@wmu.se
http://www.wmu.se/

4. REGIONAL INTERGOVERNMENTAL ORGANIZATIONS

4.1 Africa

African Organisation of Cartography and
Remote Sensing (AOCRS)
(Organisation Africaine de Cartographie et
Télédétection–OACT)
BP 102
16040 Hussein Dey
Algiers, Algeria
Contact: Chairman
Tel: 213 21 23 1717
Fax: 213 21 23 3339

E-mail: oact@wissal.dz
http://www.oact.dz/

Bay of Bengal Programme Inter-
governmental Organization (BOBP-IGO)
91 Saint Mary's Road
Abhiramapuram, Chennai - 600 018
Tamil Nadu, India
Tel: 91 44 24936188
Fax: 91 44 24936102
E-mail: bobpysy@md2.vsnl.net.in
http://www.bobpigo.org/

Benguela Current Large Marine Ecosystem
(BCLME) Programme
PO Box 40728
Ausspanplatz
Windhoek, Namibia
Tel: 264 61 2053095
Fax: 264 61 246803
E-mail: cathy@bclmenamibia.org
http://www.bclme.org/

Benguela Environment Fisheries Interaction
and Training Programme (BENEFIT)
c/o NatMirc
Strand Street
P.O.Box 912
Swakopmund, Namibia
Contact: Secretariat
Tel: 264 64 4101162
Fax: 264 64 405913
E-mail: nsweijd@benguela.org
http://www.benefit.org.na/

Conférence Ministérielle sur la Coopération
Halieutique des Etats Africains Riverains
de l'Océan Atlantique (COMHAFAT)
(Ministerial Conference on Fisheries
Cooperation Among African States
Bordering the Atlantic Ocean)
Ministère des Pêches Maritimes
BP 476, Nouvelle cité administrative
Agdal, Rabat, Morocco
Contact: Permanent Secretariat
Tel: 212 37 68 83 28
Fax: 212 37 68 83 29
E-mail: comhafat@mpm.gov.ma
http://www.comhafat.org/

FAO Regional Office for Africa (RAF)
FAO Building #2
Gamel Abdul Nasser Road
PO Box 1628

Accra, Ghana
Tel: 233 21 675000
Fax: 233 21 668427
E-mail: fao-raf@field.fao.org
http://www.fao.org/world/regional/raf/
    index_en.htm

FAO Regional Office for the Near East
    (RNE)
11 El Eslah El Zerai Street Dokki
PO Box 2223
Cairo, Egypt
Tel: 20 2 331 6001
Fax: 20 2 749 5981
E-mail: fao-rne@fao.org
http://www.fao.org/world/Regional/RNE/
    index_en.htm

FAO Subregional Office for North Africa
    (SNEA)
PO Box 300
Tunis, Tunisia
Tel: 216 1 847 553
Fax: 216 1 791 859
E-mail: fao-snea@fao.org

FAO Subregional Office for Southern and
    East Africa
PO Box 3730
Harare, Zimbabwe
Tel: 263 4 791407
Fax: 263 4 703497
E-mail: fao-safr.registry@field.fao.org

Fishery Committee for Eastern Central
    Atlantic (CECAF)
c/o FAO Regional Office for Africa
PO Box 1628
Accra, Ghana
Contact: Assistant Director-General
Tel: 233 21 675000
Fax: 233 21 668427
E-mail: fao-raf@field.fao.org
http://www.fao.org/fi/body/rfb/CECAF/
    cecaf_home.html

Indian Ocean Commission
Q4, avenue Sir Guy Forget
Quatre Bornes, Mauritius
Contact: Secretary General
Tel: 230 425 1652
Fax: 230 425 2709
E-mail: coi7@intnet.mu
http://www.coi-info.org/

INFOPECHE (Intergovernmental
    Organization for Marketing Information
    and Technical Advisory Services for
    Fishery Products in Africa)
Tour C, 19éme étage, Cité Administrative
Abidjan 01, Côte d'Ivoire
Contact: Director
Tel: 225 2022 8980
Fax: 225 2021 8054
E-mail: infopech@africaonline.co.ci
http://www.globefish.org/index.php?id=1113

INFOSAMAK (Centre for Marketing
    Information & Advisory Services For
    Fishery Products in the Arab Region)
71, boulevard Rahal El Meskini
16243, Casablanca, Morocco
Tel: 212 22 540856
Fax: 212 22 540855
E-mail: info@infosamak.org
http://www.infosamak.org/

Intergovernmental Authority on
    Development (IGAD)
PO Box 2653
Djibouti, Republic of Djibouti
Contact: Secretariat
Tel: 253 354050
Fax: 253 356994
E-mail: igad@intnet.dj
http://www.igad.org/

IOC Regional Committee for the
    Cooperative Investigation in the North
    and Central Western Indian Ocean
    (IOCINCWIO)
PO Box 95832
Mombasa 80106, Kenya
Contact: IOCINCWIO Project Office
Tel: 254 11 472527
Fax: 254 11 475157
E-mail: m.odido@unesco.org
http://ioc.unesco.org/iocincwio/

Maritime Organisation of West and Central
    Africa (MOWCA)
BP V 257
Abidjan, Côte d'Ivoire
Contact: Secretary General
Tel: 225 0 22 7115
Fax: 225 0 21 6554
E-mail: info@mowca
http://www.marineafric.com/mowca/omaoc/
    default3.htm

Niger Basin Authority (NBA)
BP 729
Niamey, Niger
Contact: Executive Secretary
Tel: 227 723102
Fax: 227 724208
E-mail: abnsec@intnet.ne
http://www.abn.ne/

Port Management Association of West and
   Central Africa (PMAWCA/AGPAOC)
12 Park Lane
Box 1113
Apapa, Lagos, Nigeria
Contact: Secretary General
Tel: 234 1 587 4108
http://www.pmawca-agpaoc.org/home.asp

Port Management Association of Eastern
   and Southern Africa
   (PMAESA/AGPAEA)
PO Box 99209
Mombassa, Kenya
Contact: Secretary General
Tel: 254 11 223245
Fax: 254 11 228344
E-mail: pmaesa@africaonline.co.ke
http://www.pmaesa.org/

Regional Activity Centre for Specially
   Protected Areas (RAC/SPA)
Boulevard du Leader Yasser Arafat
PB 337 Cedex
1080 Tunis, Tunisia
Contact: Director
Tel: 216 71 206649
Fax: 216 71 206490
E-mail: car-asp@rac-spa.org
http://www.rac-spa.org/

Regional Co-ordinating Unit of the Eastern
   African Region (EAF/RCU)
PO Box 487, Promenade House
Victoria, Mahé, Seychelles
Tel: 248 67 0429
Fax: 248 61 0647
E-mail: rolph@seychelles.sc
http://www.unep.org/eastafrica/;
http://hq.unep.org/easternafrica/

Regional Fisheries Committee for the Gulf
   of Guinea (COREP)
BP 161
Libreville, Gabon

Contact: Secretariat
Fax: 241 73 7149
http://www.fao.org/fi/body/rfb/COREP/
   corep_home.htm

Southeast Atlantic Fisheries Organisation
   (SEAFO)
133 Nangolo Mbumba Drive
Walvisbay, Namibia
Contact: Interim Secretariat
Tel: 264 64 220387
Fax: 264 64 22039
E-mail: info@seafo.org
http://www.seafo.org/

Southern African Development Community
   (SADC)
SADC House
Private Bag 0095
Gaborone, Botswana
Tel: 267 3951 863
Fax: 267 3972 848
E-mail: registry@sadc.int
http://www.sadc.int/

Sub-Regional Commission on
   Fisheries–SRCF
(La Commission sous-régionale des
   pêches–CSRP)
Km 10 Boulevard de Centenaire de la
   Commune de Dakar-Senegal
BP 20505
Dakar, Senegal
Contact: Secretariat
Tel: 221 345580
Fax: 221 238720
http://www.csrp-afrique.org/

UNEP Regional Office for Africa (ROA)
PO Box 30552
Nairobi, Kenya
Contact: Director
Tel: 254 20 624292
Fax: 254 20 623928
E-mail: sekou.toure@unep.org
http://www.unep.org/roa/

West and Central African Regional
   Coordinating Unit (UNEP
   WACAF/RCU)
Abidjan Convention
c/o Ministry of Environment and Forests
20 BP 650
Abidjan 20, Côte d'Ivoire

Contact: Coordinator
Tel: 225 2021 1183
Fax: 225 2022 2050
E-mail: biodiv@africaonline.co.ci
http://www.unep.ch/seas/dumwacaf.html

4.2 The Americas

Caribbean Community (CARICOM)
PO Box 10827
Georgetown, Guyana
Contact: Secretariat
Tel: 592 222 0001–75
Fax: 592 222 0171
E-mail: info@caricom.org
http://www.caricom.org/

Caribbean Environment Programme
    Regional Coordinating Unit
    (CAR/RCU)
14–20 Port Royal Street
Kingston, Jamaica
Contact: Coordinator
Tel: 1 876 922–9267
Fax: 1 876 922–9292
E-mail: uneprcuja@cwjamaica.com
http://www.cep.unep.org/

Caribbean Regional Fisheries Mechanism
PO Box 642
Princess Marquaret Dr.
Belize City, Belize
Tel: 501 234 444
Fax: 501 234 446
http://www.caricom-fisheries.com/

Central American Commission on Maritime
    Transport
(Comisión Centroamericana de Transporte
    Marítimo–COCATRAM)
Contiguo a Mansíon de Teodolinda
Managua, Nicaragua
Contact: Executive Director
Tel: 505 222 2754
Fax: 505 222 2759
E-mail: drojas@cocatram.org.ni
http://www.cocatram.org.ni/

Centro del Agua del Trópico Húmedo
    para América Latina y el Caribe
    (CATHALAC)
(Water Center for the Humid Tropics of
    Latin America and the Caribbean)
801 City of Knowledge
Clayton, Panama
PO Box 873372
7 Panama
Contact: Director
Tel: 507 317 1640
Fax: 507 317 0127
E-mail: cathalac@cathalac.org
http://www.cathalac.org/

Comisión de Pesca Continental para
    América Latina (COPESCAL)
c/o FAO Regional Office for Latin
    America and the Caribbean
Avenida Dag Hammarskjold 3241
Vitacura
Casilla 10095
Santiago, Chile
Tel: 56 2 337 2100
Fax: 56 2 337 2101
E-mail: francisco.pereira@fao.org
http://www.fao.org/regional/lamerica/
    organos/copescal/default.htm

Comisión Permanente del Pacífico Sur
    (CPPS)
Edificio Inmaral, ler piso
Av. Carlos Julio Arosemena, Km. 3
Guayaquil, Ecuador
Contact: Secretariat
Tel: 593 4 2221 202
Fax: 593 4 2221 201
http://www.cpps-int.org/

FAO Regional Office for Latin America
    and the Caribbean
Avenida Dag Hammarskjold 3241
Vitacura
Santiago, Chile
Contact: Director General
Tel: 56 2 337 2100
Fax: 56 2 337 2101
E-mail: gustavo.gordillodeanda@fao.org
http://www.fao.org/Regional/LAmerica/

FAO Subregional Office for the Caribbean
    (SLAC)
PO Box 631-C

Bridgetown, Barbados
Tel: 1. 246 426 7110
Fax: 1 246 427 6075
E-mail: fao-slac@fao.org

Gulf of Maine Council on the Marine
  Environment
c/o naturesource communications
PO Box 3019
Boscawen, NH, 03303–3019, USA
Contact: Council Coordinator
Tel: 1 603 796–2615
Fax: 1 603 796–2600
E-mail: info@gulfofmaine.org
http://gulfofmaine.org/

INFOPESCA (Centro para los servicios de
  información y asesoramiento sobre la
  comercialización de los productos
  pesqueros en América Latina y el
  Caribe)
Julio Herrera y Obes 1296
Casilla de Correo 7086
CP 11200
Montevideo, Uruguay
Tel: 598 2 902 8701
Fax: 598 2 903 0501
E-mail: infopesca@infopesca.org
http://www.infopesca.org/

Inter-American Institute for Global Change
  Research (IAI)
Av. dos Astronautas, 1758
CEP 12227–010 Sao José dos Campos
Sao Paulo, Brazil
Contact: IAI Directorate
Tel: 55 12 3945 6855
Fax: 55 12 3941 4410
E-mail: iaibr@dir.iai.int
http://www.iai.int/

Inter-American Committee on Ports
Organization of American States
1889 F St., NW, 773
Washington, D.C., 20006, USA
Contact: Secretariat
Tel: 1 202 458–3871
Fax: 1 202 458–3517
E-mail: cip@oas.org
http://www.oas.org/cip/defaulte.asp

Inter-American Tropical Tuna Commission
  (IATTC)
8604 La Jolla Shores Drive

La Jolla, CA, 92037–1508, USA
Contact: Secretariat
Tel: 1 858 546–7100
Fax: 1 858 546–7133
E-mail: webmaster@iattc.org
http://www.iattc.org/

International Association of Fish and
  Wildlife Agencies (IAFWA)
444 North Capitol Street NW, Suite 725
Washington, DC, 20001, USA
Contact: Executive VP
Tel: 1 202 624–7890
Fax: 1 202 624–7891
E-mail: info@iafwa.org
http://www.iafwa.org/

International Pacific Halibut Commission
  (IPHC)
PO Box 95009
Seattle, WA, 98145–2009, USA
Contact: Director
Tel: 1 206 634–1838
Fax: 1 206 632–2983
E-mail: info@iphc.washington.edu
http://www.iphc.washington.edu/

IOC Sub-Commission for the Caribbean
  and Adjacent Regions (IOCARIBE)
Casa del Marqués de Valdehoyos
Calle de la Factoría No. 36–57
Apartado Aéreo 1108
Cartagena de Indias, Colombia
Contact: Senior Assistant
Tel: 57 5 664 6399
Fax: 57 5 660 0407
E-mail: iocaribe@col3.telecom.com.co;
iocaribe@cartagena.cetcol.net.co
http://ioc.unesco.org/regcar/

North American Commission for
  Environmental Cooperation (CEC)
393, rue St-Jacques Ouest, Suite 200
Montréal, QC, H2Y 1N9, Canada
Contact: Executive Director
Tel: 1 514 350–4300
Fax: 1 514 350–4314
E-mail: info@cec.org
http://www.cec.org/

North Atlantic Treaty Organization
  (NATO)
CCMAR HQ
Northwood Atlantic Building

Northwood Headquarters
Northwood
Middlesex, HA6 3HP, United Kingdom
Tel: 44 1923 84 3763
Fax: 44 1923 84 3762
E-mail: pio@manw.nato.int
http://www.manw.nato.int/

North East Pacific Action Plan
Secretario del Plan de Acción del Pacífico
    Nordeste
Central American Commission for Maritime
    Transport
Contiguo Hotel a Mansíon de Teodolinda
Bolonia
Artado Postal 2423
Managua, Nicaragua
Tel/Fax: 505 222 2759
E-mail: geinfrae@ibw.com.ni
http://www.unep.ch/seas/rshome.html

North Pacific Anadromous Fish
    Commission (NPAFC)
889 West Pender Street, Suite 502
Vancouver, BC, V6C 3B2, Canada
Contact: Executive Director
Tel: 1 604 775–5550
Fax: 1 604 775–5577
E-mail: secretariat@npafc.org
http://www.npafc.org/

North Pacific Marine Science Organization
    (PICES)
c/o Institute of Ocean Sciences
PO Box 6000
Sidney, BC, V6L 4B2, Canada
Contact: PICES Secretariat
Tel: 1 250 363–6366
Fax: 1 250 363–6827
E-mail: secretariat@pices.int
http://www.pices.int/

Northwest Atlantic Fisheries Organization
    (NAFO)
PO Box 638
Dartmouth, NS, B2Y 3Y9, Canada
Contact: Executive Secretary
Tel: 1 902 468–5590
Fax: 1 902 468–5538
E-mail: info@nafo.int
http://www.nafo.ca/

Organización Latinoamericana de
    Desarrollo Pesquero (OLDEPESCA)
(Latin American Organization for Fisheries
    Development)
Avenida Petit Thouars 115
Tercer piso
Lima 1, Peru
Contact: Executive Director
Tel: 511 330 8741
Fax: 511 332 2480
E-mail: asist@oldepesca.org
http://www.oldepesca.org/

Pacific Salmon Commission (PSC)
1155 Robson Street, Suite 600
Vancouver, BC, V6E 1B5, Canada
Contact: Executive Secretary
Tel: 1 604 684–8081
Fax: 1 604 666–8707
E-mail: info@psc.org
http://www.psc.org/

Programa Hidrológico Internacional (PHI)
Dr. Luis Piera 1992, 2o piso
11200 Montevideo, Uruguay
Tel: 598 2 413 2075
Fax: 598 2 413 2099
E-mail: phi@unesco.org.uy
http://www.unesco.org.uy/phi/

Protección Ambiental del Río de la Plata y
    su Frente Marítimo: Prevención y
    Control de la Contaminación y
    Restauración de Hábitats (FREPLATA)
''Casa de los Ximénez''
Rbla. 25 de Agosto de 1825 N° 580
CP 11.000
Montevideo, Uruguay
Contact: International Coordinator
Tel.: 598 2 916 66 35
Fax: 598 2 915 83 35
E-mail: peter.muck@freplata.org
http://www.freplata.org/

South East Pacific Action Plan
Comisión Permanente del Pacífico Sur
    (CPPS)
Av. Carlos Julio Arosemena, Km. 3.5
Guayaquil, Ecuador
Contact: Secretariat
Tel: 593 4 2221 202
Fax: 593 4 2221 201
E-mail: cpps_pse@cppsnet.org
http://www.cpps-int.org/

UNEP Regional Office for North America
(RONA)
1707 H Street NW, Suite 300
Washington, DC, 20006, USA
Tel: 1 202 785–0465
Fax: 1 202 785–2096
E-mail: info@rona.unep.org
http://www.rona.unep.org/

UNEP Regional Office for Latin America
and Caribbean
Boulevard de los Virreyes No. 155
Lomas de Virreyes
CP 11000
México, D.F. Mexico
Contact: Regional Representative
Tel: 52 55 5202 6394
Fax: 52 55 5202 0950
E-mail: enlace@pnuma.org
http://www.rolac.unep.mx/

United States Coast Guard International
Ice Patrol
1082 Shennecossett Road
Groton, CT, 06340–6095, USA
Contact: Commander
Tel: 1 860 441–2626
Fax: 1 860 441–2773
E-mail: iipcomms@rdc.uscg.mil
http://www.uscg.mil/lantarea/iip/

Western Central Atlantic Fisheries
Commission (WECAFC)
FAO Sub-Regional Office for Latin
American and the Caribbean
PO Box 631C
Bridgetown, Barbados
Tel: 1 246 426–7110
Fax: 1 246 426–7111
E-mail: bisessar.chakalall@fao.org
http://www.fao.org/fi/body/rfb/WECAFC/
wecafc_home.htm

4.3 Asia

ASEAN Council on Petroleum (ASCOPE)
International Business Unit, Petronas
Level 45, Tower 1, Petronas Twin Towers
50088 Kuala Lumpur, Malaysia
Tel: 60 3 233 14804
Fax: 60 3 233 11203

Contact: Secretariat
E-mail: ascopesec@petronas.com.my
http://www.ascope.com.my/

ASEAN Fisheries Federation (AFF)
Association of Southeast Asian Nations
(ASEAN)
ASEAN Secretariat Building, Ground floor
Jalan Sisingamangaraja 70A
Jakarta 12110, Indonesia
Tel: 62 21 723 7177
Fax: 62 21 725 7916
E-mail: aff@aseansec.org
http://www.aff.or.id/

ASEAN Ports Association
c/o Philippine Ports Authority
Marsman Building, South Harbour
Port Area, Manila, The Philippines
Contact: Permanent Secretariat
Tel: 632 301 9074
Fax: 632 527 4749
E-mail: aida@ppa.com.ph
http://www.ppa.com.ph/apa-
2002/default.htm

Asia-Pacific Economic Cooperation (APEC)
35 Heng Mui Keng Terrace
Singapore 119616
Contact: APEC Secretariat
Tel: 65 6775 6012
Fax: 65 6775 6023
E-mail: info@apec.org
http://www.apec.org/

Asia-Pacific Fisheries Commission (APFIC)
c/o FAO Regional Office for Asia and the
Pacific
39 Phra Atit Road
Bangkok 10200, Thailand
Contact: Secretariat
Tel: 66 2 697 4000
Fax: 66 2 280 0445
E-mail: fao-rap@fao.org
http://www.apfic.org/

Asian-African Legal Consultative
Organization (AALCO)
E-66 Vasant Marg
Vasant Vihar
New Delhi, 110057, India
Tel: 91 11 26152 251
Fax: 91 11 26152 041

E-mail: mail@aalco.org
http://www.aalco.org/

Coordinating Body on the Seas of East
 Asia (EAS/RCU)
United Nations Building, 2nd floor
Rajdamnern Nok Avenue
Bangkok 10200, Thailand
Contact: Regional Coordinating Unit
Tel: 66 2 288 1860
E-mail: kleesuwan@unescap.un.org
http://www.cobsea.org/

Coordinating Committee for Geoscience
 Programmes in East and Southeast Asia
 (CCOP)
Thai CC Tower, 24th Floor, Room 244–5
889 Sathorn Tai Road
Sathorn
Bangkok 10120, Thailand
Contact: Technical Secretariat
Tel: 66 2 672 3080–1
Fax: 66 2 672 3082
E-mail: ccopts@ccop.or.th
http://www.ccop.or.th/

FAO Regional Office for Asia and the
 Pacific (RAP)
39 Phra Atit Road
Bangkok 10200, Thailand
Tel: 66 2 697 4000
Fax: 66 2 697 4445
E-mail: fao-rap@fao.org
http://www.fao.org/world/regional/rap/

Indian Ocean Tuna Commission (IOTC)
PO Box 1011
Victoria, Mahé, Seychelles
Contact: Secretariat
Tel: 248 225 494
Fax: 248 224 364
E-mail: iotc.secretary@iotc.org
http://www.iotc.org/

INFOFISH (Intergovernmental Organization
 for Marketing Information and
 Technical Advisory Services for Fishery
 Products in the Asia and Pacific
 Region)
1st Floor, Wisma PKNS
Jalan Raja Laut
PO Box 10899
50728 Kuala Lumpur, Malaysia
Tel: 60 3 2691 4466

Fax: 60 3 2691 6804
E-mail: infish@po.jaring.my
http://www.infofish.org/

INFOYU
18 Maizidian Street, Room 203
Chaoyang District
Beijing 100026, People's Republic of China
Tel: 86 10 6419 5140
Fax: 86 10 6419 5141
E-mail: infoyu@agri.gov.cn
http://www.globefish.org/index.php?id=2074

IOC Sub-Commission for the Western
 Pacific (WESTPAC)
c/o National Research Council Thailand
196 Phaholyothin Road, Chatujak
Bangkok 10900, Thailand
Tel: 66 2 561 5118
Fax: 66 2 561 5119
E-mail: westpac@samart.co.th
http://ioc.unesco.org/westpac/

Mekong River Commission
Unit 18 Ban Sithane Neua
PO Box 6101
Sikhottabong District
Vientiane 01000, Lao PDR
Contact: Secretariat
Tel: 856 21 263 263
Fax: 856 21 263 264
E-mail: mrcs@mrcmekong.org
http://www.mrcmekong.org/

Network of Aquaculture Centres in Asia-
 Pacific (NACA)
Kasetsart Post Office Box 1040
Bangkok 10903, Thailand
Contact: Secretariat
Tel: 66 2 561 1728
Fax: 66 2 561 1727
E-mail: naca@enaca.org
http://www.enaca.org/

NOWPAP (Northwest Pacific Action Plan)
Special Monitoring and Coastal
 Environmental Assessment Regional
 Activity Centre (CEARAC)
Northwest Pacific Region Environmental
 Cooperation Centre
Tower111 Building, 6th floor
5–5 Ushijimashin-machi
Toyama City, 930–0856 Japan

Contact: Director
Tel: 81 7 6445 1571
Fax: 81 7 6445 1581
E-mail: webmaster@cearac.nowpap.org
http://cearac.nowpap.org/

NOWPAP Northwest Pacific Action Plan
Data and Information Network Regional
  Activity Center (DINRAC)
Room 909, 910, Building A,
No. 1 Yuhuinanlu, Chaoyang District
Beijing 100029, People's Republic of China
Tel: 86 10 8484 0869
Fax: 86 10 8463 0849
E-mail: dinrac@zhb.gov.cn
http://dinrac.nowpap.org/

NOWPAP Northwest Pacific Action Plan
  Marine Environmental Emergency and
  Preparedness Response Regional Activity
  Centre (MERRAC)
PO Box 23
Yusung, Taejon 305–600, Republic of Korea
Contact: Director
Tel: 82 42 868 7281
Fax: 82 42 868 7738
E-mail: nowpap@kriso.re.kr
http://merrac.nowpap.org/

NOWPAP Pollution Monitoring Activity
  Center (POMRAC)
7 Radio Street
690041 Vladivostok, Russian Federation
Tel/Fax: 7 4232 312 833
E-mail: pomrac@tig.dvo.ru
http://www.pomrac.dvo.ru/

Partnership in Environmental Management
  for the Seas of East Asia (PEMSEA)
PO Box 2502
Quezon City 1165, The Philippines
Tel: 632 920 2211
Fax: 632 926 9712
E-mail: info@pemsea.org
http://www.pemsea.org/

Regional Organisation for the Protection of
  the Marine Environment (ROPME)
PO Box 26388
13124 Safat, Kuwait
Contact: Executive Secretary
Tel: 965 531 2140
Fax: 965 533 5342

E-mail: ropme@quality.net
http://www.ropme.com/

Regional Organization for the Conservation
  of the Environment of the Red Sea
  and Gulf of Aden (PERSGA)
PO Box 53662
Jeddah, 21583, Saudi Arabia
Contact: Deputy Secretary-General
Tel: 966 2 657 3224
Fax: 966 2 652 1901
E-mail: information@persga.org
http://www.persga.org/

South Asia Co-operative Environment
  Programme (SACEP)
No. 10 Anderson Road
Colombo 5, Sri Lanka
Contact: Director
Tel: 941 125 89787
Fax: 941 125 89369
E-mail: info@sacep.org
http://www.sacep.org/

Southeast Asian Fisheries Development
  Center (SEAFDEC)
Suraswadi Building
PO Box 1046, Kasetsart Post Office
Bangkok 10903, Thailand
Tel: 66 2 940 6326
Fax: 66 2 940 6336
Contact: Secretariat
E-mail: sg@seafdec.org
http://www.seafdec.org/

UNDP/GEF Yellow Sea Project Project
  Management Office
c/o Korea Ocean Research Development
  Institute
1270 Sa2-dong Sangnok-gu, Ansan-si
  Gyeonggi-do, 426–744, Korea
Tel: 82–31–400–7829
Fax: 82–31–400–7826
E-mail: info@yslme.org
http://www.yslme.org/

UNEP Regional Office for Asia and the
  Pacific (UNEP/ROAP)
United Nations Building
Rajadamnern Nok Avenue
Bangkok 10200, Thailand
Contact: Regional Director
Tel: 66 2 288 1870–4
Fax: 66 2 280 3829

E-mail: shresthasu@un.org
http://www.roap.unep.org/

UNEP Regional Office for West Asia
    (UNEP/ROWA)
PO Box 10880
Manama, Bahrain
Contact: Regional Director
Tel: 973 826600
Fax: 973 825110/111
E-mail: www.uneprowa@unep.org.bh
http://www.unep.org.bh/

United Nations Economic and Social
    Commission for Asia and the Pacific
    (ESCAP)
United Nations Building
Rajadamnern Nok Avenue
Bangkok 10200, Thailand
Tel: 66 2 288 1234
Fax: 66 2 288 1000
http://www.unescap.org/

Western Indian Ocean Tuna Organization
    (WIOTO)
c/o Seychelles Fishing Authority
PO Box 449
Victoria, Mahé, Seychelles
Tel: 248 224 597
Fax: 248 224 508
E-mail: sfasez@seychelles.net
http://www.fao.org/fi/body/rfb/WIOTO/
    wioto_home.htm

4.4 Europe

Agreement on the Conservation of
    Cetaceans of the Black Sea
Mediterranean Sea and Contiguous Atlantic
    Area (ACCOBAMS)
Secrétariat Permanent
Jardins de l'UNESCO
Les Terrasses de Fontvieille
MC-98000 Monacco
Tel: 377 93 15 80 10
E-mail: mcvanklaveren@accobams.mc
http://www.accobams.mc/

Agreement on the Conservation of Small
    Cetaceans of the Baltic and North Seas
    (ASCOBANS)
United Nations Premises in Bonn

Martin-Luther-King-Str.
D-853175 Bonn, Germany
Tel.: 49 228 815 2416
Fax: 49 228 815 2440
http://www.ascobans.org/

Arc Manche
c/o West Sussex County Council
County Hall
Chichester, PO19 1RQ, United Kingdom
Contact: English Group Coordinator
Tel: 44 1243 77 7927
Fax: 44 1243 77 7697
E-mail: rachel.gapp@westsussex.gov.uk
http://www.arcmanche.com/intro.com

Baltic 21
PO Box 2010
SE-103 11 Stockholm, Sweden
Contact: Secretariat
Tel: 46 84 40 19 20
Fax: 46 84 40 19 44
E-mail: secretariat@baltic21.org
http://www.baltic21.org/

Baltic Environment Forum (BEF)
26/28 Peldu Street, Room 505
LV-1050, Riga, Latvia
Contact: Projects Manager
Tel: 371 7 357555
Fax: 371 7 507071
E-mail: bef@bef.lv
http://www.bef.lv/

Blue Plan Regional Activity Centre
    (BP/RAC)
15, rue Beethoven
Sophia Antipolis
F-06560 Valbonne, France
Contact: Director
Tel: 33 4 9238 7130
Fax: 33 4 9238 7131
E-mail: planbleu@planbleu.org
http://www.planbleu.org/

Bonn Agreement
New Court
48 Carey Street
London, WC2A 2JQ, United Kingdom
Contact: Secretary
Tel: 44 207 430 5200
Fax: 44 207 430 5225
E-mail: secretariat@bonnagreement.org
http://www.bonnagreement.org/

Central Commission for the Navigation of
the Rhine (CCNR)
2, place de la République
Palais du Rhin
F-67082 Strasbourg Cedex, France
Contact: President
Tel: 33 3 8852 2010
Fax: 33 3 8832 1072
E-mail: ccnr@ccr-zkr.org
http://www.ccr-zkr.org/

CIESM The Mediterranean Science
Commission
16 boulevard de Suisse
MC-98000 Monte Carlo, Principality of
Monaco
Contact: Director General
Tel: 377 93 30 38 79
Fax: 377 92 16 11 95
E-mail: fbriand@ciesm.org
http://www.ciesm.org/

Commission for the Protection of the
Black Sea Against Pollution
Dolmabahce Sarayi
11 Harekat Kosku
34353 Besiktas
Istanbul, Turkey
Contact: Permanent Secretariat
Tel: 90 212 227 9927
Fax: 90 212 227 9933
E-mail: bsc@blacksea-commission.org
http://www.blacksea-commission.org/

Committee on the Challenges of Modern
Society (CCMS)
North Atlantic Treaty Organization
(NATO)
Public Diplomacy Division
B-1110 Brussels, Belgium
Contact: CCMS Secretariat
Tel: 32 2 707 4850
Fax: 32 2 707 4232
E-mail: ccms@hq.nato.int
http://www.nato.int/ccms/

Commonwealth Secretariat
Marlborough House
Pall Mall
London, SW1Y 5HX, United Kingdom
Tel: 44 207 747 6500
Fax: 44 207 930 0827
E-mail: info@commonwealth.int
http://www.thecommonwealth.org/

Conference of Peripheral Maritime Regions
(Conférence des régions périphériques
maritimes d'Europe - CRPM)
6, rue Saint-Martin
F-35700 Rennes, France
Contact: Secretary General
Tel: 33 2 9935 4050
Fax: 33 2 9935 0919
E-mail: secretariat@crpm.org
http://www.crpm.org/

Council of Europe
Avenue de l'Europe
F-67075 Strasbourg Cedex, France
Tel: 33 3 8841 2033
Fax: 33 3 8841 2745
E-mail: infopoint@coe.int
http://www.coe.int/

Council of the Baltic Sea States (CBSS)
PO Box 2010
SE-103 11 Stockholm, Sweden
Contact: Secretariat
Tel: 46 84 40 19 20
Fax: 46 84 40 19 44
E-mail: cbss@cbss.st
http://www.cbss.st/

Danube Commission
(Donaukommission)
Benczúr utca 25
H-1068 Budapest, Hungary
Contact: General Director
Tel: 36 1 461 8010
Fax: 36 1 352 1839
E-mail: secretariat@danubecom-intern.org
http://www.danubecom-intern.org/

Directorate-General Energy and Transport
European Commission
DM28, office 2/36
B-1160 Brussels, Belgium
Contact: Maritime Transport Policy Unit
E-mail: tren-maritime-policy-and-
safety@cec.eu.int
http://europa.eu.int/comm/transport/
maritime/

Directorate-General for Environment
European Commission
Information Centre Office BU-9 01/11
200, rue de la Loi

B-1049 Brussels, Belgium
http://europa.eu.int/comm/environment/
index_en.htm

Directorate-General for Fisheries and
    Maritime Affairs
Communication and Information Unit
European Commission
200, rue de la Loi
B-1049 Brussels, Belgium
Fax: 32 2 299 30 40
http://europa.eu.int/comm/fisheries/
policy_en.htm

Environment Remote Sensing Regional
    Activity Centre (ERS/RAC)
Via F. Pecoraino, Z. I. Brancaccio
I-90124 Palermo, Italy
Tel: 39 06 85305147
Fax: 39 06 8542475
E-mail: info@ers-rac.org
http://www.ers-rac.org/

EUROFISH (ex-EASTFISH)
HC Andersens Boulevard 44–46
DK-1553 Copenhagen V, Denmark
Tel: 45 33 37 77 55
Fax: 45 33 37 77 56
E-mail: info@eurofish.dk
http://www.eurofish.dk/

European Environment Agency (EEA)
Kongens Nytorv 6
DK-1050 Copenhagen K, Denmark
Tel: 45 33 36 71 00
Fax: 45 33 36 71 99
http://www.eea.eu.int/

European Group on Ocean Stations
    (EGOS)
Christian Michelsen Research A/S
PO Box 6031 Postterminalen
N-5892 Bergen, Norway
Contact: Technical Secretariat
Tel: 47 55 57 42 64
Fax: 47 55 57 40 41
E-mail: anne.hageberg@cmr.no
http://www.meteo.shom.fr/egos/

European Inland Fisheries Commission
    (EIFAC)
Viale delle Terme di Caracalla
I-00100 Rome, Italy

Contact: Chair
Tel: 39 06 5705 2944
Fax: 39 06 5705 3020
E-mail: rudolf.mueller@eawag.ch
http://www.fao.org/fi/body/eifac/eifac.asp

European Maritime Safety Agency
12, rue de Genève
B-1049 Brussels, Belgium
Tel: 32 2 7020 200
Fax: 32 2 7020 210
E-mail: tren-emsa-info@cec.eu.int
http://www.emsa.eu.int/

European Sea Ports Organisation (ESPO)
Treurenberg 6
B 1000 Brussels, Belgium
Tel: 32 2 736 3463
Fax: 32 2 736 6325
E-mail: mail@espo.be
http://www.espo.be/

FAO Regional Office for Europe (REU)
Viale delle Terme di Caracalla
I-00100 Rome, Italy
Tel: 39 06 5705 4963
Fax: 39 06 5705 5634
E-mail: REUD-RegRep@fao.org
http://www.fao.org/world/Regional/REU/
index_en.htm

FAO Subregional Office for Central and
    Eastern Europe (SEUR)
Benczur utca 34
H-1068 Budapest, Hungary
Tel: 36 1 461 2000
Fax: 36 1 351 7029
E-mail: fao-seur@fao.org
http://www.fao.org/regional/SEUR/
index_en.htm

General Fisheries Commission for the
    Mediterranean (GFCM)
FAO
Viale delle Terme di Caracalla
I-00100 Rome, Italy
Contact: Secretary
Tel: 39 6 5705 6441
Fax: 39 6 5705 6500
E-mail: alain.bonzon@fao.org
http://www.faogfcm.org/

Helsinki Commission (HELCOM)
Baltic Marine Environment Protection
   Commission
Katajanokanlaituri 6 B
FI-00160 Helsinki, Finland
Contact: Information Secretary
Tel: 358 9 6220 2235
Fax: 358 9 6220 2239
E-mail: nikolay.vlasov@helcom.fi
http://www.helcom.fi/

Institute for Environment and Sustainability
Joint Research Centre of the European
   Commission
Via E. Fermi 1
I-21020 Ispra (VA), Italy
Contact: Inland and Marine Waters Unit
Tel: 39 0332 789111
Fax: 39 0332 789001
E-mail: ies-contact@jrc.it
http://ies.jrc.cec.eu.int/

International Baltic Sea Fishery Commission
   (IBSFC)
Hozastrasse 20
PL-00–528 Warsaw, Poland
Contact: Secretariat
Tel: 48 22 628 8647
Fax: 48 22 625 3372
E-mail: ibsfc@ibsfc.x.pl
http://www.ibsfc.org/

International Commission for the
   Conservation of Atlantic Tunas (ICCAT)
Calle Corazón de María, 8, 6th Floor
E-28002 Madrid, Spain
Contact: Executive Secretary
Tel: 34 91 4165 600
Fax: 34 91 4152 612
E-mail: info@iccat.int
http://www.iccat.es/

International Commission for the
   Protection of the Danube River
   (ICPDR)
Vienna International Center
D0412 PO Box 500
A-1400 Vienna, Austria
Contact: Permanent Secretariat
Tel: 43 1 26060 5738
Fax: 43 1 26060 5895
E-mail: icpdr@unvienna.org
http://www.icpdr.org/

International Commission for the
   Protection of the Rhine (ICPR)
Postfach 200253
D-56002 Koblenz, Germany
Tel: 49 261 94252 0
Fax: 49 261 94252 52
E-mail: sekretariat@iksr.de
http://www.iksr.org/

International Council for the Exploration
   of the Sea (ICES)
44–46 H.C. Andersens Boulevard
DK-1553 Copenhagen V, Denmark
Contact: General Secretary
Tel: 45 33 38 67 00
Fax: 45 33 93 42 15
E-mail: info@ices.dk
http://www.ices.dk/

Interreg IIIB–North Sea Programme
Jernbanegade 22
DK-8800 Viborg, Denmark
Tel: 45 87 27 19 99
Fax: 45 86 60 16 80
E-mail: info@interregnorthsea.org
http://www.interregnorthsea.org/

Joint Research Centre of the European
   Commission (JRC)
SDME 10/78
B-1049 Brussels, Belgium
Contact: Public Relations Unit
Tel: 32 2 295 7624
Fax: 32 2 295 6322
E-mail: jrc-info@cec.eu.int
http://www.jrc.cec.eu.int/

Kommunenes Internasjonale
   Miljoorganisasjon (KIMO)
Local Authorities International
   Environmental Organisation
Shetland Islands Council
Infrastructure Services
Grantfield
Lerwick, Shetland, ZE1 0NT, United
   Kingdom
Contact: Secretariat
Tel: 44 1595 74 4800
Fax: 44 1595 69 5887
E-mail: kimo@zetnet.co.uk
http://www.zetnet.co.uk/coms/kimo/

Marine Environment Laboratory
International Atomic Energy Agency

4, Quai Antoine Premier
MC-98000 Monaco, Principality of Monaco
Contact: Director
Tel: 377 97 97 72 72
Fax: 377 97 97 72 73
E-mail: mel@iaea.org
http://www.iaea.org/monaco/

Mediterranean Action Plan Regional
    Coordinating Unit (MEDU)
UNEP/Mediterranean Action Plan
48 Vassileos Konstantinou Avenue
GR-116 35 Athens, Greece
Tel: 30 210 727 3100
Fax: 30 210 725 3196
E-mail: unepmedu@unepmap.gr
http://www.unepmap.org/

NATO Undersea Research Centre (NURC)
Viale San Bartolomeo 400
I-19138 La Spezia, Italy
Tel: 39 0187 527 1
Fax: 39 0187 527 700
E-mail: webmaster@nurc.nato.int
http://www.saclantc.nato.int/

Nordic Council of Ministers
Store Strandstraede 18
DK-1255 Copenhagen K, Denmark
Contact: Senior Advisor for Fisheries Affairs
Tel: 45 33 96 02 55
Fax: 45 33 93 20 47
E-mail: ag@norden.org
http://www.norden.org/fisk/

North Atlantic Marine Mammal
    Commission (NAMMCO)
Polar Environmental Centre
N-99296 Tromso, Norway
Contact: General Secretary
Tel: 47 77 75 01 80
Fax: 47 77 75 01 81
E-mail: nammco-sec@nammco.no
http://www.nammco.no/

North Atlantic Salmon Conservation
    Organization (NASCO)
11 Rutland Square
Edinburgh, Scotland, EH1 2AS, United
    Kingdom
Tel: 44 131 228 2551
Fax: 44 131 228 4384
E-mail: hq@nasco.int
http://www.nasco.int/

North-East Atlantic Fisheries Commission
    (NEAFC)
22 Berners Street
London, W1T 3DY, United Kingdom
Tel: 44 207 631 0016
Fax: 44 207 636 9225
E-mail: info@neafc.org
http://www.neafc.org/

Organisation for Economic Cooperation
    and Development (OECD)
2, rue André Pascal
F-75775 Paris Cedex 16, France
Tel: 33 1 4524 8200
Fax: 33 1 4524 8500
E-mail: webmaster@oecd.org
http://www.oecd.org/

OSPAR Commission for the Protection of
    the Marine Environment of the North-
    East Atlantic
New Court
48 Carey Street
London, WC2A 2JQ, United Kingdom
Contact: Secretariat
Tel: 44 207 430 5200
Fax: 44 207 430 5225
E-mail: secretariat@ospar.org
http://www.ospar.org/

Priority Actions Programme Regional
    Activity Centre (PAP/RCU)
Kraj sv. Ivana 11
HR-21000 Split, Croatia
Contact: Director
Tel: 385 21 340 470
Fax: 385 21 340 490
E-mail: pap@gradst.hr
http://www.pap-thecoastcentre.org/

Regional Activity Centre for Cleaner
    Production (CP/RAC)
C/París, 184–3a planta
E-08036 Barcelona, Spain
Contact: Director
Tel: 34 93 4151 112
Fax: 34 93 2370 286
E-mail: cema@cema-sa.org
http://www.cema-sa.org/

Regional Marine Pollution Emergency
    Response Centre for the Mediterranean
    Sea (REMPEC)
Manoel Island

Gzira GZR 03, Malta
Contact: Director
Tel: 356 21 337296
Fax: 356 21 339951
E-mail: rempec@rempec.org
http://www.rempec.org/

Security Through Science Programme
Public Diplomacy Division
North Atlantic Treaty Organization
    (NATO)
Bd. Leopold III
B-1110 Brussels, Belgium
Tel: 32 2 707 4111
Fax: 32 2 707 4232
E-mail: science@hq.nato.int
http://www.nato.int/science/

The North Sea Conference
Ministry of Sustainable Development
SE-103 33 Stockholm, Sweden
Contact: North Sea Secretariat
Tel: 46 84 05 10 00
E-mail: registrator@sustainable.ministry.se
http://www.dep.no/md/nsc/

UNEP Regional Office for Europe (ROE)
International Environment House
11–13, chemin des Anémones, 6th floor
CH-1219 Châtelaine, Geneva, Switzerland
Tel: 41 22 917 8279
Fax: 41 22 917 8024
E-mail: roe@unep.ch
http://www.unep.ch/roe/

Vision and Strategies Around the Baltic
    Sea 2010 (VASAB 2010)
8–10 Dlugi Targ Strasse
PL-80 828 Gdansk, Poland
Contact: Secretariat
Tel: 48 58 301 8255
Fax: 48 58 305 4005
E-mail: infov@vasab.org.pl
http://www.vasab.org.pl/

4.5 Australia, New Zealand and Oceania

Commission for the Conservation of
    Southern Bluefin Tuna (CCSBT)
PO Box 37
Deakin West, ACT 2600, Australia

Contact: Secretariat
Tel: 61 2 6282 8396
Fax: 61 2 6282 8407
E-mail: bmacdonald@ccsbt.org
http://www.ccsbt.org/

FAO Subregional Office for Pacific Islands
    (SAPA)
FAO Private Mail Bag
Apia, Western Samoa
Tel: 685 22127
Fax: 685 22126
E-mail: fao-sapa@fao.org
http://www.fao.or.th/

Forum Fisheries Agency (FFA)
PO Box 629
Honiara, Solomon Islands
Contact: Director
Tel: 677 21124
Fax: 677 23995
E-mail: info@ffa.int
http://www.ffa.int/

Marine Resources Pacific Consortium
c/o University of Guam Marine Laboratory
UOG Station
Mangilao, GU, 96913, USA
Contact: Secretariat
Tel: 671 735 2175
Fax: 671 734 6767
http://www.uog.edu/marepac/

Pacific Islands Development Program
East-West Center
1601 East-West Road
Honolulu, HI, 96848–1601, USA
Tel: 1 808 944–7778
Fax: 1 808 944–7670
E-mail: pidp@EastWestCenter.org
http://www.eastwestcenter.org/pidp-ab.asp

Pacific Islands Forum Secretariat
    (ForumSec)
Private Mail Bag
Suva, Fiji
Contact: Secretary General
Tel: 679 331 2600
Fax: 679 330 1102
E-mail: info@forumsec.org.fj
http://www.forumsec.org.fj/

Pacific Islands Marine Resources
  Information System (PIMRIS)
Marine Studies Programme
University of the South Pacific, Lower
  Campus
PO Box 1168
Suva, Fiji
Contact: Coordinator
Tel: 679 331 2934
Fax: 679 323 1426
E-mail: pimris@usp.ac.fj
http://www.usp.ac.fj/library/collection/
  pimris/pimris.htm

Secretariat of the Pacific Community (SPC)
BP D5
98848 Noumea Cedex, New Caledonia
Contact: Secretary General
Tel: 687 262000
Fax: 687 263818
E-mail: spc@spc.int
http://www.spc.org.nc/

South Pacific Applied Geoscience
  Commission (SOPAC)
Private Mail Bag GPO
Suva, Fiji
Contact: Director
Tel: 679 338 1377
Fax: 679 337 0040
E-mail: director@sopac.org
http://www.sopac.org.fj/

South Pacific Regional Environment
  Programme (SPREP)
PO Box 240
Apia, Western Samoa
Contact: Director
Tel: 685 21929
Fax: 685 20231
E-mail: sprep@sprep.org
http://www.sprep.org.ws/

South Pacific Tourism Organization
  (SPTO)
PO Box 13119
Suva, Fiji
Tel: 679 330 4177
Fax: 679 330 1995
http://www.spto.org/

Te Ohu Kaimoana (Treaty of Waitangi
  Commission)
PO Box 3277

Wellington, New Zealand
Tel: 64 4 931 9500
Fax: 64 4 931 9508
E-mail: tari@teohu.maori.nz
http://teohu.maori.nz/

Western and Central Pacific Fisheries
  Commission
PO Box 2356
Kolonia
Pohnpei, Federated States of Micronesia
E-mail: wcpfc@mail.fm
http://www.wcpfc.org/

4.6   Polar Regions

Arctic Council
c/o Ministry of Foreign Affairs of Russia
32/34 Smolenskaya-Sennaya pl.
119200, Moscow G-200, Russian Federation
Contact: Secretariat
Tel: 95 244 1239
Fax: 95 244 2559
E-mail: ac-chair@mid.ru
http://www.arctic-council.org/

Arctic Council Indigenous Peoples'
  Secretariat
Strandgade 91, 4th floor
P.O. Box 2151
DK-1016 Copenhagen K, Denmark
Tel. 45 32 83 37 90
Fax 45 32 83 37 91
E-mail: ips@ghsdk.dk
http://www.arcticpeoples.org/

Arctic Monitoring and Assessment
  Programme (AMAP)
Stromsveien 96
PO Box 8100 Dep.
N-0032 Oslo, Norway
Contact: Secretariat
Tel: 47 23 24 16 32
Fax: 47 22 67 67 06
E-mail: amap@amap.no
http://www.amap.no/

Barents Euro-Arctic Council
c/o Ministry for Foreign Affairs
PO Box 176

FIN-00171 Helsinki, Finland
Tel: 358 9 16005
Fax: 358 9 1605 6120
E-mail: anneli.puura_markala@formin.fi
  http://www.beac.st/

Commission for the Conservation of
  Antarctic Marine Living Resources
  (CCAMLR)
PO Box 213
North Hobart, TAS 7002, Australia
Tel: 61 3 6231 0366
Fax: 61 3 6234 9965
E-mail: ccamlr@ccamlr.org
http://www.ccamlr.org/

Conservation of Arctic Flora and Fauna
  (CAFF)
Hafnarstraeti 97
IS-600 Akureyri, Iceland
Contact: International Secretariat
Tel: 354 462 3350
Fax: 354 462 3390
E-mail: caff@caff.is
http://www.caff.is/

International Arctic Science Committee
  (IASC)
Middelthunsgate 29
PO Box 5156 Majorstua
N-0302 Oslo, Norway
Contact: Secretariat
Tel: 47 22 95 99 00
Fax: 47 22 95 99 01
E-mail: iasc@iasc.no
http://www.iasc.no/

Protection of the Arctic Marine
  Environment (PAME)
Hafnarstraeti 97
IS-600 Akureyri, Iceland
Contact: International Secretariat
Tel: 354 461 1355
Fax: 354 462 3390
E-mail: pame@pame.is
http://www.pame.is/

The Northern Forum
716 W 4th Avenue, Suite 100
Anchorage, AK, 99501, USA
Contact: Secretariat
Tel: 1 907 561–3280
Fax: 1 907 561 6645

E-mail: NForum@northernforum.org
http://www.northernforum.org/

5. REGIONAL NONGOVERNMENTAL ORGANIZATIONS

5.1 Africa

African Association of Remote Sensing of
  the Environment (AARSE)
Geological Survey Division, ITC
PO Box 6
NL-7500AA Enschede, The Netherlands
Contact: Secretary General
Tel: 31 53 4874 279
Fax: 31 53 4874 336
E-mail: woldai@itc.nl
http://www.itc.nl/~aarse/

Centre for Documentation, Research and
  Training on the South West Indian
  Ocean
(Centre de Documentation de Recherche
  et de Formation
  Indianocéaniques–CEDREFI)
PO Box 91
Rose-Hill, Republic of Mauritius
Contact: Director
Tel: 230 465 5036
Fax: 230 465 1422
E-mail: pynee@mu.refer.org

Empowerment for African Sustainable
  Development
14 Antrim Road
PO Box 165
Green Point
Cape Town 8051, South Africa
Contact: Director
Tel: 27 21 434 6012
Fax: 27 21 434 6134
E-mail: dave@icon.co.za
http://easd.org.za/

Fondation International du Banc d'Arguin
La Tour du valat
Le Sambuc
F-13 200 Arles, France
Tel: 33 4 9097 2926
Fax: 33 4 9097 2242
E-mail: fiba@tourduvalat.org
http://www.tourduvalat.org/news_806.htm

International Ocean Institute–Eastern Africa
Kenya Marine and Fisheries Research
    Institute (KMFRI)
Box 81651
Mombasa, Kenya
Contact: Director
Tel: 254 41 475151
Fax: 254 41 475157
E-mail: ioi-ea@kmfri.co.ke
http://www.ioinst.org/

International Ocean Institute–Senegal
Centre de Recherches Oceanographiques
    de Dakar-Thiaroye (CRODT)
BP 2241
Dakar, Senegal
Contact: Director
Tel: 221 6 834 8014
Fax: 221 8 893 0479
E-mail: dtoure-sn@yahoo.fr;
dthiam@crodt.isra.sn

International Ocean Institute–Southern
    Africa
Botany Department
University of the Western Cape
P Bag X17
Bellville 7535, Cape Town 8000, South
    Africa
Contact: Director
Tel: 27 21 959 2594
Fax: 27 21 959 1213
E-mail: kprochazka@uwc.ac.za
http://www.ioisa.org.za/

International Ocean Institute–Western
    Africa
Nigerian Institute for Oceans and Marine
    Research
Wilmot Point Road
PMB 12729
Victoria Island, Lagos, Nigeria
Tel: 234 1 261 7530
Fax: 234 1 261 7385
E-mail: niomr@linkserve.com.ng

Nature Seychelles
PO Box 1310
The Centre for Nature and Environment
Roche Caiman
Mahé, Seychelles
Tel: 248 60 1100
Fax: 248 60 1102

E-mail: nature@seychelles.net
http://www.nature.org.sc/

South African Association for Marine
    Biological Research
PO Box 10712
Marine Parade
Durban 4056, South Africa
Contact: Director
Tel: 27 31 328 8222
Fax: 27 31 328 8188
E-mail: info@saambr.org.za
http://www.saambr.org.za/

South African Network for Coastal and
    Oceanic Research (SANCOR)
c/o National Research Foundation
PO Box 2600
Pretoria 0001, South Africa
Contact: Secretariat
Tel: 27 12 481 4107
Fax: 27 12 481 4005
E-mail: annette@nrf.ac.za
http://www.botany.uwc.ac.za/sancor/

Western Indian Ocean Marine Science
    Association (WIOMSA)
PO Box 3298
Zanzibar, Tanzania
Tel: 255 24 223 3472
Fax: 255 24 223 3852
E-mail: secretary@wiomsa.org
http://www.wiomsa.org/

5.2 The Americas

Alliance for Marine Remote Sensing
    Association
PO Box 36044 RPO Spring Garden Road
Halifax, NS, B3J 3S9, Canada
Contact: Systems Manager
Tel: 1 902 820–2377
Fax: 1 902 820–2379
E-mail: amrsadmin@waterobserver.org
http://www.waterobserver.org/

American Association of Petroleum
    Geologists
PO Box 979
Tulsa, OK, 74101–0979, USA
Contact: Executive Director
Tel: 1 918 584–2555
Fax: 1 918 560–2694

E-mail: postmaster@aapg.org
http://www.aapg.org/

American Association of Port Authorities
1010 Duke Street
Alexandria, VA, 22314–3589, USA
Tel: 1 703 684–5700
Fax: 1 703 684–6321
E-mail: info@aapa-ports.org
http://www.aapa-ports.org/

American Boat and Yacht Council (ABYC)
3069 Solomons Island Road
Edgewater, MD, 21037, USA
Contact: President
Tel: 1 410 956–1050
Fax: 1 410 956–2737
http://www.abycinc.org/

American Bureau of Shipping (ABS)
ABS Plaza
16855 Northchase Drive
Houston, TX, 77060, USA
Contact: President
Tel: 1 281 877–6000
Fax: 1 281 877–5803
E-mail: abs-worldhq@eagle.org
http://www.eagle.org/

American Cetacean Society
PO Box 1391
San Pedro, CA, 90733–1391, USA
Tel: 1 310 548–6279
Fax: 1 310 548–6950
E-mail: info@acsonline.org
http://www.acsonline.org/

American Fisheries Society
5410 Grosvenor Lane
Bethesda, MD, 20814, USA
Contact: Executive Director
Tel: 1 301 897–8616
Fax: 1 301 897–8096
E-mail: main@fisheries.org
http://www.fisheries.org/

American Geological Institute (AGI)
4220 King Street
Alexandria, VA, 22302–1502, USA
Tel: 1 703 379–2480
Fax: 1 703 379–7563
http://www.agiweb.org/

American Geophysical Union (AGU)
2000 Florida Avenue NW
Washington, DC, 20009–1277, USA
Contact: Executive Director
Tel: 1 202 462–6900
Fax: 1 202 328–0566
E-mail: fspilhaus@agu.org
http://www.agu.org/

American Institute of Fishery Research
   Biologists (AIFRB)
c/o 6211 Madawaska Road
Bethesda, MD, 20816, USA
Contact: President
Tel: 1 301 320–5202
E-mail: DickSchaef@aol.com
http://www.aifrb.org/

American Littoral Society
Building 18
Sandy Hook
Highlands, NJ, 07732, USA
Contact: Executive Director
Tel: 1 732 291–0055
http://www.littoralsociety.org/

American Marinelife Dealers Association
c/o Creatures Featured
PO Box 1052
Madison, FL, 32341, USA
Contact: President
   E-mail: president@amdareef.com
http://www.amdareef.com/

American Meteorological Society
45 Beacon Street
Boston, MA, 02108–3693, USA
Contact: Executive Director
Tel: 1 617 227–2425
Fax: 1 617 742–8718
E-mail: amsinfo@ametsoc.org
http://www.ametsoc.org/

American Petroleum Institute
1220 L Street, NW
Washington, DC 20005–4070
Tel: 1 202 682–8000
http://www.api.org /

American Polar Society
PO Box 300
Searsport, ME, 04974, USA

Contact: Membership Center
E-mail: ampolars@prexar.com
http://www.oaedks.net/amerpolr.html

American Shore and Beach Preservation
    Association (ASBPA)
5460 Beaujolais Lane
Fort Myers, FL, 33919, USA
Contact: Executive Director
Tel: 1 239 489–2616
E-mail: ExDir@asbpa.org
http://www.asbpa.org/

American Society of International Law
    (ASIL)
2223 Massachusetts Avenue, NW
Washington, DC, 20008, USA
Tel: 1 202 939–6000
Fax: 1 202 797–7133
E-mail: outreach@asil.org
http://www.asil.org/

American Society of Limnology and
    Oceanography
5400 Bosque Boulevard, Suite 680
Waco, TX, 76710–4446, USA
Contact: Business Office
Tel: 1 254 399–9635
Fax: 1 254 776–3767
E-mail: business@aslo.org
http://www.aslo.org/

American Society of Naval Engineers
    (ASNE)
1452 Duke Street
Alexandria, VA, 22314–3458, USA
Tel: 1 703 836–6727
Fax: 1 703 836–7491
E-mail: asnehq@navalengineers.org
http://www.navalengineers.org/

American Sportfishing Association
225 Reinekers Lane, Suite 420
Alexandria, VA, 22314, USA
Contact: President
Tel: 1 703 519–9691
Fax: 1 703 519–1872
E-mail: info@asafishing.org
http://www.asafishing.org/

American Waterways Operators
801 North Quincy Street, Suite 200
Arlington, VA, 22203, USA
Tel: 1 703 841–9300

Fax: 1 703 841–0389
E-mail: aburns@vesselalliance.com
http://www.americanwaterways.com/

Aquacultural Engineering Society
c/o Freshwater Institute
PO Box 1889
Shepherdstown, WV, 25443, USA
Contact: Secretary/Treasurer
Tel: 1 304 876–2815
E-mail: b.vinci@freshwaterinstitute.org
http://www.aesweb.org/

Aquaculture Association of Canada
16 Lobster Lane
St. Andrews, NB, E3B 3T6, Canada
Tel: 1 506 529–4766
Fax: 1 506 529–4609
E-mail: aac@mar.dfo-mpo.gc.ca
http://www.aquacultureassociation.ca/

Association of Canadian Port Authorities
85 Albert Street, Suite 1502
Ottawa, ON, K1P 6A4, Canada
Contact: Executive Director
Tel: 1 613 232–2036
Fax: 1 613 232–9554
E-mail: leroux@acpa-ports.net
http://www.acpa-ports.net/

Association of Coastal Engineers
c/o Applied Technology and Management
    Inc.
2770 NW 43rd Street, Suite B
Gainesville, FL, 32606, USA
Contact: Executive Secretary
E-mail: pehrman@appliedtm.com
http://www.coastalengineers.org/

Association of Environmental and Resource
    Economists (AERE)
1616 P Street NW, Room 510
Washington, DC, 20036, USA
Contact: Secretary
Tel: 1 202 328–5077
Fax: 1 202 939–3460
E-mail: voigt@rff.org
http://www.aere.org/

Association of Pacific Ports
6208 N. Ensign Street
Portland, OR, 97217, USA
Contact: Executive Director
Tel: 1 503 285–5742

Fax: 1 503 285–6350
E-mail: dave@pacificports.org
http://www.associationofpacificports.com/

Association of Ship Brokers and Agents-USA, Inc.
510 Sylvan Avenue, Suite 201
Englewood Cliffs, NJ, 07632, USA
Contact: Executive Director
Tel: 1 201 569–2882
Fax: 1 201 569–9082
E-mail: asba@asba.org
http://www.asba.org/

Atlantic Coastal Zone Information Steering Committee (ACZISC)
Dalhousie University
1226 LeMarchant Street
Halifax, NS, B3H 3P7, Canada
Contact: Secretariat
Tel: 1 902 494–1977
Fax: 1 902 494–1334
E-mail: aczisc@dal.ca
http://www.dal.ca/aczisc/

Atlantic Salmon Federation
PO Box 5200
St. Andrews, NB, E5B 3S8, Canada
Contact: President
Tel: 1 506 529–1033
Fax: 1 506 529–4438
E-mail: asfweb@nbnet.nb.ca
http://www.asf.ca/

Bay of Fundy Ecosystem Partnership (BoFEP)
Acadia Centre for Estuarine Research
Acadia University
PO Box 115
Wolfville, NS, B4P 2R6, Canada
Contact: Secretariat
Tel: 1 902 585–1113
Fax: 1 902 585–1054
E-mail: secretariat@bofep.org
http://www.bofep.org/

Canadian Aquaculture Industry Alliance (CAIA)
907–75 Albert Street
Ottawa, ON, K1P 5E7, Canada
Tel: 1 613 239–0612
Fax: 1 613 239–0619
E-mail: caiaoffice@aquaculture.ca
http://www.aquaculture.ca/

Canadian Centre for Fisheries Innovation
PO Box 4920
St. John's, NL, A1C 5R3, Canada
Tel: 1 709 778–0517
Fax: 1 709 778–0516
E-mail: ccfi@mi.mun.ca
http://www.ccfi.ca/

Canadian Centre for Marine Communications
155 Ridge Road
PO Box 8454
St. John's, NL, A1B 3N9 Canada
Tel: 1 709 579–4872
Fax: 1 709 579–0495
E-mail: ccmc@ccmc.nf.ca
http://www.ccmc.nf.ca/

Canadian Coastal Science and Engineering Association (CCSEA)
c/o National Water Research Institute
Canada Centre for Inland Waters
PO Box 5050
867 Lakeshore Road
Burlington, ON, L7R 4A6, Canada
Tel: 1 905 335–4736
Fax: 1 905 336–4420
E-mail: michael.skafel@ec.gc.ca
http://www.cciw.ca/ccsea/intro.html

Canadian Council of Professional Fish Harvesters (CCPFH/CCPP)
102 Bank Street, Suite 202
Ottawa, ON, K1P 5N4, Canada
Contact: Executive Director
Tel: 1 613 235–3474
Fax: 1 613 231–4313
E-mail: fish@ccpfh-ccpp.org
http://www.ccpfh-ccpp.org/

Canadian International Freight Forwarders' Association (CIFFA)
1243 Islington Avenue, Suite 706
Toronto, ON, M8X 1Y9, Canada
Tel: 1 416 234–5100
Fax: 1 416 234–5152
E-mail: info@ciffa.com
http://www.ciffa.com/

Canadian Maritime Law Association
1155 René Levesque Blvd West, Suite 4000
Montreal, QC, H3B 3V2, Canada
Tel: 1 416 923_0333
Fax: 1 416 944_9020

E-mail: cmla@cmla.org
http://www.cmla.org/

Canadian Nautical Research Society
   (CNRS)
PO Box 511
Kingston, ON, K7L 4W5, Canada
Contact: President
E-mail: jp@post.queensu.ca
http://www.marmus.ca/cnrs/

Canadian Shipowners Association
350 Sparks Street, Suite 705
Ottawa, ON, K1R 7S8, Canada
Tel: 1 613 232–3539
Fax: 1 613 232–6211
E-mail: csa@shipowners.ca
http://www.shipowners.ca/

Canadian Water and Wastewater
   Association
11–1010 Polytek Street
Ottawa, ON, K1J 9H9, Canada
Contact: Executive Director
Tel: 1 613 747–0524
Fax: 1 613 747–0523
E-mail: admin@cwwa.ca
http://www.cwwa.ca/

Canadian Wildlife Federation
350 Michael Cowpland Drive
Kanata, ON, K2M 2W1, Canada
Tel: 1 613 599–9594
Fax: 1 613 599–4428
E-mail: info@cwf-fcf.org
http://www.cwf-fcf.org/

Caribbean Alliance for Sustainable Tourism
1000 Ponce de Leon Avenue, 5th Floor
San Juan, Puerto Rico, 00907, USA
Tel: 1 787 725–9139
Fax: 1 787 725–9108
E-mail: cast@caribbeanhotels.org
http://www.cha-cast.com/

Caribbean Conservation Association (CCA)
The Garrison
St. Michael, Barbados
Contact: Executive Director
Tel: 1 246 426–5373
Fax: 1 246 429–8483
E-mail: execdirector@ccanet.net
http://www.caribbeanconservation.org/

Caribbean Natural Resources Institute
   (CANARI)
Fernandes Industrial Centre
Administrative Building
Eastern Main Road
Laventille, Trinidad
Tel: 1 868 626–6062
Fax: 1 868 626–1788
E-mail: info@canari.org
http://www.canari.org/

CEDAM International
1 Fox Road
Croton-on-Hudson, NY, 10520, USA
Contact: President
Tel: 1 914 271–5365
Fax: 1 914 271–4723
E-mail: cedam@bestweb.net
http://www.cedam.org/

Center for Coastal Studies
PO Box 1036
Provincetown, MA, 02657, USA
Contact: Executive Director
Tel: 1 508 487–3622
Fax: 1 508 487–4495
E-mail: ccs@coastalstudies.org
http://www.coastalstudies.org/

Center for International Environmental
   Law (CIEL)
1367 Connecticut Avenue, NW, Suite 300
Washington, DC, 20036, USA
Contact: Executive Director
Tel: 1 202 785–8700
Fax: 1 202 785–8701
E-mail: info@ciel.org
http://www.ciel.org/

Centro Ecuatoriano de Derecho Ambiental
   (CEDA)
(Center for Environmental Law)
Eloy Alfaro N3Z-650 y Rusia, 3rd Floor
Quito, Ecuador
Tel: 593 2 223 1410
Fax: 593 2 223 8609
E-mail: info@ceda.org.ec
http://www.ceda.org.ec/

Chamber of Maritime Commerce
350 Sparks Street, Suite 704A
Ottawa, ON, K1R 7S8, Canada
Tel: 1 613 233–8779
Fax: 1 613 233–3743

E-mail: info@cmc-ccm.com
http://www.cmc-ccm.com/

Chamber of Shipping
100 - 1111 West Hastings Street
Vancouver, BC, V6E 2J3, Canada
Tel: 1 604 681–2351
Fax: 1 604 681–4364
E-mail: csbc@chamber-of-shipping.com
http://www.chamber-of-shipping.com/

Chilean Maritime League
(Liga Marítima de Chile)
Av. Errázuriz 471, 2o piso
Casilla Postal 117-V
Valparaíso, Chile
Tel: 56 32 235280
Fax: 56 32 255179
E-mail: ligamar@terra.cl
http://www.ligamar.cl/

Circum-Pacific Council on Energy and
    Mineral Resources (CPCEMR)
12201 Sunrise Valley Drive, MS-917
Reston, VA, 20192, USA
Contact: Secretariat
Tel: 1 703 648–6645
Fax: 1 703 648–4227
E-mail: nzeigler@usgs.gov
http://www.circum-pacificcouncil.org/

Clean Islands International
8219 Elvaton Drive
Pasadena, MD, 21122–3903, USA
Tel: 1 410 647–2500
Fax: 1 410 647–4554
E-mail: cii@islands.org
http://www.islands.org/

Coast Alliance
333 1/2 Pennsylvania Avenue, SE
Washington, DC, 20003, USA
Contact: Executive Director
Tel: 1 202 546–9554
Fax: 1 202 546–9609
E-mail: coast@coastalliance.org
http://ca.mycontent.org/

Coastal Communities Network
PO Box 1613
Pictou, NS, B0K 1H0, Canada
Contact: Executive Director
Tel: 1 902 485–4754
Fax: 1 902 752–9844

E-mail: coastalnet@ns.sympatico.ca
http://www.coastalcommunities.ns.ca/

Coastal Conservation Association (CCA)
6919 Portwest, Suite 100
Houston, TX, 77024, USA
Contact: Chairman
Tel: 1 713 626–4234
E-mail: ccantl@joincca.org
http://www.joincca.org/

Coastal Research and Education Society of
    Long Island, Inc. (CRESLI)
Division of Natural Sciences and
    Mathematics
Kramer Science Center
Dowling College
Oakdale, NY, 11769–1999, USA
Tel: 1 631 244–3352
E-mail: information@cresli.org
http://www.cresli.org/

Coastal Zone Canada Association
Bedford Institute of Oceanography
PO Box 1006
Dartmouth, NS, B2Y 4A2, Canada
Contact: Secretariat
Tel: 1 902 429–9497
Fax: 1 902 429–9491
E-mail: coastalz@mar.dfo-mpo.gc.ca
http://www.czca-azcc.org/

Consortium for Oceanographic Research
    and Education
1201 New York Avenue, NW, Suite 420
Washington, DC, 20005, USA
Tel: 1 202 332–0063
Fax: 1 202 332–8887
E-mail: core@coreocean.org
http://www.coreocean.org/

Cousteau Society
710 Settlers Landing Road
Hampton, VA, 23669, USA
Contact: President
Tel: 1 757 722–9300
Fax: 1 757 722–8185
E-mail: cousteau@cousteausociety.org
http://www.cousteau.org/

David Suzuki Foundation
2211 West 4th Avenue, Suite 219
Vancouver, BC, V6K 4S2, Canada
Tel: 1 604 732–4228

Fax: 1 604 732–0752
E-mail: contact@davidsuzuki.org
http://www.davidsuzuki.org/

Dredging Contractors of America
503 D Street, NW, Suite 150
Washington, DC, 20001, USA
Contact: Executive Director
Tel: 1 202 737–2674
Fax: 1 202 737–2677
E-mail: jimrausch@dredgingcontractors.org
http://www.dredgingcontractors.org/

Earth Island Institute
300 Broadway, Suite 28
San Francisco, CA, 94133–3312, USA
Contact: Executive Director
Tel: 1 415 788–3666
Fax: 1 415 788–7324
E-mail: johnknox@earthisland.org
http://www.earthisland.org/

Ecological Society of America
1707 H Street NW, Suite 400
Washington, DC, 20006, USA
Contact: Executive Director
Tel: 1 202 833–8773
Fax: 1 202 833–8775
E-mail: esahq@esa.org
http://www.esa.org/

Ecology Action Centre
1568 Argyle Street, Suite 31
Halifax, NS, B3J 2B3, Canada
Tel: 1 902 429–2202
Fax: 1 902 422–6410
E-mail: eac@ecologyaction.ca
http://www.ecologyaction.ca/

El Centro en Defensa de la Pesca Nacional
    (CeDePesca)
(Centre in Defence of National Fisheries)
12 de Octubre 3456 L 22
CP 7600 Mar del Plata, Argentina
Tel/Fax: 54 223 489 6397
E-mail: lared@cedepesca.org.ar
http://www.cedepesca.org.ar/

Estuarine Research Federation
PO Box 510
Port Republic, MD, 20676, USA
Tel: 1 410 586–0997
Fax: 1 410 586–9226

E-mail: webmaster@erf.org
http://www.erf.org/

Fisheries Council of Canada
900, 170 Laurier Avenue
Ottawa, ON, K1P 5V5, Canada
Contact: President
Tel: 1 613 727–7450
Fax: 1 613 727–7453
E-mail: info@fisheriescouncil.org
http://www.fisheriescouncil.ca/

Friends of the Earth (FOE)
1717 Massachusetts Avenue, NW, Suite 600
Washington, DC, 20036–2002, USA
Contact: President
Tel: 1 202 783–7400
Fax: 1 202 783–0444
E-mail: foe@foe.org
http://www.foe.org/

Geoscience Information Society
c/o Geology_Mathematics_Physics Library
University of Cincinnati
ML 0153
240 Braunstein Hall
Cincinnati, OH, 45221, USA
Contact: Secretary
Tel: 1 513 556–1582
Fax: 1 513 556–1930
E-mail: goodenam@mail.uc.edu
http://www.geoinfo.org/

Global Programme of Action Coalition for
    the Gulf of Maine (GPAC)
c/o Atlantic Coastal Action Program Saint
    John
PO Box 6878, Station A
Saint John, NB, E2L 4S3, Canada
Contact: Coordinator
Tel: 1 506 652–2227
Fax: 1 506 633–2184
E-mail: acapsj@fundy.net
http://www.gpac-gom.org/

H. John Heinz III Center for Science,
    Economics and the Environment
1001 Pennsylvania Ave, NW, Suite 735
    South
Washington, DC, 20004, USA
Contact: President
Tel: 1 202 737–6307
Fax: 1 202 737–6410

E-mail: lovejoy@heinzctr.org
http://www.heinzctr.org/

Huntsman Marine Science Centre
1 Lower Campus Road
St. Andrews, NB, E5B 2L7, Canada
Tel: 1 506 529–1200
Fax: 1 506 529–1212
E-mail: huntsman@huntsmanmarine.ca
http://www.huntsmanmarine.ca/

IEEE Geoscience and Remote Sensing
    Society
c/o IEEE Operations Centre
445 Hoes Lane
PO Box 1331
Piscataway, NJ, 08854–1331, USA
Tel: 1 732 981–0060
Fax: 1 732 981–1721
E-mail: grss@ieee.org
http://www.ieee.org/soc/grss/

IEEE Oceanic Engineering Society
13513 Crispin Way
Rockville, MD, 20853, USA
Contact: President
Tel: 1 301 460–4347
Fax: 1 301 871–3907
E-mail: j.barbera@ieee.org
http://www.oceanicengineering.org/

Institute of Navigation
3975 University Drive, Suite 390
Fairfax, VA, 22030, USA
Tel: 1 703 383–9688
Fax: 1 703 383–9689
E-mail: membership@ion.org
http://www.ion.org/

International Marina Institute
MOAA/IMI
444 North Capital Street, NW, Suite 645
Washington, DC, 20001, USA
Contact: President
Tel: 1 202 737–9776
Fax: 1 202 628–8679
E-mail: info@marineaassociation.org
http://www.marineaassociation.org/

International Ocean Institute–Canada
Dalhousie University
1226 LeMarchant Street
Halifax, NS, B3H 3P7, Canada

Contact: Programme Officer
Tel: 1 902 494–6918
Fax: 1 902 494–1334
E-mail: ioi@dal.ca
http://www.dal.ca/~ioihfx/index.html

International Ocean Institute–Costa Rica
Universidad Nacional
PO Box 86
Heredia 3000, Costa Rica
Contact: Director
Tel: 506 277 3594
Fax: 506 260 2546
E-mail: ioicos@una.ac.cr
http://www.una.ac.cr/ioi/

International Ocean Institute–South
    Western Atlantic Ocean
Centro de Estudos do Mar da UFPR
Centro Operacional papa o Atlantico
    Sudocidental
PO Box 50.002
82810_220 Pontal do Sul, PR, Brazil
Contact: Director
Tel: 55 41 455 1333
Fax: 55 41 455 1105
E-mail: edmarone@ufpr.br

Inuit Tapiriit Kanatami
170 Laurier Avenue West, Suite 510
Ottawa, ON, K1P 5V5, Canada
Tel: 1 613 238–8181
Fax: 1 613 234–1991
E-mail: info@itk.ca
http://www.tapirisat.ca/

Island Resources Foundation
Library and Island Systems Centre
H. Lavity Stoutt Community College
123 Main Street, Box 3097
Road Town, Tortola, BVI
Tel: 1 284 494–2723
E-mail: info@irf.org
http://www.irf.org/

Joint Oceanographic Institutions
1201 New York Avenue, NW, Suite 400
Washington, DC, 20005, USA
Contact: President
Tel: 1 202 232–3900
Fax: 1 202 265–4409
E-mail: info@joiscience.org
http://www.joiscience.org/

Lake Carriers' Association
614 Superior Avenue West, Suite 915
Cleveland, OH, 44113–1383, USA
Contact: President
Tel: 1 216 621–1107
Fax: 1 216 241–8262
E-mail: ggn@lcaships.com
http://www.lcaships.com/

Liberian Shipowners' Council Ltd.
99 Park Avenue, Suite 1700
New York, NY, 10016, USA
Contact: General Secretary
Tel: 1 212 973–3896
Fax: 1 212 994–6763
E-mail: jl@liberianshipowners.com
http://www.liberianshipowners.com/

Living Oceans Society
PO Box 320
Sointula, BC, V0N 3E0, Canada
Tel: 1 250 973–6580
Fax: 1 250 973–6581
E-mail: info@livingoceans.org
http://www.livingoceans.org/

Marine Conservation Biology Institute
2122 112th Ave NE, Suite B-300
Bellevue, WA, 98004, USA
Tel: 1 425 883–8914
Fax: 1 425 883–3017
E-mail: mcbiweb@mcbi.org
http://www.mcbi.org/

Marine Environment Research Institute
 (MERI)
Center for Marine Studies
55 Main Street
PO Box 1652
Blue Hill, ME, 04616, USA
Tel: 1 207 374–2135
Fax: 1 207 374–2931
E-mail: info@meriresearch.org
http://www.meriresearch.org/

Marine Retailers Association of America
 (MRAA)
PO Box 1127
Oak Park, IL, 60304, USA
Contact: President
Tel: 1 708 763–9210
Fax: 1 708 763–9236
E-mail: mraa@mraa.com
http://www.mraa.com/

Maritime Security Council
3471 N. Federal Highway, Suite 506
Fort Lauderdale, FL, 33306, USA
Tel: 1 954 567–2536
Fax: 1 954 567–2511
E-mail: mailbox@maritimesecurity.org
http://www.maritimesecurity.org/

Monterey Bay Aquarium Research Institute
7700 Sandholdt Road
Moss Landing, CA, 95039–9644, USA
Contact: President
Tel: 1 831 775–1700
Fax: 1 831 775–1620
E-mail: mcnutt@mbari.org
http://www.mbari.org/

Mote Marine Laboratory
1600 Ken Thompson Parkway
Sarasota, FL, 34236, USA
Contact: Executive Director
Tel: 1 941 388–4441
Fax: 1 941 388–4312
E-mail: director@mote.org
http://www.mote.org/

National Aquaculture Association
111 W. Washington Street, Suite 1
Charles Town, WV, 25414, USA
Tel: 1 304 728–2167
Fax: 1 304 728–2196
E-mail: naa@frontiernet.net
http://www.nationalaquaculture.org/

National Association for the Marine
 Assistance Industries (C-PORT)
619 Severn Avenue, Suite 21
PO Box 4070
Annapolis, MD, 21403, USA
Contact: Executive Director
Fax: 1 410 263–3186
E-mail: c-port@wpa.org
http://www.c-port.org/

National Association of Marine Services
 (NAMS)
5458 Wagonmaster Drive
Colorado Springs, CO, 80917, USA
Contact: Executive Director
Tel: 1 719 573–5946
Fax: 1 719 573–5952
E-mail: nams@namsshipchandler.com
http://www.namsshipchandler.com/

National Association of Marine Surveyors,
Inc. (NAMS)
PO Box 9306
Chesapeake, VA, 23321–9306, USA
Contact: Office Manager
Tel: 1 757 638–9638
Fax: 1 757 638–9639
E-mail: nationaloffice@nams-cms.org
http://www.nams-cms.org/

National Coalition for Marine Conservation
(NCMC)
4 Royal Street SE
Leesburg, VA, 20175, USA
Contact: Director of Communications
Tel: 1 703 777–0037
Fax: 1 703 777–1107
E-mail: christine@savethefish.org
http://www.savethefish.org/

National Fisheries Institute
7918 Jones Branch Drive, Suite 700
McLean, VA, 22102, USA
Contact: President
Tel: 1 703 752–8880
Fax: 1 703 752–7583
E-mail: gthomas@nfi.org
http://www.nfi.org/

National Marine Charter Association
(NMCA)
1600 Duke Street, Suite 400
Alexandria, VA, 22314, USA
Contact: Executive Director
Tel: 1 703 519–1714
Fax: 1 703 519–1716
E-mail: info@marinecharter.org
http://www.marinecharter.org/

National Marine Distributors Association
(NMDA)
37 Pratt Street
Essex, CT, 06426–1159, USA
Contact: Executive Director
Tel: 1 860 767–7898
Fax: 1 860 767–7932
E-mail: info@nmdaonline.com
http://www.nmdaonline.com/

National Marine Educators Association
PO Box 1470
Ocean Springs, MS, 39566–1470, USA

Contact: National Office
E-mail: johnette.bosarge@usm.edu
http://www.marine-ed.org/

National Marine Electronics Association
(NMEA)
7 Riggs Avenue
Severna Park, MD, 21146, USA
Contact: Executive Director
Tel: 1 410 975–9425
Fax: 1 410 975–9450
E-mail: info@nmea.org
http://www.nmea.org/

National Marine Manufacturers Association
(NMMA)
200 East Randolph Drive, Suite 5100
Chicago, IL, 60601, USA
Contact: President
Tel: 1 312 946–6200
Fax: 1 312 946–0388
http://www.nmma.org/

National Maritime Historical Society
(NMSH)
PO Box 68
5 John Walsh Boulevard
Peekskill, NY, 10566, USA
Tel: 1 914 737–7878
Fax: 1 914 737–7816
E-mail: nmhs@seahistory.org
http://www.seahistory.org/

National Ocean Industries Association
(NOIA)
1120 G Street NW, Suite 900
Washington, DC, 20005, USA
Contact: President
Tel: 1 202 347–6900
Fax: 1 202 347–8650
E-mail: kandace@noia.org
http://www.noia.org/

National Shellfisheries Association, Inc.
U.S. Environmental Prot.Agency
Narragansett, RI, 02882, USA
Contact: Secretary
Tel: 1 401 782–3155
Fax: 1 401 782–3030
http://www.shellfish.org/

Natural Resources Defense Council
40 West 20th Street
New York, NY, 10011, USA

Contact: Headquarters
Tel: 1 212 727–2700
Fax: 1 212 727–1773
E-mail: nrdcinfo@nrdc.org
http://www.nrdc.org/

Nature Canada
85 Albert Street, Suite 900
Ottawa, ON, K1P 6A4, Canada
Tel: 1 613 562–3447
Fax: 1 613 562–3371
E-mail: info@naturecanada.ca
http://www.cnf.ca/

Newfoundland Ocean Industries Association
Atlantic Place, Suite 602
215 Water Street
St. John's, NL, AIC 6C9, Canada
Contact: President
Tel: 1 709 758–6610
Fax: 1 709 758–6611
E-mail: noia@noianet.com
http://www.noianet.com/

North American Association of Fisheries
    Economics
c/o IIFET
Department of Agriculture and Resource
    Economics
Oregon State University
Corvallis, OR, 97331–3601, USA
Contact: NAAFE Business Office
Tel: 1 541 737–1416
Fax: 1 541 737–2563
E-mail: ann.l.shriver@oregonstate.edu
http://oregonstate.edu/Dept/IIFET/NAAFE/
    Home.html

North American Native Fishes Association
    (NANFA)
1107 Argonne Drive
Baltimore, MD, 21218, USA
http://www.nanfa.org/

Northwest Marine Trade Association
    (NMTA)
1900 N. Northlake Way, Suite 233
Seattle, WA, 98103–9087, USA
Contact: Executive Director
Tel: 1 206 634–0911
Fax: 1 206 632–0078
E-mail: info@nmta.net
http://www.nmta.net/

Oceanic Institute
41–202 Kalanianaole Highway
Waimanalo, HI, 96795, USA
Tel: 1 808 259–3145
Fax: 1 808 259–5971
http://www.oceanicinstitute.org/

Oceanic Society
Fort Mason Center, Building E,
San Francisco, CA, 94123–1234, USA
Tel: 1 415 441–1106
Fax: 1 415 474–3395
E-mail: office@oceanic-society.org
http://www.oceanic-society.org/

Offshore Marine Service Association
    (OMSA)
990 N. Corporate Drive, Suite 210
Harahan, LA, 70123, USA
Contact: President
Tel: 1 504 734–7622
Fax: 1 504 734–7134
E-mail: kenwells@offshoremarine.org
http://www.offshoremarine.org/

Pacific Coast Federation of Fishermen's
    Associations (PCFFA)
PO Box 29370
San Francisco, CA, 94129–0370, USA
Contact: Executive Director
Tel: 1 415 561–5080
Fax: 1 415 561–5464
E-mail: fish1ifr@aol.com
http://www.pcffa.org/

Pan-American Institute of Naval
    Engineering (IPEN)
Instituto Panamericano de Ingenieria Naval
Rua Camerino, 118 - 2o Andar
20080–010 Rio de Janeiro, Brazil
Contact: Executive Secretary
Tel/Fax: 55 21 2536263
E-mail: ipen@terra.com.br
http://www.ipen.org.br/

Passenger Vessel Association
801 North Quincy Street, Suite 200
Arlington, VA, 22203, USA
Contact: Executive Director
Tel: 1 703 807–0100
Fax: 1 703 807–0103
E-mail: pva@vesselalliance.com
http://www.passengervessel.com/

Peruvian Foundation for Nature
  Conservation (ProNaturaleza)
Av. Alberto del Campo 417
PO Box 18–1393
Lima 17, Peru
Tel: 51 1 264 2736
Fax: 51 1 264 2753
E-mail: pronaturaleza@pronaturaleza.org
http://www.pronaturaleza.org

Pew Charitable Trusts
2005 Market Street, Suite 1700
Philadelphia, PA, 19103–7077, USA
Contact: Protecting Ocean Life Program
Tel: 1 215 575–9050
Fax: 1 215 575–4939
http://www.pewtrusts.com/ideas/index.
  cfm?issue=16

Reef Care Curaçao
PO Box 676
Curaçao, Netherlands Antilles
Tel: 5999 569 2099
http://www.reefcare.org/

Reef Relief
PO Box 430
Key West, FL, 33041, USA
Tel: 1 305 294–3100
Fax: 1 305 293–9515
E-mail: info@reefrelief.org
http://www. reefrelief.org/

Restore America's Estuaries
3801 North Fairfax Drive, Suite 53
Arlington, VA, 22203, USA
Tel: 1 703 524–0248
Fax: 1 703 524–0287
E-mail: info@estuaries.org
http://www.estuaries.org/

Shipbuilders Council of America (SCA)
1455 F Street, Suite 225
Washington, DC, 20005, USA
Contact: President
Tel: 1 202 347–5462
Fax: 1 202 347–5464
E-mail: mallen@dc.bjllp.com
http://www.shipbuilders.org/

Shipping Federation of Canada
300 rue de Sacrement, Suite 326
Montreal, QC, H2Y 1X4, Canada
Tel: 1 514 849–2325

Fax: 1 514 849–8774
E-mail: info@shipfed.ca
http://www.shipfed.ca/

Sierra Club
85 Second Street, 2nd Floor
San Francisco, CA, 94105, USA
Contact: Executive Director
Tel: 1 415 977–5500
Fax: 1 415 977–5799
E-mail: information@sierraclub.org
http://www.sierraclub.org/

Sierra Club of Canada
412–1 Nicholas Street
Ottawa, ON, K1N 7B7, Canada
Tel: 1 613 241–4611
Fax: 1 613 241–2292
E-mail: info@sierraclub.ca
http://www.sierraclub.ca/

Society of Exploration Geophysicists
8801 South Yale
PO Box 702740
Tulsa, OK, 74170–2740, USA
Contact: Executive Director
Tel: 1 918 497–5500
Fax: 1 918 497–5557
E-mail: mfleming@seg.org
http://seg.org/

Taras Oceanographic Foundation
5905 Stonewood Court
Jupiter, FL 33458 USA
Tel: 1 561 743–7683
Fax: 1 561 748–0794
Email: taras@taras.org
http://www.taras.org/

The Coastal Society
PO Box 25408
Alexandria, VA, 22313–5408, USA
Contact: President
Tel: 1 703 933–1599
Fax: 1 703 933–1596
E-mail: coastalsoc@aol.com
http://www.thecoastalsociety.org/

The Ecological Society of America
1707 H Street NW, Suite 400
Washington, DC, 20006, USA
Tel: 1 202 833–8773
Fax: 1 202 833–8775

E-mail: esahq@esa.org
http://www.esa.org/

The Ocean Conservancy
2029 K Street
Washington, DC, 20006, USA
Tel: 1 202 429–5609
Fax: 1 202 872–0619
E-mail: info@oceanconservancy.org
http://www.oceanconservancy.org/

The Oceanography Society (TOS)
PO Box 1931
Rockville, MD, 20849–1931, USA
Contact: Executive Director
Tel: 1 301 251–7708
Fax: 1 301 251–7709
E-mail: info@tos.org
http://www.tos.org/

US Naval Institute (USNI)
291 Wood Road
Annapolis, MD, 21402, USA
Contact: CEO
Tel: 1 410 268–6110
Fax: 1 410 269–7940
E-mail: twilkerson@usni.org
http://www.usni.org/

Western Dredging Association
PO Box 5797
Vancouver, WA, 98668–5737, USA
Contact: Executive Director
Tel: 1 360 750–0209
Fax: 1 360 750–1445
E-mail: weda@comcast.net
http://www.westerndredging.org/

Wildlife Conservation Society
2300 Southern Boulevard
Bronx, NY, 10460, USA
Contact: President
Tel: 1 718 220–5100
http://www.wcs.org/

Women's Aquatic Network, Inc.
PO Box 4993
Washington, DC, 20008, USA
Contact: Secretariat
E-mail: info@womensaquatic.net
http://orgs.womensaquatic.net/

World Shipping Council
1015 15th Street NW, Suite 450

Washington, DC, 20005, USA
Tel: 1 202 589–1230
Fax: 1 202 589–1231
E-mail: info@worldshipping.org
http://www.worldshipping.org/

5.3 Asia

Asian Fisheries Society
PO Box 2725
Quezon City Central Post Office
1167 Quezon City, The Philippines
Tel: 63 2 921 1914
Fax: 63 2 920 2757
E-mail: info@asianfisheriessociety.org
http://www.asianfisheriessociety.org/

Coastal Development Planning Centre
25 Vasundhara Colony, Gulbai
Jkrd Ahmedabad
Gujurat, 380006, India
Tel: 91 79 656 8421
Tel: 91 79 642 0056

Eastern Dredging Association (EADA)
c/o Port Klang Association
Mail Bag Service 202
42009 Port Klang, Malaysia
Contact: Secretary General
Fax: 60 3 3157 0211
E-mail: david@pka.gov.my
http://www.woda.org/

Environmental Engineering Association of
    Thailand
122/4 Soi Rawadee, Rama VI Road
Samsen Nai, Phayathai
Bangkok 10400, Thailand
Contact: President
Tel: 66 2 617 1530
Fax: 66 2 279 9720
E-mail: info@eeat.or.th
http://www.eeat.or.th/

Federation of ASEAN Shipowners'
    Associations (FASA)
59 Tras Street
Singapore 078998
Contact: Secretary General
Tel: 65 6222 5238
Fax: 65 6222 5572

E-mail: fasa@pacific.net.sg
http://www.fasa.org.sg

Institute for Ocean Policy, Ship and Ocean
   Foundation (IOP/SOF)
1–15–16 Toranomon, Minato-ku
Tokyo 105–0001, Japan
Tel: 81 3 3502 1887
Fax: 81 3 3502 2033
E-mail: info@sof.or.jp
http://www.sof.or.jp/ocean/index.html.en

International Ocean Institute–China
c/o National Marine Data and Information
   Service (NMDIS)
State Oceanic Administration
93 Liuwei Road, Hedong District
Tianjin 300171, People's Republic of China
Contact: Director
Tel: 86 22 2430 1292
Fax: 86 22 2430 4408
E-mail: ioi@mail.nmdis.gov.cn

International Ocean Institutey–India
Department of Ocean Engineering
Indian Institute of Technology (IIT
   Madras)
IC & SR Building
Chennai 600036, India
Contact: Director
Tel: 91 44 2257 0338
Fax: 91 44 2257 0559
E-mail: ioi@vsnl.com

International Ocean Institute–Indonesia
Centre for Marine Studies, University of
   Indonesia
c/o FMIPA UI, Kampus UI Depok
Depok 16424, Indonesia
Contact: Director
Tel/Fax: 62 21 7721 1473
E-mail: cms_ui@yahoo.com

International Ocean Institute–Iran
c/o Iranian National Centre for
   Oceanography (INCO)
No. 9, Etemadzadeh Street, Fatemi Avenue
Tehran 1411813389, Republic of Iran
Tel: 98 21 694 4867
Fax: 98 21 694 4866
E-mail: nhzaker@inco.ac.ir

International Ocean Institute–Japan
c/o Intercom Inc.

403 4–20–14 Minami-Aoyama
Minato-ku
Tokyo, Japan 107–0062
Contact: Director
Tel: 81 3 5775 0181
Fax: 81 3 5775 0180
E-mail: ioijapan@qb3.so-net.ne.jp
http://www.ioi-japan.org/

International Ocean Institute–Thailand
c/o Department of Marine and Coastal
   Resources
92, Phaholyothin 7, Phaholyothin Road
SamSaen Nai, Phaya Thai
Bangkok 10400, Thailand
Tel: 66 2 579 8143
Fax: 66 2 579 8567
E-mail: cvirapat@hotmail.com

Jordan Royal Ecological Diving Society
PO Box 831051
Amman 11183, Jordan
Tel: 962 6 06 5676183
Fax: 962 6 06 5676173
http://www.jreds.org/

Malaysian Fisheries Society
(Persatuan Perikanan Malaysia)
Faculty of Veterinary Medicine
(Aquatic Animal Health Unit)
University Putra Malaysia
43400 UPM Serdang, Selangor, Malaysia
Tel/Fax: 6 03 8948 8246
E-mail: myfisoc@time.net.my
http://www.vet.upm.edu.my/~mfs/index.html

Malaysian Maritime Institute
(Institut Kelautan Malaysia–IKMAL)
No.22, Lorong Batu Nilam 3A,
Bandar Bukit Tinggi,
41200 Klang, Selangor Darul Ehsan.
Malaysia
Tel: 60 3 3324 1772
Fax: 60 3 3324 1753
E-mail: ikmalay@pd.jaring.my
http://www.ikmal.org.my/

Malaysian Shipowners' Association (MASA)
Menara Dayabumi, 17th Floor
Jalan Sultan Hishamudin
PO Box 10371
50712 Kuala Lumpur, Malaysia
Tel: 60 3 2275 2136
Fax: 60 3 2260 2575

E-mail: masa_kl@tm.net.my
http://www.malaysianshipowners.org/

Nippon Kaiji Kyokai (Class NK)
4–7 Kioi-cho
Chiyoda-ku
Tokyo 102–8567, Japan
Contact: Chairman and President
Tel: 81 3 3230 1201
Fax: 81 3 5226 2012
E-mail: bnd@classnk.or.jp
http://www.classnk.or.jp/

Small Fishers Federation of Sri Lanka
Pambala, Kakkapalliya
PO Box 01
Chilaw, Sri Lanka
Contact: Director
Tel: 94 032 48707
Fax: 94 032 47960
E-mail: sffl@sri.lanka.net
http://www.shrimpaction.com/titlessffl.html

Southeast Asia START Regional Committee
   (SARCS)
National Central University
No. 300 Johongda Road
Chung-Li 320, Taiwan, ROC
Contact: Secretariat
Tel: 886 3 426 2726
Fax: 886 3 426 2640
E-mail: sarcs@sarcs.org.tw
http://www.sarcs.org.tw/

Telapak Indonesia
Jl. Palem Putri III no. 1–3
Taman Yasmin Sektor V
Bogor, Indonesia
Tel: 62 251 715 9902
Fax: 62 251 753 7577
E-mail: info@telapak.org
http://www.telapak.org/

Yadfon Association
16/8 Rakchan Road
Tambon Tabtieng, District Muang
Trang 92000, Thailand
Tel: 66 75 219 737
Fax: 66 75 219 327

5.4   Europe

Alliance of Maritime Regional Interests in
   Europe (AMRIE)
20–22, rue de Commerce
B-1000 Brussels, Belgium
Contact: Secretariat
Tel: 32 2 736 1755
Fax: 32 2 735 2298
E-mail: info@amrie.org
http://www.amrie.org/

Association of National Organisations of
   Fishing Enterprises in the EC
   (EUROPECHE)
24 rue Montoyer
B-1040 Brussels, Belgium
Contact: Secretariat
Tel: 32 2 230 4848
Fax: 32 2 230 2680
E-mail: europeche@skynet.be
http://www.europeche.org/

Association of Port Health Authorities
   (APHA)
Dutton House
46 Church Street
Runcorn, Cheshire, WA7 1LL, United
   Kingdom
Contact: Executive Secretary
Tel: 44 8707 444505
Fax: 44 1928 581596
E-mail: apha@cieh.org.uk
http://www.apha.org.uk/

Atlantic Salmon Trust
Moulin, Pitlochry
Perthshire, Scotland, PH16 5JQ, United
   Kingdom
Contact: Director
Tel: 44 1796 47 3439
Fax: 44 1796 47 3554
E-mail: director@atlanticsalmontrust.org
http://www.atlanticsalmontrust.org/

Atlantic Whale Foundation
St Martins House
59 St Martins Lane
Covent Garden
London, WC2N 4JS, United Kingdom
Tel/Fax: 44 1162 404566
E-mail: edb@whalenation.org
http://www.whalefoundation.org.uk/

Baltic Ports Organization (BPO)
c/o Ports of Stockholm
PO Box 27314
SE-102 54 Stockholm, Sweden
Contact: Secretariat
Tel: 46 86 70 26 00
Fax: 46 86 70 26 45
E-mail: bpo@stoports.com
http://www.bpoports.com/

British Marine Life Study Society
Glaucus House
14 Corbyn Crescent
Shoreham-by-Sea, Sussex, BN43 6PQ,
    United Kingdom
Tel/Fax: 44 1273 465433
E-mail: glaucus@hotmail.com
http://www.glaucus.org.uk/

British Maritime Law Association
c/o Ince & Co.
Knolly's House
11 Byward Street
London, EC3R 5EN, United Kingdom
Contact: Secretary & Treasurer
Tel: 44 207 623 2011
Fax: 44 207 623 3225
E-mail: patrick.griggs@ince.co.uk
http://www.bmla.org.uk/

British Ports Association
Africa House
64–78 Kingsway
London, WC2B 6AH, United Kingdom
Contact: Director
Tel: 44 207 242 1200
Fax: 44 207 430 7474
E-mail: info@britishports.org.uk
http://www.britishports.org.uk/

Central Dredging Association (CEDA)
Radex Building
Rotterdamseweg183c
NL-2629 HD, Delft, The Netherlands
Contact: General Manager
Tel: 31 15 268 2575
Fax: 31 15 268 2576
E-mail: ceda@dredging.org
http://www.dredging.org/

Centre for Documentation, Research and
    Experimentation on Water Pollution
    Accidents (CEDRE)
715, rue Alain Colas

CS 41836
F-29218 Brest Cedex 2, France
Contact: Director
Tel: 33 2 9833 1010
Fax: 33 2 9844 9138
E-mail: contact@cedre.fr
http://www.le-cedre.fr/

Chamber of Shipping
Carthusian Court
12 Carthusian Street
London, EC1M 6EZ, United Kingdom
Contact: Director General
Tel: 44 207 417 2800
Fax: 44 207 600 1534
E-mail: postmaster@british-shipping.org
http://www.british-shipping.org/

Chartered Institution of Water and
    Environmental Management (CIWEM)
15 John Street
London, WC1N 2EB, United Kingdom
Tel: 44 20 7831 3110
Fax: 44 20 7405 4967
E-mail: admin@ciwem.org
http://www.ciwem.org/

Coalition Clean Baltic
Östra Ågatan 53
SE-753 22 Uppsala, Sweden
Contact: Secretariat
Tel: 46 18 71 11 70
Fax: 46 18 71 11 75
E-mail: secretariat@ccb.se
http://www.ccb.se/

Coastwatch Europe
Civil and Environmental Engineering
Trinity College, Dublin
Dublin 2, Ireland
Contact: International Coordination
Tel: 353 55 25843
E-mail: coastwatch@eircom.net
http://www.coastwatch.org/

Community of European Shipyards'
    Associations (CESA)
52–54, rue Marie de Bourgogne, 3rd floor
B-1000 Brussels, Belgium
Contact: Secretary General
Tel: 32 2 230 2791
Fax: 32 2 230 4332
E-mail: info@cesa-shipbuilding.org
http://www.cesa-shipbuilding.org/

Deltalinqs–Ports and Industries' Association
Rotterdam
PO Box 54200
NL-3008 JE Rotterdam, The Netherlands
Tel: 31 10 4020 399
Fax: 31 10 4120 687
E-mail: info@deltalinqs.nl
http://www.deltalinqs.nl/

ESF Marine Board
European Science Foundation
BP 90015
1, quai Lezay Marnésia
F-67080 Strasbourg, France
Contact: Secretariat
Tel: 33 3 8876 7141
Fax: 33 3 8825 1954
http://www.esf.org/marineboard/

Estuarine and Coastal Sciences Association
(ECSA)
Department of Zoology
Trinity College
Dublin 2, Ireland
Contact: Secretary
Tel: 353 1608 1640
E-mail: jwilson@tcd.ie
http://www.ecsa-coast.org/

EUCC–The Coastal Union
PO Box 11232
NL-2301 EE Leiden, Netherlands
Contact: International Secretariat
Tel: 31 71 512 2900
Fax: 31 71 512 4069
E-mail: admin@eucc.nl
http://www.eucc.nl/

European Aquaculture Society (EAS)
Slijkensesteenweg 4
B-8400 Oostende, Belgium
Tel: 32 59 323 859
Fax: 32 59 321 005
E-mail: eas@aquaculture.cc
http://www.easonline.org/

European Association for Aquatic Mammals
c/o St. Andrews University
Sea Mammal Research Unit
The Gatty
St. Andrews, KY16 8LB, Scotland, United
Kingdom
Contact: Secretary/Treasurer
Tel: 44 1334 650400

E-mail: info@eaam.org
http://www.eaam.org/

European Association of Fisheries
Economists
c/o Danish Research Institute of Food
Economics
Rolighedsvej 25
DK-1958 Fredericksberg, Denmark
Contact: Secretary
Tel: 45 35 28 68 95
Fax: 45 35 28 68 01
E-mail: e_lindebo@seafish.co.uk
http://www.eafe-fish.org/

European Association of Remote Sensing
Laboratories (EARSeL)
c/o Institute of Photography and
GeoInformation
Technical University of Hanover
Nienburger Strasse 1
D-30167 Hanover, Germany
Contact: Secretariat
Tel: 49 511 762 2482
Fax: 49 511 762 2483
E-mail: boettcher@ipi.uni-hanover.de
http://www.earsel.org/

European Cetacean Society
c/o Laboratoire de Biologie et
Environnement Marins
Université de La Rochelle
Institut de la Mer et du Littoral Port des
Minimes
F-17000 La Rochelle, France
Contact: Secretary
Tel: 33 546 500291
E-mail: florence.caurant@univ-lr.fr
http://web.inter.nl.net/users/J.W.Broekema/ecs/

European Coastal Association for Science
and Technology (EUROCOAST)
Department of Earth Sciences
Cardiff University
PO Box 914
Cardiff, Wales, CF10 3YE, United Kingdom
Contact: Secretariat
Tel: 44 2920 874830
Fax: 44 2920 874326
E-mail: eurocoast@cardiff.ac.uk
http://www.eurocoast.org/

European Community Shipowners'
  Associations (ECSA)
45 rue Ducale
B-1000 Brussels, Belgium
Contact: Secretariat
Tel: 32 2 511 3940
Fax: 32 2 511 8092
E-mail: mail@ecsa.be
http://www.ecsa.be/

European Desalination Association
Science Park of Abruzzo
via Antica Arischia, 1
I-67100 L'Aquila, Italy
Contact: Secretariat
Tel: 39 348 8848 406
Fax: 39 0862 3475 213
E-mail: eds@desline.info
http://www.edsoc.com/

European Dredging Association (EuDA)
2–4 rue de Praetere
B-1000 Brussels, Belgium
Contact: Secretariat
Tel: 32 2 646 8183
Fax: 32 2 646 6063
E-mail: info@euda.be
http://www.european-dredging.info/in.html

European Federation of Sea Anglers
  (EFSA)
Inglewood, Braal Road
Halkirk, Caithness, KW12 6XE, United
  Kingdom
Contact: Secretary
Tel/Fax: 44 1847 831985
E-mail: enquiries@efsa.co.uk
http://www.efsa.co.uk/

European Geosciences Union (EGU)
Max Planck Strasse 13
D-37191 Katlenburg-Lindau, Germany
Contact: Executive Secretary
Tel: 49 5556 1440
Fax: 49 5556 4709
E-mail: egu@copernicus.org
http://www.copernicus.org/EGU/

European Institute–Denmark
(Det Danske Europa Institut A/S)
Boldhusgade 6
DK-1062 Copenhagen K, Denmark
Tel: 45 33 33 91 00
Fax: 45 33 33 91 20

E-mail: euroinst@euroinst.dk
http://www.euroinst.dk/

European Maritime Pilots' Association
  (EMPA)
St. Aldegondiskaai 36–38
B-2000 Antwerp, Belgium
Contact: Secretary General
Tel: 32 3 205 9436
Fax: 32 3 205 9437
E-mail: empa@skynet.be
http://www.empa-pilots.org/

European Science Foundation (ESF)
1, quai Lezay-Marnésia
BP 90015
F-67080 Strasbourg, France
Contact: Secretary General
Tel: 33 3 8876 7100
Fax: 33 3 8837 0532
http://www.esf.org/

European Sea Ports Organisation (ESPO)
Treurenberg 6
B-1000 Brussels, Belgium
Contact: Secretary General
Tel: 32 2 736 3463
Fax: 32 2 736 6325
E-mail: mail@espo.be
http://www.espo.be/

European Shippers' Council (ESC)
Park Leopold
Rue Wiertz 50
B-1050 Brussels, Belgium
Contact: Secretary General
Tel: 32 2 230 2113
Fax: 32 2 230 4140
E-mail:
nicolettevdjagt@europeanshippers.com
http://www.europeanshippers.com/

European Society for Marine Biotechnology
c/o Burgess Laboratory
Centre for Marine Biodiversity and
  Biotechnology
Division of Life Sciences
Heriot-Watt University
Edinburgh, EH14 4AS, United Kingdom
Contact: Secretariat
E-mail: m.searle@hw.ac.uk
http://www.esmb.org/

European Water Association
Theodor-Heuss-Allee 17
D-53773 Hennef, Germany
Contact: Chairman
Tel: 49 22 42 872189
Fax: 49 22 42 872135
E-mail: ewa@dwa.de
http://www.ewaonline.de/

Federation of European Aquaculture
   Producers (FEAP)
30, rue Vivaldi
B-4100 Boncelles, Belgium
Contact: Secretary General
Tel: 32 4 338 2995
Fax: 32 4 337 9846
E-mail: secretariat@feap.info
http://www.feap.info/feap/

Federation of European Microbiological
   Societies (FEMS)
Keverling Buismanweg 4
NL-2628 CL Delft, The Netherlands
Contact: Central Office
Tel: 31 15 269 3920
Fax: 31 15 269 3921
E-mail: info@fems-microbiology.org
http://www.fems-microbiology.org/

Fisheries Society of the British Isles
c/o Granta Information Systems
82A High Street
Sawston, Cambridge, CB2 4HJ, United
   Kingdom
Contact: President
Tel: 44 1223 830665
Fax: 44 1223 839804
E-mail: president@fsbi.org.uk
http://www.fsbi.org.uk/

Fridtjof Nansen Institute
PO Box 326
N-1326 Lysaker, Norway
Contact: Director
Tel: 47 67 11 19 00
Fax: 47 67 11 19 10
E-mail: post@fni.no
http://www.fni.no/

Geographical Information Systems (GISIG)
   International Group
Via Piacenza 54
I-16138 Genova, Italy
Tel: 39 010 8355 588

Fax: 39 010 8357 190
E-mail: gisig@gisig.it
http://www.gisig.it/

German Institute of Navigation (DGON)
Kölnstrasse 70
D-53111 Bonn, Germany
Tel: 49 228 201970
Fax: 49 228 2019719
E-mail: dgon.bonn@t-online.de
http://www.dgon.de/

German Shipbuilding and Ocean Industries
   Association
(Verband für Schiffbau und
   Meerestechnik–VSM)
An der Alster 1
D-20099 Hamburg, Germany
Tel: 49 40 28 01520
Fax: 49 40 28 015230
E-mail: info@vsm.de
http://www.vsm.de/

Hellenic Marine Environment Protection
   Association (HELMEPA)
5 Pergamou Street
GR-17121 Athens, Greece
Tel: 3 210 9343088
Fax: 3 210 9353847
E-mail: helmepa@helmepa.gr
http://www.helmepa.gr/

Institute of Fisheries Management
22 Rushworth Avenue
West Bridgford, Nottingham, NG2 7LF,
   United Kindom
Tel: 44 11 5982 2317
Fax: 44 11 5982 6150
E-mail: v.holt@ifm.org.uk
http://www.ifm.org.uk/

Institute of Shipping Economics and
   Logistics
(Institut für Seeverkhvswirtschaft und
   Logistik–ISL)
Universitätallee GW 1, Block A
D-28359 Bremen, Germany
Tel: 49 421 220960
Fax: 49 421 2209655
E-mail: info@isl.org
http://www.isl.uni-bremen.de/

International Association for the Rhine
  Vessels Register (IVR)
Vasteland 12E
NL-3011 BL, Rotterdam, Netherlands
Tel: 31 10 411 6070
Fax: 31 10 412 9091
E-mail: info@ivr.nl
http://www.ivr.nl/

International Commission for Protection of
  the Rhine Against Pollution (ICPR)
(Internationale Kommission zum Schutze
  des Rheins Gegon
  Verunreinizung–IKSR)
Postfach 200253
D-56002 Koblenz, Germany
Tel: 49 261 942520
Fax: 49 261 9425252
E-mail: sekretariat@iksr.de
http://www.iksr.de/

International Marine Certification Institute
  (IMCI)
3, rue Abbé Cuypers
B-1040 Brussels, Belgium
Tel: 32 2 741 6836
Fax: 32 2 741 2418
E-mail: info@imci.org
http://www.imci.org/

International Ocean Institute–Baltic Sea
c/o Department of Biology and
  Environment
University of Kalmar
Kalmarsundslaboratoriet
Landgangen 3
SE-391 82 Kalmar, Sweden
Contact: Director
Tel: 46 480 44 73 00
Fax: 46 480 44 73 05
E-mail: ulf.lidman@hik.se

International Ocean Institute–Black Sea
National Institute for Marine Research and
  Development GEOECOMAR
Str. Dimitrie Oncvil 23–25
RO-024053 Bucharest, Sector 2, Romania
Contact: Director
Tel: 40 252 2594
E-mail: gion@geoecomar.ro

International Ocean Institute–Caspian Sea
c/o Astrakhan State Technical University
No. 16, Tatischeva Street

414025 Astrakhan, Russian Federation
Contact: Director
Tel: 7 8512 549 103
Fax: 7 8512 549 102
E-mail: ioi_csac@astu.org

International Ocean Institute–Germany
c/o Zentrum fur Marine Tropenokologie
Fahrenheitstrasse 6
D-28359 Bremen, Germany
Contact: Director
Tel: 49 421 238 0023
Fax: 49 421 238 0030
E-mail: wekau@zmt.uni-bremen.de

International Ocean Institute–Malta
University of Malta
c/o 43, Flat 1, Valley Road
B'kara, Malta
Contact: Director
Tel/Fax: 356 21 440 972
E-mail: aldo.drago@um.edu.mt

International Ocean Institute–Slovenia
c/o Marine Biology Station Piran
Unit of the National Institute of Biology
  Piran, Ljubljana
Fornace 41
6330 Piran, Slovenia
Contact: Director
Tel: 386 5674 6369
Fax: 386 5674 6367
E-mail: malej@mbss.org

International Ocean Institute–Ukraine
c/o Biotesting Department
Institute of Biology of the Southern Seas
2 Nakhimov Street
Sevastopol 99011, Ukraine
Tel: 380 692 525 249
Fax: 380 692 555 477
E-mail: radalpin@ibss.iuf.net

International Ocean Institute–Volga
c/o Nizhny Novgorod State University of
  Architecture and Civil Engineering
  (NNSUACE)
65, Iiyinskaya Street
603950 Nizhny Novgorod, Russian
  Federation
Contact: Director
Tel: 7 8312 305 492
Fax: 7 8312 300 986
E-mail: iro@nngasu.ru

Marine Biological Association of the
United Kingdom
The Laboratory
Citadel Hill
Plymouth, Devon PL1 2PB, United
Kingdom
Contact: Director
Tel: 44 1752 633207
Fax: 44 1752 633102
E-mail: sec@mba.ac.uk
http://www.mba.ac.uk/

Marine Conservation Society
Unit 3, Wolt Business Park
Alton Road
Ross-on-Wye
Herefordshire, HR9 5MB, United Kingdom
Contact: Secretary
Tel: 44 1989 566017
Fax: 44 1989 567815
http://www.mcsuk.org/

Marine Mammal Council
Nachimovskiy Avenue 36
117218 Moscow, Russian Federation
Tel/Fax: 7 095 124 7579
http://www.2mn.org/

Marine Studies Group
The Geological Society of London
c/o British Geological Survey
Murchison House
West Mains Road
Edinburgh, EH9 3LA, United Kingdom
Contact: Secretary
Tel: 44 131667 1000
Fax: 44 131 667 4140
E-mail: agst@bgs.ac.uk
http://www.ocean.cf.ac.uk/people/neil/MSG/

Maritime Development Center of Europe
Amaliegade 33
DK-1256 Copenhagen K, Denmark
Tel: 45 33 33 74 88
Fax: 45 33 33 75 88
E-mail: info@maritimecenter.dk
http://www.maritimecenter.dk/

Mediterranean Association to Save the Sea
Turtles (MEDASSET)
c/o Park Towers
2 Brick Street
London, W1J 7DD, United Kingdom
E-mail: medasset@medasset.org

Tel/Fax: 44 20 7629 0654
http://www.euroturtle.org/medasset/

National Federation of Fishermen's
Organisations (NFFO)
Marsden Road
Grimsby, DN31 3SG, United Kingdom
Contact: Secretary
Tel: 44 1472 3 52141
Fax: 44 1472 242486
E-mail: dbevan@nffo.org
http://www.nffo.org.uk/

National Union of Marine, Aviation and
Shipping Transport Officers (NUMAST)
Oceanair House
750–760 High Road
Leytonstone, E11 3BB, United Kingdom
Contact: General Secretary
Tel: 44 208 989 6677
E-mail: enquiries@numast.org
http://www.numast.org/

Netherlands Institute of Navigation
Seattleweg 7 (Haven 2801)
NL-3195 ND Pernis, The Netherlands
Contact: Director
Tel: 31 010 498 7518
Fax: 31 010 498 7560
E-mail: r.vanrhee@loodswezen.nl
http://www.nlr.nl/nin/

Northern Shipowners' Defence Club
(Nordisk Skipsrederforening)
Kristinelundveien 22
Postboks 3033 Elisenberg
N-0207 Oslo, Norway
Contact: General Manager
Tel: 47 22 13 56 00
Fax: 47 22 43 00 35
E-mail: post@nordisk.no
http://www.nordisk.org/

Offshore Pollution Liability Association
Bank Chambers
29 High Street
Ewell, Surrey, KT17 1SB, United Kingdom
Contact: Managing Director
Tel: 44 208 786 3640
Fax: 44 208 786 3641
E-mail: r.segal@opol.org.uk
http://www.opol.org.uk/

Royal Institute of Navigation
1 Kensington Gore
London, SW7 2AT, United Kingdom
Contact: Director
Tel: 44 207 591 3130
Fax: 44 207 591 3131
E-mail: info@rin.org.uk
http://www.rin.org.uk/

Royal Institution of Naval Architects
10 Upper Belgrave Street
London, SW1X 8BQ, United Kingdom
Contact: Secretary
Tel: 44 207 235 4622
Fax: 44 207 259 5912
E-mail: hq@rina.org.uk
http://www.rina.org.uk/

Royal Meteorological Society
104 Oxford Road
Reading, Berkshire, RG1 7LL, United
  Kingdom
Contact: Executive Director
Tel: 44 1189 568500
Fax: 44 1189 568571
E-mail: execdir@rmets.org
http://www.royal-met-soc.org.uk/

Scottish Fishermen's Federation
24 Rubislaw Terrace
Aberdeen, AB10 1XE, United Kingdom
Tel: 44 1224 646944
Fax: 44 1224 647058
E-mail: sff@sff.co.uk
http://www.sff.co.uk/

Sea Watch Foundation
11 Jersey Road
Oxford, OX4 4RT, United Kingdom
Contact: Director
Tel/Fax: 44 1865 717276
E-mail: info@seawatchfoundation.org.uk
http://www.seawatchfoundation.org.uk/

Seas at Risk Federation
Drieharingstraat 25
NL-3511 BH Utrecht, Netherlands
Contact: Secretariat
Tel: 31 30 670 1291
Fax: 31 30 670 1292
E-mail: secretariat@seas-at-risk.org
http://www.seas-at-risk.org/

Shetland Salmon Farmers' Association
Shetland Seafood Centre
Stewart Building
Lerwick, Shetland, ZE1 0LL, United
  Kingdom
Contact: Chairman
Tel: 44 1595 69 5579
Fax: 44 1595 69 4494
E-mail: info@shetlandaquaculture.com
http://www.shetlandaquaculture.com/

Shipbuilders and Shiprepairers' Association
  (SSA)
Meadlake Place
Thorpe Lea Road
Egham, Surrey, TW20 8BF, United
  Kingdom
Contact: Director
Tel: 44 1784 223770
Fax: 44 1784 223775
E-mail: office@ssa.org.uk
http://www.ssa.org.uk/

Sir Alister Hardy Foundation for Ocean
  Science (SAHFOS)
The Laboratory
Citadel Hill
Plymouth, PL1 2PB, United Kingdom
Tel: 44 1752 63 3288
Fax: 44 1752 63 3271
E-mail: sahfos@sahfos.ac.uk
http://www.sahfos.org/

Society for Nautical Research (SNR)
c/o National Maritime Museum
Park Row
Greenwich, London, SE10 9NF, United
  Kingdom
Contact: Honorary Secretary
Tel: 44 2 8312 6502
Fax: 44 2 8312 6632
http://www.snr.org/

Society of Consulting Marine Engineers
  and Ship Surveyors (SCMES)
202 Lambeth Road
London, SE1 7JW, United Kingdom
Contact: Secretary
Tel: 44 207 261 0869
Fax: 44 207 261 0871
E-mail: sec@scmshq.org
http://www.scmshq.org/

Society of International Law (Singapore)
c/o Faculty of Law
National University of Singapore
39 Law Link
Singapore 117589
Contact: Secretary
http://www.sils.org/

Society of Maritime Industries
30 Great Guildford Street, 4th Floor
London, SE1 0HS, United Kingdom
Tel: 44 207 928 9199
Fax: 44 207 928 6599
E-mail: info@maritimeindustries.org
http://www.maritimeindustries.org/

Station biologique de la Tour du Valat
Le Sambuc
FR-13200 Arles, France
Tel: 33 4 9097 2013
Fax: 33 4 9097 2019
E-mail: secretariat@tourduvalat.org
http://www.tourduvalat.org/

Swedish Shipowner Employers' Association
Box 1621
SE-111 86 Stockholm, Sweden
Tel: 46 87 62 71 00
Fax: 46 86 11 46 99
E-mail: info@transportgruppen.se
http://www.transportgruppen.se/

Tethys Research Institute
c/o Acquario Civico
via Pompeo Lenoi 2
I-20141 Milano, Italy
Tel: 39 02 5831 4889
Fax: 39 02 5831 5345
E-mail: tethys@tethys.org
http://www.tethys.org/

The Netherlands Shipbuilding Industry
    Association (VNSI)
PO Box 138
NL-2700 AC, Zoetermeer, The Netherlands
Tel: 31 79 353 11 65
Fax: 31 79 353 11 55
E-mail: info@vnsi.nl
http://www.vnsi.nl/

Whale and Dolphin Conservation Society
Brookfield House
38 St. Paul Street

Chippenham, Wiltshire, SN15 1LY, United
    Kingdom
Tel: 44 1249 449500
Fax: 44 1249 449501
E-mail: info@wdcs.org
http://www.wdcs.org/

5.5 Australia, New Zealand and Oceania

Australian Conservation Foundation
60 Leicester Street, Floor 1
Carlton, VIC 3053, Australia
Tel: 61 03 9345 1111
Fax: 61 03 9345 1166
http://www.acfonline.org.au/

Australian Coral Reef Society
c/o Centre for Marine Studies
Level 7 Gerhmann Building
University of Queensland
St. Lucia, QLD 4072, Australia
Contact: Secretary
Tel: 61 07 3365 4333
Fax: 61 07 3365 4755
E-mail: acrs@jcu.edu.au
http://www.australiancoralreefsociety.org/

Australian Marine Conservation Society
PO Box 5136
Manly, QLD 4179, Australia
Contact: National Coordinator
Tel: 61 7 3393 5811
Fax: 61 7 3393 5833
E-mail: amcs@amcs.org.au
http://www.amcs.org.au/

Australian Marine Sciences Association
    (AMSA)
PO Box 8
Kilkvan, QLD 4600, Australia
Tel/Fax: 61 7 4772 4858
E-mail: secretary@amsa.asn.au
http://www.amsa.asn.au/

Cawthron Institute
98 Halifax Street East
Nelson, New Zealand
Tel: 64 3 548 2319
Fax: 64 3 546 9464
E-mail: info@cawthron.org.nz
http://www.cawthron.org.nz/

International Ocean Institute–Australia
International Marine Projects Activities
  Centre
Level 6, Northtown Tower
280 Flinders Mall
PO Box 772
Townsville, QLD 4810, Australia
Tel: 61 07 4729 8452
Fax: 61 07 4729 8449
E-mail: robin.south@impac.org.au
http://www.impac.org.au/associates/ioi.htm

International Ocean Institute–Pacific Islands
c/o Marine Studies Programme
University of the South Pacific
PO Box 1168
Suva, Fiji
Contact: Director
Tel: 679 321 2960
Fax: 679 330 1490
E-mail: veitayaki_j@usp.ac.fj
http://www.usp.ac.fj/marine/IOI/index.htm

Marine and Coastal Community Network
  (MCCN)
PO Box 5136
Manly, QLD 4179, Australia
Contact: National Coordinator
Tel: 61 07 3393 5822
Fax: 61 07 3393 5833
E-mail: nat-off@mccn.org.au
http://www.mccn.org.au/

Maritime Union of Australia
365 Sussex Street, Level 2
Sydney, NSW 2000, Australia
Contact: General Secretary
Tel: 61 02 9267 9134
Fax: 61 02 9261 3481
E-mail: muano@mua.org.au
http://www.mua.org.au/

New Zealand Marine Sciences Society
c/o NIWA
PO Box 14–901
Wellington, New Zealand
Contact: Secretary
E-mail: secretary@nzmss.rsnz.org
http://nzmss.rsnz.org/

Oceania Project
PO Box 7306
Urangan Hervey Bay, QLD 4655, Australia
Tel: 61 7 4125 1333

Fax: 61 2 9225 9176
E-mail: trish.wally@oceania.org.au
http://oceania.org.au/

Pacific Whale Foundation
300 Maalaea Road, Suite 211
Wailuku, HI, 96793, USA
Contact: Chairman
Tel: 1 808 249–8811
Fax: 1 808 249–9021
E-mail: education@pacificwhale.org
http://www.pacificwhale.org/

PACON International
University of Hawaii
2525 Correa Road HIG 407A
Honolulu, HI, 96822, USA
Tel: 1 808 956–6163
Fax: 1 808 956–2580
E-mail: pacon@hawaii.edu
http://www.hawaii.edu/pacon/

5.6 Polar Regions

Antarctic and Southern Ocean Coalition
  (ASOC)
The Antarctica Project
1630 Connecticut Avenue, NW, 3rd Floor
Washington, DC, 20009, USA
Contact: Director
Tel: 1 202 234–2480
Fax: 1 202 387–4823
E-mail: info@asoc.org
http://www.asoc.org/

Antarctic Institute of Canada
PO Box 1223, Main Post Office
Edmonton, AB, T5J 2M4, Canada
Contact: Executive Officer
Tel/Fax: 1 780 452–7392
E-mail: mardon@freenet.edmonton.ab.ca

Arctic Ocean Science Board (AOSB)
Goethestrasse 5
D-61440 Oberursel, Germany
Contact: Secretariat
Tel: 49 6171 6338 40
Fax: 49 6171 6338 39
E-mail: bowden@patriot.net
http://www.aosb.org/

Barrow Arctic Science Consortium
PO Box 577
Barrow, AK, 99723, USA
Contact: Executive Director
Tel: 1 907 852–4881
Fax: 1 907 852–4882
E-mail: basc@arcticscience.org
http://www.arcticscience.org/

Canadian Arctic Resources Committee
  (CARC)
1276 Wellington Street, 2nd floor
Ottawa, ON, K1Y 3A7, Canada
Contact: Executive Director
Tel: 1 613 759–4284
Fax: 1 613 759–4581
E-mail: info@carc.org
http://www.carc.org/

European Polar Board (EPB)
European Science Foundation
1, quai Lezay-Marnésia
F-67080 Strasbourg, France
Contact: Secretariat
Tel: 33 3 8876 7166
Fax: 33 3 8876 7181
http://www.esf.org/esf_genericpage.php?
  language=0&section=2&domain=3&
  genericpage=1876

International Polar Heritage Committee
c/o Directorate for Cultural Heritage
PO Box 8196 Dep
N-0034 Oslo, Norway
Contact: Secretary General
Tel: 47 22 94 04 00
Fax: 47 22 94 04 04
E-mail: susan.barr@ra.no
http://www.polarhertiage.com/

Inuit Circumpolar Conference (ICC)
c/o ICC (Greenland)
PO Box 204
3900 Nuuk, Greenland
Contact: President
Tel: 299 3 23632
Fax: 299 3 23001
E-mail: aqqaluk@inuit.org
http://www.inuit.org/

6. REGIONAL ACADEMIC ORGANIZATIONS

6.1 Africa

Arab Academy for Science and Technology
  and Maritime Transport
Gamal Abdel Naser Street
PO Box 1029
Alexandria, Egypt
Contact: Director General
Tel: 20 3 556 1497
Fax: 20 3 548 7786
E-mail: imomou@aast.edu
http://www.aast.edu/

Benguela Environment Fisheries Interaction
  and Training Programme (BENEFIT)
c/o Nat Mirc
Strand Street
PO Box 912
Swakopmund, Namibia
Contact: Director
Tel: 264 64 4101164
Fax: 264 64 405913
E-mail: nsweijd@benguela.org
http://www.benefit.org.na/

Centre for Environmental Management
School of Environmental Sciences
Howard College Campus
University of KwaZulu-Natal
Durban 4041, South Africa
Tel: 27 31 260 2653
Fax: 27 31 260 1391
E-mail: philpk@ukzn.ac.za
http://www.geography.ukzn.ac.za/cem/

Centre for Marine Studies
University of Cape Town
Oceanography Annexe
Residence Road
Private Bag
Rondebosch 7701, South Africa
Contact: Director
Tel: 27 21 650 3283
E-mail: cms@physci.uct.ac.za

Department of Environmental and
  Geographical Science
University of Cape Town
UCT Private Bag

Rondebosch 7701, South Africa
Tel: 27 21 650 2873/4
Fax: 27 21 650 3791
E-mail: postgrad@enviro.uct.ac.za
http://www.egs.uct.ac.za/

Department of Ichthyology and Fisheries
    Science
Rhodes University
PO Box 94
Grahamstown 6140, South Africa
Tel: 27 46 603 8415
Fax: 27 46 622 4827
E-mail: difs@ru.ac.za
http://www.ru.ac.za/academic/
    departments/difs/

Department of Natural Resources and
    Conservation
Faculty of Agriculture and Natural
    Resources
University of Namibia
Private Bag 13301
Windhoek, Namibia
Tel: 264 61 206 3890
Fax 264 61 206 3013
E-mail: lkandjengo@unam.na
http://www.unam.na/faculties/agriculture/
    conservation.html

Department of Oceanography
University of Cape Town
RW James Building, Residence Road,
    Upper Campus
UCT Private Bag
Rondebosch 7701, South Africa
Tel: 27 21 650 3278
Fax: 27 21 650 3979
E-mail: hodsea@ocean.uct.ac.za
http://www.sea.uct.ac.za/

Department of Zoology and Entomology
Rhodes University
PO Box 94
Grahamstown 6140, South Africa
Tel: 27 46 603 8525
E-mail: zoosec@ru.ac.za
http://www.ru.ac.za/academic/departments/
    zooento/

Faculty of Aquatic Sciences and
    Technology (FAST)
University of Dar es Salaam
PO Box 35064

Dar es Salaam, Tanzania
Tel: 255 22 2410462
Fax: 255 22 2410480
E-mail: deanfast@udsm.ac.tz
http://www.fast.udsm.ac.tz/

Henties Bay Marine and Coastal Resources
    Research Centre
University of Namibia
PO Box 462
Henties Bay, Namibia
Contact: Director
Tel: 264 64 502600
Fax: 264 64 502608
E-mail: odmwandemele@unam.na
http://www.unam.na/research/henties/

Institut des Sciences de la Mer et de
    l'Aménagement du Littoral (ISMAL)
BP 54
Sidi-Fredj
42321 d'Alger, Algeria
Tel/Fax: 213 21 363636
E-mail: info@ismal.net
http://www.ismal.net/

Institut Fondamental d'Afrique Noire
    (IFAN)
Cheikh Anta Diop University
BP 5005
Dakar, Senegal
Contact: Marine Biology Lab
Tel: 221 825 7528
Fax: 221 825 3724
E-mail: info@ucad.sn
http://www.ucad.sn/

Institut Scientifique
Université Mohammed V
Ave Ibn Batouta
BP 703 Rabat-Agdal
10106 Rabat, Morocco
Contact: Directeur
Tel: 212 37 77 45 48
Fax: 212 37 77 45 40
http://www.israbat.ac.ma/

Institute of Marine and Environmental Law
University of Cape Town
UCT Private Bag
Rondebosch 7701, South Africa
Contact: Director
Tel: 27 21 650 5642
Fax: 27 21 650 5607

E-mail: lawmar@law.uct.ac.za
http://web.uct.ac.za/depts/pbl/imel/
   intro.htm

Institute of Marine Biology and
   Oceanography
Fourah Bay College
University of Sierra Leone
PO Box 87
Mount Aureol
Freetown, Sierra Leone
Contact: Director
Tel: 232 22 227 924
Fax: 232 22 224 260
E-mail: fbcadmin@sierratel.sl
http://fbcusl.8k.com/index.html

Institute of Marine Sciences
University of Dar es Salaam
PO Box 668
Zanzibar, Tanzania
Contact: Director
Tel: 255 24 2232128
E-mail: director@ims.udsm.ac.tz
http://www.ims.udsm.ac.tz/

Institute of Oceanography
University of Calabar
PMB 1115
Calabar, Cross River State, Nigeria
Contact: Director
Tel: 234 222855
Fax: 234 224996
E-mail: aobiekezie@yahoo.com
http://www.fish-research.net/

Nigerian Institute for Oceanography and
   Marine Research (NIOMR)
Wilmot Point Road
Bar Beach
PO Box 12729
Lagos, Nigeria
Tel/Fax: 234 1 617385
E-mail: niomr@linkserve.com.ng

Regional Maritime Academy
PO Box 1115
Accra, Ghana
Contact: Director General
Tel: 233 21 712343
Fax: 233 21 712047
E-mail: prinerma@africaonline.com.gh
http://www.rma-edu.com/

School of Maritime Studies
University of KwaZulu-Natal
Durban, 4041, South Africa
Tel: 27 31 260 2994
Fax: 27 31 260 3163
E-mail: maritime@ukzn.ac.za
http://www.maritime.ukzn.ac.za/

Shipping Law Unit
Faculty of Law
University of Cape Town
UCT Private Bag
Rondebosch 7701, South Africa
Contact: Director
Tel: 27 21 650 3087
Fax: 27 21 650 5662
E-mail: shiplaw@law.uct.ac.za
http://www.uctshiplaw.com/

UNESCO Chair in Integrated Coastal
   Management and Sustainable
   Development
Departement de Geographie
Faculté des Lettres et des Sciences
   Humaines
Cheikh Anta Diop Université
BP 5005
Dakar-Fann, Senegal
Contact: Chef de Departement
Tel: 221 825 7528
Fax: 221 825 3724
E-mail: geo@ucad.sn
http://www.ucad.sn/

6.2   The Americas

Acadia Centre for Estuarine Research
Acadia University
23 Westwood Avenue
Campus Box 115
Wolfville, NS, B4P 2R6, Canada
Contact: Director
Tel: 1 902 585–1113
Fax: 1 902 585–1054
E-mail: donna.porter@acadiau.ca
http://ace.acadiau.ca/science/cer/home.htm

AquaNet
c/o Ocean Sciences Centre
Memorial University of Newfoundland
St. John's, NL, A1C 5S7, Canada

Contact: Administrative Centre
Tel: 1 709 737–3245
Fax: 1 709 737–3500
E-mail: info@aquanet.ca
http://www.aquanet.mun.ca/

Association of Marine Laboratories of the
    Caribbean (AMLC)
Mote Marine Laboratory
1600 Ken Thompson Parkway
Sarasota, FL, 34236, USA
Contact: Executive Director
Tel: 1 941 388–4441
Fax: 1 941 388–4312
E-mail: slegore@mindspring.com
http://amlc.uvi.edu/

Bamfield Marine Sciences Centre
Bamfield, BC, V0R 1B0, Canada
Contact: Director
Tel: 1 250 728–3301
Fax: 1 250 728–3452
E-mail: info@bms.bc.ca
http://www.bms.bc.ca/

Bellairs Research Institute
Holetown, St. James, Barbados
Tel: 1 246 422–2087
Fax: 1 246 422–0692
E-mail: bellairs@caribsurf.com
http://www.mcgill.ca/bellairs/

Belle W. Baruch Institute for Marine and
    Coastal Sciences
University of South Carolina
607 EWS Building
Columbia, SC, 29208, USA
Contact: Director
Tel: 1 803 777–5288
Fax: 1 803 777–3935
E-mail: fletcher@sc.edu
http://inlet.geol.sc.edu/

Bermuda Biological Station for Research
17 Biological Station Lane
Ferry Reach
St. George's, GE01, Bermuda
Contact: Director
Tel: 1 441 297–1880
Fax: 1 441 297–8143
E-mail: webmaster@bbsr.edu
http://www.bbsr.edu/

Bodega Marine Laboratory
University of California at Davis
2099 Westside Road
PO Box 247
Bodega Bay, CA, 94923–0247, USA
Tel: 1 707 875–2211
Fax: 1 707 875–2009
E-mail: ucdbml@ucdavis.edu
http://www.bml.ucdavis.edu/

Canadian Coast Guard College
PO Box 4500
Sydney, NS, B1P 6L1, Canada
Tel: 1 902 567–3208
Fax: 1 902 567–3233
E-mail: cosey1@dfo-mpo.gc.ca
http://www.cgc.ns.ca/

Canadian Institute for Climate Studies
University of Victoria
C199 Sedgwick Building
PO Box 1700 Sta CSC
Victoria, BC, V8W 2Y2, Canada
Tel: 1 250 472–4337
Fax: 1 250 472–4830
E-mail: climate@uvic.ca
http://www.cics.uvic.ca/

Canadian Institute of Fisheries Technology
    (CIFT)
Faculty of Engineering
Dalhousie University
PO Box 1000
1360 Barrington Street
Halifax, NS, B3J 2X4, Canada
Tel: 1 902 494–6030
Fax: 1 902 420–0219
E-mail: food.science@dal.ca
http://www.dal.ca/~cift/

Center for Coastal and Land-Margin
    Research (CCALMR)
Department of Environmental and
    Biomolecular Systems
OGI School of Science and Engineering
Oregon Health & Science University
20000 NW Walker Road
Beaverton, OR, 97006, USA
Contact: Director
Tel: 1 503 748–1147
Fax: 1 503 748–1273
E-mail: baptista@ccalmr.ogi.edu
http://www.ccalmr.ogi.edu/

Center for Coastal Studies
Scripps Institution of Oceanography
University of California, San Diego
La Jolla, CA, 92093–0209, USA
Contact: Director
Tel: 1 858 534–4333
Fax: 1 858 534–0300
E-mail: rtg@coast.ucsd.edu
http://www.ccs.ucsd.edu/

Center for Ocean-Atmospheric Prediction
  Studies
Florida State University
Tallahassee, FL, 32306 2840, USA
Contact: Director
Tel: 1 850 644 4581
Fax: 1 850 644 4841
E-mail: jim.obrien@coaps.fsu.edu
http://www.coaps.fsu.edu/

Center for Oceans Law and Policy
University of Virginia School of Law
580 Massie Road
Charlottesville, VA, 22903, USA
Contact: Director
Tel: 1 434 924–7441
Fax: 1 434 924–7362
E-mail: colp@virginia.edu
http://www.virginia.edu/colp/

Centre for Asian Legal Studies
Faculty of Law
University of British Columbia
1822 East Mall
Vancouver, BC, V6T 1Z1, Canada
Tel: 1 604 822–3151
Fax: 1 604 822–8108
E-mail: borthwick@law.ubc.ca
http://www.law.ubc.ca/centres/index.htm

Centre for Community-based Management
St. Francis Xavier University
PO Box 5000
Antigonish, NS, B2G 2W5, Canada
Tel: 1 902 867–2433
E-mail: ccbm@stfx.ca
http://www.stfx.ca/institutes/ccbm/

Centre for Earth and Ocean Research
  (CEOR)
University of Victoria
Technology Enterprise Facility, Room 130
PO Box 1700, STN CSC
Victoria, BC, V8W 2Y2, Canada

Contact: Director
Tel: 1 250 721–8848
Fax: 1 250 472–4100
E-mail: ceor@uvic.ca
http://web.uvic.ca/ceor

Centre for Indigenous Peoples' Nutrition
  and Environment (CINE)
Macdonald Campus of McGill University
21,111 Lakeshore Road
Ste-Anne-de-Bellevue, QC, H9X 3V9,
  Canada
Tel: 1 514 398–7544
Fax: 1 514 398–1020
E-mail: cine.macdonald@mcgill.ca
http://cine.mcgill.ca/

Centre for Marine Sciences
University of the West Indies, Mona
  Campus
Mona, Kingston 7, Jamaica
Tel: 1 876 977–0262
Fax: 1 876 977–1033
E-mail: cms@uwimona.edu.jm
http://www.uwimona.edu.jm/cms/

Centre for Ocean Studies
(Centro de Estudos do Mar)
Federal University of Paraná
Av. Beira-mar s/n Caixa Postal/P.O.Box
  50002
CEP: 83255–000–Pontal do Sul
Pontal do Paraná–PR–Brazil
Contact: Director
Tel: 55 41 455 1333
Fax: 55 41 455 1105
E-mail: edmarone@ufpr.br
http://www.cem.ufpr.br/

Centre for Tourism Policy and Research
Simon Fraser University
8888 University Drive
Burnaby, BC, V5A 1S6, Canada
Contact: Director
Tel: 1 604 291–3074
Fax: 1 604 291–4968
E-mail: peterw@sfu.ca
http://www.sfu.ca/%7edossa/

Centro de Investigaciones Marinas
Calle 16 #114, entre 1era y 3era
Miramar Playa.
Ciudad de la Habana, Cuba
Tel: 537 23 0617

Fax: 537 24 2087
E-mail: cim@nova.uh.cu
http://www.uh.cu/centros/cim/index.htm

Centro de Investigaciones Oceanográficas
    Pesqueras (CIOP)
(Fisheries Oceanography Research Centre)
Facultad de Ingeniería Marítima y Ciencias
    del Mar
Escuela Superior Politécnica del Litoral
    (ESPOL)
PO Box 09–01–4382
Guayaquil, Ecuador
Tel: 593 4 2269 456
Fax: 593 4 2269 468
E-mail: ciop@espoltel.net
http://www.ciopespol.edu.ec

Charles Darwin Research Station
Puerto Ayora, Santa Cruz, Galapagos
    Islands, Ecuador
Contact: Director
Tel: 593 5526 147/8
E-mail: cdrs@fcdarwin.org.ec
http://www.darwinfoundation.org/

Chesapeake Biological Laboratory
Center for Environmental Science
University of Maryland
PO Box 38
1 Williams Street
Solomons, MD, 20688, USA
Contact: Director
Tel: 1 410 326–4241
Fax: 1 410 326–7264
E-mail: palmer@cbl.umces.edu
http://www.cbl.umces.edu/

Coastal and Ocean Engineering Division
Department of Civil Engineering
Texas A&M University
3136 TAMU
College Station, TX, 77843–3136, USA
Tel: 1 979 845–4515
Fax: 1 979 862–8162
E-mail: lori@civil.tamu.edu
http://oceaneng.civil.tamu.edu/

Coastal and Oceanic Geological Research
    Centre
(Centro de Estudos de Geologia Costeira e
    Oceânica–CECO)
Universidade Federal do Rio Grande do
    Sul

Av. Bento Gonçalves, 9500 Prédio 43125
Porto Alegre, RS, Brazil
Tel: 55 3316 6373
Fax: 55 3316 7302
E-mail: ceco@ufrgs.br
http://www.ufrgs.br/ceco/

Coastal Fisheries Institute
School of the Coast and Environment
Louisiana State University
2179 Energy, Coast and Environment
    Building
Baton Rouge, LA, 70803, USA
Tel: 1 255 578–6455
Fax: 1 255 578–6513
E-mail: kjone57@lsu.edu
http://www.cfi.lsu.edu/

Coastal Institute
Narragansett Bay Campus, Room 124
University of Rhode Island
Narragansett, RI, 02882, USA
Tel: 1 401 874–6513
Fax: 1 401 874–6869
E-mail: ci@edc.uri.edu
http://www.ci.uri.edu/

Coastal Resources Center
Narragansett Bay Campus
University of Rhode Island
Narragansett, RI, 02882, USA
Tel: 1 401 874–6224
Fax: 1 401 789–4670
E-mail: info@crc.uri.edu
http://www.crc.uri.edu/

Coastal Resources Institute
ECMAR-UNA
Universidad Nacional
Facultad de Ciencias Exactas y Naturales
Heredia, Costa Rica
Tel: 506 277 3313
Fax: 506 277 3485
Tel/Fax: 506 661 2394
E-mail: ecmar@una.ac.cr
http://www.una.ac.cr/ecmar/

College of Ocean and Fishery Sciences
University of Washington
PO Box 355350
Seattle, WA, 98195–5350, USA
Contact: Dean
Tel: 1 206 543–6605
Fax: 1 206 543–6393

E-mail: webmaster@cofs.washington.edu
http://www.cofs.washington.edu/

College of Oceanic and Atmospheric
  Sciences
Oregon State University
104 COAS Administration Building
Corvallis, OR, 97331–5503, USA
Contact: Dean
Tel: 1 541 737–3504
Fax: 1 541 737–2064
E-mail: mark@coas.oregonstate.edu
http://www.coas.oregonstate.edu/

Cooperative Institute for Arctic Research
  (CIFAR)
University of Alaska Fairbanks
PO Box 757740
Fairbanks, AK, 99775–7740, USA
Contact: Administrator
Tel: 1 907 474–5818
Fax: 1 907 474–6722
E-mail: cifar@iarc.uaf.edu
http://www.cifar.uaf.edu/

Darling Marine Center
University of Maine
193 Clark's Cove Road
Walpole, ME, 04573, USA
Contact: Director
Tel: 1 207 563–3146
Fax: 1 207 563–3119
E-mail: kevine@maine.edu
http://www.dmc.maine.edu/

Department of Atmospheric and Oceanic
  Sciences
McGill University
Burnside Hall, Room 945
805 Sherbrooke Street West
Montreal, QC, H3A 2K6, Canada
Contact: Chair
Tel: 1 514 398–3764
Fax: 1 514 398–6115
E-mail: ornella@zephyr.meteo.mcgill.ca
http://www.mcgill.ca/meteo/

Department of Earth and Ocean Sciences
University of British Columbia
6339 Stores Road
Vancouver, BC, V6T 1Z4, Canada
Contact: Department Head
Tel: 1 604 822–2449
Fax: 1 604 822–6088

E-mail: inquiries@eos.ubc.ca
http://www.eos.ubc.ca/

Department of Marine Sciences
University of North Carolina
12–7 Venable Hall, CB# 3300
Chapel Hill, NC, 27599–3300, USA
Contact: Director
Tel: 1 919 962–1252
Fax: 1 919 962–1254
E-mail: cisco@unc.edu
http://www.marine.unc.edu/

Department of Marine Sciences
Marine Sciences Building
University of Georgia
Athens, GA, 30602–3636, USA
Contact: Director
Tel: 1 706 542–7671
Fax: 1 706 542–5888
E-mail: agnadoc@uga.edu
http://alpha.marsci.uga.edu/

Department of Oceanography
Dalhousie University
1355 Oxford Street
Halifax, NS, B3H 4J1, Canada
Tel: 1 902 494–3557
Fax: 1 902 494–3877
E-mail: oceanography@dal.ca
http://www.dal.ca/~wwwocean/

Department of Oceanography
College of Geosciences
Texas A&M University
3146 TAMU
College Station, TX, 77843–3146, USA
Tel: 1 979 845–7211
Fax: 1 979 845–6331
E-mail: info@oceanography.tamu.edu
http://www-ocean.tamu.edu/

Department of Oceanography
0102 OSB, West Call Street
Florida State University
Tallahassee, FL, 32306–4320, USA
Contact: Academic Coordinator
Tel: 1 850 644–6700
Fax: 1 850 644–2581
E-mail: admissions@ocean.fsu.edu
http://www.ocean.fsu.edu/

Department of Oceanography
Fundaçao Universidade do Rio Grande

Caixa Postal, 474
96201–900, Rio Grande, RS, Brazil
Tel: 55 532 33 6534
Fax: 55 532 33 6601
E-mail: docosta@super.furg.br
http://www.furg.br/ciencias.marinhas

Escuela Nacional de Marina Mercante
  (ENAMM)
Av. Progreso 632
Chucuito-Callao, Peru
Tel: 511 4298210
Fax: 511 4298218
E-mail: informes@enamm.edu.pe
http://www.enamm.edu.pe/

Faculty of Law
University of Victoria
PO Box 2400, STN CSC
Victoria, BC, V8W 3H7, Canada
Tel: 1 250 721–8150
Fax: 1 250 721–6390
E-mail: lawrecep@uvic.ca
http://www.law.uvic.ca/

Faculty of Marine Engineering and Marine
  Sciences
Escuela Superior Politécnica del Litoral
Campus Gustavo Galindo Velasco
Km. 30,5 Via Perimetral
Apartado: 09–01–5863
Guayaquil, Ecuador
Tel: 593 4 2 269269
Fax: 593 4 2 854560
E-mail: info@cenaim.espol.edu.ec
http://fimcm.espol.edu.ec/

Faculty of Marine Sciences
(Facultad del Mar y de Recursos)
Universidad de Valparaíso
Av. Borgoño 16344, Montemar
Casilla 13-D
Viña de Mar
Valparaíso, Chile
Tel: 56 32 507820
http://www.uv.cl/

Faculty of Marine Sciences
(Facultad de Ciencias del Mar)
Universidad Católica del Norte
Campus Guayacán
Larrondo 1281
Casilla 117

Coquimbo, Chile
Tel: 56 51 209736
Fax: 56 51 209750
E-mail: faculmar@ucn.cl
http://www.ucn.cl/DeptoCsMar/default.asp

Fisheries Centre
University of British Columbia
Lower Mall Research Station
2259 Lower Mall
Vancouver, BC, V6T 1Z4, Canada
Contact: Director
Tel: 1 604 822–2731
Fax: 1 604 822–8934
E-mail: office@fisheries.ubc.ca
http://www.fisheries.ubc.ca/

Five College Coastal and Marine Sciences
  Program
Clark Science Center
Smith College
Northampton, MA, 01063, USA
Tel: 1 413 585–3799
E-mail: marinesci@smith.edu
http://www.fivecolleges.edu/sites/marine/

Gerald G. Mangone Center for Marine
  Policy
Graduate College of Marine Studies
University of Delaware
301 Robinson Hall
Newark, DE, 19716, USA
Contact: Director
Tel: 1 302 831–8086
Fax: 1 302 831–3668
E-mail: bcs@udel.edu
http://www.ocean.udel.edu/cmp/

Graduate College of Marine Studies
University of Delaware
111 Robinson Hall
Newark, DE, 19716–3501, USA
Contact: Office of the Dean
Tel: 1 302 831–2841
Fax: 1 302 831–4389
E-mail: info@cms.udel.edu
http://www.ocean.udel.edu/

Graduate School of Oceanography
University of Rhode Island
South Ferry Road
URI Bay Campus Box 52
Narragansett, RI, 02882–1197, USA

Contact: Dean
Tel: 1 401 874–6222
Fax: 1 401 874–6889
E-mail: TheDean@gso.uri.edu
http://www.gso.uri.edu/

Gulf and Caribbean Fisheries Institute
c/o Florida Fish and Wildlife Conservation
    Commission
Marine Research Institute
2796 Overseas Highway, Station 119
Marathon, FL, 33050, USA
Contact: Executive Secretary
Tel: 1 305 289–2330
Fax: 1 305 289–2334
E-mail: leroy.creswell@gcfi.org
http://www.gcfi.org/

Harbor Branch Oceanographic Institution
5600 US 1 North
Fort Pierce, FL, 34946, USA
Contact: President
Tel: 1 772 465–2400
Fax: 1 772 465–2446
E-mail: epomponi@hboi.edu
http://www.hboi.edu/

Hopkins Marine Station of Stanford
    University
Oceanview Boulevard
Pacific Grove, CA, 93950–3094, USA
Tel: 1 831 655–6200
Fax: 1 831 375–0793
E-mail: information@marine.stanford.edu
http://www-marine.stanford.edu/

Institut des sciences de la mer de
    Rimouski (ISMER)
Université du Québec à Rimouski
300, allée des Ursulines
C.P. 3300
Rimouski, QC, G5L 3A1, Canada
Tel: 1 418 724–1650
Fax: 1 418 724–1842
E-mail: ismer@uqar.qc.ca
http://www.pqm.net/ismer/

Institut maritime du Québec
53, rue Saint-Germain Ouest
Rimouski, QC, G5L 4B4, Canada
Tel: 1 418 724–2822
Fax: 1 418 724–0606
E-mail: institut@imq.qc.ca
http://www.imq.qc.ca/

Institute of Marine Sciences
University of North Carolina at Chapel Hill
3431 Arendell Street
Morehead City, NC, 28557, USA
Contact: Director
Tel: 1 252 726–6841
Fax: 1 252 726–2426
E-mail: ims@unc.edu
http://www.marine.unc.edu/IMS/

Institute of Nautical Archaeology
PO Drawer HG
College Station, TX, 77841–5137, USA
Tel: 1 979 845–6694
Fax: 1 979 847–9260
E-mail: ina@tamu.edu
http://ina.tamu.edu/

Interdisciplinary Studies in Aquatic
    Resources (ISAR)
St. Francis Xavier University
PO Box 5000
Antigonish, NS, B2G 2W5, Canada
Contact: Program Officer
Tel: 1 902 867–3905
Fax: 1 902 867–5256
E-mail: lpatters@stfx.ca
http://iago.stfx.ca/academic/
    aquatic_resources/

Maine Maritime Academy
Castine, ME, 04420–5000, USA
Tel: 1 207 326–2206
E-mail: admissions@mma.edu
http://www.mainemaritime.edu/

Marine Affairs Program
Dalhousie University
Kenneth C. Rowe Management Building
6100 University Avenue
Halifax, NS, B3H 3J5, Canada
Contact: Coordinator
Tel: 1 902 494–3555
Fax: 1 902 494–1001
E-mail: marine.affairs@dal.ca
http://www.dal.ca/mmm/

Marine and Environmental Law Institute
Dalhousie Law School
6061 University Avenue
Halifax, NS, B3H 4H9, Canada
Contact: Director
Tel: 1 902 494–1988
Fax: 1 902 494–1316

E-mail: melaw@dal.ca
http://www.dal.ca/law/MELAW/

Marine and Environmental Programs
Woodward Hall
University of Rhode Island
Kingston, RI, 02881, USA
Contact: Office of Marine Programs
Tel: 1 401 874–2957
Fax: 1 401 874–4017
E-mail: omp@gso.uri.edu
http://omp.gso.uri.edu/urime/

Marine Institute
Memorial University of Newfoundland
PO Box 4920
St. John's, NL, A1C 5R3, Canada
Tel: 1 709 778–0200
Fax: 1 709 778–0346
http://www.mi.mun.ca/

Marine Law Institute
University of Maine
School of Law
246 Deering Avenue
Portland, ME, 04102, USA
Contact: Director
Tel: 1 207 780–4442
Fax: 1 207 780–4239
E-mail: reiser@maine.edu
http://www.mainelaw.maine.edu/mli/

Marine Policy Center
Woods Hole Oceanographic Institution
Crowell House, MS #41
Woods Hole, MA, 02543–1138, USA
Contact: Director
Tel: 1 508 289–2449
Fax: 1 508 457–2184
E-mail: egately@whoi.edu
http://www.whoi.edu/mpcweb/

Marine Resource Management Program
College of Oceanic and Atmospheric
    Sciences
Oregon State University
104 Ocean Administration Building
Corvallis, OR, 97331–5033, USA
Contact: Coordinator
Tel: 1 541 737–1339
Fax: 1 541 737–2064
E-mail: good@coas.oregonstate.edu
http://www.oce.orst.edu/mrm/

Marine Science Center
Northeastern University
430 Nahant Road
Nahant, MA, 01908, USA
Contact: Director
Tel: 1 781 581–7370
Fax: 1 781 581–6076
E-mail: e.maney@neu.edu
http://www.marinescience.neu.edu/

Marine Science Institute
Department of Marine Science
University of Texas at Austin
750 Channel View Drive
Port Aransas, TX, 78373–5015, USA
Contact: Director
Tel: 1 361 749–6711
Fax: 1 361 749–6777
E-mail: quade@utmsi.utexas.edu
http://www.utmsi.utexas.edu/

Marine Sciences Research Center
Stony Brook University
Endeavour Hall, Room 145
Stony Brook, NY, 11794–5000, USA
Tel: 1 631 632–8700
Fax: 1 631 632–8915
E-mail: jcosgrove@notes.cc.sunysb.edu
http://www.msrc.sunysb.edu/

National Sea Grant Law Center
University of Mississippi
Kinard Hall, Wing E, Room 262
PO Box 1848
University, MS, 38677–1848, USA
Contact: Director
Tel: 1 662 915–7775
Fax: 1 662 915–5267
E-mail: sealaw@olemiss.edu
http://www.olemiss.edu/orgs/SGLC/

Naval Postgraduate School
Public Affairs Office, Code 004
1 University Circle
Monterey, CA, 93943–3164, USA
Tel: 1 831 656–2023
Fax: 1 831 656–3238
E-mail: pao@nps.edu
http://www.nps.edu/

Naval War College
686 Cushing Avenue
Newport, RI, 02841, USA
Tel: 1 401 841–1310

E-mail: qdeck@nwc.navy.mil
http://www.nwc.navy.mil/

Nicholas School of the Environment and
    Earth Sciences
Duke University
PO Box 90328
Durham, NC, 27708, USA
Contact: Dean
Tel: 1 919 613–8000
Fax: 1 919 684–8741
E-mail: admin@env.duke.edu
http://www.env.duke.edu/

Ocean and Coastal Law Program
University of Miami School of Law
PO Box 248087
Coral Gables, FL, 33124, USA
Contact: Director, International and
    Foreign Law Programs
Tel: 1 305 284–5402
Fax: 1 305 284–2349
E-mail: intl-llm@law.miami.edu
http://www.law.miami.edu/ifp/

Ocean and Coastal Law Center
School of Law
1221 University of Oregon
Eugene, OR, 97403–1221, USA
Contact: Director
Tel: 1 541 346–3845
Fax: 1 541 346–1564
E-mail: dbass@law.uoregon.edu
http://oceanlaw.uoregon.edu/

Ocean Sciences Centre
Memorial University of Newfoundland
St. John's, NL, A1C 5S7 Canada
Contact: Director
Tel: 1 709 737–3709
Fax: 1 709 737–3220
E-mail: wsparkes@mun.ca
http://www.osc.mun.ca/

Office of Marine Programs
University of Rhode Island
Narragansett Bay Campus
Narragansett, RI, 02882–1197, USA
Tel: 1 401 874–6211
Fax: 1 401 874–6486
E-mail: omp@gso.uri.edu
http://omp.gso.uri.edu/

Perry Institute for Marine Science
100N US Highway 1, Suite 202
Jupiter, FL, 33477–5122, USA
Tel: 1 561 741–0192
Fax: 1 561 741–0193
E-mail: pims@perryinstitute.org
http://www.perryinstitute.org/

Pew Institute for Ocean Science
Rosenstiel School of Marine and
    Atmospheric Science
University of Miami
4600 Rickenbacker Causeway
Miami, FL, 33149, USA
Tel: 1 305 421–4165
Fax: 1 305 421–4077
http://www.pewoceanscience.org/

Rosenstiel School of Marine and
    Atmospheric Science (RSMAS)
University of Miami
4600 Rickenbacker Causeway
Miami, FL, 33149–1098, USA
Contact: Dean
Tel: 1 305 421–4000
Fax: 1 305 421–4711
E-mail: dean@rsmas.miami.edu
http://www.rsmas.miami.edu/

School for Field Studies
10 Federal Street, Ste. 24
Salem, MA, 01970–3876, USA
Contact: President
Tel: 1 978 741–3544
Fax: 1 978 741–3551
E-mail: admissions@fieldstudies.org
http://www.fieldstudies.org/

School of Aquatic and Fisheries Sciences
University of Washington
Box 355020
Seattle, WA, 98195–5020, USA
Tel: 1 206 543–4270
Fax: 1 206 685–7471
E-mail: frontdesk@fish.washington.edu
http://www.fish.washington.edu/

School of Fisheries and Ocean Sciences
University of Alaska Fairbanks
245 O'Neill Building
Fairbanks, AK, 99775–7220, USA
Tel: 1 907 474–7824
Fax: 1 907 474–7204

E-mail: info@sfos.uaf.edu
http://www.sfos.uaf.edu/

School of Marine Affairs
University of Washington
3707 Brooklyn Avenue, NE
Seattle, WA, 98105–6715, USA
Tel: 1 206 543–7004
Fax: 1 206 543–1417
E-mail: uwsma@u.washington.edu
http://www.sma.washington.edu/

School of Marine Sciences
University of Maine
341 Aubert Hall
Orono, ME, 04469–5741, USA
Contact: Director
Tel: 1 207 581–4367
Fax: 1 207 581–4388
E-mail: davidt@maine.edu
http://www.marine.maine.edu/

School of Oceanography
University of Washington
Box 357940
Seattle, WA, 98195–7940, USA
Contact: Director
Tel: 1 206 543–5060
Fax: 1 206 543–0275
http://www.ocean.washington.edu/

School of the Coast and Environment
Louisiana State University
1002-Q Energy, Coast and Environment
  Building
Baton Rouge, LA, 70803, USA
Contact: Dean
Tel: 1 225 578–6316
Fax: 1 225 578–5328
E-mail: edlaws@lsu.edu
http://www.sc&e.lsu.edu/

Scotiabank Marine Geology Research
  Laboratory
Department of Geology
University of Toronto
22 Russell Street
Toronto, ON, M5S 3B1, Canada
Tel: 1 416 978–5424
Fax: 1 416 978–3938
E-mail: scottsd@geology.utoronto.ca
http://www.geology.utoronto.ca/marinelab/

Scripps Institution of Oceanography
University of California, San Diego
9500 Gilman Drive
La Jolla, CA, 92093–2827, USA
Contact: Director
Tel: 1 858 534–2827
Fax: 1 858 453–0167
E-mail: ckennel@sio.ucsd.edu
http://sio.ucsd.edu/

Sea Education Association
PO Box 6
Woods Hole, MA, 02543, USA
Contact: Dean
Tel: 1 508 540–3954
Fax: 1 508 457–4673
E-mail: dean@sea.edu
http://www.sea.edu/

Shoals Marine Laboratory
Cornell University
G-14 Stimson Hall
Ithaca, NY, 14853, USA
Contact: Director
Tel: 1 607 255–3717
Fax: 1 607 255–0742
E-mail: shoals-lab@cornell.edu
http://www.sml.cornell.edu/

Smithsonian Environmental Research
  Center
PO Box 28
647 Contees Wharf Road
Edgewater, MD, 21037–0028, USA
Tel: 1 443 482–2200
Fax: 1 443 482–2380
E-mail: jiacinto@si.edu
http://www.serc.si.edu/

Smithsonian Tropical Research Institute
Roosevelt Avenue, Building 401
PO Box 0843–03092
Balboa, Ancon, Republic of Panama
Contact: Director
Tel: 507 212 8000
Fax: 507 212 8148
E-mail: webmaster@stri.org
http://www.stri.org/

Tulane Law School
Weinmann Hall
6329 Freret Street
New Orleans, LA, 70118–6231, USA
Tel: 1 504 865–5939

Fax: 1 504 865–6710
E-mail: admissions@law.tulane.edu
http://www.law.tulane.edu/

Urban Harbors Institute
University of Massachusetts Boston
100 Morrissey Boulevard
Boston, MA, 02125, USA
Tel: 1 617 287–5570
Fax: 1 617 287–5575
E-mail: urban.harbors@umb.edu
http://www.uhi.umb.edu/

Virginia Institute of Marine Science
College of William and Mary
PO Box 1346
Gloucester Point, VA, 23062, USA
Contact: Director
Tel: 1 804 684–7000
Fax: 1 804 684–7097
E-mail: wells@vims.edu
http://www.vims.edu/

Whale Research Lab
Department of Geography
University of Victoria
Box 3050 SIN CSC
Victoria, BC, V8W 3P5, Canada
Tel: 1 250 472–4746
E-mail: whalelab@office.geog.uvic.ca
http://office.geog.uvic.ca/dept/whale/
    wrlmp.html

Woods Hole Oceanographic Institution
Co-op Building, MS #16
Woods Hole, MA, 02543–1050, USA
Contact: Information Office
Tel: 1 508 548–1400
Fax: 1 508 457–2034
E-mail: information@whoi.edu
http://www.whoi.edu/

6.3 Asia

Akademi Laut Malaysia (ALAM)
(Malaysian Maritime Academy)
Window Delivery 2051, Masjid Tanah
78300 Melaka, Malaysia
Tel: 60 6 387 6201
Fax: 60 6 387 6700
E-mail: mma@alam.edu.my
http://www.alam.edu.my/

Aquaculture Department
College of Agriculture and Forestry
Hue University
102 Phung Hung Street
Hue, Viet Nam
Tel: 84 54 525049
Fax: 84 54 524923
E-mail: huaf@dng.vnn.vn
http://www.hueuni.edu.vn/en/agriculture.htm

Aquatic Resources Research Institute
9th floor, Institute Building No.3
Chulalongkorn University
Phayathai Road, Pathumwan,
Bangkok 10330, Thailand
Tel: 662 218 8160
Fax: 662 254 4259
E-mail: arri@chula.ac.th
http://www.arri.chula.ac.th/

Asia-Pacific Centre for Environmental Law
Faculty of Law
National University of Singapore
13 Law Link
Singapore 117590
Tel: 65 6 874 6246
Fax: 65 6 872 1937
E-mail: lawapcel@nus.edu.sg
http://law.nus.edu.sg/apcel/

Asian Institute of Tourism
University of the Philippines
Commonwealth Avenue
Diliman, Quezon City, The Philippines
Contact: Dean
Tel/Fax: 632 922 3894
E-mail: dean.ait@up.edu.ph
http://www.upd.edu.ph/~ait/

Centre for Coastal Pollution and
    Conservation
City University of Hong Kong
83 Tat Chee Avenue, Kowloon Tong
Kowloon, Hong Kong
Tel: 852 2788 7404
Fax: 852 2788 7406
E-mail: bhrolin@cityu.edu.hk
http://www.cityu.edu.hk/bch/rcp/

Centre for Transportation Research
Faculty of Engineering
National University of Singapore
10 Kent Ridge Crescent

Singapore 119260
Tel: 65 6874 2185
Fax: 65 6777 0994
E-mail: cvefwatf@nus.edu.sg
http://www.eng.nus.edu.sg/civil/C_CTR/

Centre of Excellence in Marine Biology
University of Karachi
Karachi 75270, Pakistan
Contact: Director
Tel: 92 21 924 3230
Fax: 92 21 924 3677
E-mail: huss@cyber.net.pk
http://www.ku.edu.pk/research/cemb/
    intro.html

Coastal Resources Institute (CORIN)
Prince of Songkhla University
Hat Yai
Songkhla 90112, Thailand
Tel: 66 74 212800
Fax: 66 74 212782
E-mail: psu-corin@psu.ac.th
http://www.psu.ac.th/corin/

College of Environmental and Marine
    Science and Technology
Pukong National University
599–1 Daeyun-dong, Nam-gu
Busan 608–737, Republic of Korea
Contact: Dean
Tel: 82 51 620 6233
Fax: 82 51 628 7431
E-mail: choul@pknu.ac.kr
http://www.pknu.ac.kr/pknu%5Fen/aca_
    under/cnvi.aspx

College of Fisheries
Central Luzon State University
Nueva Ecija 3120, The Philippines
Tel/Fax: 63 44 456 5202
http://www.clsu.edu.ph/

College of Fisheries and Ocean Sciences
University of the Philippines in the Visayas
Miag-ao, Iloilo, The Philippines
Contact: Dean
Tel/Fax: 63 33 3158143
E-mail: upv_cfos@yahoo.com
http://www.upv.edu.ph/academicinfo/
    cfos/cfos.htm

College of Fisheries Sciences
Pukong National University

599–1 Daeyun-dong, Nam-gu
Busan 608–737, Republic of Korea
Contact: Dean
Tel: 82 51 620 6114
Fax: 82 51 628 7430
E-mail: cjh@pknu.ac.kr
http://www.pknu.ac.kr/pknu%5Fen/aca_
    under/fish.aspx

College of Marine Aquaculture and
    Fisheries
Can Tho University, Campus II
3/2 Street
Can Tho City, Vietnam
Tel: 84 71 838237
E-mail: webmaster@ctu.edu.vn
http://www.ctu.edu.vn/index_e.htm

College of Ocean Science and Technology
Kunsan National University
san 68, Miryong-dong
Kunsan Jeollabuk-do 573–701 Korea
Tel: 63 469 4114
E-mail: webmaster@kunsan.ac.kr
http://www.kunsan.ac.kr/english/

Dalian Maritime University
1 Linghai Road
Dalian 116026, People's Republic of China
Tel: 86 41 1472 7874
Fax: 86 41 1472 7395
E-mail: faodmu@dlmu.edu.cn
http://www.dlmu.edu.cn/

Department of Marine Science
Science Faculty
Chulalongkorn University
Bangkok 10330, Thailand
Contact: President
Tel: 662 218 5394
Fax: 662 255 0780
E-mail: marine@chula.com
http://www.marine.sc.chula.ac.th/

Faculty of Fisheries
Kasetsart University
Chatuchak, Bangkok 10900, Thailand
Tel: 66 2 5795578
Fax: 66 2 9428364
http://www.fish.ku.ac.th/

Faculty of Fisheries
Bangladesh Agricultural University

Mymensingh 2202, Bangladesh
Tel: 880 91 52236
Fax: 880 91 55810
E-mail: ffbau@mymensingh.net
http://agri-varsity.tripod.com/fish/fis-
fac.html

Faculty of Marine Sciences and Fisheries
Universitas Hasanuddin
Jalan Perintis Kemerdekaan km 10
Kampus Tamalanrea
Makassar, Indonesia
Tel: 62 411 584002
Fax: 62 411 585188
E-mail: cio@unhas.ac.id
http://www.unhas.ac.id/

Faculty of Marine Sciences
Cochin University of Science and
    Technology
City Lakeside Campus
Kochi 16 682 022, India
Contact: Dean
Tel: 91 484 235 1957
Fax: 91 484 277 7463
http://www.cusat.ac.in/

Faculty of Maritime Sciences
Kobe University
Academic Exchange Center, 6th floor
5–1–1, Fukae-minami-machi, Higashiada
Kobe 658–0022, Japan
Tel: 81 78 431 6200
Fax: 81 78 431 6355
E-mail: koho3@maritime.kobe-u.ac.jp
http://www.maritime.kobe-u.ac.jp/

Faculty of Ocean Technology
Sepuluh Nopember Institute of Technology
Jl. Arief Rahman Hakim
Kampus ITS Sukolilo
Surabaya 60111, Indonesia
Tel. 62 31 5927939
Fax. 62 31 5923411
http://www.its.ac.id/

Fisheries University
2 Nguyen Dinh Chieu
Nha Trang City, Khanh
Hoa Province, Vietnam
Tel: 84 58 831145
Fax: 84 58 831147
E-mail: dhtsnt@dng.vnn.vn

Indian Ocean Research Group
Centre for the Study of Geopolitics
Department of Political Science
Arts Block VI
Panjab University
160 014, India
Tel: 91 172 253 4757
Fax: 1 172 278 4695
E-mail: iorg@pu.ac.in
http://www.iorgroup.org/

Institute of Fisheries Science
College of Science
National Taiwan Ocean University
1, Sec. 4, Roosevelt Road
Taipei, Taiwan, ROC
Tel: 886 2 3366 2872
Fax: 886 2 3366 5864
E-mail: fishing@ntu.edu.tw
http://www.ntu.edu.tw/

Institute of Marine Science
University of Karachi
Karachi 75270, Pakistan
Contact: Acting Director
Tel: 92 43131 2378
http://www.ku.edu.pk/research/marinesc.html

Institute of Marine Sciences
University of Chittagong
University Post Office
Chittagong 4331, Bangladesh
Contact: Director
Tel: 88 031 710347
Fax: 88 031 726310
E-mail: info@imscu.ac.bd
http://www.imscu.ac.bd/

Institution of Oceanography
College of Science
National Taiwan Ocean University
1, Sec. 4, Roosevelt Road
Taipei, Taiwan, ROC
Tel: 886 2 2363 7562 ext 2305
Fax: 886 2 2362 2005
E-mail: cus@ms.ntu.edu.tw
http://www.oc.ntu.edu.tw/

Korea Inter-University Institute of Ocean
    Sciences
Pukong National University
599–1 Daeyun-dong, Nam-gu
Busan 608–737, Republic of Korea

Contact: Dean
Tel: 82 51 620 6292
Fax: 82 51 624 5387
E-mail: yunk@pknu.ac.kr
http://www.pknu.ac.kr/pknu%5Fen/
organi/rese_01.aspx

Korea Maritime University
1 Dongsam-dong Yengdo-Gu
Busan 606791, Korea
Tel: 82 51 410 4771
Fax: 82 51 404 3984
E-mail: webmaster@hhu.ac.kr
http://www.kmaritime.ac.kr/

Law of the Sea Program
Institute of International Legal Studies
3/F Bocobo Hall
U.P. Law Center
University of the Philippines
Diliman, Quezon City 1100, The
Philippines
Contact: Dean
Tel: 63 2 920 53 01
Fax: 63 2 927 71 80
E-mail: iils.claw@up.edu.ph
http://www.upd.edu.ph/~iils/

Marine Science Institute
College of Science
University of the Philippines
Diliman, Quezon City, 1101, The
Philippines
Tel: 63 2 922 3962
E-mail: admin@upmsi.ph
http://www.msi.upd.edu.ph/

Maritime Research Centre
Nanyang Technicla University
School of CEE, MRC
N1-B3b-29
50 Nanyang Avenue
639798, Singapore
Tel: 65 6790 5321
Fax: 65 6790 6620
E-mail: d-mrc@ntu.edu.sg
http://www.ntu.edu.sg/mrc/

Mokpo National Maritime University
571-2 Chukyo-dong
Mokpo, Jeonnam, 530-729, Korea
Tel: 82 61 240 7114
Fax: 82 61 242 5176

E-mail: ryujb@mmu.ac.kr
http://www.mmu.ac.kr/

National Fisheries University
2-7-1 Nagata-Honmachi
Shimonoseki 759-6595, Japan
Tel: 81 832 86 5111
Fax: 81 832 86 2292
E-mail: zenpan@fish-u.ac.jp
http://www.fish-u.ac.jp/e-index.html

National Institute of Ocean Technology
Velacherry-Tambaram main road
Narayanapuram
Chennai, Tamil Nadu, 601 302, India
Contact: Director
Tel: 91 44 5578 3300
Fax: 91 44 2246 0645
E-mail: postmaster@niot.res.in
http://www.niot.res.in/

Ocean Research Institute
University of Tokyo
1-15-1 Minamidai, Nakano-ku
Tokyo 164-8639, Japan
Contact: Director
Tel: 81 3 5351 6342
Fax: 81 3 5351 6836
E-mail: koike@ori.u-tokyo.ac.jp
http://www.ori.u-tokyo.ac.jp/

Ocean University of China
5 Yushan Road
Qingdao 266003, People's Republic of
China
Tel: 86 53 2203 2173
Fax: 86 53 2203 2799
E-mail: xzbgs@mail.ouc.edu.cn
http://www.ouc.edu.cn/

School of Environment, Resources and
Development (SERD)
Asian Institute of Technology
PO Box 4, Klong Luang
Pathumthani 12120, Thailand
Tel: 66 2 524 6069
Fax: 66 2 524 6398
E-mail: deanserd@ait.ac.th
http://www.serd.ait.ac.th/

School of Environmental Science and
Management
University of the Philippines Los Baños
College

Laguna 4031, The Philippines
Tel: 63 49 536 2553
Fax: 63 49 536 3673
E-mail: dkv@mudspring.uplb.edu.ph
http://www.uplb.edu.ph/academics/schools/
sesam/

Shanghai Fisheries University
334 Jungong Road
Shanghai 200090, People's Republic of
China
Tel: 86 21 6571 0296
Fax: 86 21 6802 1296
E-mail: xzxx@shfu.edu.cn
http://www.shfu.edu.cn/

Shanghai Maritime University
1550 Pu Dong Da Dao
Shanghai 200134, People's Republic of
China
Tel: 86 21 5885 5200
Fax: 86 21 5885 3909
E-mail: smupo@shmtu.edu.cn
http://www.shmtu.edu.cn/

Silliman University-Angelo King Centre for
Research and Environmental
Management
2nd floor, Silliman University Marine
Laboratory Building
Bantayan, Dumaguete City, Negros Oriental
6200, The Philippines
Tel/Fax: 63 35 422 5648
E-mail: suakcrem@yahoo.com
http://www.su.edu.ph/suakcrem/index.htm

South China Sea Institute of Oceanology
Chinese Academy of Sciences
164 West Xingang Road
Guangzhou 510301, People's Republic of
China
Tel: 86 20 8445 2227
Fax: 86 20 8445 1672
E-mail: scsio@scsio.ac.cn
http://www.scsio.ac.cn/

Tokyo University of Marine Science and
Technology
4–5–7 Konan
Minato-ku
Tokyo 108–8477, Japan
Tel: 81 3 5463 0358
Fax: 81 3 5463 0359

E-mail: kk-gaku@s.kaiyo.dai.ac.jp
http://www.kaiodai.ac.jp/English/index.html

Transportation Institute
6th floor, Prajadhipok-Rambhaibarni
Building
Chulalongkorn University
Phayathai Road
Bangkok 10330, Thailand
Tel: 66 2 218 7450
Fax: 66 2 214 2417
E-mail: tri@chula.ac.th
http://www.tri.chula.ac.th/

Tropical Marine Science Institute (TMSI)
National University of Singapore
14 Kent Ridge Road
Singapore 119223
Contact: Director
Tel: 65 6 774 9659
Fax: 65 6 774 9654
E-mail: tmsdir@nus.edu.sg
http://www.tmsi.nus.edu.sg/

6.4 Europe

AKVAFORSK–The Institute of Aquaculture
Research
PO Box 5010
N-1432 Ås, Norway
Contact: Research Director
Tel: 47 64 94 95 00
Fax: 47 64 94 95 02
E-mail: akvaforsk@akvaforsk.no
http://www.akvaforsk.no/

Archipelago Research Institute
University of Turku
Luonnontieteidentalo II
FI-20014 Turku, Finland
Contact: Secretariat
Tel: 358 2 333 5933
Fax: 358 2 333 6592
E-mail: paula.rasanen@utu.fi
http://www.utu.fi/erill/saarmeri/en/

Cambridge Coastal Research Unit (CCRU)
Department of Geography
University of Cambridge
Downing Place
Cambridge, CB2 3EN, United Kingdom
Tel: 44 1223 339775
Fax: 44 1223 355674

E-mail: ccru@geog.cam.ac.uk
http://ccru.geog.cam.ac.uk/

Center for Ecological Modelling (CEM)
(IMAR–Centro de Modelaçao Ecológica)
Department of Environmental Sciences and
    Engineering
Faculty of Sciences and Technology
Universidade Nova de Lisboa
Quinta da Torre
PT-2829–516 Monte de Caparica, Portugal
Tel: 351 21 2948300
Fax: 351 21 2948554
E-mail: frg@mail.fct.unl.pt
http://www.cem.fct.unl.pt/

Center for Marine and Environmental
    Research
(Centro de Investigaçao Marinha e
    Ambiental–CIMA)
Faculdade de Ciências do Mar e do
    Ambiente
Universidade do Algarve
Campus de Gambelas
PT-8005–139 Faro, Portugal
Tel: 351 289 800 995
Fax: 351 289 818 353
E-mail: cima@ualg.pt
http://www.ualg.pt/cima/

Center for Maritime Research (MARE)
Nieuwe Prinsengracht 130, Room G.2.05
NL-1018 VZ, Amsterdam, The Netherlands
Tel: 31 20 525 4143
Fax: 31 20 525 4051
E-mail: info@marecentre.nl
http://www.marecentre.nl/

Centre de Formation et de Recherche sur
    l'Environnement Marin (CEFREM)
CNRS-UMR 5110
Université de Perpignan
52 avenue de Paul Alduy
F-66860 Perpignan Cedex, France
Contact: Director
Tel: 33 4 6866 2090
Fax: 33 4 6866 2096
E-mail: cefrem@univ-perp.fr
http://www.univ-
perp.fr/see/rch/lsgm/index.htm

Centre de Recherche en Histoire
    Atlantique et Littorale (CRHAEL)
Université du Littoral Côte d'Opale

17 rue du Puits d'Amour
F-62200 Boulogne sur Mer, France
Tel: 33 3 2199 4560
Fax: 33 3 2199 4561
E-mail: crhael@univ-littoral.fr
http://www.univ_littoral.fr/rch/labo/
    crhael.htm

Centre for Coastal and Marine Research
    (CCMR)
School of Environmental Sciences
University of Ulster
Cromore Road
Coleraine, Northern Ireland, BT52 1SA,
    United Kingdom
Contact: Director
Tel: 44 28 7032 4429
Fax: 44 28 7032 4911
E-mail: jag.cooper@ulster.ac.uk
http://www.science.ulster.ac.uk/ccmr/

Centre for Development and the
    Environment
University of Oslo
Box 1116 Blindern
N-0317 Oslo, Norway
Tel: 47 22 85 89 00
Fax: 47 22 85 89 20
E-mail: info@sum.uio.no
http://www.sum.uio.no/

Centre for Energy, Petroleum and Mineral
    Law and Policy (CEPMLP)
University of Dundee
Dundee, Scotland, DD1 4HN, United
    Kingdom
Contact: Director
Tel: 44 1382 344300
Fax: 44 1382 322578
E-mail: cepmlp@dundee.ac.uk
http://www.dundee.ac.uk/cepmlp/

Centre for Environment and Sustainability
(Göteborgs Miljö Vetenskapliga
    Centrum–GMV)
Chalmers/Göteborg University
Vera Sandbergs Allé 513
SE-412 96 Göteborg, Sweden
Tel: 46 31 772 49 50
Fax: 46 31 772 49 58
E-mail: office@miljo.chalmers.se
http://www.miljo.chalmers.se/

Centre for Fisheries, Aquaculture
  Management, and Economics
Faculty of Social Sciences
University of Southern Denmark
Campusvej 55
DK-5230 Odense M, Denmark
Tel: 45 65 50 10 00
Fax: 45 65 93 56 92
E-mail: fame@sam.sdu.dk
http://www.sam.sdu.dk/fame/

Centre for Fisheries Economics
Institute for Research in Economics and
  Business Administration (SNF)
Norwegian School of Economics and
  Business Administration
Breiviksveinen 40
N-5045 Bergen, Norway
Contact: Research Director
Tel: 47 55 95 92 60
Fax: 47 55 95 95 43
E-mail: trond.bjorndal@snf.no
http://www.snf.no/

Centre for International Economics and
  Shipping
(Senter for Internasjonal Okonomi og
  Skipsfart)
Institute for Research in Economics and
  Business Administration (SNF)
Norwegian School of Economics and
  Business Administration
Breiviksveinen 40
N-5045 Bergen, Norway
Contact: Research Director
Tel: 47 55 95 95 00
Fax: 47 55 95 93 50
E-mail: guttorm.schjelderup@nhh.no
http://www.snf.no/

Centre for Marine and Atmospheric
  Sciences
(Zentrum für Marine and Atmosphärische
  Wissenschaften–ZMAW)
Max Planck Institut für Meteorologie
Bundesstrasse 53
D-20146 Hamburg, Germany
Tel: 49 40 41173 440
Fax: 49 40 41173 298
E-mail: info@zmaw.de
http://www.zmaw.de/

Centre for Marine and Climate Research
(Zentrum für Meeres- und
  Klimaforschung–ZMK)
University of Hamburg
Bundesstrasse 53
D-20146 Hamburg, Germany
Contact: ZMK Office
Tel: 49 40 428 38 4206
Fax: 49 40 428 38 5235
E-mail: harms@ifm.uni-hamburg.de
http://www.zmk.uni-hamburg.de/

Centre for Marine and Coastal Zone
  Managment
Department of Geography & Environment
University of Aberdeen
Elphinstone Road
Aberdeen, Scotland, AB24 3UF, United
  Kingdom
Tel: 44 1224 272324
Fax: 44 1224 272331
E-mail: d.r.green@abdn.ac.uk
http://www.abdn.ac.uk/cmczm/

Centre for Marine Environmental Sciences
(Zentrum für Marine
  Umweltwissenschaften–MARUM)
Der Universität Bremen
Leobener
D-28359 Bremen, Germany
Tel: 49 421 218 65500
Fax: 49 421 218 65506
E-mail: gwefer@marum.de
http://www.marum.de/

Centre for Maritime and Oceanic Law
(Centre de droit maritime et
  océanique–CDMO)
University of Nantes
Faculty of Law
Chemin de la Censive du Tertre
BP 81307
F-44313 Nantes, Cedex 3, France
Contact: Director
Tel: 33 2 4014 1570
Fax: 33 2 4014 1500
E-mail: jean-pierre.beurier@univ-nantes.fr
http://www.univ-nantes.fr/

Centre for Maritime Studies
(Merenkulkualan Koulut–MKK)
University of Turku
WTC-Building, Veistämönaukio 1–3
FI-20100 Turku, Finland

Contact: Director
Tel: 358 2 281 3300
Fax: 358 2 281 3311
E-mail: juhani.vainio@utu.fi
http://mkk.utu.fi/

Centre for Ships and Ocean Structures
Norwegian University of Science and
    Technology
(Nordisk Teknisk-Naturvitenskapelige
    Universitet)
Marine Technology Centre
Otto Nielsens vei 10
N-7491 Trondheim, Norway
Contact: Director
Tel: 47 73 59 55 35
Fax: 47 73 59 55 28
E-mail: coe@marin.ntnu.no
http://www.cesos.ntnu.no/

Centre for the Economics and
    Management of Aquatic Resources
    (CEMARE)
University of Portsmouth
Boathouse No. 6
College Road, HM Naval Base
Portsmouth, PO1 3LJ, United Kingdom
Contact: Director
Tel: 44 23 9284 4082
Fax: 44 23 9284 4614
E-mail: cemare.library@port.ac.uk
http://www.port.ac.uk/research/cemare/

Centre for Tropical Marine Ecology
(Zentrum für Marine
    Troppenökologie–ZMT)
University of Bremen
Fahrenheitstrasse 6
D-28359 Bremen, Germany
Contact: Director
Tel: 49 421 23800 21
Fax: 49 421 23800 30
E-mail: contact@zmt-bremen.de
http://www.zmt.uni-bremen.de/

Challenger Society for Marine Science
Room 251/20
Southampton Oceanography Centre
Waterfront Campus
Southampton, SO14 3ZH, United Kingdom
Contact: Executive Secretary
E-mail: jxj@soc.soton.ac.uk
http://www.soc.soton.ac.uk/OTHERS/CSMS/

Coastal and Marine Environment Research
    Centre
(Centro de Investigaçao dos Ambientes
    Costeiros e Marinhos–CIACOMAR)
Universidade do Algarve
Avenida 16 de Junno s/n
PT-8700–311 Olhao, Portugal
Tel: 351 289 707 087
Fax: 351 289 706 972
E-mail: webmaster.ciacomar@ualg.pt
http://www.ualg.pt/ciacomar/

Coastal Research and Planning Institute
    (CORPI)
Klaipēda University
H. Mantog. 84
LT-92294 Klaipeda, Lithuania
Tel: 370 46 398846
Fax: 370 46 398845
E-mail: simona@corpi.ku.lt
http://www.corpi.ku.lt/

Coastal Research Laboratory (CORELAB)
Research and Technical Center Būsam
Christian Albrechts University
Otto-Hahn-Platz 3
D-24118 Kiel, Germany
Tel: 49 431 880 3643
Fax: 49 431 880 7303
E-mail: info@corelab.uni-kiel.de
http://www.corelab.uni-kiel.de/

DEA européen en modélisation de
    l'environnement marin
(European DEA in Modeling of the
    Marine Environment)
GeoHydrodynamics and Environmental
    Research (GHER)
Université de Liège
Sart Tilman, B5
B-4000 Liège, Belgium
Contact: Director
Tel: 32 4 366 3350
Fax: 32 4 366 2355
E-mail: J.Nihoul@ulg.ac.be
http://www.ulg.ac.be/deamodel/

Department of Earth and Ocean Sciences
University of Liverpool
4 Brownlow Street
Liverpool, L69 3GP, United Kingdom
Tel: 44 151 794 5146
Fax: 44 151 794 5196
E-mail: h.kokelaar@liv.ac.uk

http://www.liv.ac.uk/earth_sciences/dept/
index.html

Department of Fisheries and Marine
   Biology
(Institutt for Fisheri og Marinbiologi–IFM)
University of Bergen
PO Box 7800
N-5020 Bergen, Norway
Tel: 47 55 58 44 00
Fax: 47 55 58 44 50
E-mail: epost@ifm.uib.no
http://www.ifm.uib.no/

Department of Geological, Environmental
   and Marine Sciences
Università delgi Studi di Trieste
Via E. Weiss 2, Building Q
I-34127 Trieste, Italy
Tel: 39 40 558 2045
Fax: 39 40 558 2048
E-mail: disgam@units.it
http://www.units.it/disgam/

Department of Marine Biology
Vienna Ecology Centre
University of Vienna
Althanstrasse 14
A-1090 Vienna, Austria
Contact: Head
Tel: 43 1 42775 4331
Fax: 43 1 42779 542
E-mail: meersbiologie@gmx.at
http://www.univie.ac.at/marine-biology/

Department of Mechanical Engineering
Technical University of Denmark
Nils Koppels Allé, Building 403
DK-2800 Kgs. Lyngby, Denmark
Contact: Head, Maritime Engineering
   Section
Tel: 45 45 25 19 60
Fax: 45 45 88 43 25
E-mail: info@mek.dtu.dk
http://www.mek.dtu.dk/

Department of Oceanography
Göteborg University
Earth Sciences Centre
PO Box 460
SE-405 30 Göteborg, Sweden
Contact: Head
Tel: 46 31 77 31 000
Fax: 46 31 77 32 888

E-mail: joro@oce.gu.se
http://www.gvc.gu.se/oceanografi/english/
   Index/index.htm

Department of Oceanography and Fisheries
University of the Azores
PT-9901–892 Horta, Portugal
Tel: 351 292 200400
Fax: 351 292 200411
http://www.horta.uac.pt/

Estonian Marine Institute (EMI)
(Eesti Mereinstituut)
University of Tartu
10a Mäealuse
12618 Tallinn, Estonia
Contact: Director
Tel: 372 6718 901
Fax: 372 6718 900
E-mail: meri@sea.ee
http://www.sea.ee/

Euro-Mediterranean Centre on Insular
   Coastal Dynamics (ICoD)
Foundation for International Studies
University of Malta
St. Paul Street
Valletta VLT 07, Malta
Contact: Director
Tel: 356 21 240 746
Fax: 356 21 230 551
E-mail: icod@icod.org.mt
http://www.icod.org.mt/

European Institute for Marine Studies
(Institut Universitaire Européen de la
   mer–IUEM)
Technopôle Brest-Iroise
Place Nicolas Copernic
F-29280 Plouzane, France
Contact: Director
Tel: 33 02 9849 8603
Fax: 33 02 9849 8609
E-mail: Direction.iuem@univ-brest.fr
http://www.univ-brest.fr/IUEM/

Faculty of Marine Sciences
(Facultad de Ciencias del Mar)
Edificio de Ciencias Básicas
Campus Universitario de Tafira
Universidad de Las Palmas de Gran
   Canaria
E-35013 Las Palmas, Grand Canary, Spain

Contact: Dean
Tel: 34 928 451 280
Fax: 34 928 451 022
http://www.fcm.ulpgc.es/

Flanders Marine Institute
(Vlaams Instituut voor de Zee–VLIZ)
Wandelaarkaai 7
B-8400 Oostende, Belgium
Contact: Director
Tel: 32 59 34 21 30
Fax: 32 59 34 21 31
E-mail: info@vliz.be
http://www.vliz.be/

Gdynia Maritime University
Morska 81–87
PL-81–225 Gdynia, Poland
Tel: 48 58 621 7041
Fax: 48 58 620 6701
E-mail: intercol@wsm.gdynia.pl
http://www.wsm.gdynia.pl/

Geohydrodynamics and Environmental
    Research (GHER)
Université de Liège
Sart Tilman, B5
B-4000 Liège, Belgium
Contact: Director
Tel: 32 4 366 3339
Fax: 32 4 366 2355
E-mail: gher@ulg.ac.be
http://modb.oce.ulg.ac.be/

Göteborg Universitets Marina
    Forskningscentrum (GMF)
(Göteborg University Marine Research
    Centre)
Earth Sciences Centre
Göteborg University
PO Box 460
SE-405 30 Göteborg, Sweden
Contact: Director
Tel: 46 31 773 1000
Fax: 46 31 773 4839
E-mail: joro@oce.gu.se
http://www.gmf.gu.se/

Graduate Institute of International Studies
(Institut universitaire de hautés études
    internationales, Genève)
132, rue de Lausanne
CH-1211 Geneva, Switzerland
Tel: 41 22 908 57 00

Fax: 41 22 908 57 10
E-mail: info@hei.unige.ch
http://heiwww.unige.ch/

Institute for Marine and Atmospheric
    Research Utrecht (IMAU)
University of Utrecht
PO Box 80000
NL-3508 TA, Utrecht, The Netherlands
Tel: 31 30 253 3275
Fax: 31 30 254 3163
E-mail: imau@phys.uu.nl
http://www.phys.uu.nl/~wwwimau/

Institute of Aquaculture
University of Stirling
Pathfoot Building
Stirling, FK9 4LA, United Kingdom
Contact: Director
Tel: 44 17 8646 77847
Fax: 44 17 8646 72133
E-mail: aquaculture@stir.ac.uk
http://www.stir.ac.uk/aqua/

Institute of Estuarine and Coastal Studies
    (IECS)
University of Hull
Cottingham Road
Hull, HU6 7RX, United Kingdom
Contact: Director
Tel: 44 1482 465667
Fax: 44 1482 465001
E-mail: iecs@hull.ac.uk
http://www.hull.ac.uk/iecs/

Institute of Hydrobiology and Fisheries
    Science
(Institut für Hydrobiologie und
    Fischereiwissenschaft)
University of Hamburg
Olbersweg 24
D-22767 Hamburg, Germany
Tel: 49 40 428 38 6601
E-mail: ihf-office@uni-hamburg.de
http://www.biologie.uni-hamburg.de/ihf/

Institute of Law of the Sea and Maritime
    Law
(Institut für Seerecht und
    Seehandelsrechti–ISSR)
University of Hamburg
Heimhuder Strasse 71
D-20148 Hamburg, Germany
Tel: 49 40 42838 2240

Fax: 49 40 42838 6271
E-mail: seerecht@jura.uni-hamburg.de
http://www2.jura.uni-hamburg.de/issr/

Institute of Marine Research (IMAR)
(Centro Interdisciplinar de Coimbra)
c/o Department of Zoology
University of Coimbra
PT-3000 Coimbra, Portugal
Tel: 351 239 836386
Fax: 351 239 823603
E-mail: imar@cygnus.ic.uc.pt
http://www.imar.pt/

Institute of Marine Sciences and
    Management
University of Istanbul
34470 Vefa Istanbul, Turkey
Tel: 90 212 528 2539
Fax: 90 212 526 8433
E-mail: cemga@istanbul.edu.tr
http://www.istanbul.edu.tr/enstituler/
    denizbilimleri/denizbilimleri.htm

Institute of Maritime Law
School of Law
University of Southampton
Highfield, Southampton, SO17 1BJ, United
    Kingdom
Contact: Institute Secretary
Tel: 44 2380 593449
Fax: 44 2380 593789
E-mail: iml@soton.ac.uk
http://www.iml.soton.ac.uk/

Institute of Oceanography
(Institut für Meereskunde)
Zentrum für Meeres- und Klimaforshung
University of Hamburg
Bundestrasse 53
D-20146 Hamburg, Germany
Tel: 49 40 42838 5052
Fax: 49 40 42560 7477
E-mail: stammer@ifm.zmaw.de
http://www.ifm.uni-hamburg.de/

Institute of Oceanography and Fisheries
Setaliste Iva Mestrovica 63
HR-21000 Split, Croatia
Tel: 385 21 358688
Fax: 385 21 358650
E-mail: office@izor.hr
http://www.izor.hr/eng/intro.html

Institute of Oceanology
Polish Academy of Sciences
PO Box 68
Powstancow Warszawy 55
PL-81–712 Sopot, Poland
Tel: 48 58 551 7281
Fax: 48 58 551 2130
E-mail: office@iopan.gda.pl
http://www.iopan.gda.pl/

Institute of Transport and Maritime
    Management Antwerp (ITMMA)
University of Antwerp
ITMMA House
Keizerstraat 64
B-2000 Antwerp, Belgium
Tel: 32 3 275 51 51
Fax: 32 3 275 51 50
E-mail: itmma@ua.ac.be
http://www.itmma.com/

International Association of Maritime
    Institutions
Faculty of Nautical Science
South Tyneside College
St. George's Avenue
Tyne and Wear, NE34 6ET, United
    Kingdom
Contact: Honorary Secretary
Tel: 44 1914 273584
Fax: 44 1914 273646
E-mail: phil.stone@iami.info
http://www.iami.info/

International Boundaries Research Unit
    (IBRU)
Department of Geography
University of Durham
South Road
Durham, DH1 3LE, United Kingdom
Tel: 44 191 334 1961
Fax: 44 191 334 1962
E-mail: ibru@durham.ac.uk
http://www-ibru.dur.ac.uk/

International Centre for Coastal Resources
    Research
(Centre Internacional d'Investigació dels
    Recursos Costaners–CIIRC)
Campus Nord
Universitat Politecnica de Catalunya
Jordi Girona, 1–3, Edif. D-1
E-08034 Barcelona, Spain
Tel: 34 932 806 400

Fax: 34 932 806 019
E-mail: ciirc@upc.es
http://lim-ciirc.upc.es/

International Geosphere-Biosphere
   Programme (IGBP)
Royal Swedish Academy of Sciences
Box 50005
SE-104 05 Stockholm, Sweden
Contact: Executive Director
Tel: 46 8 16 64 48
Fax: 46 8 16 64 05
E-mail: kevin@igbp.kva.se
http://www.igbp.kva.se/

International Studies in Aquatic Tropical
   Ecology
Zentrum für Marine Tropenökologie
   (ZMT)
Fahrenheitstrasse 6
D-28 359 Bremen, Germany
Tel: 49 421 23800 42
Fax: 49 421 23800 30
E-mail: isatec@uni-bremen.de
http://www.isatec.uni-bremen.de/

Islands and Small States Institute
Foundation for International Studies
St. Paul Street
Valletta VLT 07, Malta
Tel/Fax: 356 21 248 218
E-mail: islands@um.edu.mt
http://home.um.edu.mt/islands/

Laboratoire d'Océanologie
Département des Sciences et Gestion de
   l'Environnement
Université de Liège (ULG, Bât B6c)
B-4000 Sart Tilman, Belgium
Tel: 32 4 366 3329
Fax: 32 4 366 3325
http://www.ulg.ac.be/oceanbio/

Laboratoire Environnement Marin Littoral
Université de Nice-Sophia Antipolis
Faculté des Sciences
Parc Valrose
F-06108 Nice Cedex 2, France
Tel: 33 4 9207 6846
Fax: 33 4 9207 6849
E-mail: meinesz@unice.fr
http://www.unice.fr/LEML/

Legal Aspects of Marine Affairs Program
Cardiff Law School
Cardiff University
Law Building, Museum Road
Cardiff, Wales, CF10 3XJ, United Kingdom
Contact: Director
Tel: 44 29 2087 6705
Fax: 44 29 2087 4097
E-mail: churchill@cardiff.ac.uk
http://www.cf.ac.uk/claws/

Leibniz Institute of Marine Sciences
(Leibniz Institut für Meereswissenschaften
   an der Universitaet Kiel–IFM-GEOMAR)
East Shore Campus
Wischhofstrasse 1–3
D-24148 Kiel, Germany
Contact: Directorate
Tel: 49 431 600 2800
Fax: 49 431 600 2805
E-mail: pherzig@ifm-geomar.de
http://www.ifm-geomar.de/

Marine Law and Ocean Policy Centre
National University of Ireland
Galway, University Road
Galway, Ireland
Tel: 353 91 512439
Fax: 353 91 525005
E-mail: marinelaw@nuigalway.ie
http://mri.nuigalway.ie/marinelaw/

Maritime Institute
(Maritiem Instituut)
Universiteit Gent
Universiteitstraat 6
B-9000 Gent, Belgium
Tel: 32 9 264 6897
Fax: 32 9 264 6989
E-mail: lydie.demaerteleire@rug.ac.be
http://www.maritieminstituut.be/

Marseille Oceanology Institute
(Centre d'Océanologie de Marseille
   (COM))
Université de la Méditerranée Station
Station Marine d'Endoume
Chemin de la Batterie des Lions
F-13007 Marseille, France
Tel: 33 4 9104 1600
Fax: 33 4 9104 1608
http://www.com.univ-mrs.fr/

Martin Ryan Institute
National University of Ireland
Galway, University Road
Galway, Ireland
Tel: 353 91 492325
Fax: 353 91 525005
E-mail: siobhan.cunningham@nuigalway.ie
http://mri.nuigalway.ie/

Max Planck Institute for Meteorology
(Max-Planck-Institut für Meterologie)
Bundesstrasse 53
D-20146 Hamburg, Germany
Contact: Executive Director
Tel: 49 40 41173 0
Fax: 49 40 41173 298
E-mail: marotzke@dkrz.de
http://www.mpimet.mpg.de/

Max Planck Institute for Marine
    Microbiology Bremen
(Max-Planck-Institut für Marine
    Mikrobiologie Bremen)
Celsiusstrasse 1
D-28359 Bremen, Germany
Contact: Director
Tel: 49 421 202850
Fax: 49 421 2028580
E-mail: contact@mpi-bremen.de
http://www.mpi-bremen.de/

Mediterranean Programme for International
    Environmental Law and Negotiation
    (MEPIELAN)
Panteion University of Athens
136 Syngrou Avenue
GR-17671 Athens, Greece
Tel: 30 210 9201841
Fax: 30 210 9610591
E-mail: info@mepielan.gr
http://www.mepielan.gr/

Nansen Environmental and Remote
    Sensing Center (NERSC)
Thormohlensgate 47
N-5006 Bergen, Norway
Tel: 47 55 20 58 00
Fax: 47 55 20 58 01
E-mail: admin@nersc.no
http://www.nersc.no/

National Oceanography Centre,
    Southampton
University of Southampton

Waterfront Campus
European Way
Southampton, SO14 3ZH, United Kingdom
Tel: 44 2380 596666
http://www.soc.soton.ac.uk/

Nautical Science Program
Facoltà di Scienze e Technologie
Università delgi Studi di Napoli
    "Parthenope"
Via Amm. F. Acton 38
I-80133 Naples, Italy
Tel: 39 081 552 4342
Fax: 39 081 552 7126
E-mail: preside.scienze@uniparthenope.it
http://www.scienzeetecnologie.uniparthenope.
    it/index.php

Netherlands Institute for Fisheries Research
(Nederlands Instituut voor Visserji
    Onderzoek–RIVO)
Haringkade 1, 1976 CP IJmuiden
PO Box 68
NL-1970 AB IJmuiden, The Netherlands
Tel: 31 255 56 46 46
Fax: 31 255 56 46 44
E-mail: visserijonderzoek.asg@wur.nl
http://www.rivo.wag-ur.nl/

Netherlands Institute for the Law of the
    Sea (NILOS)
Utrecht University
Faculty of Law
Achter Sint Pieter 200
NL-3512 HT Utrecht, The Netherlands
Contact: Director
Tel: 31 30 253 7060
Fax: 31 30 253 7073
E-mail: nilos@law.uu.nl
http://www.uu.nl/uupublish/homerechtsgeleer/
    onderzoek/onderzoekscholen/centru
    mvooromgev/informationineng/23884
    main.html

North Atlantic Fisheries College
Port Arthur
Scalloway, Shetlands, ZE1 0UN, United
    Kingdom
Tel: 44 1595 772000
Fax: 44 1595 772001
E-mail: info@nafc.uhi.ac.uk
http://www.nafc.ac.uk/

Norwegian College of Fishery Science
(Norges Fiskerihogskole)
University of Tromso
N-9037 Tromso, Norway
Contact: Rector
Tel: 47 77 64 60 00
E-mail: knuth@nfh.uit.no
http://www.nfh.uit.no/

Oceanographic Institute
(Institut océanographique)
195, rue Saint Jacques
F-75005 Paris, France
Tel: 33 1 4432 1070
Fax: 33 1 4051 7316
http://www.oceano.org/

Oceanographic Institute of the Western
    Mediterranean Sea
(Instituto Oceanografico del Mediterraneo
    Occidental–IOMO)
San Juan, 9
Vespella de Gaia
E-43763 Tarragona, Spain
Contact: President
Tel: 34 977 655 214
Fax: 34 977 655 584
E-mail: iomo@tinet.fut.es
http://www.fut.es/~iomo/

Plymouth Marine Laboratory
Prospect Place, The Hoe
Plymouth, PL1 3DH, United Kingdom
Tel: 44 1752 63 3100
Fax: 44 1752 63 3101
E-mail: forinfo@pml.ac.uk
http://www.pml.ac.uk/

Proudman Oceanographic Laboratory
Joseph Proudman Building
6 Brownlow Street
Liverpool, L3 5DA, United Kingdom
Tel: 44 151 795 4800
Fax: 44 151 795 4801
E-mail: polenquiries@pol.ac.uk
http://www.pol.ac.uk/

SARS International Center for Marine
    Molecular Biology
Bergen High Technology Center
Thormohlensgate 55
N-5008 Bergen, Norway
Tel: 47 55 58 43 44

Fax: 47 55 58 43 05
http://www.uib.no/fa/sars/

Scandinavian Institute of Maritime Law
(Nordisk Institutt for Sjorett)
University of Oslo
PO Box 6706, St. Olavs plass
N-0130 Oslo, Norway
Contact: Director
Tel: 47 22 85 97 48
Fax: 47 22 85 97 50
E-mail: sjorett-adm@jus.uio.no
http://www.jus.uio.no/nifs/

Scarborough Centre for Coastal Studies
University of Hull
Scarborough Campus
Filey Road
Scarborough, YO11 3AZ, United Kingdom
Contact: CCS Centre Administrator
Tel: 44 1723 357229
Fax: 44 1723 370815
E-mail: l.j.scott@hull.ac.uk
http://coastal-studies.org/contact.html

School of Conservation Sciences
Bournemouth University
Fern Barrow
Poole, Dorset, BH12 5BB, United Kingdom
Tel: 44 1202 524111
Fax: 44 1202 962736
E-mail: enquiries@bournemouth.ac.uk
http://www.bournemouth.ac.uk/conservation/

School of Earth, Ocean and Environmental
    Sciences
University of Plymouth
Drake Circus
Plymouth, PL4 8AA, United Kingdom
Tel: 44 1752 232407
Fax: 44 1752 232406
E-mail: science@plymouth.ac.uk
http://plym.ac.uk/pages/view.asp?page=6159

School of Earth, Ocean and Planetary
    Sciences
Cardiff University
Main Building, Park Place
Cardiff, Wales, CF10 3YE, United Kingdom
Tel: 44 29 2087 4830
Fax: 44 29 2087 4326
E-mail: earth-ug@cardiff.ac.uk
http://www.earth.cardiff.ac.uk/

School of Environmental Sciences
University of East Anglia
Norwich, NR4 7TJ, United Kingdom
Tel: 44 1603 592542
Fax: 44 1603 591327
E-mail: env.web@uea.ac.uk
http://www.uea.ac.uk/env/

School of Geography
Faculty of Social Sciences and Business
University of Plymouth
Plymouth, Devon, PL4 8AA, United
    Kingdom
Tel: 44 1752 232864
Fax: 44 1752 232853
E-mail: ssb.admissions@plymouth.ac.uk
http://www.geog.plym.ac.uk/

School of Marine Science and Technology
Armstrong Building
University of Newcastle upon Tyne
Newcastle Upon Tyne, NE1 7RU, United
    Kingdom
Tel: 44 191 222 6718
Fax: 44 191 222 5491
E-mail: atilla.incecik@ncl.ac.uk
http://www.ncl.ac.uk/marine/

School of Maritime and Coastal Studies
Southampton Solent University
East Park Terrace
Southampton, Hampshire, SO14 0YN,
    United Kingdom
Tel: 44 2380 319000
Fax: 44 2380 314161
E-mail: ft.admissions@solent.ac.uk
http://www.solent.ac.uk/technology/
    technology_home.aspx

School of Ocean Sciences
University of Wales, Bangor
Menai Bridge
Anglesey, North Wales, LL59 5AB, United
    Kingdom
Tel: 44 1248 382846
Fax: 44 1248 716367
E-mail: enquiries@sos.bangor.ac.uk
http://www.sos.bangor.ac.uk/

Scottish Association for Marine Science
    (SAMS)
Dunstaffnage Marine Laboratory
Oban, Argyll, Scotland, PA37 1QA, United
    Kingdom

Tel: 44 1631 559000
Fax: 44 1631 559001
E-mail: info@sams.ac.uk
http://www.sams.ac.uk/

Sea Mammal Research Unit
Gatty Marine Laboratory
University of St Andrews
St Andrews, Fife, KY16 8LB, United
    Kingdom
Tel: 44 1334 462630
Fax: 441334 462632
E-mail: ajp7@st-andrews.ac.uk
http://smub.st-and.ac.uk/

Seafarers International Research Centre
    (SIRC)
Cardiff University
52 Park Place
Cardiff, Wales, CF10 3AT, United Kingdom
Contact: Secretariat
Tel: 44 29 2087 4620
Fax: 44 29 2087 4619
E-mail: sirc@cardiff.ac.uk
http://www.sirc.cf.ac.uk/

Stazione Zoologica Anton Dohrn
Villa Comunale
I-80121 Naples, Italy
Tel: 39 81 583 3111
Fax: 39 81 764 1355
http://www.szn.it/

Stockholm Marine Research Centre
(Stockholms Marina Forskningcentrum)
Stockholm University
SE-106 91 Stockholm, Sweden
Contact: Director
Tel: 46 8 16 37 18
Fax: 46 8 16 16 20
E-mail: smf@smf.su.se
http://www.smf.su.se/

Transport and Shipping Research Group
Cardiff Business School
Cardiff University
Aberconway Building, Column Drive
Cardiff, Wales, CF10 3EU, United Kingdom
Tel: 44 29 2087 6764
Fax: 44 29 2087 4301
E-mail: marlow@cardiff.ac.uk
http://www.cf.ac.uk/carbs/lom/tsrg/

Umeå Marine Sciences Centre
(Umeå Marina Forskningscentrum–UMF)
University of Umeå
Norrbyn
SE-910 20 Hörnefors, Sweden
Contact: Secretariat
Tel: 46 90 7 86 79 74
Fax: 46 90 7 86 79 95
E-mail: info@umf.umu.se
http://www.umf.umu.se/

6.5   Australia, New Zealand and Oceania

Australian Maritime College
PO Box 986
Launceston, TAS 7250, Australia
Tel: 61 3 6335 4711
Fax: 61 3 6326 6493
http://www.amc.edu.au/

Centre for Coral Reef Biodiversity
School of Marine Biology and Aquaculture
James Cook University
Townsville, QLD 4811, Australia
Tel: 61 7 4781 4222
Fax: 61 7 4725 1570
E-mail: ccrbio@jcu.edu.au
http://www.jcu.edu.au/school/mbiolaq/ccrbio/

Centre for Marine Science
University of Tasmania
Hobart Campus, Geography-Geology
   Building, Room 323
Private Bag 49
Hobart, TAS 7053, Australia
Tel: 61 3 6226 2108
Fax: 61 3 6226 2989
E-mail: enquiries@cms.utas.edu.au
http://www.utas.edu.au/cms/

Centre for Marine Science and Technology
Curtin University of Technology
GPO Box U1987
Perth, WA 6845, Australia
Tel: 61 8 9266 7380
Fax: 61 8 9266 4799
E-mail: info@cmst.curtin.edu.au
http://www.cmst.curtin.edu.au/

Centre for Marine Studies
University of Queensland

Brisbane, QLD 4072, Australia
Tel: 61 7 3365 4333
Fax: 61 7 3365 4755
E-mail: cms@uq.edu.au
http://www.marine.uq.edu.au/

Centre for Maritime Policy
University of Wollongong
Wollongong, NSW 2522, Australia
Tel: 61 2 4221 4883
Fax: 61 2 4226 5544
E-mail: myree@uow.edu.au
http://www.uow.edu.au/law/cmp/

East-West Center
1601 East-West Road
Honolulu, HI, 96848–1601, USA
Contact: President
Tel: 1 808 944–7111
Fax: 1 808 944–7376
http://www.eastwestcenter.org/

Environmental Law Program
William S. Richardson School of Law
University of Hawaii
2515 Dole Street
Honolulu, HI, 96822–2328, USA
Tel: 1 808 956–7966
Fax: 1 808 956–3813
E-mail: elp@hawaii.edu
http://www.hawaii.edu/elp/

Faculty of Earth and Environmental
   Sciences
University of Wollongong
Wollongong, NSW 2522, Australia
Contact: Chair
Tel: 61 2 4221 4419
Fax: 61 2 4221 4240
E-mail: cwallace@uow.edu.au
http://www.uow.edu.au/science/eesc/

Institute of Marine Resources
University of the South Pacific
Laucala Campus
Private Mail Bag
Suva, Fij
Tel: 679 321 2995
Fax: 679 330 9494
E-mail: imr@usp.ac.fj
http://www.usp.ac.fj/imr/

Lincoln Marine Science Centre
Flinders University of Southern Australia

PO Box 2023
Port Lincoln, SA 5606, Australia
Tel: 61 8 8683 2500
Fax: 61 8 8683 2525
E-mail: lmsc@flinders.edu.au
http://www.scieng.flinders.edu.au/biology/
    lmsc/

Marine Affairs Programme
University of the South Pacific
Laucala Campus
Private Mail Bag
Suva, Fiji
Contact: Coordinator
Tel: 679 321 2995
Fax: 679 330 9494
E-mail: veitayaki_j@usp.ac.fj
http://www.usp.ac.fj/marineaf/

Marine and Shipping Law Unit
TC Beirne School of Law
University of Queensland
Forgan Smith Building
St. Lucia, QLD 4072, Australia
Tel: 61 7 3365 3320
Fax: 61 7 3365 1454
E-mail: s.derrington@law.uq.edu.au
http://www.law.uq.edu.au/maslu/

Marine Laboratory
University of Guam
UOG Station
Mangilao, GU, 96913, USA
Contact: Director
Tel: 671 735 2175
Fax: 671 734 6767
E-mail: bdsmith@uog9.uog.edu
http://www.uog.edu/marinelab/

Marine Research Laboratories
University of Tasmania
Hobart Campus
Private Bag 49
Hobart, TAS 7053, Australia
Tel: 61 3 6227 7277
Fax: 61 3 6227 8035
E-mail: leane.bleathman@utas.edu.au
http://www.utas.edu.au/scieng/mrl/

Marine Studies Programme
University of the South Pacific
Laucala Campus
Private Mail Bag

Suva, Fiji
Tel: 679 323 2930
Fax: 679 323 1526
E-mail: zann_l@usp.ac.fj
http://www.usp.ac.fj/marine/

New Zealand Centre for Environmental
    Law
Faculty of Law
University of Auckland
Private Bag 92019
Auckland, New Zealand
Tel: 64 9 373 7599 ext. 87827
Fax: 64 9 373 7473
E-mail: k.bosselmann@auckland.ac.nz
http://www.law.auckland.ac.nz/groups/cel/
    index.html

School of Aquaculture
University of Tasmania
Launceston Campus, Science Building
    Room 27–306
Locked Bag 1370
Launceston, TAS 7250, Australia
Tel: 61 3 6324 3801
Fax: 61 3 6324 3804
E-mail: enquiries@aqua.utas.edu.au
http://www.utas.edu.au/aqua

School of Biological Sciences
Victoria University of Wellington
PO Box 600
Wellington, New Zealand
Tel: 64 4 463 5339
Fax: 64 4 463 5331
E-mail: biosci@vuw.ac.nz
http://www.vuw.ac.nz/sbs/

School of Geography and Environmental
    Science
University of Auckland, Tamaki Campus
Private Bag 92019
Auckland, New Zealand
Tel: 64 9 373 7599
Fax: 64 9 373 7042
E-mail: sges@auckland.ac.nz
http://sems.auckland.ac.nz/

School of Marine Biology and Aquaculture
James Cook University
Townsville, QLD 4811, Australia
Tel: 61 7 4781 4345
Fax: 61 7 4781 5511

E-mail: mbiolaq@jcu.edu.au
http://www.jcu.edu.au/school/mbiolaq/

School of Ocean and Earth Science and
Technology (SOEST)
University of Hawaii
1680 East-West Road, POST 802
Honolulu, HI, 96822, USA
Contact: Office of the Dean
Tel: 1 808 956–6182
Fax: 1 808 956–9152
E-mail: kkikuta@soest.hawaii.edu
http://www.soest.hawaii.edu/

School of Tropical Environment Studies
and Geography
James Cook University
Townsville, QLD 4811, Australia
Contact: Head of School
Tel: 61 7 4781 4325
Fax: 61 7 4781 5581
E-mail: peter.valentine@jcu.edu.au
http://www.tesag.jcu.edu.au/

Tasmanian Aquaculture and Fisheries
Institute
University of Tasmania
Hobart Campus
Private Bag 49
Hobart, TAS 7053, Australia
Tel: 61 3 6227 7277
Fax: 61 3 6227 8035
E-mail: tafi@utas.edu.au
http://www.utas.edu.au/tafi/TAFI_
Homepage.html

The International Global Change Institute
The University of Waikato
Private Bag 3105
Hamilton, New Zealand
Tel: 64 7 858 5647
Fax: 64 7 858 5689
E-mail: igci@waikato.ac.nz
http://www.waikato.ac.nz/igci/

Tourism Management Program
School of Business
James Cook University
Townsville, QLD 4811, Australia
Tel: 61 7 4781 5133
Fax: 61 7 4781 4019
E-mail: schoolofbusiness@jcu.edu.au
http://www.jcu.edu.au/fac1/public/business/
tourism.shtml

Water and Environmental Institute of the
Western Pacific (WERI)
University of Guam
UOG Station
Mangilao, GU, 96913, USA
Contact: Director
Tel: 671 735 2175
Fax: 671 734 6767
E-mail: lheitz@uog.edu
http://www.weriguam.org/

6.6 Polar Regions

Arctic Centre
University of Groningen
PO Box 716
NL-9700 AS, Groningen, The Netherlands
Tel: 31 50 363 6834
Fax: 31 50 363 4900
E-mail: arctisch@let.rug.nl
http://odin.let.rug.nl/arctic/

Arctic Centre
University of Lapland
PO Box 122
FI-96101 Rovaniemi, Finland
Tel: 358 16 341 2758
Fax: 358 16 341 2777
E-mail: paula.kankaanpää@ulapland.fi
http://www.arcticcentre.org/

Arctic Institute of North America
University of Calgary
2500 University Drive NW
Calgary, AB, T2N 1N4, Canada
Contact: Executive Director
Tel: 1 403 220–7515
Fax: 1 403 282–4609
E-mail: bbeaucha@ucalgary.ca
http://www.ucalgary.ca/aina/

Canadian Circumpolar Institute
8625–112 Street, Suite 308, Campus Tower
University of Alberta
Edmonton, AB, T6G 0H1, Canada
Contact: Director
Tel: 1 780 492–4512
Fax: 1 780 492–1153
E-mail: ccinst@gpu.srv.ualberta.ca
http://www.ualberta.ca/~ccinst/

Gateway Antarctica
Centre for Antarctic Studies and Research
University of Canterbury
Private Bag 4800
Christchurch 8020, New Zealand
Tel: 64 3 364 2136
Fax: 64 3 364 2197
E-mail: gateway-antarctica@canterbury.ac.nz
http://www.anta.canterbury.ac.nz/

Institute of Antarctic and Southern Ocean
    Studies
University of Tasmania
Hobart Campus, Centenary Building, Room
    204
Private Bag 77
Hobart, TAS 7001, Australia
Contact: Director
Tel: 61 3 6226 2971
Fax: 61 3 6226 2973
E-mail: secretary@iasos.utas.edu.au
http://www.utas.edu.au/iasos/

Scott Polar Research Institute
University of Cambridge
Lensfield Road
Cambridge, CB2 1ER, United Kingdom
Tel: 44 1223 336540
Fax: 44 1223 336549
E-mail: enquiries@spri.cam.ac.uk
http://www.spri.cam.ac.uk/

7.0 NATIONAL GOVERNMENT ORGANIZATIONS

Alfred Wegener Institute for Polar and
    Marine Research
Postfach 12 0161
D-27515 Bremerhaven, Germany
Contact: Director
Tel: 49 471 4831 1101
Fax: 49 471 4831 1389
E-mail: awi-pr@awi-bremerhaven.de
http://www.awi-bremerhaven.de/

Antarctic Climate and Ecosystems
    Cooperative Research Centre (ACE
    CRC)
Private Mail Bag 80
Hobart, TAS 7001, Australia
Contact: Communications Manager
Tel: 61 3 6226 7888

Fax: 61 3 6226 2440
E-mail: enquiries@acecrc.org.au
http://www.acecrc.org.au/

Aquafin Cooperative Research Centre
c/o South Australian R&D Institute
PO Box 120
Henley Beach, SA 5022, Australia
Contact: Chief Executive Officer
Tel: 61 8 8207 5302
Fax: 61 8 8207 5406
E-mail: peter.montague@aquafincrc.com.au
http://www.aquafincrc.com.au/

Arctic and Antarctic Research Institute
8 Bering Street
St. Petersburg, 199397, Russian Federation
Tel: 7 812 3521520
Fax: 7 812 3522688
E-mail: aaricoop@aari.nw.ru
http://www.aari.nw.ru/

Asociacíon Argentina de Ingeniería
    Sanitaria y Ciencias del Ambiente
    (AIDIS Argentina)
Av. Belgrano 1580 Piso 3
1093 Buenos Aires, Argentina
Contact: Chairman
Tel/Fax: 54 11 4381 5832/5093
E-mail: aidisar@aidisar.org
http://www.aidisar.org/

Atlantic Coastal Action Program
Environment Canada
45 Alderney Drive
Dartmouth, NS, B2Y 2N6, Canada
Contact: Project Officer
Tel: 1 902 426–8679
http://www.ns.ec.gc.ca/community/acap/

Atlantic States Marine Fisheries
    Commission (ASMFC)
1444 Eye Street NW, 6th floor
Washington, DC, 20005, USA
Contact: Executive Director
Tel: 1 202 289–6400
Fax: 1 202 289–6051
E-mail: comments@asmfc.org
http://www.asmfc.org/

Australian Institute of Marine Science
PMB No. 3
Townsville MC, QLD 4810, Australia

Contact: Chief Scientist
Tel: 61 7 4753 4444
Fax: 61 7 4772 5852
E-mail: reception@aims.gov.au
http://www.aims.gov.au/

Australian Maritime Safety Authority
GPO Box 2181
Canberra, ACT 2601, Australia
Tel: 61 2 6279 5000
Fax: 61 2 6279 5950
http://www.amsa.gov.au/

Bangladesh Fisheries Research Institute
Mymensingh 2201, Bangladesh
Tel: 880 91 54874
Fax: 880 91 55259
http://www.bangladeshgov.bd/mofl/fri/
fritop.htm

Bedford Institute of Oceanography
1 Challenger Drive
PO Box 1006
Dartmouth, NS, B2Y 4A2, Canada
Contact: Director, Oceans and Habitat
Branch
Tel: 1 902 426–3825
Fax: 1 902 426–9909
E-mail: roseca@mar.dfo-mpo.gc.ca
http://www.bio.gc.ca/

British Geological Survey
Kingsley Dunham Centre
Keyworth
Nottingham, NG12 5GG, United Kingdom
Contact: Headquarters
Tel: 44 115 936 3143
Fax: 44 115 936 3276
E-mail: enquiries@bgs.ac.uk
http://www.bgs.ac.uk/

Bureau of Fisheries and Aquatic Resources
Department of Agriculture
Arcadia Building
860 Quezon Avenue
1103 Quezon City, The Philippines
Contact: Director
Tel: 632 372 5043
Fax: 632 372 5048
E-mail: info@bfar.da.gov.ph
http://www.bfar.da.gov.ph/

Bureau of Ocean and International
Environmental and Scientific Affairs
US Department of State
2201 C Street, NW, Room 7831
Washington, DC, 20520, USA
Contact: Assistant Secretary of State
Tel: 1 202 647–1554
http://www.state.gov/g/oes/

Canada-Newfoundland and Labrador
Offshore Petroleum Board
5th Floor TD Place, 140 Water Street
St. John's, NL, A1C 6H6, Canada
Tel: 1 709 778–1400
E-mail: postmaster@cnlopb.nl.ca
http://www.cnlopb.nl.ca/

Canada-Nova Scotia Offshore Petroleum
Board
6th Floor TD Centre, 1791 Barrington
Street
Halifax, NS, B3J 3K9, Canada
Tel: 1 902 422–5588
Fax: 1 902 422–1799
E-mail: postmaster@cnsopb.ns.ca
http://www.cnsopb.ns.ca/

Canadian Environmental Assessment Agency
Place Bell, 22nd floor
160 Elgin Street
Ottawa, ON, K1A 0H3, Canada
Tel: 1 613 957–0700
Fax: 1 613 957–0935
E-mail: info@ceaa-acee.gc.ca
http://www.ceaa.gc.ca/

Canadian Polar Commission
Suite 1710, Constitution Square
360 Albert Street
Ottawa, ON, K1R 7X7, Canada
Tel: 1 613 943–8605
Fax: 1 613 943–8607
E-mail: mail@polarcom.gc.ca
http://www.polarcom.gc.ca/

Caribbean Fishery Management Council
US Department of Commerce
268 Muñoz Rivera Avenue, Suite 1108
San Juan, Puerto Rico, 00918–2577, USA
Contact: Executive Director
Tel: 1 787 766–5926
Fax: 1 787 766–6239
E-mail: miguel.a.rolon@noaa.gov
http://www.caribbeanfmc.com/

Center of Marine Research
Lithuanian Ministry of the Environment
Taikos pr.26
LT-91149 Klaipeda, Lithuania
Tel: 370 46 41 04 50
Fax: 370 46 41 04 60
E-mail: CMR@klaipeda.omnitel.net
http://www.am.lt/EN/VI/

Centre de Recherches Océanographiques
    de Dakar-Thiaroye (CRODT)
BP 2241
Dakar, Senegal
Contact: Directeur
Tel: 221 834 8041
Fax: 221 834 2792
E-mail: tdiouf@crodt.isra.sn;
crodt@crodt.isra.sn
http://www.isra.sn/crodt.htm

Centre de Recherches Oceanologiques
    (CRO)
BP V18
Rue ses Pêcheurs–Zone 3
Abidjan, Côté d'Ivoire
Contact: Directeur
Tel: 225 21 355014
Fax: 225 21 351155
http://www.ird.ci/ird/cro.html

Centre for Environment, Fisheries and
    Aquaculture Science (CEFAS)
Lowestoft Laboratory
Pakefield Road
Lowestoft, Suffolk, NR33 0HT, United
    Kingdom
Tel: 44 1502 5244210
Fax: 44 1502 524525
E-mail: lowlibrary@cefas.co.uk
http://www.cefas.co.uk/

Centre Océanologique du Pacifique,
    IFREMER
BP 7004
98719 Taravao, Tahiti, French Polynesia
Tel: 689 546000
Fax: 689 546099
E-mail: dominique.buestel@ifremer.fr
http://www.ifremer.fr/cop/

Centro Tecnológico del Mar, Fundación
    (CETMAR)
c/ Eduardo Cabello s/n

E-36208 Bouzas, Vigo, Spain
Tel: 34 986 247 047
Fax: 34 986 294 587
E-mail: info@cetmar.org
http://www.cetmar.org/

China Institute for Marine Affairs
State Oceanic Administration
1 Fuxingmenwai Avenue
Beijing 100860, People's Republic of China
Contact: Executive Director
Tel: 86 10 6803 0767
E-mail: mjli@cima.gov.cn
http://www.cima.gov.cn/

Coastal America
300 7th Street, SW Suite 680
Washington, DC, 20250, USA
Contact: Director
Tel: 1 202 401–9928
Fax: 1 202 401–9821
E-mail: virginia.tippie@usda.gov
http://www.coastalamerica.gov/

Coastal States Organization
Hall of States, Suite 322
444 N. Capitol Street NW
Washington, DC, 20001, USA
Contact: Executive Director
Tel: 1 202 508–3860
Fax: 1 202 508–3843
E-mail: ageiger@sso.org
http://www.coastalstates.org/

Coastal Zone Management Centre (CZM
    Centre)
PO Box 20907
NL-2500 EX, The Hague, Netherlands
Tel: 31 70 311 4311
Fax: 31 70 311 4380
E-mail: czmc@rikz.rws.minvenw.nl
http://www.netcoast.nl/

Commonwealth Scientific Industrial
    Research Organization (CSIRO)
CSIRO Marine and Atmospheric Research
GPO Box 1538
Hobart, TAS 7001, Australia
Tel: 61 3 6232 5222
Fax: 61 3 6232 5000
E-mail: reception@marine.csiro.au
http://www.cmar.csiro.au/

Council for Scientific and Industrial
Research (CSIR)
PO Box 395
Pretoria 0001, South Africa
Contact: Coast Program Manager
Tel: 27 12 841 2911
Fax: 27 12 349 1153
http://www.csir.co.za/

Countryside Council for Wales
Maes-y-Ffynnon
Penrhosgarnedd, Bangor
Gwynedd, Wales, LL57 2DW, United
Kingdom
Contact: Head Office
Tel: 44 0845 1306 229
E-mail: enquiries@ccw.gov.uk
http://www.ccw.gov.uk/

CRC for Coastal Zone, Estuary and
Waterway Management
Indooroopilly Sciences Centre, QCCA
Building
80 Meiers Road
Indooroopilly, QLD 4068, Australia
Contact: Chief Executive Officer
Tel: 61 7 3362 9399
Fax: 61 7 3362 9372
E-mail: coastal.crc@nrm.qld.gov.au
http://www.coastal.crc.org.au/

CRC Reef Research Centre
PO Box 772
Townsville, QLD 4810, Australia
Contact: Secretariat
Tel: 61 7 4729 8400
Fax: 61 7 4729 8499
E-mail: info@crcreef.com
http://www.reef.crc.org.au/

Danish Directorate of Fisheries
Nyropsgade 30
DK-1480 Copenhagen V, Denmark
Tel: 45 33 96 30 00
Fax: 45 33 96 39 03
E-mail: fd@fd.dk
http://www.fd.dk/

Danish Institute for Fisheries Research
(Danmarks Fiskeriundersogelser)
Jägersborg vej 64–66
DK-2800 Lyngby, Denmark
Tel: 45 33 96 33 00
Fax: 45 33 96 33 49

E-mail: info@dfu.min.dk
http://www.dfu.min.dk/

Danish Institute of Agricultural and
Fisheries Economics
(Fodevareokonomisk Institut)
Rolighedsvej 25
DK-1958 Frederiksberg C, Denmark
Contact: Director
Tel: 45 35 28 68 00
Fax: 45 35 28 68 01
E-mail: foi@foi.dk
http://www.sjfi.dk/

Danish Maritime Authority (DMA)
Ministry of Economics and Business Affairs
38C, Vermundsgade
PO Box 2605
DK-2100 Copenhagen O, Denmark
Tel: 45 39 17 44 00
Fax: 45 39 17 44 01
E-mail: dma@dma.dk
http://www.dma.dk/

Danish Polar Center
Strandgade 100H
DK-1401 Copenhagen K, Denmark
Tel: 45 32 88 01 00
Fax: 45 32 88 01 01
E-mail: dpc@dpc.dk
http://www.dpc.dk/

Department of Agriculture, Fisheries and
Forestry
GPO Box 858
Canberra, ACT 2601, Australia
Tel: 61 2 6272 5030
Fax: 61 2 6272 4875
E-mail: fisheries@affa.gov.au
http://www.affa.gov.au/

Department of Communications, Marine
and Natural Resources
29–31 Adelaide Road
Dublin 2, Ireland
Tel: 353 1 678 2000
Fax: 353 1 678 2449
E-mail: webmaster@dcmnr.gov.ie
http://www.dcmnr.gov.ie/Marine/

Department of Conservation
PO Box 10420
Wellington, New Zealand

Contact: Marine and Coastal Conservation
Tel: 64 04 471 3286
Fax: 64 04 471 3279
http://www.doc.govt.nz/Conservation/Marine-and-Coastal/

Department of Fisheries
Kasetlang, Chatuchak
Bangkok 10900, Thailand
Contact: Director-General
Tel: 66 2 562 0600 15
Fax: 66 2 562 9406 203
E-mail: sitdhitb@fisheries.go.th
http://www.fisheries.go.th/

Department of Ocean Development
Block No. 12, CGO Complex
Lodhi Road
New Delhi 110003, India
Fax: 91 11 24360336
E-mail: dodsec@dod.delhi.nic.in
http://www.dod.nic.in/

Department of Oceanology and
    Environmental Geophysics (OGA)
Instituto Nationale di Oceanografia
Borgo Grotta Gigante 42/c
I-34010 Sgonico (TS), Italy
Tel: 39 040 2140 1
Fax: 39 040 2140 266
E-mail: mailbox@ogs.trieste.it
http://doga.ogs.trieste.it/index.html

Department of the Environment and
    Heritage
Land, Water and Coasts Division
GPO Box 787
Canberra, ACT 2601, Australia
Tel: 61 2 6274 1111
Fax: 61 2 6274 1006
http://www.deh.gov.au/wcd/index.html
    #water

Dirección Nacional de Recursos Acuáticos
    (DINARA)
Constituyente 1497
CP 11200
PO Box 1612
Montevideo, Uruguay
Tel: 598 2 409 2969
http://www.dinara.gub.uy/

English Nature
Northminster House

Peterborough, PE1 1UA, United Kingdom
Tel: 44 17 3345 5101
Fax: 44 17 3356 8834
E-mail: enquiries@english-nature.org.uk
http://www.english-nature.org.uk/

Environment Canada
70 Crémazie Street
Gatineau, QC, K1A 0H3, Canada
Contact: Inquiry Centre
Tel: 1 819 997–2800
Fax: 1 819 994–1412
E-mail: enviroinfo@ec.gc.ca
http://www.ec.gc.ca/

Federal Research Centre for Fisheries
    (Bundesforschungsanstalt für Fischerei)
Palmaille 9
D-22767 Hamburg, Germany
Tel: 49 40 38905–0
Fax: 49 40 38905–200
E-mail: iud@bfa-fisch.de
http://www.bfa-fisch.de/

Finnish Institute of Marine Research
    (Merentutkimuslaitos)
PO Box 2
FI-00561 Helsinki, Finland
Tel: 358 9 6139 41
Fax: 358 9 323 2970
E-mail: info@fimr.fi
http://www.fimr.fi/

Finnish Maritime Administration
PO Box 171
FI-00181 Helsinki, Finland
Tel: 358 204 481
Fax: 358 204 48 4355
E-mail: keskushallinto@fma.fi
http://www.fma.fi/

Fish and Wildlife Research Institute
100 Eighth Avenue SE
St. Petersburg, FL, 33701–5095, USA
Tel: 1 727 896–8626
http://research.myfwc.com/

Fisheries and Oceans Canada (DFO)
200 Kent Street, 13th Floor Station 13228
Ottawa, ON, K1A 0E6, Canada
Contact: Communications Branch
Tel: 1 613 993–0999
Fax: 1 613 990–1866

E-mail: info@dfo-mpo.gc.ca
http://www.dfo-mpo.gc.ca/

Fisheries Conservation and Control Division
Malta Centre for Fisheries Sciences
Fort San Lucjan
Marsaxlokk BBG 06, Malta
Tel: 356 216 55 525
Fax: 356 216 59 380
E-mail: malta.fisheries@gov.mt
http://www.maltafisheries.gov.mt/

Fisheries Directorate
Department for Environment, Food &
    Rural Affairs
3–8 Whitehall Place
London, SW1A 2HH, United Kingdom
Tel: 44 207 238 6015
Fax: 44 207 238 6609
http://www.defra.gov.uk/fish/fishindx.htm

Fisheries Information Center (FICen)
Ministry of Fisheries
10 Nguyen Cong Hoan Street
Ba Dinh District, Hanoi, Vietnam
Tel/Fax: 84 4 7716578
E-mail: ttam.bts@hn.vnn.vn
http://www.fistenet.gov.vn/index_En.asp

Fisheries Research Agency
Queen's Tower B, 15F
2–3–3 Minatomirai
Nishi-ku, Yokohama-shi, Kanagawa,
    220–6115, Japan
Tel: 81 45 227 2600
http://www.fra.affrc.go.jp/

Fisheries Resource Conservation Council
PO Box 2001 Station D
Ottawa, ON, K1P 5W3, Canada
Contact: Secretariat
Tel: 1 613 998–0433
Fax: 1 613 998–1146
E-mail: info@frcc-ccrh.ca
http://www.frcc-ccrh.ca/

Geological Survey of Canada (Atlantic)
Bedford Institute of Oceanography
1 Challenger Drive
PO Box 1006
Dartmouth, NS, B2Y 4A2, Canada
Contact: Director
Tel: 1 902 426–3448
Fax: 1 902 426–1466

E-mail: jverhoef@nrcan.gc.ca
http://agcwww.bio.ns.ca/

Great Barrier Reef Marine Park Authority
2–68 Flinders Street
PO Box 1379
Townsville, QLD 4810, Australia
Tel: 61 7 4750 0700
Fax: 61 7 4772 6093
http://www.gbrmpa.gov.au/

Gulf of Guinea Large Marine Ecosystem
    Project (GOGLME) Regional
    Coordination Centre
c/o CRO
BP V18
Abidjan, Côte d'Ivoire
Tel: 225 355014
Fax: 225 351155
E-mail: gog-lme@africaonline.co.ci
http://www.africaonline.co.ci/AfricaOnline/
    societes/goglme/goglme2.html

Gulf of Mexico Fishery Management
    Council
2203 N. Lois Avenue, Suite 1100
Tampa, FL 33607–2389, USA
Contact: Executive Director
Tel: 1 813 348–1630
Fax: 1 813 348–1711
E-mail: wayne.swingle@gulfcouncil.org
http://www.gulfcouncil.org/

Hellenic Centre for Marine Research
PO Box 712
GR-19013 Anavissos, Attika, Greece
Contact: Director's Office
Tel.: 30 22910 76466
Fax: 30 22910 76323
E-mail: jgeorg@ath.hcmr.gr
http://www.hcmr.gr/

Icelandic Fisheries Laboratories
(Rannsóknastofnun Fiskidnadarins)
Skulagata 4
IS-101 Reykjavik, Iceland
Tel: 354 530 8600
Fax: 354 530 8601
E-mail: info@rf.is
http://www.rfisk.is/

Icelandic Marine Research Institute
(Hafrannsóknastofnunin–HAFRO)
Skulagata 4

IS-121 Reykjavik, Iceland
Contact: Director General
Tel: 354 575 2000
Fax: 354 575 2001
E-mail: hafro@hafro.is
http://www.hafro.is/

Institut de Recherche pour le
    Développement (IRD)
213, rue la Fayette
F-75480 Paris Cedex 10, France
Contact: Headquarters
Tel: 331 1 4803 7777
Fax: 331 1 4803 0829
E-mail: corlay@paris.ird.fr
http://www.ird.fr/

Institut Français de Recherche pour
    l'Exploitation de la Mer (IFREMER)
(French Research Institute for Exploitaton
    of the Sea)
155 rue Jean-Jacques Rousseau
F-92138 Issy-les-Moulineaux Cedex, France
Contact: CEO
Tel: 33 1 4648 2100
Fax: 33 1 4648 2248
http://www.ifremer.fr/

Institut für Ostseeforschung Warnemünde
    (IOW)
(Baltic Sea Research Institute
    Warnemünde)
Seestrasse 15
D-18119 Rostock, Germany
Contact: Director
Tel: 49 381 5197 100
Fax: 49 381 5197 105
E-mail: bodo.bodungen@io-warnemuende.de
http://www.io-warnemuende.de/

Institut National de Recherches Halieutique
    (INRH)
2, rue de Tiznit
Casablanca 01, Morocco
Contact: Directeur
Tel: 212 22 26 81 92
Fax: 212 22 26 69 67
E-mail: inrh@inrh.org.ma
http://www.inrh.org.ma/

Institut National des Sciences et
    Technologies de la Mer (INSTM)
28, rue du 2 mars 1934

2035 Salammbô, Tunisia
Tel: 216 71 730 420
Fax: 216 71 732 622
http://www.universites.tn/instm/fr/
    accueil.php

Institute for Baltic Sea Fisheries
(Institut für Ostseeforschung–IOR)
An der Jägerbäk 2
D-18069 Rostock, Germany
Tel: 49 381 810344
Fax: 49 381 810445
E-mail: info@ior.bfa-fisch.de
http://www.bfa-fisch.de/ior/

Institute for Coastal Research
(Institut für Küstenforschung–IfK)
GKSS-Forschungszentrum
Max-Planck-Straße 1
D-21502 Geesthacht, Germany
Tel: 49 4152 87 1533
Fax: 49 4152 87 2020
E-mail: colijn@gkss.de
http://coast.gkss.de/

Institute for Marine Biosciences
National Research Council of Canada
1411 Oxford Street
Halifax, NS, B3H 3Z1, Canada
Contact: Director
Tel: 1 902 426–8332
Fax: 1 902 426–9413
E-mail: communications.imb@nrc-cnrc.gc.ca
http://www.imb.nrc.ca/

Institute for Sea Fisheries
(Institut für Seefischerei–ISH)
Palmaille 9
D-22767 Hamburg, Germany
Tel: 49 40 38905 177
Fax: 49 40 38905 263
E-mail: info@ish.bfa-fisch.de
http://www.bfa-fisch.de/ish/

Institute of Biology of the Southern Seas
National Academy of Sciences of the
    Ukraine
2 Nakhimov Avenue
Sebastopol 99011 Crimea, Ukraine
Tel: 380 692 544 110
Fax: 380 692 557 813
E-mail: ibss@ibss.iuf.net
http://www.ibss.iuf.net/

Institute of Marine Affairs (IMA)
Hilltop Lane
PO Box 3160
Carenage Post Office
Chaguaramas, Trinidad and Tobago
Tel: 1 868 634–4291
Fax: 1 868 634–4433
E-mail: director@ima.gov.tt
http://www.ima.gov.tt/

Institute of Marine Research (IMR)
(Havforskningsinstituttet)
PO Box 1870 Nordnes
N-5817 Bergen, Norway
Tel: 47 55 23 85 00
Fax: 47 55 23 85 31
E-mail: post@imr.no
http://www.imr.no/

Institute of Ocean Sciences
9860 West Saanich Road
PO Box 6000
Sidney, BC, V8L 4B2, Canada
Tel: 1 250 363–6517
http://www-sci.pac.dfo-
mpo.gc.ca/sci/facilities/ios_e.htm

Instituto de Fomento Pesquero (IFOP)
(Fishery Research Institute)
Blanco 839
Valparaíso, Chile
Tel: 56 32 322 000
Fax: 56 32 322 345
E-mail: info@ifop.cl
http://www.ifop.cl/

Instituto de Investigaciones Marinas
Eduardo Cabello 6
E-36208 Vigo, Spain
Tel: 34 986 231 930
Fax: 34 986 292 762
E-mail: dir_iim@iim.csic.es
http://www.iim.csic.es/

Instituto de Investigaciones Marinas y
    Costeras (INVEMAR)
Cerro Punta de Betín, Santa Marta
Apartado aéreo1016 y 873, Santa Marta,
    Colombia
Tel: 57 5 421 4775
Fax: 57 5 431 2986
E-mail: srinconc@invemar.org.co
http://www.invemar.org.co/

Instituto de Mar del Perú (IMARPE)
(Peruvian Marine Institute)
Esquina de Gamarra y General Valle S/N
    Chuciuto
Callao, Peru
Tel: 51 420 2000
http://www.imarpe.gob.pe/

Instituto de Oceanología de Cuba
(Institute of Oceanology)
Calle 1ra No. 18406 esquina 184 y 186
Reparto Flores, Playa
Havana 12100, Cuba
Contact: Director
Tel: 537 21 1380
Fax: 537 33 9112
E-mail: jperez@unepnet.inf.cu
http://www.cuba.cu/ciencia/citma/AMA/
    p_a.html

Instituto Oceanográfico de la Armada del
    Ecuador (INOCAR)
(Naval Oceanographic Institute)
Avda 25 de Julio (Base Naval Sur)
via al Puerto Marítimo
Guyaquil, Ecuador
Tel: 593 4 2481 300
Fax: 593 4 2485 166
E-mail: inocar@inocar.mil.ec
http://www.inocar.mil.ec/

Inter-Agency Committee on Marine Science
    and Technology (IACMST)
National Oceanography Centre,
    Southampton
European Way
Empress Dock
Southampton, SO14 3ZH, United Kingdom
Tel: 44 2380 596611
Fax: 44 2380 596395
E-mail: iacmst@noc.soton.ac.uk
http://www.marine.gov.uk/

International Association of Fish and
    Wildlife Agencies
444 Capitol Street, NW, Suite 725
Washington, DC, 20001, USA
Contact: Executive Vice President
Tel: 1 202 624–7890
Fax: 1 202 624–7891
E-mail: info@iafwa.org
http://www.iafwa.org/

Joint Nature Conservation Committee
 (JNCC)
Monkstone House, City Road
Peterborough, PE1 1JY, United Kingdom
Contact: Headquarters
Tel: 44 1733 562626
Fax: 44 1733 555948
E-mail: comment@jncc.gov.uk
http://www.jncc.gov.uk/marine/

Kenya Wildlife Service
Marine National Parks and Reserves
PO Box 82144
Mombasa, Kenya
Contact: Assistant Director
Tel: 254 041 312744/5
Fax: 254 041 22774
E-mail: kws@kws.org
http://www.kws.org/marine.html

Korea Ocean Research and Development
 Institute (KORDI)
Ansan PO Box 29
425–600 Korea
Tel: 82 31 400 6000
Fax: 82 31 408 5820
E-mail: webmaster@kordi.re.kr
http://www.kordi.re.kr/

Maine Atlantic Salmon Commission
161 Capital Street
Augusta, ME, 04333–0172, USA
Contact: Executive Director
Tel: 1 207 287–9972
Fax: 1 207 287–9975
E-mail: patrick.keliher@maine.gov
http://www.state.me.us/asa/

Maine Department of Marine Resources
21 State House Station
Augusta, ME, 04333, USA
Tel: 1 207 624–6550
Fax: 1 207 624–6024
http://www.maine.gov/dmr/

Marine and Coastal Management Branch
Department of Environmental Affairs and
 Tourism
Private Bag X2
Roggebaai 8012, South Africa
Contact: Deputy Director-General
Tel: 27 12 402 3401
Fax: 27 12 419 6942
http://www.environment.gov.za/

Marine Board
Transportation Research Board
Keck Center of the National Academies
500 Fifth Street NW
Washington, DC, 20001, USA
Contact: Director
Tel: 1 202 334–2934
Fax: 1 202 334–2003
http://www4.nationalacademies.org/trb/
 homepage.nsf/web/marine_board

Marine Department Malaysia
(Jabatan Laut Malaysia)
Peti Surat 12
Jalan Limbungan
42007 Pelabuhan Klang, Malaysia
Contact: Director General
Tel: 60 3 3346 7777
Fax: 60 3 3168 5289
E-mail: kpgr@marine.gov.my
http://www.marine.gov.my/

Marine Environment Protection Directorate
Department of Environment, Food & Rural
 Affairs
Nobel House
17 Smith Square
London, SW1P 3JR, United Kingdom
Tel: 44 207 238 6015
Fax: 44 207 238 6609
E-mail: marine.environment@defra.gsi.gov.uk
http://www.defra.gov.uk/environment/water/
 marine/index.htm

Marine Institute
Galway Technical Park
Parkmore, Galway, Ireland
Contact: Headquarters
Tel: 353 91 730 400
Fax: 353 91 730 470
E-mail: institute.mail@marine.ie
http://www.marine.ie/

Maritime Administration
U.S. Department of Transportation
400 Seventh Street SW
Washington, DC, 20590, USA
Contact: Office of Congressional and
 Public Affairs
Tel: 1 202 366–5807
E-mail: marad.pao@marad.dot.gov
http://www.marad.dot.gov/

Maritime and Coastguard Agency
Tutt Head, Mumbles
Swansea, West Glamorgan, SA3 4HW,
    United Kingdom
Tel: 44 23 870 600 6505
E-mail: infoline@mcga.gov.uk
http://www.mcga.gov.uk/

Maritime and Ocean Engineering Institute
    (MOERI)
PO Box 23
Yusong, Daejon, 305–600 Korea
Tel: 82 42 868 77011
Fax: 82 42 868 7711
http://www.moeri.re.kr/

Maritime and Port Authority of Singapore
460 Alexandra Road
#18–00 PSA Building
119963, Singapore
Tel: 65 6375 1600
Fax: 65 6275 9247
E-mail: mpa@mpa.gov.sg
http://www.mpa.gov.sg/

Maritime Industry Authority
Department of Transportation and
    Communications
PPL Building
1000 UN Avenue cor. San Marcelino Street
Manila, The Philippines
Tel: 63 2 523 8651
Fax: 63 2 524 2746
E-mail: oadm@marina.gov.ph
http://www.marina.gov.ph/

Maritime Institute of Malaysia (MIMA)
B-06–08 Megan Avenue II
12 Yap Kwan Seng
50450 Kuala Lumpur, Malaysia
Contact: Director General
Tel: 60 3 2161 2960
Fax: 60 3 2161 4035
E-mail: mima@mima.gov.my
http://www.mima.gov.my/

Maurice Lamontagne Institute
Fisheries and Oceans Canada
850, route de la Mer
PO Box 1000
Mont-Joli, QC, G5H 3Z4, Canada
Tel: 1 418 775–0500
Fax: 1 418 775–0542

E-mail: info@dfo-mpo.gc.ca
http://www.qc.dfo-mpo.gc.ca/iml/

Mauritius Oceanography Institute
France Centre, Victoria Avenue
Quatre-Bornes, Mauritius
Tel: 230 427 4428
Fax: 230 427 4433
E-mail: moi@intnet.mu
http://moi.gov.mu/index.htm

Mid-Atlantic Fisheries Management Council
Room 2115 Federal Building
300 S. New Street
Dover, DE, 19904, USA
Contact: Executive Director
Tel: 1 302 674–2331
Fax: 1 302 674–5399
E-mail: info@mafmc.org
http://www.mafmc.org/

Ministry of Environment and National
    Development Unit
Ken Lee Tower, Cnr Barracks & St
    Georges Streets
Port Louis, Republic of Mauritius
Tel: 230 211 3658
Fax: 230 211 9524
E-mail: menv@mail.gov.mu
http://environment.gov.mu/

Ministry of Fisheries
ASB Bank House
101–103 The Terrace
PO Box 1020
Wellington, New Zealand
Tel: 64 4 470 2600
Fax: 64 4 470 2601
E-mail: info@fish.govt.nz
http://www.fish.govt.nz/

Ministry of Fisheries
Head Office, 4th Floor, L.I.C. Building
President John Kennedy Street
Port Louis, Republic of Mauritius
Tel: 230 2112470
Fax: 230 2081929
E-mail: fisheries@mail.gov.mu
http://fisheries.gov.mu/

Ministry of Fisheries and Marine Resources
Private Bag X 13355
Windhoek, Namibia

Contact: Permanent Secretary
Tel: 264 61 2059
Fax: 264 61 233 286
E-mail: nmbako@mfmr.gov.na
http://www.mfmr.gov.na/

Ministry of Marine Fisheries
(Ministère des Pêches Maritimes)
BP 475, Quartier administratif
Agdal, Rabat, Morocco
Tel: 212 37 688000
Fax: 212 37 688135
http://www.mpm.gov.ma/

Ministry of Maritime Affairs and Fisheries
(MOMAF)
140–2 Gye-Dong, Jongo-Gu
Seoul 110–793, Korea
Tel: 82 2 3674 6114
Fax: 82 2 3674 6044
E-mail: webmaster@momaf.go.kr
http://www.momaf.go.kr/

Ministry of Maritime Economy
(Ministère de l'Economie maritime)
Building Administratif
BP 4050
Dakar, Senegal
Tel: 221 849 7000
Fax: 221 823 8720
E-mail: abdoumbodj@yahoo.fr
http://www.ecomaritime.gouv.sn/

Ministry of the Environment
PO Box 35
FI-00023 Helsinki, Finland
Tel: 358 9 1600 07
Fax: 358 9 1603 9545
http://www.miljo.fi/

National Environment and Planning
Agency
John McIntosh Building
10 Caledonia Avenue
Kingston 5, Jamaica
Tel: 876 754 7540
Fax: 876 754 7595
E-mail: pubed@nepa.gov.jm
http://www.nrca.org/

National Environmental Research Institute
(NERI)
(Danmarks Miljoundersogelser)
PO Box 358

Frederiksborgvej 399
DK-4000 Roskilde, Denmark
Tel: 45 46 30 12 00
Fax: 45 46 30 11 14
E-mail: dmu@dmu.dk
http://www.dmu.dk/

National Institiute of Oceanography (NIO)
Dona Paula
403 004, Goa, India
Tel: 91 832 2450450
Fax: 91 832 2450602
E-mail: ocean@darya.nio.org
http://www.nio.org/

National Institute for Marine Research and
Development Agrigore Antipa
Boulevard Mamaia 300
RO-900581 Constanta, Romania
Tel: 40 241 543288
Fax: 40 241 831274
E-mail: rmri@alpha.rmri.ro
http://www.rmri.ro/

National Institute of Oceanography and
Fisheries (NIOF)
101 Kasr El Ainy Street
Cairo, Egypt
Tel: 20 2 792 1342
Fax: 20 2 792 1339
E-mail: awwade@niof.sci.eg
http://www.niof.sci.eg/

National Institute of Water and
Atmospheric Research
Private Bag 99940
369 Khyber Pass Road
Newmarket, Auckland, New Zealand
Tel: 64 9 375 2090
Fax: 64 9 375 2091
E-mail: webmaster@niwa.co.nz
http://www.niwa.cri.nz/

National Marine Data & Information
Service
93 Qiwei Road
Hedong District, Tianjin 300171, People's
Republic of China
Contact: Director
Tel: 86 22 2401 0801
Fax: 86 22 2401 0926
E-mail: webmaster@mail.nmdis.gov.cn
http://www.nmdis.gov.cn/

National Marine Fisheries Service (NMFS)
National Oceanic and Atmospheric
  Administration (NOAA)
1315 East-West Highway, 9th floor
Silver Spring, MD, 20910, USA
Tel: 1 301 713–2379
Fax: 1 301 713–2385
E-mail: cyber.fish@noaa.gov
http://www.nmfs.noaa.gov/

National Ocean Service
National Oceanic and Atmospheric
  Administration (NOAA)
SSMC4 Room 13317, 1305 East-West
  Highway
Silver Spring, MD, 20910, USA
Tel: 1 301 713–3060
E-mail: nos.info@noaa.gov
http://www.nos.noaa.gov/

National Oceans Office
GPO Box 2139
Hobart, Tasmania 7000, Australia
Tel: 61 3 6221 5000
Fax: 61 3 6221 5050
E-mail: office@oceans.gov.au
http://www.oceans.gov.au/

National Sea Grant College Program
National Oceanic and Atmospheric
  Administration (NOAA)
SSMC3, 11th floor, 1315 East-West Highway
Sea Grant, RSG
Silver Spring, MD, 20910, USA
Contact: Director
Tel: 1 301 713–2431
Fax: 1 301 713–0799
E-mail: ronald.baird@noaa.gov
http://www.nsgo.seagrant.org/

Natural Environment Research Council
  (NERC)
Polaris House
North Star Avenue
Swindon, SN2 1EU, United Kingdom
Tel: 44 01793 411500
Fax: 44 01793 411501
http://www.nerc.ac.uk/

New England Fishery Management Council
50 Water Street, Mill 2
Newburyport, MA, 01950, USA
Tel: 1 978 465–0492
Fax: 1 978 465–3116

E-mail: pfiorelli@nefmc.org
http://www.nefmc.org/

Nigerian Institute of Oceanography and
  Marine Research (NIOMR)
Wilmot Point Road, Bar-Beach
Private Mail Bag 12729
Lagos, Nigeria
Contact: Director
Tel/Fax: 234 1 261 9517
Fax: 234 1 617385
E-mail: niomr@linkserve.com.ng

North Pacific Fishery Management Council
605 West 4th, Suite 306
Anchorage, AK, 99501–2252, USA
Contact: Executive Director
Tel: 1 907 271–2809
Fax: 1 907 271–2817
E-mail: Chris.Oliver@noaa.gov
http://www.fakr.noaa.gov/npfmc/default.htm

Norwegian Institute for Water Research
(Norsk Institutt for Vannforskning)
Postboks 173 Kjelsås
N-0411 Oslo, Norway
Tel: 47 22 18 51 00
Fax: 47 22 18 52 00
E-mail: niva@niva.no
http://www.niva.no/

Norwegian Polar Institute
(Norsk Polarinstitutt–NPI)
Polar Environmental Centre
N-9296 Tromso, Norway
Tel: 47 77 75 05 00
Fax: 47 77 75 05 01
E-mail: postmottak@npolar.no
http://www.npolar.no/

Norwegian Pollution Control Authority
PO Box 8100 Dep.
N-0032 Oslo, Norway
Tel: 47 22 57 34 00
Tel: 47 22 67 67 06
E-mail: miljostatus@sft.no
http://www.environment.no/

NRC Institute for Ocean Technology
  (IOT)
PO Box 12093
St. John's, NL, A1B 3T5, Canada
Tel: 1 709 772–4939
Fax: 1 709 772–2462

E-mail: trish.leblanc@nrc-cnrc.gc.ca
http://iot-ito.nrc-cnrc.gc.ca/

Observatoire Océanologique Villefranche
    sur Mer
BP 28
F-06234 Villefranche Sur Mer Cedex,
    France
Contact: Secretary General
Tel: 33 4 9376 3803
Fax: 33 4 9376 3834
E-mail: michele.etienne@obs-vlfr.fr
http://www.obs-vlfr.fr/

Ocean Studies Board
The National Academies
500 5th Street, NW
Keck Building, Room K-752
Washington, DC, 20001, USA
Contact: Board Director
Tel: 1 202 334–2714
Fax: 1 202 334–2885
E-mail: sroberts@nas.edu
http://dels.nas.edu/osb/

Oceans Policy Secretariat
Ministry for the Environment
PO Box 10362
Wellington, New Zealand
Tel: 64 4 917 7400
Fax: 64 4 917 7521
E-mail: oceans@mfe.govt.nz
http://www.mfe.govt.nz/issues/oceans/

Office of Naval Research
One Liberty Center
875 North Randolph Street, Ste. 1425
Arlington, VA, 22203–1995, USA
Tel: 1 703 696–5358
Fax: 1 703 696–5940
E-mail: onrpao@onr.navy.mil
http://www.onr.navy.mil/

Office of Wetlands, Oceans and Watersheds
    (450 IT)
U.S. Environmental Protection Agency
1200 Pennsylvania Ave, NW
Washington, DC, 20460, USA
Contact: Administrator
Tel: 1 202 566–1300
E-mail: ow-owow-internet-comments@epa.gov
http://www.epa.gov/owow/

Pacific Biological Station
3190 Hammond Bay Road
Nanaimo, BC, V6RT 5K6, Canada
Tel: 1 250 756–7000
Fax: 1 250 756–7053
E-mail: info@dfo-mpo.gc.ca
http://www.pac.dfo-mpo.gc-ca/sci/pbs/

Pacific Fisheries Research Center (TINRO-
    Center)
4 Shevchenko Alley
Vladivostok, 690950, Russian Federation
Contact: Director
Tel: 8 4232 400921
Fax: 8 4232 300751
E-mail: tinro@tinro.ru
http://www.tinro.ru/

Pacific Fishery Management Council
7700 NE Ambassador Place, Suite 200
Portland, OR, 97220–1384, USA
Contact: Executive Director
Tel: 1 503 820–2280
Fax: 1 503 820–2299
E-mail: pfmc.comments@noaa.gov
http://www.pcouncil.org/

Pacific States Marine Fisheries Commission
    (PSMFC)
205 SE Spokane Street
Portland, OR, 97202, USA
Contact: Executive Director
Tel: 1 503 595–3100
Fax: 1 503 595–3232
E-mail: info@psmfc.org
http://www.psmfc.org/

Philippine Council for Aquatic and Marine
    Research and Development (PCAMRD)
Jamboree Road, Brgy. Timugan
Los Baños, Laguna, 4030, The Philippines
Tel: 63 49 536 1574
Fax: 63 49 536 5578
E-mail: dedo@laguna.net
http://www.pcamrd.dost.gov.ph/

Protected Areas Conservation Trust (PACT)
2 Mango Street
Belmopan, Cayo, Belize
Tel: 501 822–3637
Fax: 501 822–3759
E-mail: info@pactbelize.org
http://www.pactbelize.org/

Royal Netherlands Institute for Sea
  Research
(Nederlands Instituut voor Onderzoek der
  Zee NIOZ)
PO Box 59
NL-1790 AB, Den Burg, Texel, The
  Netherlands
Tel: 31 222 369300
Fax: 31 222 319674
http://www.nioz.nl/

Scottish Coastal Forum
Mail Point 7,
1 H North, Victoria Quay,
Edinburgh, EH6 6QQ, United Kingdom
Tel: 0131 244 1540
Fax: 0131 244 4071
E-mail: coastalforum@scotland.gov.uk
http://www.scotland.gov.uk/environment/
  coastalforum/default.asp

Scottish Natural Heritage
12 Hope Terrace
Edinburgh, Scotland, EH9 2AS, United
  Kingdom
Tel: 44 131 447 4784
Fax: 44 131 446 2277
E-mail: enquiries@snh.gov.uk
http://www.snh.org.uk/

Servicio Hidrográfico y Oceanográfico de
  la Armade de Chile (SHOA)
(Hydrographic and Oceanographic Service
  of the Chilean Navy)
Errázuriz 254, Playa Ancha
237–0168 Valparaíso, Chile
Tel: 56 32 266666
Fax: 56 32 266542
E-mail: shoa@shoa.cl
http://www.shoa.cl/

South African Maritime Safety Authority
Hatfield Gardens–Block E
PO Box 13186
Hatfield. 0028, Gauteng, South Africa
Tel: 27 12 342 3049
Fax: 27 12 342 3160
E-mail: pro@samsa.org.za
http://www.samsa.org.za

South Atlantic Fishery Management
  Council
One Southpark Circle, Suite 306

Charleston, SC, 29407–4699, USA
Tel: 1 843 571–4366
Fax: 1 843 769–4520
E-mail: safmc@safmc.net
http://www.safmc.net/

South Australian Research and
  Development Institute (SARDI)
2 Hamra Avenue West Beach
South Australia Aquatics Sciences Centre
Adelaide, SA 5001, Australia
Contact: Aquatic Sciences Research
  Programme
Tel: 61 8 8200 5400
Fax: 61 8 8200 5481
E-mail: cheshire.anthony@saugov.sa.gov.au
http://www.sardi.sa.gov.au/aquatic/index.html

Southeastern Association of Fish and
  Wildlife Agencies
8005 Freshwater Farms Road
Tallahassee, FL, 32308, USA
Contact: Executive Secretary
Tel: 1 850 893–1204
Fax: 1 850 893–6204
E-mail: seafwa@aol.com
http://www.seafwa.org/

Spanish Institute of Oceanography
(Instituto Español de Oceanografía–IEO)
Avenida de Brasil, No. 31
E-28020 Madrid, Spain
Tel: 34 915 974 443
Fax: 34 915 974 770
E-mail: ieo@md.ieo.es
http://www.ieo.es/

State Oceanic Administration
93 Livwei Road
Hedong District
Tianjin 300171, People's Republic of China
Contact: Chief
Tel: 86 10 6853 2211
Fax: 86 10 6853 3515
E-mail: webmaster@mail.nmdis.gov.cn
http://www.soa.gov.cn/

Sustainable Tourism CRC (STCRC)
Griffith University
PMB 50
Gold Coast Mail Centre, QLD 9726,
  Australia
Tel: 61 7 5552 8172
Fax: 61 7 5552 8171

E-mail: info@crctourism.com.au
http://www.crctourism.com.au/

Swedish Board of Fisheries
Ekelundsgatan 1
Box 423
SE-401 26 Göteborg, Sweden
Contact: Head Office
Tel: 46 31 743 03 00
Fax: 46 31 743 04 44
E-mail: fiskeriverket@fiskeriverket.se
http://www.fiskeriverket.se/

Swedish Polar Research Secretariat
PO Box 50 003
SE-104 05 Stockholm, Sweden
Tel: 46 86 73 96 00
Fax: 46 8 15 20 57
E-mail: office@polar.se
http://www.polar.se/

Transport Canada–Marine Safety
330 Sparks Street
Mail Stop: AMS
Ottawa, ON, K1A 0N5, Canada
Tel: 1 613 991–3135
Fax: 1 613 990–6191
E-mail: marinesafety@tc.gc.ca
http://www.tc.gc.ca/marinesafety/

Ukrainian Scientific Center of Marine
    Ecology of Sea (UkrSCES)
89, Frantsuzky Boulevard
Odessa 65009, Ukraine
Contact: Director
Tel: 380 482 636622
Fax: 380 482 636673
E-mail: accem@te.net.ua
http://www.sea.gov.ua/

United States Army Corps of Engineers
Cold Regions Research and Engineering
    Laboratory
CECRL-PP
72 Lyme Road
Hanover, NH, 03755–1290, USA
Tel: 1 603 646–4100
Fax: 1 603 646–4448
E-mail: info@crrel.usace.army.mil
http://www.crrel.usace.army.mil/

United States Coast Guard
2100 Second Street SW
Washington, DC, 20593, USA
Contact: Headquarters
Tel: 1 202 267–1587
http://www.uscg.mil/

V.I. Il'ichev Pacific Oceanological Institute
Russian Academy of Sciences, Far Eastern
    Branch
POI FEB RAS
43, Baltiyskaya Street
Vladivostok 690041, Russian Federation
Contact: Project Leader
E-mail: rostov@pacificinfo.ru
Tel: 7 4232 311 420
Fax: 7 4232 312 573
http://www.pacificinfo.ru/

Western Pacific Regional Fishery
    Management Council (WPRFMC)
1164 Bishop Street, Suite 1400
Honolulu, HI, 96813, USA
Tel: 1 808 522–8220
Fax: 1 808 522–8226
E-mail: info.wpcouncil@noaa.gov
http://www.wpcouncil.org/

Sam Bateman retired from full-time service in the Royal Australian Navy with the rank of commodore (one-star) in 1993, and became the first director of the Centre for Maritime Policy at the University of Wollongong in New South Wales where he is now a professorial research fellow. Dr. Bateman has written extensively on defence and maritime issues in Australia, the Asia-Pacific and Indian Ocean, and completed his doctorate at the University of New South Wales in 2001. He is co-chair of the Council for Security Cooperation in the Asia Pacific (CSCAP) Study Group on Capacity Building for Maritime Security Cooperation in the Asia Pacific, and currently also a senior fellow and adviser to the Maritime Security Program at the Institute of Defence and Strategic Studies (IDSS) in Singapore. The original research on which this article is based was undertaken during a visiting fellowship at the East-West Center in Honolulu in 2002.

Jay L. Batongbacal is a lawyer from the Philippines who specializes in marine policy. His previous work in the field has spanned a wide variety of subjects, such as community-based coastal resource management, marine environmental protection, shipping and seafaring, maritime boundary delimitations, and maritime security. He has undertaken research for government offices, non-governmental organizations, and for the private sector. He holds a Master of Marine Management (MMM) degree from Dalhousie University's Marine Affairs Program, and is currently undertaking further studies for a Doctor in the Science of Law (JSD) at the Dalhousie Law School.

Awni Behnam assumed the responsibility of the president of the International Ocean Institute in 2004. He joined UNCTAD in 1977 after a career in the navy and as lecturer at the University of Wales in the Department of Maritime Studies. He held executive posts in the Shipping Division of UNCTAD before assuming responsibility as the chief of liaison with developing countries for the Secretary-General of UNCTAD. In 1992, he assumed the responsibility of Secretary of the Trade and Development Board of UNCTAD, and in 1999 he was appointed as secretary of the quadrennial United Nations Conference on Trade and Development (UNCTAD). In 2001, he was promoted to the post of senior advisor to the Secretary-General, which he left in 2004. He holds a B.A. in business administration and an M.Sc. and a Ph.D. in development economics from the University of Wales.

Roger G. Bennett has recently retired from his lectureship at the University of Bergen. Educated in Cambridge, he received his first post in physical geography at the University of Oslo in 1965 and moved to the Department of Geography, University of Bergen in 1973, where he served as Head of Department, 1981–1983 and 1996–1998. In 2000 he was seconded to the Centre for Studies of Environment and Resources, where he was chief architect for an interdisciplinary master degree in Water Resources and Coastal Management. He has taught courses in geographical methods, theory and philosophy of science, and public planning. His research interests include planning processes, conflicts, discourses and power relations in Norwegian coastal management. He does consultancy work and still teaches classes in coastal management and planning.

Alexandru S. Bologa, former director of the International Ocean Institute's Black Sea Operational Centre (1997–2004), received his Ph.D. from Bucharest University in 1980. Bologa is a biologist, a senior scientist, and scientific director at the National Institute for Marine Research and Development "Grigore Antipa" in Constanta. He is a Member of the Romanian National Committee of Oceanography/Romanian National Commission to UNESCO and expert at UNESCO/IOC Special Court of Referees in "marine scientific research." He is a representative to the International Commission for the Scientific Exploration of the Mediterranean Sea (CIESM) and International Union of the History of Philosophy of Science/Commission of Oceanography (IUHPS/CO). His professional memberships include the International Phycological Society, the European Society for Radiation Biology, and the International Association of Radioecology. He is editor-in-chief of *Cercetari marine-Recherches marines* and a member of the editorial board of *Noesis* at the Romanian Academy. He is also an associate professor at the University "Ovidius" of Constanta. His fields of interest include marine biology (macrophytobenthos, planktonic primary production), radioactivity and radioecology, history of science, Black Sea research and management programmes, Black Sea bibliographies and databases.

Laurence Cordonnery (Ph.D. University of Tasmania, 1998) is a visiting fellow at the East-West Center in Hawaii. Her current research interests involve the management of marine resources in the Pacific region and the law of the sea, with a specific focus on Western and Central Pacific Tuna Fisheries and the development of high seas marine protected areas. While at the East-West Center, the Secrétariat Permanent pour le Pacifique has mandated her to promote research collaboration between the French Pacific Territories and Hawaii. Prior to her current appointment, she was a lecturer in law at the University of the South Pacific in Vanuatu from 1998 to 2003. She also maintains a research interest in Antarctic and Sub-

Antarctic environmental management and policy, after focusing her Ph.D. on the implementation of the Protocol on Environmental Protection to the Antarctic Treaty and the management of protected areas.

Robert O. Fournier received his master's and doctoral degrees in biological oceanography from the College of William and Mary, and the University of Rhode Island. In addition, Dr. Fournier held fellowships in Norway and England before joining the faculty of the University of Hawaii in 1969. In 1971, he joined Dalhousie University where he is presently professor of oceanography. His research interests have included studies of the physical and chemical processes that contribute to the high biological productivity on continental shelves. From 1985 to 2000, Dr. Fournier served as associate vice-president (Research & International Relations), and executive director of Ocean Studies. At the present time Dr. Fournier is director of a CIDA project to develop a masters program in coastal zone management at the University of the Republic in Montevideo, Uruguay.

Fernando González-Laxe has a Ph.D. in economics (1982) from the University of Santiago de Compostela, Spain. He is currently professor of applied economics and director of the University Institute of Maritime Studies, University of A Coruña, Spain and director of the M.A. in Maritime Administration and Port Management. He is also a member of several national and international associations of economic studies. He served as director-general for fisheries with the Spanish Ministry of Agriculture, Fisheries and Food (1982–1985) and as president of the Fisheries Commission, Parliamentary Assembly of the Council of Europe (1997–2000). He publishes articles relating to the economics of maritime transport, ports and harbours, and fisheries management.

Denise Gorfinkiel, M.Sc., is a research professor at the Faculty of Social Science, University of the Republic, Uruguay. She holds a masters of science in environmental economics from the University of the Republic and a bachelor of arts in international relations from Florida International University, Florida, U.S.A. Currently, she is a candidate for a Ph.D. in economics at the University of the Republic. Professor Gorfinkiel has research interests in the economic valuation of environmental goods and services and environmental policy instruments. She is a senior researcher at Ecoplata, an integrated coastal management program, where she has been working in the economic valuation of coastal and marine resources. At the macroeconomic level, her work has been on how environment and economy can be linked and more easily studied by establishing a set of environmental waste and resource flow satellite accounts, valued in physical terms, within the input-output model and, at the ecosystem level, work has been done to approach the economic valuation of marine and coastal ecosystems using non-market economic valuation methods to improve decision-making. Gorfinkiel's recent project includes the study of the costs and benefits of implementing a management plan in a coastal lagoon protected area.

Montserrat Gorina-Ysern specializes in public international law and ocean policy, human rights, international fisheries goverenance, and marine biotechnology law. She holds three degrees in law (Universitat Autonoma de Barcelona, Civil Law Degree, 1979; Universitat de Barcelona, L.L.M. Shipping Law, 1984; and University of New South Wales, Ph.D. International-al Law, 1996). Dr. Gorina practiced law in Spain and founded *Spainlaw* in Sydney, where she lectured at various Australian universities. She has served as an adviser to the US Department of State, U.S. Commission on Ocean Policy, and Conservation International; and as a private consultant on ISPS Code implementation in telecommunications as applied in Central American countries. She was *Rapporteur* for the Bureau of Intelligence & Research (USDOS) in symposia on *Perspectives on International Oceanographic Research, Hydrogen Based Economy,* and *Capacity Building,* respectively. Currently she provides assistance to the government of Timor Leste and is affiliated with the School of International Service, American University (USA). Her legal writings in English and Spanish have been published by Transnational Publishers, Editorial Bosch, *Golden Gate University Law Review, Marine Policy, Australian Journal of International Law, New South Wales Law Journal, Maritime Studies,* and *American Society of International Law Insights.*

John R. Hansen will receive his master's degree in 2006 from the University of Washington after completing two years of study at the School of Marine Affairs. While attending the University of Washington, Mr. Hansen focused his areas of work and study on U.S. ocean policy matters at the federal and State level. In addition to working with Professor Marc Hershman on the article published here, Mr. Hansen has also worked a regional ocean governance pilot project for the northwest U.S., as well as working for the Washington State Ocean Policy Advisory Council as a research assistant to Professor Hershman. Mr. Hansen, a California native, received his B.S. in aquatic biology from the University of California at Santa Barbara in 2003. Mr. Hansen's master's thesis topic is focused on nascent State ocean management initiatives as a response to the U.S. Commission on Ocean Policy. Mr. Hansen hopes to continue working on ocean policy issues in the U.S. at the federal or State level following his graduation from the School of Marine Affairs in spring 2006.

Marc J. Hershman is a professor in the School of Marine Affairs at the University of Washington, and adjunct Professor in the School of Law. He leads faculty and students engaged in teaching and research on integrated coastal zone management, ports and transportation, living marine resource management, marine protected areas, impacts of climate change, and other ocean issues. Professor Hershman has more than 30 years' experience in the study of ocean and coastal law and policy. In 1972, he founded the journal *Coastal Management* and continues to serve as its editor-in-chief. He has served as president of The Coastal Society, is a co-founder of the Marine Affairs and Policy Association, and is an active member of the Ocean Governance Study Group. He is the founder and a board member of Odyssey Maritime Discovery Center on Seattle's central waterfront.

Cheryle Hislop is a Ph.D. candidate enrolled with the School of Government, University of Tasmania. Majoring in political science and public policy as an undergraduate, Hislop has applied these disciplines to postgraduate research and analysis of marine resource and habitat conservation policies and management practices in Australia, Canada, and the high seas. Her Ph.D. research project explores the feasibility of creating marine protected areas in oceans beyond national jurisdiction and she has presented her research at universities and conferences in Australia and the United States. Awarded a Fulbright postgraduate scholarship, Hislop has been in the U.S. since July 2004. The first six months were spent at the Centre for Marine Policy at the University of Delaware, and since January 2005 she has been a guest scholar at the Marine Policy Centre, Woods Hole Oceanographic Institution. She returns home at the end of July 2005 to complete her dissertation and plan her post-Ph.D. life.

David E. Johnson is head of maritime and coastal studies and professor of coastal management at Southampton Solent University, United Kingdom. He is a visiting professor at the World Maritime University and a former short-term Caird Fellow of the National Maritime Museum. His Ph.D. is in conserving intertidal wetlands and he is a both a chartered geographer and scientist. In 2002, he co-ordinated the Wadden Sea Particularly Sensitive Sea Area (PSSA) Feasibility Study and is retained as a consultant on marine issues to WWF-UK. Current research interests in the marine environment include sustainable tourism, environmental impact assessment and public outreach.

Captain Joseph H. Jones retired as a Senior U.S. Coast Guard Officer with an exceptionally meritorious record at sea in command of three different Coast Guard cutters and ashore in various posts. He is the recipient of several prestigious military awards (1972–2004). He is a graduate of the USGG Academy (B.S. nuclear engineering 1972), Yale University (MBA strategic analysis and game theory, 1984), the Naval War College (M.A. Strategic Studies and National Security, 1993), and a fellow in the Strategic Studies Group (National Security and Global Strategy of the Chief of Naval

Operations, 1994). He was the Senior Homeland Security & Maritime Affairs Attaché at the US Embassy in Mexico City (2001–2003), and an expert on the International Ship and Port Facility Security Code (ISPS) of the U.N. International Maritime Organization. He is the founder of the think-tank *Captain Jones' Maritime Experts.*

Ole Martin Lund completed his master degree in geography at the University of Bergen in 2004 with a thesis on flexibility in coastal planning and the spatial regulation of sea farming. He is now a professional planner in the county administration of Rogaland, Southwest Norway.

Lesley Anne MacDougall has a B.Sc. in biology (University of Victoria, 1998) and a Master's of Marine Management (Dalhousie University, 2004). Since 1998, she has been a biologist in the Science Branch of Fisheries and Oceans Canada (DFO), Pacific Region. Past research endeavours include subtidal habitat survey and classification, juvenile salmonid habitat and diet studies, pelagic life history and population dynamics. She is currently conducting a study of science-management communication within DFO, and coordinating a small-scale simulation project to improve information sharing and decision-making frameworks with respect to groundfish management in the Pacific Region.

Denzil G. M. Miller, the executive secretary of CCAMLR since 2002, he has a Ph.D. from the University of Cape Town. A recipient of the South African Antarctic Medal (1996) for his contribution to "Antarctic conservation and management," Miller serves on a number of international committees dealing with fisheries, environmental and Antarctic matters. He has published extensively on Antarctic science, fisheries management, marine biology and marine policy in general. Miller is an honorary research professor in the Institute of Antarctic and Southern Ocean Studies at the University of Tasmania and serves on the OECD Inter-Ministerial Taskforce on IUU fishing.

Erik Jaap Molenaar studied Netherlands law, specializing in international law, at Utrecht University in the Netherlands. He completed his Ph.D. on coastal state jurisdiction over vessel-source pollution in 1998. His research has shifted more towards international fisheries law and his current research focuses on curbing the impact of third State actors in fishing and tourism in Antarctica. Dr. Molenaar has been employed as a senior research associate with the Netherlands Institute for the Law of the Sea (NILOS) since 1994.

Iouri Oliounine graduated from the State University of Leningrad in 1968 with a M.Sc. diploma in oceanography. Dr. Oliounine dedicated 40 years of his life to the service of the oceans, as a scientist of the Arctic and Antarctic

Research Institute in Leningrad working in the areas of ocean physics and dynamics. In 1977, he received a Ph.D. in marine geophysics. During the first 20 years of his career he worked onboard research vessels as an engineer, head of an oceanographic group, and chief of expeditions. He participated in or led more than 20 expeditions in the Atlantic, Pacific and Southern Oceans. The last 20 years he served as a staff member of such international governmental and non-governmental organizations as Intergovernmental Oceanographic Commission (IOC) of UNESCO (deputy executive secretary at retirement) and the International Ocean Institute as the executive director. In the IOC his sphere of responsibility covered the programmes related to oceanographic data collection and management, capacity building and marine natural disasters mitigation. In 1998, he was appointed as a coordinator of the United Nations' International Year of the Ocean. During his career he published almost 100 articles and was a co-author on three monographs. He organized dozens of international meetings and training courses, chaired and was a key/guest speaker of a number of international fora.

Nilüfer Oral obtained her B.A. from the University of Berkeley, JD from Santa Clara Law School and a DEA in private international law from the Universite of Paris I. She is currently a member of the law faculty at the Istanbul Bilgi University where she teaches several courses, including a course on the law of the sea. She is also assistant director of the Bilgi University Marine Law Research Center. In addition, she has served as an advisor to the Turkish Foreign Ministry as legal counsel at the International Maritime Organization. She has also lectured at the Rhodes Academy of Law of the Sea and spoken at various international conferences. Her publications include articles on environmental challenges of transport of oil through the Turkish Straits and the Black Sea.

Jonathan S. Potts (Ph.D. Cardiff University) is the senior specialist for marine policy at the United Kingdom's National Maritime Museum in Greenwich. In this capacity he leads the Museum's research, education, display and corporate activities that relate to contemporary maritime issues. His research focuses on shoreline management, coastal hazards and the public interpretation of marine environmental issues. He has published widely on these subjects and carried out work for a number of organisations, including the National Rivers Authority, the Environment Agency, the Ministry of Agriculture, Fisheries and Food, the Countryside Council for Wales, the Department of Culture, Media and Sport, and the Local Government Association. Most recently, he was co-editor of the book *Managing Britain's Marine and Coastal Environment—Towards a Sustainable Future*, published in 2005 by Routledge. Dr Potts is also a chartered geographer of the Royal Geographical Society and a chartered marine scientist of the Institute of Marine Engineering, Science and Technology.

Johanna Rosier, MNZPI, MPIA, is a senior lecturer in Massey University's Resource and Environmental Planning Programme at Palmerston North, New Zealand. Before joining the Massey planning programme, she was a researcher at the University of Queensland in Australia where she received her Ph.D. Her research is focused on evaluation of coastal planning in New Zealand, across all levels of planning. Current topics of interest include public access provisions in the coastal environment and interpreting the concept of "public interest" in relation to managing coastal development offshore. She is also researching the use of pre-hearing meetings in the restricted coastal activity resource consent processes adopted by regional councils. In 2004, she completed an independent review of the New Zealand Coastal Policy Statement for the Minister of Conservation. Rosier lectures in the areas of planning theory, conservation policy and natural resource planning in both the undergraduate and postgraduate planning courses. Generally, she supervises theses and projects that relate to coastal management and conservation policy.

Daniel Blake Rubenstein, CA, MA is currently a senior research associate with the Canadian Comprehensive Auditing Foundation focusing on the complex issues of how to reconcile the principles of shared, collaborative governance with the foundation principles of a parliamentary democracy. He brings to this challenge 21 years as a legislative auditor. During this period, he worked for seven years for the Commissioner of the Environment and Sustainable Development as a principal. Rubenstein's previous research focus has been on accounting for environmental and sustainable development issues. He is the author of numerous articles on this subject, and the book *Environmental Accounting for the Sustainable Corporation, Strategies and Techniques* (Greenwood Publishing). He is most interested in ensuring that oceans under stress receive more than palliative care.

Jens-Uwe Schröder graduated from the University of Rostock, Germany with an M.Sc. in Transport Engineering (Dipl-Ing.). In 2003, he completed his Ph.D. (Dr.-Ing.) in Safety Science at the University of Wuppertal, Germany. His thesis was about causes of marine casualties and underlying factors. As a former seafarer, Dr. Schröder obtained practical experience on board chemical tankers as a holder of a Master Mariner Licence (Kapitän AG). After finishing his seafaring career, he joined the classification society Germanischer Lloyd, working in the head office in Hamburg, Germany. He dealt with ship safety tasks and was engaged in manning and qualification matters. He also worked as project manager for customer-related services and as a consultant for European flag state administrations. In October

2000, he joined the World Maritime University (WMU), Malmö, Sweden. Dr. Schröder currently holds a position as Assistant Professor, lecturing and researching on marine risk assessment and management related topics. He is actively involved in WMU's efforts to provide services in maritime security. He is also assistant editor of the *WMU Journal of Maritime Affairs.*

Christopher T. Taggart has been associate professor (fisheries oceanography) in the Oceanography Department at Dalhousie University since 1995. Prior to that he was a research scientist with the Northwest Atlantic Fisheries Centre; an assistant professor (NSERC-URF) in oceanography at Dalhouise; an NSERC-PDF with Dalhousie and the Marine Ecology Laboratory at the Bedford Institute of Oceanography. He received his Ph.D. (Dean's Honours) at McGill University where he was an NSERC and McConnell Fellow and won the American Fisheries Society Student Award of Merit and the Canadian Society of Zoology's Outstanding Ph.D. Thesis Award. As principal investigator in many multi-institutional research initiatives, he conducts research with undergraduate and graduate students, PDFs, and RAs on physical, biochemical, genetic and ecological influences on recruitment, early life history and population structure and distribution in marine systems. Study organisms range from zooplankton to fishes and whales in systems ranging from the Bay of Fundy to the Coral Sea. He has co-authored 50+ primary publications, 40+ research reports and contributed 150+ conference, workshop and seminar presentations, many as invited contributions or keynote addresses.

Yoshifumi Tanaka majored in international law at Hitotsubashi University, Tokyo, as well as the Graduate Institute of International Studies, Geneva. He obtained his Ph.D. at the Graduate Institute of International Studies, Geneva, in 2002. The subject of the Ph.D. dissertation is *Predictability and Flexibility in the Law of Maritime Delimitation.* In 2002, Dr. Tanaka was awarded a postdoctoral research fellowship by the National University of Ireland Galway under the Higher Education Programme for Research in Third Level Institutions in Ireland. He is currently based in the Marine Law and Ocean Policy Centre, Martin Ryan Institute, National University of Ireland, Galway. He has published articles on international law of the sea in *International and Comparative Law Quarterly, Netherlands International Law Review, International Journal of Marine and Coastal Law,* and *Revue Belge de Droit International.*

Uwe Tietze was borne in Cuxhaven, Germany, in 1950. He took a masters degree in economic and social sciences at the University of Goettingen, Germany, in 1974, obtained a masters degree in educational sciences at the University of Kassel, Germany in 1976, and was awarded a Ph.D. in economic and social sciences at the University of Kassel in 1979. From 1975 to 1980, he worked as researcher, lecturer and social scientist at the University of Kassel and at the Technical University of Berlin. He joined the Food and Agriculture Organization (FAO) of the United Nations in 1980 as training and extension officer of the FAO Bay of Bengal Programme for the development of small-scale fisheries. In 1986, he moved to the Fisheries Department of FAO, Rome, Italy, as fishery industry officer (small-scale fisheries / fisheries socio-economics). He organized and coordinated global and regional conferences and studies and authored/co-authored major FAO publications on fisheries economics, small-scale fisheries and the use of socio-economic indicators in fisheries and coastal resources management. He also contributed to the biannual FAO Reports on the Status of World Fisheries and Aquaculture and to the UN World Fisheries and Aquaculture Atlas.

Index for Ocean Yearbook Volume 20